V!VA TRAVEL GUIDES

COLOMBIA

Bogotá - Valle del Cauca - Zona Cafetera - Tierra Paisa - Magdalena River - Cartagena - Caribbean and Pacific Coasts - Eastern Colombia - Llanos and Selva

1st Edition
September 2008

V!VA Travel Guides' Guarantee:
We guarantee our guidebook to be the most up-to-date printed guidebook available. Visit www.vivatravelguides.com/guarantee to learn more.

V!VA Travel Guides Colombia.

ISBN-10: 0-9791264-4-4
ISBN-13: 978-0-9791264-4-4

Voice: (970) 744-4244
Fax: (612) 605-5720
Website: www.vivatravelguides.com
Information: info@vivatravelguides.com

www.vivatravelguides.com

Travel is inherently dangerous. While we use a superior process for updating guidebooks and have made every effort to ensure accuracy of facts in this book, Viva Publishing Network, its owners, members, employees, contributors and the authors cannot be held liable for events outside their control and we make no guarantee as to the accuracy of published information. V!VA encourages travelers to keep abreast of the news in order to know the safety situation of the country. Please travel safely, be alert and let us know how your vacation went!

Political Position
Viva Travel Guides takes no position on the internal affairs of Colombia. We do not support one faction or another in the country's on-going civil war. The colors and sizes of maps or other features of this guidebook have no political or moral significance.

◇ Cover Design: Jason Halberstadt and Laura Granfortuna ◇
◇ Cover Photo: (Desierto de Tatacoa) Manuela & J.C. Surateau ◇
◇ Cover Photo: "Colombia, the only risk is wanting to stay." Luz A. Villa ◇
◇ Title Page Photo: Freyja Ellis ◇

CONTENTS

About V!VA Travel Guides

V!VA Travel Guides is a new approach to travel guides. We have taken the travel guide and re-designed it from the ground up using the internet, geographic databases, community participation, and the latest in printing technology which allows us to print our guidebooks one at a time when they are ordered. Reversing the general progression, we have started with a website, gathered user ratings and reviews, and then compiled the community's favorites into a book. Every time you see the V!VA insignia you know that the location is a favorite of the V!VA Travel Community. For you, the reader, this means more accurate and up-to-date travel information and more ratings by travelers like yourself.

Community and Free Membership:

The accuracy and quality of the information in this book is largely thanks to our online community of travelers. If you would like to join them go to www.vivatravelguides.com/members/ to get more information and to sign up for free.

Your Opinions, Experiences and Travels:

Did you love a place? Will you never return to another? Every destination in this guidebook is listed on our web site with space for user ratings and reviews. Share your experiences, help out other travelers and let the world know what you think.

Updates & Registering:

We update our books at least twice a year. By purchasing this book you are entitled to one year of free electronic updates. Go to www.vivatravelguides.com/updates/ to register for your free updates. Feedback on our book to get a free ebook by registering your views at www.vivatravelguides.com/register.

Corrections & suggestions:

We are committed to bringing you the most accurate and up-to-date information. However, places change, prices rise, businesses close down, and information, no matter how accurate it once was, inevitably changes. Thus we ask for your help: If you find an error in this book or something that has changed, go to www.vivatravelguides.com/corrections and report them (oh, and unlike the other guidebooks, we'll incorporate them into our information within a few days).

If you think we have missed something, or want to see something in our next book go to www.vivatravelguides.com/suggestions/ and let us know. As a small token of our thanks for correcting an error or submitting a suggestion we'll send you a coupon for 50 percent off any of our eBooks or 20 percent off any of our printed books.

Coming soon on www.vivatravelguides.com

This is just the beginning. We're busy adding new features that our users have requested to our books and website. A few coming attractions are:

- Improved Community Functions: join groups, find travel partners, participate in forums.
- Write travel blogs and share travel photos from your trip
- And more!

How to Use This Book

This book is a best-of Colombia taken straight from our website. You can check out the website to read user reviews, rate your favorite hotels and restaurants, and add information you think we are missing. The book also features highlighted sections on haciendas, eco-tourism and adventure travel. While you are out and about in Colombia, use our helpful tear-out sheet, complete with emergency contact details and helpful numbers.

Photos by Mark Hentze

Many Thanks To:

Karen Harburn, Troy Shaheen, Elizabeth Kersjes and **Leslie Brown** who helped to no end with the editing of this book. Thanks also to **Crit Minster, Tom Bacon** and **Daniel Johnson** for their input. Also, thanks to the **Techie Team**, the programming masterminds who keep our parent website www.vivatravelguides.com running smoothly and always lend a hand to the not-always-computer-savvy staff. A big thank you to the whole **Metamorf** team for their support.

Thanks also to **Germán, Shaun, René, Felipe, José, Oscar** and so many others for their tips, suggestions and information; the poet in the hotel, **Juan** and **Juan Gabriel; Jayariyú, Katy, Karmen, Amelia** and the other Wayuu women who taught us so much about their culture; **Tom** from Haifa, **Yo** and **Zora** from Japan and all the dozens of other travelers who took the challenge to know Colombia.

Most of all, to the hundreds of Colombians who shared their history and culture, and who even after three generations of civil war, continue to receive travelers with such gracious hospitality. Hasta el próximo tintico que nos provoque, this guide is for you.

ABOUT THE AUTHORS AND EDITORS

Upon re-declaring her independence at age 29, Lorraine Caputo packed her trusty Rocinante (so her knapsack's called) and began traipsing throughout the Americas, from Alaska to Patagonia. This United Statien's works has been published in a wide variety of publications in the U.S., Canada and Latin America. As the lead writer, Lorraine spent many months exploring Colombia, to share the very best that this country has to offer for the book.

Paula Newton is V!VA's operations expert. With an MBA and a background in New Media, Paula is the Editor-in-Chief and the organizing force behind the team. With an insatiable thirst for off-the-beaten-track travel, Paula has traveled extensively, especially in Europe and Asia, and has explored more than 25 countries. She currently lives in Quito.

With over five years traveling and working in Latin America, Richard McColl feels most at home on the big continent. From the former Scottish settlements of Surinam to the pristine beaches of Colombia and the glaciers of Patagonia, Richard has traveled it all. Now making his home in Colombia, Richard contributed to many sections of the book, including the Pacific Coast, Valle de Cauca, Tierra Paisa, Magdalena River Valley and Bogotá.

Brenda Yun, a freelance writer based in Honolulu, is an avid world traveler who once believed in seeing everything first and then returning to the select places that were most interesting. She fell in love with Colombia on her assignment for V!VA and vows to return sooner rather than later. She continues to write travel-related articles for print and online magazines and is currently completing a book-length memoir about her tumultuous twenties.

Lorena Fernández discovered V!VA in the same way a traveler to Colombia would discover this book: with perfect timing. With a journalism degree from Ball State University and endless curiosity about quotidian habits of virtually every culture, this Ecuadorian prides herself to have written, designed and edited the content of this book and being part of the V!VA family. The journeys ahead promise to guide even better adventures.

Staff writer Nili Larish hails from the big apple, with a background in book publishing. Upon receiving a degree in creative writing from Binghamton University in 2005, Nili backpacked through South America for 7 months. Along the way, she got to know South American hospitals better than she would have liked to. Unable to shake her wanderlust, Nili left New York and headed to Ecuador to combine her twin passions of travel and writing.

After graduating from UNC-CH with degrees in journalism and international studies, Laura Granfortuna's search for knowledge and adventure swiftly led her to Quito. Although she signed on with V!VA as a writer, Laura's artistic eye soon earned her a position as the company's designer. In addition to her regular duties handling ads, photos and graphics, she has spent countless hours building and editing the maps for this book.

This Missouri Journalism School graduate worked for V!VA to introduce her passion (travel) to her ambition (writing and editing). She has slept in the Sahara, bungee jumped in Switzerland and fed bears in Puerto Vallarta. She was born and raised in Houston and currently works there in communications. Look for Tammy in future editing endeavors—if she ever edits your work then be sure to know the difference when using the words "which" and "that."

Ricardo Segreda graduated with Departmental Honors from Manhattanville College in Purchase, New York, earning a B.A. in Religious Studies and Literature. Following a spell managing a hostel for Hostelling International in Washington State, and serving on its Board of Directors, Segreda relocated to Ecuador. In Quito, he divides his time between film critiquing for Ecuador's largest daily, La Hora and serving as a staff writer for V!VA.

Cartagena

Often referred to as one of the most beautiful cities in South America, Cartagena has plenty to offer travelers in the way of sights and sounds.

Parque Nacional Natural Ensenada de Utría

With amazing topographical features, this park is home to hundreds of marine species as well as cultural reserves.

Santa Fé de Antioquia

An architectural jewel of the 16th, 17th and 18th Centuries, this city is a must-see day trip from Medellín.

Parque Nacional del Café

Located west of Bogotá, this park is a blend of mechanical attractions, ecotourism, family entertainment and all things coffee.

La Candelaria, Bogota

With a colonial flavor, cobblestone streets, eclectic bookstores, museums and restaurants, La Candelaria is the beating heart of old Bogotá.

San Agustín

The archaeological capital of Colombia, with pre-Columbian statues guarding the verdant valleys that are laced with waterfalls and caverns.

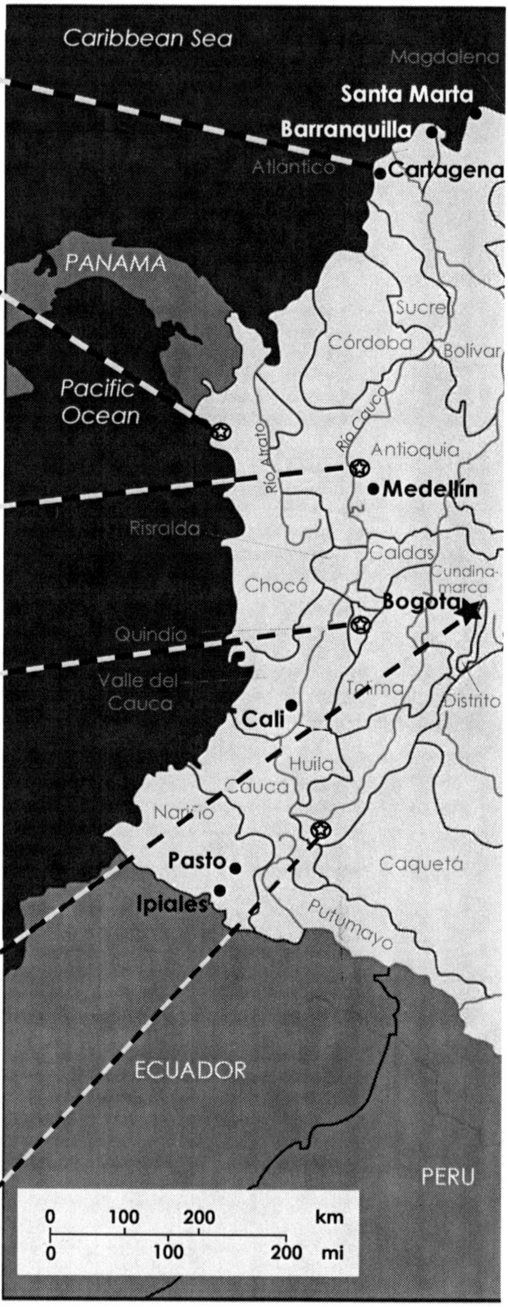

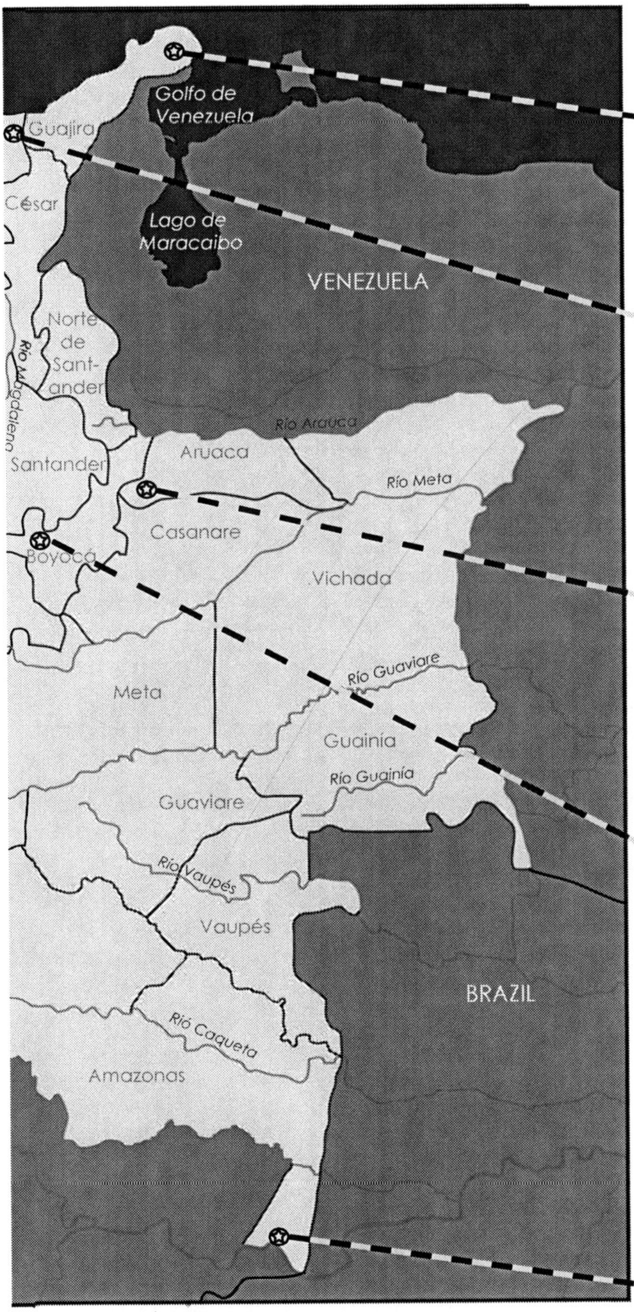

Guajira

Embark on a journey far northeast to discover the Land of Dreams and Death, as the Wayuu call their homeland.

La Ciudad Perdida

Built over 1,000 years ago by the Tayrona Indians, the journey to this lost city offers exciting trekking opportunities.

Parque Nacional Natural El Cocuy Hiking

A series of old trails traverse the wind-swept landscape rimmed with snow-covered mountains. The solitude makes this a wonderful experience.

Villa de Leyva

A quaint town that is a national historic monument, with beautifully preserved colonial buildings built with the rammed earth technique.

Puerto Nariño

The cradle of the Amazon holds ample ethnic and biological diversity, including the mystical pink dolphin.

Colombia Highlights

1. Museo de Oro (Bogotá) p.88

Housing the most impressive collection of pre-Colombian gold shaped in thousands of decoration pieces, the Gold Museum has preserved all sorts of metal objects of the pre-hispanic era as a cultural heritage treasure. The museum also leads investigations to fill-in the social context of the archeological findings. Entrance is free and museum hours are Monday and Wednesday to Saturday from 9 a.m. to 7 p.m.

2. La Ciudad Perdida (Sierra Nevada de Santa Marta) p.259

Deemed a World Heritage Site by UNESCO, the Lost City of the Tayrona people has not ceased to amaze archeologists and visitors since it was "discovered" in 1976 by a team from the Colombian Institute of Anthropology.

3. Cartagena de Indias p.216

A cultural and tourist district since 1991, Cartagena peaks as one of the most romantic and historically rich cities on the Caribbean coast. During the colonial era, this port was one of the most important of America because of all the gold and precious metal shipments departing from here to Spain. Naturally, the port was attacked by pirates several times, which is why the city had to be build into a fortress. Nowadays Cartagena has a well-developed urban zone and conserved old town.

4. Parque Nacional del Café (Quindío) p.138

Founded by the National Federation of Coffee Growers in Colombia, this theme park exhibits folkloric Colombian architecture, offers plenty of foods based on coffee, and includes attractions like a cable car and a roller coaster. The Park of Coffee Culture Fund runs this non-profit operation with the mission of preserving cultural heritage and promoting ecotourism in the region.

5. San Agustín p.428

A World Heritage Site since 1995, San Agustín housed several of the most important South American cultures, thus making this a significant archeological center of the continent. Hundreds of stone statues claim the territory where a pre-Colombian civilization once marked their tombs. On the outskirts of San Agustín one can find the archeological park, where most of the monumental statues can be found.

6. Tayrona National Park (Santa Marta) p.274

One of the most important parks of Colombia, this 15,000-hectare space–out of which 3,000 hectare is marine territory–contains over 350 species of algae and over 770 species of land plants. There are also archeological ruins left by the Tayrona civilization, which occupied the area from pre-Colombian times until well into the colonization.

7. Santa Fe de Antioquia p.153

With eight churches and plenty of colonial houses from the 16th, 17th and 18th centuries, Santa Fe de Antioquia is an architectural jewel, and has been recognized as such by Colombians and foreign visitors. Tourists from all over increasingly improve the local economy with weekend business as they visit the Bridge of Occident, the Metropolitan Cathedral and the Plaza Mayor, among others.

8. Plaza de Bolívar (Bogotá) p.93

Walking through the most historically charged plaza of the country gives pedestrians the sense of becoming part of history itself. Plaza de Bolívar is surrounded by the Palace of Justice, Capitolio Nacional, the Primary Cathedral of Bogotá and the Lievano building, which currently houses Bogotá's major City Hall. In the center of the plaza you will find the first public statue erected in the city, representing Simón Bolívar.

Regional Summaries

Bogotá P.77

Bogotá, Colombia's largest city and one of South America's most happening metropolitan areas, is a region in itself. However, technically speaking, it is located on the border of Colombia's Huila and Cundinamarca regional departments. This enormous metropolis has everything—the nation's most comprehensive museums, bohemian and trendy nightlife, and everything in between. Both art and business are booming in this capital, and, although crime and violence is still a part of life here, so is rapid development and tourism. The locals are the most cosmopolitan in the country, but are some of the friendliest and most helpful. As an essential port of international arrival and departure, the city is a sophisticated and increasingly safe and hospitable place to spend a few days. The city itself is situated on the *sabana de Bogotá*, the nation's highest plateau, making for cool year-round climate and wet conditions in the winter. After you've had a proper introduction to the country with a visit to its impressive National Museum, escape is not too far away. For a break from the quick, urban pace of Bogotá and a taste of slower-paced suburban life, head an hour north to Zipaquirá. Tour the underground cathedral and salt mine, where the country still gets most of its salt.

Valle del Cauca P.106

The Valle del Cauca is uniquely situated between the Pacific Ocean and the western ridge of the Andes, allowing for climate that is perfect for farming and agriculture. The heart of this region is Santiago de Cali, Colombia's third-largest city and often-considered salsa capital of Latin America. Visitors regard Cali as a shocking mixture of a maze-like streets, as a happening home to some of the prettiest girls in the Colombia, and, finally, as the mecca for some of the most coordinated hips in the southern hemisphere. If Colombia were three bears and Cartagena is hot and Bogotá is cold, then Cali is "just right"—both in terms of the climate and the people. There's a general feel-good nature to this part of the country. There is plenty to see and do in Cali, especially at night when the Avenida Sexta lights up like the Las Vegas Strip. Yet there are plenty of opportunities to relax and enjoy down-time by the Río Cali, which runs its way straight across the city. If you prefer something more tropical, though, head to the San Cipriano jungle and enjoy a ride on their unique open train car. Or, if you're looking for a place to cool off, then take the tourist train inland towards the hills and Risaralda, stopping off in the small towns of Buga and La Tebaida to snap photos of colonial churches and architecture.

Zona Cafetera P.128

Colombia's *zona cafetera* (coffee zone) is the newest and fastest growing tourist attraction in the country. Comprised of three lush regions—Risaraldas, Quindío and Caldas—it stretches across mountainous terrain at over 1,000 meters above sea level. Raspberries, coffee, potatoes and oranges grow naturally among green bamboo and dense forest. This region's Parque Nacional Natural Los Nevados also offers some of the most postcard-perfect scenes of high-altitude fauna and natural life. The strange-looking cactus called the *frailejones* grows upward like a tall pineapple tree and only survives in the most arid and cold climates. On the other end of the spectrum, the national tree called *palma de cera* (wax palm) gracefully towers over the Valle de Cocora near Salento, where the river microclimate explodes with bird and plant life. The coffee zone's three major cities—Pereira, Armenia, and Manizales—all buzz with urban life, while tranquil nature is just a short bus ride away.

Tierra Paisa - Antioquia P.146

Inhabitants of Medellín, Santa Fe de Antioquia, Pereira, and Manizales are referred to as *paisas*. They are known throughout Colombia for being a hardworking bunch and are bold in nature. A perfect example would be the country's president, Alvaro Uribe Velez, who has, within one decade, turned crime-ridden and struggling Colombia into a far safer and prosperous place. Indeed, paisas have proven to be the country's most industrious, business-oriented and economically wealthy members of the nation. At the same time, paisas know how to have a good time and share a unique lingo. For instance, when asking a fellow paisa how it's going, one would say, "*Qué hubo pues?*". Medellín is really the heart of Tierra Paisa. In the 1990s this violent city was the murder capital of the world, taking center stage as the home to Colombia's infamous Pablo Escobar and, along with him, the shady underpinnings of the drug cartel. Within a mere decade, however, Medellín has almost completely reversed its image, highlighting its artistic and vibrant cultural life. In recent years, paisas have actively promoted their land for tourism, and for good reason: the region is spotted with delightful, whitewashed colonial towns and conservative yet accommodating citizens with a desire to maintain their cultural heritage. There are several sites worth visiting in Tierra Paisa, such as the Gulf of Urabá on the Caribbean coast and the colonial masterpiece of Santa Fe de Antioquia.

Magdalena River Valley (Upper and Lower) upper p.182, lower p.194

Shaped by the Magdalena River and stretching nearly 1,000 miles across the interior of Colombia from south to north, the Magdalena River Valley runs from the lower extremes of the Andes (at the river's source in Huila), through the arid badlands of the Tatacoa Desert, past the towering snow-capped mountain of Nevado del Tolima in Ibagué and the hot and sticky swamps of Mompós to the Caribbean seaport of Barranquilla. Willing travelers to this area will be pleasantly surprised by the contrasts and the differences in each town. Starting at Honda, known as both the City of Bridges and Cartagena of the Interior (thanks to its narrow colonial streets), travelers can venture on to Ibague, Colombia's music capital. Here you can explore verdant canyons nearby and try to catch a glimpse of a spectacled bear. Then, follow the main cattle route to the Caribbean coast, passing through humid, hot and flat terrain where cattle farming remains the dominant industry. Enormous ranches extend out from towns along the Magdalena River and any journey will undoubtedly be delayed by a passing cattle train ambling along a major byway. You won't want to miss the smoke stacks, nodding donkeys that dot the horizons, or the Nazarenes on procession in the austere Semana Santa of Mompos, a sleepy UNESCO World Heritage Site.

Caribbean Coast p.207

In the great spirit of regionalism that defines Colombia, most people along the Caribbean coastal area are referred to as *costeños* (people from the coast). These coastal dwellers are full of a zest for life. The low-lying Caribbean is certainly Colombia's tropical heart and soul, and costeños take to the pursuit of leisure with great ease and delight. Whether you visit the dense jungles in the Darien Gap on the Panamanian border or you visit Tolú, Cartagena, Barranquilla, Santa Marta to Tayrona, the pace of life is slower than the urban centers in Colombia's interior. Yet the area is equally as vibrant as metropolitan areas. This coast is, after all, where colonization started back in 1525 with the first European settlers arriving on the shores of Santa Marta. For three centuries, pirates and plunderers plagued the coastal cities; slavery was a part of life. Impressive stone walls and fortresses were built to protect important ports. In particular, Cartagena remains one of Colombia's best-preserved colonial cities. In addition, Barranquilla's Carnaval should not be missed. Of course, Parque Tayrona near Santa Marta is a tropical paradise like no other and a place where many choose to spend their entire vacation relaxing in private bungalows beside the tranquil sea. Finally, a six-day trek to the archeological ruins of Ciudad Perdida (lost city) is a rare opportunity to see an old city in the middle of a cloud forest, meet the indigenous Kogis who live in thatched huts and live as they had centuries ago.

La Guajira p.297

The arid salt plains of the Guajira Peninsula make for a remote yet rewarding travel destination. Its capital, Riohacha, is cradled by the desert peninsula and Caribbean Sea, and used to be a convenient location to export drugs. The area has since cleaned up significantly, and poses little danger to tourists hunting for adventure, not trouble. In reality, Riohacha is just the launching point for the rest of the region. The southern and inland section of Guajira reaches the Sierra Nevada de Santa Marta, where there is heavy farming and cattle raising. Media Guajira, the northwestern section, is hot yet dry. The third section borders Venezuela and includes the scenic deserts of Cabo de Vela and Nazareth. The eastern oasis of Macuira is the most remote area in Guajira, where even the most adventurous travelers have difficulty reaching. To be certain, the heat and lack of good roads in La Guajira make it Colombia's "no-man's land." However, the fruits of rugged travel could prove most rewarding.

Eastern Colombia P.321

The central Andean regions of Boyacá, Cundinamarca and Santander are at the geographical, cultural, and historical epicenter of Colombia itself. The gold-worshipping pre-Colombian Muisca indians played an important role in forging Colombia's national identity. It was near Tunja, one of the nation's oldest cities, where Bolívar defeated the Spanish army in 1819, clearing the way for independence. Just two hours from Tunja is Villa de Leyva, a well-preserved colonial town that serves as the weekend hotspot for city dwellers. The town center boasts the largest cobblestone plaza in the country. An amazing pre-historic crocodile is on display in the archaeological museum just outside town. Farther east lies the impressive Chicamocha Canyons on the way to San Gil, the nation's adventure capital, where adrenaline junkies can enjoy whitewater rafting, rappelling, kayaking and paragliding. Then, just 20 minutes by bus and up the hill from San Gil is charming Barichara, a small colonial town with colonial architecture. On the border with Venezuela lies Cúcuta, where ties were forged between Colombia, Ecuador and Venezuela in 1821.

Southern Colombia P.406

If you're on your way out of or in to Ecuador, then Pasto will serve as the best arriving or departing city. Two short hours from the Ecuadorian border, visitors can get their first or last taste of Colombian life. Although the city itself bustles with activity by day, the real delights are found farther abroad, like atop Volcán Galeras or swimming in Laguna de la Cocha. Both are a short 30-minute bus ride away. Close by is the lovely, colonial town of Popayán, Colombia's *joya blanca* (white jewel), which serves as the perfect launching point for grand adventures in the must-see sites in San Agustín and Tierradentro. You will have to endure a rough and bumpy six-hour bus ride to either locale, but the rewards upon arrival are worth the pain in the neck. San Agustín's enigmatic stone monoliths—some twice the size of humans—are scattered around its well-kept archaeological park. Riding horses in the countryside is another enjoyable pastime for visitors with time to kill. Then, the fascinating burial tombs in Tierradentro, dug under the ground and decorated with symbols of moons, salamanders and human faces provide yet another intriguing glimpse into pre-Colombian times. Both locales are steeped in myth and legend, and situated among gorgeous mountains and clouds. Travelers often spend weeks wandering in the cloudy mists and exploring the rolling hills.

Llanos and Selva P.462

A stone's throw from Brazil and Peru, Leticia and its surrounding Amazon jungle are two great reasons to hop over to the exceedingly remote, southernmost tip of Colombia. This is Colombia's only yet often-overlooked gateway to the Amazon. The pint-sized town of Leticia was settled by Peruvians in the mid-19th Century but passed into Colombian hands about a century later. Despite past tensions, Colombia enjoys friendly relations with its Peruvian and Brazilian neighbors. A mythical indigenous group still wanders the surrounding jungle and has yet to make contact with civilization in Leticia. Leticia, which is only reachable by plane three times a week from Bogotá, is adjacent by land to the Brazilian town of Tabatinga and by boat to the Peruvian village Santa Rosa. Travelers seeking a unique Amazon experience don't need to venture far to witness the jungle wildlife in action.

Suggested Itineraries

Treasure Hunt

With its pirate past, pre-Colombian history, and indigenous presence, Colombia has some of the most fascinating cultural and archaeological sites in South America. Traveling through this country can be like embarking on a treasure hunt. To ground yourself in Colombia's rich past, begin your journey in Bogotá, visiting such emblematic museums as the Museo Nacional, Museo del Oro and Donación Botero. Hop on a bus and head one hour north to Zipaquirá, where the nation's largest supply of salt sits in a mine so immense that, in 1995, a cathedral was erected underground, inside the mine. The world's largest underground cross is here. Next stop: Villa de Leyva, a short four hours farther north, where a fascinating pre-historic alligator is on display in the Museo Paleontológico. The Saturday market in town is also a colorful sight to behold. Make your way southwest by bus or plane to Popayán, which only a few years ago was named one of the world's gastronomical centers. Here, delight yourself with tasty Colombian cuisine, or try out the Italian, French and vegetarian restaurants. Two hours away is adorable Silvia, where on Tuesdays you will find a fantastic indigenous market full of traditional wares and goods. Head to Tierradentro from here. One of Colombia's most fascinating pre-Colombian burial tombs is found under the ground. Spend at least one full day touring these cave-like tombs that still have their original colorful decorations. Finish your treasure hunt in San Agustín, exploring its gorgeously preserved Parque Arqueológico, where life-size zoologic statues protect burial mounds on the hillside.

Hips Don't Lie

Shakira, Colombia's very own pop-rock queen, says it best in her salsa-infused song: "I am on tonight and my hips don't lie and I am starting to feel it's right. The attraction, the tension. Baby, like this is perfection." Colombia is a lively center for nightlife and pure fun. It's not too surprising if you've come here more for play than for cultural exploration. If that's the case, head to the country's major cities for a taste of the good life: Latin dance and clubbing. You might as well start off in what many consider the Latin American capital of salsa dancing, Cali. Avenida Sexta is full of crazy Vegas-like salsa bars and clubs. The Cali girls, many say, are the prettiest in the country. However, Medellín girls are a bit more sophisticated, and this city, the second-largest in Colombia, really knows how to throw a party. The Zona Rosa in El Poblado lights up at night, and foam parties or other crazy, late-night antics are a part of weekend nightlife. If you're looking for something with a more colorful, Caribbean flair, then you won't have to look any farther than Cartagena. The best bars and clubs are found along Avenida del Arsenal. If you time your visit right and visit in January, then bus your way to Barranquilla for the city's crazy four-day Carnaval. With just a little more energy left in that dancing body of yours, head to Colombia's capital, Bogotá. The city's really modern and hip zona rosa in the north is packed with chic lounges, bars and clubs.

A Country of Contrasts

Colombia is certainly a country of contrasts. You may find yourself paragliding off of an enormous mountain one day and sunbathing on the beach the next. If you're searching for a blend of both, try some of these pairings:

Desierto Tatacoa & Isla Gorgona—Do you prefer dry or wet conditions? You're in luck, because Colombia offers both extremes. Tatacoa offers a glimpse of dry desert with cactus, sand and wildflowers, while Isla Gorgona, the country's largest Pacific island, is covered with lush, tropical rainforest, and you can spot humpback and sperm whale.

Salento & Coveñas—Both of these small towns are perfectly secluded, and offer tourists with privacy, but in very different settings. In Salento, visitors delight in the crisp air and gorgeous Valle de Cocora, where the hillside is dotted with *palmas de cera*, the Colombia's tall, skinny national tree. Then, in Coveñas, the warm, tropical beach is yours for the taking.

Ciudad Perdida & Parque Tayrona—Three full days of hiking in the northern Sierra Nevada will take you to an abandoned pre-Colombian town in the clouds, Ciudad Perdida (the lost city). At 1,000 meters above sea level, tourists who have endured the trek will bask in the glory of old times. Then, at sea level, on the way back to Santa Marta, is the equally lovely and relaxing Parque Tayrona, another home to the Tayrona Indians, set in calm bays and palm trees.

San Gil & Barichara—One of the country's centers for eco-adventure is San Gil, where rappelling, whitewater rafting and paragliding over the stunning Chicamocha Canyons shouldn't be missed. Just 20 minutes by bus from San Gil is the sleepy colonial town of Barichara, where the buildings are perfectly painted white with green trim. Walking along the cobblestone streets, listening to the patter of horse hooves, and observing the men donned in cowboy boots and bush knives leaves little to the imagination of how life used to be.

Leticia & Providencia—The most extreme of contrasts is the immense Amazon jungle setting in Leticia with the small, Caribbean island life in Providencia. There's nothing more Colombian about both: in Leticia, you laze around in small villages camped along the Amazon River; in Providencia, you walk or bike your way around, chatting it up with locals. The opportunity to interact with locals abound, and both cities are great ports to further exploration of Latin America. Leticia borders both Brazil and Peru, and Providencia is a very short plane ride to Nicaragua.

Introduction

Say "Colombia" and most people will immediately think of something negative: drugs, guerrilla warfare, corruption, kidnappings or crime. This is hardly surprising, since international press regularly features these facts about Colombia.

In truth, Colombia is one of the most beautiful countries in Latin America, and many places are just as safe to visit as other destinations on the continent. So, if you don't stray too far from the main tourist areas and heed current safety advice, there is no reason why you shouldn't include Colombia in your itinerary. You will be well rewarded if you do. Caribbean beaches, Andean highlands and fertile rainforest claim the highest diversity of flora and fauna on the continent after Brazil, making it a perfect spot for nature lovers. Yet even those places deemed safe and developed for tourism have hardly been touched by outside visitors. It's not, however, just natural wonders that draw the few that come here; good food, great bars and fantastic coffee are a Colombian trademark, while the locals are reputed to be some of the friendliest and most welcoming in the world, and certainly haven't lost their party spirit. Updated: Feb 06, 2008.

Geography

Colombia is virtually all coasts to the west, and all valleys and basins to the east. The northernmost tip of the Andes range mountains, which extend all along the west coast of South America, can be found in Colombia, and they stretch out in three directions known as the Cordillera Occidental, Cordillera Central, and Cordillera Oriental.

The Cordillera Oriental, on the east, varies from short, finite ridges descending into the Amazon basin to summits high enough for snow. The capital city of Bogotá, at an altitude of 2,640 meters (8,661 ft), sits on one of the high basins in this region.

The Cordillera Central offers the highest peak at its northern end, Cristóbal Colón, at 5,776 meters (18,950 ft), and many active volcanoes, including the Tolima at 5,215 meters (17,109 ft). Some valleys here host small communities, but the region overall is unpopulated.

The Cordillera Occidental runs parallel to the Pacific coast and peaks at only 3,048 meters (10,000 ft) while its hills slide into the coasts and through river deposits create thick sediment beds under the waters of the coasts.

The coastal section east of the Panama isthmus is a low-level plain born of sediment deposits, and intermingled with some hills, streaming through various rivers, especially the Magdalena River. This area contains major port cities as Cartagena and Barranquilla.

The territories that border Venezuela, Brazil, Peru, and Ecuador comprise almost two-thirds of Colombia and vary in geography from floodplains and great rivers, along which one will find most of the region's populace, as well as the spurs of the Guiana Highlands. Updated: Jan 15, 2008.

Climate

Colombia has two seasons: wet and dry, though you can experience each more than once in a calendar year depending on where you are. In Bogotá, for example, there are two rainy seasons (from April to June and October to December), while the coastal town of Cartagena typically has one rainy season from May to November. Colombia's temperatures, on the other hand, are generally dictated by altitude, with temperatures in the eastern lowlands among the hottest in South America and temperatures in the Andean range that can fall well below freezing. Temperatures in Cartagena, for example, are what you might expect from a tropical beach town, with highs around 30°C (85°F). Temperatures in Bogotá average around 14°C (57°F). Generally, expect to wear a sweater at night along the coast and a jacket in higher elevations. Also be aware that precipitation tends to be heavier on the Pacific coast and in the Andes, with annual rainfall in excess of 100 inches. Updated: Jan 11, 2008.

Flora and Fauna

Colombia is the second most diverse country in the world in terms of its concentration of flora and fauna species. Indeed, 10 percent of the entire world's species live in Colombia, many of which can be found in Amacayacu National Park. Colombia even has the largest number of land mammals on the planet. This includes such creatures as jaguar, pumas, tapirs, anteaters, sloths, armadillos, monkeys and red deer. There are 456 species total, of which 22 percent are at risk of extinction. The spectacled bear, named for the light fur around its eyes that gives it the appearance of wearing glasses, is currently being challenged. Its habitat is decreasing due to deforestation, and hunters seek these bears to obtain their claws, believed to provide fertility and vigor.

Phot by Mark Hentze

In addition to reptiles and amphibians, Colombia is home to an almost uncountable number of bird species, including toucans, cockatoos, storks, cranes, parrots, vultures and hummingbirds, with the largest being the Andean Condor. Notable as well are the huge Yubarta whales on the Pacific coast and the piranhas in rivers.

Colombia also has over 130,000 species of plants, including 55,000 autochthonous species. Hot and humid regions in the Amazon Basin give rise to high trees and dense vegetation, while drier coastal regions are home to mangroves. Foliage similarly varies according to climate throughout the country.

Unfortunately, with most farm land owned by a handful of citizens, poor farmers must seek new earth to cultivate, which is often the very habitat of at-risk species of plants and animals. The drug war has also contributed to the ecological crisis. Coca, marijuana and poppy growers have escaped into virgin territory to grow their crops. This problem is further exacerbated by the government's plans to develop its economy through using its natural resources, resulting in massive deforestation. Updated: Feb 06, 2008.

History

Pre-Conquest

The geographical area of present-day Colombia has been inhabited for centuries, since at least 10,000 BC. Various cultures came and went, many of them centered in the Magdalena River Valley. At the time of the Spanish conquest, the two most important ethnic groups were the Muisca culture, which was an advanced but small culture near Bogotá, and the Tayrona people on the Caribbean coast.

The Conquest

The Tayrona wasn't able to hold off the Spanish conquest for long, and subsequent revolts by the Tayrona caused the Spanish to almost completely stamp out the group. When Spanish forces under the command of Sebastián de Benalcázar and Gonzalo Jiménez de Quesada arrived in the area in the late 1530s, the Muisca people were feuding. Rival Zipa and Zaque people were fighting over land and salt mines. Because of this division, the Muisca culture was easily divided and conquered. The Muisca, in spite of years of repression, have managed to maintain some of their original culture.

The Colonial Era

By 1549, the strategic location of Colombia had been recognized by Spain, and Santa Fe de Bogotá was named an *audiencia*, which was a sort of legal district with a court. It thus became the most important city in the region, which was then referred to as New Granada. New Granada contained Colombia, Venezuela, Panama and part of Ecuador, and was elevated to the status of Viceroyalty in the early 18th Century. Even when it was raised to the status of Viceroyalty, New Granada was considered something of a backwater place in comparison with the wealthier Lima and Mexico cities.

INTRO & INFO

Independence

Bogotá was one of the first places in the Americas to declare independence from Spain, in July of 1810. The definitive moment for Colombian independence came in August 1819. A large force of Colombians and Venezuelans, and the British Legion of almost 1,000 British and Irish volunteers clashed with royalist forces at the Battle of Boyacá and defeated them.

Gran Colombia

In 1819, the historic Congress of Angostura established the nation of Gran Colombia, which included all of present-day Colombia, Venezuela, Ecuador and Panama, and parts of Brazil, Costa Rica, Peru and Guyana. Gran Colombia was the brainchild of Simón Bolívar, who saw it as the first step to his dream of a united South America that would compete with the United States and Europe as a world power. Unfortunately for Bolívar, communication difficulties and the petty ambitions of local leaders doomed Gran Colombia from the start. By 1831 it had dissolved into the smaller nations that we see on the map today.

The Republican Era

From 1831 to 1863, the new nation was known as the Republic of New Granada. It changed its name in 1863 to The United States of Colombia, and in 1886 it changed once again to The Republic of Colombia, a name it retains to this day. During the 19th Century, the citizens of Colombia fractured into two competing ideologies. The Conservatives believed in a strong central government, limited voting rights for citizens, and strong ties to the Catholic Church. The Liberals were just the opposite. They wanted voting opportunities for all citizens, an absolute division between church and state, and stronger regional government. The Liberals had strong support from the big coffee ranchers, who favored their looser taxes and controls.

The conflict between Conservatives and Liberals would become a long-running and violent one. The first Civil War fought between the two factions was the Thousand Days War in 1899-1902. By some estimates, as many as 100,000 people were killed as Liberal and Conservative armies fought each other all over the nation. Nominally, the Conservatives victored, but in reality the war simply devastated the nation.

The Twentieth Century

In 1902, the U.S. picked up the Panama Canal project abandoned by the French a few years earlier. When Colombia rejected their terms for future administration of the canal, the United States encouraged wealthy Panamenian families to separate from Colombia and backed them up with a war ship. At that time Colombia was still wounded from the Thousand Days War and had little choice. Panama formally became independent from Colombia in November 1903, though Colombia did not officially recognize this until 1921.

El Bogotazo

Tensions between Conservatives and Liberals continued to smolder during the first half of the 20th Century. They erupted once more in 1948, after extremely popular liberal presidential candidate Jorge Eliécer Gaitán was assassinated in Bogotá. Much like other political assassinations, conspiracy theories abound as to the architects of the murder. Among the common "culprits" are the C.I.A., the Soviet Union, Colombian Conservatives and even Fidel Castro, who had a meeting scheduled with Gaitán on the day he was killed.

The city, already swollen with impoverished people from the countryside who saw Gaitán as a savior, went mad. Radio stations urged listeners to take the streets, blaming Mariano Ospina Pérez' Conservative government for the murder. The crowd broke into hardware stores and even police stations looking for weapons. Liberal leaders and the Conservative government tried to work together to stop the violence, which by then had spread to all of Colombia's large cities. By dawn, the city was in ruins, and many institutions and buildings had been burned to the ground. Almost every store in the city had been looted, and informal markets had spring up on the outskirts of the city. All in all, over 3,000 people were killed in the riot, launching the period known as "La Violencia."

La Violencia

Following the murder of Gaitán and the Bogotazo, Colombia descended even further into chaos. The Conservative government clamped down on civil liberties, and every major political entity began forming its own death squads. These squads operated in every city, town and village in Colombia, murdering any and all who disagreed with them. The weapons of choice were clubs, knives and machetes and it was common to find hacked-up bodies in the streets. Institutions such as the press were afraid to speak up against the violence for fear of reprisal, and the church was openly siding with the Conservatives, telling followers to kill Liberals.

By the time La Violencia came to an end around 1958, between 180,000 and 300,000 Colombians had died. This horrific period closed when a military administration was replaced by a moderate compromise government formed by Liberals and Conservatives. In a way, Colombia is still suffering the effects of La Violencia. It was during this time that the FARC, an armed insurgency group still operating in Colombia, formed.

The 1990s to present time

The 1990s brought about a period of relative peace for Colombia. Many of the smaller rebel groups, including the once-feared M-19, laid down their arms in favor of legal change, although other groups (most notably the FARC) remained. With Escobar dead, the cartels lost a lot of their power and fought among themselves. The era was far from utopian as election fraud and government corruption were still present. Since the late 1990s, Colombian leaders have been trying to modernize the economy, crush the drug cartels and improve human rights in Colombia. The U.S. has been a vital partner in their efforts, giving billions of dollars in aid to help destroy the drug lords and the FARC.

Current president Álvaro Uribe has initiated a tough campaign against the drug lords and the FARC. Some accuse him of going too far, and trampling basic human rights in his quest to bring down the criminals and rebels. In early 2008 he ordered a military strike inside of neighboring Ecuador in order to capture rebel members. The raid killed several important FARC leaders but caused an ugly international incident. Updated: Apr 04, 2008.

Political System

Colombia's political structure is divided into executive, judicial, and legislative branches of government, with the latter divided into a Senate and a House of Representatives. Senators are elected via a national ballot, while representatives are elected by their local constituents. Congress convenes twice annually, and the president can summon a special session when necessary. However, unlike the American system, the Colombian president is chosen directly by the electorate, without the intervention of an electoral college. He then serves as both head of state and head of government, overseeing a multi-party representative democracy. There are two high courts in Colombia that serve separate functions. The Constitutional Court interprets the constitution and monitors observance of laws. The Supreme Court consists of 23 judges who are appointed by the legislature for eight-year terms. It's divided into a civil-agrarian chamber, a labor chamber and a penal chamber. The constitution was reformed in 1991 to allow for greater civil liberties, such as divorce and dual citizenship, and, most importantly, the right to request a tribunal if a citizen can provide evidence that his or her constitutional rights are not being honored. Updated: Jan 18, 2008.

Current Political Situation

As with many Latin American countries, Colombia's political history has been one of civil wars, social injustice, corruption, and violence. In the latter half of the 20th Century high-profile kidnappings, right-wing, left-wing, and criminal terrorism have pretty much defined this nation.

The gravest threat to Colombian stability came about through the rise of drug cartels in the 1970s and 1980s. Exploiting the increasingly high demand for cocaine in North America and Europe, their lucrative operations enabled them to bribe and/or coerce police and politicians, as well as ordinary (and usually) poor citizens. They combined their buying-off with barbarity; apart from their own pattern of abductions and violence, they also financed both right-wing paramilitaries and left-wing guerrillas, all in the service of undermining law enforcement.

In 1999, President Andrés Pastrana began Plan Colombia, an aggressive effort to fight the drug trade, along with minor attempts to address the underlying social issues that sustain it. The military facet of the plan

The Legend of Pablo Escobar

Cocaine-legend Pablo Escobar (1949—1993) began his criminal career inauspiciously as a grave robber, ripping up tombstones and re-selling them. Through underworld connections, he soon began smuggling cocaine, a job that proved to be lucrative. A series of conspicuous moves led him to become head honcho of the Medellín Cartel, earning $1 million a day in cocaine money by controlling charter-flight deliveries to the U.S. In the 1980s, Colombia controlled 75-80 percent of the cocaine trade and of that, Escobar's cartel ran the majority of it. Coca soon became the biggest cash crop in Latin America as international cocaine use exploded.

A drug baron worth $3 billion, Escobar's power and fame was widespread. He was fierce and ruled through intimidating, threatening or murdering anyone in his path, be it man, woman or child. Politicians were offered two alternatives: pay-off or death (*plata o plomo*). Despite his corrupt character, El Patrón—as Escobar was also known—won the hearts and minds of Colombia's disenfranchised by financing charity works "a la Robin Hood." He built churches and football fields, quickly winning support from the Catholic Church and the working class.

He is credited with several political assassinations and the bombing of Avianca flight 203. The crash killed several Americans who were on board, spurring D.E.A. involvement in Colombia. In order to stop a law from being passed that would allow narco-traffickers to be extradited, Pablo's men—the M-19—turned a November 6, 1985 Supreme Court meeting into a bloodbath, killing half the senators. The granddaddy of the cocaine industry also created his own political party and was elected to congress, establishing himself as head of a veritable mafia.

Eventually international pressure, primarily from the United States, forced Colombia to bring Escobar down. In 1991 he agreed to go to prison, but only if he could build his own. La Catedral, as the prision came to be known, was part of a deal with the government; in exchange for giving himself up to the authorities, he was granted immunity from extradition to the U.S. When Escobar escaped from his plush, private jail in 1992, government teams, both Colombian and American, joined hands with the vigilante group Los Pepes (People Persecuted by Pablo Escobar) to track him down. The manhunt ended in a shootout between Pablo and a U.S. army contingent on the rooftops of a Medellín neighborhood in 1993.

A Hollywood production of the life and legend of Escobar is expected to debut in 2009 with the title "Killing Pablo," starring Christian Bale. The legend of Pablo is also featured in the 2001 movie "Blow," starring Johnny Depp. Updated: Jan 11, 2008.

1811: On November 11, 1811, the province of Cartagena was the first territory of New Granada to declare independence.

1815: Spanish king Fernando VII orders the reconquest of New Granada and sends 10,000 soldiers under the command of Pablo Morillo. Tired of fighting, the Criollos quickly gave up.

1819: Great Colombia was formed, containing the territories of Venezuela (at which point included modern-day Panama), Colombia and Ecuador.

1832: The end of Great Colombia resulted in the creation of a new country, the Republic of New Granada. The first president of this unitarian republic was Santander.

1853: Once again the Constitution changed, now into a federal regime in which slavery was eliminated and the right to vote was given to men older than 21 years of age.

was backed by the U.S., with money and arms. Plan Colombia, however, failed to effect much change. The next president, Álvaro Uribe, enacted an aggressive hard line against guerrilla groups, which has reduced crime and violence, and in turn produced notable economic growth. However, major social problems such as poverty, illiteracy, class and political polarization remain. Updated: Mar 25, 2008.

The Banana Companies

On November of 1928 a unionized banana worker's strike was put down by the Colombian government in the town of Ciénaga, outside of Santa Marta, on the northern coast. Military forces rolled in and began the most gruesome employee massacre in the history of United Fruit (now known as Chiquita). The government was afraid unions would give way to communism because workers were appealing for eight-hour days, written contracts, the abolition of food coupons (to be spent only in company stores), and no more than six work days per week. The army barricaded the plaza and then proceeded to machine-gun down hundreds of workers from the rooftops.

The Colombian government claimed the violent incident was necessary to avoid an American intervention on behalf of the United Fruit Company's interests. The true number of deaths is unknown, and most figures claim between 47 and 2,000. This was a pivotal event in Colombian politics, which bolstered support for the left.

The history of United Fruit doesn't stop there: Chiquita was fined $25 million upon discovery that it had made 100 monthly payments totaling $1.7 million to the United Self-Defense Forces of Colombia (AUC), a Colombian right-wing terrorist group, between 1997 and 2004. While the company claims the payments were made to protect its workers, union organizers were targeted by the very same groups financed by Chiquita.

Oddly enough, Colombia's Urabá plantation was the most lucrative of all of Chiquita's global properties during the payment period. Additional reports allege that Chiquita boats have carried cocaine and smuggled in machine guns for the AUC. A civil lawsuit filed on behalf of hundreds of Colombian families asserts that Chiquita's payments financed both torture and murder.

Colombia's current Attorney General even demanded that Chiquita executives be extradited and tried for their crimes. The U.S. refused. Updated: Nov 13, 2007.

Economy

Colombia's economy has for decades been among the best in Latin America, thanks in large part to steady agricultural production, a healthy textile industry and a wealth of natural resources. In particular, Colombia is among the world leaders in the production of coffee, petroleum, textiles and flowers, and is South America's leading producer of gold, nickel and coal.

These and other growing sectors have in recent years helped Colombia's economy grow

1886
A new constitution finally cancelled out federalism in the now-called Republic of Colombia. A movement of "regeneration" brought another civil war named Thousand Days Civil War (1899-1902).

1903
Just as Colombians were beginning to recover from the last civil war, came the most traumatizing event of the century for the nation: the separation of Panama, which was encouraged and coordinated by the United States

1921
After a drawn-out negotiation between the U.S. and Colombia, the U.S. finally rectified the 6 of April Treaty, giving Colombia $25 million as indemnification for the loss of Panama.

1928
A worker strike broke out on the Caribbean coast and national armies were sent in to control the over 11,000 United Fruit workers protesting. The army opened fire on the crowd, killing a number of people that was never officially determined. As a result of the scandal, president Miguel Abadía Méndez was voted out of office in 1930.

1948
The murder of presidential candidate Jorge Eliécer Gaitán untied a series of conflicts that lasted until the early 1950s. The period, known as The Violence began that same night with riots in Bogotá that would later on be named El Bogotazo.

by an average of 6.8 percent a year, some two percentage points higher than the Latin American average. President Álvaro Uribe's recent efforts to increase security in Colombia have certainly helped, going a long way in rebuilding trust in the country's economy. As killings and abductions have declined, foreign investment from multinational corporations has soared, flooding Colombia's economy with money and industries geared toward future growth.

Other signs of economic strength abound. Declining inflation and unemployment have improved the country's quality of life, tourism to Colombia has nearly tripled in the last five years, and real estate is once again a stable investment. Taken together, it's not surprising to see once-dangerous or impoverished neighborhoods and districts beginning to turn around.

Yet despite its relative strength in the region, Colombia is still largely dependent on the U.S. In the last five years alone, Colombia has received some $5 billion in U.S. aid, more than all other countries in the world except Iraq, Egypt, Israel and Afghanistan.

Economy: Past and Present

With the emergence of cocaine as a major international commodity, probably no other country in the world has suffered the slings and arrows of outrageous economic fortune as much as Colombia. A country rich in natural resources, Colombia nonetheless suffered from grave economic inequalities among its population. From the very beginning, the majority of the population—people of mestizo and indigenous heritage—experienced the most marginalization in terms of low-wages and few opportunities for advancement.

This conflict between a mostly poor majority and a limited affluent minority had been an ongoing source of political conflict and economic instability, but the new cocaine market brought Colombia to the verge of financial and social chaos in the last few decades. Starting in the late 1960s, when a new global demand for illegal recreational drugs emerged, Colombia stepped up as the producer of the highest quality marijuana and cocaine in the world. Cocaine accounted for 25 percent of all foreign, albeit criminal, revenue.

This new wealth was a boom for the already affluent. Many eagerly laundered these ill-gotten gains into real estate, construction, and other investment ventures. Although the investments provided lucrative jobs, and more marginal benefits for the middle-class and to a lesser extent, the poor, it also wreaked havoc on the overall economy. The influx of foreign currency like the U.S. dollar accelerated inflation. The economy's state resulted in decades of extreme violence that profoundly damaged Colombia's infrastructure. Drug cartels not only had the firepower to wage war on law enforcement and society, they also financed left and right-wing terrorist groups. The unstable climate, which included guerrilla attacks and paramilitary attacks on petroleum drilling operations, discouraged foreign investment.

Despite this, Colombia's economy was remarkably stable and productive in compari-

1953
After five years of civil war, General Gustavo Rojas led a coup d'etat to throw out president Laureano Gómez, and granted amnesty to over 5,000 liberal guerrilla members who, in returnm dropped their weapons.

1958
Rojas' dictatorship, filled with police abuse, media censorship and raw violence, came to an end. After nine years the National Congress was reinstituted. Although The Violence was over, organized guerrilla groups began to develop.

1964
What started as a small communist guerrilla group in 1949 grew stronger despite the national army's efforts. The group came together as the Southern Bloc and then renamed themselves Fuerzas Armadas Revolucionarias de Colombia (FARC).

1974
Liberal presidential candidate Alfonso López Michelsen won the first free election since 1958 by a margin of three million votes.

1983
The newly-elected conservative president Belisario Betancur initiated peace talks with representatives of FARC.

son to that of its Latin neighbors. Colombia had a wealth of organic resources (cacao, coffee, bananas, sugarcane, palm oil, cotton, tobacco, potatoes, beans, grains, fruit and flowers) and minerals (petroleum, coal, natural gas, iron ore, copper, gold, nickel, platinum and emerald). It was committed to a free and open market, which at the time was steadily growing. During the 1980s Colombia was the only Latin country not to default on its international loans.

During the 1970s, in an ambitious attempt to improve the quality of life for Colombia's poor while maintaining a strong economy, President Alfonso López initiated a development plan centered on exports, farming, regional growth and manufacturing. In comparison, a later president, Julio César Turbay, invested public resources in Colombia's energy and mining sector. He focused on improving communication and transportation services, while decentralizing the economy and increasing public works.

However, by 1982 the growing social disorder wrought by the drug trade partly kicked the country into an economic crisis. The crisis forced President Belisario Betancur to issue decrees revising banking and fiscal guidelines to reduce unemployment while promoting economic growth.

In 1990, President César Gaviria Trujillo reduced tariffs, deregulated many private markets, and privatized state-owned industries. Gaviria privatized airports, seaports, power plants, banks and even highways as a means of drawing foreign investors. He actively sought the cooperation of his neighboring states in developing regional trading blocs, and forcefully advocated a hemispheric free-trade zone. Colombia joined the Latin American Integration Association (LAIA), a joint free-trade agreement with Chile and the G-3, which apart from Colombia included Mexico and Venezuela.

Economic Stats:

Unemployment: 11.1% (as of 2006)
Inflation Rate: 4.6% (as of 2006)
GDP Per Capita: $3,246 (as of 2006)
Population below poverty line: 14.7% (as of 2005)
Public Debt: 45.3% of GDP
Chief Agricultural Exports: Colombian coffee, cut flowers, bananas, rice, tobacco, corn, sugar cane, cocoa beans, oilseed, vegetables, forest products, shrimp.
Export Commodities: petroleum, coffee, coal, nickel, emeralds, apparel, bananas, cut flowers.
Main Industries: textiles, food processing, oil, clothing and footwear, beverages, chemicals, cement, gold, coal, emeralds.
Updated: Nov 14, 2007.

With tariffs lowered, Colombia imported soybeans, wheat and corn from the U.S., while continuing to export flowers, coffee, and petroleum, its three most valued goods. Jobs were lost in certain sectors, but this also kept the food prices low, and the economy grew at a rate of 4.5 percent.

A later president, Ernesto Samper, inaugurated more progressive social policies to improve the life of the poor. However, higher public spending expanded the fiscal deficit,

1986
Chief of the Medellín cartel, Pablo Escobar, orders the death of Guillermo Cano, director of the newspaper El Espectador. The event unleashes a war against drug trafficking.

1994
The liberal presidential candidate Ernesto Samper wins the election, and his opponent shows recordings that implicate Samper's campaign to have been funded by drug cartels. The scandal, later dubbed Process 8,000, takes two years to resolve, and after countless investigations, interrogations and many murders, Samper gets off the hook in 1996.

2002
The independent liberal candidate Álvaro Uribe won the presidential election by promising to put military pressure on the biggest guerrilla organization in the country, FARC. The security policy implemented by Uribe kept the public happy.

2004
Governmental data shows that in two years homicides, kidnappings and terrorist attacks in Colombia have decreased by 50 percent. Some thought Uribe a bit authoritarian, since he supported a congressional modification in the constitution to introduce reelection.

2006
Álvaro Uribe was reelected to serve another term until 2010.

which led to a recession and unemployment rose to 20 percent. The following president, Andrés Pastrana Arango, devalued the peso and accepted a $2.7 billion International Monetary Fund loan. The loan was given on the condition that the government use greater spending restraint and restructure spending policies. By the end of 1999 Colombia's total foreign debt was $34.5 billion, and credit rating organizations ranked the country as a poor-risk investment.

The influx of borrowed money, the new austerity policies, and the competitive price of its exports, particularly petroleum, reversed the downward trend of Colombia's economy in the late 1990s. In 2000 the U.S. loaned Colombia $1.3 billion in military aid against the drug cartels and leftist rebels, but right-wing, left-wing, and criminal violence still prevailed in 40 percent of the country.

It was against this background of fear that Álvaro Uribe was elected president in 2002. He promised to restore peace and security. In his first term, defense spending, which included 10,000 new law enforcement officers and 16,000 "peasant soldiers," nearly tripled. American troops were also sent in to guard the country's largest pipeline. The following year, with loans from the World Bank, the Inter-American Development Bank, and the Andean Development Corporation, social spending was raised. The increase necessitated cutting pensions and other social programs in order to moderate the deficit.

These reforms have been enthusiastically praised by financial institutions. Uribe was ultimately able to bring down the public-sector deficit to 1.5 percent of the Gross Domestic Product (GDP). By 2003, GDP growth reached as high as 4 percent, and has continued going up ever since. This, along with increased security, has improved investor and business confidence.

On the downside, a vast number of Colombians still live in extreme poverty—11 million live on less than a dollar a day. Meanwhile, working conditions, particularly in sectors such as mining, are difficult and dangerous. Right-wing paramilitaries have been reported to routinely assassinate men and women who attempt to form worker's unions. While the powerful Medellín and Cali cartels have experienced significant losses in the last 20 years, the very lucrative cocaine trade is still active.

However, overall foreign investment in this South American nation reached record proportions of $5 billion in 2007. Consumer spending among the middle- and upper-classes, improved credit conditions, rising employment, and improved security have created a more optimistic future for Colombia's economy. Updated: Mar 24, 2008.

Language

While Spanish is the official language of Colombia, many of the indigenous languages (there are over 180) are constitutionally recognized as official languages within their respective territories. Bilingual education is mandatory in these territories, however, so most Colombians speak Spanish as either their first or second language. Not all Colombians speak the same, however, as the spoken Spanish varies (sometimes dramatically) from region to region. In Bogotá, for example, people speak what is called the Rolo dialect (also referred to as *cachaco*, meaning educated or refined). Those from northwest Colombia speak with the "hissing S" usually recognized as the Spanish of Spain. Other dialects include Cundiboyacense, which still uses a variant of the archaic language.

If traveling to Colombia, it is recommended that you brush up on your Spanish. English is taught in schools, but not exceptionally well. Most Colombians understand much more English than one might imagine, but relatively few are fluent. Updated: Jan 11, 2008.

Religion

When it comes to religion in Colombia, Roman Catholicism is far and away the most prevalent. Brought from Spain in the early 1500s, Catholicism is popularly thought to have been spread by fear, intimidation and bribery. The truth is a little more complex. While some missionaries relied on such tactics, others, such as Fray Bartolomé de las Casas, were instrumental in the defense of the indigenous and in promoting a religion of love. Either way, Catholicism became firmly established and for centuries was the official religion of Colombia.

By hosting the Medellín Conference in 1968, Colombia also played an important role in the development and dissemination of Liberation Theology, the idea of utilizing the Christian mission to bring justice to the poor. Despite these developments, the Catholic Church in Colombia has seen its influence wane in recent years. In 1973, Colombia officially changed Catholicism from the country's official religion to "the religion of the great majority of Colombians." Perhaps more damning, the Colombian government revoked some of the church's power. In particular, Catholic missionaries no longer possessed greater influence than the government over education and health care in the Colombia's mission territories (land with primarily indigenous populations). The church was forced to surrender any right to censor public university texts and enforce the use of the Catholic doctrine in public schools. For good measure, Colombians were also granted the right to contract civil marriages without renouncing their Catholic faith.

Colombia's government expanded religious tolerance in 1991, when it guaranteed its citizens freedom of religion. Other religions have grown in Colombia as a result (Christian evangelicals and Mormons have made inroads here in recent years), though they still pale in comparison to the reach of Catholicism. According to most polls on the subject, approximately 90 percent of Colombians identify themselves as Catholic.

But signs also point to a decline in Catholic faith. A 2001 poll conducted by one of Colombia's premier newspapers indicated that as many as 60 percent of Colombians did not actively practice their faith, and more recently, Colombia overturned a long-standing law prohibiting some forms of abortion despite opposition from the Catholic Church.

For travelers, religion likely won't affect your visit. Though obviously important in Colombia, religious practice is still largely a personal experience. Updated: Feb 29, 2008.

Culture

Culturally, Colombia is one of the richest countries in South America, integrating three continents worth of tradition in music, dance, painting, sculpture, folk craft and literature.

The first cultures to arise out of this region were from pre-Columbian peoples who, with ancestral roots stretching back to Asia, inhabited the region over 10,000 years ago.

The Spanish conquest brought the florid passions of Catholicism to the region—lavish cathedrals and the iconic image of the martyred, emaciated, bleeding Christ, as well as the Holy Virgin, often adorned with gold-encrusted attire, a crown, and an equally elegant baby Jesus on her arm.

With colonization also came the tradition of secular European painting, literature, and music. The Spanish also imported African slaves, whose own culture mingled with the locals, resulting in such percussion-heavy musical genres of Cumbia, Vallenato, Porro and Champeta. The Carnival of Barranquilla, serves as a large-scale celebration of the many dimensions of Colombian music and dance, and its multi-racial, multi-ethnic roots.

In 1871 Colombia established the Academy of Spanish Language, the very first in South America, and beginning with Simón Bolívar, Colombia has one of the most noteworthy literary traditions on the continent, such as historical chronicles, poetry and fiction.

Gabriel García Márquez, who won the Nobel Prize for literature, is Colombia's most famous writer and an exponent of the modernist "magical realism" genre.

Much of modern Colombian culture—movies, television programs, music—has been strongly influenced by Hollywood, European cinema and American popular music. Singer-songwriter Shakira, from Barranquilla is an international superstar, while another artist, Juanes, from Medellín, is one of the biggest rock stars in Latin America. Meanwhile, Estefano, from Cali, has become famous both for his own music as part of the duo Donato and Estefano, and as a songwriter for such Latin artists as Gloria Estefan, Ricky Martin and Jennifer Lopez. Colombia is also noteworthy for its high number of beauty pageants as well as the highest number of museums of any Latin American country.

Sociologically, Colombia is conservative, with the family of key importance in the lives of its citizens, though it has recently become more liberal in the area of divorce and gay rights. Updated: Jan 29, 2008.

Art

The history of art in Colombia divides into four time periods: pre-Columbian, colonial, post-independence, and modern.

There is evidence of pre-Columbian culture going as far back as 5940 B.C., mostly by the animal, human and geometric designs on pottery dating from that age. However, the scarcity of information makes assessing the meaning of such work a challenge. Later civilizations such as the Taironas and the Muiscas were skilled metallurgists, particularly with gold. Their work—pendants, figurines—was rich with political and religious detail.

However, due to this work being made of gold, much of it was looted on behalf of the Spanish crown, which resulted in Spain melting down many sacred and ceremonial artifacts and sculptures.

After the Spanish conquest, Colombian art was almost entirely church-themed and derived from previous mediaeval, mannerist, and renaissance styles imported from Europe. The native Colombians who were trained in these arts retained some of their own cultural legacy in their work, particularly in the older churches in Colombia, which show elements of indigenous design.

However, at this stage in history, Spanish-born or Spanish-descendent artists prevailed on Colombian soil. The first notable artist, Alonso de Narváez, is known for a legend about a portrait he painted on cloth of the Virgin and child, flanked by two saints. Reportedly the colors quickly faded and the canvas began to rot. After it was put away in storage it was found years later to have become completely restored.

The dominant style during this time was Baroque—emotional to the point of visual melodrama. Baltasar de Figueroa, like Narváez, from Seville, integrated native influences to his European sensibility, and his legacy was continued by his sons.

The most important painter of the colonial era was Gregorio Vázquez de Arce y Ceballos. A prolific painter, his original portrait of the Trinity as a three-faced being (inverting Dante's three-faced Satan from the Divine Comedy) was later condemned as heresy partly due to its resemblance to Hindu idols. The artist responsible for a series of paintings known as the Sopo Archangels is unknown, but the paintings retained are notable for the androgynous nature of their subjects.

The 19th Century republican period, after independence, is considered negligible by most scholars. Some attribute this to Colombia's geography, which kept artists isolated from each other and the world, and thus retarded the evolution of new forms. However, two notable painters in the latter part of the century were Mercedes Delgado Mallarino

CUMBIA

The purest representation of African, indigenous and Spaniard fusion and Colombia's most significant musical art form, cumbia originated in the Caribbean coast as instrumental music created with drums, bagpipes and maracas. The word cumbia is a derivate of the African "cumbé," which means party or celebration.

Cumbia is considered by many as the queen of Afro-Caribbean rhythms, yet to get to what it is today, this musical genre has transcended race, cultural background and social class. During the 1930s cumbia rose from the working classes to the urban high-society of Colombia. It validated itself as an authentic art form and incorporated instruments such as the accordion. Today three types of cumbia prevail: classic cumbia, which is instrumental; modern cumbia, with various drums and animated lyrics; and cumbiamba, differing from cumbia in both musical instruments and dance rituals. With Spanish-inspired clothing (long skirts for women and hats and red handkerchiefs for men), the dancing portion of cumbia is a courtship ritual that follows the beat of African drums with a style of indigenous movement.

The rhythms of cumbia have spread all through Latin America, and countries such as Argentina, Chile, Mexico and Peru have developed a taste for creating and dancing the Colombian sounds. Updated: Jan 15, 2008.

de Martínez, one of the few women artists of the time, and Ricardo Acevedo Bernal, a combination painter, composer, photographer and even diplomat.

Colombia's modern art movement began in 1920, with artists such as Santiago Martínez Delgado and Pedro Nel Gómez, who imported the Mexican muralist movement to their native country. Later artists, such as Ricardo Gómez Campuzano and Carlos Correa revealed the influence of post-impressionism and cubism in their work. The Spanish-born Alejandro Obregón introduced his own expressionist romanticism, influenced by Picasso, and with a heavy environmental, political and sexual focus. Along with Eduardo Ramírez Villamizar, Édgar Negret, Enrique Grau and Fernando Botero, he was considered a member of Colombia's "Big Five" artists. Of these, Fernando Botero is considered the most famous, sharing a celebrity status rivaled only by novelist Gabriel García Márquez and singer Shakira. His "fat subject" sculptures and paintings, often humorous, are sold for millions. Yet he has not shied away from tackling any number of controversial themes, such as criticizing the church and human rights abuses committed by the American government. Updated: Feb 28, 2008.

Museums

Colombia has more museums than any other country in Latin America. You will find ample opportunities to intellectually and spiritually immerse yourself richly into the culture and geography of a region.

Some of the more notable museums in Bogotá include the Colombian National Museum. Now housed in a former prison, this museum, established in 1823, is one of the oldest and biggest museums in all of Latin America. This large and looming edifice, with arches and domes, offers no less than 20,000 collections. Former prison cells display showcases of impressive accomplishments in archaeology, ethnography, history and art. The scope of history covered goes from 10,000 years B.C. to the present, and the scope of culture ranges from European, Afro-Colombian and indigenous.

The most famous museum in this city, however, is the Museo del Oro, sponsored by Colombia's Banco de la República. Offering the largest and most impressive gold metallurgy, Bogotá's Gold Museum is one of the most memorable testaments to South America's early civilization. It includes a golden raft used in ceremonies, and ancient stoneware, shell, wood and textile archeology from the pre-Columbian period.

Other noteworthy institutions here include the Museo de Arte Colonial, the Museo de Arte Moderno, the Museo Iglesia de Santa Clara, a former and breathtakingly beautiful monastery, and the modern, interactive Maloka Museum of science.

Outside of Bogotá, other museums include the Antioquía Museum in Medellín, the second oldest in the country and one of the most important. It serves as the virtual national house gallery for world-famous painter and sculptor Fernando Botero. Over on the Caribbean, Cartagena offers a Naval Museum, a Modern Art Museum, a Museum of the Inquisition, and the San Pedro de Claver Museum, annexed to the church and plaza commemorating a 16th Century Spanish priest who advocated for the human rights of the local population. Updated: Feb 06, 2008.

Music

Melodic and multi-rhythmic, Colombia's musical genres evoke and integrate a multitude of traditions: Spanish, indigenous, African and North American. There was music in Colombia, of course, before the arrival of Spanish conquerors, and the haunting panflute melodies of Andean cultures echo in the more contemporary Bambuco, known as the "music in the interior." Integrating European waltzes set apart the music from the more purely indigenous music in Peru, Ecuador and Bolivia. It is notable for its melancholic mood.

Long popular, it peaked with the public from the 1920s to the 1930s. Pasillo, Guabina and Torbellino are similar blends of folk and European. The Spanish brought not only their tunes, both ecclesiastical and secular, but stringed instruments such as the guitar, violin, cello and bass. Through slavery, they also brought over an African population whose music added a strong element of rhythm.

Hence, Colombia's music evolved in accordance with geography and demography. Cumbia, which along with Vallenato, is Colombia's signature contribution to world music, arose on Colombia's Caribbean coast. The coast was frequently the disembarkation point for imported African slaves, many from Guinea, and Colombia's Cumbia is a variation of that country's own cumbe, from which this genre gets its name.

The Vallenato also developed in Colombia's Atlantic region, but in the valleys which gave the genre its name. A popular legend attributes its beginnings to a musician by the name of Francisco el Hombre who defeated Satan in a contest of musical skills. More probably, it is a derivation of Cumbia that spread through the region by traveling, musically skilled farmers for whom music was both a sole source of entertainment and means of bringing news to other areas.

Like Cumbia, its key components are both a stick and a drum, but the difference here is the addition of an accordion. Flutes, guitars, and other instruments have also been added over time. Another variation of Cumbia, Porro, which originated in such towns as Sucre and Córdoba, is one that blends the "big band" sound of military brass ensembles. Salsa began in Puerto Rico, but, starting in Cali, it became a Colombian genre in its own right. Champeta, popular in Cartagena and elsewhere on the Atlantic coast, is noteworthy because it has remained close to its African roots. However, it has been influenced by such other Caribbean music as Reggae, Mento, and Calypso. Currulao, which originated Colombia's Pacific coast, is also close to its African origins, using marimbas, bass drums and guasas, which are like maracas but tubular.

Música llanera (music of the plains) is a style of music popular along the Colombian/Venezuelan border. It's strong on harp and blends folk, European, and African influences. American rock, pop, funk, soul and rap have all had a tremendous impact during the last few decades. Some of the more famous musicians to emerge include Shakira and Juanes, one of the most popular singer-songwriters in all of Latin America

Dance

With Colombian music, Colombian dance evolved from European and New World traditions, culminating in a variety of unique and colorful styles of movement and dress.

Indeed, one cannot talk about Colombian dance without its accompanying costumes. For most dances, the women are barefoot, wear a short-sleeved blouse, and most importantly, wear a floor-length, multi-pleated, flowing skirt. The skirt edges are gracefully held and swayed by the dancers, both in their pas-de-deux's with their male partners and when it's only women together in a group.

The Bambuco is identified as Colombia's national dance. The music incorporates Andean and African melodies, as well as European waltzes and polkas, but with a ¾ meter. Usually, the music is sung by two voices. There are six varieties of this particular courtship dance. In all variations the groups of pairs move serenely and suggestively, and the men discreetly pursue the women who coquettishly respond. The most famous Colombian dance, as with the most famous Colombian genre of music, is Cumbia. See the Cumbia informational box on p.30.

The Sanjuanero, another courtship dance, is a variation of the Bambuco from Colombia's valley region. In this region the dancers will on occasion extend a scarf between each other as an index of the man's longing to win the object of his affection. Beginning with a series of overtures by the man toward the woman, the dance then proceeds into an ornamental series of turns, with steps backward and sideways, in which the couples come close then pull apart.

The Abozao, from Colombia's Pacific Chocó region, is a more spontaneous dance, with less-defined choreography in which moves are improvised. A group dance featuring many pairs, it can also be a courtship dance. It has a noticeably sensual elements, with the woman teasingly moving her hips, provoking the man to beg for more, which she does not offer.

The Mapalé is Colombia's sexiest dance, as well as its most overtly African, with movements that can be traced directly back to Guinea. It is one in which the woman does indeed respond to the implied proposal in the man's physical movements and gestures. Popular along Colombia's Caribbean coast, the dance is named after a fish in the Magdalena River that flows into the Atlantic, and the dancers perform with a distinctly rippling cadence meant to evoke fish.

Shakira

Whether you're in a sweaty nightclub, a dark bar, a packed bus or a local restaurant, you're likely to hear singer-songwriter Shakira, the most successful Colombian musician of all time. Known for her unique vocals, passionate lyrics and sensual belly-dance moves, Shakira is a global phenomenon.

Born in Barranquilla to parents of Colombian and Lebanese descent, Shakira began her professional singing career at age 13. After creating two commercially unsuccessful albums at a young age, Shakira released "Pies Descalzos" (bare feet) in 1996. Pies Descalzos, which sold over three million copies, featured Shakira's now signature style—a blend of Latin, Arabic and rock influences. Major singles include "Estoy Aquí," "Dónde Estás Corazón?," "Antología," "Pienso en Ti," "Un Poco de Amor," and "Se Quiere, Se Mata." During this time, Shakira also founded the Pies Descalzos Foundation to help impoverished children in Colombia (www.fundacionpiesdescalzos.com). Her 1998 follow-up record, "Dónde Están Los Ladrones?" (Where are the Thieves?), was an even bigger global success. Songs such as "Ciega, Sormuda," "Tu" and especially the heavily Arabic-influenced, Grammy-winning "Ojos Así" led Shakira to the top of the Billboard's Latin album chart, paving the way for her explosion on the American music market.

Upon enlisting Emilio Estefan (Gloria Estefan's husband) as her manager and producer, dying her hair blond and playing up her sex appeal, Shakira moved to Miami to create her first English-language album, "Laundry Service," in 2001. This album was an instant success, entering the American pop charts at number three, and selling over 200,000 copies in the first week. Hugely popular singles from this album include the hip-shaking "Whenever, Wherever," and the soulful "Underneath Your Clothes."

After an extensive tour of Laundry Service, the next few years were spent working on two albums simultaneously. The Spanish-language "Fijacion Oral, Vol. 1," won her a second Grammy Award for Best Latin Rock/Alternative Album, and the English-language "Oral Fixation, Vol. 2.," featuring her immensely popular collaboration with Wyclef Jean, "Hips Don't Lie," shot to the top of the Billboard Hot 100 chart, and became the most played song in pop-radio history during the summer of 2006. Rumor has it that Shakira is currently working on a new album, though no release date has been officially announced.

In this dance, the women often wears a short grass skirt, while the man is always shirtless. Both thrust their hips to a fast beat made of drums, hand claps and a collective vocal chant of "mapaleeé, mapaleeé!"

Other notable dances include the Joropo, which is danced with clogs. The Pasillo, adapted from Austrian waltzes, is faster, and uses more vertiginous gestures and smaller steps (which gives the dance its name). The Bunde is a religious and ceremonial dance that is often performed only by women or only by men. The music is entirely percussive, made up only of hand-slaps, drums, and vocal chants.Updated: Mar 11, 2008.

Theater

For pre-colonial peoples of Colombia, theater served as a religious ceremony celebrating gods and was related to seasons, wars and harvests. On occasions they even incorporated human sacrifices. The arrival of the Spanish introduced western theater to the New World, though apart from opera, romanticism and other European genres, it was mostly religious and pedagogical in nature.

The 19th Century, however, introduced more ambitiously secular and historical themes, especially in the genre brought over from Spain, which focused on the daily lives of the common population. Some of the more notable authors during this time include Luis Vargas Tejada, José María Samper and José María Vergara y Vergara. However, it was not until the early 20th Century that a distinctly Colombian theater came into being through the efforts of Antonio Álvarez Lleras and Luis Enrique Osorio who wrote politically-themed, realistic plays.

They also trained actors, produced theater journals and sponsored companies, all of which laid the foundations for the new direction Colombian theater would take in the years that followed. Indeed, in the period after World War II, Colombian artists felt even more emboldened to tackle ideological themes. European existentialists and the works of Antonin Artaud and Bertolt Brecht influenced Colombian theater. In addition, the events from 1948 to 1955 known as La Violencia ended the popularity of the genteel *costumbrismo* of the previous century.

In Medellín an Experimental Theater of the Institute of Fine Arts questioned the bourgeois values of Colombian culture, exploring issues as racism, class inequality, and historical oppression. It did so in an abstract manner, with characters identified as numbers or symbols as a sign of their dehumanization.

Some theater groups revived elements of pre-Columbian ceremony in theater as a means of honoring the indigenous culture. In addition to Brecht and Artaud, writers and directors imported the vanguard innovations of Stanislavski and Grotowski to Colombian culture. The art was simultaneously more realistic (especially in acting) but more experimental and modernist in its staging.

The success of the Communist revolution in Cuba was yet another notable historical factor in the evolution of Colombian theater. It inspired a generation of university-based young writers, actors and directors, many calling themselves the Nuevo Teatro, to create newer forms of community-based, cooperatively-created theater. It addressed the needs and issues of the people, particularly the poor, minorities and the disenfranchised, and became widely popular.

These works incorporated elements of folklore and revisionist views of history. One of the most popular of these works was the play, "I Took Panama," staged by the Teatro Popular de Bogotá, regarding Colombia's loss of Panama through the interventionist policies of Theodore Roosevelt. However, due to the left-leaning bent of this movement, many of the artists involved had to struggle with government censorship and harassment. Some were dismissed from their university positions, and some theater companies were shut down on charges of subversion.

The 1980s saw a resurgence of more conventionally scripted drama, particularly as paramilitary and cartel violence resulted in a decline in the popularity of activist theater. Argentinean actress Fanny Mikey successfully produced the works of Edward Albee and Neil Simon, and co-founded the Iberoamerican Theater Festival, the largest of its kind in all of South America. It attracted established repertories from all over the world, such as the Royal Shakespeare Company, and in Bogotá, as well as in Medellín, Cali, and Cartagena, a lively theatrical community still thrives. Updated: Feb 13, 2008.

Comedy

Considering the level of chaos in Colombia's history, it would have been impossible for Colombians not to have a sense of humor, but it was not until the arrival of TV in the 1950s that a distinctly Colombian comedy came into being. Shows such as Yo y Tú and Don Chinche used family life as a starting point for satirical barbs aimed at local culture and politics, often burlesquing regional dialects and attitudes.

One innovative program, "Sábados Felices," (Happy Saturdays) offered a showcase for comics from all over Colombia, along with sketches poking fun at local politicians and celebrities. A show called "No Me Lo Cambie" (Don't Change the Channel on Me) integrated bits from European and American shows along with "Candid Camera"-style jokes.

In the 1990s, Jaime Garzón initiated a more sophisticated style of political comedy, combining an opinionated acuity, often at the expense of the government, with a theatrical flair for parodying people from all walks of Colombian life. Unfortunately, his open partisanship played a hand in his death when he was assassinated on August 13, 1999, reportedly by right-wing paramilitaries.

Still, political comedy, as long as it was impartial, continued. In radio Crisanto Alfonso Vargas and Guillermo Díaz Salamanca became enormously successful with their gibes at the state and citizenry. Salamanca, particularly, lauded as the "man of a thousand voices" for his aptitude at imitating public figures in all spheres of prominence. Martín de Francisco and Santiago Moure began in TV and gained notoriety for pushing the boundaries of decorum in their humor, which later moved to radio.

In 2004 comic José Ordóñez occasioned a moment of national pride when he set the Guinness book of world records for the longest duration—65 hours—in telling continuous jokes. However, in the last decade, Colombia's two most notable contributions to world humor have come about in another comic, Andrés López, and a television *telenovela* (soap opera), "Betty la Fea." The latter not only became a massive hit across Latin America, but it inspired no less than 13 remakes in countries such as Greece, Turkey, Russia, India, Mexico, Israel, and of course, the United States, where it is known as "Ugly Betty." The telenovela is about a homely but brainy administrative assistant at a fashion agency who gets her revenge against the more easily appreciated beauties by virtue of her IQ and work ethic.

Andrés López also popularized the American tradition of stand-up and monologue comedy and achieved international renown for his one-man show "The Ball of Letters," a sardonic and observant take on generational and cultural divisions in Colombia.

John Leguizamo is a well-known actor and comedian born in Bogotá but who immigrated to the United States at the age of four. His monologues and shows have poked fun at both Latino culture in the United States as well as the popular stereotypes about Hispanics. Updated: Feb 14, 2008.

Cinema

Colombians have been trying to establish a national film industry virtually since the dawn of the medium itself. Until very recently, their success has been limited. Not only have aspiring producers, writers and directors been faced with Hollywood's domination of the market, Colombian filmmakers were also far behind Mexico and Argentina in creating a niche for themselves as a Latin film industry, even in Colombia.

Shortly after movies were introduced to Colombia at the turn of the 19th Century, the entrepreneurial Di Domenico brothers produced a historical documentary, "The Drama of October the 15th," regarding the Battle of Boyacá. Later they put out a more controversial one about the then-recent assassination of Rafael Uribe Uribe, a key political figure. For the most part, however, cinema was novelty for Colombians well until the 1920s, creative ambition did not go much further than the Lumière-like filming of everyday life.

The first full-length feature film, "María," based on a novel by native author Jorge Isaacs appeared in 1922, and in 1924 "Under the Antioquia Sky" and "The Tragedy of Silence" opened to a generally enthusiastic response. These were followed by "Claws of Gold" in 1926, a critical take on America's intervention in Colombian politics which resulted in the loss of Panama.

These sporadic efforts, however, could not compete with the flood of popular and expensively-produced cinema coming from Hollywood and Germany, and featuring such stars as Charlie Chaplin and Greta Garbo. When sound arrived in 1928, Colombian filmmakers could not afford the costly equipment needed to make their own "talkies," and were thus finished for many years. What was left of the local industry shifted entirely from production to importation.

The year 1941 saw a new beginning with the production of Colombia's first sound film. Shortly thereafter, a Bogotá businessman by the name of Oswaldo Duperly started a production company which, for a few years, made a minor incursion into the Latin market dominated by Mexico and Argentina.

In 1954, screenwriters Luis Buñuel and Salvador Dalí, novelist Gabriel García Márquez, and painter Enrique Grau collaborated on a surrealist short film, "The Blue Lobster." They hoped to manifest a renaissance in Colombian film art, but that did not happen.
In the 1970s, social problems gave rise to an exploitative genre dubbed "pornomisery." Influenced by the popularity of the lurid Mondo Cane "shockumentaries," pornomisery captured some of the worst scenes of poverty and degradation in Colombia, but without any accompanying insight or explanation. Around the same time, however, a new box office tax was instituted in order to subsidize the production of short films. Aspiring filmmakers responded to this eagerly, though few masterpieces resulted.

By the decade's end, the state sponsored a production company, FOCINE. It was a notable boom to a new generation of ambitious

INTRO & INFO

authors and actually resulted in some successes before folding due to mismanagement and an economic crisis.

The last 10 years has seen Colombian cinema recover, in part because of new government measures to finance and promote filmmaking. It is also due in part to the international success of films such as "Our Lady of the Assassins" and "María Full of Grace," which ironically were made by a Frenchman and an American, respectively. However, native filmmakers like Sergio Cabrera, Rodrigo Triana and Victor Gaviria have succeeded both at home and abroad, winning prizes and box office earnings for works that have tackled Colombia's many social problems. Colombia's film festivals in Bogotá and Cartagena are among the most well-regarded in Latin America. Updated: Mar 24, 2008.

Literature

Though for many the notion of Colombian literature immediately brings to mind Gabriel García Márquez and the style of magical realism, the literary movements and authors this country has seen are as diverse as the culture itself. The common denominator of Latin American literature can be clearly defined in Colombian authors from the colonial era, passing through the independence authors, and the styles like *costumbrismo, los nuevos, el nadaísmo* and the boom generation.

Colonial literature in Colombia was heavily influenced by religion, since only religious men were educated in the art of writing. Also, it would have been difficult to publish stories of heroes who weren't saints because the church controlled printing. By the time the people of Colombia began fighting for independence, the political discourse became the spark that ignited the fire of patriotic poetry and a general search for a national identity in narration. Antonio Nariño, a republican journalist known as the father of political journalism in Colombia, was a key figure in the literature that lead up to independence. After July 20, 1810, Nariño funded the political newspaper La Bagadela, an outlet for his centralist discourse that served him to later get elected president of Cundinamarca.

The second half of the 19th Century and the beginning of the 20th Century saw the style known as costumbrismo emerged and become the first defined mark of what we know today as Colombian literature. Costumbrismo concentrated on narrating real characters in society as a way of defining the culture and its people. The critical style acquired during the independence era continued in costumbrismo. In fact, it has continued to question quotidian rules and government throughout published pages of every literary era.

The poet Gregorio Gutiérrez Gonzáles (known as the man of the three Gs) is a particularly good example of costumbrismo, as his descriptions of romantic style gave details of everyday family life and exposed the melancholy and love of common places. León de Greiff, Luis Vidales and Tomás Carrasquilla were some of the best writers in the 1920s who belong to the literary movement referred to as *los nuevos* (the new). The style shared by this group consisted in a hidden romanticism and a negation of the past. The ugly was emphasized and the narrations were often dark and mysterious. De Greiff was the best known bohemian. His work was heavily criticized due to his constant experimentation with form, style and vocabulary. He was awarded the National Prize for Poetry in 1970.

The movement funded by Gonzálo Arango, a bohemian journalist, came to be the trend of the 1950s. Nadaísmo adhered itself to existentialist and nihilist principles. Before Arango, Fernando Gonzáles Ochoa produced the first writings that would later be catalogued as Nadaístas, as Arango was a disciple of Ochoa. Considered one of the greatest Colombian thinkers of all times, Ochoa spent his life developing original philosophies and artistic works. Though he was nominated for a Nobel Prize of Literature in 1995, he did not win the recognition. In 2006, however, Colombian president Álvaro Uribe Vélez approved a law in which the nation would remember the life and works of Ochoa and declared his house, la Casa Museo Otraparte, a cultural landmark. With the boom generation came the acclaimed Gabriel García Márquez, who achieved world admiration and the 1982 Nobel Prize for Literature with his novel "Cien Años de Soledad." Needless to say this movement advanced Colombian literature to the top of the list. However, it was followed by a generation of pessimistic authors for some years before the contemporary authors took back the characteristic commonplace descriptions and magical realism of today's publications. Updated: May 20, 2008.

Social Issues

Despite Colombia's wealth of natural resources, geographical position and advantageous climate, historical circumstances have bequeathed this Andean nation a malignant multitude of tragic social problems: high unemployment, housing shortage, malnutrition and hunger, high rates of infant mortality and abandoned children, widespread poverty, pervasive alcoholism and drug abuse, widespread juvenile delinquency, high rates of crime and violence, human rights abuses, entrenched and violently polarized guerilla factions, and inadequate health and education services.

The roots of these problems can be traced back to the legacy of Spanish colonialism and imperialism. Even after Colombia's independence from Spain, Colombia did not establish a political and social structure for the benefit of all of its citizens, but instead only for the very limited, mostly Spanish-descendent class. The effect of such institution-

Refugees of the War on Drugs

Approximately three million people have been displaced in Colombia over the last 40 years. Fifteen thousand others have disappeared and three thousand have been found in communal graves by authorities. While the rest of the world makes "recreational" use of the white powder, this country is chained to the agriculture, production, negotiation and power struggle that comes as the result of being the provider of over 80 percent of the world's cocaine.

The war in Colombia, though fueled by narcotics, is not a war on drugs, nor does it affect the substantial drug trade in the country, which accounts for almost three percent of Colombia's GDP. Confrontation between FARC guerrillas and paramilitary forces—backed by the national army and international forces—have turned Colombia into their battlefield and used civilians as tools of extortion, terror and income. Surprisingly, the paramilitaries are causing the biggest hardship on civilians. The Human Rights Watch reports paramilitary forces are responsible for 78 percent of human rights violations in Colombia, and police authorities say between 1982 and 2005 paramilitaries—who joined in a consolidated organization in 1997 called United Self-Defense Forces of Colombia, or AUC—conducted over 3,500 massacres and robbed over six million hectares of land from farmers in different areas of the country.

From 2003 until 2006, 35,353 members of the AUC were demobilized. However paramilitary groups and delinquent activities have not ceased. Today it is estimated that approximately three thousand Colombians take part in emerging groups.

Colombia has the highest number of displaced population in the world, with a significant number of refugees in its neighboring countries, Ecuador and Venezuela. In the south, Ecuadorian ONGs have adopted different strategies to handle the large amounts of Colombian families crossing the borders. As the numbers of immigrants increased from 1999, Ecuadorian organizations have periodically consulted civilians from both nations in forums and seminars.

Venezuela has also seen a significant number of refugees come in at the border, however, they have not always been received with open arms. In 1999, Human Rights Watch sent a letter to Venezuelan president, Hugo Chávez, expressing concern with the way a number of Colombian refugees were transported back to their homeland forcefully, even though there was still eminent danger from paramilitary forces circulating the area.

On February 4, 2008, thousands of people in cities across the globe put on "Colombia soy yo" (I am Colombia) T-shirts and marched for peace in the country and against the FARC. Parting from that initiative, another walk was organized for March 6 to support and remember all of the victims and refugees of the war on drugs. Economic aid is constantly passed on by world powers to ameliorate the situation of displaced Colombian families all over the world. Updated: Mar 03, 2008.

alized inequality has proven to be disastrous for the overall quality of life for Colombia's citizens. Ironically, this includes its wealthiest, who have to live in fear of being kidnapped or murdered.

In the years following World War II, the situation was exacerbated by two major factors: the new market for cocaine, and the Cold War. The U.S. and the Soviet Union subsidized opposing and often violent ideological factions in Colombia, both of whom used the other as an excuse for committing atrocities on innocent civilians. Extremists on both the right and the left also accepted funding and arms from the highly lucrative cocaine trade. The trade had an investment in undermining any form of social order which interfered with its traffic.

Colombia's rural poor, in particular, have experienced the brunt of suffering. They are often the target of extreme violence and having their territory appropriated and/or pillaged by wealthy landowners and multinational interests. For example, the Chiquita Banana corporation was exposed for subsidizing paramilitaries near their plantations, for "protection" and repressing attempts by Chiquita's low-paid workers to form unions. Guerilla warfare, paramilitaries and the narcotics trade are additional factors resulting in the displacement of millions of refugees. Many have fled to the overcrowded cities, or more frequently, left to other countries. Many go to Ecuador in search of safety and better opportunities. Women compromise 55 percent of internal refugees, and are often at high risk of sexual violence and unwanted pregnancies.
The Colombian government's response to this crisis has been criticized as being inadequate. Its Ministry of Agriculture became the subject of heated criticism when 17,000 hectares of farm land originally designated for displaced rural citizenry was to be handed over to large business interests, a plan which was eventually abandoned.

While 93 percent of Colombians over the age of 15 can read and write, education in the rural provinces is often inadequate, with poorly qualified and underpaid teachers offering only the basics of primary school, with no vocational or higher education opportunities.
During the 1990s, Colombia led the world in kidnapping rates, and was almost as high in murder rates, particularly in its cities. However, even though violence and crime still exist, it has declined in the last 10 years, due in part to the decline in the power of drug cartels and the government's hardline stance. Furthermore, in the last few years, Colombia's GDP growth has been constant, unemployment has not risen, and rates of poverty, including rates of extreme poverty, have dropped several percentage points. All this has attracted increasing national and international investments. Updated: Feb 20, 2008.

Environmental Issues

Colombia has one of the richest ecosystems in the world. The country is roughly 51 percent rainforest, and 68 percent forest in total, producing a significant amount of the Earth's oxygen. A UNESCO study ranks Colombia at number four in the world with regards to water reserves per area unit.

Unfortunately, widespread poverty, greed and corruption have taken their toll on this paradise. Deforestation, soil erosion, pesticides and the contamination wrought by inadequately monitored drilling and mining have imperiled many of its native species. The Colombian grebe and the Caribbean monk seal have already become extinct. Another 114 creatures and 429 plant species are currently at risk. This is partly a consequence of up to 600,000 hectares (1482.632 acres) of forest that have disappeared each year for the last several decades.

By the early 1990's, out of 194 countries in the world, Colombia ranked 43rd in industrial carbon emissions, totaling 63.3 million metric tons by 1996, not including vehicle emissions. While drinkable water is available to 99 percent of city residents, only 70 percent of the rural populace enjoys this privilege.

An environmental consciousness has emerged in Colombia, but it has been slow to evolve, and has been hampered by political and economic turbulence. By 1959, the government had passed measures protecting forests and the Pacific coast. In 1969 the Institute for Development of Renewable Natural Resources and the Environment (INDERENA) was established with the intention of training government employees working in conservation, forestry, and fishing. In 1973 saw the National Resources and Environment Code was created. In 1982, the Colombia Sanitary Code instituted pollution control standards.

However, though the government has set aside nine percent of the country as protected national park territory, effective safeguarding of the land has been hindered by the exhaustion of law enforcement in fighting drug trafficking, which in itself has contributed heavily to ecological damage through the chemicals used in the manufacture of cocaine, as well as the retaliatory fumigation of coca crops by the government.

Some of the private environmental groups that have emerged in the last few decades include Ecofondo, Censat Agua Viva and Semillas. These organizations often work with or alongside international environmental organizations such as Greenpeace and the World Wildlife Fund, as well as with non-environmental organizations such as the Centre for Indigenous Cooperation, in advising rural communities who often engage in illegal logging as a means of survival, in cultivating environmental awareness.

In 2006 the Colombian government adopted a controversial General Forestry Law, whose intent is to provide state support for commercial logging in areas of Colombia that are not officially authorized as protected regions. The administration of President Álvaro Uribe argued that such a measure was necessary to stimulate employment and economic growth. Opponents argued that the bill received was backed by multinational corporations, such as the paper and pulp manufacturer Smurfit Carton, and that the communities (mostly indigenous and Afro-Colombian) who live in the areas most impacted by the law were not consulted. Surprisingly, a joint 2008 Yale/Columbia University study placed Colombia

Holidays and Festivals

January 1: New Year's Day

January 6: Epiphany

Carnaval: Although Carnaval is widely celebrated in all Latin America, make a point to celebrate the fiesta in Barranquilla, Colombia. The Carnaval de Barranquilla is the most important in Colombia and possibly the second most important in all South America, after that in Brazil. Pre-celebration can start as early as the second weekend in January, but the actual celebration goes for four days, from Saturday to the eve of Ash Wednesday. Expect to see colorful costumes, huge parades and folk dancing to regional music.

Semana Santa: Semana Santa (Easter/Holy Week) is celebrated all over Colombia but Popayán is especially famous for its colonial celebration.

May 26: Corpus Christi

May 1: Labor Day

June: Fiestas de San Juan and San Pedro— toward the end of June, Colombians celebrate old traditions.

July 20: Independence Day

August 7: Batalla de Boyaca. This day marks one of the most important battles in the fight for independence.

August 15: Asunción de la Virgen María

October 12: Columbus Day

November: First Monday marks All Saints' Day.

November 17: Independence of Cartagena.

December 8: Day of the Candles. Families all over Colombia light candles to put in windows and outside doors to light the path for miles and miles.

Christmas: Most Colombians get together with their families to start celebrating Christmas on the 24th December with a large dinner. The night is filled with food, drinks, music and dancing until midnight when family members share gifts. On the morning of the 25th children open presents delivered overnight by "el niño Dios." The family celebration lasts at least four days but usually goes on until New Year's Eve.

December 28: Fools' Day. Similar to April Fool's Day in the U.S., be careful not to be tricked. News stations also participate in the holiday and create humorous specials.

December 31: New Year's Eve. This fiesta may be even more spectacular than Christmas Eve dinner. Families gather to drink aguardiente or rum, dance, and celebrate the coming of a new year. In some regions, families make a doll out of old cloth and some sort of flammable material. At midnight, when everyone is hugging and cheering, they light the doll on fire to say goodbye to the past year.

among the world's top 10 countries in terms of management of natural resources and pollution control. Updated: Feb 15, 2008.

Visas

Residents of Latin American countries, the U.S., Canada, Western Europe, and several others in Asia and the Middle East (a total of 69 nations around the world) do not need a tourist visa to enter Colombia. When a resident of the aforementioned nations comes to Colombia, an immigration officer will stamp an entry seal in their passport which will say how many days the person is allowed to stay. Although the maximum amount of days for a tourist to visit Colombia is 90, the officer generally will stamp 30 or 60 days, so be sure to ask for more if you need it. For residents of nations who do need a tourist visa (check with the local Colombian consulate) the most important thing to know is that your visa will take approximately 15 days to process. You will need three passport pictures, a valid passport, a filled application form, a photocopy of your passport, bank statement, round-trip ticket and information on the place where you plan to stay. An appointment and a $40 fee will complete the transaction. Please note that while usual visa requirements have been detailed below, it is essential that you check on the details with your closest consulate, as requirements change frequently and can vary from place to place.

Business Visa

To conduct business in Colombia or perform marketing studies, it is necessary to apply for a business visa, which can last for a maximum of three years. The visa does not allow the business person to live in the country, thus every visit should last no longer than six months. In order to apply for this visa, applicants will need three passport pictures, a valid passport, a filled application form, a photocopy of the passport, and a letter from the company the person works for describing the operations its employee will carry out in Colombia or a letter from the applicant if he or she is self employed explaining the purpose of the visit.

If these last two options don't apply to your situation, then the letter must come from the Colombian entity—private of public—inviting you, as they will be responsible for your stay. Lastly, you must present a certificate of incorporation and legal representation issued no more than three months previously. Note that the letter and the certificate you present must be notarized and certified from the secretary of the state where it was issued.

Independent business people must show a non-refundable round-trip ticket and bank statements for the three months previous to the visa application date. Though the applicant must go to a consulate for the request, the visa takes about three working days to come through for U.S. citizens and it can take up to two weeks for other nationalities. The cost of application for a business visa is $150, and it is necessary to make an appointment at the consulate.

Work Visa

To be eligible for a Colombian work visa, an applicant must meet one of the following criteria: be employed by a Colombian company; work in Colombia under an academic agreement between countries; get transferred by a multinational to a Colombian subsidiary; get hired by a news agency to as a correspondent in Colombia; participate in an artistic or cultural group coming for a performance or work as a volunteer or missioner for a religious organization.

For any of these circumstances, the applicant needs three passport pictures, a valid passport, a filled application form, a photocopy of passport, a letter of the company that is employing the applicant, a certificate of incorporation and legal representation issued no more than three months previous, a certificate of proportionality, which must be issued by the Ministry of Work and Social Security of Colombia, proof that the applicant is qualified for the position (diplomas, licenses or certificates), and a police report translated into Spanish. The cost to apply for a work visa is $205; the applicant must make an appointment at the nearest consulate for the request.

Student Visa

The student visa can be requested by someone planning to attend a private or public educational organization recognized by the national government. The applicant must sustain a minimum of 10 hours per week schedule in the institution to be eligible for the visa. It is also possible to ask for a student visa if you are completing an internship as part of an academic program or if you are participating in an exchange program recognized by the government.

A student visa in Colombia lasts for a maximum time of one year, however, one may renew the visa as many times as needed to complete an educational program, after which, if the person intends to stay in Colombia, the visa can be exchanged for another of a category that applies. To apply, you need a valid passport, a filled form, three passport photos, an authorization from parents or legal guardians (if applicant is under 18), a medical certificate stating the physical and mental health of the applicant, a certificate of acceptance from the Colombian educational institute the applicant is planning to attend, and certificates of economic solvency from parents or person who will be responsible for the expenses of the applicant.

Before You Go

Colombia can be a tumultuous country, therefore it is recommendable to check news updates on political and guerrilla situations and make sure the areas you are visiting are safe. Pack a small first aid kit with any medicine you take on a regular basis, plus some anti-diarrhea pills, aspirin, insect repellent and sunscreen. Most of these items are available in cities all around Colombia, however, if you prefer or require a certain type or brand–hypoallergenic, for example–it is best to bring it from home than to risk not finding what you want.

Insurance

Call your health insurance before you leave so you know what your coverage is like in other countries, and make sure to bring a copy of your insurance card. Insurance companies recommend taking written records of any medical conditions and proper names of any medication you are taking, plus a prescription just in case.

Maps

Buying maps in Colombia can be a difficult process and some suppliers provide out-of -date copies. The best source of maps is the Instituto Geográfico Agustín Codazzi. Oficina Sede Central Bogotá. Carrera 30, 48-51. Tel: 1-368-3443, Website: www.igac.gov.co, E-mail: cig@igac.gov.co. Open Monday-Friday 8.00 a.m.–4.30 p.m. Here you can obtain copies of a variety of national, departmental, regional and city maps ranging from $2-5 per sheet.

It is always worth visiting the local tourist information center and asking in your hotel or hostel if they have, or know where best to obtain, local maps. Most Colombian cities are structured around the grid system thus making it relatively easy to find your way around. Updated: Apr 10, 2008.

Getting To and Away from Colombia

Entering Colombia is not a difficult transition. A valid passport—for some a visa—and a return ticket to wherever you came from will be enough to get you inside. To ensure your departure is as trouble-free as the entry, keep the custom form you'll be given when you come in with your passport, it will save you some money on the departure fee.

Plane

The only international Colombian airline is Avianca, which is also the biggest operator for domestic flights. Other airlines, however, like Continental Airlines, American Airlines, Mexicana de Aviación and Aerolienas Argentinas frequently go to Colombia. Main airports include El Dorado in Bogotá, Rafael Núñez in Cartagena, José María Córdova in Medellín, Alfonso Bonilla Aragón in Cali and Ernesto Cortissoz in Barranquilla. Traveling inside of Colombia by plane is a comfortable and safe way to arriving at all your destinations, though you could be sacrificing landscape views.

Departure Tax

Before you can begin your return home you must pay a tax of US$30 for international flights, if you visited for 60 days or less. If you stayed longer, the fee is $50, which can be paid in dollars or pesos, but not by credit card. Updated: May 20, 2008.

Getting Around

Air

Flights are expensive in Colombia. Taxes on ticket sales are high, accounting for about 30% of the price. The major domestic carriers are:

AeroRepública ► www.aerorepublica.com
Aires ► www.aires.aero
Avianca ► www.avianca.com
Satena ► www.satena.com

Embassies in Colombia

Argentina

Bogotá: Avenida 40A, 13-09, 16th floor. Tel: 1-288-0900, Fax: 1-288-8868, E-mail: embargentina@etb.net.co.

Bolivia

Bogotá: Transversal, 118A–26, Santa Barbara Neighborhood. Tel: 1-629-8252, Fax: 1-619-4940, E-mail: embolivia-bogota@rree.gov.bo, ebolivia@elsitio.net.co.

Brazil

Bogotá: Calle 93, 14-20, 8th floor. Tel: 1-218-0800, Fax: 1-218-8393, URL: www.brasil.org.co.

Canada

Bogotá: Carrera 7, 115-33, 14th Floor. Tel: 1-657-9800, Fax: 1-657-9912, E-mail: bgota@international.gc.ca, URL: www.dfait-maeci.gc.ca/colombia/menu-es.asp.

Chile

Bogotá: Calle 100, 11B-44. Tel: 1-620-6613, Fax: 1-619-3863, E-mail: embajadadechile@colomsat.net.co. URL: www.embajadadechile.com.co.

China

Bogotá: Carrera 16, 98-30. Tel: 1-622-3215, Fax: 1-622-3114, E-mail: embchina@andinet.com, embchina@uol.com.co.

Costa Rica

Bogotá: Calle 103, 16-60. Tel: 1-636-2681, Fax: 1-636-1803, E-mail: embacosta@andinet.com, URL: www.embajadacostarica.netfirms.com.

Cuba

Bogotá: Carrera 9, 92-54. Tel: 1-257-3353. Fax: 1-611-4382.

Dominican Republic

Bogotá: Calle 100, 19-61, office 402. Tel: 1-635-3627, Fax: 1-635-3884, E-mail: embajado@cable.net.co.

Finland

Bogotá: Calle 116, 13-35. Tel: 1-213-2762, Fax: 1-213-2762.

France

Bogotá: Carrera 11, 93–12. Tel: 1-638-1400, Fax: 1-638-1555.

Germany

Bogotá: Carrera 69, 25B-44, 7th floor. Tel: 1-423-2600, Fax: 1-429-3145, E-mail: info@bogota.diplo.de, URL: www.auswaertiges-amt.de.

Guatemala

Bogotá: Calle 87, 20-27, office 302. Tel: 1-636-1724, E-mail: embcolombia@minex.gob.gt.

Honduras

Bogotá: Calle 121, 13A-59. Tel: 1-215-4259. Fax: 1-313-2301, E-mail: emhondcol@.andinet.lat.net.

Israel

Bogotá: Calle 35, 7-25, 14th floor. Tel: 1-327-7500, Fax: 1-327-7555, E-mail: info@bogota.mfa.gov.il, URL: www.bogota.mfa.gov.il.

Italy

Bogotá: Calle 93 B, 9-92. Tel: 1-218-6604, Fax: 1-610-5886, E-mail: ambitbog@inter.net.co.

Japan

Bogotá: Carrera 7, 71-21, Torre B, 11th floor. Tel: 1-317-5001, Fax: 1-317-5007, E-mail: emb.japon@etb.net.co, URL: www.colombia.emb-japan.go.jp.

Korea

Bogotá: Calle 94, 9-39. Tel: 1-616-7200, Fax: 1-610-0338, E-mail embacorea@mofat.go.kr.

Lithuania

Bogotá: Carrera 9, 74-08, office 805. Tel: 310-310-2660, Fax: 310-235-0757, E-mail: gkatilius@cable.net.co.

Mexico

Bogotá: Calle 114, 9-01 Torre A Oficina 204, Santa Ana Neighborhood. Tel: 1-629-4989, Fax: 1-629-5121, E-mail: emcolmex@cable.net.co, URL: www.sre.gob.mx/colombia.

Netherlands

Bogotá: Carrera 13, 93-40, 5th floor. Tel: 1-638-4200, Fax: 1-623-3020, E-mail: nlgovbog@etb.net.co,URL: www.mfa.nl/bog.

Panama

Bogotá: Calle 92, 7 A-40. Tel: 1-257-4452, Fax: 571-257-5067, E-mail: empanamacolombia@yahoo.com.

Peru

Bogotá: Calle 80A, 6-50. Tel: 1-249-8581, E-mail: lbogota@cable.net.co, URL: www.embajadadelperu.org.co.

Russia

Bogotá: Carrera 4, 75-02. Tel: 1-212-1881, Fax: 1-210-4694, E-mail: embajadarusia@cable.net.co, URL: www.colombia.mid.ru.

Spain

Bogotá: Calle 92, 12-68. Tel: 1-621-0809, E-mail: embespco@correo.mae.es.

Sweden

Bogotá: Calle 72, 5-83 9th floor, Edificio Avenida de Chile. Tel: 1-325-2165, Fax: 1-325-2166, E-mail: embswbog@col-online.com.

Switzerland

Bogotá: Carrera 9, 74-08, office 1101. Tel: 1-349-7230, Fax: 1-349-7195, E-mail: vertretung@bog.rep.admin.ch, URL: www.eda.admin.ch/bogota.

United Kingdom

Bogotá: Torre Propaganda Sancho, Calle 98, 9-03 4th floor. Tel: 1-317-6690, Fax: 1-317-6265, E-mail: britain@cable.net.co.

United States of America

Bogotá: Calle 24, 48-50. Tel: 1-315-0811, Fax: 1-315-2197, URL: www.usembassy.state.gov/bogota.

Uruguay

Bogotá: Carrera 9, 80-15, 11th floor. Tel: 1-235-2968, Fax: 1-248-3734, E-mail: urucolom@etb.net.co.

Venezuela

Bogotá: Carrera 11, 87-51, 5th floor. Tel: 1-640-1213, Fax: 1-640-1242, E-mail: evenezu3@gaitana.interred.net.co. Updated: May 21, 2008.

Bus

Colombian buses are some of the best in South America. Often, companies will have several levels of service, from *corriente* (average) to *lujo* (luxury). Bus terminals will display the safety record of all carriers, with the monthly and yearly accident, injury and death figures. Many companies issue baggage claim tickets.

By law, bus outfits have a maximum fare they can charge during the high season. In the low season there are substantial reductions, particularly with buses to or from Caribbean coast destinations. The trick is to arrive some 10 or 15 minutes before the bus leaves, and when told the price of the fare, ask (ever so sweetly) for a discount. Colombians also recommend talking directly with the driver about a cheaper rate.

At holidays, you may have to reserve your ticket at least several days in advance; some companies have online reservations, requiring a credit card. Websites for the major lines are:

Berlinas ► www.berlinasdelfonce.com
Bolivariano ► www.bolivariano.com.co
Brasilia ► www.expresobrasilia.com
Coomotor ► www.coomotor.com.co
Copetrán ► www.copetran.com.co
Flota Magdalena ► www.magdalena.com.co

As far as traveling at night, in the past Colombians would either advise against it or at least say it's a risk. These days highways are heavily patrolled by the Colombia military and the only persons likely to be stopping your bus in the middle of the night are young regimented soldiers. Colombians now feel more confident traveling after dark. Still in some parts of the country, companies are not running buses between dusk and dawn due to safety concerns.

Train

Most trains in Colombia are now tourist-oriented and run only on weekends and holidays. The La Sabana steam train chugs from Bogotá to Zipaquirá. Cali has a variety of tourist trains: the Tren Turístico Azúcar y Café and the Tren Rumbero. The Tren Ecoturístico de las Flores rattles and sways from Barranquilla to Las Bocas de Cenizas at the mouth of the Magdalena River. See under the principal cities for more information on schedules and fares. The much-ballyhooed Ruta de Maconda, from Santa Marta to Aracataca, is presently on hold until the Magdalena Department government can assure clearance of the tracks.

The only normal passenger service still in operation is the Barrancabermeja-Puerto Berrío twice-daily train. Residents of San Cipriano near Cali are running a small operation to maintain contact with the outside world.

Taxi

Not all cities enforce the use of taxi meters, so whether you catch a cab with or without it, check fares with your hostel concierge before going out. If the cab has no meter, negotiate a price with the driver before boarding the cab. Although more expensive, ask your hotel to phone for a taxi to the station or airport instead of trying to hail one on the street. Use licensed taxis. Do not enter one if someone else is in it. Keep your baggage with you. To borders, collective taxis (*collectivos*, or *por puesto* in cities neighboring Venezuela) are the norm. For short jaunts around town, mototaxis are cheaper.

Car or Motorcycle

In Colombia gas prices are on average $3.50 per gallon. For both car and motorcycle travelers, an international drivers license and insurance are obligatory, as is vehicle registration. Highways in general are in excellent condition. Motorcycles do not pay tolls. Night driving and riding are not recommended.

Check with DIAN (the customs office) for the latest procedures for entering and exiting Colombia with your own vehicle. Cars pay a tax, motorcycles do not. When you leave the country, turn in the permit document. Although DIAN might not ask motorcyclists for proof of insurance, if you are stopped you could be asked to show your proof of insurance.

A recommended website for those traveling in their own vehicle is www.liveyourdreams.com, which even has information on vehicle shipping from South to Central America.

Motorcyclists can get their bikes from Central America to Colombia in several ways:

- Some bikers join together to share shipping by private sailboat from Portobello, Panama to Cartagena, but there is no insurance or warranty. The sea can be rough with big waves. The cost for both you and your bike is $500.

- Cargo ship is another option, but captains don't like to take passengers along.

- You can ship your motorcycle by cargo airlines to Bogotá (drain gasoline and disconnect battery; $550) and travel yourself by passenger plane ($296). With this option, your bike is insured.

Motorcyclists must purchase a reflective vest with their license plate number emblazoned on it, as well as have the number put on the back of their helmets (cost for both comes to $8 in any given shop). Helmet use is mandatory by law for both rider & passenger. If you have to order parts from overseas, it can take 45 days or more. Most foreigners take off-road bikes because parts are easier to find. Bogotá has several small part shops where you can get just about anything you might need. Accommodations that accept motorcycles are common (free parking), especially in small towns. A few, like Casa Kiwi in Medellín, give a discount to motorcyclists.

Boat

The most popular routes for crossing from Colombia to Panama are by sailboat out of Cartagena or by *chalupa* (barge) along the North Coast from Turbo to Puerto Obaldía, Panama. Other launches run along the Pacific coast, though this is a less-taken route due to the nation's civil war.

River travel is the norm in the Amazon, whether heading to other Colombian villages or traveling downstream to Manaus, Brazil, or upstream to Iquitos, Peru. It is also possible to navigate rivers from Colombia to Venezuela; even though these are now heavily patrolled by Colombian military. Accessing the waterways' ports is difficult, as the roads pass through the war zone.

If you are sailing on your own to Colombia, the major Caribbean Sea ports—Cartagena, Barranquilla and Santa Marta—all have marinas. You can also drop anchor in such places as Taganga, Riohacha or Cabo de Vela.

Bike

Bicycling is quite common in Colombia. Even small villages have repair shops. Most bicyclists advise to stay on the main roads, avoid going into jungle areas and don't travel at night. All admit the biggest security issue is not with factions of the country's civil war, but with ordinary theft. Remember Colombia has three mountain ranges with passes of up to 4,000 meters (13,129 feet). Many cyclists have their own websites detailing their adventures: www.roundtheworldbybike.com/reports_americas.asp, www.rideforclimate.com/journals, www.bicicletos.com, www.pedaleandoelglobo.com.

Fun Facts

- Colombia borders **Brazil, Venezuela, Panama, Peru, and Ecuador.**
- Total landmass of Colombia is roughly **1,140,000 square kilometers**, which is slightly less than twice the size of Texas or France.
- Highest point: **Pico Cristóbal Colón**, 5,775m (note: nearby Pico Simón Bolívar has the same elevation).
- Colombia is the **oldest democracy** in Latin America.
- Colombia is the world's third-leading producer of **women's lingerie.**
- Experts believe there are 14,000 species of **butterflies** in the world: about 3,000 of them are found in Colombia.
- Colombia has the world's greatest diversity of **orchid species** (3,500) and birds (1,754 species). It also takes second place for amphibians and third for reptiles.
- Ninety-five percent of the world's **emeralds** come from Colombia.
- There are **32** departments (states) in Colombia.
- Colombian María Isabel Urrutia is the only South American to win **Olympic gold** in weightlifting.
- There are **80 different indigenous** tribes in Colombia, and they speak 64 differ ent languages.
- Colombia has been to the **FIFA World Cup four times**.
- In 2007, the Economist magazine ranked 121 countries according to how peaceful they were and how hard they strived for peace. Norway was first, Iraq was 121st. Colombia was ranked **116th**, last in Latin America, behind countries like Uganda, Pakistan and Lebanon (in case you're curious, the USA came in 96th, between Yemen and Iran).
- Tourism in Colombia **fell 21 percent** between 1995 and 1999 and **rose 48 percent** between 2005 and 2006.
- In 2002, the World Markets Research Center ranked Colombia the **riskiest country** to suffer a terrorist attack.
- It is estimated that **15 percent** of Colombia's population lives **below the poverty line (as of 2005).**
- Colombia's **literacy rate** is 92.5 percent.
- According to the International Union for Conservation of Nature and Natural Resources, Colombia is **home to 593 endangered species**, which puts them 8th on the international list. Ecuador is first, with 2,151 species.
- Some experts estimate that Colombia can produce **545 metric tons of pure cocaine** annually. The country is the **world's largest grower of the coca plant.**
- Brazil produces the most coffee annually in the world; **Colombia is second.**
- It is estimated that people drink **400 billion cups of coffee each year,** second only to water.
- After petroleum, coffee is the world's second most traded commodity.
- Colombia provides **12 percent** of the world's coffee. Updated: Oct 15, 2007.

Hitchhiking

As always, hitchhiking is an iffy proposition in terms of success and safety. Male-female couples say they encounter few problems in traversing Colombia this way. Solo males report poor luck. Lone females should probably dispose of this option for travel. Always trust your gut instinct about a prospective ride; another vehicle will eventually come along. Truck drivers are likely to be looking for a passenger (illegal), if nothing else than to help keep them awake with conversation.

BORDER CROSSINGS

NOTE: For information on crossing to Brazil and Peru, please refer to the chapter Llanos y Selva, p.485.

COLOMBIA-VENEZUELA

The most common border crossings between Colombia and Venezuela are at Cúcuta, through the cordillera, and at Maicao, the coastal route. Other crossings exist in the Llanos region, at Puerto Carreño, Colombia, Puerto Páez, Venezuela and Casuarito, Colombia, Puerto Ayacucho, Venezuela. Neverless, these crossings cannot be recommended at this time due to civil war fighting. Additionally, the few travelers that have attempted these routes report immigration facilities for either country were non-existent. *NOTE: Venezuela is a half-hour ahead of Colombian time.*

Vía Cúcuta

From Cúcuta, the highway winds 16 kilometers (9.6 miles) to Villa del Rosario, and another four kilometers (2.5 miles) to the Puente Internacional. This is the most common border crossing between the two countries. Local transportation is more geared toward these nations' citizens' comings and goings and not needing to stop at immigration to deal with bureaucracy. This makes it a bit trying for foreigners, since buses and collective taxis will not wait for you. For those travelers needing passport procedures, this border is only open 8 a.m.-6 p.m. on either side.

Take a bus as far as the border, get off at the Colombian side of the international bridge ($0.80); a taxi waiting for you to go through the rigmarole will cost about $25. On the left side of the road is DAS in the white house. Then cross back over the road and flag down a bus heading to San Antonio del Táchira, Venezuela, at the other end of the bridge. Tell the driver you are going to the DIEX (a.k.a ONIDEX) or immigration office. If you are feeling energetic, you could also cross the bridge on foot; however, be very aware of your surroundings, since robberies are possible. Six blocks from the San Antonio side of the bridge is the Venezuelan immigration office. There is about 1 kilometer (0.6 miles) between the two immigration posts.

Immediately on the Venezuelan side is a tourism information booth on the side of the road. At San Antonio del Táchira there is frequent transportation to San Cristóbal del Táchira. From there you can travel to Mérida, Maracaibo, Caracas and other points in Venezuela.

For journeyers traveling with their own vehicle, check with the Venezuelan consulate in Cúcuta or the Colombian Consulate in San Antonio for the complete procedures. In general, from Colombia to Venezuela the process will be: DIAN (customs) and then DAS (immigration). The DIAN office is a distance from the border, near the airport. See Cúcuta for addresses of the consulate and Colombian customs and other offices. If leaving Venezuela, the exit tax is approximately $20 at official rate, less at black market rates.

Vía Maicao

Despite the safety issues Maicao has, in some aspects this is a preferable Colombia-Venezuela border crossing than the one at Cúcuta. Here the immigration posts for both countries are next to each other, just like the customs offices (for those traveling with their own vehicle), and there is direct international bus service. Venezuela has consulates in Colombia's principal Caribbean coast cities, including Riohacha.

If traveling with local transport, take a bus to Maicao. At the terminal you can exchange your pesos into Venezuelan bolívares fuertes. Por puestos (collective taxis) leave when full for Maracaibo ($3). *Note: be sure the driver understands that you must go through immigration and that he waits for you.*

Berlinas has an international service connecting Cartagena, Barranquilla, Santa Marta, Riohacha and Maicao, Colombia, with

Maracaibo, Valencia and Caracas, Venezuela (check the Colombian cities' Getting to and Away sections). When the bus arrives at the border, it drops passengers off at the immigration post of the country of departure. While travelers go through procedures, the vehicle passes through customs and waits at the bus office on the other side. You then continue on to your destination.

This border crossing is properly called Parguachón in Colombia and Guarero in Venezuela. The border is supposedly open 24-hours a day. If leaving Venezuela, you'll have to pay an exit tax of $16 at the official rate, less at black market rates. Updated: May 13, 2008.

Colombia-Ecuador

Land: Rumichaca

Rumichaca, on the Pan-American Highway south of Ipiales, is the principle border crossing between Colombia and Ecuador. From Ipiales, catch a combi ($0.80) or taxi ($3) from Calle 14, near Carrera 10. You will be dropped off at DAS, Colombian immigration.

The complex also houses the offices for those crossing in their own vehicles, a exchange house, bathrooms and an Ecuadorian consulate. Colombian immigration has one line for entry stamps and another for exit.

The process is usually quick. If entering Colombia, you might receive only 60 days—though you may get lucky if you ask for 90.

Money changers work in the parking lots on either side of the bridge. If you use their services, check all calculations and bills, and count your money carefully. As you cross the modern bridge, to the west you will see the natural rock bridge Rumichaca is named for.

For centuries travelers used that stone to cross the Río Carchi—even Simón Bolívar and his minions. On the other side of the river is Ecuador's immigration. From the parking lot across the road leave mini-buses ($0.75) and taxis (collective, $0.85; private, $3). The mini-buses and collective taxis will drop you off at Parque Ayora in Tulcán (Calle Venezuela and Avenida Coral); to arrive at Tulcan's bus terminal, take a city bus ($0.75) or walk the ten blocks. A private taxi from the border will take you directly to the station.

Immigration for both countries is open 6 a.m. to 10 p.m. Transportation fares on either side can be paid in dollars or pesos.

Sea: Tumaco to Esmeraldas

For a different adventure in making the journey to Ecuador, consider going by sea. Services have improved significantly in recent years. The journey in a launch through mangroves and into the open sea has now been replaced by cargo-passenger boats.

Servimar runs a ship from Tumaco's marine port on Isla El Morro to Esmeraldas every Friday evening, arriving in Ecuador Saturday morning; the trip takes 10 to 12 hours. Buy your passage from Servimar's office across from the maritime port, where the two palm trees are (Monday-Friday, 8 a.m.-noon, 2-6 p.m.). Tickets are sold all day Thursday and Friday until 6 p.m., and cost is $15 one way.

Reportedly the DAS office in Tumaco is now authorized to give entry and exit stamps. Its offices are located about 1.5 kilometers from the port, towards Isla Tumaco; it is the green-trimmed, yellow-ochre building opposite and just past the military base. You are responsible for going there before departure to get your exit stamp (or, if arriving to Colombia, for your entry stamp). These regulations can change, so ask around, as you may have to go to Ipiales for the entry/exit stamp.

Boarding of passengers on the ship begins at 7 p.m. on Friday nights, and departure is at around 8 p.m. You will receive a bed (*camarote*) in a nine-bunk room. No food or drink is provided or sold; bring your own. Upon arrival in Esmeraldas, Ecuadorian immigration and customs will greet you dockside. Expect a very thorough search of your belongings.

From Esmeraldas to Tumaco, the boat leaves on Wednesday night, arriving in Tumaco on Thursday morning. The Esmeraldas agent is Sarjento Campaña. Whether departing or arriving to Colombia with this ship, it is more convenient to stay at Playa El Morro, just one kilometer from the maritime port.

A third way to cross from Colombia into Ecuador is through Puerto Asís to San Miguel, then down river to Puerto Colón and La Punta, from where buses depart to Lago Agrio. However, this route is unadvisable at present time, due to the war between Colombian military and FARC forces. It was near here that in March 2008, the Colombian forces bombed a FARC base camp. Furthermore, one traveler who succeeded in crossing here reported he could not find the DAS office, and so was illegally in Colombia. Perhaps in the future, as the situation once more becomes stable, foreigners can safely go through this region. Updated: May 06, 2008.

Colombia-Panama

No overland route connects Panama with Colombia; in the debate of building a highway, the jungle—known as the Darien Gap— won. The famous crossing of the Gap on foot is prohibitively dangerous now, due to guerillas, paramilitaries, drug labs and other hazards. Even missionary groups and the rangers at Los Katíos National Park have pulled out, thus leaving the potential adventurer without the traditional safety nets. The most secure border crossings between the two countries are on the Caribbean coast side of the isthmus. Other routes exist on the Pacific side, but these are rarely used due to the dangers.

Colombia does not require an onward ticket for those arriving by land or sea. Many airlines are hesitant to sell a one-way ticket from Panama to Colombia since they claim they will be fined if you are called on it. Depending on your luck, you may get a flight between the two countries for $150-300. Panama requires a demonstration of sufficient funds ($500) and an onward ticket. However, for travelers from "first-world" countries, the sufficient funds and/or credit card usually suffices. Citizens from many Eastern European countries need a visa to enter Panama. For specific requirements check: http://www.migracion.gob.pa/eng/servicio.php?cont=paisvisa.

Panama has consulates all along the coast, including in Capurganá for those going up the coast, as well as in Bogotá.

Rumors have always abounded about hitching a ride with a cargo boat out of Cartagena, Barranquilla or another Caribbean coast port to Panama. Such opportunities are, quite frankly, a pie-in-the-sky dream. Ships must use only licensed crew. Additionally, there are many contraband-running ships that are hesitant to carry passengers. If the boat is caught doing illegal activities, you and the captain will have a whole lot of explaining to do. Better to spend a bit more and get to Panama or Colombia safely and legally.

Sailboat

The most popular way now to journey between Colombia and Panama is by sailboat, plying the waves between Cartagena and Portobello (or, less frequently now, Colón) by way of the San Blas Islands, home of the Kuna indigenous. The trip takes four to six days and includes transportation, food and water, as well as customs and immigration procedures. The entire package costs approximately $275. Most boats will take only five to seven passengers. The best sources of information are Casa Viena in Cartagena or Voyager Hostal in Panama City.

Be warned that the sea can be rough at times and people frequently complain of seasickness. It is recommended to avoid boats under 37 feet, since they are not as stable. Sailboats of 37 to 44 feet high are better. Best is a 44 to 66 footer. Travelers have made positive reports of the following sailboats: Marc and Paula with the Melody; Hernando Higuera with the Marie Jo; and the Swede Mat who has the Da Capo (information from Hostal Mamallena in Panama City). Travelers have warned about are Jimy who runs the boat Mildre and Capitán Ángel de Costa with the Windsurfer (name may have been changed).

Travelers who have taken this route report Panama immigration officials are usually more lenient on the entrance requirements, figuring if the tourist can afford the passage on a sailboat, then she or he has the financial means to visit their country.

Caribbean Coastal Route

The traditional route for backpackers traversing the isthmus from Colombia to Panama has been along the North Coast from Turbo to Puerto Obaldía, Panama. As long as you stay in the villages along the way and do not wander out, you should be safe. There is a trail that runs between Aguacate to Acandí, Capurganá, Sapzurró and over the brow of the hill to Puerto Obaldía; it is unwise to attempt this route and locals will probably stop you from even trying. Be safe, be wise and you will see one of the most beautiful parts of Colombia.

Your journey begins at Turbo, the main port on the Golfo de Urabá. It is accessible by bus from Medellín. You can also reach Turbo from Cartagena, by way of Montería. Turbo is an ugly port with many safety issues. If you can, get out as soon as possible. If not, a hotel repeatedly recommended over the years has been Residencia Marcela. It is difficult to find a place to change money here. The chalupas, or boats, up the coast will take payment in either Colombian pesos or U.S. dollars.

From Turbo, twin-engined speedboats leave almost daily (usually in the early morning when the sea is calmer) for villages along the coast, including Acandí and Capurganá, and sometimes even to Puerto Obaldía. If you go directly to the Panamenian entry, you will have to get your exit stamp in Turbo. If not, head for Capurganá ($31, 2.5 hours). The journey is very wet; be sure to cover yourself and your belongings with a plastic tarp and wear a life jacket.

Capurganá has for many years been a resort town for those moneyed Colombians looking for the ultimate in white-sand beaches and amazingly colored sea. Still, there are affordable inns in this village, e.g. Capurganá Guesthouse ($10, with private bath). The DAS (Colombian immigration) office is an 8 to 10-minute walk from the jetty; here you get your passport stamped. It is difficult to change money in Capurganá; the grocery shop reportedly gives poor rates. There is no ATM.

From Capurganá chalupas go to Puerto Obaldía, Panamá ($12). Your boat will be met by the Panamenian immigration and customs officials, who are quite stringent on fulfilling the entry requirements. On the up-turned hull of a fishing boat, all your belongings will be searched, and you will have to show sufficient funds and outward ticket (a credit card may suffice in lieu of a ticket). If you do not meet the requirements, you will be sent back, especially if you are not from a "first-world" country.

In Puerto Obaldía there is lodging. The internet café gives good rates of exchange. There are four weekly flights to Panama City ($70, including taxes). Alternately, you can await a Kuna merchant ship to take you to Colón, the Atlantic terminal of the Panama Canal ($25-35, 4-5 days). The journey is rudimentary, with only wooden benches and small servings of food; bring a hammock and extra food and water. A recommended ship is the Tabualá 2 and a a fun activity is to take a launch going to San Blas Islands ($60). Updated: May 07, 2008.

Tours in Colombia

With the expansion of the tourist industry in Colombia, the number of organized travel options continues to grow. Various types of tours are available that encompass many of Colombia's historical and natural delights. Whether it is hiking through the Andes, being guided through one of Colombia's principal cities, visiting ancient landmarks or taking a boat trip down the Amazon, the opportunities available are extensive. Although low demand previously restricted tours to either being short-duration or solely in Spanish, the development of the industry is constantly opening new horizons. Updated: Apr 10, 2008.

Pre-arranged Tours

There is currently a growth of organized packages throughout parts of the country. The options of packages available vary in duration, from one week inside Colombia, to six months throughout various South America countries. Considering the higher price of the packages, these tours include most costs including accommodation and transportation. However, they are rarely fully inclusive and you should enquire about hidden costs beforehand. Not best for those searching for a relaxing break, these types of tours usually encompass a host of activities and visits to multiple locations. As well as general tours, more specific adventure travel trips and nature-orientated visits can be found. Although without as many guarantees, it is often cheaper and can be more liberating to organize trips once inside Colombia. Updated: Apr 11, 2008.

Amazon Tours

The vast expanse of the Amazon jungle provides an ideal location for various day and multi-day guided tours. Most tours leave from Leticia (p.465) in the southeastern pinnacle of Colombia and generally include trips along parts of the Amazon River and some of its multiple tributaries. Often an excellent way to see the extensive elements of jungle life, Amazon tours not only enable you to see incredible varieties of flora and fauna but can also provide an insight into indigenous lifestyles. English-speaking guides are available at numerous organizations and some tours include visits to the Parque Nacional Amacayacu. Updated: Apr 10, 2008.

Andes Tours

Like its southern neighbor, Ecuador, Colombia is intersected by the presence of the empowering Andes mountains. Split into three sections, the Occidental, Central and Oriental, Colombia's Andean mountains host various touring groups. Providing perfect terrain for mountain biking, trekking and both rock and ice climbing, it is also possible to visit the Andes with less energetic aspirations. The Parque Nacional Cocuy (p.393) encompasses snow-peaked mountains and vast lakes as well as great walking and birdwatching possibilities. Distributed throughout the Andes are a host of volcanic structures, glacial formations and impressive lakes. Whether it be sports and physical challenges or a more relaxed enjoyment of natural delights that appeals to you, it is likely that there will be an Andean tour to fit your interests. Updated: Apr 10, 2008.

Special Ruins / Landmark Tours

Guided tours to special landmarks are easy to book and usually depart from Bogotá. If, for example, you are planning to visit the Salt Cathedral in Zipaquirá—one of the seven Wonders of Colombia— (p.104) and are also interested in the enchanted lagoon of Guativita nearby, the best way to learn the history and maximize your time is probably to let a tour guide lead and arrange transportation. From Bogotá you can also hire a tour to Villa de Leyva (p.333), one of the oldest towns in Colombia, or leave for the famous archeological park San Agustín (p.428), though you will probably need to book a hotel, as this UNESCO site is large and contains much history and many myths. For a more complex tour, like going around Zona Cafetera (p.128), air transportation and extra time is necessary. Updated: Apr 10, 2008.

City Tours

Most of Colombia's principal cities have organized city tours. While some bus tours are available, seeing a city by foot is often the best way to get around and take in the location's atmosphere. It is best to visit the local tourist office to discover what type of tours a city has on offer. In Bogotá for example, walking tours are available that encompass enchanting strolls around the delights of La Candelaria (p.93) and Plaza de Bolívar (p.93).

Chivas

Although still an important means of transport across some parts of Colombia, the life of the chiva has taken a new meaning in many Colombian cities. An open bus with bands and free-flowing drinks on-board, rides on the chivas have become a popular means of nightlife entertainment. Often organized by travel agents, night time chiva tours can include numerous stops at a city's top party spots, various samples of *aguardiente* (sugar cane alcohol) and great live music. If the party lifestyle is one you enjoy, a trip on a chiva will provide guaranteed fun.

Others

Numerous other organized trips are available throughout Colombia. With some of the world's top sites for diving, many companies are organizing tours to see Colombia's underwater delights. As well being home to incredible coral reefs and collections of maritime wildlife, organized excursions to parts of Colombia's coastline can also include whale-watching, eco-lodge stays, surfing and some relaxation on the country's beautiful beaches. Tours are also organized throughout Colombia's famous coffee region and can stretch from two days to one week in duration. Updated: Apr 10, 2008.

SPORTS AND RECREATION

Colombia's collection of natural wonders makes it an excellent place for adventure travel and sports. Although its sport and recreation industry is still growing, Colombia's Pacific and Caribbean coastline, Andean mountains, vast natural expanses and extensive rivers all cater to those keen on outdoor activities.

The incredible scenery and beautiful lakes at Túquerres and the waterfall at La Chorrera are popular with hikers while visits to the marvelous Aguacate Tombs are frequently combined with long walks. For the more extreme walker, Colombia also hosts a variety of inviting yet challenging summits. There are various trekking routes that are combined with the possibility of rock or ice climbing. Suesca is a haven for climbing fans as it has diverse rock formations that are suitable for different level climbers. Colombia has an impressive collection of caves and some incredible stalagmite and stalactite formations. When caving and going on long treks it is advisable to always go with a guide. In instances of day trips, at the very least speak to someone in the know about the safety of the area. Mountain biking and parapenting are alternative ways of witnessing Colombia's natural beauty and diverse flora and fauna. The Reserva Natural Laguna de Sonso is a great site for birdwatching as over 100 different species can be seen.

Photo by Dan Anderson

Its numerous rivers make Colombia an attractive place for rafting and kayaking and its lakes are great for different water sports and fishing. Windsurfing is growing in Colombia and both off-shore and lake sailing are also becoming increasingly popular. Colombia's coastline attracts surfers and divers of all levels. The Pacific Coast (p.161) is considered best for surfing and many diving enthusiasts are flocking to experience the wonders hidden beneath the country's waters.

As well as being a fantastic location to participate in sports, Colombia can also be extremely enjoyable for the spectator. Although somewhat tarnished by the happenings of the 1994 World Cup, football is exceptionally popular both to play and to watch. Watching one of Colombia's top teams is guaranteed to provide an electric atmosphere. Baseball, polo, basketball and bull fighting can also be found throughout major cities. As increasing numbers of competitions come to Colombia's shores, surfing is riding the wave of national enthusiasm. Try and find somewhere to watch *tejo*, a national sport that is over 500 years old. Be sure to keep your distance, however, as tejo involves throwing a metallic plate towards a target filled with clay and gunpowder. Updated: Apr 14, 2008.

Hiking

The notorious reputation of Colombia's mountains and jungles as the province of terrorists, armed revolutionaries, paramilitaries, drug cartels, and even ordinary kidnappers and thieves makes the very idea of venturing beyond Colombia's cities seem brave and/or foolish. While a decades-long civil war has made many of Colombia's rural areas dangerous, a high portion of Colombia's breathtaking mountains are now safely accessible. The most popular destination for foreign hiking enthusiasts, who make up 80 percent of its visitors, is the Sierra Nevada of Santa Marta (p.265), the highest coastal mountain in the world. Its most famous attraction, the pre-Columbian Ciudad Perdida, or Lost City (p.259), was a secret to the western world until 1975. Located halfway up the mountain at 1,000 meters on the northern side, facing the Caribbean, it can only be reached on foot, and only through the agency TurCol, who make agreements with the paramilitaries and with indigenous communities to permit tour groups to visit the famous archaeological site. The entire journey takes about three or four days to walk up, and two days to return. TurCol also provides mules, food, and hammocks, all at a cost of about $300. The risk of dangerous confrontations is about less than five percent, but there is a greater risk of malaria, so travelers are advised to bring repellent and wear long-sleeved shirts at night. The degree of humidity is also very high, and visitors to the Sierra de Santa Marta during the rainy season—which runs from April to June, and later from October to December—have nicknamed it "the Green Hell."

On the southwestern side of the pyramid-like Santa Marta lies the town Valledupar, from which many intrepid trekkers begin their hike up to Santa Marta's peak, passing through various indigenous villages along the way.

Parque Tayrona (p.274), in the coastal foothills of Sierra de Santa Marta, is notable not only for its beaches, but for some pleasant hiking opportunities in the region, not to mention a local museum.

Further south, along the northeastern border with Venezuela, the Cordillera Oriental has the Sierra Nevada del Cocuy, and its Parque Nacional de Cocuy (p.393). At a 5,000-meter (16,404 feet) altitude, getting there can take up to ten days of hiking leading to a multitude of snow-covered peaks. This region is well-guarded by the Colombian army, with no reported guerilla activity. Continuing south along the Venezuelan border, the village of Puerto Inirida offers rock-climbing opportunities as well as jungle trails.

Heading inland, Bogotá (p.77) is surrounded by mountains that offer many safe one, two, and three-day hikes, as do the cities of Medellín (p.148) and Manizales (p.140), both of which border Parque Nevados, ranging anywhere from four to eight hours a day, and guides are generally available for $20 a day.

The Parque Arqueológico San Agustín at the lower end of Huila province is one of the rich repositories of pre-Columbian culture, and it even includes its own zoo, but it is also a starting point for many hikes and treks outside the park area. The level of risk here is higher; a 30 percent chance of an encounter with a guerilla or criminal, but the well-patrolled park itself is safe. Professional guides can not only take you through the park, but to the source of the Río Magdalena, which stretches nearly the length of Colombia itself. The latter is a four-to-five day walking trip.

On the southern Pacific coast, Gorgona Island (p.171), which for fifty years served as a penal colony, offers both the pleasures associated with an island, as well as many hiking paths. Boats going to Gorgona routinely depart from the port city of Buenaventura. Updated: May 14, 2008.

Surfing

Foaming at the top, they rise high and move fast towards the wide Colombian shore, which expands over 3,000 kilometers (1864 miles) in the Pacific Ocean and the Caribbean Sea. Long ignored by surfers, Colombian waves are increasingly gaining attention from both locals and tourists at every skill level who want to ride the clear water on long boards. The best surfing spots in the country are on the Pacific Coast, particularly the Department of Chocó, however, surfing is also popular in Cartagena de Indias in the Caribbean.

Surfing in Colombia has surpassed an amateur point and is now a major competitive sport at a national level, not to mention a popular destination often recommended by international surfing publications. Particularly, the city of Nuquí (p.173) has become a major surfing destination because of its deserted beaches and diverse lodging options. Hotels like El Cantil organize surfing tours of two-to-five nights in which parties are taken in a motorboat to specific isolated surfing spots. They also have alliances with surfing schools like Olaviento Indoor, where beginners can learn to balance themselves on simulators before going out into the ocean.

El Chocó is the poorest department of Colombia; the rainfall of the land (considered one of the heaviest in the world) does not allow for much agriculture, and industrial development has lagged behind in the department. The potential for tourism is what gives locals an incentive of income, and as a result surfing tours and lessons have become popular.

The surfing culture of Colombia is blooming with talent as new generations learn the sport at earlier ages than they did 10 years ago. Kids of ages 5 and 6 are picking up boards and stroking up to waves, whereas the previous generations would start surfing at ages 15 and up. Events like the Circuito Nacional de Surf OP PRO 2008, have pulled considerable crowds to places like Cartagena, Parque Tayrona and Barrranquilla in order to proclaim a national champion, who is considered an elite athlete in the nation.

In the last decade over 40 national surfing competitions and three Latin American tournaments have taken place on the beaches of Colombia. Beginners or travelers looking for a lesson usually go to Terquito beach in Nuquí or La V beach in Puerto Colombia. Intermediate-level surfers have a wide range of beaches from Mendihuaca and Los Naranjos in the department of Magdalena to Bahía Solano in Chocó to El Bolsillo in Puerto Colombia. Finally, experts looking for a challenge go to Pela Pela or Pico de Loro in Nuquí.

If you plan to surf in Magdalena, note that the best months to surf on the Caribbean coastline are December through March and July through September. The Pacific, however, is considered a higher quality surf coast. Although surfing as a competitive sport is not widely known to be a South American specialty, most countries in the continent train and participate at national and international levels. Colombia holds some of the best surfing spots and is therefore developing a well-respected community and getting Colombian surfers on the wavelength of world-renowned board riders. Updated: Mar 03, 2008.

Rafting

Colombia has some excellent rivers for rafting, and some reliable operators to take you there. The rafting industry in Colombia is centered in and around San Gil (p.348), where local operators generally will take you to one of three nearby rivers: Fonce, Chicamocha, or Suárez.

The Fonce River has a good mix of rapids, with long sections of everything from class II to class IV rapids. Short trips can be made to the slower parts, a good option for novices or mixed groups. The Fonce can get a bit rough, too, in other sections: up to class IV, suitable for intermediate and advanced rafters.

The Chicamocha River is generally a bit rougher than the Fonce, and rafting trips pass through the scenic Chicamocha canyon. The Suárez is the roughest of them all. One reputable operator in the region is Colombia Rafting Expeditions (http://www.colombiarafting.com/) located in San Gil.

If you're in Bogotá, there is some rafting to be had on the Río Negro, not far outside of town. This class III river is good for beginners.

For a slightly different rafting experience, Paisa Travel (http://www.paisatravel.com/) offers a trip on a balsawood raft through Colombia's coffee-growing region on the La Vieja River. The river is not particularly rough and participants are encouraged to swim off the raft as it makes its way along the river. Updated: Oct 26, 2007.

Horseback Riding

Horseback riding is a popular sport in Colombia, and the the country's Andean sierras provide an ideal climate for equestrian enthusiasts. However, as can be expected, the degree of safety varies from region to region in Colombia. The Llanos region in the northeast is the most well-known destination for horseback riding, but unfortunately it is not the safest, and tour agencies will generally recommend Popayan's (p.409) outlying areas, inside the southwest province of Cauca, where many adventure outfits will rent horses and lead guided tours. The "Circuito Ancestral," in particular, has a world-famous reputation for its scenic and historical value. East of Popayán, one can visit the ancient rock sculptures of San Agustín; best reached by horse.

Many towns have their own equestrian festivals, most notably Cali, from Christmas to New Year's Eve—in 2007, drunken residents mistreated the horses to the point that "Cabalgatas," or horse processions, were canceled. There has been less controversy with traveling horse shows sponsored by local restaurants, that feature actual dancing horses. Finally, having a shot of the potent aguardiente while on a horse is common custom.

Mountain Biking

The most popular mountain biking routes for foreigners who travel to Colombia are located around Bogotá or in such places as Villa de Leyva (p.333) near Boyacá and along the Venezuela border. Due to safety reasons, most routes are one-day only, though in the Parque de Los Nevados (p.143) in Manizales, both two and three-day routes are available. North of Bogotá, mountain biking is very popular in the city of Suesca, where you will find many shops renting bikes, offering tours, as well as many specially designed routes and trails.

There are also relatively safe mountain biking areas in Santa Marta, near Tayrona, as well as in the Zona Cafetera. The best times to visit, that is, the months with the least amount of rainfall, are from November to December, and from July to August.

Due to the high risk of theft, there are only a handful of places in Colombia where you can rent a bicycle. The cost is generally $40 per day, and you can hire a guide for an additional $35. However, group tours generally charge only $15 per person.

For those willing to brave it, and use precautions, Colombia offers some of the most spectacular scenery in the world on sierras as high as 4,000 meters (13,000 feet). The country sponsors a variety of mountain biking, cross-country, downhill, and biking marathons, and there are a number of successful biking Colombians, such as María Luisa Calle, Olympic Bronze Medal Velodrome winner in 2004, and Fabio Parra, who came in third at the 1998 Tour de France.

BIRDWATCHING

A trip to Colombia should be at the top of every devoted birdwatcher's list. It is one of the most biodiverse countries in the world, especially where birds are concerned. To give you an idea, a quarter of the 800 bird species of Colombia's Chocó department are unique to that area. Colombia is home to more than 1,800 species of birds, about 150 of which are considered rare or endangered. Roughly an additional 1,000 species more also come through on their annual migration path.

Granted, some of the best birding locations require a little sense of adventure and an affinity for off-the-beaten-path travel. But there are still amazing birdwatching opportunities for those who prefer to stick to more heavily-trafficked areas. Whatever you chose, you will most likely need to make some arrangements in advance or hire a guide. Many of the national parks require visitors to first obtain a permit from local authorities before entering.

In recent years Colombian tourist infrastructure has improved significantly, and generally you will face little risk at the reserves (although don't expect any luxury accommodations). Nevertheless, don't think you can just go wandering around by yourself – there have been a few instances of birdwatchers getting kidnapped. Do make sure to inquire about possible risks before entering an area, and stay abreast of safety developments. Here are a few of Colombia's birding highlights by region:

Around Medellín (p.148)

Yellow-Eared Parrot Reserve

The Yellow-Eared Parrot is a critically endangered species now found only in a few small areas in the Colombian Andes. In addition to being a haven for these rare parrots, the 130 hectare reserve is also home to Tawny-breasted Tinamou, Purple-throated Woodstars, Yellow-vented Woodpeckers, Spillman's Tapaculo, Handsome Flycatchers, Chestnut-crested Cotingas, Black-tipped Cotingas, Sharpe's Wren, Indigo Flowerpierce and Tanager Finches.

Chestnut-capped Piha reserve

Besides the Piha, you may encounter Stile's Tapaculo, Red-bellied Grackle, Multicolored Tanager, Black-and-gold Tanager, Parker's Antbird. Black Tinamou, Blue-fronted Parrotlet, Colombian Screech Owl, Red-faced Spinetail, Striped Woodhaunter, Purplish-mantled Tanager, Scarlet and White Tanager, Sharp-tailed Streamcreeper, Fulvous-breasted Flatbill and Chestnut-breasted Wren.

Around Cali (p.108)

El 18

This forest habitat, with its many varieties of tanager, is a good place to get your feet wet. The Multicolored Tanager is the most sought after, but you are also likely to see Beryl-spangled, Saffron-crowned, Golden, Blue-capped, Golden-naped, Metallic-green, Scrub, Fawn-breasted, Purplish-mantled and Blue-necked Tanagers, as well as several species of woodpecker and hummingbird. There are around 140 different species in total, although in one visit you'll probably only see about half of that. The habitat is 18 kilometers from Cali, heading down Buenaventura to the village of Dapa. It is an unmarked area of forest, so it is better to hire a guide or at least ask a cab driver who knows the area rather than attempting to go it alone.

La Planada

This private, 3,200 hectare reserve is one of the most prominent in the country, and protects several species of rare birds, including the White-Face Nunbird. The reserve, which forms part of the Chocó region, is also home to the Dark-backed Wood Quail, Semicollared Hawk, Black-and-Chestnut Eagle, Colombian Screech-owl, Cloud-Forest Pygmy Owl, Velvet-purple Coronet, Crimson-rumped Toucanet, Orange-breasted Fruiteater, Plate-billed Mountain-toucan, Violet-tailed Sylph and Crimson-rumped Toucanet, as well as an assortment of Tanagers.

Reserva Natural Laguna de Sonso, Cali

There are about 160 species of bird inhabit this wet land area.

Pacific Coast (p.161)

Río Ñambi

This reserve sits between Altaquer and Junín on the Pasto-Tumaco highway at El Barro. It has around 300 documented species of birds, among which are some of the rarest on earth. Some of these species include the Dark-backed Wood-quail, Plumbeous Hawk and Forest-falcon, Pale-eyed Thrush, Rufous-brown Solitaire, Toucan Barbet, Beautiful Jay, Torrent Duck and Fasciated Tiger-heron. You can get to the reserve on any bus coming from Ipiales or Pasto to Tumaco. From the entrance it is a 4-kilometer walk to the reserve center. Lodging can be arranged on the reserve, and it is best to book in advance.

Pueblo Nuevo

Of all the places listed, this birding area may be the most difficult to access. Also located along the Pasto-Tumaco highway, the little village of Pueblo Nuevo is a six-hour walk through the woods (although you do not necessarily need to walk all the way to the village to see flapping beauties). The best way to get there is to hire a guide nearby at Altaquer or Río Ñambi. Count on only the most basic lodging. Despite its frustrating obscurity, Pueblo Nuevo is worth the trouble for a determined birder. Species in this area include a variety of tanagers (including, if you're very lucky, the Yellow-green Bush-tanager), woodpeckers, toucans, antbirds, Stripe-billed Araçari, Chestnut-headed Oropendola, Purple Honeycreeper, Purple-crowned Fairy, Spot-crowned Antvireo and a great number of Five-coloured Barbet.

Other reserves and areas to visit:

Amacayacu National Park (p.470)

This reserve, which is comprised of both swampland and forest, is made up of different zones, each with its own distinct list of bird species. From the reserve center itself you can see several species of tanager and parrots, as well as others including the Black-fronted Nunbird, Black-crested Ant-shrike, Boat-billed Flycatcher, Golden-tailed Sapphire and Southern Beardless-tyrannulet. Another fruitful region of the park for birdwatchers is Isla Mocagua. This is a good location for viewing waterbirds, especially the Hoatzin, or Stinkbird. You may also see a few varieties of hawk, heron and vulture. To visit Amacayacu, it is mandatory you go with a guide. To get the most out of the park, it is best to go during the wet season.

Tayrona National Park (p.274)

This 37,000-acre park outside Santa Marta is home to more than 200 species of birds.

Santa Marta Mts(Minca Road) (p.265)

A good place to become familiar with Colombia's many endemic birds. Take the Minca road up to San Lorenzo (and further, if you like) in a 4x4 vehicle.

Ucumarí & Los Nevados

This is located in the Central Cordillera on the edge of Los Nevados National Park. A permit is required. This park has an incredible amount of species.

Bosque Yotoco

Located in the Western Cordillera, this reserve is especially notable for having Cauca Guan, Turquoise Dacnis-tanager and Multicoloured Tanager. You must request permission from the Corporación Autonoma Regional del Valle del Cauca (CVC) in Buga Efrén to be able to visit. Tel: 2-227-8347, Fax: 2-228-6172.

Photo by: Mark Hentze

Sanctuario Los Flamencos

Made up of two areas—Perico and Camarones—both located near Riohacha. At the sanctuario reside Rufous-vented Chachalaca as well as a variety of acquatic birds, including the Greater Flamingo.

Volcán Chiles
An inactive volcano on the Colombia / Ecuador border where it is possible to spot the famous Andean Condor.

Studying Spanish

Out of all the places in Latin America to study Spanish, Colombia is not the ideal option. Someone beginning to learn Spanish may find the Colombian accents difficult to understand. In addition, there is not the abundance of Spanish language schools that are found in other countries. If you choose to study in Colombia, make sure you obtain a student visa prior to your arrival. Overall, when looking for a place to study Spanish, Bogotá, Medellín and Barranquilla provide the best options. Schools arrange airport pick-up, housing and offer a variety of excursions and activities in addition to language classes, such as cooking classes or field trips to local museums and historical sites. Many of these extracurricular activities will be offered for an additional, yet low, cost.

Nueva Lengua (www.nuevalengua.com) has locations in Cartagena, Bogotá and Medellín. Aside from intensive language classes, Nueva Lengua also offers specialties such as medical Spanish, or combination courses, like Spanish and scuba diving. The course prices vary depending on location.

In Bogotá, High Technology Learning, or HTL, as is commonly known, has three-, five- or ten-week courses. The longer courses offer fewer classes per week.

Foreign students coming to learn Spanish at the Universidad del Norte in Barranquilla (www.uninorte.edu.co) can choose between month-long sessions according to the school sessions or private classes. The university partners foreign with university students and offers foreign students the opportunity to attend all activities provided by the university.

Lastly, at EAFIT University in Medellín (www.eafit.edu.co) the Spanish language classes are guaranteed to have a maximum of 10 students to a class and one-on-one conversational programs are set up for extra practice. Updated: Apr 08, 2008.

Living in Colombia

Life can be relatively straightforward in Colombia, but of course, Latin American bureaucracy can raise its ugly head at any given time. For the most part, tourists arrive on a regular three-month tourist visa and either prefer to leave the country in order to obtain an extension or run through the demands required of them by the DAS office.

If you have the means and the visa to stay longer, such as by working for an NGO or working as a journalist, the ideal situation would be to organize a visa in your home country and then to request a Cédula de Extranjería from the DAS office once you have arrived.

Volunteering

While the opportunities to volunteer in Colombia are increasing, there is still a long way to go for the country to reach the levels now experienced in Ecuador or Costa Rica. Given that many places in Colombia are still very much "out of bounds," charities can be forgiven for not sending people into the *zona roja*. Things are changing, however, and foreign-run NGOs, as well as local outfits, are beginning to recognize the value that willing volunteers can bring.

Aside from showing up and lending your services, it is worthwhile doing some research and perhaps organizing your volunteering stint from your home country so as to be sure of what you are getting yourself into.

As with most Latin American countries, there are a host of organizations out there needing volunteers. Obviously most will need a voluntary contribution and a minimum commitment period. In order to work with children it is recommended that you make your enquiries from your home country and provide the chosen organization with a background check to ensure the safety and security of the children with whom you intend to work. Below is a list of organizations where you can find opportunities:

Globalteer–www.globalteer.org
Healing Colombia–www.healingcolombia.org
Idealist–www.idealist.org
Let's Go Volunteer–www.letsgovolunteer.com
United Planet–www.unitedplanet.org

CULINARY VOCABULARY

Aborrajados ▶ Banana dessert.

Almojábana ▶ Type of bread made with cheese and flour.

Arepa ▶ Corn flour pattie that can come plain or stuffed with other ingredients. Popular as a breakfast food, can also be found in Venezuela.

Arequipe ▶ Caramel made out of milk and cinnamon.

Arracacha ▶ Elongated tuber that is brown on the outside and yellow on the inside.

Auyama ▶ Though in the dictionary it means pumpkin, Colombians call auyama a type of squash with green peel and orange insides.

Batata ▶ Sweet potato.

Bocadillo ▶ A sweet made out of the guayaba fruit. Sometimes people call bocadillo a small snack.

Buñuelo ▶ A deep-fried dough served as dessert with syrup.

Caldo corto ▶ Broth made out of legumes and herbs. It is used to cook fish and seafood.

Cañón ▶ Pork meat.

Caspiroleta ▶ Drink made out of milk, eggs, brandy, cinnamon and sugar.

Champús ▶ Traditional beverage prepared with fruits, corn meal, corn, pineapple, *lulo*, cinnamon and *panela*.

Changua ▶ Soup made out of milk, onion, cilantro and egg.

Chicharrón ▶ Fried pig's skin.

Cuchuco ▶ Barley and pork meat soup.

Curuba ▶ Acid fruit of yellow skin and lots of small seeds.

Guasca ▶ Edible leaf.

Malta ▶ Sweet drink made out of barley, not fermented.

Marranitas ▶ Little balls prepared with pork rind and plantain.

Merengues ▶ Also known as *besitos*, or kisses, these sweets are a combination of egg whites and sugar beet, baked. They are found all over Latin America.

Muchacho relleno ▶ Literally "stuffed boy," the dish is actually stuffed beef.

Oblea ▶ Thin sheet made of flour and water, baked in a round mold. It's served with jams and sweet sauces or caramel.

Pasabocas ▶ Finger foods served in social gatherings. Generally come on a toothpick or over a small cracker.

Patacón ▶ Found in other adjacent countries, this side dish is made from plantains cut and squashed before going to the fryer.

Pocillo Tintero ▶ A small cup of coffee.

Ponqué ▶ Basic cake made out of flour, butter, eggs and sugar.

Salpicón ▶ Drink made out of juice of varying flavor with diced fruit. It can also mean a beef or fish stew.

Tinto ▶ Black, strong coffee.

Zapote ▶ A fruit of green peel and fibrous, orange insides with one big seed in the middle. Updated: Jan 15, 2008.

WORKING

Most people residing and working in Colombia have come here sponsored by an international private school or a multinational firm. For these individuals, securing the correct documents is straightforward. For others this is not the case. It is fundamental to have your papers in order. To do this one must have a legitimate reason for being here, be it teaching English, starting a business or being of some obvious benefit to the country. The last thing that the Colombian authorities want is a number of drug-addled dropouts drifting around their country, hence the stringent measures. In order to have everything correct you must first contact the Ministry of Foreign Affairs (www.minrelext.gov.co) and have all your forms approved there before getting your ID card at your local DAS office.

Renting an apartment outright is a tricky issue. Should you go through a licensed agent and receive the security and legal sureness offered you will need a proof of income, a Colombian national to countersign your contract and then to have the documents notarized. Unfortunately most Colombian apartments to let are unfurnished as well. The easiest way around this is searching the web for people offering private furnished properties.

A great number of people end up coming to Colombia and falling in love with the country and its oft-flaunted attractions. These folk usually enter on a three-month tourist visa and then continue renewing their visitor status at the DAS office when required. For those who intend to live in Colombia, there are a number of ways of doing so:

1. **Become an Investor:** Check with the Ministry of Foreign Affairs to see what is required of an investor in Colombia to receive a visa. There is a minimum investment fee that frees up a lot of paperwork.

2. **Teach English:** The pay is notoriously low, but most English teachers supplement their income by offering private classes in addition to being affiliated to a language school. It is fundamental to have a TESL or TEFL.

3. **Study:** There are a number of world-class universities in Colombia, all of which accept foreign students. Check their websites. If you are already in the country and thinking of this option, it is worthwhile to visit the university or academic institution to find out enrolment requirements.

Any of these listed options should present you with a good opportunity to live, earn and fully enjoy Colombia. We strongly advise against people attempting to slip under the radar and go about their business without the correct paperwork. Colombian bureaucracy is substantial. A failure to comply with the required norms is frowned upon and could result in deportation, a hefty fine and/or some time in a particularly unpleasant Colombian prison. Updated: Feb 27, 2008.

Lodging

From a shared room in a hostel to renting a country house, the lodging options in Colombia have the capacity to satisfy every need and budget. Cities like Bogotá, Medellín and Cartagena are equipped with hotel chains of standard services, however, as you venture into the country and more desolated beaches you are bound to find lodging options such as finca hotels (ranches turned into lodges), country hotels and eco-hotels. Currently the majority of environmently-friendly options are not so budget-friendly, yet they are unique places worth your money, if you are willing to spring for it. There are also apartments in big cities, a good option for an extended stay. Make sure to take precautions if you are staying in a hostel, particularly if you are sharing a room, as some travelers who find themselves in need may find your belongings helpful.

Hotels and Hostels

As the image of Colombia improves in the eyes of international travelers and tourism takes on a bigger role in the economy of the country, the quality of hotels becomes a priority for those in the tourism industry. The cities receiving the majority of tourists—over 10 cities throughout Colombia—all have lodging options of international standards and several franchises for those more comfortable with the familiar. There are, however, plenty of unique hotels set in historical buildings, ranches, residential areas and even protected natural areas that enhance the experience of visiting Colombia. As far as hostels go, there are plenty of affordable options in urban areas, prices averaging at about $10 for a shared room. A great deal of people staying at hostels are university students—some major institutions don't have housing—who have not been able to find a host family to stay with.

Eco-Lodges

In 2006, Colombian President Álvaro Uribe opened the first 20 eco-lodges in the Sierra Nevada for a program called "Fostering Families," which helps the families highly affected by cocaine production. Now, the government promotes eco-tourism throughout the Sierra Nevada in places that people avoided walking for fear of landmines surrounding coca fields, like Parque Nacional Tayrona near Santa Marta, which also has some of the most pristine beaches.

These days, focus is more on whale-watching rather than watching out for drug smuggling. Most eco-lodges in Colombia have package (sometimes all-inclusive) deals that can be arranged through travel agents. Look for packages that specialize in relaxation, whale-watching, surfing, scuba diving, birdwatching, fishing or jungle walks. The Chocó region along the Pacific Ocean provides some of the best choices for environmentally -friendly eco-lodges. Pijiba Lodge near Nuquí offers transportation in a glass-bottom boat. El Almejal in El Valle really focuses on conservation and teaching.

Chocolate Bogotano

A unique version of hot chocolate in which the white floating pieces in your cup will not be marshmallows, but actually mozzarella or criollo cheese, chocolate Bogotano—or Santafereño—is a traditional delicacy enjoyed at breakfast or during a cold afternoon. Follow your nose to one of many *chocolaterías* in the city for a taste of this slow-cooked combination of milk, water, chocolate and cinnamon. The drink is usually served with toast and the pieces of cheese can come on the side or already in the drink. Although for some it may seem cheese is not the best ingredient to add to a steaming cup of chocolate, this drink is very popular and often regarded as a great discovery among foreigners. If you find yourself a new fan of chocolate bogotano-style, here is the recipe to enjoy after your trip:

1 chocolate tablet
½ cup of water
½ cup of milk
Cinnamon
4 pieces of diced mozzarella cheese

In a high pot pour in the water, milk and chocolate tablet and place onto medium heat. Stir to help dissolve the chocolate evenly, and once it has come to a boil move the pot from the fire. Beat the mix energetically, then place the pot back on the heat. Let it boil two more times, beating the mixture in between. Serve in a large cup, adding the cinnamon and the cheese. Updated: Jan 15, 2008.

Taste the organic fruits grown in the garden at Playa Koralia, on Colombia's Caribbean side, but leave the laptop at home, or it could be confiscated. They're serious about being one with nature.

Also, check out El Refugio de Mr. Jerry, Lodge Piedra Piedra, Hotel Kipara, Finca Raval Jardín Ecológico, El Cantil or Estado Natural. Updated: Apr 21, 2008.

Spas

Colombia offers many variations on the stereotypical relaxing and tranquil spa vacation. There's the spa getaway of a quick facelift or tummy tuck, but if you want to indulge in the local specialty, cacao, try the choco-therapy at the Thermaé Spa at the Hotel Opera (1-336-2066) in Bogotá. The New York Times calls Casa Boutique Veranera (5-664-1111) in Cartagena "a jewel box of a hotel with a spa and yoga studio." Many of the Radisson Hotels throughout the country, especially in Bogotá, have massage rooms. Take care of any medical or wellness treatments at the Skin Medspa (1-758-2813) in Bogotá. Soak in the scenery and the hot springs at the Termales de Santa Rosa de Cabal (096-364-5500), west of Bogotá, though spa treatments are only offered on the weekends. Don't skimp on the insect repellent during beachside massages or meditation sessions at Playa Koralia (310-642-2574). Lastly, while in Medellín, don't miss out on treating your tootsies—for free—to the foot spas in the Parque de los Pies Descalzos. Updated: Apr 10, 2008.

Camping

If interested in camping in Colombia, it is advisable to contact local tourist authorities for information on campsites or suitable areas to put up your tent or park your camper van. Camping, especially if unplanned, can be dangerous as it generally takes place away from safer urban centers. However, as the security situation improves and Colombia's tourism industry grows, the popularity and number of camping opportunities is expanding.

Although the number of campsites is growing throughout the country, they are rarely signposted from main roads and can often be difficult to find. In no instance should you camp on private land without permission. This is not only illegal but extremely dangerous. You should always ask permission to camp on someone's land but only do so when assured of the area's security.

A few free sites can be found throughout the country and others go from as little as $1 per person per night. Some national parks also offer the opportunity to camp and are generally safer than non-supervised camping. Hostels are increasingly catching on to the popularity of camping for budget travelers and nature lovers and are offering camping opportunities in their grounds.

NOTE: White gas (gasolina blanca) is now virtually impossible to obtain in Colombia. There are only one or two places in Bogotá where it can be bought and one place in Bucaramanga. Campers now have to use gasolina roja (i.e. regular gasoline) in their campstoves. Therefore, if going to use a campstove in Colombia, make sure it's multi-fuel equipped to use regular gas. Updated: Jun 29, 2008.

Food and Drink

Like many other Latin American nations' cuisines, Colombian food relies heavily on fresh, regionally available ingredients. While Colombian cuisine may not have the boldest or most adventurous flavors, the traveler will have no trouble finding filling and inexpensive traditional dishes, snacks, street food, and tropical produce that hit the spot.

Colombian *arepas* (fried cornmeal patties) are a street food sold and eaten all over the country, but are often breakfast, (along with hot chocolate) in the western part of Colombia. Plain arepas are rather bland and are typically eaten with cheese or butter spread on top, though several variations on the traditional arepa are also popular. Stuffed arepas include the *arepa de choclo* (corn), *arepa de huevo* (egg), *arepa de queso* (cheese) and *arepa boyacense*, filled with savory and sweet cheeses. Packaged arepas can also be bought in the supermarkets. Empanadas and *buñuelos* (refer to Culinary Vocabulary box) are more deep-fried foods quite common.

Regional specialties

An ever-popular dish you are likely to encounter, especially in Bogotá and around, is *ajiaco*, a riff on chicken soup that contains corn and potatoes. It is usually served with heavy cream and avocadoes, making it a hearty lunch on its own.

Though typical of Medellín and the northwest, another nationally-favorite dish is the *bandeja paisa*, or paisa platter, which includes rice, beans, ground beef, plantain, sausage, chicharrón (friend pork skin), arepa, avocado and a fried egg.

Sancocho, a stew that is typical of Cali and the southwest, is often prepared on special occasions or weekends. It is another hardy dish usually containing chicken, fish or oxtail, plantains, yuca, potatoes, cilantro and spices.

Both Pacific and Atlantic coastal cuisine is unsurprisingly heavy on spicy fish and lobster, often accompanied by coconut rice. Seafood is generally difficult to find inland.

In the Llanos, or eastern plains, where large ranches and *vaqueros* (cowboys) punctuate the open landscape, barbequed meat or *asado* is the main staple, and the most common dish is *ternera llanera*, barbequed veal.

Juan Valdéz

Good coffee seems to often come with the face of a mustached man accompanied by a donkey, and though Juan Valdez is a fictional character who borders the stereotypical, his face represents over 500,000 Colombian men who are part of the National Federation of Coffee Growers. Formed in 1927, the federation protects farmers from the threat of international prices falling by saving up any extra income when prices are high and therefore guaranteeing a steady salary throughout the year.

In 1981 the logo of Juan Valdez took on the new role of distinguishing 100 percent Colombian coffee from mixed brands. Thirteen years later, Juan Valdez made his first TV appearance along with his mule, Conchita, and ever since the trademark has become popular in pop culture.

A non-profit organization, the National Federation of Coffee Growers handles several programs for the economical and educational advancement of Colombian *cafeteros* and their families. Projects such as sanitation of living environments, electricity installation, potable water installation and schools for both children and adults have helped strengthen the communities of coffee growers. Updated: Jan 15, 2008.

In the department of Nariño, bordering Ecuador, adventurous meat-lovers can also try fried or roasted *cuy* (guinea pig). Though cuy is generally consumed in the household, many tourist-oriented restaurants have it on offer.

Produce

Particularly pleasing is Colombia's abundance of delicious exotic fruits, many of which do not have names in English. *Lulo* and *guanabana* make particularly good juices, and *curuba* (banana passion fruit), *feijoa*, *mamey*, *guayabamanzana* (hybrid between guava and apple), and *níspero*, among many others, are all worth a try. Vegetables are rather hard to come by in Colombian cuisine, and vegetarians may find it difficult to find satisfying options in restaurants aside from arepas, rice, beans, and potatoes.

Beverages

By far the most famous of all Colombian beverages is, of course, their internationally consumed coffee. Be warned, however, that coffee quality varies, and your *tinto* (small black coffee) may be weaker than expected. The word tinto can also mean a glass of red wine, but avoid Colombian wines—Chilean and Argentine wines are widely available and are of a much higher quality.

Other alcoholic drinks of Colombian origin that are worth trying include aguardiente, sugar cane alcohol; *guarapo*, a drink made of fermented fruits and sugar; *canelazo*, a warm, fruity drink made with aguardiente and cinnamon; *refajo*, a mixed drink of rum or beer and cream soda; and *chicha*, a fermented corn drink made by the indigenous in the Andes. Of course national beers are also widely available.

If alcohol isn't your thing, there are many non-alcoholic drink options worth a try. Colombian hot chocolate is made with a special pitcher and a *molinillo* for stirring, and is often served with cinnamon and cheese. *Aguapanela* is a drink of dissolved sugar cane in hot water with lime juice and sometimes cheese added in for flavor. Both *champús* and *lulada* are thick drinks that utilize Colombia's wondrous spread of unique fruits, and *salpicón*, which translates into large splash, is a refreshing drink of soda and chopped fruit. Coca-cola and other sodas are available everywhere as well.

Where to eat on the cheap

As in its neighboring countries, many restaurants in Colombia offer inexpensive multi-course set lunches, which usually include soup, meat, rice, a small salad and fried plantains. This is the best way for the traveler on a budget to fill up on hearty, hot food. These and other restaurants do not usually have printed menus, so if your Spanish is rusty, it might be useful to have a pocket dictionary handy while the server gives you the run-down on what is available. Colombians tend to take siesta in the afternoon, so most lunch spots serve meals between noon and 2:00 p.m.

For a sweet, cheap dessert, street vendors sell *obleas*, large circular wafers, with *arequipe* or fruit sauces to spread on, then another wafer on top. Mangos, watermelon, pineapple and coconuts are commonly sold on the street.

International fare

Should you tire of Colombian food and require something different, the three big cities of Bogotá, Cartagena and Medellín offer quite a few nice restaurants with international fare to choose from. Updated: Jun 29, 2008.

Shopping

Traveling through the variegated land of Colombia, you will find plenty of souvenirs that represent the rich culture and resources of this country. From a miniature figure of a chiva to a *vueltiao sombrero* or an emerald pair of earrings, there are endless choices at every price range and often with the possibility of bargaining. Generally, shopping hours are subject to the weather of each city; colder places like Bogotá are usually open for business from Monday through Saturday 11 a.m. to 9p.m., while warmer cities tend to close at lunch hours (11 a.m. to 3 p.m.) yet open at around 9 a.m.

What to Buy

Aside from being the largest producer of emeralds in the world, which you can get the best bargains for in Bogotá and Muzo, Colombia is known for making arguably the best quality coffee. Pick some up at the Zona Cafetera, along with plenty of other sweet derivatives. Crafts like baskets, 3D paintings, *tagua* (vegetable ivory) figurines and beaded necklaces vary depending on the region you are visiting, but generally can be found to be very similar throughout the weekly markets. Southern and eastern towns in the country hold weekly markets, however cities in the Caribbean coast, Guajira, Llanos or the jungle rely on craftsman shops and strip malls. For wool clothing items try to get to Concepción on your way to Málaga, where you are bound to find elaborate woodwork and delicious candy. *Ruanas* (short ponchos) are a popular item, one you can certainly bargain for almost everywhere you go. Gaita flutes, woven hammocks and leather in every color, shape and size are some of the things almost all travelers are destined to fall in love with in Colombia.

What Not to Buy

Aside from animal and plant products, it is not possible to export cocaine from Colombia, and most nations reject the importation of any of these three products. Avoid buying products made out of insects, feathers or endangered species of flora and fauna.

How to Buy

Practice your bargaining skills all over Colombia when you are buying souvenirs and other goods. Businesses like grocery stores and malls are not up for the bargaining game, however, if you are in a market, a souvenir shop in a small town or a crafts fair, prepare to offer about half of what the asking price is and start negotiating. Try to keep good humor as you settle on a price and consider the effort and time it may have taken to create the piece you have your eyes on.

Store Hours and Payment Information

In general businesses open Monday through Friday 8 a.m.-noon and 2-6 p.m., yet commercial stores stay open for a bit longer and a lot of them open on Saturdays. Remember Colombians consider Sundays, holidays and lunchtimes personal time. All major credit cards are accepted in urban areas, however, as you get further away from major cities, it will be more difficult to find both businesses that accept credit cards and places to cash travelers' checks and currency exchange houses.

Where to Buy

Although some crafts and traditional artifacts can be found throughout the country (and even international boutiques, as Colombians have migrated in considerable numbers taking their culture with them), different towns and regions specialize in typical Colombian goods. Villavicencio, for example, offers magnificent musical instruments ranging from gaita flutes to harps. Beautiful ruanas are found in Cumbal and other southern towns. Ráquira is known for its pottery, the district of La Candelaria in Bogotá holds some of the cheapest emeralds and the indigenous groups of Sierra Nevada de Santa Marta are known for making resistant woven bags and clothing.

Places to Shop in Bogotá

Almacén de Antiguedades Leonardo F

A good bet for quality antiques. Carrera 4 No. 12-34. Tel: 1-334-8312.

Anticuarios Gilberto F. Hernández

Antique shops are found mainly in the northern districts of Chapinero, Chicó, and Usaquén. One of the best is Anticuarios Gilberto F. Hernández. Calle 79B No. 7-48. Tel: 1-249-0041 / 248-7572.

Artesanías El Zaque

Artesanías El Zaque offers especially good buys on hammocks. Centro Internacional, Carrera 10 No. 26-71. Tel: 1-342-7883.

Centro Andino

Stylish boutiques dominate the chic Centro Andino, an anchor of the Zona Rosa since 1993. Tower Records, the only major chain store, is a good place to buy English-language magazines and newspapers. There's a U.S.-style food court and a movie theater on the fourth floor. Carrera 11 No. 82-71. Tel: 1-636-0012.

El Balay

El Balay stocks the city's widest selection of souvenirs from around Colombia. Carrera 15 No. 75-63. Tel: 1-248-5833.

Flea Markets

The flea market in the Centro Internacional takes over a parking lot alongside the Museo de Arte Moderno, on Sunday. It is a good place to hunt for antiques, handicrafts, and just plain junk. Calle 24, half a block east of Carrera 7. An upscale Sunday flea market in Usaquén has a good selection of high-quality local crafts. Carrera 7 No. 119B-33.

Galería Cano

Both the Centro Internacional and the Centro Comercial Andino sell emeralds as well as gold jewelry using striking pre-Columbian designs taken from the Museo de Oro. Edificio Banco Mercantil, Carrera 12 No. 84-07. Tel: 1-635-0529. Edificio Bavaria, Carrera 13 No. 27-98. Tel: 1-336-3255

H. Stern
There are countless jewelry shops in the Centro Internacional along Carreras 6 between Calles 10 and 13. H. Stern sells all kinds of precious gems. Tequendama Hotel, Carrera 10 No. 26-21. Tel: 1-283-2819.

Hacienda Santa Bárbara
The upscale Hacienda Santa Bárbara was constructed as an extension of a colonial-era plantation home. Carrera 7 No. 115-60. Tel: 1-612-0388.

María Cancino
The two branches of María Cancino stock both Colombian antiques and European pieces. Calle 63 No. 9-54. Tel: 1-212-6353.

Museo de Artes y Tradiciones Populares
The shop at the Museo de Artes y Tradiciones Populares carries handmade items. Carrera 8 No. 7-21. Tel: 1-342-1266.

Pasaje Rivas indoor market
In the warren of stalls at the daily Pasaje Rivas indoor market look for bargain-price ponchos, blankets, leather goods, and crafts. Carrera 10 at Calle 10.

Unicentro Shopping Center
The massive Unicentro Shopping Center in Bogotá's affluent north is one of South America's largest air-conditioned malls and has a huge selection of stores. Av. 15 No. 123-30. Tel: 1-213-8800. Updated: May 22, 2008.

Health and Safety

Many people prior to travel get too preoccupied with the dangers associated with tropical diseases and what they will do if they fall sick. Other than the somewhat inevitable and rarely threatening diarrhea associated with changes in diet, very few travelers suffer serious illness in Colombia. A key to avoiding sickness while abroad is preparation. Although less equipped in rural areas, most Colombian cities have good health facilities and numerous pharmacies that will provide medicines in the eventuality that you become ill during your travels. As an obvious precautionary measure, you should take out travel insurance that covers medical necessities.

If you are undertaking travel for an extensive period of time, there are a few recommendations to consider before departing your home country. A dental check-up could prove useful and for those who suffer from diabetes, heart trouble/cardio-pulmonary disease, high blood pressure or cholesterol problems consultation with your doctor is highly advised. If you are on regular medication take extras in the eventuality of loss and document all necessary information including generic medical names.

Minor Health Problems

Altitude Sickness

When traveling in the Colombian Andes it is important to rest for the first few days and drink lots of bottled water. Should you suffer from a severe headache, drowsiness, confusion, dry cough, and/or breathlessness, drink lots of water and rest. If the symptoms continue, it is advisable to move to a lower altitude. Anyone planning to hike at high altitudes is advised to relax in high altitude locations for a few days before any physical exertion. Note that altitude sickness, locally called *soroche*, can come on suddenly if you experience a sudden change of altitude. You may suffer from it when traveling to the likes of Parque Nacional Natural El Cocuy or Volcán Puracé. Sickness can also affect locals so be prepared and take care.

Sunburn / Heat Exhaustion

Even at high altitudes where cool breezes constantly blow and snow can accumulate, the sun is incredibly strong. Apply sunscreen with at least an SPF of 30 every few hours spent outside. The sun on the coast is particularly strong and unprepared visitors can get badly burned. If you get severe sunburn, treat it with a cream and stay out of the sun for a while. To avoid overheating, wear a hat and sunglasses and drink lots of water. Overweight people are more susceptible to sun stroke. The symptoms of heat exhaustion are profuse sweating, weakness, exhaustion, muscle cramps, rapid pulse and vomiting. If you experience heat stroke, go to a cool, shaded area until your body temperature normalizes and drink lots of water. If the symptoms continue, consult a doctor.

Motion Sickness

Even the hardiest of travelers can be hit by motion sickness on the buses in the Andes or boat trips along the coast or to Malpelo Island. Sit near the front of the bus or stay above deck on the boat and focus on the horizon. If you are prone to motion sickness, eat light, non-greasy food before traveling and avoid drinking too much, particularly alcohol. If you're prone to motion sickness, over-the-counter medications such as Dramamine can prevent it. If you suffer from severe motion sickness, you may want consult a pharmacist to get a prescription for something stronger.

Traveler's Diarrhea

This is probably the most common illness that travelers suffer from. There is no vaccine to protect you from traveler's diarrhea; it is avoided by eating sensibly. Contrary to popular belief, it is usually transmitted by food, not contaminated water. Eat only steaming hot food that has been cooked all the way through in clean establishments. Avoid raw lettuce and fruit that cannot be peeled, like strawberries. Vegetables are usually safer than meat. Some supermarkets stock vegetable wash and this can be a good way to ensure clean fruit and vegetables if you are cooking your own meals.

Make sure any milk you drink has been boiled. Avoid ice cream that could have melted and refrozen, such as anything for sale in the street. If you do get diarrhea, it is best to let it run its course while staying hydrated with clear soups, lemon tea, a Gatorade-type drink and soda that has gone flat. Bananas are also a good source of potassium and help stop diarrhea. Coconut water can also prove an effective remedy. If in an isolated location, mixing one teaspoon of salt and one tablespoon of sugar to a liter of water can reduce the severity of diarrhea. If you need to travel and can't afford to let the illness run its course, any pharmacy will give you something that will make you comfortable enough for a bus trip. If the diarrhea persists for more than five days, see a doctor.

Frostbite

Frostbite is simply the freezing of the skin and is more commonly suffered at higher altitude zones. This can usually be avoided if you wear proper clothing—double thick socks, gloves, and a ski-mask can all help. Try to wear water-resistant clothing and change out of wet clothes immediately if you can. Smoking and drinking alcohol also raise your risk because they decrease your circulation. The most common places to get frostbite are on the hands and feet, although exposed facial areas like the ears, nose and cheeks are also vulnerable areas. The first signs of frostbite are usually tingling, numbness, and discoloration of the skin to white or yellow. When you begin to warm up you will start feeling pain in the affected area, and it may turn red and swell. The best way to treat frostbite is to soak the skin in warm, but not hot water until feeling returns. Only begin treatment when you are safely out of the cold.

Fungal Infections

These are most common in hot and humid areas and generally accumulate between the toes or fingers or around the groin. Spread by infected animals or people, fungal infections thrive in moist conditions. If you suffer from a fungal infection it is best to ensure the affected area is kept dry and clean and avoid scratching. Wear loose clothing and avoid artificial materials. Treating with antifungal cream or powder can also assist the infection.

More Serious Health Problems

Hepatitis

It is advisable to be vaccinated against hepatitis A and B. Avoid situations where you could be punctured by a dirty needle. Needless to say, it is a good idea to stay away from any sort of questionable injection. It is also not a good idea to get a piercing while traveling, especially at the popular outdoor markets.

Malaria

Most doctors around the world will tell you that if you travel anywhere in Colombia, you must take pills to prevent malaria. This is not true as there are parts of Colombia where malaria is not present. If you are only traveling above 2,500 meters, where mosquitoes do not thrive, you do not need to take preventative medicine. However, if you plan to spend time along the Eastern Llanos, Colombia's coastline, inland river valleys or in Amazonía, it is a good idea to take the proper measures to prevent the disease. Mosquitoes carrying malaria are evening and nighttime biters. In terms of preventative medical measures, you are advised to consult a pharmacist prior to travel as various malarial medicines are available. You are generally required to begin your prophylactic regime a few days prior to arrival in a malarial zone and, dependent on the prescribed medicine, two to six weeks after leaving.

If you are planning to go to the Amazon Rainforest for a couple of days, you may want to ask the accommodation staff for recommendations. Thoroughly apply insect repellent with at least 30 percent DEET. Applying it to your hair a is good way to make the scent stay on your body longer. Sleep under a mosquito net, preferably elevated off the ground. Wear light-colored clothes and avoid shiny jewelry. It is advisable to wear long-sleeved clothing during the evening. Avoid using scented soaps or perfumes. Pregnant women are particularly vulnerable to catching malaria and should be vigilant with their preventative regime.

The general initial symptoms of malaria are high fever, shivering, sweats, headaches, body pains and possible diarrhea or vomiting. In the instance that you suffer some of these symptoms, you should seek immediate medical assistance.

Rabies

There are stray dogs throughout Colombia that are usually harmless. Avoid all dogs that are behaving strangely. Some home owners train guard dogs to attack trespassers. On long hikes in rural areas, always carry a walking stick to defend yourself if a dog starts to attack. In the Llanos and Amazonía regions ensure you are covered at night, especially on the feet, as some vampire bats can bite. In case you are bitten by a dog or a wild animal, clean the wound thoroughly and seek immediate medical consultation. If required, rabies vaccinations are readily available in most major cities. Try to identify the animal or its owner and inform the relevant authorities. If you are planning to visit particularly isolated areas or will be working in a field that involves contact with animals it is advisable to consult a doctor and think about having the rabies vaccination prior to travel.

Typhoid

An oral capsule or injection should be taken before taking off if you are planning to travel in Colombia or South America for an extended period of time (six months or more). The injection needs boosting every three years.

Yellow Fever

This mosquito-born disease is not endemic to Colombia but there is a risk of it, especially in the rainforest. Talk to your doctor before taking the vaccine, as it is not recommended for people with certain allergies, pregnant women, children under nine months and other special cases. The vaccine lasts for ten years and has minimal, if any, side effects. When vaccinated you will be given a Certificate of Yellow Fever Vaccination you should carry on your travels, as some places in South America may ask for it.

Cholera

Although the risks of cholera in Colombia are small and vaccinations are generally not necessary for international travel, there are some precautionary measures that can be taken to avoid contracting this potentially fatal disease. As cholera is an intestinal disease contracted from contaminated food or water, it is advisable to undertake similar precautions to those relating to diarrhea. Cholera triggers a watery diarrhea that can lead to severe dehydration. If contracted you should seek immediate medical attention.

Dengue Fever

As being experienced in some other parts of South America, cases of dengue fever in Colombia have increased over the past year, especially along the northern coast. Dengue fever is a mosquito-transmitted viral infection that is most common in densely populated urban areas. The best prevention is avoiding insect bites through means mentioned above with regard to malaria.

The symptoms of dengue fever are severe flu-like conditions. These include intense joint and muscle pains, fever, vomiting and headaches; conditions often followed by a rash. There is no immediate cure for dengue and, as well as seeking to replenish lost fluids, medical assistance should be sought in the unlikely eventuality of contracting the disease.

Pulmonary Edema

Associated with a rapid climb in altitude and a severe deterioration of altitude sickness, some people can suffer from the potentially fatal pulmonary edema. As well as those associated with altitude sickness, symptoms of pulmonary edema can be a persistent cough, bloody phlegm, wheezing, a sensation of drowning and blue or bruised lips. The illness can also trigger a loss of orientation and hallucinations. An assisted descent in altitude is essential to avoid the intensification of these conditions and possible death.

Water Borne Infections

Before swimming in local waters you should always enquire about their safety. Be extremely careful if thinking about swimming in piranha or caribe-infested rivers. Do not swim naked as some waters are populated by Candiru fish, which trace urine currents and can enter bodily orifices. When bathing wear sandals as some tropical fish eject venom if trodden on.

AIDS (SIDA)

As in many parts of the world, AIDS infections are increasing. The virus, HIV is transmitted through injection by unsterilized needles previously used by an HIV sufferer and, via unprotected sex. Contrary to popular belief, HIV in Colombia is more commonly transmitted by heterosexuals rather than homosexuals. It is worth avoiding the likes of acupuncture and tattooing unless certain of the location's hygiene standards and safety. As is the case with any sexually transmitted disease, you should always practice safe sex. The HIV infection does not always trigger an automatic illness and can only be certified from a blood test. Updated: Apr 17, 2008.

Hospitals

Though adequate medical care is available in Colombia's major cities, it can be more difficult to obtain if you stray from these hubs. In the capital city of Bogotá, many travelers choose to go to the Fundación Santa Fe de Bogotá (Calle 119 No. 9-33. Tel: 1-603-0303.) Another good option in Bogotá is the Clínica Del Country (Carrera 16 No. 82-57. Tel: 1-530-0470 / 530-1270; URL: www.clinicadelcountry.com.

Several other well-appointed hospitals also exist in Cartagena and Barranquilla. In Cartagena: Medihelp Services, (Tel: 5-665-2255); Bocagrande Hospital, (Tel: 5-665-5270); and Naval Hospital (Tel: 5-655-5759.) In Barranquilla: Clínica del Caribe, (Tel: 4-356-4861); Clínica La Asunción (Tel: 4-368-1148); and Clínica Bautista (Tel: 4-360-2200).

Should a life-threatening medical problem arise, you may have to be evacuated to a country with more developed facilities. Check with your health insurance provider to make sure you are covered should this occur.

It is important to note that while "medical tourism" has become increasingly popular in Colombia, (particularly elective, aesthetic surgeries) these surgeries are inherently dangerous. Should you choose to undergo this kind of procedure in Colombia, be sure to thoroughly investigate the facilities and your surgeon beforehand. Updated: Mar 31, 2008.

Doctors

Pharmacy chains recommended by the U.S. Embassy in Bogotá include Cafam, Colsubsidio and Olímpica, and Sideral (most connected to major supermarkets). All of these offer delivery service.

AMI (Asistencia Médica Inmediata), a medical service in Bogotá, Barranquilla and Cartagena provides ambulance service, 24-hour house calls and pharmacy service. Updated: May 22, 2008.

Safety

The security situation in the country is generally safe. However, there are areas where it is more "fluid" and others that remain in the red zone of the nation's civil war. These include parts of the Pacific coast, Río Magdalena valley, the Llanos and the interior (Southern and Eastern) jungles. We have, as much as possible, pointed these out in the text. At the time our correspondents went to places, it was safe to do so. If you are considering going off the beaten track or into one of the problematic zones, check the news and ask local advice. Updated: Feb 22, 2008.

Keeping in Touch

Mail and Packages

The national postal service is Correos de Colombia, also called Adpostal. Most towns have an office. Letters and packages take up to a week for national delivery, 8-12 days for addresses in the Americas and about two weeks for other overseas destinations. All overseas post, even to neighboring countries, is sent via air mail. There have been reports of letters arriving opened and taped back shut. Prices for letters and packages is quite high.

Weight Normal Certified South America to Rest of World	
0 - 20g	$2.70 - $5.85
21 - 100g	$8.95 - $12.15
10 1- 500g	$20.00 - $26.50
501-1000g	$30.30 - $36.50

Courier companies are common throughout Colombia as well. The major ones are Servientrega Internacional, DHL, Deprisa (Avianca Airlines) and Federal Express.

You can have mail sent to you by way of the post office's general delivery. Have your post marked: your full name (as it appears in your passport, last name in capitals), Poste Restante, Lista de Correos, Correo Central, city or town, Colombia. If you hold an American Express credit card, you can also receive your mail at one of its offices (www.americanexpress.com). These days, very few embassies hold mail for their citizens.

Telephone Calls

Colombia's telephone country code is 57. In many smaller towns, Telecom has an office with phone service to local, national and international numbers. To make a local or national phone call, you can also go to a shop with a sign stating "Minutos" or "Llamadas."

Local phone calls have eight digits and begin with a number from 1 to 8; 9 is reserved for pay phones. For domestic long distance, Colombia has three carriers covering specific cities and regions of the country. Only ETB is nation-wide. Domestic long distance calls are prefixed with "0," followed by the code for the carrier: 5 for Orbitel, 7 for ETB and 9 for Telefónica. The third number in the initial series is the region code.

Phone Code	Department	Capital
1	Cudinamarca	Bogotá
2	Cauca	Popayán
2	Nariño	Pasto
2	Valle del Cauca	Cali

Phone Code	Department	Capital
4	Antioquía	Medellín
4	Chocó	Quibdó
4	Córdoba	Montería
5	Atlántico	Barranquilla
5	Bolívar	Cartagena
5	César	Valledupar
5	La Guajira	Riocacha
5	Magdalena	Santa Marta
5	Sucre	Sincelejo
6	Caldas	Manizales
6	Quindío	Armenia
6	Risalda	Pereira
7	Arauca	Arauca
7	Norte de Santander	Cúcuta
7	Santander	Bucaramanga
8	Amazonas	Leticia
8	Bocayá	Tunja
8	Caquetá	Florencia
8	Casanare	Yopal
8	Guainía	Puerto Inírida
8	Guaviare	San José de Guaviare
8	Huila	Neiva
8	Meta	Villavicencio
8	Putumayo	Mocoa
8	San Andrés y Providencia	San Andrés
8	Tolima	Ibagué
8	Vaupés	Mitú
8	Vichada	Puerto Carreño

National emergency numbers are 112 in Bogotá and 123 for Medellín.

To make an overseas call, numbers are prefixed with "00." Some internet and phone cafés have international phone service, charging $0.15-0.30 per minute to the U.S. and more for other countries. Skype is a more affordable option, though in some parts of the country it is unavailable (especially in the southern and eastern regions). It is also possible to make collect calls.

Cell Phone

Some travelers, especially if they are staying long-term in Colombia, pick up a cellular phone to keep in touch. Shop around, as the three companies here are quite competitive. In the major cities many small shops specialize in the sale of refurbished cell phones. Cards to recharge your *saldo* (account) come in 5,000, 10,000 and 20,000 COP. Many businesses also have mobile phones. The area codes for each of the three carriers are:

Tigo ▶ 300, 301, 302, 304
Comcel ▶ 310, 311, 312, 313, 314
Movistar ▶ 315, 316, 317

Internet

Internet cafés are found in towns of any significant size. Connections are usually fast (most have broadband) and charge $0.80-1.55 per hour. There are still many small villages where the populace does not have access to the internet. A trend throughout Colombia is to boycott Microsoft programs, instead using Open Office. Only hostels geared towards international or higher-budgeted travelers have on-site internet. WiFi is still uncommon in much of the country and is frequently charged for. Before sitting down with your laptop and logging in, make sure you will not be charged for this connection. Updated: Jul 10, 2008.

MEDIA

Colombia is a tough country for journalism. Human rights organizations like Amnesty International and Human Rights First, as well as professional journalist organizations such as Committee to Protect Journalists and Reporters Without Borders, rank Colombia as one of the four most dangerous countries for journalists. They also report that Colombia suffers one of the highest assassination and exile rates of any country in the world.

Gabriel García Márquez and other Latin American journalists have established the Fundación para un Nuevo Periodismo Iberoamericano to train the new generation of journalists. The institute has regular seminars, workshops and other programs. Calle San Juán de Dios 3-121, Cartagena de Indias, Tel.: 5-664-5890, Fax: 5-664-5904, URL: www.fnpi.org.

The established media in Colombia play a major role in the Uribe government's anti-terrorism program. Below is listed some of the independent media of the country. More listings for Colombia media may be found at Internet Public Library (www.ipl.org) or at World Press (www.worldpress.org/newspapers/AMERICAS/Colombia.cfm).

Newspapers

El Espectador (Independent, Bogotá)
www.elespectador.com
El Heraldo (Liberal, Barranquilla)
www.elheraldo.com.co
El Mundo (Liberal, Medellín)
www.elmundo.com
El País (Conservative, Cali)
www.elpais.com.co/paisonline
El Tiempo (Centrist, Bogotá)
www.eltiempo.com
El Universal (Liberal, Cartagena)
www.eluniversal.com.co

Magazines

Cromos (Centrist, news)
www.cromos.com.co
El Malpensante (Literary)
www.elmalpensante.com
Número (Left-wing, cultural)
www.revistanumero.com
Revista Cambio (Liberal)
www.revistacambio.com/html/index.php
Semana (Centrist, news)
www.semana.com

Television and Radio

Caracola — www.canalcaracol.com
RCN — www.canalrcn.com
Televisión Telesur — Colombia is not officially part of the Telesur consortia, but it can be received in some parts of the country. www.telesurtv.net

Online

Colombia Indy Media
http://colombia.indymedia.org
CM andamp; la Noticia
www.cmi.com.co
Colombian Journal (journalist Gary Leech) http://colombianjournal.org
El YesQuero (lawyer-journalist Rafael Rincón) http://elyesquero.blogspot.com
Updated: Jul 10, 2008.

Money and Costs

Costs

In Colombia, prices (particularly for hotels and transportation) as a rule increase 5.5-6 percent at the beginning of each year. Since research began for this guide, the dollar has decreased in value about 15 percent against the Colombia peso (COP).

Budget travelers can easily get by on about $17 per person per day, including the occasional national park visit and meal at a fancy restaurant. With a bit of an eye on expenses, though, you could survive on $15 per day. In much of the country, basic lodging can be had for $6-8 per night. Set meals of the day cost $2 on average. Transportation is the major expense. See the Budget Travelers section in this chapter for ways you can travel for less money in Colombia.

Mid-range travelers should allow $40-50 per day for basic expenses. Hotel rooms in this class cost $20-25 per night (less per person for couples), and have private bath (with hot water in cold climates, with only cold water in hotter parts of the country), cable TV and air conditioning. Meals usually cost about $8-10, including a drink.

Luxury travelers will find Colombia to be quite a bargain, especially if you are from Europe. Very nice hotels go for $70 on up. Count on having private bathroom with hot water in all climates, air conditioning, swimming pool, sauna and other amenities. You can enjoy a dinner with wine for $20-30, at the least. Be sure to add to your itinerary an Amazon jungle lodge, a Llanos hotel campestre and national park accommodations at Tayrona, Gorgona or Amacayacu. Updated: Jul 10, 2008.

Money

The official currency of Colombia is the peso (abbreviated COP). There are 50, 100 and 500 peso coins; the 10 and 20 pesos coins are rarely used now. Bills come in denominations of 1,000, 2,000, 5,000, 10,000, 20,000 and 50,000 COP. The symbol used before

Eco-tourism in Colombia

By the end of 2007 the Colombian Ministry of Commerce, Industry and Tourism reported approximately 1,260,000 tourists visited Colombia that year, a major improvement in the industry. Colombia is a variegated nation that offers visitors a wide range of eco-tourism options. Under Colombian law, eco-tourism is defined as a specialized type of tourism developed in areas with a unique natural environment that fits within parameters of sustainable human development. Ultimately, eco-tourism looks to entertain and educate the visitor through observation, study of natural resources and cultural aspects related to a place.

The Natural National Parks System contains 16 areas with an eco-tourism vocation and activities that respect nature and show visitors unique fauna and flora. Many of these places have camping grounds, restaurants, information centers, trails, etc. The system is set to offer tourists hiking excursions along designated trails in both jungle and highlands. The three Andes mountain ranges have spots for rock and ice climbing, camping, and hiking. Sailing on lagoons and rivers in search for dolphins, caimans and other aquatic creatures is also a possibility within eco-friendly boundaries as part of the national parks' activities. Furthermore, protected areas inside the parks often have museums and archeological sites to give visitors cultural contact with pre-Columbian groups.

Eco-tourism is an important tool to strengthen the park system. It generates financial resources through concessions, services and fees, allowing redistribution throughout the system. Although controlled eco-tourism can represent an improvement in the lives of people living in unique areas, it is essential to consider that some places are not designed for any kind of tourism. Don't push yourself into people's homes or privacy, and don't trespass limits of trails in parks. Colombia has organized eco-tourism and looks to conserve its natural areas; taking advantage of the opportunities that are available will expose you to a variety of sights and activities valuable to any traveler, in addition to allowing you to help with contributions to maintain the parks and communities. Updated: Mar 03, 2008.

prices is $. Even though most people travel only with a bank card, a variety of money options should be employed.

Cash

Carry some U.S. dollars in perfect condition for changing at border crossings or for areas where ATMs may not be available. *Casas de cambio* (exchange houses) in major cities will change Euros. Currencies of other countries are difficult to change into pesos anywhere.

Banks

These are the only institutions that cash travelers checks (see below). ATMS are common, connected with both Latin American and international networks (redes), including Cirrus and Plus. ATM machines are said to give better rates and have a higher daily withdrawal limit.

Credit Cards

High-end businesses accept credit cards. Mastercard and Visa are the most common; some also take Diners or American Express. Many bank ATMs take credit cards as well. Visa cash advances can be obtained at Banco de Bogotá and Banco Popular.

Travelers Checks

Bancolombia and some branches of Banco Santander exchange U.S. or Euro American Express Travelers checks. Go prepared with your passport. You will also have to fill out a form and give your right index finger print. Few casas de cambio and businesses accept travelers checks.

Wiring Money

Some travelers find they need to have folks back home wire them money through Western Union (www.westernunion.com) or MoneyGram (www.moneygram.com). You receive it in pesos, though you can buy U.S. dollars, if they are available. Branches of money wiring services at banks typically handle transactions only for Colombians. Foreigners will have to go to Giros y Finanzas (www.girosyfinanzas.com) for Western Union wires and Cambiamos (www.cambiamos.com) for MoneyGram. Check the websites for office locations. Updated: Jul 10, 2008.

Etiquette and Dress

Colombia is an extremely courteous country. When addressing strangers, a Colombian calls someone *primo(a)* (cousin) or *vecino(a)* (neighbor). In the countryside, a high form of respect you can show to a *campesino* is to call him *don* or her *doña*. To address someone with these titles is considered a bit old-fashioned in the cities, where you should stick with *señor* and *señora*. In eastern Colombia, particularly the Boyacá Department, the very formal *su merced* is used instead of *usted*. In greeting people, men shake hands with men, and women receive barely a kiss on the right cheek.

Dress in Colombia is conservative, with plain, simple lines. For business encounters, men should wear suits with tie; women can wear a dress, skirt or pants. The key for both genders is well-tailored, well-pressed clothing. Even on the Caribbean coast, fashions are a bit conservative, with the *guayabera* (short-sleeve shirt) being considered almost formal. Updated: Jul 11, 2008.

Officialdom and Business

Colombia has a very business-oriented society. Arrive to appointments on time, even though the other party may not. When dealing with public officials, be courteous. Usually they are patient—if you are. When going to an office, greet the person from the doorway. It is considered rude to enter uninvited.

When stopped by the military on the highways, remember these recruits are only doing their job. Usually only men are asked to step off the bus. Women stay on board. However, documents of all passengers are checked. Men may be patted down, in the search for weapons. Updated: Jul 11, 2008.

Responsible Tourism

Tourism in Colombia is experiencing rapid growth that is hoped will bring considerable benefits to the country. Unfortunately, some aspects of tourism can have negative social, environmental and even economic consequences. Responsible tourism benefits both the traveler and the local community alike. The traveler gets an insight into local cultures while the local community gains from low-impact, sustainable income. Sustainable, responsible actions are crucial to the future of the industry and we all play an essential part. Problems associated with drugs in Colombia are well documented. Aside from being vigilant of dangers direct and indirect dangers associated with the drugs industry, it is vital to act responsibly to avoid serious punishment. Certain principles can be identified to ensure that both you, and the local community can simultaneously benefit from your visit.

Do:

► Research your location prior to traveling and upon arrival visit the local information center or tourist office to discover any potential hidden delights. Try and learn at least the basics of Spanish as this will not only make things easier and more enjoyable but can also leave a positive impression with locals.

► Inquire about the environmental records of tour operators and, when appropriate, give preferential treatment to local guides, restaurants and accommodation over multinational firms that have a poor ecological reputation. This will enhance your experience and often ensures that your money goes directly to local people.

► Respect cultural and religious traditions. Colombia is a Catholic country and always act with consideration when in the vicinity of religious establishments.

► Be courteous and considerate when taking photos of people and always ask for their permission beforehand.

► Practice safe sex. The consequences of not doing so can be severe for both parties.

Do Not:

► Abuse privileges such as water and electricity, especially in smaller communities where resources are scarce. Some more expensive hotels provide the option of having your linen and towels washed daily. This is an unnecessary luxury that uses considerable energy and water.

► Drop litter. Although rubbish dropping may be a more common problem in Colombia than where you are from it is not ok to join this trend. Provide a good example, pack a plastic bag for trash and recycle when possible.

► Interfere in local ecology. However beautiful a flower may be, do not pick any and avoid interfering in wildlife habitats. Small actions can have devastating, long-term impacts on local environments. Updated: Apr 10, 2008.

PHOTOGRAPHY

Film

At the Airport

Take all your film with you in your carry-on luggage. The scanning process for checked luggage will damage your film. Passing your film more than five times through the X-ray can also damage it, but in this unlikely situation you can just ask for a hand check.

What Kind of Film to Buy

Fuji Velvia slide film is known for producing rich colors and good sharpness and contrast —great for vacation photos. The downside: it's a little pricey, and if you want the pictures in something other than slide format you'll have to get the slides scanned or scan them yourself.

Colombian Photography

If you are interested in looking at photos and not just taking them, Colombia has a lot to offer. The national photography museum in Bogotá, Photomuseo, is an innovative nonprofit that brings photography to all levels of society through its outdoor exhibitions. It holds five annual street exhibitions of national and international photographs in three different areas of the city, with each exhibit lasting 45 days. In doing this, Photomueso hopes to share the value of this art form with the public without elitism or pretention.

The museum holds two other events during the year—photomarathon, which brings together the works of professional, amateur and student photographers from Colombia and neighboring countries, and Fotográfica Bogotá, which involves street and gallery exhibitions of work from the most important national and international photographers. This occurs twice a year.

Colombia has produced several notable photographers, among them Leo Matiz, Saúl Orduz Vega, Abdú Eljaiek, Sady González Moreno and Gabriel Carvajal Pérez. (You can view their work at fotographoscolombianos.com).

Purchase, Repair and Develop

Bogotá

ABC Digital Center Servicio Técnico
Camera and video camera repair. Ca. 9, 37-40 L-2015/2016. Tel: 1-247-5589.

Artecámaras Reparaciones
Camera sale and repair. Carrera 9, 18-51 L-101. Tel: 1-282-7195.

Almacenes Super Foto Digital
Film developing. Ca. 23, 4-22. Tel: 1-281-6112.

Medellín
Electronippon Asistencia Técnica Integral LTDA. Authorized service for: Sony, Samsung, JVC, Toshiba and Sharp. Camera and camera accessory sale, camera and video camera repair. Ca. 46, 79-64.

COLORMATIC S.A.
Film developing. Carrera 43, A 28-18. Tel: 4-232-2822.

Cali
A.AB Centro Electrónico Digital
Camera repair. Autop Sur Oriental 65 A-36, Valle del Cauca. Tel: 2-524-2488 / 339-3300.

Universal Fotográfica
Develop all brands and types of film, transfer to CD, slides. Ca. 13, 3-29, Valle del Cauca. Tel: 2-880-5050 / 411-1085, E-Mail: info@universalfotografica.com, URL: www.universalfotografica.com. Updated: Apr 11, 2008.

Women Travelers

Colombia is a good country for the lone woman traveler. They are hassled less here by the stereotypical Latino whistling and cat-calling. However, if you do experience any such treatment, the best course of action is to ignore it and walk right on by. You may be considered a bit of an oddity, though, as most Colombians of either gender travel in groups. If it makes you feel more comfortable, use the old ploys: that a friend is nearby, carrying a photo of your "friend," wearing a wedding ring or travel with a companion. Wearing a cross or Star of David (which many Christians wear) does wonders to change people's attitudes, as they seem to believe you are a "good girl." Birth control and tampons are expensive and difficult to buy outside the major cities, so stock up before you leave.

Gay and Lesbian Travelers

Colombia has one of the more accepting scenes for gay and lesbians travelers—at least legally. In 2007 the National Legislature passed a law guaranteeing equal rights for same-sex couples in issues of finances, insurance and inheritance. It is estimated that 300,000 same-sex couples live in this country. Having said this, society in general is yet a bit up-tight about open expressions of love. The large cities, like Bogotá, Cali and Medellín, and Caribbean port towns have quite large GLBT communities that celebrate annual Gay Pride Day. A source of information about gay-friendly businesses is: www.guiagaycolombia.com.

Senior Travelers

As Colombia becomes safer, more retirees are heading to this country to explore the jungle, trek to Ciudad Perdida or just relax on the beach. Senior citizens (*tercera edad*) as they say in Colombia—will find Colombia to be quite enjoyable. Discounts on everything from bus fares to museum entries are given to those over 65 years (and in some places, even younger). As in other Latin cultures, much respect is shown to older adults.

Disabled Travelers

Travel for disabled persons is a mixed bag in Colombia. Much understanding is lent to these travelers, as quite a high percentage of the nation's population is disabled, due to landmines and other incidences of the civil war. However, the infrastructure is not quite designed for persons with disabilities. Newer constructions and more upscale businesses are trying to be more conscious of this population's special needs. If you are sojourning in a wheelchair, keep an upbeat attitude. Travel with a companion who can help you get over that doorstep or wherever you might need a hand. Phone hotels and restaurants beforehand to inquire about their accessibility.

Traveling with Children

Because families are the center of Colombian society, you will find you receive different—if not better—treatment when traveling with children. When Colombians travel, the whole family goes. It is common that mid-range and above hotels have a kiddie pool, playground or other special amenities for children. Some of the more upscale inns even have suites with a bedding area just for the young ones. Often the Banco de la República cultural centers have story hour or other programs for kids. On buses, fares for children are cheaper if they ride in a parent's lap. At hotels, ask about the children's rate or bargain for one. It is acceptable to share a meal with a young one. Teach your kids to say simple niceties like *gracias* and *por favor*. Updated: Jul 10, 2008.

Budget Travelers

Colombia is a "swing" country for travelers spending six months to two years traveling in the Americas, from Argentina to Mexico. Many will be flying out of an expensive country like the U.S., Mexico, Chile or Brazil. It is important to save money, otherwise you may have to find yourself cutting your journey, having to work or going into debt. Here are some tips to help you experience Colombia more economically.

Lodging

Cheaper hostels include *hospedajes* and residencies, often located near the markets; skip the extras, like private bath, air conditioning and TV. If staying for more than a few nights, ask about a possible discount. Room prices are generally cheaper per person for couples than for the solo traveler. Camp or sleep in hammocks wherever offered. If you feel comfortable with new cheap alternatives younger travelers are relying on, there is couch surfing (www.couchsurfing.com) and artisan crash pads.

Food and Drink

Breakfast is a poor-value meal; fix it in. Inexpensive meals are the comida corriente, or set meal available at lunch and dinner ($1.30-3) and those found in the dinning room section of the public market. Buy a portable heating element to warm water for tea or coffee. Look for hostels that have cooking facilities. Purify your own water by filter or drops (some pharmacies sell Aquasafe).

Going out to Colombian nightclubs is almost prohibitively expensive to the shoestring traveler. Consider that often the cover charge alone is about $10, plus your drinks on top of it. Save such activities for a special occasion. Buying beer at the store is relatively cheap; wine is quite pricey.

Transportation

Journeying long legs is cheaper than short ones in Colombia. Outside the high season, ask for a discount. Couples report success hitchhiking, though remember that this is not without its risks.

Activities

Many museums and archaeological sites in Colombia are free. Discounts are frequently given to those with an ISIC card, and often with your university's own ID. Children and seniors get substantial reductions. For free entertainment, check out exhibits, concerts, movies and other events at cultural centers or universities. Some active sports are absolutely free, like swimming, snorkeling and hiking *caminos de herradura*, or stone roads that lace the Colombian countryside.

General

Avoid prime Colombian destinations during holidays, when prices for lodging and food at least double, and in some places up to quadruple. Limit travel at these times. Although it may seem tedious, keep a daily accounting of your expenses. You can then see how you are spending your money, and know where to cut back if you find you are overspending. An additional advantage to this is you will always have handy the figures of hotels and transport to pass along to other travelers. Updated: Jul 10, 2008.

Colombia Bibliography

If you cannot find these books at your local vendor, ask your public library if you can obtain them through interlibrary loan (there may be a small fee for this service). This is just a sample of books about Colombia:

"The Darkest Jungle: The True Story of the Darién Expedition and America's Ill-fated Race to Connect the Seas." Todd Balf. (Crown Publishers, 2003)—About the 1850s expedition through the Darien Gap to find a suitable place to build a canal.

"Until Death Do Us Part: My Struggle to Reclaim Colombia." Ingrid Betancourt. (Ecco, 2002)—The former presidential candidate's memoir about fighting against the drug cartels and corruption in her country.

"Killing Pablo: The Hunt for the World's Greatest Outlaw." Mark Borden. (Atlantic Monthly Press, 2001)—The rise and fall of Pablo Escobar.

"The Assassination of Gaitán: Public Life and Urban Violence in Colombia." Herbert Braun. (University of Wisconsin Press, 1986)—How the assassination of presiden-

INTRO & INFO

tial candidate Jorge Eliécer Gaitán affected the course of Colombian history.

"Camilo Torres: A Biography of the Priest Guerrillero." Walter Broderick. (Doubleday, 1975)—A biography of the priest-turned-guerrilla-fighter Camilo Torres.

"The Making of Modern Colombia: A Nation in Spite of Itself." David Bushnell. (University of California Press, 1993) – The first book on Colombian history published in English.

"Walking Ghosts: Murder and Guerrilla Politics in Colombia." Steven S. Dudley. (Routledge, 2004)—Chronicles based on Dudley's five years reporting from Colombia for National Public Radio.

"Heart of the World: The Elder Brothers." Alan Ereira. (Knopf, 1992)—About the Kogui beliefs and way of life deep in the Sierra Nevada de Santa Marta.

"1928 La masacre en las Bananeras." Jorge Eliécer Gaitán. (Editorial Cometa de Papel, 1997)—Gaitán's presentation of eyewitness reports of the 1928 banana worker massacre in Ciénaga.

"One Hundred Years of Solitude." Gabriel García Márquez—Well-known for his novels and short stories, García Márquez is a must-read for anyone attempting to understand Colombian culture.

"The Heart that Bleeds: Latin America Now." Alma Guillermoprieto. (Knopf, 1994) and Looking for History: Dispatches from Latin America (Vintage Books, 2002)—A collection of this Mexican journalist's articles for the New Yorker magazine.

"María." Jorge Isaacs. A piece of classic Colombian literature.

"Simón Bolívar: A Life." John Lynch. (Yale University Press, 2006)—The first biography in English of the Great Liberator in over 50 years.
"Reflections on Mining in Colombia: When 'Development Creates Deprivation". Suzanne MacNeil. Colombia Journal Online, August 13, 2007 (www.colombiajournal.org/colombia262.htm).

"The Dispossessed: Chronicles of the Desterrados of Colombia." Lafredo Molano. (Haymarket Books, 2005)—Testimonies from internal refugees of Colombia's civil war.

"Colombia and the United States: War, Terrorism and Destabilization." Mario Murillo. (Seven Stories Press, 2003)—The effects on Colombian civilians of the U.S. War on Drugs.

"Chambacu: Black Slum." Manuel Zapata Olivella. (Latin American Literary Review Press, 1989) and "A Saint is Born In Chima" (University of Texas Press, 1991)—Zapata Olivella was one of the most important Afro-Colombian writers and ethnographers.

Reuters Alert Net: Colombia Displacement—An excellent series of articles about the effects of the War on Drugs, narcotrafficking and refugees (www.alertnet.org/printable.htm?URL=/db/crisisprofiles/CO_DIS.htm).

"Colombia: Fragmented Land, Divided Society." Frank Safford and Marco Palacios. (Oxford University Press, 2001)—Colombian history and culture from before Columbus to the modern day.

"Our Lady of the Assassins." Fernando Vallejo. (Consortium Book Sales)—The novel upon which the movie was based.

For Children

"Colombia." Jill DuBois. (Marshall Cavendish, 2002)—A primer on Colombia.

"Encantado: Pink Dolphin of the Amazon." Sy Montgomery (Houghton Mifflin, 2002)—An invitation to learn about the magic and diversity of Colombia's Amazon.
"The Orinoco River." Carol Rawlins. (Franklin Watts, 1999)—Getting to know the second greatest river of South America, the Orinico.

"Colombia: A question and Answer Book." Kremena Spengler. (Capstone Press, 2006)—An introduction to Colombia's history, geography and culture. Updated: Jul 10, 2008.

Information Resources

Government Pages

Colombia:
http://web.presidencia.gov.co,
http://www.gobiernoenlinea.gov.co
U.S. Embassy, Bogotá:
http://bogota.usembassy.gov

British Embassy:
http://www.britishembassy.gov.uk
Canadian Embassy:
http://www.dfait-maeci.gc.ca/Colombia/about-en.asp
Ministerio de Relaciones Exteriores:
http://www.minrelext.gov.co (addresses of embassies andamp; consulates)
Ejército Nacional, Republica de Colombia: http://www.ejercito.mil.co

Factions

Autodefensas Unidas de Colombia (AUC): http://www.colombialibre.org
Ejército de Liberación Nacional de Colombia **(ELN):** http://www.nodo50.org/patrialibre
Fuerzas Armadas Revolucionarias de Colombia (FARC): http://www.farcep.org

Media

Print
El Espectador (Bogotá):
http://www.elespectador.com
El Tiempo:
http://eltiempo.terra.com.co
El Heraldo (Barranquilla):
http://www.elheraldo.com.co
El Mundo (Medellín):
http://www.elmundo.com
El País (Cali):
http://www.elpais.com.co/paisonline
El Universal (Cartagena):
http://www.eluniversal.com.co
Television Telesur:
http://www.telesurtv.net/
Online
Colombia Indy Media:
http://colombia.indymedia.org
CMI:
http://www.cmi.com.co
Reuters Alert Net: Colombia Displacement:
http://www.alertnet.org/printable.htm URL=/db/crisisprofiles/CO_DIS.htm,
Colombian Journal (journalist Gary Leech): http://colombianjournal.org
More listed at Internet Public Library: www.ipl.org

Tourism

Colombia.com:
http://www.colombia.com
Fondo de Promoción Turístico Colombia: http://www.turismocolombia.com/prehome.asp
Instituto Nacional de Vías:
http://www.invias.gov.co (road conditions, maps, etc.)
Instituto de Hidrología, Meteorología y Estudios Ambientales:
http://www.ideam.gov.co
Instituto Geográfico Agustín Codazzi:
http://www.igac.gov.co

Blogs and Other Sites

Poor But Happy:
http://poorbuthappy.com/colombia
Couch Surfing:
http://www.couchsurfing.com (recommended by a traveler from Colombia)
Hospitality Club:
http://www.hospitalityclub.org (recommended by a traveler from Colombia)
Platypus:
http://platypusbogota.com/info.php
Third World Traveller:
http://www.thirdworldtraveller.com
Mochileros.org:
http://www.mochileros.org
Plan B Bogota: http://planb.com.co
Gringo (in Hebrew):
http://www.gringo.co.il/country_page.asp?countryID=9

Human Rights Organizations and Other NGO's

CODHES (Consultoria para los Derechos Humanos y el Desplazamiento): http://www.codhes.org/
Witness for Peace: http://www.witness-forpeace.org
Peace Brigades International:
http://www.pbi-colombia.org/pbi-colombia.html
Fellowship of Reconciliation:
http://www.forcolombia.org
United Nations High Commission on Refugees:
http://www.unhcr.org/cgi-bin/texis/vtx/country?iso=col
Amnesty International:
http://web.amnesty.org/web/content.nsf/pages/gbr_colombia
Amnesty International (USA):
www.amnestyusa.org/By_Country/Colombia

Human Rights Watch:
http://hrw.org/spanish/informes/1998/guerra7.html

Refugees International:
http://www.refugeesinternational.org/content/country/detail/2934
Global Exchange:
http://www.globalexchange.org/countries/americas/Colombia

Indigenous Rights

General Indigenous Actualidad Ética:
http://www.etniasdecolombia.org/actualidadetnica/index.asp
Organización Nacional Indígena de Colombia: http://www.onic.org.co
Survival:
http://www.survival-international.org/tribes/arhuaco (Arhuaco: http://www.survival-international.org/tribes/arhuaco)
Nukak:
http://www.survival-international.org/tribes/nukak

Specific Nations
U'wa Colombia:
http://www.uwacolombia.org/
Wayuunaiki:
http://wayuunaiki.com
NotiWayúu:
http://www.notiwayuu.blogspot.com. Updated: Jun 29, 2008.

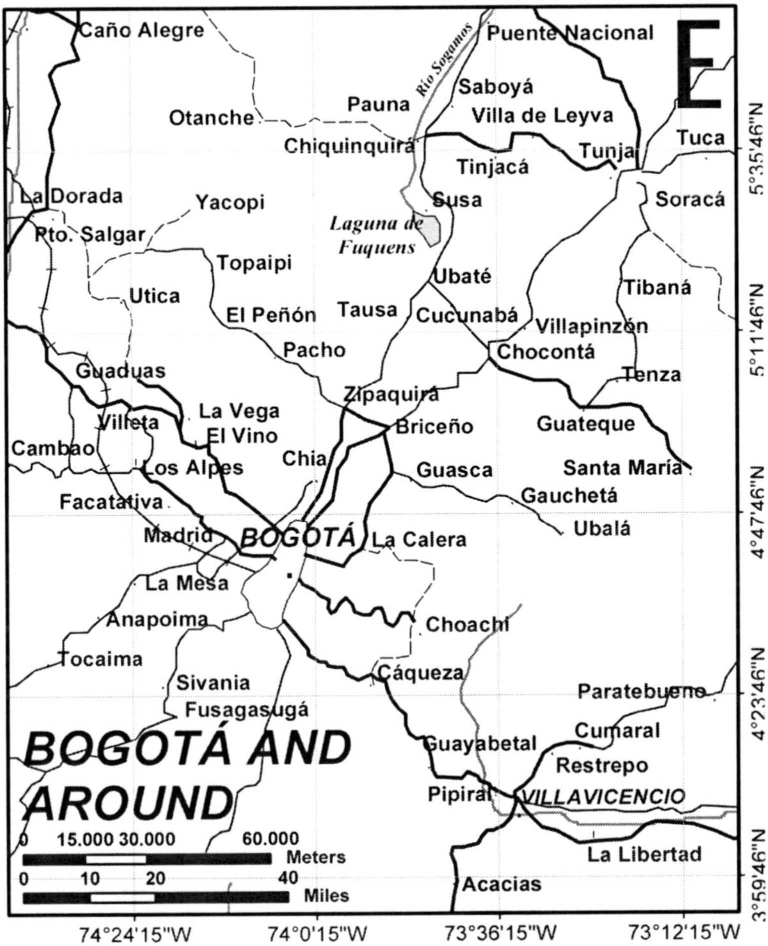

BOGOTÁ

Alt: 2,600m Pop: 6,779,000 City Code: 1

Perhaps the quintessential Latin American city, Bogotá is a place of sharp contrasts. Combining history with modernity and luxury with poverty, this is a varied and fascinating destination for travelers. With preserved colonial architecture, luxurious high-rise hotels and quaint bohemian cafés, Bogotá has a range of highlights and attractions that can satisfy the desires of backpackers and high-end tourists alike.

Located in the center of Colombia atop an Andean plateau, Bogotá is flanked by the Cordillera Oriente to the east and smaller mountain ranges to the west. With an altitude of 2,600 meters (8530 feet) above sea level, the capital takes third place for highest major city in the world. Travelers will find Bogotá, once considered too dangerous and dirty, has recently undergone a serious makeover. With increased security, infrastructure, and maintenence the Colombian capital now thrives as a cultural case study in South America. Despite these recent advances, crime is still prevalent and visitors should be alert around tourist areas and government buildings.

The colonial region of Bogotá is alternately called La Candelaria and Centro Histórico. This area provides travelers with a pleasant sense of history and a great selection of cafés, theatres and museums. Considered by many the intellectual and cultural center of Bogotá, La Candelaria is a must-see district. A strong university presence here results in low prices and a prevalent bohemian culture.

In contrast to the historic La Candelaria, the north of Bogotá offers a far more modern, commercial and capitalist atmosphere. Luxury hotels, glitzy apartments and swanky shopping malls bring the city out of the colonial era and into the modern age. Thought to be reasonably safe, this area is great for high-end accommodation and shopping. Hacienda Santa Bárbara provides all the services of a comprehensive shopping mall and the Museo Mercedes de Pérez offers a wide array of 18th-Century art.

Day trips outside of the city are also popular due to Bogotá's central location. Restless travelers can stretch their legs as they explore the surrounding landscape. The cliffs of Suesca offer world-class rock climbing, while short journeys to Laguna de Guativa provide great views of the Cundinamarca countryside.

Highlights

Visit the **Jardín Botánico**—Botanical Garden—(p.89) for a mini national park experience.

Stroll through the exhibitions of the **Gold Museum (p.88).**

Become part of the lively atmosphere in the cafés of **La Candelaria (p.93)**.

Aside from dancing and walking in the city parks, stay fit by taking a bike ride through the street of Bogotá on the **Ciclovía (p.89)**.

Take a ride to the stunning **Cerro de Monserrate (p.94)** for a spectacular view of the city.

Visit the **Centro Cultural Gabriel García Márquez (p.94)**, a new museum chronicling the life and art of the Colombian literary legend. Updated: Jun 6, 2008.

History

Standing high on its plain, Bogotá was originally inhabited by one of the region's most advanced pre-Columbian civilizations, the Muisca. In the 16th Century, the Spanish conquistador Gonzalo Jiménez de Quesada reached the Muisca capital of Bacatá. Struck by it's location, the prevalence of rivers, and by the legend of El Dorado–the Muisca were master goldsmiths–Quesada attacked, defeating the tribe and christening the location Santa Fe de Bogotá.

With the passage of riches moving from current-day Ecuador and Peru up through Colombia, Bogotá grew rapidly as an important administrative center. In 1740 the city was declared the capital of the Viceroyalty of New Granada, an area including what is now Colombia, Venezuela, Ecuador and Panama. In the following years, Bogotá both heralded the arrival of South America's Liberator Simón Bolívar and shunned him from the city limits. The city became defined by its remarkable and ornate Republican architecture, all of which can be seen in and around the Plaza de Bolívar.

Despite considerable growth by the turn of the 20th Century, Bogotá still only contained a population of about 100,000. It wasn't until the middle of the century, in a drive for industrialization, that the city began to thrive.

In an unfortunate turn of events that has resulted in the socially fractured Colombia we know today, Liberal leader Jorge Eliécer Gaitán was assassinated on April 9, 1948, in Bogotá. What ensued is known as the *Bogotazo*–a period of mayhem when the city was literally under attack from within. Churches, public offices and buildings were sacked and burned during this time. A tenuously organized mob took control and thousands of people lost their lives. Since, Bogotá has been regaining its confidence and evolving into a vibrant capital city. Updated: Feb 26, 2008.

When to Go

Often referred to by its polite and well-educated citizenry as the "Athens of South America," Bogotá virtually always has culturally stimulating events. Check local listings, bill stickers on the walls of La Candelaria or the directories in the newspaper, El Tiempo (www.eltiempo.com) for continuously updated event listings. Given the city's altitude and location on the altiplano, it should come as no surprise that the average temperature in Bogotá is roughly 13°C (55°F). It can drop to a low of 6°C (42°F) on especially cold evenings, and on some occasions has been known to reach a high of around 19ºC (66ºF). Be warned that it rains a good deal in Bogotá. Updated: Feb 26, 2008.

Holidays and Festivals

Month	Event
January	Arrival of the Three Kings in the Barrio Egipto
February	Bull fighting season starts
March/ April	Iboamerican Theater Festival (2008 and every other year)
April	Feria del Libro
August	Summer Festival, Bogotá's Birthday, Salsa in the Park
September	Jazz in the Park
October	Bogotá Film Festival, Rock in the Park
November	Opera in the Park
December	Christmas Lights Festival

Updated: Feb 6, 2008.

Getting To and Away from Bogotá

Air

International and internal flights with Aeropública leave from and arrive to the Aeropuerto El Dorado (Avenida El Dorado, 93-30. Tel: 1-425-1000). A newer terminal has been built about a half-mile from El Dorado and is called the Aeropuente. All Avianca internal flights leave from here. When traveling by taxi, the driver will ask you to specify which airport, El Dorado or the Aeropuente.

Land

Terminal de Transportes (Diagonal 23, 69-60. Tel: 1-423-3630 / 416-3951) is the main hub for land travel aside from closer destinations such as Zipaquirá, Guatavita, Suesca and Villa de Leyva. These areas can be reached by taking the Transmilenio to the final station north (Portal del Norte) and then catching small interurban buses from there. You will need to familiarize yourself with the Terminal de Transportes, since buses leave from here for every part of Colombia. Bear in mind that you can negotiate bus fares in Colombia. Do not accept the first rate offered.

Train

(To Zipaquirá and around)–The Turistren, which runs its course to Zipaquirá and the surrounding area, leaves from the Sabana Station only on Saturdays, Sundays and holidays. This is not a regular transport train but a tourist activity. More information can be found at www.turistren.com.co. Updated: Feb 26, 2008.

Getting Around Bogotá

At first glance Bogotá seems disorganized, but actually it is pretty easy to navigate. The most important thing to remember is that Avenidas and Carreras run North to South, and Calles run East to West. Once you have your bearings, you will see that the mountains in Bogotá are at the extreme eastern edge of the city and that the major thoroughfares are Carrera 7 and Carrera 10.

There are three ways to get around the city. The easiest is by taxi, since taxis are prevalent throughout Bogotá and are inexpensive. Late at night try to catch an official taxi to avoid being cheated. All taxis run on meters that should comply with a set-rate chart visible to the passenger. Fares after 8 p.m., on holidays, Sundays, and to and from the airport have special surcharges. One recommended taxi company is Taxis Express, Tel: 1-411-1111.

Bogotá's aging buses careen around street corners, race to beat the change of traffic lights and belch out thick fumes. In the front window of each bus you'll find the listed destination. The cost of a fare is normally around $0.60. If you are in doubt about anything ask a fellow traveler. Buses do not necessarily stop at conventional bus stops—they can stop everywhere.

The Transmilenio is a new bus system that is fast and convenient. Beware of peak hours, when the service is saddled with delays, overcrowded vehicles and pickpockets (otherwise it can be a delight). Also, be warned that the Transmilenio maps are not particularly clear and often the buses are poorly labeled. There are plans to extend the service and include a new route to the airport. Single fare is $0.70. Tel: 1-364-9400. Updated: Feb 26,2008.

Safety in Bogotá

For a city of its size, Bogotá is remarkably safe. Gone are the days when travelers feared

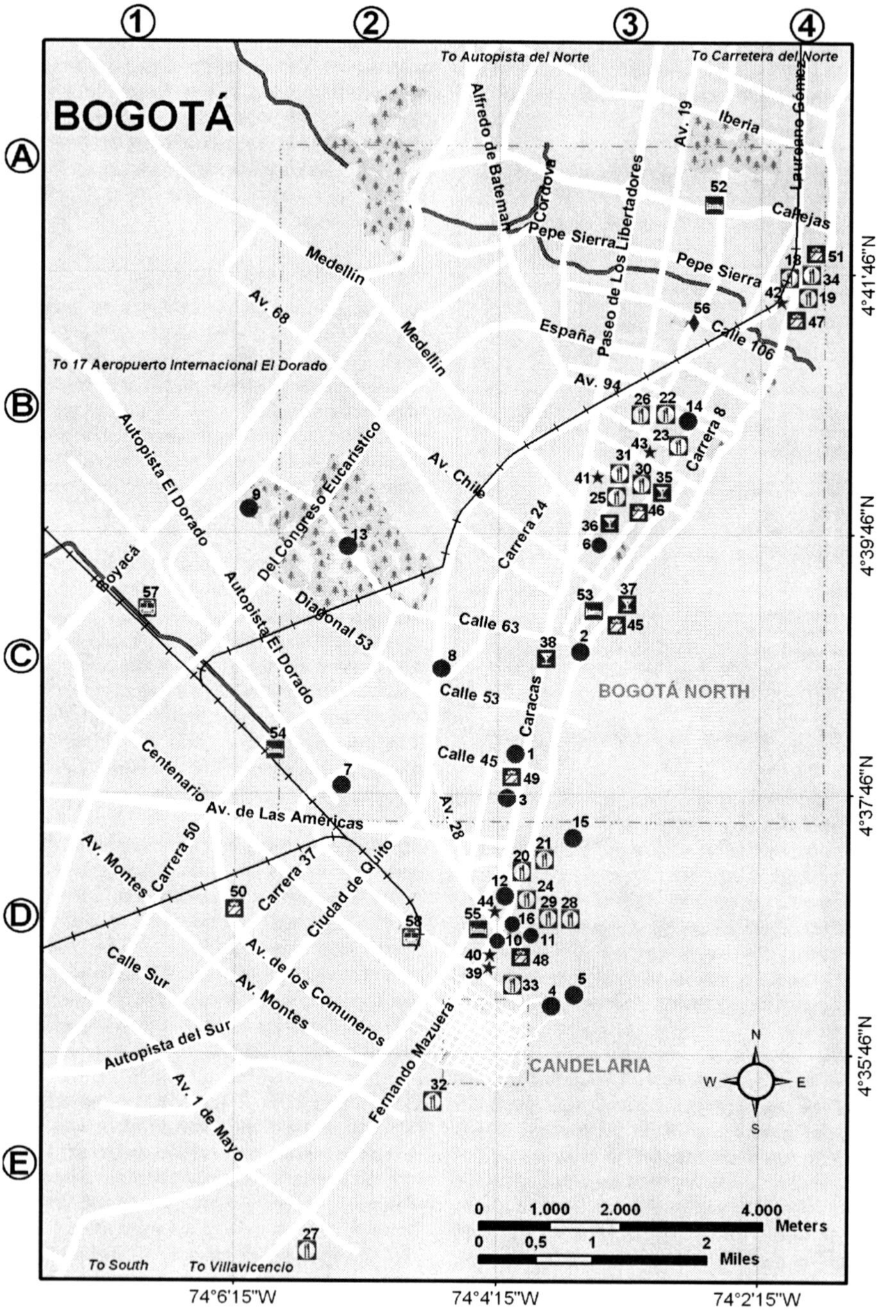

Activities ●

1 Body Care Gym C4
2 BodyTech C4
3 Casa Museo Jorge Eliecer Gaitán C4
4 Casa Quinta de Bolívar D4
5 Cerro de Monserrate D4
6 Cinema C4
7 Corferias C3
8 El Campin C3
9 Jardín Botánico José Celestino B3

10 Museo de Arte Moderno D4
11 Museo de Bogotá D4
12 Museo Nacional D4
13 Parque Central Simón Bolívar C3
14 Parque de la 93 B4
15 Parque Nacional Olaya Herrera D4
16 Plaza de Toros la Santamaría D4

Airport

17 Aeropuerto Internacional El Dorado B1

Eating

18 80 Sillas B5
19 Alfredo's Bistro B5
20 Cha Cha D4
21 El Cafecito D4
22 El Salto del Angel B4
23 El Sitio B4
24 Frida D4
25 Gótica B4
26 Kukaranakara B4
27 La Cocina y Cava E3
28 La Hamburgueseria D4
29 La Juguetería B4
30 Luna B4
31 Penélope B4
32 Pizza al Paso B3
33 Sanzinnis D4
34 Zhang China Gourmet B5

Nightlife

35 Alma B4
36 Bar 201 B4
37 Café Internet Bar C4
38 Monkey Pub C4

Services ★

39 Camera Repair Almacén Buitriago D3
40 Camera Repair Local 231 D3
41 Hospital Clínica del Country B4
42 Hosptital Santa Fe de Bogotá B5
43 Mac Tools B4
44 Policía Turismo D4

Shopping

45 Author Books C4
46 Centro Comercial el Andino B4
47 Centro Comercial Hacienda de Santa Bárbara B5
48 Flea Market D4
49 Nomada C4
50 San Andresito D3
51 Usaquen Flea Market A5

Sleeping

52 Estelar la Fontana A4
53 La Casona del Patio Amarillo C4
54 Martha's Place C3
55 Tequendama International D3

Tours ♦

56 Tesoro Tours A4
57 Bus Terminal C2

Transportation

58 Steam Train to Zipaquirá D3

walking at daytime through La Candelaria and would hurry back to their accommodation at dusk. Begging is prevalent, especially in La Candelaria, and tourists should be advised not to stray west of Carrera 10 in this area. Caution should be exercised as in other big cities. Be especially diligent with your personal belongings on buses and on the Transmilenio. If you are the victim of any crime, you can report the incident to the Policía de Turismo (Hotel Tequendama, Carrera 13, 26-62. Tel: 1-337-4413 / 1-243-1175). Updated: Feb 26, 2008.

Bogotá Services

Tourism Office

In the southwest corner of the Plaza de Bolivar in La Candelaria there is an informed and helpful Tourist Information office. Open 8 a.m. - 6 p.m. Plaza de Bolívar Carerra 8, 9-83. Tel: 1-327-4916. You can also find Tourism Offices in the Terminal de Transportes (1-295-4460) and in the airport (1-413-9053).

Money

The Carrera 7 running north from the Plaza de Bolívar is the most convenient place to locate any and all of the banks and financial institutions that you might need. There are a number of ATH (*A Toda Hora*—at all times) ATMs that work with every type of card. There are also a couple of well-policed ATMs close to the Museo de Oro. Money changers jostle for position on street corners near the Avenida de Jiménez Transmilenio station. Do not change money in the street. Go to one of the official offices nearby instead.

Keeping in touch

In Bogotá, and in particular in La Candelaria, the traveler has many choices of internet cafés and telephone cabins. International calls can be made easily and cheaply while an hour on the internet should cost no more than $1.

Medical

Pharmacies can be found on almost every block along the Carrera 7 and inside most major supermarket chains (Exito, Carrulla and Carrefour).

Hospitals:

Fundación Santa Fe de Bogotá. Calle 116, 9-02. Tel: 1-629-0766.

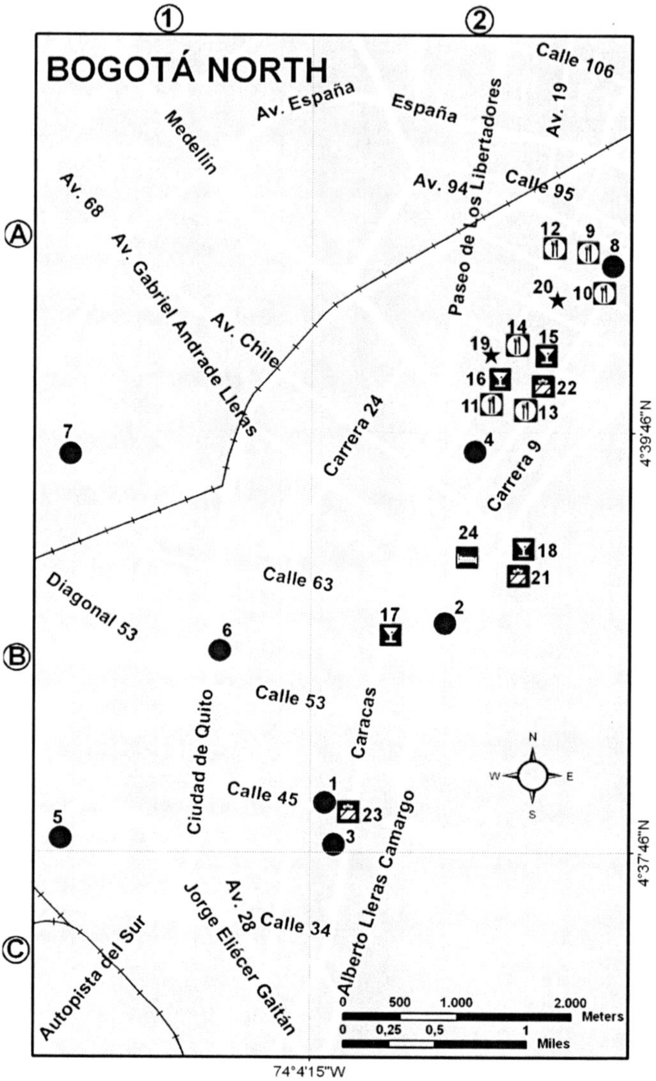

Activities ●

1 Body Care Gym B2
2 BodyTech B2
3 Casa Museo Jorge Eliecer Gaitán B2
4 Cinema B2
5 Corferias B1
6 El Campin B1
7 Parque Central Simon Bolívar B1
8 Parque de la 93 A2

Eating

9 El Salto del Angel A2
10 El Sitio A2
11 Gótica A2
12 Kukaranakara A2
13 Luna A2
14 Penélope A2

Nightlife

15 Alma A2
16 Bar 201 A2
17 Café Internet Bar B2
18 Monkey Pub B2

Service ★

19 Hospital Clínica del Country A2
20 Mac Tools A2

Shopping

21 Author Books B2
22 Centro Comercial el Andino A2
23 Nomada B2
24 La Casona del Patio Amarillo B2

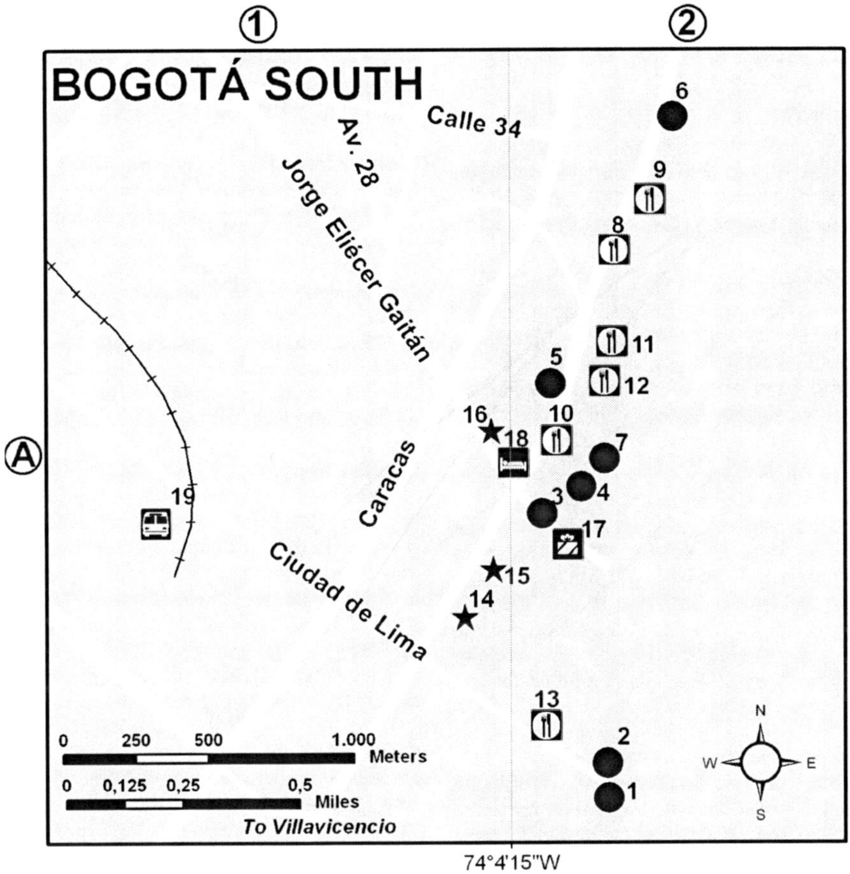

Activities ●

1 Casa Quinta de Bolívar A2
2 Cerro de Monserrate A2
3 Museo de Arte Moderno A2
4 Museo de Bogotá A2
5 Museo Nacional A2
6 Parque Nacional Olaya Herrera A2
7 Plaza de Toros la Santamaría A2

Eating

8 Cha Cha A2
9 El Cafecito A2
10 Frida A2
11 La Hamburgueseria A2
12 La Juguetería A2
13 Sanzinnis A2

Service ★

14 Camera Repair Foto Almacén Buitriago A1
15 Camera Repair Local 231 A1
16 Policía Turismo A1

Shopping

17 Flea Market A2

Sleeping

18 Tequendama International A2

Transportation

19 Steam Train to Zipaquirá A1

Clínica del Country. Carrera 16, 82-57. Tel: 1-530-0470, E-mail: www.clinicadelcountry.com.

Laundry

Most accommodation options will have a laundry service you can use. However, for those in La Candelaria that don't, try Lavaseco La Colonial. Carrera 3, 13-88.

Camera Repair

Foto Almacén Buitrago, 9:00 a.m.-2:30 p.m. Monday-Friday. Located on Carrera 7, 21-65, second floor.
Camera repairs, Local 231, Carrera 7 22-31. Tel: 1-286-3369. Updated: Feb 26, 2008.

Shopping

From the polished marble surfaces in the ultra-modern shopping malls to the street markets in San Andresito, there is plenty of shopping in Bogotá. Should you need hiking equipment, new books written in English, repairs for your iPod or if you simply wish to pick up some locally ground coffee and Colombian keepsakes, all can be found here in Bogotá with relative ease.

Centro Comercial el Andino
An incredibly popular shopping center in the heart of the Zona Rosa, Centro Comercial el Andino offers everything from quality clothing stores to designer sunglass emporiums. What makes this mall a destination for the visitor is its six-screen cinema and enormous food court. Just a few streets over, on Calle 81, is the Atlantis Plaza. This is another mall with more cinemas and similarly styled stores. Carrera 11, 82-71. Tel: 1-621-3111.

Herencias de Artesanías y Café de Colombia
Although you can find tourist trinkets and ground coffee for cheaper in nearby galleries, this shop is a convenient option. If you are in a hurry and need some high-quality and nicely-packaged goods, Herencias de Artesanías will not disappoint. The shop stocks high-quality coffee and interestingly crafted Colombian *artesanías*. Calle 16, 4-92. Tel: 1-243-0195, E-mail: herencias_artesanias@hotmail.com.

Authors Books
In addition to its attractive café, Authors Books stocks new releases, classics and a healthy variety of English-language magazines, though books are marked up significantly. If the prices are too steep, try your luck in Tower Records in Atlantis Plaza and Centro Comercial Andino. Carrera 7, 70, 5-23. Tel: 1-217-7788, E-mail: www.authors.com.co.

San Andresito
More a collection of warehouses than a store, San Andresito is spread over four or five square blocks and sells just about everything from knock-off shoes and clothes to the latest electronic devices. Cheap alcohol, cheaper DVDs and vendors at every turn are the sum of San Andresito. Bargaining is a necessity and be sure to compare prices between stalls before making a final purchase. Be advised to watch your belongings here. Carrera 38, 6.

MacTools
Since almost every traveler or someone they know has an iPod, iTouch or iPhone of some shape and description, it is worth noting that there is an Apple Certified Technician in Bogotá who can tend to any problems and glitches. Of course they also stock all the new software for Apple products. Calle 90, 13-53. Tel: 1-622-3188, E-mail: camilovega@cable.net.co, URL: www.applemactools.com.

Hacienda Santa Bárbara
Yet another enormous shopping center in Bogotá, the Hacienda Santa Bárbara is located in Usaquén in the northern part of the city. Part of the shopping mall has been fashioned out of what remains of a vast colonial building. This structure would have been a weekend retreat for wealthy bogotanos in the past. The number of shops, cafés and eateries is astounding. Any trip to Usaquén should include a gander through the Hacienda Santa Bárbara. Carrera 7, 115-60. Tel: 1-612-0388.

Usaquén Flea Market
The Usaquén Flea Market is not far from the amenities of the Hacienda Santa Bárbara and the delightful Usaquén plaza, and is surrounded by restaurants and artsy cafés. Designers and craftsmen all display their curios here. T-shirts, shawls, carvings, organics and other items are up for negotiation. Calle 119B.

Nómada
While some of the larger supermarkets, such as Exito in Chapinero, stock some items supplied by specialist camping stores, it is worth knowing that there is a specific camping sup-

Gay Bogotá

Although an amendment ensuring equal rights for gay citizens passed in 1991, homophobia is still quite prevalent throughout the machista culture of Colombia. Bogotá is the exception. Although most rural regions of the country maintain strictly traditional notions of gender and sexuality, Bogotá has developed a progressive gay culture with a variety of clubs, bars and social networks. The Colombian capital has come a long way in terms of tolerance and acceptance. Nine years ago, the first annual Gay Pride Parade attracted just 32 participants. This year, the number was estimated at 3,750. Today, Bogotá is one of Latin America's leaders in the acceptance and celebration of LGBT culture.

The gay scene is primarily in the north of Bogotá. The Chapinero district–affectionately nicknamed "gay ghetto," "gay hills" and "bodygay,"–features a majority of the city's gay-friendly establishments. Dance clubs like Theatron (Calle 58, 10-34. Tel: 1-249-2092, URL: www.theatrondepelicula.com) and Lottus (Calle 58 10-42, piso 3) provide lively rumbas for the gay traveler within the Chapinero. Both have a cover charge of $7 that usually includes several drinks along with a wild night of partying. Be aware that Lottus is open to male patrons only. Outside of the Chapinero, Cats (Calle 74, 15-51. Cel: 310-555-4699) and Club G (Carrera 17, 14-68 Sur. Tel: 1-278-3030) are also popular spots. For the high-end traveler looking to venture a bit outside the city, El Closet Lounge (Km5 Via Calera. Tel: 1-520-7126, URL: www.elclosetbogota.com) is a luxurious club with a great view of Bogotá and a well-equipped sound system. These are only a few of Bogotá's plethora of gay bars and clubs.

Bogotá also offers hotels geared toward homosexual guests. High Park Hotel (Carrera 4, 58-58. Tel: 1-753-7724) advertises itself as 100 percent gay and lesbian. Other lodging options include Residencias Gays (Carrera 15, 86A-42 Apt. 201. Cell: 315-613-3670) and Green House (Avenida Caracas, 55-52. Tel: 1-346-0461).

Gay travelers will also find restaurants, gyms and tour agencies specifically geared toward LGBT patrons. For a complete listing of gay services, communities and entertainment in Bogotá, visit www.guiagaycolombia.com/bogota.

ply store in Bogotá. Aside from stocking climbing, hiking and camping equipment, Nómada also has lists of credible mountain guides and can offer advice on treks and hikes throughout Colombia. It's probably worth your while to check here before heading out. Calle 45 and Avenida Caracas, 2nd Floor.

Flea Market
This flea market occupies a parking lot near Museo Nacional on Sundays and offers general bric-a-brac. Flea market enthusiasts can find some real steals here, or just while away a few hours sieving through antiques and trinkets. Carrera 7 and Calle 24.

Emeralds
Gathered like children with dirty secrets, the famed emerald vendors of Bogotá fill the corners of Avenida de Jiménez and Carrera 7, Monday to Saturday. Walk down this street and you will likely be approached by a number of salesmen with folded slips of paper proffering green slivers of the stone. It's best not to get involved or purchase emeralds here, but it is worth standing back and observing all the same. If you are keen on buying an emerald, head to Carrera 6 between Calles 10 and 12. Avenida Jiménez and Carrera 7. Updated: Feb 29, 2008.

Camping

After a long flight, you arrive in Bogotá and discover that in those hurried last-minutes packing you've forgotten the tent. Or hearing the tales of other travelers, you've learned Colombia is a great place to camp (and it'll help your budget out a bit). No sweat. Bogotá has a number of stores carrying everything you need to sleep under the stars and to outfit you for scaling its grand mountains:

Acampar / Camping Vive—Diagonal 5A 73C-16, Barrio Mandalay. Tel: 1-608-7457 / 1-452-8731.

Acampar Guías y Mapas—Calle 57, 9-29, office 301. Tel: 1-217-4480 / 1-211-8082.

Acampemos Iglu Ltda—Carrera 24, 48-24. Tel: 1- 245-2369; Calle 140, 23-61, local 13. Tel: 1-214- 3721 / 1-259-4536, URL: www.iglu.com.co.

Aventura Almacenes—Carrera 13, 67-26. Tel: 1-248-1679 / 1-313-3219.

Manglares (for cycling and kayaking equipment and dry bags)—Carrera 5, 55-68. Tel: 1-346-4132 / 1-310-565-5352.

Montaña Accesorios—Carrera 13A, 79-46, Tel: 1-530-6103.

Montaña Rescate—Calle 100, 41-40, local 501. Tel: 1-482-4509 / 1-533-3826 / 1-613-1771. Calle 95A, 51-11. La Floresta. Tel: 1-277-7257.

Tatoo, Outdoors & Travel—Carrera 15, 96-67. Tel: 1-218-1125, URL: www.tatoo.ws.

White gas (*gasolina blanca*) is next to impossible to encounter in Colombia, as its sales have been restricted. One place that still carries it is on Calle 7, 3-65.

Bogotano Bookshops

For acquiring just about any book you would ever want, whether current bestsellers or those long-out of print, there's a place you can go in Bogotá. Spend hours (or even days) browsing the hundreds of shops sprawling for several square blocks and tucked into commercial centers (indeed, entire malls jammed with stalls). Bogotá even has books in English and other foreign languages. In many places you can bargain a bit. For bookworms interested in collectors and antiquarian items, check out Merlín. Carrera 8A, 15-70. Tel: 1-284-4008 / 4301, E-mail: merlinlibros@hotmail.com. Updated: May 19, 2008.

Things to See and Do

No trip to Bogotá is complete without a few hours spent gaping at the riches and craftsmanship on display at the world renowned Museo del Oro. This in turn can be combined with wandering through the colonial streets of La Candelaria, spending some time in the Donación Botero, and heading into the striking and imposing Plaza de Bolívar. If there is any event taking place at the elegant Teatro Colón, you are strongly advised to make space in your itinerary to marvel at the décor found within. Updated: Feb 29, 2008.

Casa Museo Jorge Eliécer Gaitán

Casa Museo Jorge Eliécer Gaitán preserves the home and office of the most important social leader in modern Colombian history. Shortly after graduating from law school, Gaitán became a progressive Congressman of the *Partido Liberal* (Liberal Party) in the 1920s. Before the legislature, Gaitán presented testimony he compiled from survivors of the 1928 Ciénaga banana massacre. This stunning documentation is still widely available. His entire career was focused on

Tertulia (Literary Reading) Hot Spots

Casa de Poesía Silva—Calle 14, 3-41. Tel: 1-286-5710, URL: www.casadepoesiasilva.com.

Academia de la Lengua—Carrera 3, 17-34. Tel: 1-334-3152.

Centro Cultural Gabriel García Márquez— Calle 11, 5-60, La Candelaria. URL: www.fce.com.co/index.asp.

Prólogo Café y Libros—Tertulias Thursdays. Calle 96, 11A-46. Tel: 1-757-8069.

Loto Azul—Open mic music and poetry, Friday 6-11 p.m. Carrera 5, 14-00. Tel: 1-334-2346.

Museo de Museos—Tertulias Fridays. Calle 36, 5A-19, La Merced. Tel: 1-245-3780 / 1-245-4492.

Arte Letra Librería Café—Carrera 7, 70-18.

Atrio Café Bar—Carrera 11, 67-34, Chapinero. Tel: 1-249-5828.

Authors Bookstore and Café— Calle 70, 5-23. Tel: 1-217-7788, Fax: 1-217-7790, E-mail: info@authors.com.co, URL: www.authors.com.co.

Biblos Librería—Avenida 82, 12A-21. Tel: 1-218-1831.

Café Gaitán—Calle 23, 7-73. Tel: 1-480-1325.

Casa de las Citas—Carrera 3, 13-35. Updated: May 19, 2008.

improving the social rights of his country's people, which made him a tremendously popular presidential candidate in 1948. He was assassinated before the election on Calle 7, near Avenida Jiménez, in downtown Bogotá. His killing sparked the present-day civil war that has now lasted more than 60 years. Casa Museo Jorge Eliécer Gaitán teaches visitors about the life, work and philosophy of this illustrious Colombian. Calle 42, 15-23. Tel: 1-572-0070 / 0071 / 0072, Fax: 1-245-3626, E-mail: casagaitan@unal.edu.co, URL: www.unal.edu.co/diracad/catsede/catsede.html / www.colarte.arts.co/Museos/JorgeEliecerGaitan/general.htm. Updated: May 19, 2008.

Museo de Arte Moderno

The MAMBo was opened in 1976 and has emerged as a frontrunner in Latin American modern art. Here you can enjoy cinematic arts, the avant garde two and three dimensional art. The MAMBo also collaborates with the opera to create sets and help put the works together for shows in the Teatro Colón. Taking a taxi is recommended. Calle 24, 6-00. Tel: 1-286-0466, Fax: 1-281-7710, E-mail: mambogota@mambogota.com, URL: www.mambogota.com. Updated: Feb 07, 2008.

Museo Nacional

Ten blocks north of La Candelaria and in the shadow of the Plaza de Toros stands the Museo Nacional, which resembles a fortress and once served as a prison. With more than 20,000 objects and 17 permanent exhibition galleries, the Museo Nacional is well funded and maintained. Be sure to check out the exhibits on AfroColombian history and ethnology and one of the many fabulous temporary exhibitions as well. In previous years, the museum has displayed the Terracotta Army and also the jewels of Sipán. Worth looking into are the free talks on weeknights that discuss points of historical interest. Carrera 7 between Calles 28 and 29. Tel: 1-334-8366, Fax: 1-337-4134, E-mail: info@museonacional.gov.co. Updated: Feb 08, 2008.

Museo de Bogotá

Just up the hill from the Museo Nacional is the Museo de Bogotá, illuminating the city of Bogotá and its inhabitants. The place is often frequented by screaming hordes of schoolchildren who are unleashed at the Planetarium. Quieter is the section on the urban

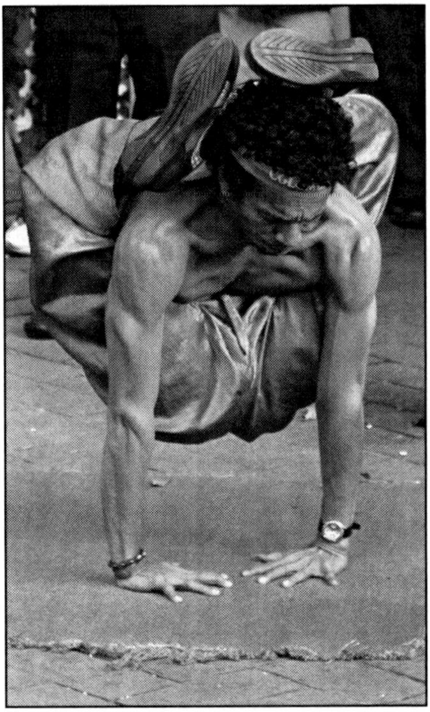

Photo by Dan Anderson

development of Bogotá. There are various exhibitions erected all through the year, and your best bet is to check the website to see what is coming up. Calle 26, 6-07. Tel: 1-281-4150, Fax: 1- 283-6309, E-mail: mdb@scrd.gov.co, URL: www.museodebogota.gov.co. Updated: Feb 08, 2008.

Corferías

Corferías is a huge conference and exhibition center. Whether you are a literature fanatic who needs a fix at the book fair or you would like to see the finest crafts that Colombia has to offer at the Exportesanias, this place is worth checking out. Events and exhibits are publicized on the web. Carrera 37, 24-67. Tel: 1-381-0000, URL: www.corferias.com.
February ► Travel Fair
April ► Book Fair
August ► Health and Beauty
September ► Home Show
November ► Food Show
December ► Expoartesanias
Updated: Feb 07, 2008.

Bogotá's Literary Scene

It's typical for many of Colombia's writers to spend some time in the nation's capital. Hit up Bogotá's blossoming literary café scene and hear the latest words scribed by the modern poets and authors. Some venues even open the microphone up to the public, giving the opportunity to share some verses. For a schedule visit www.goguiadelocio.com.

Steam train to Zipaquirá

A great way to get out to the Salt Cathedral at Zipaquirá is to travel on the Sabana Steam train from central Bogotá. The train only runs on Saturdays, Sundays and public holidays, and it is imperative that you head to the Estación de La Saban a couple of days in advance to secure your seat. There is a buffet carriage on the train, but purchases here are not included in the price of your ticket. Saddle up, settle down and let the touring papayera band play their tunes as you roll out to Zipaquirá. Taking a taxi to the station is recommended. Estación de La Sabana, Calle 13, 18-24. Tel: 1-375-0557, URL: www.turistren.com.co. Updated: Feb 07, 2008.

Parque Central Simón Bolívar

The veritable lungs of Colombia's capital city, Parque Central Simón Bolívar offers the largest area (more than 400 hectares) of green-

The Gold Museum

By Wilson Lievano, V!VA List contributor, 2007

Legend tells that when the Muiscas, the native civilization of what is today Bogotá, had to crown a new *cacique*, or chief, they congregated at the nearby Guatavita lagoon. Their candidate was then covered in gold dust, and he and the tribe's shamans would sail to the center of the lagoon in a raft loaded with offerings of gold, emeralds and other precious objects. As the shamans offered the precious objects to the god of the lagoon, the would-be cacique would jump into the icy waters. If he emerged unharmed, he became their new leader.

This legend, which later came to be known as the myth of El Dorado, lured many greedy Spaniards to Muisca territory with the promise of incredible wealth, but aside from some pieces of gold and jewelry found at Guatavita lagoon, no one has ever found the mythical place. In 1939, to honor the memory of the Muisca and to preserve Colombian archeological heritage, the Colombian government created its own Dorado: El Museo del Oro, (the Gold Museum) a permanent collection of more than 35,000 ornaments, tools and art pieces made of gold by all the native prehispanic cultures of Colombia.

One of the most famous pieces of the exhibit is a representation of the legend of El Dorado. It is a raft with figures that represent the cacique and his priests made in solid gold. The level of detail of this piece and its historic significance have made it the museum's image. There are other fascinating pieces, such as the Poporo Quimbaya, a golden urn decorated with perfectly round spheres, an impressive achievement since these cultures didn't know the metallurgical techniques used in Europe at the time.

The museum, located in downtown Bogotá, has three floors; the first floor houses temporary exhibitions. The second floor displays the main collection: a voyage through the history and customs of the tribes that lived in the center, south and north of Colombia organized by the types of metallurgical processes they used. The third floor contains a history of gold and its significance to prehispanic cultures, along with an exhibit of pieces made by cultures originally from the Colombian southwest. While walking through the museum, visitors will hear the legends, myths and stories that are associated with these pieces. Other pieces were made during the Spanish conquest and tell the story of the native resistance and defeat at the hands of the Spanish invaders.

The museum has its own stop on the Transmilenio, Bogotá's mass transportation system. To visit, get off the Avenida Jiménez line at the station Museo del Oro and walk two blocks to the museum. Entrance to the museum is $2 Monday - Saturday. Entrance is free on Sunday.

ery in Bogotá. Open from the early morning to the early evening, on a sunny day this park is a great place to wander around the lake, participate in water sports, jog, cycle, or have picnic. The park also hosts concerts and has welcomed international stars like Roger Waters and Iron Maiden onto its verdant grounds. Calle 63 and 53 between Carreras 48 and 68. Updated: Feb 07, 2008.

Jardín Botánico José Celestino Mutis

For anyone who does not have the time to see all of Colombia's diverse regions, or for those who just want to escape the bustle and mayhem of downtown Bogotá, a trip to the Jardín Botánico should be high up on the list of things to do. Wide lawns and snaking pathways lead the visitor through the flora that adorns Colombia. Throughout the year various exhibitions are held, the most popular being the butterfly house that attracts hundreds of visitors and schoolchildren every day. Arriving by taxi is recommended. Calle 63, 68-95. Tel: 1-437-7060, Fax: 1-630-5075, E-mail: bogotanico@jbb.gov.co, URL: www.jbb.gov.co. Updated: Feb 08, 2008.

Parque Nacional Olaya Herrera

If the Parque Central Simón Bolívar is too far away, an easier option is to head to the Parque Nacional Olaya Herrera located in Chapinero. Not as large or as scenic as Parque Central Simón Bolívar, it is still very popular with bogotanos. There are fountains, plazoletas, football pitches, tennis courts and play areas for children. On weekends (Sundays in particular) the park is very well attended. Avoid at night. Between calles 36 to 39 and Carreras Séptima to Quinta. Updated: Feb 08, 2008.

Ciclovía

Every Sunday, as with other major Colombian cities, many of Bogotá's major roads and arteries are blocked off and given over to joggers, cyclists and bladers. People are out with their dogs, taking a stroll, meeting friends, heading to the park for an aerobics workout, or just people-watching. The ciclovía starts early in the morning and continues until 2 p.m. If you are keen on getting some high altitude exercise or just taking a stroll, feel free to join in. There are also state sponsored bike mechanics all along the route. Updated: Feb 07, 2008.

Keeping Fit in Bogotá

Aside from the Ciclovía that takes place every Sunday morning, there are other options that allow the visitor to keep fit while in the capital, including several decent gyms with day pass entries. In La Candelaria there is a cheap and relatively respectable gym at the corner of the Parque de los Periodistas and the Avenida Jiménez. The cheapest of the lot in La Candelaria is on the Avenida 19 but we cannot recommend it as the equipment is severely lacking. Further north and into the area of Chapinero is Body Care Gym on Calle 45, 15-38. This is a far better option than those previously mentioned. If you must have the best, head to any of the branches of BodyTech based around the city—the closest to downtown is on Carrera 7 and Calle 62. Bring your own towel. Updated: Feb 07, 2008.

El Campin

If you can, try to get to a soccer game between the two city rivals, Santa Fe and Millonarios. Even better, get to an international match at the Nemesio Camacho Stadium (otherwise known as El Campin). See almost 50,000 rabid fans cheering in true Latin American style, complete with whistles, fireworks, toilet paper rolls and enthusiasm. Take the Transmilenio bus to the El Campin stop. Best enjoyed with friends while seated in the Colombia section. Avenida Norte-Quito-Sur (NQS) with Calle 57, Teusaquillo. Updated: Feb 07, 2008.

Rumba Bogotaña

Bogotá may have some of Latin America's greatest party spots. No visit to the city would be complete without a night on the town. Your options are vast and varied, from clubbing the night away in the Zona Rosa, La Candelaria or Usaquén to something more refined like a night at the theater or a trip to the movies. Locals will recommend that you try and get involved in a night time chiva tour, where old, refashioned high school buses are decked out with loud music and alcohol is served . Updated: Feb 07, 2008.

Studying Spanish

To study Spanish in depth, sign up for a course offered at any one of the following Universities in Bogotá. All have internationally recognized courses and can offer differing levels of instruction:

Religion in Bogotá

Bogotá has become quite a religiously diverse community. There are representations of many Protestant sects and non-Christian faiths. The mainstream Protestant churches, the Baptists (Bautista), Lutheran (Luterana), Presbyterian (Presbiteriana), Methodists (Weysleyana), Disciples of Christ (Discípulos de Cristo) and Menonites (Menonita) all have houses of worship.

Colombian Episcopalians and Anglicans have their own website to help orientate visitors (www.iglesiaepiscopal.org.co). There is even an Orthodox church (Iglesia Ortodoxa). For addresses of these temples, check the Páginas Amarillas under "Iglesias Bautistas." Bogotá also has a Monthly Friends Meeting. The capital's synagogue is Bet Chabad (Calle 94 9-52. Tel.: 1-635-8261/8251). For Islamic travelers there is Centro Cultural Islámico (Monday-Friday, 9 a.m.-noon, 2-5 p.m. Diagonal 22B, 43A-13. Tel.: 1-335-0364, Fax: 1-244-9824, E-mail: centroculturalislamicocolombia@yahoo.com). Also, there are a number of Buddhist temples; consult www.budismo.cl/dir/colombia.html for listings. Updated: May 19, 2008.

Universidad Javeriana–www.puj.edu.co
Universidad Externado–www.uexternado.edu.co.
Universidad de la Sabana–www.unisabana.edu.co.
Universidad Nacional de Colombia–www.unal.edu.co. Updated: Feb 26, 2008.

Volunteering in Bogotá

Volunteering opportunities in Colombia are not as available as in Ecuador or Costa Rica. There are volunteer opportunities, but with the political climate here, a lot of this is looked upon with suspicion and doubt. In the past, unwanted visitors to Colombia have entered the country using NGO visas or by claiming to be volunteers. The best way to find out where one can volunteer is to contact the Catholic Church, which has a list of credible and effective charitable organizations. In addition, some hostels have established relationships with long running charities and can offer help in finding placements. Updated: Feb 26, 2008.

Bogotá Tours

There are dozens of tour outfits in Bogotá with all kinds of tours available. Popular tours include Rumba tours in a chiva and tours to Zipaquirá and Villa de Leyva. For a complete list of tour companies go to www.bogotaturismo.gov.co. Updated: Feb 26, 2008.

Cultural Tours in La Candelaria

Covering the many sites of interest in Bogotá's colonial Candelaria center, this company offers a variety of tours in both English and Spanish for groups and individuals. Carrera 8, 11-39. Tel: 1-281-5569, E-mail: info@lacandelaria.info, URL: www.lacandelaria.info. Updated: Feb 26, 2008.

Tesoro Tours

Tesoro tours have been operating for a few years and specialize in everything that Bogotá and the surrounding area have to offer. Available tours include a night tour, a shopping tour, a city tour or a trip as far out as Zipaquirá. They also provide custom tours. Ave. 15, 106-50. URL: www.tesorotours.com/eng/index.php. Updated: Feb 26, 2008.

Bogotá Lodging

From the slick boutique hotels found in the north to the rough yet homey backpacker digs of the south, Bogotá caters to every budget. What you get depends on what you are prepared to spend. Recently, the number of options for the traveler in La Candelaria has increased threefold, most of the additions are backpacker hostels. Family-run establishments and luxury options are concentrated in the historic center. Updated: Feb 26, 2008.

Hotel Zaragoza

(BED: $13-16) The Hotel Zaragoza has become the haunt among European non-backpacker, budget travelers. A four-story, green and hot-pink building that blends into the modern architecture of Avenida Jiménez, this hotel offers medium-sized rooms with cable TV and private, hot water baths. Some rooms have balconies that look out over the avenue. The good beds come with several blankets to keep you warm on those chilly bogotano nights. Word of this hotel is spreading among those "done with dorms" and as a result, this place is often full. Avenida Jiménez, 4-56. Tel: 1-284-5411 / 1-608-8290. Updated: May 19, 2008.

Martha's Place

(ROOM: $18-79) This is a fully furnished three-bedroom vacation rental, which can be rented by room or fully. Each room has a TV and WiFi. Martha's Place is two blocks from the US Embassy and a ten minute walk to the largest mall in South America. Cheaper and nicer than most hotels, Martha's Place fills a niche for budget travelers who don't want to rough it. Calle 22, 48-65 Conjunto Salitre Pijao. URL: www.apartmentinbogota.com. Updated: Jan 01, 2008.

Bogotá Restaurants

Whether you have a rigid budget of $5 per day, or have all the money to spend on a gluttonous feast, Bogotá is the place for you. Small restaurants all over the city run lunch deals starting around $2 that will fill your stomach with hearty fare (typically a soup followed by meat with rice, potatoes and beans). If you fancy something more chic, newer establishments in La Candelaria and the Macarena will probably fit the bill. In the Zona Rosa and Parque la 93 the restaurants look like California transplants.

Like most capital cities, Bogotá offers a wealth of nightlife options. Fashionable clubs line the streets in the north and student hangouts riddle the colonial mayhem of La Candelaria. Most clubs close between 2 a.m. and 3 a.m., but those with an appetite for more can go on to "after parties." Bogotá's arts scene is a lively one too, with art-house cinemas, theaters and live music venues continually playing to rapturous audiences. Updated: Feb 26, 2008.

Donde Tatiana

(LUNCH: $1.60) Donde Tatiana is where many bogotanos go to have the lunch or dinner special. Choose from a variety of meats that include beef, *sobrebarriga* (stuffed roasted beef) and fish. The plates come heaping with salad, *patacones* (fried plantains), French fries, rice and beans. The mealtime spread starts with the customary soup and a drink goes along with the ensemble. The restaurant is just blocks from La Candelaria, which makes it a good place to fuel up after a long day of traveling into the capital. Monday-Saturday 11 a.m.-8 p.m. Carrera 4, 16-63. Updated: May 19, 2008.

Sanzzini's

With a large brick furnace visible in the kitchen, Sanzzini's obviously specializes in all things Italian. Reasonably sized pizzas and excellent calzones are enough to make the first-time visitor a frequent diner here. Located on the corner of Calle 19, it can be hard to find, but once you do, Sanzzini's makes for an excellent escape from the noise, bustle and excesses outside. Carrera 5 and Calle 19. Tel: 1-283-0287. Updated: Dec 19, 2007.

Capachos Asadero

(ENTREES: $7.25-8.25) If your itinerary doesn't include a hop down to Villavicencio and the Colombian plains, you can still try mamona at Capachos, the typical barbecue from the Llanos. A young calf, not yet weaned, is split and placed on *varas* (stakes) and slow cooked to succulent perfection. Capachos also grills pork and mojarra fish. Your plank of meat comes with roasted plantains, potatoes and yucca, and various sauces to dunk your meat. From Thursday to Sunday there's live *llanera* music. Open daily 11:30 a.m.-5 p.m., Friday and Saturday until 7 p.m. Calle 18, 4-68. Tel: 1-243-4607, URL: www.asaderocapachos.com. Updated: May 19, 2008.

El Café Internet Bar

El Café Internet Bar is a popular, queer-friendly hangout with loud music, stiff drinks, fast computers, cute boys (and a few girls), and comfy seats. It's busy most evenings. El Café is open 10:00 a.m. to midnight, Sunday through Wednesday, and until 2:00 a.m. Thursday through Saturday. Calle 59, 13-32. Tel: 1-249-6512. Updated: Feb 07, 2008.

The Monkey Pub !

With conviviality, impressive beers, great food, good music and modern design elements, The Monkey Pub is a bar with an English twist. It's a popular place to have a business lunch, drink a quick pint after work or watch the big match. The pub shows as many sporting events as it can handle, premiership soccer on Saturday mornings and the NFL playoffs. The Monkey, or "El Mon-key" as it

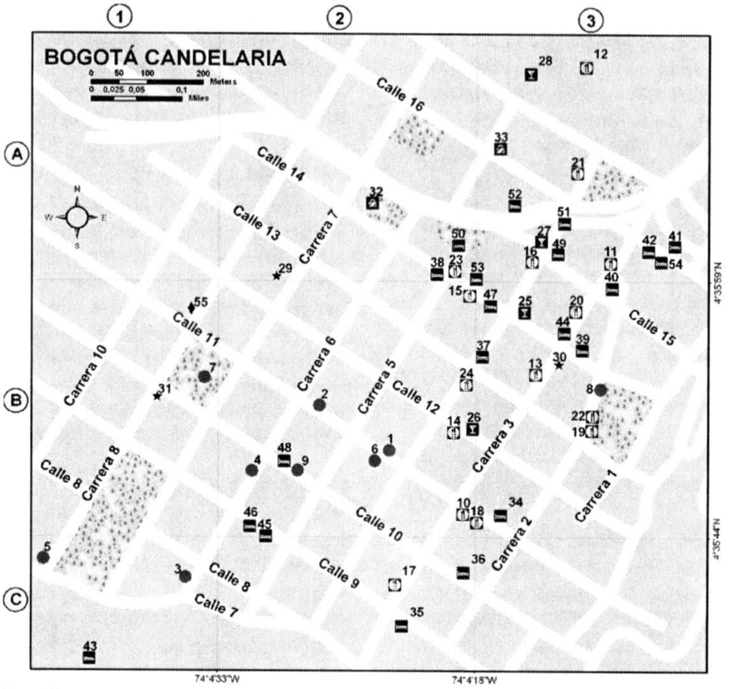

Activities ●

1 Biblioteca Luis Ángel Arango B2
2 Centro Cultural Garbriel García Márquez B2
3 Museo Arqueológico C1
4 Museo de Arte Colonial B2
5 Museo de Artes y Tradiciones Populares C1
6 Museo Donación Botero B2
7 Plaza Bolívar B1
8 Plaza del Chorro de Quevedo B3
9 Teatro Colón B2

Eating

10 An Anandantee Ma Non Troppo B2
11 Café Sue A3
12 Capachos Asadero A3
13 Casa de Citas B3
14 El Santo Viático B2
15 La Vida en Rosa B2
16 Pastelería Organización Gers A3
17 Pimienta y Café C2
18 Quinua y Amaranto B2
19 Restaurante Bolón de Verde B3
20 Restaurante Café Israelí L´Jai B3
21 Restaurante Donde Tatiana A3
22 Restaurante Plaza de Chorro B3
23 Restaurante Vegetariano Loto A A2
24 Salabha B2

Nightlife

25 Café del Sol B3
26 Café para dos B2
27 Escobar y Rosas A3
28 Quiebra Canto A3

Services

29 Adpostal / Correos de Colombia A2
30 Lavaseco la Colonial B3
31 Tourist Information Office B1

Shopping

32 Emerald Center A2
33 Herencias de Artesanías y Café A3

Sleeping

34 Abadía Colonial B3
35 Anandamayi C2
36 ApartaEstudios C2
37 Centro Plaza Hotel B3
38 Dorantes A2
39 Fátima Hostal B3
40 Hospedaje Cacique Sugamaxi B3
41 Hostal La Candelaria A3
42 Hostal Sue A3
43 Hostelling International Bogotá C1
44 Hotel Aragón B3
45 Hotel Casa de la Bótica B2
46 Hotel Casa Medina A3
47 Hotel Dann Colonial B3
48 Hotel de la Opera B2
49 Hotel El Dorado A3
50 Hotel Internacional A2
51 Hotel San Sebastian A3
52 Hotel Zaragoza A3
53 Oceania Hotels B3
54 Platypus Hotel A3

Tour ♦

55 Cultural Tours in Candelaria B1

is affectionately known by its regulars, opens at 7 a.m. for breakfast (including Full English). Its lunch menu is mostly salads, with pub grub in the evenings to accompany an excellent selection of draft beer and more than 50 types of bottled beer from around the world. Carrera 5, 71-45, 2nd floor. Tel: 1-756-1253. Updated: Feb 24, 2008.

La Candelaria

With a colonial flavor, cobblestone streets, eclectic bookstores, dance academies, museums and restaurants, La Candelaria is the beating heart of old Bogotá. One could spend several days wandering the streets of La Candelaria, exploring the Plaza de Bolívar overshadowed by the opulent Presidential Palace and Cathedral, the museums and many other points of interest on Calle 10.

With a handful of universities in the district, there is a considerable student presence that keeps the prices down, the level of bohemia high and the number of bars and cheap restaurants at a premium. Most, if not all, affordable accommodations and some luxury options are located in La Candelaria. In terms of nightlife, there are a few options in Escobar y Rosas (Carrera 5 with 14) and Quiebracanto (Carrera 5, 17-76). Updated: Feb 13, 2008.

Things to See and Do

Museo de Arte Colonial

Originally the seat of the Colegio Máximo de la Compañía de Jesús in the late 17th Century, this Spanish colonial-style building was converted into a museum in the 1940s. Visitors will be impressed, as a renovation to the building in the late 1990s brought the place up to standard. The museum houses unforgettable works by Vásquez and Figeroa and portraits of key players in the colonial period. There are scattered antiquities and furniture from the colonial era as well. To get there, go up the hill one street from Carrera 7 and one block over from the Plaza de Bolívar. Carrera 6a, 9-77, La Candelaria. Tel: 1-341-6017, URL: www.bogota.gov.co/vis/museoarte/museoartec.html. Updated: Feb 08, 2008.

Museo de Artes y Tradiciones Populares

Built in 1583 and formerly an Augustinian cloister, this is certainly one of the oldest surviving buildings in Bogotá. The museum has a fantastic collection of wares crafted by Colombia's vast array of indigenous tribes. If you can't make it to the various parts of Colombia where arts and crafts are made, then you might enjoy the museum's gift shop. Carrera 8, 7-21, La Candelaria. Tel: 1-284-2670. Updated: Feb 08, 2008.

Museo Donación Botero

This museum should be at the top of the to-do list for anyone interested in art. Of the Museo Donación Botero's two sections, the first is dedicated to the famous Colombian artist Fernando Botero, who, in the words of most Colombians, "paints fat people." This wing displays 123 examples of Botero's work. As the museum's name suggests, Botero donated many of his own private pieces to the collection. The second section of the museum displays 85 works by internationally renowned artists from the 19th Century, such as Renoir, Chagall, Picasso, Bacon and Moore. The museum is located just three blocks up from the Plaza Bolívar. Calle 11, 4-41, La Candelaria. Tel: 1-343-1340, URL: www.lablaa.org/museobotero.htm. Updated: Feb 08, 2008.

Museo Arqueológico

The Museo Arqueológico, or MUSA, has an overwhelming permanent collection of pre-Columbian ceramics housed in a staggering 17th-Century mansion. The history of the mansion is a fascinating story. For a period of time, it belonged to the Marquís de San Jorge, a viceroy only recognized for his cruelty. Opened to the public in 1973, the museum offers exhibitions of ceramics, colonial art, and seasonally changing works. Close to the Plaza Bolívar. Carrera 6, 7 - 43. Tel: 1-243-0465, Fax: 1-243-0442, E-mail: fpc-direccion@etb.net.co, URL: www.museoarqueologico.com. Updated: Feb 08, 2008.

Plaza Bolívar

The grandeur upon entering the unashamed opulence of Bogotá's Plaza de Bolívar is overwhelming. Tall stately buildings rise up on all four sides, from the Capitol building and the Palacio de Nariño to the Cathedral and the Palacio de Justicia. This plaza, complete with a statue of Simón Bolívar in the center, was the location where Bogotá was declared the seat of Nueva Granada's colonial government. The Presidential Palace, or Palacio de Nariño, was rebuilt in 1949 after the fallout of the Bogotazo. The Palacio de Justicia had some renovations done after the siege of the building in

1985 by the M-19 guerrilla group. Today, the plaza is a place where all demonstrations end, where children chase pigeons and photographers vie for your business. Avoid the plaza after dark. Carrera 7 between Calles 10 and 11. Updated: Feb 08, 2008.

Casa Quinta de Bolívar

The Quinta, not far from the Universidad de los Andes in La Candelaria, is perhaps best known as Simón Bolívar's longest-running residence in his adult life. He spent 423 days here, though not continuously. The elegant hillside mansion, with its well-preserved gardens, european architecture and courtyards was a gift to Bolívar from the Colombian state and remained his for 10 years. The Quinta then changed hands and was even owned by a brewery before being bought back by the state to create the museum. Tours take in the key rooms, pointing out interesting antiquities like Bolívar's bed and other objects from that era. Tours are only given in Spanish. Calle 20, 2-91, La Candelaria. Tel: 1-336-6419, Fax: 1-336-6410, URL: www.quintadebolivar.gov.co. Updated: Feb 08, 2008.

Teatro Colón

Right in the thick of things on Calle 10 (across the road from the Ministry of Foreign Relations) and one block up the hill from the Plaza de Bolívar is the delightfully ornate and decorative Teatro Colón. This is really Colombia's centerpiece theater. Opened in 1892, it can seat up to 900 people. Plan your visit to coincide with a performance or concert that will allow you to fully appreciate one of the continent's most beautiful theaters. To get there, simply find Calle 10 from Plaza de Bolívar and climb one block. Calle 10, 5-32, La Candelaria. Tel: 1-284-7420. Updated: Feb 08, 2008.

Plazoleta del Chorro de Quevedo

Deep in the student heartland of La Candelaria is a small plaza with bars, restaurants and ecclectic shops that appeal to an off-beat crowd. Here in the Plazoleta del Chorro de Quevedo is where Gonzalo Jimenez de Quesada—the founder of Bogotá—stopped and drank from a stream in his push south. On weeknights the place buzzes with music, storytellers and people of all kinds. During the week, when students are out and about, the area is safer. Plazoleta del Chorro de Quevedo, Calle 13 and Carrera 2, La Candelaria. Updated: Feb 08, 2008.

Centro Cultural Gabriel García Márquez

Nobel prize-winning author Gabriel García Márquez was born in Aracataca, Colombia. Although his most famous piece of work, "One Hundred Years of Solitude" is set in the author's homeland, it was born in México, where he has resided for many years. As a gift from the Aztec nation to Colombia, the Fondo Cultura Económico (a major Mexican publisher) created the Centro Cultural Gabriel García Márquez. Inaugurated in 2008, the design by Rogelio Salmona lends the building a feeling of intermeshing circles where the spaces (the bookstore, record shop, auditorium, exhibition hall, restaurant and café) revolve around two patios. The ground level displays García Márquez' life in large panels. The center frequently hosts literary readings and other cultural events. Calle 11 (Calle de la Enseñanza), 5-60. URL: www.fce.com.co/index.asp. Updated: May 19, 2008.

Biblioteca Luis Ángel Arango

Bogotanos proudly declare that their library, Luis Angel Arango, is one of the most visited in the world, with more people walking through its doors per week than the New York Public Library. While these claims may not be accurate, there is no doubt the universities in La Candelaria contribute a steady flow of students to this location. The library is worth visiting for its often-changing exhibits and occasional recitals. Calle 11, 4-14, La Candelaria. Tel: 1-343-1212, Fax: 1-286-3551, URL: www.lablaa.org. Updated: Feb 08, 2008.

Cerro de Monserrate

If you would like a truly impressive view of the city, it is imperative that you head up to the top of the Cerro de Monserrate, 3,152m above sea level. The view on a clear day is breathtaking. Opened in 1929, the Cerro is a site for pilgrims, some of whom decide to make the journey to the top of the mountain on their knees. Since there have been robberies here, especially when the pathway is deserted, it is not recommended that you walk to the top. If you must walk the route, do so on the weekend or on a religious holiday, when the number of visitors increases. There are two other forms of reaching the top: In the cable car or on the funicular. Often, if one of the aforementioned is running and in service, the other is not. The Cerro is open every day and also in the evenings. Taking a taxi is recommended. Carrera 2, 21-48 Paseo Bolívar. Tel: 1-284-5700, URL: www.cerromonserrate.com. Updated: Feb 08, 2008.

La Candelaria Lodging Budget

Oceanía Hotels

(BED: $3-25) An addition to the lodging scene since 2007, the Oceanía is clean and well managed. Its rooms fit up to five people. Downstairs there is a reasonable restaurant that serves inexpensive lunchtime set meals. A good option for those eager to escape a dormitory and enjoy a snore-free night. To get there, take any bus running into La Candelaria en route to the Biblioteca Luis Angel Arango and get off on Carrera 4 with Calle 14. Calle 14, 4-48. Tel: 1-342-0650 / 0561 / 0562, Fax: 1-342-1879. Updated: Oct 02, 2007.

Hostal Sue

(BED: $5-10) Definitely a worthy backpacker's rival to the mighty neighbouring Platypus, Hostal Sue boasts a lively social atmosphere, exhaustive DVD collection and heated terrace. Dormitories and private rooms available in either Sue 1 or just two short blocks away in Sue 2. Calle 16, 2-55. Tel: 1-334-8894, Cell: 3-10-877-5381, E-mail: reservations@hostalsue.com, URL: www.hostalsue.com. Updated: Dec 19, 2007.

V!VA Member Review-Hostal Sue

The shower is the best one in South America! The atmosphere is very Colombian—warm, friendly and relaxed. The hostal is in the center, close to good bars, clubs, and museums. Belgium, Dec 07, 2007

Hotel Aragon

(BED: $5-10) For those seeking a cheap bed far from the noise, bustle or dormitories of a regular hostel, the Hotel Aragon is an understandable option. Be warned, last we checked it appeared as though the management hadn't invested in hotel upkeep since the 1950s. Still, private rooms are available for bargain basement prices. The hotel is an easy stroll from Las Aguas or Museo del Oro Transmilenio stops. Carrera 3, 14-13. Tel: 1-342-5239. Updated: Oct 02, 2007.

Hotel El Dorado

(BED: $5.30-21) While among some journeyers the Hotel Dorado has earned a reputation for poor security, it is nonetheless a cheap lodging option in this neighborhood. The rooms are basic, if a bit small, and most of the quarters have windows. The headless showers spew hot water. Rooms on the terrace have beautiful views over the city and of Montserrate, but share a common bath. Carrera 4, 15-00. Tel: 1-334-3988 / 1-281-7271, E-mail: doradohotel@hotmail.com. Updated: May 19, 2008.

Hostal Fátima

(ROOM: $6-37) Opened in September 2007, the Hostal Fátima has other hostal owners in La Candelaria reaching for their checkbooks to update and improve their facilities. The ownership has placed special emphasis on comfort and security. Brand-spanking-new bathrooms complete with Jacuzzi, included breakfast, a sauna and solarium are just some of the treats available. Located about five minutes by foot from the Las Aguas Transmilenio Station. Calle 14, 2-24. Tel: 1-281-6389 / 1-283-6411, Cell: 315-601-4816, URL: www.hostalfatima.com. Updated: Feb 13, 2008.

Hostelling International Bogotá

(BED: $7) With so many options exhausted before reaching the Hostelling International building located on Plaza Bolívar, this vast 105 bed establishment suffers from its location. Very few travelers make it this far, but if they do, they are pleasantly suprised by what they find. Although not equipped with amenities like other established hostels in La Candelaria, the Hostelling International building caters to groups and has a restaurant offering cheap eats. Dorms are single sex, and there is a midnight curfew. Carrera 7, 6-10. Tel: 1-280-3202, Fax: 1-280-3460, E-mail: hostelling@fcaj.org.co, URL: www.fcaj.org.co. Updated: Jan 11, 2008.

Hotel Internacional

(BED: $8.50-22) The business card for Hotel Internacional states, "We are the second most happy country in the world." Upon arriving in Colombia to see if this might be true, many travelers, especially young Israelis, check into this hotel. Several floors, with common or private bath and hot water, await the weary journeyer. Budget traveler conveniences, like a common kitchen and book exchange, make stays here comfortable. There's even free coffee to sip while making a Skype call. Carrera 5, 14-45. Tel: 1-341-3151 / 8731, 1-342-3768, E-mail: hotelinternacionalbogota@hotmail.com, URL: es.geocities.com/hotelinternacionalbogota. Updated: May 19, 2008.

Hospedaje Cacique Sugamuxi !

(BED: $9-24) Open since 2008, Hospedaje Cacique Sugamuxi is La Candelaria's newest hostel. Many of the rooms are small but are furnished for the traveler who needs to relax and catch up on journal writing. The kitchen is well-equipped and has a sunny eating area, and common baths are marked by gender. Hospedaje Cacique Sugamuxi also offers its guests the cheapest in-house internet ($0.50 per hour) and laundry service ($1.05 per kilogram) around. Corner of Carrera 3 and Calle 15A, above a restaurant and fruit shop. Tel: 1-337-4326 / 317-331-1071, E-mail: caciquesugamuxi@hotmail.com, URL: www.caciquesugamuxi.com. Updated: May 19, 2008.

Platypus !

(BED: $9-27) The front of this hostel has no sign announcing its name, only a drawing of the animal to greet its guests. Enormously popular among travelers, Platypus offers all the comforts anyone could want. Germán Escobar, the owner, is a backpacker who has traveled around the world and understands the traveler's needs. There is free coffee and tea all day long, a kitchen to use, laundry service, and a great common room with wood-burning fireplace. Other services include a free book exchange and travel information books. Escobar is a tremendous source of information regarding what to see in Colombia, his native land. He speaks Spanish, English, German, French and Italian. If there are no rooms available, the staff will gladly call around to other hotels for you. Reservations are highly recommended. Calle 16, 2-43. Tel: 1-341-3104 / 2874, Fax: 1-352-0127, E-mail: platypushotel@yahoo.com, URL: www.platypusbogota.com. Updated: May 19, 2008.

Anandamayi

(ROOM: $10-50) One of the newest additions to La Candelaria, the Anandamayi has arrived and added much needed substance and style to the area. Rambling internal patios lend themselves to idle days spent in hammocks, and the spacious dormitories and country-style kitchen get positive reviews from patrons. With an open plan and a verdant garden out back, this is one of the more relaxing hostels in Bogotá. Calle 9, 2-81. Tel: 1-341-7208, Cel: 3-15-215-5778, E-mail: anandamayihostel@yahoo.com, URL: www.anandamayihostel.com. Updated: Oct 02, 2007.

Hotel Centro Plaza

(BED: $12-32) The Star of David subtly adorning the entrance to Hotel Centro Plaza marks its popularity with Israeli travelers. This hostel has dorms furnished with single beds (no bunks here) as well as large private rooms with 24-hour hot water baths. Hotel Centro Plaza also has special features, like a game room with billiards and ping pong tables, a fruit shop and a kosher restaurant. Carrera 4, 13-12. Tel: 1-243-3818 / 286-1580, E-mail: hotelcentralplaza@hotmail.com, URL: www.hotelcentralplaza.com. Updated: May 19, 2008.

Hotel San Sebastián

(ROOM: $12-25) Definitely better than the Aragon but nowhere near as cheap, the San Sebastián is a safe and decent hotel located in La Candelaria. Rooms are clean and include cable TV. Situated between the Transmilenio stops of Las Aguas and Museo del Oro in La Candelaria, the hotel is a few minutes walk from each. Any bus heading along Carrera 7 to the Luis Angel Arango Library will drop you right outside. Av. Jiménez, 3-97. Tel: 1-334-6041. Updated: Oct 02, 2007.

MID-RANGE

Hostal La Candelaria

(ROOM: $18-35) La Candelaria hostel is made up of four apartments arranged around a large central courtyard. Each apartment is completely independent and is rented separately. The spacious accomodations allow for a very comfortable stay. The hostel only rents apartments for one to four people. Calle 16, 2-50 La Candelaria District Historic Center. Tel: 1-482-2760, E-mail: reservations@hostallacandelaria.com, URL: www.hostallacandelaria.com. Updated: Jan 01, 2008.

Hotel Dorantes

(BED: $21-32) In the mid-19th Century, Hotel Dorantes was a family mansion. The woodwork and parquet floors still exhibit that elegance. Original art adorns the lobby, hallways and staircases. The rooms, some with balconies, are airy and come with a private, hot water bathrooms and cable TV. Before starting your day's sightseeing, you can relax in the lobby and read the newspapers. The staff speaks some English. Calle 13, 5-07. Tel: 1-334-6640, Cell: 310-320-8503, Fax: 1-341-5365, E-mail: administradora@hoteldorentes.com, URL: www.hoteldorantes.com. Updated: May 19, 2008.

Hotel Dann Colonial

(ROOM: $25-50) An outdated 1970s relic, both architecturally and stylistically, the Hotel Dann Colonial fits perfectly into La Candelaria's landscape. Service could use an upgrade. In fact, the hotel should undergo a complete makeover as the rooms feel worn despite the obvious conveniences of cable TV and minibar. Monday-Friday there is an inexpensive buffet lunch. Calle 14, 4-21. Tel: 1-341-1680 / 1681. Updated: Dec 19, 2007.

HIGH-END

Abadia Colonial

(ROOM:$50-75) Do not be put off by the raucous student bars opposite Abacadia. This hotel's boutique rooms are all at the back of the building and remain unaffected by the noise. Care and details have been employed to make this a charming place in the heart of Bogotá's bohemia. Calle 11, 2 - 32. Tel: 1-341-1884, Fax: 1-342-2672, E-mail: abadiacolonial@gmail.com, URL: www.abadiacolonial.com. Updated: Oct 02, 2007.

Hotel Casa de la Botica

(ROOM: $100-125) Not as showy as the Hotel de la Ópera and one block further south, the Hotel Casa de la Botica is a wonderful high-end hotel with a special touch. Craftsmanship and design have been employed in every facet of the hotel, from the airy courtyard and salon that seats 120 people to the fireplaces, balconies and fountains. Pricing comes in two options, standard and suite, for which you get a stylish room in a restored republican house. You also get access to a pizzeria, French bakery and a snazzy restaurant. If you're looking for a luxury hotel, you can't do much better than this. Calle 9, 6-45. Tel: 1-281-0811, E-mail: ventas@hotelcasadelabotica.com, URL: www.hotelcasadelabotica.com. Updated: Oct 03, 2007.

Hotel de la Ópera

(ROOM: $143-210) Set in two beautifully restored houses next door to the Presidential Plaza on one side and the opulent Teatro Colón on the other, Hotel de la Ópera is La Candelaria's most luxurious lodging option. Everything about this hotel oozes romance. From the elegant dining rooms to the Italian-styled suites, every detail is in perfect order. Amenities include an on-site pool, spa, restaurants with magnificent views of colonial Bogotá and a business center with free internet. If money is no object, this option is a can't miss. Calle 10, 5-72. Tel: 1-336-2066 / 5285, Fax: 1-336-2066, E-mail: sales@hotelopera.com.co, URL: www.hotelopera.com.co. Updated: Oct 09, 2007.

ApartaEstudios La Candelaria

(APT: $370-775) If Bogotá is more than just a brief stopover, consider renting a studio apartment by the week or month. With four types of apartments to choose from (the cheapest are simple studios and the most expensive decked out with spiraling staicases, chimneys and stylish kitchens), you should be able to fit one of these apartments into your budget. All apartments are fully furnished and come with wireless internet. Any bus can get you close but it is an uphill walk from the station. Calle 10, 2-40. Tel: 1-281-6923, Cel: 313-442-1805, E-mail: contactenos@apartaestudioslacandelaria.com, URL: www.apartaestudioslacandelaria.com. Updated: Oct 09, 2007.

LA CANDELARIA RESTAURANTS

BUDGET

Café Sue

(LUNCH: $2.65) This intimate restaurant serves delicious blue-plate special lunches. These lunches include a small glass of wine to awaken the taste buds for the meal to follow: savory soup, a main dish with generous portions, great salads, and home-made dessert. In the evenings Café Sue serves up a variety of drinks and coffees to accompany crêpes and *pica palos* (snacks). The small tables are candle-lit and adorned with flowers. There is seating on a small interior balcony and a rear room is spread with floor pillows. Carrera 3, 15-45. Tel: 1-281-9716. Updated: May 19, 2008.

Pastelería Organización Gers

This bakery shop may have an unusual name, but it certainly creates some mighty delicious temptations. Just walking along Carrera 4, your wandering eye will latch onto the desserts gleaming in the glass case. There are the usual goodies, like *milhojas* (cake made with puff pastry) and *alfajores* (soft cookie filled with caramel), as well as some different creations. Try the raspberry-filled, lemon-iced chocolate cake. But Pastelería Organización Gers doesn't just make sweets. Baskets overflow with fine breads, some standard, and some not so (such as the rye with raisins and seeds). Open Monday-Saturday, 7 a.m.-10 p.m., Sunday, 7 a.m.-6 p.m. Carrera 4, 14-95. Tel: 1-482-0742. Updated: May 19, 2008.

Quinua y Amaranto

One of two excellent vegetarian restaurants in La Candelaria. Due to its popularity, this charming and atmospheric place gets pretty packed—arrive early to avoid disappointment. You can watch the staff creating meals up in front, including a great tortilla Española and tasty set menus. Calle 11, 2-95. Updated: Dec 19, 2007.

Salabha

An excellent vegetarian option. Lunchtime specials are well-balanced. Do not be put off by the location in a galeria with a telephone center and internet café. Carrera 4, 12-78. Updated: Dec 19, 2007.

Mid-Range

An Andante Ma Non Troppo

(LUNCH: $6) Situated on the corner of 11th and 3rd, it would be easy to stride past this place without realizing it exists. One entrance lies at the back of a gift shop and the other is fairly nondescript. Once you do enter, the restaurant/café sprawls through four rooms. On offer is good coffee, pastries and a killer lunchtime two-course promotion for around $6. Options include such treats as Mexican soup, grilled chicken in herbs accompanied with patacones and salad, and freshly-squeezed natural fruit juice. Calle 11 and Carrera 3. Updated: Dec 19, 2007.

Café del Sol

Café del Sol's dimly lit rooms are an ideal place to conduct an affair. With atmospheric, decadent décor, the Café del Sol is intimate and meant for couples. Calle 14, 3-60. Updated: Dec 19, 2007.

Café Para Dos

On the corner from the Hotel Aragon is Café Para Dos. Behind a window of multicolored bottles lie rooms scattered with Moroccan throws and cushions. Upstairs there is an open fire, making this café an ideal place to sit back, drag on a hookah, enjoy a coffee or cocktail and decompress. Carrera 3 with Calle 12. Updated: Dec 19, 2007.

Casa de Citas

Formerly a brothel, hence the name, the Casa de Citas has converted itself into a cool hangout for live music and easy bites. Don't let the cover charge put you off. Once inside, knock back a rum or aguardiente and listen to Cumbia, Bolero or Cuban Son. Check out the balcony where women *de la vida alegre* (prostitutes) once stood to promote themselves to potential customers. Carrera 3, 13-35. Updated: Jan 11, 2008.

Escobar y Rosas

From Wednesday night onwards, there are lines of people left in the cold as this wildly popular bar/club reaches capacity. Inside, loads of fashionably-dressed people are crammed into two tiny floors while the DJ plays funky tunes. Before you ask, the name has nothing to do with the former head of the Medellin Cartel, but refers to a pharmacy that was formerly situated where the club is now. Only cash is accepted here. Carrera 4, 15-01. Tel: 1-341-7903. Updated: Jan 11, 2008.

La Vida en Rosa

La Vida en Rosa has an extraordinarily large menu and appears to have an enormous turnover, filling all five of its rooms at lunchtime. The set menu looks of particular quality and the lasagnas are enormous. Busy staff run between tables taking orders. A popular joint for brisk lunchtime service. Calle 14, 4-38. Updated: Dec 19, 2007.

Pimienta y Café

For a couple of dollars one can feast on a set lunch menu that would fill even the most vacuous stomach. Pimienta y Café is clean, friendly and large and is often frequented by politicians climbing up the hill from Congress. The service is fast and the food is substantial and flavorful. Carrera 3, 9-27. Updated: Dec 19, 2007.

Plaza del Chorro de Quevedo

In the heart of La Candelaria, at the steep end of the hill is the Plaza del Chorro de Quevedo. On any given evening one can find a host of interesting and eclectic bars to frequent. In front of the small chapel there is normally a *cuentero* (storyteller) regaling a crowd for his dinner. Recommended bars are Pequeña Santa Fe, El Gato Gris and Merlín. Plaza del Chorro de Quevedo, Calle 13 with Carrera 2. Updated: Jan 11, 2008.

Quiebra Canto

Quiebra Canto is the brainchild of a group of students from the Universidad Nacional. Twenty-nine years ago they decided to create a place to play Silvio Rodríguez songs and start the revolution. Very little of that original theme remains, but nonetheless Quiebra Canto is one of Bogotá's most popular haunts. Here, funk is mixed in with salsa and often washed down with a healthy dose of samba. Students dance the night away and loners stand at the bar looking moody. For a bird's eye view of the dancefloor, head to the second level. Carrera 5, 17 -76. Tel: 1-243-1630. Updated: Jan 11, 2008.

Restaurante Vegetariano Loto Azul

For more than two decades, Restaurante Vegetariano Loto Azul has been serving bogotanos and foreigners delicious vegetarian food. Besides whipping up breakfasts and lunches accompanied by a nice salad bar, Loto Azul also prepares lasagnas, sandwiches and buffets. Several times per week it also prepares specials. In addition, the restaurant offers cooking courses, Bakhti yoga sessions (Tuesday, 5:00 p.m.), videos (Thursday 6:15 p.m.), and open mic poetry and music (Friday 6:00-11 p.m.) Open Monday-Saturday. Carrera 5A, 14-00. Tel: 1-334-2346. Updated: May 19, 2008.

Restaurante Café Israelí L'Jaim

Hummus, matbuja, falafel, shawarma (lamb, veal or chicken), lafa, zoarim, shakshuka — this place has any Middle Eastern comfort food that your stomach aches for. Made from millennia-old recipes, L'Jaim prepares traditional Israeli food for the discerning public. If you can't quite make up your mind, then you and a companion can try a combination plate. Vegetarian plates are also on the menu. Most dishes come with French fries. Don't forget to take home some pita, lafa or hummus. Open Sunday-Friday 11 a.m.-5:30 p.m. Carrera 3, 14-79. Tel: 1-281-8635, E-mail: ljaim.restaurante@hotmail.com, URL: restauranteljaim.tripod.com. Updated: May 19, 2008.

HIGH-END

El Bolón Verde !

(ENTREES: $9.50-16) Creative haute cuisine dished-up with sweet jazz awaits you at El Bolón Verde. The eats cannot get more inspired than at this bistro. Choose from seafood such as shrimp, squid and octopus, or beef tenderloin and pork served in curry or ground coffee and whiskey sauce. Other dishes include the julienned mango, bread with eggplant butter and meat platters accompanied by mashed potatoes, salad and bread. Don't forget to try the homebrewed beers. From Thursday to Saturday nights there's live jazz music. There are public jams on Fridays or Saturdays. Open Wednesday-Sunday from noon, Wednesday until 11:30 p.m., Thursday 1:30 a.m., Friday and Saturday 3 a.m., Sunday 10 p.m. Carrera 1A (Callejón de las Brujas), 13-20, Plazoleta de El Chorro de Quevedo. Tel: 1-561-0237, E-mail: bolondeverde@hotmail.com. Updated: May 19, 2008

El Santo Viático

An upmarket feed in La Candelaria, El Santo Viático is a good option housed in the cloisters of what looks like a former church. This place is romantic and the menu features largely Italian dishes. An ideal place to splurge with a loved one. Calle 12, 3-55. Updated: Jan 11, 2008.

CHAPINERO

Two years from now the Chapinero district will likely look like a different neighborhood. Traditionally popular with students and young couples as it is close to both centers of business and universities, all of the old apartment buildings are being knocked down to make way for new constructions. Any bus from La Candelaria running north on Carrera Séptima will take you through Chapinero. There are choices of restaurants and nightclubs here, but for the backpacker this will remain largely a transit area between La Candelaria and Zona T. Updated: Dec 05, 2007.

Chapinero Lodging

El Cafecito

(ROOM: $12-29) The owners of the El Cafecito brand (with branches in Quito and Cuenca, Ecuador) have opened the newest addition to Bogotá's growing list of fine hostals. One block from the Parque Nacional, a 20 minute walk from La Candelaria, and perhaps 10 minutes from the Macarena, El Cafecito is a traveler hub. The hostel is a beautifully restored Bogotá townhouse with large rooms, wooden floors, an ample garden and a downstairs café and bar. Most rooms are dormitories but the hostal also has one double room and one private room. As the only neighbors are office buildings, there is no problem should your evening BBQ or party in the garden get a little raucous. Carrera 6, 34-70. Tel: 1-285-8308, E-mail: bogota@cafecito.net, URL: www.cafecito.net. Updated: Feb 08, 2008.

La Casona del Patio Amarillo

(ROOM: $35-50) Positioned almost equidistant between La Candelaria and the Zona Rosa, La Casona has long been a favorite for those with a little more cash and a desire to escape the traditional gringo scene. Attentive staff, a great breakfast, well-cared-for rooms and communal areas make La Casona arguably the best value mid-range option in Bogotá. Carrera 8, 69–24. Tel: 1-212-8805 / 1991, Fax: 1-212-3507, E-mail: casona@telecom.com.co, URL: http://www.lacasonadelpatio.net. Updated: Dec 19, 2007.

Chapinero Restaurants

Cha Cha Bar

The winning ticket for Cha Cha is its lofty location on the 41st floor of an otherwise nondespcript Bogotá skyscraper. With views over all of Bogotá, clubbers can enjoy electronica music and chill out on open-air patios. The club is available to rent for private functions during the week and then becomes a proper club from Thursday night onwards with a total capacity nudging 900 dancing bodies. Carrera 7, 32-26, Floor 41. Tel: 1-350-5074, E-mail: info@elchacha.com, URL: www.elchacha.com. Updated: Dec 19, 2007.

Zona T

So-called for its two pedestrian streets that meet in a "T", the Zona T has some of Bogotá's best shopping and nightlife. Rival restaurants and bars blast music in efforts to drown each other out and lure in patrons. Fine restaurants as well as staple favorites such as Crepes and Waffles and the Irish Bar are located here. If you're not interested in the bars, restaurants or clubs, there are three enormous shopping malls in the immediate vicinity. Atlantis and Andino have multiscreen cinemas and El Retiro is considered a luxury mall. Updated: Dec 05, 2007.

Zona T Restaurants

Bogotá Beer Company

The Bogotá Beer Company molds itself on various American-style micro-breweries. It offers artesanal beers in a pub setting as well as large screen TVs are permanently tuned into sporting events. There are other franchises in Usaquén, Parque la 93 and the Zona T. URL: www.bogotabeercompany.com. Updated: Dec 19, 2007.

The Irish Pub

Popular with young Colombians, the Irish Pub really does not resemble an Irish establishment at all. However, on weekends the forecourt that spills onto the pedestrianised section of the Zona T is full with revellers. For a pint and some traditional pub food you could do a lot worse. Updated: Dec 19, 2007.

Luna

In the heart of the Zona T, Luna, along with many of its neighbors in the area, is an upmarket Italian restaurant, specializing in risotto and pastas. The decor sets it apart from the rest and the food will have you purring appreciatively. Calle 83, 12-20. Tel: 1-257-2088. Updated: Dec 19, 2007.

V!VA Member Review-Luna

My favorite restaurant in Bogotá. Each time I eat here the food is perfect! Netherlands, Feb 07, 2008

Parque de la 93

Along with Zona T, Parque de la 93 is a key area in Bogotá for merrymaking. With a plethora of restaurants, bars and clubs, the area has transformed from a residential district into a commercial one. This area appeals to a more mature crowd than the Zona T, evident when you compare prices. For an excellent night out you should head to Salto del Ángel on the western edge of the park, where you can enjoy dinner and watch the restaurant morph into a late night bar and nightclub.

You would be hard pressed to call Parque de la 93 a real park. It is more of an upmarket grassy tree-lined plaza. The Parque 93 is somewhere to go when you have had your fill of colonial buildings and the mayhem of La Candelaria. Here you can spy on how the other half lives; this area is full of luxury appartments and expensive restaurants. There are a couple of places that accommodate the traveler's budget, namely the Bogotá Beer Company on the corner of Juan Valdéz. If money is not an issue, you can indulge in many places here. Updated: Feb 06, 2008.

El Salto del Ángel Bar

Mainly appealing to young, moneyed professionals, El Salto del Ángel is filled with beautiful people every Friday and Saturday, and often during midweek. Tables are moved aside as 80s music, electronica and contemporary latin beats are turned up. Carrera 13, 93a-45. Tel: 4-635-9307. Updated: Dec 19, 2007.

Kukaramakara Bar

This tongue-twisting bar is another effervescent option in northern Bogotá. The house band plays live Latin music, with a DJ spinning booty-shaking records during their breaks. Serious party people won't want to get off the dance floor until they're good and sweaty, and their glasses are empty. Arrive early to secure a table. Carrera 15, 93-57. Tel: 1-642-3170, URL: www.kukaramakara.com. Updated: Dec 19, 2007.

Samper

If you take the Hotel Tequendama as a reference point or are visiting the Museo Nacional, then you are standing in the small but perfectly located district of Samper. Samper is filled with fancy restaurants that cater to a highly-paid clientele on weekdays, while La Macarena is up the hill behind the Museo Nacional and beyond the Plaza de Toros. In La Macarena you can find eclectic, artsy shops and funky restaurants and bars. Residents of La Macarena are probably what one describes as "alternative," and they are battling to keep their area this way. Bohemian and funky alike head here for a chilled glass of wine or cocktail before wandering in and out of local art galleries. Updated: Dec 05, 2007.

Things to See and Do

Plaza de Toros la Santamaría

If you think you can handle it, head to the bull ring in the early morning during the months of January and February to glimpse young toreros training. The Plaza de Toros la Santamaría routinely fills to capacity during these months. Carrera 6 with Calle 26, La Macarena. Tel: 1-334-1482. Updated: Feb 08, 2008.

Samper Lodging

Tequendama Intercontinental Hotel

Don't let the 50s-era architecture fool you—Tequendama is all luxury on the inside. Rooms come in various sizes, from standard and business to junior and presidential suites. At the lowest level, rooms come with cable TV, mini-bar, 24-hour room service, a tub or Jacuzzi and a daily paper (amenities increase as you climb the ladder). On-site restaurants offer Colombian and international cuisine (mostly Italian), and the well-stocked hotel bar is quite chic. Other amenities include a business center with internet access, a putting green and an on-site sauna and spa. Another advantage to this hotel is its close proximity to the historical center and the Plaza de Toros. It also has easy travel options to the airport, the fashionable Zona Rosa and Parque 93. Carrera 10, 26-21. Tel: 1-382-2930, Fax: 1-282-2860, E-mail: bogharsv@interconti.com, URL: www.inter-tequendama.com.co. Updated: Oct 03, 2007.

Samper Restaurants

La Juguetería

Where else can you dine on fine steaks while surrounded by toys? Dozens of slightly creepy dolls are suspended from the beams and rafters here, nonethless it is hard to be distracted from the scrumptious food on offer. Bring along some old toys and receive a discount. Calle 27, 4ª-03. Updated: Dec 19, 2007.

La Hamburguesería

Small and brightly decorated, with a street-side heated patio, La Hamburguesería is a good option if you are craving a succulent burger. Medallions of beef and the *calentao* are recommended. Carrera 4a, 27-27. Tel: 1-281-1286, URL: www.lahamburgueseria.com. Updated: Dec 19, 2007.

Frida

Though out of reach for most budget travelers, Frida's is quite simply the best Mexican restaurant in town. The flavorsome pork ribs bathed in a *rosa de jamaica* (Jamaican rose) salsa are a must-try. For more traditional meals, try fajitas or the sopa azteca. Beautifully decorated and with incredible service, this is the place to come for Mexican. Carrera 10, 26-40. Tel: 1-562-0606, E-mail: eliasmendoza@hotmail.com. Updated: Dec 19, 2007.

Leo Cocina y Cava

Quite simply the most exclusive and expensive restaurant in Bogotá, and with good reason. Chef Leonor Espinosa has dedicated this establishment to Colombian coastal food with a gourmet twist. If you can make a reservation and secure a table then be sure to try the tuna cut, encrusted with santanderean ants. Come well dressed—you'll be brushing shoulders with the highest ranking politicians. Calle 27B, 6-75. Tel: 1-286-7091 / 281-6267 Updated: Dec 19, 2007.

Rosales

Young professionals in Chapinero dream of upgrading to Rosales. Here the streets are tree-lined, security is high and the beautiful people drift from cafés to design stores to award-winning restaurants. New bars such as Dar Papaya (69 A, 4-78) are springing up to great aclaim, and theaters and fancy shops can be found around every street corner. This is not a backpacker destination, but if you feel like leaving behind the dirt-encrusted cargo pants and fleece and taking a few more pesos out with you, Rosales is a fun place to dress up. Updated: Dec 05, 2007.

Rosales Lodging

Estelar La Fontana

(ROOM: $100-250) Located in the north, next to the shops and restaurants of the Unicentro mall is Estelar Fontana. With 193 rooms and high-end amenities, this stately construction is a sight to behold. From standard rooms to the Estelar Suite, spaces are decorated along the lines of high-end U.S. hotel chains. The on-site restaurant features live music and a rotating buffet. The English-style bar is also a great place to end the day. Av. 127, 15A-10. Tel: 1-615-4400, Fax: 1-216-0449, E-mail: reservas@hotelesestelar.com, URL: www.hotelesestelar.com. Updated: Oct 03, 2007.

Hotel Casa Medina

(ROOM: $310-600) Located in the heart of Bogotá's business district and within short walking distance of some of Rosales' fashionable bars and restaurants, Casa Medina is an ideal destination for business travelers. Built in 1945 and displaying a blend of Spanish and French influences, its rooms boast a modern-chic ambiance without sacrificing comfort. Casa Medina's restaurant isn't lacking in elegance either, with international cuisine available in a sophisticated dining area. Menu options include Thai chicken supreme, salmon medallions in a citric fruit sauce, and broiled veal escalope in a cherry sauce. If work is on the menu, the hotel offers a fax, copy center, translation services, a secretary center and audiovisual equipment. Try the on-site gym or massage room when work gets you down. Carrera 7, 69A–22. Tel: 1-217-0288 / 312-0299, Fax: 1-312-3769, E-mail: centralreservation@hoteles-charleston.com, URL: www.hoteles-charleston.com/casamedina. Updated: Oct 09, 2007.

Zona Rosa

Located between streets 79 and 85 and Carreras 11 and 15, this lively area on the northern part of the city is a trendy night spot where younger crowds meet and party along the streets lined with fine restaurants and hot night clubs. Updated: Jun 03, 2008.

Nightlife in Zona Rosa

Bar 201

(COVER: $5) Designed to look like a singleton's apartment, complete with paintings, sofas and table lamps, Bar 201 is a fun place to listen to tunes and have a drink. On occasion there is live music. The cover charge is $5 and there is usually no line to get in. Calle 82, 13-26. Tel: 1-530-4051. Updated: Dec 19, 2007.

Gótica

A favorite in Bogotá for its seemingly endless list of world-class DJs, Gótica's three rooms are sure to get you dancing. On Friday and Saturday nights, the club blasts electronica, crossover or hip hop. Prices are steep, but for one evening you can enjoy enough to forget about the money. Carrera 14, 82-50. Tel: 1-218-0727. Updated: Dec 19, 2007.

Penélope

(COVER: $10) While other clubs are succumbing to the fad of minimalist themes and furnishing, Penélope, a classic club in Bogotá, refuses to be bullied and maintains its glam style and purpose. The music here, electronica and crossover, is excellent and can be heard in the two dance rooms. Entry is roughly $10 and a bottle of whisky will set you back around $50. Carrera 14a, 83-49. Tel: 1- 606-3568, E-mail: info@club-penelope.com, URL: www.club-penelope.com. Updated: Dec 19, 2007.

El Sitio

El Sitio—The Place—is exactly that if you want to do some good, old-fashioned partying, Colombian style. This bar/club is the spot to buy a bottle with some friends, kick back to some live music, then leap up and dance energetically with the rest of the patrons. Arrive early to avoid long lines. Carrera 11a, 93-52. Tel: 1-530-5050, URL: www.elsitiobar.com. Updated: Dec 19, 2007.

Cinema

Routinely lauded as the best place to get your fix of progressive house and electronic music, Cinema boasts vast rooms and thundering beats. Between 2 a.m. and 4 a.m., long lines extend around the block as traditional haunts close down. Partyers continue the festivities well past dawn in Cinema. Carrera 14, 75-46. Tel: 1-310-5968. Updated: Dec 19, 2007.

Alma

New in July 2007, Alma has quickly converted itself into the most happening club in Bogotá. Entry is tough but not impossible—best to find friends in high places who can guarantee your entry. If that's not possible, arrive early. People call weeks ahead of time to reserve the VIP sofas. Wednesday night is strictly salsa, Thursday is 80s night with a sprinkling of Latin rock. On Fridays and Saturdays, the three rooms are split into funk, soul and acid jazz. Calle 85, 12-51. Tel: 1-622-8289. Updated: Dec 19, 2007.

Usaquén

Usaquén, at one time a separate village on the outskirts of Bogotá, has subsequently been consumed by the capital's unrelenting sprawl. Now Usaquén resembles a village within Bogotá with chic boutiques, quality restaurants and some equally enticing bars. These businesses are all clustered around an attractive plaza in an area inhabited by wealthier residents. A great day to visit is Sunday, when the Usaquén flea market is in full flow with interesting bric a brac. Updated: Feb 08, 2008.

Usaquén Restaurants

Zhang China Gourmet

(ENTREES: $10) Good chinese restaurants in Bogotá are pretty hard to come by, so the discovery of this eatery in Usaquén is well received. The setting is ideal, right on the corner of the plaza and the interior is modern and stylish. Dishes come in at roughly $10 and will quench the desire for Asian food. Carrera 6, 119-01. Tel: 1-213-3979. Updated: Dec 19, 2007.

80 Sillas

80 Sillas lists itself as an "informal restaurant." However, at first glance it appears to be anything but that. This seafood restaurant is fast becoming a hot favorite for yuppies working in the area of Usaquén. The ceviche is very good and the staff is insistent that the ingredients arrived fresh that morning from the coast. Calle 118, 7-09. Tel: 1-619-2471. Updated: Feb 13, 2008.

Alfredo's Bistro

Alfredo's Bistro, right in the heart of the village-like district of Usaquén, is a perfect place to settle down to a long lunch after a shopping excursion in the Hacienda Santa Bárbara. When the weather holds, the place to be is on the patio, otherwise there are plenty of tables indoors. The Thai chicken salad is good value for its size at $10, also recommended are the dill salmon and the grilled chicken in a blue cheese sauce. Carrera 6a, 117-35. Tel: 1-213-3246. Updated: Dec 19, 2007.

V!VA Member Review-Alfredo's Bistro

I'm from Bogotá and this is one of my favorite restaurants. The food has real flavor, the pasta is very well made with traditional sauces. It's a great opportunity to try different entrees. Bogotá, Mar 14, 2008.

BOGOTÁ

Salt Cathedral

By Wilson Lievano, V!VA List Contributor, 2007

Dark passages beneath mountains traditionally have been associated with hell and the devil in the Christian culture. However, a group of miners in Zipaquirá transformed their workplace into a place of worship which became a symbol of their devotion.

For more than 500 years the salt mountains surrounding the town of Zipaquirá have been exploited, first by the Muiscas, the region's indigenous culture, and later by the Spaniards and their descendants. After Christianity was introduced into the region, the miners started to hang religious images on the walls of the mine for protection. The fervor of the workers inspired the government to build a shrine in the mines. The project was completed in 1954 and soon began to attract visitors.

The salt cathedral is a must-see for Catholics who visit Bogotá (Zipaquirá is just 15.5 miles from Bogotá and is accessible by car or train), but the architecture and the fine carving of statues and religious symbols appeal to all kinds of visitors.

The current cathedral is not the original. As time passed, water seeping in from outside (rain is frequent in the region) started to damage the cathedral, which posed a threat to visitors. In 1990 the government closed the shrine and started to build a new one 197 feet (about 60 meters) below the old cathedral. The project was completed in 1995 and now covers 2.1 acres of underground tunnels and chambers.

Entrance to the cathedral is $5 for adults and $2.50 for kids under 12. There are no religious requirements for admittance. People with heart conditions or fears of darkness or enclosed spaces are not encouraged to take the tour. For the rest, the experience of descending into the darkness may just bring a few closer to God.

Near Bogotá

Zipaquirá

Alt.: 2,600m Pop: 62,000 City Code: 1

Zipaquirá is mostly known for its enormous, underground salt cathedral. What visitors don't necessarily know is that this is one of the more attractive colonial towns in the country. It is worth spending a day or two here to bask in the sun and surrounding greenery. The main plaza boasts the history of this salt mining town, and the wealth of Zipaquirá is immediately evident in a brief glance at the immense cathedral on the square and the immaculately clean conditions of the narrow surrounding streets.

In pre-Columbian times, this town was home to the Muisca people. Zipaquirá, which in Chibcha, the Muiscan language, means "the land of the zipa (king)," suggests that this was a prosperous region, likely due to the region's salt supplies. The Muisca people would sell salt or trade it for goods.

The salt, which is still being mined from the mountainside to this day, was formed thousands of years ago when Zipaquirá was once under water.

Photo by Freyja Ellis

Zipaquirá Lodging

Hotel Colonial

(BED:$7-15) A fantastic find in the center of town (just two blocks from the main plaza and another two blocks from the salt cathedral), Hotel Colonial has everything you are looking for in an economic yet stylish and comfortable hotel. With fifty rooms among two well-manicured courtyards and a cozy, green backyard, you're sure to find the right setting and accommodation. All rooms (except the dorm) have a private bathroom with hot water and cable television. $7 dorm bed, $12 single room, $15 double room. Facing the mountain from the main plaza, walk one street to the left and then take the first street to the right. Hotel Colonial is the yellow hotel on the left side of the street. Updated: May 28, 2008.

Zipaquirá Restaurants

Sakura Japonés

(LUNCH: $3.50) Although Sakura Japonés doesn't serve the most authentic Japanese cuisine in the country, you can still count on having a complete meal in a pleasant atmosphere. There is a set lunch menu that includes juice, soup, salad, vegetables, meat or chicken, rice or potatoes and a pastry dessert for just $3.50. You can always order á la carte from the general menu, where noodle soups and basic sushi items are freshly prepared in the tiny kitchen out back. Catering or take-out service is also available upon request. Calle 4, 12-37, in front of Parque la Esperanza. Tel: 2-851-0261, Cell 313-244-8555 / 4197. Updated: May 28, 2008.

Restaurante Sabor a Leña

With so many similar restaurants to choose from, it would be easy to skip Sabor a Leña. However, it shouldn't be overlooked, as its great prices, tasty local food and convenient location make it perfect for travelers needing a good, quick meal. The menu, which changes daily, can be found outside the main entrance. Sabor a Leña is across the square from the archaeological museum, at the foot of the hill of the salt cathedral. Calle 1, 7-00. Tel: 2-852-7406. Updated: May 28, 2008.

Suesca

Suesca is a rock climber's wonderland. There are rocks of all shapes and sizes that cater to experts, beginners and those in between. Not only can you have fun on the rocks, but you can also try your hand at rafting, mountain biking, camping and hiking. Suesca makes for an excellent weekend break from Bogotá and can be combined with trips to Guatavita and perhaps Villa de Leyva. There is a fair amount of guesthouses and restaurants throughout the area. Getting there: Take the Transmilenio to the Portal del Norte station (the northern end of the line) and then catch any bus within the station heading to Suesca (40 minutes to 1 hour). Updated: May 16,2008.

Guatavita

Guatavita is a pleasant day-trip destination from Bogotá, a place where travelers can escape the city fumes and explore a little of the Cundinamarca countryside. The original Laguna de Guatavita was a sacred site to the local Muisca people, who were known to have enormous reserves of gold. Here in the lake the leader of the Muisca would bathe covered in gold. This most likely gave rise to the idea held by Spanish conquistadors, in particular Gonzalo Jiménez de Quesada who discovered the lake in 1537, that the lake was one of the possible sites of the mythical El Dorado. There is a wedge cut out of the side of the lake where the Spanish attempted to drain it to extract its riches. Over the years there have been several attempts to recover gold from the lake and all have ended in failure.

The town as it is today was built in a traditional colonial fashion but is obviously articificial. It was moved to its present location in 1970 after the waters from the River Bogotá flooded. There are some decent restaurants and plenty of stalls to purchase Colombian gifts. Some brave souls go into the chilly lake waters for aquatic sports. From Bogotá, take the Transmilenio to the Portal del Norte station and then catch a bus from within the station. Updated: May 16,2008.

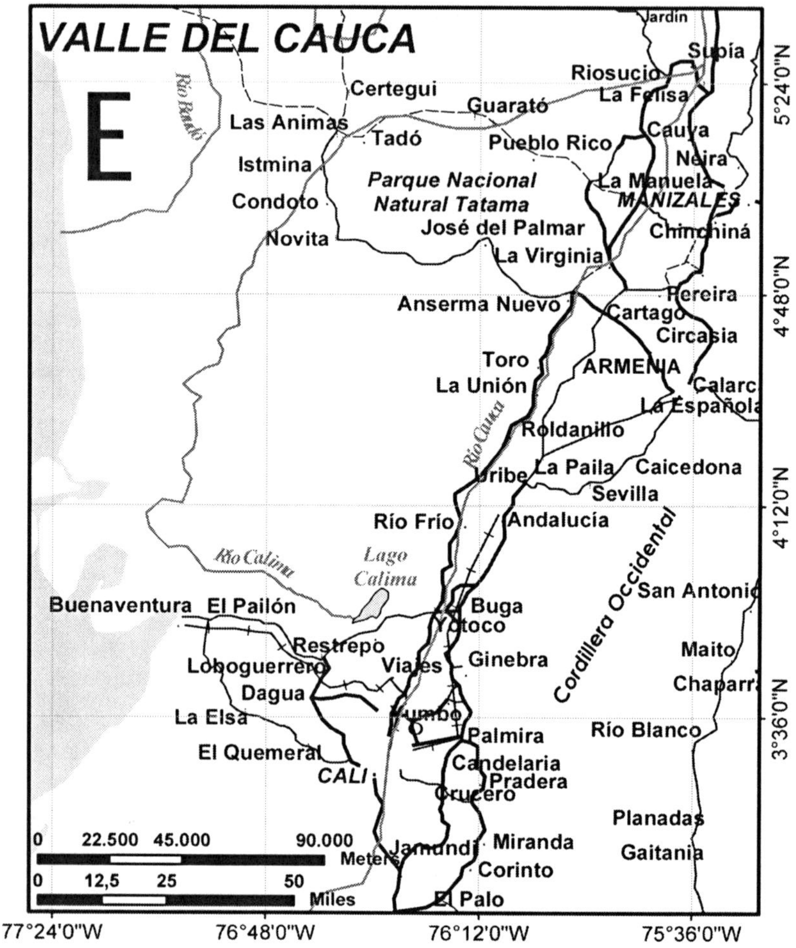

Valle del Cauca

The raucous epicenter of Cali makes the department of Valle del Cauca the powerhouse of southwestern Colombia. Throughout the region, the average altitude is roughly 1,000m above sea level. In Valle de Cauca's extreme west one confronts Cali's ugly sister, Buenaventura, a port city flanked by the waters of the Pacific Ocean. The department's other boundaries are defined by the mountain ranges that make up the central and western ridges of the Andes. The Cauca, one of Colombia's most powerful and longest rivers, flows throughout these mountains.

The department has always been strategically important for overland travel and import/export, so there is no shortage of interesting sites to visit. Starting in the north from Cartago, bordering the neighboring department of Risaralda, there is a steady line of religious monuments that follow the Cauca River and span south. Notable churches can be found in Cartago, Toro, Roldanillo, Bugalagrande, Guacari, Guadalajara de Buga and Jamundí.

If following the route of the river, take time to check out the traditional *vallecaucana estancias*, coffee farms, adventure sports and natural sights in Calima, El Cerrito and Palmira. Also, don't miss an opportunity to check out locally woven crafts made from plantain fibers or try the nationally famous vallecaucana *champús* (traditional fruit and herbs drink) , *marranitas* (fried plantain balls) and *aborrajados* (banana dessert) dishes. Updated: Dec 04, 2007.

Highlights

Camping, hiking and watersports around Cali can be enjoyed at **Lago de Calima** and **Parque Nacional Natural Los Farallones de Cali (p.127)**.

If you are in Cali in December, don't miss the **Feria de Cali (p.109)**. Updated: Dec 04, 2007.

History

Until the arrival of the Spanish, the territory now called Valle del Cauca was inhabited by hunter-gatherer tribes mostly prevalent in and around the Calima River. The Spanish empire grew and in 1536 the Conquistador Sebastián de Benalcázar founded Popayán and later Cali.

During this colonial period the area fell under the auspices of the governing body in Quito, Ecuador. Later, after independence and the annexation of the Valle del Cauca, the territory was split between Popayán and Buenaventura. In 1857, a state was created that included the departments of Chocó, Caquetá and Pasto. However, in 1908 these territories were divided, creating Valle del Cauca as we know it today.

During the industrialization of the 20th Century, a deteriorating economy and violence pushed people toward the major urban areas of Cali, Cartago and Palmira, which influenced the growth of the department. To this day Cali and other towns suffer from ill distribution of wealth, mass migration due to conflict, and the destruction that accompanies the rise and fall of powerful cocaine cartels. Updated: Dec 04, 2007.

When to go

During just about every month of the year there is a festival or *feria* taking place somewhere in the Valle del Cauca, from the remotest hamlet to downtown Cali. The *Feria de Cali* in December should not be missed. In June, the town of Ginebra holds its festival of Andean music. The festival of sugarcane held each March is worth a peek.

It is difficult to predict weather conditions along the coast. A squall can blow up at any time, but the two defined rainy seasons take place from March to May and then again from October to November. During these seasons, Cali is badly affected—escape closer to the mountain ranges for a cooler climate.

Average temperatures hover around 24°C (75°F). Updated: Dec 04, 2007.

Safety in Valle del Cauca

Travel in Valle del Cauca is generally safe.You should be aware, however, of the red zone in the southeastern corner of the region, which is a disputed area by the government and the FARC rebels. The FARC has suggested that the government create a demilitarized zone to negotiate prisoner exchanges near the towns of Florida and Pradera. In Cali, standard precautions are advised, as for any major city.

The only place where caution should be applied at all times is Buenaventura. The port city is wrenched in a continual power struggle among government forces, paramilitaries and leftist guerrillas, who are all intent on securing this strategic city. The drug trade in Buenaventura is visible and violence is prevalent. Updated: Dec 04, 2007.

Things to See and Do

Should you tire of dancing salsa in Cali (the self-proclaimed salsa capital of the world), put your feet to work outdoors where there are many activities to partake in while visiting Lake Calima or any national park in the department. Any type of natural attraction is available in this southwestern Colombia department, given the region's varied geography that includes plains, mountains, cloud forest, jungle and coast. Updated: Dec 04, 2007.

Parque Nacional Natural Mapelo

If you love diving, marine wildlife and exploring untouched nature, then it is worth your time to arrange transportation from Buenaventura to the rocky island of Mapelo. Two hundred miles off the coast, the island is only 0.25mi by 2mi, but the surrounding water is recognized as one of the best diving sites in the world (many say that it is similar to Cocos, Costa Rica). The diving sites include the Three Musketeers, *La Gringa* and the Altar of the Virgin. Divers have the opportunity to see dolphins, manta rays, white-tipped reef sharks, hammerheads, starfish, whales and many other sea creatures.

In addition to life under the sea, Mapelo's volcanic formations make it a wonder to behold and it is easy to believe why it's referred to as one of Colombia's treasures. The island is also home to a quarter of the world's population of Nazca Boobies.

Fishing is illegal within a 25-mile radius. In 2006 Mapelo was declared an UNESCO World Heritage Site, however, the wildlife, especially the sharks, are still endangered.

For more information about Malpelo's surrounding waters, check out www.fundacionmalpelo.org. Updated: May 21, 2008.

Valle del Cauca Tours

For tours close to Cali, contact the Centro Cultural de Cali, Tel: 2-885-8855, E-mail: oficinadeturismo@cali.gov.co. For Valle del Cauca tours call the Fondo Mixto de Promoción del Valle del Cauca, Tel: 2-886-1300, ext 500. Updated: May 05, 2007.

Valle del Cauca Lodging

Tourism is growing in the Valle del Cauca. This growth is reflected in the prevalence of decent, if not above-average, accommodation options. If you are happy with a cheap and cheerful backpacker haunt, then you will not be disappointed with the offerings available in Cali. One step up and you can find family-run places that make you feel at home. There are also stylishly rustic haciendas—usually kept in the family for eons—that have been thoughtfully restored and converted into tourist attractions and wonderful guest houses. Of course, if money is no object, look for boutique hotels and luxury chains in most of the major cities. Updated: Dec 05, 2007.

Cali

Alt: 757m Pop: 2,100,000 City Code: 2

Colombia's third largest city is one of many contrasts. Protected by the statue of the Cristo Rey and the monument of the Tres Cruces, the capital of the Valle del Cauca region is the industrial heart Colombia's southwest. Cali entices all who visit with promises of balmy nights spent in the company of beguiling caleñas with salsa rhythms setting the mood. Days can be spent idly wandering through neighborhoods lined with boutiques or historic districts steeped in art and culture.

In the outlying areas of Cali there are many recommended sights that include the zoo, Buga, Sonso, Parque Nacional Natural los Farallones and the Ecoparque Río Pance. Cali has much more to offer beyond its renowned nightlife and it is gradually becoming a well-rounded tourist destination. Nonetheless, it is the contagious desire to shake those hips that brings people together in the packed *discotecas* of the Colombian salsa capital.

Cali is coming to terms with its violent past and unruly present. Unlike other Colombian cities of its size, Cali's geography means that poorer *barrios* are mixed in with richer ones to a greater extent than Bogotá or Medellín.

It may not be a city to everybody's liking, but given Cali's geographical location, there is no denying its importance for those travelling to or from Ecuador. There are attractions here and in the surrounding areas that can keep the visitor entertained for a few days or more. Updated: Mar 06, 2008.

Highlights

Put some salsa rhythm to your trip at the endless dance clubs of chic neighborhoods like **El Peñón** and **Granada (p.113)**.

The colonial neighborhood of **San Antonio** provides a beautiful view of the city and is the cultural center of Cali.

If you intend to ever learn **salsa**, this is the place! Take advantage of the wide range of schools available in the city. Updated: Mar 06, 2008.

History

Santiago de Cali was founded on July 25, 1536 in a fertile valley of the Lili River by the Spanish conquistador Sebastián de Benalcázar (also the founder of Ecuador's capital city, Quito). The original site of the city is in the southern end of the current metropolis. The city was moved roughly 17km away from the original site due to interference from the native Jamundí people.

During this period, Cali played second fiddle to Popayán and long into the 18th Century the city was more or less dominated by the existence of large *fincas*. In 1810, Cali declared its independence from Popayán, which led to several battles between royalists and the local militia.

Cali is a city near the frontline of the current Colombian conflict due to its location within close range of some of Antioquia's main industrial areas, the ports of the Pacific and the eastern edge of the Andes. Throughout the 1980s, the infamous Cali cartel was the major rival of their better-publicized Medellín brethren (of Pablo Escobar fame) in the North.

Cali suffers on account of the guerrilla activity in neighboring areas. There have been guerilla reports as recent as April 2007, when a Cali police station was destroyed by a bomb attributed to the FARC. Updated: Feb 13, 2008.

When to Go

Cali is blessed with favorable weather patterns. The temperature averages of 24-30°C (75-85°F) year round. Cali has two rainy seasons, and though you can expect the showers to be short, they are tremendous in volume. The first wet season runs from March into May and the second, briefer, takes place October to November. Updated: Feb 18, 2008.

Holidays and Festivals

Although there are Easter processions in Cali, they are not particularly notable. You would be better served to head a couple of hours away to Popayán.

Shortly after the Feria de Cali (see below), the *Carnaval de Juanchito* is held in the municipality of Candelaria at the beginning of every year. Salsa dancing is yet again on display here, as well as vallecaucan sights, tastes and sounds.

The *Feria Nacional de la Caña de Azúcar* is yet another important festival held in Florida. The sweet taste of sugarcane is celebrated and locals parade wearing native costumes.

Prices generally increase in Cali around and during *Semana Santa*—when all Colombians travel—and during the famous Feria de Cali. Updated: Feb 18, 2008.

Feria de Cali

The well-known Feria de Cali takes place December 25-30. It has been a yearly event since 1957. Work ceases as the partying starts—this event is the city's version of Carnaval. Nights are made livelier with salsa concerts, horse races, parades and exhibitions.

As the salsa dancing capital of Colombia, this rythmically rich event is the biggest festival in the country and one of the most important in the Americas. For one week at the end of every year, there are bull fights, beauty and fashion pageants, food festivals, sports events and city-wide street festivities. To close the year on December 31, there is always a huge concert on the hill in Plaza San Antonio, where song and dance is the center of the New Year's party. Updated: Apr 28, 2008.

Getting to and Away from Cali

Bus

The Terminal de Transportes de Cali is a sprawling three-story monument to cement and could appear somewhat daunting at first glance. It is well policed and fairly easy to negotiate. All bus companies are on the second floor. Calle 30N, 2AN-29. Tel: 2-668- 3655.

Palmira, Coopetrán and Bolivariano have services to Bogotá.

Cali – Bogotá leaving at 1:30 p.m. (check times) $25 for 10 hours.

A variety of companies run frequent buses along the route to Popayán from Puerto Tejada ($6) and Palmira ($5).

Cali – Medellín (8 hours) is served by Coopetrán ($20), Expreso Trejos ($17) and Palmira ($15). Most companies have various buses making the journey everyday starting at 3:30 a.m., then subsequently every two hours.

Train

The tourist train runs at various times—take it to Cumbre, Buga and La Tebaida. This services is not just transport, but includes live music and partying. Avenida Vásquez Cobo, 23N-47. Tel: 2-666-6899 / 2-620-2324, E-mail: trenturistico@ert.com.co, URL: www.trenturisticocafeyazucar.com.

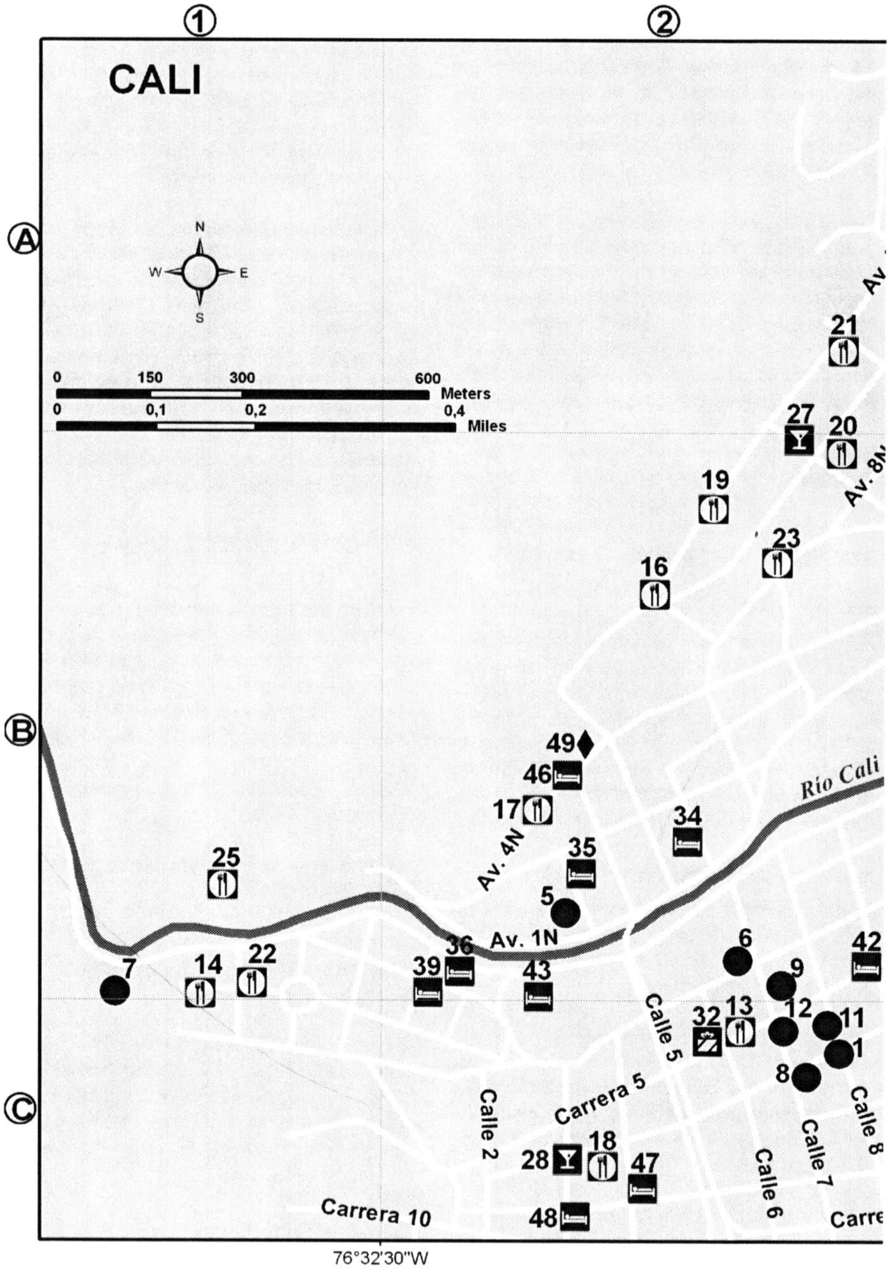
CALI
1
2
A
B
C
N
W
E
S
0
150
300
600
Meters
0
0,1
0,2
0,4
Miles
Río Cali
Av. 4N
Av. 1N
Av. 8N
Calle 2
Calle 5
Calle 6
Calle 7
Calle 8
Carrera 5
Carrera 10
76°32'30"W
1
5
6
7
8
9
11
12
13
14
16
17
18
19
20
21
22
23
25
27
28
32
34
35
36
39
42
43
46
47
48
49

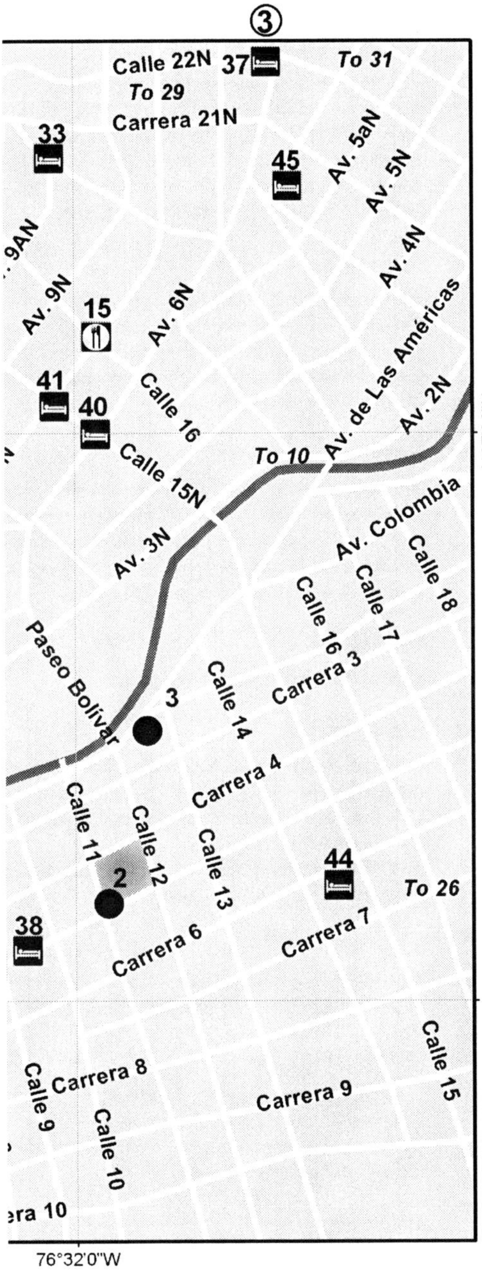

Activities ●

1 Capilla de la Inmaculada D2
2 Iglesia San Pedro C3
3 La Ermita C3
4 Loma de la Cruz Artisan Park D2
5 Los Gatos C2
6 Museo Arqueológico La Merced C2
7 Museo de Arte Moderno D2
8 Museo de Oro Calima D2
9 Museo Religioso y Colonial San Francisco C2
10 Nuestra Señora de los Remedios B4
11 Plaza San Francisco D2
12 Teatro Municipal Enrique Buena D2

Eating

13 Arte y Cocina C2
14 Cafe Mulatto C1
15 Cathay B3
16 La Antorcha C2
17 La Joroba de Camello C2
18 Macondo D2
19 Matiz C2
20 Pacífico C2
21 Palo Alto B2
22 PIccolo Pomadoro C1
23 San Borondón C2
24 Soneros D2
25 Vinos del Río C1

Nightlife

26 El Habañero C4
27 Faro 2004 C2
28 Greco D2

Services ★

29 Correos de Colombia A3
30 Hospital San Juan de Dios C3
31 I.S.S. B4

Shopping

32 Centro Cultural de Cali D2

Sleeping

33 Calidad House B2
34 Centenario C2
35 Centenario Suites C2
36 Design Hotel Austral C2
37 Hostal Iguana B3
38 Hotel Camino Real C2
39 Hotel Dann C2
40 Hotel Don Jaime B3
41 Hotel Granada Real B2
42 Hotel Imperial C2
43 Hotel Intercontinental C2
44 Hotel Posada Colonial C3
45 Hotel Sartor B3
46 Kaffee Erde C2
47 Posada de San Antonio D2
48 Sabor I Arte D2

Tours ♦

49 Christian Dojoseba C2

Air

Alfonso Bonilla Aragon airport (also known as Palmaseca airport) is located outside of Cali, Tel: 2-418-5000. Some international flights and internal flights land here.

A taxi from the city to the airport, and visa versa, will set you back more than $25. The cheapest way to get here from the center is to go to the bus terminal first and head to Lineas Consul, which has vans leaving every 15 minutes for the 30-minute ride. The cost for one passenger is $1.75. To get from the airport to the city center is the same – go to the exit point for national flights and from there you can catch a similar van for the same price. Updated: Feb 13, 2008.

Getting Around

Cali is a confusing city, as street numbers appear to have little rhyme or reason. Use the river and the Intercontinental Hotel as major landmarks. Or, look up at the hills to see statue of the Cristo Rey and the monument of the Tres Cruces—this will go some way toward helping you gain your bearings.

Wherever you are going, be sure to have the address written correctly, since Avenida 4 is not the same thing as Avenida 4 Norte. The best way to avoid such problems is by finding out exactly which barrio it is you want.

Buses are fairly straightforward and have their destinations plastered across the front window. For the most part, they travel on the main roads and each journey costs $0.70. There is a new mass-transit system, the Transmilenio (referred to as the *Mio*, here), being put together in Cali. Once this is up and running transport around town will become much easier. Updated: Feb 13, 2008.

Safety in Cali

Cali, as with any large city of similar ilk, is beset with problems. Colombia's unrest has led many displaced people to the city in search of security and access to money.

Panhandlers are common in the downtown area. In Granada and El Peñón you won't be bothered too much. Pay attention to your belongings and heed local advice. Cali beggars are not persistent—they'll ask for money once and then move on. Updated: Feb 13, 2008.

Cali Services

Tourism Office

There is a helpful tourist information office in the bus terminal (ground floor). For more detailed information, go to the Centro Cultural de Cali, Calle 6 and Carrera 5. Tel: 2-885-8855, ext. 122, E-mail: oficinadeturismo@cali.gov.co, URL: www.caliturismo.com.

Money

Banks and cash machines are prevalent in the city. On Avenida Sexta (the city's major thoroughfare) as well as in the Plaza de Caizedo and downtown, you can easily find all the major banks.

Keeping in Touch

You are never more than a few blocks from an internet café or telephone call center. Avenida Sexta has them by the dozen. Cyberphone Club is recommended on Av. 6, 4-52 Barrio San Fernando, Tel: 2-514-6563.

Post Office

Correos de Colombia Av. 6, 30-21.

Medical

Clínica Fundacion Valle de Lili–Carrera 98, 18-49. Tel: 2-331-7474 / 2-331-9090.
Clínica de Occidente–Calle 18 Norte, 5N-34. Tel: 2-660-3000.
Hospital Universitario del Valle–Calle 6, 36-08. Tel: 2-558-6355.

Laundry

Laundry places are common. There is certain to be at least one near any accommodation.

Camera Repair

Edicameras on Avenida Sexta, 30-11, Tel: 2-558- 3893, or Tecno Cameras on Avenida Sexta, 24-84, opposite the Biblioteca Departamental. Updated: 03/06/2008.

Shopping

Cali is considered a fantastic place for shopping. A few of very well-regarded shopping centers are Palmetto Plaza, Jardín Plaza, Cosmocentro, Unicentro, Chipichape and Centenario. Cali offers everything that a shopaholic craves, including chic boutiques in the barrios of La Granada and El Peñón.

Granada and El Peñón
Both of these neighborhoods are famous for art galleries, antique shops, fashion boutiques, artisan stores and restaurants. In Granada, the Galería café has good food and sculptures by local artist Emilio Hernández. Across the river from El Peñón, you can admire the dozen of cat sculptures in the park (see "Los Gatos" in Things to See and Do).

Jardín Plaza
This well-stocked shopping center in the southern part of Cali has a wide range of modern clothing and electronics stores. You are certain to find all of the major brand-name accessories here, and there's even a movie theater. It is also one of the few places with Wi-Fi access. Carrera 98, 16-200.

Chipichape
Chipichape, located in the north, is currently THE mall of choice. Shoppers come in hordes in search of the latest bargain or to sit on the benches and watch people go by. Chipichape's eateries are popular at lunchtime. Throughout the day, caleños come to watch a movie at one of the 12 screens in-house. Come nighttime, then head to the cool reggae and pop bar or other hip nightspots to salsa until late. Avenida Sexta, 35-47.

Loma de la Cruz
Little stores line the streets around Loma de la Cruz, making this area your best bet for purchasing artisan goods. There is a strange legend locally known as *mano del negro* (the black hand) surrounding this part of town. Long ago, it was here that a black slave was unjustly killed. The legend says that if you pass through the area late at night you can see the slave's hand emerge from the ground.

Centro Comercial Único
If you are looking for quality goods at a discounted price, this is the outlet mall for you. It is the only place in the city where leading brands are sold at 50 percent off the retail price. If you get tired of shopping, you can rest your feet while watching a movie at the 12-screen cinema. Calle 52 between Carrera 3 and 4. Updated: Apr 27, 2008.

SALSA IN CALI
Ride in a public bus, sit in a bar or walk down Avenida Sexta in Barrio La Granada and you will know that this city is all about salsa. There are dozens of salsa schools in Cali where a novice can learn a few steps to impress friends back home. In addition, there are many clubs where the irresistible urge to get up and strut one's stuff will be too overwhelming to rebuff.

No one should pass through Cali without attempting to salsa with a local at least once. Salsa is the pulsating heart of this city, and from cab drivers listening to the tinny beats on their vehicle radios to live performances in public spaces and theatres, you can't avoid it. At the 2008 International Salsa Championships, the top three places in the group dancing category all went to dance troupes from Cali. Pick up some of the champion steps at one of the salsa schools, where even the most lead-footed foreigner will be left eager to give it a go.

If you left your dancing shoes at home, head to the chic barrios of El Peñón or Granada to browse the boutiques for a solid pair. Afterward, stick around and enjoy a sumptuous meal in one of the city's most exclusive restaurants. Updated: Mar 06, 2008.

SALSA SCHOOLS IN CALI

Academia Combinación Rumbera
Calle 28B, 33E-70.Tel: 2-438-1810.

Fundación Artística Nueva Dimensión
Calle 36, 41A-10. Autopista Simón Bolívar. Tel: 2-681-1749.

Fundación Escuela de Baile Swing Latino
Carrera 33, 29-11. Tel: 2-336-6784.

Escuela de Baile Impacto Latino
Carrera 41, 38-75. Tel: 2-336-3146.

Constelación Latina
Carrera 26ª, 76-47. Tel: 2-422-5034.

Things to See and Do

Cali can easily keep travelers occupied for a number of days. Don't pass up an amble through the colonial neighborhood of San Antonio. Walk until you reach the San Antonio chapel at the top of the hill, where you can catch a great view of the city. Then, wander down the hill into the old part of the center, lined with both modern and colonial theatres and museums.

The historic center has a plethora of museums. In the north, the barrios of Granada and El Peñón boast upscale restaurants and shops that could be found easily in Los Angeles or Miami. Updated: Feb 13, 2008.

Museums

Start at the imposing Teatro Municipal Enrique Buenaventura. The yellow Baroque architecture on Calle Sexta and Carrera 6 is hard to miss. From here, head to the Museo Religioso y Colonial San Francisco to see more than 350 pieces of priceless religious works of art. Carrera 4, 6N-117.

Your next stop should be the Museo Arqueológico La Merced, Carrera 4, 6-59. Then take the short stroll over to the Museo de Oro Calima. Carrera 4, 7-14. Updated: Nov 15, 2007.

Museo Nacional del Transporte

If you have time on the way to or from the airport, it's well worth stopping in for a quick whirl around the national museum of transportation. This museum has an impressive collection of classic cars, historical planes, steam trains, motorcycles, bicycles, combustible engines, model cars, helicopters and other modes of transportation.

There is a coffee shop if you need a bite to eat, as well as free parking for visitors. To get here by bus, Rápido Aeropuerto goes to and from the terminal and the airport past the museum every 15 minutes. Monday-Friday, 8 a.m.-4 p.m., Saturday-Sunday and Holidays, 10 a.m. - 5 p.m. Next to the Alfonso Bonilla Aragón airport in the Zona Franca de Palmaseca. Tel: 2-651-1154, E-mail: museodetransporte@yahoo.com, URL: www.museodetransporte.org. Updated: Apr 27, 2008.

Museo del Oro Calima

A respectable collection of gold and ceramics is housed in the Banco de la República building. This is a fairly recent collection of Calima cultural artifacts (Calima is the name of the original indigenous group in the Valle de Cauca), which dates back nearly 9,000 years. Unlike the Quimbayá collection in Armenia, this museum does not have an English translation along each panel to guide you through the room. There is, however, a helpful English brochure that outlines the history of the Calima people and their customs. After you are finished browsing the Calima artifacts, head down the hall into the second exhibition room. There are several paintings and works of art that describe and illustrate the six stages of development of Latin American art and are well worth a look. Tuesday-Friday, 9 a.m.-5 p.m., Saturday, 10 a.m.-5 p.m. Calle 7a. Tel: 2-684-7754 / 55, URL: www.banrep.org/museo. Updated: Apr 28, 2008.

Museo La Tertulia

For a little taste of modern art, your best bet is Museo La Tertulia. Much more than just an art museum, there is also an outdoor auditorium where you can catch musical performances, especially at the beginning and end of every month. Next to it is the Cinemateca art house, which plays independent films and frequently hosts passing film festivals. Behind the theater is the XV Salón de Arte BBVA, a bank-sponsored art hall designed to support children's education through modern art. Finally, there are temporary and permanent exhibitions on display in two separate buildings. Monday-Saturday, 10 a.m.-6 p.m. Avenida Colombia, 5-105 Oeste. Tel: 2-893-2941 / 2939, Fax: 2-893-2961, E-mail: museolatertulia@telesat.com.co. Updated: Apr 29, 2008.

La Merced and Museo de Arte Colonial

The Museo de Arte Colonial in the convent of La Merced houses pottery and pre-colonial relics. Built in 1545, this is the oldest church in Cali. The church is a well-preserved colonial-style building, a nice contrast to the blander, more modern city buildings in the neighborhood. Monday-Saturday, 9 a.m.-1 p.m., 2 p.m.-6 p.m. Sunday and Holidays 9 a.m.-12 p.m. Updated: Apr 28, 2008.

La Ermita

The small Baroque chapel's original name, before it was destroyed in 1787, was Ermita de Nuestra Señora de la Soledad del Río. Today stands a very different, very beautiful Gothic structure that was built in 1942 and modeled after the cathedral in Cologne, Germany. La Ermita's intricate construction as well as its attractive pale blue and white coloring make it a city symbol, and certainly the most photographed church in all of Cali. Updated: Apr 28, 2008.

Iglesia San Pedro

First erected for the Priest of Quito in 1539, then later torn down and rebuilt in 1772, again in 1841, and one last time in 1930, this church has undergone several alterations. Inside and out, it is simple and understated, with stark white walls and ceilings, accentuated by seven gorgeous crystal chandeliers above the center aisle and an enormous wooden organ on the second floor. Take some time to admire the nice marble image of Jesus seated next to St. Peter. The side chapel is also a solemn place to pay homage to the Virgin Mary. On the way out, look at the bronze work by artist William Echeverría on the doors. Calle 11, 5-53. Tel: 2-881-1378. Updated: Apr 29, 2008.

Capilla de la Inmaculada

Built in 1762, the Capilla de la Inmaculada has a modern and modest interior, but is worth a quick peek because it remains the church of choice at midday. This narrow and long chapel is an homage to the Virgin Mary, who solemnly stands at the front altar. The interior is accented with seven arcs and several white columns with a blue and gold trim. Mass is held at 6:30 a.m., 10 a.m., 3 p.m., 6 p.m., and 8:30 p.m. Updated: Apr 28, 2008.

Casa Proartes

This great little neoclassic style building, next door to the Teatro Municipal, is yet another center for the arts in Cali. Built in 1871 and beautifully restored in 1991, free temporary art exhibits and performances are its biggest draw. There is a small cinema on the ground floor and across the way there is a pleasant cafeteria open for lunch on weekdays. Check the front entrance for the latest evening performances and daytime exhibits. Carrera 5, 7-02. Tel: 2-885-1179. Updated: Apr 28, 2008.

Plaza de Caicedo

This plaza is the best place to people watch during lunchtime. Plaza de Caicedo has always been the center of public, commercial and political life in Cali. During the colonial period it was called the Plaza Mayor. Between 1674 and 1897, the park was used for public markets. In 1813, it took the name of Plaza de la Constitución. In 1913, the name was changed to Plaza de Caicedo to honor caleño Joaquín de Caicedo, a martyr of the nation's independence. There is a stunning white judicial building on the northern edge of the plaza, a few small fountains around the perimeter and Caicedo's bronze statue in the center. Updated: May 13, 2008.

Plaza San Francisco

Destroyed in 1960 and rebuilt in 1969, this enormous brick plaza is one of the largest in Cali. People gather here to catch some rays and chill out. Be sure to check out the black fountain near the entrance to Capilla de la Inmaculada. This modern monument was erected in 1970 to honor the reverend father Damián González. Updated: Apr 28, 2008.

Monumento de las Tres Cruces

Standing at 1,500 meters above sea level, the three crosses that comprise this high-altitude monument were constructed in 1837. On May 3 (Colombia's Labor Day), caleños climb to the top of this hill to pay homage to Santa Cruz and celebrate their city's independence from Spain. There's a good view of the city from the top. An interesting fact to keep in mind is that the center cross is 26 meters tall and 22 meters wide. You can safely walk to the monument on a path from barrio Normandia. Or, simply flag one of the taxi jeeps marked "Las Cruces" that bus sightseers to and from Normandía Plaza and the monument. Updated: May 13, 2008.

Los Gatos

In 1996, renowned painter and sculptor Hernando Tejada began what came to be a collection of a dozen cat sculptures along the Cali River, close to El Peñón. Tejada's original cat, "El Gato del Río," is the largest of the collection. The subsequent cats are half its size but some have twice the charisma. These latter felines were painted by other significant Colombian artists and are all decorated to match—examples include "Magic Cat,"

"Coquette Cat" and "Seven Lives Cat." This is a great place to stroll along the river and appreciate some interesting modern Colombian art. Updated: Apr 29, 2008.

Teatro Municipal

On April 9, 1918 construction of this beautiful theater began. Ten years later it was completed, then remodeled in the 1950s. Designed like an Italian opera theater, this Neoclassical, stylish, elaborate theater holds up to 1,200 people. It was declared a national monument in June 2002. The ticket office is open in the afternoons. When it's closed, the guard can normally give you free tickets to private performances or let you take a look at the stage. Updated: May 13, 2008.

Lake Calima

Spanning an area of 7,000 hectares, Lake Calima is the largest artificial body of water in Colombia. The lake was created in 1964 when the Government undertook a massive dam project to provide energy for the region. Just 90 kilometers from Cali, it has become one of the top weekend destinations for residents of Cali and lovers of watersports. Visitors can either rent a cabin or camp. Sports include windsurfing, kite surfing, sailing, canoeing and water-skiing. Nearby, there are options for parasailing and canopy tours. El Darién, Calima. Updated: Nov 26, 2007.

Ecoparque Río Pance

The Río Pance runs south of Cali, by the city garden and the university district. A very popular spot that sees hundreds of city folk on the weekends, the Ecoparque Río Pance is a convenient place to relax by the river. The park has open-air gym stations, a lake for fishing, a botanical garden, and food and bathroom facilities. There are wonderful views of the Cali countryside throughout the park. Buses to Ecoparque Río Pance leave the bus terminal every 30 minutes and cost $1.50, one way. Updated: May 13, 2008.

Tren Turístico

Much like the Sabana train that runs from Bogotá, the Tren Turístico Café y Azúcar runs trips from the station in downtown Cali to points in the Valle del Cauca countryside and beyond. Choose from a variety of journeys that leave in the morning and return late afternoon, from Cali to Buga, the recreational park La Cumbre, Finca Villa Karen or Finca Turística La Gran Bélgica. Trips can have a party atmosphere, complete with a papayera band that plays in the carriages and stewardesses who attend to all of your eating and drinking needs. If you buy a package on any of the above trips, lunch and park entries are included.

An option for the true reveler is the Tren Rumbero (the party train). This train makes a round trip from Cali to the club Hostal del Pipe and includes entry to the club and a DJ on board. It leaves for Cali at 2 a.m. from Estación del Ferrocarril. This train does not run on a daily basis — check well beforehand to be sure that it is operating that day. During rainy season the train is often cancelled since the tracks become covered by small landslides. To get there, catch a bus to the bus terminal, the train station is next door. Avenida Vásquez Cobo, 23N-47, Piso 2. Tel: 2-666-6899, E-mail: trenturistico@ert.com.co, URL: www.trenturisticocafeyazucar.com. Updated: Nov 26, 2007.

Cali Teatro

One of the few places in the city where you can get fresh air and a fine view of Cali is atop the hill in barrio San Antonio. Here you will find an 18th Century chapel and a park. The Cali Teatro, a block from the park, has seasonal performances that could be worth an evening out if you're Spanish is strong enough to understand the dialogue. Visit the Cali Teatro website for upcoming events. URL: www.caliteatro.com. Updated: May 13, 2008.

Reserva Natural Laguna de Sonso

Roughly 10 kilometers southwest of the municipality of Buga, the Reserva Natural Laguna de Sonso is a wetland reserve that will delight avid birdwatchers. The eastern margins of the Cauca River pour into this area, also known as the Laguna de Chircal. The area consists of 2,045 hectares, 90 percent of which are wetland. Recent studies have revealed that up to 162 species of birds make these wetlands their migratory resting point or home. Of these 162 species, 55 are aquatic birds and in mating season up to 15,000 members of the Greyish Piculet descend into the area. Other prevalent species in the area are the Blue-winged Teal and the Apical Flycatcher.

To get there, catch a bus from the Terminal de Transportes to Buga (every 15 minutes, journey time roughly 45 minutes). Then, from the terminal in Buga, catch a local bus that is heading southwest. The journey should take 30 minutes.

Zoológico de Cali

The best place in Colombia to see a wide variety of animal life resides in the western portion of Cali, in barrio Santa Teresita. The Zoológico de Cali is a surprisingly clean and well-organized spread, with every imaginable mammal (lions, tigers, pumas, jaguars and spectacled bears—oh my!), native birds, which include condors and parrots, and snakes from the Valle de Cauca.

Free transportation to and from the zoo is available in northern and southern city routes (see below). The zoo transportation is available at 11 a.m., noon, 1 p.m. From the zoo, it is available at 11:30 a.m., 12:30 p.m., 3:30 p.m., 4:30 p.m., 5:30 p.m.

NORTH ► La 14 de Calima - Sameco - Menga - Chipichape - Av. Vásquez Cobo - Av. Las Américas - CAM - Av. Del Río - Portada al Mar - Zoo.
SOUTH ► Cosmocentro - Calle 5 - La Tertulia - Zoo.
9 a.m.-6 p.m. Carrera 2 Oeste and Calle 14 in Barrio Santa Teresita. Tel: 2-892-7474, URL: www.zoologicodecali.com.co.

Fútbol

Catching a *fútbol* game in any city in Colombia is nothing short of a religious experience. The hordes come to their version of a cathedral to utter furious chants at the opposition, while heaping praise on their side. Cali has two teams that call the Estadio Pascual Guerrero home. America de Cali (red) and Deportivo Cali (green) have their tribes of supporters—for your safety do not get the two confused! Perhaps the most extreme fútbol experience you can have is to go to a local game between the two bitter city rivals. You would be advised to go with someone knowledgeable, since more than 40,000 fans show up to these games. It's best not to take valuables or large amounts of money. To get there, take any bus that runs down the Calle 5. Get off when you see the flags in front of the stadium. Updated: Nov 15, 2007.

Studying Spanish in Cali

When it comes to Spanish schools, Cali is not as developed as Bogotá, Medellín and Cartagena. However, the big city universities have established language learning centers and offer courses almost all year round.

Javeriana University

Javeriana University, a fairly new Jesuit school located in southern Cali, offers a special "Functional Spanish for Foreigners" language and culture program through their humanities and social science department. This program aims to immerse foreign students in practical, social and cultural interactions in class and through various activities and excursions around the city. Colombian culture is the focus of the course—you will attain more fluency with the Spanish language, and a better understanding of the country. Calle 18, 118-250, Avenida Cañasgordas. Tel: 2-321-8200. Updated: May 13, 2008.

Universidad Santiago de Cali

Specifically designed for foreigners, the Universidad Santiago de Cali offers a Spanish language course with a good deal of social interaction and cultural activity. Placing students in three levels (basic, intermediate and advanced) to focus on improving their verbal communication as well as developing written fluency. Cultural trips go out to the Valle de Cauca. Of course, there are also salsa dance outings and lively *rumba* excursions. 120 hours of lessons cost $690. Calle 5, Carrera 62, Campus Pampalinda. Tel: 2-518-3000, ext. 421, URL: http://virtual.usc.edu.co/espaextranjeros. Updated: May 13, 2008.

International Student Services Organization

For a shorter Spanish language program, you could opt for the one offered at ISSO, which provides online, small group and private lessons. You can start the online program anytime. Semi-private lessons begin every two weeks and include materials and 40 hours of lessons for just $250. Private lessons can be arranged by the hour for $14 or a 25-hour program costs $350. Homestays, furnished apartments or hotel accommodations can be arranged for an additional fee. Avenida Sexta C Norte, 23DN-86 - Office 301. Tel: 2-680-2001 / 2-660-1798, E-mail: isso@estudiosexterior.com. Updated: May 13, 2008.

Cali Tours

Chivas Tour

Cali is a great place to take a chiva tour—a tour of the city on an open-air party bus. By day, this company will show you around the city, indicating the important sights. A Spanish-speaking guide can provide you with historical information and general orientation. Then, at night, get your boogie on and ride around on the party chiva to the numerous salsa hotspots. $50 will get you a full-day chiva tour with a Spanish-speaking guide and evening transport along Avenida Sexta. The night chiva costs $10, but does not include nightclub cover charge. Calle 8, 10-70. Tel: 2-680-3535. Updated: May 13, 2008.

Christian Dojoseba

Christian, the owner of Kaffee Erde Hostal, is a very accommodating tour operator who is more than happy to take you on a jungle trip to San Cipriano or to closer locales, like Ecoparque Río Pance. Having lived in Cali for several years, he takes tourists on informative strolls around the city. He'll often stop to buy fresh fruit on the way and will take you back to his hostel and make you fresh juice, while telling you about the joys of living in Cali. Tel: 301-400-0914. Updated: Apr 27, 2008.

Max Viedmon

Frequently referred by travelers passing through Cali and beyond, Max is a great reference should you speak Spanish and want to experience the region like a local. If you would rather he pick you up on the other side of Colombia and show you around, he is happy to accommodate and personalize a countrywide tour. He takes security and safety very seriously and guarantees discounted rates and a wealth of information. His affiliate, Jenny, provides horseback riding tours on fast-trotting Colombian horses (called *caballo de paso Colombiano*). She even accommodates for physical rehabilitation programs and camping trips by horse. These services cost approximately $40 per day. E-mail: maxviedman@hotmail.com, URL: www.maxviedman.blogspot.com. Updated: May 13, 2008.

Neighborhoods of Cali

The three barrios of San Fernando, El Peñón and La Granada were originally residential areas that have slowly morphed into high-rent, trendy zones. In San Fernando, you will find the Parque del Perro—a statue of a dog in the middle—lined with small bars and more than a dozen restaurants. This park appeals to a young crowd and during the weekends it is bursting with people.

El Peñón, on the other hand, is behind the Intercontinental Hotel and close to the Tertulia Museum of Modern Art. Its bars, shops and restaurants appeal to a more mature clientele, who are intent on eating well and being seen in the right place.

La Granada is the largest of the three areas and stretches for 10 city blocks. Dining in this barrio is expensive and exclusive, though budget places also exist. The beautiful people frequent the bars prior to heading out for a night of dancing.

San Antonio is Cali's bohemian center. Across the road and up the hill from the museums, its streets are lined with small and independent theaters, interesting cafés and artists workshops. At night, caleños come to the park beneath the San Antonio Chapel (constructed in 1747). Up here, they enjoy the breeze and occasional live music while watching the sparkling lights of Cali down below—this makes a great evening out.

Cali Lodging

Cali's reputation as a tourist destination is growing and every type of accommodation possibility now exists. In San Antonio, Miraflores and near Granada there are hostels and guesthouses for traveler's on a budget, and the most exclusive hotels are in El Peñón. Toward the center of town there are out-of-style 1970s accommodations, which add mid-range options to the area. A good number of guesthouses and B&Bs list themselves as hostels, but are nothing of the sort, so be aware. Updated: Feb 13, 2008.

Budget

Hotel Posada Colonial

(ROOM: $5-20) Quickly becoming a hotspot for budget travelers, Hotel Posada Colonial is a curious establishment that has 22 rooms, each with a different quality and price. One room is like a closet with a tiny twin bed and tiny bathroom squeezed inside, for $6 a night (not recommended). Others are more spacious and have large, private bathrooms. There is little natural light, so the place feels a bit more like a prison than a hotel. However, it is conveniently located, since it is half a block from Avenida Sexta. Plus, there is a decent restaurant next door that is nice to use as your lounge. Calle 14, 6–42. Tel: 2-661-2925. Updated: Apr 28, 2008.

Calidad House

(BED: $7-8.50) This place offers eight simple, comfortable rooms, including three four-bed dormitories with shared bathroom. Private rooms sleep between one and three people. Hot water is hard to come by, but the hostel's location at the heart of the exclusive La Granada is unrivaled. Calle 17 Norte, 9AN-39, La Granada. Tel: 2-661- 2338, E-mail: calidadhouse@yahoo.com, URL: www.calidadhouse.com. Updated: Nov 12, 2007.

Iguana

(BED: $8-10) This self-proclaimed destination of choice for all backpackers who pass through Cali is a great place to settle down to spend a few days. Dorm rooms and communal areas are the name of the game here. This is a value option for a place located in the one of the choicest neighborhoods of Cali and near exclusive restaurants and bars. Calle 21N, 9N - 22. Tel: 2-661-3522, E-mail: iguana_cali@yahoo.com, URL: www.iguana.com.co. Updated: Nov 12, 2007.

Kaffee Erde

(BED: $8-11) One of the newer additions to the scene, Kaffee Erde has quickly become a good alternative to the two other backpacker hostels in Cali. This converted house in barrio Centenario makes guests feel right at home and Christian, the owner of the place, makes you to feel like part of his family. Although the house itself is a little lackluster and in need of some updating, there is a very redeeming living room and outdoor lounge area. Also, dorm rooms have only three beds, which gives the dorms an airy feel. There are separate male and female bathrooms. You are more than welcome to use the kitchen or drink all the free premium Colombian coffee you like. Christian's sister provides free salsa lessons in the evenings, and on the weekends Christian will escort his guests to the best salsa clubs in town or serve as your guide on a jungle trip. Av. 4 Norte, 4n79. Tel: 2-661-5475. Updated: Apr 27, 2008.

Hotel Sartor

(ROOM: $10-25) Hotel Sartor offers pretty decent accommodations close to the Avenida Sexta nightlife and has been on the backpacker trail for some time now. This is a good option for travelers seeking a convenient location and a good value. All rooms have private baths and surround a little courtyard. There is a computer with internet available for $1 per hour, and an Italian restaurant attached to the lobby. Avenida 8 Norte, 20-50. Tel: 2-668-7443 / 6482, Fax: 2-661-5037. Updated: Apr 29, 2008.

MID-RANGE

Hotel Camino Real 1A

(ROOM: $15-20) This is another option in the hustle and bustle of downtown, which is cheaper than the Hotel Imperial. There are 50 rooms, so reservations aren't an issue. Each room comes with cable TV, private bathroom and fan. Calle 9, 3-54. Tel: 2- 680-2626, Fax: 2- 684-1175, E-mail: caminoreal1a@hotmail.com, URL: www.hotelcaminoreal1a.com. Updated: Nov 12, 2007.

Casa Aguacanela !

(ROOM: $15-30) Run by the delightful Esperanza, the Casa Aguacanela is a true home away from home in the safe residential area of Miraflores. The guesthouse has three rooms. Two rooms are dormitories with three beds each and the last room is a private double. Limited sleeping capacity makes this a calm retreat in the mayhem of Cali. There is a communal kitchen and a pleasant balcony with views over the city. Carrera 24A, 2A-55, Miraflores. Tel: 2-556-8382, E-mail: etrujil@yahoo.com, URL: www.casaaguacanelacali.com. Updated: Nov 09, 2007.

Hotel del Puente

(ROOM: $20-30) Smack dab on the bridge bordering barrio San Antonio and El Centro, this four-story hotel has an unfortunate view of one of the busiest byways in the city. The rooms here are basic—just a bed, window and private bath. The advantage to staying here is the location just steps away from all of the major sites in Cali. As the hotel is technically in the Barrio San Antonio, good cafés and restaurants are also just around the corner. Calle 5, 4-36. Tel: 2-893-8484. Updated: Apr 27, 2008.

Hotel Nevada

(ROOM $20-50) Founded in 1991, Hotel Nevada was built for tourists seeking refuge in the city's busy, yet safe and heavily patrolled Zona Rosa. Just one block from the nightlife on Avenida Sexta and within 15 minutes from El Centro, Nevada has 21 comfortable guest rooms with luxuries like a sauna, steam room and Jacuzzi. All rooms are tastefully decorated and have a private bath with hot water and cable TV. Avenida 8 Norte, 14N-19. Tel: 2-667-9693, 2-668-5330, 2-661-2143. Fax: 2-660-3689, E-mail: hotel_nevada@etb.net.co. Updated: May 13, 2008.

Hostal Santa Rita

(ROOM: $25-50) A delightful place for families or for those just passing through, in northern Cali the Santa Rita is one block from the river of the same name in a colonial style house that dates back to 1945. The seven rooms are immaculate and have private bathrooms, hot water, A/C, internet and cable TV. Guests are treated to a hearty breakfast. Avenida 3 Oeste, 7-131. Tel: 2-892-6143, Fax: 572 892 0021, E-mail: info@hostalsantarita.com, URL: www.hostalsantarita.com. Updated: Dec 19, 2007.

Centenario Suites

(BED: $25-70) These offer apartment-style accommodations for executives and tourists visiting Cali. Guests enjoy the privacy and comfort of ample suites on a quiet side street in the peaceful barrio Centenario. There are eight tastefully decorated suites that sleep up to six people, making it an ideal place for a family to stay. There are significant discounts if you plan to stay longer than 10 or 20 days. In addition, a 24-hour, secure, covered parking garage is available for guest use. Calle 4N-41, barrio Centenario. Tel: 2-660-3459, Cell: 315- 415-6766. Updated: Apr 29, 2008.

Hostal San Fernando

(ROOM: $29-39) Just up the hill and within a block of the Parque del Perro is the Hostal San Fernando. The 12 rooms are all equipped with A/C and private bathrooms, but are a little dark. It is a decent place, but perhaps not ideal for those traveling with a partner—all the room windows open onto the central courtyard and it's easy to hear conversations in other quarters. Calle 3, 27-87. Tel: 2-556-2226, E-mail: calihotel@hotmail.com, URL: www.calihotel.com. Updated: Nov 15, 2007.

Posada de San Antonio

(ROOM: $30-40) Located in a beautifully restored colonial mansion in the historic barrio of San Antonio, this Posada has been open for years. Its familiar style and relaxed ambience have made it a favorite with those wishing to stay in an establishment a step up from backpacker digs. The Posada has 14 rooms and room for 45 people. The helpful staff will move or add beds to accommodate groups. Each room has its own bathroom with hot water, cable TV and a fan. Breakfast is included. Carrera 5, 3-37. Tel: 2-893- 7413, Fax: 2-893-7413, E-mail: posada.sanantonio@hotmail.com, URL: www.posadadesanantonio.com. Updated: Nov 12, 2007.

Hotel Imperial

(ROOM: $32-45) There are plenty of reasons not to stay downtown, but if you must, you may find yourself checking into one of a number of hotels that now seem dated and claustrophobic. The Hotel Imperial may have been stylish in the '70s, but has aged badly. For your money, you'll get a room in a 50-room high-rise close to the city's museums. Breakfast is included, as are all taxes. Calle 9, 3-93. Tel: 2-889-9571, E-mail: hotelimperialdecali@hotmail.com, URL: www.hotelimperialdecali.com. Updated: Dec 19, 2007.

Sabor I Arte

(ROOM: $42-62) Accommodations in a separate building and rooms named after fruits makes the Sabor I Arte into an artist's concept of how accommodations should be run. The owner prepares meals while you sit and relax in his tranquil colonial house in the Barrio San Antonio. There's no sign outside, so use the Posada de San Antonio as your reference point and the Sabor I Arte will be next door. Carrera 5, 3-23, Barrio San Antonio. Tel: 2-893-7064, Fax: 2-893-7064. E-mail: soniaserna7@yahoo.com, URL: www.saboriarte.com. Updated: Dec 19, 2007.

Hotel Granada Real

(ROOM: $57-86) Definitely a place for patrons in town for a conference, the Hotel Granada Real is alone on Avenida 8 Norte, but near the amenities and nightlife attractions of the Avenida Sexta and Barrio Granada. The 61 rooms are all equipped with A/C, cable TV, mini-bar and refrigerator. You could be anywhere in the world while staying here. The hotel conveniently offers private parking and front-desk safe boxes. Avenida 8 Norte, 15AN-31. Tel: 2-661-4920, Fax: 2-668-0166, E-mail: hotelgranadareal@telesat.com.co, URL: www.hotelgranadareal.com. Updated: Dec 19, 2007.

HIGH-END

Hotel Don Jaime

(ROOM: $65-75) Hotel Don Jaime seems to appeal to business types and it bares all the hallmarks of an establishment of this ilk. The recently renovated hotel has 29 rooms with A/C, WiFi, cable TV, mini-bar, refrigerator and clock radio. There is a restaurant open to the public on the ground floor and a terrace bar on the top floor. Conference rooms are also available. Avenida Sexta Norte, 15N-25. Tel: 2-667-2828, Fax: 2- 668-7098, E-mail: reservas@hoteldonjaime.com, URL: www.hoteldonjaime.com. Updated: Nov 12, 2007.

Cali Plaza Hotel

(ROOM: $80-200) Cali Plaza Hotel is a very popular and centrally-located meeting place, which just so happens to have one and three bedroom apartments available for its guests. The café is one of the only places in town where you can get free Wi-Fi reception, which makes this a perfect place to socialize with locals and foreigners. It is right off Avenida Sexta, so guests can easily stumble to their Cali home after visiting their nightclub of choice. Calle 15 Norte, 6N-37. Tel: 2-668-2611, Cell: 312 -287-9840, E-mail: Claude@Ledbetter.com, URL: www.CaliPlaza.com. Updated: May 13, 2008.

Design Hotel Austral

(ROOM: $95-105) Aimed at those interested in boutique accommodations, this hotel creates that environment with 19 rooms. Open since October 2007, the whole place has a sparkling new feel with simplistic designs and a spartan décor. Rooms have all the conveniences one would expect. Although with a fine variety of quality restaurants and bars in the barrio El Peñón, you will not be spending too much time indoors. Calle 1 Oeste, 2-18. Tel: 2-892-2828, Fax: 2-893- 3697, E-mail: reservas@hotel-austral.com, URL: www.hotel-austral.com. Updated: Nov 12, 2007.

Hotel Dann and Dann Carlton

(ROOM: $100-200) Two towers stretching across Calle 2 connected by a third-floor footbridge make up the very large and luxurious Hotel Dann and Dann Carlton. The Carlton tower is the newer, noticeably more modern and shiny, with a gorgeous, covered third-floor pool and bar. Together, the brick towers provide nearly 200 guest quarters complete with mini bar, internet, and flat-screen TV. If that's not enough to tickle your fancy, there is also a fully-stocked convention center, a Tony Roma's restaurant and free guest parking garage. Avenida Colombia, 1-40. Tel: 2-886-2000, E-mail: reservas@hotelesdanncali.com.co, URL: www.hotelesdann.com. Updated: Apr 29, 2008.

Hotel Intercontinental

(ROOM: $100-200) An enormous luxury hotel conveniently located by the river and very close to El Centro, Intercontinental is part of the Hotel Estelar chain spread throughout Colombia. This one features almost 300 spacious guest rooms and suites. Despite its immense size, this hotel offers surprisingly personalized service and impeccable amenities, such as three restaurants, a spa, travel agency, an attractive courtyard and high-class shops. Avenida Colombia, 2-72. Tel: 2-882-3225, E-mail: cali@interconti.com. Updated: Apr 29, 2008.

CALI RESTAURANTS

Cali offers enough quality places to eat to rival most major cities. For a western-style dining, head to the upper-class neighborhoods of El Peñón and La Granada. Otherwise, a little bit of hunting around will uncover decent budget locales. They spring up and close down routinely. Restaurants offering set meals and reasonable prices are usually within a few of blocks of the ultra-posh and expensive places.

BUDGET

El Canelazo

(LUNCH: $2.25) About a block from the Parque del Perro is a cheap, family-run establishment that specializes in home-cooked set meals. Here at El Canelazo the menu changes daily. You can fill up on a soup as a starter and a healthy main course for $2.25. Expect grilled chicken breast or pork chop, preceded by plantain soup. Calle 34, 35-38. Updated: Nov 15, 2007.

Romani

(LUNCH: $2.75) Romani is another bargain restaurant along the Parque del Perro. This Colombian-Italian fusion place offers home-cooked set meals at lunchtime. It is popular with office workers and students. For your hard-earned $2.75, you get a choice of soup or spaghetti as a starter, one of two types of meat accompanied by rice, salad, potatoes and fresh juice to wash it down. Calle 3A, 34-57. Tel: 2-556-1341. Updated: Nov 15, 2007.

Nutricentro

(LUNCH: $3.50) This gourmet café is perfectly situated down the street from Teatro Municipal in El Centro. You can grab a healthy and hearty vegetarian buffet for $3.50. Get here early enough—or before they run out—to order the *special* plate for $1 more. A meal comes with juice or soy milk, fruit, salad, vegetarian side dishes and a small dessert. There are two other branches north and south of the city that offer more specialized health treatments, like therapeutic massage, reflexology, shiatsu, relaxation gym, yoga and Arabic dance lessons. North: Calle 23A Norte, 3-66. Tel: 2-660-3794. South: Carrera 39, 5A-69. Tel: 2-556-0875. Updated: Apr 29, 2008.

Arte Nativa

This cute tea house in barrio Santa Rita prepares exclusive tea cocktails and delicious Mediterranean plates at a very reasonable price (tea $2; food $5). Tea comes in great flavors like vanilla, mango, mint and other creative herbal, black and green combinations. Wooden and ceramic artisan crafts, as well as colorful lamps and household goods, are for sale in the front room. There is pleasant outdoor seating, where on Thursdays between 7 p.m. and 11 p.m. patrons can enjoy live jazz. Avenida 3 Oeste, 7-75 across from the Carulla Supermarket in La Portada al Mar. Tel: 2-892-6068, E-mail: artenativa1@hotmail.com. Updated: Apr 28, 2008.

Arte y Cocina

(LUNCH: $4) Around back of the Centro Cultural de Cali is an ideal place to escape the heat of downtown after picking up tourist information. Restaurant Arte y Cocina, at the back of the courtyard, provides much needed tranquility and respite from the heat and traffic of the centro. You can get 10 empanadas for $4 or a buffet lunch for the same price. On Thursdays there are Tango lessons from 6:30-8:30 p.m. and on Tuesdays Bolero/Paso Doble. Carrera 5 and Calle 7, Centro. Tel: 2-896-1992. Updated: Nov 13, 2007.

Café Mulatto

Up the hill, a few blocks the from the Tertulia Museum of Modern Art is the Café Mulato. This place clearly takes pride in the quality of its ground beans and its tranquil ambience. Light music wafts from speakers as patrons sip on strong organic roasts, making this place a chilled-out retreat. Wraps, salads and other options are also available. Calle 5 Oeste, 3-05, El Peñón. Tel: 2-893-2963. Updated: Nov 13, 2007.

Cathay

Like many Chinese restaurants, the menu at Cathay is not merely dishes from the Orient, but fried local platters and French fries as well. Nonetheless, if you are in the neighborhood and hankering for some quality dim sum or sweet and sour pork, then this is the place to come. Avenida 8 Norte, 16-70. Tel: 2-660-1654. Updated: Nov 13, 2007.

La Joroba de Camello

This joint above a jazz club is a place only a local would know. The Joroba de Camello (camel's hump) is dark, moody with loud music, cold beers and great slices of pizza. You can pile up the toppings on your slice for $2. The cocktails are killer, and make a great appeal to the younger crowd. Avenida 4A Oeste, 1-65. Updated: Dec 19, 2007.

Macondo

Macondo caters to the bohemian crowd that frequents the barrio of San Antonio. At this café, patrons arrive fresh from theater workshops and art studios to enjoy booze fortified coffees, sandwiches and cocktails. A veggie sandwich will set you back around $3 and is full of mushrooms, cheese and other goodies. Carrera 6, 3-03. Updated: Nov 13, 2007.

Palo Alto

Less chic than the surrounding places in La Granada, yet far from a dump, Palo Alto is where you come if you need a good coffee, a wrap or juice after browsing boutiques in the surrounding area. In addition to the above, Palo Alto serves pita sandwiches and salads and has a great terrace. Avenida 9 Norte, 14N-73. Tel: 2-653-5390, E-mail: cafepaloalto@gmail.com. Updated: Nov 13, 2007.

Al Lado del Camino

Cheap and cheerful, Al Lado del Camino (on the side of the road) is frequented by droves of medical students from the nearby hospital. The restaurant has a menu that changes daily but that sticks to one rule—the set menu will have three choices for starters and three choices for a main course. Vegetable soups and grilled chicken breast are the norm, but the high turnover of patrons and bustle make this an entertaining place for lunch. Calle 5, 4B-18. Updated: Nov 15, 2007.

Vinos del Río

Across from Los Gatos Park and the river is a nice wine store that offers free wine tasting with snacks. The wine is primarily from Argentina, but there are also some selections from Chile and Spain. Tasting is professional and obligation-free, making it a nice place to rest your feet, sip on award-winning wine and have a snack. Monday-Saturday 10 a.m.-8 p.m. Avenida 4 Oeste, 3-88. Tel: 2-892-0343, Cell: 315-570-7733, Fax: 2-893-1874, E-mail: megatrading@cable.net.com, URL: www.vinosdelrio.com. Updated: Apr 27, 2008.

MID-RANGE

Café Tostaky

In addition to a French-Colombian fusion café, travelers can rent rooms, too. It is no surprise that a French and Colombian couple owns this café/hostel in the colonial district of San Antonio. Tostaky is a place where you relax and taste a little of the two cultures. For more information, feel free to contact the couple. Prices range from $18 to $30. Carrera 10, 1-76. Tel: 2-893-0651, E-mail: cafetostaky@gmail.com, URL: www.cafetostaky.blogspot.com. Updated: May 26, 2008.

Greco

Passing by in their cars, most caleños wouldn't have any idea that the Greco even exists. Inside there are beds, mattresses, cushions and sofas strewn haphazardly; areas of wall have been artfully stripped to the brick and curiosities line the lintels and ceilings throughout the two floors. This is a place for the cool kids. Beers are sold by the pitcher and the cocktails are recommended as well. Outside, if you don't mind the noise from the road, there are also hammocks strung between palms for relaxing. 2-116 El Peñón, behind the Torre Estelar. Updated: Nov 13, 2007.

La Antorcha

How La Antorcha can ever hope to fill every seat is a mystery. This vast restaurant is another in the zone that specializes in *parrillas* but live music on Friday and Saturday nights definitely sets it apart from the rest. Patrons should try the *portobello antorcha*, a specialty of the house. Avenida 9A Norte, 9-69. Tel: 2-653-6131. Updated: Dec 19, 2007.

Patio Valluca

This pleasantly decorated café and restaurant is one of the classier places to try authentic caleño cuisine. More of a dinner spot than for lunch, Valluca has a variety of special regional dishes. A popular dish here is the *arroz atoyado*, a delicious casserole that resembles a risotto with chicken, sausage and potatoes. All of the main plates are filling and reasonably priced. Everyday, 7:30 a.m.-11 p.m. Calle 2 Oeste, 1-07. Tel: 2- 893-3322. Updated: May 13, 2008.

Piccolo Pomodoro

A very cozy Italian eatery, Piccolo Pomodoro aims to please, and does so effortlessly. All of the food here, including several different types of ravioli (even asparagus), is homemade and delicious. There are some yummy appetizers like carpaccio salad. You can cap it all off with a big slice of tiramisu. Monday-Saturday, 12-3 p.m. and 7:00 p.m.-1:00 a.m.

Carrera 2a Oeste, 2-34, El Peñón. Tel: 2-893-0780. Updated:Apr 28, 2008.

Restaurante Pizca Arte y Sabor

(ENTREES: $10-18) Up the hill of the ever-hip El Peñón is a trendy Mediterranean lunch and dinner spot. The place is rather artsy, modern paintings on the walls, nice décor, stylish furniture and warm-colored walls. The food here isn't bad, though you'll need deep pockets. Appetizers are between $6-8 and mains like seafood and pasta, are between $10-18. Monday-Friday, 11:30 a.m.-2 p.m., Tuesday-Saturday, 6 p.m. until around 11 p.m. Carrera 3a Oeste, 2-05, El Peñón. Tel: 2-893-9659. Updated: May 13, 2008.

San Borondón

Claiming to offer the flavor of two worlds, San Borondón caters to caleños who cannot decide whether they want sushi or Argentine parrillada. The terrace, with its cooling breeze, is the place to settle down to a *punta de anca* steak or a platter of sushi options. Calle 10 Norte, 8N-43. Tel: 2-668-3326, E-mail: restaurante@sanborondonrestaurante.com, URL: www.sanborondonrestaurante.com. Updated: Nov 12, 2007.

Matiz

The darkened lighting and wine racks stocked with fine European and South American bottles are enough to draw the tannon enthusiast through the doors of Matiz. For the veggie connoisseur, on Mondays this decidedly Euro-dining establishment, in the heart of Cali's Granada district, specializes in salads. Fridays are set aside for *ceviche* and Saturdays for *paella*. Calle 10 Norte, 9N-22. Tel: 2-661- 5198, E-mail: matizvinoysabor@gmail.com, URL: www.matizvinoysabor.com. Updated: Nov 12, 2007.

HIGH-END

Cali Viejo

Find the city's premier Valle del Cauca dining spot in a sprawling *finca* (1870), next to the Cali River and near the zoo. A musical trio wanders among the tables playing traditional Colombian Andean music. The wait staff is dressed in 19th-Century garb. You may feel that you have stepped back in time, except for the modern-day steep prices. The food is typical of the region, the helpings are enormous and the location is incredible. Try the traditional *champus* (an Indian beverage prepared with corn meal, corn, pineapple, *lulo*, cinnamon and *panela*) and follow it with a hearty grill accompanied by a *marranita* (a little ball prepared with Pork rind and plantain). Casona Vieja Bosque Municipal, 200 meters beyond the zoo. Tel: 2-893-4927, Fax: 2-893-4927, E-mail: comercialcaliviejo@telesat.com.co, URL: www.restaurantecaliviejo.com. Updated: Dec 19, 2007.

Granada Faró

Customers frequent Granada Faró for the sophisticated ambiance. The restaurant features three distinct dining rooms: a principal salon with windows facing the street, a private salon specially designed for private engagements and an airy salon for socializing with friends. The fresh food is primarily of the Mediterranean. There is another branch of the same restaurant in Jardín Plaza, in the southern part of the city. Avenida 9 Norte, 15AN-02. Tel: 2-667-4625 / 2-661-782. C.C. Jardín Plaza, Torre del Campanario. Tel: 2-324-7261 / 7262. Updated: Apr 29, 2008.

Pacífico

Hidden from the street by potted palms, the Pacífico is a decidedly elegant establishment that specializes in seafood. While out for an ideal romantic dinner, try the *cazuela del Pacífico,* which includes shrimp, squid, clams, crab, paingua clam and coconut. Otherwise go for the *guiso de piangua*, a local dish from the southwest made with clams harvested from the roots of mangroves. Avenida 9N, 12-18. Tel: 2- 653-3753, URL: www.pacificorestaurante.com. Updated: Nov 12, 2007.

Petite France

This warm, cozy restaurant in El Peñón serves what is arguably the best French cuisine in Cali. Including crab bisque, quiche and fondue, the dishes at Petite France bring a little bit of Paris to Cali. The food here is not cheap, but it is tasty and authentic. Behind the Colegio Sagrada Familia, Carrera 3A Oeste, 3-53. Tel: 2-893-3079, E-mail: petitefracecali@yahoo.com. Updated: My 13, 2008.

CALI NIGHTLIFE

Known for salsa dancing, Cali becomes alive at night. Ask around for the most fashionable dancing spots, though you are sure to bump into salsa wherever you go. If you crave a more relaxed atmosphere—or need a night off from dancing—trendy lounges are springing up in La Granada and Parque del Perro. Or, check out the eclectic bars in the barrio San Antonio. Updated: Feb 13, 2008.

Tin Tin Deo

Routinely described as one of the best places to go for salsa music and dancing in Cali, come here to watch in awe as the beautiful people strut their stuff. Calle 5, 38 – 71. Tel: 2-514-1537. Updated: Dec 19, 2007.

El Habanero

Spicy, hot and tingling are all sensations likely felt after being worn out by a night of salsa at El Habanero, just like the name warns. Expect a variety of music here, especially Cuban. Calle 23A, 7A – 01. Tel: 2-557-4390. Updated: Dec 19, 2007.

Soneros

Often equipped with a live salsa band, Soneros has a different vibe from other salsa haunts. It is hard to put your finger on it —the dancing is first rate, the ambience is excellent and any night spent here will be one to remember. Av. 6A Norte, 12A - 119. Tel: 2-660-4074. Updated: Dec 19, 2007.

La Matraca

La Matraca is a salsoteca with a longstanding tradition of playing *salsa dura,* but also Cuban *son* and *bolero*. On Sundays the place changes somewhat and offers revelers a taste of tango. Carrera 11, 22 - 80 Barrio Obrero. Tel: 2-885-7113. Updated: Nov 15, 2007.

Kukaramakara

(COVER: $6) Always a good bet during the weekends, Kukaramakara pumps salsa, rock and pop music from open to close. Don't be surprised late in the evening when locals start to dance on chairs and tables in this rowdy place. Occasionally, the house band will play live Latin pop songs. Drinks are by the bottle. Servers are always circulating around, keeping a drink in your hand as you dance the night away. $6 cover, aguardiente $35 (bottle) and rum $45 (bottle). Thursday-Saturday, 6p.m.-2 a.m. Calle 28N, 2Bis-97. Tel: 2-653-5389. Updated: May 13, 2008.

Faro 2004

Faro 2004 occupies a prime location on a corner in the trendy Granada barrio. Live music on weekend evenings in the expansive front courtyard makes this an ideal place for a cocktail from their extensive list. More a bar than a restaurant, the food is nonetheless sizeable and flavorsome. This is not a place for a quiet meal, but somewhere to begin the evening's festivities. Avenida 9 Norte, 12-76. Tel: 2-409-6518. Updated: Nov 12, 2007.

Around Cali

Yotoco

Some 18 kilometers from Buga, the natural reserve of Yotoco measures 560 hectares and its altitude oscillates between 1,200 meters and 1,600 meters above sea level.

The town of Yotoco itself was founded in 1622 by Captain Diego Rengifo Salazar, who took full advantage of the Yotoco settlement already in place. What you find today is a small town with some interesting colonial buildings, but a more fascinating range of flora and fauna. All the flora that covers the eastern edge of the Andean cordillera is represented. Fishing opportunities, as well as bird watching, abounds. Aside from fishing in the Escondite and Picapiedra rivers, go for a swim in the pools of the Los Chorros river. Only 56 kilometers from Cali, this makes for a great day trip. Updated: Nov 15, 2007.

Señor de Los Milagros

On Sundays and public holidays, masses of devout Colombian Catholics make their way from Cali and neighboring towns to the town of Guadalajara de Buga to pay their respects and ask favors of the Señor de los Milagros in the Basílica in Buga. Buga, also known as the *Cuidad Señora,* has a history that dates back as far as 1555, which makes it one of the oldest Spanish settlements in the country. Although completed in the 18th Century and later destroyed by an earthquake, the Ermita was bestowed with the title of Basílica in August 1937 by Pope Pius XI. This place has now become a central point for Catholics in Colombia and pilgrimages. An estimated two million people a year come to the Basílica.

From Cali, through several companies you can catch a van from the main bus terminal for around $2-$3 that takes 40 minutes. It

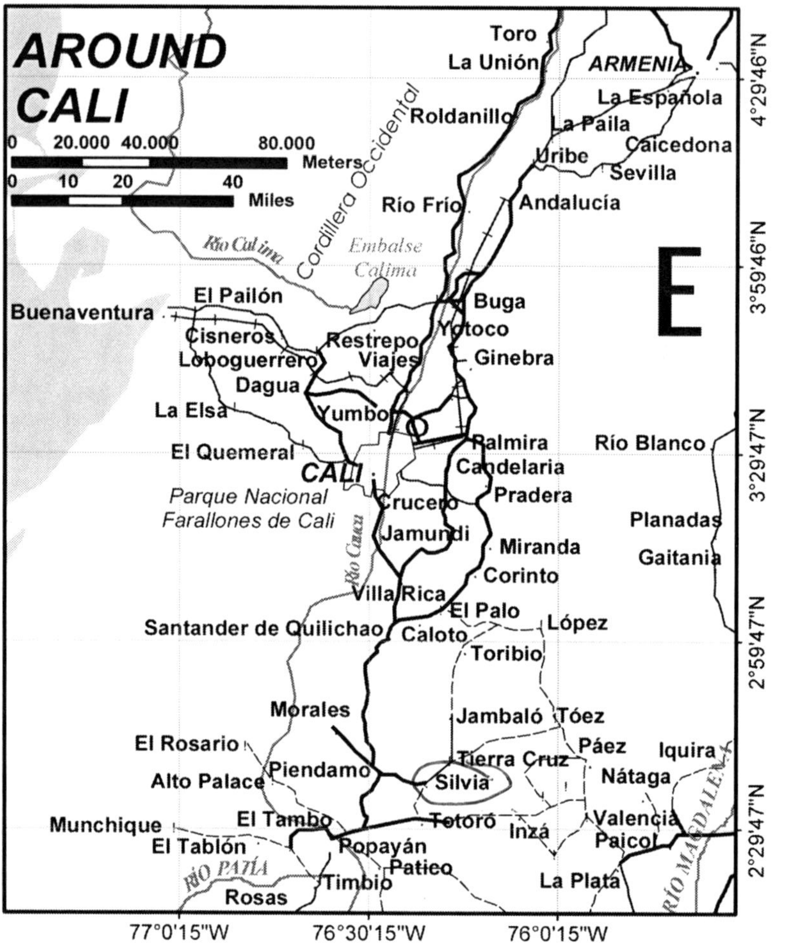

will drop you at the terminal in Buga. From there, it is a straight 10-minute walk to the town center and the Basílica. Carrera 14, 3-62. Tel: 2-228-2823, URL: www.milagros-debuga.com. Updated: Nov 15, 2007.

San Cipriano

San Cipriano is fast becoming a must-do activity for all those adventure-seeking travelers. What you find here is this: at Córdoba (two hours from Cali on the road to Buenaventura) there are train tracks where trains no longer run. The town of San Cipriano has effectively been cut off from civilization. Except, the locals have devised an ingenious way of attracting visitors. They have created their own carts that travel the train tracks. You can choose to ride either a hand-pumped cart or one attached to a motorcycle. Hop aboard and take in the stunning, lush scenery on the way to San Cipriano.

When you finally arrive to San Cipriano, you'll find a very small town with rope bridges, a few streets and a beautiful river. The river has some rapids that make it fun to hire inner tubes and spend an afternoon drifting down the river.

To get there, catch a bus from Cali going to Buenaventura and ask to be dropped off at Córdoba (two hours). From Córdoba, wander down the hill, avoiding the unnecessary touts, and pick out your cart of choice. Fifteen minutes later you are in San Cipriano. Updated: Nov 15, 2007.

Parque de los Farallones

The Parque de los Farallones is a sight to behold. Only 20 minutes from Cali's city limits, it is bordered by the slopes of the Pacific coast, the eastern cordillera of the Andes and the Cauca River. Created in 1968, its ecosystems include the Andes, the Chocó and everything in between, which means that it ranges from 1,600 meters above sea level to over 4,000 meters. Spanning 150,000 hectares, the park includes steep mountain ranges, cloud forests, numerous water sources and rainforests, as well as lowland jungle. Due to the variety of altitudes, precipitation and temperatures found within the park, the environment hosts around 700 species of birds, 200 species of snakes, peccary, deer, pumas and monkeys. There are visitor centers and campsites, but permission to enter the park must be sought prior to arrival. To get there, take the road to Piedras Blancas and Pichinde 28 kilometers from Cali. Tel: 2-664-9334, URL: http://www.cali.gov.co/publico2/ecocali.htm. Updated: Nov 15, 2007.

Zona Cafetera

The smell of tangy oranges, the taste of coffee and the sound of bird songs—all of this and more can be found in the impressive green lands of the Zona Cafetera, a region made up of the provincial departments of Caldas, Risaralda and Quindío. This part of Colombia is rich in rolling landscapes, valleys filled with bamboo and mountain peaks that tickle the sky. The coffee-growing region is a throbbing heart, pumping with natural life, tranquility and adventure.

Colombia's coffee zone only has two million inhabitants. Its major cities, Manizales (p.140), Pereira (p.137) and Armenia (p.130), are all less than 200 years old, illustrating how this part of the country is richer in rural cultivation and natural beauty than urban growth and prosperity. Coffee is just one of many reasons why this region has recently gained popularity. Other draws are its large natural parks, like Los Nevados and Valle de Cocora, and the thermal springs in Santa Rosa de Cabal. The inhabitants here undoubtedly value tradition and a slower-paced rural lifestyle. Still, with modern citites close by, the traveler who hungers for peace and quiet but still wants to be near the action can be satisfied.

History

Two thousand years before the Spanish conquest, the Cauca Medio region (or Zona Cafetera) was populated by agricultural workers, gold and salt miners, ceramic artists and farmers. Gold and ceramic art were highly valued in these early societies, and the abundance of gold and clay spurred a great proliferation of art for centuries. Metal works were created with unique methods combining gold and copper, and ceramics depict simple yet beautiful zoomorphic and anthropomorphic figures.

Until 1540, there were so many different indigenous customs, traditions and languages here that European settlers classified the cultures into provinces: Caramanta, Anserma, Arma, Picara, Carrapa, Quimbaya, Quindío and others. Among all of these groups, the most impressive gold and masterful art came from the Quimbaya.

As the nation's green region, Zona Cafetera has a perfect microclimate for plant life, with active agricultural trade and development of coffee, berries, potatoes, and many other fruits and vegetables that grow here almost effortlessly. These industries developed as populations in the area flourished.

In the late 1500s, the indigenous and native people in metropolitan centers like Manizales and Pereira moved to a quiet, more comfortable mountain village. This is why there are so many lovely colonial *pueblos* and buildings in this region. Rural farm life continues to hold value for the people here, and traditional customs are still practiced in the more remote parts of Risaralda and Quindío.

When to Go

The rich, fertile land of the Zona Cafetera is 1,000 meters above sea level. Therefore, the climate in this region is almost always cool or cold, especially in the mountains. The rainy seasons (March-May, September-November) can be downright depressing, sometimes with pounding rain all day. The drier seasons are quite temperate and tend toward warmer temperatures.

The *feria* in Manizales is one of the largest festivals in Colombia and always draws quite a crowd of locals and tourists alike. Salento's population seems to double every weekend, as food tents and artisan stalls pop up on the main square. In January, Salento also has a very popular, raucous celebration in remembrance of the town's founding. Updated: May 27, 2008.

Safety in Zona Cafetera

The Zona Cafetera is a very laid-back part of Colombia. Travelers will feel particularly safe and secure in the smaller towns. The larger cities are generally safe, even at night. However, the usual precautions are advised.

Recent reports tell of adolescent students in Pereira carrying guns to class, so there is still a sense of danger in urban areas. Pijao, a town near Armenia, is also known by locals as a base for the FARC.

Always ask tourist information offices about areas to avoid, or ask your hotel which are the city's more dangerous neighborhoods. These locations change fairly frequently, as both rural and urban areas in this region are experiencing growth. Updated: May 27, 2008.

Things to See and Do

The Zona Cafetera is a place to indulge the senses—from hot thermal springs to the cold Cocora Valley; sweet berries to bitterly rich coffee. Manizales, Pereira and Armenia are the capitals of the departments that make up the Zona Cafetera, and each provide a different take on the many riches Colombia has to offer.

In Manizales, a treacherous trip to the top of La Basílica is not to be missed. Near Pereira, travelers should set aside a full day in the Parque del Café or spend a few hours basking in the hot thermal springs of Santa Rosa. The Museo del Oro Quimbaya in Armenia remains one of Colombia's best preserved and organized gold collections. Also of note is Salento, a small town tucked neatly in the skirt of a mountain, where farm-grown trout is deliciously prepared on a large *patacón* (fried plantain).

Zona Cafetera Tours

This region is the ideal place to enjoy the gorgeous Colombian countryside, and to do so fully you will certainly need a guide. In fact, Los Nevados Park requires visitors be accompanied by a park ranger or guide. This is not only for your safety but also to help navigate you through the high, winding park roads.

Cocora Valley near Salento is another place where you might benefit from a tour guide. While trails into the valley are well-marked, a good guide can help you get the most out of your experience.

Finally, if you're coming to this region you should not miss stopping by a coffee farm. You are, after all, in Colombia, where the highest grade and richest coffee is produced and exported throughout the world. You will find there is a great deal to learn, and it is well worth the extra money to hire a local farmer to show you around and teach you the tricks of the trade. Many tours and guides can be found upon arrival in your destination of choice. In the case of Los Nevados, it may be wise to arrange a tour in Manizales that includes transportation to and from the park. Horseback riding is also a very popular activity in this region. It costs about $20 for a day tour (4-6 hours) in the countryside.

Zona Cafetera Lodging

In general, the municipalities in the Zona Cafetera have a wide range of accommodation options for foreigners. Manizales and Salento in particular have good, low-cost backpacking hostels that draw travelers year-round. There are only a handful of places that offer dorm beds, the cheapest option for budget travelers. You will be surprised, though, how far your cash can go if you break from the backpacker route and search for your own accommodations in town. Los Sauces in Manizales, for example, provides you with a private room for less than a dorm bed in the popular Mountain House, and Los Sauces is two blocks from Plaza Bolívar.

It is a little more difficult to find cheap accommodation in Armenia and Pereira, as these cities have less developed tourist infrastructures. If you plan on spending a night or two in either of these places, first go to the information booth at the bus terminal. This is the best place to get some good suggestions for accommodation and pick up some business cards. It will also give you a chance to get your bearings and learn which neighborhoods are safe and which to avoid. As the entire region is temperate and often cool, you will appreciate that all accommodations have 24-hour hot water.

Armenia

Alt: 1,500m Pop: 273,000 City Code: 6

Armenia was founded on October 14, 1889 by Jesús María Ocampo, also known as "Tigrero" (or the "Tiger Killer") because of his love of hunting jaguars (known locally as tigers). Ocampo came to Armenia, which is advantageously located on the Río Quindío, looking for shelter in the mountains. He paid 100 pesos in gold coins for the land, planning to build a trade center he and other colonists from the surrounding areas could use. He proceeded to sell land for settlement. Six months after its founding, the settlement had reached a population of 100 people, earning it legal recognition by the government. The city was named "Armenia" to honor the people murdered in the Hamidian massacres of 1894-96.

Armenia's fortunate geography at 1,500 meters above sea level, near two rivers and within just a few hours of the country's three largest cities (Bogotá, Medellín, and Cali) made it a commercial hub during the 20th Century. In January 1999, Armenia experienced a devastating earthquake that left 200,000 people homeless. Fortunately, with international aid the city's modern infrastructure was quickly rebuilt, and even came to include a brand new bus terminal and a contemporary pedestrian mall in the center of town. A collection of gold, often regarded as the best in the country, is located in the north of the city at the Museo del Oro Quimbaya.

Getting To and Away From Armenia

Armenia is conveniently situated between many of Colombia's largest cities. Bogotá and Medellín are just six hours away by bus, Cali and Ibagué are three hours away and Pereira and Manizales are one and two hours away respectively. Getting to and away from Armenia by bus is the easiest and safest option. The city's new, secure bus terminal is located at the southern edge of the city, a short five-minute taxi ride ($1.50) from Plaza Bolívar at the city's center.

Walking from the terminal to Plaza Bolívar is not advised. You can take any local bus from the terminal to "Centro" ($0.75), which will pass through the center on its route around the city. There is very little reason to fly here. If you do decide to fly, the Pereira airport services Armenia by airport shuttle on the hour. Updated: May 27, 2008.

When to Go

Armenia's temperate climate often allows for pleasant days and cool evenings. As in other areas of the Quindío, Armenia tends to be wetter in April and October.

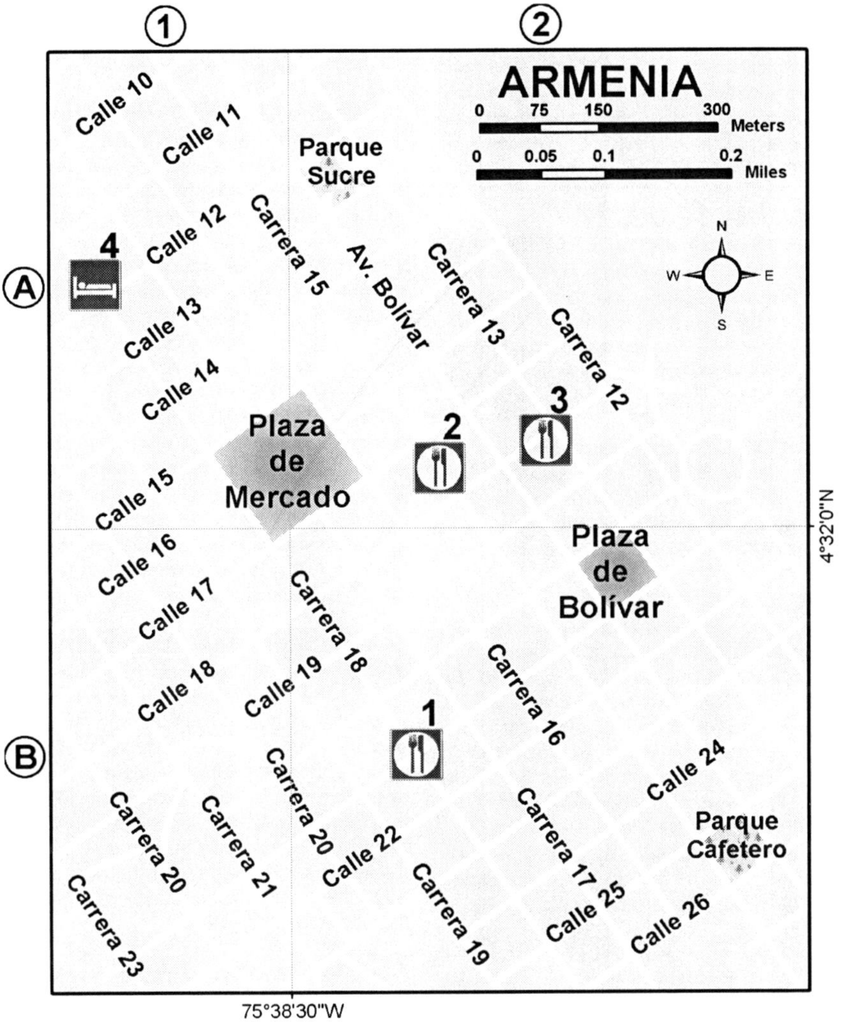

Eating

1 El Toque Pizzería

2 Home

3 Rincón Vegetariano

Sleeping

4 Hotel Alpino

Holidays and Festivals

In February, a festival worth catching is Armenia's unique Yipao, or Jeep Parade. Jeeps, which have become the beloved symbol of the coffee culture in this part of Colombia, are driven in an immense procession around the city, loaded with heaps of colorful fruits and vegetables. The cars carrying the most harmonious arrangements of produce win prizes. In 2006, Armenia and nearby Calarcá were inaugurated into the Guinness Book of World Records for a caravan of nearly 400 jeeps.

Getting Around Armenia

Armenia's new pedestrian mall through the center of the city makes getting around by foot the best option. Yellow taxis also buzz around town at all hours, should you need one (minimum day $1.50, night $2.50). Red buses run along Armenia's main thoroughfares for $0.75 per ride and are the best transportation option if you plan to visit the Museo del Oro Quimbaya, to the north of the city. Updated: May 27, 2008.

Safety in Armenia

Armenia is a surprisingly clean and safe city. Only the few blocks around Plaza Bolívar can get a bit shady at night. There is little crime to speak of in this town, but the usual precautions apply when wandering the city alone or after dusk. Updated: May 27, 2008.

Armenia Services

The best place to go for tourist information is the booth in the bus terminal, which is at the top of the stairs when you arrive. The agents here are very attentive and helpful. They will provide you with maps, handouts and all the other information you need to enjoy the fruits of the city.

Banks, ATMs, postal services, pharmacies and internet hubs are best found around Plaza Bolívar or along the pedestrian mall. The city's best hospital is a short ten blocks from Plaza Bolívar to the north. Updated: May 27, 2008.

Pedestrian Mall

There is plenty of shopping to be had along the pedestrian walkway, extending from Plaza Bolívar (cross street, Calle 21) to the hospital (on Calle 9)—about a dozen blocks. On weekends, this street is packed with people in need of some retail therapy. Artisan shops, drugstores, clothing boutiques and bigger malls line both sides of the street, so you'll be sure to find what you're looking for. Pedestrians are the privileged ones here, as cars cross the road slowly, giving shoppers the right of way. Updated: Apr 24, 2008.

Things to See and Do

Armenia is a passageway to the rich Quindío region, but the city itself offers few attractions. Other than the Museo del Oro Quimbaya and the Parque Nacional del Café close by, most visitors head to the hills to experience nature. Hiking, rafting and fishing opportunities are plentiful outside the city, should you choose to stay here for a couple of days. Updated: Jun 09, 2008.

Museo del Oro Quimbaya !

The most impressive permanent gold collection in the Zona Cafetera is found at the northern edge of Armenia on the way to Salento and Pereira. This museum is the primary reason travelers pass through the city. It is housed in a fantastic brick structure, surrounded by green courtyards and complete with a kid's library and lecture hall, cafeteria, temporary exhibition hall and two rooms holding Quimbaya gold and pottery.

The first room begins with the history of the Quimbaya, the indigenous people who occupied the mid-Cauca region (the departments of Caldas, Risaralda and Quindío) long before the Spanish conquered this area in the early 16th Century. The gold on display is a fascinating collection of body ornaments, musical instruments, tools and objects used to check coca leaves. The pottery is mostly comprised of human figures and pumpkwin-shaped urns and pots. Animal, female and pumpkin shapes dominate the gold and clay objects because they represent life, reproduction and fertility—three important Quimbaya values. The pinkish glow to the gold comes from a mixture of gold and copper alloy—gold symbolizes males and copper, females. The second room details the importance of ceremony and the conservation of tradition after the Spanish conquest.

To date, there have been two significant discoveries of Quimbaya gold. The first, called the "Quimbaya Treasure," was a collection of over 200 golden objects and numerous pieces of pottery. The entire collection was regrettably given to Spain as a gift and is now on display in the Museum of America in Madrid. A second group of objects was uncovered in the Antioquia region and is on display in a traveling exhibition through the Banco de la República. Check its website to find its current location.

Admission is free, and both rooms have English translation guides that you can carry with you. The museum is open Tuesday-Saturday, 10 a.m.-5 p.m. and closed on Mondays and public holidays. Take any bus to Circasia and get off at the rotary with the black steam train in the center. Avenida Bolívar, 40 Norte - 80. Tel: 6-749-8433, E-mail: museoquimbaya@banrep.org, URL: www.banrep.org/museo. Updated: Apr 24, 2008.

Territorio Aventura

Natural wonders are within arm's reach in Armenia. Just 30 minutes from the city, you can visit a natural park, try your hand at fishing, go kayaking or rafting, or see the world from great heights as you rappel or parasail above the Quindío countryside. Territorio Aventura is ready to plan the perfect adventurous trip for you. Longer trips include *finca* (farm) stays in peaceful haciendas outside the city. Carrera 14, 14n – 6 Edificio Acuarium, Local 1. Tel: 6-749-5448 / 3352, Cell: 310-422-0596 / 504-3555, URL: www.territorio-aventura.com.co. Updated: Apr 24, 2008.

Armenia Lodging

There are some good, economical hotels a few blocks from the city's pedestrian mall along Avenida Bolívar between Calle 21 and 9. Basic accommodations include a clean, well-lit room with private bath, and usually a fan. It never gets hot enough in Armenia to justify A/C. It's best to stick to the bustling area next to the pedestrian mall, as there are a few sketchy parts of town that would be best to avoid (like Simón Bolívar, which is not to be mistaken with Plaza de Bolívar). Updated: Jun 09, 2008.

Hotel Alpino de Armenia

(ROOM: $10-25) Hotel Alpino is a good budget option at the northern end of the city. Although this place is a little farther away from the pedestrian mall, Plaza Bolívar and busy Carrera 19, it can still be rather loud. But with a clean room that includes private bath, hot water and TV for just $10 a night, who's complaining? You can negotiate to have breakfast included. Carrera 19, 12-41. Tel: 6-745-4040. Updated: Apr 24, 2008.

HC Comfortel

(ROOM: $15-25) Manager Rubiel keeps this ten-room hotel spic and span and makes sure his guests are happy during their stay. The rooms here are spacious with private bath and cable TV. For convenience and comfort on a budget, Comfortel's location, (a few blocks from Plaza Bolívar,) and its prices will hit the spot. Calle 22, 17-30. Tel: 6- 741-4852, Cell: 311-777-7133. Updated: Apr 24, 2008.

Hotel El Eden Country Inn

(ROOM: $30-50) This neat and colorful inn between Armenia and Circasia is the perfect place to experience the major sites in Quindío—namely, the Museo del Oro Quimbaya, Parque Nacionál del Café and Valle de Cocora. Set in a few brightly colored colonial buildings, this inn has 15 guest rooms (11 standard rooms, two family suites and two presidential suites). It also has a pool, Jacuzzi, gym and a restaurant open to the public (Monday-Saturday, 12-9 p.m., Sunday 12-6 p.m.). The living room fits 100 people and is occasionally used for social events and meetings. Take any bus to Circasia, Salento and Pereira and have the driver drop you off at the entrance to the hotel—on your left, up the hill. Kilometer 4 outside Armenia. Cell: 315-547-5347 / 316-527-8558 / 314-635-3228, E-mail: country@telesat.com.co. Updated: Apr 24, 2008.

Finca Cafetera El Balso

(ROOMS: $60-100) The gentle climate in this region makes it an ideal environment for cultivating rich, Colombian coffee. It also makes the Finca Cafetera El Balso one of the most attractive destinations to stay in outside of the city. Located 5 kilometers outside of Armenia, here you can enjoy privacy coupled with the treasures of the coffee country. This hacienda offers five comfortable rooms with a total capacity of 14 guests. You'll want to stay for a while to fully enjoy the farm's beautiful gardens, green fields, coffee and fruit crops. Updated: May 29, 2008.

Armenia Restaurants

As the capital city of the Quindío region, delectable, fresh treats can be found on nearly every street corner in Armenia. This area of the country is the leading producer of flour, apples, potatoes and berries. The city is also big on fresh meat and fish. There are several decent eateries right in the center of town that serve vegetarian food, traditional Colombian dishes, and more. Updated: Dec 19, 2007.

Rincón Vegetariano

Serving what is arguably the best vegetarian food in all of Colombia, Rincón Vegetariano is a fantastic find in the heart of Armenia. The menu is set every day, but includes juice and milk, fruit, soup, four small vegetarian dishes and a dessert. Service is quick and the second-floor balcony seating is ideal. For just $3.50 in house and $4.00 take-out, you really can't go wrong here. They also deliver. Highly recomended. Calle 18, 13-24. Tel: 6-744-5055, Cell: 311-634-7767. Updated: Apr 24, 2008.

El Toque Pizzeria

This clean, blue-themed pizzeria next to Plaza Bolívar prepares hearty pizzas for a good price. There is free delivery service as ıline menu if you wish to order . Small (1 slice), medium (per-ı) and large (8 slices) orders are generous and, more importantly, u. . Calle 18 and Avenida Bolívar. Tel: 6-741-0134, URL: www.eltoquepizzeria.com. Updated: Apr 24, 2008.

Home

A nice establishment with an enormous flat screen TV in the front room, a buzzing kitchen and a pleasant back patio, Home does in fact offer the comforts of home—Colombia style. The name of the game here is meat—lots and lots of *churrasco*, *chorizo* and pork. There's also trout, but in this kind of hearty setting you'll be more inspired to order a big plate of churrasco and potatoes with a Colombian beer. Prices are a bit expensive ($7-10 per plate). Carrera 15 between Calle 17 and 18. Updated: Apr 24, 2008.

SALENTO

Alt:1,800m Pop: 7,000 City Code: 6

On January 5, 1830, Simón Bolívar passed through the original town of Barcinales on his "Camino Nacional," which took him from Cartago to Ibagué. Twelve years later, the townsfolk moved to Salento's current location higher in the mountains at 1,800 meters and the area was named "Villa de Nuevo Salento." In time, just Salento stuck. Salento was officially declared its own municipality much later, in 1908.

Despite its relative newness, Salento is still considered the "Father of Quindío," and you will fully understand the term upon visiting this beautifully scenic town. With just 7,000 residents, infinite natural beauty and architectural uniformity, as well as a general adherence to and appreciation for tradition and culture, it is no wonder Colombians and foreigners fall in love with this place. The colorful two-story buildings along Carrera 6, from the main plaza to the stairs of the *mirador*, have been excellently preserved. Aside from the occasional car or motorcycle passing through, and the fact that nearly every building along this street has been converted into a restaurant or artisan store, not much has changed here. Walk into a local bar and you'll find men in their traditional gear playing cards or billiards.

Salento, encircled by folds of green hills, is the perfect place to explore nature at its finest, whether it's by horseback along the Quindío River, by foot along dozens of mountain paths, or by jeep in the gorgeous Cocora Valley. Don't forget to snap a photo of the national tree, the Palma de Cera, which is a very tall, thin palm native to this area of the country. And, of course, your trip to Salento is not complete without *trucha con patacón* (trout with fried plantains). Updated: Jun 16, 2008.

When to Go

Like the other 12 municipalities in the department of Quindío, the weather in Salento is always temperate if not cool. There is more rain in March, April, September and October. Other times of the year a T-shirt and jeans will suit you fine.

Holidays and Festivals

There is a major festival called Palma de Cera, named for Colombia's national tree, which is common to this area. The festival is held every year on January 5-12 in celebration of the founding of the city. Some interesting contests are held, as well as theater performances and other cultural events. During this festival you may also lay eyes on the biggest fried patacón you'll ever see. Updated: Apr 23, 2008.

Getting To and Away From Salento

Buses converge in the main square. There are three buses that leave to and from Pereira per day. Buses to Armenia come and go hourly. If you're heading to the Valle de Cocora for the day, there are three departures by jeep on the other side of the square. There are several buses back to Salento, with the last bus leaving from the valley at 5 p.m. It takes about one hour to get to each of these destinations. Updated: Apr 23, 2008.

Getting Around Salento

Salento is a very small town, fully manageable by foot. You could always try to hitch a ride from one end to the other, but there are no local buses or taxis. If you'd like to visit the restaurants down by the river, you can hop on any bus heading out of town. The road to Salento is windy, and cars zoom by at an alarming rate, so it's best to travel out of town by bus even if you're just going down the hill. Updated: Apr 23, 2008.

Safety in Salento

The 4,200 residents of Salento's small urban center are used to seeing both national and international visitors year-round. Locals are helpful and accommodating and you don't have to worry excessively about crime or theft. In addition, the tap water here comes from the mountains and is fresh enough to drink! While you're here, you can say goodbye to bottled water and fill up straight from the faucet. Updated: Apr 23, 2008.

Salento Services

Tourism Office

The information office at the mirador has useful tips about activities around Salento.

Money

There is an ATM in the main square on Carrera 7 in the yellow and blue building. There is no sign, so you have to look for it or just ask. Sometimes the machine is also out of money, so be sure to stock up on cash in Pereira or Armenia before coming. Some restaurants and stores accept Visa and MasterCard, but most of the hotels in town do not.

Keeping in Touch

There are two decent internet cafés on Carrera 6 that charge $1 per hour.

Medical

The hospital is at the corner of Carrera 7 and Calle 7. Updated: Apr 23, 2008.

Things to See and Do

Coming to Salento means taking a deep breath of fresh mountain air and enjoying the peace and tranquility of a slow-paced lifestyle. The things to see and do in Salento are all outside; take a walk, ride a horse, or climb a mountain. There are beautiful natural sights within arm's reach. Cocora Valley, with its diverse cloud forest and beautiful river, is a must-see. So too is the town's mirador. Browse the artisan shops on Calle de Real on your way there. Updated: Jun 09, 2008.

El Mirador de Salento

The Mirador de Salento is much more than a look-out point. First, you must climb 200 stairs to the big cross at the top. Along the way, you will find signs that tell the story of Jesus. Follow the path to your left to the mirador, which is a covered lookout with a grand view of Cocora Valley. There is a tourist office here providing all the information you need to know about the Cocora Valley, Salento, Armenia and other sites in the department of Quindío. The path by the parking lot will lead you down to the river and to other trails in the valley. Updated: Apr 23, 2008.

Valle de Cocora

Cocora Valley is a great launching point for nature hikes and wildlife spotting. There are several trails leading up the mountain, along the river and farther into the valley. A peaceful cloudforest with little man-made pedestrian bridges over the river is about an hour away by foot. Another 30 minutes up the valley will take you to Acaime, a small home with dozens of native hummingbirds. You can sleep here for $5 a night, or enjoy a refreshment and snack for $1. Another trail on the hillside takes you back to Cocora, or you can hoof it up the hill five more kilometers to another lookout. If you don't want to walk the trail, a horse and guide will take you wherever you want for $8 an hour.

To get to Cocora Valley, hop in a jeep from the main plaza at 7:30 a.m., 11:30 a.m., or 4 p.m. ($2 per person, one way, one hour). Head back to Salento from the valley at 8:30 a.m., 12:30 p.m. or 5 p.m. Updated: Apr 23, 2008.

Horseback Riding

Another great way to see the vast, beautiful countryside around Salento is by horse. Paulino, a local cowboy, has 35 willing horses and a crew of cowboys ready to take you on trails up the mountain or along the Río Cocora. Trips range from 1.5 hours up to six hours and Paulino charges $5-20, depending on the length and difficulty of the ride. Bigger groups receive discounted rates. White house with red trim at the corner of Calle 7 and Carrera 8 in barrio Boquerón. Contact Paulino Callejas. Cell: 313-320-4277. Updated: Apr 23, 2008.

Salento Lodging

There are several hostels and hotels along Calle 6 and Carrera 6. You will be much happier staying closer to the plaza, and there is always a room available somewhere unless you're coming for festival week in

January. All accommodations are about the same price ($18 per room per night) and provide the same amenities: private bath with hot water, plenty of blankets and, if you're lucky, a window with a view of the landscape. If you arrive mid-week or during low season, you can bargain for a better rate. Updated: Jun 09, 2008.

Plantation House

(ROOM: $7.50+) Most backpackers in Salento stay in Plantation House, and often linger longer than expected. It's easy to see why; beautiful views, comfortable accommodation and hammocks, knowledgeable and well-connected English-speaking staff, and the very tranquil atmosphere all beckon you to stay just one more night. Get off the bus by the fire house (*Estación de Bomberos*) in Salento. Facing the main square, follow the street on your right. It's on the left, two blocks up. Anyone who lives in town will know where it is as well. Alto de Coronel, Calle 7, 1-04. Tel: 6-759-3403, E-mail: theplantationhousesalento@yahoo.co.uk. Updated: Jun 16, 2008.

Posada del Angel !

(ROOM: $15-20) This hostel is the best find in town and just a few paces from the main plaza. Most tourists don't know about this place because it is not in an obvious location. Upon arrival at the plaza, instead of heading back through town whence you came, head down the hill half a block on Calle 6, where on the left you will find this cute white hostel with blue trim. Elsa, the owner, resident and local expert, is a sweet lady who will make you feel right at home. Her house has four bright, airy rooms—each with cable TV and a private bath. The room next to the kitchen has a nice balcony looking out over the countryside. Elsa will cook breakfast for you for $2.50, or you are free to use the kitchen. Calle 6, 7-47. Tel: 6-759-3507, Cell: 311-609-0977 / 317-257-7314. Updated: Apr 23, 2008.

Balcones de Ayer

(ROOM: $18-20) This attractive colonial home provides basic but modern accommodations half a block from the plaza. All six rooms are the same—cable TV, a clean, private bath (with hot water) and a big, comfortable queen-size bed. The $18-room includes breakfast in the first-floor restaurant, which also serves traditional lunches and dinners (meat and fish) for $8-10 per plate. Calle 6a, 5-40. Tel: 6-759-3273, Cell: 312-226-2921. Updated: Apr 23, 2008.

Salento Restaurants

All of Salento's restaurants are located around the plaza and along Carrera 6. There are enough restaurants to last you a week without going back to the same one, though most serve up the same dishes, so it's a good idea to ask the locals which are popular. The specialty here is fresh trout, available eight different ways, and served with a large patacón. Typical Paisa dishes are also common menu items. Updated: Apr 23, 2008.

Super Patacón con Trucha

Its name deserves a prize, as does its monstrously delicious trout and patacón. This place is no secret to either locals or tourists. If you ask anyone where to go for the best trout in town, you'll wind up here. Super Patacón is right on the square and its food is enormous and tasty. Depending on how you order the trout, it will come in a bubbling soup with garlic and mushrooms, or sit right on top of the big yellow fried plantain. Use pieces of patacón to scoop up your fish and enjoy! Updated: Apr 23, 2008.

Las Mariposas !

This artisan store has a lovely restaurant in the back garden serving traditional Colombian cuisine, including regular and half portions of trout with patacón. Trout plates can be prepared in eight ways—all of which include a fresh salad with tangy dressing. The restaurant has a perfect view of the colorful stairs to the mirador, making it an ideal lunch spot. Updated: Apr 23, 2008.

Las Tapias

This classic Italian and French eatery is a tasty option if you're seeking something other than trout or fried meat. It just moved to this central spot in the middle of Carrera 6 and is brightly decorated with heavy wooden tables and chairs. The crepes, pizza and pasta here are all cheap and delicious. Updated: Apr 23, 2008.

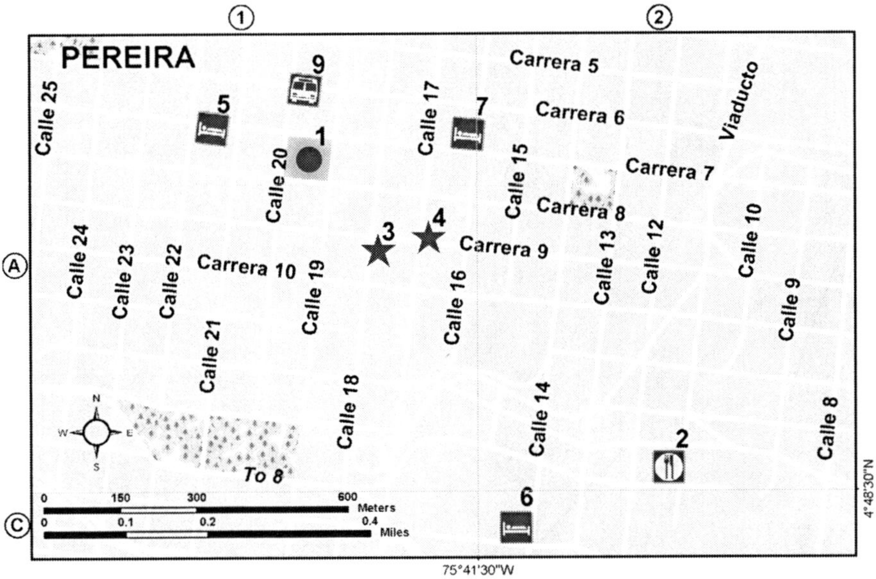

Activity ●
1 Plaza Bolívar B3
Eating
2 Kilaba B4
Service ★
3 Banco de la República B3
4 Fomento del Turismo B3
Sleeping
5 Hotel Abadía Plaza B3
6 Hotel Santa Rosa C4
7 Hotel Suite Center B3
8 Laureucio House B1
Transportation
9 Estación Central B3

Pereira

Alt: 1,500m Pop: 428,000 City Code: 6

Pereira, originally the town of Cartago, was moved to its present-day location in 1691 after becoming the capital of the Risaralda. The Cartago-Pereira area was culturally influenced by the fierce Quimbaya tribes. The Quimbaya people are famous for their gold work, considered some of the best representations of pre-Columbian culture. Similar to its metropolitan neighbor Manizales, this area was occupied by settlers from Antioquia during an expansion that developed much of Colombia. Because of its economically strategic location, fertile soil and good weather, Pereira experienced significant growth during the time of colonization. Settlers grew large quantities of coffee, still the most important crop produced in the area.

Unlike Manizales, Pereira had many settlers from Valle del Cauca, Bogotá and other major Colombian cities, and even today the city boasts a diverse population. In 1921, with the arrival of the locomotive train, Pereira quickly became known as the "Prodigious City," experiencing quick economic growth. Over the course of 50 years, the city doubled in population, and now holds 428,000 residents. Today, it continues to buzz with agro-industrial, manufacturing and financial activity. Pereira is still in need, however, of infrastructure for foreign travelers. The two tourist offices in town are more like bookshelves with flyers and business cards, and the hotels cater to business travelers rather than backpackers. Still, if you set aside a day in Pereira, chances are you will find a suitable place to sleep and decent city-based activities.

When to Go

Pereira is the warmest city in the Zona Cafetera and sees a fair amount of sunshine. Still, it can be a bit cooler and rainier in April and October. Small food festivals are held in the Plaza Bolívar three times a year to celebrate a variety of local foods such as *mazamorra* (a dessert made from corn, milk and *agua de panela*). For about

Parque Nacional del Café

By Wilson Lievano, Viva List Contributor, 2007

If Juan Valdéz, the image of Colombian coffee through the world, had a farm, it would probably be on the grounds of the Parque Nacional del Café, the theme park for all things coffee related.

Located in the town of Montenegro, Quindío, 160 miles west of Bogotá, in the heart of the coffee growing region of Colombia, the park is a blend of mechanical attractions, eco-tourism, and family entertainment. All pay homage to the production of the smoothest, tastiest coffee in the world.

The park sits in a small valley. To get there, visitors can take a cable car which gives a broad view of the park and its surroundings or a path that allows them to see and touch all the varieties of coffee plants that are grown in Colombia, along with several other varieties from around the world. The path forks, one way leading to the auditorium where twice a day a dance troupe performs the typical dances of the region. The other arm leads to several stations where park officials explain step-by-step how the coffee goes from the Colombian highlands to your favorite mug.

Both paths converge on a big colonial-style square filled with statues and stores. During the Christmas season, the square has a large tree and live re-enactments of the Nativity. From the square, visitors can walk to the mechanical attractions area that has everything from carousels for the kids to roller coasters and go-karts for the grown-ups. A little further down the road is the lake of the legends, a place that offers boat rides and several tales of the myths and legends of the original inhabitants of the region.

There are buses that take visitors to the park, but for convenience visitors are encouraged to rent a car and drive there. No visit to the park is complete without taking some time to sit in one of the many coffee houses scattered all over the park to enjoy a tinto (the name that locals give to a cup of regular coffee). These shops also offer a wide variety of candy, made from coffee (of course).

The Parque Nacional del Café is a tribute to one of the products that make Colombians proud. Families, nature enthusiasts and wide-eyed java-heads will enjoy themselves here. While you are in the park keep an eye open for Juan Valdez and his trusted mule Conchita: they will gladly invite you for a cup of coffee.

It is easier to get to the park from Armenia than from Pereira. Take any bus from Armenia to Cicasia (15 minute ride for $1, leaves the terminal every 15 minutes), where you can ask to be dropped off near the park entrance. Additionally, buses from Salento to Armenia (20-minute ride for $1, leaving every half hour) pass through Cicasia. Updated: Apr 25, 2008.

five days at the end of August, the city holds its annual Fiestas de la Cosecha, which celebrates the harvest season with food and drink. Updated: May 29, 2008.

Getting To and Away From Pereira

Pereira's international airport, the largest in the region, is located 20 minutes from the city center (about $5 by taxi). The city's bus terminal is new and clean, and it's a safe, 20-minute walk from Plaza Bolívar. Pereira is just an hour from Salento, Armenia and Manizales, about four hours from Cali and six from Bogotá. Updated: May 29, 2008.

Getting Around

The city is easily navigated on foot, but taxis are readily available all over town. There is a minimum $1.50 day rate and $2.50 night rate for a taxi ride. City buses run along the main thoroughfares to all the major destinations ($0.75 per ride). There is also a brand new Megabús system with routes running in the center, north to south and east to west. ($1.00 per ride). Updated: May 29, 2008.

Safety in Pereira

As in all larger cities, it's best to use caution when walking alone in Pereira at night. Some streets even in the center of town are not particularly well-lit in the evening, so it would be wise to take a cab if you are walking long distances. There have been recent reports of students carrying weapons, despite the seeming lack of crime in Pereira. Stick to the city center around Plaza Bolívar and you will feel safe, but you should still be aware of pickpockets and use basic common sense. Updated: May 29, 2008.

Pereira Services

Tourism Office

There are two tourism offices in Pereira just two blocks from one another. The Fomento del Turismo, located in the big mall on Calle 17 and Carrera 9, has brochures and maps to choose from, but no office attendant. The other office is located in the city's government building two blocks down the hill, where staff can help you make local calls to arrange accommodations or tours.

Other Services

There is a variety of pharmacies, banks, ATMs and internet cafés on the main Plaza Bolívar, but the main hospital and medical clinics are located just outside of the city's center by the bus terminal. Updated: June 09, 2008.

Shopping

Estacíon Central
This brand new shopping mall just a block from the Plaza Bolívar is being filled up with modern stores and food stalls. Retail and electronics stores are on the top three floors, and there's a variety of food options (fast food, bakery goods, Russian desserts and sweets) downstairs. There is free WiFi in the downstairs atrium and plenty of tables and chairs for resting your feet. Updated: Apr 25, 2008.

Things to See and Do

There is nothing special for foreigners to see or do in the city other than walk around the city center. If you find yourself passing by the obscure Fomento de Turismo or the Banco de la República, pop in to find out about current events or local activities. Pereira is mainly a commercial center and a transportation hub between Manizales, Armenia and northern and southern Colombia. There are some nice thermal springs worth visiting about 20 minutes from Pereira in Santa Rosa de Cabal. Parque Nacional Ucumarí is 2 hours away in the direction of La Florida. Updated: Dec 19, 2007.

Banco de la República

The city's very modern library and cultural center is worth stopping by if only to catch up on current events in the city. The bulletin board on the first floor will tell you the latest temporary exhibits, afternoon lectures, educational talks or evening concerts that are held on-site. The third floor has a good collection of Colombian magazines, newspapers and literature, which, if you're Spanish is good enough, could prove to be an afternoon well spent. The third floor also has a nice reading area with desks and a pleasant outdoor terrace with tables and chairs that visitors are encouraged to use. Calle 18bis, 9-57. URL: www.banrep.org. Updated: Apr 25, 2008.

Ucumarí Park

Ucumarí National Park is one of Colombia's best locations to spot birds, animals and plant life. The variations in altitude in this area are what make Ucumarí so biologically diverse.

Because the park covers some 10 miles in diameter, the best and practically the only way to experience it is to hire a tour guide, who can take you to the park via *chiva* bus. With a guide you can visit waterfalls, hike in the forest, spy unique birds, and if you're lucky, Andean Spectacled Bears, which dwell in this region.

Dormitories and camping sites are available in the park, and there are accommodations and tourist services to Ucumarí in nearby Los Nevados National Park. Accommodations are 30 minutes by foot from the entrance to the park.

If you are serious about visiting Ucumarí, plan on spending at least a full day in the park with a guide and be sure to account for the time needed to travel to and from Pereira (two hours each way). Updated: May 29, 2008.

Pereira Lodging

As of yet, there are no cheap hotels and certainly no hostels in Pereira worth recommending. The city's best accommodations are within a three block radius of Plaza Bolívar. These hotels are expensive and modern. Cheaper family homestays and other lodges are located out of town on the way to Manizales. Updated: Dec 19, 2007.

Hotel Suite Center !

(ROOMS: $17-40) Smack dab in the center of Pereira, Hotel Suite Center is likely the most affordable and comfortable option. Rooms range from a bit shabby (with metal bunk beds) to pretty posh (canopy bed, large screen TV and a bathtub in the bedroom), but all have hot water and a fair share of comfort and security. The restaurant on the main floor serves decent Colombian fare. Calle 16, 7-56. Tel: 6-333-0989, Cell: 310-388-1520, Fax: 6-333-9018. Updated: May 29, 2008.

Hotel Santa Rosa

(ROOMS: $60-100) Travel 15 minutes out of town to Santa Rosa de Cabal and you will find this comfortable, luxurious hotel, complete with a naturally heated pool filled with fresh water from the thermal springs. The hotel boasts decadent furnishings and includes two private Jacuzzis, secure parking, a massage parlor, restaurant and bar. A 15-minute walk down the surrounding trails leads you to mountain waterfalls or the town of Santa Rosa. The hotel's 30 guest rooms situated in one of two buildings are comfortable and family-friendly. The hotel can accommodate meetings or special events in its 60-person conference room. Tents are available to rent for those interested in camping on the grounds. Calle 14, 15-41. Tel: 6-363-4966, Fax: 6-364-1490, E-mail: ventas@termalesantarosadecabal.com. Updated: May 29, 2008.

Hotel Abadia Plaza

(ROOM: $100-120) The best of the best in Pereira, Hotel Abadia is a high-end establishment in the heart of the city. The 50 modern, tastefully decorated rooms have first-class amenities, including flat screen TV. There is a large meeting space on the first floor, as well as a 60-car parking lot in the building. Breakfast in the hotel's restaurant is included in your stay, and guests are also free to use the hotel gym and sauna. Carrera 8, 21-67. Tel: 6-335-8398, Fax: 6-334-2471, E-mail: gerencia@hotelabadiaplaza.com/Reservas@hotelabadiaplaza.com, URL: www.hotelabadiaplaza.com. Updated: Apr 25, 2008.

Pereira Restaurants

There is little variety to speak of when it comes to cuisine in Pereira. You'll find typical *arepas*, *empanadas* and Colombian plates. As in Manizales, head to the restaurant of one of the nicer hotels in town if you are looking for more creative dishes. Food stalls offering a variety of options are also found in shopping mall food courts. There, at least, you will be able to choose from a greater selection of small menus. Updated: Dec 19, 2007.

La Catorce !

If passing through Pereira, a convenient option is La Catorce shopping mall across the street from the bus terminal. Inside is a food court with fast food as well as a variety of restaurants. Since there is little to no atmosphere at La Catorce, this place is best for travelers on the go, or those who plan on doing some retail shopping in addition to having a quick bite to eat. Updated: May 29, 2008.

Kilaba

This unique eatery, with an Arabian take on Colombian cuisine, serves up *bandeja paisa* and other traditional dishes with some Middle Eastern flair. In addition to Colombian fare, you can also order some unique dishes and desserts, like stuffed grape leaves or baklava. This is one of the few nice establishments that stays open until late in the evening. The restaurant is a few blocks from Plaza Bolívar and comfortably seats 30 guests in its warmly decorated dining hall. Calle 11, 12B-27 Circunvalar. Tel: 6-334-5121 / 9207. Updated: May 29, 2008.

Manizales

Alt:2,150m Pop: 368,000 City Code:6

Manizales was founded by a group of 20 Antioquians on October 12, 1849, in the middle of a civil war. Even though it is the capital city of the department of Caldas and the most important city in the nation's coffee region, Manizales is still physically a part of Antioquia, the region where Medellín reigns supreme. This

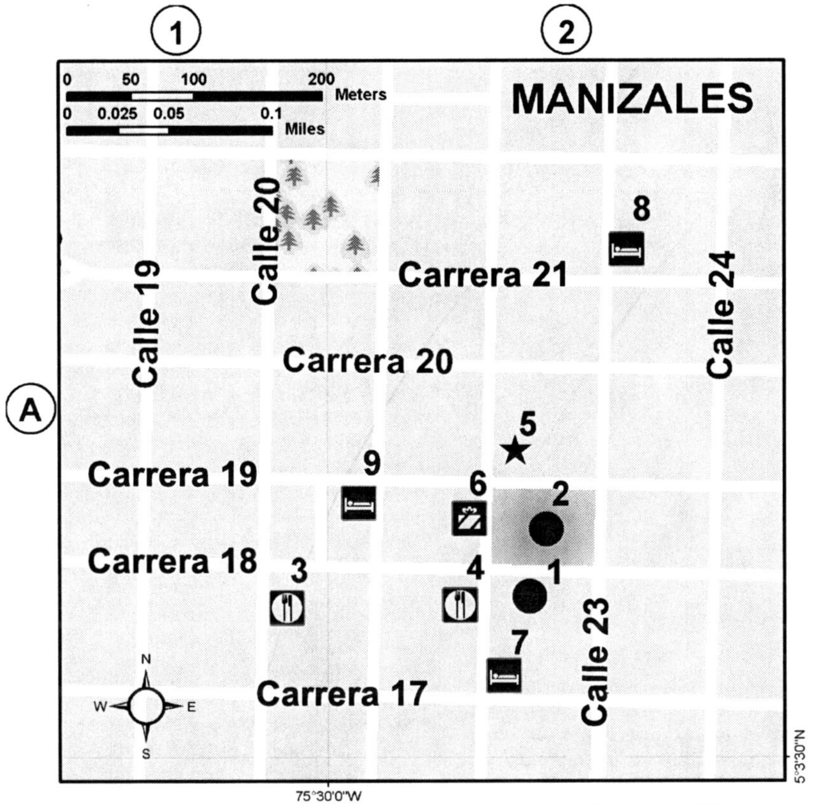

Activities ●
1 La Basílica A2
2 Plaza Bolívar A2

Eating
3 El Murál Restaurante A1
4 Plaza 22 A2

Services ★
5 Tourism Office A2

Shopping
6 Cafam (market) A2

Sleeping
7 Hotel Bolívar Plaza A2
8 Hotel Escorial A2
9 Hotel Los Sauces A2

city's culture has a strong Spanish influence, but its initial homogeneity has been tempered by other ethnic groups migrating to the city to attend its outstanding universities. Tango or rumba is the dance of choice here, and jazz is widely enjoyed as well.

Because of the climate, culture and landscape, Manizales resembles San Francisco, California, with its trendy eateries, chilled-out lifestyle and proximity to the outdoors. At 2,150 meters, this city has a cool factor all its own. While the city's commercial center around Plaza Bolívar is a historical area, the newer university district and zona rosa keep Manizales hip. The city's harmonious blending of old and new makes it a pleasant place to spend a few days.

When to Go

Because of its elevation, temperatures are cool year-round. Expect more rain from March to May and September to November.

Holidays and Festivals

The biggest festival is the Feria de Manizales, which takes place in January. There are parades, craft fairs, arts and literature events, and a beauty pageant where the coffee queen is crowned. Bullfighting is also an important aspect of this festival. The Festival Latinoamericano de Teatro takes place in late September, when there are free concerts in Plaza de Bolívar and special theater events throughout the city. Updated: Apr 24, 2008.

Photo by Dan Anderson

Getting To and Away from Manizales

Manizales is the perfect stopover between Bogotá and Medellín. Buses to Pereira and onward to Armenia and Cali leave every 15 minutes. The road to Manizales is very curvy, so you will be much more comfortable riding in a bigger bus rather than a van or *collectivo* (smaller bus).

From Manizales

Arrive	Time	Price
Pereira	1 hour	$4.50
Armenia	2 hours	$9
Cali	5 hours	$15
Medellín	5 hours	$15
Bogotá	5 hours	$15

Getting Around

Manizales' city center is best managed on foot. The zona rosa is about 10 minutes from Plaza Bolívar by car. You can hail a cab, which should cost you about $2.50, or flag down any bus with a sign for "Av. Santander" and either "Estadio" or "Cable" in the window. All municipal buses cost $0.75 per ride. Updated: Apr 24, 2008.

Safety in Manizales

There have been reports of theft in Manizales, especially in the city center between the bus terminal and Plaza Bolívar. The sidewalks are not particularly well-lit at night. It is not advisable to walk around the city alone after dark. Updated: Apr 24, 2008.

Manizales Services

A small yet informative tourist office is located on the Plaza Bolívar by La Basílica. Here you can pick up a map, get other relevant info about the city and look into the activities Manziales has to offer. The area around the Plaza is also considered the commercial center of the city, so it is the best place to find ATMs, cheap internet and postal services. Hospitals and universities, however, are located outside of the historical center along Avenida Santander on the way to the zona rosa, so head in that direction if you are looking for pharmacies, laundry services or grocery stores. Updated: May 29, 2008.

Shopping

Cable Plaza !

Looking for some good old-fashioned shopping, eating and movie viewing? This modern mall has it all: a supermarket downstairs, fashionable clothing stores on three floors, a deck with nice views of the greater Manizales countryside, a food court with free WiFi and a six-screen cinema playing recently released films in English with Spanish subtitles. On Tuesdays, movies are only $3.50. On other days catch one for $4.50. Take the bus on Avenida Santander toward El Estadio or El Cable and get off at Calle 65. Updated: Apr 24, 2008.

Cafam (Supermarket)

This centrally located supermarket is a great place to stock up on food or supplies, especially if you plan to do some camping in the area. Just minutes from the bus terminal, take advantage of the bakery and fresh produce. Calle 22, 21-51. Walk four blocks toward Plaza Bolívar. Updated: Apr 24, 2008.

Things to See and Do

Most of the best sights and activities in the area involve being outdoors in the crisp, cool air. There are several parks spread around this hilly city where you can spend a few hours if the weather is nice. The Parque Nacional Natural Los Nevados should be high on your list of activities—time your visit on a sunny or clear day.

La Basílica

The two bronze doors at the front entrance of La Basílica tell the story of this Neo-Gothic church. Originally built in 1854, it was first destroyed in 1878 by an earthquake, rebuilt from wood, and then devastated again in a fire in 1925. Construction of the current basílica began four years later, and now it is an impressive building both inside and out, with dazzling stained glass windows on every side. You can walk up the main tower, which is 106 meters high—the highest in the country—for $3. The stairway to the top is winding and steep, so it's not for the faint-hearted. The tower is open Tuesday-Sunday, 9 a.m.-5 p.m. Purchase your ticket from the western entrance. Updated: May 29, 2008.

Río Blanco Ecological Reserve

This well organized eco-park is ready for a high volume of tourists, but few foreigners make time to visit. The water of Río Blanco is considered some of the purest in the world, and 35 percent of the water used by Manizales comes from here.

Start your visit at the museum by gathering info about the surrounding natural sites. Then, follow a well-mapped route and walk along any of the four distinct trails in the park. Observe the flora and fauna in the cloud forest, and visit expositions and environmental workshops. There is a pair of spectacled bears here, as well as 256 species of birds and 350 species of butterflies. Bring your raincoat and wear your sneakers or boots. It is also best to wear dark-colored clothing to blend in better with the surroundings. Bring binoculars, if you have them. Updated: May 29, 2008.

Botanical Garden

Yet another great place to spend a clear, sunny day is the botanical garden in the university district of Manizales. There are plenty of colorful flowers to admire, or you can sit on the benches to read or people-watch. The park is smaller than the others in the city, but the free entrance into the garden is a major draw, as well as the peace and quiet. Updated: May 29, 2008.

Recinto el Pensamiento

Just 20 minutes from Plaza Bolívar and the hustle and bustle of city life is the beautiful Recinto el Pensamiento. At this cloudforest park you can take several ecological trails to the butterfly farm, orchid garden or the gorgeous bamboo pavilion. The café in the park sells Buendía (locally farmed) coffee and other local products. The park is closed on Mondays. Updated: May 29, 2008.

Los Yarumos Ecological Park

Situated in the city's surrounding cloudforest is Los Yarumos Ecological Park, a lush, green forest reserve where you can enjoy trails and lovely views of the countryside. The park is home to nearly 30 species of birds and hundreds of endemic flowers and trees. Visitors can even participate in extreme sports, such as rock climbing, canopy tours or rappelling. Outdoor concerts or cinema functions are held on weekends in the park's amphitheater. While you're here, you might as well take a quick peek at the park library and natural history museum, too. Updated: May 29, 2008.

Tierra Viva

This new agricultural and ecological park offers a lot of great outdoor activities, such as thermal baths, horseback riding, park tours and farm tours. Tierra Viva is a private park where you can rest, enjoy yourself, and also learn about nature and the cultural values associated with this area of the country. Once you've had your fill of the park's activities, feel free just to lounge and sip on a cup of Colombian coffee as you take in the views from its comfortable café-restaurant. Updated: May 29, 2008.

Parque Nacional Natural Los Nevados

Nevado del Ruíz, Crater de la Olleta, Nevado de Santa Isabel, Laguna Verde and Valle del Silencio are just a few of the reasons to visit Parque Nacional Natural Los Nevados.

The trip to Los Nevados, which means "snow-capped mountains," starts in Manizales at 2,150 meters (7053 feet) above sea level and covers almost 59,000 hectares of territory. In the midst of the Colombian central mountain chain, snow and sand live side by side, and small spouts of water surge to supply nearby towns. You can pass through desert landscapes with bright red rocks at Ruiz, photograph wild flowers and evergreens of Santa Isabel or admire the glittering snow of Laguna Verde.

Lodging is available at El Cisne Visitors Center or you can camp at one of the park's two designated camping areas. Lodging fees at El Cisne are $45-90. Tours of the park require a guide, which will cost about $30 a day. If you plan on walking up Nevado del Ruíz, be sure to drink a lot of water the day before—even so, you still may experience altitude sickness up top. Choose a sunny or clear day to visit, and bring cold weather gear as it can get quite chilly at this elevation. The park is located about 45 minutes from Manizales. Buses to the park lodge and entrance leave from the terminal every hour, but guides are required upon entrance to the park. The altitude increases quickly, so on the way up, keep the windows open. Updated: May 29, 2008.

Manizales Lodging

The best hotels in Manizales are located within two blocks of Plaza Bolívar. The cheap hotels are down the hill, a few more blocks along the new tunnel to the city (which is currently undergoing major renovation and construction). The other option is to stay in the newer part of the city near the zona rosa, which is 10 minutes away by bus along Avenida Santander. Accommodations in this part of town are modern and quiet. They are also closer to Manizales' nightlife, the stadium and the main shopping malls. Updated: Jun 09, 2008.

Budget

Hotel Los Sauces

(ROOM: $8-12) A decent, economical option in El Centro, Los Sauces has 22 rooms, all with a private bath with hot water, TV and radio. The bathrooms are tiny but functional, and the beds here are very soft. Although it is located in the industrial heart of the city, this is a clean and comfortable option for travelers on a budget. It is close to all the major city sites as well as the bus terminal. From Plaza Bolívar, walk downhill three blocks on Calle 23. The hotel is on your right. Calle 23, 18-55. Tel: 6-882-1228 / 884-9881. Updated: Apr 23, 2008.

Mountain House !

(ROOM: $9-18) This lively hostel in the zona rosa, 15 minutes from El Centro by bus, has been open for almost five years and is already a well-oiled machine. The owners, both named Christina, run a tight ship when it comes to service. There are two private rooms and four dorm rooms that sleep up to eight people. The spotless 24-hour kitchen is available for preparing breakfast, which is included in the price, and you can also use the BBQ out back to cook up a hearty dinner. Cesar, a biology major at the university, keeps fantastic company when he is on duty at the house and can tell you all about nature excursions and birdwatching in the area. The other members of staff are equally amiable local experts. To get here, hop on any bus that goes to El Estadio or El Cable and get off at Calle 66. Calle 66, 23B-137 (Avenida Paralela in barrio Guayacanes). Tel: 6-887-4736, Cell: 315-230-6986 / 311-745-3761, URL: www.mountainhousemanizales.com. Updated: Apr 23, 2008.

Mid-Range

Hacienda Guayabal !

(ROOM: $45) This gorgeous coffee farm and homestay is just 15 minutes outside of Chinchina, one of Colombia's coffee centers. Hacienda Guayabal is a totally self-sufficient farm that exports its coffee oversease to places like Japan and Spain. For $8 you can take a three-hour tour and learn everything you'll need to know about the production of coffee. If you work on the farm, you can sleep on-site for free. Or, just relax here for $45 per night (all inclusive). From Manizales, take the bus to Chinchina ($2, 30 minutes). Catch another bus in front of the main church to Guayabal ($.50, 10 minutes). Get off at Guayabal and walk through the town and up the hill to the hacienda (10 minutes). Carrera 3, 15-72 in Chinchina. Tel: 4-840-1463, Cell: 315-540-7639, E-mail: haciendaguayabal@hotmail.com, URL: www.guayabal.tripod.com. Updated: May 29, 2008.

High-End

Hotel Bolívar Plaza

(ROOM: $90-100) You can't beat the location, price, atmosphere or view of Hotel Bolívar Plaza. This clean hotel has 18 rooms, all of which include cable TV, internet, breakfast and a private bath with hot water. Ask for a room facing the Basílica. It will be a bit noisier, but the view is worth it. Calle 22, 22-40. Tel: 6-884-7777, Cell: 313-684-7246, Fax: 6-884-7396, E-mail: bolivarplaza@hotmail.com. Updated: Apr 24, 2008.

Regine's Hotel

(ROOM: $60-80) Regine's motto, "A tranquil place for all your needs," perfectly describes this small European-style accommodation near the zona rosa. This hotel has just 10 rooms that are elegantly decorated with a mini-bar and sophisticated wooden furnishings. The cushy, spotless common areas are great for reading and relaxing. Although this hotel is close to night clubs and bars, it is tucked away on a quiet street, so you can easily spend a peaceful evening here if you so desire. Calle 65a, 23B-113. Tel: 6-887-5360, Cell: 311-762-1572, Fax: 6-887-5686, E-mail: regineshotel@hotmail.com, URL: www.ciudadeje.com. Updated: Apr 24, 2008.

Hotel Escorial

(ROOM: $60-90) This upscale hotel is a great option for travelers with a heavier wallet. Uniformed staff members roam about all day making sure guests feel at home. With about 60 rooms including all major amenities as well as a parking lot for guests, this conveniently located hotel (just one block from Plaza Bolívar and outgoing local buses) will satisfy even the fussiest customers. Restaurante Los Vitrales on the third floor is set in a pleasant, colorful courtyard. The menu is the same for breakfast, lunch and dinner (appetizers $3, entrees $15), but the food is meticulously prepared. Calle 21, 21-11. Tel: 6-884-7646 / 8271, Fax: 6-884-7722, E-mail: escorial@une.net.co, URL: www.hotelesmanizales.com. Updated: Apr 24, 2008.

Manizales Restaurants

When it comes to restaurants in Manizales, there is not much variety to speak of. Most restaurants are fast food joints with typical Colombian fair. Exceptions are best found in the nicer hotels in the city, but you have to be willing to pay up to three times the price for a special dish. Manizales is still considered *paisa* country, so *bandeja paisa* (varieties of meat served with avocado, egg, beans and grilled banana) is worth a try if it's on the menu. The *cazuela* (seafood or meat stew) is also very tasty in this part of the country. Updated: Jun 09, 2008.

Don Juaco Snaks

If you're looking for a hearty meal at a reasonable price, Don Juaco will deliver. This is a great little find with warm, comfortable indoor and outdoor seating. Traditional dishes served in generous portions. Main plates (like the lasagna and cazuela) are served in clay bowls with plenty of melted cheese on top. Complete meals come with salad, French fries and half of a canned peach. A local dish to try is the *mazamorra con panela* ($3), which is a corn and milk soup with a caramel cookie on the side. Address: Calle 65, 23A-44. Tel: 6-855-0610, Cell: 310-830-2218, E-mail: bervigo@epm.net.co. Updated: Apr 24, 2008.

Plaza 22

This three-in-one restaurant, café and *cevichería* has every snack or big meal your belly could desire. Downstairs houses a cafeteria serving bread, fruit and refreshments, while the upstairs is a restaurant serving seafood, meat and local plates in a pleasant setting. You could also opt for the $4 lunch special that changes every day. At the corner of Plaza Bolívar on Calle 22. Updated: Apr 24, 2008.

El Mural

On the third floor of the Estelar Las Colinas Hotel, El Mural is pricey but quality option if you are in need of a break from typical Colombian cuisine. Here, you can order some nicely prepared seafood or pasta dishes. The $10 buffet available on weekdays is perfect for those who want to splash out. Estelar Las Colinas Hotel Carrera 22, 20-20. Tel: 6-884-2009, Fax: 6-884-1590, E-mail: reservas@hotelesestelar.com. Updated: Apr 24, 2008.

El Bistro

Particularly popular among foreigners, this sweltering bakery serves up some of the tastiest breads, desserts, pastas, salads and sandwiches in the area. Despite its lack of A/C, customers sit amid whirling fans to sip coffee and read something from El Bistro's small multi-language bookshelf. If you can't bear the heat, order take-out or have the food delivered. Expect to pay about $6, $8 and $10 respectively for breakfast, lunch and dinner specials, which are posted outside on a chalkboard. Centro Calle de Ayos, 4-46. Tel: 5-664-1799. Updated: Apr 14, 2008.

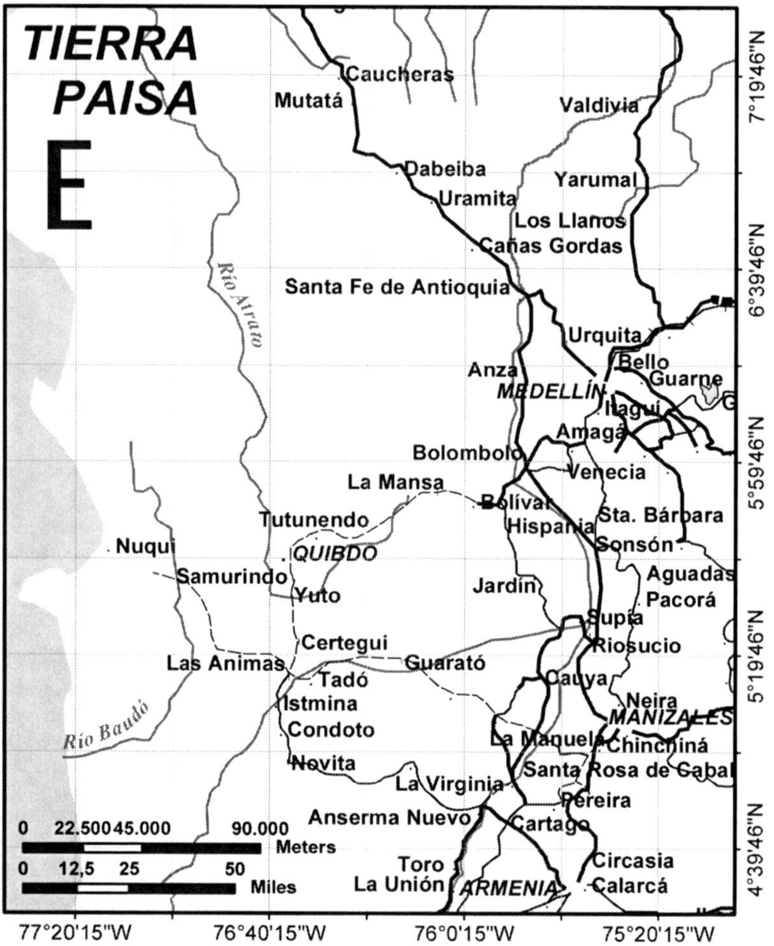

Tierra Paisa

Tierra Paisa is a fertile and verdant swath of land that includes not only the massive department of Antioquia, but also Caldas, Risaralda and Quindío, taking up most of the area known as the Eje Cafetero.

As you would expect, inhabitants of the Tierra Paisa are referred to as *paisas*, and they are considered among the friendliest and hardest working of Colombia's residents. In fact, paisas are known throughout Colombia for their proactive business sense, including arguably the most famous of the paisas, current President Álvaro Uribe Vélez.

In keeping with their nature, paisas have successfully established all types of high-yield industries in the region, such as agriculture (coffee), mining (coal) and commerce, making it a powerful economic force within Colombia.

In recent years paisas have actively promoted their land as one for tourism, and with good reason: the area is strewn with beautiful colonial villages striving to keep their cultural heritage alive.

Medellín is the region's capital, but there are other sites near here worth a visit, such as the Gulf of Urabá on the Caribbean coast, the scenery in and about the coffee town of Salento in Quindío, the colonial masterpiece of Santa Fe de Antioquia, and the towns of Manizales, Pereira and Armenia. Updated: Jan 11, 2008.

History

The first tribes encountered in the Tierra Paisa were the Nutabes and their allies the Catíos, neither of which took the arrival of the Spanish *conquistadores* particularly well—as evidenced by continuous battles waged against the first colonial capital, Santa Fe de Antioquia.

Tierra Paisa was first discovered in 1541 by the conquistador Jorge Robledo, who was responsible for founding Santa Fe de Antioquia. The region's history has since been characterized by violence and power struggles, including calls for and acts of independence from both the Spanish Crown and Colombia itself. This can easily be understood given the rising wealth of the region.

Throughout the 18th, 19th and 20th Centuries, the economy of Tierra Paisa flourished. It suffered a major setback in the 1970s, however, allowing for the rise of the Medellín cartel that put the city and the region on the map for all the wrong reasons. With drug lord Pablo Escobar's death in 1993, a relative peace settled on Medellín, and the city has since turned itself around. Updated: Dec 04, 2007.

When to Go

In terms of climate, there is no right or wrong time to go to Tierra Paisa—the region's varied terrain, ranging from the tropical Caribbean coast in the north to the cooler Andes running from north to south, allows for a wide variety of temperatures at any time of year. On the western slopes of the Andes, the mountain terrain transitions into the humid jungle of the Chocó, and on the northeastern frontiers reaching Puerto Berrío the land is flat, humid and hot. Updated: Dec 04, 2007.

Safety in Tierra Paisa

In the major cities such as Medellín, the visitor will be pleasantly surprised at the overriding sense of security, but you are advised to exercise caution at night, especially in the downtown areas.

Road travel for the most part is safe, although travel is not recommended in the western parts of Risaralda that lead to the Chocó. On occasion, night travel on buses from Medellín east into Santander (through the Magdalena Medio region) can be suspended due to activities by one or another of the armed groups rife in Colombia. Updated: Dec 04 ,2007.

Things to See and Do

The Tierra Paisa could stand as a tourist destination in its own right. It has everything from captivating colonial villages to pre-Columbian historical sites, beaches in the north around Apartadó and Turbo, and jungles in the west as you reach the Chocó. All of these are complemented by nearby destinations offering something completely different. Head in one direction and you are in the heart of the coffee producing region near Pereira. Head in another and you could reach the Nevado del Ruiz near Manizales, ideal for climbing and trekking. Conveniently, adventure seekers can also temper physical exertion with cultural activities and nights out in Medellín. Updated: Dec 04, 2007.

Tierra Paisa Tours

There is no doubt that the capital is also the seat of business, so many tour companies can be found in Medellín that offer routes through the region. The Corporación Turístico del Suroeste Antioqueño (Carrera 65, 8B-91 / Oficina 248 C.C Terminal del Sur, Tel: 4-361-2022, E-mail: ctdelsuroeste@yahoo.com) is a good place to start, as they offer rafting trips, coffee tours through Jardín, tours into the Eje Cafetero, trips to Jericó, horseback excursions through the southwest and other options. Updated: Dec 04, 2007.

Lodging

Given that the paisas are expert businesspeople, it should come as no surprise that there are many accommodation options for every budget in Tierra Paisa. In Medellín you can find Colombia's finest hotels, the ubiquitous backpacker digs—complete with travelers chilling in hammocks and gearing up for another night out—and everything in between.

Often, if you are organizing trips through a company in Medellín or another city, it will have its own choice of accommodation on offer. The quality can vary massively, but for the most part these lodgings should be decent.

Out and about in the region there are many family-run guesthouses that specialize in home cooking and first rate service, but they may require some warning that you're planning to stop in. Updated: Dec 04, 2007.

Medellín

Alt: 1,495m Pop: 2,750,000 City Code:5

Medellín, the second largest city in Colombia, is continually transforming itself into a place where people come to visit and end up staying far longer than they ever intended. Rely on the highly accessible and excellent metro to shuttle you from the sights of downtown's sculpture-filled Parque Berrío to the exclusive bars, restaurants and hotels of El Poblado. There is also the cable car, which takes you high over the less affluent *barrios* in Medellín, offering a bird's eye view of the expanse of the city. If nightlife isn't your thing—although Medellín and the beguiling nature of the paisas may convert you—then there are frequent free concerts in the Teatro Metropolitano and a lively arts scene to quench any cultural thirst. If you can arrive for July and August be certain to catch the flower festival, then stroll to the Parque de los Pies Descalzos to marvel at the dazzling modern architecture. Updated: Jan 03, 2008.

Highlights

One of the seven Cerros Tutelares, **Cerro Nutibara (p.152)** is arguably the most interesting for visitors. The oversized mount houses the allegory to the areas of the region, Pueblito Paisa, the 3,800-capacity outdoor theater "Carlos Vieco" and the park of sculptures, a permanent exhibition of the work of 11 renowned artists from Colombia and around the world.

A **walking tour (p.152)** of the city is the best way to appreciate the art of Medellín. Downtown has the biggest concentration of sculptures, along with Poblado avenue and the park of sculptures.

Santa Fe de Antioquia (p.153) is a town that is a national monument, with quaint cobbled streets and historical churches.
Updated: Nov 23, 2007.

History

Lying deep in the Valle de Aburrá, Medellín was founded in 1616 by Spanish explorer and conquistador Francisco Herrera y Campuzano. The city's name was changed from the original San Lorenzo de Aburrá to Villa de Nuestra Señora de la Candelaria de Medellín in 1675 and was subsequently granted city status in 1813.

Populated for the most part by Spanish settlers from the province of Extremadura, known for their work ethic and hardy lifestyles, Medellín, over the years, became a major center for commerce and industry, particularly in textiles, making the city one of the fashion centers of South America.

In spite of Medellín's best efforts to alter its image, it has been a city tainted by death. One of the most infamous incidents was the murder of the Colombian soccer player Andrés Escobar in 1994. Escobar was gunned down in front of a nightclub for failing to save the goal that resulted in the national team's elimination from the World Cup.

In a history that remains, unfortunately, too well known throughout the world, Medellín gained a justifiably terrible reputation in the 1980s and 1990s as the world capital of murder, kidnapping and crime. Pablo Escobar's cartel and its rivals were responsible for countless deaths, making the city one of the most dangerous on earth.

In December 1993, this godfather of the international cocaine trade was hunted down and shot in his hometown of Medellín. In the years since, violence in the city has decreased considerably. Updated: Jan 03, 2008.

When to Go

Known as "the city of eternal spring," Medellín maintains a warm temperature between 27 and 28°C (81 - 82°F) throughout the year. A constant, refreshing breeze runs through the city, but every once in a while (usually in the second half of the calendar year) a rainy season reduces overall temperatures. The lowest temperature in Medellín oscillates around 16°C (61°F).

Holidays and Fiestas

June–Festival Internacional de Poesía.

July / August–Feria de las Flores.

August–Feria Nacional de las Artesanías, Colombiamoda.

September–Medellín Medio Maratón.
Updated: Nov 23, 2007.

Photo by Carolina Fonseca

Getting To and Away From Medellín

Air

Medellín has two airports: Aeropuerto Olaya Herrera (Carrera 65, 13-157. Tel: 4-285-9999) is located downtown and is the older of the two. This airport is equipped to receive only small aircraft and therefore is limited to internal flights. Flights to Chocó are available from here.

Aeropuerto Jose Maria Cordova (Tel: 574-562-2828) located outside Medellín in the neighboring municipality of Río Negro is larger and therefore the international hub. Getting here from downtown takes 30 minutes or more.

Bus

Medellín also has two bus terminals, the Terminal de Transportes Norte Mariano Ospina Pérez and the Terminal de Transportes Sur. As you would imagine, the north terminal is located in the north of the city, connected to the Caribe metro station, and the south terminal is close to the Olaya Herrera Airport.

Terminal de Transportes Norte: Buses to and from Bogotá and the North Coast and surrounding towns.

Gómez Hernández and **Sotrauraba** work on alternate days, running buses every hour to Santa Fe de Antioquia for $4-4.50. Trips last 1.5 hours.

Coonorte runs buses to Puerto Berrío at 4.15 p.m. and 11.30 p.m. for $10.50.

Cootransmagdalena does the same route –and with connections to El Banco and Magangue (if going to Mompós) leaving at noon for $10.

Rapido Tolima–12 daily buses to Bogotá for $20, 8-9 hours.

Expreso Arauca–Nine daily buses to Bogotá for $25.

Fronteras–To Cartagena at 9:15 p.m., 12 hours, $48.

Brasilia–Six daily to Cartagena for $45 and two daily to Bogotá leaving at 8:45 p.m. and 10 p.m. for $25. Updated: Nov 23, 2007.

Getting Around

The city of Medellín may still be paying for the metro system built in 1995, but it is dazzlingly new, easy to use and gets you just about everywhere. For a $0.70 fare you are able to reach 25 stations on lines A and B and the connecting lines to the cable car, which run from Acevedo Station to the Barrio Santo Domingo Savio.

Buses are frequent and have their destinations plastered on the front windscreen. Taxis are inexpensive and efficient. Updated: Nov 25, 2007.

Safety in Medellín

Modern-day Medellín may lull the traveler into a false sense of security, but every big city has its problems. Gone are the dark days of Escobarian terror, but drug trafficking is still an issue, and visitors should be wary in the evening, especially downtown. Security is tight in El Poblado where most hostels and hotels are located. Updated: Nov 25, 2007.

Medellín Services

Tourism Office

There is an extremely helpful, well-informed tourist information booth in the Parque Berrío near to the station. Otherwise, information booths are located in both airports and both bus terminals.

Money

Every bank and ATM can be found in El Poblado, particularly in the big shopping centers.

Keeping in Touch

Locating telephone exchanges and internet cafés is not a problem in any sector of Medellín.

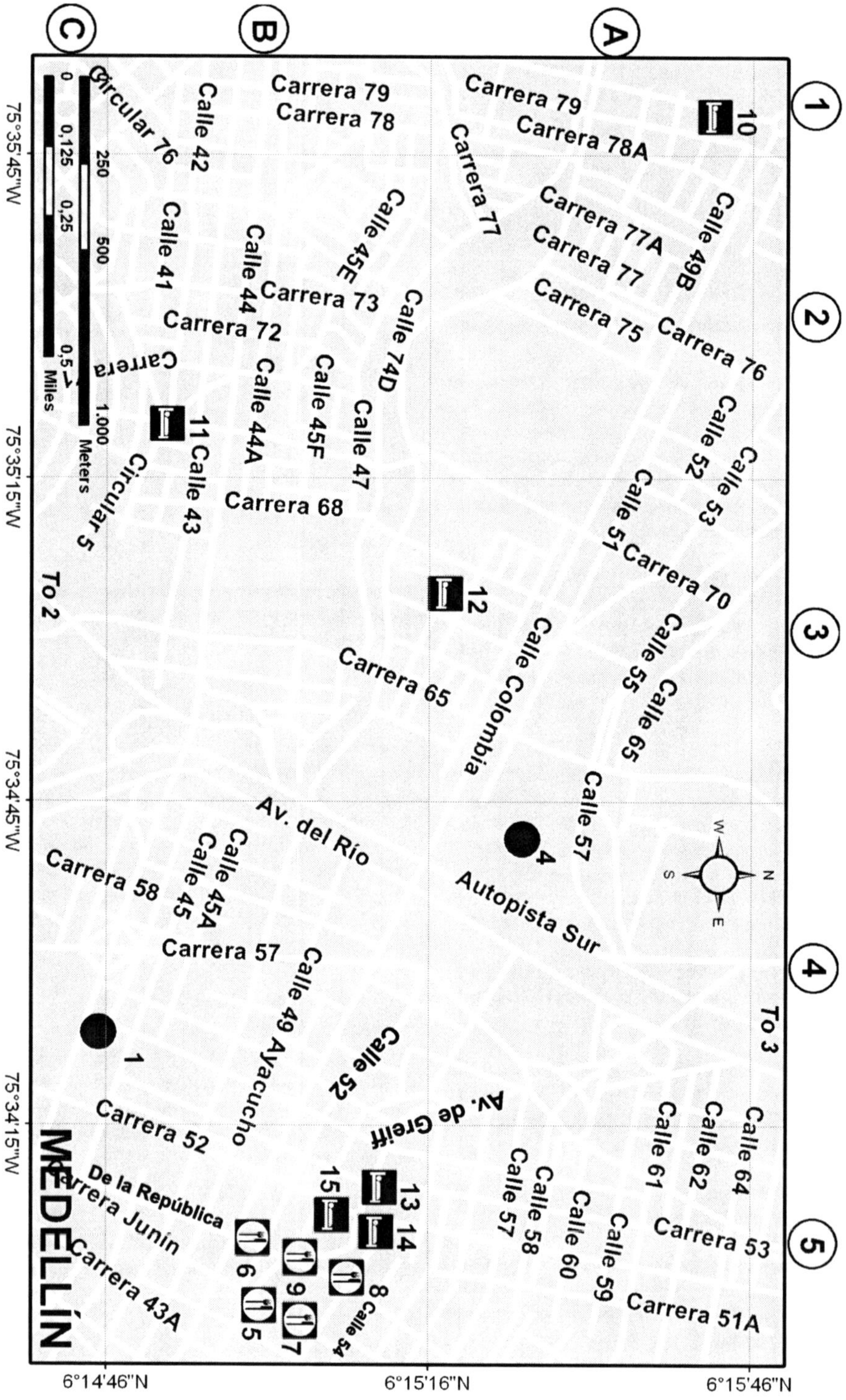
MEDELLÍN
A
B
C
1
2
3
4
5
Carrera 79
Carrera 78
Carrera 78A
Carrera 77
Carrera 77A
Carrera 76
Carrera 75
Carrera 73
Carrera 72
Carrera 70
Carrera 68
Carrera 65
Carrera 58
Carrera 57
Carrera 53
Carrera 52
Carrera 51A
Carrera 43A
Carrera Junín
Carrera
Circular 76
Circular 5
Calle 42
Calle 41
Calle 43
Calle 44
Calle 44A
Calle 45
Calle 45A
Calle 45E
Calle 45F
Calle 47
Calle 49 Ayacucho
Calle 49B
Calle 51
Calle 52
Calle 53
Calle 54
Calle 55
Calle 57
Calle 58
Calle 59
Calle 60
Calle 61
Calle 62
Calle 64
Calle 65
Calle 74D
Calle Colombia
Av. del Río
Av. de Greiff
Autopista Sur
De la República
To 2
To 3
0 250 500 1.000 Meters
0 0,125 0,25 0,5 Miles
N S E W
75°35'45"W
75°35'15"W
75°34'45"W
75°34'15"W
6°14'46"N
6°15'16"N
6°15'46"N

Activities
1 Feria de las Flores D5
2 International Poetry Festival E3
3 Jardín Botánico B6
4 Museo de Arte Moderno C5

Eating
5 Agua Clara D6
6 El Rincón Antioqueño D6
7 Hacienda Real D6
8 Las Cazuelas D6
9 Lating Coffee D6

Sleeping
10 Casa del Sol C2
11 Hotel Eupacla D3
12 Hotel Los Almendros C4
13 Hotel Nutibara D6
14 La Bella Villa D6
15 Palm Tree D6

Medical

Hospital General de Medellín–Carrera 48, 32-102. Tel: 4-384-7300.

Clinica El Rosario–Carrera 20, 2 Sur-185. Tel: 4-326-9216.

Laundry

Most, if not all, hotels and hostels have a laundry service.

Camera

Camera repair shops are located in the Centro.

Shopping

Medellín, perhaps more than any other major Colombian cities, is a veritable treasure-trove for shopaholics. Because it's a hub of the textile and fashion industry, major-name brands are available here at bargain prices. Vast shopping malls now take up areas of hillside and have rapidly become major meeting points for people of all ages.

Centro Comercial San Diego–Calle 34, 43-66. Tel: 4-232-0624.

Parque Comercial El Tesoro–Loma del Tesoro with Transversal superior. Tel: 4-321-1010.

Cuidadela Comercial Unicentro–Carrera 66B, 34ª-76. Tel: 4-265-1116.

Centro Comercial Oviedo–Calle Sur, 43ª-127. Tel: 4-321-6116.

Centro Comercial Mayorca–Calle 51 Sur, 48-57. Tel: 4-373-0335. Updated: Nov 25, 2007.

Things to See And Do

Medellín has a wealth of diversions to offer the visitor, from the luxury nightspots of Parque Lleras to curious activities such as riding the cable car over the city's shanty towns. Popular tourist attractions include the Cerro Nutibara with the Pueblito Paisa and the botanical gardens.

Medellín's thriving arts scene alone makes it a place worth exploring. The city has an excellent selection of museums, and you can frequently find a free concert in one the city's theaters, or just catch an improvised performance in the streets near El Poblado.

If you are interested in further activities, then Medellín is a fantastic destination for adventure sports. Just on the city limits one can locate opportunities for rock climbing, parapenting, trekking and rafting. Updated: Nov 25, 2007.

Pablo Escobar

It may seem a particularly macabre or even an inappropriate activity, but some choose to make the pilgrimage of sorts out to the cementery of Jardines de Montesacro.

Pablo Escobar's name is not going to go away. His notoriety sells books and magazines and inspires Hollywood. In short, fame is a curious thing, and for this reason travelers make the trip out past the final metro stop to pay their respects to the former head of the Medellín Cartel.

In the space of 20 minutes, you can chat with many well-wishers from the poorer barrios of Medellín who continue to see Pablo Escobar as the "papa de los pobres," or father of the poor. Talking to these people is in itself a revealing experience.

To get to Cementerio Jardines de Montesacro take the metro to Itagüí, alight, and continue walking for 15-20 minutes as if you were heading out of town—the cementary will appear on the right. If you don't fancy the walk, either take a cab or catch a bus along the roadside.

If you visit the cementary, remain respectful. Remember, Pablo Escobar still means a great deal to a great many people here. Updated: Dec 19, 2007.

Jardín Botánico de Medellín

Considered the lungs of Medellín, the Jardín Botánico Joaquín Antonio Uribe is a delightful leafy and tranquil destination within the confines of the bustling city.

The verdant wealth contained within the garden's 14 hectares ranges from a spectacular orchid collection (the country's national flower) to flora found all throughout Colombia. Aside from being a pleasant place to escape from the rigors of city life, there is an emphasis here on ecology, education and entertainment. Schools frequently visit the garden to learn the importance of environmental preservation, and researchers regularly visit the garden's library. Concerts are often performed in the garden as well, so be sure to check listings.

To get here, catch the metro to the Universidad station and follow the signs. Cra 52, 73-298. Tel: 4-444-5500, Fax: 4-571-8967. E-mail: comunicaciones@jbotanicomedellin.org, URL: www.jbmed.org. Updated: Dec 19, 2007.

Walking Tour

In a day the visitor can cover most of what the old center of Medellín has to offer by foot—and there is no better nor more relaxing way to see this part of town.

Start the day at the Basílica Metropolitana de Medellín located at the far end of the Carrera Junín. Enjoy a *tinto* coffee in the park while admiring this immense brick structure.

From here you can then walk along the Carrera Junín, browsing the shops and businesses in the downtown sector. As you reach the end, cross over the road and make your way to the Basilica de Nuestra Señora de La Candelaría. A colonial-style building, it stands at odds with its environment of 1970s high-rise office blocks.

Just a few blocks from here on the other side of the metro station you can find the attractions of Parque Berrío with its museums and Botero sculptures. The Museo de Antioquia is the large building towards the back of the square and holds a permanent collection of 119 pieces donated by Fernando Botero himself. Pose for photos in front of the grotesque, reclining lady before moving south a few more blocks.

The Parque San Antonio really isn't a park at all. It more resembles an enormous parking lot in front of a shopping mall. But, of interest to the visitor are the two Botero sculptures here. The original bird of peace sculpture was placed here by Botero and was subsequently blown up by a suspected FARC bomb, tragically killing a dozen or so passersby. Instead of replacing or moving the mangled sculpture, in brave defiance Botero created an identical sculpture to the original and placed it alongside its disfigured predecessor.

Move down from the Parque San Antonio to the Estación Central where historically all rail travel passed into Medellín. Now a visitor center, you can relax at the Estación with a cold juice or another coffee before moving through the large buildings that make up the town hall of Medellín and finally passing by the Plaza de Cisneros in front of the city library.

From here you will be able to see the Edificio Inteligente—literally the intelligent building—which was built with environmental concerns in mind. Before reaching this building, pass through the Parque de los Pies Descalzos (park of the bare feet) where kids like to come to play in the cool fountain jets after visiting the nearby children's museum.

The only notable geographic feature in this part of the Aburra Valley, the Cerro Nutibara, should now be easily visible. From this 80-meter high hill you can gain a nice view of the downtown area and Pueblito Paisa, constructed here to show what a typical antioquian village should resemble. To get to Cerro Nutibara, first catch the metro to Parque Berrío, then do the rest on foot or by taxi. Don't forget to bring your camera and some cash. Centro, Medellín. Dec 19, 2007.

International Poetry Festival

From its inception in 1991 amidst a backdrop of extreme violence, the Medellín international poetry festival has grown from a small event to a national phenomenon. In 2007 it celebrated its 17th anniversary with poets from all over the world participating in readings at Medellín's theaters and parks. The Festival takes place every July and is well worth checking out. Especially worthwhile is the opening ceremony, held every year in the theater on the Cerro Nutibara. Transversal 39A, 72-52. Tel: 4-541-2944, Fax: 4-412-8822, E-mail: festivalpoesiamedellin@yahoo.es, URL: www.festivaldepoesiademedellin.org. Updated: Dec 19, 2007.

Santa Fe de Antioquia

When the city planners of Medellín came up with the idea of creating a Pueblito Paisa replica—a typical antioquian village—on the Nutibara hill, Santa Fe de Antioquia was what they had in mind.

A bus journey of 1.5 - 2 hours from Medellín's Terminal del Norte bus station takes you out of the Aburra valley and into the heartland of the region. At the station, head to either Gomez Hernandez or Sotrauraba companies, which run to Santa Fe about once an hour on alternating days (van $4.50, bus $4).

Also known as "Ciudad Madre," the town is a national monument recognized for its antiquated but well-maintained cobbled streets, white-washed walls, historical churches and breezy plazas.

The first Spanish settlement in the area was founded in 1541 by Mariscal Jorge Robledo and was an agricultural and mining village.

Aside from wandering the streets, you can visit the Museo de Arte Religioso, Museo Juan del Corral and the Casa del Niño Tomás. Some six kilometers away there is the famous Puente de Occidente, or east bridge, measuring 291 meters in length, which was constructed in 1895. E-mail: turismo@antioquia.gov.co, URL: www.antioquia.gov.co. Updated: Dec 19, 2007.

Museo de Arte Moderno

The pride and joy of Medellín artists is the Museo de Arte Moderno (MAMM). And so it should be: by placing an emphasis on homegrown Colombian talent, it effectively displays the high quality of art this nation produces. Exhibiting in the realm of 1,400 pieces of art, including works by recognized Colombian artists such as painter Debora Arango and sculptor Hernando Tejada, the MAMM is well worth a peek. Spend a morning or afternoon exploring the museum and the surrounding Suramericana district. If this leaves you hungry for more art, then stroll your way through the ever-changing exhibits of photos, videos, design, architecture and recordings. To get to the museum catch the metro to the Suramericana station, and from there walk along Carrera 65 before turning right on the major road and walking a few blocks down. Cra 64B, 51-64 Barrio Carlos E. Restrepo. Tel: 4-230-2622, Fax: 4-230-2723, E-mail: museodearte@une.net.co, URL: www.mammedellin.org. Updated: Dec 19, 2007.

Marinilla, El Peñol, Guatapé

Marinilla, El Peñol and Guatapé are small municipalities roughly 50 kilometers from Medellín, making them easily reachable from the Terminal del Norte.

Marinilla is of great importance in the region of Antioquia as a site of historical and artistic interest. Founded in 1690, it bears all the hallmarks of a religiously motivated town with ornate and austere churches open for visits. It is said that despite the introduction of black slaves into the community and the existence of indigenous peoples, the colonial settlers never intermarried, and, to this day, their descendants are still fair-haired.

El Peñol was founded in 1714, and in contemporary times has risen to prominence as a tourist haven. When a damn was built nearby, a massive artificial lake was formed, making this a great place to practice water sports.

Guatapé, which neighbors El Peñol, is also a major destination for people from Medellín looking to enjoy the lake. Visitors to the area can join the fray, participating in everything from eco-tourism, exploring the religious sites, boarding or trekking. From the northern bus terminal in Medellín buses leave every 15 minutes and take anything from 30 minutes to an hour to arrive. Oriente Antioqueño. Updated: May 19, 2008.

The Medellín Cable Car

It is hard to imagine a more delightful and relaxing way to make your daily commute to work than drifting over the rooftops in a cable car. But this mode of transport was not developed to help businessmen unwind —building a metro to run up the valley wall into the poorer barrios of the city was a lo-

gistical impossibility. So, the powers that be in Medellín came up with a novel idea—they built a cable car that connects these districts with the main metro line at Acevedo station. From Acevedo the cable car runs through two stations, Andalusia and Popular, before reaching the end of the line at Santo Domingo Savio and then commencing the return journey. The trip over the less affluent barrios of Medellín is a great introduction to the troubles that still haunt the city. Hop on or off, and you will find a willing local ready to chat, share some wisdom, and point out the sights of the city from up high. Take a camera and snap some shots of the city from Santo Domingo Savio. Acevedo station. Updated: Dec 19, 2007.

Feria de las Flores

It is no secret that 80 percent of all cut flowers grown in Colombia are sold to the United States, and the Feria de las Flores shows why. Recognized as the most important and traditional feria in Medellín, this festival brings the city to a halt in a sweet-scented, brightly colored gridlock for a week in August. Parades of garlands float through the city streets, but it is the Silleteros parade (2007 marked the 50th year of this competition) that defines the whole week, when elaborate tableaus of flowers are paraded and judged. Also to be enjoyed are the classic car, mule and orchid parades. Alcaldia de Medellín, Calle 44, 52-165. Piso 7. Tel: 4-385-5097, E-mail: feriadeflores@medellin.gov.co, URL: www.feriadelasfloresmedellin.gov.co. Updated: Dec 19, 2007.

Studying Spanish in Medellín

Due to its favorable climate, cultural activities and unstoppable nightlife, Medellín is fast becoming a firm favorite for those wishing to study Spanish. Several good language schools have been established here and are making a name for themselves.

Nueva Lengua Escuela de Español
E-mail: contactenos@nuevalengua.com, URL: www.nuevalengua.com/spanish/medellin.htm.

Medellín Spanish School
Connected to the Black Sheep Hostal. E-mail: info@blacksheepmedellin.com, URL: www.spanishinmedellin.com.

EAFIT University
E-mail: abotero@eafit.edu.co, URL: www.eafit.edu.co/EafitCn/Idiomas/spanishprogram/Index.htm. Updated: Mar 14, 2008.

Medellín Tours

A few years ago Medellín had still to realize its tourism potential, but these days there are tour operators in existence—though not as many as you would imagine given all that Medellín has to offer.

Expediciones Makondo Expeditions

Expediciones Makondo Expeditions (EME) offers a wide variety of tours and activities including: eco-tours, horseback riding, city tours, night tours, archaeological ruins, climbing, rafting, hiking, birdwatching, trekking, water sports, whale watching, wildlife tours and coffee landscape tours. Spanish, English, Danish, German, French, Italian and Quechua are spoken. Calle 9, 39-09, Parque Lleras. Cell: 310-373-1176, Fax: 4-266-7790, E-mail: amigosdelparque@gmail.com, URL: www.expedicionesmakondoexpeditions.com. Updated: Apr 14, 2008.

Medellín Experience

The Medellín Experience caters to small groups and arranges tailor-made travel plans. They will give you personal attention and advice as well as a free quote. They offer horseback riding trips, parascending, rafting, treks, coffee tours, city tours and advice on hotels and other trips in the region. Cel: 312-220-2047, E-mail: andrespuldain@hotmail.com, URL: www.medellinexperience.com. Updated: Nov 25, 2007.

Turibus

Turibus runs city tours all day from 9 a.m. until 5 p.m. They hit the major city sights such as Parque el Poblado, Plaza Botero and the Parque de los Pies Descalzados, making Turibus a good solution for those who do no have a lot of time. The company also offers party buses for night tours, and once booked on the tour you will gain discounts to various restaurants and bars. URL: www.seditrans.com. Updated: Nov 25, 2007.

Turixmo Receptivo Medellín

Offering a metro tour of the city, a regular city tour, a shopping tour, a *chiva* party tour, tours to the east of Antioquia and tours to the west of Antioquia, Turixmo is perhaps the most comprehensive tour agency in Medellín. Tel: 4-266-2846, E-mail: turixmo@geo.net.co. Updated: Nov 25, 2007.

Medellín Lodging

As a tourist and business destination Medellín has a great variety of accommodation options. There are cheap backpacker digs in desirable areas with a good nightlife scene—fine places to go back to and recover from a night of serious partying. Business options abound in El Poblado and the barrio of Laureles, making the decision of where to stay a difficult one. Mid-range hotels can be found in converted townhouses should you wish to vary from the norm.

Budget

Casa del Sol

(BED: $8-12) Run by a Colombian couple who, after traveling for a number of years, decided to settle down and open up a hostel of their own in their hometown of Medellín. The Casa del Sol has a couple of mixed dormitories and a few private rooms. Breakfast is included and the owners offer lunch and dinner at reasonable prices. As with most hostels there is internet access, a large communal TV room and well-maintained communal areas. Catch the metro to the Floresta station and walk towards the Parque de los Enamorados before heading down Calle 81 for a couple of blocks. Calle 49, 81A-24, Calasanz. Tel: 4-422-0531, URL: www.hostalcasadelsol.com. Updated: Dec 19, 2007.

Palm Tree

(BED: $8.50-16) Perhaps the grandame of Medellín hostels, the Palm Tree has maintained a steady record over the years as a popular backpacker haunt. This townhouse sits in a residential barrio close to cheap restaurants and next door to a massive supermarket stocked with everything. Good dorms, free internet, communal kitchen, hammocks, BBQ, bar area—what more could you ask for. Catch a metro to the Suramericana station and head towards the large Exito supermarket. The Palm Tree is located behind this and is visible due to a great deal of flags outside. Cra 67, 48D-63. Tel: 4-260-2805, URL: www.palmtreemedellin.com. Updated: Dec 19, 2007.

The Black Sheep Hostal

(BED: $8.50-17) The Black Sheep hostel is an excellent place, delivering on every front. Thirty-four beds, double rooms, dorms, hammocks, computers with Skype, mega—Argentine BBQ, Spanish courses, hot water and a laundry service. Kelvin, the owner, is also a great resource who can inform you on all things Colombian. Be sure to book in advance if you're arriving on a Thursday or Friday, as the place tends to fill up for the weekend and empty out on Monday. If you are coming in a taxi, tell the driver to head to the Patio Bonito area of El Poblado. Otherwise, catch the metro to Poblado station, walk out to the right, and at the major crossings, head as if to the Exito supermarket, then right. Transversal 5a, 45-133. Tel: 4-311-1589, E-mail: kelvin@blacksheepmedellin.com, URL: www.blacksheepmedellin.com. Updated: Dec 19, 2007.

Hostal Tamarindo

(BED: $8.50-20) With a maximum capacity of 16 people, the Hostal Tamarindo is one of the smaller choices for accommodation in El Poblado. There are two cleanly kept and well-maintained mixed dormitories of six and eight beds respectively, as well as one double room. The Tamarindo comes with a communal TV room, book exchange and a small terrace. Take the metro to the Pobaldo station and hike up the hill for about 20 minutes and you'll find the hostel with ease. Calle 7, 35-36. Tel: 4-268-9828, E-mail: hostaltamarindo@gmail.com. Updated: Dec 19, 2007.

Casa Kiwi

(BED: $8.50-50) The Casa Kiwi is becoming a real institution in Medellín, especially when you only have to walk five blocks (downhill) to get to the buzzing nightlife of Parque Lleras. The hostel has dorm rooms, luxury dorm rooms, private rooms, and it recently added a new wing. In addition to a big screen TV, the communal area is equipped with sofas, hammocks and a pool table. Just a few blocks from Parque Lleras the hostel is easy to find—if coming by metro, get off at Poblado, walk up the hill for 10-15 minutes and then hang a right past the pizza place. Cra 36, 7-10. Tel: 4-268-2668, E-mail: casakiwi@gmail.com, URL: www.casakiwihostel.com. Updated: Dec 19, 2007.

Mid-Range

La Bella Villa

(BED: $14-20) In the same mold as the Hotel Eupacla, the Bella Villa has seen more prosperous days. The hotel has been a bit neglected of late, with travelers now leaning toward the more desirable areas of El Poblado and Laureles. The inside of the hotel can make you feel a bit claustrophobic—low ceilings and heavy drapery do not help. If every other hotel in Medellín is occupied and the Bella Villa meets your budgetary requirements, then this place is suitable. Calle 53, 50-28. Tel: 4-511-4915, Fax: 4-512-9477, E-mail: bellavillahotel@hotmail.com. Updated: Dec 19, 2007.

Provenza Hostal

(BED: $15-45) Open for scarcely two years, this well-maintained hostel still has a new feel about it. The management's major desire is to take good care of their patrons, and so the rooms (private and dorms) are spotless, the communal areas are well-kept, and, in short, the place is spic and span. From Poblado metro station you will need to walk up the hill for 20 minutes past Parque el Poblado and Parque Lleras, then hang a right on Carerra 35. Cra 35, 7-2. Tel: 4-326-5600, E-mail: provenzahostal@gmail.com, URL:www.provenzahostal.com. Updated: Dec 19, 2007.

Hotel Eupacla

(ROOM: $26-75) If you're really keen on being in the Centro rather than Laureles or El Pobaldo, then this is a reasonable option. The hotel has dated furnishing and an overall worn and used feel to it, but if you need to be downtown for business or by preference, then so be it. With over 60 rooms, the only time this hotel is likely to be filled to capacity is when there is a massive conference in town. Get off the metro at Parque Berrío and walk beyond and behind the Hotel Nutibara and you will find the Eupacla easily. Cra 50, 53-16. Tel: 4-231-1765, Fax: 4-251-6969, E-mail: hoteleuplacla@eupacla.lalianxa.net. Updated: Dec 19, 2007.

Hotel Los Almendros

(ROOM: $30-35) A new family-run venture in the executive district of Laureles, Hotel Los Almendros has 25 comfortably furnished rooms for those not wishing to spend a fortune in the area. Breakfast comes included, and the staff endeavors to make your stay enjoyable. Internet access has not yet been installed in the rooms, but as of November 2007 the management was working on it. Your best bet is to hail a taxi, as the roads in Laureles can be misleading. Calle 41A, 70-78. Tel: 4-412-9002. Updated: Nov 22, 2007.

Alcazar de Patio Bonito

(ROOM: $40-75) A family-run bed and breakfast with few rooms but plenty of charm. Ideally located close to the Poblado metro station, the Exito supermarket, the Oviedo shopping center and the active nightlife of Parque Lleras. The rooms may need a little modernizing, but they are clean, and each has its own private bathroom, cable TV, refrigerator and constant hot water. From the Poblado metro station ask directions from the Exito parking lot. You are within three blocks. Cra 45, 6-68. Tel: 4- 266-2583, E-mail: carmensofic_16@hotmail.com, URL: www.hotelalcazardepatiobonito.com. Updated: Dec 19,2007.

Apartments-Medellín

(ROOM: $40-100) A good alternative to some of the more expensive hotels in Medellín. Rent apartments on a daily, weekly or monthly basis. Calle 5 Sur, 37 - 128. Torre Granada, Apt 802, Poblado, Medellín. E-mail: info@apartments-medellin.com, URL: http://www.apartments-medellin.com.

Hotel Nutibara

(ROOM: $48-65) Opened in 1945, this behemoth of a hotel in the downtown area was built at a time when the Centro was the height of fashion and security. Things have changed somewhat, but the Nutibara still maintains high standards. With 137 rooms it is the largest hotel of its type in this part of Medellín. Each conventionally furnished room comes with cable TV, mini-bar, private bathroom and A/C. It is not a bad choice if you've got the cash and need to be in this part of town. Prices include tax. You can get to Nutibara easily by taxi, but another option is to catch the metro to the Parque Berrío and walk the two blocks from there. Calle 52A, 50-46. Tel: 4-511-5111, Fax: 4-512-4693, E-mail: info@hotelnutibara.com, URL: www.hotelnutibara.com. Updated: Dec 19 ,2007.

Palma 70

(ROOM $52-65) The Palma 70 is one of the many hotels looking to cash in on the relatively new conference center in Medellín, and by all accounts it appears to be doing a good job. Rooms are standard fare with the traditional hotel furnishing and are kept clean and in good condition. Prices are negotiable if paying in cash. Take a taxi into the Laureles district. Circular 5, 70-37. Tel: 4-409-1020, Fax: 4-412-5751, E-mail: hotelpalma70@gmail.com. Updated: Dec 19, 2007.

High-End

Hotel Cabo de la Vela

(ROOM: $62-70) Another hotel in Laureles aimed at the executive market, Hotel Cabo de la Vela is clean, modern and well-located on a tree-lined residential street. In addition to rooms fully equipped with all the conveniences you would expect, the hotel offers a large conference room, a restaurant and a staff knowledgeable in all facets of life in Medellín. To get here on the metro alight at Estadio Station and walk down Carrera 70 until you meet Circular 4. Otherwise catch a taxi from the station so as not to get lost. Circular 4, 70-72. Tel: 4-413-8400, Fax: 4-413-8410, E-mail: cabo@epm.net.co, URL: hotelcabodelavela.com. Updated: Dec 19, 2007.

Hotel Laureles 70

(ROOM:$65-85) In an area flooded with hotels for the "executive," this is another choice that is comfortable, newly decorated and equipped with helpful staff. With 38 rooms ranging from a junior suite to single and double options, the Laureles 70 is a fine option for a short stay. A taxi will get you here no problems. Circular 5, 70-15. Tel: 4-411-2828, Fax: 4-411-7268, E-mail: la70@une.net.co, URL: www.hotellaureles70.com. Updated: Dec 19, 2007.

Mediterraneo Hotel

(ROOM: $70-85) Modern and sleek, this hotel is banking on its Swiss modern style to attract clientele. The 32-room novelty offers everything that the executive might need. From WiFi, sauna, gym, breakfast and parking, the owners place a premium on service. Discounts are offered should you stay for more than two days. The same goes if you decide to pay in cash. A taxi is the most convenient way to reach this hotel. Cra 10, C5-23. Tel: 4-410-2510, Fax: 4-250-5059, E-mail: info@mediterraneoMedellín.com, URL: www.mediterraneoMedellín.com. Updated: Dec 19, 2007.

Hotel Pobaldo Plaza

(ROOM: $124-162) Right next door to the Oviedo mall, the Hotel Estelar Poblado Plaza is a luxury hotel for those with no limit on their budget. Its 84 rooms range from suites with two private bathrooms to superior rooms with twin beds. In truth, if you were to stay here you could be forgiven if you forgot which country you were in. In addition to WiFi access in the rooms, there are free computers on every floor for those who failed to bring their laptop with them. Should you book to stay on a weekend, when it's quieter, the prices drop to $80 per person. Cra 43A, 4 Sur 75. Tel: 4-268-5555, Fax: 4-268-6949, E-mail: info@hotelpobladoplaza.com, URL: www.hotelpobladoplaza.com. Updated: Dec 19, 2007.

Medellín Restaurants

There are world-class eateries in Medellín ranging from locales that can offer the finest and freshest seafood, flown in that day from the Pacific, to vast cavernous steakhouses and specialist sushi restaurants. For those on a budget a short foray into the areas around Parque el Poblado will reveal various locations that can provide set lunchtime meals for around the $2 mark. The same goes for restaurants in the Centro. Updated: Nov 28, 2007.

Budget

Donde Paco

For people staying at the Casa Kiwi or the Provenza Hostal, Donde Paco will be very familiar. As a reasonably cheap and very cheerful restaurant located close to these hostels, it is always popular. Servings are a good size, the food is tasty, and for those suffering from the effects of the night before it is only a short walk to get here. Cra 35N, 8A-80. Tel: 4-311-9097, E-mail: dondepaco@hotmail.com. Updated: Dec 19, 2007.

MID-RANGE

Amazonia

Amazonia sits pretty in the hot nightlife area of Parque Lleras, the heart of Medellín's Zona Rosa. The restaurant offers exotic foods from lesser known regions of Colombia. While Amazonia claims to offer bites from the Amazon and beyond, if these are not to your liking there are many traditional dishes such as ajiaco and parrilla with which you can feed your inner monster. Cra 8a - 32 Parque Lleras. Tel: 4-266-6307. Updated: Dec 19, 2007.

Las Cazuelas

A decent and reasonably priced restaurant downtown where you can sample a whole load of culinary delights from the Antioquia region. If you are hankering for a paisa stew —beans, pork scratchings, salsa, avocado, rice, arepa and plantain—then for $3.50 this is the place for you. Cra 49, 52-107. Tel: 4-293-2180. Updated: Dec 19, 2007.

Latin Coffee

With set-lunch menus at $3.25 in a clean and calm area in the Centro, you won't do a great deal better than Latin Coffee if you're in this part of town. All lunches come with a soup, then either roast chicken or grilled beef with rice, salad, arepa and a juice to wash it down. Union Centro Comercial Local 217 Cra 52-107. Updated: Dec 19, 2007.

El Rincón Antioqueño

In the same food court as Latin Coffee and Las Cazuelas, El Rincón Antioqueño is another option set back from the bustle of the Carrera Junín and above the mayhem on the second floor. Offering standard fare from this area, you can sink your teeth into a set menu with beef for $4 or a breakfast for $2.40. Union Centro Comercial, Balcon de Comidas, Local 221, Cra 49, 52-107. Updated: Dec 19, 2007.

Hacienda Real

If your curiosity is piqued by talk of the famed dish from Antioquia—the bandeja paisa—this is one place you should check out in the historical district of the Centro. The Hacienda Real is located on the second floor conveniently above the noise and hurried existence of the street vendors on the Carrera Junín. The dish is well prepared and large, enough to keep you full for the rest of the day. Cra Junín, 52-98. Updated: Dec 19, 2007.

Agua Clara

This is another good option located above the Carrera Junín in the Centro. You can get a set menu lunch for $4, and that's never bad. The servings are generous, flavorsome and the locale is clean and welcoming. You know what you're getting here...beef or chicken accompanied by rice, beans and potatoes with some garnish. Cra Junín, 52-141. Updated: Dec 19, 2007.

BANDEJA PAISA

Perhaps the most terrifying dish available in Colombia comes from this region. Not terrifying in the nature of the food—not toasted ants, brains or the like—in truth it's similar to a full English breakfast, but it is eaten in the heat, and with every mouthful you can feel your arteries thickening.

A bandeja paisa consists of beans, ground beef, rice, chorizo, blood sausage, pork scratchings, avocado, arepa, plantain and topped off with an arepa and a fried egg on top.

If that doesn't make your heart skip a beat in fear then nothing will. And if you can finish this hearty platter you are doing better than most. With any luck the sugar and grease rush will make you feel superhuman and not on the verge of suffering a heart attack.

You can find this dish in any restaurant downtown. If you want to give it a try, make sure you don't eat breakfast beforehand—come to the table with an empty stomach.Updated: Dec 19, 2007.

HIGH-END

La Grappa

La Grappa, a chic offering in the continually buzzing Parque Lleras, specializes in mediterranean cooking, pastas and meats. Perhaps its setting attracts revelers more so than diners: tall glass windows and a deck on the second floor make this a very stylish place to drop some money on a cocktail before heading out for the evening. Calle 8a, 37A-01. Tel: 4-312-7266, URL: www.acomerafuera.com. Updated: Dec 19, 2007.

MEDELLÍN NIGHTLIFE

Medellín's nightlife centers around the bright lights of the bars and clubs in El Poblado. The place to go, without a doubt, is the Parque Lleras, and from there see where the crowd and your new-found friends will lead you. Certainly it will be an entertaining evening. You can find anything from clubs playing electronica to traditional salsa haunts. Choose something on a whim and you won't be disappointed.

Discoteca Mango's

Located on the road out of town, Mango's is immensely popular despite its wild west theme. The hordes come out to this institution week-in-week-out and dance the night away to the sounds spun by excellent DJs. Catch a cab out to Mango's with some friends and you probably won't regret it. Cra 42, 67A-151. Tel: 4-277-6123, URL: www.discotecamangos.com. Updated: Dec 19, 2007.

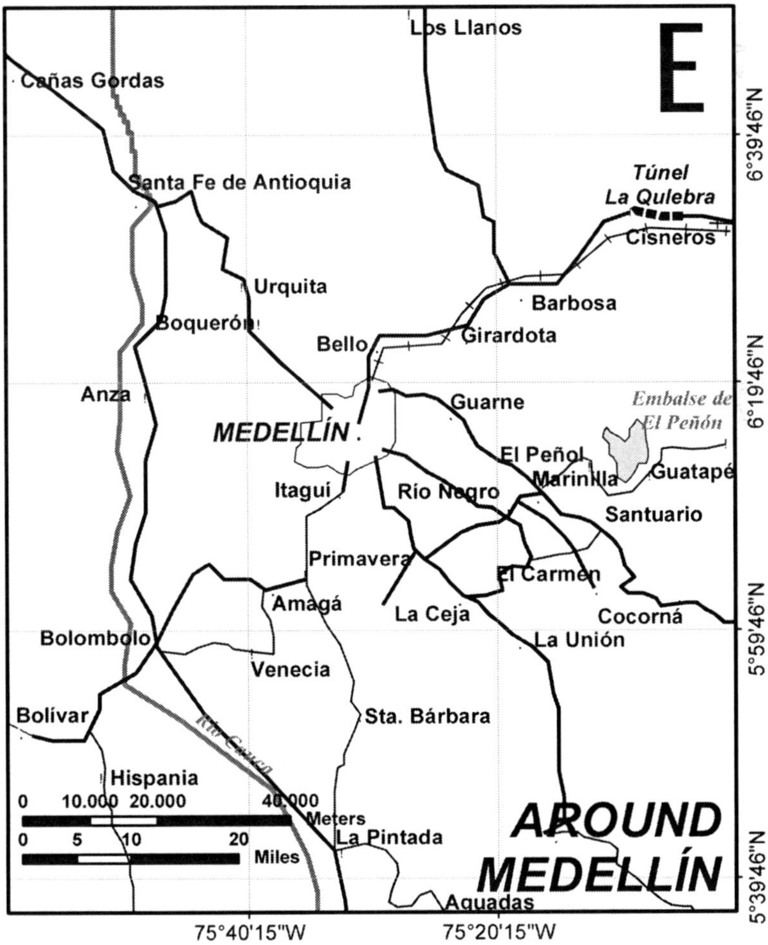

Berlin 1930

Berlin 1930 appears to have been around as long as Medellín itself. No one knows when it opened, but one thing remains a constant: its popularity. A great place for an early evening beer or cocktail and a game of pool, located very close to the clubs and other nightspots of the Parque Lleras. Calle 10, 41-65. Updated: Dec 19, 2007.

Blue

Recognised as being the place to go on a Thursday night, Blue is a Medellín institution, and very popular with backpackers. Electronica flows out of massive speakers as Paisas dance along. Capacity is often reached here, such is its reputation among the traveling crowd, so you might want to get in early. Cra 41 with Calle 10. Updated: Dec 19, 2007.

Rincón Chocoano

A small establishment located on the main road through El Poblado, Rincón Chocoano is easily missed—unless of course you were specifically looking for it. The restaurant may seem an odd choice, but in truth Chocoano food is very tasty, and those who frequent the bar know how to party. You'll make friends rapidly and will probably have to toast with a few shots of the lethal local firewater—platino. Calle 10 with Cra 38. Tel: 4-268-9205. Updated: Dec 19, 2007.

Oz

Becoming increasingly popular with travelers, Oz delivers loud music in a variety of rooms through enormous, booming speakers. Not only popular with visitors to the city, Oz is a firm favorite with many of the beautiful people of Medellín. Cra. 38, 8-8. Tel: 4-311-5781. Updated: Dec 19, 2007.

Sam Pues

If you are itching to dance, then Sam Pues may be the place for you. Tables and chairs lay scattered about as people, normally relatively dormant by nature, spring up and start to strut their stuff. Located close to Parque Lleras, Sam Pues has been around for some years and has solidly established itself on Medellín's nightlife map. Calle 10a, 40 -37. Tel: 4-266-9404. Updated: Dec 19, 2007.

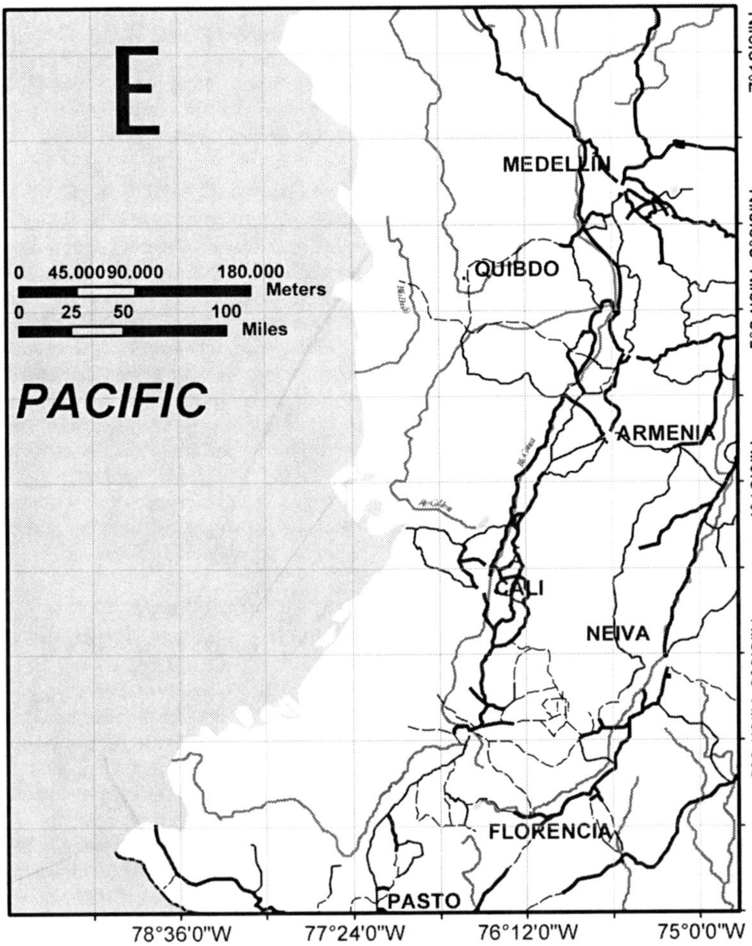

The Pacific Coast

The Colombian Pacific region remains a largely unvisited and unknown part of Colombia. Don't let this dissuade you from visiting the regions of Chocó, Valle del Cauca, Cauca and Nariño. The religious and colonial splendor of Popayán, the steamy nightlife of modern Cali and eco-tourism opportunities throughout the region ensure that travelers will have a wide variety of things to do in Western Colombia. The region itself is dominated by two rivers, the Atrato in the north and the San Juan in the south. It is roped off from the rest of the country by the Andes' spine in the east. In the far north, the Panamanian border is defined by the Darien Gap.

Although a small number of the roads into the more unknown areas are being paved, many journeys to this part of Colombia, including trips to eco-lodges on the Chocó coast, require costly national flights followed by boat trips. Most of the roads wind toward important ports, and the tangle and mesh of rivers serve as highways for *chalupas* and canoes. The jungle is so dense and has such extreme climatic conditions that it seems highly unlikely that jungle roads will be constructed anytime soon.

Security remains an issue throughout different parts of the Pacific Coast, especially in the land extending from the ports of Tumaco and Buenaventura. The inhabitants of this region, mostly descendants of African slaves and Embera Indians, increasingly find themselves in the crossfire between the government troops and FARC guerrillas. For this reason, it is advisable to plan ahead, always use common sense and travel with caution. Updated: Apr 16, 2008.

Highlights

Isla Gorgona (p.171) is a fantastic place for outdoor activities, particularly watersports.

While in **Bahía Solano (p.177)** and **Nuquí (p.173)**, watch for humpback whales, go on wreck dives and hike in virgin rainforests. Updated: Nov 19, 2007.

History

Chocó's history sets it apart from Nariño, Cauca and Valle del Cauca.

Chocó has remained a relatively unexplored region, due to its distance from Bogotá, hostile environment for travelers and poor infrastructure. Until recently, this region and its people have been left alone, but the violence now has created a disturbance.

Nariño, Valle del Cauca and Cauca have an altogether different history. Originally home to hunters and gatherers, the area evolved into a thoroughfare by the Spaniards en route to Quito during the colonial era. As a result, these departments have seen a lot of Colombia's troubles throughout history. Cauca, in particular, suffered in the Colombian Civil War of 1860–62. Nowadays, trouble still lingers. Major ports, such as Buenaventura and Tumaco, are coveted by both the government and the guerrillas. Fights break out regularly in these places. Updated: Nov 19, 2007.

When to Go

The humidity along the coast is nothing short of staggering. The official wet season runs from May through October.

Holidays and Festivals

June and July are good for sport fishing in Bahía Solano. Come between late July to late September to see the migration of the Humpback whales. December is when the Feria de Cali takes place, a party rivaled only by Barranquilla. Updated: Nov 19, 2007.

Things to See and Do

Cultural curiosities, natural wonders, colonial opulence and adventure sports are just some of the attractions available along Colombia's Pacific Coast. Visit Isla Gorgona, Ladrilleros, Juanchaco, Nuquí or Bahía Solano to marvel at Humpback whales. From Nuquí, make the short trip south to Cabo Corrientes, where surfers claim to find the best surf conditions on the Pacific coast. Finally, make your way to Sanquianga National Park to watch enormous sea turtles haul their bodies up the beach to lay eggs. If you can't make it to that, arrive to see the offspring hatch and strike out on their own for the ocean. Updated: Nov 19, 2007.

Pacific Coast Tours

If whale watching is on your itinerary, professional tours are a must, especially to places like the Utría National Park. To get to Isla Gorgona, it may be necessary to organize a tour through Aviatur (the only tour company with access to national parks). So many sightseeing opportunities on the Pacific Coast are available through big package tours. It's cheaper to sign up with one company for a tour that includes meals and accommodations. Updated: Nov 19, 2007.

Pacific Coast Lodging

Cali and Popayán offer a wealth of accommodation options, with everything from ultra-sleek and modern hotels to regular backpacker haunts. Infrastructure remains an issue outside of major cities. Shop around for lodging in this region of Colombia. Instead of always looking for the cheapest option, it is often better to pay a few dollars more for a place where you and your belongings are safe. Because tourists in Chocó are sparse, places like Quibdó are short on good hotels, and hostels are all but impossible to find. Along coastal destinations in the Chocó, choices among award-winning eco-hotels are abundant, a special mention goes to the Pijiba Lodge. Natural luxury is provided by all-inclusive lodges that take a special pride in service. Most of these places are package deals that can be arranged from Medellín. Updated: Nov 19, 2007.

TUMACO

Alt: 2m	Pop:161,000	City Code: 2

San Andrés de Tumaco, 304 kilometers from Pasto, is one of two major ports on the Pacific Coast and consists of the Tumaco, Viciosa and El Morro islands. Each island is connected by a bridge. Isla Tumaco is the most populated. Seen from the air, it looks like a coast-to-coast blanket of populated area. The city's air and maritime ports are on Isla El Morro, as well as a major military base.

Tumaco is called *La Perla del Pacífico* (the Pearl of the Pacific). Despite the name, its luster is a bit dulled in certain spots. The chaotic bustle, streets under repair and the smell of the polluted sea strikes visitors upon arrival. The growth it has sustained in the past decade, primarily due to internal refugees from Colombia's civil war, has stretched the city beyond its already limited infrastructure. Street signs on Islas Tumaco are scarce and they use the numbered calle-carrera system. Locals use different names for the streets. Barrio Puentes and other neighborhoods in tsunami-risk areas are soon to be a thing of the past because they are being relocated to safer grounds.

Tumaco has been declared a special industrial port, eco-tourism and Biodiversity District. This status has invigorated improvements in infrastructure and promoted tourism. Tumaco's most distinctive feature is its mangroves, which are especially prominent in the Parque Nacional Sanquianga on the northern coast.

The clean beaches of Islas El Morro and Bocagrande provide escapes from the bedlam of Isla Tumaco. Afro-Colombian and Tuma indigenous cultures still thrive along this coast.

Besides its beach resorts, mangrove reserves and unique cultures, Tumaco has yet another interesting attraction—the coastal town can provide sea transportation to Ecuador. Updated: Oct 19, 2007.

HISTORY

The Tumaco region was settled over 4,000 years ago by the Tumaco-La Tolita people. Their reign stretched along the Pacific Coast from northern Ecuador to southern Colombia. This civilization's history remains largely unstudied and untouched.

Francisco Pizarro arrived on the islands in 1526. Father Onofre Esteban founded the present city in 1610. Several times, the Tuma community attempted to drive off the Spanish. The Tuma were eventually forced to escape into the protection of the mangroves. By 1628, Tumaco became an important port between Panama and Callao, which developed a mixture of people and cultures.

During the 18th Century, Tumaco served as a base camp for the defense of Spain's Pacific-American ports. English and Dutch pirates attacked the port in the late 17th Century. Raids continued until the early 19th Century. Legend has it that Henry Morgan hid his loot in the Isla del Morro caves.

Out of the water and on land, the *Comuneros de Tumaco* revolted against Spanish rule in 1781. The rebellion was suppressed the following year. Slaves escaped during the uprising into the swamps. Those slaves, known as Maroons, form the base of modern Tumaco's Afro-Colombian culture.

Twentieth-century Tumaco was destroyed by tsunamis in 1906 and 1979. The latter storm left more than 400 people dead and 1,000 missing. Updated: Oct 04, 2007.

When to go

Tumaco is said to be one of the rainiest places on earth. The wettest months are May to July and the driest are April and August. Temperatures range from 25-35°C (77-95°F).

Tumaco has become popular with vacationing Colombians. Beaches get pretty crowded during holidays. Christmas-New Year, Easter week (*Semana Santa*) and July to August are especially crowded. Prices go down out of these seasons. Updated: Oct 04, 2007.

Getting To and Away from Tumaco

Tumaco has two city bus routes: Ruta 1 to Playa El Morro (about 30 minutes) and Ruta 2 to the airport. Fares are $0.75. The last bus from downtown to El Morro leaves at about 7:45 p.m. and from El Morro to town at 8 p.m.

Taxis charge $3 between Isla Tumaco and Isla El Morro. Intercity buses have their of-

PACIFIC COAST

fices on Calle 13, including Transipiales (Tel: 2-727-2426), Cootranar (Tel: 2-727-2562) and SuperTaxis.

For launches to Bocagrande and various small villages in the coastal mangroves, go to Transmart on the dock (*muelle*) at Calle San Carlos and Calle de Comercio (Tel: 316-682-7243, cel). The *puerto marítimo* (seaport) is on Isla El Morro, about one kilometer from Playa El Morro. Boats to Esmeraldas, Ecuador also depart from this port. See the "Tumaco-Esmeraldas Border Crossing" article for more information. Updated: Oct 04, 2007.

From Tumaco

Arrive	Departure	Time	Price
Cali	5 a.m., 1 p.m., 7:30 p.m., 8:30 p.m.	14-15 hours	$26 -29
Pasto	hourly 4 a.m. to 4 p.m.	6 hours	$12
Ipiales	4 daily super-taxis	5 hours	$11

SAFETY

Keep in mind that Tumaco is a poor port town. Be careful during the day and, especially, at night. If you're hitting the clubs at night, always take a taxi home.

The road to Tumaco is in a zone with sporadic activity by armed factions of the civil war and narcotraffickers. Despite the location, the situation has significantly improved due to the increased military presence in the area. Check up on the safety conditions before embarking on your journey.

Tsunamis are taken seriously in Tumaco. If there is an earthquake, follow instructions and get to higher ground.

Because of the excessive rain, it is prudent to take precautions against malaria and dengue fever. Many hotels have screened windows to protect against bugs. Hotels in Playa El Morro also have *toldillos* (mosquito nets that cover the beds).

Take particular care when it comes to food and water. Tap water contains mangrove matter so is not safe. Updated: Oct 04, 2007.

SERVICES

Tourism Office

Tumaco's tourism office is on the third floor of the Alcaldía building (Monday - Friday, 8 a.m.-noon, 2-5 p.m. Calle 11/Caldas and Carrera 9/Calle Mosquera). If it is not open, try the very helpful Cámara de Comercio (Monday-Friday, 8 a.m.-noon, 2-5 p.m. Calle Sucre, a half-block from Calle Mosquera).

Money

Calle Sucre is nicknamed *Calle de los Bancos* (Street of the Banks), because there are branches of all of Colombia's major banks. None, however, change travelers checks or cash. There are ATMs. Bancolombia handles any type of bank card. A few agencies exchange US dollars, but only if the manager is around. For cash exchange, head to Viaje Turismo (Monday-Friday, 8 a.m.-noon, 2-6 p.m. Calle Sucre, two blocks from Calle del Comercio) and Giros and Finanzas/Western Union (Monday-Friday, 8 a.m.-noon, 2-5:30 p.m., Saturday, 8 a.m.-noon. Calle Mosquera, half a block from the Cathedral, in Centro Comercial La Sultana).

Keeping in Touch

Internet cafés can be found throughout Isla Tumaco. Service is basic—don't expect to make a Skype call or burn photos onto a CD. Internet costs around $1.50 per hour. Make local and national calls from any store or street stall announcing *llamadas*. They charge $0.10 per minute.

Pacific Net (Monday-Saturday, 8:30 a.m.-1:30 p.m., 2-10 p.m. Calle Ovando/Carrera 9B, 11-55, next to Hotel Las Lajas) offers international phone calls at $0.25 per minute to North America and $0.90 to Europe.

Avianca Depris (Monday-Friday, 8 a.m.-noon, 2-6 p.m., Saturday, 8 a.m.-noon. Calle Caldas/Calle 11, near Carrera 9) ships certified packages and letters. It will cost you a pricey $30 for a letter to the US.

At the El Morro beach it is quite a bit harder to keep in touch. Local and national calls are $0.15 per minute. There are no international or internet services.

Medical

Hospital San Andrés is a level-two hospital with many emergency care services. However, be advised that it does not have a hyperbolic chamber, making scuba diving a risky activity in these parts. (Calle 7 de Agosto and Carrera 12B, Tel: 2-727-1099). Pharmacies are found on Calle 13 and Calle 9B (Calle Ovando). Updated: Oct 04, 2007.

Things to See and Do

Don't let your first impression of Tumaco put you off from spending a bit of time here. If the streets get too chaotic, seek refuge in the Catedral or stroll about Parque Colón. Or, face the chaos head on and battle the market street madness in search of fresh fish or souvenirs. Walk around until you reach the home of Virgen de la Merced, Tumaco's patron saint, on Parque Nariño.

The Casa de la Cultura has a small museum and library (Monday-Friday, 8 a.m.-noon, 2-6 p.m. Calle Bolívar and Calle San Carlos).

These islands offer plenty of beach escapes. Playa El Bajito, on Isla Viciosa just before Puente El Morro, is in the process of reclamation. Despite the improvements, the waters are still too polluted for swimming. Another beach is across the bridge, at the end of Isla El Morro, which has tranquil waters and black sands. If you can, take the trip through the mangroves to Isla Bocagrande, where you'll find the region's best beaches.

Anyone who loves nature should check out Parque Nacional Sanquianga, which is home to waterfowl, sea turtles and 30 percent of Colombia's Pacific Coast mangroves. It lies four hours north on the coast.

If you can't be in Tumaco for one of the interesting festivals, you can still catch performances of the traditional Afro-Colombian dances. Every Wednesday and Thursday (from 7-9 p.m.), rehearsals are held at the Cancha on Calle San Judas and Calle de los Estudiantes. Updated: Oct 04, 2007.

Playa El Morro

The Isla Tumaco - Isla El Morro road ends in a loop at a glistening, black-sand beach with warm waters. Just offshore is the unique El Morro rock formation. At the far end of the road is the famed Arco del Morro; as the tide lowers, its tranquil pool drains to the ocean. Beyond the arch, the low tide exposes a long beach. Because of the mangrove sediment, the swimming here is not great, but the beachcombing and birdwatching are rewarding. During low tide is also the best time to visit the caves, where legend says Pirate Henry Morgan hid his treasure. Frequent buses run between Isla Tumaco and Playa El Morro (5 a.m.-7:45 p.m. from Tumaco, until 8 p.m. from El Morro, $0.75, 30 minutes). Don't go swimming at low tide when poisonous stingrays surface (Entry: $1.10).

Take in the sunset at the beach, and then head in for a fresh seafood dinner. Afterward, hit one of the beach's disco-bar kiosks. Chill beneath the palm trees to the tune of jazz, foreign oldies, salsa and *vallenato*.

Spending the night at Playa El Morro is much more peaceful than in the main town of Tumaco. It's also a more convenient option for those doing crossing by boat to and from Ecuador. The entire loop of beach road is lined with hotels for every pocketbook. Do not camp on the beaches. The tide gets high and there is a strong possibility of theft. Although, the town itself is securely patrolled. Updated: Dec 19, 2007.

Playa Bocagrande

Bocagrande is a small island, tucked into the mangrove estuaries near Tumaco. A magical place to spend a few days, the crystalline sea washes upon fine silvery sand and soft breezes interrupt the warm day. The temperature averages 27°C (81°F). Great for birdwatchers, waterfowl abound. The fishing in Bocagrande is also astounding. This beach is great for those hoping to escape civilization for a few days and bask in the warm waters and sunshine. However, scuba diving is almost nonexistent due to the lack of coral reef. Launches to Bocagrande leave at high tide. In high season, there are launches daily. In the low season, trips leave on demand. Passage costs $5.25 per person. Transmart (in Tumaco, along the dock at the end of Calle la Merced, and Calle del Comercio. Tel: 316-682-7243. Updated: May 19, 2008.

Parque Nacional Sanquianga

On the Pacific Coast in northwestern Nariño, Parque Nacional Sanquianga contains 30 percent of Colombia's Pacific mangrove forests.

This 80,000-hectare park protects a complex estuary delta system formed by the Sanquianga, Patía, La Tola, Aguacatal and Tapaje Rivers. The ecosystem also includes 60 kilometers of sandy beaches, swamps and *guandal* (giant bamboo) forests. A great diversity of marine species, including sponges, mollusks, crabs and *pianguam*, live within the shelter of the red mangrove. This sanctuary has the highest concentration of shore and seabirds on the Colombian Pacific. It is a primary nesting ground for brown woodrail (*Aramides Wolfi*), gull-billed tern (*Sterna nilotica*), Sporophila insulata and neotropical cormorant (*Phalacrocorax brasilianus*). It also is known for its Caguama sea turtles. Other fauna include sloths, iguanas and babillas. The labyrinths of Sanquianga harbor small indigenous and Afro-Colombian communities, with a total population of about 11,000.

Canoe through the mangroves to observe the flora and fauna of Parque Nacional Sanquianga and experience one of the best preserved mangrove forests in Colombia. Interpretive trails at El Secadero and El Carboncillo allow you to penetrate the verdant forest. On Playas Guascama, Barrera, Tasquita, Mulatos, Amarales and Vigía, you can swim and play soccer or beach volleyball. From Tumaco, check the various boating companies located on the pier at the end of Calle La Merced, near Calle Comercio, for launches to the National Park. The trip takes four hours. Updated: May 19, 2008.

Asociación de Artesanos José el Artesano

A small, nondescript building stands alone on a lot at the bend of Playa El Morro's beach road. Peer into the windows to glimpse drums, baskets and jewelry. Once inside, you are fully exposed to the creative world of Tumaco. These artists craft their wares with natural materials from the islands. There are earrings made out of coconut, jewelry made from seashells and hand-made *conuno* drums and *marimba*. Tetera and other plants are woven into bowls and other containers. If the shop is not open, talk to Doña Clara at the workshop on the corner of the other side of the road. From Tumaco, take a combi to Playa El Morro. It is across from the Hotel Reynolds. Updated: Dec 19, 2007.

Tumaco Tours

There are presently no tour operators in Tumaco. A handful of travel agencies will help you buy flights or tour packages from here to other, more popular Colombian destinations. But, for now, everything is pretty much do-it-yourself. SENA (Servicio Nacional de Apredizaje) is training people in lower economic brackets as guides. This is just one of the steps being taken to develop the local tourist industry. Updated: Oct 04, 2007.

Viaje Turismo

If you decide to fly from here to your next Colombian destination, this office can sell you tickets for major airlines from Tumaco's La Florida Airport. Viaje Turismo also handles the airlines' tourist packages to Cartagena, Medellín and other resorts. In addition, they take care of mail services. When the owner is in, you can change cash US dollars for pesos. This is one of the few places in Tumaco where you can do so. Monday-Friday 8 a.m.-noon, 2-6 p.m. Calle Sucre, one and a half blocks from Calle Comercio. Updated: Oct 19, 2007.

Guía T.P. Viajes y Turismo-SENA

Guía T.P. Viajes y Turismo (part of SENA's tourism development efforts) is a travel agency run by students. It guides you to major attractions throughout the city, Playa El Morro and Bocagrande. They also offer trips to small indigenous and Afro-Colombian settlements deep within the mangroves. Some tours have private vehicles to chauffeur you to the sites. Negotiate with your individual student-guide for the cost of your excursion. Tel: 315-447-1973 (cel), Professor Lida Villota, Tel: 316-692-3389 (cel). E-mail: adilvim@yahoo.es. Updated: Oct 19, 2007.

Tumaco Lodging

Tumaco has every type of accommodation. Many of the high-end hotels are booked long-term by military personnel. Keep in mind the smell of the polluted water when staying at a seafront hotel. Playa El Morro has better options for budget travelers or couples looking for a romantic getaway. If coming from, or going to, Ecuador by the weekly ship, then it's better to stay here because the port and immigration (DAS) offices are nearby. Panorama Kioss provides shaded campsites for $2.60-4.20 (back loop of beach road, up from Hotel El Morro. Tel: 311-766-2401. Once

PACIFIC COAST

again, beach camping is not recommended for safety reasons, due to high tides and robberies. Updated: Oct 04, 2007.

Hotel Guaduales del Pacífico

(BED $5.30) Hotel Guaduales, built from giant bamboo, is an example of the traditional architecture found in this region. The rooms are simple — a bit rough, but adequate — with a private bath (cold water only) and mosquito nets over the beds. The screened windows make the rooms light and airy. The common upstairs balcony has a tranquil sea view. The restaurant has seating on the front veranda and serves *comida corriente* (daily special) for $2.65. They also serve beer. Owner Doña Yolanda, a jolly but no-nonsense woman, is always ready to ask you, "¿Le provoca un tinto?" ("Would you like a coffee?") Beachside road, Playa El Morro. Tel: 2-727-2927. Updated: Dec 19, 2007.

Hotel El Dorado

(BED: $5-8) El Dorado is one of the oldest lodging options in Tumaco, it has served travelers for more than 35 years. The second-floor rooms share common baths (cold water only) for $5.30 per person per night. On the roof, surrounding a garden patio, are nice cabañas for one to three people with private (cold water) bathrooms and TV. These cost $8 per person. The front cabins have a balcony over the street. The back cabins have a sea view. Remember since this hotel is on the seafront, the polluted sea is easily smelled. Prices include tax. Calle El Comercio, between Calle La Merced and Calle Parque Colón. Tel: 2-727-2565. Updated: Dec 19, 2007.

Hotel Barranquilla

(ROOM: $32-48) The most luxurious hotel at Playa El Morro. Hotel Barranquilla is a high-rise with well-equipped rooms, which include A/C, private bath, hot water, fridge and cable TV. Some rooms sport a balcony and sea view. If you'd like to explore nearby sights, the owners of Hotel Barranquilla can arrange tours. Be sure to check out the top-floor restaurant and the kiosk disco on the beach. Beachside road, Playa El Morro. Tel: 2-727-1760, E-mail: hotelbarranquilla@hotmail.com. Updated: Dec 19, 2007.

Tumaco Restaurants

Food prices in Tumaco tend to be higher than those in inland cities. A comida corriente costs about $2.60. Fish and seafood are the town's specialties. Try the *encocados* (dishes prepared in coconut milk) and the *ceviche.* A local drink to cool sultry afternoons is *champú* (a non-alcoholic brew of fermented corn, tropical fruits and raw sugar).

The food vendors bustle daily on many of the streets of Tumaco, especially Calle de Comercio and Calle de la Merced to Plaza Nariño.

Tumaco has a number of dance spots where locals and military personnel relax at night. A cluster of clubs line Calle de los Estudiantes near the playground, but the most happening scenes are at the El Morro bridge. There are clubs with kiosk bars, tables beneath palm trees and a lawn-tent dance floor with pulsating lights. Most clubs close at 1 a.m. No matter where you decide to rumba the night away, take a taxi home (unless you are staying at El Morro). Updated: Oct 04, 2007.

Restaurante Coma Bien

(LUNCH: $2.35) Near the bus stations, Restaurante Coma Bien is a convenient place to grab lunch before or after hitting the road. The cheapest in Tumaco, it offers not only the usual chicken or beef dishes, but also fish and, even, the occasional shrimp or crab ($2.35 soup, main dish and drink; $1.85 main dish only). The bandeja with eggs ($1.30) is available for vegetarians. The service is quick and friendly. Calle 13 (Calle La Merced), in front of the Cootranar bus station. Tel: 314-671-0295. Updated: Dec 19, 2007.

Restaurante La Corvina

(LUNCH: $2.65) At the bend of the beach road, not too far from the Arco del Morro, is a double row of kiosk restaurants. Each kiosk serves a fish lunch for $2.65. The menu at La Corvina sticks out from the rest. Not only does its proprietor, Doña Nata, prepare à la carte seafood dishes like crayfish, oysters, squid, shrimp, clams, crabs ($4.20-13) and lobster ($11-21), she also offers other wild game meats. These *animales del monte* include familiar animals (rabbit and venison) as well as exotic ones (fox, wild pig and *guatín*). Prices include tax. The set meals at lunch and dinner are an economical alternative to the à la carte selections. Fourth restaurant on right, Kiosk Row, Playa El Morro. Updated: Dec 19, 2007.

Restaurante Alta Mar

(LUNCH: $4.20) The open-sided dining room at Restaurante Alta Mar gives a commanding view of the sea. The fresh morning breeze creates an enjoyable breakfast experience from 7-9 a.m. ($2.65). The excellently prepared lunch special, served 11 a.m.-2 p.m., includes soup, a main dish of fish or meat, rice, *patacones* (fried plaintains), salad and a large fresh fruit drink. The lunch costs $4.20. The seafood á la carte menu ($9.50-19.50) is served until 9 p.m., which offers the opportunity to watch the sunset and enjoy the evening breeze. Hotel Barranquilla, Beachside road, Playa del Morro. Updated: Dec 19, 2007.

Tumaco Nightlife

Punto Baré

For the best rumba in Tumaco, locals recommend Punto Baré without hesitation. The party begins at 7 p.m. and lasts until 3 a.m. The music is salsa with a bit of merengue and reggaeton thrown into the mix. Hit that huge dance floor and sway under the pulsating lights, or sidle up to the long bar for a drink. If you're looking for something non-alcoholic, you're out of luck. No door charge, but there is a steep minimum consumption of $11. The place is elegant, which means men aren't allowed in shorts. Subida del Puente del Morro, fifth from the bridge on the left side of the road. Updated: Dec 19, 2007.

Kiosko El Caído del Sol

At a table beneath palm trees at Kiosko El Caído del Sol, friends nurse beers over a quiet conversation. The cool blue light of the dance floor gleams on a couples swaying to the sensual rhythm of Cuban Son. There's no hassle here at the Kiosko El Caído del Sol, no door charge (well, this beach bar has no door) and no minimum consumption. Just chill with a cold drink and some salsa, son and jazz. Open daily 8 p.m.-1 a.m. Across from Hotel Barranquilla, Playa del Morro. Updated: Dec 19, 2007.

Buenaventura

Alt: 7m	Pop: 324,000	City Code: 2

Buenaventura is 128 kilometers from Cali. It is a sweltering port on the Colombian Pacific Coast, with its center built mainly on the island of Cascajal. The port is a pivotally important communication and transportation hub, which makes it lucrative to guerrillas, paramilitaries and the government, and hence a dangerous place. Tourists are here because they are lost or they are making a connection to the nearby tourist areas and whale-watching retreats of Juanchaco and Ladrilleros.

If you wind up with some time to kill, check out the shops, hotels and restaurants along Calle 1. With a few hours, be sure to visit the San Andresito area of town for bargain shopping. Afterward, head to the Muelle Turístico to have a fresh-squeezed fruit juice and watch the massive tankers power their way out into the open ocean. Updated: Nov 15, 2007.

History

Founded in the 16th Century, Buenaventura was a major world player before the creation of the Panama Canal. Ships going to and from the California Gold Rush would pass through these waters, increasing the city's importance. Currently, Buenaventura is Colombia's leading port on the Pacific Coast and is crucial for importing cargo to surrounding areas, particularly Cali. Updated: Nov 15, 2007.

When to Go

Between late July and late September, people descend on the resorts of Juanchaco and Ladrilleros to catch a glimpse of the migrating humpback whales. Updated: Nov 15, 2007.

Getting To and Away from Buenaventura

Air

The airport is a 25-minute drive from downtown Buenaventura; a taxi ride costs $7. Satena has flights here several times a week.

Bus

The Terminal de Transportes is downtown. To get there, even though it is close to the hotels on Calle 1, it is recommended that you always take a taxi ($1.50-2). Vans from the terminal leave for Cali approximately every 20 minutes. Given the areas the journey passes through, it would be wise to go during daylight hours. The road to Cali winds through valleys and tunnels. It has been blocked on occasion after landslides from heavy rains. There are numerous companies that run vans to Cali from Buenaventura. Two reputable companies are Palmira and Transmar. Vans cost $7-8 per person. Taxis, which leave when full, cost $10 per person. The journey takes three to four hours.

Boat

From the *Muelle Turístico,* organize transport by boat to Juanchaco, Ladrilleros, Guapi and Charco. There are half a dozen boat operators, and most leave for their destinations from 9 a.m. - 11 a.m. Two recommended companies are Pacifico Express and Transmilenio. Updated: Nov 15, 2007.

From Buenaventura

Arrive	Price
Bocana	$14
Charco	$38
Guapi	$35
Juanchaco	$24
La Cangreja	$9
Pianguita	$15
Timbiquí	$40

Safety in Buenaventura

Any visitor to Buenaventura should never take safety lightly. This is ground zero for turf wars between the paramilitaries and the guerrillas who want control over the area's drug trade. The murder rate in the city is startling high. Tourists should not stray from Calle 1 at night. Because of rampant unemployment, there are a lot of delinquency problems, as well. Updated: Nov 15, 2007.

Buenaventura Services

Tourism Office

For tourist information, head to the Muelle Turístico. The office there can provide you with maps and trip ideas.

Money

Bancolombia (Calle 1) has an ATM that accepts Visa. Or you can go to Davivienda on Calle 2 and Carrera 3.

Keeping in Touch

Cyber Pacífico (Calle 2 – 11) is best for internet. It is opposite the Olímpica supermarket.

Medical

Clínica Buenaventura can be found on Calle 6, 16-24. Tel: 2-554-755.

Shopping

For knock-off sports shoes, clothes and alcohol, head to San Andresito to bargain for various items. San Andresito is located on Calle 9 and Carrera 6. Updated: Nov 15, 2007.

Buenaventura Tours

As previously said, unemployment is rife in Buenaventura. When you arrive at the Muelle Turístico, various individuals confront you who claim to be official tour guides. Head straight to the tourism office (the yellow building located off to the left) to make sure you get an accredited guide. The office staff can provide you with maps and prices. Whale-watching tours should cost about $10 per person. A tour that covers all of Cascajal Island will cost $42. Updated: Nov 15, 2007.

Buenaventura Lodging

Hotel Titanic

(ROOM: $15-25) This hotel is a respectable establishment on Calle 1 in the safer part of Buenaventura. The hotel has 37 rooms with cable TV, mini-bar, private bathroom, A/C and telephone. The hotel also has a restaurant and bar. Calle 1a, 2A-55, in front of the park. Tel: 2-241-2046. Updated: Dec 19, 2007.

Hotel Capilla del Sol

(ROOM: $25-45) Nine floors of hotel rooms provide visitors with plenty of options for ocean views on Cascajal Island. All rooms have A/C, a private bathroom, mini-bar, balcony and WiFi. The rooms are clean and comfortable. On the roof terrace, there is a well-regarded restaurant that stays open until 10 p.m. From the airport, the taxi ride is roughly 25 minutes and costs about $7. The hotel is near the Olímpica supermarket. Calle 1a, Carrera 2a Esquina, second floor. Tel: 2-242-3000, E-mail: hotelcapilladelsol@gmail.com. Updated: Dec 19, 2007.

Gran Hotel

(ROOM: $27-38) Twenty-eight rooms with private bathroom, A/C, cable TV, WiFi and a mini-bar makes the Gran Hotel in a great place to spend a night. The staff is very helpful and friendly and the hotel has its own restaurant. If you are coming from the Muelle Turístico, cross the road and walk one block along the street to the right on Calle 1. Calle 1a, 2A-71. Tel: 2-241-8028, Fax: 2-243-4846, E-mail: granhotel@mibuenaventura.com. Updated: Dec 19, 2007.

Hotel Estelar Estación

(ROOM: $100-175) Built during an era when decadence and class meant everything, the Hotel Estelar Estación cuts an awkard gait in today's Buenaventura. Truly the only luxury hotel in the city, its stucco-front balconies set it apart from all of the other lodging options. If it's luxury you're after, then pick any one of the 75 suites, bathe in the pool or dine at one of its restaurants. Calle 2, 1A-08. Tel: 2-243-4070, Fax: 2-243-4118, E-mail: recepcion.hestacion@hotelesestelar.com, URL: www.hotelesestelar.com. Updated: Dec 19, 2007.

Buenaventura Restaurants

La Casa

Enviably situated with an ocean view and a cooling breeze, the restaurant La Casa is a welcoming place to eat in town. Set menus at lunch appeal to the budget-minded traveler. Those looking for something more substantial will find the á la carte menu eye-catching. Shrimp platters and fish grilled in garlic cost about $9. Calle 1, 5A-46. Tel: 2-241-0056. Updated: Dec 19, 2007.

Primos

Although it lacks the quality and setting of some other places in the neighborhood, Primos is another decent option on Calle 1. There are generous helpings of typical coastal fare, including fried fish and different cuts of meat. Calle 1, 3. Tel: 2-242-3109. Updated: Dec 19, 2007.

Soles

On the 11th floor of the Capilla del Sol Hotel, Soles makes for a pleasant respite from the noise of cars along the Zona Rosa strip. Standard eats are available. Although the food is better than passable, the main reason to come here is the view of the city lights overlooking the Pacific. Calle 1a, Carrera 2a, 11th floor. Tel: 2-242-3000. Updated: Dec 19, 2007.

Rapy Taylor

One of six fast food stalls on the shore side of Calle 1 in the Zona Rosa, Rapy Taylor delivers exactly what you would expect. Pizza, hamburgers, hot dogs and other fast food fare is available for diners in a hurry. Calle 1, opposite the hotels. Updated: Dec 19, 2007.

Sabrosuras del Pacífico

Strategically positioned on a second story facing the sea, Sabrosuras del Pacífico specializes in seafood dishes native to the area. Although this is an ideal place for lunch, it may not be to everyone's liking for dinner, when the neighboring club opens and smothers the restaurant with loud music. Calle 1, opposite Hotel los Delifines. Tel: 2-241-7944. Updated: Dec 19, 2007.

Leños y Mariscos

In the heart of Buenaventura's Zona Rosa on Calle 1, Leños y Mariscos is an upscale eatery that offers fairly standard fish, chicken and beef dishes. However, the helpings are sizeable and accompanied at lunchtime by a salad and small dessert. Calle 1, 5B-13. Tel: 2-242-2089. Updated: Dec 19, 2007.

Buenaventura Nightlife

Because it is a major port, Buenaventura has a colorful nightlife, to put it mildly. As a tourist, you are recommended to stick to the Zona Rosa on Calle 1, which extends from the Muelle Turístico up the hill to the Mirador Azul bar. Between these two landmarks you should be less likely to run into problems. Rumba the night away in one of dozens of places, like Krypton or Chaplins. Updated: Nov 15, 2007.

Near Buenaventura

Juanchaco and Ladrilleros

Both areas are swamped during the whale-watching season, which runs from late July into the early weeks of October. Every long weekend or public holiday brings hordes of vacationers from Cali eager to reach the coast and catch a glimpse of the migrating humpbacks. Juanchaco's beach is littered with driftwood and is not a place you would spread out a towel to catch some sun. But, beaches in Ladrilleros are much more suitable for sunbathers. When the tide is out, the beach widens enormously and vendors set up their stalls. They provide everything from fortified coconut cocktails to fried fish lunches. There are places to stay in both areas, many of which are arranged through pre-packaged deals. There are also a number of smaller residences that rent out rooms in both of the towns.

Gorgona Island

Gorgona was a prison island before being converted into a national park. Thirty kilometers off the coast, it is home to a large variety of venomous snakes and migrating birds. The waters are a favorite destination for migrating humpback whales. Diving is high quality; there are opportunities to see marine turtles, sharks and many species of fish. You can arrange to get to Isla Gorgona from the Muelle Turístico in Buenaventura. There is a $10 park entrance fee, payable prior to arrival. Most people organize trips to Gorgona through the Aviatur company, which sells packages that include meals and transport. Updated: May 19, 2008.

Quibdó

Alt: 50m Pop: 109,000 City Code: 4

Quibdó's skyline is dominated by the immense San Francisco de Asís Cathedral. This landmark towers over the banks of the Atrato River. The river is the city's most important means of transportation, aside from flights into the airport. Two ill-maintained roads are Quibdó's only other real connection to the outside world.

To put it bluntly, Quibdó is an unattractive place. The infrastructure suffers from the harsh climatic conditions that leave the streets with potholes and stained buildings. It almost looks as if they were burnt by the humidity. For the intrepid traveler, these descriptions should offer no obstacle. You will likely be the only tourist. The friendly people, mainly Embera Indians and descendants of African slaves, adopt visitors as one of their own, in due time.

Accommodation is not as developed or established as it is in other places. This is because Quibdó mainly hosts soldiers and officials from Médicos Sin Fronteras (Doctors Without Borders). Updated: Nov 15, 2007.

History

The early city's history is largely uncharted. In 1648, the Franciscan order was granted the lands in the area by Embera Indians. While the city was destroyed under subsequent attacks by hostile tribes, in 1654 it was rebuilt under the watch of the Jesuits Pedro Cáceres and Francisco de Orta. Later Quibdó declared its independence in February 1813 and in 1825 the city was officially named San Francisco de Quibdó.

In 1948, when the department of Chocó was created, Quibdó was named its capital. In 1966, the city was once more ravaged by fire. Currently, it is better known as being in the heart of the Zona Roja and suffering from urban forms of malaria and poverty.

When to Go

Quibdó is a hot and wet city. There is no effective wet or dry season, since the rain is likely to fall at any time of the year. The rainiest month is August, the driest is February, but in reality there is little to differentiate between the months. Chocó is said to receive up to six meters of rainfall every year. Meteorologists have found that it rains at least 20 days out of the month.

Holidays and Fiestas

In April, there is a celebration for typical chocoano dances and foods. In September, check out the *Fiesta of San Francisco de Asís.* Updated: Nov 15, 2007.

Getting To and Away from Quibdó

Satena and Aires have regular flights from Quibdó's Al Carano Airport to Bogotá, Medellín and Pereira, and vice versa. From Quibdó, flights can be bought to Nuquí and Bahía Solano. Airport Tel: 4-671-9048.

Traveling here by road from Risaralda or Medellín is strongly discouraged, despite the beautiful scenery. The western regions of Antioquía, Risaralda and Quindío that border the Chocó are dangerous. However, if you decide to waive caution, Rápido Ochoa has buses that leave three times a day from Medellín to Quibdó. River travel is not recommended either. Your best option is to fly. Updated: Nov 15, 2007.

Safety in Quibdó

The people in Quibdó are very polite and helpful, but as in all cities there are dangers. Avoid unlit streets at night or going off main roads. Remember that Quibdó is a port town, and comes with typical port disturbances.

Since Quibdó sometimes seems like a major garrison town, and hardly a tourist destination, the police and military will regard you with suspicion. Be sure to keep cameras hidden. Do not even look like you are taking photos of military personnel or buildings. The DAS (Departamento Administrativo de Seguridad) officers will be curious about who you are, so be sure to have all of your papers in order. Updated: Nov 15, 2007.

Quibdó Services

Tourism Office

Government of Chocó. Tel: 4-671-1415.

Money

There are a lot of ATMs that accept Visa in Quibdó. One is in Bancolombia, Calle 24 with Carrera 2. The other is Av. Villas, Carrera 3 with Calle 26.

Keeping in touch

There is a decent internet café with telephone booths at Calle 25 and Carrera 5.

Medical

San Francisco de Asís Hospital. Carrera 1, 31-25. Tel: 4-671-1160.
Hospital Local Ismael Roldan Valencia. Tel: 4-671-0101.

If you develop a dire medical condition but you are well enough to travel, then it is best to get on the earliest flight to Medellín.

Shopping

For everyday goods, the street behind the port can provide most things, like toiletries, cheap clothes and medical supplies. For more touristy pieces such as Indian weaves and the like, the airport has a couple of good stalls. Although, Quibdó is really not a shopping destination. Updated: Nov 15, 2007.

Things to See and Do

There are no obvious attractions in Quibdó, but it does make for an interesting couple of days spent off the beaten track. Until the security situation gets better and tourism increases, Quibdó is a place to mix it up with the locals, stroll along the riverfront and spend time at the market.

Atrato River

This vast river flowing alongside Quibdó is worth a look. It runs 750 kilometers further north to the Gulf of Uraba.

The San Francisco de Asís Cathedral

Spend some time marvelling at the enormity of this grand riverside cathedral in Quibdó. Updated: Nov 15, 2007.

Quibdó Lodging

Quibdó's tourism infrastructure has remained undeveloped to the point of despair. Given the low number of visitors, this is to be understood. Updated: Nov 15, 2007.

Hotel Malecón

(ROOM: $30-45) The Hotel Malecón is recommended for its helpful staff, clean rooms and security. As the name suggests, this hotel is located right next to the port in Quibdó, which straddles the Atrato River. Its drab stairwell is hard to miss. Don't let the facade put you off, Hotel Malecón is a good option. It is safe, its 25 rooms are clean and Ramón, the concierge, is a great source for information about the area and city. Rooms are equipped with either a fan or A/C and come with a mini-bar and private bathroom. There is no hot water, but this is hardly a necessity in Quibdó. (Do not mistake the Hotel Malecón with the Hotel Central, which is reached by the same flight of stairs and rents rooms by the hour.) From the airport, any taxi costs roughly $2.50. For a collectivo bus, ask to be dropped off at the Convent. The Hotel Malecón is across the road. Tel: 4-671-4662 / 2725. Updated: Dec 19, 2007.

Quibdó Restaurants

There are a number of restaurants to choose from in Quibdó. If you want some true fish from the Chocó, then head to the market, pick out what you want, and pick a stall to prepare it. Otherwise, La Terraza is a good option. Along the riverfront, get any type of fresh-squeezed, cheap fruit juices.

The Mercado

Although not an official restaurant, the mercado is a great place for fresh fish. Here, locals fry up the morning's catch and accompany it with the ubiquitous plantain and rice. Cheap and cheerful, if you are looking for a true Quibdó experience, this is it. Atrato Riverfront. Updated: Dec 19, 2007.

Pizzería Maestro Pierro

Pizzería Maestro Pierro is Quibdó's first pizzería. It has decent pizza, some varied pasta dishes and the usual Colombian lunches. Carrera 3, Calle 31. Updated: Dec 19, 2007.

Rapi-Pollo

Although this is not the healthiest option, Rapi-Pollo is a good option for a quick bite to eat. Hunks of fried or roasted chicken come with side orders of salted potatoes at reasonable prices. Carrera 4, behind the Banco de la República. Updated: Dec 19, 2007.

La Terraza

On the first floor of a nondescript corner building, La Terraza is a great place to gorge in Quibdó. The restaurant offers large servings of typical dishes, such as fried fish with patacones and rice or the wildly popular and artery-clogging *bandeja paisa* (steak, *chicharrón*, red beans, rice, sausage, fried egg and *arepas*, usually with plantains and avocado). La Terraza is warm, welcoming and very popular with the locals. If you aren't up for a big meal, come in for a *sancocho* soup and a cheap Poker beer. Carrera 4, 24 - 197. Tel: 4-671-1940. Updated: Dec 19, 2007.

Quibdó Nightlife

Claims among locals declare Quibdó the party capital of Chocó, if not Colombia. There is a small Zona Rosa, along Calle 31 on Carreras 2 and 3, that caters to those who want to dance and drink. Updated: Nov 15, 2007.

Nuquí

Alt: 5m Pop: 6,300 City Code: 4

Nuquí has some services that cater to tourism but it is better known as the base for excursions into the surrounding area. Nuquí's beach front looks out into the vast Gulf of Tribuga. The beach is expansive and strewn with driftwood. If you have arranged to spend your time at one of the nearby award-winning eco-lodges, then you'll likely be picked up at the airport on the eastern end of town. After registering with the DAS official and paying the tourist tax ($1.50), a motorboat will take you to your chosen destination. There are no banks in Nuquí and electricity is scarce. The hotels are in the northern sector, a five-minute walk from the airport. Aside from these, Nuquí itself offers little.

As previously stated, the local surroundings are the major attraction. People come to the area to see the mangroves in Coquí, the hot springs at Termales, the surf at Cabo Corrientes, and the waterfalls and wonder at the Utría National Park. Updated: Nov 15, 2007.

History

One-hundred-twenty kilometers from the capital of Chocó, Nuquí was established as a town in 1917 by Juanito Castro. The area was historically used by hunter-gatherers and Embera Indians, and is now populated by the descendants of African slaves. A few Paisas from Medellín also live in Nuquí, hoping to cash in on the tourist industry as it develops. Updated: Nov 16, 2007.

When to go

Nuquí is a year-round destination. However, to catch the real flavor of the Chocó and the natural sights, it's best to get there for the whale-watching season. This lasts from late July into October.

It will rain during your time in Nuquí. That is a given, but it is unlikely you will ever get cold, since the average year-round temperature is 28°C (82°F). Updated: Nov 16, 2007.

Getting To and Away from Nuquí

It is best to arrive to Nuquí by either sea or air. From Medellín, Aexpa and Satena have flights directly to Nuquí. Both airlines also have flights from Bahía Solano and Quibdó. In addition, Aexpa covers the route from Pereira to Nuquí.

Boats come in frequently, bringing supplies from Buenaventura. If you are an adventurer, get a seat in a fisherman's vessel coming or going from El Valle or Bahía Solano. This journey is not made frequently due to shortages of gasoline. Updated: Nov 16, 2007.

Safety in Nuquí

Nuquí is a safe town and the surrounding areas are unaffected by conflict. Leave your worries behind, as much as you can while in Colombia. Focus most of your angst on riptides and sunburns. Updated: Nov 16, 2007.

Nuquí Services

Money

There are no banks or ATMs in Nuquí. Come prepared with plenty of cash.

Keeping in touch

The main lodges have radio contact with Medellín. Often the phone lines and/or electricity is down. There is no internet. If necessary, you can make calls from rented cell phones.

Shopping

Next to the airport, there are some decent shops that sell goods created by Embera Indians. These goods include paddles and woven baskets. Necessities should be bought before leaving major cities. Updated: Nov 16, 2007.

Things to See and Do

Guachalito and the Southern Beaches are beautiful beaches reached via boat ride to the south of Nuquí. Check out Coquí, the amazing mangroves near an indigenous village.

Termales are the town and the beach that go by the same name. Take a short walk through the town to get to the hot springs.

At Cabo Corrientes, surf in the company of turtles, lobsters and abundant species of fish. Utría National Park is a stunning natural reserve located north of Nuquí.

Go whale watching between late July and October. Marvel at the annual migration of the humpback whales as they swim south with their young. Updated: Nov 15, 2007.

Ensenada de Utría National Park

The park covers an area of 338 kilometers in the department of Chocó. This park has amazing topographical features such as the Utría Fjord and the Baudó Hills. The year-round temperature hovers around 28°C (82°F) and is always humid.

The park environment is made up of rainforest, tangles of mangrove swamps, coral reefs and 17 hectares of Pacific Coastline. It is home to the increasingly rare Chocó Tinamou bird and very diverse marine fauna, including 105 species of crustaceans and several species of whales that visit the coral reefs, including the famous humpback whales. In addition, there are two Indian reserves within the park. Experience all that Chocó has to offer through hiking, kayaking or purely enjoying the abundance of life in the park. To get there, fly into Bahía Solano and arrange transport south on the one road that leads to El Valle and cross the bridge south. Otherwise, contract a boat from Nuquí and enjoy the two-hour ride to the peninsula. It is advisable to bring your own water. If you have any worries, it is easy enough to contract a local guide. Be sure to advise the park authorities of your whereabouts. Updated: May 19, 2008.

Water Activities

Nuquí offers a cornucopia of delights for the adventurous traveler, particularly in the realm of watersports. Each eco-hotel that lines the rugged, dramatic coast near the town of Nuquí has its own kayaks. Grab one to explore the rocky bluffs for yourself and maybe even see some whales. If kayaking is not your thing, rent a surf board and have a guide tow you out to the good surfing areas near Cabo Corrientes. You can also join one of the diving and snorkeling excursions, which offer the opportunity to spot large groupers or green turtles. Unless you have arranged for a trip on a cargo boat north from Buenaventura, the only way of getting here is to fly in from Medellín, Pereira or Quibdó. Check all equipment before heading out and familiarize yourself with the tidal movements in the area. Do not attempt to touch the wildlife. Updated: Dec 19, 2007.

Nuquí Lodging

Visitors are spoiled with choices in the environs of Nuquí. There are a couple of good options in the town itself that can organize tours and offer half-board, but it is beyond the town's limits that one reaches paradise.

Eco-lodges such as the Morromico, Pijiba and Piedra Piedra are not cheap by any measure but all thoughts of cost are quickly banished when you reach their lush settings. Private cabanas stocked with everything you might need are complimented by delicious full-board catering. Updated: Nov 15, 2007.

Hostal La Nena

(ROOM: $9-12) This is the absolute budget option in Nuquí. Follow the road from the airport toward the beach and turn right on the last paved road. Hostal La Nena is rustic and family-run. Noise may be an issue from the mechanics working on boat engines out front. Although the four rooms available are clean and newly furnished, they suffer from a lack of security. The walk from the airport takes no longer than five minutes. Calle 7-94. Tel: 4-683-6224. Updated: Dec 19, 2007.

Palmas del Pacífico

(ROOM: $25-30) The Palmas del Pacífico is a block behind the other accommodation choices in Nuquí. It is a definite step up from the Hostal La Nena. The cabañas are comfortable, yet dated, and guests enjoy the sea breeze from the terraces. As with most hotels in the region, the Palmas del Pacífico relies on tourists coming from Medellín on package trips. It includes two meals in the price. Walk toward the beach and turn right on the second-to-last block. Palmas is just before the military football field and one block back from the Iraka del Mar Eco-Hotel. Tel: 4-683-6010 / 6127. Updated: Dec 19, 2007.

Pijiba Lodge

(ROOM: $35-85) Pijiba Lodge is hands down the most environmentally friendly lodge on this stretch of coast. In fact, it recently won an award from Conservation International. The three cabañas are each split into two rooms, and there is some overflow accommodation. The maximum occupancy in the lodge is 18. Each room has a private bathroom and comes equipped with mosquito nets and candles. All meals are included in the price, as are various excursions. A pre-booked package to the Pijiba Lodge includes airport pick up and boat ride. If you do not have reservations, then catch a colectivo boat south. Tel: 4-474-5221, E- mail: info@pijibalodge.com, URL: www.pijibalodge.com. Updated: Dec 19, 2007.

Iraka del Mar Eco-Hotel

(ROOM: $35-59) The brightly-painted Iraka del Mar Eco Hotel is the best in Nuquí. The hotel provides 12 inviting cabins, all equipped with private bathrooms and decks with hammocks. The staff can arrange tours and transport to other parts of Chocó, including trips to the thermal springs, Utría park and whale watching. The package deals include two meals a day. Iraka del Mar Eco Hotel is down the main road from the airport, toward the beach, and on the right at the last opportunity. To find them, look for the brightly colored cabañas in front of the Palmas del Pacífico Hotel. Tel: 4-683-6016, E-mail: info@nuqui.com. Updated: Dec 19, 2007.

V!VA Member Review-Iraka del Mar Eco Hotel

The balconies have hammocks and look out over the Pacific Ocean, and you can see magnificient sunsets! We paid 30,000 pesos per person per night. Electricity in Nuquí only comes on between 6 p.m. to 11 p.m., so charge your camera batteries in the evening. The staff is extremely friendly and helpful. They can help you set up boat rides to the termales. During the boat ride you might see whales, sea turtles or sharks — I did! Good plumbing and comfortable beds. Take a walk north on the beach for a day trip, but bring lots of water to drink and wear sunscreen. Visit Nuquí for a peaceful, clean, naturalist vacation. May 13, 2008. Ottawa, Canada

Piedra Piedra

(ROOM: $40-80) Perched on top of a rocky bluff that looks out onto the Pacific Ocean, Piedra Piedra has a stunning location. With a capacity for 17 people in its four rooms, the owners at Piedra Piedra are insistent on keeping their operation small to safeguard the natural beauty of the area. Available tours include scuba diving and kayaking. However, if you fancy just laying around, there's also a tanning deck. All meals are included in the price. Meet the boat driver in Nuquí to be taken 40 minutes south. Otherwise, wait for the colectivo boat for a ride. Tel: 4-311-2358, E-mail: info@piedrapiedra.com, URL: www.piedrapiedra.com. Updated: Dec 19, 2007.

El Cantil

(ROOM: $40-80) El Cantil Eco-Lodge is right next door to the Pijiba Lodge. The lodge's seven cabins each sleep up to six people. Rooms are self-contained, independent units spread evenly on the hillside to ensure that each has an ocean view. All deals include three meals. El Cantil has surfboards, kayaks and offers scuba diving excursions. Your journey, if pre-arranged, will include transport from the airport. If not, you will need to secure a place on a south-bound colectivo boat. Tel: 4-252-0707, 4-352-0729, E-mail: elcantil@elcantil.com, URL: www.elcantil.com. Updated: Dec 19, 2007.

Morromico

(ROOM: $60-75) With four rooms that in total sleep a maximum of 12, Morromico Hotel is definitely a quiet place to kick back and enjoy the Chocó. The emphasis is on harmony with nature as well as with one another. Ample communal areas for relaxing means you will make friends quickly. Meals, airport and boat transportation 45 minutes to the north of Nuquí are included. Tel: 8-521-4172, E-mail: playa@morromico.com, URL: www.morromico.com. Updated: Dec 19, 2007.

Nuquí Restaurants

Nuquí has a few basic restaurants that specialize in fish dishes. Near the airport, there are places that offer cheap fish empanadas and arepas. Most likely, wherever you stay will provide you with meals.

Nuquí Nightlife

There are discos in Nuquí, albeit very basic ones, including one that offers a striptease show at an entry cost of $2.50. For something more relaxing, kick back on someone's front porch with a beer. Updated: Nov 15, 2007.

El Valle

Alt: 5m Pop: 1,000 City Code: 4

Take the only road south from Bahía Solano for about 20 kilometers to reach El Valle. Contrary to what its name would suggest, the town is distinctly un-valley like. El Valle is gradually stepping out of the shadow of its larger neighbor to the north, Bahía Solano, and El Almejal Nature Reserve is helping it become a destination in its own right.

For now, the town consists of two roads and a pathway to Playa Almejal. There has been a massive construction push along this beach, which looks like it could have some great effects in the future.

Electricity cuts and communication problems are the norm. If you desperately need medical attention, or just want to run an errand, you must head north to Bahía Solano. When the weather is at its worst, provisions in El Valle become scarce. During one recent October, torrential rain caused several places to run out of beer!

Soak in everything, as little as that might be, that El Valle has to offer. The town's skyline displays the spurs of the Baudo mountainous region and a variety of species of migrating birds. El Valle is also great for whale-watching trips. Hop on a launch from the expansive stretch of beach, which runs south from the town into the Utría National Park, and is populated by lazy dogs and coconut harvesters. Updated: Feb 12, 2008.

History

El Valle's history is one defined by the river and its exit into the Pacific Ocean. El Valle is inhabited by Embera Indians, who survive on small-scale hunting and fishing, and descendants of African slaves brought in during the period of Spanish rule.

When to Go

Late July to October is whale-watching season. From June to July, there are sport fishing tournaments. Updated: Feb 12, 2008.

Getting To and Away from El Valle

Unless you arrive to El Valle by sea, you must first fly into Bahía Solano. It is about an hour flight from Medellín, Pereira or Cali. From the airport it should be easy enough to hire a jeep or *chiva* for the 20 kilometer-journey (one hour) south from Bahía Solano to El Valle on the only stretch of road in El Chocó. Be warned, during the wetter seasons there are parts of the road that are impassable. When rivers burst their banks, the mud on the road can be very deep. Authorities have been attempting to pave the route. Updated: Feb 12, 2008.

Safety in El Valle

El Valle is generally safe, though usual precautions do apply. People are friendly and willing to help, should you require assistance.Updated: Feb 18, 2008.

Things to See and Do

Take walks to the beaches of Cuevita and Almejal. There are plenty of ecological tours into the nearby Utría National Park. Take a canoe trip through the mangroves of the Tundo River or visit the waterfalls by Playa Larga, El Tigre, Chado River and Juna River. The best time for a trip to the turtle conservation project is in September, when the hatchlings emerge. Updated: Feb 12, 2008.

Playa El Almejal

One of Colombia's most environmentally expressive beaches is El Almejal. The beach stretches two kilometers and ends dramatically as the ocean's fury makes a meal of the surrounding rocks. Here, you have nature in all its glory, along with the opportunity to surf, swim or just relax in the shallow waters.

El Almejal also represents a good indication of the future development. In recent years, diggers and trucks trundled along the beach collecting rocks and sand for nearby resorts. Sadly, that which is most precious to El Almejal—its tranquility—may be lost in the coming years. Visit now before the hordes discover one of Colombia's best kept secrets! Walk a few of kilometers north from the town; you can't miss El Almejal. Out of season the beach is deserted and many of the guesthouses are closed. Updated: Apr 14, 2008.

El Valle Lodging

In the actual town of El Valle, there are few tourist accommodation options. Sleeping choices are north of town along the fringes of Playa El Almejal. Here, there is a massive drive to promote and increase tourism. Away from the construction work, there are some pleasant eco-lodges. Updated: Feb 12, 2008.

Hotel Valle

(BED: $4-8) The Hotel Valle offers a roof to go over the traveler's head, some food and little more. This is not a destination in its own right, but a place offering shelter. Double rooms are cramped, with sheets that don't fully cover the mattresses. Towels are provided and rooms are available with private bathrooms. There are two pleasant terraces on the second level. The *ají* sauce prepared by the owner, Lorena, is only for those with a high-chili tolerance! If arriving from the south, cross the long bridge from the agricultural college and follow the road. Otherwise, ask for directions to the main crossroads. Tel: 4-682-7907, E-mail: hotelvalle@hotmail.com.Updated: Dec 19, 2007.

Kipara Hotel

(ROOM: $40-50) An attractive swimming pool and a pleasant location near the stunning El Almejal beach makes the Kipara Hotel a choice escape for people from Medellín. A restaurant and bar are also on-site, though the family-run Kipara is no luxury resort. Updated: Dec 19, 2007.

El Almejal Rainforest and Beach Lodge

This lodge is a destination all on its own. It offers all-inclusive per-person packages for a minimum of three nights and a maximum of seven. A three-night stay at the lodge ($432) includes all of the amenities and one of three expedition choices: a low-impact tour, a pure adventure tour or a whale-watching tour, depending on the season. The sustainable eco-lodge features hammocks surrounded by palm trees, twelve open-air lodges, each with their own bathroom, butterfly gardens and hiking paths. Although the prices are steep, eco-tourism packages include everything from transport, meals, rooms, expeditions and even taxes. Fly into Bahía Solano, then take a jeep to El Valle and down the road to the lodge. Tel: 4-230-6060, URL: www.almejal.com.co. Updated: Mar 12, 2008.

El Valle Restaurants

Most of the lodges and hotels are package deals that include meals. Most likely, you will end up eating where you stay. Food is basic, but enough to stick to your ribs and keep you satiated. Expect fish preceded by fish soup. There are few options in town. The restaurant at the Hotel Valle serves roast chicken, and also doubles as a bakery.

El Valle Nightlife

Nightlife in the area is next to non-existent. Your best bet is to settle down for a few beers with the locals. However, this is not always an option. Remember the town has been known to run out of beers when the roads are closed and supplies can't get through. Updated: Feb 12, 2008.

Bahía Solano

Alt: 5m Pop: 9,000 City Code: 4

Bahía Solano is poised to take advantage of its location to become the Pacific Coast's major tourist destination. The town, protected by a vast bay, is descended upon by hundreds of tourists during the whale-watching and sport-fishing seasons.

The town itself is similar to others along the Pacific Coast, as the tourist aspect is kept separate from the daily life of the locals. All hotels in Bahía Solano are located in the southern end of the town. Use the massive Hotel Balboa Plaza as a reference point and it'll be highly unlikely that you'll get lost. There are just a few restaurants and places to stay, so a great deal of vacationers head to the next beach along the coast, Huina.

The polite and captivating people of Bahía Solano dedicate themselves to various industries: fishing, cattle, agriculture, tourism and the more sinister industry of cocaine fishing. The DAS office and military have a significant presence here. Do not, under any circumstances, attempt to photograph military installations or involve yourself in any way in the drug trade. Updated: Feb 08, 2008.

Highlights

Plunge into one of the **waterfalls** bursting with *agua dulce* (fresh water) located near the town.

Watch from the shore as a **whale** breaches.

Take a dive to the **Sebastián de Benalcázar wreck** **(p.179)**.

Stroll down the uninterrupted and unspoiled **beaches**.

History

Founded in 1935, the original name of Bahía Solano was Puerto Mutis, but over time this name fell by the wayside. As with the rest of the Pacific Coast, the original settlers were the Embera Indians whose territory reaches north into Panama.

Today, the majority of the population is a mix of descendants of African slaves and people who moved from Medellín about 50 years ago. Those from Medellín came expecting Bahía Solano to explode on the tourist circuit, because at the time there were plans to build the Pan-American highway through this area. The plans changed and the highway's route has effectively cut Bahía Solano adrift. Both guerillas and Colombia's armed forces covet Bahía Solano for its strategic geographic location. Updated: Feb 08, 2008.

When to Go

The year-round average temperature is 28°C (82°F). It rains less in the early part of the year, though precipitation is expected daily. Chocó is considered one of the wettest places on earth. Updated: Feb 08, 2008.

Getting To and Away from Bahía Solano

Boat and Air

Ways of getting to Bahía Solano are limited to air transport, unless you arrive by cargo boat from Buenaventura or hire a boat from El Valle or Nuquí. There are frequent flights with Satena and Aexpa to Medellín, and connecting flights can be picked up from there.

Road

The only road in this stretch of the Colombian Pacific connects Bahía Solano to El Valle. Large portions of the road are unpaved making delays inevitable. Four-by-fours make the 20-kilometer journey in the morning for $5 per person. Updated: Feb 08, 2008.

Safety in Bahía Solano

The military presence is strong in Bahía Solano. Any suspicious activities are reported and recorded. Since the conflict is an issue to the north of Bahía Solano, the military checks each hotel and hostel every day to receive updates on guests. Hotel owners are expected to attend security update briefings at least once every fortnight. If you plan on spending any time in Bahía Solano, or traveling in the region, it is recommended you register with the DAS office. Registered travelers will receive updates about security issues in the area. Updated: Mar 10, 2008.

Services

Money

There is one bank in Bahía Solano and it accepts Visa. It is located at the main crossroads, opposite the DAS office.

Keeping in Touch

Only some cell phone companies receive coverage here. Many kiosks and individuals will rent cell phones that charge by the minute.

There is a Telecom office opposite the Hotel Bahía that has internet access. However, Bahía Solano's frequent energy shortages mean the internet is not always functioning.

Medical

Get all your vaccinations before going. There is a clinic in Bahía Solano, but for any emergencies go to Medellín.

Shopping

Your shopping opportunities are limited to a few places off the main strip, which sell T-shirts and sandals. Updated: Mar 10, 2008.

Things to See and Do

Visit the deserted beaches of Huina to the south and Mecana to the north. These are great places for diving and observing marine life. Take a fishing trip off the coast if you are interested in snaring some bluefin tuna. Hike to the waterfalls, just past the military checkpoints along the coast, which explode with agua dulce. Dive to the bottom of the sea to see the Sebastián de Benalcázar, a sunken ship that survived Pearl Harbor and later became a Colombian naval vessel. Contact Rodrigo at the Hostal del Mar, he runs all diving trips from Bahía Solano. During May and September, migrating humpback whales are so abundant that they are easily visible from the shore. Hikes up to the statue of the Virgin offer inspirational views of the city and the bay. For more trip or activity ideas, contact Enrique at the Hotel Rocas de Cabo Marzo. Updated: Feb 11, 2008.

Diving in Bahía Solano

Almost 34 meters below the sea, the wreck of the former Colombian Navy vessel, the Sebastián de Benalcázar, is a mystical attraction. The site is out of reach to open-water divers, but remains an enticing destination for more advanced divers. The ship, scuttled to provide a haven for marine life, has an incredibly interesting history. Originally a US Navy boat that survived Pearl Harbor, it was decommissioned by the US, sold to Colombia and named after a Spanish conquistador. At that time, the vessel and crew were responsible for intercepting the largest shipment of weapons destined for the M19 guerrilla group. Today, experienced divers glide over the ship's hull, view into the control room and massive snappers, groupers and the occasional shark. For very experienced divers, if the conditions are appropriate, there are possibilities of exploring within. For more information on diving, contact Rodrigo Fajardo at the Hostal del Mar. Tel: 4-682-7415, E-mail: rfajardo@bis.com.co. Updated: Mar 10, 2008.

V!VA Member Review-Sebastián de Benalcázar

The diving was incredible. Although we saw no sharks, there were enormous groupers, snapper and just before immersion we spotted a turtle and a pair of whales. Nov. 05, 2007, London.

Sport Fishing

Every June and July fishing enthusiasts descend onto the murky Pacific waters in Bahía Solano, Cupica and Tribuga for catch and release tournaments. The reward isn't really the money as much as the bragging rights that come with snagging a marlin. People also haul in tuna, barracuda and sharks. Remember that trips of this nature will be costly, given the nature of the sport. Plus, gasoline needs to be stockpiled. Contact expert fisherman Enrique García Reyes. Tel: 4-682-7525, E-mail: bahiatebada@hotmail.com, URL: www.maparacrab.com. Updated: Mar 10, 2008.

Bahía Solano Lodging

There are a variety of accommodations in Bahía Solano that include the opulent, like the Hotel Balboa Plaza, and places that clearly rent by the hour. During high season, you'll want to book a room in advance, especially on the longer holiday weekends when the town comes under siege by Colombian vacationers. Updated: Feb 11, 2008.

Hostal del Mar

(BED: $10-15) These are self-contained cabañas run by the town's dive center, meaning this hostal caters to the backpacking and diving crowd. It's comfortable, friendly and the best budget choice. Rodrigo, the owner, has been in Bahía Solano for many years, knows all the dive spots and points of interest, and can regale you with tales of adventure. Find the Hotel Balboa Plaza, then head south for two blocks. The next building after the Satena office is the Hostal del Mar. Tel: 4-682-7415, E-mail: hostaldelmarbahiasolano@yahoo.com. Updated: Mar 11, 2008.

Hotel Bahía

(ROOM: $12-25) This 15-room hotel is the better of the two opposing buildings on the so-called *Calle de Comercio*. Rooms are unimpressive, but are clean and come with private bathroom. The hotel has a decent restaurant on the ground floor and a small kiosk for making phone calls. Ask any taxi driver from the airport, he'll have you there within 15 minutes. Otherwise, just look for the towering Hotel Balboa Plaza, head for that and the Hotel Bahía is across the way. Calle 3, 2-34, Tel: 4-682-7047 / 7048. Updated: Mar 11, 2008.

Hotel Rocas de Cabo Marzo

(ROOM: $25-50) Hotel Las Rocas de Cabo Marzo is a posada right on the coast, ensconced by the jungle. Hotel owners Nancy and Enrique have lived in Bahía Solano for almost two decades. They know everything there is to know, and open their home to travelers in order to share their vast knowledge of the area. They also will put together special package tours. With only five rooms, the hotel is effectively a family-run guesthouse. Rooms come with double beds, private bathrooms and mosquito nets. Enrique is a committed sports fisherman and diver, and Nancy is a phenomenal cook. They make the Rocas de Cabo Marzo among the best places to stay in Bahía Solano. Get a taxi at the airport and tell the driver to take you to the Balboa Plaza Hotel, turn left and head south from there. Tel: 4-682-7525, E-mail: bahiatebada@hotmail.com, URL: www.maparacrab.com. Updated: Mar 11, 2008.

Hotel Balboa Plaza

(ROOM: $35-60) In the hands of its original owner and creator, Pablo Escobar, this hotel must have been truly opulent. Now, its glory has faded considerably and the external features need some attention. Torn, stained awnings flutter in tatters over the windows. The garden—a nice place to enjoy a beer—has seen better days and the mural beside the pool is weathering into nothingness. The restaurant is passable. The hotel has plans to renovate many of the rooms. Tel: 4-682-7075, Fax: 4-682-7401, E-mail: hotelbalboap@telecom.com.co. Updated: Mar 11, 2008.

El Refugio de Mr. Jerry

(ROOM: $50-80) A 10-minute boat ride around the bay from Bahía Solano to Huina reveals another beach with more accommodations. One of these is what is known simply as Mr. Jerry's. The building could use some superficial work, but Mr. Jerry's can comfortably sleep 50. The hotel works mostly with package tours, which include three meals, flights and transfer to Huina. If not, contract a fisherman to take you to Mr. Jerry's. Tel: 4-682-7233, E-mail: mrjerrybahiasolano@telesat.com.co. Updated: Mar 10, 2008.

Playa de Oro Lodge

The Playa de Oro Lodge is a massive construction on Huina beach that caters to package tourists from Medellín. The resort is made up of four blocks, each with eight rooms. All have private bathrooms, fans and a hammock on a private terrace. The package

The Cocaine Industry in Bahía Solano

Bahía Solano's pivotal location in the transportation of narcotics has made local involvement inevitable. Although there is no obvious consumption of the product in Bahía Solano, the industry, made lucrative by the US and Europe, certainly makes waves here.

In recent years, fishermen no longer fish as much for the traditional catch, but instead for 25-kilo parcels of cocaine thrown overboard from drug boats on their way north, under threat of capture by the Colombian authorities. A fisherman stands to gain $25,000 by collecting the parcel, hiding it on a secluded beach, informing a buyer and essentially selling it back to its owner. The profit margins are so great that neither party is particularly upset.

One strange side-effect of the cocaine industry is that Bahía Solano—with an oceanfront abundant in fish—is often left without fish to buy. Restaurants are void of fish to prepare. The supply aircrafts from Medellín stop making trips to the area since they make the return route without fish to sell. Updated: Feb 08, 2008.

deal includes transportation from the airport in Bahía Solano and a transfer to Huina. Tel: 4-682-7481, E-mail: info@hotelesdecostaa-costa.com, URL: www.hotelesdecostaacosta.com. Updated: Mar 10, 2008.

Bahía Solano Restaurants

The restaurants in Bahía Solano offer the standard fare of the region—fried fish, patacones and rice. Remember, sometimes the fishermen are distracted by the prominent drug industry and restaurants could run low on fresh catch. The majority of restaurants also offer set meals as an alternative.

Bahía Solano Nightlife

The discos and bars in Bahía Solano are for the locals. Grab a beer, sit down and you'll make friends. At the crossroads beyond the DAS office, there is typically a small crowd enjoying excessively loud music, at any hour of the day. Updated: Feb 11, 2008.

Balboa Plaza Restaurant

One peek inside the hotel shows off the typical restaurant décor; it could be anywhere in the world. The food is standard, but since numbers of visitors are low, the establishment does not see fit to replenish dwindling provisions. Sometimes tuna can be the only thing on the menu for multiple nights in a row. The Hotel Balboa Plaza. Tel: 4-682-7075, E-mail: hotelbalboap@telecom.com.co. Updated: Mar 10, 2008.

Las Palmas

The expression "cheap and cheerful" could not apply to a nicer, more pleasant place in Bahía Solano. This restaurant is family run and owned. Las Palmas has set menus for lunch and dinner that price out at roughly $4. A dish of fried fish, rice and plantains is preceded by soup. They also stock cuts of beef and chicken. It is next door to the Hotel Bahía. Updated: Mar 10, 2008.

O Sole Mío

Run by Enrique at the Rocas de Cabo Marzo Hotel, this pizzeria offers more than just pizza. His wife, Nancy, conjures up tasty delights from the Pacific Region, especially incredible fish dishes. There is a family-like, relaxing atmosphere. Tel: 4-682-7525, E-mail: bahiatebada@hotmail.com, URL: www.maparacrab.com. Updated: Mar 10, 2008.

Hotel Bahía restaurant

Offering standard set meals at lunch and dinner, the Hotel Bahía's restaurant is a good budget option. Fish, of course, is the most prevalent dish on the menu, but cuts of pork, beef and chicken are also available. All is freshly prepared and accompanied with rice, salad and patacones. Calle 3, 2-34. Tel: 4-682-7047. Updated: Mar 10, 2008.

Puerto Ventura

One of two fast food restaurants in Bahía Solano. The Puerto Ventura does a brisk trade in hamburgers, hot dogs and other ubiquitous fast-food items. They also squeeze an excellent, fresh fruit juice. The juice may seem pricey, but rest assured it is large and refreshing. Updated: Mar 10, 2008.

Jimmy's

The other fast food restaurant in town, Jimmy's is at the end of the main road past the DAS office. Pizza and hamburgers are the house specialities, and the dining experience is enhanced by a lovely sea view. The place does a roaring trade on weekends and is a fine spot to have a beer while watching the sunset. Updated: Mar 10, 2008.

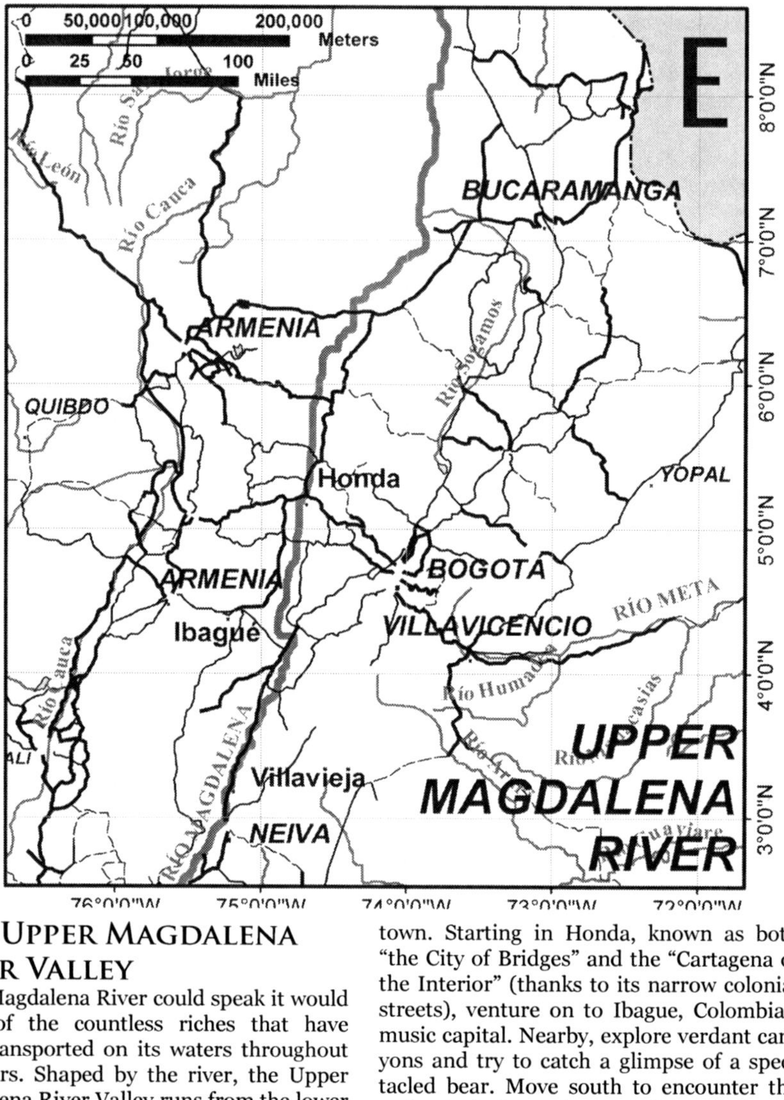

The Upper Magdalena River Valley

If the Magdalena River could speak it would boast of the countless riches that have been transported on its waters throughout the years. Shaped by the river, the Upper Magdalena River Valley runs from the lower extremes of the Andes (at the river's source in Huila) to the well-preserved statues of San Agustín. It continues its run through the arid badlands of the Tatacoa Desert and past Nevado del Tolima, a towering snow-capped mountain standing 5,200m. over the departmental capital of Ibague. The Magdalena then encounters the last navigable point from the coast inland, Honda.

Travelers to this area should be pleasantly surprised by the unique offerings in each town. Starting in Honda, known as both "the City of Bridges" and the "Cartagena of the Interior" (thanks to its narrow colonial streets), venture on to Ibague, Colombia's music capital. Nearby, explore verdant canyons and try to catch a glimpse of a spectacled bear. Move south to encounter the archeological wonder of Neiva, which will whet the appetite for the wonders further down the road at San Agustín.

Many of these towns and settlements date back to earlier than 1,000 B.C. So, given their history and the importance of the river as one of Colombia's principal highways, it is no wonder that they have played a major significance in Colombia. Updated: Mar 14, 2008.

Highlights

Visit the magnificent **anthropomorphic statues** on display in the parks around San Agustín.

Lesser known, but well worth a visit, are the badlands of the **Tatacoa Desert (p.186)**, which are perfect for camping.

Lush, sunny valleys and charming towns create a must-experience environment around **Ibagué (p.188).**
Updated: Apr 14,2008

History

Antigua Taberna Queirolo,the departments of Tolima and Huila, which make up the majority of the Upper Magdalena River Valley, has played host to a fascinating past. This includes advanced pre-Columbian tribes who created the wonders found around San Agustín. The history of the region is full of tales of indigenous royalty martyred by the Spanish. Indigenous tribes flourished until the arrival of the Spanish conquistadors in 1538. Records show numerous successful communities along the Magdalena that violently opposed the invaders and made Spanish settlement of this region difficult, to say the least. Eventually the Spanish influence grew and the local opposition abated. During the Colonial and Republican eras, the Magdalena turned into a major commercial and transit route through Colombia. Honda, in particular, rose to prominence as Colombia's wealth passed through this inland port. Updated: Apr 14, 2008.

When to Go

December to March are the driest months around Upper Magdalena. In order to really enjoy the cities around the region it is worth keeping a rain jacket handy and knowing the dates of the local festivals. Consider timing your trip to coincide with Honda's Festival de la Subienda in February or Neiva's Reinado del Bambuco and Ibague's Folkloric Festival, which both take place in June. Updated: Mar 14, 2008.

Safety in Upper Magdalena

Although the Upper Magdalena River Valley is considered an overall safe place for traveling, it is worth noting that in 2007 there were two attempts in Neiva to assassinate the then-mayor. Neiva is the gateway to the regions of Caquetá and Putumayo, which are considered the red zone. So, there is always a possibility that some violence, normally restricted around Neiva, may spill over. Updated: Mar 14, 2008.

Things to See and Do

Taveling around the Upper Magdalena River Valley is typically an unconventional route. But, it is one that will not disappoint. In the same day it is possible to revel in the striking contrasts between the Tatacoa Desert and the rock sculptures in San Agustín. For walkers, hikers, climbers and rafters, the region includes the Combeima Canyon, the Nevado del Tolima and the rapids on the Magdalena. For the non-outdoorsy types, there are plenty of cultural indulgences around—many of these can be found in Ibague. Those who appreciate good food shouldn't pass up trying a *tamale tolimense.* Updated: Dec 19,2007.

Upper Magdalena Tours

Tourism is still in a fledgling state in this region. For the best and most up-to-date details, contact the following:

Ibagué	Proyectos de promoción Turística. Tel: 8-267-8906
Nevado de Tolima	Fundación Yulima. Tel: 8-261-2902
Tolima (general)	Gobernación de Tolima. Tel: 1-288-2349, casatolima@etb.net.co, turismotolima@gov.co, www.tolima.gov.co
Huila (general)	Secretaría de Cultura y Turismo del Huila. Tel: 8-874-1198
Tatacoa	Secretaría de Cultura y Turismo Villavieja, Tel: 8-879-7744 (ext. 110)

Updated: Dec 19, 2007.

Upper Magdalena Lodging

Accommodation options in the Upper Magdalena River Valley are surprisingly varied and, on the whole, pretty good quality. Since it has been on the tourist map for a few years, traditional backpacker and trav-

UPPER MAGDALENA

eler haunts are readily available in in San Agustín. In Ibagué and Neiva, however, expect cheap hotel options with little character or sense of community. And, if you decide to visit the Tatacoa Desert, your accommodation options are limited to camping. Updated: Dec 19, 2007.

NEIVA

Alt: 442m Pop: 331,000 City Code: 8

Neiva is a city moving ahead in tourism. A key intermediary city in this part of the country, Neiva has traditionally connected conventional tourist destinations like Popayán and San Agustín to more off-the-beaten-track places like Caquetá and Putumayo. These days, major efforts are being made to make the city more than that and more aesthetically pleasing.

Neiva offers a variety of activities, including the shady Parque Santander in the heart of the city and the Malecón del Río Magdalena at the river's edge. If the city doesn't capture your fancy, then it makes a perfect base to explore the attractions in the surrounding parts of the region, such as the Tatacoa Desert to the north and Parque Isla on the opposite side of the Magdalena. If you can, be sure to get to Neiva in June for the notoriously riotous festivals that take place. Updated: Feb 27, 2008.

HISTORY

Prior to the arrival of the Spanish in 1538, there existed a complex and developed indigenous civilization around the Huila region. (There have been numerous archeological artifacts found in the area.) Between 1000 B.C. and 1650 A.D. the Agustinian culture reigned supreme, before petering away—though not without a fight. Famed sites, like those in San Agustín, are what's left of the culture today. Local tribes, like the Pijao, the Andiquie, the Yalcones, the Paeces and the Tamas, all fiercely opposed the conquistadores. They made life and imperial expansion difficult in this region. Neiva was first founded in 1539 by Juan de Cabrera, but was subsequently destroyed. The city was founded a second time by Juan Alonso on the present-day site of Villavieja to the north, though this too was destroyed. Finally, in May 1612, Diego de Ospina y Medinilla, chancellor of Nueva Granada, founded "Limpia Concepcion del Valle de Neiva," where Neiva has stood ever since. Updated: Feb 27, 2008.

When to Go

Given its relatively low altitude and the fact that it is near the equator, Neiva is always hot, with temperatures continually in the 30s.

Holidays and Fiestas
May ▶ Birthday of Neiva
June ▶ Festival of Folklore and Senorita Neiva
June ▶ Fiesta de San Pedro .
Updated: Feb 27, 2008.

Getting To and Away From Neiva

Aeropuerto Benito Sala de Neiva is a five-minute taxi ride from downtown. Buses to Bogotá ($10) with Cootranshuila and Coomotor leave at 1 p.m. and take five hours. Neiva is also a key connection point for buses into the lesser known regions of Caquetá and Putumayo. To get to the Tatacoa desert, take the Coomotor collectivo van at the far end of the Terminal to Villavieja ($2.50, 1 hour). Updated: Feb 27, 2008.

SAFETY IN NEIVA

Neiva is safe. There really is no feeling of personal danger or aggression toward tourists. However, there were two attempts in 2007 on the then-mayor's life. There were two car bombs found, possibly placed by the FARC. One bomb was deactivated and the other detonated, causing a great deal of damage. Updated: Feb 27, 2008.

NEIVA SERVICES

Tourism Office

There is a good tourist info booth in the Terminal de Transportes. For further information, contact the Secretaria de Cultura y Turismo de Huila, Cra 5, 21-81, Tel: 8-875-3042.

Money

Around the Parque Santander you will find every bank and cash machine you could need.

Medical

Hospital Universitario Hernando Moncaleano—Calle 9, 15-25, 8-871-5907.
Clinica Nueva—Cra 4, 9-46, Tel: 8-871-0998.

Shopping

Although there are some shopping centers around Neiva, this is not a shopaholic's destination. To pick up some trinkets and souvenirs from the region, head to the Malecón del Río Magdalena for a number of artisan stalls.

Centro Comercial Metropolitano—Cra 5, 6-28.

Centro Comercial La Decima—Ca. 4, 5-41.

Updated: Feb 27, 2008.

Things to See and Do

Neiva offers enough options to keep a traveler busy, including the arid Tatacoa desert in the north and the attractions along the Magdalena, like the bars, restaurants, clubs and the ecological park. Don't forget that though these might not seem like the biggest and best attractions, Neiva is a completely different kind of place in June. The riotous partying that happens during the festival is recognized as among Colombia's best. Updated: Feb 27, 2008.

Termales de Rivera/Rivera Hot Springs

About a half hour south of Neiva, the Rivera Hot Springs make for a good day trip or overnight excursion, especially for families. The natural hot springs have been made into a water park, of sorts. There are well-designed warm and cool pools, some pools have slides and there is a spa. The hot springs offer other activities like horseback riding and hiking. This place tends to not be frequented by tourists, but is very popular with Colombians. The park is reasonably priced, and there is an on-site hotel and restaurant. Just outside of the town of Rivera, about 30 km south of Neiva. Tel: 8-838-7147, E-mail: recreacion@comfamiliarhuila.com.Updated: Apr 21, 2008.

Piedra Pintada Aipe

At more than 6m long and 3m high, it is a wonder that the Piedra Pintada (Painted Rock) has survived the ages. Try to make meaning of the carvings and marks made by both the Paeces and Pijaos tribes. Experts believe this was likely a meeting point for commerce and trade. In the immediate vicinity archeologists have found burial grounds and ceramic utensils. It is thought that perhaps proves that this was once a sizeable community. Updated: Feb 06, 2008

Neiva Tours

For the Tatacoa desert, you can easily contract a guide as you enter the town of Villavieja. To hire one in advance, contact the Alcaldia at 8-879-7744 (ext 110). Updated: Feb 27, 2008

Neiva Lodging

One thing to bear in mind in Neiva is that any establishment listing itself as a "hostel" is actually a place that rents its rooms by the hour and is not a hotel. On the whole, there are decent options in Neiva for those on a budget, such as the Hotel Andino. If money is not a consideration then the Hotel Khalifa is not a bad choice. Rooms will book up fast in June for the festival, so booking in advance is recommended. Updated: Feb 27, 2008.

Hotel Andino

(ROOM: $13-20) Set back from the noisy Calle 9, the Hotel Andino is the budget destination of choice in Neiva. The 20 rooms are newly painted, all have a fan, private bathroom, cable TV and telephone. You are not getting luxury, but you are in a secure place in the center of town. You can walk to all sites of interest and are very close to all the major banks. Calle 9, 5-82. Tel: 8-871-7844, Fax: 8-871-3853. Updated: Feb 06, 2008.

Hotel Géminis

(ROOM: $20-25) The proprietors at Hotel Géminis, in front of the Concha Acustica, have made significant efforts to clean the place up. This hotel caters to both the rent-by-the-hour crowd and those who wish to stay several nights. Rooms are accommodating, with all the usual amenities. The only aspect that could remind you about the hotel's other, less salubrious side is that most rooms have mirrors on the ceiling! Calle 7, 8-37. Tel: 8-871-4954. Updated: Feb 06, 2008.

Hotel Khalifa

(ROOM: $24-33) This is Neiva's more regal option, if your budget is up to it. You can negotiate the price down by paying in cash. Hotel Khalifa has 48 rooms comfortably equipped; rooms with fans instead of A/C are cheaper. The place is unlikely to fill up, apart from during Neiva's fiestas and any conferences. Cra 6, 8-76. Tel: 8-871-2021, Fax: 8-871 0023. Updated: Feb 06, 2008.

Hotel Casa Pablo

(ROOM: $24-40) The Hotel Casa Pablo is up the hill, out of the hubub of central Neiva. This three-floor hotel has plenty of rooms that range from cheaper ones on the ground floor with fans and no A/C to more luxurious ones on higher levels. All rooms have private en-suite bathrooms and cable TV. Plus, the owner is very knowledgeable about things to see and do in and around Neiva. Calle 5, 12-45. Tel: 8-872-3100, Fax: 8-871-2807, E-mail: hotelcasapablo@gmail.com. Updated: Feb 06, 2008.

Neiva Restaurants

If downing a chilled, freshly blended juice is your vice, then you have come to the right city—Neiva has a vast quantity of *fruterias*. Along the Magdalena River's main boardwalk there are a dozen or so options for dining that all more or less offer the same fare, so take your pick. The mayor's office set this area aside to promote tourism and increase nightlife options in Neiva.

Things are pretty low-key during the week. But, during the weekends Neiva's nightlife really kicks off along the Magdalena. Open-air bars and clubs all tend to get pretty lively. Otherwise, the Neiva Plaza Hotel on the Parque Santander claims to have the best nightclub in town. It wouldn't be unheard of to try out all the options and then decide what you like best. Updated: Feb 27, 2008.

Super Jugos La Ñapa

It might not look like much at first glance, but this is where the locals come, and often, for a cooling fruit juice and cheap, filling snacks. Fruits of all shapes and sizes are blended up here into juices. Sip on a concoction of tropical flavors, which are untranslatable into English, for as little as $0.65. If you're hungry, grab a sandwich for a $1. Cra 5, 12-54. Updated: Feb 06, 2008.

Brasas del Río

The Brasas del Río is one of the establishments along the Magdalena River. In this pleasant riverside setting, surrounded by abundant greenery and artesans stalls, feast on a *Huilense Parilla* (pork) or more traditional fare such as grilled beef, chicken or fish. Prices are reasonable and the restaurant is a nice place to enjoy a cold beer and people watch. Malecón del Río Magdalena. Updated: Feb 06, 2008.

Tijuana

Wedged between a Renault dealership on one side and a garage on the other, the proprietors of Tijuana could have chosen a more tranquil spot for ther restaurant and bar. Despite this, the adobe-style architecture, Mexican flags and good food make this somewhere to enjoy something different than the usual fare in Neiva. Prices are reasonable and the margaritas are perfect for those who want to cool off from the equatorial heat. Cra 5, between Calles 11 and 12. Updated: Feb 06, 2008.

Frutería y Heladería Alaska

Clearly a cool place—a juice bar with the name of the States' most northern state in the hot region of Neiva. Here is an exhaustive list of fruit juices and some interesting house concoctions such as "El Boxeador," which includes fruit and a raw egg, or the "Explosivo," which includes crab! Some creations may not be to your liking, but the conventional and the random (*curuba, cebada, chulupa, borojo*) are all here, for low prices. Cra 6, 8-36. Updated: Feb 06, 2008.

Huila Café

On the second floor of an elegant hall with high ceilings, swooshing fans and ample space, Huila is more than just your average café. Couples canoodle in private corners, the coffee is excellent, and the location is among Neiva's best. If you are peckish, a croissant will set you back $1.50. Opposite the Post Office, 6-59 on the second floor. Updated: Feb 06, 2008.

Desierto de la Tatacoa

In the northern part of Huila, people have rarely heard of or visited the Tatacoa Desert. It should really be on every traveler's list of things to do in Colombia. It rates highly with all those who do manage to get out to the 33,000 hectares of red and gray rock. In addition to an incredible scenery that is remiscent of a Spaghetti Western, with towering cacti and interesting rock formations, the Tatacoa Desert is a huge paleontological cemetery. Visit the area around Villavieja, approximately 40 minutes from Neiva, to camp out for free under the stars. When heading out from Neiva, don't forget to pack plenty of water, sun block and look for the Coomotor collectivo vans at the far end of the bus terminal, which leave when full. Updated: Feb 06, 2008.

Villavieja

Alt: 347m Pop: 2,000 City Code: 8

Villavieja is a tiny village, with closest proximity to the Tatacoa desert. Nearby Villavieja is Aipe, which is across the river and on the main highway that runs between Neiva and Bogotá. Be aware that Villlaviejans don't like residents of Aipe. They believe people from Aipe are thieves. Neither town wants to build a bridge to make transportation easier for each other or visitors to the Tatacoa Desert. Based on the bad blood between these two towns, some say it may be safer to bypass Aipe altogether. That said, it does not feel dangerous. Updated: Feb 06,2008.

Getting To and Away from Villavieja

If you're heading to Villavieja from Ibagué or Bogotá and you prefer not to travel to Neiva and backtrack to Villavieja, then take any bus to Neiva and get dropped off on the highway in Aipe. Walk through Aipe and down the hill to the river bank. It should take about 20 minutes (1.6km). There is a motorized canoe that shuttles people back and forth across the river between Aipe and Villavieja every half an hour during the day ($1, 15 minutes). From the drop-off point on the other side of the river, it's a short 10 minute walk to Villavieja. The easiest way to get to Villavieja is from Neiva (1 hour, $3). Collectivos run hourly from 9 a.m. - 6 p.m. A morning bus to Bogotá (5 hours, $12) leaves Villavieja at 5 a.m.

Things to See and Do

Piscina Orfanda

Not quite an oasis, but certainly a perfect location for a pool, Piscina Orfanda is a private pool about 10km into the desert. It provides visitors with perfect freshwater relaxation amid idyllic gray sand and green cacti. The water comes from a natural spring just up the hill from the pool. It's crystal clear and just the right temperature. The pool is on the small side (you can't swim laps). It is a popular spot for locals on the weekend, so head there early (before 10 a.m.) if you want it all to yourself. $2 for adults, $1.50 for kids. Updated: May 28, 2008.

Villavieja Tours

Chopo Taxi !

Chopo, a most enthusiastic local Villaviejan, is more than happy to serve as your local guide and taxi driver during your visit to the Tatacoa Desert and around. He knows the best places to go and best times to visit the different places in the desert. Know ahead of time that Chopo will drive his blue taxi around town and wave at nearly every person on the street. His family also owns a small store in Villavieja. Cost: $1 for a ride around town, $5 to the observatory and $20 for a full five-hour excursion in the desert. Tel: 313 865 8710. E-mail: chopotaxi@hotmail.com. Updated: May 28, 2008.

Villavieja Lodging

El Observatorio

(BED: $6-10) The observatory at the entrance of the Tatacoa Desert isn't just for watching the sunset, the moon rise and the world turn. Owners Pisco and Alberto also provide a variety of accommodations for sleeping under the stars in the desert. They hang hammocks on the front porch, rent tents and have two cabanas with private bathrooms. The idea here is to really get the desert experience from dusk 'til dawn. There are mosquitoes and other invisible biting bugs at night, so bring repellent or a net.

No need to call ahead for reservations. Hire a local taxi (a small tri-wheel *tuk tuk*) to take you to the desert along the paved road from Villavieja. The observatory will be on the left just before the road becomes unpaved. Updated: May 28, 2008.

Hospedaje La Cason

(BED: $8-12) La Cason is the only local, official accomodation. It has three enormous dorm rooms; one can sleep more than 10 people. Its huge backyard serves as the restaurant. There is even an empty, dry swimming pool that might be functioning someday or might not. Since there are so few visitors to Villavieja, reserving a room in this one-hotel town is not currently necessary. Updated: May 28, 2008.

Villavieja Nightlife

El Tizón

If you're looking for some good, old-fashioned, live country music, dancing and fun, El Tizón has got just that. This place gets packed in the evenings and stays open until the country folk decide to ride their horses (or motorcycles) home, which is often when the sun rises the next morning. The *vallenatos* and *rancheras* music—complete with accordion, acoustic guitar, drumming and twangy vocals—booms from this happening nightspot at the edge of town. There is a five-piece live band that plays on the weekends.Updated: May 28, 2008.

Parque Nacional Natural Nevado del Huila

The Parque de los Nevados (Nevados National Park) attracts thousands of trekkers, hikers and climbers each year. (It is definitely recommended to hire a guide and to bring your warmest hiking clothes.) Bird watchers might find this park especially interesting, since it is home to birds like the Golden Eagle, Andes Condor, Bull Pisco, tanagers and hummingbirds. Founded in 1977, the 158,000 hectare park close to the Magdalena River is broken up throughout Colombia's departments of Huila, Tolima and Cauca.

The park features indigenous ruins, Laguna Paez and an area of volcanic wasteland, which includes Colombia's highest, and not-so-dormant, volcano. The snow-capped Nevado del Huila stands at 17,602ft (5,364 m) and is 241.4km southwest of Bogotá. Dormant for more than 400 years, the volcano woke up in 2007 and, as of May 2008, had already erupted numerous times. According to the Smithsonian Institution's Global Volcanism Program, the eruptions have caused damaging mudslides and thousands of residents were evacuated from their homes. Please check with government agencies and/or the Smithsonian, before traveling to this area.

Keep in mind, when heading out to the park that the closest hospital is in Neiva. So, please, when going hiking, bring along a first aid kit and keep altitude sickness and frostbite in mind. Hours: 8 a.m. — 4 p.m. Accommodations: Camping is the only sleeping option inside the park. Updated: Jun 02, 2008.

Ibagué

Alt: 1,285m Pop: 440,000 City Code:8

Ibagué resembles Bucaramanga, only smaller. Ibagué's recent growth reflects its growth in importance. Multinational chain stores even have sprung up on the city's edge. As if trapped in a breathless valley, temperatures average out at 24°C, keeping Ibagué a pleasant year-round destination. As the capital of the Tolima department, it also plays an important role in the cultural development of the country by hosting the Colombian Festival of Folklore. For more than 30 years the Tolimenses have been blending music, dance and gastronomy beneath the towering Nevado del Tolima and welcoming all to participate. Updated: Feb 27, 2008.

History

Andrés López de Galarza originally founded Ibagué in 1550 on the current-day site of Cajamarca. The town was originally called Villa de San Bonifacio de Ibagué del Valle de las Lanzas. It was moved a year later to escape the spears and continuing attacks of the Pijao Indians. The town grew steadily and was drawn into the spotlight for a brief spell as the capital of Nueva Granada after a Coup d'Etat in 1854. Updated: Feb 27, 2008.

When to Go

Holidays and Fiestas

Month	Event
March	National Duets Competition
June	Colombia Festival of Folklore
June	Fiestas of San Pablo

Updated: Feb 27, 2008.

Getting To and Away From Ibagué

Plane

Aeropuerto Perales de Ibagué—8-267-5662, 8-268-5600.

Bus

Terminal de Transporte de Ibagué—Cra 2, 20-86, 8-261-8122.
There are bus connections to all over Colombia at the Terminal de Transportes.
Updated: Feb 27, 2008.

Safety in Ibagué

Exercise caution when walking in the city center around Carrera 1, the several abandoned areas make for some sketchy spots. The tourist office in the bus station does not recommend walking from the Terminal Transporte to the town center, since the path goes through an abandoned park. A taxi to a hotel in the center from the bus terminal should cost no more than $1.50. Aside from these tips, Ibagué is a safe place to visit. Updated: Feb 27, 2008.

Ibagué Services

Tourism Office

There is a helpful tourism information booth in the bus terminal. For further details, contact the Camara de Comercio on 8-263-1784.

Medical

Hospital Federico Lleras Acosta—Calle 33, 4A-50, 8-264-0888.
Clinica Tolima—Cra 1, 12-22, 8-261-0367
Updated: Feb 27, 2008.

Shopping

The city is well known for its music. There are several music shops just off Cra 3 in downtown. Since Ibagué is a large city, it has a few good shopping centers:
Centro Comercial Multicentro—Av El Jordan Calle 64 Centro.
Comercial La Quinta— Cra 5, 29-32.
Centro Comercial Combeima—Cra 3, 12-54. Updated: Feb 27, 2008.

Things to See and Do

Ibagué, Colombia's Musical City, places a strong emphasis on the arts. The downtown bars and restaurants reflect this, as well as the Teatro Tolima. In addition to the draw of art and culture, the valley surrounding Ibagué also provides a unique pull. Outdoor pursuits in the Combeima Canyon are becoming increasingly popular. Maybe you could conquer the Nevado del Tolima peak. Updated: Mar 04, 2008.

Teatro Tolima

Ibague's love of the arts is most apparent at the Teatro Tolima. Originally built in 1915, the theater was later renovated and constructed in an imposing Art Deco style. Get your ticket to one of the many shows listed on the theater window. The theater can house up to 1,000 people. Teatro Tolima, Cra. 3, 11-76. Tel: 8-261-1608, Fax: 8-261-0328, E-mail: info@teatrotolima.com, URL: www.teatrotolima.com. Updated: Feb 06, 2008.

Combeima Canyon

The Combeima Canyon is the gateway to the Nevado del Tolima and a favorite getaway for ibaguereños during long weekends. The Canyon is known for its clean air, beautiful scenery and interesting flora and fauna. Roughly 30km from the city of Ibagué, around the Canyon, are the towns of Chapeton, Tres Esquinas, Llanitos, Pastales, Villerestrepo and Juntas. Things to enjoy around here are typical dishes from the region, bathing in waterfalls, biking or rock climbing. The town of El Rancho is closer to the mountains. It has medicinal hot springs recognized for healing properties, which could be great after the gruelling ascent of the Nevado del Tolima. Updated: Feb 06, 2008.

Climbing the Nevado del Tolima

The snowcapped peak of the Nevado del Tolima presents a challenge that hikers, climbing enthusiasts and adventure sports junkies should not miss. At 5,200m, the Nevado del Tolima is both one of the most difficult and beautiful peaks in Colombia. The route up is steep and rocky and at any moment you are at the mercy of a downpour. In order to truly appreciate the ascent and descent of the mountain, factor a trip of three days. Bring as much of your own equipment as possible to make the trip more economical. Also, start looking into about guides and information at least two days before you want to make the climb, to find the best resources. Updated: Feb 06, 2008.

Ibagué Tours

Ibagué has yet to fully grasp the tourism bull by the horns, but slowly and surely the potential for growth in this field is being recognized. For further information on tours and packages, contact Jaime Gutierrez of JM Logistica y Eventos. Cell: 315-213-9176, E-mail: jmturismolocal@yahoo.es, jmturismolocal@hotmail.com, URL: www.jmlogisticayeventoszzn.com. Updated: Feb 27, 2008.

Ibagué Lodging

You can find most budget and mid-range hotels downtown. Standards vary from the de-

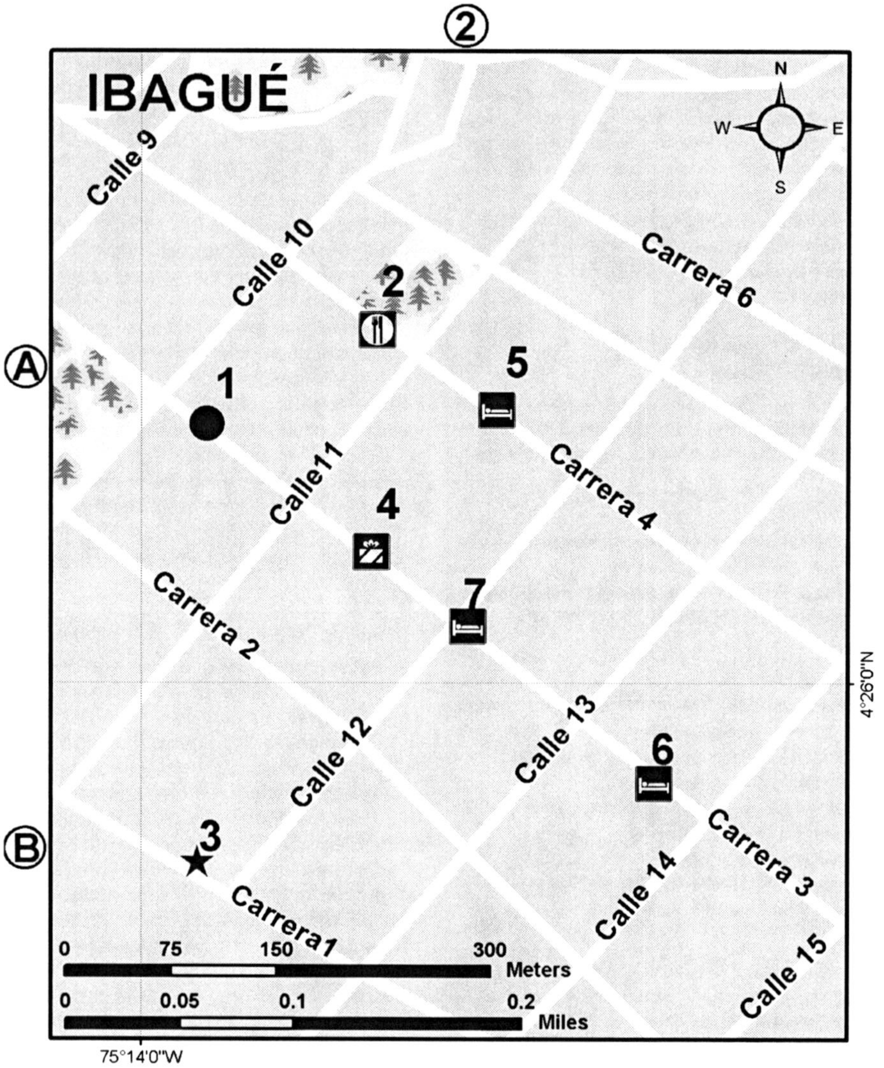

Activities ●
1 Teatro Tolima A2

Eating
2 Chuzo Restaurante A2

Services ★
3 Clínica Tolima B2

Shopping
4 Centro Comercial Combeima A2

Sleeping
5 Hotel Center A2
6 Hotel Lafont A2
7 Nelson's Inn Hotel B2

cidedly seedy to the passable to outright value. Worthy of note for their low prices, hospitality and helpfulness are Nelson's Inn and the Hotel Center. Updated: Feb 27, 2008.

Hotel Center

(ROOM: $15-25) In a perfect world, every hotel would be a little more like the Hotel Center. The location in the center of Ibagué is unrivaled; great restaurants are nearby. Additionally, it has clean, comfortable rooms with WiFi, cable TV and a private bathroom with hot water. More to the point, it is affordable. The staff do everything within their power to make your stay a pleasant one. They offer advice on sites of interest and connect you with tour companies. Cra 4, 12-52. Tel: 8-263-7181, Fax: 8-263-7186, URL: www.hotelcenteribague.com. Updated: Feb 06, 2008.

Hotel Lafont

(ROOM: $15-20) The Hotel Lafont is in a shabby 1970s-style building right in the heart of Ibagué. Upon entry you're greeted by a cracked stairwell, poor paintwork and worn decór, which offers an insight into how the establishment is run. However, these are only surface flaws. This really is a decent, cheap option in the center of town. The hotel has 22 rooms, all with private bathrooms and cable TV. In the lobby there is a restaurant, laundry, conference room and a few computers for Internet use. Calle 14, 3-19. Tel: 8-263-1519. Updated: Feb 06, 2008.

Nelson's Inn Hotel

(ROOM: $36-50) A step up from the Hotel Center, Nelson's Inn has nothing to do with the English Naval hero and is called this simply because it's the owner's name. It is right on the doorstep of Ibagué's pedestrian-only Cra 3 and close to restaurants, bars and shops. Nelson's Inn is a fine place, especially if passing though Ibagué on business. The hotel has 41 rooms, all with a fan, cable TV, a private bathroom with hot water and some rooms have balconies. Internet is not yet available in the rooms, but the hotel's foyer has WiFi and some computers for free guest use. Calle 13, 2-94. Tel: 8-261-1867, Fax: 8-261-1810, E-mail: nelsonsinnhotel@latinmail.com. Updated: Feb 06, 2008.

Ibagué Restaurants

The region of Tolima is recognized throughout Colombia for tasty pork dishes and flavorful tamales, neither of which are hard to come by anywhere in Ibagué. Ask a local, they'll happily direct you to their favorite eatery in the downtown area. Updated: Feb 27, 2008.

Chuzo Restaurante

Chuzo's finely polished red awning singles it out as a landmark in downtown Ibagué. The neatly arranged and stylishly decorated interior make it an uppercrust eatery. The menu is full of sophisticated takes on hamburgers and steaks. Or, customers can feast on hearty patties in mushroom sauces or delicately grilled skewers of beef or chicken all in a WiFi hotspot. Calle 11, 4-29. Tel: 8-263-3104. Updated: Feb 06, 2008.

Honda

Alt: 229m Pop: 40,000 City Code:8

Honda mainly exists because for a long, long time it has been the last stop on the river journey to Bogotá. From Honda, conquistadors and royalty had to rough the rest of their journey overland. The city was declared a national monument based on its historically significant location.

Honda is also known as the "City of Bridges" due to the 29 bridges that cross back and forth over the Magdalena River. Some architecturally interesting buildings remain on the bridges from the colonial era.

In addition to the last stop along the river, all bus lines that run in from the Caribbean Coast come through Honda and pause briefly to let a few passengers off. So, to most travelers Honda represents little more than a hot and nameless stop on an overnight bus to Bogotá. There is no central terminal, so in the darkness it just looks like a confusing crossroads on the highway.

Others also know Honda as the "City of Peace," because it avoided the violence in the 1950s that affected so many of Colombia's major cities. As a whole, the city has a worn and used-up feel and has definitely known better days. Updated: Feb 27, 2008.

History

Founded in August 1539 by the Conquistador Francisco Nuñez Pedroso, Honda grew into its golden age during the latter half of the 19th Century thanks to the steam boats that traversed the Magdalena. The elegant and imposing structures that still exist from this era hark to a time of expansion and hope. Unfortunately the same thing that happened to Mompós happened to Honda—the river changed its course and steam travel became a thing of the past. Honda was left to flounder without purpose as a major transshipment route. Updated: Feb 27, 2008.

When to Go

Honda is hot all year round. Temperatures are almost always in the 30sC. If you are around in February, check out the plundering of the river during the Subienda Fishing Festival. Updated: Feb 27, 2008.

Getting To and Away From Honda

There is no official bus terminal. The stretch of the highway that cuts through Honda is used by all the bus companies. Brasilia, Copetrans, Rapido Ochoa, Omega, Bolivariano and others all have offices here. Bogotá is a mere four hours away and Ibagué, three. Updated: Feb 27, 2008.

Safety in Honda

Honda does not feel unsafe. Keep your normal traveler's wits about you. There is the potential that a possible bag snatching or mugging could take place near the bus stops. Updated: Feb 27, 2008.

Honda Services

Tourism Office

The office is located in the Alcaldia and can be reached at 8-251-4145 or 8-251-3500.

Medical

Hospital San Juan de Dios—Calle 9, 16-38, 8-251-3577.
Clinica Honda—Ca. 11, 17-66.
Updated: Feb 27, 2008.

Things to See and Do

Honda is a incredible destination for history enthusiasts and fishermen. There is the famous fishing festival in February and the colonial-era buildings, which pay tribute to the first attempts at settlement in northern South America. Beyond these attractions, Honda generally can be found lacking. Updated: Feb 27, 2008.

Colonial Buildings in Honda

For insight and understanding into the expansion of Colombia, Honda is a good place to start. Pretty much all travel from the early years of the conquest into the Republican era came through Honda via the Magdalena River. Honda, sometimes referred to as the "Cartagena of the Interior," due to its colonial buildings and narrow alleys also has a few notable buildings. If you have a couple of hours to spare in Honda, then take a stroll over the 29 bridges in town that span the Magdalena River. Check out the historic buildings still remaining over the water. Updated: Feb 06, 2008.

Subienda Fishing Festival

Every February Honda's population swells to nearly 60,000. Tourists and fishing enthusiasts yearn to glimpse the famous Festival de la Subienda. During the festival, participants fish the waters of the mighty Magdalena River. Fish like Nicuro, Bagre, Kapax, Bocachico and Tolomba are caught in abundance and offered to all to share. Although the main focus of the festival is the fish, other events take place. One lucky lady wins a beauty pageant and is elected to the *Reinado de la Subienda* (the festival's royal court). There are also rodeos and parades. The Festival de la Subienda is Honda's main event of the year. It transforms a decaying city into a party location, so don't forget to book a room far enough in advance. Updated: Feb 06, 2008.

Honda Lodging

Hit the road to the suburbs outside of Honda proper to find nicer hotels that cater to Colombian families. A big plus for this hot city is that the resorts in the suburbs and the surrounding countryside typically have pools. Otherwise, options near the center of the city tend to be much seedier. Most look as if they have not been updated since the 1960s and still use the same bedding. During the festival in February all rooms book up fast. Updated: Feb 27, 2008.

Hotel Villa Real

(BED: $5-11) You are not getting luxury, but the Villa Real is decent and safe. If you are here for the fishing festival, then check out this hotel. It is located away from the mayhem of the crossroads of the Pan-American Highway, behind the cathedral up the hill. All of the dozen rooms have A/C, and there is a pool. Updated: Feb 06, 2008.

Honda Restaurants

This river town doesn't have a huge amount of eating options. Close to the highway that cuts the town in two, there are a handful of mediocre bakeries and cafés that serve pastries and coffee. Up the hill, across the Magdalena River there are more choices that offer better fare. Head to the large market building to take your pick.

Honda still has the reputation of being overrun by whiskeries and brothels. Perhaps the town has never recovered from the colonial era, when sailors docked and those places were pretty typical. These days, there are a couple of bars and clubs that thump out loud music just up the hill from the bus stop. However, exercise caution when visiting this area. Updated: Feb 27, 2008.

!!!!!

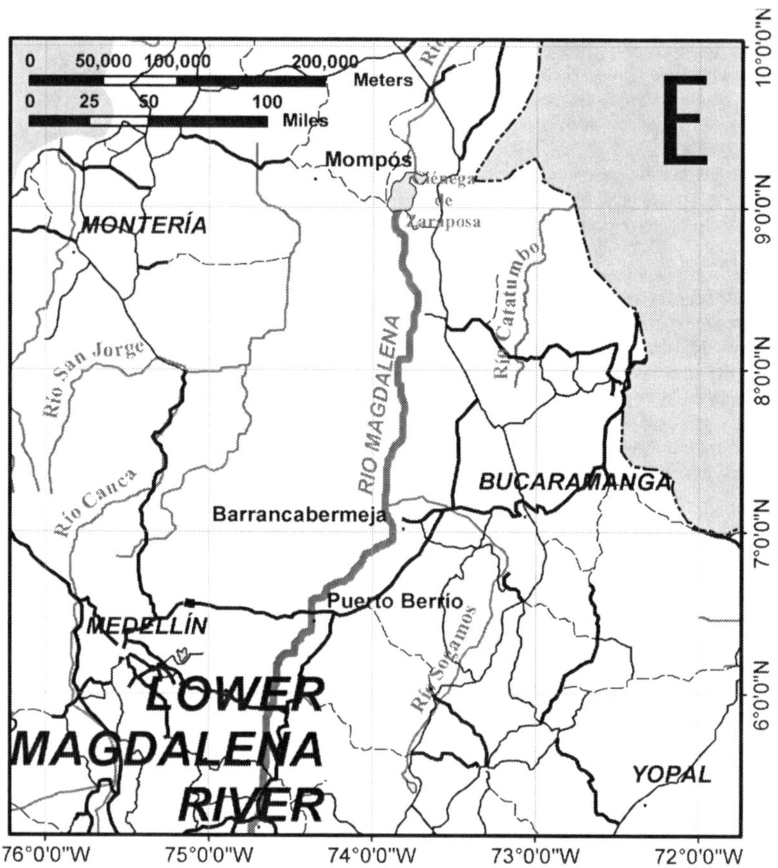

Lower Magdalena

Strategic and fertile are two words that describe the vast stretches of flood plain comprising the Lower Magdalena River Valley. This area, originally a strategic main route from the coast to the interior of Colombia, now prospers with some of the nation's largest cattle ranches. Spend any time here and you'll see that cattle farming is the dominant industry. Enormous ranches extend out of the towns along the river, and any journey you make will undoubtedly be delayed by a passing cattle train ambling along a major byway. As ranching is life to the people here, town festivals often resemble rodeos. The bull riding and drinking evoke scenes reminiscent of a long-disappeared American West.

In the spirit of Colombian regionalism, most people in this area are referred to by other Colombians as *costeños* (from the coast). This name comes despite the fact that towns like Mompós, Puerto Berrío and Barrancabermeja are located several hundred kilometers from the nearest shore. The relative misnomer is justified when you learn that residents of these towns are defined by the freshwater of the Magdalena River.

From the smoke stacks and nodding donkeys in Barrancabermeja to the silversmiths and Nazarenes in the austere Semana Santa of Mompós, the Lower Magdalena River Valley is an area you will not want to miss. The García Márquez-like idiosyncrasies and welcoming inhabitants will leave a lasting impression on any traveler. Updated: Mar 05, 2008.

Highlights

Well kept in its hard-to-reach location, **Mompós (p.202)** is one of the colonial jewels in Colombia's opulent crown.

The only one of its kind in Latin America, the **Oil Museum (p.199)** of Barrancabermeja is a good resource for understanding the importance of the oil industry in Colombia.

Take a ride on a **speed boat (p.200)** up the Magdalena River for the full experience of this region's activities. Updated: Mar 05, 2008.

History

Prior to Spanish occupation, this area was solely inhabited by indigenous tribes. Despite the injustices that have ocurred on their land, the current settlements in this part of the Magdalena River Valley are distinctly defined by their lack of hostility toward intruders.

As the Spanish colonial empire flourished, the main highway from principal towns and ports was directly connected to the river. Everything, including silver from the mines in Potosí and contraband from the Caribbean Islands, passed through these waters. During the drive for independence, the towns along the Lower Magdalena were pivotal in Simón Bolívar's push for separation from Spain. Since Mompós and other settlements gained more income through contraband, which the Spanish crown was intent on curtailing, locals quickly sided with the Venezuelan-born liberator to join the fight against Spain.

Toward the end of the Republican era in Colombia, the Magdalena River started to change its course. Silt levels rose and many branches of the river became impassable by way of the old paddle steam boats. The importance of the river as a major highway diminished and towns formerly at the heart of trade routes became bare-boned and isolated.

In contemporary years, the Lower Magdalena has seen its fair share of violence from both paramilitaries and left-wing guerrillas. Barrancabermeja, in particular, has been at the heart struggles. Updated: Jan 21, 2008.

When to Go

When planning your trip to Lower Magdalena, take into consideration the unrelenting heat that rarely dips below high 20°C (68° F). Travelers should be aware of when rainy seasons hit, since there is widespread flooding in the Lower Magdalena, and journeys can be delayed. Keep an eye out for floods during January and from April to May. Updated: Jan 21, 2008.

Safety in Lower Magdalena

Since the Uribe government has made special efforts to secure all major highways, most routes in the Lower Magdalena are safe. However, you are advised not to travel on the road from Medellín via Puerto Berrío to other destinations at night, since the paramilitaries have a large presence in these areas. Updated: Jan 21, 2008.

Things to See and Do

No visit to the Lower Magdalena is complete without some time spent interacting with the river. The Magdalena River is intrinsic to Colombian identity and has characterized Colombia's history through thick and thin. The town of Mompós is the river's main attraction. With handsome churches and curious histories, the outgoing traveler can explore beyond simple tourism and delve deep into the heart of Colombia. Updated: Jan 21, 2008.

Lower Magdalena Tours

Hostal Dona Manuela

Hostal Dona Manuela is the one of the finest tour operators in Mompós. They offer city and wildlife tours of the local ciénagas, which let visitors marvel at the abundance of birds. Doña Manuela also runs a finca outside of Mompós that has a swimming pool and horses. Tel: 5-685-5142, E-mail: mabe642@hotmail.com. Updated: Jan 21, 2008.

Mompós Tour

Mompós Tour takes tourists from Cartagena to Mompós on Tuesdays, Thursdays and Fridays in a fully air-conditioned minivan. Prices are steep, but if you only have a few precious days, this is a good choice. All the transportation is organized for you. Tel: 5-685-5142. Updated: Jan 21, 2008.

Lower Magdalena Lodging

Accommodation quality varies considerably from town to town. Small port towns, such as Puerto Berrío and Puerto Boyaca, offer decent and relatively inexpensive hotels. These are much better than the cheapest, brothel-like options. Mompós has a selection of overpriced hotels, with a few reasonable places as well. Barrancabermeja is an industrial capital and its hotels, though plentiful, cater to engineers sent to the city on a work ticket. Nonetheless, decent options are possible to find. Updated: Jan 21, 2008.

Puerto Berrío

Alt: 125m Pop: 38,000 City Code: 4

The first thing you notice upon arriving in Puerto Berrío is the staggering heat and humidity. Temperatures average above 30° C (87°F). Once you have become more accustomed to the dank humidity that leaves everyone covered in a shimmer of sweat, you note the obvious absence of the typical hills. Puerto Berrío and the surrounding region are quite flat.

Formerly, Puerto Berrío had greater significance as a transport hub for the rail network, moving coal and other products through Colombia. Now, the railroad service is gone and the town is little more than a vital port on the Magdalena River. All that remains are some forlorn tracks and a historic engine in front of the military base.

In the past, Puerto Berrío was renowned for its bawdy *whiskerías* (brothels) and *chicas de la vida alegre* (prostitutes). These aspects of the town helped fill the role of transit hub, linking river and rail networks. This is still the case around the port area, where these establishments can still be found. Updated: Nov 26, 2007.

History

On the banks of the Magdalena River and the border between the departments of Antioquia and Santander, Puerto Berrío occupies a region known to Colombians as the Magdalena Medio. It has little in common with the rest of its department, but more in common with other settlements along the Magdalena.

Founded in 1875 by Pedro Javier Cisneros, Puerto Berrío's fate has been inextricably linked to business drawn there by its port and railway hub. In 1925, the town was all but destroyed by a fire. Due to the loss of the railway and the shifting river, Puerto Berrío is no longer the important hub that it once was. Updated: Nov 27, 2007.

Getting To and Away Puerto Berrío

Bus

There is no terminal per se, but all buses come to a halt in the main plaza in Puerto Berrío. This leaves you close to all hotels, banks and restaurants. There are three main transportation companies that make the trip to Puerto Berrío: Cootransmagdalena, Rápido Ochoa (mainly to Medellín) and Rápido Tolima (taxi services).

From Puerto Berrío:

Per day	Arrive	Price
6 buses	Bucaramanga	$13
7 buses	Barrancabermeja	$8
1 taxi	Honda	$9
6 taxis	Ibagué	$12.50
26 buses	Medellín	$9-10.50
2 taxis	Puerto Boyaca	$5

River

Cootransfluviales Unidos has an office right in the port and runs *chalupas* (fast boats) to Barrancabermeja (2.5 hours) at 9 a.m. and 2:30 a.m. for $10. Tel: 4-833-3238.

Trans Fluvial runs boats from Puerto Berrío to La Sierra at 7:30 a.m., 10:30 a.m., 1:30 p.m., and 4 p.m. Updated: Nov 27, 2007.

Safety in Puerto Berrío

Puerto Berrío is a relatively safe town. As long as you stay away from the port after dark, you should encounter little trouble. The most dangerous moments of any visitor's trip is the time spent on public transportation. From time to time, the roads to and from Medellín and Barrancabermeja are closed due to military or guerrilla operations in the area. As of late 2007, there was no cause for alarm and everything was running smoothly and according to schedule. Updated: Nov 27, 2007.

Puerto Berrío Services

Tourism Office

There is no tourism office in Puerto Berrío. On that principal, it is suspect whether there is much of a tourism industry at all. Even hotel managers have been rumored to say that "in reality there's nothing."

Money

The BBVA, in the Plaza Mayor, has cash machines. Adjacent is a Bancolombia with similar facilities.

Keeping in touch

There are plenty of call centers for making international calls. There are three internet cafés: Edetel (in front of the military base), Enter.Net (Calle 54 between Carreras 4 and 5) and Mundo Digital (on the corner of Calle 54 and Carrera 5).

Medical

Pharmacies abound in Puerto Berrío. There is a recommended clinic next door to Bancolombia. Updated: Nov 26, 2007.

Puerto Berrío Tours

There are plenty of side-trips and activities from Puerto Berrío. Go to Puerto Olaya, where you can enjoy a plate of fish served with fried macho plantain and rice. El Zuam has one of the most beautiful places to swim. Take a nice trip in a *lancha* on the Magdalena river or just relax with a beer at La Malena.

Puerto Berrío Lodging

Puerto Berrío has hotels of all shapes, sizes and costs. Visitors should stay within a few blocks of Plaza Mayor and, if possible, avoid the cheaper options near the port where security comes into question. Many of the cheap, port motels rent rooms by the hour. The hotels listed here are credible establishments that do not cater to the rent-by-the-hour crowd. Updated: Nov 26, 2007.

Las Golondrinas

(ROOM: $15-35) Las Golondrinas, right on the corner of the main square, is one of the recommended hotels in town. Rooms come with A/C, refrigerator, cable TV and darkened windows that keep out the blazing sunshine. Each room has a private bathroom (without hot water, since it's unecessary here). Calle 51 with Carrera 4. Updated: Mar 27, 2008.

Hotel Las Dos Palmas

(ROOM: $20-25) Hotel Las Dos Palmas, four blocks from the Puerto Berrío bus stop, is one of the best options in town. A few blocks from the seedy port area and main square, the hotel has 20 rooms. Each room is equipped with A/C (an absolute necessity in this sweltering town). A one-bed room goes for $20 and a two-bed room for $25. Calle 53, Carrera 2. Tel: 4-833-3339. Updated: Mar 27, 2008.

Puerto Berrío Restaurants

Those easily satisfied with an enormous and freshly blended fruit juice from a market stall ($0.50) will be more than happy in Puerto Berrío. There are many levels of restaurants to choose from, but keep in mind that the quality does not match that of Medellín. Cheap eats and lunchtime deals abound. Updated: Nov 26, 2007.

Fresas y Moras Fruteria

If you have never tried *níspero*, *uchuva* or *corozo*, then take advantage of the chance at Fresas y Moras Frutería. Get your hands on a fine, fresh-squeezed fruit juice, fruit salad or a breakfast omlette. The staff at this street-corner restaurant are helpful and accommodating. They will advise you about the best seasonal fruits. Calle 7, 3-36. Tel: 4-833-2679. Updated: Mar 27, 2008.

Chara

(LUNCH: $2) Located beneath the Residencias Bahia, about a block back from the town square, Restaurante Chara is a functional and clean establishment. It won't win any Michelin stars, but it will provide the traveler with a hearty and reasonably priced meal. A breakfast of calentao-rice, beans and meat goes for only $1.25 and you can enjoy a set lunch for roughly $2. Calle 52, Carrera 4. Updated: Mar 27, 2008.

Las Dos Palmas

(LUNCH: $2) On the ground floor of the hotel by the same name, this restaurant is a decent option for a quick breakfast. Lunch is a set menu ($2) and drinks are an additional $0.60. The restaurant is clean, the staff are attentive, the fans go some way to cooling you off and the TV blares at all hours. Calle 53 with Carrera 2. Tel: 4-833-3339. Updated: Mar 27, 2008.

El Portón de los Frijoles

This is one of the best places to eat in Puerto Berrío. The extensive menu and the quality of the food have few rivals in town. Sit out in the still, humid air while sipping a cold beer and attacking a steak, or retreat to the dining room with soothing A/C. The restaurant specializes in grilled food. There is an emphasis on beef and fish dishes. The grilled river fish is particularly appetizing. Calle 49, behind Bancolombia. Updated: Mar 27, 2008.

Casa Vieja

On the corner next to Bancolombia, Casa Vieja sets out to be the elegant dining option in Puerto Berrío. It does reasonably well, too. The restaurant boasts shaded tables out front and a very keen eye for detail and decor. The dishes are not cheap, but you will find them to your liking if you are into seafood. Almost all speciality dishes include some sort of river fish, bagre in particular. Calle 50 beside Bancolombia. Updated: Mar 27, 2008.

BARRANCABERMEJA

Alt: 126m Pop: 300,000 City Code: 7

Barrancabermeja is, first and foremost, an oil town. This detail is not lost on the visitor as a massive refinery looms large over this sweltering settlement on the Magdalena River. Temperatures rarely dip below 30°C (85°F) and are more often edging near 40°C (105°F). Barrancabermeja was the first city in Colombia with an international airport, since its refinery drew in prospectors from all over the world.

To this day, the citizens talk of three different Barrancabermejas. The first being the refinery that is pretty much its own city, the second being the leafy and pleasant middle class neighborhoods and the third being the poor barrios on the other side of the tracks.

In addition to its tourism, Barrancabermeja is a great place to mix it up with the locals. People are friendly and accommodating. Visitors will find themselves invited on day trips to nearby ciénagas. Swim in the cooling waters, enjoy various aquatic sports and lunch on freshwater fish. Updated: Feb 08, 2008.

HISTORY

Although Barrancabermeja has many remnants of small indigenous settlements, the town as it is now known was not created until the Spanish came along. Explorer Gonzalo Jimenez de Quesada named the area on account of the ravines (*barranca* means ravine in Spanish). Nowadays, Barrancabermeja is commonly called Barranca. The city expanded rapidly with the oil boom of the 1920s. During this time, Standard Oil moved in to occupy the highly profitable area.

In addition to its petroleum history, the city has long been in the crossfire of the long-running Colombian conflict with the ELN. This organization staked their claim to the region in the 1970s and 1980s, and later in the 1990s when the FARC arrived. In 1998, Barrancabermeja suffered a massacre signaling the paramilitary forces' intent on making its presence felt. Updated: Feb 08, 2008.

When to Go

Barrancabermeja is inextricably associated with oppressive heat. Temperatures rarely drop below 30°C (85°F). The rainy season in September and October hardly alters the heat. Breeze is also hard to come by.

Holidays and Festivals

April—Reina Internacional de Petróleo pageant.
August—Fiesta del Petróleo.
Updated: Feb 08, 2008.

Getting To and Away from Barrancabermeja

Road

There is no bus terminal but most bus companies have offices near or on Carrera 6 in downtown.

From Barrancabermeja:

Arrive	Departure	Price
Bucaramanga	every half hour	varies
Puerto Berrío	5:30 a.m., 6 a.m.	varies
Barranquilla	7 p.m., 9:30 p.m.	$35 -40

Arrive	Departure	Price
Bogotá	6 a.m., 10 a.m., 2:30 p.m., 9.30 p.m. 10 p.m. 10.30 p.m.	$35
Cartagena	7 a.m., 7 p.m. 8:30 p.m. 9 p.m.	$40 -46
Maicao	7 p.m.	$35
Cali	7 a.m., 3 p.m., 7 p.m. and 9 p.m.	$30
Medellín	8 a.m., 2 p.m., 10 p.m.	$35

Train

A functioning train service runs from Barrancabermeja to Puerto Berrío daily at 5 a.m. and 1 p.m. Carriages are small and the journey takes three hours ($7.50). Tel: 7-602-7684.

River

Since Barrancabermeja is on the River Magdalena, transport on the river is vital. Journeys are long and expensive. The two companies are Cootransfluviales and Transportes San Pablo.

Puerto Berrio—6:30 a.m. ($10).
Gamarra—7 a.m.
El Banco (connection from here to Mompox) —five hours ($24).
San Pablo—9 a.m., 10 a.m., 12 p.m., 12:30 p.m.
Magangue (connections to Mompós)—6 a.m., nine hours ($40).
Updated: Feb 08, 2008.

Safety in Barrancabermeja

Since the conflict has been forced out of the city limits and into other areas, Barrancabermeja has become a pretty safe place. However, visitors must use common sense. Travelers should be especially vigilant when withdrawing money from ATMs. There has been a recent surge of motorcycle-riding thieves who follow the those who just took out cash to rob them as they exit their taxi. Updated: Feb 08, 2008.

Barrancabermeja Services

Tourism Office

There is no official tourism office. For further information contact Corporacion Mixta de Promocion de Santander (Carrera 19, 35-02, Tel: 7-630-7589) or the Instituto Municipal de Cultura (Calle 30, 26-117, Tel: 7-634-1132).

Money

Banks are located throughout the city and cash machines are easily accessible.

Keeping in Touch

There are internet cafés throughout every district of the city.

Medical

Clínica Primero de Mayo, Carrera 21A, 47-30. Tel: 7-622-2468.

Shopping

All things considered, there is very little to shop for in Barrancabermeja. Due to the heat, sunblock, a hat or after-sun cream are easily found around downtown.Updated: Feb 08, 2008.

Things to See and Do

If you find youself in Barrancabermeja, there are probably one of three reasons why you have ventured to this oil town:

You are an engineer or an oil prospector brought in on a business gig.

You are making the incredible journey by river from the Colombian coast to the interior or vice versa.

You are lost or stranded.

Despite all the negative comments you might have heard about the city—the oppressive heat or the ever-present silhouette of the refinery—Barrancabermeja has a few attractions to keep tourists occupied.

The surrounding countryside, fed by the waters from the Magdalena River, is surprisingly beautiful. The large lakes nearby are good for day trips. Take a dip in the cool waters, waterski, jet ski or dine on fantastic fish dishes. During weekends, you'll find that most *barramejos* descend upon these areas to escape from the heat. Updated: Feb 08, 2008.

Oil Museum

The importance of the oil industry in Colombia becomes clear when you see the dozens of

The River Train

"Peto, peto," Doña Sorelly calls. She opens her milk can, steam from the corn drink escapes into the slightly cool morning. The toot of the autoferro's horn warns of our imminent passage. We leave Barrancabermeja, entering this new day swaying, occasionally jolting, down narrow-gauge tracks. Wheels upon rails sharply clack and rumble as we pass homes with still-sleeping families. Mango trees scrape our sides. The cloud-silhouetted dawn is just beginning to lighten. In the distance, on the banks of the Río Magdalena, refinery stack smoke and derrick flames billow. Lightning streaks the western sky. A thin rain sheens off bronze cacao leaves.

This landscape begins to define itself with waterlilied swamps and stands of bamboo. Cattle rise, the dew and drizzle glisten on their hides. Passengers come, cargo goes. Slowly these villages and settlements we visit are awakening, stalls are mounted in the light of lamps. Garzas rise from their trees, white blips winging across the grey sky. There's a hollow clatter as we cross over bridges above small rivers flowing to that great Río. Workers board, workers leave, it's just another day to labor. This land, so flat, begins to undulate. The rain ceases, though the day is yet subdued. Thin-limbed, potbellied children stand in their golden-lit doorways, lethargically watching us shudder past.

After Puerto Olaya, the Río Magdalena comes into view. Soldiers patrol the bridge we soon cross. The river glimmers silver and brown beneath us, its sandbars exposed. Swooshing, swaying, clattering past shack homes we arrive to our destination, Puerto Berrío. Updated: May 13, 2008.

oil rigs lining the coast of Barrancabermeja. The statue of Christ dedicated to oil is also a pretty telling sign. The city government recommends checking out the Oil Museum (Museo del Petroleo), reportedly the only one of its kind in Latin America, to learn the history of oil and the current progress of the industry. Updated: May 16, 2008.

Ciénaga San Silvestre

Likened to a freshwater ocean, the Ciénaga San Silvestre spans out from Barrancabermeja to Puerto Wilches. This creates a vast body of water of 9 square kilometers.

On the banks of San Silvestre, a 10-minute drive from Barrancabermeja, various water sports resorts have sprung up. At these family-friendly places, around the delectable waters of the ciénaga, you can swim, waterski, parasail and fish. Normally there is a beach volleyball court set up, a band playing on weekends and spaces to set up your own BBQ.

If that's all too much action for you, then grab a hammock, string it up in the shade of some trees and have a serious siesta in the breeze coming off the ciénaga.

To keep costs down, you could bring your own picnic food. Also, make sure to bring plenty of sun block and watch out for freshwater stingrays near the shore during dry season. Updated: Dec 19, 2007.

Barrancabermeja Lodging

The accommodation options in Barrancabermeja go from luxurious to seedy. At the high end of the scale, businessmen at the behest of oil companies lounge by swimming pools at the finer establishments. The next rung of hotels cater to the contracted engineers brought in for short-term jobs, these are typically decent and efficient places. Finally, there are the cheaper options downtown in the city's Zona Rosa. Many are just fine, but the majority cater to guests renting rooms by the hour. Updated: Feb 08, 2008.

San Cristobal

(ROOM: $11-24) Although the San Cristobal is in the city's Zona Rosa, the respectable hotel is definitely separate from the many seedy options. The price for one of the 40 rooms is cheaper if you choose a fan over A/C. The rooms are generally clean. All come with cable TV, a cooling option and telephone. To get there, catch any bus heading downtown and ask to be dropped off on Calle 50. Calle 50, 12-36. Tel: 7-622-4346, Fax: 7-621-1163. Updated: Dec 19, 2007.

Hotel Cacique

(ROOM: $36-49) Just next door to the Pipaton is the far less charming Hotel Cacique. It really does live in the shadow of its neighbor and is nothing more than a location for businessmen coming through Barrancabermeja. Rooms are standard, with TV, A/C and private bathrooms. Calle 47, 1-14. Tel: 7-622-3350, Fax: 7-622-6672, E-mail: hotelcacique-barranca@yahoo.es. Updated: Dec 19, 2007.

San Carlos

(ROOM: $51-62) Just down the hill and around the corner from the Pipaton, the San Carlos also appeals to the engineering crowd. Each of the 30 rooms and seven apartments have A/C, cable TV, minibar, WiFi and a private bathroom. San Carlos is functional but lacks character. It also loses customers to the Pipaton, as they have a pool. Calle 49, 5-104. Tel: 7-602-2010, Fax: 7-622-4372, E-mail: hsanca@yahoo.es, URL: www.suhotelsancarlos.com. Updated: Dec 19, 2007.

Hotel Bachue

(ROOM: $55-75) This hotel, in the center of town, underwent a complete renovation in August 2007. Everything, from to the tiling in the bathrooms to the linen on the beds, has been upgraded. The entryway still has a 1970s feel but the 40 rooms have been highly modernized. They each offer WiFi, A/C, a private bathroom and a refrigerator. Breakfast is included. Weekend rates are significantly lowered due to the drop in occupancy. Carrera 17, 49-12. Tel: 7-622-2599. Updated: Dec 19, 2007.

Pipaton

(ROOM: $65-85) This colonial-style building stands tall, giving great views over the Magdalena River. Once you stroll through its welcoming doors, you'll note the swimming pool and the air conditioned lobby. All rooms have WiFi, A/C, private bathroom, TV with cable, refrigerator and breakfast included. If coming in from the airport, call in advance and they will have a taxi pick you up free of charge. Avenida del Rio, 47-16. Tel: 7-602-0250, Fax: 7-602-0258, E-mail: hotelpipaton@reservashoteleras.com.co. Updated: Dec 19, 2007.

Barrancabermeja Nightlife

The Zona Rosa, a string of clubs downtown, constantly produces loud Vallenato music and salsa. Barrancabermeja does not have the same level of nightlife as Medellín or Bogotá, but prices are low and the entertainment value is premium. Updated: Feb 08, 2008.

Barrancabermeja Restaurants

The best food in Barrancabermeja comes fresh from the water. Head to the river banks, not far from the Cacique Hotel, to find a number of set-ups preparing delectable bagre and bocachica fish dishes. Go downtown to find anything else to eat.

Avenida del Río

Avenida del Río is a great stroll for anyone with an appetite. A line of unnamed and numbered stalls along the riverfront specialize in local delicacies like sancocho de pescado, bagre and bocachica fish dishes. Don't be put off by the backdrop of the massive refinery; this is the place to come to enjoy fish with the locals. On weekends, all of the stands are full to capacity. Choose a stand that suits you and settle in for a sumptuous feast. Updated: Dec 19, 2007.

Carrera 10

Often just referred to as "la 10," Barrancabermeja's Zona Rosa positively buzzes on Fridays and Saturdays. The pizzeria/bar, La Via Lactea, has an open- air section, unintrusive music and is an ideal happy hour spot. The following clubs are all found on Carrera 10 and close to the Parque de la Vida: Amnesia, Evolution, Cucaracho, Seven, Amatista and La Ciudad. All of these play a variety of music and, for the most part, entry is free and beer is cheap! Carrera 10. Updated: Dec 19, 2007.

Café y Bohemia

Small tables line this narrow establishment and take nothing away from its ambience. Come inside for the A/C and a cocktail, a coffee or a sandwich. Café y Bohemia may just be a perfect escape from Barrancebermeja within the confines of the city. Calle 49, 19-30. Tel: 7-611-2575. Updated: Feb 06, 2008.

Mompós

Alt: 18m	Pop: 31,000	City Code: 5

To visitors and locals alike, Mompós represents an older, forgotten, colonial Colombia. It is a city of tradition, family ties, and a mix of myth and religious piety. The culture remains largely untouched by the conflict found throughout the rest of the country. Some find it quiet, some find it rowdy, Mompós can be what you make it.

Two hundred kilometers east of Cartagena, this island town is difficult to reach. However, it is well worth the effort.

Colonial Mompós has been an UNESCO World Heritage Site since 1995. It is comprised of three long, whitewashed streets that run parallel to the Magdalena River.

Mompós' stifling heat and backwater status do not create the most favorable place for toursits. However, anyone interested in colonial Colombia and the European Diaspora, or in observing one of Latin America's most austere Semana Santa celebrations, should consider a visit. Updated: Feb 18, 2008.

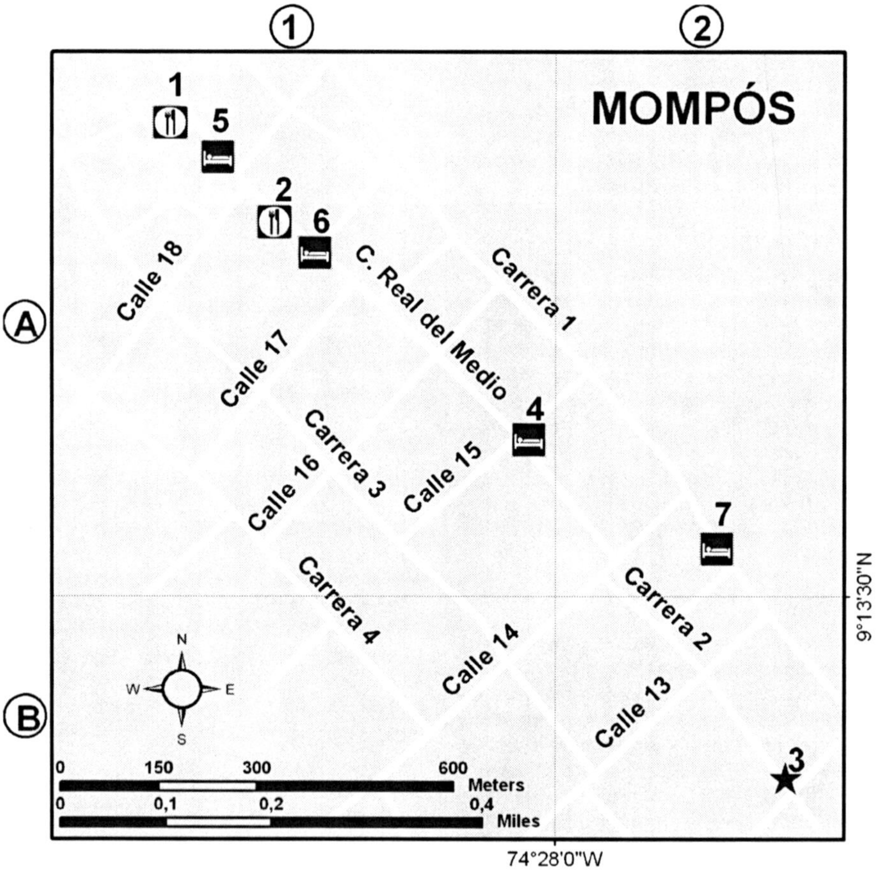

Eating

1 Asadero Patio Bonito B1

2 Crepes Helados Pan D' la Villa B1

Services ★

3 Planet Net C2

Sleeping

4 Casa Hotel La Casona B1

5 Casa Hotel Villa de Mompox B1

6 Hostal Dona Manuela B1

7 La Casa Amarilla B2

History

Like similar colonial settlements, Mompós came about due to its favorable location along the Magdalena. The absence of unfriendly indigenous tribes also helped foster a successful colony. Mompós grew considerably during the colonial era, when the river was the fastest route to Honda, and subsequently Bogotá. It is said that more money passed through Mompós than through Cartagena, thanks to the bootlegging of precious metals, tobacco and alcohol en route to and from the Ecuadorian port of Guayaquil.

Simón Bolívar's numerous stays in Mompós create another historical connection to Latin American history. While there, Bolívar raised an army of willing *mompósino* volunteers to aid in his march on Caracas. It is rumored that Gabriel García Márquez built this history into "The General and His Labyrinth" and possibly into his other books as well. Bolívar once proclaimed, "If to Caracas I owe my life, to Mompós I owe my glory."

The aforementioned are high points in the history of this colonial wonderland, but all this came to an end when the river somewhat changed its course and fluvial travel became less important. Updated: Feb 18, 2008.

When to Go

Semana Santa is Mompós' one real high season. The streets are filled with Nazarenes and tourists from throughout Colombia. The normally sleepy town receives an economic boost during December and January from family members who return for the holidays and tourists coming from the coast. Aside from these times, life in Mompós is pretty slow.

The wet season occurs during the months of April, May, and September through October. Heavy downpours can keep normally high temperatures in the upper 20°C (70°F). Outside of these months, Mompós is hot and dry.

August 6 marks the Independence of Mompós. Around this date, revelers enjoy more than a few cold ones while watching the rodeos or listening to the booming street music. Updated: Feb 18, 2008.

Getting To and Away from Mompós

Mompós is not easy to reach. However, through a combination of buses, taxis, water transportation and maybe a 4X4, any traveler can make it.

From the Caribbean Coast:

The fastest (but most expensive) way to get to Mompós is to fly into Cartagena or Barranquilla and organize an interurban taxi to Magangue. From there, catch a motorized canoe across the river, then head on from Bodega to Mompós.

Taxi

From Cartagena to / from Magangue, they leave when full and take 3 hours ($15-20).

Taxi from Bodega to / from Mompós: 1 hour ($3).

Canoe

Motorized canoe from Magangue to / from Bodega: 25 minutes ($3).

Bus

Otherwise, buses leave from Mompós every day to Barranquilla, Cartagena and Sincelejo with connections to Tolú, Coveñas and Medellín. If you are stuck in Mompós and have to leave, the best bet is to get to Magangue and try your luck there, since there are more options.

Copetran—Callejon del Cementerio, Carrera 3-74. Tel: 5-685-5768.

Coming from the Colombia's interior and Bogotá:

Omega and Copetrans have direct buses to El Banco. Although, they say this, the buses do not reach all the way to El Banco. The direct bus takes 16–18 hours, leaves Bogotá at night and drops travelers at the edge of a lake. (The reason is that the long-promised highway connecting to El Banco is currently still under construction through a swamp, and has yet to actually connect to El Banco.) At the lake, hop into a motorized canoe ($2.50) to El Banco. Then, head to the market roughly 25m. away and jump into a waiting 4x4 that runs the arduous 2-3 hour journey ($10-12) over bad roads to Mompós.

Also, there are direct minivans that run from Mompós to Cartagena, the price varies ($30-40) depending on the season.

River Travel

From Barrancabermeja and other points on the Magdalena River, there are infrequent departures to Magangue and El Banco. Be sure to ask around, since the river journey will be far more pleasant than one by road. The Colombian government has stated its intent to make the waterways in this region passable, so there should be more available long-distance river travel options in the future. Updated: Feb 18, 2008.

Safety in Mompós

Mompós itself is incredibly safe. Imagine a town where, once the sun has set, entire families bring rocking chairs onto their front porches to sit with doors left open and chat with anyone around. Due to its secluded location, Mompós has been unaffected by many of Colombia's ills. Updated: Feb 18, 2008.

Mompós Services

Tourism Office

There is no official tourist office around these parts, but for more information about Mompós ask at the Museum on Calle del Medio or at the Alcaldia. Tel: 5-685-5738.

Money

There are three ATMs in town. All are on the corner of the Parque Bolívar and the Camellon del Colegio. The ATH ATM machines provided by the Banco Popular accept all cards. The ATM provided by BBVA accepts Visa.

NOTE: During Semana Santa, demand for cash is at a premium and it has been known to run out.

Keeping in Touch

There is an internet café on the Alberrada, across the corner from the El Éxito supermarket. There is another, Planet Net, with telephones and computers on the Calle del Medio, 12-06. Both cafés charge $1 per hour.

Medical

Be aware that if you are ever in dire need of serious medical attention, there is every possibility that it will not be available in Mompós. However, you can take a chance at the pharmacies and clinics in the Plaza del Mercado.

Shopping

Taller y Joyería Jimmy

This shop offers some of the finest metal ornaments in Mompós. Calle del Medio, Carrera 2, 15-86. Tel: 5-685-5383.

Joyería William Vargas

This shop is interesting, but has the same jewelry as the other typical stores. Tel: 5-684-0453. Updated: Feb 18, 2008.

Things to See and Do

If you are not making your way to this river city for the major Semana Santa, it is good to remember that a visit to Mompós is not all about seeing and doing. The activities are slim pickings—a trip here is more about soaking up the atmosphere. The typical tourist activies include a tour of the ornate churches and a telling of the stories relating back to the mysterious Masons.

To really get a glimpse at the unique local beauty, Mompós lends itself to rising early and taking a walk. Start with looking for the howler monkeys in the park, then stroll down Calle del Medio, with a detour at the Plaza del Mercado to observe the early-morning activity. Next, head back along the shady riverfront, where the wealthier residents live in the Portales de la Marquesa.

Tours of the Ciénaga are offered at the ludicrously hot hour of 2 p.m. Some establishments rent bicycles. For those interested, cockfights are also held around town on most weekends. Updated: Feb 18, 2008.

Semana Santa in Mompós

Much like Popayán's celebrations, The Semana Santa (Easter Week) in Mompós is a wonder to behold. During this week, the streets fill with worshipers and Nazarene volunteers who, clad in purple robes and suffering in the heat, hoist weighty floats onto their shoulders for processions. These take place every day and every night.

On one night in particular—*El Alumbrado* (Wednesday)—town members head to the cemetery to visit deceased family members and friends. As a band plays, the people light candles to place on or near the tombs of loved ones. The resulting spectacle is both touching and inspiring. The whole cemetery is set aglow.

Toward the end of the week, locals erect religious images in the streets, only to be eventually trampled by the seemingly unending processions that follow. Updated: Feb 06, 2008.

Mompós Lodging

In addition to its hard-to-reach location, Mompós has suffered at the hands of hoteliers who take advantage of the distance to other tourist sites and other hotel options. Room prices here are steep, even in the off season. That said, service is good and most places offer clean accommodations topped off with A/C and efficient services.

Be Advised: Semana Santa is Mompós' only true high season. During this time, hotel prices often double or increase more than the norm. Rooms book up fast, though locals have been known to rent out their spare rooms. Book accommodation in advance. If possible, book your bus tickets in advance as well. Updated: Feb 18, 2008.

La Casa Amarilla

(BED: $10-25) Long overdue, La Casa Amarilla opened in 2008 and provides budget accomodation to travelers. It is a large, renovated colonial mansion with views over the River Magdalena. The kioskos are in a great place, where you can enjoy an ice-cold beer and watch the howler monkeys. The mansion has two dormitories (three- and four-person rooms) and each has a private bathroom. There are also two private rooms with double beds, one has a private bathroom. The British owner has tried to make this the budget traveler's choice. The prices are reasonable, apart from during Semana Santa. The second entry room has a TV and a DVD player. If you come in on the Unitransco bus, it will drop you at La Casa Amarilla. If you're coming in from El Banco, then head to the Albarrad (the road by the river) and follow it upstream to La Iglesia Santa Barbara, the hostal is one block beyond. Carrera 1, 13-59, La Albarrada with Santa Barbara. Cel: 301-362-765, E-mail: lacasaamarillamompos@gmail.com, URL: www.lacasaamarillamompos.blogspot.com. Updated: May 13, 2008.

Casa Hotel Villa de Mompox

(ROOM: $25-80) One step up from backpacker comfort and charm, the Villa de Mompox sits on the edge of everything colonial in Mompós. Prices are a bit steep for what is offered. All rooms come with A/C, ceiling fans and private bathrooms. The hotel lacks a comfortable communal area for guests. The hotel sleeps up to 43. Across the road, there are a few rooms for the overflow that inevitably happens during Semana Santa. Calle Real del Medio, 14-108. Tel: 5-685-5208, E-mail: casahotelvillademompox@yahoo.com. Updated: Feb 06, 2008.

Casa Hotel La Casona

(ROOM: $40-85) As one of the leading Hotels in Mompós, the expectation is that La Casona should be a paradise. However, the rooms are dark, the furniture could use some updating and the communal areas need work. For too long, it seems, the establishment has been resting on its laurels, knowing full well that a steady stream of tourists will stay there during Semana Santa. Although the staff are helpful and friendly, you can do better for the price. Carrera 2, 18-58. Tel: 5-685-5307, E-mail: eusedeal@yahoo.es. Updated: Feb 06, 2008.

Hostal Dona Manuela

(ROOM: $62-85) This 28-room behemoth of a colonial mansion sits proudly on the Calle del Medio, the main street in Mompós. It is quite simply the most elegant place to stay in town, and it is routinely used as a location for wealthy *momposinos* to hold special events. Prices are not cheap, but you get what you are paying for, including: A/C, cable TV, elegance and a swimming pool, which is an excellent addition in the Mompós heat. The rooms accommodate any number, from doubles all the way up to as many as six-bed rooms. There is a maximum capacity of 90 people.

The owners also have a finca on the outskirts of Mompós where guests can go to stay. The finca provides opportunity for horseback riding and swimming. For those not interested in paying to stay here, there's a $3 day pass for the pool or for $10 the pass also includes a few drinks. Real Calle del Medio, 17-41. Tel: 5-685-5142, E-mail: mabe642@hotmail.com. Updated: Feb 06, 2008.

Mompós Restaurants

Restaurants in Mompós offer Creole meals as well as standard regional fare. Be aware that Mompós is found lacking for salads or lighter fare. Most dishes consist of chicken or beef, though one place does offer crepes. If you are looking for more unusual foods, then Mompós might be the ideal destination. Locals here eat just about everything including sea turtles (Galápagos/ icotea), peccary (ponche/chiguiro) and the occasional iguana.

Along the riverfront, on the Alberrada, bars are lined up side by side. Each blasts different genres of music. The pick of the bunch and the most historic is the Luna de Mompox. Updated: Feb 18, 2008.

Asadero Patio Bonito

Asadero Patio Bonito is cheap and cheerful. This restaurant stands out from the crowd thanks to its good-size portions and inexpensive nature. The dirt floors are hardly noticeable, since the place is only open at night and the lighting is dim. All platters cost about $3. Don't forget to specify whether you want beef or chicken. Opposite the Hotel Villa de Mompox, on the Calle del Medio. Updated: Feb 06, 2008.

Dely Bross

Run by an efficient and friendly *paisa* (a native of Medellín), the Dely Bross is an unassuming restaurant near the Parque Bolívar. Locals must truly enjoy the owner's decent-sized platters of grilled chicken, beef and river fish, since almost every lunchtime and evening the crowd is near capacity. The Dely Bross seems to do an outstanding job. El Camellon del Colegio, opposite the Colegio Pinillos. Updated: Feb 07, 2008.

Crepes Helados Pan D' la Villa

The service is slow and the staff aren't very friendly. That aside, Crepes Helados Pan D' la Villa's location, right at the heart of Real Calle del Medio, makes it an ideal spot to break from the stifling heat. Enjoy a light crepé lunch at the only place where crepés are available in Mompós. Wash it all down with a sweet, chilled *jugo de corozo*. The site can seat up to 40, but keep in mind that service slows considerably with larger crowds. Real Calle del Medio 17-51. Updated: Feb 07, 2008.

Luna de Mompox

As the oldest and most established bar in Mompós, the Luna de Mompox is a classy spot. On the corner of the Alberrada de los Angeles, it has a prime spot that overlooks the Magdalena. This is a great place for a happy hour that could extend into an impromptu late-night party.

A few other bars along the Alberrada; Bar D' Rumba and Mango Biche Bar—both recent additions intent on drowning one another out with loud music. It will be interesting to see whether they make the cut. Alberrada de los Angeles. Updated: Feb 07, 2008.

LOWER MAGDALENA

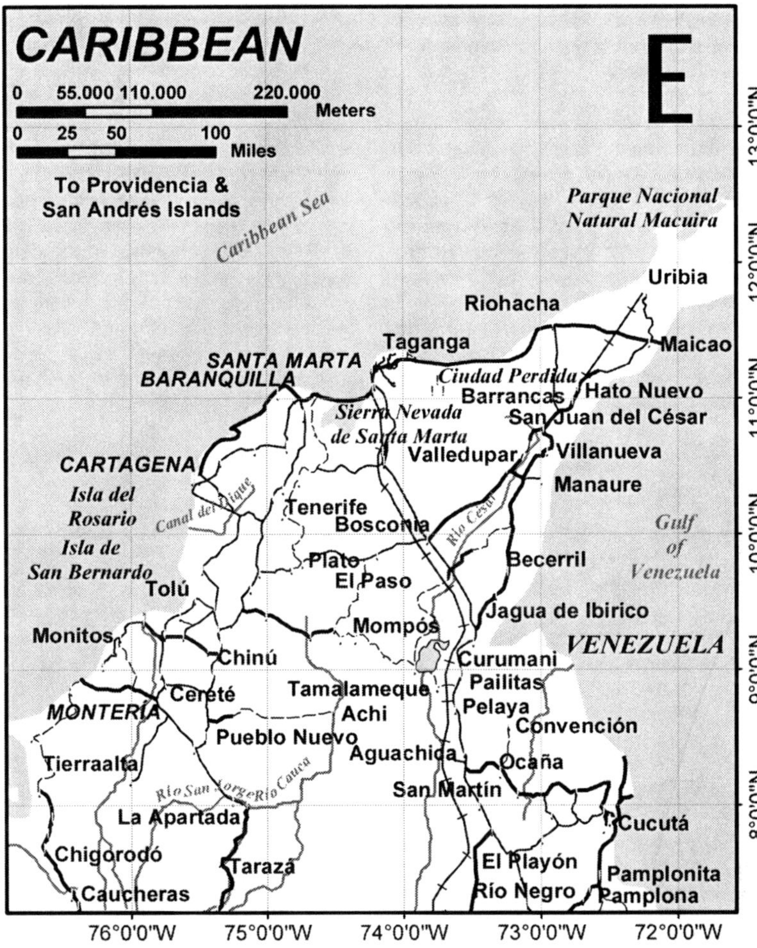

The Caribbean Coast and Islands

Colombia's Caribbean Coast features gorgeous and deserted coastlines, both on the mainland and islands. Nearly all the beaches, with a couple of notable exceptions, remain completely unspoiled.

By far the most popular visitor spot on the coast is Cartagena. Set right on the edge of the sea and surrounded by a stone wall, it has an unbeatable location. The colonial architecture in Cartagena is among the best-preserved in Latin America and coupled with the laid-back Caribbean atmosphere, food and music it's easy to see why so many people—foreigners and Colombians alike—come here for holidays. Despite Cartagena's popularity, however, it's rarely overcrowded with tourists, even in high season, and it's never a problem finding somewhere to stay. There are some hotels in the historic center, but generally the more comfortable ones are in Bocagrande, the huge, built-up resort area south of town. And, keep in mind that the beaches close to Cartagena aren't the best.

Serious beach-lovers, divers and snorkelers head to the Islas de Rosario, with wide, sandy bays, palm trees and off-shore reefs that teem with colorful sea life. There are a couple of places to stay on the islands, but they're so close that most people just go over from Cartagena for a day trip. Just up the coast from Cartagena, the fishing village of Boquilla also makes a good day trip. It's very quiet during the week, but livens up on weekends, when little wooden huts open up to serve up the catch of the day, accompanied by rice and plantains.

Further north, Santa Marta is reachable in a day from Cartagena. There's not much to do in the town itself—most people come to gain access to Parque Nacional Natural Tayrona, which arguably has Colombia's best beaches. Most of the beaches are set in deep bays surrounded by forest, and there's a good chance you'll have one all to yourself. Santa Marta is also a good base from which to organize trips to The Lost City (*Ciudad Perdida*), an ancient pre-Columbian town that remained hidden deep in the thick rainforest until it was discovered by accident in 1975. There are no roads, and the city can only be reached by foot. It's a six- to seven-day hike there and back.

Colombia also lays claim to two Caribbean Islands, San Andrés and Providencia, each of which has a completely different feel. San Andrés is the more visitor-oriented, with a resort atmosphere that attracts sun-seekers and watersport enthusiasts, many from South America. The beaches are good and the diving is said to be the best in Colombia. In contrast, Providencia is not nearly as well-developed for tourism, which, for some, is the best thing about it. It is far quieter, the beaches are pristine, and there are plenty of good dive spots here, too. Updated: Nov 20,2006.

Baseball

Take me out to the ballgame, take me out to the crowd
Buy me some perros and cerveza
I don't care if I ever...

It has often been said that you can trace US military occupations through baseball. To this rule, however, Colombia is an exception. Here, the sport was introduced by local boys who learned it in other countries and thought it would be cool to play in their Caribbean hometowns.

Gonzalo and Hibraim Zúñiga Ángel, brothers from the Chocó, went to the US to study. When they got off the ship in Cartagena in 1903, they were toting bats, balls and other strange equipment. They and Fernando Gómez and Guillermo de la Espriella began playing the sport in that city. In the case of Barranquilla, three brothers—Venancio, Abraham and José García—introduced the game in 1906 from Cuba. Two years later they formed the Barranquilla Cubans team. The first game between these two rival cities was held on November 11, 1916; Cartagena won 6 to 2.

And it's root, root, root for the home team
If they don't win it's a shame...

The professional season in Colombia depends on the major leagues in the States. This is because many players on State-side teams come down to play during the off-season. Generally, it's from October to February. Only four cities in Colombia have professional teams: Barranquilla Caimanes, Cartagena Indios, Montería Cardenales and Sincelejo Toros.

What is big in this country is the minor leagues, or Liga Menor, which runs from March to September or October. Most towns along the Caribbean Coast from the Sucre Department to the Guajira have several minor league teams, including Montería, Sincelejo, Cartagena, Barranquilla, Ciénaga and Santa Marta. Even Bogotá has a team, and Chiquinquirá will soon have one, too. Games are on Saturdays and Sundays at 3 p.m. So if you happen to be on the coast during the season, drop by the ballpark and catch the action.

So it's one, two, three strikes, you're out at the ol' ballgame....

Updated: May 23, 2008.

Highlights

The quintessential colonial port of **Cartagena (p.216)** with its white-washed buildings shields almost 500 years of history.

A six-day trek to **Teyuna (p.259)**, the Lost City, is a pleasant way to get to this mystic city deep in the jungles near Santa Marta.

Head out to the ballpark and munch down on fritos and beer while enjoying a **baseball (p.208)** game.

The annual **Vallenato** music festival in Valledupar (p.278) every April is a great opportunity to learn about the extended music culture of Colombia.

From the **San Andrés Islands (p.285)** to **Parque Nacional Natural Tayrona (p.274)**, divers can explore coral reef as well as old Spanish galleons.

History

The indigenous Arawak-Caribe were the original inhabitants of Colombia's Caribbean Coast and San Andrés Islands. Included in this group were the Tayrona, goldsmith masters and ancestors of the modern-day Kogui, who still inhabit the Sierra Nevada de Santa Marta. These nations had extensive trade networks throughout the hemisphere. (Their work has been found as far north as the Ohio River Valley.)

In 1525, Santa Marta was the first Spanish settlement in South America. Soon other ports were settled along the coast. The most important was Cartagena in 1533, which became the main storehouse and port for the riches mined in the Spanish colonies. The cities were targets for pirates for more than a century. Some of the famous seadogs who hit up this area were Sir Francis Drake and the Cote brothers.

These foundling cities played important roles in the struggle for independence from Spain. Cartagena was one of the first cities of Nueva Granada to declare freedom and under whose patronage Simón Bolívar fought. In 1830, that Great Liberator died in Santa Marta. After the breakup of Gran Colombia, the region along the Río Magdalena suffered from the civil wars that raged, including the War of 1,000 Days in the late 19th Century.

At the end of the 19th Century, the US banana companies arrived. United Fruit Company had plantations stretching across the Lower Magdalena River Valley, operating under various names, including Sevilla Fruit Company and Magdalena Fruit Company. In 1928 the workers went on strike, leading to a massacre of the *bananeros* and their families in Ciénaga. The United Fruit Company is still here (now known as Chiquita), the plantations stretch all the way to the Urubá Gulf. Dole and Fyffes also have a presence in the region.

The Magdalena River Valley, Sierra Nevada de Santa Marta and the Chocó have been hot points in the late 20th Century civil war, which still rages to this day. The ELN is the major guerrilla group in the area, but there is some FARC and a strong paramilitary presence, too. Updated: May 27, 2008.

When to Go

The Caribbean Coast and islands have a hot climate. Daytime temperatures reach the upper 20s°C to mid-30s°C (80-95°F). Typically there are two rainy seasons, May to June and August to November. Storms can be torrential and sometimes cause local flooding. From the end of the year into March, high winds come blowing out of the North. During these windy times, small craft advisories may be issued. In the San Andrés Islands you have to watch out for hurricane advisories from May to September. Although, historically, hurricanes do not strike as far south as the northern coast of South America. Updated: May 27, 2008.

Safety in the Caribbean Coast

Petty crimes occur in large tourist cities, like Cartagena, Barranquilla and Santa Marta. In these areas use common sense and leave valuables in your hotel. When out and about, be aware of your surroundings and keep an eye on your camera and backpack.

These major population areas are outside of the red zone of Colombia's civil war. Security has improved greatly in the past few years, but problems still exist in the regions along the Río Magdalena and in the Sierra Nevada de Santa Marta. For the most part, however, it is safe to visit towns in those areas, as long as you don't go wandering off into the back country. Keep informed of current situations and always ask for local advice. Updated: May 23, 2008.

Things to See and Do

The Caribbean Coast and islands aren't just about white sand beaches and scuba diving. You can delve into the depths of colonial and independence history, in such cities as Cartagena and Santa Marta, tracing the steps of Spanish explorers and Simón Bolívar. Many astounding national parks and reserves, like Tayrona, Los Flamencos, Ciénaga and Sierra Nevada de Santa Marta, provide opportunities to witness sea turtles breeding and spectacular birds. Let your footfalls echo through the ancestral ruins of The Lost City and El Pueblito. Aracataca, author Gabriel García Márquez' hometown, is the ultimate Macondo (the mythical town in "One Hundred Years of Solitude"). But along this coast, every village is a Macondo, with strange festivals to celebrate with the locals, from the caiman in Ciénaga to the donkey pageant in Sincelejo. Of course, don't forget to join the big parties here, drinking whiskey with Valledupar at the Vallenato music festival and dancing traditional *cumbia* in Barranquilla's Carnaval. The visual arts are not neglected, with world-class art museums in the major cities and Cartagena's film festival. San Andrés is the most exotic of the Colombian Caribbean jewels, with an English-based culture and the best of beaches and scuba diving.

Caribbean Coast Tours

Many agencies throughout Colombia and overseas offer package excursions to the San Andrés Islands, Cartagena and other tourist destinations. Cruise ships have begun returning to the ports here, the most popular call being Cartagena. If you make it to the coast on your own, tour operators can help you with exploring local sights or destinations like Parque Nacional Natural Tayrona and The Lost City (Ciudad Perdida). Some go even further to Cabo de la Vela and the Guajira Peninsula.

Many agencies handle the arrangements for the most popular sport in the Caribbean region—scuba diving. Whether you are an experienced diver or a novice wanting to learn, get ready to discover the world beneath these crystalline waters. You'll be swimming with colorful fishes and manta and searching sunken ships. The most popular places to study for PADI certification are Santa Marta and Taganga.

Caribbean Coast Lodging

The full gamut of lodging types exists along Colombia's Caribbean Coast, from *mala muerte* inns, which double as brothels, to five-star hotels. In villages, expect only basic accommodations. Backpacker hostels are opening up in more towns, providing safe and inexpensive options for budget travelers. Most hotels will have only showers with room temperature water, which, in these latitudes, is quite warm. Luxury resorts are the only places to have heated water. Lower-priced hostels will only have fans as cooling systems; whereas, mid-range accommodations offer the choice between a room with a fan or A/C, for a cost.

In tourist destinations (Cartagena, Barranquilla and Santa Marta) hotels have one price for the low season and a much higher price in the high. Reservations are advisable during the high seasons. During Carnaval, room rates quadruple in Barranquilla. At any hotel along the coast it is worth asking for a discount during low season, especially if you will be staying for more than a few days.

Coveñas

Alt: 0m Pop: 11,000 City Code: 5

The more amiable and interesting area of the Coveñas township is the short stretch of three beach front hotels: the resort-like yellow and blue Hotel La Fragata, apartment-style Villa Melissa and modest white and blue Hotel Los Corales. The sea in front of the first two is a horseshoe of beach protected by jetties on either side, and La Fragata's bar is on stilts in the middle of the ocean. A nice, long, white sand beach begins in front of Hotel Los Corales and extends almost a kilometer down to Punta de Piedra. In addition to the hotel, there are homes for rent along this stretch of the beach.

Mornings by the sea are calm, but the fierce sea breezes are at full gust by noon. The hot tropical sun makes the ocean feel more like a Jacuzzi. Several pleasant days can easily pass by here, since time somehow slips its way through your fingers. Weekenders mob the beach, though the weekdays often come with empty sand and sea.

The actual town of Coveñas is a few more miles down the road from the hotel and beach area. Its general services and hotel prospects are grim. If you plan to spend a few days at the beach, check your email, go to the bank and stock up on food in Tolú. Then, leave your worries behind in the town, kick back and relax in your very own coastal paradise. Updated: Apr 14,2008.

When to Go

Coveñas, has tropical weather year-round. The beach gets crowded on the weekends and during holidays. Hotels fill up on Sundays in particular, and clear out by Tuesday. If you are seeking a private plot of sand, come on a weekday. Occasionally the hotels see so few guests and are so quiet it is spooky. Updated: Apr 09, 2008.

Getting To and Away from Coveñas

Coveñas is best reached by bus from the local terminal in Tolú. It costs $1 to be dropped off at Villa Melissa (about 20 minutes) and $1.50 to get to the town of Coveñas (10 minutes more). To get back to Tolú from Coveñas, just flag down a passing bus. Buses between Tolú and Coveñas run every 20 minutes. Buses farther west to San Antero and Cispatá leave from the main road in Coveñas town. You are better off returning to Tolú if you are traveling to Cartagena, Medellín or other long distances. Updated: Apr 14, 2008.

Getting Around Coveñas

It is very easy to walk around beach side Coveñas. If you have strayed far from your hotel and need a lift, it's also very easy to hitch a ride on the main road or on the boardwalk for about $0.50. Official motorcycle drivers for hire wear dark or orange vests. There is also the slower alternative of a two-peddle cart along the boardwalk. Young schoolboys offer rides for the same price, too. Updated: Apr 09, 2008.

Safety in Coveñas

In Coveñas you will have surprisingly more to worry about during the day than at night. Well, if you spend your day on the beach, that is. Hawkers sell everything including sunglasses, beaded necklaces, massages, wind chimes, fake idols, powdered medicine for your skin, *ceviche* or ice cream. They march back and forth along the beach begging you to buy something. It doesn't get any better in the water, either. Boats loop around offering to take you on a banana boat or tube ride, and men call for you from the beach to rent rafts, tubes and other floating devices. Take this all with a grain of salt. This is their livelihood, so just respectfully decline if you are not interested. Updated: Apr 15, 2008.

Coveñas Services

Laundry service can be completed for $2 per kilo. There is an unreliable local bank with an even more unreliable ATM in Coveñas town, but internet, post and other services are not found here. You are better off heading into Tolú for services or to stock up on food. Updated: May 19, 2008.

Things to See and Do

Coveñas is all about relaxing on the beach, possibly under the shade of a thatched umbrella. There is another slightly less developed but equally pleasant beach, Playa Blanca, 20 minutes west of Coveñas, just past San Antero on the way to Cispatá. Volcán de Lodo near El Porvenir, which is 10 minutes west of Coveñas, has a natural and healing mud baths. A trip to the Manglares of Cispatá is also a worthwhile half-day excursion. Updated: Apr 14, 2008.

Playa Blanca

Very few foreigners know about Playa Blanca, 30 minutes west of Coveñas. This town has small beaches separated by jetties is where Colombians seeking sand and sun come to vacation. During the holidays, weekends and throughout the month of July, the beach fills up with people. At all other times of the year this place is completely empty and, therefore, a perfect getaway should you find Coveñas not to your liking. Hotel Playa Blanca is the only hotel in town ($40 per night), but offers clean and modern cabanas with hammocks and has a large pool. The other accommodations are homes across from the beach, which can only be reserved upon arrival. You might want to think about stocking up on snacks before you leave for this beach, since the handful of restaurants here serve

Photo by Shawn O'Bryant

plain meals at kind-of high prices ($5-10 per plate). Updated: Apr 14, 2008.

Volcán de Lodo

Treat yourself to a healing mud bath at Volcán de Lodo. The mud supposedly has special healing ingredients. The great thing about this place is the price. For just $2 you can play in the mud while watching your skin transform and soften. The facilities here are basic. Get yourself dirty, then rinse yourself off. It's a great way to break up your day on the beach. Take the bus from Coveñas to San Antero ($1) and ask the driver to drop you off at Volcán de Lodo. Updated: Apr 14, 2008.

Manglares de Cispatá

Spend an interesting half-day trip at the Manglares de Cispatá. Tour a small animal sanctuary that has turtles, alligators and crocodiles. You can touch and hold most of the animals. A guide explains the kind of preservation work currently happening in the area. If you come by boat, you also can visit a bird sanctuary with plenty of pelicans and take a tour around a sardine fish farm. There are two ways to get here: take a taxi or bus from Coveñas to Cispatá (about 30 minutes) or, if you are staying on Playa Blanca, hire a boat to show you around for $50 and make a day of it. Updated: Apr 14, 2008.

Coveñas Lodging

Coveñas beachgoers tend to stick to the three very decent beach front hotels previously listed, though you will quickly notice along the road that there are dozens of options. Nevertheless, even the most private vacationers or wildest party people will find an appropriate option from one of the three most acceptable and distinct accommodations, which are all equally in the center of the Coveñas action. Updated: Apr 14, 2008.

Los Corales !

(ROOM: $15-25) Los Corales' Swiss owner keeps a watchful eye over the hotel and can tell you firsthand how much Coveñas has changed since his hotel opened much more than a decade ago. Back then, it offered just three guest rooms and basic accommodations. Now, this place has 27 guest rooms, public shower and bathroom facilities, and a fully functioning dining hall and beach front restaurant. For half as much as you would pay at La Fragata or Villa Melissa, you get a spacious and modern room with A/C or a fan. Los Corales is still expanding, during the next few years it should have up to 40 rooms and more facilities. Avenida La Playa Segunda Ensenada. Tel: 5-288-0336, Fax: 5-288-0573. Updated: Apr 14, 2008.

Hotel Nitana

(ROOM: $25-40) The Nitana, a Spanish-owned and -run enterprise, is an excellent option for anyone considering losing a few days here on this stretch of beach. Rooms are new, clean and comfortably equipped with A/C, refrigerator, new mattresses and fine bathrooms. The beach out front is narrow and far from ideal, but a 15-minute stroll will take you to wider, sandier points. It is between Punta Piedra and Boca de la Ciénaga. If you are coming on the bus from Cartagena, ask to be dropped on the outskirts of Coveñas. Keep an eye out for the signs to the hotel, it is clearly visible on the right-hand side. Tel: 5-249-9315, E-mail: info@nitana.com, URL: www.nitana.com. Updated: Apr 14, 2008.

La Fragata

(ROOM: $50-100) La Fragata is a lively, resort-like hotel comprised of six distinct buildings. There are the three cabana-style structures, the main reception hall that includes second-floor rooms overlooking the ocean, a six-story structure that has more hotel-like accommodations and, lastly, a pool area and hut for relaxing. It is a bonus that La Fragata has almost 100 differently styled guest rooms available, but the rooms are all a bit simple and in need of updating. However, La Fragata does provide the best facilities in town—a protected beach with a bar built on stilts, shaded huts with hammocks, tables and chairs, an enormous pool with a bar, and game room and lounge on the second floor of a large thatched hut. This is definitely the best option for families and large groups. Take the bus from Tolú and get off at the Villa Melissa stop, La Fragata is next door. Tel: 5-288-0061, Cell: 312-665-8975, URL: www.hotel-lafragata.com. Updated: Apr 14, 2008.

Villa Melissa

(ROOM: $50-150) One of the best options in Coveñas. The owners are friendly workaholics who will do everything within their power to make your stay a pleasant one. Their dedication to their investment shows—a pristine clean pool welcomes guests and the rooms/apartments are large, well-furnished and accommodating. They have one-, two- and three-bedroom apartments, each has a balcony, A/C, fans and cable TV. Since it is about six kilometers outside of Coveñas, your best bet is to either ask the bus driver to let you off when you see the sign or to catch a taxi from Coveñas. Tel: 8-288-0249. E-mail: gerencia@apartahotelvillamelissa.com, URL: apartahotelvillamelissa.com. Updated: Apr 14, 2008.

V!VA Member Review- Villa Melissa

Villa Melissa is ideal for vacationers hoping to cook their own meals or have some privacy. This apartment-style hotel has 12 guest apartments that each house up to eight people. All apartments have fully-functioning kitchens as well as a living room separate from the bedrooms. There are colorful lawn ornaments lining the internal garden and a tiny pool. Guests here keep to themselves. Honolulu, Apr 14, 2008.

Estado Natural Ecolodge

(BED: $12-21) Immerse yourself in nature at Estado Natural Ecolodge, about 46 kilometers west of Coveñas. You'll find it hard not to enjoy nature being surrounded by all of the activities offered at this resort, including snorkeling and birdwatching. Stay in a two- or one-story cabana (the two-story comes with a private kitchen) that has been constructed based on indigenous, environmentally sustainable techniques. Be warned: there are compost (waterless) toilets. The closest national airport is more than an hour away in Montería. The lodge is also accessible by private car or public bus. Tel: 316-738-7874, E-mail: info@estado-natural.com, URL: www.estado-natural.com. Updated: May 29, 2008.

COVEÑAS RESTAURANTS

The few restaurant options in Coveñas are all comparable in price and quality. The typical fare at every restaurant is a plate of fish, meat or chicken with a side of salad and plantains. Notice that many of the local boys spend their time fishing on the jetties or even walking around with their fishing spears. So rest assured, the seafood is always fresh and of particularly good value. For the most part, visitors tend to eat at their respective hotel's restaurant, especially since it is so easy to charge the bill to your room. La Fragata, Villa Melissa and Los Corales each have extensive menus ($5-10 for entrees). Another good option for a midday snack is buying ceviche ($2 for a small cup) or oysters from one of the many vendors roaming the beach and boardwalk. There is very little variety between these restaurants. The most you can expect from these eateries is to leave full and satisfied. Updated: Apr 14, 2008.

Punta de Piedra

Restaurante Punta de Piedra is a peaceful place to eat while taking in the local scene. Saul, the owner, frequently hosts his friends in one corner of the dining room for a game of cards called "51," which is a form of gin rummy. The openness of this restaurant and the amiable locals make this a great place to wind down your day. The food here is decent and reasonably priced—especially the seafood. Cell: 312-668-5643. Updated: Apr 14, 2008.

Palmar

When the local youth turn up the music and chill out in the shade, Restaurante Palmar becomes a pretty lively place for lunching. The food here is just average, so come more for the atmosphere than the cuisine. There is a second-floor balcony with hammocks and seating that you are free to use even after you finished your meal. Updated: Apr 14, 2008.

Tolú

Alt: 0 m Pop: 28,000 City Code: 5

Tolú is a busy commercial port, and there's nothing particularly attractive about it aside from the warm ocean. It has friendly locals and a light-hearted feel due to the abundance of bars along the boardwalk that blast *champeta* (a mix of salsa and reggaeton). During holidays and weekends, when Colombian tourists flock here, the town doubles in size.

Tolú is the ideal launching point to see natural sights or to lounge on a white sand beach. Some interesting places are 30 minutes to an hour from Tolú, like the San Bernardo Islands, Coveñas, Caimanera, Volcán de Lodo and Playa Blanca.

There are a far greater number of Colombians here on vacation than foreigners, but backpackers are slowly discovering Tolú, too. Most people spend just a day or two in Tolú, stock up on food and basic supplies, then head further west, along the coast. Updated: Apr 14, 2008.

When to Go

Tolú, like Cartagena, has the benefit of year-round tropical weather—generally hot and clear conditions. During December, January and Semana Santa this place gets so packed that, depending on what kind of beach holiday you are looking for, it may not be worth stopping here. Updated: Apr 14, 2008.

Getting To and Away from Tolú

There are two bus terminals in Tolú. The terminal by Parque Principal serves long-distance buses to Cartagena, Medellín and beyond. Buses leave nearly every hour in the mornings, from 7:30 until noon, picking up again hourly from 5 p.m. until 9 p.m. The other terminal services closer destinations such as Sincelejo and Coveñas. These buses are more frequent—about every half-hour.

From Tolú

Arrive	Time	Price
Coveñas	30 minutes	$2
Sincecelejo	45 minutes	$3
Cartagena	3 hours	$12
Medellín	10 hours	$36

Updated: Apr 09, 2008.

Getting Around Tolú

The town of Tolú is small and manageable on foot. The major activity happens around Parque Principal and the boardwalk along the beach. If you're hard-pressed to get somewhere quickly, hitch a ride with a *bicicletero* (a man riding a bicycle with two-person cab in the back). He will take you anywhere in town for $0.50. Updated: Apr 14,2008.

Safety in Tolú

Tolú is a safe enough city. Its residents are curious about where you come from, and will want to look after you and ensure you have a good time. Still, it is best to stick to the main streets at night and not wander too far out of the city limits. Updated: Apr 14, 2008.

Tolú Services

Money

The only bank in town is Banco de Colombia, located next to the long distance bus terminal in Parque Principal—pray it is open or that the two ATM machines are working.

Keeping in Touch

The best internet café, with lightning-fast broadband at $1 per hour, is conveniently located east of the other local bus terminal at the corner of Carrera 2 and Calle 17.

Medical

The hospital is in the park on your way out of town, across the street from the gas station.

Laundry

Laundry is available at any home-for-rent or hotel, and all charge about $1 per kilo.

Shopping

The best place to stock up on groceries and goods is at the southeastern corner of Parque Principal. Updated: Apr 09, 2008.

Things to See and Do

Tolú has little to offer in terms of historical sights or tourist activities. It is easy to pass a few days around town taking a boat trip, spending time on the beach, walking or going for a ride with a bicicletero around town. Make sure you stop the at the lagoon. In the evenings, the boardwalk has a nice sea breeze, shopping, lively music and a warm atmosphere. Updated: Apr 14, 2008.

La Ciénaga de Caimanera

Just 15 minutes out of town by taxi is a pleasant, natural half-fresh and half-salt water bog, Ciénaga de Caimanera. Here, you can take a boat around the lagoon, pick and eat raw oysters, spot *jaibas* (small crabs), and see shrimp by the dozen. The eco-tour here is worth a few hours of your day. Call Nicholas (311-671-0184) to schedule a tour or just show up at La Boca de Ciénaga. Also, book tours through your hotel. Take a taxi from Parque Principal to La Boca de Ciénaga, which should cost you about $2, one way. Updated: Apr 14, 2008.

Islas de San Bernardo

In an effort to attract affluent clientele and foreign revenue, the Colombian tourism industry has recently begun actively promoting the tiny 10-island archipelago of San Bernardo, an hour boat ride from Tolú. Tours include a visit to an ill-equipped aquarium on Isla Palma, a stop at El Islote, the tiniest island with a population of its size, and Isla Mucura, for its beaches. Be warned that locals on Isla Mucura overcharge for beach chair rentals. Trips are usually offered by tour companies that are affiliated with hotels in both Tolú and neighboring Coveñas. These tour companies hike their prices up during public holidays, long weekends and the high season. You can also book your tour directly with Marina Tolunautica, Avenida Primera, 9-48, Tolu. Tel: 5-288-5775. Updated: Feb 18, 2008.

Club Náutico

The little beaches along Tolú's boardwalk provide necessary breaks from the heat. The water is quite warm and not so clean, so these are not beaches you would sit on all day to relax. The best way to experience the sea is to hire a boat and take a trip to the San Bernardo Islands. Day trips can be arranged for $35 (including lunch) through Club Náutico, which is located at the western end of the boardwalk by the boat harbor. Boats leave for the islands nearly every day. On off days, Club Náutico is happy to help you arrange a boat trip with a fisherman on request. Avenida La Playa, 11-36. Tel: 5-288-5481 / 286-0079, Cell: 310-362-6014 / 638-7648, E-mail: maradentrotolu@hotmail.com, URL: www.clubnauticomaradentro.com. Updated: Apr 14, 2008.

Tolú Lodging

You will have little trouble finding accommodation upon arrival in Tolú. On every block close to the boardwalk there are at least two or three houses, hostels, hotels and rooms for rent. Accommodations are basic but satisfactory. Places across from the ocean cost at least $5 more than the others. Loud music from bars along this stretch make the hotels on perpendicular streets a more attractive choice. Expect to pay about $10 for a room with cold water and a fan, $15 with A/C, and $20 with A/C and cable TV. Updated: Apr 11, 2008.

Hotel Caribe

(ROOM: $10-15) Although Hotel Caribe offers basic rooms, its location in the center of the boardwalk across from the beach is ideal. The rooms here are in need of updating. Nonetheless, you get what you pay for, at $10 for a room with a fan or $15 for one with A/C. Updated: Apr 14, 2008.

Hostal Rokalpa

(ROOM: $10-15) Hostal Rokalpa is a centrally-located, clean hostel worth a try. The rooms here all have cable TV but are basic and small. The airy courtyard is a nice place to relax or have breakfast (which you need to ask to be included in your stay). Bargain with the owner for no more than $10 for a room with a fan or $15 for one with A/C. Updated: Apr 09, 2008.

Hotel Darimar

(ROOM: $15-25) The exterior of Hotel Darimar makes it seem more comfortable than it actually is. Rooms are small and stuffed with three short, hard beds. The bathrooms are hardly functional. This place feels more like a hospital than a hotel, but it's quiet and conveniently located just off the boardwalk, right next to the best internet in town and the local bus terminal. Calle 17, 1-60. Tel: 5-288-5153. Updated: Apr 14, 2008.

Villa Babilla

(ROOM: $20-30) The best known hostel on the backpacker route, Villa Babilla is a bit out of the way from the town activity and charges $5 more than other centrally-located places for a room. This is a peaceful hostel though, with lots of hammocks, a nice outdoor patio, a community kitchen and clean rooms. Calle 20 3-40. Tel: 5-288-6124, Cell: 312-677-1325, E-mail: info@villababillahostel.com, villababillatolu@yahoo.com, URL: www.villababillahostel.com. Updated: Apr 14, 2008.

Tolú Restaurants

Restaurants in Tolú are consolidated along the beach front. Unfortunately, there's not a lot of variety in this town. You generally have a choice of meat, chicken, fish, lobster and shrimp, served with either plantains or rice, salad and occasionally a scoop of beans. Prices are similar everywhere you go. Lunchtime sees a conglomeration of locals at the 20 or so small food stalls that begin at the boardwalk and run along Calle 20. There are lots of juice bars by the boardwalk, as well as fresh fruit for sale around Parque Principal. Updated: Apr 11, 2008.

Varadero Restaurant and Bar

Located next to Club Náutico, Varadero serves a fantastic breakfast complete with scrambled eggs (with ham, tomato and onions), *arepa*, cheese, and your choice of hot chocolate or coffee. Prices on the menu are outdated, so be sure to find out the price of your food before you order it. Updated: Apr 09, 2008.

Restaurant Row

For a decent, cheap lunch, head to Tolú's Restaurant Row, which begins at the boardwalk and extends one block along Calle 20. Twenty great little stalls serve up fresh fish with rice and salad for just $3. Around lunchtime the stalls are packed with locals, especially the most popular one, Fonda La Gordita. Updated: Apr 09, 2008.

Terraza Restaurante La 15

This is one of the better restaurant options in Tolú. The service here is quick, the food is tasty and the prices are what they should be. You can't complain about the setting either, since Terraza is on a breezy corner of the boardwalk with tables by the beach and under a covered patio. Updated: Apr 09, 2008.

Donde Carlos

This restaurant suffers from the same problem as Hotel Darimar across the street. It looks great from the outside (clean, with peach and cream-colored decor), but the food here is expensive and not very tasty. Instead of asking for the menu, ask about the daily lunch special, which is half the price of the food on the menu. Updated: Apr 09, 2008.

Cartagena

Alt: 0m Pop: 895,000 City Code: 5

Foreboding fortresses, narrow streets, hidden patios and enchanting colonial houses characterize Cartagena, a vibrant city, rich in history and Caribbean culture. The city sits on a stretch of coastline extending from the Darién Gap to Guajira, a route lined with banana, palm plantations and swamplands. Frequent trade winds temper the heat, bestowing Cartagena with pleasant weather and an abundance of tropical fruit all year.

Often referred to as one of the most beautiful cities in South America, Cartagena has plenty to offer travelers in the way of sites and sounds. One of the best ways to enjoy this intriguing city is to amble along its historic streets (head to the small plazas centered near the San Diego quarter), exploring nooks and crannies and savoring small surprises.

A series of stone-walled forts scattered throughout the city stand as ominous reminders of Cartagena's colonial past. Among the many forts to see are San Fernando, Fuerte San José, San Sebastián, San Lorenzo and Castillo de San Felipe de Barajas, the largest Spanish fort in the Americas. The old walled city is divided into two sections, though little remains of the physical wall. Artisans once lived in the outer city where many colonial buildings still stand today, along with a number of budget hotels and restaurants. The adjacent downtown sector, La Matuno, is dominated by street vendors and a few sporadic mid-range hotels. High officials and nobility occupied the inner city, while the middle class spread across the San Diego district. Today these sections are less crowded and dotted with hotels and restaurants.

A few of the sites in the inner and outer sections include the church of Santísima Trinidad, Monastery of San Francisco, Plaza de la Independencia, Museo de Arte Moderno, Museo del Oro y Arqueológico, the Cathedral, Plaza Santo Domingo (lined with delightful pavement cafés and restaurants, a popular spot to spend the evenings), and the church and monastery of Santa Clara de Assisi (now a charming hotel). The ramparts of walls around Plaza de la Bóvedas provide a spectacular view of the city, and a lighted underground passage and drawbridge lead from here to the fortress of La Tenaza, occupying a formidable spot at the water's edge.

Day trips abound from Cartagena, including excursions to the Fortress of San Fernando and the Castillo de San Felipe de Barajas, across from the Puente Heredia. Spectacular views of the city can be had from the top of La Popa hill, where the church and monastery of Santa Cruz and restored ruins of a convent dating back to 1608 are found, along with a well-preserved image of Virgin of La Candelaria, whose festival is celebrated on February 2. Further outside the city there are a few noteworthy beaches, including Bocagrande, Marbella, Playa Blanca on Isla Barú, La Boquilla and Islas del Rosario, where you'll find Parque Nacional Corales del Rosario. If beaches aren't your bag, then head to the clay baths at Volcán Totume, reportedly more than 500 meters deep. Updated: Mar 27, 2008.

Pirates and the Sacking of Cartagena

Cartagena attracts visitors year-round, most of whom journey to this coastal hub to enjoy all that the Caribbean port town has to offer. But long before throngs of vacationers flocked here for the surf, sand and shopping, Cartagena attracted visitors of a different sort: pirates. As one of the great treasure ports of Spain's colonial conquests, Cartagena saw a fair share of gold, jewelry and gems enter through its waters. As such, the city was also one of the prime targets for English, Dutch and French buccaneers. Of course the Spanish did everything they could to deter such attacks, but as Cartagena's history suggests, they suffered many setbacks before achieving that goal.

One of the first pirate attacks of note involved Robert Baal, a pirate of French descent who in 1551 was able to wrest more than 600 pounds of gold from the governor of Cartagena as ransom for sacking the city. The King of Spain reacted swiftly, commissioning engineers from Europe to construct fortifications around the city—a task that would install some of the city's most lasting and iconic symbols. Though the fortifications helped, it took nearly 200 years to be completed, and pirates continued to successfully attack Cartagena for decades to come.

The pirates' standard operating procedure involved calculated sieges of the city followed by demands for ransom. In return, pirates promised not to completely destroy the city. French pirate Martin Cote exacted a large sum of money this way not long after Baal.

Perhaps the most famous swashbuckler to leave his mark on Cartagena, Sir Francis Drake attacked the port in 1572. Spaniards fled the city in droves, leaving the port largely unprotected. According to lore, Drake burned much of the city to the ground, including a nave of the Cathedral. He received a very large ransom, with one report estimating it at more than 100,000 ducats, a large amount of gems and jewels, artillery pieces, and other assorted goods.

By the 1600s, Spanish engineers had improved the city's fortifications enough to thwart most attempts at the city. The last successful invasion came in 1697, when Baron de Pointis was able to enter the city, thanks in large part to a slave rebellion that took place inside the city's walls. Spain again strengthened fortifications in response, leading to one of the city's greatest defensive successes in 1741, when Admiral Edward Vernon led the English Navy in an attack against Cartagena. After fierce fighting and some 350 bombs, Cartagena was able to repel the English attack. Cartagena's success proved a defining moment for the city, as it brought a halt to attacks on the city by foreign entities. Another attack would not take place until the 19th Century, when the war for Colombian independence was under way. Updated: May 19, 2008.

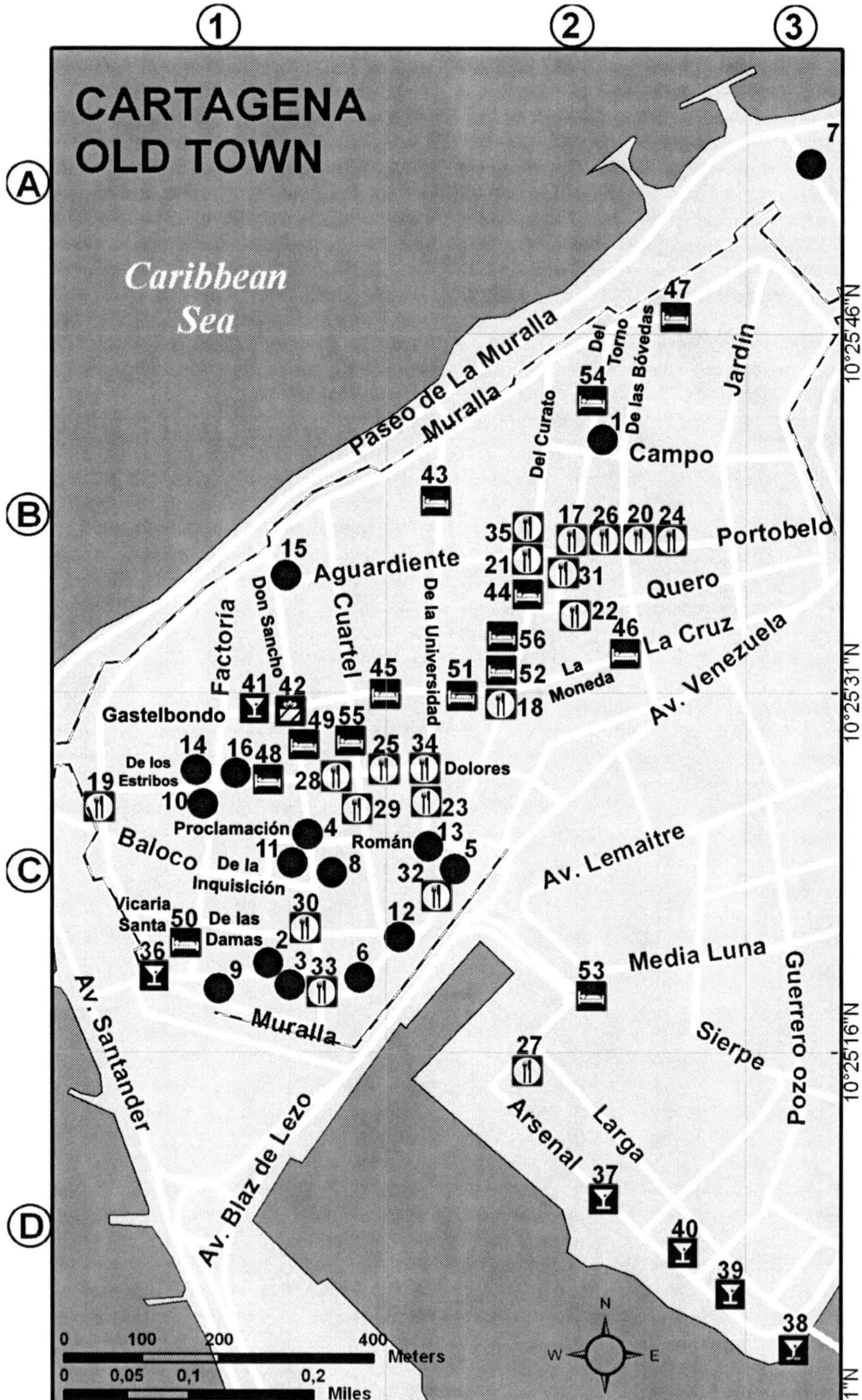

CARIBBEAN COAST

Activities
1 Casa de Gabriel García Márquez B2
2 Enoteca C1
3 Iglesia de San Pedro Claver C1
4 La Catedral C1
5 La Torre del Reloj C2
6 Museo de Arte Moderno C1
7 Museo de las Fortificaciones A3
8 Museo del Oro C1
9 Museo Naval del Caribe C1
10 Palacio de la Inquisición C1
11 Plaza de Bolívar C1
12 Plaza de la Aduana C2
13 Plaza de los Coches C2
14 Plaza Santo Domingo C1
15 Teatro de Heredia B1
16 Templo de Santo Domingo C1

Eating
17 Arepas del Santísimo B2
18 Brianzola B2
19 Cafe del Mar C1
20 Café del Santísimo B2
21 Cafetería Bocaditos Madrid B2
22 Casa Majagna B2
23 Cuero Centro Café C2
24 Da Danni's Restaurant B2
25 El Bistro C1
26 El Santísimo Restaurant and Café B2
27 La Cocina de Socorro D2
28 Mila C1
29 Moe's C1
30 Palo Santo C1
31 Pizza en el Parque B2
32 Portal de los Dulces C2
33 Restaurante San Pedro C1
34 Spezia's C1
35 Tamarindo B2

Nightlife
36 El Baluarte Tasca-Bar C1
37 La Carbonera D2
38 La Casa de la Cerveza D3
39 León de Baviera D2
40 Mister Babilla D2
41 Rincon de la Mantilla C1

Shopping
42 Bookstore C1

Sleeping
43 Casa del Tejadillo B2
44 Casa La Fé B2
45 Hospedaje Cartagena C1
46 Hostal Mar Azul B2
47 Hostal San Diego A2
48 Hostal Santo Domingo C1
49 Hotel Central C1
50 Hotel Charleston C1
51 Hotel El Viajero C2
52 Hotel los Balcones de Badillo B2
53 Hotel Monterrey C2
54 Hotel Santa Clara B2
55 Hotel Tres Banderas C1
56 Portal de San Diego B2

Highlights

Stroll through the narrow streets of the city all the way to the churches of **San Pedro**, **Santo Domingo (p.227)** and **La Catedral (p.222)**.

The **Inquisition Museum (p.227)** offers an interesting glimpse of Cartagena's fascinating history.

After sunset, head to **Plaza San Diego (p.232)** for a wide selection of restaurants, then spend the rest of your night at the clubs and bars of **Avenida Arsenal** in Getsemaní. Updated: Apr 14, 2008.

Cartagena History

Cartagena was founded by Pedro de Heredia in 1533. Within 20 years, six forts (San Fernando, San José, San Sebastián del Pastelillo, San Lorenzo, San Felipe de Barajas, and La Tenaza) were built to protect the city from invasion. Still, Cartagena experienced several sieges for 200 years. The most notable attacks were by Sir Francis Drake in 1586, Baron de Pointis and Ducasse in 1697, and Sir Edward Vernon in 1741. This latter siege was defended by the famous one-eyed, one-armed, one-legged hero Blas de Lezo, whose statue stands at the entrance of the San Felipe fortress. These severe attacks led to the building of the old city's protective wall that still stands today. Cartagena declared independence from Spain in 1811 and Bolívar used the city as a jumping-off point for his Magdalena campaign just one year later. However, the city was forced to bear the imperial burden when royalists ascended to power in 1815, under the surveillance of Pablo Morillo. The city declared full independence in 1821, thanks to the support of heroic patriots. Updated: Apr 08, 2008.

When to Go

Temperatures in Cartagena range from warm to hot—and it's usually hot. The only distinguishing factor in the weather is the humidity. Rain falls between August and November, but this doesn't detract tourists. Prices of accommodations are 20 percent higher in December and January and during Semana Santa.

Photo by Ryan Bird

Holidays and Fiestas

The city's patroness, Virgen de La Candelaria, is honored at La Popa on February 2. Nine days before the feast, thousands go up the hill by foot, horse or car, and, on the ninth day, they carry candles. There is a Caribbean music festival at the end of the year and for five days in March. Cartagena's International Film Festival is held in the spring (usually in March). The Festival of Sweets is held during Semana Santa in Plaza de los Coches. Last but not least, a great feast is held from November 11-14 to celebrate the city's independence, where men and women in masks and fancy dress dance in the streets to celebrate the independence of Cartagena. Colombia's national beauty contest is held during this festival. Updated: Apr 14, 2008.

Getting To and Away from Cartagena

Crespo airport is located one and a half kilometers from Cartagena, and offers a number of national and international flights.

A taxi stand is immediately to your right as you exit the airport terminal and will print out a ticket for the exact cost of the ride to your hotel (about $3.50 to El Centro). A bus circles around El Centro making stops along Avenida Santander before going to the bus station, which is 20 minutes away, for $1.25.

The bus terminal is 30 minutes from the walled city by taxi or bus.

From Cartagena

Arrive	Departure	Time	Price
Tolú	Hourly	3 hours	$10
Santa Marta	Hourly	4 hours	$15
Bucaramanga	Hourly mornings/ evenings	8 hours	$30
Medellín	Hourly mornings/ evenings	13 hours	$40

Updated: Apr 14, 2008.

Getting Around Cartagena

It is easy to walk around El Centro in a day. Buses run along Avenida Santander to take you to and from Laguito and Bocagrande for $0.60. Horse-drawn carriages can take you on a romantic whirl around the old city for $23 (45 minutes.)

The only reason to take the bus would be to visit Bocagrande, La Popa or Castillo de San Felipe de Barajas. Hop on a bus from Avenida Santander to Bocagrande (10 minutes) for $1. Buses to La Popa or San Felipe (10-15 minutes) frequently leave from India Catalina for $1.

Taxis are safe and cheap. In the evenings, get to and from Bocagrande and El Centro for $2. Everything between El Centro, San Diego, Matuna and Getsemaní is walkable.

The walled portion of Cartagena de Indias is broken into four neighborhoods: El Centro, San Diego, Matuna and Getsemaní. Most of the city's tourist attractions are consolidated in El Centro. San Diego has a quieter pace by day and a sophisticated buzz by night. Matuna is not worth visiting at all, as it is rather dirty and urban. Getsemaní is a bit rough around the edges, but has a lively night scene. Most tourists prefer to stay in the old city, while vacationing Colombians tend to head to Bocagrande and Laguito, located on an l-shaped peninsula just five minutes south of the old city. High-rise condos and upscale hotels are popping up on the peninsula at a heart-pounding rate. Updated: Apr 14, 2008.

Safety in Cartagena

The money changers in the old city are notorious for short-changing tourists, so you are advised to withdraw money from an ATM or exchange money at a reputable bank. El Centro is well lit at night and very safe for tourists, but travelers should always use caution when walking around alone at night. Updated: Apr 14, 2008.

Cartagena Services

Tourism Office

The newly renovated tourist office in Plaza de la Aduana is a recommended first stop before you embark on any sightseeing in Cartagena. Here, you can view a map of the whole city where sites light up based on the activities that interest you. Stock up on free tourist magazines and maps.

Money

Banks are located along Avenida Venezuela.

Keeping in Touch

Internet is readily available throughout the city for about $0.85 per hour and is particularly easy to find around Calle Santo Domingo in El Centro.

Medical

If you are in need of a doctor, the best are found outside the walled city, at the hospital in Bocagrande or Ami in Pie de la Popa.

Shopping

High-fashion Caribbean women's apparel, handicrafts and emeralds are easily found within the walls of Cartagena's old city. The clothing and shoes can be expensive along Calle Santo Domingo, but the boutiques are classy and colorful. Mementos and handicrafts make Las Bóvedas a perfect place to practice your bargaining skills. Finally, those shiny green gems are hard to pass up and might make a nice accessory for your night on the town. Updated: Apr 14, 2008.

Supermarket

Stock up on groceries or pick up some clothes or digital accessories at this three-story supermarket conveniently located on Avenida Venezuela. The first floor carries all the food you need to fill your fridge. Fresh produce, alcohol, dairy and bread are all reasonably priced. There is an orange café on the second floor that sells local lunches like rice with shrimp for just $2.85. On the third floor, you can purchase a SIM card for your phone for only $6. The corner of Avenida Venezuela and Calle del Boquete. Updated: Apr 14, 2008.

Santo Domingo Boutiques

Ladies will be impressed with the trendy boutique shopping found along Calle Santo Domingo. Loose, clean styles, creative designs, and vibrant Caribbean colors characterize Cartagena's hip and lively fashion scene. Prices (about $100 for a swimsuit, sandals or a dress) are rather high, so for better bargains, head to the stores around Calles Badillo and Moneda. Updated: Apr 14, 2008.

Emerald Shopping

El Centro, particularly along Calle del Ladrinal, houses an overwhelming selection of emerald shops, many of which sell gems found in the mountain ranges near Bogotá. Jewelry ranges in quality and size, but prices are consistently high. If you're serious about buying, expect to bargain for about 50 percent of the price quoted, which might explain why some stores have "50 percent off" slogans permanently painted on their windows. Also, don't be fooled by the elegant interior of a place—some of the cloudiest emeralds are there. Hired men will try to lure you in to their stores for you to take a look. The best plea for attention is "Museo de la Esmeralda," which you will find is a jewelry store like its competitors, and not a museum at all. Nonetheless, if you are selective, inquisitive and keen enough, you could still find that gorgeous piece you are seeking. Updated: Apr 14, 2008.

Things to See and Do

Cartagena is truly a Caribbean paradise with a long history, complete with pirates, rum, legend and lore. The best way to experience this city is to walk. Visit the churches, plazas and museums to get a taste of its history. Walk on Las Murallas, the city's famed wall, to bask in the tropical sun and enjoy the sea breezes. Take photographs of the colorful colonial buildings. Drink freshly squeezed fruit juice from a stall on a narrow street in El Centro. When your feet get tired, take a spin on a romantic horse-drawn carriage. Be warned—it is difficult not to fall in love with this magical city. Updated: Apr 07, 2008.

Las Bóvedas

The same engineer that designed Castillo San Felipe de Barajas built this structure to serve as a military quarters for the city in the late 18th Century. The 23 vaults contained within this yellow building were used to lodge military personnel and store ammunition, provisions, and tools. During the republican era, these vaults were used as jail cells. Today, they have been renovated and now house artisan shops selling Colombian and Caribbean handicrafts and souvenirs. Las Bóvedas is located at the northern perimeter of San Diego, next to Museo de las Fortificaciones. Open every day, 10 a.m.-5 p.m. Updated: Apr 14, 2008.

Castillo de San Felipe de Barajas

A statue of Blas de Lezo, who famously and successfully defended Cartagena from invasion in 1742, stands in front of Castillo de San Felipe de Barajas, Cartagena's strongest and largest military fortress. This fortress was built on San Lázaro Hill over the course of nearly 150 years and features advanced military engineering directed by Antonio de Arévalo. Wander through the underground passageways, which are now lit so that visitors can witness the impeccable design. Visitors shouldn't miss seeing this military wonder, which remains a symbol of Cartagena's history under siege and its people's long journey toward independence. The fortress is just a 20-minute walk from the old town, or take a local bus from Parque del Centenario. Open everyday, 8 a.m.-6 p.m. Av Arévalo, San Lázaro. Tel: 5-673-4790. Updated: Apr 14, 2008.

La Catedral

Built of wood and cane, La Catedral's construction began in 1575. Plans were revamped by Simón González, who worked on the greater part of its construction from 1577 until 1612. Sir Francis Drake famously destroyed it in the midst of construction in 1586. It took nearly 100 years to complete the building of this grand cathedral, and it recently underwent further renovation in 2007. The final product is a perfect blend of colonial and modern styles. It has a gaping doorway opening up to its hollow, simple interior, and contains a gilded 18th Century alter and marble pulpit. The interior is flanked by thick white columns and large arches that are tall and impressive. La Catedral is located next to Plaza Bolívar and is open everyday from 9 a.m.-5 p.m. You can purchase an audio tour for $2.50, which explains the church's history and other items found inside. Updated: Apr 14, 2008.

La Popa

Atop the highest point in the city sits Convento de la Popa, which is also known as "Stern of the Galley" because of its situation at the back end of Cartagena. "La Popa" however, takes on more humorous meaning, as many thought the hill looked like a poop deck. When the convent was originally founded in 1607, it was named Convento de Nuestra Señora de la Candelaria ("Our Lady of Candles.") An image of La Virgen de la Candelaria, the patroness of the city, still hangs inside the chapel and an important festival is held in her honor on February 2. There have been reports of armed robbers on the road leading to La Popa, so it is advisable to visit by taxi, not by foot. Open every day, 8 a.m.-5:30 p.m. Tel: 5-666-2331. Updated: Apr 14, 2008.

Muelle de los Pegasos and el Camellón de los Martires

Along the walkway separating El Centro with Getsemaní, you will find some interesting monuments marking Cartagena's independence. Three impressive bronze pegasus statues look out to the sea beside the city convention center. The centerpiece of the grand Hall of the Martyrs is a lovely white statue of a woman also looking out to sea. These monuments together come to represent the peace and independence so earnestly fought for and won here. They serve as an affirmation that the plunder that once plagued the city is long past. Updated: Apr 14, 2008.

India Catalina

This monument was sculpted by Eladio Gil Zambrana, and erected in 1974. India Catalina, an indigenous woman and supposed daughter of a chief from Colombia's Atlantic coast, accompanied Pedro de Heredia to Cartagena's shores in the 16th Century and served as his interpreter during the Spanish conquest. She was fluent in Spanish and the native language, adopted the Catholic religion, and later married Pedro de Heredia's nephew. Ironically, Heredia's conquest completely annihilated the Calamari people who had previously lived in Cartagena. Today, India Catalina symbolizes the fading pre-Columbian inhabitants. At the same time, she serves as a tribute to the Caribe culture and the original inhabitants of this region. Smaller replicas of her statue are given to award winners of the Cartagena Film Festival. Updated: Apr 14, 2008.

Museo de las Fortificaciones and Las Murallas

Construction of Las Murallas, the walls protecting Cartagena de Indias, began in 1586 when Bautista Antonelli, an Italian engineer, was hired to service the Spanish Crown. It was later fortified by Cristóbal de Roda in 1608, who worked to build the section separating the city from the open sea. From 1631-33, Francisco de Murga worked to further protect the city on the other side, in Getsemaní. Further repairs from several sieges were made in the late 17th Century and into the 18th Century. Many of the wall's old canons are in place still today, and visitors can walk around the walls to get a taste of Cartagena's military past. The museum is located next to Las Bóvedas. Tel: 5-664-4790. Updated: Apr 14, 2008.

Cartagena Water Sports

Since the city is guarded on one side by the Caribbean sea, it's not difficult to try your hand at a variety of water sports here. Sea breezes begin their usual dance into Cartagena in the early afternoon, making it a perfect time to play in the water. Kitesurfing, windsurfing, sailing, scuba diving or snorkeling are all possible. Rental gear is available at the following aqua sport shops:

Aqua Nautica
Kitesurfing and Windsurfing
E-mail: www.kitesurfcolombia.com / Aquacartagena@yahoo.com, Tel: 5-656-8243, Cell: 310-727-1110.

Diving Planet
Centro, Calle del Estanco del Aguardiente #5-94. Tel: 5-664-2171.

Cultura del Mar
Snorkeling, Scuba Diving, Canoeing
Tel: 5-664-9312, E-mail: info@culturadelmar.com, URL: www.culturadelmar.com. Updated: Apr 14, 2008.

Isla de Tierra Bomba

Just a 15-minute boat ride from the Bocagrande boardwalk, La Isla de Tierra Bomba remains steeped in history. It was through here that the first pioneers entered Cartagena. A fairly large island, most day trippers are only able to experience its southern shores, Punta Arena and Punta Luna. To experience the relaxing vibes here, hire a boat for $2.85 each way, spend the day on the beach, eat fresh island fruit and fish, drink an *aguila* (beer), then make your way back to Bocagrande at sunset. If you would like to stay on the island for a night, walk to Hotel Tres Banderas, on the eastern tip of the island (about $80 per night). Updated: Apr 14, 2008.

Studying Spanish in Cartagena

Studying Spanish in Cartagena has two advantages to studying in Medellín or Bogotá: the ocean and the Caribbean culture. Nowhere else in Colombia will you be able to study Spanish in a tropical paradise and participate in water sports later that day. Well aware of Cartagena's multitudinous draws, several Spanish language schools in the city combine work with play, offering afternoon cultural activities like dance and sports in conjunction with morning Spanish lessons. It is the perfect blend of schoolwork and recess that you wish you had as a kid. Updated: Apr 14, 2008.

Casa Cultural

The Casa Cultural Colombo Alemana, in the historic center of Cartagena and close to Teatro Heredia and the city beaches, provides a relaxed and friendly atmosphere for inter-cultural exchange and learning Spanish. Three different types of Spanish classes are taught at this small school: beginner to advanced Spanish, Spanish for tourism, and Spanish for the workplace. Individual classes or small groups provide students with a flexible schedule. In addition, afternoon cultural activities are available to enhance students' practical learning of the language. Centro Calle 38, 5-31, Calle Estanco del Aguardiente. Tel: 5-660-2522 / 664-9837 Fax: 5-664-5610, E-mail: colomboaleman@gmx.net, URL: web:www.casacolomboalemana.latinowebs.com. Updated: Apr 14, 2008.

Languages in Action

Languages in Action is part of an international organization of language schools. The school in Cartagena offers beginner, elementary, intermediate and advanced Spanish courses that focus on speaking, listening, reading and writing. Particular attention is paid to the practical use of the language in daily situations. The school also provides an assortment of more specialized programs: individual or group lessons; Spanish for business; medical Spanish; Spanish immersion; homestay with a Colombian family; Spanish with volunteering; Spanish combined with dancing; Spanish and scuba diving; Spanish and kitesurfing; Spanish and windsurfing; and Spanish and sunfishing (sailing). URL: http://www.learn4good.com/great_schools/colombia_spanish_language_immersion_courses.htm. Updated: Apr 14, 2008.

The Cactus Language School

The Cactus Language School is located in the historic part of Cartagena, and the courses are designed for people who want to improve their Spanish during holidays. The school is located five minutes from the Torre de Reloj and three blocks from El Centro, the walled center of the city. The school is spaciously situated in a colonial house that reflects the history and culture of Cartagena. Its cafeteria, internet, library, courtyard and garden are available for student use. The school works with a non-profit organization called Actuar por Bolívar to help the poorest people of Cartagena. Students are involved in social projects in association with this program to enrich their cultural experience and enhance their language skills. Course length can range from one to 12 weeks. Students have the option of staying with a host family or living in the school residence. Dance courses are also available upon request. Booking can be made online. Updated: Apr 14, 2008.

Adventure Travel Program

Founded in 1992 and in affiliation with the World's Best Language School, which has schools in Italy, New Zealand and Venezuela, the Adventure Travel Program in Cartagena is a unique combination of language learning and scuba diving. Students work independently or in groups up to 10 people to to study Spanish and learn the Colombian way of life while simultaneously discovering the mysteries of the sea in afternoon scuba diving lessons. One week courses provide 15 hours of Spanish, three scuba lessons, and either five hours of cultural activities or five hours of salsa/merengue dance lessons ($300). The two week course provides 30 hours of Spanish, a full PADI-certified open water course, and 10 hours of cultural or dance lessons ($710). General or intensive Spanish, Spanish and dancing, as well as Spanish and volunteering programs are available as well. Spanish lessons take place at the school, just five minutes from the main entrance to the old city. Students have the option to live with a family, at the school, in an apartment or hotel, or find their own accommodations. E-mail: info@learnspanishanddive.com, URL: http://www.learnspanishanddive.com/colombia.htm. Updated: Apr 14, 2008.

Voyage International

Voyage International students are immersed in a language and cultural program of their choosing in a personalized setting. With small group lessons in the mornings and dance or volunteer activities in the afternoons, students are able to fully embrace their Spanish learning academically, culturally and practically. The volunteer social work performed in the afternoon is through Funafamiliar, an NGO that arranges for young boys who have been living on the streets or who have had problems at home to have a place to go. Volunteers develop friendships with the boys so that they can begin a healthy recovery, prepare for their return home, and stay off the streets. Voyage International also offers Spanish combined with scuba diving, kitesurfing, windsurfing or sailing, when these sports are in season. E-mail: info@langage.com. Updated: Apr 14, 2008.

Cartagena Tours

If you prefer not to wither while walking in the city's sometimes unbearable tropical heat, or would like to visit the sites outside of the walled city, consider booking a tour through an operator in Cartagena. Expert guides will offer up local knowledge, history and lore. Transportation time and fees are often discounted when joining a group trip to places like Isla Tierra Bomba, Barú, Rosario, and Totume. Updated: Apr 14, 2008.

Adventure Ecotours

Adventure Ecoturismo provides superior city tours or tours in northern Colombia. Trips and excursions can be arranged for groups of two to eight people, and range from one hour to a full day in Cartagena de Indias, or up to a week with affiliated operators in the country. Adventure EcoTours can arrange a six day trek to The Lost City though the TurCol agency in Santa Marta. Other destinations include Las Islas Rosario, Playa Blanca, San Andrés, Parque Tayrona and beyond. Rates are reasonable (and negotiable), and Spanish, English and French is spoken. Calle del Santísimo #8-55. Cel: 300-558-0874 / 314-588-2378, Tel: 5- 664-8500, E-mail: Adventurecolombia@gmail.com. Updated: Apr 14, 2008.

Ocean and Land Tours

This tour operator offers exactly what its name alludes to: organized tours of land and sea. The guides speak English and Spanish, providing city tours both near and far. Here, you can also book a rumba ride in a *chiva*—a mobile party. This operator can organize boat trips, arrange for your accommodations, or book your trip to Islas del Rosario, Playa Blanca, Santa Marta or other events. Bocagrande, Cra. 2, 4-15 Local 6, Edificio Antillas. Cell: 311-681-9239 / 316-700-7943 / 311-435-9855, Tel: 5-665-7772, E-mail: oceanlandtours@yahoo.com, oceanlandtours2@hotmail.com. Updated: Apr 14, 2008.

Arrecifes Tours

Arrecifes Tours specializes in local tours and accommodations in and around Cartagena. Transportation is included for both, though the guided city tours are basic. If you are looking for a private vacation away from the crowds, they can book a nice cabana for you at beach locations close to the city. Their cabana on Isla de Tierra Bomba is well-equipped with air conditioned rooms, an airy terrace, and a spacious kitchen. In the mornings, drink Colombian coffee with a private view of the sea from the front porch. Cell: 310-611-5842 / 315-736-8693, Tel: 5-665-6477 / 6878, E-mail: Arrecifesoperadora@hotmail.com. Updated: Apr 14, 2008.

Isla del Encanto

This tour operator can help arrange an affordable visit to the Rosario Islands or Totumo volcano, plan a tour around the city (including trips to Castillo de San Felipe and La Popa), or organize a ride in a chiva party bus. Whether you'd like to rent a boat for a day, go camping, jet skiing, diving or snorkeling, Isla del Encanto will happily assist you in making your stay in Cartagena easy, enjoyable and worry-free. Visit their office in the Michel Center on Avenida San Martín in Bocagrande. Avenida San Martín in the Michel Center, 5-52, Bocagrande. Tel: 5-655-8315 / 5454, E-mail: Info@isladelencanto.info, URL: www.isladelencanto.info. Updated: Apr 14, 2008.

Cartagena Lodging

The cheapest accommodation can be found in Getsemaní, with hostels by the handful around Calle San Andrés. You will find basic rooms around here, with a stiff bed and cold water showers. Once you cross over Avenida Venezuela into El Centro and San Diego, both price and quality rise. Accommodations in El Centro are right in the thick of daily activity, while hotels in San Diego are quiet and serene. Updated: Apr 07, 2008.

Cartagena Restaurants

Whether you are grabbing a street snack or sitting down to a decadent meal, dining in Cartagena is a gastronomical treat. Caribbean ladies balancing bowls of fruit on their heads tempt you with bright colors and sweet smells. Delicious street food can be found around every corner. Take time to savor the many facets of Colombian-Caribbean cuisine. Cheaper restaurants are found on Calle de Ayos. Mid-range restaurants are consolidated between Plaza Fernández de

Madrid and Plaza San Diego. Pricier, more luxurious locales are on Calle Santo Domingo. Updated: Apr 07, 2008.

Cartagena Nightlife

The street that runs along Avenida del Arsenal from the convention center to la Casa de la Cerveza lights up and vibrates every night from 10 p.m. until dawn. You can choose from an array of pubs, bars, lounges and clubs. The streets between Plaza Santa Teresa (Babar should not be missed) and Plaza Santo Domingo (where you will find the Joy Slava Club) are popular with locals and foreigners alike. The area around Plaza San Diego and Plaza Fernández de Madrid in the old city also offers several chic hangouts, but these spots are not open quite as late. If you are looking for a more relaxed local nightlife scene, head to Avenida San Martín in the Bocagrande. Updated: Apr 14 ,2008.

Photo by Ryan Bird

Centro

All of Cartagena's major museums, plazas and churches are consolidated in El Centro. This part of the city starts at the Puerta del Reloj and extends outwards, covering roughly 50 blocks filled with colonial buildings draped with bougainvillea. If you have just one day in Cartagena, spend it in this neighborhood, as there is much to see and do here. The shopping, hotels and restaurants in El Centro are the most expensive in the city. Still, it is worth the extra cash just to meander one of the quaintest and most breathtaking city centers in all of Colombia. Updated: Apr 21, 2008.

Things to See and Do

Museo del Oro

You can't go wrong visiting this informative, free and surprisingly educational gold museum. It is nicely curated and features pre-Colombian gold from the Zenú tribes that resided in what is now central Colombia. The gold on display here was used for burial ceremonies. In the Zenú tradition, gold was placed in urns, then the urns were buried under trees to symbolize fertility and new life. One wing on the second floor explains the agricultural methods and resources used during pre-colonial times. A six-minute video in English, French or Spanish describes how canals were built for agricultural purposes. Tuesday-Friday, 10 a.m.-1 p.m. and 3-7 p.m. Saturday 10 a.m.-1 p.m. and 2-5 p.m. Sundays and Holidays ,11 a.m.-4 p.m. Banco de la República Centro, Cra. 4, 33-26. Tel: 5-660-0778. Updated: Apr 14, 2008.

Museo de Arte Moderno

Housed in two buildings—the first, built in the 17th Century, the second added during the end of the 19th Century—the Museo de Arte Moderno houses permanent and temporary exhibtions of Latin American modern art. Latin American paintings from the 1950s onward, and contemporary Colombian and Caribbean art are all on display. The museum also has a library and gift shop. Plaza San Pedro Claver Calle 30, 4-08. Tel: 5-664-8966. Updated: Apr 14, 2008.

Museo Naval del Caribe

This extensive museum recounts Cartagena's remarkable naval history. Located behind Iglesia de San Pedro Claver, this emblematic building was restored by local artisans and now includes two large aisles separated by gardens and a second floor. The first floor, known as the Republican Wing, was constructed in the 1900s and housed the first batallion. As you proceed up the stairs to the Colonial Wing, you can find naval weapons and ship parts. Artifacts such as anchors, cannons and other sea instruments are also on display. This museum is a great way to learn about and piece together the city's maritime legends and history. Calle San Juan de Dios. Tel: 5-664-9672. Updated: Apr 14, 2008.

Palacio de la Inquisición

With its large, baroque-style stone entrance, external balconies overlooking the Plaza de Bolívar and Spanish coat of arms, the Palacio de la Inquisición is one of the city's best examples of late colonial, civil architecture. Beginning in 1610, this palace used to be the site of the Punishment Tribunal of the Holy Office, but construction wasn't completed until 150 years later. Now a museum, instruments of torture, pottery, paintings, furniture, and other artifacts from both the colonial and independent eras are on display. Visitors can wander through this old palace and step back in time to chronicle the history and legend of the 17th Century Spanish Inquisition. Adults $5; Children $3.50. Open 9 a.m.-6 p.m. every day. Tel: 5-664-4113. Updated: Apr 14, 2008.

Templo de Santo Domingo

Templo de Santo Domingo was originally located in Plaza de los Coches but, after a terrible fire that consumed the city, it was destroyed and relocated to where it stands today. Construction began at the end of the 16th Century, making it the oldest church in Cartagena de Indias. This temple has a Spanish renaissance architectural style, and looks like it was carved out of a very large rock. There is one unfinished tower and the other one is twisted, according to local legend, by the devil. Inside, you will notice foreboding tombstones that pave the baroque-style, marble altar's floor. A 16th Century image of Christ carved from wood as well as an image of the Virgin with her gold and emerald crown are the centerpieces for worship. Updated: Apr 14, 2008.

Iglesia de San Pedro Claver

First constructed in the 17th Century by the Jesuits, this convent served as the residence and grounds for Saint Pedro Claver, a priest whose missionary work focused on helping slaves from Africa, often regarded as the "Slave of Slaves" or the "Apostle of the Blacks." He lived here until his death in 1654 and was the first person canonized in the New World (in 1888). The high altar is made from marble imported from Italy. Inside and under the main altar is a museum containing relics from his mission. Behind the cloister a convent for the Society of Jesus was built, which served as a hospital for the poor and for charity and later as the headquarters to republican troops. Now, the old convent is the site for the Naval Museum. Guides are available in the church, though, and they provide tours in English, Spanish, and French and charge about $3 per person, or $6 for a group of up to six people.Monday-Sunday, 8 a.m. - 5 p.m. Museum: Adults $3; Children $2. Tel: 5-664-7256. Updated: Apr 14, 2008.

Plaza de Bolívar

Plaza Bolívar is the ideal place for relaxation in the center of the old city. At lunchtime, locals (mostly men) take advantage of the shade offered around the center statue of Simón Bolívar on his horse, and travelers sit down to rest their feet and people-watch. Cheap fruit and food stalls are available around the Plaza, as well as some of the city's best known sites, such as La Catedral, the Museo de Oro and the Museo de la Inquisición. Updated: Apr 14, 2008.

Plaza Santo Domingo

The always-happening Plaza Santo Domingo is filled with classy cafés, ideal for people-watching. The brick plaza and the shops that dot the periphery of the plaza seem unchanged by time, so it is easy to imagine life back then while you enjoy a *limonada de coco* under the shade of a table umbrella. The square is set among elegant colonial houses, and the famous fat lady statue is situated in front of the church. Touching her supposedly brings you good luck. Updated: Apr 14, 2008.

Plaza de la Aduana

This is the oldest and largest plaza in Cartagena and serves as the commercial heart of the city, and the parade grounds for festival days. You will likely find people conglomerating in this plaza by day and into the evening. It is the ideal meeting place for day trippers taking the ferry to Isla Barú, or for travelers visiting the newly renovated tourist office. A few local banks and ATMs are also on the square. A statue of Colombus stands in the center of the plaza. Updated: Apr 14, 2008.

El Torre del Reloj

The yellow clock tower in Plaza de los Coches remains the primary symbol of Cartagena. Built in the beginning of the 18th Century, it was originally a clock above the main entrance gate into the walled city. It was originally referred to as the Bridge Gate because it joined Getsemaní with El Centro. Later, in 1888, the republican-style tower was added to hold the four-sided clock. The Torre del Reloj, as it is known now, continues to be a landmark meeting place for residents in the city. Updated: Apr 14, 2008.

Plaza de los Coches

Walking into El Centro through the Torre del Reloj, you must try to imagine this busy plaza that now bustles with shops and vendors as it was 300 years ago. Back then, Plaza de los Coches was the center for transportation but it was also where slaves were bartered and sold. A statue of Pedro de Heredia, the city's founder, has been erected where the slave market used to be. The large buildings with colonial arches and balconies that surround this plaza are some of the oldest in the city. Updated: Apr 14, 2008.

Teatro de Heredia

If you are a fan of interpretive arts, the Teatro de Heredia is a must-do. Located in Plaza de la Merced in the old city, this theater was built in the 19th Century on top of the ruins of a convent. Its original neo-classical style imitated the famous European theaters of the time and housed artistic and cultural activity. The theater has since been remodeled, but it remains the epicenter of theater, ballet, folkloric dance, and other performances. Updated: Apr 14, 2008.

Shopping

Bookstore
At the corner of Calle de la Mantenilla and Calle de la Iglesia, you will find the old city's only trendy café and bookstore. Nicely furnished with dark wooden chairs, tables and bookshelves, this is a great place to find a small selection of literature in English. Some people spend a whole day here, drinking freshly brewed coffee and reading the newspaper or a book pulled straight off a shelf. Monday-Saturday, 9 a.m.-8:30 p.m.; Sun/Holidays 4 p.m.-8:30 p.m. Corner of Calle de la Mantenilla and Calle de la Iglesia. Updated: Apr 14, 2008.

Portal de los Dulces
Some sticky Caribbean sweets can be found throughout the day and evening along the arched Portal de los Dulces. Chocolates, flavored rock candy, coconut delights, dried fruits and other treats like *muñecas de leche* or *bolas de panela* that will make your tooth ache are stuffed in glass jars and displayed on the multi-tiered stalls along the plaza. Some may not look appetizing, but, if you're in Cartagena, you should give at least one treat a try. The Festival de los Dulces falls in March in the Plaza and features an even stickier assortment of sweets. Updated: Apr 14, 2008.

El Centro Lodging

Budget

Hostal Mar Azul !

(BED: $10-30) By far the best value in El Centro, Hostal Mar Azul is a colorful little gem on the second floor of a colonial building on Calle de la Moneda. The walls are painted with bright Caribbean colors and the place exudes a happy vibe. Some of the 10 rooms have A/C and all have private baths. There is a computer with internet that is available for guests. The only downside to this cute hostel is that the hallways are very narrow and the rooms are a bit small. Calle de la Moneda, 7-51, 2nd floor. Cell: 300-837-0660 / 300-271-5462, Fax: 5-664-1915, E-mail: chepr1@hotmail.com. Updated: Apr 14, 2008.

Hotel Central

(BED: $12-30) A notch or two below El Viajero in quality and style, and just two blocks away on Calle de la Iglesia is Hotel Central. This run-of-the-mill hotel in El Centro has two very large dorms that each sleep eight (for $12 per person). It has 15 other basic rooms, all with private baths and cold water. You would reason staying here for the convenience of this hotel, which is steps away from all of the major sites in El Centro. Calle de la Iglesia, 35-28. Tel: 5-664-2354. Updated: Apr 14, 2008.

Mid-Range

Hospedaje Cartagena

(ROOM: $15-24) If you're not daunted by the very sketchy hourly rate at this conveniently located hostel, you might actually get some bang for your buck here. Up the hotel's steep stairs, you will come face-to-face with a lady behind a glass booth. Take a nap or stay for a night, but don't expect any fancy treatment. Hourly rates start at $4. Calle de la Soledad, 5-58. Updated: Apr 14, 2008.

Hotel El Viajero

(ROOM: $20-50) Hotel El Viajero is one of the only hotels in El Centro that you will find for under $50 per night. It features 18 basic rooms—some with A/C, all with cold showers. El Viajero has been on the Cartagena lodging scene long enough to know how to keep guests satisfied and happy. It has a sizable front lounge overlooking cute Calle Porvenir and a clean kitchen for guest use. Calle de Porvenir, 35-68, 2nd floor. Tel: 5-664-3289, E-mail: hotelviajero664@hotmail.com. Updated: Apr 14, 2008.

Hostal Santo Domingo

(ROOM: $30-50) Right in the center of Calle Santo Domingo, this small nine-room hostel is steps from nearly every major site in the old city. Set back from the street in a two-story colonial building, the place is clean and quaint with a courtyard and two-person tables in front of each room. Breakfast is included in the price. Smaller rooms just have fans and cold showers, but the location is unbeatable. Calle Santo Domingo, 33-46. Cell: 300-347-3625 / 316-799-8898, E-mail: hsantodomingopiret@yahoo.es. Updated: Apr 14, 2008.

High-End

Hotel los Balcones de Badillo

(ROOM: $50-150) If you're seeking another great alternative to often-booked Hotel Tres Banderas in San Diego, look no further than Balcones de Badillo. With a dozen white balconies overseeing the activity of the streets below, this is a great place to relax and people-watch. This hotel might look a bit shabby and maze-like from the stairwell, but the rooms here are all nicely furnished and, for the most part, worth the price. Room 303 is the best suite of the 11 rooms, with two queen size beds and an enormous wraparound balcony. During high season, you could pay upwards of $150 for this gem, but it will go for as low as $80 per night if you're a good bargainer. The price includes a hearty breakfast on a very pleasant rooftop that overlooks the city. Calle Segunda de Badillo, 36-12. Tel: 5-660-1703, Cell: 300-805-0916. E-mail: losbalconesdebadillo@hotmail.co, URL: www.hotellosbalconesdebadillo.com. Updated: Apr 14, 2008.

Portal de San Diego

(ROOM: $70-100) A lovely hotel in a central location between El Centro and San Diego, Portal de San Diego has eleven quaint rooms around a pleasant courtyard. The modern design of the place, from the clean, white stairwell up to the lobby on the second floor to the stylish paintings and decorations in the common areas give the hotel a sophisticated air. Calle Segundo de Badillo, 36-17. Tel: 5-660-1083 / 664-8615, Cell: 315-655-9529, E-mail: portaldesandiego@hotmail.com. Updated: Apr 14, 2008.

El Marqués Hotel Boutique

(ROOM: $150-300) El Marqués does an impeccable job of providing quality accommodations in the best location possible, the middle of Calle Santo Domingo. Spend a few nights in one of eight modern, spacious, beige- and wood-themed suites. Guests are treated like royalty and can enjoy the small pool, sushi bar and terrace at their leisure. This place is a dream—pure, contemporary comfort at its best. Calle Nuestra Señora del Carmen, 33-41. Tel: 5-664-4438 / 7800, Cell: 314-581-0743, Fax: 5-664-7957, E-mail: reservas@elmarqueshotelboutique.com/reservas.elmarques@gmail.com, URL: www.elmarqueshotelboutique.com. Updated: Apr 14, 2008.

Hotel Charleston

(ROOM: $150-300) A magnificently restored 17th Century convent situated in the old walled city, Hotel Charleston in Plaza Santa Teresa is one of the grandest hotels in Cartagena. Designed with impeccable taste and attention to detail, the burnt orange exterior blends perfectly with its classy interior, balancing both the colonial and republican styles evident in the city's history. The hotel features 90 guest rooms and suites, as well an enormous Presidential Suite, all of which are decorated with fine ornaments representative of Cartagena's traditional style. The rooftop pool has one of the best views of the old city—you can also sit up there for tea or a reasonably priced light lunch ($8-12). Plaza de Santa Teresa Cra. 3A, 31-23. Tel: 5-664-9494, Fax: 5-664-9447, E-mail: Info@hoteles-charleston.com, URL: www.hoteles-charleston.com. Updated: Apr 14, 2008.

El Centro Restaurants

Budget

Brianzola

For affordable pizza, coffee and ice cream, head to the main square of the university, where you'll find an always-packed, hip, and refreshingly air-conditioned joint café. Satisfy your caffeine craving at Juan Valdéz or, if you're hungry, order a pizza next door at Brianzola. If you have a sweet tooth, the 15 unique flavors of rich ice cream should do the trick. Calle San Agustín, 6-15, Esquina de la Uni. Tel: 5-664-2564, Cell: 316-616-1039. Updated: Apr 14, 2008.

Cafeteria Bocaditos Madrid

Located across from Santo Toribio Church, locals crowd this cheap café that serves traditional Colombian lunch for an unbeatable price. Pull up to a stool at the the bar and ask for the *set* lunch. For $2.50, it comes with a cup of *agua de panela* (sweet water), a bowl of soup, and a lunch plate with your choice of meat, lentils, salad and sweet plantains. If you're in the mood for lighter fare, pick up arepas and empanadas from the glass case on the counter—just $0.50 each! Calle Segundo de Badillo, 36-171. Tel: 5-664-6021. Updated: Apr 14,2008.

Cuero Centro Café

Just one block from Plaza de los Coches is this small café/leather store that serves up good, cheap lunch. Order something to nibble on and enjoy the hustle and bustle of Cartagena street life outside. The handicrafts sold at the store are a bit ordinary but worth a look. Calle del Colegio, 34-53. Tel: 5-664-5516 /4353 / 5-660-0949. Updated: Apr 14, 2008.

Enoteca

In El Centro, near San Pedro Claver Plaza, this Italian restaurant has casual outdoor dining and more formal indoor dining. Calle San Juan de Dios, 3-39. Tel: 5-664-3806, Fax: 575-664-1004. Updated: Dec 07, 2007.

Mila

At Mila, pastry chef and cook Camila Andrea Vargas bakes up delightful breads and French pastries. There is a dessert that has a chocolate chip bigger than the brownie on which it sits. Or, get a local treat, like a *churro*. The atmosphere feels like a French café. Bakery items are on display in a shiny glass case and there is an enormous hanging chalkboard with soup, salad, sandwich, wrap and drink descriptions. This is a great place for a light lunch or midday snack. Calle de Ayos (next to El Bistro). Tel: 5-664-1347, Cell: 314-516-1246 / 1247, E-mail: milacartagenacentro@hotmail.com. Updated: Apr 14, 2008.

Moe's

A chic lunch and dinner spot in the heart of El Centro, this restaurant/bar/lounge serves up very reasonable specials that include soup, salad, meat and fries. Although the food is rather basic, it is sure to fill your stomach. The blue-lit interior and overall modern feel of the place makes it a nice break from the Cartagena heat. Calle Ayos Centro Comercial. Tel: 5-664-3399, Cell: 300-814-7271, E-mail: moescoffebar@gmail.com. Updated: Apr 14, 2008.

Mid-Range

Palo Santo

Cooking up some of the most delicious Arabic and international cuisine in El Centro, Palo Santo is a great dinner spot off of Calle Santo Domingo. The *kibbeh* plate, meatballs served with pita and hummus, is a tasty and unique appetizer. Try the dinner special, which includes a soup or salad, your choice of three entreés, a dessert and glass of house wine. Take your meal in the quaint courtyard or sit inside the brightly decorated restaurant. Calle de las Damas, 3-13. Tel: 5-664-4783, E-mail: Palosanto_1@hotmail.com. Updated: Apr 14, 2008.

El Bistro

Particularly popular among foreigners, this sweltering bakery serves up some of the tastiest breads, desserts, pastas, salads and sandwiches in the area. Despite its lack of A/C, customers sit amid whirling fans to sip coffee and read something from El Bistro's small multi-language bookshelf. If you can't bear the heat, order take-out or have the food delivered. Expect to pay about $6, $8 and $10 respectively for breakfast, lunch and dinner specials, which are posted outside on a chalkboard. Centro Calle de Ayos, 4-46. Tel: 5-664-1799. Updated: Apr 14, 2008.

Spezia's

Popular among locals at lunch time, Spezia's has a pub atmosphere created by dark wooden bar stools and tables. The food is made with fresh and natural ingredients, exotic flavors, and the aroma and colors of the Caribbean and is reasonably priced. Before entering, look over the specials posted by the door. Their extensive drink menu keeps customers coming into the evening, when the place tends to wind down. Calle de Ayos, 4-32. Tel: 5-660-0118, Cell: 311-219-1017 / 310-581-6082. Updated: Apr 14, 2008.

HIGH-END

Portón de Santo Domingo

Portón de Santo Domingo is a high-class establishment that has been cooking up creative culinary masterpieces for more than 100 years. It continues to draw wealthy clientele in search of excellently prepared plates, like stuffed lobster, and decadent desserts. Choose from four different dining environments: the social lobby bar, the patio with fountains for a tropical inspiration, the wine cave for an elegant setting or the salon for a romantic evening. Live tropical and Cuban music plays in the courtyard on Monday through Saturday, starting at 8 p.m. Calle Santo Domingo, 33-66. Tel: 5-664-8897 / 8171 / 4846, URL: www.portondesantodomingo.com. Updated: Apr 14, 2008.

Restaurante San Pedro

With fantastic, flavorful food and outdoor seating directly facing the Iglesia San Pedro Claver, this enormous restaurant and café could satisfy even the most critical customers. The restaurant produces divine Asian-fusion food like sushi, nasi goreng and pad thai noodles, and the café serves an extensive list of wine, cocktails, fresh juices and beer. All the food is prepared with lovely garnishes and colorful Caribbean touches. The servers are friendly, well mannered and accommodating. Depending on the evening, you may have to wait for a seat outside on the plaza, so it would be wise to call ahead if you plan on having dinner between 7-9 p.m. Plaza San Pedro Claver, 30-11. Tel: 5-664-5121, Cell: 315-664-9675. E-mail: cafesanpedro@decameron.com. Updated: Apr 14, 2008.

EL CENTRO NIGHTLIFE

La Esquina Sandiegana

One of the only authentic salsa bars in Cartagena, the music and dancing at La Esquina Sandiegana gets going once the sun goes down and usually keeps going until the sun comes back up. If you're looking for a backpacker haunt, this is not the place—La Esquina caters to a loyal local clientele. Updated: Apr 14, 2008.

Babar

Surprisingly, Babar is one of the only successful nightclubs in El Centro. Across the street from the Naval Museum, you will find this very hip and colorful spot on the second floor, overlooking the night's activities in Plaza Santa Teresa. Many of the cocktails on the extensive menu, and the flirtatious foreigners who socialize and dance until the morning hour, have Caribbean rum in them. Updated: Apr 14, 2008.

El Baluarte Tasca-Bar

An ideal location for a cocktail is El Baluarte, located precisely on the old ramparts of the San Francisco Javier bastion in front of Plaza Santa Teresa. It is nice to watch the sunset or bask in the evening hum in the heart of Cartagena. Taste delicious grilled food and enjoy live music—all by the light of the night sky. This bar, similar to Café del Mar, is a great choice for a romantic nightcap. Calle San Juan de Dios. Tel: 5-664-2425, Cell: 315-864-3325, Fax: 5-660-0468, E-mail: Baluartesanfrancisco@yahoo.com. Updated: Apr 14, 2008.

Café del Mar

Café del Mar, on Baluarte de Santo Domingo, is one of the few long-standing night spots that continues to be a popular place to enjoy the sunset, meet new people and party on the weekends. People aren't drawn by the food or pricey drinks, they come for the great outdoor atmosphere, infectious house music, lovely evening scenery and happy-go-lucky crowd. Sometimes, especially on the weekends, this place gets so packed that guests spill out into the street. On quieter nights Café del Mar is a great place to unwind. Baluarte de Santo Domingo. Tel: 5-664-6513, URL: www.cafedelmarcolombia.com. Updated: Apr 14, 2008.

Rincón de la Mantilla

The absence of a sign outside this large, wooden restaurant and bar doesn't mean that both tourists and locals can't find Rincon de la Mantilla. Its huge draw is that it is a good spot to drink a local beer and people-watch. Anyone who appreciates the yeasty beverage, must be attracted to this lively place by the wall of refrigerators stocked with bottles of Aguila and Club Colombia beer. Help yourself and take a seat outside, inside or at the bar. Calle de la Mantilla, 3-32. Tel: 5-660-1430. Updated: Apr 14, 2008.

Plaza San Diego

San Diego is the classiest and most sophisticated part of Cartagena. There are plenty of picturesque buildings and narrow streets, just like El Centro, but there is a high concentration of fancy restaurants and luxury hotels. The pace of life in San Diego is slower and seclusion and privacy are easily found. This is also the area of the city that inspired bits of Gabriel García Márquez' "Love in the Time of Cholera." On the plaza, you are likely to brush elbows with the city's elite. Updated: Apr 21, 2008.

Things to See and Do

Casa de Gabriel García Márquez

Gabriel García Márquez' house in San Diego has not been turned into a museum or tourist attraction. If it were, it would be one of the most popular sites in Cartagena. The inspirational house still stands today at the corner of Calle del Curato and Baluarte de Santa Clara. From the fifth floor terrace of the Hotel Santa Clara you can get a peak of his old courtyard. Updated: Apr 08,2008.

Plaza San Diego Lodging

Hotel San Felipe

(ROOM: $20-40) The centrally located Hotel San Felipe seems to appeal to Colombians on holiday or business. However, its convenience and amenities are also suitable for foreign tourists. As part of the Dorado Plaza hotel group, which has hotels in Bocagrande, Isla de Tierra Bomba and Bogotá, Hotel San Felipe is an industrial hotel with basic amenities. All of the 55 rooms spread throughout five floors have cable TV and a clean bathroom with a cold shower. The 25 rooms facing the street have fans and nice balconies, though this can make them a bit noisier during the day. The 30 interior rooms have A/C and are generally quieter. There is 24-hour security in the lobby, a restaurant, a bar and the staff is very friendly and helpful. In all, it is a good and spacious alternative to the tight quarters of the hostels around the corner. Cra. 9A, 31-72, Avenida del Centenario. Tel: 5-664-5439 / 5-664-0205, Fax: 5-664-5443, E-mail: mercadeo@doradoplaza.com, URL: www.doradoplaza.com. Updated: Apr 14, 2008.

Hostal San Diego

(ROOM: $75-150) A bit overpriced for what you get—a small, room with A/C and a cold shower. And, there are certainly better options in the San Diego neighborhood. However, for the location and comfort, you won't be too disappointed at the Hostal San Diego. Its conveniently next door to an internet café and has an inviting exterior and quaint interior courtyard. It is also the closest accommodation for shopping at Las Bóvedas and watching the sunset from the bastion. Ultimately, this place has some perks as well as a handful of drawbacks, but it's one of the cheapest options in the heart of San Diego. Calle de las Bóvedas, 39-120. Tel: 5-660-1433 / 0986, E-mail: hostalsandiego@telecom.com.co, URL: www.hostalsandiego.com. Updated: Apr 14, 2008.

Hotel Tres Banderas

(ROOM: $78-132) Hotel Tres Banderas's convenient location, relaxing atmosphere and reasonable rates make it a popular accommodation for both locals and foreigners. The three rooms have earth-tone walls and a tasteful decór. There are three common areas that have free internet and WiFi—two have relaxing waterfalls. Breakfast with arepa, toast, fruit, juice, coffee and tea is complimentary. You can also enjoy a free ferry transport to the sister hotel on Isla de la Bomba, just 15 minutes from Boca Grande, and on the beach with a pool and a respite from the hustle and bustle of Cartagena de Indias. A third sister hotel is in the works about half an hour from Cartagena, set to open by June 2009. Calle Cochera de Hobo, 38-66. Tel: 5-660-2112 / 0160, E-mail: info@hotel3banderas.com, URL: www.hotel3banderas.com. Updated: Apr 14, 2008.

Casa La Fe

(ROOM: $80-120) This great little B&B in the sophisticated Plaza Fernández de Madrid will pamper you until you have to tear yourself away from Cartagena. Fifteen neatly decorated and comfortable rooms, all with private bathrooms and A/C, surround the house's lush garden courtyard, where guests are served breakfast. Don't miss an opportunity to relax in the lounge on the roof, which offers shade and WiFi. A solid alternative to Hotel Tres Banderas around the corner, La Fe is a bit pricier, but packs a punch. Calle Segundo de Badillo, 36-125. Tel: 5-664-0306, Fax: 5-660-0164, E-mail: admin@casalafe.com, URL: www.casalafe.com. Updated: Apr 14, 2008.

Casa del Tejadillo

(ROOM: $125-250) This gorgeous republican-style house was built in the 19th Century. It provides the same luxury and comfort as El Marqués Boutique Hotel, but in a quieter corner of the city. On Calle del Tejadillo, this immaculate historical home has been meticulously restored and refurbished to provide superior accommodations. Another similarity to El Marqués is that this house has just eight clean and spacious rooms. The house can be rented out for large groups. Calle del Tejadillo, 38-53. Tel: 5-664-2974, Cell: 311-221-8167 / 310-321-7701, E-mail: casadeltejadillo@gmail.com, casadeltejadillo@hotmail.com, URL: www.casadeltejadillo.com. Updated: Apr 14, 2008.

Hotel Santa Clara

(ROOM: $290-526) Don't let the Sofitel's dark orange exterior fool you. As one of Cartagena's best luxury hotels in the heart of Cartagena de Indias, this place exudes comfort and offers quality service. The Sofitel Santa Clara Hotel has 120 luxurious guest rooms, including 17 suites. There are two different kinds of rooms—colonial and republican—and either have views over the old city, the ocean, and/or the hotel's well-manicured gardens and pool. Choose from two fine-dining establishments that serve French-based cuisine infused with other international flavors. Or, grab a drink at the chic bar and café. The pool is for guest use only. Calle Del Torno, 39-29. Tel: 5-650-4700 / 5-664-8040. E-mail: reservas@hotelsantaclara.com. Updated: Apr 14, 2008.

Plaza San Diego Restaurants

Pizza en el Parque

Local late night partygoers end up at this unassuming pizza joint in Plaza Fernandéz de Madrid. Choose from 10 types of pizzas with the usual toppings, then take your pizza outside, sit in the park, and enjoy your meal under the stars. Plaza Fernandéz de Madrid. Updated: Apr 14, 2008.

Arepas del Santísimo

This small but affordable café is difficult to spot from the street. But, once you do find it, it is worth the search. Enjoy arepas with several different fillings, like cheese, ham, chicken, beef and chorizo. Grilled arepas start at $1.50, and more complex meals cost $3.50 at the most. They are made to order on one small grill. The café is minimally decorated inside a small, pleasant courtyard and has just five tables. The food here is tasty. Calle del Santísimo, 8-55. Tel: 310-305-1142. Updated: Apr 14, 2008.

Café del Santísimo

Café del Santísimo is an indoor and outdoor restaurant and house with a religious-theme that is run by a Cordon Bleu chef. Ask about the wines in the cellar and the fixed-price menu that includes unlimited drinks. Interesting and fun artwork adorns the walls. The café is about a block from Hotel Santa Clara. Calle del Santísimo, 8-19 (also called Playa de la Artillería), Tel: 5-664-3316. Updated: Dec 07, 2007.

Da Danni's Restaurant

This is the only restaurant in Cartagena that serves quality Italian pasta. Da Danni's in San Diego is a really good option for travelers who need a break from typical Caribbean / Colombian cuisine. Stepping into the restaurant feels surprisingly fitting, as if you've walked right into a restaurant in Bologna, Italy. The food here is excellent and the helpings are very large, so you get plenty of food for the price. The bread is baked fresh. Also, the quality of service is excellent, waiters are quick to bring you the food and the check. Calle de Santísimo, 8-01. Cell: 312-617-3529. (In Bocagrande: Cr. 3, 8-69; Centro Comercial La Mansión; Tel: 5-665-8979). Tel: 5-660-0030, E-mail: dadannisrestaurant@

hotmail.com, URL: www.dadannisrestaurant.com. Updated: Apr 14, 2008.

Casa Majagna

This restaurant's interesting mix of Italian and local dishes, extensive beer and wine menu, and classy, lounge setting have drawn a bunch of local loyals. The tables outside make a perfect place to meet friends for dinner and drinks. The prices and overall atmosphere here are comparable to Tamarindo, which is on the same square. Although both Majagna and Tamarindo have tasty food, Tamarindo's tiny tapas are quite different from Majagna's hearty dishes. Let your stomach and your mood decide for you. Calle de la Tablada in Plaza Fernández de Madrid. Updated: Apr 14, 2008.

Tamarindo

The happy hour at Tamarindo is the primary reason people crowd in Plaza Fernández Madrid in the early evening. This nice, little restaurant serves up two Spanish and/or local *tapas* for the price of one between 6 and 8 p.m. on weekdays. Ideally situated on the corner of the plaza, with tables outside, this mid-range restaurant is the perfect place to unwind after a long day of sightseeing. Plaza Fernández de Madrid, 36-95. Tel: 5-664-0932. Updated: Apr 14, 2008.

El Santísimo Restaurant and Cave

This popular and fancy establishment on the well-trodden Calle Santísimo offers quintessential Caribbean cuisine in a romantic, cave-like courtyard. The food and wine here come highly recommended by both locals and tourists. Santísimo's mouth-watering calamari ($10) and succulent lobster ($16) are particularly delectable. Choose from an extensive wine selection, which you can get by the glass (starting at $6). Calle el Santísimo, 8-19. Monday-Saturday 12 p.m.-3 p.m.; 7 p.m.-12 a.m., Sundays and holidays 5 p.m.-12 a.m., Tel: 5-664-3316, Cell: 315-754-9954, E-mail: restauranteelsantisimo@gmail.com. Updated: Apr 14, 2008.

La Tinaja

Dine beneath an outdoor gazebo and enjoy your delicious Colombian fare to a sweet serenade. La Matuna Cl32 Edificio Pedro, Ganem Av. D. Lemaitre. Tel: 5-664-1730. Updated: Dec 07, 2007.

Getsemaní

First-time visitors to Cartagena are often fooled by hotel propaganda that says its accommodations are "reasonably priced and conveniently located in the walled part of Cartagena de Indias." Many of the city's cheap hotels are found in Getsemaní, which is technically part of the old city, but is neither as quaint nor as enjoyable as El Centro, the real heart of Cartagena. In short, Getsemaní is a bit grungy and lackluster. There are, however, three advantages to staying in this neighborhood: 1) it's cheaper, 2) it's close to the major sights, and 3) it has the best nightlife in town (along Avenida Arsenal). Updated: Apr 21, 2008.

Gestemaní Lodging

Hotel Marlin

(BED: $8-16) Hotel Marlin has been open since 2002 and offers comfortable accommodations for backpackers, business people and tourists. Set in a colonial house, Marlin has 24 rooms, each with a private bathroom and your choice of a ceiling fan or A/C. Internet service, cable TV, laundry service, safety boxes and a common kitchen are available for guest use. The hotel also provides helpful tourist information for further destinations like Volcán Totume, Playa Blanca or the Islas del Rosario. The building also has a comfortable common room and garden. Calle de la Media Luna and Calle 30, 10-35. Updated: Apr 23, 2008.

Hostal Casa Viena

(BED: $8-20) Hands-down the most well-known hostel in Cartagena de Indias, Casa Viena continues to be the first choice for backpackers. With only nine rooms in total, however, this place simply can't meet the demand. The only way to secure a room is to call ahead, and even that doesn't guarantee they will have a bed for you. The good news is that several newer hostels are well-equipped and in some cases (Hotel Familiar and Hostal Mar Azul, for instance) are better options than Casa Viena. The dorm is the only room with A/C and sleeps eight ($8 per person). The other eight rooms range in size and start at $10. Calle San Andrés, 30-53. Tel: 5-664-6242, E-mail: Hotel@casaviena.com, URL: www.casaviena.com. Updated: Apr 14, 2008.

Hotel Familiar

(ROOM: $10-20) This large, airy hotel has basic rooms that come with a fan and with or without a private bathroom. The rooms with private bath get booked up first because the shared bathroom is out of the way and quite rudimentary—a toilet with no seat cover, plastic shower curtain and cold water. The hotel's ambiance, however, is redeeming enough to justify staying here. There are plenty of lounging options and really lovely internal balconies. The place maintains a respectable reputation and tourists usually leave satisfied with the price. Calle el Guerrero, 29-66. Tel: 5-664-2464. Updated: Apr 14, 2008.

Hospedaje y Refrequería Marta

(ROOM: $10-20) This small, 10-room hostel is not the most fantastic option. You'd better off paying a bit more and checking first at La Casona next door or Casa Viena down the street. But, if you are in a pinch, it works. The rooms are basic—each with a grainy TV and dimly-lit private bathroom. The fans look decades old and about to disintegrate. The room in front is a quad, and the rest are doubles with one or two beds. Calle Tripita y Media Carrera 10, 31-16,. Tel: 5-664-7653, Cell: 311-672-5802 / 312-693-2179, . Updated: Apr 14, 2008.

Hostal Real

(ROOM: $10-20) The location, just three blocks from El Centro in Getsemaní, is pretty good and the 20 rooms will work out fine. The rooms are a bit dank and the bathrooms are a bit tight, but they are reasonably comfortable. Altogether, the hostel has an airy feel created by the two connected courtyards that extend all the way to the back. A few rooms have A/C and all have private baths with cold water. The hostel has a nice, big dorm room upstairs that can hold larger groups without a problem. Calle Primera de la Magdalena, 9-33. Tel: 5-664-7866, Cell: 313-516-1542, E-mail: hostalreal@yahoo.com. Updated: Apr 14, 2008.

Hostal "La Casona" Getsemaní

(ROOM: $20-30) Twenty eight rooms surround a peaceful courtyard. La Casona is still a bit overpriced for its location and the quality of the rooms. The rooms are very simple with nothing more than the basic amenities like a small TV, fan or A/C and private bath. For the value and the better quality of the rooms, you are better off in a larger and air-conditioned room. Calle Tripita y Media, 31-32. Tel: 317-639-5644, Cell: 317-639-5653, Fax: 5-664-13 01, E-mail: hostallacasona@hotmail.com. Updated: Apr 14, 2008.

Hotel Monterrey

(ROOM: $80-100) Next door to the Teatro Cartagena and across the street from the convention center, the Hotel Monterrey displays a quiet colonial elegance with its stark white exterior. The hotel's design is a perfect blend of European style and 19th Century Caribbean flair. The hotel's simple interior decór and understated luxury are easy to take for granted, but the quality of service and general peaceful atmosphere are not. Guests can enjoy the Jacuzzi, relax in the comfortable lounge and make free local calls. The hotel also offers private parking. The hotel's 30 spacious rooms and suites, most of which are singles or doubles, provide a suitable break from the buzz and heat of Cartagena. Cra 8 B, 25-103. Tel: 5-664 8560. Updated: Apr 14, 2008.

Gestemaní Restaurants

La Casa de Socorro

Popular with the locals, La Casa de Socorro is a pure Caribbean delight that offers kind of eccentric cultural foods like turtle, rabbit, deer and hen. It has an extensive menu and mostly specializes in seafood and Cartagenian-Caribbean cuisine, which is orientated mostly around dishes with fish, meat and stew. La Casa can seat nearly 100 people. Customers can sit in the cozy, wooden interior or outside on the covered patio. The walls are decorated with stylish Caribbean art painted on wooden planks. This place is not for vegetarians. Open from 10 a.m.-10 p.m. every day. Calle Larga, 88-112, in front of the Centro Comercial Getsemaní. E-mail: restaurantelacasadesocorro@yahoo.com. Updated: Apr 14, 2008.

Gato Negro

The very unsuspecting black cat on a sign outside a cerulean blue building on Calle San Andrés (two doors down from Hostal Casa Viena) is the only indication that this small café exists. It specializes in vegetarian, breakfast or light lunch options, like crepes, salads and eggs for around $3. Call ahead to get your meal to go. Despite the reasonable prices, this is pretty much the spot for foreign travelers. You would be hard pressed to find locals at this little eatery. Calle San Andrés, 30-39. Tel: 317-345-3096. Updated: Apr 14, 2008.

La Cocina de Socorro

Not to be mistaken for the other restaurant in Getsemaní with the word "socorro" in it's name. La Cocina de Socorro is a fancier establishment that serves original and traditional Caribbean food. María Nelly del Socorro, the cook, fell in love with the art of cooking at a very young age when her grandmother would prepare exquisite meals. She came to Cartagena when she was 12 to study cooking and to enact her grandmother's cooking secrets. Her typical foods consist of magical Caribbean flavors blended together with the family recipes she was fond of as a child. Some specialties include seafood stew, jumbo shrimps au gratin, lobster and a fisherman's platter with creole sauce that she calls "Festival de Mariscos." This is Caribbean fine dining as you've never seen it before. There is free parking for guests. Across from the Convention Center. Tel: 5-660-2044 / 2045, Fax: 5-660- 1868, E-mail: lacocinadesocorro13@yahoo.es, URL: www.lacocinadesocorro.com. Updated: Apr 14, 2008.

Gestemaní Nightlife

León de Baviera

This hotspot is much more than just a restaurant and bar—it is Bavaria in the heart of Cartagena. This is a good place to meet fellow travelers or local weekend regulars. The bar plays rock music and serves German beer and food. The owner, Stefan Pellkofer from Germany, provides a lively atmosphere without being too "Oktoberfest" over-the-top. The bar has live rock music on Thursdays and a collection of live music from different groups on Sundays. Tuesday-Sunday 4 p.m.-4 a.m., Avenida del Arsenal, 10B-65. Tel: 5-664-4412. Updated: Apr 14, 2008.

La Casa de la Cerveza !

Perfectly perched atop the old wall of the city at the crook of Getsemaní, the hip outdoor restaurant and bar, La Casa de la Cerveza, provides lovely views of the interior lagoons and Castillo de San Felipe de Barajas. The patio has comfortable couches and pillowed sofas and Caribbean salsa music plays all night. Order from a small assortment of food and choose from a variety of colored (green, red or wheat) beer in an even wider assortment of sizes (from pint to carafe). Try the popular mojito and party the night away. Calle Arsenal, Baluarte San Lorenzo del Reducto. Tel: 5-664-9261 / 660-0811, URL: www.casadelacerveza.com.co. Updated: Apr 14, 2008.

La Carbonera

La Carbonera is reputedly the best night club and lounge in town. It has beautiful people and the best house, dance and techno music. Locals consider this hip spot in the middle of Avenida Arsenal the place to see and to be seen. People pour in late in the evening, so it's best to end the night here. There is a dress code, so dress to impress or it might be difficult to get in. 9 p.m.-4 a.m., Avenida del Arsenal, 9a-47. URL: http:/lacarbonera.com. Updated: Apr 14, 2008.

Mister Babilla !

What La Carbonera is for beautiful people, Mister Babilla, just a few doors down, is for wild ones. The colorful, Caribbean-themed bar in the front provides the perfect allure for what awaits inside. Walk down the hallway, with scantily-clad waitresses asking for your order along the way, to the back and you will understand when they say, "*Rumba en la playa.*" ("Dance on the beach.") This huge, wooden mess hall fills up late in the evening with singing and dancing maniacs. Things here can get a bit crazy, so be prepared. 8 p.m.-4 a.m., Calle 24, 8B-137, Calle del Arsenal. Tel: 5-664-8616 / 7005. Updated: Apr 14,2008.

Bocagrande

If you are in Cartagena for a few days, hit up Avenida San Martín in the Bocagrande section of town. Located about a block from the beach, this street has loads of hostels, restaurants and businesses. Bocagrande's beach is world-renowned, even though its quality is not-so-great. Due to crowdedness and persistent vendors, this beach isn't ideal, but the area is suitable to catch some rays. Bocagrande, which literally means "big mouth," is also the launching point for boat tours to the Isla del Encanto and to the historical Isla de Tierra Bomba. As for the nightlife, it's mellow. Although Bocagrande's bars are more low-key than those of Getsemaní, head to the Avenida San Martín to dance the night away.

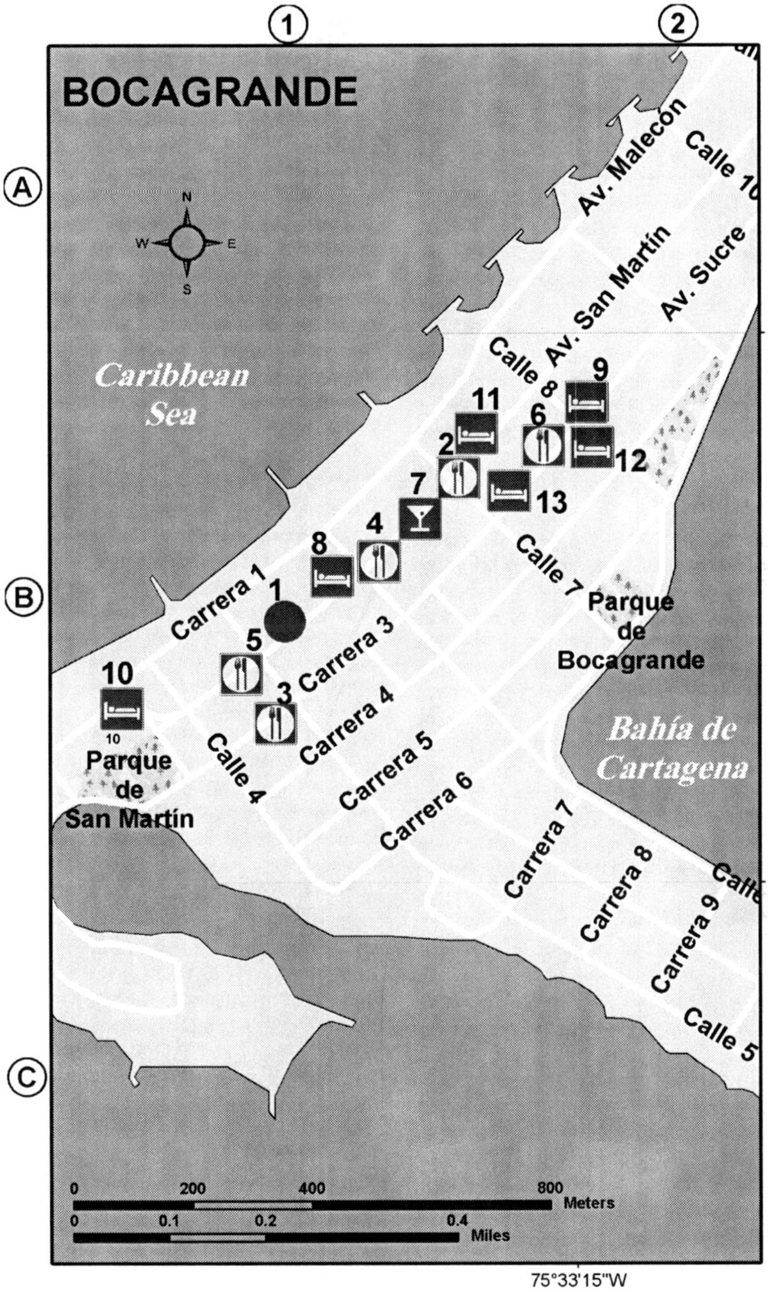

Activities
1 Río Casino B1

Eating
2 Crepes and Waffles B1
3 Da Pietro Restaurant B1
4 La Dulceria B1
5 La Olla Cartagenera B1
6 Restaurante Arabe B1

Nightlife
7 REZAK Bar Club B1

Sleeping
8 El Almirante B1
9 Hostal Leonela B1
10 Hotel Caribe B1
11 Hotel Charlotte B1
12 Hotel Parque Real B1
13 Hotel Pietty B1

CARIBBEAN COAST

Bocagrande Lodging

Hotel Pietty

(ROOM: $10-25) More of a hostel than a hotel, this small place is family-owned and operated. There are 10 basic rooms, each with TV, private bath (cold water) and fan. Restaurant Madrigal, out front, draws a local crowd in the evenings and serves basic dishes (fish, meat, or chicken with rice and salad) for about $5. Bargaining is the name of the game here as prices fluctuate greatly depending on the season, but the rooms here are worth no more than $12 a night. If there's no one at the front desk, talk to the lady at the front kiosk to get a sense of the most recent prices. Carrera 3, 7-59. Tel: 5-655-2922, Cell: 316-389-0319 / 315-778-8035. Updated: Apr 14, 2008.

Hostal Leonela

(ROOM: $15-50) With 35 years of service and helpful staff, you really can't go wrong by staying at Hostal Leonela. The hostel's 35 rooms are all situated around a calming blue courtyard, where guests are served their morning breakfast. Some rooms have fans, others have A/C, but all have private bathrooms (cold water only) and a grainy cable TV. The rooms are spacious and clean. This is a great find with a pleasant atmosphere in a convenient location. Carrera 3A, 7-142. Tel: 5-665- 8595 / 4761, Fax: 5-665-8863, E-mail: Hostaleonela@yahoo.com, URL: www.hostaleonela.com. Updated: Apr 14, 2008.

Hotel Parque Real

(ROOM: $20-50) This quiet 30-room hotel appears fancy from the outside but is a bit more basic than you might think. This place draws an older local crowd but also welcomes foreigners. Rooms are clean and simple. Prices are not negotiable, with double rooms starting at $30. Carrera 3, 7-171. Tel: 5-665-2936 / 5531 / 5507. Updated: Apr 14, 2008.

Hotel Caribe

(ROOM: $75-150) The grandame of Bocagrande, Hotel Caribe is a luxurious resort. With 363 rooms, of which 17 are suites, the elegance and comfort of the Caribbean are yours for the taking. Eat at one of the hotel's several fine-dining options, meander the gardens at your leisure, exercise in the gym, or tan by the enormous pool. Between Bocagrande and Laguito. Tel: 5-655-0155 / 0131, Fax: 5-655-4970 / 7707, E-mail: hotelcaribe@hotelcaribe.com, URL: www.hotelcaribe.com. Updated: Apr 14, 2008.

Cartagena Rental Accommodations

(ROOM: $80-150) This is a great option if you plan to stay in Cartagena for a week or longer. With studios, one- and two-bedroom apartments in the old city, Bocagrande, and Laguito, you are sure to find the right housing option for you. With six accommodation options—and more coming in the near future—guests feel at home in these convenient, modern condos. This option is ideal for traveling professionals or families on vacation. Contact Dave Jones to arrange accommodations in English.URL: www.colombiarental.net. Updated: Apr 14, 2008.

Hotel Charlotte

(ROOM: $80-200) Smack dab in the middle of Bocagrande's always-happening Avenida San Martín, Hotel Charlotte is a peaceful getaway. Just one block from the sea and set amidst a magnificent modern brick building, this hotel has 34 spacious, clean and modern guest suites. Relax by the pool or have a drink or meal at the cozy restaurant-bar downstairs. Hotel Charlotte is romantic yet family friendly. Private parking is available for guests. Av. San Martín, 7-126. Tel: 5-665-9298 / 9365, E-mail: cartagena@hotelescharlotte.com, URL: www.hotelescharlotte.com. Updated: Apr 14, 2008.

El Almirante

(ROOM:$171-301) Located in the heart of Bocagrande, El Almirante offers good breakfasts with fresh juices, a helpful staff and a central location. Calle 6 Esquina. Tel: 5-665-8811 / 01-800-051-4000, Fax: 5-665-8269, E-mail: reservas@hotelesestelar.com. Updated: Dec 19, 2007.

Bocagrande Restaurants

La Dulcería

The sweet smell of baklava lingers in this bright, little café from noon until closing. On display in glass cases are various Middle Eastern desserts, but La Dulcería (the sweet shop) doesn't just bake its own sweets. One look at their 10-page menu will quickly put any fully-fledged appetite at ease. Reasonably priced appetizers, soups, empanadas and salads can be made to order. Carrera 2, 6-53. Tel: 5-655-0281. Updated: Apr 14, 2008.

V!VA Member Review-La Dulcería

I loved everything! The service, the quality of food, the nice camaraderie, authentic recipes...it is just phenomenal. I strongly recommend it! New York, Jan 18, 2008.

Crepes and Waffles

It's utterly appropriate that a town called Bocagrande, which literally means "large mouth," has this popular food chain on busy San Martín street. With an extensive menu featuring a huge variety of crepes, pitas, salads, soup and waffles, you are certain to leave this place a few pounds heavier. The crepes come either sweet or salty and their bread bowls do too. Make your own salads at the salad bar or order delicious ones off the menu. Av. San Martín and Calle 7. Updated: Apr 14, 2008.

La Olla Cartagenera

Specializing in seafood and Middle Eastern cuisine, La Olla Cartagenera is a fine place to kick back and have a decent meal. There is seating outside on Avenida San Martín, or you can take your meal in the large dining area in the back, decorated with shells, fishing nets and equipment hung on the walls. Both food and prices here are good. Av. San Martín, 5-100. Tel: 5-665-3861, Fax: 5-665-1291. Updated: Apr 14, 2008.

Da Pietro Restaurant

The homemade pasta and pizza at this hotel's restaurant is surprisingly good and probably the best you will find in Bocagrande, if not Cartagena as a whole. The Italian food is right on par with Da Danni's in San Diego and cheaper, too. The homey decorations make for a romantic evening setting. If you're not in the mood for pizza, ravioli or lasagna, you can always opt for Colombian cuisine prepared with a bit of Italian flair, like seafood casserole and fish fillets. Cra. 3, 4-401. Tel: 5-655-2369 / 8855 / 1837, Fax: 5-665-5439. Updated: Apr 14, 2008.

Restaurante Arabe e Internacional

This is one of the few restaurants in Bocagrande that offers half portions of nearly everything on the menu. Specializing in Arabic dishes like *quibbe* and *baba ganoush*, this place cooks up mighty fine food in the quaint quarters of a courtyard and relaxing fountain. Local meat and seafood dishes are available here too. Arabic dancers perform for restaurant guests on Fridays and Saturdays. Cra. 3A, 8-83. Tel: 5-665-4365 / 3632, Fax: 5-665-2200, E-mail: Arabeinternacional@telecom.com.co. Updated: Apr 14, 2008.

Bocagrande Nightlife

REZAK Bar Club

Bocagrande is not very well known for its nightlife, so REZAK is an anomaly in this altogether quiet part of Cartagena. Usually hopping on the weekends, this hip night spot fills with locals and keeps the party going just like its counterparts on Avenida Arsenal in Getsemaní. Av. San Martín, 6-155. Tel: 5-665-4000. Updated: Apr 14, 2008.

Río Casino

Río Casino is a great place to spend an evening winning—or losing—money. This casino is part of a larger South American chain, so don't mind the name, as there is no river nearby. All of the slots, roulette and blackjack tables have much smaller minimum bets than in the U.S. What's a few dollars lost when you've had some fun? Av. San Martín and Calle 4. Updated: Apr 14, 2008.

Things to See and Do Near Cartagena

Islas del Rosario

About 25 miles southeast of Cartagena, Islas del Rosario is an archipelago made up of coral islands, with some of the best beaches and diving in Colombia. The islands were declared a protected national park in 1977. The islands' 30 designated diving and snorkeling spots have an unlimited amount of underwater delights. The diversity of sea life keeps even seasoned divers occupied for days—35 species of echinoderms (such as sea cucumbers and urchins), 45 kinds of sponges, 52 types of coral, 170 different crustaceans, 180 kinds of molluscs and 215 species of fish.

Islas del Rosario Accommodations

Most visitors begin their water adventures in Barú, which is 20 minutes by boat from Cartagena. Since there are only a few accom-

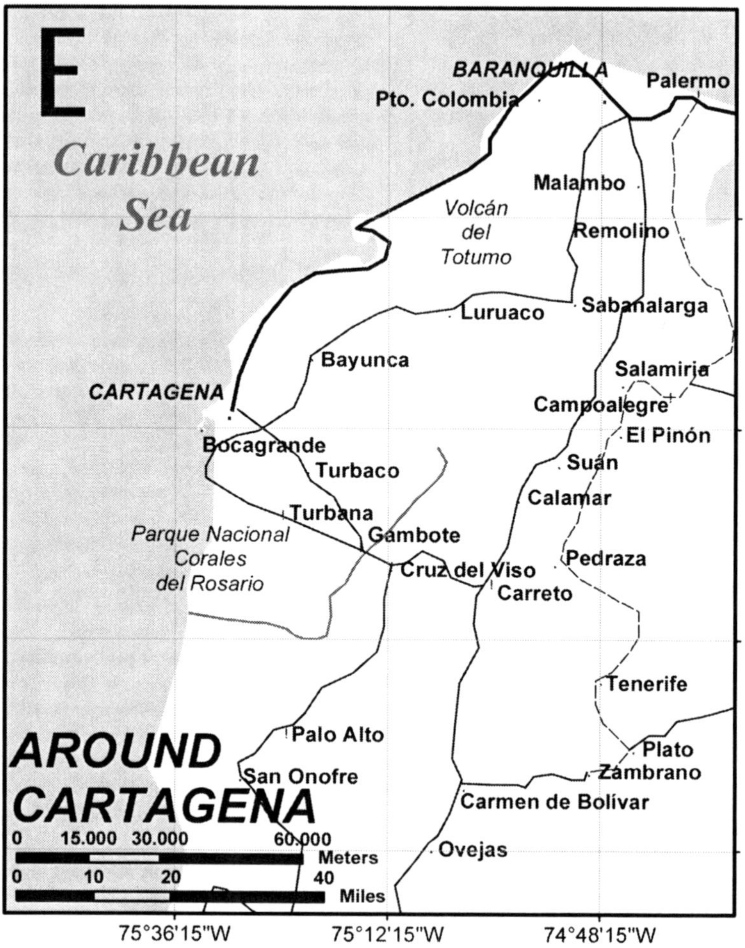

modation options on this island and the price for accommodations in the park is exorbitant, tourists prefer to arrange day trips through local tour operators. If you arrange your own transport and stay the night, expect to pay at least $28 for transport each way and at least $115 per night for a room. There is also a park entrance fee of $2 per person. Booking overnight stays through a tour operator is much easier and transportation and accommodations are of10 arranged for you. On Barú, check out the Hotel Mona Priet (www.monaprieta.com). And, on Isla Grande, look into the Hotel Majagua (www.hotelmajagua.com) or the Coco Liso Resort (www.cocolisoresort.com). Updated: Apr 09, 2008.

Volcán Totume

The natural wonder of Volcán Totume is 40 minutes northeast of Cartagena. This area has so much environmental beauty. The marsh, La Ciénaga Totumo, has intense green waters created by fresh water colliding with the sea. It provides a sanctuary for birds, and people enjoy healing mud baths at the volcano. The volcano is not what you would expect—it is more of a hill than a mountain. Climb to the top to take in the volcano's healing properties. Most tourists visit the volcano and natural spa in one day. It is best to book with a tour operator in Cartagena. Updated: Apr 09, 2008.

Barranquilla

Alt: 5m Pop: 1,112,000 City Code: 5

Barranquilla, Colombia's principal Caribbean port and capital of Atlántico Department, is midway between Cartagena and Santa Marta on the Troncal del Caribe highway. This city is on the west bank of the Río Magdalena, 22 kilometers (13 miles) from the river's mouth.

It was a backwater town for several centuries, but in the 19th Century it began to exude international commercial importance. Immigrants arrived from around the world, adding a variety of flavors to the city. It has a sizeable Middle Eastern community evident through commerce, two mosques and Arabic channels on cable TV. This segment of the population also has its famous sons and daughters, including—most notably— Shakira.

Barranquilla, known as *Puerto de Oro de Colombia* (Colombia's Gold Port) or *La Arenosa* (The Sandy One), is most famous for its pre-Lent Carnaval. But, there is much more to learn about what makes the city famous. From museums to stunning architecture and premier beaches to baseball, there is an unlimited range of ways to pass the sultry barranquillero days.

History

According to historian Alonso de la Espriella, Barranquilla is a city that was not founded, rather, simply populated. Spanish explorer Rodrigo de Bastidas discovered the mouth of the Río Magdalena in 1503, but sailed on. More than a hundred years alter, in the 1620s, Sabanitas de Camacho on the low bluffs was discovered again, and settled, by Galapa indigenous and cattle farmers (looking for pastorage during a prolonged drought). In 1774 the name was changed to Barrancas de San Nicolás. The city's official creation date is considered April 7, 1813, when it was named Villas de Barlobento. None of the names really stuck. It just became Barranquillas, the diminutive of *barrancas* (bluffs).

Barranquillas never played a big part in the journeys of the Great Liberator, Simón Bolívar. He passed through the area on several occasions, but stayed in nearby Soledad and San Nicolás (Barlobento). The places he stayed are being turned into museums.

The 1940s saw an explosion in Colombian letters in this city. Gabriel García Márquez formed the Grupo de Barranquilla, which included Enrique Grau, Cecilia Porras and Cepeda Samudio, among others. The Cueva, a former neighborhood diner and bar, was the group's meeting point. Their influence continues to be felt to this day. Updated: May 22, 2008.

When to Go

Barranquilla has a hot climate with daytime temperatures averaging between 19°C and 25°C (77-84°F). The rainy seasons are May to June and August to November. During rainy seasons creeks, known as *arroyos*, stream through the streets. These make using the high curbs, which make walking around the city such an exercise, a necessity. Then, from the end of October to the beginning of January, high winds out of the north, called *aliseos*, whip through the city.

Everyone who can comes for Carnaval and pre-Carnaval, which begins two weeks before the main event. Hotel rooms are booked months in advance and prices go up triple to quadruple in amount. Updated: May 26, 2008.

Holidays and Festivals

Barranquilla is best known for Carnaval (a moveable feast celebrated before Lent begins). However, barranquilleros invite guests to visit for other festivals, too.

Photo by Dan Anderson

Month	Event
February	**Carnaval de las Artes**—A four-day, behind-the-scenes look at the art of Carnaval. **Festival del Bollo**—An Afro-Colombian salute to the bollo (a roll made of corn, yucca or plaintain cooked in maize or banana leaves), a contribution from Africa to Barranquilla's cuisine. (February 14)
March	**Festival del Dulce**—The last two weeks of the month, an acknowledgment of Afro-Colombian sweet culinary traditions.
April	**Día de Barranquilla**—The celebration of the city's founding. There are military and folkloric parades, conferences and concerts. (April 7)
June	**Poetas del Mundo**—Features local, national and international poets, an off-shoot of Medellín's Poetry Festival.
August	**El Caribe Cuenta**—An international storytellers' fête.
September	**BarranquiJazz**—An international jazz fest and the International Contemporary Dance Festival.

Updated: May 26, 2008.

Getting To and Away From Barranquilla

Bus

Barranquilla's bus terminal is in Soledad, five kilometers (three miles) from the city. It is divided into four sections. Facilities include restaurants, shops, bakeries, bathrooms, phones, a beauty salon, casino, internet and ATMs. To catch a buseta to downtown (45 minutes) or El Prado (1 hour), walk out of the station and cross the road on the left to the corner where buses pass.

Air

Aeropuerto Ernesto Cortissoz, 10km (6mi) from the city, is one of the five airports in Colombia with international flights, connecting Barranquilla to South, Central and North America. Most airlines have offices in the El Prado district, as well as at the airport:

AeroRepública / Copa—Calle 72, 57-79, Tel: 5-369-0048.
Aires—Carrera 54, 72-27, local 13, Tel: 5-360-6629.
American—Carrera 54, 72-96, local 14, Tel: 01-800-052-2555.
Avianca—Calle 72, 57-79.
Delta—Carrera 54, 68-196, local 107, Tel: 5-369-2679.
Taca / Lacsa—Carrera 54, 68-196, office 209, Tel: 5-368-2954. Updated: May 26, 2008.

From Barranquilla

Arrive	Departure	Time	Price
Cartagena	Every 20 minutes 5 a.m. - 11 p.m.	2 hours	$5.30 - 6.35
Montería	Hourly 3 a.m. - 3 p.m., 9 p.m., 9:30 p.m.	6 hours	$16 - 22
Mompós	Daily 7:30 a.m.	5 - 6 hours	$19
Medellín	Three morning departures 6:30 - 11:30 a.m. and six buses 2:30 - 11 p.m.	13 hours	$42 - $58.30
Cali	Noon, 8:30 p.m.	24 hours	$74
Santa Marta	Every 10 minutes 5 a.m. - 6:30 p.m.	2 hours	$5.30
Riocacha /Maicao	Every 45 minutes 3 a.m. - 3 p.m., half-hourly 9 - 11:45 p.m.	5 - 6 hours	$18 - 21.60
Maracaibo	Daily 11 a.m.	8 hours	$44.75
Caracas	Daily 11 a.m.	18 hours	$92.15

Arrive	Departure	Time	Price
Valledupar	9:30 a.m., 11:30 a.m.	4 - 5 hours	$12.15
Bucaramanga	Hourly 4 a.m. - 11 p.m.	10 - 12 hours	$47.50
Cúcuta	8:45 p.m.	17 hours	$63.20

Getting Around

Barranquilla has an extensive public transportation network ($0.60-0.80, slightly higher on Sunday and holidays). To go from the Centro to El Prado, catch a Uninorte Carrera 54 buseta to the bus terminal. Then, go to Calle 45/Calle Murrillo for a Simón Bolívar or Tranalianco transport to Trupillo / Terminal de Transporte. Taxis are unmetered, so agree upon a rate before boarding. Around-town fares should run to $2.10-2.65, and from the bus station to town $4.75. Presently the Transmetro is under construction, a mass transit system similar to Bogotá's Transmilenio.

The the curbs alongside the streets are often calf- to knee-high at the corners, which makes walking through the city quite a workout. Many streets in Barranquilla are one-way. If you have own vehicle, be aware that there are non-circulation days based on license plate numbers. Updated: May 26, 2008.

Safety in Barranquilla

Barranquilla is not only a large city, but also a port. This is important to remember. Many businesses in the centro close before nightfall and others by 9 p.m. The area around the ex-Aduana and Parque Cultural del Caribe (Calle 37 to the river, below Carrera 46) is unsafe even during the day, so take a taxi directly there. The city is reclaiming this area in order to make it the downtown district once again. Updated: May 26,2008.

Barranquilla Services

Tourism Office

Barranquilla should have a tourism office in the Parque Cultural del Caribe by now (Calle 36, 46-66. Tel: 5-372-0581 / 372-0582, E-mail: comunicaciones@culturacaribe.org, URL: www.culturacaribe.org). The Comité Mixto de Promoción del Atlántico, in the Antiguo Edificio de la Aduana, has excellent free maps and brochures about Barranquilla and the Atlántico Department (Monday-Friday 8 a.m.-noon, 2-5 p.m., Vía 40, 36-135. Tel: 5-330-3300 / 330-3701). Both these places are in a rather doubtful neighborhoods, so it is better to get there by taxi. For more information, visit www.alcaldiabarranquilla.gov.co (Spanish only).

Other useful addresses:
DAS—The immigration office is open Monday - Friday 8-11:30 a.m., 2-5:30 p.m. Calle 54, 41-133. Tel: 5-371-7500.
Instituto Geográfico Agustín Codazzi—Calle 36, 45-101. Tel: 5-341-1683.

Two dozen countries have consulates in Barranquilla. European countries with representation are Austria, Belgium, Czech Republic, Denmark, Finland, France, Germany, Holland, Hungary, Italy, Norway, Poland and Romania. Check the end of the telephone directory's white pages for a complete listing.

Brazil—Monday-Friday 8:30-11:30 a.m., 2:30-5 p.m. Carrera 58, 85-215. Tel: 5-357-0356
Panama—Monday - Friday, 9:30 a.m.-noon, 2-4 p.m. Carrera 57, 72-25, oficina 207-208. Tel: 5-360-1870.
Venezuela—Monday - Friday, 7:30 a.m.-2 p.m. Carrera 52, 69-96. Tel: 5-358-0048/2832.
UK—Carrera 44, 45-57, piso 2. Tel: 5-340-6936.
US—Monday - Thursday, 8:30 a.m.-noon. Calle 77B, 57-141, office 511. Tel: 5-353-2182.

Money

All banks have their main offices in Barrio El Prado, along Calle 70, between Carreras 52 and 54. Bank branches and ATMs are available throughout the city. In the downtown area (centro), banks are on Paseo Bolívar (Calle 34).
Some of the major banks are:
Banco AV Villas—Carrera 51, 75-215.
Banco Citibank Colombia—Calle 74, 53-13.
Banco de Bogotá—Carrera 46, 44-89.
Banco GNB Sudameris—(pay DAS visa extension fee here) Calle 76, 56-71.
Banco Santander—Calle 74, 55-67.
Bancolombia—(changes American Express travelers checks) Carrera 44, 37-19.
In the airport and along Calle 76, between

Carreras 47 and 49, are a number of exchange houses. One centrally located exchange house is El Cairo, which changes US dollars, Euros and Bolívares Fuertes, as well as other currencies. Only the El Prado branch cashes travelers checks. Open 24-hours. Centro: Paseo Bolívar/Calle 34, 43-117. Tel: 5-379-9441, E-mail: cairointerms@hotmail.com. El Prado: Calle 76, 48-30, Tel: 5-368-1707.

Western Union / Giros y Finanzas has eight branches in Barranquilla. MoneyGram / Cambiamos has four. Check the telephone directory's yellow pages under Giros for the closest one.

Keeping in Touch

The mass of phone stands and shops in Barranquilla has all but done away with the major phone couriers' service offices. These charge $0.05-0.15 per minute for local and national calls. Some on Carrera 41, between Calles 39 and 40, have international calls at the bargain price of $0.10-15 per minute to the U.S. You can find internet anywhere in the city and prices range from $0.50-$1.60 per hour. Correos de Colombia has branches downtown (Monday - Friday 8 a.m.-noon, 2-6 p.m., Saturday 8 a.m.-noon. Calle 40, 44-93) and in El Prado (Monday - Friday 8 a.m. -noon, 2-5:30 p.m., Saturday 8 a.m.-noon. Carrera 53, 70-180).

Medical

The major hospitals in Barranquilla:

Hospital Universidad del Norte—Calle 30, Autopista al Aeropuerto, next to Parque Muvdi, Ciudad Rotario. Tel: 5-371-5555.

Hospital Universitario Cari E.S.E.—Calle 57, 23-100. Tel: 5-330-9000.

Hospital Universitario Metropolitano—Carrera 42F, 75B-18. Tel: 5-356-5109.

Pharmacies are plentiful throughout the city.

Camera Repair

Several camera supply stores are along Paseo Bolívar (Calle 34), between Carreras 39 and 44. For repairs, try Foto Hora (Carrera 53, 72-39. Tel: 5-358-7390), Lukkan Reparaciones (Carrera 53, 68-119. Tel: 5-368-3201) or Serge Gámez Walberto (Carrera 61, 68-76. Tel: 5-344-4737).

Activities ●

1 Antiguo Edificio de la Aduana D5
2 Catedral Municipal & Plaza de la Paz D4
3 Escuela de Bellas Artes C3
4 Estadio Tomas Arrieta C4
5 Museo Antropológico C3
6 Museo de Arte Moderno B2
7 Museo del Caribe D5
8 Museo Romántico C3
9 Planetario D2
10 Teatro Amira de la Rosa C4
11 Zoológico de Barranquilla A3

Eating

12 El Huerto C2
13 Govinda E5
14 Pepe Anca Bar and Steakhouse C1
15 Restaurante Bar La Cueva D3
16 Restaurante Country B2
17 Restaurante la Castellano E5
18 Restaurante Sarab C1

Services ★

19 Banco AV Villas B2
20 Banco Colombia E2
21 Banco de Bogotá D4
22 Banco GNB Sudameris B2
23 Banco Santander B2
24 CajaCopi D3
25 Casa de Cambio El Cairo E5
26 Casa de Cambio El Cairo C1
27 Citibank C2
28 Correos de Colombia (Centro) D5
29 Correos de Colombia (El Prado) C2
30 DAS (Inmigration) E3
31 Foto Hora B2
32 Hospital Universitario Metropolitano C1
33 Instituto Geográfico Agustín Codazzi D5
34 Panamá Consulate C3
35 Parque Cultural del Caribe D5
36 Tourism Office D5
37 UK Consulate D4
38 United States Consulate B2
39 Venezuela Consulate C2

Shopping

40 Casa del Deporte E5
41 Indio's Artesanías y Variedades C2
42 Hotel Girasol D4
43 Hotel Los Angeles E5
44 Hotel Mezzaluna C3
45 Hotel Prado C2
46 Hotel Skal E4
47 Hotel Villa Dilia C3

Tours ♦

48 Travesía Tours C2

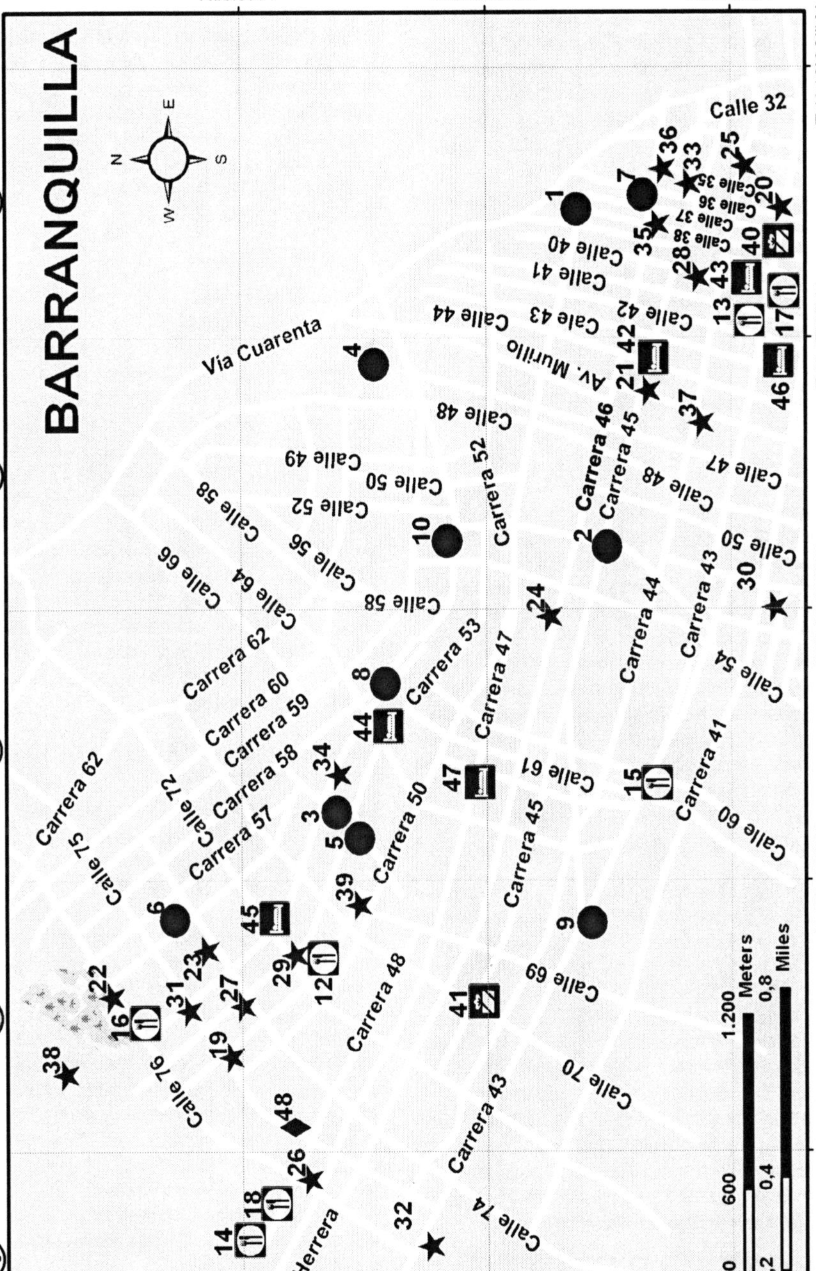
BARRANQUILLA
11°0'0"N
10°59'30"N
10°59'0"N
74°46'30"W
74°47'0"W
74°47'30"W
74°48'0"W
74°48'30"W
N
S
E
W
Vía Cuarenta
Av. Murillo
Av. Olaya Herrera
Calle 32
Calle 35
Calle 36
Calle 37
Calle 38
Calle 40
Calle 41
Calle 42
Calle 43
Calle 44
Calle 47
Calle 48
Calle 49
Calle 50
Calle 52
Calle 54
Calle 56
Calle 58
Calle 60
Calle 61
Calle 64
Calle 66
Calle 69
Calle 70
Calle 72
Calle 74
Calle 75
Calle 76
Carrera 41
Carrera 43
Carrera 44
Carrera 45
Carrera 46
Carrera 47
Carrera 48
Carrera 50
Carrera 52
Carrera 53
Carrera 57
Carrera 58
Carrera 59
Carrera 60
Carrera 62
Meters
0
300
600
1.200
Miles
0
0,2
0,4
0,8

Religion

It's true, non-Catholic Christian churches are present in Barranquilla, including a dozen Baptist and Presbyterian. For mass times and faith listings, see the end of the white pages and the yellow pages under *Iglesias* in the phone book.

Non-Christian faiths also have practicing communities in this city:
Sinagoga Bet-El—Calle 87, 42H-46, Los Nogales. Tel: 5-359-1949.
Comunidad Budista—Carrera 50, 80-273. Tel: 5-356-1982.
Asamblea Espiritual de los Bahais—Calle 50C, 3-91. Tel: 5-363-7927.
There are two mosques: one Sunni, the other Shi'ite.

Shopping

Casa del Deporte
Casa del Deporte has everything needed for sports along the Caribbean Coast. It stocks swimming gear, snorkeling equipment and fishing tackle. If your destination is a Tayrona beach campsite, purchase a two- or four-person tent, sleeping bags or backpacks. You can get just about anything here for any sport: roller blading, tennis, soccer, shooting, darts, ping pong and—even—badminton. Cra 43, 39-01, Centro, or Cra 53, 74-86, local 4, Barrio Norte. Tel: (Centro) 5-370-5781 / 8235; (Barrio Norte) 5-360-7597 / 8098. Updated: May 26, 2008.

Indio's Artesanías
Indio's Artesanías has crafts from all over the Caribbean coast. There are spoons and other items made from *totumo* and coconut bowls. To prepare for Carnaval, there are masks and wine skins. Form your own traditional *cumbia* band, pick up some gaitas, drums, flutes, maracas and guacharacas. For those lazy days, pick up a cloth hammock to string between two palm trees. And, if you have room, get some souvenirs for the folks back home. Cra 45, 70-205. Tel: 5-356-9423 / 313-599-3709 / 314-515-0205. Updated: May 27, 2008.

Things to See and Do

Don't dismiss Barranquilla as just a big port. This metropolis offers more activities than just Carnaval, such as the zoo, planetarium, and many historical and art museums. Train buffs should check out the small museum at the old Aduana building and then board the Tren Ecoturístico de las Flores to the mouth of the Río Magdalena. In addition, the city has impressive architecture, such as the Teatro Amira de la Rosa, Iglesia de San Nicolás (the original cathedral) and the Moorish-inspired El Prado neighborhood. Nor should the beaches be forgotten, like those at Puerto Colombia or villages like Tubará. Updated: Dec 19, 2007.

Jardín Zoológico

Barranquilla's Zoological Garden is said to be one of the best on the continent. The majority of the animals (there are more than 140 species) come from Colombia's Caribbean region, and others from different parts of the country and world. Among its denizens are spectacled bears, manatees, flamingos, condors, lions, chimpanzees and white-faced monkeys. For the kiddies, there's a petting zoo. But the Jardín Zoológico doesn't only present fauna species. In addition, there is a Botanical Garden, which preserves plant life from the Atlántico Department. Catch a Boston-Boston or Caldas-Recreo bus from the downtown or El Prado sections of town. Calle 76 and Cra 68. Tel: 5-368-5765. Updated: May 27, 2008.

Tren Ecoturístiso de las Flores to Las Bocas de Cenizas

The long, covered wooden cars of the Tren Ecoturístico de las Flores rock along these narrow tracks, slowly, steadily pulled by a small machine. Not many take this ride. However, be different, pass some time with others listening to folk music and waiting to see the mouth of the Magdalena River. The trip is 45 minutes one-way. In the high season, Cajacopi (Caja de Compensación Familiar) runs its train almost every day. At times the tracks are under repair, so Cajacopi won't operate. However, the independent operators will still run trains. For the Tren Ecoturístico de las Flores, make reservations with Cajacopi (Cra 46, 53-41, piso 1. Tel: 5-371-4583, URL: www.cajacopi.com). For a more rustic ride, go out to Flores, just west of Barranquilla, where the independent operators run their trains. Updated: May 27, 2008.

Museo Romántico

The Museo Romántico is in a republican-era mansion, once home to the U.S. consul in Barranquilla. The museum houses items

CARIBBEAN COAST

from the city's history, including Simón Bolívar's letters and the typewriter Gabriel García Márquez used to write "La Hojarasca" ("Leafstorm"). Special sections address the Grupo de Barranquilla literary group, the metropolis' journalistic traditions and the Jewish community. The second floor displays the gowns of the Carnaval queens, from the very first in 1918 to the present day, and other traditional Carnaval costumes. Cra 54, 59-199, El Prado. Tel: 5-344-4591. Updated: May 27, 2008.

Barranquilla Tours

Barranquilla has few tour operators. Most specialize in large group trips to local attractions, the Colombia-family-on-vacation market. SENA is an excellent agency to check out. It trains students to become professional guides, which is a good solution for travelers on a budget and interested in supporting education.

Travesías Tours

Join about 50 partiers on one of Travesías Tours' chivas rumberas tours of the city and to four of the hottest dance spots for $17 per person, including cover charges, a half bottle of aguardiente and *fritos* (fried snacks). During the daytime this tour company also offers a chiva panorámica. You'll take in the major sights of the city on a classic, old-style wooden bus. Travesía Tours also goes further out of the city to other major attractions, like Sabanalarga and Santa Verónica. Calle 75, 49-23. Tel: 5-358-0588 / 5-369-0371, E-mail: travesiastour@gmail.com. Updated: May 26, 2008.

Cajacopi

Cajacopi specializes in family tour packages to beach resorts and attractions in the Barranquilla area. The company offers packages to Centro Recreacional El Descanso and Castillo de Salgar. In conjunction with the Ministerio de Transporte, it is also the official operator of the Tren Ecoturístico de las Flores, the train that rides down to Boca de Cenizas (the mouth of the Río Magdalena). Purchase tickets in advance at Cajacopi's main office. Caereraa 46, 53-41, first floor. Tel: 5-371-4583, URL: www.cajacopi.com. Updated: May 27, 2008.

Museum	Description	Hours	Address	Contact
Museo Romántico	Full of Barranquilla's history and culture.	Monday - Friday 8: 15 a.m. - noon, 2 - 6 p.m.	Carrera 54, 59 - 199, El Prado	Tel: 5-344-4591
Museo de Arte Moderno	Temporary and permanent exhibits of nationally renowned contemporary artists.	Tuesday - Saturday 9 a.m. - 1 p.m., 3 - 7 p.m.	Carrera 56 74 - 22, El Prado	Tel: 5-360, 9952
Planetario	Learn more about the universe at Barranquilla's planetarium.	Wednesday 6:30 - 8:30 p.m., Saturday 5 - 8:30 p.m.	Carreras 43, 63B - 77	Tel: 5-351-7700 / 368-2928
Museo del Caribe	Should be open—the nature, people and culture of Colombia's Caribbean region, from the Chocó to the Guajira.	Tuesday-Sunday 9 a.m. - 5 p.m.	Calle 36, 46 - 66 Centro Rosario	Tel: 5-372-0581
Antigüo Edificio de la Aduana	This former customs house is now home to historical and musical archives.	Monday - Friday 8 a.m. - 6 p.m.	Adjacent the former Montoya railway station, now a train museum, Vía 40, 36-13	Tel: 5-330-3300 / 330-3701

Updated: May 27, 2008.

Barranquilla Lodging

Lodging is much more expensive in Barranquilla than in its coastal cousins, Santa Marta and Cartagena. The higher prices hit the solo traveler's wallet, because it's advantageous to book rooms in pairs. There are budget hotels in the downtown area. The most expensive are in El Prado and the least expensive options are in the centro. Room rates are normally in the lower mid-range. During pre-Carnaval and Carnaval prices double, triple and quadruple. For these times, make reservations several months in advance. This is definitely a time when having friends or connections to homestay organizations comes in handy.

Hotel Skal

(BED: $13-24) Hotel Skal is the most popular among backpackers in Barranquilla. It is the least expensive, decent option in the city. This hostel is in a stunning early 20th Century family home. It has large, clean rooms with private bathrooms, cable TV and a choice of a fan or A/C. Only three rooms have one bed and the rest come with two. An extra surprise is the swimming pool out back, the perfect place to cool off in this sultry city. Hotel Skal is presently undergoing renovations, so fewer rooms are available. Calle 41, 41-35. Tel: 5-351-2069 / 379-2069 / 351-0074. Updated: May 27, 2008.

Hotel Los Angeles

(ROOM: $13-27) Hotel Los Angeles is a mid-range option in the center of Barranquilla. The staff help guests best navigate the city. This four-story hotel has clean, decent-sized rooms (especially those for more than one person), with cable TV and private bathrooms. Many of the rooms surround a central patio on the second floor. The view of the city from the top floor is excellent and the free coffee is a nice plus. Calle 40, 41-64. Cell: 315-751-0456; Reservations: 5-351-3680 /3342 / 341-5115, E-mail: hlosangeles@hotmail.com, URL: www.hotellosangelesbq.com. Updated: May 27, 2008.

Hotel Girasol

(BED: $16-26.50) The Hotel Girasol is in an older building with a circular front drive. Rooms are in the main part and a newer additional section. All rooms are large, with a fan or A/C, private bath, cable TV and a minibar to keep your own beers or snacks cold. The hotel has a family environment, which guarantees a quiet stay. It also has nice amenities that include free local calls, internet and private parking. A 10 percent surcharge is added to credit card payments. Guests who stayed at the Hotel Saboy in Santa Marta receive a discount. Calle 44, 44-103, Tel: 5-379-3191 / 1891. Updated: May 27, 2008.

Hotel Mezzaluna

(ROOM: $27-32) The modern Hotel Mezzaluna is an executive hotel, geared toward businessmen and families. The administration is friendly, but the furnishings make the place seem impersonal. The rooms come equipped with good beds, A/C, cable TV, telephone, minibar (extra charge) and private bathroom. The restaurant next door serves only typical local lunches. Relax in the bar after a day of meeting business clients or sightseeing. Despite its higher-end classification, Hotel Mezzaluna doesn't accept credit cards. Cra 53, 59-28. Tel: 5-368-4092 / 4093, Fax: 5-368-3895. Updated: May 27, 2008.

Hotel Villa Dilia

(ROOM: $37-48) Hotel Villa Dilia has excellent service and pleasant rooms. This hotel is worth the few extra bucks. The rooms are simple, with the standard equipment—private bath with room-temperature water, mini-bar (extra charge) and A/C. Solid, thick wooden doors guarantee the room's security. Near the El Prado district, it is convenient for both business and leisure activities. Cra 47, 68-40. Tel: 5-358-3353 / 5368, Fax: 5-345-7320. Updated: May 27, 2008.

Hotel El Prado

(ROOM: $180-580) Greta Garbo stayed here, as well as Grace Kelly and Carlos Gardel. Their spirits still seem to roam the arcaded balcony halls and gardens of this sophisticated, five-star hotel. Hotel El Prado rolls out the red carpet for guests, whether stars or regular-joe travelers. The 1920s hotel has a large lobby furnished in bamboo that recalls a tropical elegance of times past. The rooms are large and include a sitting area and sanitized bathrooms. All rooms surround a palm-shaded patio garden and swimming pool. Every detail of this hotel conjures up one word—luxury. Who knows, maybe you'll bump into Shakira or Carlos Vives in the lobby. The hotel has special package deals at slower times, which cost about half the normal price and include taxes, insurance and breakfast. Cra 54, 70-10. Tel: 5-369-7777 / (toll free) 01-800-051-1101, E-mail: reservas@hotelelpradosa.com, URL: www.hotelelpradosa.com. Updated: May 27, 2008.

Barranquilla Restaurants

Barranquilla, Colombia's largest Caribbean port, has a smorgasbord of international foods. A lot are Middle Eastern restaurants, due to generations of Arab immigrants. Some are quite chic and have live belly dancing performances. Vegetarians have so many options that they can try a different restaurant each day of the week. Like everything else in Barranquilla, a set lunch is a little more expensive. Or, check out food options at the market that buzzes across many blocks, between Carreras 34-40 and Calles 40-42.

Restaurante El Huerto

Since 1986, Restaurante El Huerto has been preparing meals and baked goods especially for vegetarians and dieters. Its luncheon special is varied, so check the monthly menu calendar (12-3 p.m., $3). Wednesdays feature international cuisine from Mexico, China, Cuba or the Middle East, just to name a few. Tuesdays and Thursdays are free dessert days. Restaurante El Huerto's branch in El Prado has a garden dining terrace, (Cra 52, 70-139. Tel: 5-368-4573). At both bistros, the staff speaks English. The downtown restaurant is open Monday-Friday 8 a.m.-5:30 p.m., Saturday 8 a.m.-3 p.m., closed Sunday. Cra 45 and Calle 36. Cell: 310-636-1742. Updated: May 27, 2008.

Restaurante Country

Even in the ritzy El Prado neighborhood, daily set-plate specials are available at a reasonable price. At lunch time, blue- and white-collar workers crowd these picnic tables on the large front patio beneath a yellow awning. Don't be shy to ask to share a table. The food here is great, down-home Colombian cooking ($1.85-2.10 per plate). The price includes soup and drink. Á la carte is offered mornings and evenings. Open daily 6 a.m.-8 p.m. Calle 76, between Cras 53 and 54. Tel: 5-360-8568. Updated: May 27, 2008.

Restaurante La Castellana

Look for the Restaurante La Castellana tucked way back from the street and down a long hall. Locals, visitors and the guests of the neighboring Hotel Los Angeles eat here. For a good reason, too. The food is delicious and the service attentive. The set meal (for lunch or dinner) includes a choice of meats, plenty of sides and free refills on drinks, as well as the customary starter soup ($2.10-2.65). Calle 40, 41-66. Updated: May 27, 2008.

Govinda

Climb the steps to the second floor and push open the door on the right. As you step into the leaf-green room, Krishna greets you from a stained-glass window. New Age music plays low and A/C cools the heat of the Barranquilla afternoon. This Govinda, like others in Colombia, serves excellent vegetarian fare, but here it is on porcelain plates. The lunch (soup, main course, salad, drink and dessert) is served 11:30 a.m.-2 p.m. ($2.65). You can also special-order breakfast or dinner to take out. Govinda offers Hatha yoga and cooking classes, as well. Or, pick up some baked goodies on your way out. Cra 43, 41-10. Cell: 301-408-0898. Updated: May 27, 2008.

Restaurante Sarab

The menu of Restaurante Sarab is full of typical Middle Eastern dishes. Order *labne*, *fatuch*, *tahini*, *taboule*, *falafel*, kabobs, shwarma and other delicacies in full ($2.65-5.80) or half portions ($0.80-3.20) and mixed plates, including vegetarian ($5.30-7). Kabob, falafel and other sandwiches run at $5.30. Top it off with a Middle Eastern dessert. Enjoy your meal inside air-conditioned comfort or out on the shady, front patio. Open Monday 11:30 a.m.-3 p.m., Tuesday-Sunday 11:30 a.m.-9:30 p.m. Cra 49C, 76-139. Tel: 5-368-7407 / 5514. Updated: May 27, 2008.

Pepe Anca Steakhouse and Bar

Pepe Anca, Barranquilla's finest steakhouse, has everything done right, from the menu to the interior design. The inside of this restaurant has light burnt orange and ochre walls and the tables are clothed in dark blue and peach. The menu features certified Argentinean Angus beef (300 grams $17.50, 450 grams $23.50) and national beef (300 grams $13.50, 450 grams $20), which you can have plain or in a blue cheese, mustard or balsamic vinegar and red wine sauce. Or, choose from the seafood and fish plates ($14.50-19). All dishes come with two sides. Don't forget to choose a bottle from the extensive wine list. Open Monday-Saturday noon-3 p.m., 6-11 p.m., Sunday 12-4 p.m. Cra 49, C 76-164. Tel: 5-356-4637 / 6289, E-mail: pepeancasteakhouse@yahoo.com.mx. Updated: May 27, 2008.

Barranquilla Nightlife

Most of the nightclubs in town are either in the El Prado or El Norte neighborhoods. The downtown area has mainly taverns that appear to serve much more than mere liquor. So if you are staying in this part of town, be prepared to travel quite a distance to wear out your dancing shoes. Something interesting to note is that despite having a renowned annual jazz festival, throughout the rest of the year jazz is strangely absent from the city, except at La Cueva.

Bar Restaurante La Cueva

La Cueva of today is definitely not the laid-back, eating and watering hole it was back when the native writer, Gabriel García Márquez, and his literary friends, the Grupo de Barranquilla, would stay into the wee hours. Today it offers a select menu of exotic dishes with a Caribbean, Italian or Oriental flair at not-so-working-class prices. Even the full bar has some out of the ordinary drinks, like the mango margarita. Sometimes La Cueva hosts literary events and on Friday and Saturday nights there's live Cuban music or jazz (no minimum consumption or door charge). Open Monday-Thursday noon-3 p.m., 6-10:30 p.m., Friday and Saturday noon-3 p.m., 6 p.m.-1 a.m., closed Sunday. Cra 43, 59-03. Tel: 5-340-9813 / 5-379-2786, Cell: 316-313-2491, E-mail: fundacionlacuevayahoo.com. Updated: May 27, 2008.

Piche Caliche Café Bar

Piche Caliche is a serious party bar and claims to have the best rumba in the city. It has an open bar with all you can drink rum or beer for one set price ($10.50 for men, $8 for women). The clientele are mostly university students. Thursday's Happy Hour (8-10 p.m.) is free to women. Friday is the rumba universitaria—there are beer drinking contests and the bar opens at 2 p.m., to to start the weekend early. Calle 96, 46-32, second floor. Cell: 311-407-6834 / 300-478-1920. Updated: May 27, 2008.

Tubará

Alt: 200m Pop: 8,900 City Code: 5

Tubará is one of those sleepy Caribbean villages. Pastel-colored houses with palm-thatched roofs provide homes for residents of this pre-Hispanic hamlet. Its white-washed church gleams under the strong sun. Twenty three kilometers (14 miles) from Barranquilla, on the Carretera del Algodón, Tubará is one of the few places where traditional gaita flutes are made with a feather vibrator. While out this way, check out the Piedra Pintada (also called Petroglífo Mocaná), the Museo de los Coll and Parque El Mirador.

Puerto Colombia

Alt: 5m Pop: 20,000 City Code: 5

For many generations, Puerto Colombia has been the favorite beach getaway for barranquilleros. The broad, clean, dusky-beige sand beaches and warm sea, which is a bit muddy, only 13 kilometers (eight miles) is an easy trip from the city. Many restaurants line the strand, offering the best food the ocean has to offer. In the late 19th Century, Puerto Colombia was an important port. Its 1893 pier and other buildings of the period are now tourist attractions. Other places to visit include the fortress Castillo de Salgar and the beaches at Prado Mar and Sabanilla. The Lago del Cisne is a destination for watersports.

Santa Marta

Alt: 3m Pop: 415,200 City Code: 5

The second most important port along the Atlantic Coast hides many treasures. Look closely to see jumbled boulders beneath an opalescent sunset, jade-green waves, screeching parrots and the banana ships entering the harbor while local fishermen prepare to go to out to sea. Stroll along the seafront park or take a night dip in the sapphire Caribbean. Santa Marta hides her treasures well to the casual visitor who has come for the larger gems of the region: The Lost City (*Ciudad Perdida*) and Parque Nacional Natural Tayrona.

At the foot of the Sierra Nevada Mountains where they cascade to the sea, Santa Marta was founded. On a clear day, the snowy peaks of the Sierra Nevadas edge the horizon. This port city used to be repeatedly sacked by pirates and it is the place where Simón Bolívar died. He lived his last days at Quinta de San Pedro Alejandrino, which is now a museum to the Liberator.

Santa Marta is a frequent host to music, theater and other festivals. Centro Cultural San Juan Nepomuceno and the Alianza Francesa have movies, art exhibitions or lectures almost nightly. It is recommended to visit the Museo de Oro (free) before going to the Ciudad Perdida. It has a good archaeological collection and impressive vault of Tayrona gold. English-language guides are available.

South of the city, there are two towns of interest. Aracataca is the hometown of Gabriel García Márquez, the world-renowned and native author and winner of the 1982 Nobel Prize for Literature. His childhood home is now a museum. It is worth spending several hours—even several days—in this real-life Macondo. García Márquez' stories seem to leap to life. Near the old train station is a statue of Remedios (a character from "One Hundred Years of Solitude") and her yellow butterflies.

Ciénaga is a lagoon full of bird, animal and plant life. On its east shore is the town of the same name, surrounded by banana plantations. The railroad station plaza is where the 1928 banana worker massacre occurred, mentioned by García Márquez in his work.

Near Santa Marta are the beaches of Rodadero. There are services for the higher budget visitor and excursions to an off-shore aquarium and Taganga, a popular destination with backpackers and scuba divers.

The greatest pearl of this coast is Parque Nacional Natural Tayrona. White-sand beaches and emerald jungles line the crystalline waters in the park. Lost to the outside world in this paradise, many spend days snorkeling, swimming and swaying in a hammock. A pleasant walk through the jungle leads to Pueblito Chairama, a preserved Tayrona ruins.

Then, there is the most splendid jewel of all the region—Ciudad Perdida. Undiscovered until 1975, a six-day hike brings visitors to the most important ruins of the Tayrona culture.

Blinded by the gems nearby Santa Marta, many overlook her simpler pleasures. Days spent waiting for tours to Ciudad Perdida and Parque Nacional Natural Tayrona can be occupied basking in the tropical breezes, taking cooling midday siestas, wandering down narrow streets lined with colonial buildings, sitting beneath the shade of Parque Bolívar and enjoying the culture this city offers. Updated: Jun 04, 2008.

Photo by Lorraine Caputo

History

Santa Marta was the first Spanish city established in South America. Officially founded in 1525 by Rodrigo de Bastidas, it quickly developed into an important port. Despite the protection of the bay by two fortresses, 26 known pirates and countless other anonymous ones assailed Santa Marta between 1543 and 1702. These pirates included Sir Francis Drake and Martin Cote. On December 3, 1655, British Vice Admiral William Goodson attacked and burned the city.

Santa Marta is where Simón Bolívar's journey home to Caracas, Venezuela came to an abrupt end. He was forced to stop due to intense tuberculosis and was given refuge at Quinta San Pedro de Alejandrino. He died there on December 17, 1830 and was buried in the cathedral. Thirteen years later, Bolívar would finally reach his hometown, where his body now rests in the Panteón.

During the first half of the 20th Century, until 1966, the United Fruit Company had its headquarters in Santa Marta. Remnants of its *Barrio Gringo* still exist. Updated: May 27, 2008.

CARIBBEAN COAST

When to Go

It is always hot in Santa Marta. Temperatures are moderated by the winds that come in from the end of December to the beginning of March. In January, those winds whipping through the streets from dusk to dawn are called *La Loca* (the crazy one). From September to the beginning of December is the rainy season. At times, storms can be very strong, turning the streets into rivers.

Santa Marta is a popular destination for vacationing Colombians, especially during the time from Christmas to New Year's, July to August and Semana Santa. Updated: May 27, 2008.

Holidays and Festivals

Like any place along the coast, Carnaval is celebrated by *samarios* (Santa Marta residents) with *comparsas* (dance troupes) and a flurry of corn starch, spray foam and water. Be ready to dance, dodge and party. Santa Marta and neighboring villages observe the feast days of the Virgen del Carmen which culminate on July 16. A special feature is a flotilla from Taganga to Santa Marta and El Rodadero. The city's patron saint, Saint Martha, is commemorated with processions on July 29. Every year Santa Marta hosts a Fiesta del Mar, which may occur in June, July or September. Updated: May 28, 2008.

Getting To and Away from Santa Marta

Air

Santa Marta's Aeropuerto Simón Bolívar is 16 kilometers (almost 10 miles) south of the city. Three airlines offer national flights, with international connections.

Aero República—To Bogotá: twice daily, with national and international connections, $200 one-way. (Monday-Friday 8 a.m.-6 p.m., Saturday 9 a.m.-1 p.m. Carrera 3, 17-27, Tel: 5-421-0120.)
Aires—To Barranquilla, Valledupar ($138) and Montería ($100) daily; also Cartagena ($100) daily, with international connections to Panama City ($418, daily; one-way tickets sold only to Panamanian residents or those travelers who have a connecting flight), Curaçoa (Tuesday, Saturday) and Aruba (Sunday, Thursday). (Carrera 3, 17-27, local 4, Tel: 5-431-7024.)
Avianca—To Medellín: daily, $191 one way; to Bogotá: daily, $201 one way. (Monday-Thursday 8 a.m.-6 p.m., Friday 8 a.m.-noon, 2-6 p.m., Saturday 9 a.m.-1 p.m. Carrera 2A, 14-17.)

Bus

Santa Marta's bus terminal is about midway between the city and El Rodadero. It has showers, bathrooms, ATM, luggage keep (7 a.m.-7 p.m.), snack stands, shops, phones and internet. The main bus companies are Ochoa, Brasilia, Berlinas, Cootragua and Copetrán.

From Santa Marta

Arrive	Departure	Time	Price
Barranquilla	Frequent departures 4:30 a.m.-8:30 p.m.	2 hours	$5
Cartagena	Half-hourly 4:30 a.m. -4 p.m.	4 hours	$11-14
Montería	10:30 a.m., 2:30 p.m., 5 p.m., 9 p.m.	7 hours	$29
Riohacha	Every half hour.	3 hours	$10-11
Maicao	Every half hour.	4-5 hours	$12-15
Venezuela*	Daily noon and 12:30 p.m.	24 hours	$124
Bucaramanga	8 a.m., 10:30 a.m. 3 p.m., 8 p.m. 8:30 p.m.	9-10 hours	$32-44
Valledupar	5 a.m., 6 a.m., 7 a.m. 9 a.m. 12:30 p.m., 2:30 p.m., 3 p.m.	4 hours	$11
Bogotá	Afternoons: 2, 4, 5, 6, 7, 8 p.m.	17-18 hours	$42-64
Medellín	Frequent departures 4:30 a.m.-8:30 p.m.	15 hours	$42-65

*Passport needed to book ticket

Train

The tourist train Ruta de Maconda, from Santa Marta to Aracataca, is presently on hold until the government of the department of Magdalena can assure that the tracks are clear. Updated: May 28, 2008.

Getting Around Santa Marta

Santa Marta has a good city bus network. Small combis or vans shuttle people around the town and to neighboring El Rodadero and Taganga. To get to the bus terminal, take a buseta marked Transporte from Avenida Bastidas ($0.50, 30 minutes).

Taxis are unmetered. Typical fares from the bus terminal are: to downtown (el centro), $2.10; to the airport, $8; to El Rodadero, $3.20; and to Taganga, $5.30. From downtown, rates are: to the airport, $8; to El Rodadero, $3.20; and to Taganga, $4.20. Updated: May 28, 2008.

Safety in Santa Marta

In general, Santa Marta is safe enough. Remember, it is a port town and a major tourist destination, so keep a close watch on your camera, daypack and other belongings. Watch your stuff on the beaches while you go swimming. Wandering down toward the port gate and old railroad station at anytime of the day or night is never the safest idea. Be careful at night if returning in the wee hours from the bars. There is an active drug scene in the city and, at times, police set foreigners up to be arrested. Usually, they are just looking to make some easy money. Updated: May 28, 2008.

Santa Marta Services

Tourism Office

The Santa Marta tourism office on the second floor of the historic Casa de Madame Agustine gives out free maps of the city, El Rodadero and Taganga (Monday-Friday 8 a.m.-6 p.m. Calle 17 and Carrera 4). Information about what to see and do in the Magdalena Department is available from the Dirección de Cultura y Turismo in the Gobernación building (Monday-Friday 8 a.m.-noon, Carrera 1, Calles 16 and 17. URL.: www.gobmagdalena.gov.co).

For maps of the region, go to the Instituto Geográfico Agustín Codazzi (Calle 15, 3-25, Edificio BCH, piso 4, Tel: 5-421-0157). Dirección Territorial Caribe de la Unidad de Parques Nacionales Naturales coordinates the national parks in Magdalena, including Tayrona, Ciénaga and Sierra Nevada de Santa Marta (Monday-Friday 8 a.m.-noon, 2-6 p.m. Calle, 17 4-06, Tel: 5-423-0704 / 0752). The immigration, or DAS, office is at Carrera 8, 26A-15. The phone number for extranjería or visa extensions is 5-423-2704. Panama, Spain, Finland, France and Italy all have consulates in Santa Marta. Check a local phone book for contact information.

Money

Many banks in Santa Marta are in the Edificio de Bancos, between Calles 14 and 15, Carreras 2A and 3, and tellers are on the second floor. Other banks are in the same neighborhood or on Calle 15 along the Parque Bolívar.

Bancolombia—Monday-Thursday 8-11:30 a.m., 2-4 p.m., Friday 8-11:30 a.m., 2-4:30 p.m. Carrera 3,
Edificio de los Bancos—Changes American Express travelers checks; ATM (on Calle 14 side of building): MasterCard, Visa, Cirrus, American Express
Banco de Occidente—ATM: ATH, Visa, Plus, MasterCard, Cirrus. Carrera 2, 15-28.
Banco AV Villas—ATM: ATH, Visa, Plus, MasterCard, Cirrus. Calle 15, 3-79.
Banco Popular—ATM: Visa, Plus, MasterCard, Cirrus. Carrera 3, Edificio de los Bancos.

City Cambios can change U.S. Dollars, Euros or Bolívares (Monday-Saturday 8 a.m.-noon, 2-6 p.m. Calle 13, 5-22).

For receiving wired money in Santa Marta: Western Union / Giros y Finanzas (Monday-Friday 8 a.m.-noon, 2-5:30 p.m., Saturday 9 a.m.-1 p.m. Calle 23, between Carreras 7 and 8, Almacén SAO); and MoneyGram / Cambiamos (Monday-Saturday 9 a.m.-7 p.m. Carrera 5 and Calle 23, Almacén Vivero, Tel: 5-423-5439).

Keeping in Touch

Telecom in Santa Marta has local calls for $0.05 per minute, national calls for $0.15 per minute and international calls starting at $0.30 per minute, plus internet at $1.05 per hour (Monday-Friday 7 a.m.-4 p.m., Saturday 8:30-11:30 a.m., closed Sunday and holidays.

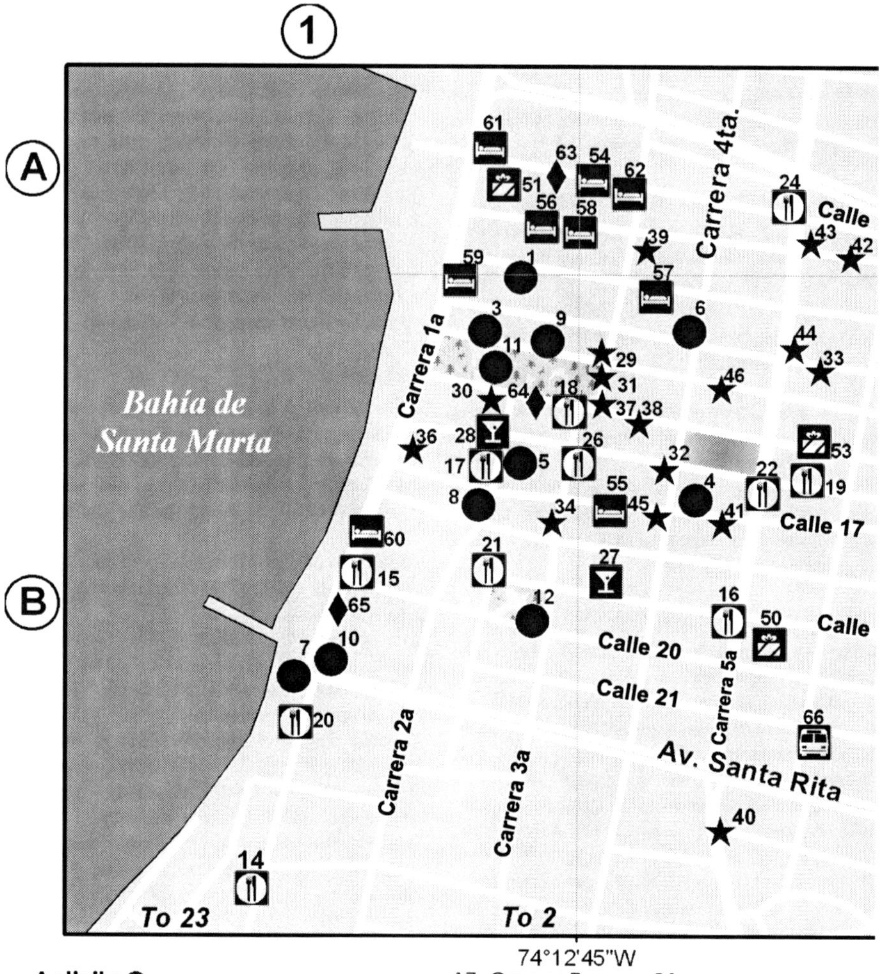

Activity ●

1 Alianza Francesa B1
2 Bananatown B1
3 Biblioteca Banco de la República B1
4 Catedral de Santa Marta B2
5 Centro Cultural San Juan B1
6 Iglesia San Francisco B2
7 Monumento a los Tairona B1
8 Museo de Arte B1
9 Museo de Oro Tairona B1
10 Museo Etnográfico de la Universidad B1
11 Parque Bolívar B1
12 Parque de los Novios B1
13 Parque San Miguel B1

Eating

14 Baguettina Café B1
15 Ben & Josep B1
16 Burundun B2
17 Crepes Express B1
18 Deli Krem B2
19 Govinda B1
20 Ostras El Juancho
21 Restaurante Donde Chucho B1
22 Restaurante Lucky Hong Kong B2
23 Restaurante Mañe Cayón C1
24 Restaurante Mi Pueblo A2
25 Ristorante-Viñería El Sabor de Italia B2
26 Tama Café B1

Nightlife

27 Bar la Puerta B2
28 Bar Lautrec B1

Shopping

29 Almacén Olímpica A2
30 Almacén SAO Olímpica A2
31 Almaneces B2
32 Callejón de los Jipis A1
33 Market area A2

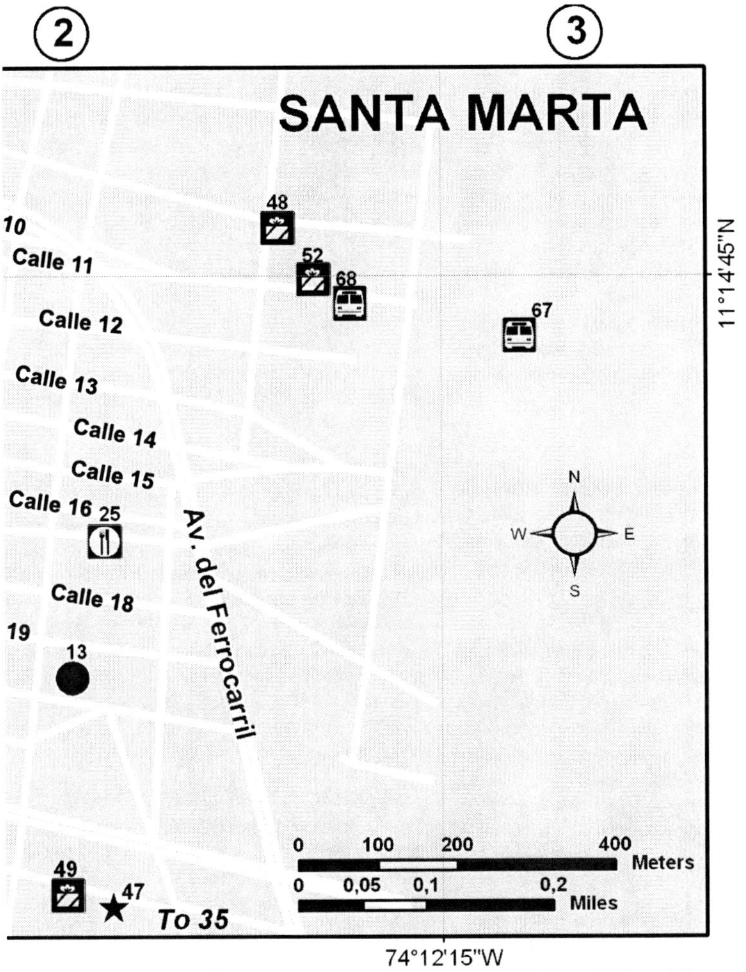

34 Señor Alberto GóngolaÆs shop B2

Service ★

35 Banco Colombia B2
36 Banco Occidente B1
37 Banco Popular B2
38 Biosierra B2
39 City Cambios B2
40 Correos de Colombia/Adpostal B1
41 DAS C2
42 Dirección de Cultura y Turismo B1
43 Edificio de Bancos B2
44 Instituto Agustín Codazzi B2
45 Lavandería A2
46 Money Gram B2
47 National Park Office B2
48 Servisony A2
49 Tayrona Net A2
50 Telecom B2
51 Tourist Information B2
52 Vestigios B2
53 Western Union B2

Sleeping

60 Hotel Casa Familiar A1
61 Hotel Imperial Caribe B2
62 Hotel Las Vegas del Caribe A1
63 Hotel Nueva Granada B2
64 Hotel Saboy A2
65 Hotel Yuldama B1
66 Park Hotel B1
67 Residencia El Titanic A1
68 Residencias San Jorge A2

Tour ♦

69 Atlantic Divers A1
70 Aviatur B1
71 Turcol B1

Transportation

72 Taxis a Ciénaga B2
73 Transportation to Minca B2
74 Transportation to Parque Tayro B2

Calle 13, 5-27). Local shops charge $0.05-0.15 per minute for local and national calls. Internet is quite common in Santa Marta, including Skype. The average price is $0.50-0.80 per hour. A one-stop option for all telecommunications needs is T@yrona.Net which has international calls starting at $0.25 per minute and internet for $0.35-0.80 per hour, depending on the time of day. Ask at the desk for the headset to make Skype calls (daily 7 a.m.-10 p.m. Calle 11, 5-05. Tel: 5-431-4997).

Mail that "wish you were here" postcard at Correo de Colombia (Monday-Friday 7:30 a.m.-noon, 2-6 p.m., Saturday 8 a.m.-noon. Calle 15, 5-31).

Medical

The most recommended medical facility is Clínica Capri, near the market in Santa Marta (Calle 11, 8-21, Tel: 5-421-0142). Several pharmacies are on Parque Bolívar and Carrera 5.

Laundry

There is no lack of laundromats in Santa Marta. Two are located right next to one another on Calle 11. Lavandería Santa Marta is the cheaper. It charges $1.30 per kilo for wash and dry and has same-day service (Monday-Saturday 7:30 a.m.-7:30 p.m., Sunday 7 a.m.-2 p.m., 4-7 p.m. Calle 11, 2-60, Tel: 5-423-5906 / 431-5040).

Camera Repair

To purchase film, digital cards, batteries or any other camera accessories, Carrera 5 has a number of shops that can fulfill your needs. Servisony (Calle 11, between Carreras 5 and 6) repairs digital cameras. For analog cameras, go to Señor Alberto Góngola's shop in the passage on Calle 15, between Carreras 5 and 6.

Religion

Santa Marta's telephone directory lists Catholic mass hours and non-Catholic churches at the end of the yellow pages. Protestant faiths in Colombia are called "Iglesias Cristianas Evangélicas." There are also several Baptist and Presbyterian churches listed.

Shopping

Vestigos

The voices of the ancients continue to speak through the T-shirts Vestigos creates. The company uses designs from petroglyphs, pottery and other artifacts to honor Mother Earth or tell the story of ancient cultures from Colombia and around the world. The 100 percent cotton T-shirts keep you cool in the tropical Caribbean heat and the price is reasonable at $5.30. Moreover, Vestigos has bags made by the present-day indigenous of Sierra Nevada de Santa Marta. Calle 14, 4-08. Tel: 5-741-8819, Cell: 316-587-1805, E-mail: yubeli_15@hotmail.com. Updated: May 28, 2008.

Biosierra

Biosierra is the storefront of Fundación Pro-Sierra Nevada de Santa Marta, which works with communities in the mountain range for environmental conservation and recuperation. Biosierra sells bags made by the Arhuaco, Kankuama, Kogui, Wayuu and Wiwa. Each nation has its own distinctive designs. The local settlements make baskets, gourds and woodwork, jewelry, T-shirts, puzzles and other artesanial work, including products like organic coffee and honey. Biosierra also sells publications. "La Sierra de Santa Marta" is available in Spanish, English, German, French or Japanese. Calle 16, 3-94. Tel: 5-431-0551 / 0552, Fax: 5-431-5589, E-mail: biosierra@prosierra.org, URL: www.prosierra.org. Updated: May 28, 2008.

Things to See and Do

Many travelers consider Santa Marta just a passing-through point on the way to Taganga, Parque Nacional Natural Tayrona or Ciudad Perdida. However, there is a lot going on beneath the surface of this port city. Travelers interested in history should head for Quinta San Pedro Alejandrina and the Bananatown. Anyone with an inkling for ruins, go to the Museo de Oro, Tayrona's El Pueblito and Bahía Neguanje's archaeological site. Art connoisseurs, take in the several museums and cultural centers, which often present free events. For the nature lovers, there is El Rodadero's aquariums, Santuario de Flora y Fauna Ciénaga Grande or Parque Nacional Natural Sierra Nevada de Santa Marta. Sports enthusiasts have a number of sporting options, including fishing and scuba diving, as well as minor league baseball. Don't forget to visit villages like Minca, Ciénaga or Aracataca or the many neighboring beaches.

Catedral

The white-washed Catedral of Santa Marta was built within a decade of the city's founding. The front façade is accented by an onion-domed bell tower. The floor plan is a Roman cross. The nave has barrel vaulting, the side aisles have quadpartite vaulting and the side chapel screens are made of marble. The front left chapel exhibits a statue of the Virgin that accompanied the Spanish founders. Within this bright, solemn space is the last resting places of founder Rodrigo de Bastidas and Bishop Celedón. For a while, the Great Liberator, Simón Bolívar, rested here before his remains were taken to Caracas in 1839. (His heart and intestines remain here.) Upon entering the cathedral, the tomb of Bastidas is to the left of the door and Bishop Celedón's to the right. To the right of the altar is Bolívar's first grave, and in front of the altar is his second burial site.Between Calles 16 and 17, with Cra 4. Updated: May 28, 2008.

Cultural Centers of Santa Marta

Just because you are traveling on a tight budget doesn't mean you can't get a fair dose of the arts while in Santa Marta. The city's cultural centers often present free events.

Banco de la República: Library (open Monday-Friday 8:30 a.m.-6 p.m., Saturday 9 a.m.-1 p.m.); occasional literary readings, concerts and art exhibits; children's programs (Calle 14, 1C-37, Parque Simón Bolívar).

Alianza Francesa: French-language library and reading room; art exhibits; free cinema most Fridays, 7 p.m. (Monday-Friday 8 a.m.-noon, 3-7 p.m., Saturday 9 a.m.-noon. Calle 12, 1C-82. Tel: 5-423-5971 / 431-6332, E-mail: santamarta@alianzafrancesa.org.co, URL: www.alianzafrancesa.org.co).

Centro Cultural San Juan Nepomuceno: Cultural core of the Universidad del Magdalena. Has an art museum, bookstore, literary readings, lectures, concerts and movies (Tuesday 7 p.m.) (Carrera 2, 16-44, Tel: 5-438-2048, E-mail: centro.cultural@unimagdalena.edu.co, URL: www.unimagdalena.edu.co). Updated: May 28, 2008.

Museo de Oro Tairona

The building that once held Santa Marta's customs office now has the Museo de Oro Tairona, a must-stop for those planning to visit El Pueblito or Ciudad Perdida. The museum gives excellent explanations about the society, culture and technology of the Tayrona peoples, including a scale model of Ciudad Perdida. The vault protects an impressive collection of Tayrona gold artifacts and throws light on the processing and forging techniques. On the second floor of the old house is the room where Simón Bolívar's body was laid for public viewing. Now, the room is almost bare save the flags of the six Bolivariana nations. Guided tours in Spanish or English are free. Calle 14, 2-07. Updated: May 28, 2008.

Quinta de San Pedro Alejandrino

The Quinta de San Pedro Alejandrino has been around since 1608, with the mission to cultivate sugar cane. More than 200 years later, the farm would leave a deep mark on the history of Latin America. At 1:03 a.m. on December 17, 1830, Simón Bolívar exhaled his last breath in a front room. Restored to its original condition, this manor preserves the Liberator's death bed, the carriage that brought him from Santa Marta to the farm and other artifacts. The grounds also house the Altar de la Patria monument, the impressive Museo Bolivariano de Arte Contemporáneo and the 22-hectar Jardín Botánico, which are all included in the price of admission. From Carrera 1 (Avenida Bastidas) in Santa Marta, take a southbound buseta heading toward Mamatoca. Tell the driver you want to get off at the Quinta de San Pedro Alejandrino ($0.50). Guides that speak Spanish and English are at hand (extra charge). Updated: May 29, 2008.

Bananatown

The United Fruit Company once based all operations out of Santa Marta. There was a company town within the city for its corporate offices and executive housing.

From Calle 25 to the Río Manzanes, between Carreras 4 and 5, was where the executives lived in a walled-in neighborhood. People had to pass through one of two guarded gates and the neighborhood had its own railway station where the company's families boarded. Vestiges of the enclave still exist. Part of the six-meter-high fortification remains near Carrera 5 and Calle 29. The streets are lined with one-story Florida Keys-style bungalows with expansive grass lawns. Nowadays local organizations have replaced the previous homes. The Colombo-American Center is in one of these. The El Prado Clinic had been the company hospital and the Atlantis Building at Carrera 5, between Calles 23 and 24, was the company's headquarters. The United Fruit Company buildings had extended to Carrera 2, where the lower-level workers lived. Although these facilities might seem impressive, the United Fruit Company's facilities in Sevilla pale in comparison—they included a casino.

To get to these old Bananatown neighborhoods, walk southward down Carrera 4 to Calle 24. From here you can start wandering around; the neighborhood will soon be obvious from its architecture.

Jimmy Porto, director of the Colombo-American Center (Monday-Friday 8 a.m.-noon, 2-6 p.m. Calle 26, 4-100), grew up in the Bananatown and is delighted to talk about what life was like in the neighborhood. Updated: May 29, 2008.

Santa Marta Beaches

Nothing surpasses the pale sand and warm waters of the Caribbean Coast. Santa Marta is no exception. There is a beach within the city, though it is a bit dirty, it is very popular with locals and tourists. The super bright city spotlight rivals the full moon during evening dips. There are several premier beaches at El Rodadero. The El Rodadero and Playa Blanca beaches rent beach chairs and water-sports gear, plus they are the only beaches in the area with lifeguards.

Launches to Playa Blanca leave from El Rodadero, from both the main beach and from the other side of the estuary at the right end of the beach (1-4 people $21, 5+ people $2.65 each). Updated: Jun 04, 2008.

Santa Marta Tours

Santa Marta has a small amount of tour agencies, despite the number of attractions in the region. Most agencies focus on one of two activities: the trek to Ciudad Perdida and scuba diving. Many also offer day trips to Parque Nacional Natural Tayrona and places on the lower slopes of the Sierra Nevada de Santa Marta. The scuba shops offer courses,

Museum	Description	Hours	Address	Contact	Price
Museo de Oro Tairona	Collections of Tayrona artifacts and information about their society.	Monday-Friday 8:30 a.m.-noon, 2-4 p.m., Saturday 9 a.m.-1 p.m.	Calle 14, 2-07		Free
Museo de Arte	Three galleries of regional and national artists, with special exhibits.	Monday-Saturday 9:30 a.m.-noon, 3-7 p.m., Sunday and holidays 3-7 p.m.	Carrera 2, 16-44	Tel.: 5-438-2048	$1-2
Museo Etnográfico	A people's history of Santa Marta and the Sierra Nevada.	Monday-Saturday 8 a.m.-6 p.m.	Carrera 1, corner of Calle 22	Tel.: 5-431-7513 / 315-742-0176	$2-3
Quinta de San Pedro Alejandrino	The death place of the Great Libertor, Simón Bolívar.	Daily 9:30 a.m.-4:30 p.m.	Av. Libertador, Santa Marta		$3-5
Museo Bolivariano de Arte Contemporáneo	Special exhibits of modern Colombian and Latin American art.	Daily 9:30 a.m.-4:30 p.m.	Quinta de San Pedro Alejandrino, Av. Libertador, Santa Marta	Tel: 5-423-7021	Included in the price of the Quinta

Updated: May 28, 2008.

as well as dives to the coral reefs that fringe the national park.

Tour to Ciudad Perdida

Learn about pre-Columbian culture, modern indigenous life and the farmers of the Sierra Nevada through a trip to Ciudad Perdida (the Lost City). Start out from Santa Marta by jeep. Two hours later you'll arrive at the entrance of the National Park. (Don't bring too much luggage, you will have to carry whatever you bring for the next six days!) The first night of the hike is spent on a farm eating dinner by candlelight. After a good night's sleep—in a hammock—the hike starts early the next morning.

On the path to Ciudad Perdida, you will pass by several Kogi (local culture) houses, a sugar cane mill and pleasant rivers. After the second night you will be hiking more in a primeval forest. You will hear birds with human-like voices, see spiders and snakes, and walk through luxuriant vegetation. That afternoon, you'll finally reach the stone stairs that lead to the peak of Ciudad Perdida. Take the time to count the stairs—there are innumerable steps until you reach where you sleep for the night.

Ciudad Perdida is a huge collection of ruins that were rediscovered in the 1970s. After being exploited by gold diggers, bandits and later by archaeologists, it was transformed into a national park. On the fourth day of the hike, your guide will show you the remains of the town and explain more about Tayrona culture. You can take a bath in the river and hang out a with a nice view of the Sierra Nevada. The return hike takes two days and brings you back through the same sites.

While on the six-day hike, remember to bring very little money, good walking shoes, a big, refillable bottle of water and a lot of energy. All of this will ensure that you should get one of the nicest nature experiences. Updated: Feb 21, 2008.

Aviatur

Aviatur is the official handler of the national park administration's locations inside Parque Nacional Natural Tayrona. The agency manages the operations of the first-class Ecohab cabañas at Cañaveral, as well as lodging and a campsite at Arrecifes. Aviatur provides horseback riding, interpretive paths, guides and other eco-tourism activities. This tour operator also offers excursions to other parts of the country, as well as hotel and air reservations. Aviatur has one office in El Rodadero (Cra 2, 6-42, Tel.: 5-422-1803 / 422-9929, E-mail: angelborja@aviatur.com.co). Calle 15, 3-20. Tel: 5-421-3848 / 423-5655, Fax: 5-421-3840, E-mail: j_polo@aviatur.com.co. Updated: Jun 04, 2008.

Turcol

Turcol is most known for taking people to Ciudad Perdida. They have a six-day, five-night all-inclusive package for $252. However, Turcol has much more on its agenda, like day trips to Parque Nacional Natural Tayrona ($32), El Pueblito in Parque Tayrona with a hike from Calabozo to Cañaveral ($80), Quebrada Valencia ($25), Buritaca ($25) and Taganga ($11). It also does a two-day, one-night excursion to Cabo de la Vela (137). For day trips, make reservations the day before, but for the Lost City make them as soon as possible. Turcol has female and male guides and English-speaking personnel. Cra 1, 20-15. Tel: 5-421-2256 / 433-3737, Cell: 310-640-1875, Email: info@buritaca2000.com / turcol_24@hotmail.com, URL: www.buritaca2000.com. Updated: Jun 04, 2008.

Atlantic Divers

Atlantic Divers is one of the oldest scuba shops in Santa Marta. It has more than 25 years experience taking explorers through the underwater wilderness of the Caribbean. Fun dives out to the El Morro shipwrecks or the coral reefs edging the coast cost $58 and a three-day, six-dive open water packet is $290 (includes transport, lunch and drinks). If you are a novice, the mini-course is $69 and the four-day course leading to PADI certification is $290. Divemaster instructors speak English. Calle 10C, 2-14. Tel: 5-421-4883, Cell: 316-544-9193. Updated: Jun 04, 2008.

Santa Marta Lodging

Santa Marta has the full spectrum of lodging options, including inexpensive hostels to luxury hotels that face the bay. Take into consideration that some of the dirt-cheap hostels have quite heavy and open drug use. For a few dollars more, you can find safer and quieter quarters. An unusual feature of Santa Marta is that budget hotels are almost any place throughout the city, though most are concentrated on Calles 10C and 11. Most places, even in the luxury price range, only have bathrooms with room temperature water which, in this climate, can be quite warm.

BUDGET

Residencias El Titantic

(BED: $4-5) Residencias El Titantic is the best option if you are traveling on a budget. This hotel is safe and well-kept, with a friendly staff. There is cable TV in the lobby or hammocks in the plant-filled courtyard. The small El Titantic has 10 basic furnished rooms, each with private bath, fan and TV. Avoid room No. 9, because it is unbearably stuffy. Some of the rooms are furnished with double beds and others are set up like dormitories. However, in the dormitories, strangers will not be placed with couples or groups of friends. The hotel has baggage storage for no extra charge. Plus, the Residencias El Titantic has a courtyard washbasin or a laundry service, in addition to an adequately equipped kitchen, which guests can ask to use. Calle 10, No. 1C-65 Santa Marta. Tel: 5-421-1947. Updated: May 15, 2008.

Residencias San Jorge

(ROOM: $6-8) An understated hotel tucked among the partying-budget traveler, shadier hotels on Calle 10C, Residencias San Jorge provides a family atmosphere. For more than 30 years Javier and Rosealba have offered the weary journeyer comfortable, secure rooms that surround their back courtyard. The 14 rooms are decent-size, clean and come with cable TV and a fan. All except one come with a private bathroom. A laundry service is available or you can wash your own clothes. Calle 10C, 2-68. Tel: 5-431-1293. Updated: Jun 04, 2008.

Hospedería Casa Familiar

(ROOM: $7-23) Hospedería Casa Familiar has long been a standby for shoestring travelers who don't want the party atmosphere of the other Calle 10C budget hostels. It's a bit pricier, but that the security and tranquility is worth the extra few dollars. To help save while spending, there's a common kitchen available for guest use. Other amenities include a book exchange, tourist information, internet and laundry service. Calle 10C ,2-14. Tel: 5-421-1697 / 4622. Updated: Jun 04, 2008.

Hotel Las Vegas del Caribe

(ROOM: $8-16) Clean, friendly, quiet and safe is an apt description of the Hotel Las Vegas del Caribe. It is a three-story green structure with mid-size rooms with private bathrooms, cable TV and a choice of fan or A/C. The front rooms have windows that face the street, but during the night the street light shines through. The hallways have murals of the town's highlights, and the second and third floors have a common balcony for lounging and watching the Calle 11 goings-on. Calle 11, 2-08. Tel: 5-421-5094 / 431-6730, Cell: 311-666-7265, Fax: 5-421-3021, E-mail: clementhv@hotmail.com. Updated: Jun 04, 2008.

Hotel Saboy

(ROOM: $8-16) Hotel Saboy is one of the many sub-mid-range options for the budget traveler, especially anyone not traveling alone. Service is good, particular attention is paid to ensuring guests receive company safely. Rooms are ample and comfortable, with private bathrooms that have room-temperature water and cable TV. Also, the hotel is quiet and provides a comfortable ambience. Calle 11, 2-22. Tel: 5-421-3799, Fax: 5-421-4388, E-mail: saboysantamarta@hotmail.com. Updated: Jun 04, 2008.

Hotel Imperial Caribe

(ROOM: $13-35) Hotel Imperial Caribe is a travel agent's favorite place to put up tourists. Frequently, buses pull up and package-tour travelers stumble out, looking in awe at their new surroundings. This hotel from the 1920s still has a lot of class that's created by the ceramic-tile floors and high ceilings. Rooms are large with private bathrooms and either ceiling fans or A/C. The space is bright from the tropical sun streaming through the long windows. This old hotel has held up well over the decades and continues to serve the journeyer well. Calle 17, 3-96. Tel: 5-421-1556 / 431-5592, Fax: 5-421-4556, E-mail: jhon_angarita@hotmail.com. Updated: Jun 04, 2008.

MID-RANGE

Hotel Nueva Granada

(ROOM: $27-48) The Hotel Nueva Granada's beautifully decorated rooms surround the garden courtyard. Comfortable and quiet, each comes with a spotless private bath and a safe. Sit in the garden and read a book from the in-house library. Or, relax in the Jacuzzi after trekking to the Lost City. The price includes American breakfast and a half-hour of free internet per day. Hotel Nueva Granada also rents bicycles to guests ($1.60 per hour, $6.35 per day). Calle 12, 3-17. Tel: 5-421-0685 / 431-2568, Fax: 5-421-1337, E-mail: hotelnuevagranada@hotmail.com, URL: www.hotelnuevagranada.com. Updated: Jun 04, 2008.

Park Hotel

(ROOM: $32-64) Since its inception in 1927, the same family has lovingly run the Park Hotel, which is a favorite of Colombian TV personalities and international journalists. The outside may have had a face lift a few decades back, but the inside has had the same elegance since conception. High-relief carvings of dancing figures and tropical vegetation cover the pilasters and stairways. The public areas are accented by paintings and stone sculptures. The tastefully decorated rooms have high ceilings, ceramic-tile floors and private bathrooms. (Here's a secret: the *turista* rooms have a sea view!) On steamy afternoons, cool off in the swimming pool and after sunset, relax in the bamboo furniture on the broad, common balcony overlooking the bay. Park Hotel pays attention to the children, too, providing a reading room and pool just for them. Thursday is movie night. Paseo Bastidas (Cra 1), 18-67. Tel: 5-421-1215 / 4939, Fax: 5-421-1574, E-mail: lgomez@dialnet.net.co. Updated: Jun 04, 2008.

Hotel Yuldama

(ROOM: $47-58) The Hotel Yuldama is a relic of late 1950s architecture. The disappointingly worn rooms have the typical amenities. There's A/C, cable TV, minibar (extra charge), telephone, closet and private bath room. The quarters facing Avenida Bastidas are a bit noisy, though they offer a wonderful view of the bay, especially at sunset. Guests of this hotel can also use the pool and sauna at the Hotel Yuldama Inn in El Rodadero. Cra 1, 12-19. Tel: 5-421-0063, E-mail: informacion@hotelyuldama.com, URL: www.hotelyuldama.com. Updated: Jun 04, 2008.

HIGH-END

Playa Koralia

(ROOM: $100-130) The Guardian's article "Colombia on a Natural High" uses Playa Koralia as an example of supreme chillness and says that Shakira booked in here to just get away from it all. Owner Jose Luis Nieto encourages relaxation, and will even confiscate laptops. Chill outside in simplistic hammocks while gazing at the beach, but once inside your cabin, you'll wish sleeping at the beach always felt like being an Arab Sheikh. The interior decoration is based on inspiration from pre-Columbian symbology, popular Mexican art, Hindi-Rajastan and the Mediterranean. Camping is also available if you have your own tent. Koralia offers the chance to observe local handicrafts being made, canoe trips, jungle hikes to waterfalls, mountain hikes, snorkeling, massages, flower baths, and more. In addition to a restaurant with a menu inspired by Caribbean, Mediterranean and Asian cuisine, there is a bar on the beach that has live music and bonfires. Playa Koralia offers a pick-up and drop-off transportation for a fee. Prices include taxes and all meals. Cell: 310-642-2574, E-mail: koralia@koralia.com, URL: www.koralia.com. Updated: Apr 22, 2008.

SANTA MARTA RESTAURANTS

Around this port town, seafood and fish make frequent appearances on menus, no matter the type of establishment. Santa Marta has a broad array of restaurants, including fine dining (less expensive than in El Rodadero) and joints with daily plate specials ($1.60-4.20). All day the stands at Calle 16 and Carrera 5 churn out fresh juices. Come sunset, vendors bloom along Avenida Bastidas and the Camellón like a garden of night flowers scenting the air with cheese arepas, shish kabobs and other delights. Many restaurants along this stretch are wonderful options for watching the sunset over the bay. For dessert, buy a *crema de arroz* (rice with milk and coconut) from a peddler.

Santa Marta's market sprawls between Avenidas del Libertador and del Ferrocarril, Calles 8 and 12. Centrally located supermarkets include Éxito (Monday-Saturday 8:30 a.m.-9 p.m., Sunday and holidays 9 a.m.-6 p.m. Carrera 5 and Calle 19) and Olímpica (Monday-Saturday 6 a.m.-8:30 p.m., Sunday and holidays 6:30 a.m.-5 p.m. Calle 11, 8-54). Aguasafe water purifying drops can be bought at Droguería Andina (Monday-Saturday 7:30 a.m.-8 p.m., Sunday 8 a.m.-2 p.m. Carrera 5, 18-34) and other pharmacies along Carrera 5.

Budget

Deli Krem

(CONE: $1.60-1.85) Sometimes the only thing that will really take away the sting of a blistery day is ice cream. Most locals come to Deli Krem, right on the Parque de Bolívar, to grab a hand-dipped cone in one of 15 flavors (double $1.60, in waffle cone $1.85). Deli Krem also whips up malts ($2.90). Grab a container of the creamy delight to take home or down to the sea wall (half-liter $3.50 to four-liter $15). Open Monday-Friday 9:30 a.m.-7 p.m., Saturday 9:30 a.m.-1 p.m., 3:30-7 p.m., closed Sundays. Calle 15 2-70. Updated: Jun 04, 2008.

Tama Café

(COFFEE: $0.40-2.90) Tama Café is a great place to slip in and chat while having an excellent, strong mug of organic coffee. If that isn't quite your cup, have a tea, *granizado* or beer ($0.40-2.90). The glass cases show off the rich desserts (those chocolate brownies are absolute killers). If you need to catch up on email, Tama Café has WiFi, or up the spiral staircase are several computers. Open Monday-Friday 8 a.m.-7 p.m., Saturday 8 a.m.-1 p.m. Calle 16 and Carrera 3. Updated: Jun 04, 2008.

Mi Pueblo

(LUNCH: $1.60) Restaurante Mi Pueblo is one of those neighborhood eateries crowded with folks at lunchtime and well into the evening. They serve classic Colombian food (several selections of meat and fish) and an ice-cold pitcher of water (safe to drink) for one of the cheapest prices in town; the complete lunch special costs only $1.60. It may look a bit worn on the outside, but the food is sure to agree with your gut. Open Monday-Saturday noon-8:30 p.m. Calle 10C, 4-70. Updated: Jun 04, 2008.

Ostras El Juancho

(ENTREES: $2.10-6.35) For more than 35 years this has been the most trusted place to get a seafood cocktail off the street. It is a mixture of shrimp, octopus, conch and manta ray for any size ($2.10-6.35). If the four benches along the wall are full (as they usually are), just take your cup over to the sea wall to watch the sunset. Serves daily 8 a.m.-8 p.m. (except on New Year's Day). Cra 1, between Calles 22 and 23, just past the Gino Passcalli store. Updated: Jun 04, 2008.

Lucky Hong Kong

(ENTREES: $2.25-11) For a different kind of typical set lunch, drop by Restaurante Lucky Hong Kong for Chinese food. The set-plate lunch special is $1.60. Of course, Lucky Hong Kong also has à la carte selections—in fact 135 dishes—that range in price from $2.25-11 and include something called 26 Ray Coling (a bandeja mixta of fried rice and stir fry). Vegetarians, you have much to choose from here. Don't forget to ask the quick staff for a pair of chopsticks. Open daily 11 a.m.-9:30 p.m. Calle 16, 5-56. Tel: 5-421-6291. Updated: Jun 04, 2008.

Baguettina Café

(BAKED GOODS: $2.65-7) Fulfill the yearning for pastrami, prosciutto, salami, tocineta or imported cheeses with the Baguettina deli. All sorts of thick sandwiches on fresh-baked baguettes, pita, round French bread or as wraps await you here, whether a meat-eater or vegetarian. Begin your meal with a salad, end it with an incredible pastry and accompany it with a fresh fruit juice, beer or wine. Cocktails are also on the menu, including the intriguing-sounding tamarind daiquiri. Cra 1C, 23-30. Tel: 5-421-6378 / 431-7666, Fax: 5-423-2057, E-mail: baguettina@gtelecom.com.co, URL: www.baguettina.com. Updated: Jun 04, 2008.

Govinda

(LUNCH: $2.35) Like its sister location in Barraquilla, the Hare Krishna's Govinda restaurant in Santa Marta is a small, upstairs affair with inside and balcony seating. Music plays low while a set lunch is served, which includes soup, a main course (beans, brown rice, soy or gluten, a vegetable side and salad), dessert and drink ($2.35). Although lunch is officially served from noon to 2 p.m., it often runs out beforehand. Just like its other locations, besides a restaurant and bakery, Govinda has a few more things on its plate. Stop by the office downstairs to find out about yoga classes or staying at the Gambhira yoga monastery ($5.30 per day, room and board). Calle 16, 5-67. Tel: 5-421-3590, Cell: 314-803-7576, URL: www.inboundtours.com. Updated: Jun 04, 2008.

Crêpes Expresso Café Bar

(ENTREES: $4.20-7.40) The crêpes at Crêpes Expresso Café Bar are named after writers and other figures from French culture. Eric and his crew mount some delicious, freshly prepared additions to Santa Marta's international menu. The *Pierre de Ronsard* (beef, Roquefort cheese sauce and mushrooms, $4.20) and the *Jules Supervielle* (curried shrimp, $7.40) are savory choices. Dessert crêpes abound, including the simple *Anna de Noailles* (butter and sugar, $1.60) and the heavenly *Madame de Sévigné* (chocolate, almonds, Chantilly crème, ice cream and strawberries, $4). Vegetarians have several options of delicious entrées, like the *Charles Baudelaire* (spinach, mushrooms and cream, $3.20). There is a full bar of alcoholic and non-alcoholic drinks. These crêpes are served on a Styrofoam plate with plastic cutlery, it is fast food, after all! Open Monday-Saturday 3 p.m. to whenever. Carrera 16-33. Updated: Jun 04, 2008.

MID-RANGE

Ben and Josep !

Ben and Josep serves other dishes, but let's talk about what has made this place famous: the steaks. Not just any steak, but the filet mignon. These are tender, even when cooked *medio crudo* (half-raw or very rare). Ben and Josep's steaks are so special because they directly purchase the animal from the rancher and butcher it themselves. You can have your chunk of meat natural or with a black pepper, BBQ or blue cheese sauce, while dining on a sidewalk table. Open Monday-Saturday 4 p.m.-1 a.m. Food service begins at 6 p.m. Cra 1, 18-67. Updated: Jun 04, 2008.

Mañe Cayón Restaurante

(ENTREES: $8.50-24) Some say that the best seafood stew in Colombia is right here at Mañe Catón Restaurante. This sand-floored, lattice-wood-sided eatery has seafood and more seafood to satisfy your taste buds, with some items you don't see on other menus: prawn, lobster, shrimp, octopus and squid. Everything comes with salad and patacones. Fish are offered too—sierra, snapper or a nice fillet. You can have your seafood solo, in one of Mañe Cayón's famous stews ($11.50-14.70), a salad, rice concoction or cocktail. Open daily 11 a.m.-8 p.m. Cra 1, 26-37 (the restaurant is one block further on than you would think by the street numbering scheme, past Calle 27.) Tel: 5-423-0812. Updated: Jun 04, 2008.

Donde Chucho

(ENTREES: $12-38) Tucked in a quiet corner across from the Parque de los Novios is Donde Chucho, one of Santa Marta's premier gourmet restaurants. It takes pride in specializing in delicacies of old Italy. Pasta plays a major role on this menu. There are six types of noodles and eight sauces, as well as cannelloni, ravioli and four versions of lasagna, plus risottos and antipastos. Seafood is also a principal actor, whether in an antipasto, pasta, risotto or rice. It can also play a solo role (as can chicken or beef), with scant potato sides. Donde Chucho also has an El Rodadero branch (Cra 2, 16-39. Tel: 5-423-7521 / 422-1752). Calle 19, 2-17. Tel: 5-421-4663, E-mail: dondechucho@hotmail.com. Updated: Jun 04, 2008.

SANTA MARTA NIGHTLIFE

Santa Marta's nightlife is driven by its port town atmosphere. The streets vibrate until dawn, with cafés with live Cuban son music, standard discos and hole-in-the-wall dance-and-brothel clubs. There is also a visible gay bar scene here, with probably more tolerance than you'll find outside of coastal Colombia.

La Puerta

Founded by the same Frenchmen who established Santa Marta's Alliance Française, La Puerta has become the spot to go—even for Ciudad Perdida hikers. This café has long been a meeting place for artists and writers, to drink and share ideas or dance a bit. La Puerta is intimate, with several rooms hung and a back patio. The music (rock of all eras and styles and Latin jazz) is never too loud. The bar has domestic and imported beers, French and Spanish wines and the house special is an organic blackberry wine made in the Sierra Nevada de Santa Marta. Open Tuesday-Wednesday 6 p.m.-1 a.m., Thursday 6 p.m.-2 p.m., Friday-Saturday 6 p.m.-3 a.m. Calle 17, 2-29. E-mail: ohlalalapuerta@hotmail.com. Updated: Jun 04, 2008.

Burundun

Burundun declares itself as Santa Marta's Bohemian hotspot. This restaurant-bar and antique shop is quite eclectic. Indeed, entering Burundun is like walking into a store of historic items. Old sewing and other machines, mechanical dolls, bottles and cans decorate the rooms. Burundun is Bohemian because most weekends it features live Cuban son music. So drop by Burundun to to eat or drink, to listen to old tropical rhythms or purchase an aged knickknack. Open Monday-Thursday, 4-8 p.m., Friday and Saturday 6 p.m. "until late." Calle 19, 4-76. Tel: 5-423-5442, Cell: 300-834-0226, E-mail: burundun.restuarante@gmail.com. Updated: Jun 04, 2008.

Laùtrec Café-Bar

Laùtrec Café Bar is a bar for everyone, it is said, from straight to gay. Bodies sweating in this tropical heat boogie to cross-over music (vallenato, salsa, reggaeton) on the two large dance floors. At times Laùtrec has live bands and fashion shows. Both alcoholic and non-alcoholic drinks are served. So, if you're ready to bop the night away until just before dawn begins painting the sky, head just a half-block from Parque de Bolívar. Open Tuesday-Sunday 7 p.m.-4 a.m. Cra 2, 16-08. Tel: 5-431-9485, Cell: 316-878-4125. Updated: Jun 04, 2008.

Ciénaga

Alt: 3m Pop: 100,000 City Code: 5

Ciénaga is a bustling coastal town set amid banana and African palm plantations. Commotion reigns its streets, with passengers boarding buses headed to the coast or deep into the heart of the Zona Bananera. If you can, get here for the town's famed Festival del Caimán in February, when the mythical man-beast comes to party down.

The former railroad station and plaza where the December 6, 1928 massacre of striking banana workers occurred is in Ciénaga, at Calle 17 and Carrera 15. In the middle of the market stands the statue of Juan el Machete, silently commemorating the untold number of victims.

On the way to Ciénaga are the Aguas Termales de Ciénaga, or Cordobita, whose waters and mud are said to be curative. (Open daily 9 a.m.-4 p.m., not safe after dark. Entry: $2.65. 20km [12mi] from Santa Marta). Between Ciénaga and Barranquilla is Santuario de Flora y Fauna Ciénaga Grande de Santa Marta, a complex of over 100 swamps in the Magdalena River delta. Updated: Jun 05, 2008.

Getting To and Away From Ciénaga

Frequent buses leave from Santa Marta (every five minutes, 4:30 a.m.-7:00 p.m., $1.05, 30 minutes) and Barranquilla. If coming south from Valledupar or Aracataca, take a Barranquilla-bound bus and get off at Ciénaga.

To get to Aguas Termales de Ciénaga from Santa Marta, hop off at the Cordobita bridge. The entrance to the hot springs is near the gas station. Updated: Jun 05, 2008.

Things to See and Do

Santuario de Flora y Fauna Ciénaga Grande de Santa Marta

Santuario de Flora y Fauna Ciénaga Grande de Santa Marta is a 23,000-hectare mangrove ecosystem within the deltas of the Río Magdalena and rivers streaming from the Sierra Nevada de Santa Marta. Created in 1977, it was declared a Ramsar site in 1998 and a UNESCO Human and Biosphere Reserve in 2000. Its swamps are refuge for mangrove fox (Procyon lotor), several types of monkeys (Alouatta seniculus, Cebus albifrons), chigüiro (Hydrochaerys hydrochaeris), manati, babillas (Caiman crocodilus fuscus) and caiman (Crocodilus acutus), boas, rattlesnakes and slider turtles (Trachemys scripta). The mangrove ecosystem was almost totally destroyed by the Troncal del Caribe highway's construction, which cut off its connection with the sea. However, thanks to conservation efforts it is becoming a haven for flamingos and other waterfowl and a birdwatcher's heaven once more. Presently the only activities permitted in the sanctuary are research and conservation.

At El Jobo, La Conda and Cabaña de Cangarú there are basic lodgings and campsites. Due to the swampy ground, camping is impossible anywhere else. The abundance of mosquitoes makes sleeping in a hammock difficult.

To get there from Santa Marta or Barranquilla, travel as far as the Puente de la Barra, where you can hire a boat to take you south through the Ciénaga Grande de Santa Marta to the mouth of the Río Fundación and the El Jobo canal.

For more information about the Santuario de Flora y Fauna Ciénaga Grande de Santa Marta, stop by the national park office in Santa Marta. Calle 2A-33. Tel: 5-423-0752. Updated: Jun 05, 2008.

Minca

If you're getting tired of the heat, sun and the salty sea, you could head to where *samarios* go—Minca. This is a small village on the slopes of the Sierra Nevada de Santa Marta and has a temperate climate, with clouds swirling around the forested mountains. The air is scented with coffee blossoms on the fincas and crystalline pools of cool, sweet water await. Several farms and country houses lodge guests looking to enjoy this magical landscape for a bit longer. Updated: Jun 05, 2008.

Getting To and Away from Minca

Pick-up trucks and other transport leave from Calle 11 and Carrera 12 in Santa Marta (every 1.5 hours 9 a.m.-4 p.m., last return to Santa Marta 5 p.m., $2.10, 1 hour).

Parque Nacional Natural Sierra Nevada De Santa Marta

On a clear day, the snow-streaked peaks of the Sierra Nevada de Santa Marta can be seen from the city of Santa Marta. This cordillera is the highest coastal range on the planet, only 45 kilometers (27 miles) from the sea. Its three crown jewels are Pico Cristóbal Colón (5,775m / 18,942ft), Pico Bolívar (5,775m / 18,942ft) and Pico Codazzi (5,375m / 17,630 ft). Much of the area—383,000 hectares of it—are protected lands, the Parque Nacional Natural Sierra Nevada de Santa Marta, spreads out between the Magdalena, Guajira and Cesar Departments. It is the birthplace of 30 rivers. Wildlife like jaguar, mountain tapir, condor, páramo deer, paujil and mountain parrot inhabit the forests. Arhuaco, Kogi and other indigenous nations also call this home.

Most of the Sierra Nevada is closed to outsiders. The deeply folded terrain of the Sierra Nevada is no place to go alone; the security situation is uncertain, and many locals state the civil war is still being waged there. Likewise, the indigenous are fiercely protective of these mountains, which they consider sacred land, and resent outsiders intruding into its depths. There are, however, several places to visit, including Ciudad Perdida of Teyuna, the research station at San Lorenzo and the agro-ecological community of Los Cocos.

Getting To and Away from PNN Sierra Nevada de Santa Marta (north sector)

Public transportation for various villages on the slopes of the range leaves from Santa Marta's market area on Calle 11.

For more information or to make a reservation to stay at the San Lorenzo research station, visit the National Park office in Santa Marta. Some tour operators in Santa Marta and Taganga offer excursions into this part of the PNN Sierra Nevada de Santa Marta. Also, it may be possible to find a guide in Palomino to take you there.

The southern sector of the park is accessible from Valledupar. From there, Pueblo Bello and Nabusimake are easily reached indigenous villages.

Things to See and Do

La Ciudad Perdida (Lost City)

See p.259 for details of this trip, which only two tour operators, Turcol in Santa Marta and Sierra Tours in Taganga, are licensed to take groups on.

Aracataca

Alt: 40m Pop: 34,000 City Code: 5

All along the coast, when recounting some strange occurrence, a local will undoubtedly say, "*pues, es un Macondo*" (well, it's a Macondo). The original fictional town of Macondo, though, is a town deep in the heart of plantations: Aracataca. It was here where Nobel-winning novelist Gabriel García Márquez was born and raised on the tales of his grandmother. A few short blocks away is the Casa Museo, his childhood home (Monday-Saturday, 8 a.m.-noon, 2-6 p.m., Sunday and holidays 8 a.m.-2 p.m. Entry by donation). If you've read one or more of García's novels, a tour of this town will take you right back to his magical tales, like the Casa del Telegrafista (featured in some of García's works) is at Calle 9, 5-30. If you want to stay in Aracataca for a while and check out what makes it Macondo, there are several basic inns. Catequeros are friendly—and great storytellers. Updated: Jun 05, 2008.

Getting To and Away From Aracataca

From Santa Marta, take any Fundación-bound bus as far as Aracataca (every half-hour, $2.65-3.20, 1.5 hours). You'll be let off at the roadside. To get to the center of town, take a mototaxi ($0.50) or walk the kilometer.

El Rodadero

The road from Santa Marta undulates southward through dry hills forested with small-leafed trees and cardoon cacti. From the crest you see the high-rise condos and hotels of the port's richer half-sister, El Rodadero. This is where Colombian families come to spend the holidays enjoying the warm sea and clean beaches. Colombian musicians and actors have their vacation homes along the coast. At the mouth of the cove is Pelican Island, privately owned by the family of an ex-governor of Magdalena Department. Everything in this resort town is geared to tourism—there's a water sport theme park and aquariums where you can feed the fish and swim with the dolphins. Travelers on excursions with more exclusive tour groups will stay in this part of town. However, there are still places for journeyers with more modest budgets. Updated: Jun 05, 2008.

History

El Rodadero was just a sparsely populated beach until the first eatery opened in the 1950s. Hotel Tamacá, built in 1959, was the first hotel. Since then, El Rodadero has grown into the large-moneyed resort it is today.

When to Go

El Rodadero is even more sultry than Santa Marta. It experiences winds from the end of December to the beginning of March and rains from September to the beginning of December. Like Santa Marta, El Rodadero is a trendy vacation destination during Semana Santa, July, August and the Christmas and New Year holidays. Updated: Jun 05, 2008.

Holidays and Festivals

El Rodadero participates in the celebration of the Virgen del Carmen's feast days during the second week of July and the flotilla from Taganga to Santa Marta and El Rodadero.

Getting To and Away From El Rodadero

El Rodadero is on Santa Marta's city bus network. Its *combis* (vans) carry people back and forth from here to the main town; many pass by the bus terminal ($0.50). The typical taxi fare from the bus terminal to El Rodadero is $3.20; to downtown Santa Marta, also $3.20.

Coming in from out of town, many long-distance buses pass through or near El Rodadero—ask the driver if he will be doing so. Several companies have offices in El Rodadero where you can advance purchase tickets. Updated: Jun 05, 2008.

Safety in El Rodadero

Because it is a wealthier vacationer's resort, El Rodadero has better security than other towns in this area. On the beach there are posted suggestions to the tourist about steps to take for personal safety, both in Spanish and English. The beaches here have lifeguards. Updated: Jun 05, 2008.

El Rodadero Services

Tourism Office

The Fondo de Promoción Turística de Santa Marta dispenses excellent brochures and other information. Monday-Friday 8 a.m.-noon, 2-6 p.m., Saturday 8 a.m.-noon. Calle 10, 3-10. Tel: 5-422-7548, E-mail: fondoturisticasantamarta@gmail.com, URL: www.santamartaturistica.com.

Money

Most of the banks are located on Calle 9, between Carreras 1 and 3:

AV Villas, Calle 9, 1-47. ATM accepts ATH, MasterCard, Visa, Plus, Cirrus.
Servibanco, Carrera 3 and Calle 9. ATM accepts Visa, Plus.
Bancolombia, Carrera 1A and Calle 6. ATM accepts MasterCard, Visa, Plus.
Colmena, Carrera 2, between Calles 6 and 7, next to the Hotel Arhuaco. ATM accepts Visa, Plus, MasterCard, Cirrus.

Keeping in Touch

Phone shops are all over this town; internet is bit more difficult to find. Correos de Colombia is on the corner of Calle 7 and Carrera 2.

Shopping

Callejón de los Jipis

This alley connecting Carrera 2 and the beach is still popularly called Callejón de los Jipis (Hippie Alley), though they left long ago. Officially its name is now Callejón de los Artesanos, where 47 families have booths set up to sell their creations. You can pick up items such as clothing, bags and jewels, made from diverse materials ranging from lowly bamboo to elegant emeralds. They can also repair your broken chain or watch. Shopping is best during the high season, though local artisans open shop on the weekends as well. Carrera 2, between Calles 11 and 12. Updated: Jun 05, 2008.

Things to See and Do

El Rodadero has plenty to see and do in the way of traditional Caribbean beach towns. You can relax in a lounge chair across the beach, ride a giant banana across the bay, drop a line for marlin or scubadive to see the world below the waves. If you prefer to see the creatures of the briny deep from the comfort of dry land, visit one of the two aquariums here. For those who consider shopping a sport, there are plenty of shops to explore in this resort town.

Acuario y Museo del Mar del Rodadero

A small boat takes you across the deep blue-green bay to Ensenada Inca Inca, 10 minutes away. On the cove's shores is Latin America's first aquarium, founded in 1966. Its 15 tanks and six sea pools house angel fish, barracudas, sharks, starfish, corals and other natives to this corner of the Caribbean Sea. The guides, a few of whom speak English, will teach you about them. Canela and Manuela, the sea lions, will put on a show for you, as will the bottle-nose dolphins. You can even swim with these magical mammals. The adjacent Museo del Mar gives a fascinating historical and biological glimpse of this sea. The aquarium is open daily 9:30 a.m.-5 p.m. It is 10 minutes away by launch. Buy your combined ticket (boat ride and entry) from the Acuario's office in El Rodadero. Entry costs $8 for adults and $4.75 for children between 4-10 years old. Cra 1 and Calle 8, Edificio Fuentemar. Tel: 5-422-7222 / 2405, E-mail: acuariorodadero@gmail.com, URL: www.acuariorodadero.org.

Mundo Marino

Twenty-five panoramic aquariums and a marine tunnel display more than 700 organisms local to the region's ecosystem. Mundo Marino also has fish, sea turtle and shark feedings. Daily 8 a.m.-noon, 2-6 p.m. Entry costs $4.75 for adults, $3.70 for children ages 2-12 and senior citizens. Cra 2, 11-68. Tel: 5-422-9334, E-mail: mundomarino@utadeo.edu.co. Updated: Jun 05, 2008.

Aquatic Sports in El Rodadero

Where there is a sea resort, there will be water sports. Scuba diving is popular in these parts, and many dive shops are eager to help plan an excursion. There's more to do besides diving, though. Rent a kayak or a jet ski to skim across the crystalline waters. Take a fun, jostling ride on a *gusano*, or a water banana. Be sure to wear a life jacket if zipping across the bay.

To purchase your own snorkel or scuba gear, stop by the main office of the Acuario y Museo del Mar. Cra 1 and Calle 8, Edif. Fuentemar.

If you're a bit timid of the big pond, Parque Acuático El Rodadero is an aquatic amusement park with corkscrewing slides and pools. The park is located at the left end of the beach. Entry costs $6.35 for anyone over the age of 3. Open Saturday and Sunday 9 a.m.-5 p.m. during low season, daily during high season. Tel: 5-422-7706 / 1113.

El Rodadero Lodging

Most of the lodging in El Rodadero consists of resort hotels. Cheap accommodations, however, can be found, especially in the off season when you can negotiate a cheaper rate. Renting an apartment or condo is another option for those looking to save money. Ask around with locals or check the newspapers for possibilities. El Rodadero also has several campsites. Updated: Jun 05, 2008.

Camping Cantamar

(ROOM: $4-5) If you happen to be traveling with your own tent, this is the place to go. Camping Cantamar is located on the farther end of the bay, with basic sites only 200 meters (700ft) from the seaside. No sign marks the gate, just a palm-thatched shack at the entrance. Cooking is allowed, though there are no grills. In season, a restaurant serves *comidas corrientes* ($2.35). A watchman patrols the small grounds. Don Jairo also has a few simple cabaña rooms to let. Calle 21, 1-16. Tel: 316-273-3081, E-mail: campingcantamar@hotmail.com, URL: www.cantamarviajes.com / www.campingcantamar.com.

Tima Uraka Hospedaje

(ROOM: $13-32) Now El Rodadero is possible on a budget traveler's funds. Tima Uraka Hospedaje, or The House of the Moon, is a new backpackers' hostel. The beautiful courtyard garden has hammocks to lounge in and the community kitchen is well-equipped. All the rooms are nicely decorated and have TV and private bath. You can use the laundry facilities to wash your clothes, or if you're too busy relaxing, give them to the laundry service. Discount in the low season with Hostelling International card. Calle 18, 2-59. Tel: 5-422-8433, Cell: 300-801-6833, E-mail: casalunahostal@hotmail.com, URL: www.timauraka.com. Updated: Jun 05, 2008.

Hotel Arrecifes Caribeño

(ROOM: $10.50-24) Hotel Arrecifes Caribeño is a perfect lodging choice for travelers in a group. This four-story hostel has rooms for four to eight people, and there are special prices for groups in the low season: $13.15 per person, including breakfast and dinner. Solo travelers and couples can stay in rooms with private, cold-water baths. The entire inside of Hotel Arrecifes Caribeño is covered with murals by a Colombian artist. Prices double in the high season. The inn is about seven blocks from the beach, on the other side of the main highway through El Rodadero. Calle 19, 6-54. Tel: 5-422-3265, Fax: 5-422-3028. Updated: Jun 09, 2008.

Hotel El Rodadero

(ROOM: $48-59) The modern Hotel El Rodadero's reception area greets its guests with sea-themed stained glass and sand-filled pillars. Rooms come with cable TV, phone, air conditioning, a tepid-water bath and a mini bar (extra charge). The rooms, even those facing the beach, are quiet. The hotel also has a pool with a kids section and a playground. The inn is partially handicap accessible—there are ramps throughout the hotel but the bathrooms have no handrails. Prices include breakfast and dinner. Calle 11, 1-29. Tel: 5-422-8323 / 4649, Fax: 5-422-8295, E-mail: hotelrodadero@paginasamrillas.com / bertony12@hotmail.com, URL: www.hotelrodadero.com. Updated: Jun 09, 2008.

Hotel Arhuaco

(ROOM: $108-215) Every detail in the Hotel Arhuaco is perfect, down to the floral arrangements in the lobby. The rooms are spotless with A/C, satellite TV, personal safe deposit box, mini bar and private bath. The baths have a real luxury in this climate: hot water. This is a perfect getaway for couples or families, with a spa and a swimming pool. The Hotel Arhuaco also caters to business travelers. With two fully-equipped conference rooms, it is the ideal place for business meetings and other conferences. Prices include tax, insurance and U.S.-style breakfast. Cra 2, 6-49. Tel: 5-422-7166, Fax: 5-422-7235, E-mail: reservas.sarh@solarhoteles.com, URL: www.solarhoteles.com. Updated: Jun 10, 2008.

El Rodadero Restaurants

Some of Santa Marta's finest restaurants are located in El Rodadero. Here you will find everything from Argentine *parrillas* (BBQs) to Italian bistros, so folks come all the way from Barranquilla to dine. Of course prices reflect the wealthier tourists who frequent El Rodadero, but that doesn't mean there isn't a fair selection of *comida corriente* restaurants here. Try along Carrera 4 (the main highway through this town), where such a plate will cost about $2.65. A massive Olímpico supermarket is on Carrera 4, between Calles 12 and 13.

Nader Delicias Árabes

(ENTREES: $3.20-7.65) Labne, garbanzo and eggplant tahini, tabboule, fattuch and chanclish are just some of the Arabian delicacies you'll find at Nader, but what makes this restaurant stand out is the roasted lamb. Other typical Middle Eastern dishes include stuffed eggplant, grape leaf and cabbage, shish kabobs and shawarmas (gyros). A mixed plate will fulfill the undecided stomach. Oddly, though, Nader Delicias Árabes does not serve falafel. Prices include tax; tip is voluntary. Open Monday-Saturday 6 a.m.-10 p.m., Sunday, 10 a.m.-10 p.m. Cra 3, 8-07. Tel: 5-422-2700, Cell: 316-491-5884. Updated: Jun 05, 2008.

Restaurante El Pibe

(ENTREES: $5-8.50) At this Argentine sidewalk restaurant you can get empanadas and other dishes from the Southern Cone. Specialties include *churrasco* (fried meat with a fried egg on top), ravioli, *carne a la plancha* (grilled beef), and *lomito a la parrilla* (beef loin). You also can get a good, down-pampa BBQ. Options for larger appetites include churrasco, chicken, *ubre* (udder), *chinchulín* (cow intestine), *morcilla* (blood sausage), chorizo sausages and potatoes, all heaped onto a plate with condiments on the side. Calle 6, 1-30. Updated: Jun 09, 2008.

Ristorante-Viñería El Sabor de Italia

(ENTREES: $8.50-13.70) Only true Italian ingredients are used at El Sabor de Italia to guarantee authentic Italian flavors. Antipastos start the meal off with a traditional touch. Next choose pasta largo (spaghetti) or corto (fusseli) with one of 14 freshly-made sauces. Lucas, the owner, may be from the north of Italy, but his creations come from all regions of the nation, including Sicilian cannolis and cassatta cake, though only on the weekends. The only non-Italian items on the menu are the Chilean and Argentine wines. Prices include tax, but not the 10 percent "voluntary" tip (though the service is so excellent, it is merited). Open Wednesday-Monday, noon-2 p.m., 7-10 p.m.; closed Tuesdays. Calle 17, 1A-77, Edificio Tamacá Country II. Tel: 5-422-7259, E-mail: meorrea21@yahoo.com. Updated: Jun 05, 2008.

El Rodadero Nightlife

The nightlife scene in El Rodadero is tailored towards the more well-heeled clientele of this beach resort. Get out your finest dancing clothes if you are coming out here to shake your hips, as most clubs have dress codes. Of course, the life cycle of these discos follows the seasons of the tourist—there is more action on weekends and during the vacation high seasons.

Taganga

Alt: 0m	Pop: 5,000	City Code: 5

Located just 5 kilometers (3 miles) from Santa Marta, this once-upon-a-time small fishing village has become a backpacker's haven. Steep desert hills meet a palm tree-fringed horseshoe bay. On one side of the bay the fishing boats bob in the sunset, on the other side bathers enjoy the cool waters. Taganga has become a premier center for scuba diving in the region and excursions to reefs off neighboring Parque Nacional Natural Tayrona (PNN Tayrona) are popular. Tranquility and laid-back partying reigns here, something that many travelers, both foreign and Colombian, find appealing. Taganga is an escape from the bustling ports and tourist towns of this Caribbean coast, a place where an increasing number of expats find a home. The town is rapidly growing, with increasing services available to its visitors. Whether this village continues to maintain its peaceful ambiance or becomes the next El Rodadero is yet to be seen, but a scarcity of water may help to preserve Taganga's charm. Updated: Apr 29, 2008.

History

Until the mid-1990s, Taganga was just a small, typical fishing village. Then shoestring travelers looking for a cheap place off the beaten track discovered Taganga's charms. The rest, we can say, is history. Quickly, the buzz hit the backpacker grapevine and every year more and more arrive. The town has experienced a seemingly unstoppable boom, especially since the turn of the millennium. Updated: Apr 29, 2008.

When to Go

Taganga has a hot climate, much like Santa Marta, though Taganga is a bit dryer. The La Loca wind drops in from December to January, helping to moderate temperatures. It rains from September to early December.

Taganga is popular amongst Colombians as well as foreigners, so expect large crowds during holidays. It is best to make reservations in advance for Easter Week, July-August, Christmas to New Year and three-day holidays. Updated: Apr 29, 2008.

Holidays and Festivals

Taganga celebrates Carnaval with costume parades at dusk, music and dancing. Get your disguise prepared and join in the fun—just don't forget the *maicena* (corn starch) to throw.

Along with Santa Marta and El Rodadero, Taganga honors the Virgen del Carmen, the patroness of fishermen and sailors. This village is the starting point of the fleet of boats on July 16. Updated: Apr 29, 2008.

Getting To and Away From Taganga

Busetas to Taganga pass by Avenida de Bastidas, along Santa Marta's water front, every 10-15 minutes from 6 a.m.-9 p.m. (15 minutes) and direct from the bus terminal (50 minutes); either costs $0.50. Taxis charge $3.70 from Taganga to Santa Marta and $4.20 from Taganga to the bus terminal. Moto-taxis are a way to get around Taganga ($0.50); they can also take you all the way to Santa Marta, if you like ($1.60).

If you want to reach Taganga on your own bike or vehicle, follow Carerra 11 across the railroad tracks and out of town, up the hill and then down the other side to the beach town. Updated: Apr 29, 2008.

Safety in Taganga

All told, Taganga is a pretty safe place to hang out. Nevertheless, locals warn to be careful walking to Playa Grande and other beaches. To avoid robberies, don't leave your things alone on the beach. Beware of glass and the steep drop just off-shore at the in-town beach.

Since 2006, a number of travelers have reported contracting dengue in this area; it remains unclear whether the contagion zone is Taganga or PNN Tayrona. Take proper precautions in both areas.

When the La Loca winds come calling, seas become rough and small-craft advisories are issued. Keep this in mind when planning boating expeditions. Updated: Apr 29, 2008.

Taganga Services

Keeping in Touch

Mojito Net Internet

Mojito Net Internet Cocktail Bar is a veritable swiss army knife for travelers in Taganga. A few meters from the beach, it has a friendly staff and the fastest internet in town. Their 16 computers cost $1 per hour, they have 2-for-1 drinks from 2 p.m. to 9 p.m. and three or four nights a week they have a wide variety of live music in the bar area, which stays open until 3 a.m. daily. The food is good, too, though not particularly cheap. The delicious fruit, grain and yogurt breakfast is particularly tasty, with six kinds of fruit and berries. Walk along the beach until you see the sign or ask any local. Calle 14, 1B-61. Tel: 5-421-9149, E-mail: mojitonet@dialnet.net.co. Updated: Feb 06, 2008.

Shopping

Literar-té

Head to Literar-té to find just the right book for those lazy hours. With books in 16 different languages, you're bound to find just the right thing. Swiss-native Diana even has guidebooks to help you plan your journey. Literar-té offers more than just books—it has salsa classes, bikes to rent, a cabaña and campsites, and can arrange fishing excursions. Diana keeps no set hours, though she usually opens the shop Monday-Friday mornings. If the shop isn't open, just drop by and call from the gate. Literar-té is uphill and to the right from the soccer field; follow the signs to the seashell-covered house on the right. Cell: 317-273-2862. Updated: Apr 29, 2008.

Things to See and Do

Taganga is a great place to kick back. Work on your suntan, go swimming, swing in the hammock, eat fresh fish, take a siesta, watch the sunset or go to Parque Nacional Natural Tayrona to do some more major relaxation. Hike or boat out to other beaches. Study Spanish or scuba dive. Go on a fishing safari. Make an excursion into Santa Marta or El Rodadero to take in a museum, or head up to Ciudad Perdida for the ultimate jungle trip. Updated: May 20, 2008.

Playa Grande and Playa Cristal

If the beach in town gets too familiar, try one of the other stretches of sand nearby. The knoll to the right of Taganga Bay shelters the pale gold Playa Grande. Be aware that restaurants out on Playa Grande are quite pricey. Be careful walking out to the beach, and don't leave any personal belongings unattended on the shore. To get to Playa Grande, walk up Taganga Beach to Hotel Bahía Taganga and take the trail begins behind it (20 minutes). Updated: May 05, 2008.

Alternatively, you can take a launch from the village to PNN Tayrona's closest beach, Playa Cristal, formerly named Playa de Muerte (10 minutes, $2.10-2.65 round trip).

During the week both beaches are tranquil, though be wary of weekends and vacation times when Colombians come flocking for some sun and sea.

Scuba Diving

This area of Colombia's Caribbean hides many wonders beneath the sea, from coral reefs to old Spanish galleons. As such, Taganga has become a hot spot to explore. About a half-dozen dive shops currently operate out of this small village, and many offer courses from basic to divemaster levels. You can choose daytime diving excursions, fun dives or night dives from more than 30 different sites. One outfitter even does scuba safaris to more distant locales, including Cabo de la Vela in the Guajira. Always check your scuba gear to make sure it is in good condition and that the outfit is PADI-certified. Ask other travelers about their experiences with different dive shops. There is no hyperbaric chamber on this stretch of the coast. Updated: May 05, 2008.

Fishing

Every morning and afternoon local men head out to go fishing, the traditional craft of Taganga. To try your hand at catching some *bonito pargo rojo* (red snapper), albacore, barracuda or shark, talk with a local fisherman about taking you out. Or, contact Caracol about arranging a fishing trip in his boat, followed by a beach BBQ to grill your catch. Cell: 317-273-2862. Either way, you'll be doing it as the locals do, with just a fishing line on a roll, and you'll get to learn about the Caribbean artisanal fishing culture. The fishing port is on the right-hand side of the bay. You can also drop by Literar-té to contact Caracol. Be warned that from December to January high winds (*La Loca*) blow in, causing small craft advisories to be issued. Updated: May 05, 2008.

Studying Spanish In Taganga

Academia Latina !

There is a Spanish school in this village, allowing foreign visitors to study the language while taking in the sand and sea. The teachers at Academia Latina are all Colombian and are certified Spanish teachers. Part of the proceeds go to Foundación Más, an organization which works on local projects for poor children. Calle 14, 3-41. Tel: 5-421-9261, Cell: 316-600-6410, E-mail: edwin@academia-latina.com, URL: www.academia-latina.com. Updated: Apr 29, 2008.

V!VA Member Review-Academia Latina

The free grammar list is very good idea. Everything was good. The laid-back atmosphere made learning fun. Loved the free coffee. UK, Jul 2, 2008.

Taganga Tours

Most of the tour operators in Taganga are scuba dive centers. Ask other travelers about their experience with these shops before settling for one. Inquire with local fishermen about going on a fishing expedition. The few tour agencies in the village can help you plan your trip to Ciudad Perdida, Tayrona or further afield without having to go all the way to Santa Marta.

Be aware that Taganga is blowing up with fly-by-night salesmen and guide organizations, and scams are all too common. Get some honest advice from Felipe or the owners of El Miramar in Taganga and Santa Marta before paying any money anywhere. Ask at Tsunami on Calle 17 in Taganga or go to Calle 10 in Santa Marta and talk to one of the owners or a guide. They have years of experience. Updated: Dec 19, 2007.

Poseidón Dive Center

Poseidón Dive Center is the oldest and most frequently recommended scuba shop in Taganga. Poseidon offers mini-courses for those who don't have much time but want a little taste of the briny deeps ($95, half-day, two dives). It provides full courses in open water (four-day, $337, four immersions), advanced, rescue, divemaster and assistant instructor levels. The PADI-certified teachers speak Spanish, English, French and German. Tour options include night dives, underwater photography, deep dives and wreck dives. All Poseidón's packages include scuba equipment (cheaper if you have your own), boat transport, snacks and a divemaster. Calle 18, 1-69. Tel: 5-421-9224, E-mail: info@poseidondivecenter.com / poseidon@atgc.net.co, URL: www.poseidondivecenter.com. Updated: Apr 29, 2008.

Calipso Dive Center

Tempted by days of underwater exploration and romantic nights in a seaside hammock, travelers are flocking to Calipso Dive Center's unique scuba diving safaris. There are two sites: Cabo de la Vela and the "Playa del Amor" (beach of love) in Guayaca Bay. Guayaca is ideal for beginner divers and divers-to-be, with lots of easy, fun dive spots and a relaxed atmosphere. Advanced and fun divers do six-day dives and one-night dive.

In Cabo de la Vela, experienced divers can explore above and below the waves: there are amazing, rarely-seen dives and before and after dives. There's traditional food, dancing and games from the matriarchal Wayu indigenous culture. Safari-goers stay in a Wayu family's beachfront home.

Open water and advanced courses in Guayaca cost $300 (compared to $225-$250 normally), or $275 for fun divers. Trips are two or three days and one or two nights. Cabo de la Vela costs $375 for four days, three nights, and four dives.

Calipso also offers classes and fun dives out of Taganga and has free dorms for divers. In Guayaca, take advantage of Calipso's snorkeling gear, too. Calle 12, 1-40. Tel: 5-421-9146, E-mail: roberdive@hotmail.com, URL: www.calipsodivecenter.com. Updated: Apr 30, 2008.

Sierra Tours

For many years only one tour agency was authorized to lead groups to Ciudad Perdida (the Lost City). Now a second, Sierra Tours, has joined the ranks and quickly earned a name for itself. Groups of five to 10 trek into the deep folds of the Sierra Nevada heights for six-days and five-nights, though smaller parties can be accommodated. The $255 price covers transportation, food and snacks, hammock with mosquito net, blankets and an experienced guide; you carry your own pack. Sierra Nevada also goes to other points in its namesake's range: Don Diego, Nabusimake and El Congo. This agency also tours Parque NN Tayrona and Cabo de la Vela. Calle 17, 1-18. Santa Marta: Calle 22, 16-61. Tel: 5-421-9401, Cell: 317-417-1797, E-mail: info@sierratours-trekking.com, URL: www.sierratours-trekking.com. Updated: Apr 29, 2008.

Taganga Lodging

In the past few years Taganga has seen a boom in hotel construction. Most cater to backpackers, though more mid-range options are coming on the scene. Camping is possible at Diana's house (see Literar-té) or at Mónica la Argentina's house, 150 meters (500 feet) past the shop El Esquinazo. During the high season most places raise their prices, so reservations are recommended. Water is scarce in Taganga; sometimes hostels will be without water for a while. Do your part to help conserve this precious liquid. Updated: Dec 19, 2007.

El Miramar Taganga Sea-View and Tsunami Café Bar !

(ROOM: $12) El Miramar Taganga and the rooftop Tsunami Bar Café are quaint, comfortable, clean businesses one block from the beach. They offer tours, diving courses, trips to Tayrona, guided fishing trips and more. The hotel is in the center close to the beach (1.3 blocks), just above the police station and Pelican, on the second corner after entering Taganga. Calle 17, 2-36. Tel: 5-423-3276, E-mail: elmiramar_santamarta@yahoo.com, URL: myspace.com/hotelmiramar. Updated: Mar 20, 2008.

Aquantis Bed, Breakfast and Diving

Aquantis Bed, Breakfast and Diving is a small hostel and dive center located 30 meters from the beach on a quiet street. They offer PADI courses and minicourses, and package deals can be arranged that include both dives and lodging. Aquantis is on the first street from the beach, just before Hotel Ballena Azul. Calle 18, 1-39. Tel: 5-421-9344, E-mail: hostalaquantis@hotmail.com. Updated: Apr 14, 2008.

Casa de Felipe !

(BED: $5-24) Literally built by hand, Casa de Felipe is a work of many years of love. Felipe has created a spectacularly comfortable space for the budget traveler with all the important amenities, including kitchen and laundry facilities. The rooms are spacious and beautifully decorated. The shady garden terraces, hung with hammocks and scattered with tables, have fantastic views of the bay and awe-inspiring sunsets. Studios for four or six, complete with private kitchen, BBQ and terrace are available as well. Casa de Felipe is a tranquil hostel away from the beach's weekend and night insanity. The staff speaks Spanish, French and English. Some of the buses from Santa Marta turn up the road towards Casa de Felipe and let you off a block away; otherwise hop off at the road before the policía nacional post and walk up the road on the right. Casa de Felipe is 10 minutes uphill from the beach. Cra 5A, 19-13. Tel: 5-421-9101 / 9120 / 9239, Cell: 316-318-9158, E-mail: info@lacasadefelipe.com, URL: www.lacasadefelipe.com. Updated: Apr 29, 2008.

> *V!VA Member Review-Casa de Felipe*
>
> Spectacular sunsets, peaceful gardens, great staff - and Felipe and Sandra are marvelous. If any hostel ever deserves two thumbs (and two big toes) up, this is the place! USA Apr 29, 2008.

Casa El Amparo

(COTTAGE: $10-12) Casa El Amparo has fully furnished, one-bed, one-bath cottage/apartments that sleep between two and six people. More than six can be accommodated if you bring sleeping bags. Cottages can be rented by the day or week. Casa El Amparo is located in a quiet part of town, one block from the beach. Take a Collectivo bus from Santa Marta, go two blocks past the police station and turn left just before the church. Casa El Amparo has a decorative iron railing and will be the first house on your right. Calle 15, 1B-49. Cell: 301-432-1421, E-mail: vargas_amparo@yahoo.com, Updated: Nov 28, 2007.

Taganga Restaurants

Dining in Taganga is a bit more expensive than in Santa Marta. A *comida corriente* with fish at one of the beach eateries should cost $2.65-3.20. Recently several restaurants with cheaper set-meals ($2.10) have opened up on Calle 16, a half-block from the beach. To save money, look for accommodations that have kitchen facilities for its guests' use. Supertienda Taganga is the closest thing Taganga has to a supermarket; it is conveniently located on the beach road, across from the Parque de los Niños.

Los Baguettes de María

(LUNCH: $3-5.30) At Los Baguettes de María people go to get a nice hot sandwich, its sauce just beginning to seep into the soft interior of a crispy crust baguette. Its 10 different choices, all named for regional attractions, have made this shop one of the most chic eats in Taganga. All sandwiches are prepared with a cornucopia of toppings—and a lot of Doña María's love. Play a board game at one of the picnic tables or sway in a hammock while María prepares your baguette. The menu is in six languages. Open Sunday-Thursday 10 a.m.-10 p.m., Friday 10 a.m.-6 p.m., Saturday after 6 p.m., delivery only. Calle 18, 3-47, in front of the soccer field. Tel: 5-421-9328, Cell: 316-386-2720 (Spanish) / 680-6470 (English), E-mail: losbaguettesdemaria@hotmail.com, info@losbaguettesdemaria.com, URL: www.losbaguettesdemaria.com. Updated: Apr 29, 2008.

Restaurante Bitácora

(ENTREES: $6.50-9) Word is spreading fast about Restaurante Bitácora. With well-prepared foods and a seaview porch shaded by potted plants and match-stick bamboo blinds, there is plenty to recommend about this small dining place. Main dishes feature chicken breast, beef or fish with salad and French fries. Restaurante Bitácora also serves vegetarians—try the vegetarian lasagna or the Ensalada Bitácora, with roasted peppers, mushrooms, roasted eggplant, mozzarella cheese, sesame seeds and olive oil. Open daily 8 a.m.-midnight (kitchen closes at 10:30 p.m.) Cra 1, 17-13. Updated: Apr 29, 2008.

Restaurante Las Velas

(ENTREES: $6.50-60.50) One of Taganga's finest restaurants, if not the finest. It offers a full menu, including starters of soup, fruit or salads and light entrees such as seafood cocktail and *ceviche*. Full meals fresh from the sea come with rice, salad and plaintains. If dining in a group, try one of the samplers with an assortment of surf and turf goodies ($13-60.50) or a *paella* for six ($50). Open Monday-Friday 8:30 a.m.-6 p.m., Saturday and Sunday 8:30 a.m.-6:30 p.m.; groups can make special arrangements for later service. Cra 1, 18-95 (on the beach). Tel: 5-421-9072 / 420-6321. Updated: Apr 29, 2008.

Taganga Nightlife

There isn't much on the nightclub scene in Taganga. There are only two places in town to hang out and have a drink with the locals. The most popular place among backpackers is La Puerta, over in Santa Marta. Remember if you return late, your only option will be by taxi, so be sure to not drink your fare back! Updated: Apr 29, 2008.

Matasuegra

At first glance this word seems to mean "Mother-In-Law Killer" in Spanish, but this bar actually takes its name from a type of firework. This is the townspeople's bar, with locals sitting out front drinking beer. The foreigners are welcomed in, with full-volume English-language music at times and a rasta décor. There are several small rooms inside to kick back. Open almost every day from 3 p.m. on. Calle 14, between Carreras 1 and 2. Updated: Apr 29, 2008.

El Garage Bar

El Garage Bar is the oldest nightclub in Taganga. Whereas Matasuegra is more of a local hangout, Garage's clientele is almost exclusively foreigners and caters to foreign music tastes. The rumba happens only on Wednesday and Thursday nights, from 8 p.m. to 2 or 3 a.m. Calle 8 and Cra 3. Tel: 5-421-9003, E-mail: angelagarage@hotmail.com. Updated: Apr 29, 2008.

Parque Nacional Natural Tayrona

The Tayrona National Park is said to be one of the most beautiful spots in Colombia. It offers a little bit of everything, but its main appeal is peace and quiet. If you're looking for a truly secluded trip head farther into the park, as the beaches closer to town tend to fill up with locals during weekends and holidays.

The park sits on 37,000 acres of pristine beaches, coral reefs, mangrove forests, Tayrona Indian ruins, seemingly endless varieties of wildlife and more than 770 species of plants. Be careful in the water, as some areas of the ocean surrounding the park are rougher than others.

Various accommodation options are available inside the park. Book through Avitar, the only agency with permission from the government to make bookings at the *cabañas* and lodges. Or, if you prefer living on the trail, set up your hammock between two trees—just don't forget a mosquito net. As a bonus, you might be able to reach a ripe mango from the comfort of your bed. Watch for the falling coconuts while sleeping, walking, standing, sitting, etc...

It is a good idea to leave as much of your stuff in Santa Marta as possible before heading into the park. Theft isn't a big issue, but you have to carry everything you bring. Bring your own water, it gets pricey. Also, don't forget insect repellent, a flashlight and long sleeves, pants and socks—it can get cool at night and they protect you from insects.

The entry fee to PNN Tayrona is $13 for foreigners, $5 for Colombians, and $2.65 for children 5-12 years old and students with ID; visitors under five and over 65 get in free. Pay at El Zaíno (access point for Cañaveral and Arrecifes), Calabozo and Palagana (access point for Bahía Neguanje and Playa Brava). Soon, the park service will begin issuing plastic bracelets, which will allow reentry into the park.

Travelers should be aware that it is not unusual for anyone entering the park to be searched for drugs. At one time the park was a hotbed for narcotic activities. This should only happen at the entrance and you should be left alone the rest of the time in the park. Updated: May 20, 2008.

When to Go

The rainy season is from May-June and September-November. The eastern end of the park, where the Cañaveral and Arrecifes beaches are, receives up to 2000 millimeters (78 inches) of precipitation per year.

PNN Tayrona has become the place to be for foreigners and Colombians alike. During holidays the park gets crowded and can negatively impact the environment. During the Christmas-New Years holiday in 2007, the park closed to anyone else entering after it reached 3,000 overnight visitors. For more tranquility and for the sake of the wildlife, consider avoiding these peak times. Updated: May 13, 2008.

Getting To and Away From PNN Tayrona

PNN Tayrona is located along the main Caribbean highway, just east of Santa Marta.

From Santa Marta, take a Granero Super Estrella bus from the corner of Calle 11 and Carrera 11 to the park entry at El Zaíno ($2.10, 1 hour). A jeep will take you the 4 kilometers (2.4 miles) to the parking lot ($1.05 per person, 10 minutes), and from there it is a five-minute walk to the crossroads of Cañaveral and Arrecifes. Cañaveral is five minutes to the right, and Arrecifes is a 45-minute walk to the left. If you prefer to go by horse, the charge is $10.50. Bikes are also available to rent.

La Piscina is a 15-minute walk beyond Arrecifes, and Cabo San Juan del Guía is another 20 minutes. Updated: May 13, 2008.

Safety in PNN Tayrona

The more remote areas of the park are reportedly safer than they were 10 years ago. However, if hiking more isolated trails (e.g., from Calabozo to Cabo San Juan del Guía), it is more advisable to do so in a group or with a guide. Take no valuables.

Watch out for the straying, omnivorous donkeys, especially at Arrecifes. Hang all your belongings beyond their reach.

Swimming is not safe at Cañaveral and Arrecifes, due to strong surf and currents.

Take proper protection against mosquitoes. At times yellow fever is reported in the area and the park is closed entirely or entrance is restricted to those with proof of vaccination. Since 2006 a number of cases of dengue have been reported by travelers; it's unclear if the culprit zone is the park or nearby villages. Also, beware of ticks and other bloodsuckers when walking along jungle-crowded paths.

If visiting beaches or entering the park by boat, be aware of small-craft advisories issued during December and January due to high winds. Updated: May 13, 2008.

Things to See and Do

The main reason people come to PNN Tayrona is to relax, swaying in a hammock in the jungle by the sea. To stretch your legs, hike the Nueve Piedras trail at Cañaveral and visit the archaeological Museo Chairama, or climb up to the incredible ruins of El Pueblito. A longer trek is from Calabozo to Cañaveral. Snorkeling can be quite rewarding at La Piscina, a large natural sea pool. There is a special *playa nudista* (nudist beach), beyond Cabo San Juan del Guía. Other less-visited beaches are Bahía Concha and Bahía Neguanje, both easily accessible from Santa Marta. Certain zones of the park allow scuba diving and fishing; tour operators in Santa Marta and Taganga can help you plan excursions. Updated: May 20, 2008.

El Pueblito

The Tayrona nation lived up in the cool, lush forests of the mountains, escaping the harsh environment of the beaches. The ruins of Chairama, popularly known as El Pueblito, are wonderfully preserved in the park. The paved path from Cabo San Juan del Guía echoes with the footsteps of those approaching this once-great town, a mechanism which alerted its residents of approaching visitors. If you can't make it to Ciudad Perdida, El Pueblito will give you a good idea of the Tayrona's impressive civilization. From Cañaveral or Arrecifes, walk along the beach to Cabo San Juan del Guía; from there follow the sign up the mountainside. It takes 1.5 hours to climb the well-paved path through the forest. Pack all your trash out. Updated: May 13, 2008.

La Piscina

La Piscina is a natural sea pool surrounded by rock and reef. Large and tranquil with warm waters, La Piscina is home to many species of colorful fish which dart among the coral. Manta rays silently wing through the liquid blue, the white sand billowing beneath their forms. A *sendero subacuático*, or underwater trail, takes you through the coral forests and marine grass meadows. La Piscina is a 15-minute walk beyond Arrecifes. Do not touch or step on the coral, as this may kill it. Pack all your trash out. Updated: May 13, 2008.

The Other Beaches

Most visitors to PNN Tayrona go to the beaches near Cañaveral and Arrecifes in the humid forest zone of the park. Other, less-frequented beaches with different vegetation lie on the western end of Tayrona. Bahía Concha, the nearest beach to Santa Marta, has a dry, scrub forest habitat with mangrove trees at the mouth of the Quebrada Concha. The coral reefs make for excellent scuba diving. Playa Brava at the wide Bahía Neguanje also has dry scrub, mangrove forest and coral reefs, as well as an archaeological site, parking and restaurant. Camping is said to be possible at both locations.

At present, the park only charges an entry fee for Neguanje, not for Bahía Concha; this will probably change in the future. Do not touch or step on the coral, as this will kill it. No dining options are available at Concha. Pack all your trash out. Updated: May 13, 2008.

From Santa Marta, transport for Neguanje departs from the market area from 6 a.m. to 4 p.m., with the last return to Santa Marta at 4 p.m. ($2.65 one way). For Bahía Concha, vehicles leave from Barrio Fundadores ($1.60 one way).

Hike: Calabozo to Cañaveral

This humid tropical forest blankets you with its own type of silence: the hum of cicadas and the rustle of wind through leaves. In the mosaic you can catch glimpses of howler monkeys swinging overhead or of iguanas, skinkers and other lizards darting among the brush. You can sense the reverence the Tayrona ancestors felt for these places.

To see this meditative space, walk the trail from Calabozo to Cañaveral. The path takes you from the park entrance at Calabozo to Chairama, otherwise known as the ruins of El Pueblito (2 hours). Follow the stone path laid by the Tayrona, your steps echoing through the still, to Cabo San Juan del Guía (1.5 hours). Take the jungle trail to La Piscina (20 minutes), then on to Arrecifes (15 minutes) and finally to Cañaveral and the main park entry at El Zaíno.

This hike is probably best to do in a group or with a guide. Take no valuables. It is possible to do the trip in the opposite direction, from Cañaveral to Calabozo, although it is a demanding one-day trek and you must begin by 7 a.m. if leaving from Santa Marta. The walk is easier and quicker to do from Calabozo to Cañaveral, as much of it is downhill. You can dine at Cabo San Juan del Guía, Arrecifes or Cañaveral, although it is expensive. Pack all your trash out.

To get here, take a van to the Calabozo entry to the park. Follow signs and ask directions along the way, though the route is fairly easy to find. Updated: May 13, 2008.

PNN Tayrona Tours

Within PNN Tayrona there are no tour operators; guides are available at El Pueblito. Individuals at the El Zaíno-Cañaveral car park have horses for hire. Day excursions to Tayrona, including hiking from Calabozo to Cañaveral, can be arranged with tour operators in Santa Marta and Taganga. The tourist agency Aviatur in Santa Marta handles the park's cabañas at Cañaveral and Arrecifes. All scuba shops in Santa Marta and Taganga offer dives at the many bays lacing the park's coastline. Taganguero fishermen can take you on fishing expeditions to Granale in the extreme west of the park. Updated: May 06, 2008.

PNN Tayrona Lodging

Lodging in PNN Tayrona goes from one extreme to the other. At Cañaveral you have a full-luxury spa, privately operated by Aviatur; this agency also has not-too-bad cabañas at Arrecifes, as well as campsites. On the other end of the scale are hammocks spaces, campsites and simple cabins run by families at Arrecifes. All-in-all, accommodations are comparatively expensive at Tayrona, but the nature and peacefulness are priceless. Camping reportedly is also possible at Cabo San Juan del Guía. Updated: May 20, 2008.

Independent Lodging

(ROOM: $5-8) There are a few family-owned lodging options within the park. Most backpackers head to Arrecifes to sway in a hammock slung in an *enrramada* (open-sided, palm-thatch shelter). This is the ultimate Eden, with the Caribbean meters away. A family at Cabo San Juan del Guía also rents hammocks and campsites. Prices are uniform between the places—$5.30 if you bring your own hammock and $8 if you rent one from the hotel. Updated: May 13, 2008.

Concesión Tayrona !

(ROOM: $232 -290) The eco-huts at Cañaveral are based on traditional Tayrona architecture, but with all the modern comforts. The spa is first-rate, and the caviar massage has to be the most delicious of the treatments. The cabins at Arrecifes are cheaper but not as opulent. ($162 in the low season, $220 in the high season for 1-5 people, including breakfast). Aviatur also provides hammock spaces and campsites for travelers with simpler tastes and budgets. (Hammock $8.60 or $6 if you bring your own

Tayrona Culture

The Tayrona was an extensive pre-Columbian culture which lived in the northern part of the Sierra Nevada de Santa María, inside what is today the Natural National Park Tayrona. Subversive and hard-working people, the Tayrona gave Spaniard conquistadors a hard time when they tried to move into the territory.

There were several conflicts between various indigenous groups and the Spaniards between 1525 and 1599, and the Spaniards were forced to establish civilized relationships with these communities in order to survive. Tayronas began to network with French and English pirates and burned the city of Santa Marta several times during these years. In 1599 the governor, Juan Guiral Velón, conducted an intense military campaign and managed to capture and kill every indigenous chief, leaving the Tayrona people powerless and at the mercy of the Spaniards. Few managed to get away and their descendents, a group named Kogis, remain isolated from the world.

Nowadays there are plenty of archeological remants in the area, the biggest area being Ciudad Perdida (the Lost City). The 13 hectares of archeological evidence suggest 1500-2400 people lived in the city. Updated: Jan 15, 2008.

hammock, mosquito net included; camping $6). Calle 15, 3-20. Tel: 5-421-3848, 5-423-5655, Fax: 5-421-3840, E-mail: carlosrheebilcock@aviatur.com.co / reservasparques@aviatur.com.co, URL: www.aviatur.com. Updated: May 13, 2008.

PNN Tayrona Restaurants

All restaurants in Tayrona are associated with lodging establishments and can be pricey for budget travelers. A basic vegetable and rice plate costs $4.20, and a fish meal costs $7.40-10.50; a beer is $1.60-1.85 and water is $2.10. Many backpackers and shoe-string travelers prefer to buy supplies in Santa Marta. If you choose to do this, please pack all your trash (especially bottles, cans and bags) back out to civilization. Fresh water, which can be purified, is available. Updated: May 06, 2008.

Valledupar

Alt: 169m Pop: 348,000 City Code: 5

From Bucaramanga, the north highway continues to Bosconia (405 kilometers / 243 miles). There the road turns eastward, skirting the Sierra Nevada de Santa Marta. From a night bus the sunrise reflected off the snow peaks is spectacular. After another 89 kilometers (53 miles) the road arrives at Valledupar, the purported birthplace of Vallenato music. It is the capital of Colombia's newest department, César, which was carved out of the old Magdalena political district in 1967. This is the beginning of the Caribbean region of Colombia. The nearby Sierra Nevada de Santa Marta is home to four indigenous nations. The Valledupar region is the furthest south of Wayuu territory. This city's main square, Plaza Alfonso López, is a mango tree-lined island in a sea of wonderful colonial buildings with plaques proclaiming which historical figures of Valduparense, or Vallenato, lived within. The town has many streets with both numbers and letters, which are more like diagonal streets. This makes the city a bit confusing with its odd angles. Updated: Apr 24, 2008.

History

When Spaniard Hernando de Santana and his legions arrived here in 1550, Tupe and Chimila indigenous occupied this valley of the Río Guatapurí, or Cold Water River. The invaders called their new city Ciudad de los Santos Reyes del Valle del Cacique Upar—or, to make it short, Valle de Upar. This shortened to today's Valledupar. According to legend, the Tupe set Valledupar on fire and poisoned the water supplies in revenge for the Spaniards' ill treatment. The Virgen del Rosario miraculously resuscitated the Europeans. The settlement was refounded and the Spaniards promptly hung 15 Tupe chiefs on La Popa hill in retaliation. In 1813, María Concepción Loperena Fernández de Castro declared Valledupar's independence from Spain and sent 300 horses to Simón Bolívar. During the 1000-Day War (end of the 19th / beginning of the 20th Century), Valledupar was witness to some of the battles.

In the late 20th Century this region became a hot spot in the country's civil war, with clashes first between the ELN and government forces followed by a cleansing by paramilitaries. The departmental government still faces charges in connection with *paracos*, or paramilitaries. Updated: Apr 23, 2008.

When to Go

The rainy season lasts from February to April. The rest of the year is deliciously hot in this valley, with daytime temperatures reaching 32-36°C (90-97°F), and sometimes peaking above 40°C (104°F). Evening temperatures drop to a balmy 22-24°C (72-75°F). Updated: Apr 23, 2008.

Holidays and Festivals

Valledupar is most famous for its Vallenato Music Festival, but there are other *fiestas* where you can catch well-known groups live.

January 6 ► The city's founding. Civic ceremonies, marathon, free Vallenato concerts at Parque de la Leyenda Vallenata
April ► Vallenato Music Festival
July ► Cattle Fair
Updated: Apr 23, 2008.

Getting To and Away From Valledupar

The main bus terminal is about 3.5 kilometers (2 miles) from the center, at Carrera 18D (Avenida Simón Bolívar) and Calle 45, where the Cacique Upar monument is.
Valledupar's Aeropuerto Alfonso López Hangar is located on the road to Codazzi, south of the city. A taxi there costs $2.65. Avianca has direct flights to Bogotá ($130-204) and Aires has flights to Barranquilla ($129). Updated: Apr 23, 2008.

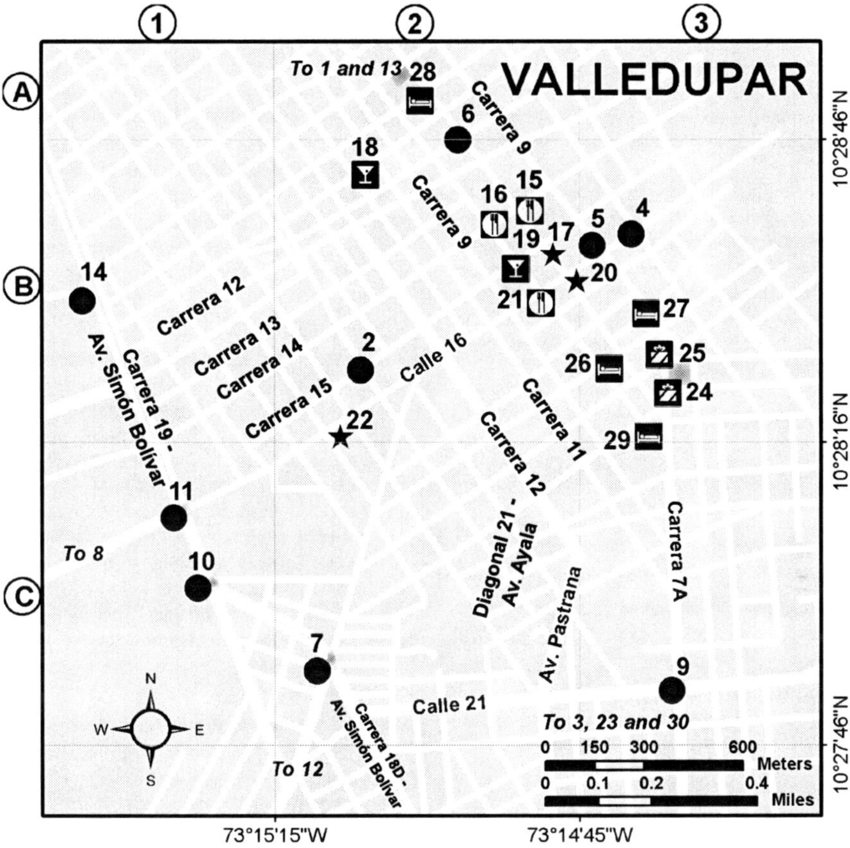

Activity ●
1 Balneario Hurtado A3
2 Biblioteca Péblica Departamental C4
3 Cacique Upar G5
4 Casa de la Cultura C5
5 Cine Royal C4
6 El Viajero B4
7 Folclor Vallenato D4
8 Guajira Cantos del Viento E1
9 Hernando de Sanatana D5
10 Los Gallos D3
11 María Mulata D3
12 Obelisco F2
13 Pedazo de Acordeón A2
14 Poporos C3

Eating
15 Panadería Arabe C4
16 Restaurante Muralla China C4
17 Restaurante Nandoburguer C4

Nightlife
18 Bartolomé C4
19 Café de las Madres C4

Service ★
20 Banco Colombia C4
21 Banco de la Repéblica C4
22 Coordinadora de Turismo, Agustina Alvarez López C4
23 Hospital Eduardo Arredond Daza G4

Shopping
24 Artesanías Ebratt C5
25 Asociación de Artesanos de Valledupar C5

Sleeping
26 Hotel Los Cardones C5
27 Hotel Vajamar C5
28 Jerusalem Express B4
29 Residencias Kennedy C5

Transportation
30 Bus Station G5

Getting Around

Taxis in Valledupar are unmetered and you negotiate prices; a trip from the bus terminal to downtown is $1.60. City buses are $0.45 a trip but are scarce on Sundays. For $0.50 you can catch a ride on the back of a motorcycle.

Bus companies that do trips to other Colombian cities are Cootracegua, Costa Line, Copetrán, Cootragua, Cootaxi, Berlinas, Libertadores and Cootracosta. Cootracegua has the largest variety of destinations, but be sure to shop around as fares and trip time can vary from company to company. Updated: Apr 23, 2008.

From Valledupar

Arrive	Departure	Time	Price
Maicao	Hourly 4:45 a.m.-2:45 p.m.	4 hours	$11
Riohacha	8:15 a.m.	4 hours	$11
El Banco	3 a.m.-12:30 p.m.	4.5 hours	$13
Mompós	5:30 a.m., 9:45 a.m.	4.5 hours	$13
Santa Marta	3 a.m.-4 p.m.	3-4 hours	$13
Barranquilla	Hourly 3 a.m.-6 p.m.	4 hours	$11 - 13
Cartagena	Hourly 4 a.m.-6 p.m.	7 hours	$21
Bucaramanga	4 a.m.-9:45 a.m.	8-9 hours	$35 -$37
Cúcuta	8:30 a.m.	14 hours	$40
Bogotá	1-8:30 p.m.	16 hours	$61

Safety in Valledupar

Take care at night, especially after 9 p.m., even in the center of the city's buzzing nightlife. Locals warn about going to Parque de la Leyenda Vallenata, the University and Balneario Hurtado at odd hours—go when there are plenty of people, such as late afternoons.

The Sierra Nevada de Santa Marta is closed to any independent trekking, due in part to the three indigenous nations' wishes (Arhuaco, Kogui and Arzario), since it is sacred land to them. Much of the mountain range is also a "hot zone" with coca cultivation and cocaine processing labs, plus the perseverance of guerrilla and paramilitary forces. On this side of the Sierra you can visit Pueblo Bello and Nabusimake, and on the Caribbean side, Ciudad Perdida—these last two only with guides. Dengue fever has occasionally been reported in Valledupar. Updated: Apr 23, 2008.

Valledupar Services

You can pick up information from the Coordinadora de Turismo, Agustina Álvarez López, on the fourth floor of the Gobernación del César (Monday-Friday 9 a.m.-noon, 3-5 p.m. Calle 16 and Carrera 13. Tel: 5-574-3860, URL: www.valledupar.gob.co). Maps of the city are very difficult to come by. For tourist card or visa extensions, go to the Extranjería office of DAS (Monday-Friday 7:30 a.m.-noon, 2-6 p.m. Carrera 11A, 15-42, Tel: 5-574-2833). However, you will receive only 30 more days, effective from the day of renewal.

Money

Many of Valledupar's banks have branches throughout the city. Below are just the principal locations of a few banks.

Bancolombia—Changes American Express travelers checks; ATM: MasterCard, Visa, Cirrus, American Express. Carrera 9, near Calle 16.

Banco Popular—ATM: ATH, Visa, Plus, MasterCard, Cirrus. Calle 16 8-20.

Banco de Bogotá—ATM: ATH, Visa, Plus, MasterCard, Cirrus. Calle 16 7-46.

Most exchange houses deal only in bank check cashing, but not travelers checks. One exception is Cambios y Negocios, which exchanges cash dollars and bolívares fuertes. Monday-Saturday 8 a.m.-noon, 2-6 p.m. Calle 16, 17-67. Giros y Finanzas is the Western Union agent. Diagonal 16, 17-67, inside Supertiendas Olímpicas.

Keeping in Touch

Edetel is your telecommunications stop—local and national calls cost $0.10 per minute with international calls from $0.25 per minute; internet is $0.75 per hour. Monday-Friday 8 a.m.-noon, 2-6 p.m., Saturday 9 a.m.-noon. Calle 15 10-17. Shops and phone stands charge $0.10-0.15 per minute for local or national calls. The going price for internet is $0.80 per hour, but it appears no one has Skype. There is a cluster of internet cafés charging as little as $0.50 per hour on Calle 16B, between Carreras 9 and 10.

Medical

Valledupar's public health facility is Hospital Eduardo Arredondo Daza, on Carrera 20, 43-63, Tel: 5-582-6784. There are other medical facilities and pharmacies on Calle 16, between Carreras 15 and 18. More pharmacies are on Carrera 7, between Calles 16 and 17.

Camera

There are several camera shops that carry digital cameras and accessories. Batteries and film are on Calles 16 and 16A, between Carreras 7 and 8. No one, however, can repair malfunctioning apparatus.

Religion

Valledupar has a small Muslim community that meets to worship, but no mosque. Updated: Jun 09, 2008.

Shopping

Asociación de Artesanos de Valledupar
More than two dozen local artisan stalls line the one-story, mall-like Asociación de Artesanos de Valledupar. Handmade wares include molded white hats of the Arhuaco indigenous community of the Sierra Nevada de Santa Marta, densely woven bags and of the Wayuu of the Guajira, black and white *sombreros de paja* (straw hats), the national symbol of Colombia, and Vallenato kitsch. You can even form your own Vallenato band here, with small accordions, modern caja drums and *guacharaca* (scraper). Calle 16, 7-32. Updated: Apr 23, 2008.

Artesanías Ebratt
The Ebratt family has been creating arts and crafts for at least three generations as a member of the Asociación de Artesanos de Valledupar. One son, Ciro, crafts Vallenato and other knickknacks. Another son paints brilliant canvasses depicting the culture and life of the town. Doña Esperanza, the mother, gives new life to old treadle sewing machines and other discarded items by turning them into works of art. The father is a cabinetmaker. The family also carries Arhuaco hats and bags, *chinchorros* (hammocks) and other craftworks. Calle 16, 7-32, local 13. Cell: 315-719-0101, 310-368-7411. Updated: Apr 23, 2008.

Panadería Árabe
Panadería Árabe is like walking into a neighborhood Mediterranean shop. It may call itself a bakery, and sure, there's pita bread and baklava, but that's only the beginning. The shelves are full of everything a native Mediterranean might miss from home, inluding green olives, artichoke hearts, stuffed eggplant, couscous, pickled vegetables, halvah and olive oil. Turkish candies, dried dates and apricots, and natural pistachios round out the selection. Cra 9 14-94. Tel: 5-570-8465. Updated: Apr 23, 2008.

Things to See and Do

Visitors arriving in the cradle of Vallenato music in other times than when the festival takes place, have the chance to experience Valledupar for what it truly is—a small town with deep artistic roots. You can visit a music school, study at one or drop by one of the city's several cultural centers. Wander the streets and take in the colonial architecture of the center and the dozen monuments. To cool off after a day of exploration, dip into the cold waters of Balneario Hurtado. The Sierra Nevada de Santa Marta on the western horizon is home to four indigenous nations. You can visit the Arhuaco villages of Pueblo Bello and Nabusimake. Updated: Dec 19, 2007.

The Monuments of Valledupar

A dozen public monuments pay tribute to Valledupar's history and culture. These statues are mostly located on roundabouts on the city's major thoroughfares. Negotiate with a taxi to take you to all the monuments in one trip, or walk to each. Be careful in the afternoon heat and sun, especially if walking. Updated: Apr 23, 2008.

Balneario Hurtado

When Valledupar's heat gets to be a bit much, do as the locals do—head for Balneario Hurtado. Here the Río Guatapurí's cool waters pool along the banks. Young men body surf the few mild rapids rushing by the boulders. Families come to swim, sit at a table or sling a hammock between the trees. There's more than a kilometer of shore to spread out, though there's no guarantee you'll be able to avoid the crowds. There are no bathrooms or changing facilities. The party goes on well into the night any day of the week, though locals warn the area can be unsafe after dark. Watch for bottlecaps and glass along the banks. North edge of the city at the Río Guatapurí. Take any van that says "Universidad," which is next door to the Balneario ($0.45). The last bus back to town is at 6 p.m. After the last bus, hail a taxi ($2.65). Updated: Apr 23, 2008.

The Cultural Centers of Valledupar

Culture in Valledupar isn't just limited to Vallenato music. Several centers provide free exhibits, literary readings and concerts:

Casa de la Cultura—Calle 16A and Carrera 6.

Banco de la República—Carrera 9, 16-13.

Biblioteca Pública Departamental Rafael Carrillo Lúquez—Calle 15 and Carrera 14.

If you are in the mood for a movie, Cine Royal shows the latest national and international films. On Thursday evenings, tickets are two-for-one. Daily 4 p.m., 7 p.m., 9 p.m. Calle 16, across from the Banco de la República. Updated: Apr 23, 2008.

Vallenato Music Schools

Vallenato music isn't confined to festival time in April. You'll hear Vallenato strains out of stereos and from the locals themselves at any time of the year. To catch the next generation learning the trade, stop by some morning or evening to one of the local music schools, such as Escuela Talento Vallenato Rafael Escalo (Cra 5, 16-50) or the famous Academia Andrés "Turco" Gil (Calle 31, 4-265, Tel: 5-582-4274). You can also sign up for classes if you would like to study the intricacies of this genre. Check a school's policies on visits before going; the schools listed here allow visitors. Updated: Apr 23, 2008.

Valledupar Lodging

Hotels in Valledupar tend to be a bit expensive. Mid-range options are fairly basic and have an impersonal feel. Upper-priced choices generally are excellent. Hotels and apartment-hotels along Calle 19 and near the bus terminal on Carrera 18D (Avenida Bolívar) guarantee a family atmosphere. Make reservations as early as December or January if you plan to visit during the April Vallenato Music Festival. Updated: Dec 19, 2007.

Residencias Kennedy

(ROOM: $4-6) Residencias Kennedy is a no-frills inn—no plants surround the brick-tile courtyard and there are no TVs in the rooms. The 17 rooms only have a double bed and night table with a ceiling fan to keep you cool. All rooms have windows. The elderly owner, doña Raquel, and her assistant, Jairo, keep it relatively clean. Doña Raquel is a bit hard-of-hearing so she may take a while to answer the door. You can ask to use the laundry basin. Calle 19, 9-102. Updated: Apr 23, 2008.

Hotel Los Cardones

(ROOM: $11-19) Hotel Los Cardones' quarters surround a back courtyard. The hotel has a restaurant and sitting room at the front of the building. Some rooms have air conditioning, others have more economical fans. All rooms have cold-water baths and cable TV. The rooms are a bit cramped with two to four beds each. If you want a room with only one bed, call ahead and the family will arrange it. Calle 17, 9-74. Tel: 5-574-3023, Fax: 5-574-2322. Updated: Apr 23, 2008.

Hotel Vajamar !

(ROOM: $53-86) One of Valledupar's finest hotels, this establishment has 20 years experience in providing comfortable, tastefully decorated rooms to the discerning traveler. Some of the suites have views over the stunning Sierra Nevada de Santa Marta, and a few have balconies where you can enjoy a meal under the moon. The bathrooms are immaculate and have hot water. The pool out back is free to guests, but nonguests must pay. A Sunday BBQ with free use of the pool is open to all. Room prices include tax and insurance, plus an American breakfast buffet. Cra 7, 16A-30. Tel: 5-574-3939, 5-580-5380, Fax: 5-574-4819, E-mail: hvajamar@tierra.com, URL: www.valledupar.com/hotelvajamar. Updated: Apr 23, 2008.

Valledupar Restaurants

A small Arabic community is quite culinarily active in Valledupar and sells Arabic food in both restaurants and shops. Chinese food is also available in the city. Otherwise, look forward to more fine Colombian cooking and rotisserie chicken. Comidas corrientes run to $1.80-3.20. Some very expensive gourmet and fusion-cuisine restaurants are on Carrera 9, especially between Calles 9 and 11.

Monuments	Description	Address
Revolución en Marcha	By Rodrigo Arenas Betancourt.	Plaza Alfonso López.
El Viajero	A traveller resting from his long journey, with his bag at his feet.	Carrera 9 and Calle 12.
Hernando de Sanatana	Homage to Valledupar's founder.	Calle 21 and Carrera 7A.
Cacique Upar	The Tupe leader for whom the town is named.	Avenida Guatapurí / Calle 44 and Avenida Simón Bolívar / Carrera 18D, in front of the bus terminal.
Obelisco	A 30-meter (100-foot) tall obelisk designed by architect Carlos García in homage to life.	Avenida Badillo / Calle 44, with Avenida Villa Olímpica / Carrera 31 and Avenida Ayala / Diagonal 21.
María Mulata	This representation of a blackbird was created by Enrique Grau for the 450th anniversary of Valledupar's founding.	Avenida Pedro Castro Monsalvo / Calle 16 and Carrera 19.
Los Gallos	Representing the strong relationship between cock fighting and Vallenato music.	Carrera 19.
Folclor Vallenato	Depicting a traditional Vallenato trio.	Diagonal 21
Poporos	To the three principle indigenous nations of the Sierra Nevada de Santa Marta, the Arhuaco, Kogui and Arzario, by Jorge Maestre.	Avenida de la Juventud, by the Coliseo del Festival.
Pedazo de Acordeón	By Gabriel Betrán, in memory of accordian master Alejandro Durán Díaz.	Calle 1 and Carrera 9, Parque de la Leyenda Vallenata.
La Sirena	Recounts the legend of a young woman who dared taboos and swam in the Río Guatapurí on Good Friday.	Balneario Hurtado.

The city's central market, Galería Popular, bustles from 6 a.m. to 4 p.m. (between Carreras 7 and 7A, Calles 18A and 18B). The public market is at Carrera 12 and Calle 21. An Olímpica supermarket is conveniently in the heart of the city. Monday-Saturday 7:30 a.m.-10 p.m., Sunday and holidays 9 a.m.-9 p.m. Carrera 9 and Calle 14.

Jerusalem Express

(ENTREES: $1.55-5.30) At Jerusalem Express, Lebanese-born Ibraham and his Colombian wife have introduced valduparenses to healthy Middle Eastern cuisine. They prepare quibbes, fatayer (meat or chicken turnovers), malfuf (stuffed cabbage leaves), parra (stuffed grape leaves), stuffed eggplant, cucumber or sweet pepper and beef or chicken shwarma. There's plenty on the menu for vegetarians as well, such as spinach fatayer, garbanzo or eggplant tahini and falafel shwarma. If you can't make up your mind, just order the combo plate. The final touch is a small bite of an Arabian dessert. Open daily 4:30-11 p.m. Cra 9, 9-30. Tel: 5-573-4288 / 7217. Updated: Apr 23, 2008.

Restaurante Nandoburguer

(ENTREES: $2.65-2.90) Despite the name, Restaurante Nandoburguer is much more well-known for its hearty home-cooked meals than for its burgers. With two rooms of indoor seating and a few tables on the front patio, the waiters are kept busy attending to the crowd. At very busy times, like Sunday afternoons, be prepared to display the patience of a saint. The comida corriente comes with over a half-dozen choices for the main course. Open daily 9 a.m.-9 p.m. Cra 9, 16B-48. Updated: Apr 23, 2008.

Restaurante Muralla China

(ENTREES: $4-14) Valledupar's resident Chinese restaurant, Muralla China, has more than 80 Chinese dishes and a few international ones. Start off your meal with egg rolls or a seafood cocktail before moving on to a classic Chinese plate, in either half or full order. Mains include chow fan (fried rice), chop suey, chow mein or lo mein prepared with chicken, beef or seafood. Vegetarian options are available as well. Open daily 11 a.m.-10 p.m. Cra 9, 14-30. Tel: 5-580-0909 / 0555 / 0338. Updated: Apr 23, 2008.

Café de las Madres !

Valduparenses head to Café de las Madres, tucked behind Parque de las Madres, when the setting sun paints the sky. The wrought-iron garden tables fill quickly with colleagues and couples meeting to have an Atardecer Vallenato (cappuccino and whiskey) or one of the creative coffee shakes, with or without a kick. Other end-of-day beverages include liquored coffees, cocktails, wine, beer and whiskey or vodka. For lovebirds, there's a special cappuccino served in vertically nestling cups, with a card and gift. Don't wait until evening to come—escape the day's heat with an iced coffee or a cool glass of white wine. Café de las Madres serves only organically grown Sierra Nevada coffee. Open Monday-Saturday 8 a.m.-11 p.m. Cra 9 and Calle 15, Parque de las Madres. Cel: 300-293-5493. Updated: Apr 23, 2008.

Valledupar Nightlife

Despite being the home of Vallenato music, very few nightclubs feature live Vallenato bands—or live music at all, for that matter. Most establishments play prerecorded music, and Vallenato is the most common, of course. As in many towns in Colombia, clubs are only open on weekends. The most common beverages are beer, aguardiente and whiskey, the liquor associated with Vallenato music. Updated: Dec 19, 2007.

Bartolomé

You don't have to come to Valledupar in April to catch live Vallenato music. During the off season Bartolomé is one of the only places in town where you can catch bands playing those down-to-earth melodies. Join the crowd by downing some *traguitos* (shots) and singing along about life and love under the roof of this open-sided nightclub. Bathed by the nocturnal breeze and the community vibes, you'll quickly discover why this music is so beloved. Open only Friday and Saturday nights. Cra 11 and Calle 13A. Apr 23, 2008.

Pueblo Bello

Alt:1,200m Pop: 17,000 City Code: 5

The village of Pueblo Bello is in the Sierra Nevada de Santa Marta, on the edge of Arhuaco territory. From here an arduous road winds up to Nabusimake (San Sebastián), a ceremonial center of this native nation. You must get permission to enter Nabusimake upon arrival or in Pueblo Bello. The indigenous community will outline where you may hike in the Sierra Nevada and assign you a guide. The land of these mountains is stunning and undisturbed, with waterfalls and good birdwatching. The Arhuaco will also arrange housing in a communal center or may give you permission to camp. Updated: May 20, 2008.

San Andrés, Providencia and Santa Catalina Islands

The Colombian islands of San Andrés, Providencia and Santa Catalina are located 800 kilometers from Cartagena and a mere 290 kilometers from Nicaragua, deep in the southern Caribbean. The department of San Andrés consists of three major islands, five atolls and several coral banks and spans a total land area of 57 kilometers (36 miles) squared.

The islands offer something for everyone from all manner of aquatic sports to lounging and kicking back on a pristine beach, exploring pirate and puritan heritage, hiking through Providencia's gnarled volcanic hills, or hitting the clubs of San Andrés after hours of early evening retail therapy in one of the many duty-free boutiques. Updated: Oct 18, 2007.

History

The islands were used as fishing grounds and minor settlements for Miskito Indians until the 17th Century. None of this history remains, since in 1620 Europeans arrived in the form of Puritans looking to create a religious society. After a decade of Puritan control, the society faltered and became a major base for slavery and privateering. This opened the islands up to other opportunists of the time, namely the pirate Henry Morgan who used Providencia as his base for years. He planned and launched the sacking of Panama from here.

Given the islands' closeness to Spanish territories in South America, they became Spanish possessions, but remained for the most part ignored by their new lords. With the separation of Gran Colombia from Spain and Colombia's subsequent independence, San Andrés, Providencia and Santa Catalina came with the package.

Despite claims by Nicaragua to the International Court of Justice claiming sovereignty, the islands remain Colombian territory. In the 1950s the Colombian Government launched an intensive "Colombianization" of the islands to promote their growth, and declared them a free-trade zone.

As a result, San Andrés has become the package holiday and weekend destination of choice for Colombians from all walks of life. Providencia and Santa Catalina, declared national parks, are protected Caribbean marvels. Updated: Oct 18, 2007.

When to Go

The islands are blessed with fine Caribbean weather year-round, although San Andrés suffers more from hurricanes than Providencia due to favorable currents protecting the smaller island. Hurricane season causes heavy rains, winds and overcast skies from late September to early December.

Accommodation rates also fluctuate throughout the year depending on holidays and weather patterns. High season goes from late December to late January and Easter Week. Mid-season lasts from mid-June to mid-August. Low season is from the end of January to mid-June (except Easter Week) and mid-August to mid-December. Updated: Oct 18, 2007.

Things to See and Do

Without a doubt, scuba diving is the most impressive activity on the islands. The water is warm, clear and bursting with life. For anyone not certified, PADI certification is not expensive. Or you can stick with snorkeling, an easy alternative.

Johnny Cay is the most popular day trip from San Andrés. A 20-minute boat ride from the island, this stunning palm-lined retreat is ideal for a day at the beach. Take water and plenty of sunscreen.

Head to South West Bay on Providencia one Saturday to see the horse races. Two horses are pitched against each other in a competition that extends the length of the beach. Millions of pesos change hands in bets and the atmosphere is nothing short of electric. Updated: Oct 18, 2007.

San Andrés, Providencia & Santa Catalina Lodging

Most accommodation options on the islands can be arranged from the mainland, since most hotels on San Andrés are parts of international chains. They range from ultra exclusive five-star resorts to relics of another era of money laundering and narco-influenced extravagance. Take a look at the gaudy Sunrise Hotel, which resembles a dam more than a hotel.

The opposite is true on Providencia, where the islanders are intent on protecting their heritage and cultural identity. Most hotels are small, family-run enterprises with few rooms. International hotel chain Decameron has affiliated itself with five hotels on the island, which ensures that the level of quality reaches international standards. Updated: Oct 18, 2007.

San Andrés Island

San Andrés is a small island in the Caribbean, less than 100 miles off the coast of Central America. The island has an interesting history, which includes pirates and legends of lost treasures. The shopping on San Andrés is particularly good, as the town itself is considered a duty-free zone, so you don't have to pay taxes on anything you buy. There are good beaches and good scuba diving too.

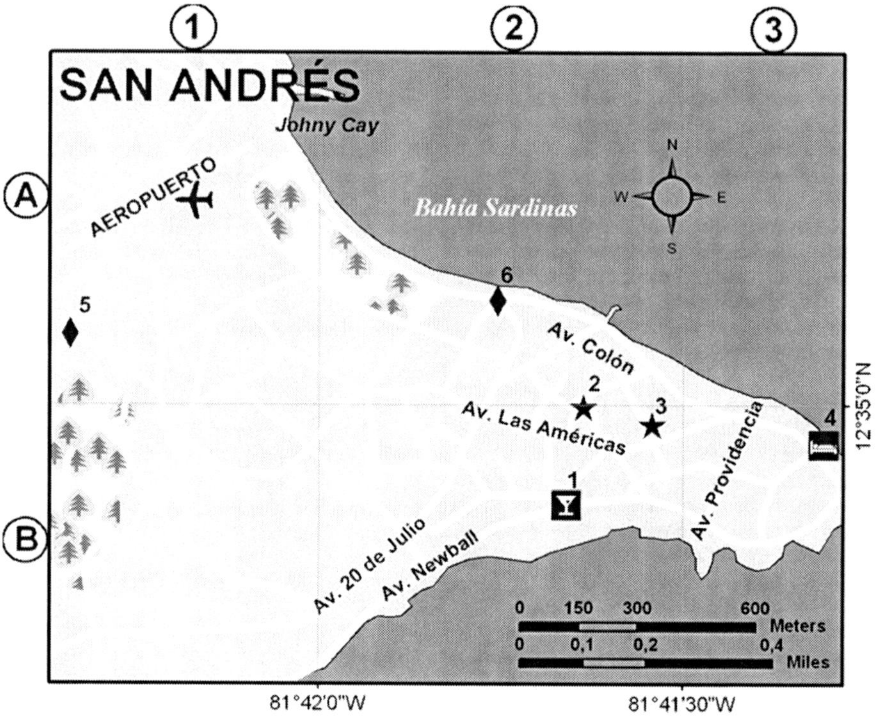

Nightlife
1 Blue Deep Discotheque C2
Service
2 Banco Colombia C2
3 Banco de Bogotá C2
Sleeping
4 Tres Casitas Apartahotel C3
Tour
5 Over Receptour B1
6 Viajes Portofino B2

San Andrés is a growing resort spot, popular with South American tourists, although for the most part North Americans have yet to discover it. The island is only about 44 square kilometers in size. Larger resorts, where most visitors stay, are scattered around the island, and there is a town at the north end with lower-budget accommodations.

There are some interesting activities for those wishing to do something besides lounge around on the beach all day. On a San Andrés island tour you'll visit the sea, traditional architecture, a restored home, and some cheesy pirates at Morgan's Cave. The tour includes snorkeling at West View and a stop at the Blowing Hole, a natural phenomenon which draws many visitors. Updated: Mar 06, 2007.

History

The first inhabitants of these Caribbean islands were Miskito Indians from the coast of Nicaragua. Later discovered by the English, the islands were nevertheless settled by the Spanish. The islands changed hands between the two powers several times during the 17th and 18th Centuries. In 1793 England formally recognized Spain's claim.

The legendary privateer Sir Henry Morgan used these islands as bases. On San Andrés you can visit Morgan's Cave, a natural cave formation where Morgan allegedly stashed treasures. As with most places once frequented by pirates, the islanders tell tales of lost loot but no one ever seems to find any.
At various times, the islands have been under British, Spanish and Dutch control, which resulted in a blend of languages and cultures. Spanish is most commonly spoken,

followed by English. Most of the native islanders speak a mixture of the two, a sort of Caribbeanized-Spanglish incomprehensible to outsiders, but they can speak standard Spanish if they wish to. Different groups of immigrants have come to the islands over the years, including American missionaries, Chinese, Arabs and mainland Colombians.

Traditional island homes are sturdy, airy, wooden structures with broad porches and old-fashioned wooden shutters. There are relatively few nowadays, however, as most residents live in North End or in squat, cement homes built in the last fifty years. One of the best places to see traditional island architecture is at the Island House Museum.

Colombia claimed the islands in 1822 when it gained independence. The United Provinces of Central America (1823-1840) and Nicaragua disputed the claim, although neither had the military to challenge Colombia. Nicaragua has never given up, however, and as recently as 2001 filed a claim with the International Court of Justice to resolve the matter. Colombia has responded by establishing military bases on the islands, although no one expects any shooting wars anytime soon. There is also a small movement of islanders seeking independence from Colombia. Updated: Nov 16, 2006.

When to Go

San Andrés has a year-round Caribbean climate oscillating between 26º and 29ºC (79º-84ºF). The island has two seasons, wet and dry. While the dry season (January-April) can last up to five months, it invariably ends with the commencement of the hurricane season in late September. From September to December it rains more, although rains only last 10-20 minutes before the sun comes back out.

High season is December to January and Easter weekend, when all accommodations and flights will increase in cost.

Holidays and Festivals

Month	Event
July	**20- Fiesta Patria.** Parades span the island and celebrate the culture of the Archipiélago.
August	**7- Fiesta Patria.** Parades and expositions of local color and gastronomy in the San Luis district.
October	**12- Día de La Raza.** Cultural activities displaying riches of the island.
November	**30- Fiestas Patronales de San Andrés.** Celebrations in honour of the island's patron Saint.

Updated: Oct 19, 2007.

Getting To and Away From San Andrés

There are flights from most major Colombian cities to San Andrés with Aero República, Avianca and Satena, from Panama City via Bogotá or direct from San José, Costa Rica (45 minutes). Prices and numbers of flights vary according to season and demand. Usually you can get from most major cities, including Bogotá, Barranquilla, Cali, Medellín, and Cartagena, on a direct flight. If flights are overbooked you'll likely have to connect in either Bogotá or Cartagena.

The International Airport Gustavo Rojas Pinilla is located at the north end of San Andrés, close to the major resorts.

A tourist card for the island is required and can be purchased upon check-in in mainland Colombia or upon arrival in San Andrés. Currently it costs $10 and must be presented at your departure from the island. Updated: Oct 19, 2007.

Getting Around

Taxis are outrageously overpriced—the three-minute journey from the airport to a downtown hotel usually costs $5. It is recommended that you seek alternative forms of transport. Renting a moped or a golf cart is a good alternative; there are dozens of shops around San Andrés.

If you are not pushed for time and want to travel with the locals, then hop on any bus on the coastal road. You'll not get lost since the road swings around the exterior of the island. Updated: Oct 19, 2007.

Safety in San Andrés

Crime is incredibly low on San Andrés. The occasional bag snatching is inevitable but hardly the norm, and beyond that you should feel very at ease. You are advised not to take valuables to the beach and to make full use of hotel safes. Updated: Oct 18, 2007.

San Andrés Services

Tourism Office

There are no tourist offices in the San Andrés airport. Most hotels are equipped to answer any queries and further information can be found at www.sanandres.gov.co.

Money

Banks in San Andrés are open Monday to Thursday 8:00-11:30 a.m. and 2-4 p.m. On Friday, the hours are the same but they stay open until 4:30 p.m. Most of the banks listed have ATMs that accept international cards.

Bancafe—Av. Costa Rica, Centro Comercial San Andrés L-10, Tel: 8-512-5575.
Banco Agrario—Av. 20 de Julio 3-76, Tel: 8-512-8332.
Banco AV Villas—Av. Providencia 1-85, Tel: 8-512-7828.
Banco de Bogotá—Av. Colón 2-156, Tel: 8-512-4173.
Banco Caja Social de Colombia—Av. Las Américas. Tel: 8-512-8791.
Banco Comercial y de Ahorros—Av. Providencia Edificio Leda 2-52, Tel: 8-512-7835.
Banco Davivienda—Av. Duarte Blum 1-110 / Av. Costa Rica 3-19, Tel: 8-512-7004 / 3753.
Banco de Occidente—Av. Providencia 2-47, Tel: 8-512-3553.
Banco Granahorrar—Av. las Américas 2-419, 2-421, Tel: 8-512-4055.
Bancolombia—Av. Atlántico 1A-35 P-1, Tel: 8-512-4195.
Banco Popular—Av. las Américas 2A-69, Tel: 8-512-3621.

Money Exchanges:
Cambios Country S.A—Av. Providencia 1A-48 L–112 Edificio Leda, Tel: 8-512-4175, URL: www.macrofinanciera.com.
Titán Intercontinental S.A.—Av. Providencia 1A-48, L-105 Edificio Leda, Tel: 8-512-6091.
Cambios y Capitales S.A.—Carrera 2, 1-35, L-118 Centro Comercial New Point Plaza, Tel: 8-512 1804.
Giros and Finanzas CFC S.A. (Western Union)—Centro Comercial San Andrés L-12, URL: www.girosyfinanzas.com.
Cambiamos S.A. (MoneyGram)— Av. Costa Rica, 3-19, Tel: 8-512-3757.

Keeping in Touch

There are dozens of internet cafés and international call centers downtown.

Medical

Hospital Timothy Britton is the main hospital on the island. It includes a decompression chamber for scuba diving problems. Av. Colombia Sarie Bay, Tel: 8-512-7392, Fax: 8-512-3443.

Other hospitals and clinics:
Hospital VillaReal—Barrio Obrero, Tel: 8-512-4385.
Hospital Seguro Social—Av. Colombia Sarie Bay, Tel: 8-512-6965.
Centro de Salud San Luis—San Luis, Tel: 8-513-2096.
Centro de Salud La Loma—La Loma, Tel: 8-513-2769.

There are pharmacies on most streets in downtown San Andrés.

Religious Services

Most islanders are Baptists, but alternative options can be found, including the following: Catholic, Adventist, Spanish Baptist, Christian Missionary, Muslim and Jehovah's Witness. For the most part, services are held in the local language.

Laundry

There are very few laundry facilities, but you can expect to find someone in your hotel offering the service.

Shopping

In an attempt at "Colombianization," the Colombian government declared San Andrés a tax-free zone. Now, along with the sea and stretches of white sand beaches, the island is a shopping destination as well.

Consumer electronics are few, although with some searching you can bargain for knock -off mp3 players and digital cameras. Large-screen TVs are available in abundance. Respectful bargaining is expected and very few items actually possess a price tag.

The real winners are those shopping for American clothes, perfumes, sunglasses, watches and alcohol. The new pedestrianized area a block from the beach in San Andrés is crammed with exclusive boutiques stocking all of these products in deliciously air-conditioned shops.

Colombians come here to buy everything from kitchen appliances to bed linens. Do not be surprised to see people wandering in and out of these stores dressed in beachwear—they may just be browsing to get out of the heat for a while.

Perfume: The perfumes come in two categories—genuine and knock-off. The vendors are quite candid about what's real and what's imitation. Ask around to make sure you're getting the real deal (or the fake deal, if that's what you're looking for).

Alcohol: If you buy alcohol, be sure you know how much you can bring back to your home country. Salespeople in some of the better stores may be aware of these limitations. Also, be sure to check out some local Colombian hooch—they make fine rums and coffee liqueurs in Colombia. The better shops will package your purchase in easy-to-carry boxes if you buy more than one bottle.

Chocolate: If you buy chocolate, be sure you get it from one of the air-conditioned stores. Otherwise it may have melted more than a few times.

Other items: There are other things for sale, such as designer clothing, scuba and snorkeling gear, a wide variety of flip-flops, water shoes and luggage. Updated: Oct 18, 2007.

Things to See and Do

Most visitors to San Andrés come to relax on white-sand beaches and to drink piña coladas beside a hotel pool. That's all well and good, but there is much more to this tiny island. Once you're done tanning and scanning, you might want to check out some of the following activities.

San Andrés is known for shopping. The best shopping can be found in the commercial district of the town of San Andrés, known to locals as North End.

Snorkelers will have many spots to choose from. Nearby Aquarium Island is a favorite among locals and tourists alike, but bring your own gear and avoid it on weekends.

An island tour is a good investment because it will take you to some of the best spots all at once. A popular stop on the island tour is the Casa Museo Isleña, or Island House Museum, a restored traditional home. No island tour is complete without a visit to the Blowing Hole, a somewhat bizarre tourist attraction which features a natural hole in the ground, out of which, occasionally, a strong puff of air bursts.

Scuba divers won't want to miss the chance to jump into the warm Caribbean and hit some local hot spots. One of the easiest and best dive sites is the sunken freighter The Blue Diamond, resting in about 12 meters (40 feet) of water off the island's eastern shore. Updated: Oct 29, 2007.

La Loma

La Loma is the central hill of the island, and many San Andrés island tours will take you there. A hotel on La Loma has the best views–you can see the beautiful Caribbean, known for its seven shades of blue and green, some mangrove swamps and the city of San Andrés at the north end. Nearby are several older homes in the traditional island architecture—wooden houses, simply framed and airy, with wooden shutters. Also on the hill is the Emanuel Baptist Church, which dates back roughly 160 years; it was founded in 1844 by evangelical missionaries from the southern United States. La Loma is home to most of the oldest island families. Updated: Oct 29, 2007.

The Blowing Hole

Only on a small Caribbean island in the middle of the ocean could a hole in the ground which occasionally blows a strong puff of air be a major tourist attraction.

There is a rocky patch of land on the southern end of the island, about ten meters from the ocean. On this patch of land there is a small hole in the ground with a diameter a little larger than a basketball. The hole is connected underground to the rocky shore. Every few minutes a wave hits the shore just right, pushing a strong draft of warm air through the tunnel and out of the hole, where there is usually a family of tourists waiting. The puff is actually quite impressive—it hits you with the force of about 50 hair dryers for a brief moment. Occasionally tides, waves and other conditions are just right, and a geyser of water will erupt from the hole (although this is uncommon).

The Blowing Hole is a popular stop on the island tour, and there are plenty of vendors on sight willing to sell you a beer, a T-shirt, a necklace, a pretty conch shell or anything else a tourist could want. The vendors aren't aggressive and are even happy to tell you just where to stand or to snap your photo when the blast of air hits your face. They seem very proud of the Blowing Hole and are more than willing to share with guests. There is no admission cost, and it is best seen as part of a larger island tour. Updated: Oct 29, 2007.

West View

West View, a short pier into the ocean, is included on most island tours. Tourists who want to stay dry feed the fish while other tourists snorkel around in the water, watching the fish eat. Everybody wins! A few slices of bread are included in the entrance fee. There is some underwater apparatus here as well—a large glass bubble you put over your head to walk around on the sea floor while a hose brings you air, similar to scuba for those who aren't certified. The water is shallow and warm, and the staff is friendly. Updated: Mar 06, 2007.

Casa Isleña Museum

This relatively new museum is a restored home, an example of traditional functional island architecture. It is decorated as it would have been decades ago, with family portraits on the walls. There is a separate kitchen and bathroom, which the islanders used to have long ago. The museum is a popular tour stop, and the place is either deserted or packed with tourists. Occasionally, young girls will start off the tour with a traditional dance. The museum boasts an ocean view and makes for a pleasant, informative visit. Av. Circunvalar, Kilometer 5. Tel: 8-512-3419. Updated: Oct 29, 2007.

Morgan's Cave/Pirate Museum

Shiver me timbers! Pirate buffs won't want to miss Morgan's Cave, believed to once have been a hiding place for pirate loot. Locals have turned this unassuming hole in the ground into one of San Andrés' main tourist attractions.

A visit starts with a trip to a small museum where a Halloween pirate displays an impressive collection of fake skulls, fake guns, old treasure-chest looking trunks, nylon pirate flags and plastic swords. Get your picture taken with the clothing-store mannequin dressed in traditional, stereotypical pirate garb. In the back of the pirate museum you'll find the "Coconut Museum," easy to miss if you're not looking for it. Next it's on to the little art gallery, a squat building notable for the number of old rum bottles built into the walls. Pirate architecture, likely—what else would a pirate build a house out of except rum bottles? The paintings feature mostly seascapes. No parrots or cannons or skulls, unfortunately.

Once you've hit the museum and the art gallery, you get to see the cave itself. According to local legend, infamous privateer Sir Henry Morgan used the cave as a place to stash stolen loot. It's a bit of a disappointment, especially if you're expecting skeletons or cannons scattered around, but it is a lovely natural cave full of fresh water. You can only descend a few feet into the cave before the water blocks your passage, and according to the pirate-guide it's quite deep. There is an old cannon mounted on concrete nearby.

There are a couple of shops near Morgan's Cave where you can get a snack or a drink (yes, you can get rum). The usual necklace vendors are there as well. One of the shops is decorated with hanging sea-turtle shells, old lanterns and a battered microscope.

The whole complex is silly fun, and just a wink away from tongue-in-cheek. You won't learn any more about real pirate lore than you would from a comic-book version of Treasure Island, but that's the fun in it. Av. Circunvalar, Kilometer 8. Tel: 8-512-2316. Updated: Oct 29, 2007.

Aquarium Island

Aquarium Island is a small key covered with palm trees, sandy beaches and tourist huts. It is a 10-20 minute boat ride off the western coast of San Andrés. It is actually two islands, one small and sandy, the other larger and covered in palm trees. Both islands feature rudimentary tourist facilities, and they are connected by a sand bar below a few feet of water.

The smaller island is popular with snorkelers because the water is warm and clear and the many native fish are easy to see. Snorkeling gear is available on the island, but prices are high. There are small lockers for rent in one of the huts. Glass-bottom boats leave from Aquarium to see shoals of fish, and you can sometimes rent jet-skis.

To get to Aquarium Island, go to the small port on the eastern side of San Andrés and ask to get on the next boat over. You can also book passage through Over Tours or one of the other tour operators on the island. If you go through a tour agency, expect to pay about $5 per person to get there and back. It's usually cheaper to make your own arrangements at the port.

On weekends, Aquarium fills up with locals from San Andrés and tourists. The fish are frightened off, lockers may fill up, locals can be rude to tourists, every square inch of shade is taken and the entire experience can be quite unpleasant. Weekends are bad, but holiday weekends are unbearable and should be avoided at all costs.

Also note that there are sea urchins in the vicinity. If you're planning on swimming or snorkeling, you'll want good water shoes for protection. Aquarium Island is often packaged together with a trip to larger Johnny Key. Updated: Oct 29, 2007.

The Blue Diamond wreck dive

According to local lore, the Blue Diamond was impounded in the 1990s by the Colombian government for running drugs before being scuttled as a dive attraction. Whatever its history, this medium-sized freighter is an enjoyable wreck, full of little nooks and crannies that divers simply love to explore.

The dive is easy and fun. The wreck rests near the eastern shore of the island in about 10 meters (35 feet) of very warm water—even those most likely to get chilly underwater will not need a wetsuit. The stern, which rests about 12 meters (40 feet) down, is the deepest part of the dive. The boat cracked and split as it sank, and there are several areas through which an adventuresome diver can swim without running much risk of getting stuck or caught. Sea life such as fans, corals and small sponges has begun to grow on the wreck, and several small, colorful reef fish make it their home.

Highlights include the massive propeller half-buried in the sandy bottom and the bow. You can swim through an open hatch in the bow and come out a hole in the side —just let the divemaster go first. Look for *barracuda* and other fish darting in and out of the wreckage.

The Blue Diamond is located in a sandy spot, but there are coral gardens and small reefs not far away. If you still have air after completing an exploration of the wreck, you may be able to look around before resurfacing. Updated: Oct 29, 2007.

San Andrés Island Tours

There are dozens of tour agencies on San Andrés, many of which work in conjunction with big hotels. They all offer the same tours for the same prices to more or less the same places—Johnny Key, Morgan's Cave, The Coconut Museum, La Piscinita and the Blowing Hole.

Viajes Insular—Av. Providencia 4-11, Tel: 8-512-1675.
Islatur L'Alianxa—Av. Newball 4B-12 Edif. Bahía Fragata, Tel: 8-512-3358.
Over Receptour—Swamp Ground Cr 9 A 10-156 Aeropuerto, Tel: 8-512-8855.
Viajes Portofino—Av. La Playa with Av 20 de Julio, Tel: 8-512- 2210. Updated: Oct 19, 2007.

San Andrés Lodging

Many visitors to San Andrés stay in one of Decameron's five massive hotels. Generally the hotels sell all-inclusive packages which allow you to dine and see shows at any of the five hotels, as long as you sleep at your own. It's a good way to get to see several restaurants and shows. There are other, non-Decameron hotels available, some of which are better (and pricier) than others. Travelers on any budget should be able to find a hotel, although budget travelers will have the most difficulty. The fanciest hotels are on the coast and have private beaches. The cheapest lodging is in the town of San Andrés and do not have beaches. Updated: Nov 20, 2006.

Hotel Cocoplum

(ROOM: $45-200) The Cocoplum is a vibrant-colored large hotel on a stretch of white sandy beach with amply-sized hammocks out front. There are 24 double rooms and 14 family suites, although the hotel feels a bit cramped. Rooms with beach views cost more than front-facing rooms. The buildings lack a little love and care and could use some modernizing. However, once you're here you are unlikely to leave. The restaurant and bar make this a fine choice for families or couples. Prices fluctuate between low and high seasons. You can get here via tax or bus. Follow the signs from San Andrés to San Luís. The Cocoplum is on the ocean side. Vía a San Luis 43-39. Tel: 8-513-2121 / 2421 / 2646, E-mail: informes@cocoplumhotel.com, URL: www.cocoplumhotel.com. Updated: Mar 12, 2008.

Portobelo Hotel

(ROOM: $50-75) The Portobelo is right on the beach in downtown San Andrés. The hotel could use some upgrades, and the most redeeming feature of the iffy-looking rooms are the sea views. However, if you are in San Andrés to get your groove on and throw back a few cold ones you can't be in a better location. Av. La Playa, 5a-69. Tel: 8-512-9077, Fax: 8-512-5105, E-mail: portobelo@sol.net.co. Updated: Mar 14, 2008.

V!VA Member Review-Portobelo Hotel

Cleanest room I have ever had in the Caribbean. Nice restaurant in front and the best beach. The staff is very friendly and helpful, transfer from the airport is less than 5 minutes, and it's a 5 minutes walk to the center. Germany, Mar 13, 2008.

Sunrise Beach Hotel

(ROOM: $60-250) This massive block of a hotel looks as if it were planted by people with little taste. The hotel caters to the package tourist crowd, with inclusive meals and activities. Ask for a room with a view of the water, as rooms without a sea view stare over forlorn, humidity-stained blocks. The pool, however, is wonderful. A taxi from the airport costs $5 and takes 5 minutes. Av. Fancisco Newball, 4-169. Tel: 8-512-3977, Fax: 8-512 -3825, E-mail: info@sunrisehotel.com, URL: www.sunrisehotel.com. Updated: Dec 19, 2007.

Sunset Hotel

Open only a few months out of the year and situated a blissful 20 minutes from downtown San Andrés, the Sunset Hotel offers a respite from the hustle and bustle of downtown. Twenty twin rooms immaculately laid out with bathroom, air conditioning, TV and fridge make the Sunset an ideal place to relax. The hotel mainly caters to the scuba diving crowd since Sharky's Dive Shop is attached. A taxi will get you here from downtown in 20 minutes and a bus will take a little longer. Just ask the driver to let you off at kilometer 13 on the coastal road. Carretera Circunvalar, Kilometer 13. Tel: 8-513-0433 / 0141, E-mail: sunsetsai@hotmail.com, URL: www.ecohotelsunset.com. Updated: Mar 12, 2008.

Tres Casitas Apartahotel

Tres Casitas has ten fully furnished and equipped apartments close to San Andrés' nightlife district. While the furnishing is somewhat dated, the location is unrivalled. The swimming pool and the balconies in every apartment are a nice touch and the communal areas are well-maintained. Right downtown, the Tres Casitas is a five minute drive from the airport. Av. Colombia, 1-60. Tel: 8-512-6944 / 5873, Fax: 8-512-5880, E-mail: 3casitas@sol.net.co, URL: www.apartahoteltrescasitas.com. Updated: Dec 19, 2007.

San Andrés Restaurants

As the majority of visitors to San Andres arrive here on all-inclusive deals, all of their dining arrangements are taken care of within the hotel. While this may be of great convenience to them and exactly what they are looking for, it has resulted in there being fewer quality restaurants available for the independent traveler.

San Andrés Nightlife

As most Colombians are here to party, there are a few good clubs. Most are located within the big hotels, often on the top floor, so ask around for the current hot spot. Both the Melon Kiss and Blue Deep are located in the Hotel Sunrise. Av. Francisco Newball, 4-169. Tel: 8-512-3977. Updated: Oct 19, 2007.

Melon Kiss Disco

Crowds at the Sunrise Hotel dance the night away to electronic beats while throwing back fancy cocktails. The Melon kiss also screen live sporting events on big televisions. Av. Francisco Newball, 4-169. Tel: 8-512-3977. Updated: Dec 19, 2007.

Blue Deep Discotheque

The Blue Deep has been classed as one of the best nightclubs in Latin America. It consists of three distinct bars, two dance floors, a light and laser show and perfect sound amplification. With a capacity for 800 revelers, be prepared for non-stop dancing. Inside the Hotel Sunrise, Av. Francisco Newball, 4-169. Tel: 8-512-3977. Updated: Dec 19, 2007.

Providencia and Santa Catalina

Alt: 360m Pop: 6,000 City Code: 8

The main settlements on Providencia are Pueblo Viejo (for businesses) and Agua Dulce (for tourism). However, since there is a main road skirting the outside edge of the island, most inhabitants live in a linear fashion along the shore. Santa Catalina, an island with an area of just 1 square mile, is accessible from Providencia by the "Lover's Bridge."

Nothing but the names and an odd cannon remain from the early Puritan, slave and pirate settlements. Pueblo Viejo has a few ramshackle streets where one can find cafés, a supermarket, banks and a cash machine. Unless you arrive at the nearby airport or need to withdraw some funds, there should be no urgent need to visit Pueblo Viejo.

Instead, stick to the island's main attractions—unspoiled beaches, charming islanders conversing in their Creole English, tours of the mangroves and hikes into the interior volcanic hills. Updated: Oct 19, 2007.

History

Providencia has seen its fair share of masters. It was originally a Miskito Indian fishing territory, but became a Puritan community in 1630 and then pirate lair where Henry Morgan made a home.

After the Puritan project failed in the mid 17th Century, the island fell into Spanish hands but remained ignored by the protectorate in Cartagena. Unbothered by the Spanish, the descendants of African slaves cemented their identity on Providencia, and they ensure that the culture remains intact. Updated: Oct 19, 2007.

When to Go

Temperatures on the islands average 25-28° C (77-82°F). October and November are the rainiest months and hurricane season can span from late September into December in a bad year. The dry season is January-April.

High season, when hotel prices shoot up, is mid-December to mid-January and Easter week. Prices can be respectfully negotiated the rest of the year.

Holidays and Fiestas

June 23—Festival Folklorico, Cultural y Deportivo de la Vieja Providencia. This is the island's most important festival, which includes sports competitions, gastronomy and a beauty pageant.

Saturdays—Gather on South West beach just after 1 p.m. to see one of the most interesting equine events in the world—the beach horse races of Providencia. Updated: Oct 19, 2007.

Getting To and Away From Providencia and Santa Catalina

Air

Local airline Satena has two public flights daily to Providencia and one flight reserved for those on packages with Decameron resorts. The 20-minute flight from San Andrés lands at the airport at Embrujo.

Sea

A small ferry runs infrequently from San Andrés. The trip takes eight hours and is not for the weak of stomach. Updated: Oct 19, 2007.

Getting Around

Collectivo taxis run the route around the island's main road, but they are expensive. Other options include renting a moped (low season $25 per day) or a golf buggy. Updated: Oct 19, 2007.

Safety in Providencia and Santa Catalina

Issues that affect other parts of Colombia are noticeably absent—the main risks here are of absent-minded drivers and motorcyclists. Updated: Oct 19, 2007.

Providencia and Santa Catalina Services

Tourism Office

Located in the airport just back from the baggage reclaim man. Open when the Satena flight lands. Most hotels in Agua Dulce will accept U.S. dollars or exchange them. Otherwise the only bank and cash machine are located in Pueblo Viejo.

Keeping in Touch

All of the larger hotels have telephone and fax facilities, although internet is harder to come by. There is an internet café in Pueblo Viejo and in the Body Contact Travel Agents offices in Agua Dulce.

Medical

The Medical Center can be found in Pueblo Viejo, but for any serious complaints a trip to San Andrés is required. There is a pharmacy in the supermarket in Pueblo Viejo.

Laundry

There are no specialist laundry facilities on Providencia, but the larger hotels have laundry services.

Religious Services

Most religious services are held in English, the local common language of Providencia. There are Baptist, Adventist, Catholic and other Protestant churches.

Shopping

There are a number of arts and crafts stores of varying quality sprinkled around the island. Unless you are terribly interested in these, you won't find much aside from excursions and dining to spend your money on. Updated: Oct 19, 2007.

Things to See and Do

Providencia is a nature lover's paradise, due to its idyllic geographical isolation and the fact that it remains largely undeveloped. Aside from being an ideal place to lie back and relax, its status as a protected area means that a short stroll away from the main areas reveals a tropical wonderland for divers, hikers and people keen on eco-tourism.

Boat Tour

Organized by Body Contact tours the boat tour takes all day and includes lunch. The tour completely circles the islands of San Andrés and Providencia, stopping at the key point of interest such as beaches that can only be reached by sea and Cabeza de Morgan.

Hike to McBean Lagoon

McBean Lagoon is in the extreme northeastern point of Providencia, between Maracaibo Hill and Iron Wood Hill. The lake was created in 1995 in an effort to conserve the natural wonders of the island. Near here you can observe a full 360-degree view of the island and the multicolored ocean that ripples over the exposed reefs.

Playa Manzanillo

Playa Manzanillo is one of the most beautiful beaches in the Colombian Caribbean, with unobstructed views of the wide-open ocean backed by lofty palms. Get here early to enjoy a full day of paradise. Roland's Bar serves a mean red snapper and some potent cocktails. Updated: Oct 19, 2007.

Santa Catalina

Santa Catalina is an island in its own right. It was connected to Providencia at one time, but it is believed that pirates, possibly Henry Morgan or the Dutchman Edward Manswelt, may have cut the links in order to create a passage for ships between the two islands. This would create an impregnable and easily defendable base around this 1 kilometer area of land. Today Santa Catalina is connected to Providencia by a causeway named "Puente de los Enamorados" or "Lover's Bridge". A short walk across this leads to a path along the waterfront. The path is interrupted with placards detailing historical curiosities and identifying where six forts have been placed over the years. What remains today of these bastions representing European imperial designs are hardened rubble and a few scattered canons. Be sure to bring along your camera and snap some photos of the views and of the delightfully painted traditional Caribbean architecture. Updated: Apr 14, 2008.

Providencia and Santa Catalina Tours

Providencia is a small island where everybody knows everybody, so it is not always necessary to sign up with a tour operator. However, in order to remain safe it is advisable. The most comprehensive operator on the island is Body Contact, located in Bahía de Agua Dulce.

Body Contact—Tel: 8-514-8118, Fax: 8-514-8283, E-mail: bodycontact2002@yahoo.com.
Caribean Dream Travel Agency—Telefax: 8-514-8871.
Viajes Providencia—Telefax: 8-514-8010. Updated: Oct 19, 2007.

Hike to El Pico, Providencia

Check the skies, consult the weather forecast, speak to some islanders and then choose the ideal day to hike up to El Pico. The highest point on the rugged island of Providencia, El Pico offers breathtaking views over the whole island, its azure bays, white sandy beaches, mangroves that are home to migratory birds, quaint settlements and McBean lagoon. Check with Body Contact tours on how to get here, and be sure to bring sunblock. Updated: Apr 14, 2008.

Diving in Providencia

Arguably with clearer and cleaner water that its larger and more frequently visited neighbor, San Andrés, Providencia is a scuba diver's dream. The island boasts clear, calm waters and an abundance of marine life. Both novice divers and seasoned professionals will enjoy diving here. In addition to this, Providencia is a perfect place to learn to dive. Don't be put off by the islanders' laid-back attitudes in their day-to-day business—the diving equipment is well cared for and the instruction is up to international standards. Body Contact, Freshwater Bay. Tel: 8-514-8283. Updated: Apr 14, 2008.

Providencia and Santa Catalina Lodging

Cabañas El Recreo

Cabañas El Recreo is not a bad choice for your visit to Providencia, though similar hotels are located right on the beach. El Recreo is close to the beach and rooms here come fully equipped with air conditioning, refrigerator and cable TV. The Happy Sailor restaurant is located on the grounds and the friendly hotel staff will book you onto trips or organize transport. Any collectivo or taxi will take you to Freshwater Bay from the airport. Tel: 311-333-0519, E-mail: capbryan@col3.telecom.com.co. Updated: Dec 19, 2007.

Posada Vicky

(ROOMS: $10-35) A short walk up the hill from the beach, Posada Vicky is a family home with two converted rooms for tourists. These rooms have air conditioning but lack a good view and sea breeze. Located on the road running down to South West beach, Posada Vicky is an option should other destinations with better locations be full. From the airport, take a collectivo taxi for 20 minutes and ask to be dropped off at the Posada Vicky, on the road leading to South West beach in South West Bay. Updated: Dec 19, 2007.

Hotel Sirius Center

(ROOM: $25-125) The Hotel Sirius Center is at the far end of South West beach. This expansive 12 room (30 bed) development is also the site of the Sirius dive center. All rooms have air conditioning, ocean views, TV and a minibar. Aside from the convenience of a dive shop on your doorstep, the hotel has a conference room and a restaurant. Prices vary greatly between low and high seasons—for more information, see their website. The collectivo will get you to the Hotel Sirius Center in 20 minutes from the airport. The hotel is located at the bottom of the road to South West Bay on the left, opposite from Miss Mary. Tel: 8-514-8213, Fax: 8-514-8808, E-mail: info@siriushotel.net, URL: www.siriusdivecenter.com/siriushotel/Caribbean/hotel.htm. Updated: Dec 19, 2007.

Miss Mary

(ROOM: $35-50) Imagine being able to stroll out of your room and onto a white sandy beach with cool turquoise Caribbean waters lapping the shore, or sipping a cool drink under shady palms in a hammock.

That, in a nutshell, is Cabañas Miss Mary. Located in the desirable and tranquil South West Bay, Miss Mary has seven rooms with a total of 14 beds. Four rooms look out onto the ocean while the other three are around the back in a much less atmospheric setting. Staying here feels like a privilege rather than a right—the rooms are comfortable and clean and there can be nothing better than sitting on your porch in a hammock watching the sun drip over the horizon. From the airport any collectivo will get you there in roughly 20 minutes for a flat fee in the region of $5 per person. If you rent your own transport, follow the island's road around (you cannot get lost) until you meet the signposted turn off. Tel: 8-514-8206, Fax: 8-514-8454. Updated: Dec 19, 2007.

Hotel Miss Elma

(ROOM: $40-65) The Hotel Miss Elma is found in the "tourist zone" of Freshwater Bay, Bahía de Agua Dulce. All four suites in the hotel have ocean views, air conditioning, minibar and cable TV. Well-kept and brightly painted, the Hotel Miss Elma is everything a Caribbean hotel should be, effortlessly charming and laid-back. Freshwater Bay is a handy location, close to reputable tour companies and with a host of restaurants nearby. From the airport, catch a collectivo to Bahía de Agua Dulce. The driver will drop you at the front door. The trip lasts about 20 minutes. Updated: Dec 19, 2007.

Hotel El Pirata Morgan

(ROOM: $45-80) The Hotel El Pirata Morgan is a 30-room hotel (60 beds) on the beach at Freshwater Bay. It's named after the famed pirate who used the island as his base on many an occasion. The hotel isn't built in the traditional Caribbean style, but don't let this put you off. Each room has an ocean view and is fully equipped with bathroom, air conditioning, minibar and Direct TV. Any collectivo from the airport will get you here in under 20 minutes for a flat fee of around $5. Tel: 8-514-8067 / 8528. Updated: Dec 19, 2007.

Providencia and Santa Catalina Restaurants

Seaflower Bakery and Coffee Shop

The Seaflower, a perfect place for a coffee break, has pastries, sandwiches, coffees and a bookstore. It's cheap, friendly and very much a local's place. Opposite the Alcaldía, Pueblo Viejo. Tel: 8-514-8584. Updated: Dec 19, 2007.

Roland's

Roland Bryan Eden and his son Jason have the best spot on the best beach in Providencia, with its shaded and sheltered homemade tables and chairs clustered in a palm grove. With views of Providencia's incredible Playa Manzanillo, Roland's is a place to come for lunch and stay until dinner. Service may be slow, but if you are here you'll not want to leave. Try the house speciality: Snapper with vegetables cooked in aluminum foil over an open fire—simply delicious. Reggae beats play at a pleasant volume and on occasion a live band plays in the evening around the burning embers of the central fire. While no credit cards are accepted here, prices are reasonable. Playa Manzanillo, Providencia. Tel: 8-514-8417, E-mail: rolandsbeach@hotmail.com. Updated: Dec 19, 2007.

El Divino Niño

(ENTREES: $5-16) Open only at lunchtime, El Divino Niño is the quintessential Caribbean beachfront eatery. Wooden tables are placed haphazardly on the sand and the menu is painted primitively on the back wall. Don't let the informality of the place put you off, the prices are reasonable for Providencia and the food is sumptuous. Seafood is, of course, the speciality, but it serves chicken as well. An order of fried fish is enough for two people. South West Bay, Providencia. Updated: Dec 19, 2007.

Richard's Place

Richard's Place is ideal for a sunset on South West Beach. Enjoy a potent piña colada or coco loco, or settle for an ice-cold beer while relaxing in the tranquil setting. Updated: Dec 19, 2007.

Donde Martín

Donde Martín is in the Hotel Cabañas Agua Dulce, at the north end of Freshwater Bay. The menu is extensive and more adventurous than other restaurants on the island. Donde Martín has a true marine feeling expressed though marine inspired décor. The use of spices and imagination has been encouraged here. Particularly recommended are the seafood specials and the chicken and crab entree. Tel: 8-514-8160. Updated: Dec 19, 2007.

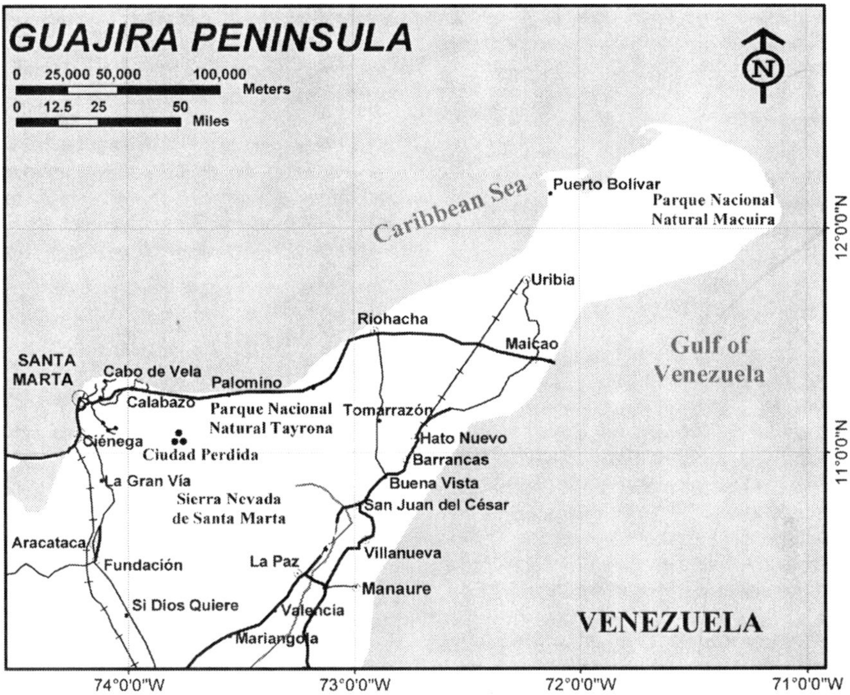

La Guajira Peninsula

For centuries, the Guajira (Wajirra in the language of the Wayuu) was a no-man's land replete with smugglers and outlaws. It was an isolated, barren corner of the earth far too dangerous to travel alone to. When you embark on a journey to this far northeastern region of Colombia, however, you will soon discover a rather different truth. Welcome to the Land of Dreams and Death, as the Wayuu call their homeland.

The Guajira is divided into three parts, each distinguished by vegetation. To the south is Baja Guajira, with lands reaching toward the Sierra Nevada de Santa Marta. It's economy is based on agriculture and cattle. The world's largest coal mine, El Cerrejón, is in the Baja Guajira. Media Guajira, the second part, includes regions Riohacha, Maicao and Manaure. It's a hot region with moderate temperatures and low-desert flora. Alta Guajira, the final region, stretches from Uribia, north to Cabo de Vela and Nazareth. Alta Guajira represents the classic image of a desolate desert. On the eastern side of this area is the Macuira mountain range. Much of this part is difficult to reach with public transport. A sliver of the Peninsula belongs to Venezuela, though for the Wayuu this border does not exist.

The Wayuu (Guajiro) is a very traditional matrilineal society. Many people are willing to teach you about their culture after the ice is broken. It is said you make a Wayuu friend for life. Even if you return 10 years later, you will be welcomed into the home. There are also significant communities of Afro-Colombians, descendents of Maroons.

Fresh water is scarce in the Media and Alta Guajira, thus affecting the price of every commodity. Hotels may have limited supplies, and "blue-plate specials" often don't include a drink. Transport is also expensive. Prepare your budget accordingly and use conservation practices.

La Guajira is accessible by the Troncal del Caribe highway and by another road from Valledupar in the south. This road parallels the coal mega-railroad from El Cerrejón to Cuatro Vías, the crossroads with the Troncal; the northern spur of the road goes to the Alta Guajira. When making your travel plans, be aware the southern highway is closed and heavily patrolled from dusk to dawn. The U.S. may establish a military base in the peninsula. Updated: Jun 09, 2008.

History

The first Spaniard to sail around the coast was Alonso de Ojeda and the first to step foot on this barren earth was Juan de la Cosa. In the 16th Century, the governments of Santa Marta and Venezuela disputed the governance of this península, since each wanted to control the wealth of the region.

The first city in the Peninsula, Cabo de la Vela, was founded by Martín Fernández de Enciso in 1526. This was the territory's capital until 1544, when the seat moved to Riohacha. In 1772, Antonio de Arévalo went to pacify the peninsula and establish homes where the indigenous were relocated. These were San José de Bahía Honda (1772), Pedraza (1774), San Bartolomé de Sinamaica (1774) and Santa Ana de Savana del Valle (1776).

The Guajira was part of Magdalena until 1871, when it was made an independent territory. In 1964, it was decreed a new department of the nation. During all these centuries of foreign domination, the Wayuu were peons in their own homeland, forced to labor in the salt and coal mines, in pearling and fishing, on cattle ranches, and in contraband running.

In the latter part of the 20th century and now into the 21st, the Wayuu, Afro-Colombians and other inhabitants of the region have seen their communities adversely affected by massive coal mining and port operations.

Highlights

Take out your binoculars and observe flamingos and other migratory birds at **Santuario Natural Nacional Los Flamencos (p.307).**

Visit **Cabo de la Vela (p.316)** for its natural wonders like the Ojo de Agua, the Pilón de Azúcar and Hoyos Sopladores, not to mention the magnificent sunsets.

Celebrate the artistry, gastronomy, music and poetry at the **Festival de Cultura Wayuu (p.312)**, the meeting of the Wayuu nation held at the end of May in Uribia.

The glittering salt flats of **Manaure (p.308)** are a perfect example of the differences between industrial and traditional extraction of this mineral.

Explore a cloud forest amidst the desert: **Parque Nacional Natural Macuira (p.315).**
Updated: Jun 10, 2008.

Responsible Travel in La Guajira

Wayuu suggest the following etiquette practices for visitors to Guajira:

► Water is very important. Use only what is necessary for showering.

► Always ask permission to take photos.

► Cemeteries are sacred grounds. You may enter, but have respect and don't touch anything.

► If you give a gift to a family you are visiting, give it to the head of the household.

► Drinking alcohol is taboo.

► Giving money to beggars is OK, if you feel so inclined. However, don't give candy or money to children.

► When eating with Wayuu, do not begin until everyone is present and seated.

► After a meal, especially lunch, it is customary to take a nap.

► Men may wear shorts. Sleeveless shirts are fine at home. In public, wear a shirt with sleeves. Going shirtless is frowned upon.

► Women may wear any type of shirt, with sleeves or without, or even showing the midriff. However, as for men, going shirtless is not accepted. Pants and shorts are OK.

► Both genders can swim in whatever atire they'd like, but no skinny dipping.
Updated: Jun 10, 2008.

Remote settlements have been victims of paramilitary attacks, even in 2008. The attacks have caused a tremendous internal refuge problem. Updated: Jun 10, 2008.

When to Go

The Guajira is hot, especially the Media and Alta; temperatures can reach over 40°C (over 100°F). The most scorching and wettest months are different depending on the region. In Riohacha and Manaure, in the Media Guajira, May-July are the hottest months, with rains coming in April and again from September-November. As you move into the Alta Guajira, patterns change. Inland, around Uribia, showers come from May-July. Cabo de la Vela, on the coast, has its rains from June-August and heat from September-November and January-February. The entire region experiences high winds in January and February. The beaches of the Guajira, like Palomino and Cabo de la Vela, have become very popular vacation destinations for Colombians. During Christmas, New Years, Semana Santa, and three-day holiday weekends the beaches get very crowded and prices rise accordingly. Updated: Jun 10, 2008.

Safety in La Guajira

Travel with public transportation is safe in the Guajira, even when alone. If traveling by private vehicle, stick to main roads, carry extra gas and water, and don't drive at night. Hitchhiking in pairs is said to be OK. Although police and locals are helpful, residents warn not to walk across the desert, whether by trail or road, for danger of robbery. Contraband (especially drugs) and paramilitary activities still occur in remote areas.

In La Guajira the sun is extremely strong. Even Wayuu women wear an earthen mask as a natural sunscreen to protect themselves. (Face paint designs also express what is going on in a Wayuu woman's life.)

Dengue is present during the rainy season. Malaria and yellow fever exist in more humid regions, most notably the coast west of Riohacha and areas toward the Sierra. In the mountain ranges watch out for Chagas, a disease caused by a parasitic bite from the so-called assassin bug. There are scorpions and snakes in the desert, especially in secluded areas. Updated: Jun 10, 2008.

Things to See and Do

Wajirra is a land of contrasts: sea and desert, colonial Riohacha and modern Uribia, untouched landscapes and exploited resources.

Sunsets and moon rises are breathtaking, especially at Cabo de la Vela, which also has stunning natural formations to explore. Beaches like Poportín and Palomino are virtually empty during the low season.

Guajira is a birdwatcher's paradise, with flamingos taking haven in lagoons like Laguna de Utta, Carrizal and Musichi. Within the region are several important national parks, among them Macuira, Sierra Nevada de Santa Marta and Santuario de Flora y Fauna Los Flamencos. The region also boasts the world's largest open-pit coal mine, El Cerrejón; one of the biggest wind-turbine electricity projects, Parque Eólico Jepirachi; and the greatest salt extraction at Manaure. You can visit all of them.

The female-centered Wayuu culture remains well-preserved. You can buy *susu* (bags), *chinchorros* (hammocks) or other weavings, spend an evening at a *ranchería* (ranch) eating typical food and drink, or attend the annual Festival de Cultura Wayuu.

La Guajira Tours

Tour companies across the Caribbean coast offer packages to Guajira. These excursions tend to be quite pricey, from $75-190. One-day trips from Riohacha are available for $27 per person (minimum of four people). Some scuba shops in Santa Marta and Taganga arrange diving safaris at Cabo de la Vela and other points off the Guajira coast. Tour operators also offer a "Tarde de Ranchería," a visit to a Wayuu community. You learn about the culture and traditions of this nation, see a dance performance, and partake in a typical Wayuu meal including *friche* (goat meat) and *chirrinchi* (the traditional alcoholic drink). On some multi-day trips you sleep in hammocks. Before deciding on an agency, make sure its vehicles are in good shape and they stock up on plenty of water. Investigate the relationship the operator has with the native communities as well, to make sure they have good relations. Updated: Jun 09, 2008.

La Guajira Lodging

Lodging costs quite a bit more in La Guajira, mostly due to high water prices. Shoestring travelers should budget for this. Camping or slinging a hammock is also possible in some areas, and may be a traveler's only choice. Large chain hotels have yet to arrive on the scene, and Wayuu communities are resisting their entrance into the market. Wayuu prefer to welcome guests traditionally, thus promoting employment and economic opportunities. In villages and rancherías, do not expect the installed shower to work. You will have to *echar el agua* (have a tossed-water shower). A large covered container is provided from which you dip water to throw over yourself. Keep the water clean and cover the container to minimize mosquito breeding.

Riohacha

Alt: 5m Pop: 169,000 City Code: 5

Historic Colombian literature paints the picture of Riohacha (Wayuu: *Süchiimma*) as a Wild West-type town, with contraband running and other shady activities going on. Upon arrival, though, you soon discover it's a pleasant town with a beautiful *malecón* (boardwalk) and great beach. This is the capital of the Guajira—the native Wayuu are prevalent. Only one hour from the Venezuelan border, Riohacha is a convenient resting point before heading to or coming from that nation. Welcome to what is considered one of the most mysterious corners of Colombia.

The Troncal del Caribe highway passes through Riohacha, cutting the city into two.

Wayuu Culture

Some describe the Wayuu of the Guajira (Wajirra) as a society where men do nothing and women do all the work. From the viewpoint of someone raised in a patriarchal culture, it may seem valid. In truth, this nomadic society is matrilineal, which means names, societal status and property pass through the mother's side of the family.

Wayuu society is divided into 12 clans, each with its own name, symbol and animal. Both group and individual identification is passed through the mother's lineage. In marriages between Wayuu and *alijuna* (non-Wayuu), the child is only Wayuu if the mother is.

Community duties follow gender lines. Women are responsible for the household and child-rearing; the men for fishing and goat-rearing. Women fetch precious water and the men get firewood. Women weave *süi* (hammocks) and *susu* (bags), and the men weave *womu* (hats) and *waireñas* (sandals). Healers may be of either sex. Some healers specialize in dreams, a discipline in which Wayuu place special significance.

The youngest daughter inherits property, as she is the nearest to life. The eldest daughter, being the closest to death, is responsible for the funeral rituals. The Wayuu have two burials: one immediately after death and a second five to 10 years later. For this, the daughter undergoes a year-long purification before unearthing and cleaning the bones for the second entombment.

At puberty, only females have a rite of passage. In the past, a female endured more than a year of isolation from the community, during which she learned songs, dances, weaving and other female customs. Because of modern-day demands like school attendance, this ritual now lasts two or three months. Only in isolated *rancherías* do females practice this tradition for longer periods.

The most important male figure to a child is the eldest maternal uncle, and it is he who disciplines. When a potential fiancé asks for a Wayuu woman's hand in marriage, he must go to the uncle, who sets the bride-price. If the husband seeks a divorce, the woman keeps the dowry. If the wife seeks a divorce, she must return half the bequest.

Yonna, or dance, is performed only for rituals. Recreational dancing, such as salsa dancing, is not part of Wayuu culture. Updated: Jun 10, 2008.

Within the city the highway is called Calle 15. In the center of this roadway, marking more or less the geographic center of the city, is a roundabout with a statue of the town's most famous figure: the legendary Vallenato accordionist Francisco el Hombre. He's immortalized in song for his duel with the Devil and in Gabriel García Márquez's "Hundred Years of Solitude." Updated: Jun 09, 2008.

History

This coastal stretch had long been a meeting ground of indigenous peoples. The Kogui descended from the Sierra Nevada to trade with the Wayuu and others. In 1535, German explorer Nikolaus Federmann established Riohacha on the west bank of the Río Ranchería. For many years the most prized pearls came from here, which made it a favorite target of pirates. Sir Francis Drake sacked the port in 1596. With the collapse of the pearl industry in the 18th Century, Riohacha became just a tropical backwater, earning the reputation of being an anything-goes town. Riohacha became the official capital of Guajira department in 1965 when the department was officially created. Updated: Jun 10, 2008.

A Few Words in Wayuunaiki

Wayuunaiki, or the Wayuu language, is of the Arawak language group. Pronunciation is similar to Spanish, except that the "r" and "rr" have a sound between that of an "r" and an "l"; and "sh" is pronounced as in English. The language reflects the matrilineal aspect of Wayuu society. Many family relationships are distinguished between that by way of the mother and that by father, for example *ashi* (paternal uncle) and *alaüla* (maternal uncle). The language also has 21 terms for the position of the sun.

Kasashi punuria ► What's your name?
Tanoria ► My name is
Jamaa pia? ► How are you?
Watta'a mal ► Good morning
Anas aipa'a ► Good night
Ounshi way'a ► See you later
Miyaasüütaya ► I'm thirsty
Oushutaya jamü ► I'm hungry
Wüin ► fresh water
aa ► yes
nnojo ► no
ei ► mother
ashi ► father
jierü ► woman
toolo ► man
alijuna ► a non-indigenous person
kusina ► from other indigenous nation
Updated: Jun 10, 2008.

When to Go

Expect rains in Riohacha and the surrounding region from September to November, and in April. January winds play with the sea and rough waters may incite small craft advisories and put the kibosh on scuba diving. May, June and July are the hottest months, with temperatures reaching 39°C (102°F). Updated: Jun 10, 2008.

Holidays and Festivals

Like every town along the Caribbean coast, Riohacha observes the pre-Lent feast of Carnaval beginning the Saturday before Ash Wednesday. Locals claim Riohacha's Carnaval is the oldest in Colombia. Around 3 a.m. on Sunday morning, men cover themselves with mud and enter town dancing the *cumbia de pilón*. Everyone joins the Queen of Carnaval in the procession to the sea, where the men wash themselves off. Look forward to lots of *maicena* (corn starch) and water being tossed.

The feast days of the Virgen de los Remedios, Riohacha's patron saint, commemorate May 14, 1663, when she saved the city from a surging tide. The Festival del Dividivi, June 29-July 1, is a salute to the arbor symbol of the Guajira department. Updated: Jun 10, 2008.

Getting To and Away From Riohacha

There are a variety of ways to get to Riohacha: *busetas* or small buses ($0.35), taxis ($1.30-1.60) and mototaxis ($0.50).

The bus terminal, at Calle 15 and Carrera 11A, has restaurants, a phone, shops and bathrooms. Alternately, you can flag down a bus to your destination as it passes through town on Calle 15. To go to Palomino, take a Santa Marta bus.

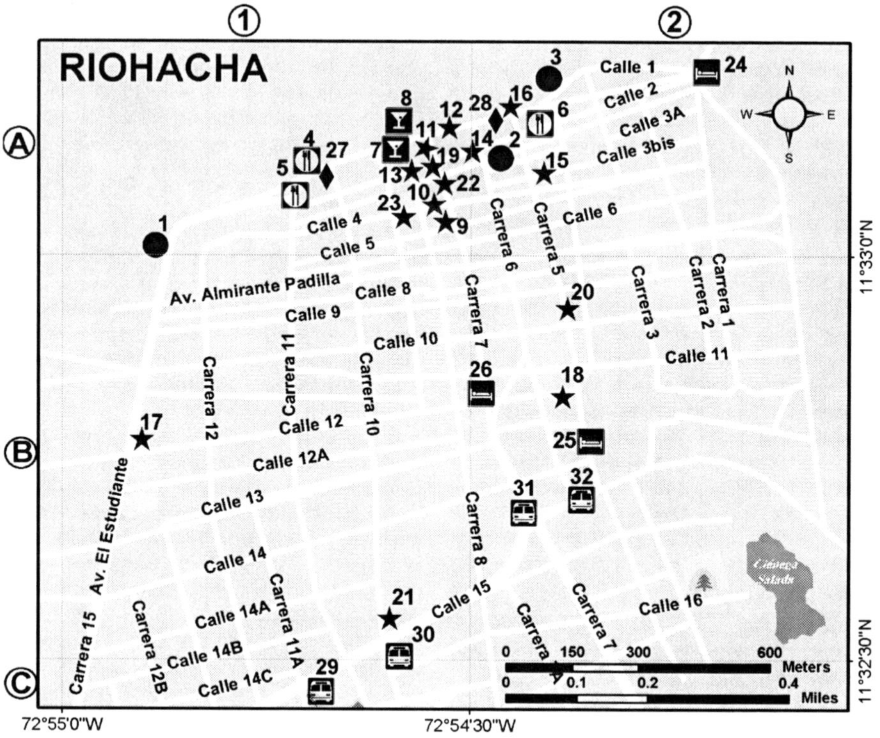

Activity ●
1 Casa de la Cultura A1
2 Centro Cultural Municipal Enrique Lallemand A2
3 The Malecón and Beach A2

Eating
4 Asados Don Pepe A1
5 Marino's Junior A1
6 Restaurante Bar La Tinaja A2

Nightlife
7 Casa Vieja Galería Bar A1
8 Mariano's Bar A1

Service ★
9 Banco AV Villas A1
10 Banco Colombia A1
11 Banco de la República A1
12 Banco Popular A1
13 BBVA A1
14 Correos de Colombia A1
15 DAS A2
16 Dirección de Turismo de la Guajira A2
17 Hospital Nuestra Señora de los Remedios B1
18 Instituto Geográfico Agustín Codazzi B2
19 National Park Office A1
20 Spumas Lavandería y Servicios B2
21 Telecom B1
22 Venezuelan Consulate A1
23 Yejogi Internet A1

Sleeping
24 Hotel Gimaura A2
25 Hotel Panorama B2
26 Hotel Yalconia del Mar B2

Tour ♦
27 Cabo de la Vela Operadora Turística A1
28 Luna Guajira A2

Transportation
29 Bus Terminal C1
30 Collective taxis for Valledupar B1
31 Collective taxis to Camarones B2
32 Collective taxis to Maicao, Uribia and Manaure B2

From Riohacha

Arrive	Departure	Time	Price
Maicao	5 a.m.-10 p.m.	1 hour	$2.65
Maracaibo	3:30 p.m.	2-3 hours	$24
Caracas	3:30 p.m.	18 hours	$76
Santa Marta	every half hour	2-3 hours	$8-13
Barranquilla	every half hour	4-5 hours	$11-17
Cartagena	every half hour	6-7 hours	$19-24
Valledupar	4 p.m.	4 hours	$8
Bucaramanga	4 p.m.	12 hours	$49
Bogotá	3 p.m., 3:15 p.m.	20-24 hours	$69

Shared taxis to Maicao leave from Calle 15 and Carrera 5 (5:30 a.m.-5 p.m.), and the last taxi from Maicao to Riohacha leaves at 6 p.m. ($3). To get to Manaure and Uribia taxis take off from the same neighborhood. Collective taxis for Valledupar depart from Calle 15 and Carrera 10, across from the phone company. To reach Camarones, catch a ride from Calle 15 and Carrera 7.

Camionetas (pick-up trucks) to Manaure and Uribia leave from the large municipal market on Carrera 7, about five long blocks south of Calle 15.

Aeropuerto Almirante Padilla provides service to Bogotá (end of Carrera 11, south of Calle 15, Tel: 5-727-3854). Updated: Jun 10, 2008.

Safety in Riohacha

The central part of Riohacha is said to be safe at night, but not the barrios on the far side of Calle 15. Care should be taken on more secluded parts of the beach during dark hours. During the rainy season, you should take precautions against disease-carrying mosquitoes. Updated: Jun 10, 2008.

Riohacha Services

Tourism Office

Dirección de Turismo de La Guajira is on the boardwalk. It dispenses basic information on what to see and do in all the Guajira. Daily, 8 a.m.-noon, 2-6 p.m., but may close earlier on weekends. Calle 1 and Carrera 5. Tel: 5-727-1015, E-mail: lourdesmarevalo@yahoo.es.

Other offices of importance are:
DAS—Monday-Friday, 7-11:30 a.m., 2-3:30 p.m. Calle 5 4-48. Tel: 5-727-2407.
Instituto Geográfico Agustín Codazzi—Calle 12 5-25. Tel: 5-727-3930.
National Park office—Carrera 7 2-15. Tel: 5-728-2636.
Venezuelan Consulate—Carrera 7 3-08, P-7B, Edificio Ejecutivo (next to Banco AV Villas). Tel: 5-727-4076.

Money

As money facilities such as banks, ATMs and *casas de cambio* are nonexistent in the peninsula, it is best to stock up on pesos in Riohacha before heading into the hinterlands.
BBVA ATM—MasterCard, Visa, Plus. Calle 2 and Carrera 8, across from the church.
Banco Popular ATH—Visa, MasterCard, Cirrus, Plus. Calle 1 and Carrera 7. ATM on Carrera 7.
Banco AV Villas ATM—ATH, Plus, Cirrus, MasterCard, Visa. Carrera 7 3-16.
Bancolombia—Exchanges: American Express travelers checks; ATM—MasterCard, Visa, Cirrus, American Express. Monday-Thursday, 8 a.m.-4 p.m., Friday 8 a.m.-4:30 p.m. Carrera 8 3-09.

Keeping in Touch

Telecom has local, national and international phone services. Monday-Friday, 8 a.m.-noon, 2-6 p.m., Saturday 8 a.m.-noon.

Shops and street stands charge $0.10 per minute for local or national calls.

Correos de Colombia has an outpost on Calle 2, 6-46. Monday-Friday 7:30 a.m.-noon, 2-6 p.m., Saturday 8 a.m.-noon.

Internet is a bit difficult to find but the average price is $0.80 per hour. Yejogi Internet has a special price of $0.50 per hour from noon-2 p.m. Monday-Saturday 9 a.m.-9 p.m., closed Sunday. Calle 4 8-29.

Medical

Hospital Nuestra Señora de los Remedios serves Riohacha's medical needs. Calle 12, Avenida de los Estudiantes. Tel: 5-727-1374 / 3077. Pharmacies are found throughout the city; several are on Calle 7, near Carrera 7.

Laundry

Spumas Lavandería y Servicios is the place to do your laundry. At $2.35 per kilo it is more expensive than in other parts of Colombia, owing to the scarcity of water in these parts. Monday-Saturday, 8 a.m.-7 p.m., closed Sunday and holidays. Carrera 5 9-27. Tel: 5-727-4514 / 749-1064.

Camera

A trio of camera shops offering processing, print films (Kodak, Fuji and Konica), cameras (both analog and digital) and accessories, as well as other photographic services, are located on Calle 3, between Carreras 6 and 7.

Shopping

Tienda de Carnaval

Happen to be in Riohacha just in time for Carnaval? Stop by Tienda de Carnaval to pick up necessities to join riohacheros in this yearly event. Spend a few pesos on rainbow-colored wigs and masks, glittery T-shirts, silly hats, and, of course, cans of spritz foam. During the off-season, Tienda de Carnaval sells all sorts of items for any festivity. Carrera 8 7-16. Tel: 5-727-2884. Updated: Jun 10, 2008.

Wayuu Artesanas

Every day, Wayuu women come from their rancherías with their communities' craftwork. They pass the day on the south side of the Avenida la Marina, in the shade of buildings, chatting with other women while crocheting bags. In the evening, when the burning sun begins to set beyond the Caribbean Sea, they all pack up and move to the other side of the road, setting up on the arcades of the boardwalk. Their bags, hammocks and other goods hang from palm trees and spread on the ground. Buying from these women means you are purchasing direct from the producers, cutting out the middleman. Updated: Jun 10, 2008.

Things to See and Do

Strolling down the malecón is a pleasurable way to spend a few hours exploring the many facets of riohachero life. Take a breather from the burning sun by hiding in one of the cultural centers or beneath the shady trees of Parque de Almirante Padilla, the main plaza. Just to the west of the city is Camarones village and Santuario de Flora y Fauna Los Flamencos, a wonderful spot for bird watching. On the way to Santa Marta is a little-known gem, Palomino, with deserted beaches.

The Malecón and Beach

Riohacha's malecón hugs the shell-strewn, pale beige sand. Depending on the season, the sea is the color of milky coffee or turquoise. Do not underestimate the sun here. Be sure to keep yourself hydrated and take frequent rests in the shade or someplace cool. Along its length are little plazas where you can rest and buy Wayuu crafts. Try your hand at fishing from the long wharf at the foot of Carrera 6. Between Carreras 7 and 9 is a grove of palm trees. String up your hammock for a siesta. Just past Carrera 11 are juice and seafood cocktail stands, and down on the beach, fishermen sell their catch in the late afternoon. The malecón runs from the tourism office, at Calle 1 and Carrera 5, and ends at the new Casa de la Cultura.

Cultural Centers of Riohacha

The afternoon heat and sun are quite strong in Riohacha. For a respite from the glare, check out the latest art exhibits at one of the cultural centers. Some centers have evening events.

Centro Cultural Municipal Enrique Lallemand—Art exhibits, movies, dance performances, classes. Monday-Friday, 8 a.m.- noon, 2-8 p.m. Calle 3 5-49.

Banco de la República—Art exhibits, library. Monday-Friday, 8-11:30 p.m., 2-6 p.m., Saturday, 9 a.m.-1 p.m. Carrera 7 between Calles 1 and 2.

Casa de la Cultura—Art exhibits, concerts, dance, theater, literary readings, library and internet access. Calle 1 and Carrera 15. Updated: Jun 10, 2008.

Riohacha Tours

Many tour operators are eager to take you into the deep regions of the Guajira. Trips usually include the Salinas de Manaure, Uribia, Parque Eológico Jepirach and sights around

Cabo de la Vela. Three-day outings take you to Nazareth and Parque Nacional Natural Macuira, or to the world's end at Punta Gallina (the most northern point of South America, where desert meets sea). In the past, some agencies additionally offered boating excursions upriver to virgin mangrove jungles. However, these stopped due to insecurity from the civil war. It's possible that companies may resume trips as stability returns.

Luna Guajira

Luna Guajira presents a variety of packages to get to know Wayuu culture and the beauty of the Guajira Peninsula. One-day packages take you in the Santuario Los Flamencos, Cabo de la Vela or the El Cerrón coalmine ($29 including transportation, guide and entries). Longer excursions, from two days/one night to seven days/six nights, visit a combination of attractions ($75-365). This agency also goes to Punta Gallinas and Parque Nacional Natural Macuira (five days/four nights $395). All trips require a four-person minimum. Luna Guajira also has a gift shop with Wayuu crafts. Calle 1 5-01. Tel: 5-728-6223 / 300-809-5191, E-mail: lunaguajira@gmail.com. Updated: Jun 10, 2008.

Cabo de la Vela Operadora Turística

Cabo de la Vela Tours can take you to Cabo de la Vela and other area sites, like the salt mines of Manaure and Uribia (one-day to three day/two night packages $47.50-111, minimum four persons). A visit to a Wayuu community to learn about the culture and sample a typical meal is $26.50. Cabo de la Vela also offers one-day tours to Santuario Los Flamencos and El Cerrejón mine. A five-day/four-night excursion goes into the Guajira Alta, including Punta Gallina and Macuira ($343 per person, minimum four, all inclusive). Calle 1 and Carrera 10. Tel: 5-728-3654, Cell: 300-343-0169 / 310-707-1560, E-mail: turismoyelisgomez@hotmail.com. Updated: Jun 10, 2008.

Riohacha Lodging

Accommodations in Riohacha are more expensive than in other areas, primarily due to competition and the short supply of water. Even the cheaper inns, however, are of fairly good quality. Solo travelers will definitely feel the bite here. If you can, journey with a partner to cut costs, or budget for it. In an effort to conserve water, supplies are cut off during the day at the beginning of each week (Monday and/or Tuesday).

Hotel Panorama

(ROOM: $13-21) The rooms at the two-story Hotel Panorama are spacious enough, with built-in concrete platform beds that sport comfortable mattresses. Other amenities in these quarters are private baths with cold water, cable TV and your choice of fan or air conditioning. A common balcony on the second floor overlooks Carrera 5, a nice place to watch the sunset. Hotel Panorama has parking in a locked lot next door and is convenient for the collective taxis to Maicao, Manaure and Uribia. The Ariza family is friendly. Prices are negotiable. Carrera 5 13-35. Tel: 5-727-6580. Updated: Jun 10, 2008.

Hotel Yalconia del Mar

(ROOM: $16-27) Hotel Yalconia del Mar has upgraded over the years from being a basic hotel to one now providing the traveler with comfortable, elegant rooms at a mid-range price. The rooms are large, with private bath (cold-water shower), cable TV, and air conditioning or fan. Doña Amanda knows the Guajira region well and has been providing lodging with a homey atmosphere for many years. This inn is on the other side of Calle 12, the broad boulevard that divides the center of Riohacha, making it close to restaurants and nightclubs. Carrera 7 11-26. Tel: 5-727-3487 / 728-0044. Updated: Jun 10, 2008.

Hotel Gimaura

(ROOM: $58-69) Undoubtedly, Hotel Gimaura is a great lodging choice in Riohacha. Located at the eastern end of Avenida la Marina, this two-story lodge has generous rooms set around a garden or overlooking a field where the heliport used to be. All accommodations have air conditioning to keep you comfortable in this blistering climate, cable TV and private bathroom (cold water only). The swimming pool is another place to cool down and relax. This hotel is also family-friendly—children can amuse themselves on the hotel's private playground. Prices include American-style breakfast, tax and insurance. Calle 1, Avenida la Marina. Tel: 5-727-0009 / 0019 / 4546, E-mail: hotelgimaura@hotmail.com. Updated: Jun 10, 2008.

Riohacha Restaurants

Riohacha has a surprising variety of restaurants. Many offer fresh fish and seafood dishes, but also some alternatives. *Comidas corrientes* are difficult to find and cost $2.10-2.65, without drink. Carreras 8 and 9, from Calles 13 to 14, buzz with market activity. A larger municipal market is about five blocks south of Calle 15 on Carrera 7. Supermarket Cumaná Express is conveniently downtown (Monday-Saturday, 8-11 a.m., 2-9 p.m., Sunday 8a.m.-1 p.m., 5-9 p.m. Calle 2 7-46). On the beach at the foot of Carrera 11, fishermen sell their catch in the late afternoon.

Asados Don Pepe !

(ENTREES: $1.30-3.20) At 4 p.m., Don Pepe begins firing up the grill under a tarp along Avenida la Marina. By 6 p.m., the line of people throng in. This *asadero* (grill), though basic, serves up some of the best barbecue you'll find along this coast — and at a very good price. Choose between chorizo sausage ($1.30), chicken ($2.10), goat ($2.65) or beef or pork cutlet ($3.20). All plates come heaping with salad, *bollitos* (boiled corn-dough rolls), yucca or potatoes and huge slabs of meat. Open daily, from 6-10 p.m. Calle 1 and Carrera 10. Updated: Jun 10, 2008.

Marino's Junior

How many ways can you fix a hotdog? Marino's Junior has over 50 of them. The best of the charcoal-grilled sausages is the Suizo, 10 inches of pure beef. They also have six other types of dogs with a variety of fixings: Italian (with mozzarella cheese), Scottish, ranchero, Mexican and Hawaiian. All come with fries. Open daily from 4 p.m. until they run out of steam, often until dawn. Calle 1 10-97. Cel: 310-705-0117. Updated: Jun 10, 2008.

Restaurante-Bar La Tinaja

Restaurante-Bar La Tinaja's menu includes typical Colombian and Guajiran dishes. However, its specialty is seafood—specifically the *cazuela de mariscos*, a stew made with select fish and shellfish ($10.50). The staff will eagerly explain the recipe to you. It comes served with yummy coconut rice or white rice and *patacones* (fried plantains). The restaurant has a sea view and the service is stellar. Open daily, 7 a.m.-10 p.m. Calle 1 4-59. Tel: 5-727-3929, Fax: 5-727-2731. Updated: Jun 10, 2008.

Riohacha Nightlife

Along Avenida la Marina several bars open until late at night, where you can sit at a sidewalk table nursing a beer, watching the riohachero night and singing along with the gang to Vallenatos. Discos are almost exclusively a Thursday to Friday night affair.

Marianos Bar

At the corner of Avenida la Marina and the pedestrian street Carrera 8 are many yellow tables full of people. An intense strobe light show plays across the ceiling of the second floor, where you can spot other clubbers lean against the balcony, watching the night scene below. There is no real dance floor here. Relax, enjoy the breeze coming off the sea and talk with friends. There's a full bar, as well as several national beers ($1.60-2.65). Open 1 p.m.-1:30 a.m. Calle 1 and Carrera 8. Tel: 317-410-2936. Updated: Jun 10, 2008.

Casa Vieja Galería Bar

Inside, a small dance floor invites you to groove to the music playing at just the right volume. Nooks and crannies conceal couples chatting over a drink. Original paintings by local artists decorate the walls. A few tables and a bar out on the pedestrian street is where you can have your brew, taking in the sea breeze and nightlife. A beer here costs $1.30-1.60. Cocktails of various types run from $2.65-4.20. Open daily, 4-11 p.m. Carrera 8, between Calles 1 and 2. Updated: Jun 10, 2008.

Palomino

Here's a little Colombian secret, one that few foreigners have heard about. It's called Palomino and it is mid-way between Riohacha and Santa Marta, flanked by the San Salvador and Palomino Rivers. Buses pass through the town straddling the coastal highway. But head to the beach where the Caribbean lies wide open, waves crumpling ashore. In the dawn light, fishermen push their boats to sea. Comb these amber sands for shells or observe birds in the rivers' mangroves. On clear mornings the snowy peaks of Sierra Nevada de Santa Marta backdrop the palm trees. Sea turtles nest here in season. Updated: Jun 10, 2008.

When to Go

Palomino, like the rest of coastal Guajira, is hot, especially from May to July. January winds are brisk. September-November is the rainy season, as is April.

Palomino is a popular vacation destination for Colombians. If you want the beach to yourself, avoid Christmas-New Years, Semana Santa and three-day holiday weekends. Updated: Jun 10, 2008.

Getting To and Away from Palomino

Take any Riohacha-Santa Marta bus and ask the driver to let you off at Palomino (from Riohacha, bus $6.35; to Santa Marta buseta $3.70, bus $3.70-6.35; 1.5 hours in either direction). The beach, where most lodging is located, is a kilometer (0.6 miles) away. As the way is confusing and access difficult, it is best to phone the hostel you'll be staying at for directions. Updated: Jun 11, 2008.

Safety in Palomino

Most lodging is in fenced grounds where the administrator-family also lives, providing some security. Beach camping is not recommended, except possibly during holiday times when others pitch their tents too.

There are strong currents along the shore and at the mouth of the rivers. Most locals go swimming upstream of the rivers, where the water is more placid. During the rainy season, take precautions against mosquitoes, which carry dengue, malaria and yellow fever (for which you should be vaccinated). Updated: Jun 10, 2008.

Palomino Lodging

On the beach are a half dozen or more inns but most close during the off season. There are camping and hammock places, and romantic cabaña get-aways. Expect your shower to be a toss-water affair. Electricity is a bit scarce along here, so be sure you have a flashlight and extra candles with you. As the nearest restaurants are up by the highway 1 kilometer (0.6 miles) away, some hostels have cooking facilities. Call the hotel where you will be staying beforehand so it may arrange for your visit accordingly.

La Casa de Rosa

(BED: $3-5) Eugenio and his young family run this wonderful backpacker retreat on a wooded ground just 50 meters from the beach. Lodging is either camping, a hammock in the *enramada* (open sided palm-thatch shelter) or front porch of the guesthouse, or a room with a bed in the hostel. A rustic shower hut is where you take a toss-water bath. Porcelain latrines service your other needs. Prepare your meals in the outdoor kitchen. There is no electricity, though candles are provided. If you're looking for something more luxurious, ask Eugenio for a room with electricity and other amenities. Call for directions. Tel: 315-752-6287 / 311-680-6821. Updated: Jun 10, 2008.

Near Palomino

Santuario de Flora y Fauna Los Flamencos

With the collapse of the fishing industry on this coast, Santuario de Flora y Fauna Los Flamencos was established in 1977 to recover the ecosystem and provide alternative income to locals. The park encompasses 7,000 hectares, protecting four coastal lagoons. It is home to 237 bird species, including flamingo, roseate spoonbill, black ibis and cari cari. Four species are endemic, 78 resident and 39 migratory. The best months for sighting flamingos and other migratory fowl are October and November. Besides sail-canoe tours through the lagoons and mangroves, several paths wind through the desert forests to lookout towers where you can observe wildlife.

Grupo Asociativo El Santuario, formed by the community within the Santuario, has basic lodging at the reserve, near the ranger hut (per person: camping $2.65, your own hammock in a cabaña $3.70, hammock rental in cabaña $6.35). Meals are available (breakfast $2.65, lunch or dinner $5.30-8). The bathrooms are nice but have toss-water showers, and there is no electricity. From Riohacha, collective taxis for Camarones leave from Calle 15 and Carerra 7 (last bus back from Camarones at 6 p.m., $1.05 to Camarones village, $1.60 to the mouth of Río Camarones if enough passengers, 15 minutes). Twenty kilometers (12 miles) west of Riohacha, 165 kilometers (99 miles) east of Santa Marta. Tel: 310-369-7763, E-mail: ecoturismosantuario@yahoo.es, redcimarron21@hotmail.com. Updated: Jun 10, 2008.

Photo by Lorraine Caputo

Manaure

Alt: 3m Pop: 68,000 City Code: 5

Amid a flat landscape where small-leafed trees and cacti meet the blue-green sea is the small village of Manaure. Northeast of Riohacha, it is called La Novia Blanca (White Bride) of Colombia, for the important salt flats that have been exploited here since long before the Spaniards arrived to these shores. The main plaza has a sculpture commemorating the salt worker. Manaure's Catholic church has an impressive mosaic of Wayuu cosmology on its façade. Updated: Jun 10, 2008.

History

For centuries, this part of the coast was an important sea salt cultivation spot for Wayuu. The present town, San Agustín de Manaure, was founded in 1723 by Capuchin missionary friars. The namesake, Manaure, was a revered Wayuu warrior of the region. Like its neighbor Riohacha, Manaure was visited by pirates in search of salt as well as riches. Legend says the great Henry Morgan hid part of his booty here. Updated: Jun 10, 2008.

When to Go

As in the rest of Guajira, it is hot here and even more so for the salt flats. The most searing time of the year is May-July. Temperatures range from 28ºC-38ºC (82-101ºF). Short, torrential downpours descend on the city during May-June and again from October to November. Refreshing winds are common.

During vacation times, Manaure experiences some increased tourism by Colombians seeking to experience a beautiful and exotic part of their country. It is the Wayuu village closest to major population areas and the easiest to get to.

Holidays and Festivals

The big festival in Manuare occurs in June, giving salute to all the things most important to its economy: Festival de la Sal, Gas y Flamencos. In addition to being Colombia's greatest producer of marine salt, Manuare also has great reserves of natural gas. The third honoree, flamencos, of course refers to the pink flamingos that reside at Musichi.

Getting To and Away from Manaure

Manaure is a fairly small town, so it is easy to get around on foot. In the hottest part of the day, though, you might consider taking a covered bicycle taxi ($0.50).

All transportation in Manaure leaves from the various company offices in the street market district, on Carrera 4 between Calles 6 and 9. Mostly, they are shared taxis that depart when full.

From Manure

Arrive	Departure	Time	Price
Rioacha	5 a.m. -5 p.m.	2 hours	$6
Uribia*	6 a.m. -5 p.m.	20 mins	$2
Maicao	5 a.m. -5 p.m.	1 hour	$4

*NOTE: For safety and time reasons it is better to transport to Uribia from sunrise to sunset.*Updated: Jun 10, 2008.

Safety in Manaure

When asked about how safe Manaure is, especially when staying overnight in the beach kiosks, the response from locals is, "It's too safe." Of course, to side with caution, keep valuables well protected and an eye on belongings. Updated: Jun 10, 2008.

Manaure Services

Tourism Office

The village does not have a tourism office, but it does have a website where you can learn more about this destination: http://manaure-laguajira.gov.co.

Money

Manuare has a Banco Agrario, though no ATMs or services for non-residents. Some shops handle transactions for major banks, but again nothing for the traveler. Cachaco Carto, in the two story green building down in the market area, will reportedly change U.S. dollars (Carrera 4, between Calles 8 and 9).

Keeping in Touch

The Telecom office in Manaure closed a while back, and the village has no post office. Shops and stands charge $0.10-0.15 per minute for local and national calls. Several internet cafés are around the plaza but most close for lunch. Internet is more expensive here, costing $1.60-2.10 per hour.

Medical

The public hospital is E.S.E. Hospital Armando Pabón López (Calle 1 6-35, Tel.: 5-717-8020. There are three pharmacies on Carrera 4, between Calles 4 and 7.

Shopping

Artesanías Wayuu Jalianaya

Jalianaya is an *asociación de trabajo* (labor association) comprised of Wayuu women. Walking into its shop, you'll see them seated around the edge of the front showroom, crocheting, talking and buying bundles of yarn. On the walls hang a rainbow of bags (beginning from $19). Most of these, made of strong acrylic string, are of traditional design, though some are more modern. In a back room hang hammocks, woven in synthetic or cotton fiber on an upright loom (from $210). Calle 2 2-07. Tel: 5-717-8516 / Sales (Manaure) 311-442-1017 (Bogotá) 314-470-7034, E-mail: mariacristina@jalianaya.com, URL: www.jalianaya.com. Updated: Jun 10, 2008.

Artesanía Wayuu Mutsia

The wall to one side of Artesanía Wayuu Mutsia's front patio is like a picture dictionary, giving you an introduction to the Wayuu language. Inside, typical items await you, like *wayuusheein* (natural fiber robes) *wayuusupatsu* (sandals with pompoms) and *waireñas* (regular cloth sandals). There are also *susu* (bags), *süi* (hammocks) and ceramics. All items are made by Wayuu. Original paintings by Chicho Ruiz Ortiz are available. During the high season, Artesanía Wayuu Mutsia is also open Saturdays. Calle 3, on the Plaza Principal. Tel: 5-728-1553 / 310-745-3092 / 3331. Updated: Jun 10, 2008.

Things to See and Do

Manaure has few activities, but all of them are worth doing. Musichi, Carrizal, Poportín and other near-by coastal lagoons are fruitful grounds for birdwatchers. The salt works are the largest of the country, permitting you to see the contrast between the age-old methods of the indigenous Wayuu and the modern-day massive extraction by big industry. Several women's cooperatives sell everyday articles made by hand as well as invite you to know about the Wayuu way of life. The beaches are clean and the sea is beautiful, perfect for taking a break from the heat. Updated: Jun 10, 2008.

The Salt Works

The road along the beach connects the two salt works in town. To the east is the industrial one, with high, white mountains glistening in the sun. It is the largest salt extraction in Colombia, covering 4,200 hectares and garnering up to 700,000 tons of this mineral per year. Guides are available for hire to take you through the site.

At the opposite end of the beach road, just past the barrio popular are the salt flats of the local Wayuu community. Rectangular plots are carved into the sand. As the water within them evaporates, they turn a brilliant fuchsia rimmed with crystallizing salt.

It is easy to walk to both of these salt works, or you can hire a bike or motor taxi to take you. Tours to the Guajira make an obligatory stop at the *salinas* (salt flats). Do not underestimate the power of the sun here. Cover up well, drink plenty of fluids and rest in the shade. Updated: Jun 10, 2008.

Musichi

A spectacular sight is watching a flock of flamingos wading through shallow waters, bending their serpentine necks to sieve food through their bills. A perfect place to observe these majestic, rose-colored birds is at Musichi, 14 kilometers from Manaure. Here the sea forms a lagoon which is a rendezvous point for them, even outside the rainy season. There is also a beach where you can soak up the sun and dip into the fine water. The best time to see the flamingos is 5-7 a.m. and 3-5 p.m. There is a lookout tower from which to observe them. As they are easily spooked, do not use a motor launch in their vicinity. You can arrive at Musichi by mototaxi ($16) or by 10-person launch ($42 for two-hour trip, takes a half hour to arrive). Updated: Jun 10, 2008.

Beaches near Manaure

In and near Manaure are a number of lagoons where you can observe flamingos and other waterfowl. Many also have beaches where you can cool down. In Manaure itself the beach is a shadeless, pale-gray expanse and the sea a deep teal. Pájaro and Mayapo beaches have kiosks providing shade and food. Northeast of Manaure is Poportín with white sand beaches and shallow, clear waters. Here, as well as at Cordón and Carrizal further up the coast, birdwatching is excellent. To get to these other beaches without your own transportation is a bit difficult. You can make arrangements with the tour operators in Manaure and Uribia, or hire a taxi. Updated: Jun 10, 2008.

Manaure Tours

Manaure has only one official tour operator, run by a group of Wayuu women. Most agencies in Riohacha and elsewhere include the salinas in their itinerary of the Guajira, but not Musichi. Your hotel may be able to help you locate a launch or mototaxi to take you out there. One recommended ride is Antonio de la Rosa, who can take you to both the salinas and Musichi for $16 with a two-hour wait at the latter. Tel: 2-606-1987, or through Hotel Palaaima.

Coopmur

Coopmur, Cooperativa Multiactiva de Trabajo Asociado de Mujeres Rurales, is a cooperative of 12 local Wayuu women with the vision of sharing their world with outsiders. Through guided tours to the salinas, Musichi, local beaches, fishing coops and Ruinas de Santa Rosa, you can get to know corners of the Manaure countryside few other tour agencies go to. These women are eager to share their culture and legends with visitors in an effort to dispel misunderstandings of their unique society. Coopmur also supports the creation of traditional Wayuu crafts, such as bags and hammocks. Cel: 313-502-6496 / 311-276-8484, E-mail: coopmur@hotmail.com. Updated: Jun 10, 2008.

Manaure Lodging

Surprisingly, Manaure has more places to stay than Uribia does. For the most part, they are basic, well-kept places. Problems with the water supply exist here. Showers are provided with a large container of water from which you take a toss-water bath. On the west end of the beach are a dozen open-sided public kiosks where you can stay overnight, camping or sleeping in a hammock. No facilities are provided at these, and the only security provided is the large spotlight in the center of the grouping.

Hotel Unuuipa

(BED: $6-21) Hotel Unuuipa wears the colors of these desert lands: salmon, ochre and melon. Inside are two courtyards around which somewhat cramped rooms are arranged. All have private bath, though for your shower you have to scoop water out of the provided barrel and toss it over yourself. With a variety of lodging options, you can choose the level of comforts you want and money you want to spend. The staff can help you arrange travel to nearby sites. Carrera 7 4-12. Tel: 316-888-2156. Updated: Jun 10, 2008.

Cabañas Manaure Beach

(BED: $10.50) Cabañas Manaure Beach is a basic, four-room hostel: two quarters have three beds each and the other two, four beds each. The windows have shutters, but no glass or nets. Even though the private baths have showers set up, they may not work. A large barrel of water is provided from which to do a toss bath. Don Orlando also rents hammocks if you want to stay in the public cabañas ($5.30), and he can arrange a visit to Musichi by boat for you. Tel: 5-728-3678 / 310-372-2160 / 455-5287. Updated: Jun 10, 2008.

Hotel Palaaima

(ROOM: $15-32) For many years Doña Iris has been welcoming visitors to Manaure. Her Hotel Palaaima is the best lodging option in the village. The beautiful building has 14 airy rooms, simply decorated, with private bath, TV and fan or air conditioning. She is knowledgeable about the Guajira and can help you arrange outings. In the courtyard of this inn is a tile-floored, thatched shelter restaurant that serves breakfast, lunch and dinner ($2.10-2.65). Carrera 6 7-34. Tel: 5-717-8455 / 8195, E-mail: hotelpalaaima@hotmail.com / irisfaep@hotmail.com. Updated: Jun 10, 2008.

Manaure Restaurants

Manaure doesn't have very many restaurants, and they close relatively early. Past the west end of the beach are some basic shacks that serve blue-plate specials and fish. Along Carrera 4, between Calles 6 and 9, there is a street market and grocery stores. The formal mercado municipal is on Calle 9 between Carreras 2 and 3. As well as food, check here for Wayuu robes, bags and hammocks. Market day is Saturday.

There is not much in the way of nightlife in Manaure. Wayuu society frowns on drinking establishments, and its culture does not include any dancing other than for ceremonies.

Heladería y Refresquería Marce

To seek refuge from the ardent Manaure sun, pull up a seat at one of the tables on the front walk of Heladería y Refresquería Marce to enjoy a cup of ice cream. No, doña Marce doesn't mess with cones. It is all served in cups, from two scoops on up. She also sells other ice cream treats, milk shakes, sodas, sandwiches and snacks. This place is open Monday-Saturday, 8 a.m. until whenever, Sunday, from 2 p.m. until, well, whenever. Calle 3, next to Banco Agrario on the main plaza. Updated: Jun 10, 2008.

Restaurante La Negra

Restaurante La Negra is one of the very few real restaurants in Manaure. At lunch time, the tables inside and out on the sidewalk are crowded with people chowing down on the set lunch, which includes soup, choice of meat, beans or lentils, salad and yucca (beef $2.65, fish $3.20-3.70). An unusual feature in these parts is the accompanying drink. At dinner hour, only the main course is served. Open daily, 6:30 a.m.-6:30 p.m. Carrera 7-67. Updated: Jun 10, 2008.

Restaurante Manaure Beach

Restaurante Manaure Beach is, as you can expect, right on the shore. The main restaurant is a large, open-sided kiosk with a deck extending out over the sand. The menu is almost exclusively seafood. A meal with fish comes with coconut rice, fried plantains and salad (from $6.35). Also on the menu is *cazuela de mariscos* (soup prepared with shrimp, conch, squid and octopus) with rice and fried plantains on the side ($13.10). Open daily, 8 a.m.-6 p.m. If you are staying at the cabañas, you can order for later. Manaure Abajo (west end of beach). Tel: 5-728-3678 / 301-372-2160 / 455-5287. Updated: Jun 10, 2008.

Uribia

Alt: 29m Pop: 116,000 City Code: 5

The road heads north from Cuatro Vías to the Uribia-Manaure turn-offs (one tollbooth). To the left is Manaure. Turning right, after four kilometers (2.4 miles) you come to the Indigenous Capital of Colom-

Festival de Cultura Wayuu

The three-day festival draws participants from both Colombia and Venezuela. In Uribia's plaza, three-sided huts called *enramadas* exhibit weavings, and townsfolk serve gastronomic delights. In the evenings are various programs, like the *yonna*, a dance performed for socially or spiritually important occasions; its different movements are named for the region's fauna. Contestants out-vie each other in *jayeishi*, a sung poem relating personal experiences and Wayuu culture. They play traditional instruments like *kasha* (a drum made of goat or cow hide), *totoroy* (flute) and *wahawai* (a wind instrument that imitates birdsong). The festival's culmination is the election of the *Majayut*, or queen, who must demonstrate a profound knowledge of Wayuu traditions. Updated: Jun 10, 2008.

bia, Uribia. Here is the heart of Guajira, the land of the Wayuu. All roads lead to Uribia. It is the hub of transportation for the Guajira Alta. You must come here first to go to Cabo de la Vela and Nazareth, gateway to Parque Nacional Natural Macuira. This young city is laid out like Paris, France, in that The Plaza Parque Colombia is octagonal. This is the center of village life. Here are an obelisk, gazebo, playground, basketball court and bandstand. Around the perimeter are the important buildings, such as the mayor's office and church, as well as restaurants and other businesses. From the plaza all streets radiate out. All of the streets have at least three names, making it a bit difficult to give directions. Updated: Jun 10, 2008.

Uribia History

Uribia is a 20th Century city, founded on March 1, 1935, by Capitán Eduardo Londoño Villegas. It is named in memory of General Rafael Uribe, one of the leaders during the Guerra de 1,000 Días, the civil war that racked Colombia at the end of the 19th Century. For a while, Uribia was the capital of Guajira Territory, until the Department was established in 1954 and the capital moved to Riohacha. This city then became the center for indigenous affairs. Updated: Jun 10, 2008.

When to Go

Uribia is hot all year. During the daytime, temperatures climb to 30-35°C (86-95°F). Nights are a cooler 28°C (82°F). In January and February winds moderate the heat a little. Rains can be expected from May to July.

The Festival de Cultura Wayuu is a big event in the region, with participants arriving from all over the Guajira. It draws many national tourists as well. If planning on visiting the area during this time, advance reservations should be made at the established hotels.

Holidays and Festivals

The biggest event in Uribia is the annual Festival de la Cultura Wayuu, held the last week of May, highlighting all aspects of this indigenous nation's traditions and the election of their *Majayut de Oro* (Miss Gold).

Pre-Carnaval is celebrated for two weeks before Carnaval, on Friday and Saturday nights. At dusk, the townspeople, dressed in costumes, dance through the streets to the rhythm of bands. Then comes the pre-Lenten party. Updated: Jun 10, 2008.

Getting To and Away From Uribia

Bicycle rickshaws ply the streets of Uribia. Transportation leaves from Avenida Fundador, the street on which the market is, or you can ask the company to pick you up at your lodging. Fare depends on the distance.

Arrive	Departure	Time	Price
Maicao	pick-up truck 6-8:30 a.m.	1 hour	$3
Rioacha	6 a.m.-4 p.m.	2 hours	$6
Manaure	6 a.m.-5 p.m.	20 mins	$2
Cabo de la Vela	9-11 a.m., 4 p.m.	1-2 hours	$5-8
Nazareth	Sunday 8 a.m. or earlier	8-10 hours	$16 -19

A cheaper way to arrive to Uribia is to take a bus as far as the Cuatro Vías crossroads ($2.10), and from there a collective taxi or pick up truck ($2.65). Updated: Jun 10, 2008.

Safety in Uribia

Residents of Uribia say the city is very safe. They counsel that if you are going out into the desert, you should go with someone who knows the area, and, if going on a tour, make sure the company has a back-up plan in case the vehicle breaks down. Take plenty of water with you if going into the Alta Guajira.

Uribia Services

Tourism Office

There is no tourism office at present, but once the new Palacio Municipal on the corner of the plaza and Avenida Fundador is finished, the city plans to have an Oficina de Cultura y Turismo. URL: www.uribia-laguajira.gov.co.

Money

On the plaza, between Avenida La Marina and Avenida Hospital is a Bancolombia ATM (MasterCard, Visa, Cirrus, American Express, ATH). The ATM doesn't work all the time. It is best to play it safe and stock up on pesos in Riohacha or Maicao. Apparently, a store down in the market area changes U.S. dollars and bolívares fuertes.

Keeping in Touch

Thanks to the predominance of cellular phones, Uribia's Telecom has closed. Plenty of shops offer local and national calls for $0.15 per minute. It is difficult to make international calls. Luckily, Compartel, the only trustworthy internet provider in town, has Skype. Sit down at a computer for $1 per hour. Monday-Friday, 8:30 a.m.-12:30 p.m., 3-9 p.m., Saturday 9 a.m.-12:30 p.m., 3-9 p.m. Next to Ludoteca on the plaza, near the corner of the street to Hotel Juyasirian. Uribia has no post office.

Medical

Avenida Hospital leads straight to Hospital de Nuestra Señora del Perpetuo Socorro (Transversal 8 6-45, Tel: 5-717-7033). There is only a handful of pharmacies in Uribia: Droguería El David (Diagonal 7 5-77) and Droguería Keyris (Diagonal 8B 8-32).

Camera

Foto Wayuu stocks only batteries and Fuji ASA 100 color film. Monday-Friday, 7 a.m.-9 p.m., irregular hours Saturday and Sunday. Avenida Fundador, half block from the plaza, on the right-hand side.

Shopping

Cecilia Bonivento

At her home in Barrio Abuchairre, Doña Cecilia of the Jusayú clan sits in an open-sided hut. A colleague shows her a new technique for weaving drawstrings for bags. From a line, in the shade of another hut, hang an assortment of the bags in earthen and brighter colors, mostly in traditional designs. Also strung from pole to pole is a double-faced hammock, thick yet cool and comfortable, woven by her and other women out at the ranchería. Her work is certified by Artesanías de Colombia in Bogotá and carries the Icontec seal of quality. Barrio Abuchairre. Tel: 312-607-8644. Updated: Jun 10, 2008.

Things to See and Do

Uribia is not a destination in and of itself, except as the Capital Indígena de Colombia and its annual Festival de la Cultural Wayuu. From here roads weave like threads across the desert into the Alta Guajira: to Cabo de la Vela, Nazareth and the cloud forest reserve Parque Nacional Natural Macuira, or to mythical places, like the Rock of Destiny, the lost city of Puerto López and the end of the world at Punta Gallina.

Uribia Tours

There are two tour operators in Uribia ready to take you on adventures into the Alta Guajira. Both have connections with the indigenous Wayuu communities, thus providing excursions as seen through the eyes of the people of this land. SENA has a program here in Uribia to train local youths to be guides. Tel: 311-264-6903 / 421-1833 / 672-4115.

Kai Ecotravel

Kai Ecotravel is a network of Wayuu communities welcoming visitors into the Alta Guajira, providing guides, translators (Spanish and Wayuunaiki), vehicle rental with drivers, lodging and meals. Kai offers an eight-day package to Wosopo, Castilletes, Puerto López, Punta Espada (Piedra del Destino), Nazareth and Macuira, Punta Gallinas, Parque Eólico and Cabo de la Vela. Cost depends on group size and includes driver, guides, lodging and meals. Alternately, hire a vehicle and guide for a two-day/one-night excursion to Punta Gallinas (1-5 persons $160, lodging and meals extra) or a one-day outing to El Cardón, Carrizal, Cabo de la Vela and Parque Eólico (1-5 persons $80). Avenida Bogotá (Diagonal 1B) 8-68. Tel: 312-626-8121 / 311-436-2830, E-mail: info@kaiecotravel.com, URL: www.kaiecotravel.com. Updated: Jun 13, 2008.

Kaishi

Owned and operated by Andrés Delgado and Ericka Brujes, who is Wayuu and the former tourism officer for Uribia. Specializing in eco and ethnotourism, they offer tours to Cabo de la Vela, Manaure, Maicao Minas de El Cerrejón and Tardes de Ranchería en Cabo de la Vela or Riohacha. On longer excursions, they will take you to Cabo de la Vela, or to some of the harder-to-reach destinations of the Alta Guajira, like Piedra del Destino, Nazareth, Parque Nacional Natural Macuira and Punta Gallinas. Birdwatching trips can be arranged. Kaishi has bilingual guides. Plaza Principal, between Avenida la Marina and the avenue without a name, next to Asados Mana. Tel: 5-717-7306 / 7008 / 311-429-6315, E-mail: kaishiturismo@yahoo.co.uk / adelgadorozco@yahoo.com, URL: www.kaishitravel.com. Updated: Jun 13, 2008.

Uribia Lodging

For many years Uribia was a one-hotel town, but now it has two decent inns. In the market district is a tumble-down *residencia*. During the Festival de Cultura Wayuu, places to stay are difficult to find. Updated: Jun 13, 2008.

Hospedaje Villa María

(ROOM: $8-21) Hospedaje Villa María is the new kid in town, owned and operated by Kaishi tours. Along one side of the bare interior patio, which also serves as secure parking for its guests, there is a corridor for hammock sleeping (yours or theirs, $8). In this area, guests share the common bath. This is the least expensive option in Uribia. Off this area are rooms decorated simply with A/C and private bath ($21 per person). From the Plaza, follow Avenida la Marina (where the new Alcaldía Municipal is being built) up one block. Take a left and the inn is about four houses down on your left. Phone or drop by tour operator Kaishi's office. One block up from the Plaza Parque Colombia, a half-block to the left of Avenida la Marina. Tel: 5-717-7306 / 7008 / 311-429-6315, E-mail: kaishiturismo@yahoo.co.uk / adelgadorozco@yahoo.com. Updated: Jun 13, 2008.

> **Travel Tips**
>
> Be prepared to spend time and money if traveling on your own, due to infrequent transportation. The most important thing to take is plenty of water. Also pack emergency food supplies, sun block, a hat or other items to protect you from the sun, and a tent or hammock. Along the way you should be able to find shelter and food. In Punta Gallinas one of the only inns where you can spend the night and eat is Hospedaje y Comidas Luzmila. Tel.: 5-521-5005 / 312-647-9881 / 626-8121. Updated: Jun 17, 2008.

Hotel Juyasirian !

(ROOM: $16-21) Walking into Hotel Juyasirian, you can tell it was built specifically for high-ranking government officials and others important people. The architecture has refinements that whisper of its former existence. But now anyone can stay here in these spacious rooms, most with central A/C and private bath. The staff is friendly and attentive. Anytime of the day it is a pleasure to sit out on the front veranda or the gazebo, sipping on a free cup of wine and chatting with whoever walks by. Hotel Juyasirian is a favorite with tour groups. From the Plaza Parque Colombia, behind the stage, follow the unnamed street that is between the library and the *ludoteca* (children's store) for one block. The hotel is at the next intersection. Calle 14A 9-06. Tel: 5-717-7284 / 310-734-0654. Updated: Jun 13, 2008.

Uribia Restaurants

Uribia has very few restaurants. A couple hole-in-the-walls are in the market district on Avenida Fundador, where the majority of general stores are as well. Buy plenty of water here if going into the Alta Guajira, as it is much more expensive elsewhere ($1.60 for a five-liter jug). Uribia's water is brackish and not suitable for purification.

Goat is a main staple of Wayuu cuisine—the dish to try is *friche* (stewed goat). *Sahpulana*, a soup made of beans, corn and squash, is a traditional dish. *Chinchirri*, a strong alcoholic beverage made from *panela* (raw sugar) and water is a common drink of choice.

Due to the presence of the military and other non-Wayuu, a few dance clubs and drinking establishments do operate, despite such customs not being part of the Wayuu way of life. They are mostly the evening operations of restaurants. Updated: Jun 13, 2008.

Asados Mana

(ENTREE: $2.10) Just before dusk, a few tables are put out on the sidewalk and the ever-present BBQ grill is fired up. Soon the chickens are put on the rotisserie, their dripping grease sizzling as it hits the hot coals. By night, the smell of *pollo asado* drifts across the park as plates of poultry and potatoes are served to eager diners ($2.10 for a quarter of a chicken). Another name for Asados Mana is Mana Restaurante y Disco Licores, as the back room is a bar serving cocktails, as well as national and international liquors. In the plaza, three doors to the right of Avenida La Marina. Updated: Jun 13, 2008.

No-name Restaurant

(LUNCH: $2.65) This simple building with leaf-green roll-up doors is one of the few dining choices in Uribia. For breakfast, you can have eggs with arepa and coffee or chocolate ($1.85), or the standard Colombian stewed or grilled beef platter ($2.65). From 11 a.m. on is time for almuerzo ($2.65). As in much of the Guajira, a drink is not included. Evenings, the tables are pushed back to make way for the dance floor of the town's only regular disco, playing whatever the clientele want to hear. The restaurant is open daily 7 a.m.-4 p.m.; the disco is open Monday-Thursday, 5-10 p.m., Friday-Saturday 5 p.m.-1 a.m. On the plaza, at the corner of Avenida Fundador. Updated: Jun 13, 2008.

Restaurante Juyasirian

(LUNCH: $3.70) In the cool shade of an enramada on the back patio is the restaurant at Hotel Juyasirian. Parrots and macaws roam freely on the rafters overhead. In a cage, a mico monkey sways in a hammock, taking interest in female diners. It's not the cheapest place (breakfast $2.65, luncheon comida corrientes with drink $3.70, à la carte dishes from $5.30), but doña Eugenia and her staff provide excellent food and good service. Open 7 a.m.-9 p.m. Calle 14A 9-06. Tel: 5-717-7284 / 310-734-0654. Updated: Jun 13, 2008.

The Alta Guajira

The Alta Guajira has many impressive sites. On the road to Nazareth is Puerto López, which was once an important port but is now a ghost town abandoned to the desert. Petroglyphs decorate Piedra de Alas at Siapana, a holy spring. Punta Espada, or Piedra del Destino, is a mythical rock that reveals the future of the visitor.

Along the north coast are other places of interest, such as Puerto Bolívar, the port where the El Cerrón mine railway arrives; Bahía Portete, another important port with beaches, mangroves and the only sea crocodiles in the world; Bahía Honda with fortress ruins; and Punta Gallina, the northern-most point of South America, where golden dunes tumble to a deep-blue sea.

Getting To and Away from the Alta Guajira

Places in the Upper Guajira are difficult to reach, except by private car or on a tour. You could wait for next week's truck to possibly make it to the places along the road to Nazareth. You can also ask around in Nazareth and other villages to see if anyone is heading for the north coast. Updated: Jun 17, 2008.

Nazareth and Parque Nacional Natural Macuira

Alt: 65m Pop: 7,000 City Code: 5

Nazareth serves as the gateway into Parque Nacional Natural Macuira, a unique biological island that is a cloud forest within the desert. Its 25,000 hectares encompass the Serranía de Macuira, an ancient mountain range that reaches to 865 meters (2,837 feet). Among the 249 flora species are mosses and orchids. Fauna include monkeys, tigrillo, deer, guacharaca and 22 endemic species of birds. Entrance to the national park is free. Updated: Jun 10, 2008.

Getting To and Away From Nazareth and PNN Macuira

Early Sunday morning an unsheltered truck leaves from Maicao, swinging through Uribia, for Nazareth ($18.65-21). In the high season, there may also be a truck that leaves on Wednesdays. It is best to arrive in Uribia at least one day in advance to verify if the truck will be going.

The truck returns to Uribia and Maicao on Thursday or Friday. Transportation is only once weekly (twice in high season).

An alternative way to reach Nazareth and Parque Nacional Natural Macuira is with one of the tour agencies in Uribia and Riohacha. Guides in Nazareth charge $5.30-32 per group for trips into the park, depending on the hike. The national park office is in Nazareth. Updated: Jun 10, 2008.

Safety in Nazareth and PNN Macuira

There are many snakes in the park. Yellow fever is endemic in this area, so get the vaccine well before arriving. Updated: Jun 13, 2008.

Cabo de la Vela

Alt: 3m Pop: 1,500 City Code: 5

North of the Manaure-Uribia crossroads, the highway continues to parallel the coal railway northward, to the turn-off for Cabo de la Vela and eventually passing the Parque Eólico and ending at Puerto Bolívar. The road is rough and low clearance vehicles will have a difficult time. From the turn-off for Cabo de la Vela, a well-worn track cuts 17 kilometers across the desert to the coastal hamlet. Several creeks have to be crossed.

Cabo de la Vela is on a bay. Along the south shore, a road edges the waterfront. On the right side are mostly cane-slat buildings serving as restaurants, shops and hostels. On the seaside of the strip are enramadas rented out for hanging a hammock or pitching a tent. The beach road continues to the desert, then curves westward giving access to inns along the north coast of the bay and ending at El Faro. Updated: Jun 13, 2008.

History

Even though Alonso de Ojeda was the first Spaniard to sail around this cape in 1498, the first to set foot on this land was Juan de la Cosa. In 1526, Martín Fernández de Enciso founded Nuestra Señora Santa María de los Remedios del Cabo de la Vela as the capital of the Guajira Territory. Later the administrative seat would be moved farther south. Updated: Jun 13, 2008.

When to Go

The hottest months in Cabo de la Vela are September-November, with more cooling winds in January and February. The wet season is from June to August.

Cabo de la Vela is a popular vacation destination. Colombians warn that if you want the tranquility Cabo de la Vela has to offer, do not come during the December-January holidays and Semana Santa. The beach is packed with campers and music blares until after dawn. Everyone sleeps until mid-morning and the party resumes. Updated: Jun 13, 2008.

Holidays and Festivals

Most of the holidays in Cabo de la Vela are the same as in the rest of Colombia, the most important being December 8, the Velorio de la Virgen; Christmas Eve; and 31 December, New Years Eve with the burning of effigies representing Old Year Man. A special date is July 16, the feast day of the Virgen del Carmen, when all the hamlet's newborns are baptized. Updated: Jun 13, 2008.

Getting To and Away From Cabo de la Vela

To get to anyplace out of Cabo de la Vela via public transportation, you must first go to Uribia. Three pick-ups leave daily 4-4:30 a.m., and another possibly at 7 a.m. ($5.30); two of these continue to Maicao ($8). It is best to advise the driver the afternoon or evening before that you will want to travel the next day, so he stops to pick you up.

From Maicao a pick-up leaves at about noon, arriving in Uribia at about 4 p.m., then making its way to Cabo de la Vela at about dusk. Updated: Jun 13, 2008.

Safety in Cabo de la Vela

Safety in Cabo de la Vela and to the nearest sites is OK. Be mindful of personal belongings if staying in a beach enramada. These businesses usually have a place where you can stow your pack. Locals say walking away from the village to the highway is unsafe.

Be mindful that you are in a desert with very strong sun. Drink plenty of fluids, use sunscreen, and keep in the shade during the fiercest part of the day. On the north side of the bay are jellyfish (*aguas malas)* and coral reefs. Strong currents exist at Pilón de Azúcar. Updated: Jun 13, 2008.

Cabo de la Vela Services

Money

There are no banking or exchange services here. The nearest reliable ATM or place to cash travelers checks is in Riohacha.

Keeping in Touch

The village's Telecom is in Hotel Jarrinapi. It charges $0.25 per minute for local or national cellphone calls and $0.30 per minute to land lines; international calls begin at $0.60 per minute ($0.80 to U.S.). (Daily 8 a.m.-noon, 2-8 p.m.) Local shops charge $0.30-50 per minute for local and national calls. There is no internet café or post office.

Medical

The Centro de Salud is near the entrance to town. The only pharmacy is next door.

Camera

Tienda El Jhor, the bright blue concrete block building before Hotel Jarrinapi, sells Kodak color print film. Otherwise, you're out of luck. Updated: Jun 17, 2008.

Shopping

Donde Rosita Sánchez

Next to Restaurant y Hospedaje Miramar 2, Donde Rosita Sánchez is a community shop specializing in crafts. The small front-entry patio is hung with a wide assortment of the bags and hammocks for which the Wayuu are famous. On the racks inside is a selection of *wayuusheein* (the typical manta dresses of the women), some with traditional designs, others hand-painted. Shelves hold baskets of time-honored medicinal herbs. For $2.65 you can have your photo taken dressed in a wayuusheein and your face painted with Wayuu designs. Next to Restaurant y Hospedaje Miramar 2. Updated: Jun 13, 2008.

Artesanía Wayuu

The sunlight dapples through the cane slats of this small stand and onto the miscellaneous crafts exhibited. A small selection of bags and hand-painted covers sway in the wind. These necklaces, earrings, shell key chains and sculptures are created by the younger artisans of the village. Also for sale are home remedies like *aceite de tiburón* (oils for coughs and all that ails you) and powdered mother of pearl (for sunburn, which you are likely to suffer from here). Two lots past the Hotel Jarrinapi. Updated: Jun 13, 2008.

Things to See and Do

The biggest activity in Cabo de la Vela is getting relief from the sun, whether swinging in a hammock or swimming in the teal-blue sea. Walks to natural features along the coast are best done at dawn or late afternoon, to avoid the sun. The main road follows the curve of the bay. On the way, to the right horizon are El Pilón de Azúcar, Hoyos Sopladores (blow holes), Ojo de Agua (a natural pool) and caves. Ask around for a guide to take you to the more hidden treasures. Between the town and El Pilón de Azúcar is Laguna de Utta, a waterfowl refuge. Updated: Jun 13, 2008.

El Pilón de Azúcar

Out on the northeastern horizon you see an odd triangular-shaped rock rising out of the flat landscape. This is Kamainshi (Kamaici), the Lord of the Things of the Sea. El Pilón de Azúcar has always been a sacred site, believed to be Jepira, where the spirits of the dead arrive. Now a Virgin of Fátima shrine perches atop the white and pale green stone. From that vantage point, you can see the windmills of Parque Eólico Jepirachi twirling in the distance. At the western foot of Kamainshi is a small, golden-sand beach where you can cool off before continuing your hike.

A loose-gravel path zig-zags to the top. It can be quite windy on the summit. If with young children, hold onto them tight. It is a steep drop down to the sea. Take the walk in the early morning or late afternoon to avoid the heat. Families sell soft drinks and water in the parking lot at El Pilón de Azúcar. Swimming is fine near the beach, but further offshore there is a strong current.

Follow the road northwards out of town. When you get to the T crossroads, turn right. This will take you directly to El Pilón de Azúcar. From the main part of the village on the south shore, it takes about an hour one way. The apex is only 2.5-3 meters (7-10 feet) wide. Updated: Jun 13, 2008.

Laguna de Utta

A virtually unexplored birding paradise awaits you: Laguna de Utta, stretching across the desert just east of Cabo de la Vela, between the village and El Pilón de Azúcar. Not many visit this lagoon, which is a seasonal haven for waterfowl, such as flamingos and herons, as well as for shorebirds like sandpipers. Despite the immense size of this lagoon, its mangrove ecosystem has been little studied. Laguna de Utta has not yet been designated a protected area, either.

To avoid the heat, do the walk in the early morning or late afternoon. Be careful walking around the shore, as it is marshy. Also beware of snakes. Ask around in the village to see if someone has a launch to hire for boating around the lagoon. Follow the road northwards out of town. When you get to the T crossroads, turn right. You will begin seeing the lagoon's shore about 100 meters to the right of the road. From the main part of the village on the south shore, it takes around 30-45 minutes. Updated: Jun 13, 2008.

El Faro

The lighthouse is located on the very tip of the cape, warning those at sea of the imminent danger of these rocky shores. These days, it is a modern device keeping watch for sailors. The walk through this desert landscape or along the shore strewn with washed up fragments of large shells and sea urchins is the main appeal to this spot, as is the view of the sea stretching to an indistinct horizon.

Do the walk in the early morning or late afternoon, to avoid the heat. If staying to watch the sunset, do not begin the trip back too late. Follow the road northwards out of town. When you get to the T crossroads, turn left. This will take you directly to El Faro. From the main part of the village on the south shore, it takes 45 minutes to one hour, one way. Updated: Jun 13, 2008.

Snorkeling

The north side of the bay is rocky with coral reefs. Combined with the clear waters, this is a good place to do a bit of snorkeling. Beneath the surface are a variety of colorful tropical fish and other marine life among the coral reef and plant life. The water is a bit warmer on this side, with slightly more wave action and the occasional jellyfish. The sun is very strong. Wear a shirt to prevent sunburn. To get there, just walk along the shore, or follow the road out towards El Faro. The sea nears the road just before you arrive to the lighthouse. Updated: Jun 13, 2008.

Aquatic Sports

During Semana Santa (Easter Week) and the December-January holidays, locals open sites renting equipment for different aquatic sports. How about skipping across these crystalline waters on a *velero* (sailing boat), or windsurfing? *Gusanos* (giant inflatable rubber raft) are another way to enjoy a trip across the bay. Folks also rent out snorkeling gear and offer boat tours around the cape. However, to enjoy most of these activities, you'll have to come when everyone else does. Updated: Jun 13, 2008.

Parque Eólico Jepirachi

Like giant stoic soldiers lined up across the flat barren lands, awaiting the charge of a Quijote, hundreds of windmills reel their three arms against the clear azure sky. This is one of the largest electrical projects in the world, Parque Eólico Jepirachi, generating a good portion of Colombia's energy needs. Here there is a visitor center, various paths, a botanical garden and the Parque de Leyendas, explaining Wayuu mythology, as well as Saanain Woumain, an artisan association.

Most tours from Riohacha or Uribia include this on their itineraries. In Cabo de la Vela you can hire someone to drive you there and back, with a 30-minute wait ($26.50). Along the main north-south road, midway between the Manaure-Uribia crossroads and Puerto Bolívar, not too far from the turn-off for Cabo de la Vela. Cell: 310-718-6802 / 312-831-8955, E-mail: parqueolico@yahoo.es. Updated: Jun 13, 2008.

Cabo de la Vela Tours

Most tours that come pulling into Cabo de la Vela in big buses originate in Riohacha or Santa Marta. This town has no operators of its own. Ask around to see if anyone is interested in chauffeuring you out to Pilón de Azúcar or Parque Eólico Jepirachi, or in taking you for a boat ride along the coast or on Laguna de Utta. You will have to negotiate the price for these services. Updated: Jun 13, 2008.

Andrés Gómez

Señor Gómez is the only person who formally hires out his car and launch for trips to attractions. The land vehicle fits up to six people and the launch, seven. To Pilón de Azúcar or El Faro is $2.65 (minimum of four people).

He will pick you up at the time you specify for the return journey. To Parque Eólico, with a 30-minute wait, is $26.50 round trip, minimum six persons. By sea to Pilón is $37 for the whole boat. To both El Faro and Pilón de Azúcar, a three-hour trip, is $10.50 per person (up to seven) or $75 for all. Left of the *ferretería* (hardware store), before coming to the curve of the cove. Updated: Jun 13, 2008.

Cabo de la Vela Lodging

All of the lodging options in Cabo de la Vela are local family-run establishments. For the most part, it is sleeping in hammocks in an enramada (an open-sided, palm-thatched shelter) on the beach. There are a few standard hotels, some quite expensive. The village has no electricity, but some establishments have generators they fire up only for a few hours at night. Bring a good strong flashlight and candles. Due to the scarcity of water, most inns charge extra for a toss-water shower, and some charge for using the restroom facilities, which you flush with water scooped out of the provided reservoir. Updated: Jun 13, 2008.

Rosita

(BED: $2-8) Doña Rosita is just one of dozens of restaurants along the south side of the bay as you enter Cabo de la Vela that also rent hammock space. On the beach across from her place are three enramadas where you can pass the night in the cooler air or pitch a tent. Behind the restaurant, in the family's living compound, is a cabaña for let if you prefer to hammock sleep in an enclosed space. Four lots down to the left from the church. Cell: 313-595-6111. Updated: Jun 13, 2008.

Hotel Jarrinapi

(BED: $5-16) Popular Hotel Jarrinapi provides cabañas with hammock or a bed, private bath with 24-hour water and fan. Common sitting areas provide refuge during the heat of day and places to relax after a day of hiking. It has its own generator, providing its guests with electricity from 5 p.m. - 6 a.m. As well as having a restaurant, this hotel also operates a store and the village's Telecom office. Cell: 311-683-4281. Updated: Jun 13, 2008.

Kayuusipaa

(BED: $6-13) Many moons ago, doña Conchita opened up one of the very first inns in Cabo de la Vela. She is a bit of a legend, known to spend evenings teaching the mythology and ways of her people. In rustic cabañas, her guests sleep in hammocks, and use the clean common baths out back. The lodge is more isolated and closer to the many natural wonders in the area, making it a perfect choice for those who wish to spend time meditating and hiking. The inn is open only when doña Conchita is here, so call beforehand. Tell the driver of the pick-up truck from Uribia that you are going to "Donde Conchita;" he will take you to the head of the drive at the roadside. From there it is about a 100-meter (350-foot) walk down to the compound. On the north shore of the bay, almost to the very end. Cell: 3111-442-0427 / 5-726-4463 (Maicao) / 1-347-9294 (Bogotá). Updated: Jun 13, 2008.

Cabo de la Vela Restaurants

As you can expect, the most common items on the menus of Cabo de la Vela's restaurants are fish and seafood. The second-most popular meat is goat. Exotic dishes like chicken and beef cost a bit more. Few places have blue-plate specials, which do not include soup due to the shortage of water. Beverages are a separate charge and, yes, it is true: a beer is cheaper than water here. A few small shops sell canned goods and water, all of which is more expensive than elsewhere. Purchase several jugs of water to take with you before leaving Uribia. The water in Cabo de la Vela is salty, thus unsuitable for purification. Updated: Jun 13, 2008.

Restaurant Isa

(ENTREES: $3.70-8) A cane-slat picket fence zigzags around a sand-floored restaurant. Within this small space are only two tables. Here the señora lends personalized service and dishes up generous portions at the most excellent prices. It's a simple menu she offers: goat stew ($3.70), shrimp with rice ($3.70), fish ($5.30), langostinos ($6.35) and lobster ($8). All come with a tomato-onion salad, rice and patacones. Open daily 6 a.m.-8 p.m. Two doors to the left of the church. Updated: Jun 13, 2008.

Restaurante El Wuashi

(LUNCH: $4.20) Restaurante El Wuashi may have one of the most expensive, modern hotels in Cabo de la Vela, but its restaurant does have blue-plate specials. The breakfast (with eggs) is $3.20; the set-lunch meal includes fish, chicken or beef for the same price ($4.20). The menu also includes à la carte fish and seafood dishes ($5-30-26.50). Open for breakfast, 7-9 a.m., lunch, 11 a.m.-1 p.m. and dinner, 6-10 p.m. Near the entrance to town, before the church. Cell: 311-400-7515 / 686-0195. Updated: Jun 13, 2008.

Restaurante Donde Mamiche

(ENTREES: $6.35) One of the more popular eateries for tour groups and vacationing families is Donde Mamiche. This blue and white restaurant has a large open-sided patio and an even larger enclosed room where service is rendered. It has a wonderful, unobstructed view of the sea. The menu is primarily fish and seafood, with dishes beginning at $6.35, and accompanied with a simple salad, rice and patacones. The wait staff is young and leaves the service a bit to be desired. Open daily 6 a.m.-8 p.m. Three doors down from Restaurant Rosita. Updated: Jun 13, 2008.

Near Cabo De La Vela Maicao

Alt: 20m Pop: 103,000 City Code: 5

Mention you'll be crossing the border at Maicao, and the first response of Colombians and Venezuelans is silence. Then they'll advise you, "Get in and out as fast as possible." Many Maicao natives take offense to this negative characterization. They'll be quick to point out attractions like the beautiful mosque, which is the second-most important in Latin America. Its negative reputation is based on years of contraband running, drug smuggling and robbery. The paramilitary presence since the 1990s has caused a great migration from the city, especially of the Muslim community. Even though its citizens claim it has become a more tranquil place, you are still counseled to be inside before nightfall. Despite all its problems, Maicao continues to be an important land port between Colombia and Venezuela for both legitimate and "other" commerce.

!!!!!

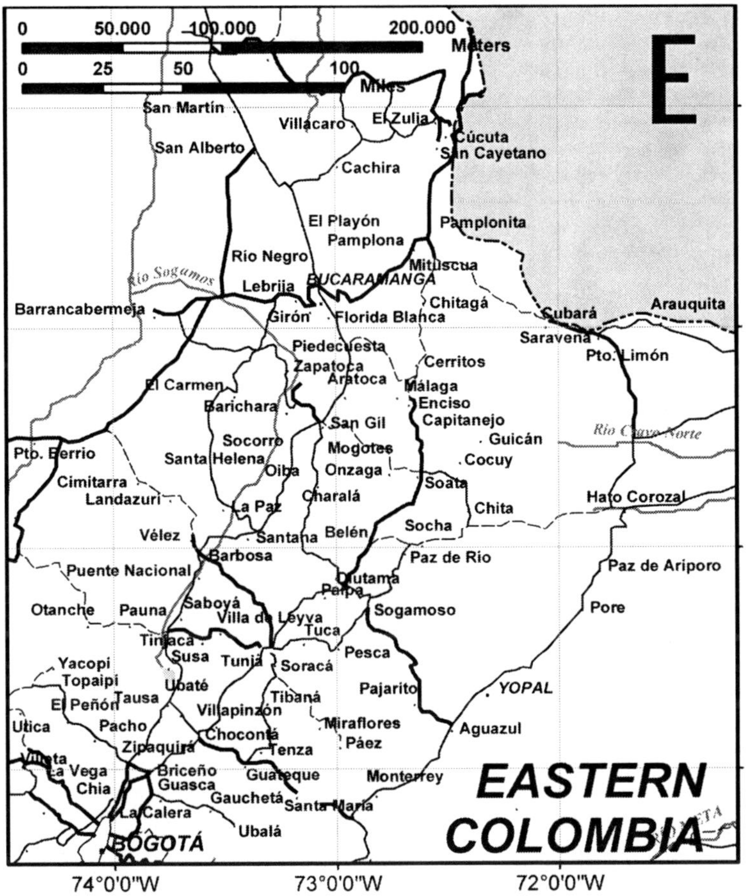

Eastern Colombia

Eastern Colombia encompasses the land northeast of the nation's capital. This area is embraced by the broad lowlands of the Lower Magdalena River Valley to the west and the towering heights of the Cordillera Oriental to the east. Within Eastern Colombia are the departments of Boyacá, Santander and Norte de Santander. A major highway connects Bogotá and Santa Marta, passing through Tunja and Bucaramanga—there are 13 *peajes* (tollbooths) along the way. From Bucaramanga another thoroughfare heads east to Pamplona, Cúcuta and the Venezuelan border. An older, tollbooth-free road twists through the mountains from Tunja to Capitanejo, Málaga and down to Pamplona, connecting with the Bucaramanga-Cúcuta highway. This is the preferred route for buses and trucks, and the fastest way to get to Parque Nacional Natural El Cocuy and El Cocuy and Güicán.

The physical and cultural beauty of Eastern Colombia surpasses the imaginable. Colonial villages abound, as do the reminders of former inhabitants, including prehistoric sea creatures and the pre-conquistador Muisca and Guane nations. In the Cocuy region (p.398), the modern-day U'wa indigenous hang on to their lifestyle, struggling to protect their land from oil companies. The Cordillera Oriental has three peaks that surpass 5,300 meters (17,000 feet) and it shelters the largest snow field in South America north of the Equator.

Eastern Colombians have an ultra courteous reputation, especially people in Boyacá. Don't be surprised if locals around the department of Boyacá address you with the medieval titles. They often call visitors *vecino* (neighbor). Updated: Dec 19, 2007.

History

Long before humans left their footprints in Eastern Colombia, marks were made in the form of fossils deposited by a vast inland sea that covered the region. Eons after the prehistoric sea, great indigenous nations flourished. The most important were the Muisca and the Guane. The gold mines and ports of trade flourished for a while near Bucaramanga during the Spanish reign.

There was a lot of activity seen around these parts during Gran Granada's struggle for independence from Spain. Some of the sparks from the independence movement ignited in villages around San Gil. In 1819 Simón Bolívar and Francisco de Paula Santander led a decisive, winning battle for independence at Puente de Boyacá near Tunja. When Gran Colombia (Venezuela, Colombia and Ecuador) was formed in 1821, the Villa del Rosario was the seat for the constitutional congress and the first Gran Colombia convention was held in Villa de Leyva.

The 1,000 Day War took place at the end of the 19th Century in Colombia. One of the main foci of fighting was the department of Santander, in Eastern Colombia. Then, the last—and bloodiest—battle of this war was fought at Palonegro, near Bucaramanga.

In the 1980s, both the FARC and ELN guerrilla groups began occupying a good part of Eastern Colombia, especially between the principal north-south highway and the Río Magdalena, the Sierra Nevada del Cocuy (including the national park) and the less-populated areas along the Venezuelan border, particularly in the Norte de Santander Department. The mid-1990s brought paramilitary forces into the region and some villages, like Málaga and Capitanejo, had many killed during what the locals call "a reign of terror." Many fled. Populations of principal towns, above all Bucaramanga and Cúcuta, swelled with these *desplazados* (displaced). During the third millennium and with a new president power, military forces commenced driving the guerrillas out of populated areas. Soldiers continue to occupy villages to this day. Remote zones still see armed confrontations between the government, guerrilla and paramilitary armies. Updated: May 13, 2008.

Photo by Blandine Mingret

When to Go

In general, Eastern Colombia experiences two rainy seasons per year, typically from March to May and September to November. The drier months are June, July, December, January and February. Although, due to the region's diverse topography, some areas, like San Gil and Barichara, receive very little rain year round. Other areas of the region, like Cúcuta and Capitanejo, get downright scorching during the dry months, with temperatures reaching into the upper 30s °C (upper 90s °F). The best time to visit Parque Nacional Natural El Cocuy and the neighboring villages is during the dry season from December to February. However, be aware that this is also when temperatures get the coldest—it can get below freezing in the park.

Malagá and Pamplona are both college towns. When the universities are in session (January to June and August to the beginning of December), the towns have a energetic and youthful atmosphere. Once the students leave on break, these cities become quiet villages.

Among vacationing Colombians, Villa de Leyva, Barichara, San Gil and Pamplona are extremely popular during major holidays and three-day weekends (*puentes*). Hotel prices rise substantially at these times and reservations are necessary. Parque Nacional Natural El Cocuy is becoming a trendy spot to visit for the extended December into January vacation. Updated: May 13, 2008.

Safety in Eastern Colombia

Eastern Colombia is much safer than it was before 2003. Since President Uribe's program to demobilize paramilitary forces and neutralize the guerrilla armies, roads are now heavily patrolled by the Colombia military. Expect frequent checkpoints, especially traveling toward the Río Magdalena, the less-frequented areas bordering Venezuela and into the Sierra Nevada del Cocuy. If journeying to Barrancabermeja, El Banco and other towns on the Río Magdalena, stay on the main roads and in the villages, because the surrounding countryside may still be unsafe.

Trips along the Venezuelan border cannot be recommended at this time. It is still considered a hot zone and there are many conflicts taking place between Colombia's civil war factions. The exception to this is Cúcuta, the major crossing between the two countries. Updated: May 13, 2008.

Things to See and Do

The breadth of things to do and see in Eastern Colombia includes everything imaginable, including culture and high-octane sports. Tunja has many beautiful churches, most notably the Iglesia de Santa Bárbara, which displays embroidery done by Juana la Loca (the "mad" mother of Emperor Carlos V). Villa de Leyva and Barichara are both colonial towns on the national register of historic villages. The countryside surrounding Villa de Leyva bears the fossilized marks of its denizens from more than 160 million years ago. San Gil is the adventure sports capital of the nation, go whitewater rafting, spelunking (cave exploring) or something else extreme.

Between San Gil and the bustling Bucaramanga are the Cañón de Chicamocha and Mesa de Ruitoque, the nation's best places for paragliding. In the deep folds of the Cordillera Oriental there are small villages that have diverse climates and customs, like Málaga, Concepción (the wool capital of Colombia) and Capitanejo (the goat, tobacco and melon capital). At the apex of these mountains is the Parque Nacional Natural El Cocuy, which has superb mountain and rock climbing, and trekking. Updated: Dec 19, 2007.

Eastern Colombia Tours

As a major tourist destination, many of the cities in Eastern Colombia have tour operators to help with traveling and itineraries. The agencies in San Gil specialize in taking visitors on high-adrenaline adventures, like whitewater rafting, paragliding, rappelling, spelunking, horseback riding and other such sports. Guides in Parque Nacional Natural El Cocuy are mostly from the local community and have been specially trained in tourism. They specialize in trekking and mountain climbing and some rent out pack mules. Another place to look for inexpensive guides is at the local SENA program, which is training low-income residents in tourism. Even villages as small as Capitanejo have SENA training programs. Also, many tour agencies in Bogotá can arrange outings to Eastern Colombia, especially to Villa de Leyva and Parque Nacional Natural El Cocuy. Updated: Dec 19, 2007.

Eastern Colombia Lodging

Eastern Colombia has a broad assortment of types and quality of hotels. Smaller villages have homier, simple hostels. In the rural areas, near Málaga and Villa de Leyva, are working farms where you can stay for a completely different kind of experience than a hostel. To get in touch with your spiritual side, check out the Hare Krishna retreat center close to Bucaramanga. In the warmer zones, hot water is only available at luxury accommodations and most other places come with room temperature water — though the sun heats the water to a refreshing degree. In popular vacation destinations like San Gil, Villa de Leyva and Barichara, there is a no-

Photo by Blandine Mingret

ticeable difference in room prices during the low season and high season. If you go at peak time, make reservations well in advance. During other times, bargaining for the price of a room shouldn't be difficult. Also, camping is possible in most of Eastern Colombia. Updated: Dec 19, 2007.

TUNJA

Alt: 2,746m Pop: 152,000 City Code: 8

Tunja is on the main highway heading north from Bogotá, about 135 kilometers (81 miles) to Santa Marta along the Atlantic coast. The capital of the department of Boyacá is on a high-altitude plateau surrounded by mountains. The name of the city comes from the Muisca language (of the Chibcha linguistic group) and means "Land of Blankets" or "Royal Mantle." Some Colombians may tell you there's nothing to see in Tunja, but you should decide for yourself. The city has managed to preserve much of its colonial past, including what is said to be the only remaining house in Latin America of the Conquistador Gonzalo Suárez Rendón. Many of the Catholic temples share a gold-leaf-on-red motif, which is most stunningly displayed in the Iglesia de Santo Domingo. A few fragments of the indigenous Muisca culture also remain. However, the Wars of Independence are the most important parts of Tunjano history. The monumental Batalla de Boyacá was fought 15 kilometers (8 miles) to the south. This battle showed the viceroy of Nueva Granada that the end of the Spanish reign was at hand. Updated: Dec 17, 2007.

HISTORY

For centuries the Muisca lived in the Boyacá region. Tunja was then known as Hunza, which was the principal political seat to the 800,000 to one million inhabitants — considered the most advanced civilization of that time. The Muisca fought hard to keep the Spanish out, but in 1539, the Spaniards succeeded in their conquest of this region. Gonzalo Suárez Rendón established Tunja on the site of Hunza. The city declared its liberty from Spanish rule centuries later in 1811. Updated: Dec 17, 2007.

When to Go

Like other areas of the Colombian Andes, Tunja experiences a three-month cycle of wet and dry seasons. Tunja has a number of civic, cultural and religious celebrations. No matter what time of year you visit, you will undoubtedly be here for one. For exact dates visit the tourism office's websites.

Month	Event
March/ April	Semana Santa
June	Fiestas de la Virgen del Milagro
August	Fiestas de San Bartolomé Founding of Tunja/Semana de la Cultura Tunjana (August 6)
September	Fiestas del Señor de la Columna Festival Internacional de la Cultura and Fiestas de San Lázaro I
October	Festival del Frío
November	Feria Artesana
December	Fiestas de San Lázaro II Aguinaldo Boyacense (December 16-22)

Getting To and Away From Tunja

Tunja has a fine network of city buses. The fare is $0.40 ($0.45 Sunday and holidays). The bus terminal is at Carrera 7 and Calle 17. There are two levels: buses on the lower floor go to distant cities and on the upper floor go to Villa de Leyva and surrounding villages.

From Tunja:

Arrive	Departure	Time	Price
Villa de Leyva	Half-hourly 6 a.m.- 6 p.m.	45 mins	$2.40
Puente de Bocayá	Half-hourly 6 a.m.- 6 p.m.	20 mins	$1.30
Paipa	Every 10 minutes	30 mins	$2.60
Bogotá	Every 10 minutes	2 hours	$7
Málaga	8 a.m., 11 p.m.	8 hours	$16

Arrive	Departure	Time	Price
Güicán	10 a.m., 10 p.m.	10 hours	$19
San Gil	9 a.m.- 11 p.m.	6 hours	$25
Cúcuta	9 a.m., 4 p.m., 6 p.m., 8 p.m., 10 p.m., 11:30 p.m.	12 hours	$32
Santa Marta	12:30 p.m.	19 hours	$58
Cartagena	12:30 p.m.	22 hours	$69
Riohacha	1 p.m., 3 p.m., 11 p.m.	21 hours	$69

Updated: Dec 17, 2007.

SAFETY IN TUNJA

The areas around the bus terminal and the Iglesia del Carmen neighborhood are dangerous, especially at night. Locals also describe the Los Cojines de Zaque archaeological site as ugly and dangerous. The Centro Histórico is patrolled by the tourism police and considered very safe. As in most places around the country, the tap water is not safe to drink. Updated: Dec 17, 2007.

TUNJA SERVICES

Tourism Office

The tourism office, Dirección de Cultura y Turismo de Tunja, has excellent maps of the city and information on hotels (Monday-Friday 8 a.m.-noon, 2-6 p.m. Closed Saturday and Sunday. Carrera 9, 19-70, Casa del Fundador, Plaza Bolívar. Tel: 8-742-3272). On the other side of the plaza is the Secretería de Cultura y Turismo of Boyacá Department, which has information on festivals, other cultural events and attractions all over Boyacá (Carrera 10, 19-17. Tel: 8-742-6547, E-mail: cultura.turismo@boyaca.gov.co). You can obtain maps at the Instituto Geográfico Agustín Codazzi (Monday-Friday, 8-11:15 a.m., 1:30-4 p.m. Calle 18, 11-31 Banco Agrario building).

The immigration, or DAS, has an office in Tunja where you can get visa extensions (Monday-Friday 8 a.m.-noon , 2-5 p.m. Calle 20, 7-38). Updated: Dec 17, 2007.

Money

Major banks have branches in Tunja; many have 24-hour ATMs:

Bancolombia—(AmEx travelers checks; ATM: MasterCard, Visa, Cirrus) Monday-Friday 8-11:30 a.m., 2-4:30 p.m. Carrera 10, 22-35, near Iglesia San Francisco.

Santander—(AmEx travelers checks; ATM) Monday-Friday 8-11:30 a.m., 2-4:30 p.m. Carrera 10, 18-16.

AV Villas—(ATM: Visa, Plus, MasterCard, Cirrus) Monday-Friday 8 a.m.-7 p.m., Saturday 9 a.m.-3 p.m. Calle 19, 10-83.

BBVA—(ATM: MasterCard, Cirrus) Monday-Friday 8-11:30 a.m., 2-4:30 p.m. Carrera 11, 18-41.

The Western Union agent in Tunja is at Giros and Finanzas (Monday-Friday 8:30 a.m.-5 p.m., Saturday 8:30 a.m.-1 p.m. Carrera 10, 16-81, inside Almacén Comfaboy. Tel: 8-740-9877); the MoneyGram agent is in the Davivienda bank (Monday-Friday 8 a.m.-4:30 p.m., Saturday 9 a.m.-3 p.m. Carrera 10 and Calle 14. Tel: 8-742-4898). Updated: Dec 17, 2007.

Keeping in Touch

Many shops have local and national service for $0.10-0.20 per minute. Telecom is located on the corner of Calle 19 and Carrera 9. International calls start at $0.45 per minute. Monday-Friday 8 a.m.-8:30 p.m., Saturday 8a.m.-noon. A cheaper option for international calls is Meg@.net, $0.20 per minute. Carrera 10, 21-42, Centro Comercial Pinal.

A plethora of internet cafés populate Tunja and charge between $0.50 and $1.30 per hour. Benicnet is one of the only cheap places open on Sundays and holidays (Monday-Saturday 8 a.m.-8 p.m., Sunday and holidays 9 a.m.-5 p.m. Calle 19, 12-69). Adpostal, the post office, is on Calle 18, 11-79 (Monday-Friday 8 a.m.-noon, 2-6 p.m., Saturday 8 a.m.-noon). Updated: Dec 17, 2007.

Medical

The public health facility, Hospital San Rafael, is a full-service center (Carrera 11, 27-27. Tel: 8-742-2041). There are also a number of private clinics. The main *droguerías*, or pharmacies, are on Calle 19. Updated: Dec 17, 2007.

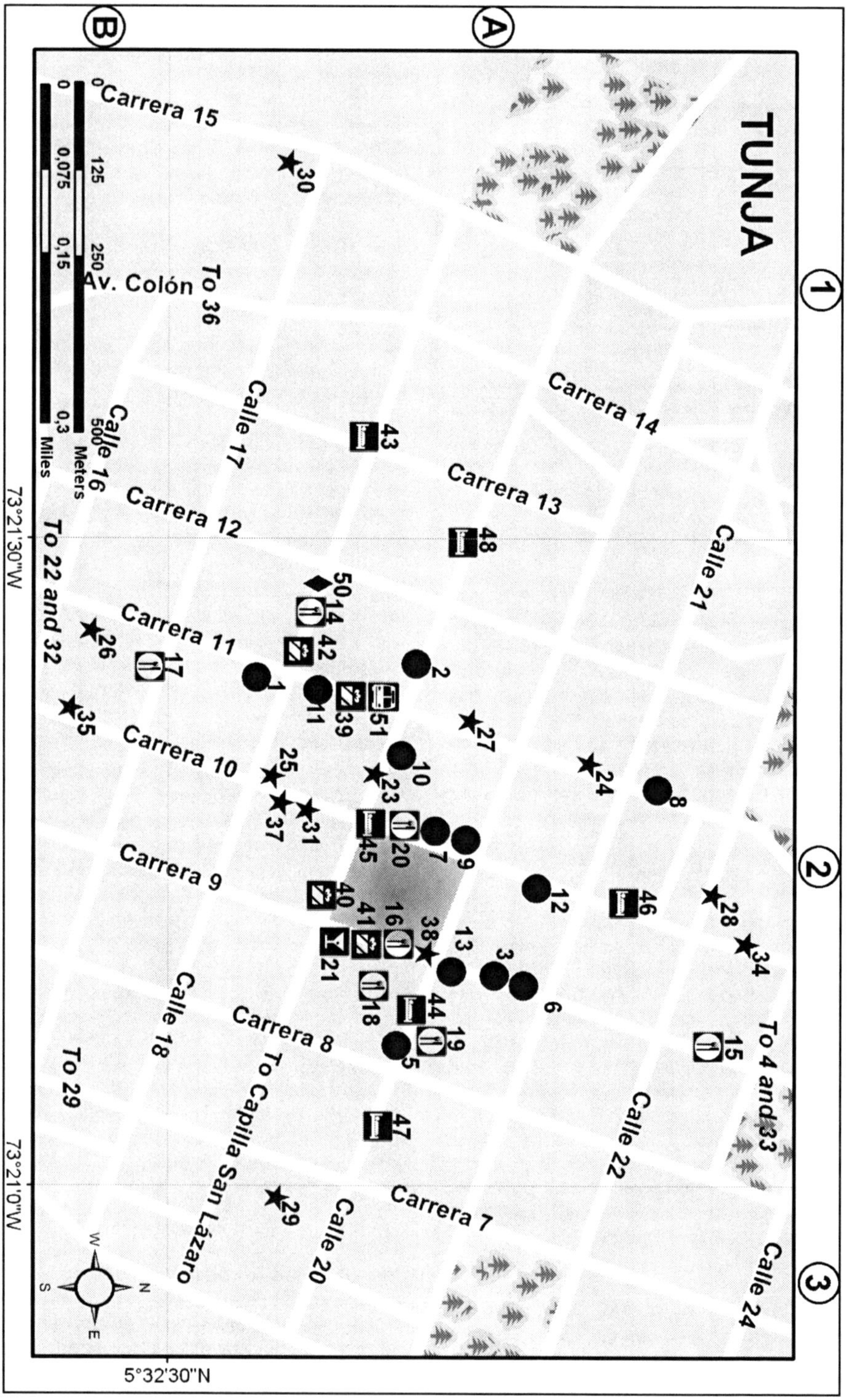

TUNJA
A
B
1
2
3
Carrera 15
Carrera 14
Carrera 13
Carrera 12
Carrera 11
Carrera 10
Carrera 9
Carrera 8
Carrera 7
Calle 16
Calle 17
Calle 18
Calle 20
Calle 21
Calle 22
Calle 24
Av. Colón
To 36
To 22 and 32
To 29
To 4 and 33
To Capilla San Lázaro
0 125 250 500 Meters
0 0,075 0,15 0,3 Miles
73°21'30"W
73°21'0"W
5°32'30"N
N
S
E
W

Activity ●
1 Capilla y Convento de Santa Clara
La Real B3
2 Casa de la Familia Niño y Capitán Martín Rojas B2
3 Casa del Escríbano del Rey Don Juan de Vargas B2
4 Casa del Fundador B2
5 Casa del Presidente General Gustavo Rojas Pinilla C2
6 Catedral Santiago de Tunja B2
7 Iglesia San Francisco B2
8 Iglesia San Ignacio B2
9 Iglesia San Laureano C2
10 Iglesia Santa Bárbara C2
11 Iglesia Santa Clara B2
12 Iglesia Santo Domingo B2
13 Iglesia y Monasterio de El Topo B1
Eating
14 Parrilla y Son B2
15 Pussini Café-Bar B2
16 Restaurante China B2
17 Restaurante Pila del Mono B2
18 Restaurante Vegetariano Roma B2
19 Ristorante-Caffe La Buona Vita B2
20 Trigos B2
Nightlife
21 Macondo B2
Sleeping
22 Hotel American B2
23 Hotel Boyacá Plaza B2
24 Hotel Conquistador de América B2
25 Hotel Don Camilo B2
26 Hotel Dux B2
27 Hotel El Cid B2
Service ★
28 Adpostal B2
29 AV Villas B2
30 Banco Colombia B2
31 BBVA (bank) B2
32 Benicnet B2
33 DAS B2
34 Foto Veracruz B2
35 Hospital San Rafael A2
36 Instituto Geográfico Agustín Codazzi B2
37 Levandería Nuevo Milenio C2
38 Meg@.net B2
39 MoneyGram C1
40 Santander B2
41 Telecom B2
42 Tourism Office (Boyacá) B2
43 Tourism Office (Tunja) B2
44 Western Union C2
Shopping
45 Artesanías de Mi Tierra B2
46 Supermarket Ley B2
47 Taller Galería Artesanal Ambar B1
48 Tunja Artesanal B2
Tour ♦
49 Piri Company Tours B2
50 Viajes Naturaleza y Vida B2
Transportation
51 Bus Terminal C2

Laundry

Several laundry places are scattered away from the downtown area. One you might try is Lavandería Nuevo Milenio, across from Parque Bosque de la República (Monday-Friday 7:30 a.m.-1 p.m., 3-7 p.m., Saturday 8 a.m.-7 p.m. Carrera 10, 13-20. Tel: 8-743-6857, Cell: 310-333-3508). Updated: Dec 17, 2007.

Camera

Like all other services in Tunja, camera shops are not all in one area of town. None, apparently, repair cameras. However, the best one-stop option seems to be Foto Veracruz. It has all sorts of batteries and battery chargers, black-and-white and color films (Kodak, Fuji, Konica, AGFA in 100, 200, 400 ASA), all types of digital camera cards, and analog and digital cameras for sale, as well as film processing (Monday-Friday 8 a.m.-7:30 p.m., Saturday 9 a.m.-7:30 p.m., Sunday and holidays 9 a.m.-1 p.m. Carrera 10, 18-24. Tel: 8-742-3982). Updated: Dec 17, 2007.

Shopping

Taller-Galería Artesanal Ambar

Craftman Rafael Piñeros Bonilla creates simple to extravagant jewelry. Whether your taste runs from seeds, shells and stones to sterling silver, there's a ring, necklace or pair of earrings that await. A unique item is his *Botero* ring collection: thick and round, some with emerald or semi-precious gems. If you can't reach Rafael Piñeros Bonilla, you can check out his work as Tunja Artesanal in the Casa del Fundador. Calle 18, 13-03. Cell: 312-483-3813. Updated: Feb 06, 2008.

Artesanías de Mi Tierra

In this two-level store, crafts hang from ceilings, crowd the shelves and are piled in mounds on the floor. There is pottery from Ráquira and ceramic miniatures of houses, basketry, woolen *ruanas* (short ponchos) and scarves, net bags, hammocks and cane furniture from other villages in the Boyacá Department. There's even honey and scrumptious honey caramel. Everything comes from family workshops, but if you can't make it to the villages, then Artesanías de Mi Tierra brings it all to you in one shop just a half-block from the main plaza. Calle 20, 8-79 (also Carrera 19-92). Cell: 311-264-3803 / 316-472-6003. Updated: Feb 06, 2008.

Tunja Artesanal

This new shop presently offers artesian work from family workshops in Tunja. Pick up a wool sweater, ruana or scarf, a piece of jewelry or a net bag. Tunja Artesanal offers a tasteful selection. To send greetings home, choose a card of handmade paper or sheets of *fique* paper. The store is realizing its dream of also carrying crafts from neighboring villages, including baskets from Tenza. Back patio, Casa del Fundador. Updated: Feb 06, 2008.

Things to See and Do

Despite having once been the capital of the Muisca in this region (the Cojines del Zaque and the Pozo de Hunzahúa), little remains of the culture in Tunja. Evidence of the colonial era is still prevalent however, including preserved mansions, many of which are now museums. Other colonial buildings available to visitors include the Casa de la Familia Niño y Capitán Martín de Rojas (now the Boyacá tourism office) and the Paredón de los Mártires in Parque de la República, which still has the bullet holes from the executions of independence fighters. For movie buffs, Tunja has three cinemas. If you are in the mood to shoot 18 holes, there are also several golf courses in the area. Sports fans should check out bullfighting or soccer matches, depending on the season. Updated: Dec 17, 2007.

The Churches of Tunja

Tunja's Catholic churches have unusual architectural features that are seldom seen elsewhere. As previously mentioned, a common theme in many are the gold-leaf-on-red furnishings. There are open mass hours, except where noted. No photos are allowed of any of the church interiors.

Catedral Santiago de Tunja—(Basílica Metropolitana de Santiago el Mayor de España) Contains the tomb of Gonzalo Suárez Rendón, founder of Tunja. It is possible to make an appointment to visit the office of Cultura and Turismo. Carrera 9.

San Laureano—Carrera 10, between Calles 13 and 14.

Santa Clara—Carrera 11, between Calles 20 and 21.

San Ignacio—This church has a stunningly simple interior with bare adobe and whitewashed walls. There's also a fully gilded chapel and altar screens. Also open Thursday evenings for concerts. Carrera 10, between Calles 18 and 19.

Santa Bárbara—Carrera 11, between Calles 16 and 17.

San Francisco—Carrera 10, between Calles 22 and 23.

Santo Domingo—Impressive red interior with gold-leaf and nacre (mother-of-pearl) accents. The Capilla de la Virgen del Rosario is considered Latin America's "Sistine Chapel." Carrera 11, between Calles 18 and 19. Open daily 8 a.m.-noon, 2-6 p.m.

Capilla y Convento de Santa Clara La Real—Also houses the Museo de Arte Religioso. Free. Carrera 7, 19-17. Open daily 9 a.m.-12:30 p.m., 2-6 p.m.

Iglesia y Monasterio de El Topo—Visits can be arranged with the tourism office. Carrera 15, 17-99. Updated: Feb 06, 2008.

Iglesia de Santa Bárbara

Iglesia Santa Bárbara is perhaps the most unusual of Tunja's churches. Upon entering the atrium, there is a room full of niche tombs on the right. Steps then lead from the atrium down into the nave. The color scheme of the sanctuary is impressive: the walls are dark blue-grey accented with gilt-wood orchid flowers. The designs are simpler up to the transept chapel arches, this part was restored after a 1927 earthquake. Beyond this section, the richness and the intricacy of the wall treatment, done in silver and gold paint, is very noticeable. The ceiling is intertwined with flowering-vine murals. The apse arch is covered in bright gold leaf with basket-weave pilasters and capitals, people burning in hell and a vegetative motif.

Remember, one of the key sites in town that has been mentioned before is found in this church. In the left transept chapel is the treasure of this temple: red silk vestments embroidered in gold and silver thread created by Juana la Loca, mother of Emperor Charles V. Carrera 11, between Calles 16 and 17. Updated: Feb 06, 2008.

V!VA Member Review-Iglesia de Santa Bárbara

Wow, this church is really rad and those cloths done up by Joan the Mad! (Have you seen the movie about her?) The only bad thing about it is trying to find it open. Gotta go to mass, if you want to see this gem! USA, Jun 11, 2008.

Casa del Fundador Gonzalo Suárez Rendón

Casa del Fundador was the home of Gonzalo Suárez Rendón, founder of Tunja. It is claimed to be the only surviving home of the conquistador in Latin America. Built in the mid-16th Century by Spanish and indigenous laborers, the mansion has Mudéjar and Andalusian features. The upstairs quarters give you an insight into Spanish life during the colonial period, including austere furnishings and imaginative ceiling murals that depict a nobleman's favorite pastime: hunting. Guided tours in Spanish or English (if available). No photos of the second floor are allowed. Carrera 9, Plaza de Bolívar. Updated: Feb 06, 2008.

Puente de Boyacá

This large white monument to the Battle of Boyacá is easily spotted alongside the highway between Tunja and Bogotá. On August 7, 1819 a small liberation force under the direct command of General Francisco de Paula Santander defeated a large column of Spanish troops. (Simón Bolívar was overseeing the entire military campaign that day.) The hallmark of this site is an 18-meter (59 feet) high monument dedicated to Bolívar, designed by Ferdinand von Müller. Other structures include a triumphal arch, an obelisk dedicated to the Liberator and the Boyacá Bridge (Puente de Boyacá). Every Saturday a different Boyancense village leads the commemorative ceremonies, complete with honor guards (8 a.m.-5 p.m.). Busetas leave from the upper level of Tunja's bus terminal every half-hour ($1.30 each way), 15 minutes south, vía Bogotá. Updated: Feb 06, 2008.

Pozo de Hunzahúa

The Muisca leader who founded Hunza (Tunja), Hunzahúa, fell in love with his beautiful sister Noncetá, who was much beloved by her people. During a journey taken together, they consummated their love and became husband and wife. When their mother, Faravita, discovered the act, she beat Noncetá with the *chicha*-making paddle. The chicha urn broke, spilling its endless contents, thus forming this little lake now known as Pozo de Hunzahúa. For the Muisca, it was a holy place; gold was offered to the depths of the lake. Their leader Quemuenchatocha ordered all gold and emeralds to be thrown in to save them from the avaricious Spanish conquerors. An early colonizer, Jerónimo Donato, had the little lake drained to retrieve the treasure — but to no avail. On Carrera 12, downtown, take a Muiscas bus. Get off at the pedestrian overpass at Iglesia Santa Inés, just past the railroad station ($0.45 one way). The Pozo is on the other side of Avenida Norte, next to the Universidad Pedagógica y Tecnológica de Colombia (UPTC). Updated: Feb 06, 2008.

Jardín Botánico José Joaquín Camacho Lago

The new Jardín Botánico José Joaquín Camacho Lago, on the southeast side of the city, is a center for the study and preservation of Andean endangered flora species. Stroll through these 33 hectares (81 acres) that have been set aside to learn about the ecosystems of the Colombian Andes. This is a good introduction before trekking in Parque Nacional Natural El Cocuy or other parts of the region. No city buses pass this way. A taxi costs $1.30-1.60 per vehicle one way. Vía Soracá, just past the *circunvalar* (city bypass). Updated: Feb 06, 2008.

TUNJA TOURS

Tunja has more tour operators than many other small cities. The pride in the riches of the Boyacá Department is a good explanation for the recent growth in the tourism industry here. Besides the obligatory tours to Villa de Leyva and Paipa, there are additional trips to villages and natural sites or arrange a trip to Parque Nacional Natural El Cocuy from Tunja. The majority of guides only speak Spanish but it is possible, yet expensive, to hire a translator. Updated: Dec 17, 2007.

Viajes Naturaleza y Vida

Viajes Naturaleza y Vida offers all-inclusive, multi-day tour packages to some of the region's highlights. Experience Semana Santa in Tunja, extreme sports in San Gil ($200) or the virgin nature of Iguaque and Cocuy National Parks ($79 and $226, respectively). Trips occur at set times throughout the year, which is great for solo travelers. Guides are Spanish-speaking, but Naturaleza y Vida can obtain translators at an extra charge. Naturaleza y Vida has trips to other parts of Colombia, like the Zona Cafetera, the Caribbean Coast and the Llanos. There are additional offices in Bogotá and Villavicencio. Carrera 9, 22-47. Tel: 8-743-0255 / 743-0276, E-mail: viajesnaturalezayvidatunja@yahoo.com, viajesnaturalezayvidatunja@hotmail.com. Updated: Jan 14, 2008.

Piri Company

Piri Company is one of several companies that offer tours around the department of Boyacá. The one-day trips follow the Anillo de Hinojosa, visiting the *páramo* (highlands), waterfalls, mountains and villages of the area. Of course, there are several options for Villa de Leyva: one focuses on museums, another on the pottery village of Ráquira and the Candelaria monastery, and a third on hiking in Parque National Sanctuary. If the group is less than 10 participants, transportation costs extra. A translator costs an additional $37. Casa del Fundador, back patio. Tel: 8-743-1286, Cell: 310-209-3894, E-mail: turism@piricompany.com, URL: www.piricompany.com. Updated: Jan 14, 2008.

Tunja Lodging

Good, inexpensive lodging is difficult to find in Tunja. The cheapest hostels are near the bus terminal — an area that is said to be unsafe and have a lot of prostitution and drugs. Better hotels are found after a steep, up-hill climb to the center of the city, though expect to pay a few dollars more. There are also several more expensive hotels that could still be under renovation. Updated: Dec 17, 2007.

Budget

Hotel Don Camilo

(ROOM: $5-19) One of the least expensive hotels in Tunja is right on the main plaza. A small sign announces Hotel Don Camilo, walk down the long entry hall and up the steps. The rooms are a bit worn, but seem clean enough. All rooms have windows and a desk. Shared and private bathrooms both come with hot water. Carrera 10, 19-57, Plaza de Bolívar. Tel: 8-740-9309. Updated: Feb 22, 2008.

Museums of Tunja

All of Tunja's museums are housed in colonial or Republican-era former homes, which are some of the oldest in Latin America. While on the Tunja museum circuit, don't miss Santa Clara La Real's religious art museum (see churches).

Museum	Description	Hours	Address	Price
Casa del Fundador Gonzalo Suárez Rendón	It is claimed as the only surviving home of the Tunja founder in Latin America.	Daily 8 a.m.-noon, 2-6 p.m.	Carrera 9, Plaza de Bolívar.	$0.50 -1
Casa del Escribano del Rey don Juan de Vargas	Built at the end of the 16th Century, this colonial mansion portrays Mozarab, Andalusian and Toscan influences.	Tuesday-Sunday 8 a.m.-noon, 2-6 p.m.	Calle 20 8-52	$0.50 -1
Casa del Presidente General Gustavo Rojas Pinilla	Now the Casa de la Cultura, with galleries that salute poetry, music and three Colombian presidents.	Daily 8 a.m.-noon, 2-6 p.m.	Calle 17 10-73	Free
Casa de la Familia Niño y Capitán Martín de Rojas	Home of the Instituto de Cultura y Turismo de Boyacá (ICTBA) and the Museo de Arte Contemporáneo.	Monday-Friday 8 a.m.-noon, 2-6 p.m.	Carrera 10 19-17	Free

Updated: Feb 06, 2008.

Hotel Dux

(ROOM: $8-16) The Hotel Dux is a creaky, classic building where the same, friendly family has greeted visitors for several generations. Rooms are large with at least two beds. All, save one, have private bathrooms and a TV. Ask permission, and you can wash your clothes. At the front entrance is a café run by Marta, who serves one dynamite cup of coffee. Marta and her sisters, Luzalba and Edilma, manage the hotel and are always ready to chat. Calle 19, 10-78. Tel: 8-742-5736. Updated: Feb 22, 2008.

Hotel American

(ROOM: $7-19) Another hostel found up a flight of stairs, Hotel American offers respectable rooms at a comfortable price. Some have private, hot water bathrooms and TVs, but others are more basic, with shared bathrooms and cold water. The on-site restaurant is on the covered front patio. In the back courtyard is a seating area with couches and overstuffed chairs. Carrera 11, 18-70. Tel: 8-742-2471. Updated: Feb 22, 2008.

Hotel Conquistador de América

(ROOM: 13-21) Right on the corner of the Plaza de Bolívar, the Hotel Conquistador de América is a budget lodging option in the heart of Tunja. Out of the two stories of rooms, some of the rooms upstairs have balconies that look over the pedestrian street. All rooms have private bathrooms with gas-heated hot water, a TV, phone and shabby carpeting. The first-floor courtyard is quite large and filled with plants and seating areas. Calle 20, 8-92 (corner, Plaza de Bolívar). Tel: 8-742-3534, Cell: 310-321-1506, Fax: 8-742-3534. Updated: Feb 22, 2008.

Mid-Range

Hotel El Cid

(ROOM: $24-35) The Hotel El Cid is located on the second floor, above a shopping mall (the manager assures it's quiet after 8 p.m.). All conservatively decorated rooms have private bath with hot water, cable TV, mini-bar and a telephone. The larger rooms have balconies overlooking the street. The restaurant only prepares breakfast ($2.65). Carrera 10, 20-78. Tel: 8-742-3458 / 744-4179, Fax: 8-744-4417, E-mail: Alfonso_736@hotmail.com. Updated: Feb 22, 2008.

High-End

Hotel Boyacá Plaza

(ROOM: $52-57) Hotel Boyacá Plaza offers Tunja's finest accommodation option, in a quieter part of the city. An elevator will whisk you to your carpeted room completed by a view of the city. All of the rooms have a private bathroom with hot water and a mini-bar. Smoking and non-smoking rooms are available. The hotel has as many amenities as you can expect from a place of this caliber: security, room service, internet, WiFi and parking. Calle 18, 11-22. Tel: 8-740-1116 / 1117, Fax: 8-742-7635, E-mail: hotelboyacaplaza@hotmail.com. Updated: Feb 22, 2008.

Tunja Restaurants

Tunja doesn't offer much in the way of formal dining establishments. Although, no visitor will starve in this city. There are plenty of places to purchase your own food. Tunja has two markets on either side of the city. Market days at the southern one are Thursday and Friday, and Saturday and Sunday at the northern one. Several supermarkets are on Carrera 10, between Calles 18 and 19, e.g. Ley (Monday - Saturday 9 a.m.-9 p.m., Sunday and holidays 9:30 a.m.-7 p.m.). Check out one of Tunja's several scores of pastry shops that bake all sorts of delights, which include *pan integral* (multi-grain) and three-seed breads. If you want to sit and be served, the average price of a daily set lunch is $1.85 at a local restaurant. Updated: Dec 17, 2007.

Trigos

Grab a basket and tongs and prepare for tackling the bakery. Trigos has an incredible selection of fresh-baked breads — raisin, cheeses, whole wheat, white, three-seed and a mouth-satisfying six-grain with nuts. There are also tempting desserts, like ice creams of 24 flavors, made according to an Italian recipe with milk and fresh fruit that's served in a large waffle cone with a dollop of whipped cream. Kick back at one of the downstairs tables or in the spacious dining area upstairs. Go ahead, indulge in something sinfully sweet. Open Monday-Saturday 7 a.m.-9 p.m., Sunday and holidays 7 a.m.-7 p.m. Calle 19, 11-35. Tel: 8-742-3870, E-mail: trigosmch@hotmail.com.co. Updated: Feb 06, 2008.

Restaurante Vegetariano Roma

(ENTREES: $2-3.70) If it doesn't seem clear from the name, Restaurante Vegetariano

Roma is a good option for traveling vegetarians in need of a respite from the lack of options. Walk right and the restaurant appears small, but head up to the second floor where two rooms offer a larger dining experience. The tables set with linen cloths and napkins and the attentive service add to the relaxing meal. The lunch menu has two choices for the main dish, gluten or soy, with brown rice and a choice of either a fresh fruit drink or soy milk ($2-3.70). À la carte pasta dishes, with bread and dessert ($2.35-3.70) and breakfast ($1.35-1.85) are also available. Open daily 9 a.m.-4 p.m. Carrera 9, 20-69. Tel: 8-743-1368. Updated: Feb 22, 2008.

Ristorante-Caffe La Buona Vita

(ENTREES: $3.95-13.70) The Ristorante-Caffe La Buona Vita has a refined feel that pervades the dining rooms and the patio. Many of Tunja's wealthier citizens and visitors are drawn by the distinguished service or, possibly, the homemade pastas created by the Italian-trained chef. Begin the meal in *paisano* fashion with an antipasto ($3.70-10.50). Then, move on to pasta ($7.40-10.50), a wood-fire-oven-baked pizza ($3.95-13.70, depending on size) or one of the numerous meat and seafood entrees ($8.15-14.20). Unfortunately, there are no suitable vegetarian dishes. There is, however, a variety of non-alcoholic and alcoholic drinks and wine is sold only by the bottle. Open Monday-Saturday 10 a.m.-10 p.m., Sunday and holidays 10 a.m.-4 p.m. Carrera 9, 23-45. Tel: 8-742-2198, E-mail: labuonavitarestaurant@yahoo.com.mx. Updated: Feb 22, 2008.

Parrilla y Son Restaurante-Bar

(ENTREES: $4.75-7.95) The second floor of one of Tunja's historic colonial buildings has been converted into a popular restaurant. The main breakfast and lunch area is out on a sky-lit patio and the large, front room is the principal nighttime gathering place. Perhaps it is the savory lunches ($2.10) that draw the clientele. Check out the unusual menu item; lamb hamburgers. There is a variety of chicken and beef dishes ($1.70-3.95), shish kabobs ($2.35) and meats hot from the grill ($4.75-7.95). Some foods are grilled with unusual preparations, like the tropical au gratin. During the evenings, the full bar is a nice addition. Open daily 7 a.m.-10 p.m. Carrera 9, 20-27, second floor. Tel: 8-742-3483, Cell: 314-237-0099. Updated: Feb 22, 2008.

Restaurante China

(ENTREES: $3.70-8.50) The delivery men at Restaurante Chine really hustle, picking up orders and running out to their motorbikes. Even at an early lunch hour, a third of the tables at Restaurante China are full. The medium-size restaurant is dimly lit and decorated with typical Chinese ornaments. There is no set lunch special, everything is à la carte. The usual Chinese fare includes fish, pork, chicken, beef or seafood, chow fan, or fried rice ($3.70-8.50), chop suey ($4.75-8.50), noodles ($6.35-8.50), sweet and sour ($5.80-6.90), chow mein ($5.45-8.50), a variety of stir fries ($5.30-20.10) and combination plates ($4.75-9). Vegetarians have few choices — either chop suey or chow mein. Sodas, lemonade, Pony Malta and beer are the wash-down options. Open daily 11 a.m.-10 p.m. Carrera 11, 17-83. Tel: 8-740-1878 / 9423. Updated: Feb 22, 2008.

Restaurante Pila del Mono

(ENTREES: $6.35-15.25) A monkey in a fountain guards one of Tunja's other fine dining establishments, Restaurante Pila del Mono. Take a seat at one of the linen-draped tables set with napkins tucked into water goblets. The menu includes Boyancense dishes, like beef, pork or chicken dishes ($6.35-9.50) or, perhaps, fish or seafood, ($6.90-$15.25). Everything comes with rice or potatoes and salad. For something a bit cheaper, there are pastas, which come accompanied by garlic bread and a salad ($3.70-6.35). Open Monday-Saturday 10 a.m.-10 p.m., Sunday and Holidays 11:30 a.m.-4 p.m. Calle 20, 8-19. Tel: 8-744-7750, Cell: 300-264-3808 / 310-550-5983. Updated: Feb 06, 2008.

Tunja Nightlife

When in Tunja, do as the tunjanos do and start a weekend night at a café around the plaza for a small bite and a bit of liquor. The locals turn into dance machines after a week at work, so make sure you drink plenty of water if you want to keep up with them. After 10 at night, everyone heads to a nightclub. The most happening discos are in the zona rosa and around the university on the north side of the city. Updated: Dec 17, 2007.

Pussini Café-Bar

Come to Pussini Café-Bar to find a friendly dancer to teach you the *rumba*. The lights are soft and the music low, in the bar and up on the balcony people sip on cocktails (typical, classic or special, $3.20-8.50) at the small tables or have a cold brew (national $0.90-1.50, import $2.65). For the non-alcohol drinkers, there are plenty of special coffee choices or tea ($1.30-2). A good place to chill out and get ready before heading to a *discoteca*. Open Monday-Saturday 8 a.m.-midnight, Sunday and holidays 10 a.m.-10 p.m. Carrera 10, 19-53, Plaza de Bolívar. Tel: 8-743-2047. Updated: Feb 22, 2008.

Macondo

The discoteca Los Cien Años de Macondo is more commonly known around Tunja as just Macondo. Since the club features pre-1980 bohemian music, it might seem like it is more for the older crowd, but the young folk come, too. In addition, the music includes salsa and tropical, *boleros* and ballads. Age doesn't matter, anyone will enjoy a trip back in time via music. Open Friday and Saturday only, from 7 p.m.-1 a.m. Carrera 11, 21-47. Tel: 8-742-4036. Updated: Feb 22, 2008.

PAIPA

Alt: 2,250 Pop: 27,000 City Code: 8

Paipa is in a valley surrounded by high mountains and softly rolling hills, 45 kilometers (28 miles) from Tunja and 184 kilometers (114 miles) from Bogotá. Throughout Colombia, Paipa is renowned for its bodies of water. At the thermal springs, there are large and small public pools, and 10 private pools ($5.30). Then there is Lago Sochagota, outside of Paipa, a man-made lake for fishing, waterskiing or other water sports. Also around Paipa, there are several haciendas. El Salitre is three kilometers (1.8 miles) away and Bonza 10 kilometers (6 miles). The last notable bodies of water to mention are the swimming pools at many of the principal hotels in Paipa. The city is 45 kilometers (28 miles) north of Tunja and 184 kilometers (114 miles) from Bogotá. Combi buses leave for Paipa from the upper level of Tunja's bus terminal every 10 minutes ($2.60, 30 minutes). Updated: May 20, 2008.

VILLA DE LEYVA

Alt: 2,149 Pop: 12,000 City Code: 8

The road to Villa de Leyva winds downhill 39 kilometers (23.5 miles) from Tunja through rocky hills. The incredible folds of strata tilt almost vertical to reveal a fascinating geological history. The road is decent, a good blacktop, though some parts are subject to flooding and rock slides and the route passes through Cucaita, a 450-year old village. Villa de Leyva is big on the destination list for both Colombian and foreign vacationers. The town is a national historic monument that has beautifully preserved the colonial buildings constructed with the *tapia pisada* (rammed earth) technique. Attractions include the white-washed buildings that hug cobblestone lanes, the many shops and cultural activities. Villa de Leyva has excellent services and fine restaurants. Although, some visitors might find it a bit too touristy. Attractions outside the village, though, are definitely worth exploring. There is a bit of everything for any type of explorer, including indigenous and colonial ruins, vineyards, horse racing, the desert and páramo landscapes. Updated: Jun 16, 2008.

HISTORY

Fossils from descendants of the Mesozoic Era (160-180 million years ago) now pepper the Villa de Leyva Desert. Eons later, the Muisca (1000-1550 AD), a Chibcha nation called this valley home. An important ceremonial center, El Infiernito testifies to the culture's presence. Then, the Spaniards founded Villa de Nuestra Señora de Santa Marís de Leyva on June 12, 1572. The official founder, Andrés Díaz Venero de Leyva, also was the first president of Nuevo Reino de Granada. Villa de Leyva played an important role in the struggle for independence from Spain. It was the home of the revolutionary heroes Antonio Nariño and Antonio Ricuarte. The village also hosted the first convention of the United Provinces of Nueva Granada. Much further down the line, in 1954, the town was declared a national monument in an effort to preserve its colonial architecture. Updated: Jun 17, 2008.

When to Go

Villa de Leyva enjoys a dry climate. Temperatures average 18° C (65° F). The days can get pretty warm, but the evenings are chilly. January and February are the driest months of the year and October is the wettest.

Holidays and Festivals

It seems like everyone flocks to Villa de Leyva for the national holidays, thanks to its prox-

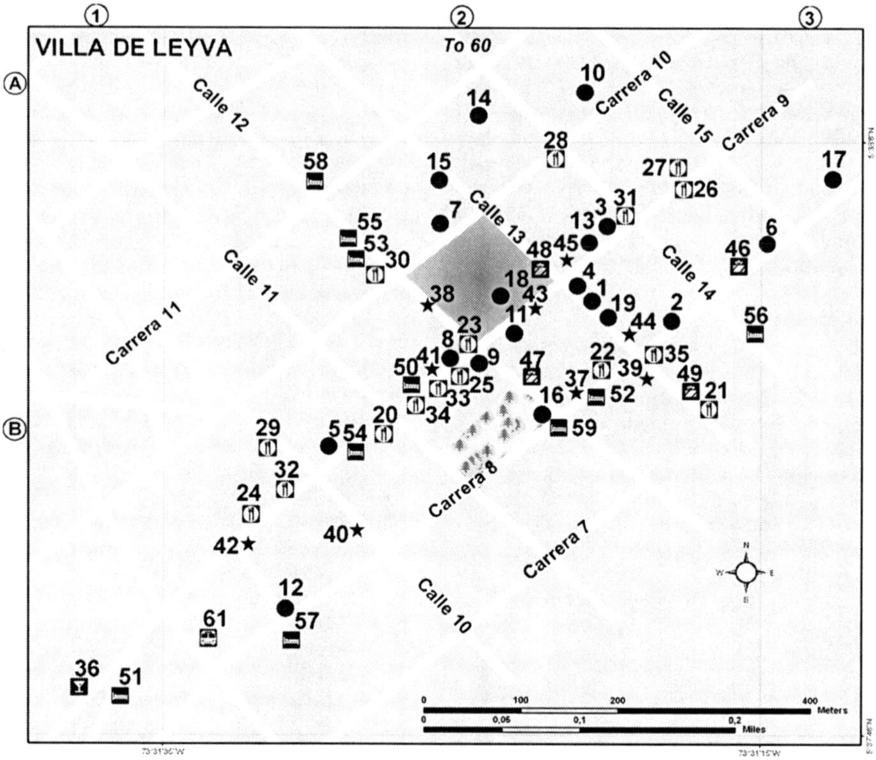

Activity ●

1 Arquería del Jardín de los Próceres B2
2 Asociación Humboldt B2
3 Casa de Juan de Cast allanos B2
4 Casa del Primer Con greso B2
5 Museo Antonio Nariño B2
6 Museo Antonio Ricaurte B2
7 Casa Museo Luis Alberto Acuña B2
8 Casa Quintero B2
9 Cine Bar El Patriarca B2
10 Iglesia el Carmen A2
11 Iglesia Parroquial B2
12 Iglesia San Francisco B2
13 La Guaca B2
14 Museo de Arte A2
15 Museo Prehistórico B2
16 Parque Nariño B2
17 Parque Ricaurte B3
18 Plaza Mayor B2
19 Fábrica de Licores B2

Eating

20 Asadero La Villa B2
21 Casa Blanca B2
22 Chepa Chaves B2
23 Chichería El Pote B2
24 El Fogón de la Gallina B2
25 Hechizo de la Luna B2
26 Heladería Los Indios B2
27 La Alcazaba B2
28 La Tienda de Teresa B2
29 Pastelería Francesa B2
30 Pizzería Olivas y Espe cias B2
31 Restaurante Don Quijote B2
32 Restaurante La Parilla B2
33 Restaurante Xirrus B2
34 Restaurante Zarina B2
35 Té y Café B2

Nightlife

36 Guarapos B1

Service ★

37 Azul Internet B2
38 Banco Popular B2
39 Correo B2
40 Lavandería Milán B2
41 QuinteroNet B2
42 Red si B2
43 Telecom B2
44 Telecom B2
45 Tourism Office B2

Shopping

46 Creaciones Bertha B2
47 M Manos Mujer B2
48 Manos Colombianos B2
49 Taller de Joyería Oro y Plata B2

Sleeping

50 Casa Campesina/El Solar Camp B2
51 Hospedaje El Mirador B1
52 Hospedaje Sol de la Villa B2
53 Hospedaría La Villa B2
54 Hospedería Antonio Nariño B2
55 Hospedería Colonial B2
56 Hospedería Don Paulino B2
57 Hostal San Francisco B2
58 Hotel Boutique la Espa ñola B2
59 Hotel La Posada de San Antonio B2

Tour ♦

60 La Tasca B2

Transportation

70 Bus Station B2

imity to Bogotá. The village even hosts some of its own festivals, pretty great ones, too. Like most tourist destinations, expect significantly higher prices and a lot more people — as well as longer waits at the restaurants during the high season. Updated: Jun 17, 2008.

Month	Event
January	Astronomy Festival
March/ April	Semana Santa
July	Fiestas de la Virgen del Carmen (the patron saint of Villa de Leyva) with gastronomic fairs.
August	Kite Festival
October	National Tree Festival
December	Festival de las Luces y Concurso de Pesebres is celebrated with a riotous burst of fireworks and a crèche, or manger scene, contest.

Updated: Jun 17,2008

Getting Around Villa de Levya

Keep in mind, if you are bringing your own car, street parking is prohibited and the speed limit is 5 kilometers per hour in the center of the village. In addition, the streets are paved with uneven stone, making walking difficult.

Getting To and Away From Villa de Leyva

Hire a taxi at the bus station to take you to visit sights throughout the area. Depending on the route, a four-hour excursion will cost $37-42 per vehicle. Updated: Jun 17, 2008.

Arrive	Departure	Time	Price
Tunja	every 15 minutes 5:30 a.m. - 6 p.m.	45 mins	$2
La Periquera	6 buses, 6:45 a.m.-5 p.m.	40 mins	$2
Santa Sofía	6:45 a.m., 7 a.m., 9 a.m., 1 p.m., 4 p.m.	30 mins	$2
Ráquira	7:30 a.m., 8:30 a.m., 12:30 p.m., 4:30 p.m.	30 mins	$2
Ganchantivá	6:45 a.m., 9 a.m., 2 p.m., 4:30 p.m., 5 p.m., 5:30 p.m.	1 hour	$2
Bogotá	daily 5 a.m., 1 p.m., Sunday and holidays 3 p.m.	3 - 5 hours	$9
Iguaque Park	7 buses 6 a.m.-5:30 p.m.	40 mins	$2
Arcabuco	7 buses 6 a.m.-5:30 p.m.	1 hour	$2
Chinquiquirá	hourly 6 a.m.-5:30 p.m.	1 hour	$3
Sutamarchán	5 buses 7 a.m.-4 p.m.	20 mins	$1

Safety in Villa de Leyva

Wealthy tourists are constant visitors to Villa de Leyva, meaning that security here is pretty tight. It is rare to hear about the guerrillas or other forces ever harassing the town. The streets are patrolled by soldiers, especially between dusk and dawn.

In terms of natural dangers, the region has a species of scorpion that's easily encountered. Its bite is said to feel like a bee sting and can cause muscle cramping at the spot of injection. If camping while staying in a rural area or living in rustic conditions, be sure to shake out clothes and footwear before dressing. Updated: Jun 17, 2008.

Villa de Leyva Services

Tourism Office

The tourism office in Villa de Leyva has good maps of the city and information about all there is to see and do (Tuesday- Friday, 8:30 a.m.-12:30 p.m., 2-6p.m., Saturday 10 a.m.-5 p.m., Sunday 10 a.m.-2 p.m., closed Monday. Carrera 9, near corner Calle 13. Tel: 7-732-0232). On weekends a tourism information kiosk operates at the bus station. The town has several websites as well with information about attractions and services: www.villadeleyva.net / www.expovilla.com.

Money

Villa de Leyva has two banks, both on Calle 12, on the Plaza Mayor. Neither cashes traveler's checks. Banco Popular does cash advances on international Visa credit cards and its ATM handles Visa, Plus, Cirrus and MasterCard (Monday-Thursday 8 a.m.-1:30 p.m., Friday 8 a.m.-2 p.m. Calle 12 9-49). The Comcel a few doors down from the church sometimes changes U.S. dollars.

Keeping in Touch

Telecom has two offices in Villa de Leyva. The main one has international phone service beginning at $0.45 per minute, as well as local and national calls (daily 8 a.m.-10 p.m. Calle 13 and Carrera 8). A branch office is on the main plaza, down from the cathedral (Monday-Sunday 7:30 a.m.-10 p.m., Tuesday and Wednesday closed 12:30-1:30 p.m. Carrera 9 12-36). Many shops have phone service as well; look for the Minutos sign ($0.10-0.20 per minute). Villa de Leyva's post office is in Papelería Librería Comercial Fabio (Monday-Friday 8 a.m.-noon, 2-8 p.m. Calle 13 7-87). There are only a few internet cafés in this town. QuinteroNet (daily 10:30 a.m.-1 p.m., 3-9 p.m., closed Wednesday mornings. Carrera 9, 11-75, $1.05 per hour) and Redsi (daily 8 a.m.-8 p.m. Carrera 9, 9-99, $1.05 per hour) have Skype. Azul Internet is the least expensive, charging $0.95 per hour (Monday-Saturday 8 a.m.-noon, 2-8 p.m. Carrera 8 12-39).

Medical

Hospital San Francisco is at Calle 9 and Carrera 8, next to Iglesia San Francisco (Tel: 7-732-0516 / 732-0244). Pharmacies are distributed throughout the town.

Laundry

Lavandería Milán does mainly dry cleaning, though it also does wet wash. A pound of shirts, underclothing and such is $1.30. Pants and jackets are charged per piece. Calle 10, 8-27. Tel: 7-732-1374.

Camera

The two camera shops on Carrera 9, between the Plaza Mayor and the bus station, carry basic supplies. They also sell cameras, including disposable ones. Updated: Jun 17, 2008.

Shopping

Villa de Leyva is a place for shopaholics. On the portal side of the Plaza Principal, there are three stores dispensing tons of souvenirs. For unique crafts, stroll down Carrera 9 and Calle 13, both pedestrian malls.

On Carrera 9, between the plaza (Calle 13) and Puente El Real are many boutiques selling weavings. There is also an antique shop. On the left side of this lane is Casa don Juan de Castellanos with eight artisan shops, including Manos Colombianas and several jewelers. A few doors down is La Guaca with gourmet bistros, woven goods and an antique store.

Many of the artisans on Calle 13 between Carrera 7 and 8 also specialize in weaving, though there are other shops of interest. Maestro Reinaldo López, one of the village's most noted painters, has a gallery (Calle 13, 7-97). For leathers, visit Ricardo Luna (Calle 13, 7-54). For fine home details, check out Decorando (Calle 13, 7-35). Taller de Joyería Oro y Plata has exquisite silver and gold jewelry. Calle 13, 7-52.

Creaciones Bertha

Creaciones Bertha is an association of families producing fine hand-made woven and knitted goods. The entire process is in their hands, from the carding of the wool to the dying to the weaving on upright looms. Using mostly virgin sheep yarn, but also cotton and alpaca, they fashion hats, vests and hooded ponchos, all exclusively designed. Other creations are avant-garde wall hangings and rugs. If you don't find what you're looking for, Creaciones Bertha does special orders. Carrera 8, 14-81. Tel: 7-732-0527, Cell: 312-442-2365, E-mail: creacionesbertha1@hotmail.com. Updated: Jun 17, 2008.

M. Manos Mujer

Walking into M. Manos Mujeres (*manos mujeres* means women's hands), you are blasted with color and novelty. Within this space, a collective of 20 women from eight families bring together their handiwork. Through the sales of these cards, hand-made paper, jew-

EASTERN COLOMBIA

elry, batiks and weavings, they are supporting their families with their imaginations and long-hidden skills. One home-distills floral essences, lotions and oils. Some even delve into arts that for women are non-traditional, like woodworking and sculpture. Also for sale at very reasonable prices are original watercolors. Calle 12, between Carreras 8 and 9, Parque Nariño. Cell: 315-318-0968. Updated: Jun 17, 2008.

Manos Colombianas
If you can't make it to the far corners of Colombia, drop by Manos Colombianas. Here you'll find crafts from near and far, by Colombia's diverse indigenous nations. By the Kuna of the Chocó are colorful, hand-stitched molas. By the Wayuu of the Guajira and the Arhuaco of the Sierra Nevada de Santa Marta, are their famous bags. Artisan work comes all the way over the Cordillera Oriental and from the deep Amazon and Llanos regions as well. Fine Boyacense weavings and Ráquira pottery are also for sale. Casa San Juan de Castellanos, second floor. Carrera 9 and Calle 13. Updated: Jun 18, 2008.

Taller de Joyería Oro y Plata
Now that you've picked up a new woolen shawl from one of the local weavers, it's time to stop by Taller de Joyería Oro y Plata to pick up the perfect accessory. For over 20 years, the master jeweler of this workshop, Luis Eugenio Guerrero, has been fashioning beautiful rings, pendants, intricate bracelets and necklaces from .950 sterling silver and gold. Some of the pieces feature stones, such as agates, quartzes, zircon as well as others. Señor Guerrero also does repairs. Calle 13, 7-52. Cell: 310-556-5522. Updated: Jun 17, 2008.

Things to See and Do

Villa de Leyva has a richness of activities. The village is a masterpiece of colonial architecture and has artisan workshops and history, art and science museums. The surrounding countryside is full of fossils, petroglyphs, ancient ruins, vineyards and religious centers. The intense natural beauty of the area spreads across deserts, tropical forests and páramo. Natural sites include 112 waterfalls and the Santuario de Flora y Fauna de Iguaque. For something different, if you like betting on the ponies, catch the thoroughbred racing at the Hipódromo. Updated: Jun 16, 2008.

Museo Paleontológico

Museo Paleontológico, in conjunction with the science department of the Universidad Nacional de Colombia, presents impressive exhibitions on the geology and paleontology of what we today call the desert of Villa de Leyva. The extensive collection, housed in the old Molina de Losada (one of the first mills in the region) includes fossils of creatures from the Mesozoic sea, like bivalves, gastropods, ammonites, fishes and sea dinosaurs, as well as of plants. You can even adopt a fossil as part of a project to keep finds in their original places. Walk east along Carrera 9 or 10, both intersect before becoming the Vía Arcabuco. After a kilometer (0.6 miles), the museum is on the left. Kilometer 1, Vía Arcabuco. Tel: 8-732-0466, URL: www.unal.edu.co/museopale. Updated: Jun 16, 2008.

The Churches of Villa de Leyva

The cathedral in the Plaza Mayor was first built between 1604 to 1665. It was reconstructed after an earthquake in 1845. A few blocks away, Carrera 10 and Calle 14, is the relatively new Iglesia del Carmen (1845). There is also a colonial-era church built by the Carmelitas in 1642.

A few of Villa de Leyva's religious sites have taken on a new life. The cloister of San Agustín is now the Asociación Humboldt, an environmental studies research center. Carrera 8, between Calles 13 and 14. Tel: 8-732-0174. At the Iglesia de San Francisco it is necessary to peek through the cracks in the door to get a glimpse of the church built in 1613, but there are plans to restore it. Calle 9 and Carrera 8. The Catholic churches in Villa de Leyva are open only during mass hours. To visit Asociación Humboldt and see the cloisters of San Agustín, phone first. Updated: Jun 17, 2008.

Casas Coloniales of Villa de Leyva

In addition to the colonial houses in town that have been turned into museums, there are a few others that are possible to visit.

The building **Casa del Primer Congreso** held the first convention of the United Provinces of Nueva Granada. Open Tuesday-Thursday, Saturday 8 a.m.-1 p.m., 2-5 p.m. Carrera 9 and Calle 13.

Arquería del Jardín de los Próceres. Calle 13, between Carreras 8 and 9.

Real Fábrica de Licores (1736) was the Spanish Crown's first official liquor maker in Nueva Granada. To see the excavated building, ask at the Telecom office next door. Calle 13, between Carreras 8 and 9.
Casa don Juan de Castellanos was built from 1585 to 1607. It has an art gallery with a permanent exhibit on the second floor. Friday-Sunday, holidays 10 a.m.-9 p.m. Carrera 9 and Calle 13.

Molina Mesopotamia (1568) existed even before the village was founded. It is currently an upscale hotel. Ask at the reception for permission to see the mill (now a restaurant) and the pond in the back, where you can also go swimming ($2.65 for non-guests). Carrera 8, near Vía Arcabuco.

Molina de Losada was another one of the first mills in town. One kilometer (0.6 miles) from town, on Vía Arcabuco, the old mill is now home to the Museo Paleontológico.

In addition, several of the classic colonial mansions have been turned into malls.
Casa Quintero has gourmet restaurants. Wednesday-Monday 10 a.m.-11 p.m., closed the Wednesday after three-day holidays. Carrera 9 and Calle 12.

La Guaca has artesian shops and gourmet restaurants. Daily 10 a.m.-9 p.m. Carrera 13-57. Updated: Jun 17, 2008.

Casa Museo Luis Alberto Acuña

Luis Alberto Acuña (1904-1993) is considered one of Colombia's most important 20th

Museum	Description	Hours	Address	Contact	Prices
Casa Museo Antonio Nariño	This once-home of a major Independence leader was constructed in 1600	Thursday-Tuesday 8 a.m.-noon, 2-6 p.m.	Carrera 9, 10-21	Tel.: 8-732-0342	$0.50-1.60
Casa Museo Luis Alberto Acuña	Houses the works of this 20th Century painter and muralist	daily 9 a.m.-6 p.m.	Carrera 10, 12-83	Tel.: 8-732-0422	$0.50 -1
Museo Prehistórico	Acuña's small private collection of fossils and related paintings, with a Jurassic park in the garden	daily 9 a.m.-6 p.m.	Calle 13 and Carrera 10.	Tel: 8-732-0422	$0.50 -1
Museo del Arte Religioso del Carmen	Considered one of Colombia's finest collections of religious art	Saturday, Sunday, holidays 10 a.m.-1 p.m., 2-5 p.m.	Calle 14, 10-73	Tel.: 8-732-0214	$0.50 -0.80
Casa Museo Ricaurte	Home of a local Independence War hero who fought with Bolívar	Wednesday-Friday 9 a.m.-noon, 2-5 p.m., Saturday, Sunday, holidays 9 a.m.-1 p.m., 2-6 p.m.	Calle 15, 8-19	Tel: 8-732-0876	$0.50 -0.80
Museo Paleontológico	An impressive collection of the area's fossils	Tuesday-Saturday 9 a.m.-noon, 2-5 p.m., Sunday and holidays 9 a.m.-3 p.m.	Puente. Km 1, Vía Arcabuco / Carrera 9	Tel: 8-732-0466	$0.50 -1

Updated: Jun 17, 2008

Century artists. In 1979 he established this museum to exhibit his own artwork as well as the art of others. There are also antiquities and decorations on display. The main gallery exhibits Acuña's works in painting and ceramics. The Sala de Antigüidades presents antiques from all periods, especially from the period of Nueva Granada. In the patio are Acuña's sculptures, masks and murals that depict indigenous legends. The building has been under restoration, but the museum has been open. Carrera 10, 12-83. Tel: 8-732-0422, URL: www.gratisweb.com/museoacuna. Updated: Jun 18, 2008.

Viñedo Guananí

Viñedo Guananí wines are in high demand by Colombian wine connoisseurs. There are tours of the vineyard, including the three hectares where Carbernet Sauvignon, Isabela and Chardonnay grapes are organically grown. The tour goes on to present the fermentation and aging vats. At the end of the tour there is a complimentary glass. Tours are given only Saturday, Sunday and holidays at 10 a.m. and 2 p.m., with a minimum of six people ($2.10). Aside from the winery, Viñedo Guananí also has a hotel. Vía Casa Fundador. Tel: 8-732-0398, Fax: 8-732-1788, E-mail: guanani30@hotmail.com. Updated: Jun 17, 2008.

Road to Santa Sofía

The 18-kilometer (10.8-mile) stretch of road from Villa de Leyva to Santa Sofía holds many attractions for visitors en route to the Desierto de Villa de Leyva. Pozos Azules, three kilometers (1.8 miles) outside of the city, has sapphire pools like an oasis in the desert. One kilometer (0.6 miles) further is the Amonita, a large fossil that is set in a monument at the crossroads. At the Amonita is the left-hand turn-off for Criadero de Avestruces, an ostrich farm (daily 9 a.m.-5 p.m., entry: $2.65). Also just past the Amonita, on the right side of the road, is Fibas Jardín Botánico del Desierto. Wednesday-Sunday 8:30 a.m.-5:30 p.m., entry costs $1.05.

Another site one kilometer (0.6 miles) down the road is Museo El Fósil, which has an on-site Kronosaurus fossil. Daily 9 a.m.-5 p.m., entry: adults $1.30, children $0.80.

Continuing on the road, you pass the Ruinas de Monquirá. These are vestiges of a church built by Fray Bartolomé de Ojeda in 1533, 6 kilometers (3.6 miles) from Villa de Leyva. Not too far beyond these is the track leading to the enigmatic statues in Parque Arqueológico de Monquirá El Infiernito (Tuesday-Sunday 9 a.m.-noon, 2-5 p.m., closed Tuesday after three-day holidays, entry: adults $1.70, students and children $1.05).

Another three kilometers (2 miles) along the Santa Sofía road is the turnoff for Viñedo Aim Karin (entry: $2.65), go 600 more meters for the entrance.

The last major attraction on this route is the 17th Century Monasterio Santo Ecce Homo (daily 8 a.m.-5 p.m., entry: $1.30). It is almost 12 kilometers (7.2 miles) from Villa de Leyva, and one kilometer off the main road.

Tour agencies in Villa de Leyva offer half and full day trips to these sites (entry fees not included) or you can hire a taxi at the bus station to take you on this route ($37 for four hours). For a good walk, take a Santa Sofía bus as far as Monaste and walk the rest of the way. Updated: Jun 23, 2008.

Fibas Jardín del Desierto

Fibas Jardín del Desierto is more than just a botanical garden. In the Muisca language, *fibas* means wind. This garden is a project to recover a piece of land that winds have eroded. Through this recovery process, Fibas hopes to teach others about cultivation in desert climates (xero-culture). Two labyrinths of indigenous geometric designs lead you through a maze that represents our relationship with the universe and instructs us how we should care for the environment. Kilometer 4, Vía Santa Sofía, just past Monumento Amonite. Cell: 311-222-2399, E-mail: jaimerodriguez@fibas.org / jrrpu@yahoo.com, URL: www.fibas.org. Updated: Jun 23, 2008.

El Fósil

In 1977, in a hamlet outside of Villa de Leyva, some farmers found the skeletal remains of one former inhabitant of this valley — a Kronosaurus who perished some 110 to 115 million years earlier. This discovery was tremendous because it is one of the few nearly complete fossils of this dinosaur in the world (the others are in Australia). The 12-meter (39-foot) long creature is joined by other former inhabitants like the Ictiosaurus and the Elasmosaurus. Price includes guide services (Spanish only), from 8 a.m.-noon, 2-5 p.m.

No flash photos are allowed. Five kilometers (three miles) from Villa de Leyva, Vía Santa Sofía. Updated: Jun 23, 2008.

El Infiernito

The official name is Parque Arqueológico de Monquirá, though it is more commonly known as El Infiernito (small hell). This was an astronomical center for the Muisca. Although, according to archaeologists, the Muisca believed that when the sun cast no shadow on the observatory's identical lines of 36 stones, then it was busy fertilizing the earth and the planting would begin. Additionally at this time, the women would be fertile. At El Infiernito, they would perform rituals among the forest of phallic statues, hugging and caressing them to ensure pregnancy. Due east of this is Laguna de Iguaque, the birthplace of humans, according to Muisca mythology. Recent excavations have revealed a tomb and a 4,000-year-old proto-Muisca altar. It is 7 kilometers (4.2 miles) from Villa de Leyva, Vía Santa Sofía. Updated: Jun 23, 2008.

Monasterio Santo Ecce Homo

On a spread of boulder-strewn land, four Dominican monks established a monastery in 1620. Inside this fossil-studded stone edifice, tour the original chapel (note the moon and sun in the apse arch) and a dozen galleries that exhibit religious art and portraits of the monks' daily life. The choir loft displays parchment musical manuscripts. The cloister patio arcade has 33 columns, which represent the years Jesus lived and has a passage of the dead. Members of the donor's family and abbots are buried under these bricks. Peeking from beneath the whitewashed walls are murals that were covered in the 18th Century. If the door isn't open during the set hours, ring the bell. It is also possible to do retreats at the monastery and live within the monk's community. Public mass is in the chapel Sundays at 5 p.m. Almost 12 kilometers (7.2 miles) from Villa de Leyva, Vía Santa Sofía. Updated: Jun 23, 2008.

Beyond Santa Sofía

If the road to Santa Sofía is imprinted by the past and present occupants of the Desierto de Villa de Leyva, then the road beyond this small village is sculpted purely by nature. Waterfalls drape the bluff, like the Cascada Guatoque that stands at 80 meters (262.5 feet) and Cascadas de Sorocota, which is made up of three cascades, the tallest is 30 meters (98.5 feet). Carved within the auburn earth are caverns and caves, among these are the Cueva del Indio and Cueva de la Chapa. All the elements come together at Hayal in the Cascada Hayal, which stands 70 meters (229.5 feet) tall, Cueva del Hayal and Gruta del Hayal. Then there is the Paso del Ángel, a narrow ridge between two deep canyons. The Páramo del Merchán tops off the whole landscape. It is difficult to reach most of these sights without a private car. Tour agencies in Villa de Leyva offer half and full day trips. Updated: Jun 23, 2008.

To Gachantivá

Explore one of the many caves that pockmark the land, like the Cueva del Indio and Cueva la Furatena. There are also many creeks and cascades. Practice *torrentismo* (rappelling) over the Cascadas la Periquera; camp on the banks of Quebrada la Honda; or, hike to Laguna las Coloradas. To wash the sweat off after a long day of adventuring, dip into the Pozo de la Vieja on the banks of Río de la Cebada. The ruins of the old viceroy's residence, Gachantivá Viejo, should not be missed, with its graveyard segregated by class and race, the old church and other notable buildings. Updated: Jun 23, 2008.

Santuario de Flora y Fauna de Iguaque

Amid the chilly mists swirling across this páramo, the goddess Bachue rose from the crystalline waters of Laguna de Iguaque. According to Muisca legend, this is how mankind was born. It is believed a pilgrimage to this sacred place cleanses the soul and purifies the spirit. The Laguna lies in the midst of the 6,800-hectare Santuario de Flora y Fauna de Iguaque. This park cradles wetland forests and páramo lands between 2,440 and 3,660 meters (8,000 and 12,000 feet) tall and eight lagoons. A hiking path to Laguna de Iguaque has signs that describe the special environment of this sanctuary.

Tour agents in Villa de Leyva and Tunja make day trips to the Santuario de Flora y Fauna Iguaque. If on your own, take a bus heading toward Arcabuco and get off at the park entrance. The road at the entrance is rough and the walk to Laguna de Iguaque takes three and a half hours there and three back.

Accommodation within the park is available. The Furachiougua cabin (Muisca meaning "good woman") sleeps six to eight people ($14 per person, per night). Camping is only allowed in the designated site near the administrative center. Bring all equipment with you (low season: one-time charge of $2.15 for site, plus $2.15 per night per person / high season: $3.70 for site plus $3.70 per person per night). There is also a restaurant within the park. Vía Arcabuco. E-mail: norandin@col1.telecom.com.co, URL: www.parquesnacionales.gov.co/areas/lasareas/iguaque/iguaintro.htm. Updated: Jun 23, 2008.

Villa de Leyva Tours

There are quite a few tour agencies in Villa de Leyva for city tours, trips out to the local sights or a *chiva* ride around town. This village has some premier experts available to teach you about the ecology of this region, which spreads from desert to páramo, or to take you on adventure excursions, like rappelling into canyons, caves and waterfalls. Bold adventurers rent horses along Avenida Circunvalar. Updated: Jun 16, 2008.

Guianzas Pierre LaCour

Pierre LaCour is a professional, French rafter experienced in torrentismo and sustainable agriculture. LaCour offers adventure trips in the Villa de Leyva area, including hiking and horseback riding. However, rappelling is his specialty. Imagine leaping on a rope down a waterfall or a canyon. Depending on the excursion, it costs $10.50 to $42 per person per day. Pierre also has package tours for groups interested in learning about biodynamic and organic agriculture. Cell: 310-773-1556, E-mail: elarcaverde@gmail.com / elarcaverde@hotmail.com. Updated: Jun 16, 2008.

Colombia Highlands

Colombia Highlands has a variety of half- and full-day outings to the standard Villa de Leyva sights and adventure tours, which include rappelling and caving. Owner, Oscar Gilède, offers something special to visitors: scientific tourism. This biologist and eco-instructor can specially tailor outings for birdwatching, entomology (including spiders), geology, botany or amphibians. He also leads nighttime excursions on foot or horseback into the desert for stargazing. Carrera 9, 11-02. Tel: 8-732-1379, Cell: 311-308-3739, E-mail: colombianhighlands@hotmail.com, URL: www.colombianhighlands.com / www.algo-diferente.net / www.expovilla.com. Updated: Jun 17, 2008.

Guías y Travesías

Focusing on guided walking tours for all ages, Guías y Travesías offers short and long hikes to 70 attractions in the Villa de Leyva area. Trace the footsteps of the past to El Fósil, Monasterio de Santo Ecce Homo and El Infiernito or take in the dessert in Ráquira and Monsterio de la Candelaria (either tour: adults $21, children $17.50, four hours). Head out to Santa Sofía for caves, rivers and roads of adventure (adults $21, children $17.50, six hours). Or, hike to sacred Laguna de Iguaque (adults $24, children $20, 9 hours). All excursions include guide, transport and entry fees. Guías y Travesías also rents bicycles ($3.20 / hour, $10.50 / half-day, $18.50 / full day). Calle 11, 8A-30. Tel: 8-732-0742, Cell: 311-461-1298. E-mail: guiadevilladeleyva@yahoo.com. Updated: Jun 17, 2008.

Villa de Leyva Lodging

Despite the vast amount of hotels in Villa de Leyva, lodging is difficult on the shoestring traveler's budget. You'll be hard-pressed to find a room for under $8 per night. Slim-budget travelers might consider not visiting during the high season, when prices double or more. However, if you are so equipped, camping is a viable alternative. Most hotels are mid-range and charge up to $40 per night. Villa de Leyva has few spectacular luxury hotels, which are complete with packages for couples who want the ultimate in weddings.

The high season includes all national holidays, three-day weekends, July and August, Semana Santa and December 20 to January 15. Reservations are necessary during high season. Hotels are not allowed to charge higher prices outside of the dates mandated by the tourism office. Feel free to report the establishment, if you find out otherwise. Updated: Jun 23, 2008.

Budget

Hostal Renacer

(ROOM: $3-37) Hostal Renacer is a place for rejuvenation after a day of strenuous sightseeing. Just outside of Villa de Leyva, Oscar has created the place for backpackers to relax and rest. There is something to fit every budget — a dorm, room or camping and common bathroom or private. The upstairs suite is perfect for a romantic getaway. There is also a laundry area, kitchen and brick oven, as well as a common room with a fireplace. Lay in a hammock on the portico surrounding and watch hummingbirds. Follow Carrera 9 / Vía Arcabuco East out of town. After the bridge, go on Vía Colorado on the right for 600 meters (2,000 feet) to the road that leads to the front gate of Hostal Renacer. Tel: 8-732-1379, Cell: 311-308-3739, E-mail: colombianhighlands@hotmail.com, URL: www.colombianhighlands.com / www.algo-diferente.net / www.expovilla.com. Updated: Jun 23, 2008.

Zona de Camping San Jorge

(BED: $4) A common complaint about campgrounds in Villa de Leyva is that they are like warehouses of people. Although, Camping San Jorge is said to be the best in Villa de Leyva, and includes proper facilities. These grounds have good-size camp sites, bathhouses with hot showers, fire pits and a place to wash your dishes. Private security and parking are other pluses. Besides camping, San Jorge offers a two-bedroom apartment for six people with a private bath, cable TV, a dining nook and kitchenette. Vereda roble Kilometer 1, Vía Arcabuco, in front of the fire station, 1.5 kilometers from town. Tel: 8-732-0328, Cell: 311-213-1125; Reservations (Bogotá): 1-625-2612 / 612-3130. E-mail: campingsanjorge@gmail.com. Updated: Jun 23, 2008.

Hospedería Colonial

(ROOM: $8-21) Just half a block from the main plaza is Hospedería Colonial. The family who runs the place lives in the main part of the house. Off their living room are simple rooms for one or two people, which share the family's bathroom. The backyard has a terrace and the portico porch has bamboo chairs. Around the first level of the patio are attractively decorated rooms with private, hot-water baths. Some even come with Jacuzzi. All rooms come with cable TV. Calle 12, 10-81. Updated: Jun 23, 2008.

Hospedaje El Mirador

Hospedaje El Mirador is not too far from the bus station, on a quiet side street. This hostel is geared toward groups of travelers, each room comes with at least two beds, a private bathroom and cable TV. One thing that sets this place apart is the riotous courtyard garden filled with plants and pottery fauna from nearby Ráquira. Calle 8A, 6-94. Tel: 8-732-0941. Updated: Jun 23, 2008.

Casa Campesina / El Solar Camping

(BED: $5-11) Casa Campesina, near the corner of the main plaza, has a very home-like atmosphere. The owner, Martha de León, has become the surrogate mother to many younger travelers. She sits down over a complimentary tea, coffee or juice during breakfast to listen to their travel tales. The rooms have comfy beds and share common bathrooms, with hot water. A seating area is out on the covered back patio, which includes a BBQ, fireplace and hammocks. For those on a budget, camping is available in the large garden. Besides Doña Martha, other permanent residents include a dog and *morrocoy* turtle. Carrera 9, 11-44. Cell: 311-832-7919, E-mail: campingfamiliar@hotmail.com. Updated: Jun 23, 2008.

El Arca Verde

(ROOM: $5-11) El Arca Verde (The Green Ark) is an organic, biodynamic farm outside of Villa de Leyva. Guests lodge in the maloka, a traditional, round indigenous hut made of earth, stone and reused materials. The restaurant serves dishes prepared with the farm's produce. The common room serves as a dorm, with beds around the perimeter of the space. Upstairs, there are two private rooms. A fireplace keeps the house warm on cool evenings and showers are solar heated. The owners, Mariela and Pierre, teach visitors about agricultural biodynamics. Take into consideration that it is possible to trade working on the farm for lodging. Take the road to Santa Sofía, at Carcamo take a right and follow the signs for 8 kilometers to El Arca Verde (4.8 miles). It is past Posada San Javier. A taxi costs $10.50.Valle Escondido, Vereda Las Vegas, 15 kilometers (9 miles) from Villa de Leyva. E-mail: elarcaverde@gmail.com / elarcaverde@hotmail.com. Updated: Jun 23, 2008.

Hospedería Don Paulino

(ROOM: $8-11) Don Paulino and Doña Olga have established a wonderful hotel on a tranquil street just a few blocks from the Plaza Principal. It has a second-story balcony with a great view of the sunset over the valley's hills. The rooms are nicely decorated with clean bathrooms and a TV. In the mornings, the doña greets guests with fresh orange juice and coffee. The kitchen is open for guests to prepare their own food. The owners are retired teachers and are very knowledgeable about the region. Calle 14, 7-46. Tel: 8-732-1227 / 315-235-9447 / 313-323-2975. Updated: Jun 23, 2008.

Hospedería La Villa

(BED: $8-37) Hospedería La Villa, a half block from the Plaza Principal, is a colonial-era house with a rambling maze of rooms, which all have windows facing the courtyard off the street. Many of the quarters are quite basic and a bit cramped. Some come with a TV and private bath with hot water. There is a special room separate from the main building for six people that includes a seating area ($47.50 low season, $95 high season). Calle 12, 10-11. Tel: 8-732-0848, Cell: 311-852-4038. Updated: Jun 23, 2008.

MID-RANGE

Casa Hotel Villa Cristina

(ROOM: $21-48) On a quiet dirt road far from the center of town, the Casa Hotel Villa Christina is a white, multi-story house with a red-tile roof, cobblestone interior courtyards and terrace, and kiosks with hammocks. This is an intimate B&B that has 10 rooms with private bathrooms, hot water and cable TV. In addition to a tourism information desk, Villa Christina provides express tours with guides to local sites and horseback rides. Prices are per person, and include American breakfast, parking and tourism information. Calle 10, 3-78. Tel: 8-732-0594, Cell: 300-568-6828, E-mail: chvillachristina@yahoo.es, URL: www.villadeleyva.com.co/contenido/hoteles/Otros_alojamientos/Casa_Hotel_villac.htm. Updated: Jun 23, 2008.

Hotel Boutique La Española

(ROOM: $24-32) Hotel Boutique La Española is a new and very special hotel on the crowded Villa de Leyva hotel scene. The Soler family's ancient home has been transformed into an intimate hotel with beautiful tile accents. The water flowing through the courtyard is just one example of the Feng Shui principles used to design every inch of this space. The 15 rooms are simply furnished, but include a TV and a spectacular private bathroom with hot water. If you get a suite, it comes with a Jacuzzi. The comfortable common room has a TV and a fireplace.Calle 12, 11-06. Tel: 8-732-0464, Cell: 300-564-6502, E-mail: hotel.laespanola@hotmail.com, URL: www.laespanola.villadeleyva.com.co. Updated: Jun 23, 2008.

Hospedaje Sol de la Villa

(ROOM: $24-32) Hospedaje Sol de la Villa is off of Parque Nariño, a few blocks from the bus station. This modest B&B provides tastefully decorated, clean rooms with private, hot water bathrooms. Smoking is not allowed. Reservations are highly recommended. Hospedaje Sol de la Villa accepts credit cards, but with a surcharge. Prices include an American breakfast, tax and insurance. Carrera 8, 12-28. Tel: 8-732-0224, Fax: 8-732-0932. Updated: Jun 23, 2008.

Hospedería Antonio Nariño

(ROOM: $27-63)Hospedería Antonio Nariño was recently built in the heart of Villa de Leyva, but with historic architecture and techniques. Fountains spray the large, cobblestone courtyards that are surrounded by second-floor balconies. The spacious rooms have double beds, private bathrooms with hot water and cable TV. A special feature is the deluxe suite, which comes with a Jacuzzi, mini-bar and a fireplace ($132 low season, $158 high season). Despite the elegance of this hotel, it doesn't offer other amenities, such as laundry, breakfast or a restaurant. Carrera 9, 10-34, Tel: 8-732-0211, Cell: 311-440-3901, E-mail: hospenarino@hotmail.com, URL: www.villadeleyva.net/hot_antonio_narinio.php. Updated: Jun 23, 2008.

HIGH-END

Hostería del Molina La Mesopotamia

(ROOM: $58-237) This is the hotel mentioned previously in this chapter in reference to interesting, old buildings. Built in 1568 as a wheat mill, Hostería del Molina La Mesopotamia is now one of Villa de Leyva's finest hotels. Slip back in time as you fall off to sleep in the rooms furnished with period pieces — including four-poster beds. Heavy, embroidered curtains keep the quarters warm at night. Each room has a private bathroom with hot water. The actual mill is now the restaurant. The millionaire Vanderbilt family and actor Ernest Borgnine are some of the famous people who have stayed here. Non-guests can ask permission at the reception to stroll through the immaculate grounds or swim in the warm pond fed by a medicinal spring ($2.65). Room prices include breakfast, tax and insurance. Carrera 8, near Vía Arcabuco. Tel: 8-732-0235, E-mail: hosteriamesopotamia@hotmail.com, URL: www.hosterialamesopotamia.addr.com Updated: Jun 23, 2008.

Hotel La Posada de San Antonio

(ROOM: $95-106) Hotel La Posada de San Antonio is a converted mid-19th Century mansion on Parque Nariño. It has the feel of a country mansion, with a pool table in the library, a chapel, many antiques and a conservative décor. All rooms are spacious with king-size beds and private bathrooms. The hotel has a location in the country that provides conference facilities, a swimming pool and horseback riding. The rooms here are bright and airy, for one to three people. There is also wedding and honeymoon packages. Carrera 8, 11-61. Tel: 8-732-0538 / 0390, Cell: 310-280-7326, E-mail: padelgo@hotmail.com. Updated: Jun 23, 2008.

Hotel Casa de los Fundadores

(ROOM: $125-150) Casa de los Fundadores is a different kind of hotel — a project of the Dominican nuns. Many years ago, the nuns had lived on this land, but now the sisters have built an exclusive hotel with all the imaginable luxuries, including a sauna, chocolate therapy massage, guided tours on horseback and their very own chapel, of course. Other special touches are the fire pit, bicycle rentals, a game room and playground. The guest rooms are immaculately decorated, with private bathrooms. Special vacation packages are available, as well as all-inclusive weddings. Kilometer 1, Vía Viñedo de Guananí. Tel: 8-732-0880 / 732-0878, Fax: 8-732-0839, E-mail: admin@casadelosfundadores.com, URL: www.casadelosfundadores.com. Bogotá: Carrera 11, 77-20, local 4. Tel: 1-211-2720 / 530-4602, Fax: 1-210-2392, Updated: Jun 23, 2008.

Villa de Leyva Restaurants

Eating in Villa de Leyva tends to be on the high end, both in the level of gastronomy and price. Many of the nicer restaurants are closed on Wednesdays, including those in the Centro Comercial Quintero. After a three-day holiday weekend, many restaurants are closed on Tuesday, too. Generous daily plate specials are always available, for about $2.10. If you are on a budget, some of the cheaper hostels have common kitchens to do your own cooking. And, on Saturdays the market plaza is a flurry of sights and smells when farmers and other producers come in from all over the countryside to sell their goods (Calle 12 and 13, Carrera 5 and 6).

Heladería Los Indios

Heladería Los Indios is said to have the best ice cream of Villa de Leyva. Even the wooden Indian statues that stand out front are licking cones. There are dozens of flavors, and one scoop is a cool $0.85. If you're going for something more, have a sundae ($2), a coke float ($1.85) or a milk shake ($1.85). Open Sunday-Friday 11:30 a.m.-8 p.m., Saturday 10:30 a.m.-10 p.m. Carrera 9, 14-54. Updated: Jun 23, 2008.

Pastelería Francesa

Leave Colombia—for a moment—in the Pastelería Francesa. This small café has old-fashioned wooden display cases, photos of early-to-mid-20th Century France and French magazines that create a very French ambience. Master baker Patrice Rio creates French pastries. Try the croissant de *almendras* (pastry filled with almond crème), a *feijao* tart (made from a local fruit) or a mini-quiche. *Oui*, there are also baguettes, white or whole wheat. Open Thursday-Monday 8 a.m.-6:30 p.m. (until 7 p.m. for carry out). Closed Tuesday and Wednesday. Calle 10, 9-41. Updated: Jun 23, 2008.

Restaurante La Parrilla

Restaurante La Parrilla is a popular budget choice for locals. The five tables are often full of diners eating set-plate meals (breakfast $2.10; lunch or dinner $2.10 complete, $1.85 main course and drink only). The midday and evening portions are generous and come with meat, rice, beans, several vegetables and a salad. So much food, in fact, you might leave with a doggie bag. Substitute the meat with eggs for a lower price. Open daily 6:30 a.m.-9 p.m. Carrera 9, 9-17. Updated: Jun 23, 2008.

El Fogón de la Gallina

El Fogón de la Gallina is a few doors down and similar to Restaurante La Parrilla. El Fogón serves good set-plate specials of Colombian classics, though the portions aren't as generous and the prices are a wee bit more than those of its neighbor. Another difference is that the interior of El Fogón de la Gallina is a bit snazzier than La Parrilla. It is one of the cheaper places to eat well in town. Carrera 9, 9-23. Updated: Jun 23, 2008.

Restaurant Xirrus

Restaurant Xirrus specializes in vegetarian, vegan and organic cuisine with novo-Colombian flair. À la carte dishes include wraps with banana cake and house salad ($7.40-10.50), salads ($3.20-8.50) and pastas ($6.35-9.50). There is miso soup, chicken and seafood, like the shrimp salad prepared with avocado and mango ($8.50). A full bar of hot, alcoholic and non-alcoholic drinks makes the grade. A plaque commemorates the last concert former Elvis Presley drummer Bill (Rueda) Lynn gave before dying in Villa de Leyva. Open Friday 4-10 p.m., Saturday, Sunday and Monday holidays 10 a.m.-10 p.m. Centro Comercial Casa Quintero. Updated: Jun 23, 2008.

Asadero La Villa

At the entrance to Asadero La Villa an enclosed fire pit has meats roasting on an upright spit. Inside the restaurant, there is a large space with many long wooden tables that can accommodate groups of diners. Delicious lunch and dinner plate specials include a choice of meat and soda ($2.35, set meal $1.60). Beer is also available to go with your BBQ ($0.60). Thursday-Sunday and holidays 7 a.m.-7 p.m. Carrera 9, 10-58. Cell: 314-488-2380 / 325-8128. Updated: Jun 23, 2008.

Té y Café Saloom

Té y Café Saloom is good for a quick breakfast, a snack or a nighttime tea. (Despite being called a saloom, er saloon, no alcohol is served.) Everything at the small café is homemade, including the cookies to dip in your coffee ($0.50-0.80) and the rich cakes and brownies ($1.30-2.40). There are also savory goodies, like *arepas* ($1.85-3.70). The beef or chicken with mushrooms and cheese arepa is worth a taste. Open Monday-Thursday 8 a.m.-9 p.m., Friday-Sunday 8 a.m.-10 p.m. Carrera 8, 13-00. Tel: 8-732-0177, Cell: 312-480-5486. Updated: Jun 23, 2008.

Restaurante Casa Blanca

Many hostels in Villa de Leyva recommend Restaurante Casa Blanca to their guests for an inexpensive dining choice. The establishment has earned a reputation after many years of serving classic Colombian dishes and — it is said — the best *cazuela boyacense* around ($2.40). They also serve set meals for breakfast ($2.60), lunch and dinner ($3.20), Casa Blanca has daily featured plates. These special entrees are beef, chicken, fish (including trout) or *longaniza* sausage, accompanied by yucca, potatoes and salad. Open daily 8 a.m.-9 p.m. Calle 13, 7-02. Tel: 8-732-0821. Updated: Jun 23, 2008.

Chepa Chaves

The legend says that Chepa Chaves was a charming young woman who arrived one day at the turn of the 20th Century in Villa de Leyva. Many men fell in love with her, and her cooking. The tradition of fine Colombian cuisine continues at this restaurant named after her, with a small selection of distinctive dishes. The chef creates special house sauces to accompany grilled trout or chicken and braises rounds of beef or pork in red wine. Red snapper and goulash are also on the menu, both come with salad, rice or vegetable cake and French fries ($8.20-10.30). Chepa Chaves also has an executive lunch ($4.25). Open Tuesday-Sunday and holidays noon-9 p.m. Carrera 8, between Carreras 12 and 13. Updated: Jun 23, 2008.

Hechizo de la Luna

Hechizo de la Luna, (moonstruck) is one of Villa de Leyva's best pizzerias. The moon theme threads throughout the dining experience, decorating the stained-glass hurricane lamp on the tables, the wine glasses with the Man in the Moon amid stars and the check that comes on the crescent moon platter. Unique combinations of thin crust pizzas really stand out, like the Pizza de la Luna (smoked ham, prosciutto, salami, mushrooms, roasted peppers, olives, eggplant) or the Sweet Temptation (mozzarella, cherries, apple, smoked bacon, Vienna sausage). Choose between a small ($4.20-7.40) or medium ($8.50-13.15). Open Thursday-Monday 11 a.m.-9 p.m. Centro Comercial Casa de Quintero, local 13. Tel: 8-732-1774. Updated: Jun 23, 2008.

Restaurante Zarina

Restaurante Zarina is an intimate bistro that only has four tables, a perfect place for a romantic candlelit dinner. Its Colombian-Lebanese proprietors are experts in Arab, Mediterranean and vegetarian cooking. Some of the menu's highlights are the anti-pasto, like the á la Charly with Serrano ham, Paipa cheese, olives, dried tomatoes, peppers and eggplant in olive oil, served with whole wheat bread ($9.50). The mixed Arab and vegetarian plates ($10-11) are another house specialty. Beef, trout and chicken dishes are also served ($10-12). Open Thursday-Monday 11 a.m.-11 p.m. Centro Comercial Casa de Quintero. Updated: Jun 23, 2008.

Pizzería Olivas y Especias

On the corner of the main plaza is one of the other recommended pizzerias in Villa de Leyva. This rather large bistro also serves Italian dishes and crepes. The pizzas come with a smorgasbord of toppings, in three sizes ($7-14.75). Pizzería Olivas y Especias Pasta offers lasagna dishes that come only with bread ($5.50-7) and vegetarians have several dishes available as well. The restaurant has alcoholic drinks, including *canelazo*, and fresh juices. Open daily 4-10 p.m. Carrera 10, 11-99. Tel: 8-732-1261, Cell: 310-262-0664. Updated: Jun 23, 2008.

Restaurante Don Quijote

At Restaurante Don Quijote, seating is available on the patio or in the kitchen of the 400-year-old colonial house. The eclectic menu offers dishes of beef, chicken, trout, squid or shrimp accompanied by pesto pasta and salad ($8-9) and Thai pasta or rice ($9). Stir-fried vegetables with noodles or the *tortilla española* might fit the bill for a hungry vegetarian. The roasted lamb plate ($18.65) is definitely a task for two. On weekdays, Restaurante Don Quijote serves set plates ($4.20), but on weekends it's only à la carte. Open daily noon-9 p.m. Centro Comercial Guaca (Carrera 9, Calle 13). Cell: 313-225-2406. Updated: Jun 23, 2008.

La Tienda de Teresa

Tienda de Teresa is a good place to fuel up on a hearty boyacense breakfast ($1.40-2.60) or cazuela boyacense ($2.30) before heading out for a day hike. Teresa's is a good place to drop by any time of day. Try one of the arepas stuffed with anything and everything, including vegetarian options ($1.35-3.70). In the evening, warm up with a canelazo, chocolate or other hot drink. Teresa also bakes some of the region's typical desserts ($0.30-$1.60). Open daily 8 a.m.-8 p.m. Carrera 10, 13-72. Updated: Jun 23, 2008.

Restaurante Guananí

Restaurante Guananí provides a break from the standard Colombian and haute cuisine eateries in town. This bistro specializes in German cooking, especially authentic sausages. Cold platters of ham, cheese or sausage and bread ($5.30-6.85) are on the menu. Among the main dishes are German hamburger, veal or pork scallopini, chicken goulash and trout. These come with a German potato salad or fried potatoes. Have a glass — or bottle — of the house wine (from Guananí's vineyard) with your meal. Open weekdays by reservation; Saturday, Sunday and holidays 8 a.m.-7 p.m. Viñedo Guananí, Vía Casa Fundador. Fax: 8-732-1788, E-mail: guanani30@hotmail.com. Updated: Jun 23, 2008.

Chichería El Pote

The scent of crushed eucalyptus wafts within the small space of Chichería El Pote. Pull up a rough-hewn wooden table and settle down to your favorite drink. National and international brands are on hand ($1.60-3.70) as well as wines, cocktails and a variety of hard liquors by shot, half-bottle or bottle. The traditional drinks include canelazo and, yes, *chicha* (a traditional corn drink). Leave your mark on the walls, guests have been doing it for years. Open Thursday-Tuesday noon-midnight or 1 a.m., depending on the number of people hanging out. Centro Comercial Casa Quintero, first floor. Updated: Jun 23, 2008.

Villa de Leyva Nightlife

The dance scene in Villa de Leyva only really exists when the tourists come on weekends and holidays. During the week some of the cafés and restaurants around the plaza have musicians. Your chances of catching live concerts are better during the high season and holidays. Updated: Jun 23, 2008.

Cine Bar El Patriarca

It's show time in Villa de Leyva! Sink into one of the comfy chairs with a beer, soda and a hotdog or popcorn. El Patriarca shows mostly international and Colombian films, with the occasional Hollywood flick. Movies are shown when at least six viewers are present. Buy tickets in advance downstairs at QuinteroNet ($3.20). Centro Comercial Casa Quintero, second floor. Updated: Jun 23, 2008.

La Alcazaba

La Alcazaba is the center of the bohemian scene in Villa de Leyva. Intellectuals, writers and artists meet up at this café-bar. The antique-filled space has spiral staircases that lead to seating areas with fireplaces and balconies. Classic Spanish tapas ($2.65-8), fondues ($5.30-8) and *empanaditas* ($1.60-3.70) go nicely with coffee or liquor. During the week, the house music is *bolero*, *cha cha* and other classic, smooth Latin music. Saturdays and Sundays feature live guitar or Cuban son (minimum consumption, $8 per person). There are literary events as well. Open daily 10 a.m.-midnight. Carrera 9, 14-57. Tel: 8-732-0190, Cell: 311-217-7442, E-mail: la.alcazaba@hotmail.com / la.alcazaba@yahoo.com. Updated: Jun 23, 2008.

La Tasca

Locals and tourists all shake it at La Tasca. Massive green wooden gates lead to the front courtyard of this large hall with stain-glass windows. The club is a way out of town, about 300 meters beyond the cemetery, but that doesn't seem to hurt its popularity much. Check the posters around town for information on what's shaking at La Tasca. During high seasons, La Tasca has live mu-

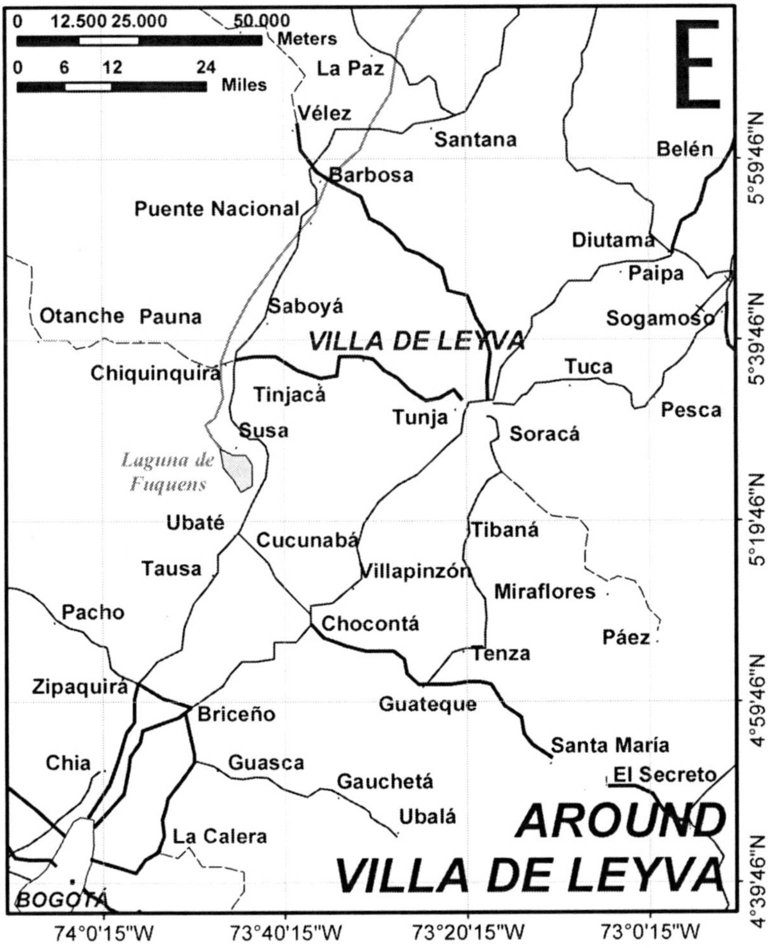

sic. This is also a popular place for organizations to have fundraising balls. Open only Friday and Saturday nights. Entry is $2.70. Calle 15 (Avenida Circunvalar), 12A-25, past the cemetery. Updated: Jun 23, 2008.

Guarapos

Guarapos takes pride in having the best sound system and light show of any nightspot in this popular tourist town. The club also claims to bring in the best groups and events. There is live music during the high seasons and special holidays, though the cover charge is a bit pricey at $27. Buy tickets in advance in several neighboring towns, as well as in Villa de Leyva. Check Guarapos' website for more information. Carrera 9, 7-25. URL: www.guaraposvilladeleyva.com. Updated: Jun 17, 2008.

Near Villa de Leyva Ráquira

Alt: 2,200 m Pop: 12,300 City Code: 8

Ráquira in Chibcha means "The City of Pots." To this day, the workshops of this village give credence to the name by making the animal-shaped ceramics for which they are famous. Most visitors come for the Sunday market, but any time is pleasant. The narrow streets are lined with colorful houses and gardens. Ráquira's main temple dates from about 1600 AD. Six kilometers (3.5 miles) away in the Desierto de la Candelaria is Convento Monasterio Nuestra Señora de la Candelaria, an Agustinian monastery founded in 1597. Its museum of religious art and antiques is open to the public ($2.65). The monastery additionally has a restaurant and hostel (Cell: 315-257-4152 / 310-261-3135. In Bogotá: Calle 73A, 69A-69. Tel: 1-251-6886 / 252-9954, Fax: 1-430-1075). Updated: June 23, 2008.

San Gil

Alt: 1,114 m Pop: 49,500 City Code: 7

San Gil is great for extreme sports or just for relaxing. San Gil has long been popular with Colombians as a weekend and holiday escape. Travelers have just recently come to know of this colonial town in Santander, only six hours from Bogotá.

There are several private nature preserves, the most famous being Parque Gallineral, with guided nature tours and swimming pool, on the banks of the Río Fonce.

Numerous travel agencies offer "extreme sports" tours, including paragliding, rappelling, kayaking, caving, biking, horseback riding and day walks. Also there is whitewater rafting down several local rivers or through the Chicamocha Canyon. Prices for these tours are regulated.

Nearby are several historical towns. Barichara has virtually untouched colonial architecture and the Parque de las Aguas. In Guane there is a paleontology museum, and good rock and fossil hunting. Updated: May 06, 2008.

History

In pre-Spanish conquest times, the Guanes lived in the San Gil area. They were related to the Muisca, of the Chibcha linguistic family. The Guanes were still here when the Spaniards arrived but were quickly exterminated by the conquering forces. Only 351 survived and were relocated to the village of Guanes.

San Gil as we know it today was founded in 1689 by don Gil Cabrera y Dávalos, by decree of the Spanish king. The town was originally named for don Gil and later for the saint of the same moniker.

The sparks of independence ignited in the villages near this colonial town. In 1781 mestizo José Antonio Golán led the comunero revolt in Charalá; similar uprisings occurred in Mogotes, Onzaga and Socorro. A number of important battles occurred in this region. The Batalla de Pienta of 1819 resulted in heavy losses to the viceregal troops, which helped the rebels later win the Battle of Boyacá.

San Gil and surrounding towns were flashpoints of the 20th Century civil wars, especially the Guerra de Mil Días at the beginning of the millennium and the disruptions that arose after Liberal presidential candidate Jorge Eliécer Gaitan's assassination in 1948. Updated: Jan 07, 2008.

When to Go

The weather in San Gil is pretty much the same all year long. There is no real rainy season as in other parts of the country. Temperatures average 25°C (77°F). It is very popular with vacationing Colombians, especially during December-January holidays, Semana Santa (Easter week), July-August holidays and three-day weekends. Hotel prices rise substantially at these times and reservations are necessary. Updated: Jan 07, 2008.

Getting To and Away from San Gil

You can arrive to San Gil from Bogotá or Tunja. If in Villa de Leyva, you have to return to Tunja, or take the back roads, which is cheaper: go by way of Arcabuco, which is on the main Bogotá-Bucaramanga road. If arriving from the coast, first go to Bucaramanga, then transfer.

San Gil has a good public transportation system (daily 5 a.m.-9 p.m. $0.40). For the long-distance bus terminal, catch one that says "Terminal" from Calle 10 and Carrera 11. Taxis cost $1.40.

The long-distance bus terminal, handling traffic to Bogotá, Cucuta and the coast, is located on Carrera 12 and Calle 31, about two kilometers from town. Most routes to Santa Marta and other coastal points and to Cucuta transfer in Bucaramanga. It is better to go to Bucaramanga from where there is cheaper and more frequent transport. Minivans to villages near San Gil leave from the depot at Carrera 11 and Calle 15. For Guanes, first go to Barichara and transfer there.

Direct services are listed below. Primary bus companies include Berlinas, Brasilia, Copetran and Cotrasangil. Schedules and prices vary among companies, so be sure to check them out for yourself, and bear in mind that usually the last bus making the return trip to San Gil will leave earlier than the last bus departing from San Gil to the same destination.

From San Gil

Arrive	Departures	Time	Price
Bogotá	Every hour	6 hours	$16 -$24
Cartagena	5p.m., 7:30 p.m.	14-15 hours	$37 -$48
Mogotes	7 buses / day	2 hours	$3.20
Barichara	6:10 a.m. - 6:30 p.m.	0.5 hours	$1.60

Arrive	Departures	Time	Price
Cabrera	Mon. - Fri. 5:45 a.m. - 11:30 a.m.; Sat. -Sun. 9 a.m., 11:30 a.m., 5:45 p.m.	1 hour	$2.10
Charalá	Every half hour 6 a.m. - 6:30 p.m.	45 mins.	$2.10
Curití	Every 15 min. 6 a.m. - 7p.m.	20 mins.	$0.80
Bucaramanga	Every half hour 4:30 - 8 p.m.	2.5 hours	$7.40
Páramo	6 a.m. - 7:15 p.m.	0.5 hours	$1.50
Villanueva	Every 20 min., 6 a.m. - 6:50 p.m.	0.5 hours	$1.30

Updated: Jan 07, 2008.

Holidays and Festivals

The Fiesta de San Gil on 17 March is celebrated with civic acts and parades. Other civil holidays include 20 July, Fiesta de la Patria, and 7 August, the Batalla de Boyacá. Semana Santa, Easter Week, has religious processions on Maundy Thursday, Good Friday and Holy Saturday. This same week is the Festival de Música Colombiana Andina y Religiosa. The feast of the Immaculate Conception is marked with candlelight ceremonies, especially in homes. On any national holiday or three-day weekend expect San Gil to be jammed with Colombians chilling out. Updated: Jan 07, 2008.

Safety in San Gil

San Gil is a safe place to spend a while. When participating in any extreme sport, be sure that the company provides you with proper safety equipment and well-trained guides. Do not swim in the Fonce River, which flows through Parque Gallineral and town, as it has very strong currents. People have drowned in it. The tap water is chlorinated and said to be OK to drink. As in other parts of lowland Colombia, dengue is present in San Gil. Updated: Jan 07, 2008.

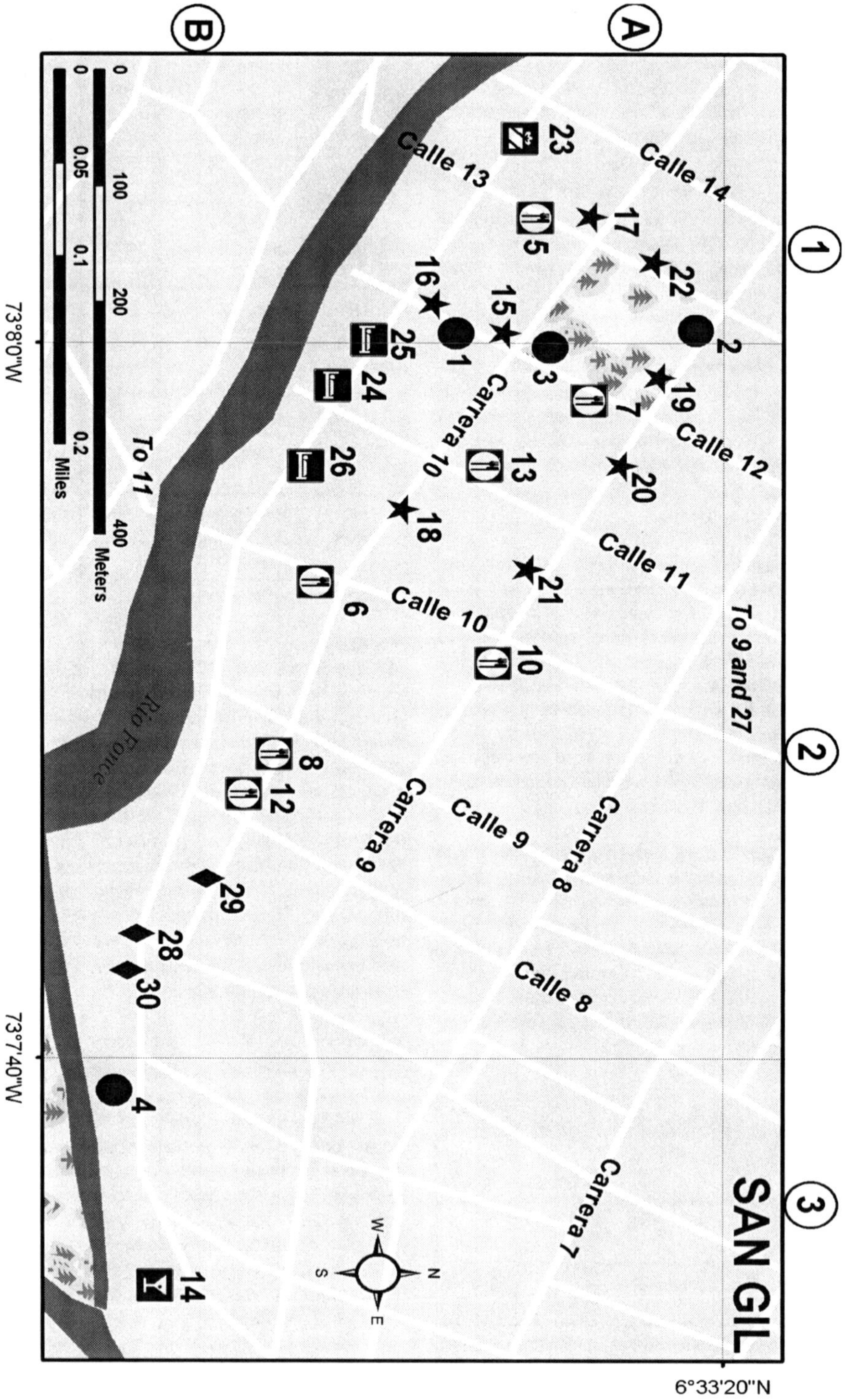
SAN GIL
Calle 14
Calle 13
Calle 12
Calle 11
Calle 10
Calle 9
Calle 8
Carrera 10
Carrera 9
Carrera 8
Carrera 7
To 9 and 27
To 11
Rio Fonce
0 100 200 400 Meters
0 0.05 0.1 0.2 Miles
73°8'0"W
73°7'40"W
6°33'20"N
A
B
1
2
3

Activity ●
1 Casa de la Cultura B2
2 Catedral B2
3 Parque La Independencia B2
4 Parque Natural El Gallinero C3

Eating
5 Restaurante Carnes y Carnes B2
6 De Santander Tienda Café B3
7 La Polita B2
8 La Posada Familiar A3
9 La Ricotta Pizza B2
10 Restaurant La Casona Criolla B3
11 Restaurante KowLoon Dragones C3
12 Restaurante Regelia B3
13 Restaurante Saludable Delicia B2

Nightlife
14 Masai Mara (night) B4

Service ★
16 Banco Colmena (Western Union) B2
17 Banco Colombia B2
18 Banco Popular B2
19 Cayasan B2
20 Comcel B2
21 MegaRed (Banco de Bogotá) B2
22 Puerto PC B3
23 Telecom B2

Shopping
15 Mercado B2

Sleeping
24 Hotel El Viajero B2
25 Hotel San Carlos B2
26 Hotel Victoria B3
27 Macondo Guesthouse B2

Tour ♦
27 Aventura Total B2
28 Colombia Rafting Expediciones B3
29 Planeta Azul B2

San Gil Services

Tourism Office

San Gil's Oficina de Turismo is located at the front gate of Parque Gallineral (daily 8 a.m.-6 p.m., Tel: 7-724-4372). Unfortunately, it only provides basic information, none of which is directed to the independent traveler, and a very small, error-filled map. Many hotels have information on hand for their guests. You can read more on what San Gil has to offer at www.sangil.com.co. Updated: Jan 07, 2008.

Money

Several banks in San Gil have ATMs. Bancolombia has the highest withdrawal limit of $400. It accepts MasterCard, Visa, American Express and Cirrus (Calle 12, 10-44). ATH, or multi-network ATMs, also take Plus cards. You can find these at Mega Banco / Banco de Bogotá (Carrera 9, 11-56) and Banco Popular (Calle 13, 10-34). There is no official place to exchange traveler's checks or cash dollars. The local Western Union branch in Banco Colmena performs transactions only for Colombians (Monday-Friday 8-11:30 a.m., 2-4 p.m. Corner Carrera 10 with Calle 12, Parque la Libertad). Updated: Jan 07, 2008.

Keeping in Touch

Colombia's national phone carrier, Telecom, charges $0.10 per minute for local and national calls, and from $0.30 per minute for international calls (daily 6 a.m.-10 p.m. Calle 13, 9-70, Parque La Libertad). A national or local call from shops cost on average $0.15 per minute. Throughout San Gil you can find internet cafés; most charge $0.80 per hour. One that costs only $0.60 per hour is Puerto PC, which also has special discounts, Skype and inexpensive international calls, at $0.25 per minute (Monday-Saturday 8 a.m.-12:30 p.m., 2-8:30 p.m.; Sunday, holidays 8:30 a.m.-1 p.m. Carrera 9, 10-65, local 107, Edifico Venecia). Correos de Colombia /Adpostal is in the Cajasan mall on Carrera 10, between Calles 10 and 11 (Monday-Friday 8 a.m.-noon, 2-6 p.m., Saturday 8 a.m.-noon). Updated: Jan 07, 2008.

Medical

The main public hospital in San Gil is Hospital Regional San Juan de Dios (Carrera 5 9-102, Tel: 7-723-5513 / 723-5549). The private Clínica Santa Cruz de la Loma is recommended. An English-speaking doctor is available for emergency cases (Calle 12, 12-20, Tel: 7-724-2100). Pharmacies can be found everywhere in the mid-town area, about one every block; Carrera 11 has a number between Calles 10 and 13. Updated: Jan 07, 2008.

Camera

Only a handful of camera shops are found in San Gil. Besides providing one-hour film processing, Fotos Peñaloza has all types of batteries; digital camera cards; 100 and 200 ASA color, 110 and black-and-white films; and disposable, underwater and other cameras for sale. It can also connect you to a camera repairperson. (Monday-Friday 8 a.m.-noon, 2-7 p.m., Saturday 8 a.m.-1p.m., 3-7 p.m., Sunday and holidays 8:30 a.m.-

12:30 p.m. Carrera 10, 10-101. Tel: 7-724-2879.) Updated: Jan 07, 2008.

Shopping

Feria Artesanal

It had begun as a holiday crafts fair but now is a permanent affair. In the large front sala of San Gil's Casa de la Cultura, 17 Santandereano artesanos—mostly women—bedeck their stalls and tables with their work. To shade yourself during an outing, take along a hat made of palm or plaintain leaf. Shod your feet with sandals or buy napkin holders, placemats or other items made of this plant fiber (*fique*) to decorate the dining room table. And, of course, there's jewelry. If your sweet tooth starts to ache, then take home a bag of the honey caramels. Casa de la Cultura, Calle 12, between Carreras 10 and 11, half-block from the main plaza. Updated: May 13, 2008.

Arte y Naturaleza

Showing off a Santandereano pride, Arte y Naturaleza crochets fashion accessories and other items from natural-colored cotton. You'll need a hat that's guaranteed to keep you cool in these warm lands, especially if you are heading for the Caribbean coast. To make your ensemble complete, don't forget a belt with metal or wooden buckle and a shoulder bag. Besides having its home workshop, Arte y Naturaleza also has a stall at the Feria Artesanal in the Casa de la Cultura. Address: Calle 15, 2-60. Tel: 7-724-4086, Fax: 7-724-6315, E-mail: arteynaturalezasangil@yahoo.es. Updated: May 13, 2008.

De Santander Tienda Café

De Santander Tienda has gathered the best in Santander's artistry and showcases it all in this small corner shop. Everything is for sale, from the paintings on the wall to the hammock chairs hanging from the ceiling. Shawls, ponchos and bags crafted from fique and linen fill the shelves. As its names implies, De Santander isn't just a shop, additionally it is a café that serves regional coffee, *tamales* and sweets, which you can purchase to take on the road with you. On Saturdays, the café hosts lectures, poetry readings, concerts and other events. Carrera 10, 10-103. Tel: 7-724-3655. Updated: May 13, 2008.

Things to See and Do

San Gil has much to offer those looking for an adrenaline rush—raft or kayak on rivers with class II to V rapids. If you'd like something very different, try *hydrospeeding* (body boarding down the Río Fonce), rappelling, or *torrentismo* (rappelling in waterfalls). Soar like a condor, paragliding from the new Parque Nacional Chicamocha. Or crawl through some remarkable caves. Stroll and picnic in the botanical gardens of Parque Natural El Gallineral. For those who are more culture-minded, there are villages to check out, like Barichara with colonial architecture and a resident artist community, or Curití, where fique artisans practice their trade. Updated: Jan 07, 2008.

Parque Natural El Gallineral

Long tendrils of moss hang from ancient trees and sway in the slight breeze. Sunlight dapples on the torrent of the Río Fonce. This is Parque Natural El Gallineral, four hectares of botanical gardens where the creek Quebrada Curití meets that robust river. Within this park, nine *plazoletas* are connected by a network of paths through foliage so dense you will not meet another soul. After an enchanting afternoon of wandering through these thickets, bathe in the refreshing spring waters of the pool. Do not swim in the Río Fonce, as it has dangerous currents. The swimming pool is closed for cleaning every two weeks, usually on a Tuesday. There are lockers and showers in an adjoining bathhouse. The restaurant and cafeteria are expensive. Updated: May 13, 2008.

The Camino Real from San Gil to the Río Magdalena

Go trekking on the old road Camino de los Guanes to the Río Magdalena. You can follow the footsteps of the Guane ancestors, who had laid down this path, later used by the Spaniards. The stone road originally extended from Girón, near Bucaramanga, to Barrancabermeja on the river. In this modern era, the intrepid trekker begins the journey at Cabrera, from there it is a two-hour walk to Barichara. From Barichara to Guane is the most-trodden part of the road (1.5-two hours). The trail then continues to Villanueva (three hours). Now comes the toughest part through the Chicamocha River Canyon with a 1,000-meter (3,280-foot) descent and ascent in over 35°C (95°F) heat. From Villanueva, the road plunges to the ghost town of Jordán at the base of the canyon (three hours). A four-hour climb brings one to Mesa de los Santos on the other side of the abyss.

The camino originally went further, to the Río Magdalena. According to all sources, it is impossible to continue on from Mesa de los Santos. Some say it is because of safety issues, especially with civil war fighting, but others say it is because bridges no longer exist past this point. Because of the on-going civil war in the region, be sure to ask about safety in each village before beginning the next leg. A guide is not necessary, though you will have to ask directions frequently. The entire trek will take two or three days. Accommodation and food are available in all the villages. Buses leave from San Gil to all the towns on the route, save for Jordán.
Updated: May 13, 2008.

Waterfalls and Torrentismo

Waterfalls drape the river canyons slicing the countryside around San Gil. At some of the cascades, not only can you gaze upon these natural wonders, but also practice a sport offered by the good folk of this area: torrentismo (rappelling in waterfalls). Get ready to zip down a slick rock face, misted by tumbling waters. This has got to be the most extreme you can get of the wild adventures San Gil offers (well, save hydrospeeding). The easiest fall to get to on your own is 150-meter (500-foot) high Juan Curí, out near Charalá, which has a delightfully cool pool at its base. Contact local tour operators;, as they offer excursions to several different waterfalls. If doing torrentismo, check the quality of equipment. At Juan Curí, there are two entry points through private property. The first is cheaper ($1.05), though the second includes a tour of the cacao farm ($2.65). To rappel is extra.

To get to Juan Curí on your own, catch a Bucaramanga-bound bus or one to Charalá ($1.60). Tell the driver you're going to Juan Curí. Updated: May 06, 2008.

Whitewater Rafting

San Gil has become renowned for its whitewater rafting. Three principal rivers, all with different characteristics, offer adventures for novices and experts alike. The Río Fonce has Class II rapids (and higher) you can experience on the 1.5-hour trip, which is especially good for beginners and families ($13.25 per person). Río Suárez is considered the best, with class IV to V rapids, depending on the time of year. The six-hour trip includes three hours on-river ($63 per person). Through Cañón Chicamocha is the river of the same name, which has class II to IV rapids. You can arrange special five-day expeditions down this river. Be sure the rafting company has adequate equipment and safety measures. Updated: Feb 06, 2008.

Other Water Sports

Besides whitewater rafting, there are other aquatic sports in San Gil. Check with tour operators in the town for these excursions.

Kayaking: There are eight rivers to run, though commercial trips are offered only on three of the rivers. Multi-day expeditions may be arranged, but be warned that the water temperature of the rivers is 14-18°C (57-64°F). Check the quality of safety equipment.

Torrentismo: Rappelling in waterfalls is a specialty in the San Gil area.

Hydrospeeding: This is an intense adventure of surfing down 10 kilometers (6 miles) of the Río Fonce's rapids. You receive instruction and are outfitted with board, flippers, life jacket and a helmet. A kayak accompanies you for security. The standard price is $19 per person. Updated: May 13, 2008.

Caving

Delving into the bowels of the earth (a.k.a caving) is another adventure you can undertake while in San Gil. You can only visit a few of the many caves that gouge the landscape.

Cueva del Indio: This cave out in Páramo is the easiest to spelunk, suitable for the whole family. A special feature is ziplining or jumping 5 meters (16.4 feet) into a pool, then swimming out along a rope.

Cueva la Antigua: This cave is more demanding and hands-on, calling for a lot of crawling through mud. This is not for the claustrophobic.

Ojo de Pájaros: This 100-meter (328-foot) deep and 20-meter (65.5-foot) wide cave near Mogotes earns its name from the thousands of oil birds that reside in it.

Other caverns of interest include Cueva del Yeso and Cueva de la Vaca. All caves are on private property and each has only one tour company authorized to lead expeditions. It is illegal to go on your own. Contact the tour operators in town to go caving. Check the quality of safety equipment. Updated: May 13, 2008.

San Gil Tours

Most tour agencies that exist in San Gil are actually booking agents, arranging your excursion with one of the four tour operators in the town. All offer rafting on the smaller rivers, paragliding, caving, rappelling, and guided tours to Barichara and the waterfalls. San Gil is an OK place to paraglide if you have some experience; however, if you want to take courses, keep in mind that present teachers speak only Spanish. There is an English-speaking *parapente* guide and instructor in Bucaramanga. All tour operators charge the same for any excursion, as prices are regulated by the city government. Updated: Jan 07, 2008.

Planeta Azul

Planeta Azul has rafting excursions on the various rivers in the region. The company also offers tours into Cuevas del Yeso, de la Vaca, Antigua and del Indio and rappelling and torretismo to Pescaderito, Pinchote and Páramo. Or, you can choose paragliding (parapente) at Cañón del Chicamocha and Curití or horseback riding with an *almuerzo típico* (typical lunch) to Villa Nueva, Curití and Valle de San José. As if all the above weren't enough, Planeta Azul will also zip you around on a chiva tour or suit you all up for a good old-fashioned paintball battle. Planeta Azul's guide who specializes in hikes to Casacada de Juan Curí and the Camino Real from Barichara to Guane also speaks English. Entrance of Parque Natural el Gallineral. Tel: 7-724-0000, Cell: 310-771-7586 / 315-823-4796, Fax: 7-724-7679, E-mail: info@planetaazulcolombia.com, URL: www.planetaazulcolombia.com. Updated: May 13, 2008.

Aventura Total

Aventura Total lives up to its name. The company offers all types of adventures in the San Gil region, from whitewater rafting on the all three main rivers (Fonce, Suárez and Chicamocha) to rappelling at Pinchote and torrentismo at Cascada Juan Curí to caving at Cuevas Antigua, de la Vaca and del Yeso or horseback riding trips (*cabalgatas*) to Hacienda Santa Bárbara or Curití ($27 per person, all inclusive). Aventura Total's fame rests in its notoriety as one of San Gil's better operators for paragliding. However, some do not recommend the company for rafting. Malecón, in front of Parque Natural el Gallineral. Tel: 7-723-8888, Cell: 310-551-5254, E-mail: info@aventuratotal.com.co, URL: www.aventuratotal.com.co. Updated: May 13, 2008.

Colombia Rafting Expeditions

Whether your interest is simple rafting or any of the other adventure sports to partake in San Gil, like caving or hydrospeeding, Colombia Rafting Expeditions can make it happen. Considered by some to be the best rafting operator in San Gil, Colombia Rafting Expeditions' guides have international experience and many also speak English. This company offers expeditions on all three principal rivers, in raft or kayak, as well as kayaking courses ($50-185). Personnel in another raft or kayak accompany you for security. The only cave that Colombia Rafting visits is Cueva Antigua. Carrera 10, 7-83. Cell: 311-283-8647 / 291-2870, Fax: 7-724-5800, E-mail: info@colombiarafting.com, URL: www.colombiarafting.com. Updated: May 13, 2008.

San Gil Lodging

Accommodation in San Gil is surprisingly inexpensive and provides good-quality service. Cheaper hostels are generally found on Carrera 11 between Calles 10 and 13. These generally run from $5-8 for one person. By law, hotels must display their prices and may not charge more than the highest shown. Bargain in low season, or *temporada baja*. Most inns double or triple rates in the high season (*temporada alta*) so make reservations at these times. There are several camping options outside San Gil. A recommended, free site is Pescadarito, near Curití. Updated: Jan 07, 2008.

Hotel San Carlos !

(ROOM: $4 - 16) The Hotel San Carlos is one of the budget options in San Gil. It is close to the Parque Central, the central market and Parque Natural Gallineral. A variety of rooms are provided, for one to three persons or families, some with private bath and TV. The reception area has cable TV. There is a laundry area to wash your own clothes, and an area for motorcycle parking. Carrera 11, 11-25. Tel: 7-724-2542. Updated: May 06, 2008.

Mesón del Cuchicute

(BED: $5.40-35) As one of San Gil's finest hotels, Mesón del Cuchicute is still remarkably affordable. A country-club-styled inn with park-like grounds, the Mesón has all the comforts that make up a luxury vacation: swimming pool, playground, Jacuzzi, sauna, gymnasium and game room. The brick-floored rooms have fan, cable TV, mini-bar (separate charge) and private balcony. The hand basins in the hot-water baths are made of rough marble, copper and brass. Mesón del Cuchicute also is ecologically conscious—it recycles and has a composting refuse. This has to be one of the best bargains in Colombia. Camping is $5.40 per person, with right to facilities, including cold-water bathhouse but not grills. Cabañas or rooms run $21 per person (low season, Monday-Thursday), $27 (low season, Friday-Sunday) and $35 (high season). Non-guests can use the pool 10 a.m.-5 p.m.: $3 adults, $2 children under 11 years old (swimming cap required).

Mesón del Cuchicute is located one kilometer from town, past the long-distance bus terminal. Some of the city buses go right to the front gate of the complex, e.g. the one marked "Mesón" ($0.40). A taxi from the center costs $1.40. Km. 1 Vía San Gil-Socorro. Tel: 7-724-2042, Cell: 312-480-2509. Reservations: 7-724-2041 / 8104 / 8069. Fax: 7-724-3171, E-mail: mesondelcuchicute@comfenalcosantander.com.co, URL: www.comfenalcosantander.com.co. Updated: May 13, 2008.

Macondo Guesthouse !

(ROOM: $6-13) Macondo Guesthouse has become the place to stay in San Gil. Australian-born Shaun opens the doors of this colonial house just a few blocks from Parque La Libertad to backpackers and other travelers. He offers both dorms and private rooms, all sharing baths. Amenities include kitchen, laundry facilities (or use the convenient laundry service), hammocks in the front courtyard, book exchange and much more. Shaun is the best source of information in town, and can help you organize any adventure activity. Prices stay the same in high and low season. Calle 12, 7-26. Cell: 311-828-2905, E-mail: macondohostal@hotmail.com, URL: www.hosteltrail.com/macondo. Updated: Feb 06, 2008.

V!VA Member Review- Macondo Guesthouse

A very friendly place. If you're a couple, try to get a room out back. There are great views, and downstairs doubles aren't the nicest. Dorm rooms looked nice enough and had new mattresses. Perfect place if you want to do activities – there are always people around wanting to do stuff. Good nightlife too, thanks to great locals.Sean is extremely helpful and seems to know a lot. I recommend his rafting and paragliding trips, too. Febuary 19, 2008, England.

Hotel El Viajero

(ROOM: $8-19) Conveniently located on Carrera 11, just a few blocks from Parque Gallineral and the market, the Hotel El Viajero provides comfortable accommodations. All rooms have windows, private bath (room-temperature water) and cable TV, as well as a table and chair for catching up on your journal writing. The first floor has a bright, plant-filled courtyard and a balcony overlooking the Río Fonce. The inn guarantees a comfortable atmosphere, suitable for families as well the solo backpacker. In low season, a single room is $8 and a double is $13; in high season, rooms cost $13 and $19, respectively. Carrera 11, 11-07. Tel: 7-724-4817, E-mail: hotelelviajero2@hotmail.com. Updated: May 13, 2008.

Hotel Victoria

(ROOM: $9-35) The Hotel Victoria is a picturesque, family-owned hotel near the major attractions of San Gil. The beautiful courtyard has several different sitting areas, all protected from the rain. Several different types of rooms are offered, for one to five persons: basic ones with private bath, fan, reading lamp and television; those with air conditioning, stereo, refrigerator and large-screen TV; and suites with bathtub. After a pleasant night's sleep on firm mattresses, the family serves morning coffee to their guests. Like most hotels in San Gil, prices double during the high season. Carrera 11, 10-40. Tel: 7-724-2347, Fax: 7-724-5955, E-mail: fora30m@yahoo.es. Updated: May 06, 2008.

La Posada Familiar

(ROOM: $16-37) A small, family-run inn, La Posada Familiar has six rooms with extra touches. The quarters are simply decorated, but come with a ceiling fan, stocked mini-fridge (extra charge for what you consume) and cable TV with a remote control. The private baths are gleaming white, with room temperature water. All the rooms are outfitted for more than one person, though in the low season the lone traveler can check in too. La Posada Familiar has a small interior patio with a fountain and it also has a garden, an outside balcony and many other areas to sit and relax after an adrenaline-pumping day rafting or caving. Carrera 10, 8-55. Tel: 7-724-8136. Updated: May 13, 2008.

San Gil Restaurants

Comida corrientes in San Gil cost $2.10-3.70. Cheaper restaurants are found on Carrera 11, between Calles 9 and 10. The municipal market is a good place to grab breakfast or lunch (daily 6 a.m.-2 p.m., Carrera 11 between Calles 13 and 14). The market is busiest on Wednesdays and weekends.

Some of the typical dishes you may want to check out are *cabro* (goat), *pipitoria* (rice prepared with finely chopped goat innards and goat's blood), *ubre* (cow udder), *carne oleada* (beef marinated in beer, sun-dried, then grilled) and *hormigas culonas tostadas* (roasted flying ants). Updated: Jan 07, 2008.

Budget

Galería y Cafetería La Polita

Considered by some to have the best coffee in San Gil, La Polita is much more than just a stiff cup of joe. At any time of the day you can come in to have a bit of the hair of the dog that nipped you, a stiff shot of any kind of liquor. It seems everyone comes to La Polita, so at times it can be tough to find a table. Check out the paintings strewn across the walls, which showcase the region's best talents. Monday-Thursday 7 a.m.-7 p.m., Friday and Saturday 7 a.m.-1 a.m., Sunday 7 a.m.-noon. Calle 12, 9-35. Tel: 7-724-4259, E-mail: linasare@latinmail.com. Updated: May 13, 2008.

La Casona Criolla

For heaped helpings of good ol' Colombian food, drop by the very popular La Casona Criolla. Pull up a table on what was once the interior patio of a colonial home, now covered with red *tejas*. In the center is a fountain and there are potted plants scattered around. The sides are colonnaded, creating intimate dining spaces. The place is softly lit with chandeliers. The family is friendly and the set meal is good value ($2.10). Open daily 6 a.m.-9 p.m. Carrera 9, 9-96. Tel: 7-724-8080, Cell: 313-326-2284. Updated: May 13, 2008.

Pizzaría La Ricotta

Located up the hill, near several schools and the university, Pizzaría La Ricotta serves up oven-hot pizza at student prices. Whether ordering by the slice ($1.30-1.70) or an extra-large pie ($12-14), you can take care of that evening hunger here. A local specialty is the Sangileña, topped with cheese, sausage, corn, cilantro and tomatoes. La Ricotta also has several vegetarian pizzas, like the tropical with an assortment of fruits and cheese and, of course, a plain old-fashioned vegetarian one. If pizza doesn't quite fit the bill, try the lasagna ($3.20-3.70) or a panzerotti (calzone, $2.35-3.70). Open Monday-Saturday 3-10 p.m., Sunday 5-10 p.m. Carrera 7, 14-05. Tel: 7-724-7283. Updated: May 13, 2008.

Restaurante Vegetariano Saludable Delicia

Saludable Delicia lives up to its name, providing delicious, healthy meals to traveling vegetarians. Mornings, the shop sells baked goods, teas, supplements, tahini and peanut butter. The set-meal lunch is from 11 a.m. to 2 p.m. and costs $2.35. Thereafter until close, only á la carte dishes are available. All is served with brown rice. The dining areas are tranquil and airy and the staff soft-spoken. If adventure sporting has left you a bit twisted, come and have a massage (Sunday-Friday 8-10:30 a.m., 3-7 p.m. $3.70-10.50). Saludable Delicia is open Sunday-Friday 7 a.m.-7:30 p.m. Calle 11, 8-40. Tel: 7-724-3539, Cell: 312-263-1928. Updated: Feb 06, 2008.

Restaurante Rogelia

Restaurante Rogelia presents typical dishes of the Santander region, including cabro con pipatoria and carne orneada. The *bistec de res a caballo* is not horse meat, but rather a beef steak topped with an egg. To sample a bit of everything, ask for a *picada platter* ($8-10.50). The comida corriente costs $2.35; only the *bandeja* (main dish) is $2.10. After 4 p.m. you can order a pizza hot out of the oven.

Restaurante Rogelia also serves breakfast. Open daily 7 a.m.-8 p.m. Carrera 10, 8-09. Tel: 7-724-0823. Updated: May 07, 2008.

Mid-Range

Restaurante Kowloon Dragones

You can find Chinese restaurants in every corner of Colombia, even in San Gil. Restaurante Kowloon Dragones presents the visitor with a full menu of Sino classics prepared with a variety of meats and sauces. Also on the menu are a few choices for the vegetarian, as well as some international dishes. If a group of you are dining together, split one of the *menus familiares*, which include everything from wine to appetizers and soup, plus several types of Chinese fare ($16 for two up to $52 for six). Open daily 10 a.m.-10 p.m. Carrera 12, 5-82, La Playa (on the other side of the Río Fonce from the main part of town). Tel: 7-724-2034 / 724-8444. Updated: May 13, 2008.

High-End

Bar-Restaurante Carnes y Carnes

Nothing more than a mere a banner pronounces Carnes y Carnes. Unbeknown to the casual passerby, beyond the gate is one of San Gil's classier eateries. Within the large roofed garden is the restaurant that has a large brick grill in the center. At the grill, the chef prepares your entrée: chicken, perhaps with an intriguing sauce ($7-8.25), pork ($9-10), beef ($10-13.50), or fish or seafood ($8.50-14). Only rice and potatoes accompany the dishes—but then, the name of this bistro is Meat and Meat. While waiting for your repast, read the menu full of tales of the origins and legends of the region's foods. Open daily 10 a.m.-10 p.m. Calle 11, 10-27, Tel: 7-724-7008. Updated: May 13, 2008.

San Gil Nightlife

Any night of the week, you can join *sangileños* and Colombians who sit in front of shops for a beer (or something stronger). The most popular places are along Parque la Libertad. Nightclubs and karaoke joints within the city are required, by law, to close at 1 a.m. No such restrictions hold for those outside the city limits. These businesses are open weekends until day break or when the rumba fizzles, whichever comes first. If heading for the out-of-town hotspots, be sure to keep some money back for the cab fare home. Updated: Jan 07, 2008.

Masai Mara Safari Discoteca-Bar

Ask locals what the most happening dance spot is in San Gil, many will tell you Masai Mara. Join the crowd at this large club and chill with a beer or something stronger while grooving to the throbbing beats of merengue, salsa, vallenato and reggaetón. Open only on Fridays and Saturdays, beginning at 8 p.m., but the scene doesn't start to get hot until after 9:30 p.m. and can go on until dawn's first light. Vía a Bella Isla. Tel: 7-724-0296. Updated: May 13, 2008.

Curití

Curití is a typical Santandereano village of narrow streets lined with white-washed homes. Its residents are famous for their *artesanía* in fique, or *agave sisal*. This hamlet offers more to the casual visitor than just shopping. Here you can scrabble underground in Cueva de la Vaca and Cueva del Yeso, or go horseback riding. Near Curití are the crystalline swimming holes Balneario Pescaditos, where you can camp for free (said to be safe) and rappel the cliffs. Updated: May 20, 2008.

Getting To and Away from Curití

Curití is seven kilometers (4.2 miles) north of San Gil, off the main highway to Bucaramanga. Take a bus from the terminal at Carrera 11 and 15 ($0.80). Updated: May 06, 2008.

Parque Nacional del Chicamocha !

Founded in 2006, Parque Nacional del Chicamocha protects part of the rim of the Río Chicamocha's canyon. This national park proffers much for the amusement of its visitors. The culture connoisseur can partake the Museo Guane, Plaza de los Costumbres and the Salón de Exposiciones. The adrenaline junkie can paraglide or zip down the *cablevuelo* (zipline). For the whole family, there are walking trails, lookouts over the gorge, buggy cars and an ostrich farm. Construction has begun on a cable car that will descend to the ghost town of Jordán at the base of the canyon, and is expected to open the end of 2008. Entry: $4.20 adults, $2.10 children. The buggies, cable-vuelo and ostrich farm are extra. Updated: May 06, 2008.

Note: In Colombia, a Parque Nacional (national park) is one that belongs to the nation and not necessarily a wildlife reserve.

Protected areas are called Parque Nacional Natural. Updated: May 06, 2008.

Baríchara

Alt: 1,336m Pop: 10,000 City Code: 7

Barichara is the get-away of choice for better-heeled Colombian vacationers seeking to escape metropolitan hassles. This town perches on a plateau overlooking the Río Suárez, 20 kilometers (14 miles) from San Gil, 118 kilometers (80 miles) from Bucaramanga and 307 kilometers (200 miles) from Bogotá. Its well-preserved colonial architecture, made of *tapia pisada* or rammed earth, earns Barichara a place on the national register of historical sites. Traditionally this is a village of stone carvers, but in recent years artists of other media have come, inspired by its tranquility and beauty. Whereas neighboring San Gil is for the adventure sports enthusiast, Barichara is for the cultural tourist. Due to the immemorial buildings, the Parque para las Artes, the stone workshops and work of Colombia's premier painters, you can pass days here soaking in Barichara's bohemian atmosphere. Its inhabitants are called *patiamarillas*, for the golden-rust colored soil of their land. Updated: Dec 19, 2007.

History

Bahia-chala (meaning "at the heights of a resting stop") was inhabited by the indigenous Guane people. The Spanish city, Barichara, was founded by Capitán Francisco Pradilla y Ayerbe in 1714. An image of the Immaculate Conception was seen on a rock in 1702. A chapel built to protect it became the nucleus of the new town. In the 18th Century, the Guane were rounded up from the region and relocated to Guane village, near Barichara. A dependency of San Gil until 1800, Patiamarillos petitioned for independence; nonetheless, this was not granted until 1821. In 1975 Barichara was proclaimed the most beautiful village in Colombia and in 1978 declared a national monument. Updated: Apr 23, 2008.

When to Go

Barichara enjoys a delightfully warm, dry climate year-round with average temperatures of 22°C / 72°F. As a trendy get-away for Colombians, you'll encounter more crowds at holiday times. During an ordinary week, you'll find Baricahara to be almost sleepy. Many artisan shops and studios are closed, as are local branches of tour operators, and clubs and cafés providing an evening's entertainment. Updated: Apr 23, 2008.

Holidays and Festivals

A hamlet as ancient as Barichara of course has a number of festivals. Some are religious and many celebrate the arts for which this town is renowned. Every other year, in odd years, is the Festival de la Talla en Piedra, or the Stone Carvers Festival.

Month	Event
Easter Week	**Semana Santa** – Celebrated with processions.
August	**10: San Lorenzo Mártir** – Patron saint of Barichara.
January	**Patrimonio Cultural Patiamarillo** – This festival, which has a focus on the stonecarvers, occurs the last Sunday of the month.
February	**11: Virgen de la Piedra** – The patron saint of carvers.
October	**12: Fiestas Culturales de la Solidaridad y el Retorno** – Cultural festivals of solidarity and return.
November / December	**Olimpiados Campesinos** – The country folks' Olympic Games.
December	**8: Inmaculada Concepción** – The other patron saint of the village. **16-24: Aguinaldo Patiamarillo** The Christmas novena celebrated in Patiamarillo style, with music, theater, poetry and art. **28: Día de los Angelitos Pichones** – Akin to April Fool's Day. **31: Quemado del Viejo** – The burning of effigies representing the Old Year.

Updated: Apr 23, 2008.

Getting To and Away from Barichara

Although a poor camino winds from Socorro to Barichara, the better route is from San Gil. This road is paved the entire way. For good views, sit on the driver's side. Buses ply between San Gil and Barichara every half hour daily, from 5:15 a.m. to 6:30 p.m. ($1.60). Direct busetas leave from Bucaramanga during the week. Updated: Apr 23, 2008.

Safety in Barichara

Barichara has no untoward problems with personal safety, so swear the locals. No paramilitary or guerrilla presence is reported.

Barichara Services

Tourism Office

Barichara's tourism office, Oficina de Cultura, Turismo y Deportes, is located on the second floor of the alcaldía building on the main square. It is very helpful and provides excellent, bilingual maps of that town and of Guane (Monday-Thursday 7:30 a.m.-noon, 2-6 p.m., Friday 7:30 a.m.-noon, 2-4 p.m. Calle 5, 6-39, Tel: 7-726-7052, URL: www.baricharavive.com/www.patiamarillo.com). On weekends, a tourism information booth is set up across the street at the base of the flagpoles.

Money

On the church side of the plaza is an ATH / Megared ATM machine, accepting all cards (save American Express). If you are relying on traveler's checks, your nearest provider for this service is in Bucaramanga or Tunja. There are no official exchange houses.

Keeping in Touch

The main Telecom office, providing phone service for local, national and international calls, is a half-block from the Templo de la Inmaculada Concepción (Monday-Saturday 7 a.m.-10 p.m., Sunday and holidays 7 a.m.-9 p.m. Carrera 7, 4-73). Telecom's internet service is three blocks away, near the Casa del Mercado. It charges $1.05 per hour (Monday-Saturday 9 a.m.-9 p.m., Sunday 9 a.m.-2 p.m. Calle 7, between Carreras 6 and 7). Adpostal, the post office, is also a half-block from the main plaza, at Carrera 6, 4-90 (Monday-Friday 8 a.m.-noon, 2-6 p.m.).

Medical

Barichara's Hospital Integrado San Juan de Dios is on Carrera 2, between Calles 3 and 4 (Tel: 7-726-7400). Several pharmacies are found on or near the main square. Updated: May 20, 2008.

Shopping

El Almacencito de Margoth

Right on the plaza, in the Casa de la Cultura, Margarita (Margoth) Bermúdez has a shop. This space features not only her creations, but also those of other artisans of the village. Here you can purchase stone and wood carvings, boxes, fique fashion accessories, paintings and candies, for which this town has some renowned pieces (the alfajores are simply divine). A special item doña Margoth carries is ceramics by the only living Guane indigenous that follows traditional designs and techniques. Calle 5, 6-29. Cell: 315-379-0217. Updated: Apr 23, 2008.

Añil, Tienda de Artes Plásticas

Artists Carlos Santamaría and Yasmith Beltrán have joined up with their colleagues to offer a showcase of their appetizers. Some are Barichara natives and others have come here to live and create. The 20 of them—about half women—decorate Añil's airy space with colorful canvasses and modern sculptures in both stone and wood. If you fall in love with their inspirations, but just can't carry something bulky or heavy, check the racks of hand-painted T-shirts. Each one is an original work of art and costs $19. Calle 6, 10-46. Cell: 311-470-1175 / 316-886-7394, E-mail: anilartesplasticas@yahoo.com. Updated: Apr 23, 2008.

Los Tiestesitos

Tiestesitos: diminutive of *tiesto*, a plant or flowerpot. Indeed, the front patio porch and large interior anteroom of Los Tiestesitos is full of such bittersweet-orange-colored pottery. Shaped from the golden earth by doña Alicia and her clan, these vessels come in all sizes and shapes, from the mundane to animal. And they're not just for potting. They have many purposes (how about a lamp?). To fill that planter you just bought, check out Los Tiestesitos' *vivero*, or greenhouse, for just the right flora. Carrera 5, 7-62, Tel: 7-726-7224. Updated: Apr 23, 2008.

Things to See and Do

The main attraction of Barichara is this ageless village itself. Most stone-carver workshops are on Carrera 5, near the entrance to

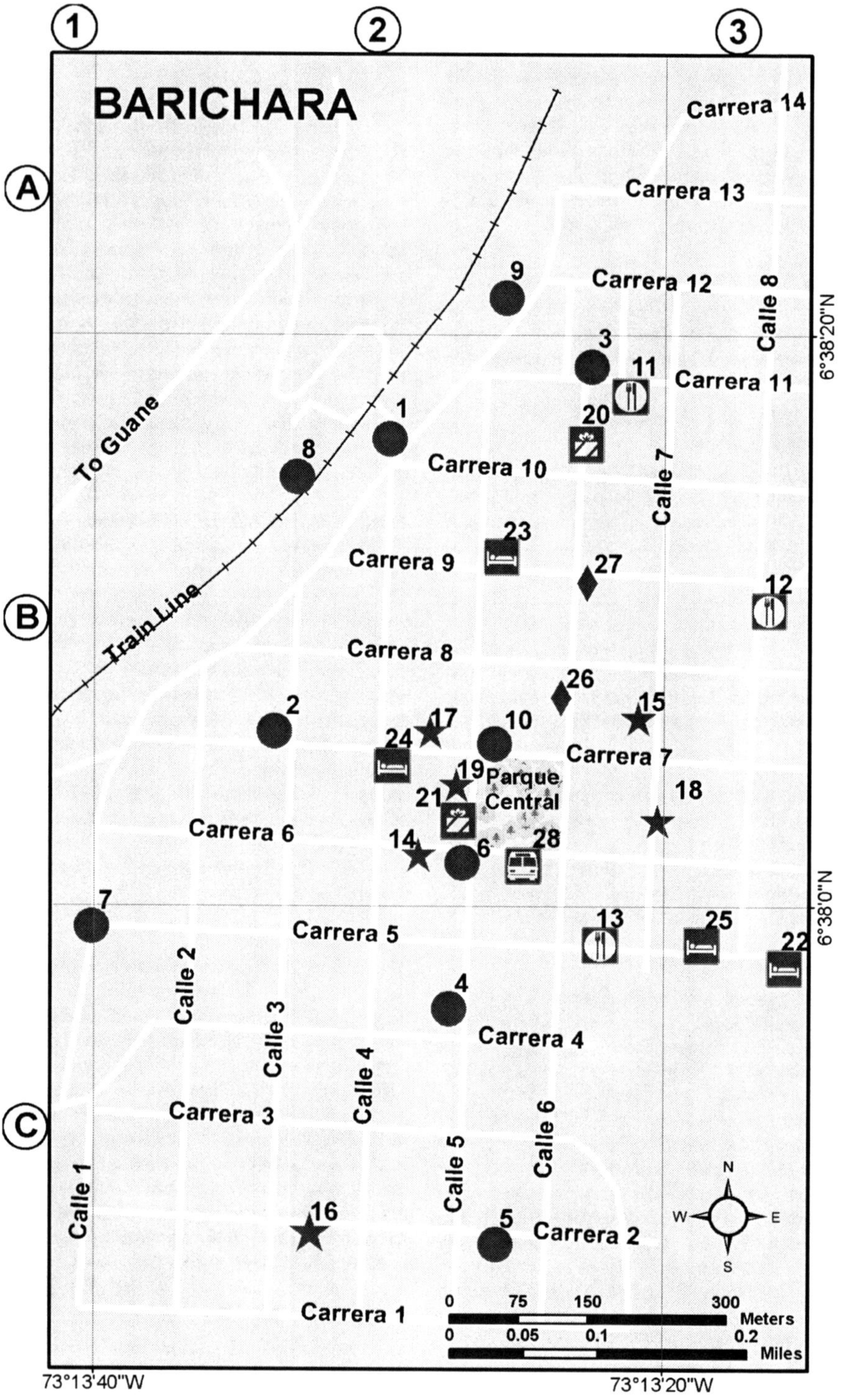
BARICHARA
1
2
3
A
B
C
To Guane
Train Line
Carrera 14
Carrera 13
Carrera 12
Carrera 11
Carrera 10
Carrera 9
Carrera 8
Carrera 7
Carrera 6
Carrera 5
Carrera 4
Carrera 3
Carrera 2
Carrera 1
Calle 1
Calle 2
Calle 3
Calle 4
Calle 5
Calle 6
Calle 7
Calle 8
Parque Central
1
2
3
4
5
6
7
8
9
10
11
12
13
14
15
16
17
18
19
20
21
22
23
24
25
26
27
28
6°38'20"N
6°38'0"N
73°13'40"W
73°13'20"W
N
S
E
W
0 75 150 300 Meters
0 0.05 0.1 0.2 Miles

Activities ●
1 Camino Real to Guane A2
2 Capilla de Jesús A1
3 Capilla de Santa Bárbara A2
4 Capilla San Antonio B2
5 Casa Aquileo Parra B2
6 Casa de la Cultura A2
7 Gordelia Tobacos B1
8 Mirador A1
9 Parque para las Artes A2
10 Templo Inmaculada A2

Eating
11 Restaurante Algarabia A2
12 Restaurante Color de Hormiga A2
13 Restaurante Patiamarilla B2

Services ★
14 Adpostal A2
15 ATM: ATH / Mega Red A2
16 Hospital Integrado San Juan de Dios A2
17 Telecom A2
18 Telecom Internet A2
19 Tourism Office A2

Shopping
20 Añil, Tienda de Artes Plásticas A2
21 El Almanecito de Margoth A2

Sleeping
22 Hospedaje Los Tiestesitos B2
23 Hostal Misión Santa Bárbara A2
24 Hotel Coratá A2
25 Los Tiestesitos B2

Tours ♦
26 Barichara Cultura y Aventura A2
27 Guanecito (Colombia Rafting Expeditions) A2

Transportation
28 Buses to San Gil and Guane A2

the town. Rock isn't the only material worked here. There are also fique artisans, painters and cigar makers. To pick up a hand-rolled cigar, stop by Gordelia Tabacos for a free tour (weekends and holidays 9 a.m.-noon, 2-4 p.m. Carrera 5, 0-84, Tel: 7-726-7684, Cell: 311-531-4771, E-mail: gerencia@gordelia.com, URL: www.gordelia.com). The Parque para las Artes is another must-do for the culturally minded visitor. To stretch your legs, hike up to the *mirador* overlooking the Río Suárez canyon, or to Salto de Mico, 30 minutes along the Barichara bluffs, before hitting the camino real to Guane, with an impressive palaeontological and archaeological museum. Updated: Dec 19, 2007.

A Walking Tour of Colonial Barichara

The real treasure of Barichara is its pristine colonial architecture. Many come to this town just to wander its flagstone lanes, snapping photos of the white-washed, red-tile roofed buildings. Start your exploration at the Templo de la Inmaculada Concepción y San Lorenzo on the main square. It is built of local stone carved by the village's artisans. Walking West on Carrera 7 to the corner of Calle 3, you come to the Capilla de San Juan de Dios with a noteworthy cemetery. South three blocks on Calle 3 to Carrera 4, then left two blocks to Calle 5 brings you to Capilla de San Antonio, with a small, shaded plaza. Another two blocks South, on Carrera 2, between Calles 5 and 6, is Casa Aquileo Parra. This once-home of a former Colombian president (1876-78) is presently a museum. Returning northward along Calle 6, you will pass the plaza once more and arrive to Capilla Santa Bárbara, now used for cultural events. Updated: Apr 23, 2008.

Parque para las Artes

Uphill from the Capilla de Santa Bárbara is Parque para las Artes, a small park dedicated to the main art form Barichara is known for: stone sculpture. Founded after the second Festival Internacional de la Talla en Piedra, it features 27 statues carved by artists of 11 countries. Some are based on European or indigenous American mythology, others are abstract. Small brooks pass through the landscape, around these modern sentinels guarding a staggering view over the Río Suárez canyon. The park is also conveniently located next door to a public swimming pool. To reach the park, walk up Calle 6 to Capilla de Santa Bárbara, then turn left. About 300 meters (180 feet) on the right-hand side is the entry. Updated: Apr 23, 2008.

Camino Real to Guane

The camino real to Guane is part of the old *camino de herradura* (horseshoe road) that traversed the countryside from Girón, near Bucaramanga, to Barrancabermeja on the banks of the Río Magdalena. It was originally built by the Guane indigenous, and later used by the Spaniards. From Barichara to Guane is the most trodden stretch these days, having been rebuilt in 1864 by the German George von Lenguerke. The stone-paved trail gently slopes downhill nine kilometers (six miles), passing through a convulsing landscape, the thick stone strata revealing the geologic history of this region, once part of great sea 60 million years ago.

From the Parque para las Artes, walk down the path along the rim of the canyon. A sign on the right marks the beginning of the trail. It takes 1.5-two hours to hike to Guane. The last bus back to Barichara is at 5:30 p.m. ($0.65, 15 minutes). Be sure to pace yourself, unless you want to spend the night in Guane at its simple inn. Updated: Apr 23, 2008.

Barichara Tours

Two tour operators exist in Barichara. Both are branch offices of San Gil-based outfits. These offices are closed during the off-season. It may be better to book any activity through the main office. See the San Gil listings for contact information there.

Guanecito (Colombia Rafting Expeditions)—Carrera 9, 6-02. Cell: 311-202-4391 / 313-365-7755, URL: www.baricharaguanecito.com.

Barichara Cultura y Aventura—Calle 6, 7-72. Cell: 310-809-9784. Updated: Dec 19, 2007.

Barichara Lodging

Most visitors to Barichara come only for the day. If you're looking for some true peace, then spend a night or two, and learn why so many Colombians escape to this town caught in time. Although Barichara has a reputation for being expensive, it does have a full range of lodging options, from simple hospedajes to luxury inns. Prices rise in the high season. During the this time, many families open their homes to the traveler for $10.50 per night per person. For a list of providers, stop by the tourism office. Updated: Dec 19, 2007.

Hospedaje Los Tiestesitos

(ROOM: $6-8) On the outside, Hospedaje Los Tiestesitos is a pottery workshop. But back behind a small courtyard, doña Alicia has three rooms to let, all with private, cold-water bath. Some have one bed and others two. The simply furnished rooms are snug, kept warm by the thick walls. These quarters have the earthen aroma of the tapia pisada (rammed-earth) construction of this house. This much-recommended hostel is probably the cheapest in Barichara. Carrera 5, 7-62. Tel: 7-726-7224. Updated: Apr 24, 2008.

Hotel Coratá

(ROOM: $21-35) Just a block from Barichara's main plaza, is an old casona that has taken on the life of a hotel. On its first floor, around a corridor porch, are nine spacious rooms for its guests' rest, all adequately furnished. These rooms come with TV and private, cold-water bathroom. Stairs lead from the porch to the sunken interior patio, where you can relax. In the morning, you can order typical Santandereano breakfast ($3.20) before heading out to check out more of what Barichara has to offer. Carrera 7, 4-08. Tel: 7-726-7110, Cell: 311-481-3195, Fax: 7-726-7071. Updated: Apr 23, 2008.

Hostal Misión Santa Bárbara

(ROOM: $45-$74) This former family mansion is now one of Barichara's most prestigious inns, without being pretentious. The older part of this large house is one story, with a grape-harbor-covered patio. The newer section is two-story, with a five-stroke swimming pool in which to cool down after hiking. Throughout, gardens proliferate, with hammocks strung beneath the foliage. The rooms are large, many with an alcove—a favorite sleeping place for kids. The bathrooms are spotless and have hot water. To while away the evenings are a game room (complete with ping pong table). Children even have their own part of the grounds. Calle 5, 9-12. Tel: 7-726-7163 / 726-7373, E-mail: reservas@hostalmisionsantabarbara.info, URL: www.hostalmisionsantabarbara.info. Bogotá: Calle 40A, 13-59. 1-288-4949 / 232-2846. Bucaramanga: Tel: 7-635-1432, Fax: 7-726-7060. Updated: Apr 24, 2008.

Barichara Restaurants

Barichara has an impressive array of food, from classic Colombian cooking to down-home Spanish. Even nouveau cuisine based on fat-bottomed ants, a regional delicacy, makes the platter. During the week in the low season, many restaurants have limited hours. At the corner of Carrera 6 and Calle 7 is the Casa del Mercado where you can stock up. Panadería Barichara bakes superb breads and desserts (Calle 5 5-33).

Restaurante Patiamarilla

Restaurante Patiamarilla is a clean, well-lit space, with clothed tables and wooden chairs awaiting its dining clientele. The white walls are hung with a motley collection of pictures, including even a very young Clint Eastwood. A simple eating establishment, Patiamarilla serves up Colombian and Santandereano dishes, guaranteed to give you enough fuel for a day's worth of Barichara sightseeing. The comida corriente is a bargain in this town, costing only $1.60. Breakfasts are also prepared. Open 7 a.m.-8 p.m. Carrera 5 6-25. Updated: Apr 23, 2008.

Restaurante Color de Hormiga

Color de Hormiga proclaims itself as Comida Atípica. And that is precisely what you'll find here. Much of its menu is prepared with a regional delicacy: *hormigas culonas*, or fat-bottomed ants. Try the beef tenderloin in ant sauce, or if you're not such the adventurous sort, in a blue cheese sauce. Color de Hormiga also presents beef kabob and a few chicken platters. To accompany your meal, choose a fresh fruit juice, beer or wine ($16 per bottle). Pull up a table on the covered patio after taking a dip in the pool, then dive into one of these unforgettable dishes. Open daily noon-4 p.m., longer hours at holiday times. Calle 8, 8-44, Tel: 7-726-7156. Updated: Apr 23, 2008.

Restaurante Algarabia

Restaurante Algarabia imparts traditional Spanish cooking to the Barichara tourist. From *tortilla española* ($3.70) to rice dishes ($14), and every Iberian classic in between appears on the menu, including *jamón serrano, queso machego, pavo de castilla* and *calamares romana*. Claro, there's wine and sangria to complement your repast, and desserts to put the final touch on the evening. Travelers rave about Algarabia's food, but their reports on service are mixed. Open Thursday to Sunday noon-9 p.m. Calle 6, 10-96. Tel: 7-726-7414, Cell: 313-364-8726 / 311-239-5184, E-mail: francon.mira@gmail.com. Updated: Apr 24, 2008.

Barichara Nightlife

If you come to Barichara during the off-season, you may find it a bit boring come evenings. The village has few nightclubs, most of which are cafés featuring live music. They are open only on weekends and at holidays. Updated: Dec 19, 2007.

Guane

Alt: 1,573m Pop: 170 City Code: 7

Long before the Spaniards' arrival, the Guane people lived atop a narrow mesa above the Río Suárez. It was to here, Guane pueblo, that all surviving Guane were relocated in the 17th Century. This entire hamlet, from its fossils to its tapia pisada architecture, is a museum. On the main square is a statue of the last Guane *cacique* (chief), Guanenta. On the south side is an attractive stone church; on the east side of the plaza is the Museo de Paleontología y Arqueología, containing over 10,000 fossils of fish, ammonites, shells and petrified wood, as well as an indigenous mummy, ceramics and religious art (some from the Quiteña School).

Be sure to pace yourself, unless you want to spend the night in Guane. There is basic lodging. The village produces many products from goat's milk. Try the *sabajón*, a delicious, slightly alcoholic drink in various flavors.

Guane's feast days are Virgen de la Candelaria (2 February), San Isidro Labrador (September) and Santa Lucia (13 December).

In the Guane region are a number of petroglyphs and cave paintings: Piedra de Lubigara and Cueva del Pino (near Guane); Hato Viejo (Villanueva); La Custodia, Los Pozos and Cueva de Cartagena (Mesa de los Santos); Cueva Rica (Mogotes), and others along the Río Chicamocha. Updated: Apr 30, 2008.

Getting To and Away from Guane

Buses leave from Barichara's main square at 6 a.m., 11:30 a.m., 5 p.m. and leave Guane for Barichara at 6:30 a.m., 11:45 a.m. and 5:30 p.m. ($0.65, 15 minutes). Also, you can walk the Camino Real. Updated: Apr 30, 2008.

Things to See and Do

Museo de Paleontología y Arqueología

Entry to the Museo de Paleontología y Arqueología is $1.05 for adults and $0.50 for children. Updated: Apr 30, 2008.

Bucaramanga

Alt: 960m Pop: 550,000 City Code: 7

Continuing north on the main highway to the coast is Bucaramanga, 273 kilometers (164 miles) from Tunja. The paved road is in good condition, with four tollbooths and several military checkpoints. It is a major transportation hub between the nation's capital and the coast or the Colombo-Venezuelan border at Cúcuta. Built amid a much-eroded landscape, Bucaramanga's hills are like a crushed paper bag. This capital of Santander Department is one of Colombia's largest cities, and is home to 10 universities.

Bucaramanga's appellation, *La Ciudad de Parques* (city of parks), is apt; unfortunately, the ones in the center are in poor repair. Only upon entering the residential areas do you find the more well-kept green spaces. Parque García Rovira was the heart of colonial Bucaramanga, whereas Parque Santander is the modern-day center. Several once-upon villages have become bedroom communities of Bucaramanga. Floridablanca, Girón and Piedecuesta are home to museums, botanical gardens and zoological parks that make for great escapes from the city. Bucaramanga is an alternative place to base yourself for rafting and paragliding adventures on the Río Chicamocha or to visit the Parque Nacional Chicamocha, though San Gil is a more logistic spot from which to do these activities. Updated: May 06, 2008.

History

Real Minas de Bucaramanga (royal mines of Bucaramanga), was founded on June 3, 1539, by Martín Galeano, some 83 years before the village of the same name was founded by Capitán Andrés Páez de Sotomayor and Father Miguel Trujillo. Ultimately these mines along the Río de Oro ceased. Spanish descendents and *mestizos* replaced the largely indigenous population and the residents turned to agriculture. However, they continued to reap the benefits as a provider of gold to the Spanish Crown. The fraud was eventually unveiled. In 1857 Bucaramanga became the capital of Santander Department; four years later it lost this position to Socorro but regained it in 1896. The 1000-Day War at the end of the 19th Century caused economic duress for Bucaramanga, from which it did not recuperate until a century later. The decisive battle of this civil war was fought at Palonegro near the city. Updated: Apr 09, 2008.

When to Go

Ask *bucaramanguenses* (or *búcaros*, after their soccer team) when it is best to visit their city and the response is usually, "Oh, you know..." Some say the rains come between March and May, others in September. No one seems to have a definitive answer. But they all agree that almost any month is a fine time to visit. Updated: Apr 09, 2008.

Holiday and Festivals

Besides celebrating national holidays, Bucaramanga plays host to festivities of its own:

Month	Event
April 1	**Día de la Santandereanidad** — A celebration of the Santander identity.
August	**Festival Internacional de Piano** — last week of the month
October	**Feria Bonita** — Celebration and display of cattle, artisan crafts and other commercial wares that takes place in the second half of the month.
October — November	**Festival Iberoamericano de Cuenteros** — Ibero-American Storytellers Festival
November	**Festival de Música Andina Colombiana** — second half of the month.

Neighboring towns' fiestas:

Month	Event
June	**Feria Ganadera**—Cattle Fair in Piedecuesta in the first half of the month.
August	**Reinado Departamental del Turismo**—In Girón the second half of the month.

Month	Event
October	**Fiestas del Señor de los Milagros** — Processions and celebrations in Girón during the first half of the month.
November	**Festival de Cultura, Aire y Dulce** — Cultural festival in Floridablanca the second week of November.

Updated: Apr 11, 2008.

Getting To and Away from Bucaramanga

The modern bus terminal is southwest of downtown, on the Girón road. The station is divided into four modules and has several ATMs (outside Module 3), restaurants, phones, elevator, information booth (outside Module 3) and even billiards to pass the time. Bus companies include Cotramagdalena, Cotrasangil, Extrarápidos Los Motilones, Copetrán, Omega, Cotaxi, Cotranal, Cooptimotilon, Bolivariano, Cootrasaravita, Transander, Concorde, Costa, Cotrans, Crasilia and Berlinas. Cotrans, Cootrasaravita and Cotranal have offices conveniently located near the center of the city.

From Bucaramanga

Arrive	Departures	Time	Price
Barrancabermeja	Every half hour	2 hours	$8
El Banco		6 hours	$24.20
Pamplona / Cúcuta	Every half hour	4 / 6 hours	$12.10 / 18.10
Málaga / Capitanejo	4:30 a.m., noon	7 / 8 hours	$17 / $18
San Gil	Every half hour	2 hours	$8
Bogotá	6:30 a.m., 8:30 a.m.-11:30 p.m. every half hour	9 hours	$34
Medellín	8 a.m., 9 a.m., five afternoon / night buses	9 hours	$37
Cali / Ipiales		15 hours / 26 hours	$51 / $64
Valledupar	6 a.m., 9 a.m., 11 a.m., six afternoon / night buses	10 hours	$37
Santa Marta	Evening buses	9 hours	$40
Barranquilla / Cartagena	9:30 p.m.-12:30 p.m.	9 hours / 12 hours	$43 / $49

Bucaramanga's Aeropuerto Palonegro, west of Girón, has direct flights to Cúcuta, Medellín and Bogotá. Parque Santander Taxi Aeropuerto leaves from a kiosk on Calle 35, (Open 4 a.m.-6 p.m., Tel: 7-642-5250, Cell: 310-273-2552). Reserve at least two hours before; shared $3.20, solo $ 5.30). Public busetas ($0.85) towards the airport leave you quite a distance away, but reportedly taxis shuttle the last leg. Avianca, Satena and Copa have offices on Calle 36, between Carreras 13 and 19. Updated: Apr 11, 2008.

Getting Around

Bucaramanga has good public transportation that runs not only throughout the city, but also connects to the neighboring towns of Floridablanca, Girón and Piedecuesta. In the center, most buses pass Parque de Santos (Carrera 22 and Calle 31). In-city taxis are metered. Metrolínea, a new mass transit system like Bogotá's Transmilenio, is currently under construction. If traveling with your own vehicle, be aware of no-drive days that correspond to your plate's last digit. Updated: Apr 11, 2008.

Safety in Bucaramanga

Bucaramanga is one of Colombia's five most dangerous cities. Always be street-savvy and be sure to take a taxi after dark. The area just north of Parque Santander, between Calles 33 and 30, Carreras 15 and 21, is one in which to have particular care at night. Neighbors say with a wave of the hand that during the day it's *más o menos*. Immediately outside it are some of the city's best hotels. Calle 35 is both a market street and where most of the banks are. Take care. Most central city parks have 24-hour Policia Nacional kiosks. Updated: Apr 11, 2008.

Bucaramanga Services

Tourism Office

Bucaramanga has no tourism office. The Parque Santander Policia Nacional kiosk gives only general information on sites. The Cámara de Comercio has free, hard-to-read maps (Monday-Friday 8 a.m.-noon, 1-5 p.m. Carrera 19, 36-20). These websites can orientate you on Bucaramanga and Santander Department: www.bucaros.com and santandertierradeaventurs.com.co.

Other useful addresses include:
DAS—Open Monday-Friday, 8 a.m.-noon, 1-4:30 p.m. Carrera 11, 41-13. Tel: (extranjería) 7-630-2050.
National Park Office—Avenida Quebrada Seca 30-44, piso 1. Tel: 7-645-4868 / 634-5251.
Instituto Geográfico Agustín Codazzi—URL: http://www.igac.gov.co.
Venezuelan Consulate—Calle 37, 52-75. Tel: 7-643-6621 / 643-8942, Fax: 7-643-6389.

France, Italy, Belgium and Spain all have honorary consuls here. Check the end of the telephone directory's white pages for contact information. Updated: Apr 14, 2008.

Money

Downtown the major banks are along the pedestrian street Calle 35. Most have usual bankers' hours, Monday-Friday, 8-11:30 a.m., 2-4:30 p.m. For traveler's checks exchanges, go to Bancolombia or Santander.
Bancolombia—ATM accepts Visa, Plus, MasterCard, Cirrus, American Express. Carrera 18, 35-02.
Santander—ATM accepts Visa, Plus, MasterCard, Cirrus. Calle 35, 17-87.
Banco de Bogotá—ATM accepts all cards. Calle 35 and Carrera 17.
AV Villas—ATM accepts all cards. Calle 35, 17-45.
In Centro Comercial Rosedal (Calle 35, 18-65) are several casas de cambio. **Cambios Internacionales Euro-Dolar** changes cash US dollars, Pound Sterling, Euros and Bolívares (Monday-Friday 8 a.m.-noon, 2- 6 p.m., Saturday 8 a.m.-noon. Local 121, Tel: 7-630-3614).

For wired money:
Western Union / Giros y Finanzas—Centro Comercial Cañaveral, local 01, Carrera 25, 29-57, Floridablanca.
MoneyGram / Cambiamos—Centro Comercial Cabacera, Etapa 4, Local 104, Carrera 35ª, 49-07. Tel: 7-643-8826. Updated: Apr 14, 2008.

Keeping in Touch

The main Telecom branch has local and national calls at $0.05 per minute, international calls from $0.40 per minute and private-booth internet at $1.05 per hour (Monday-Friday 8 a.m.-7 p.m., Saturday 8-11 a.m., closed holidays. Calle 36, 17-75). Shops offer local and national services for $0.10-0.15 per minute. Several Comcel agents around Parque de Santos (Calle 33 and Carrera 22) have inexpensive international calls at $0.15 per minute.

Most internet cafés cost $0.80 per hour, including Barichar@ On-Line, which also has Skype (7:30 a.m.-7 p.m. Carrera 20, 33-34, Tel: 7-652-0982).

To send letters and packages go to Adpostal (Monday-Friday 7:30 a.m.-noon, 2-6 p.m., Saturday 8 a.m.-noon. Carrera 16, 37-106). Updated: May 20, 2008.

Medical

As to be expected in a city the size of Bucaramanga, there are a number of public and private medical facilities. The main one is Hospital Universitario de Santander, a.k.a. Hospital Ramón González Valencia (Carrera 33, 28-126, Tel: 7-634-6110). Pharmacies are common throughout the metropolitan area. Updated: Apr 14, 2008.

Photo by Lorraine Caputo

Shopping

María

While out in Girón on a daytrip, you may want to take back a reminder of your visit. Look up María Pinto. With hands scarred from the resilient material she works with, she'll show you the hats, belts, bags, shoes and sandals she crafts from fique, a palm fiber. All are her own original, innovative designs. Call first before arriving at her workshop, if you don't find her stall set up on Girón's main square. Calle 19, 25-95, Portal Campestre, I Etapa, Girón. Tel: 7-659-3082, Cell: 311-895-2116, E-mail: artesantandermaria@hotmail.com. Updated: Apr 14, 2008.

Acampemos

Before heading up to Parque Nacional El Cocuy, you might want to stop by Acampemos to pick up on camping gear and supplies. Not only does it stock packs, tents, sleeping bags and pads, and rain-proof clothing at whole-sale prices, it manufactures it. If you don't see what you need, Acampemos can make it for you. Also on-hand are climbing ropes and clamps. It is also one of the few places left in Colombia where you can purchase white gas. Calle 48, 24-57. Tel: 7-647-4194, Cell: 300-556-5645. Updated: Apr 14, 2008.

The Malls

Need a dose of U.S. culture (or a reminder of why you might have left there)? Hop on a bus towards the suburbs. Straddling either side of the highway are *centros comerciales* (shopping malls), all conveniently connected by pedestrian overpass bridges. Spend hours in these air conditioned, glittering palaces of consumerism, window shopping and munching down at the food courts. You'll see some familiar "faces" in these places. There are even movie theaters showing the latest Hollywood blockbusters (or duds); Cañaveral has a Muiltplex cinema and La Florida has a Cinemark theater. If you need more pocket money, Cañaveral has bank branches and ATMs. To get there, catch a buseta that says Cañaveral or Autopista($0.55) from Parque de Santos (Calle 22). Autopista a Floridablanca. Updated: Apr 14, 2008.

Plaza Central

Now that you have had your taste of US culture, it's time to have a real Colombian shopping experience. Head to Plaza Central, Bucaramanga's municipal market which is said to be the largest in Colombia. Enter at Calle 34 and grab a shopping cart to begin exploring this crazy world of Colombia's answer to the mall. These four floors are the best of Colombia's products and produce. The first story is where to pick up vegetables and get your watch repaired. Up the ramp to the second level are fruits, juice bars, bakeries, spices and eggs. Third floor is the cheese and meat department. Lastly the fourth level is where you'll find hats, drinking gourds, hammocks, basketry and other artesanía for your trip or gifts. Need colored candles, incenses, soaps or essential oils for your spiritual needs? You get them here, also. Now for some refueling at the food court (including a vegetarian restaurant) with a great view over the crags surrounding the city. Carrera 16, between Calles 33 and 34. Updated: Apr 14, 2008.

Camera

A number of camera shops are found on Calle 36, between Parque Santander and Parque García Rovira. All offer film processing; various types of print film and digital camera cards, and camera accessories. Fotografía Colombia (Calle 36, 17-31) can put you in touch with someone who does repairs. Updated: May 20, 2008.

Religion

Bucaramanga is a religiously diverse city. The Hare Krishnas have a strong presence here, with a restaurant and a retreat center. Bahai'is have a home here also (Calle 35, 21-47, Tel: 7-645-3203). Purportedly there is a mosque serving Bucaramanga's significant Muslim community. Updated: Apr 14, 2008.

Things to See and Do

If you find yourself caught, Bucaramanga presents visitors various escapes from the eroded metropolis. Of course, La Ciudad de Jardines has many parks—city, recreational, botanical and zoological—as well as a surprising colonial nugget. The museums cover a range of topics, from the historical Casa de Bolívar and the archaeological Pierda del Sol to the Museo de Arte Moderno and the Universidad Industrial de Santander's natural history. Neighboring Floridablanca, Piedecuesta and Girón are charming villages and host to some of Bucaramanga's attractions. Updated: Apr 11, 2008.

The Churches Of Bucaramanga

Only a few of Bucaramanga's churches are open outside of mass hours, which are listed in the telephone directory. Some of the city's more interesting Catholic temples are:

Catedral de la Sagrada Familia—Calle 36, 19-56, Parque Santander.

Capilla de los Dolores—The oldest sanctuary in Bucaramanga. Calle 35 and Carrera 10, corner of Parque García Rovira.

Iglesia de San Laureano—Carrera 12, 36-08, Parque García Rovira.

Iglesia de San Pío X—Carrera 22, 17-49.

Templo Gótico de San Francisco: Carrera 22, 17-49.

Iglesia del Sagrado Corazón de Jesús—Calle 45, 27A-55. Updated: Apr 09, 2008.

Museo de Arte Moderno de Bucaramanga

The Museo de Arte Moderno de Bucaramanga, or MAMB, is in a Republican-styled house built in the 1940s. Three rooms, one devoted to sculpture by contemporary creators, await your perusal. The museum specializes in bimestral itinerant exhibits of mostly national artists. It currently has no permanent collection, but future plans are to extend the building in order to display its growing compilation of impressive works. Check out what is showing this month, but remember at times the Museum may be closed in preparation for the next exhibit. Calle 37, 26-16. Tel: 7-645-0483.Updated: Apr 14, 2008.

Cultural Centers of Bucaramanga

Besides attractions like its churches, parks, la Casa de Bolívar and Museo de Arte Moderno, this city has several other foci of culture:

Casa de la Cultura—with special exhibits and events (Calle 37, 12-46. Tel: 7-630-2046).

Casa Mexicana—whose mission is bringing Mexican art, literature and cinema to Colombia (Tuesday-Saturday 10 a.m.-noon, 4-7 p.m. Carrera 28, 49-40. Tel: 7-647-4869, URL: www.casamexicana.blogspot.com).

Casa Luis Perú de la Croix—home of the 19th-Century writer, soon to become a library (Calle 37, 11-18).

Banco de la República—with free exhibits and concerts (Carrera 19, 34-93. Tel: 7-630-3174 / 630-3133, ext. 221, E-mail: sbucaramanga@banrep.gov.co, URL: www.lablaa.org). Updated: Apr 14, 2008.

Casa de Bolívar

This wasn't exactly the Liberator's home, but Simón Bolívar did stay here for some 70 days in 1828. In the principal sala are exhibited the belongings he left behind—as well as the mantilla and comb of a woman who had danced with him. Better said, the Casa de Bolívar is the home of the History Academy of Santander, displaying other interesting items of the Department's history. Among them is an excellent collection of indigenous Guane textiles. On the back patio are explanations and artifacts of the Batalla of Palonegro, the last and bloodiest battle of the 1000-Day War. Calle 37, 12-15. Updated: Apr 14, 2008.

The Parks of Bucaramanga

Bucaramanguenses are proud of their Ciudad de Parques, a well-deserved nickname for this city of almost two dozen parks. Parque Santander is the modern downtown. Down the bustling streets you'll find Plaza Cívica Luis Carlos Galán, around which are governmental buildings, and Parque García Rovira, the hub of the colonial town; here is the oldest church of this metropolis. Heading towards Floridablanca is Parque Los Lagos, a popular recreational area. Floridablanca has the Jardín Botánico Eloy Valenzuela. Piedecuesta is home to the zoo. On the northeast edge of Bucaramanga, on the road to Cúcuta, is Parque Morrorico with pleasant views. Updated: Apr 14, 2008.

Paragliding

Have you ever wished you could fly? Well, you can't quite get fitted with a permanent set of wings in Bucaramanga, but nearby Mesa de Ruitoque offers you the next best thing. Those heights are considered to be the best place to practice *parapente*, or paragliding. Soaring over river valleys and ancient stone roads, you will see Colombia from a vantage point few will ever witness. You needn't worry about being experienced, as agencies offer tandem flights. You will take wing with the pilot riding piggyback. So strap the sail on and take off to see the countryside unfold below you. However, be certain the equipment and agency is up to certification. Updated: Apr 17, 2008.

Bucaramanga Tours

Tour operators in Bucaramanga are few and far between. Most businesses catering to journeyers are either travel agencies or airline offices. For most adventure sports, such as rafting, go to San Gil. A few specializing in paragliding, or parapente, are located at Mesa de Ruitoque, the premier place in Colombia to do this sport. However, make sure the operator does have proper equipment and certification. Few speak any language other than Spanish. In recent years accidents leading to permanent injury and even death have occurred. Updated: Dec 19, 2007.

Bucaramanga Lodging

Bucaramanga has the full range of lodging options, from extremely cheap, yet decent hotels to fine business class hotels. The cheapest options are located downtown, mainly around Calle 31 and Carrera 20. Be forewarned, however, that inns here double as brothels. To sift that chaff from the wheat, look for signs that say *ambiente familiar* (meaning the place is decent enough for the whole family to stay there). More upscale hotels are between the zona rosa and Cabecera areas of the city. Updated: Dec 19, 2007.

Budget

Hotel Amparo

(ROOM: $4-8) A friendly, family-run inn, Hotel Amparo provides its guests with no-frill rooms with or without TV. All have private, cold-water baths and fan to keep you cool in the hot Bucaramanga climate. The beds are OK. The rooms are cleaned daily. In the main lobby of this two-story hotel is a television, and on the front patio there is a restaurant offering inexpensive breakfasts and comida corrientes. If you arrive on motorbike, there's parking inside. This is definitely one of the cheapest hostels with the ambiente familiar. Calle 31, 20-29. Tel: 7-630-4098 / 652-5394. Updated: Apr 14, 2008.

Residencias Las Tres Margaritas

(ROOM: $5-11) Another family-atmosphere hotel in the city's center that promises three important basics: safety, cleanliness and cheap prices, is Residencias Las Tres Margaritas. This is a new, four-story building with amply-sized rooms that are clean with private, cold-water baths and cable TV. Some of the rooms have balconies overlooking the main street. All is kept clean. The family ensures its guests will have a peaceful stay without incident in their inn. With such service, Las Tres Margaritas is often full. Calle 31, 20-40. Tel: 7-630-0029. Updated: Apr 14, 2008.

Hospedaje D'Kpri

(ROOM: $8-13) Hospedaje D'Kpri is essentially a boarding house for university students. However, some rooms are let for travelers. The small quarters have all furniture built-in, from the platform bed to the night table. The attached bath is clean and has hot water. If you are planning to stay a while in the city, ask about the special monthly rates (about $100 per month). The D'Kpri is located between the zona rosa and Cabecera districts of Bucaramanga, not too far from the night clubs. Calle 34, 30-47. Cell: 301-407-9513. Updated: Apr 14, 2008.

Mid-Range

Hotel Balmoral

(ROOM: $13-21) Conveniently located in the center of the city, Hotel Balmoral is a mid-range option for your visit to Bucaramanga. The hostel is a bit worn, but clean. It offers four floors of accommodation, all with windows and some with balconies. The large rooms come equipped with firm beds, air conditioning, cable TV, closet, mini-bar (extra charge) and private bath with hot showers. Hotel Balmoral is the inn of choice for Colombian families and budget businesspersons. Carrera 21, 34-75. Tel: 630-4136 / 3723, Fax: 7-630-4663. Updated: Apr 14, 2008.

Finca Raval Jardín Ecológico

(ROOM: $15-20) Pamper your physical and spiritual selves at Finca Raval Jardín Ecológico, a Hare Krishna-run spa located 25 kilometers (15 miles) from Bucaramanga. Besides providing simple lodging and vegetarian food, it has a natural swimming pool, volleyball court and hammocks. The price also includes classes on meditation, spirituality, nutrition and yoga. For an extra charge, go for the Finnish-styled sauna or a massage. You may also come for the day to enjoy the facilities. A room with three meals is $20 per person; It is $16 for children six-10 years old, and kids under six stay for free.

You can also camp for $17.60 per person, or $14.70 per person if you bring your own tent. Camping also includes three meals. Special packages are available. A sauna with herbs is $16 and a relaxation massage is $8 and a total massage is $16. The finca is in Raval, about nine kilometers (5.4 miles) from Piedecuesta. From Bucaramanga, board a Trans-Piedecuesta buseta. From that village's market, catch a "Ruta a Curos" bus and alight at Restaurante Caracolí. Ask directions, then, for the Hare Krishna finca. Tel: 7-680-2045 / 2075, Cell: 312-351-0209, E-mail: govindap@intercable.net.co. Updated: May 20, 2008.

HIGH-END

Hotel Chicamocha

(ROOM: $58-112) One of Bucaramanga's finest hostels is Hotel Chicamocha. Providing the best in services to upscale and corporate business travelers, Hotel Chicamocha provides luxuries few other inns do. Courtesy of the house are a welcoming cocktail, breakfast buffet, a pillow menu (yes, you read correctly), medical assistance, swimming pool, sauna, Turkish bath and gym. Also on-site are event rooms, an internet café, a beauty salon, masseuses, restaurant, bars and a travel agent. The spacious, well-appointed rooms have air conditioning and private bath with hot water. Prices include tax and insurance. Rooms in the Torre Norte are less expensive than those in the Torre Sur. Calle 34, 31-24. Tel: 7-634-3000 / 01-8000-511-723 (national toll-free), Fax: 7-635-1809, E-mail: reservas.mcch@solarhoteles.com, URL: www.hotelchicamocha.com. Updated: Apr 14, 2008.

BUCARAMANGA RESTAURANTS

Bucaramanga has some mighty fine eats at good prices. A comida corriente, the set-menu, costs $1.60-2.65 at most establishments. Even a premium meal needn't cost you an arm and a leg; a repast with wine will set you back about $10. The variety of foods reflects the internationally diverse population of this city. For those staying downtown and eating meals in, an Éxito Vecino is at the corner of Calle 36 and Carrera 16. Also be sure to embark on the adventure through Plaza Central, Bucaramanga's market, reputed to be the largest in Colombia.

Govindas

Govindas is an Indian vegetarian delight, brought courtesy of the Hare Krishnas. For a healthy, flavorful lunch pull up a table in one of the three rooms and relax to ragas softly playing. Soon your three-course lunch will be served: soup and multi-grain bread, the main course with drink, then an herbal tea and dessert ($2.20). During non-midday hours, there's veggie fast food. Adjoining shops sell incense, literature and other items. The bakery has soy cheese, meat, milk and yogurt, as well as natural grain breads, granola and flours. You're sure to leave with your stomach chanting the names of the Lord. Open Monday-Saturday 9 a.m.-7:30 p.m. Carrera 20, 34-65. Tel: 7-630-2045 / 4154, Cell: 312-351-0209. Updated: Apr 14, 2008.

La Cocina de la Abuela

If you're craving some of grandma's cooking hot off the stove, even if it's the middle of the night, then head over to her kitchen. La Cocina de la Abuela prepares Colombian culinary classics, like *carne oreada* (dried beef cooked in beer) and *cabro con pipitoria* (goat with a side of rice prepared with finely chopped goat viscera and blood). Lunchtime is busy—and for good reason. Grandma serves up huge portions in this four-course affair (appetizer, soup, entrée and dessert) ($2.65). Grandpa gets into the action too, firing up his grill a few doors down at La Parrilla del Abuelo. Open daily around the clock. Calle 34, 32-23. Tel: 645-6083, E-mail: lacocinadela.abuela@hotmail.com, Updated: Apr 14, 2008.

Repostería Berna

Swiss-owned Repostería Berna is a time-honored place to have a morning treat or afternoon tea. Select a table on one of the three stories (or on the second-floor balcony facing the pedestrian street), and try to decide which of the tasty sweets you'll try this day. Will it be petits-fours, cakes or cookies? Perhaps ice cream—whether solo or as a sundae or banana split. To complement your treat, choose coffee, tea, juice or soda. For something a bit more substantial, there are tamales, sandwiches, empanadas and other goodies. Stop off at the bakery to take home some bread, goat-milk cheese or yogurt. Open Monday-Friday 8 a.m.-noon, 2-6:30 p.m., Saturday 8 a.m.-6:30 p.m., closed Sunday and holidays. Calle 35, 18-22. Tel: 7-630-3371 / 642-3895. Updated: Apr 14, 2008.

Restaurante Toy San

Along pedestrian Calle 35 you'll see the street vendors munching down on some okay-looking Chinese food. Ask where they got it from, and someone might have handy a card from Restaurante Toy San. There you'll find all the tables full of folks enjoying the lunch special ($1.85). Well, fight your way to the counter for carry out and eat your meal on a park bench instead. Á la carte meat or vegetarian chow mein, chop suey and other Chinese dishes cost $6.35-8 for a full order, $4.20-5.80 for a half. Open daily 11 a.m.-9 p.m. Carrera 18, 37-44. Tel: 7-642-4625 / 0549. Updated: Apr 14, 2008.

Pizzaría Asturias

At Pizzaría Asturias it's hard to decide which of the 14 pies to order ($2.50-14), almost half of which are vegetarian, including one of *bocadillo* (guava paste) and cheese, and the Tutifruti, adorned with apple, peach, plum, pineapple and cheese. The marinera is delightful—*chipi-chipi* and róbalo fish, squid, shrimp and clams. Pizzaría Asturias isn't just about pizzas though—it also prepares breakfasts ($2-4), *almuerzos ejecutivos* ($3.20) and à la carte dishes ($5.50-17). Open daily 8 a.m.-10 p.m. Carrera 22, 35-01, Hotel Asturias. Tel: 7-645-7565 / 635-1914. Updated: Apr 14, 2008.

Calle de los Mariachis

Calle 33 is one of the busiest avenues and there's no street-side cafés to sit and nurse a beer while listening to the strolling ensembles. About 5 p.m., in the open windows of upstairs greenrooms, men dress in *charro* outfits. A trumpet's music waltzes down to the street, heard above the rush hour traffic. Those who are ready drink a *tinto* (coffee), waiting for the night's first customer to hire their services. Twenty conjuntos will be here until 2 a.m., in case you want to serenade a sweet Colombian. Several clubs—Garibaldi, El Venado del Oro and El Sombrero—have mariachi shows beginning at 10 p.m. every night. Carrera 33, between Calles 37 and 39. Updated: Apr 14, 2008.

Bucaramanga Nightlife

Bucaramanga has quite a lively nightlife on weekends. Bars near the universities, though, are open every night. The once-fashionable zona rosa (between downtown and Carrera 30) is now lined with strip joints. The happening scene has now shifted to the neighboring Cabecera district, most clubs are along Carrera 33. Highly recommended ones these days include La Calle, which features mainly Colombian music and merengue, and Mi País. Updated: May 06, 2008.

Floridablanca

Floridablanca, one of Bucaramanga's bedroom communities eight kilometers (five miles) away, is a popular place to seek refuge from the city, especially on Sundays. A fountain is surrounded by vendors who sell *raspado* (flavored shaved ice) and *oblea* (wafer and caramel sandwich). A few blocks away is the Piedra del Sol, a massive boulder with spirals and circles carved by Guane ancestors a millenium or more ago. A modern casa de cultura with an archaeological museum surrounds it. About a kilometer away is the Jardín Botánico Eloy Valenzuela, once owned by El Paragüitas tobacco company. Updated: May 20, 2008.

Jardín Botánico Eloy Valenzuela

On the banks of the Río Frío is the Jardín Botánico Eloy Valenzuela. Paths wind through its nine, lake-dotted hectares ablaze with mini-gardens of orchids, bamboos, palms, aquatic plants, medicinal herbs and other flora. There is even a Japanese meditation garden—a perfect place to do a session of aikido or tai chi. Keep an eye out for the red and black squirrels, birds (including ducks and woodpeckers) and turtles that make this parcel their abode. The serenity of the Jardín Botánico Eloy Valenzuela is refreshing. However, if you want to remember this peaceful place, you'll have to juice up your memory. Photographs of the flora are forbidden. Updated: Apr 09, 2008.

Casa de la Cultura Piedra del Sol and Archaeological Museum

The Casa de la Cultura Piedra del Sol takes its name from a mysterious piece sheltered within its courtyard: a boulder carved with spirals and circles. The creators of this work were the Guane, a Chibcha-speaking nation that occupied the Santander region from the seventh Century BC to the 16th Century AD. Inside, the Museo Arqueológico Regional Piedra del Sol, also known as Museo Arqueológico de los Guanes, presents an impressive collection of textiles, pottery, jewelry and others objects in well-displayed exhibits with excellent explanations on their use and significance. Carrera 7, 4-35. Updated: Apr 14, 2008.

Girón

On the banks of the Río de Oro, amid tobacco country is San Juan de Girón, nine kilometers (5.4 miles) southwest of Bucaramanga. This 17th Century village of white-washed buildings and narrow cobblestone streets is another well-liked get-away. The palm-shaded main plaza has artisan booths and a plaque noting how many times Bolívar passed through. Visit the over-400-year-old Mansión del Fraile, a museum of various knickknacks and a room where the Libertador had stayed, and the Museo de Arte Religioso Benedicto XVI. Down by the river you can try your hand at knitting and munch down on local cuisine. Updated: May 20, 2008.

Fritanga

Beneath a centuries-old almond tree, you'll find a market-like place. In today's zephyr, the signs wave, whispering Donde Lola, Donde Maragrita, La Favorita, La Tía Gloria. If you follow a vegetarian, kosher, halal or low-cholesterol diet, ignore the calls. What these women serve up is a traditional must-try for visitors to Girón: the *fritanga*, a plate heaping with sausages, *rellena* (stuffed pork loin) and other pork delicacies, all deep-fried and served hot with a toothpick to your white-tile table. You only need a soda or beer to wash it all down. Riverfront malecón (Calle 27) and Carrera 28. Updated: Apr 14, 2008.

Pamplona

Alt: 2,287m Pop: 77,000 City Code: 7

A good highway leaves eastward from Bucaramanga, climbs to the settlement of Berlín on the páramo, and then descends to Pamplona (120 kilometers / 72 miles). Pamplona can also be reached from Málaga to the south. At a relatively high altitude, Pamplona enjoys a pleasant spring-like climate year-round, thus making it a popular get-away for Colombians and Venezuelans alike. It is a cultural mecca, hosting a number of music, dance and cinematographic festivals, and possessing some excellent museums.

This small town has produced poets (Jorge Gaitán Durán, Augusto Ramírez Villamizar, Francisco Valencia) and artists (Eduardo Ramírez Villamizar), as well as military leaders and a president (Rafael Faría Bermúdez).

Pamplona's Semana Santa, or Easter Week, is rated as one of the top three in Colombia, along with Popayán and Mompós. Other Colombian cities can't match Pamplona for the number of nicknames it has garnered over its 450 years of existence: Founder City of Cities, Patriotic City, The Mitered City, First Capital of the Sovereign State of Santander, The City Spoiled by the Mists, Student Capital of Eastern Colombia. University education has become the basis of Pamplona's economy. Updated: Feb 18, 2008.

History

Pamplona was established in 1549 by Pedro de Urgúa and Ortún Velasco, who promptly enslaved the indigenous Chitarero nation. A few years later, this new town developed into a gold and silver mining center, one of the richest in the Spanish colonies. Pamplona also became the base for the founding of many cities in both Colombia and Venezuela (Mérida, San Cristóbal and La Grita), thus earning it the monicker Ciudad Fundadora de Ciudades (founding city of cities). With the rise of the comunero movement against Spanish rule in the late 18th Century, Pamplona turned into an important center of rebellion. In 1810 it declared its independence. Between 1817 and 1819, a reign of terror gripped it, meriting another alias, this from Simón Bolívar: Pamplona, Ciudad Patriótica. Once the Colombian Republic was formed, Pamplona was designated the first capital of Santander Department, in 1857. Updated: Jan 11, 2008.

When to Go

The wettest months are usually March to April and October; the driest is December. The town is especially crowded with tourists during Semana Santa and the 4th of July festivities. The city's beat pulses with its university. When there are classes—January to June and August to the beginning of December—Pamplona hops with many cultural events and a vibrant nightclub scene. But, as with college towns wherever, once the students go on break, the city becomes sleepier, with fewer services. Updated: Jan 11, 2008.

Holidays and Festivals
Many of Pamplona's holidays have one-week, free cultural festivals associated with them:

Month	Event
January	**Fiesta del Niño Huertanito** — last Sunday of the month.
March / April	**Semana Santa (Easter Week) and the Festival Internacional de Música Sacra Coral** — Easter week and the International Sacred Choral Music Festival.
July	**4: Grito de la Independencia de Pamplona** and the **Festival Nacional de Danza Folclórica** — Cry of Pamplona's Independence, in 1810 and the National Folk Dance Festival. **16: Fiesta de la Virgen del Cármen**
September	**14: Fiesta del Señor del Humilladero**
November	**Founding of Pamplona** and the **Film Festival**

Updated: Jan 11, 2008.

Getting To and Away from Pamplona

The Pamplona bus terminal is at the end of Calle 4, one block past the bridge, across from the Policia Nacional base. On the main level of the station are bathrooms, snack shops and phones; on the upper level are restaurants. Updated: Jan 11, 2008.

From Pamplona

Arrive	Departures	Time	Price
Silos	7 a.m., 11 a.m., 4 p.m.	1.5-2 hours	$3.70
Cácota	hourly 7 a.m.-4 p.m.	40 mins	$2.65
Chitagá	Last return 4 p.m.		$3.70
Málaga	8 a.m. - 8 p.m.	5 hours	$12
Capitanejo	2 p.m., 5 p.m., 6 p.m., 8 p.m.	6-7 hours	$14
Cúcuta	Every half hour 11 a.m. - 6 p.m.	2.5 hours.	$4 -6
Bucaramanga	Hourly	5 hours	$12
El Banco	8 p.m.	12 hours	$37
Bogotá	9 a.m. -9:30 p.m.	12 hours	$29 -46
Cali	11 a.m. -8 p.m.	20 hours	$58 -$59
Medellín	5 p.m., 8:30 p.m.	12-14 hours	$45 -57
Santa Marta	10:30 p.m.	14 hours	$51
Barranquilla	3p.m. -7:30 p.m.	15 hours	$45 -56
Sincelejo	4:30 p.m	18 hours	$53
Montería	2:30 p.m., 5:30 p.m	18 hours	$63
Cartagena	3p.m. -7:30 p.m.	18 hours	$48 -63

Safety in Pamplona

Pamplona is a relatively safe town. However, locals do advise to stay on the more trafficked streets, like Carrera 6 (which goes down to the main night club district) after dark. Updated: Jan 11, 2008.

Pamplona Services

Tourism Office

The Instituto de Cultura y Turismo de Pamplona, or Pamplona's Culture and Tourism Institute, has its office in the Museo Casa Colonial (Monday-Friday 8 a.m.-noon, 2-6 p.m. Calle 6, 2-56, Tel: 7-568-2043, URL: www.ictp.gov.co). The Centro Cultural Municipal Ramón González Valencia also supplies informative maps of the city (Monday-Friday 8 a.m.-noon, 2-6 p.m. Carrera 7, 5-52).

Money

None of the banks in Pamplona cash traveller's checks. The following have ATMs:

Bancolombia—Accepts MasterCard, Visa, Cirrus, American Express. Calle 7, 5-76.

Banco de Bogotá—ATH—accepts Visa, MasterCard, Cirrus, Plus. Carrera 6, 5-47.

BBVA—Accepts Visa, MasterCard, Plus. Carrera 6, 5-71, main plaza.

There are no casas de cambio, nor does either Western Union or MoneyGram have agents here.

Keeping in Touch

Telecom/Telefónica charge $0.15 per minute for local and national calls, from $0.30 per minute for international calls, and $1.05 per hour for internet (Monday-Saturday 8 a.m.-noon, 2-8 p.m. Corner Calle 7 and Carrera 5A). A national or local call from a shop costs about $0.10 per minute. Generally, internet cafés charge $0.60-0.80 per hour, though some have special hours costing only $0.50. Shop around. Don't bother looking for Skype, as it seems no-one has it (let alone know what it is).

For letter writers, the post office, Correos de Colombia/Adpostal is the place to go (Monday-Friday 7:30 a.m.-noon, 2-6 p.m., Saturday 8 a.m.-noon. Calle 6, 6-36).

Medical

Hospital San Juan de Dios is at the end of Calle 5, just over the river (Tel: 7-568-2482). Carrera 6, between Parque Águeda Gallardo (the main plaza) and Plazuela Almeida (where the obelisk is) is home to most of the city's pharmacies.

Laundry

That entity that is few and far between in Colombia, Pamplona happens to have two of, for the convenience of both frazzled university students and travelers: the laundromat Lavoexpress can wash your clothes for $0.50 per kilo, or wash and dry them for $1.05 per kilo. If you get your dirty duds in during the morning, they can be done by close the same day (Monday-Saturday 8 a.m.-noon, 2-6 p.m. Calle 5, 4-09, Tel: 7-568-2554). Lavaexpress has another outlet at Calle 9, 7-89, which has the same hours.

Camera

There are several camera shops in town, two right on the main square, Parque Águeda Gallardo. All are pretty basic, mostly dedicated to photo processing and digital camera sales. Film is hard to find. Try one of the drugstores. Updated: Jan 11, 2008.

Things to See and Do

Pamplona preserves the beauty of its colonial buildings, unlike many Colombian cities. Several colonial homes have become museums, like the Museo de Arte and the Casa Colonial. Other edifices of the era not to miss on your stroll around Pamplona are Casa de Doña Agueda Gallardo (Calle 5 and Carrera 6), Casa de las Cajas Reales (Carrera 5, between Calles 4 and 5) and the Casa del Mercado, formerly a Jesuit School (Calle 6 and Carrera 5). Around Pamplona are a number of villages offering crafts, museums, hot springs and natural beauty that are worthy of day trips. Among these are Silos, Cácota, Chitagá, Mutiscua and Pamplonita. Updated: Jan 11, 2008.

The Churches of Pamplona

Pamplona, renowned for not only its colonial architecture but for its Semana Santa and other religious traditions, has a fine selection of churches. Most are open only during mass.

The Museums of Pamplona

One of the city's appellations is "La Ciudad de Museos." Although few in number, Pamplona's museums cover a spectrum of themes.

Museo de Arte Ramírez Villamizar

An impressive collection of art by native Eduardo Ramírez Villamizar, and modern Colombian and Venezuelan artists. Originally the home of Juan de Maldonado, founder of

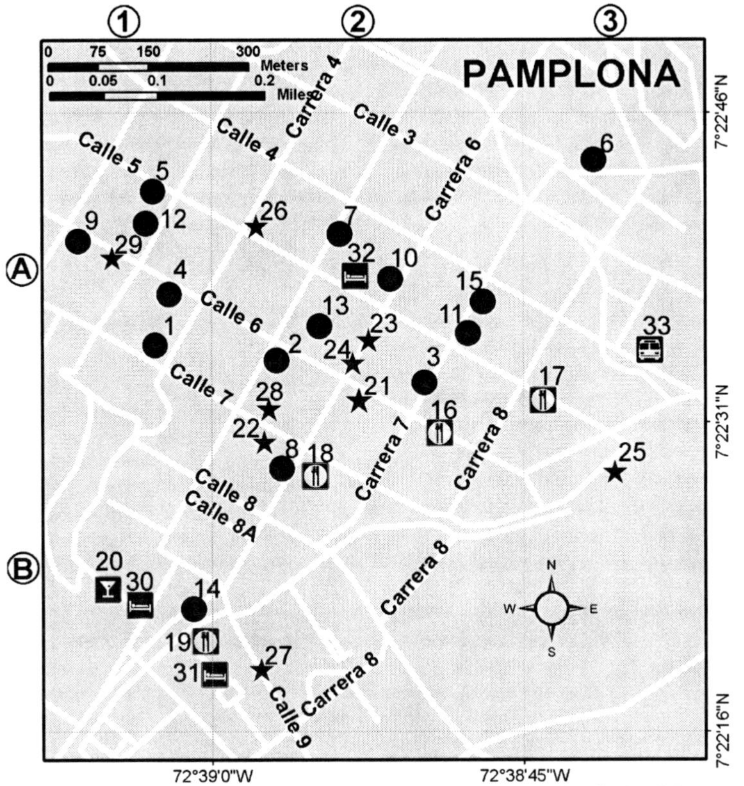

Activities

1 Capilla de San Juan de Dios B1
2 Catedral Santa Clara B2
3 Centro Cultural Municipal B2
4 Convento de Santa Clara B1
5 Ermita de las Nieves B1
6 Ermita del Señor del Humilladero B3
7 Museo Arquidiocesano B2
8 Museo Casa Azoátegui C2
9 Museo Casa Colonial B1
10 Museo de Arte Ramírez Villamiz B2
11 Nuestra Señora de las Nieves B2
12 Nuestra Señora del Carmen B1
13 Parque Aqueda Gallardo B2
14 Plazuela Almeida C1
15 San José B2

Eating

16 Restaurante El Arreiro C2
17 Restaurante El Solar B3
18 Restaurante Govinda C2
19 Siux Coffee Bar C1
20 Discoteca, Hotel Carionga C1

Services

21 Adpostal B2
22 Banco Colombia C2
23 Banco de Bogotá B2
24 BBVA B2
25 Hospital San Juan de Dios C3
26 Lavo Express 1 B2
27 Lavo Express 2 C2
28 Telecom B2
29 Tourism Office C1

Sleeping

30 Carionga Hotel C1
31 Hotel El Llano C1
32 Hotel Ursua B2

Transportation

33 Bus Terminal B2

San Cristóbal de Táchira, this was also once a convent and a brothel—hence La Casa de las Marías. (Tuesday-Sunday 9 a.m.-noon, 2-6 p.m. Calle 5, 5-45, Parque Águeda Gallardo, Tel: 7-568-2999. Entry: $0.50 children, $0.80 adults).

Museo Arquidiocesano de Arte Religioso

The treasures of Pamplona's churches, including paintings by some of the most important colonial artists (Monday-Saturday 10 a.m.-noon, 3-5 p.m., Sunday and holidays 10 a.m.-noon, closed Tuesdays. Carrera 5, 4-53, Tel: 7-568-0960. Entry: $0.50).

Museo Casa Azoátegui

The once-home of Venezuela-born independence general José Antonio Anzoátegui is now a museum and archives (Monday-Saturday 9 a.m.-noon, 2-5:30 p.m. Carrera 6, 7-48, Tel: 7-568-0960, E-mail: museoanzoategui@gmail.com / museoanzoategui@yahoo.com, URL: www.museoanzoategui.blogspot.com. Entry: $0.50).

Museo Casa Colonial

Also known as the Museo de Pamplona, this museum exhibits small collections of archaeological, palaeontological, religious and historical artefacts (Monday-Friday 8 a.m.-noon, 2-6 p.m. Calle 6, 2-56, Tel: 7-568-2043, Entry: $0.50). Updated: Feb 06, 2008.

El Huerfanito

In the 17th Century, an earthquake devastated Pamplona. Only three buildings were left standing. Upon remembering that the statue of the infant Christ was up in the choir loft of the chapel, the nuns of Santa Clara convent cried out, *"Se quedó Huerfanito El Niño!"* The child has been left an orphan! Searching for him, a beam fell on one of the sisters, killing her. Removing the debris, her colleagues found the Christ child unharmed and with one arm raised, as if giving a last benediction to the fallen nun. Since then, he has resided in a spacial place in the rebuilt temple. Updated: Jan 11, 2008.

Corporación de Turismo de Pamplona

On weekends you can join the Corporación de Turismo de Pamplona's several tours to explore the richness of nearby villages. How about a day in Silos, visiting indigenous tombs, dipping into thermal pools and shopping for a new poncho? Or to Cácota to pick up on some ceramics and to canoe across the Laguna de Cácota? You can also drop a fishing line into Laguna del Salado, spend

Cathedral	Description	Address
Catedral Santa Clara	Formerly the chapel of Santa Clara convent, the current-day cathedral was built in 1587 by the daughter of one of Pamplona's co-founders.	Calle 6, between Carreras 5 and 6, Parque Águeda Gallardo.
Nuestra Señora de las Nieves	Parts of this temple are from the original Convento de Santo Domingo, built in 1563 and destroyed by earthquake in 1875.	Carrera 7 and Calle 5.
San José	A more modern building constructed on the former site of Santo Domingo monastery.	Carrera 7, between Calles 4 and 5.
Ermita del Señor del Humilladero	This shrine of Pamplona's most holy relic was built shortly after the city's founding, and expanded in 1605.	Calle 2, between Carreras 7 and 8.
Convento de Santa Clara	This convent chapel is home to another important Christ representation, El Huerfanito, which survived a 17th century earthquake.	Calle 6, between Carreras 3 and 4.
Capilla de San Juan de Dios	A simple, white-washed parish church erected in 1665.	Carrera 4, between Calles 6 and 7.
Ermita de las Nieves	Pamplona's first church, dating from 1550.	Calle 5 and Carrera 3.
Nuestra Señora del Carmen	A younger edifice neighboring the Ermite de las Nieves.	Carrera 3, between Calles 5 and 6.

Updated: Feb 18, 2008.

a while in the Casa de Bolívar and snack on cheese, cakes and peaches while in Chitagá. The Corporación de Turismo de Pamplona also has outings to Mutiscua and Pamplonita. All trips include transportation and lunch, and most a guide, at very reasonable prices ($8-18.65 per person, depending on excursion destination). Tel: 7-756-0960, Cell: 310-278-6994. Updated: Jan 11, 2008.

Silos

Between Pamplona and Bucaramanga is a spur road at La Laguna that goes south to the small village of Silos. Surrounded by the foothills of the Cordillera Oriental, Silos is rich in minerals, including marble, coal and limestone. Its inhabitants also weave woolen blankets and *ruanas* (short ponchos). The countryside is dotted with lagoons, some of which offer the fisher a try at trout. Other attractions include pre-Columbian tombs, the Museo Cacique Magará and hot springs. Horseback riding is another possible activity for the visitor.

Getting there: Extra Rápidos de Motilones has daily buses at 7 a.m., 11 a.m. and 4 p.m. ($3.70, 1.5-2 hours); the last departure from Silos to Pamplona is at 1 p.m. You can also go on tour, but only on weekends. Updated: May 20, 2008.

Pamplona Lodging

Hotels in Pamplona range from basic to time-worn resorts. Cheaper residencias and hospedajes are on the east side of the river, between Calles 7 and 9. On weekends rooms may be a bit more difficult to find due to families making a quick escape to this sphere of culture. Reservations are highly recommended for the high season, especially Semana Santa and the July 4 festivities. Updated: Feb 18, 2008.

Hotel El Llano

(ROOM: $4-11) Located a half-block from the obelisk in Plazuela Almeida, the Hotel El Llano is one of Pamplona's cheapest inns promising an *ambiente familiar*, or family atmosphere. Most of the small, brick-block rooms have windows facing onto the central patio. The better options and common bath are on the newer second story. All share the common, hot water baths, save one that has a private bathroom. The smell of cleanliness pervades the air. Something uncommon about this Colombian hostel: no rooms have television, thus allowing it to charge such an economical price. Guests can use the laundry area to wash clothes. Calle 9, 7-30. Tel: 7-568-3441. Updated: Feb 06, 2008.

Hotel Ursua

(ROOM: $8-16) The Hotel Ursua is like your country grandmother's house: big, overstuffed beds and mismatched furniture in the rooms, and generations of now-antique sewing machines, irons, phonographs and other items scattered throughout (be sure to check out the LP record collection—you'll be impressed by her wide selection such as Seals and Croft and a very young Joan Serrat). Now a third generation of this family's women is greeting the weary traveler to this eclectic but comfortable lodge that is in part of the over-400-year-old house of Juan de Maldonado. All rooms have private, hot water baths. Opt for TV or not. The restaurant serves good food. Calle 5, 5-67, Parque Águeda Gallardo. Tel: 7-568-2470. Updated: Feb 18, 2008.

Carionga Hotel

(ROOM: $27-74) A time-worn resort built in 1960s architecture of glass and metal, Hotel Carionga still provides the best service to the journeyer to Pamplona. It caters primarily to businesspeople, excursion groups and families. The era-theme continues into the large rooms, in classic 1960s simplicity. Hotel Carionga has many of the usual amenities, plus a few more: audio-visual equipped rooms for conferences, BBQ patio and a playground. The parking lot is fenced and guarded. Carrera 5 and Calle 9, Plazuela Almeida. Tel: 7-568-1515, E-mail: hotelcarionga2005@yahoo.es. Updated: Feb 06, 2008.

Pamplona Restaurants

Like other tourist-oriented services in Pamplona, restaurants are affected when the university is not in session. They tend to close earlier and have a more limited menu. Mostly you will find *criollo* (typical *nortesantansereano* dishes). The municipal market occupies the entire block between Calles 6 and 7, Carreras 4 and 5. The entrance to the *comedores* (eateries) is on Calle 7. Here you'll find cheap breakfasts and lunches (open 6:30 a.m.-2 p.m.). For inexpensive evening meals, drop by one of the small restaurants down Calle 6, between Carreras 6 and 8. As you can expect in a gown-town, Pamplona has quite a happening night club scene, with bohemian cafés with live trova music, bars to sit 'round talking theories with friends over a few drinks and discoteques galore. Many are concentrated around Plazuela Almeida, where the obelisk is. This is the service sector that is most affected when the university is not in session; many are closed. The few that remain open during this downtime do so with limited hours and/or only on weekends. Updated: Jan 11, 2008.

Restaurante Govinda

In the courtyard of the Hare Krishna-run Hostal Santa Clara in the fourth chakra of Pamplona is Restaurante Govinda, providing this town with well-prepared, nutritious vegetarian food—as is the Hare Krishna tradition. Good soups, mains and fresh fruit juice—a colorful ensemble for your physical and spiritual selves. Sometimes the "meat" is soy, others it is gluten. The price of the comida corriente is just right for the poor student or budget traveler: $1.60. Open 7 a.m.-10 p.m. when the university students are in town; out of term, open only for lunch noon-2 p.m. Carrera 6, 7-21. Tel: 7-568-4105. Updated: Feb 20, 2008.

Restaurante Desayunadero El Arreiro

An airy restaurant constructed of plaited bamboo slat walls, Restaurante Desayunadero El Arreiro prepares simple criolla dishes. Sit down at one of the clothed tables to a basic, two-course comida corriente (with drink, $1.60) or one of the many à la carte entrées on the menu ($3.20). The señora is friendly and the service quick. After your meal, kick back and chat with her while the soap operas flash on the TV. Open daily 9 a.m.-8 p.m. Calle 6, 7-14. Updated: Feb 06, 2008.

Restaurante El Solar

This classy, yet rustic dining hall of worn brick and wood is a pleasing atmosphere in which to sit down and enjoy an excellent meal. With a menu aimed at the carnivorous crowd, Restaurante El Solar brings sizzling steaks to your table, including what it promises to be an authentic T-bone Americano ($7-13). There are also several chicken breast and fish platters ($7.40-8 and $10.50-14.70, respectively). In season, the strands of live vallenato music drift through the large space, adding to the ambience. Calle 5, 8-18. Cell: 312-568-2966 / 522-9225 / 527-2395. Updated: Feb 06, 2008.

Siux Coffee Bar

A comfortable, dimly-lit establishment that serves mostly liquor and little coffee. Despite the canned music that at times can be a bit too loud, it's still one of the favorite places to hang out, chew the fat, expound on a professor's lecture and have a few drinks. If you're a more solitary soul—or want to be a fly on the wall and watch the unfolding scene—just take a corner table. But be forewarned: they are also sought out by those there with their someone-specials. During the academic calendar, live music is slated at times. Open off-season Friday and Saturday only, 8 p.m.-2 a.m. Calle 9 7-16. Updated: Feb 18, 2008.

Pamplona Nightlife

Discoteca, Hotel Carionga

On Friday and Saturday nights, *pamploneses* head here for some elegant dancing. Many make this part of the circuit of hitting the night clubs down near the Plazuela Almeida. There's no cover charge and no minimum consumption. Merengue, salsa, vallenato and reggaetón (yes, even reggaetón) throbs this dance hall until the morning's wee hours. Only rum and aguardiente are on hand, though if what you want isn't, the staff can scare up something. Open Friday and Saturday 8:30 p.m.-2 a.m. Carrera 5 and Calle 9, Plazuela Almeida. Updated: Feb 06, 2008.

Cúcuta

Alt: 320m Pop: 920,000 City Code: 7

Two hours (72 kilometers/43 miles) from Pamplona is San José de Cúcuta, capital of Norte de Santander Department. The twisting paved road has one tollbooth and a military checkpoint. You may at times feel like you are already in Venezuela--with the slang of cucuteños, the fashions and all the cars with Venezuelan plates--but you are yet some 20 kilometers (12 miles) from the official border.

Cúcuta is also a principle commercial center between the two countries, whether of legitimate wares or contraband (especially gasoline). A popular shopping destination for Venezuelans, everything in Cúcuta is geared towards this: numerous ATMs and casas de cambio, shops specializing in clothing and shoes, and fast-food restaurants to fuel frenzied shoppers. Traffic is insane. Two lanes become three or more. Motorcycles disregard what few stoplights there are and use the sidewalk to bypass snarls. Commerce spills from stores into the littered streets. Those traveling in their own vehicles may find the bustle a bit beyond their experience and prefer to spend the night in Pamplona. Cúcuta is a bit more than a gateway to Venezuela and a commercial capital. It is also a city steeped in independence history. Nearby Villa del Rosario preserves important symbols for the *bolivariano* nations. Updated: Feb 06, 2008.

History

Cúcuta is a relatively modern city, in Colombian terms, having been founded in 1734. The city played significant roles during the Wars of Independence from Spain. It was captured by Simón Bolívar during his Magdalena campaign of 1813. The first congress of Grand Colombia (1821), to unite Venezuela, Colombia and Ecuador, was held in neighboring Villa del Rosario. Bolívar was elected president and General Francisco de Paula Santander vice president. In 1875 this town was destroyed by an earthquake and subsequently rebuilt. In recent years, Cúcuta has seen much settlement by *desplazados*, or internal refugees from the war-torn areas in the immediate region. Updated: Feb 07, 2008.

When to Go

It's always hot and sunny in Cúcuta. June and July can see temperatures reaching up to 40°C (104°F). August and September are windy. The rainy season comes in November and December with brief daily showers. The city is even more crowded with vacationers and shoppers in July, August and December. Updated: Feb 07, 2008.

Holidays and Festivals

Apart from the national holidays, Cúcuta has its own observances. February 28 is the commemoration of the Battle of Cúcuta; parades wend up to Loma de Bolívar (Bolívar Hill). Cucuteños celebrate San José, the patron saint, on 19 March with processions and fireworks. The city's birthday, 17 June, is another occasion for *pólvora* (fireworks), as well as civic events.

One holiday that is observed on a different day than the rest of the country is Mother's Day, normally the second Sunday of May. The reason, of course, is commerce. In the early 20th Century, goods arrived through Maracaibo Lake ports.

One year the special goodies for Día de la Madre were delayed. So that the merchants wouldn't be stuck with the merchandise, the date for this holiday was changed to the last Sunday of May, and has remained so ever since. Updated: Feb 07, 2008.

Getting To and Away from Cúcuta

Taxis are unmetered, so negotiate a price before boarding. Minimum fare is $1.60 and transport to the airport costs $3.70. Note that in Cúcuta carreras are called avenidas.

Cúcuta has an extensive public bus system. To go to the Venzuelan consulate or DIAN, catch the "Consulado" buseta from Calle 10 and Avenida 1 ($0.60).

Cúcuta's bus terminal is a madhouse located on Avenida 7 between Calles 2 and 0. Its reputation is notorious (see Safety). Plans are underway to build a new facility. If you are heading to the border, Pamplona or other nearby destinations, it is better to head straight out to the bus lot and talk directly with the driver.

Bus companies running trips to other major cities include Cotrans, Concorde, Copetrán, Omega, Brasilia, Cootransmagdalena and Bolivariana. Prices and trip times vary.

From Cúcuta

Arrive	Departure	Time	Price
Pamplona	Every half hour	2 hours	$4
Bucaramanga	Every half hour	6 hours	$18
Capitanejo (by way of Málaga)	6 a.m., noon, 3 p.m., 8 p.m.	8 hours	$20
Bogotá	5 a.m. 9:30 p.m.	15 -18 hours	$40 -69

Arrive	Departure	Time	Price
Mompós	1 p.m., 8 p.m.	13 hours	$37
Cali	9 a.m.- 6 p.m.	21 hours	$65 -70
Medellín	11:30 a.m. - 7:30 p.m.	14 hours	$48 -52
Barran-quilla	9 a.m.-5:30 p.m.	16 hours	$53 -64
Cartagena	9 a.m.-5:30 p.m.	18 hours	$58 -69

To Border: Frequent buses, $0.80. See Border Crossings for more information. Avianca and Aires fly out of Cúcuta's Aeropuerto Camilo Daza, with departures direct to Bogotá ($140-185, plus taxes). Updated: Feb 07, 2008.

Safety in Cúcuta

Like any other port—whether land or waterway—Cúcuta has serious problems with security. The streets bustle with commerce and the constant movement all make it easy for a thief to do his/her deed and easily disappear. The entire city is considered to be unsafe after 9 p.m., until daybreak. If needing to move at these hours, take a registered taxi. Otherwise, keep your activities to daylight hours.

The bus terminal has a long history of people working the traveler trying to navigate the confusion that reigns therein. Some of the tricks in the past were to have you turn over your valuables for "safe keeping" in the bus office, and the selling of fake tickets. Do not fall for any of this. It is better to go to the bus office window or the bus driver and buy your tickets directly from these personnel.

Recently whenever tensions between Venezuela and Colombia that could affect trade in Cúcuta have flared, the border crossing has seen demonstrations and has even been shut down at times. Keep an eye on the news for any such activities. Updated: Feb 07, 2008.

Cúcuta Services

Tourism Office

The tourism office in Cúcuta, the Corporación Mixta de Promoción de Norte de Santander, has information on sites throughout the department and sells maps of the city ($1.60). (Monday-Friday 8-11:45 a.m., 2-6 p.m., Saturday 8 a.m.-noon. Calle 10, 0-30, Edificio Rosetal, Tel: 7-571-3395).

DIAN, or the customs (*aduana*) headquarters is on Avenida Aeropuerto, just past the Venezuelan consulate. Those travelers entering or leaving Colombia in their own vehicles will have to pay a visit here.

DAS (immigration) has two offices in Cúcuta: one for extensions and other such business (Avenida 1, 28-53, Tel: 7-583-6964) and the other for receiving your entry or exit stamp for Colombia (at the Puente Internacional). If you need a visa for Venezuela or are traveling with your own vehicle, drop by the Venezuelan consulate (Avenida Aeropuerto 17N-73, Zona Industrial, Tel: 7-579-1954).

Money

Most financial institutions in Cúcuta are around the main plaza, Parque Santander:

AV Villas—ATM: multi-network ATH. Avenida 5, next to the Catedral.
Bancolombia—American Express traveler's checks; ATM takes MasterCard, Visa, Cirrus, American Express. Avenida 5, 9-80.
Banco de Bogotá—ATM: multi-network ATH. Avenida 6, 10-82.

Additionally, you can find ATMs in just about any nook of the city. Avenida 6 holds a number of casas de cambio. As this service is needed by the masses of Venezuelan shoppers, you can actually find exchange houses all over, as well as at the bus terminal and airport.

Both major international money wiring services have main branches in the downtown area: Western Union/Giros y Finanzas (Monday-Friday 8:30 a.m.-5:30 p.m., Saturday 9 a.m.-3 p.m. Calle 10 3-42, Edificio Suramareicana) and MoneyGram/Cambiamos (Monday-Saturday 8 a.m.-6 p.m. Calle 12, 4-47, Centro Comercial Internacional).

Keeping in Touch

Telecom charges $0.05 per minute for local and national calls, from $0.40 per minute for international calls, and $1.05 per hour for internet (Monday-Saturday 8 a.m.-8 p.m. Calle 10 and Avenida 0). Local / national calls from shops and street stalls are $0.05-0.10 per minute, and to Venezuela

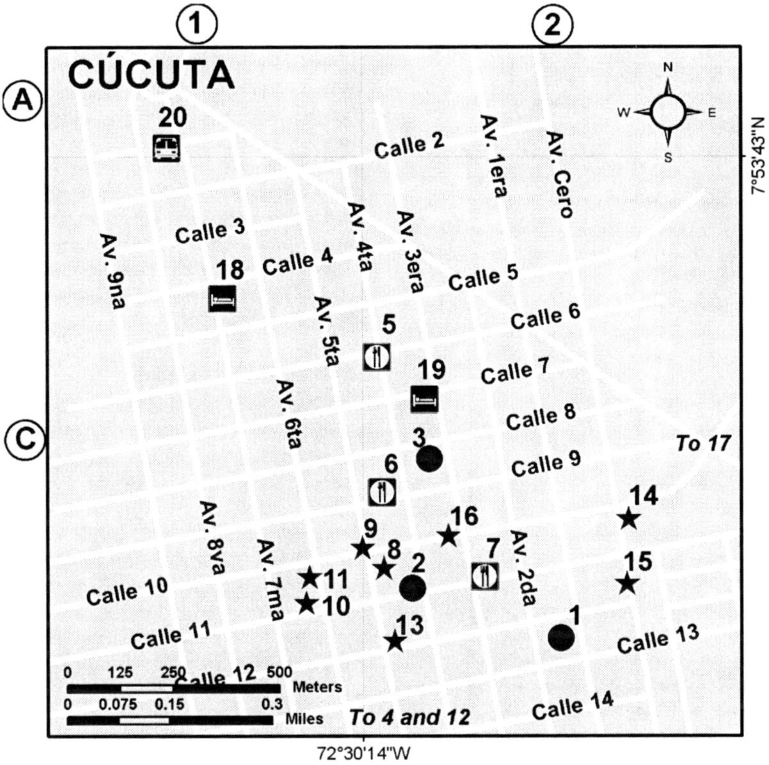

Activities ●
1 Biblioteca Julio Pérez Ferrero B2
2 Catedral San José B2
3 Correos de Colombia Adpostal B2
4 Monumento Cristo Rey C2

Eating
5 El Castillo de Job B2
6 Pastelería La Araña de Oro B2
7 Restaurante Vegetariano Jiarit B2

Services ★
8 AV Villas B2
9 Banco Colombia B1
10 Banco de Bogotá B1
11 Banco Santander B1
12 DAS C2
13 Moneygram B2
14 Telecom B2
15 Tourism Office B2
16 Western Union B2

Sleeping
17 Hotel Bolívar B3
18 Hotel Casa Real Cúcuta B1
19 Hotel Las Pirámides B2

Transportation
20 Bus Terminal A1

$0.20 per minute.
Internet is surprisingly hard to find in Cúcuta. A centrally located shop is in the Centro Comercial Llanomar, to the left of the Catedral.

Correo de Colombia is on the Parque Nacional (Monday-Friday 8 a.m.-noon, 2-6 p.m., Saturday 8 a.m.-noon. Calle 8 and Avendia 3, Edificio Santander.

Medical

Cúcuta's two main hospitals neighbor each other on the east side of the city: Hospital Erasmo Moez (Avenida 11E, 5AN-71, Tel: 7-574-6888) and S.E.S. Francisco de Paula Santander (Avenida 11E, 5AN-1511, Tel: 7-574-1722). Pharmacies are plentiful. A number of them are concentrated on Calle 9, as well as on Avenida 5.

Camera

Your camera needs can be met at any of the several shops along Calle 10, between Avenidas 3 and 6. Updated: Feb 07, 2008.

Things to See and Do

Cúcuta does have some historic buildings of note. The Biblioteca Pública Julio Pérez Ferrero was built in 1786 and served as the city's first hospital; in 2000 it took on its present duty as the public library, providing many children's and cultural activities (Avenida 1, Calle 12). A block away on the other side of Parque is the Torre del Reloj, with the distinction of being the only clock in Colombia that tolls the national anthem each hour. It is now home to the department's Cultural Secretariat, with exhibits and cultural events. Quinta Teresa, designed at the end of the 19th Century by Domingo Díaz, served as an educational institution. It is presently under restoration.

The city's cathedral on Parque Santander is one of almost a dozen Catholic churches you can visit. The Monumento Cristo Rey, executed by Marco León Mariño, affords good views. It is 35 meters (174 feet) high with 82 steps to the top (Avenida 4 and Calle 19).

Along the Río Pamplona are the city's most luxurious hotels and several shopping malls. On the road towards the border is Villa del Rosario, where the Congreso Constituyente met in 1821 to form Gran Colombia (Venezuela, Colombia and Ecuador). Sites of interest here include the Templo Histórico, meeting place of the Congress, and the Casa-Museo General Santander, home of one the Independence leaders and the first vice president of Gran Colombia. Updated: Feb 07, 2008.

Cúcuta Lodging

Cúcuta has the whole gamut of lodging choices from dubious residencies to full-luxury hotels. However, due to the safety issues of the city, it might be more advisable to pass the night in Pamplona, two hours away. For those traveling with their own transportation, it is better to stay away from the city center and its nightmare traffic. Many cheap options are on Avenida 7, near the bus terminal; some are questionable, but those proclaiming ambiente familiar are usually decent enough for the whole family to stay in. Only high-end establishments will have hot water. Updated: Feb 07, 2008.

Hotel Casa Real Cúcuta

(ROOM: $7-16) Just a few blocks from the bus terminal, Hotel Casa Real Cúcuta is one of the few places along Avenida 7 that has that ambiente familiar. It doesn't quite have the shine as in days past, and honestly some of the rooms have become quite shabby (ask to see several before deciding). But it is clean enough for a night's stay. With the children, it can be a bit noisy come evenings, but thankfully Colombian kids have an early bedtime. All rooms have private, cold water bathrooms. You can choose between having a TV or not, or having a fan or air conditioning. Avenida 7, 4-45. Tel: 7-583-1249, Cell: 315-853-9738. Updated: Apr 14, 2008.

Hotel Las Pirámides

ROOM: $11-27) Located between the bus terminal and downtown, Hotel Las Pirámides is a good mid-range choice for the journeyer needing to spend a night in Cúcuta. The modern building proffers well-appointed rooms with private bath (cold water only), double beds, TV and fan or air conditioning (there is one room without TV that costs the same for one or two persons, a good choice for budget travelers). The Pérez family is attentive to its guests. Cash only is accepted. Calle 7, 3-73. Tel: 7-571-9831 / 583-2299. Updated: Apr 14, 2008.

Hotel Bolívar !

(ROOM: $72) A member of the Spanish Celuisma hotel chain, Hotel Bolívar is probably the smartest place you can stay in Cúcuta. It was built with a Mediterranean architecture and it has three swimming pools set within a tropical garden. All 127 tile-floored rooms are very spacious and have air conditioning, satellite TV, a mini-bar, sitting area and internet. Prices include a buffet breakfast. Hotel Bolívar is located in one of the city's most important commercial zones, only 15 minutes from the airport. With its easy access to the road to the border and security, this makes it a good choice for those traveling in their own vehicle. The room price for one and two people is around $72, and you pay $24 for each additional person. Avenida Demetrio Mendoza, Vía San Luis, next to Centro Comercial Bolívar. Tel: 7-576-0764, Fax: 7-576-3349, E-mail: reservas@hotel-bolivar.com, URL: reservas@hotel-bolivar.com. Updated: May 26, 2008.

V!VA Member Review-Hotel Bolívar

Our stay was extended to almost four weeks. We enjoyed the hotel, the staff, and the children especially enjoyed the pool. We highly recommend this hotel. Our only complaint is that laundry services in the hotel are extremely expensive, but we needed clean clothes. We took to washing most of our clothes in the shower and hanging them to dry. 23 May 2008, Alaska, USA.

Cúcuta Restaurants

Although the restaurant scene may not be as diverse when school's not in session and students overrun the city, there are still quality options available. Luckily, some of the restaurants in this college town have college prices. The comida corriente is tasty and cheap, and ready to be washed down with a glass of beer or liquor. Unlike the ample supply of restaurants with lunch specials, cafés with real coffee are more elusive. Searching for a cup of brewed coffee may feel like a scavenger hunt at first, but there are some key spots to refuel. Head downtown to feed your caffeine and pastry needs. If you're into a whole-grain, fresh-fruit breakfast instead of a cup of leaded coffee, several cafés offer delicious, healthy dishes. Many have vegetarian options at good prices, too. Updated: Feb 07, 2008.

Pastelería y Biscochería La Araña de Oro

Soothe your caffeine-deprived nerves at one of the few cafés in the downtown area that serves fresh coffee. Its glass cases display a luscious assortment of cakes and cookies. But for breakfast, something *salado* (savory): a chicken or meat empanada, perhaps, a flaky turnover. Open Monday-Saturday 8 a.m.-7 p.m., Sunday 8 a.m.-noon. Calle 9, 5-20. Tel: 7-571-2651, Updated: Apr 14, 2008.

El Castillo de Job

In the front courtyard of an old castle, beneath the shade of a large tree, doña Claudia grills up fish, chicken and steak for the á la carte entrées ($1.85-2.65). In the small kitchen, the comida corrientes—rice, beans, salad, yucca or potatoes and meat—are dished up ($1.30). All is served with a pint of *agua de panela*. Expect to share one of the nine tables, as this is an extremely popular lunch place. The dining experience, with that subtle *cucuteña* breeze, is a refreshing alternative to hot, stuffy restaurants. Open daily 7 a.m.-2 p.m.; lunch 10:30 a.m.-whenever the food runs out. Corner of Calle 6 and Avenida 4. Updated: Apr 14, 2008.

Restaurante Vegetariano y Tienda Naturalista Jiarit

Does Cúcuta have a surprise for you, vegetarians—over a half-dozen restaurants to feed your needs. Jiarit is one of the choices, serving breakfast and lunch ($2.10). The fruit salad is massive, with a generous sprinkling of granola ($1.85). Also on the menu are soy and oat yogurt, and natural fruit juices. A shop provides baked and other goods. You can also get a massage or steam bath. Open Monday-Friday 7 a.m.-6:30 p.m., Sunday 7 a.m.-4 p.m. A sister restaurant, Salud y Vida, is at Avenida 4, 6-40. Calle 11, 2-81. Tel: 7-571-8629, Cell: 312-853-8620. Updated: Apr 14, 2008.

Málaga

Alt: 1,400m Pop: 15,182 City Code: 7

The *carretera central*, the favored route of truck drivers to Cúcuta, continues north 35 kilometers (21 miles) from Capitanejo to Málaga. The road is paved but has potholes and is subject to landslides. The east side affords views of the cordillera.

Málaga is home to several small universities and to a growing adventure and agro-tourism industry. You can opt to stay in one of the very reasonably priced hotels or in a *granja* (working farm). Surrounded by mountains and *páramo* (tundra plains) carved by waterfalls and caves, the traveler looking for some excitement in practicing spelunking or *torrestismo* (rappelling in waterfalls) will not be amiss in spending a few days here. There are also enjoyable hikes to lagoons and small villages. At the end of the outing, take a refreshing dip in a pool. The surrounding mountains are also home to many *duendes* (elves)—or so legends say.

Departing from Málaga, you have two choices for your north-bound journey: the narrow carretera central, which sharply curves down to Pamplona and then joins the main highway to Cúcuta; or another, partially paved road that proceeds through San Andrés and Guacas before joining the major north-south highway to Bucaramanga. Both highways are prone to landslides and have several military checkpoints. Updated: Jan 15, 2008.

History

Hernán Pérez de Quesada and a small group of Spaniards in search of the *Casa del Sol* (house of the sun), rumored to be made of gold, came across the Valle de los Cercados. They called the valley this because the indigenous Chitareros encircled their *bohíos* (huts) with cane poles. Upon hearing of this discovery, Gonzalo Suárez Rendón, Governor of Tunja and originally from Málaga, Spain, ordered Jerónimo de Aguayo to establish a settlement there. On March 10, 1542, Málaga was founded and named in honor of Suárez Rendón's hometown. In 1549, with the creation of Pamplona, Málaga fell under its jurisdiction. In the present era, paramilitary forces entered Málaga around 2000, causing an exodus of the population. Colombian military entered approximately three years later, securing the town. The people have since returned, once more making it vibrant. Updated: Jan 15, 2008.

When to Go

The rainy season in the Málaga area is from April to May and September to November, with the wettest months being May, October and November. Typically, January, June and December are drier and warmer. The city hosts several universities, which are in session January to June and August to the beginning of December. Updated: Jan 15, 2008.

Holidays and Festivals

Málaga commemorates its patron saint, San Jerónimo, the first week of January. Besides the usual masses and processions, there is a *carrazo* (car float) competition pitting different sectors of population against each other, as well as elections of kings, dog and cattle shows and bull fights.

During the *aguinaldos* (the novena leading up to Christmas), 16-24 December, do not be startled by the sight of masked, Cousin-It-looking creatures prowling the streets, swinging a brightly painted, inflated cow's bladder at anyone who dares to challenge them. Nowadays it's young boys (and even a few girls) carrying on the tradition—but it has much changed. In the past, grown men dressed like this, with much competition among them for the best costume. Money would be collected from would-be wallop victim; those funds were then used to finance the carrazos at the beginning of January.

To finish off the year is the Festival de Carrancios, or the burning of Old Man Year, on 31 December. Updated: Jan 15 ,2008.

Getting To and Away from Málaga

Málaga has no city bus system and local taxis are virtually non-existent. There is no central bus terminal. Major companies include Copetrán, Cotrans and Concorde. Also, shared taxis leave when full from the corner of Carrera 8 and Calle 12, on Parque García Rovira.

From Málaga:

Arrive	Departure	Time	Price
Capitanejo	3 a.m. -11 p.m.	1 hour	$3
Pamplona	4 a.m. -11 p.m.	5 hours	$13
Bucaramanga	4 a.m. -5 p.m.	7 hours	$19
Bogotá	3 a.m. -11 p.m.	9 hours	$24
Cúcuta	4 a.m. -11 p.m.	7 hours	$18

Málaga's airport, Aeropuerto Jerónimo de Aguayo, is one kilometer from town. Región Air is the only carrier, with flights once or twice a week to Bucaramanga ($80, 25 minutes). Updated: Jan 15, 2008.

Safety in Málaga

Málaga, everyone says, is a very safe place to stay and that there's no problem at all at night. Updated: Jan 15, 2008.

Málaga Services

Tourism Office

The Oficina de Información Turística de los Andes, Málaga's tourism office, is in the Casa de la Cultura Simón González Reyes (Monday-Friday 8 a.m.-noon, 2-6 p.m. Corner,

Calle 13 and Carrera 10). Saturdays and vacation times you can find the staff, composed largely of SENA tourism students, at a booth on the main square, dispensing information about not only Málaga, but also Capitanejo and neighboring villages.

Money

The two major banks in town, Bancolombia and Banco Popular, are located across from each other on Calle 12, between Carreras 7 and 8. Their ATMs handle MasterCard, Visa, Cirrus, Plus. An ATH, multi-network ATM is at Carrera 8, 13-38. There is no place to cash traveler's checks, nor any casas de cambio, nor branches of Western Union or MoneyGram.

Keeping in Touch

Telecom provides local and national phone calls for $0.10 per minute and international from $0.25 per minute (Monday-Saturday 8 .am.-noon, 2-7 p.m. Calle 12, between Carreras 6 and 7). Adpostal, the post office, is located in the same building (Monday-Friday 7 a.m.-noon, 2-6 p.m., Saturday 7 a.m.-noon). Internet cafés are a bit scarce in Málaga. All charge $0.80 per hour. None have Skype. The largest one, and with the most reliable service, is in Cafetería y Frutería El Virrey. Monday-Saturday 8:30 a.m.-noon, 2:30-9:30 p.m., Sunday 6-9 p.m. Carrera 8, 12-30, Parque García Rovira.

Medical

Málaga's main medical facility is Hospital Santo Domingo. Calle 16 and Carrera 7, Tel: 7-660-7475 / 660-7494. Around Parque García Rovira are several major-brand pharmacies; others can be found on Carrera 8.

Camera

There are scant camera stores to be found in Málaga. None repairs cameras, and film is limited. Most shops are devoted to taking *cédula* (ID card) photos or processing. Foto Art has some camera accessories and 100 ASA color and black-and-white *rollitos* (film). Carrera 9, between Calles 13 and 12. Some drugstores also carry film. Updated: Jan 15, 2008.

Shopping

Panuchas

You see them for sale all over Colombia, these malagueño sweets. Now you can get them direct from Panucha's main store: candies lemon or mandarin rind, or a *breva* (fig) wrapped around a ball of pure arequipe; *cocadas* (coconut nuggets), *alfajores* (a delicate cookie sandwich filled with arequipe and edged with coconut) or sugar-coated gummies in a variety of fruit and other flavors (even celery!) What's a *panucha*? Arequipe whipped with coconut to a soft delectable bit of heaven. There are even jars of homemade *arequipe* (soft caramel) and jams. If you can't quite make up your mind, choose a sample of goodies. Carrera 9, 13-64. Tel: 7-660-7080, URL: www.panuchas.com. Updated: Feb 15, 2008.

Mundo Artesanal Titis

Mundo Artesanal Titis is a ma-pa-son operation crafting a variety of useful goods right in their own home. Doña Mariela (ma) will show you around the shop. She makes the small ceramic cups and saucers, candlesticks and candles. Her menfolk create the small

Photo by Lorraine Caputo

wooden boxes. The family also mixes essential oils and incenses. The necklaces and earrings are by a young man in this same village and the fique-cotton sandals by a woman in a nearby settlement. Carrera 9, 13-35. Cell: 312-359-9497. Updated: Feb 15, 2008.

Artesanía Colombia

Artesanía Colombia is another family workshop, this one concentrating on making wooden household items: boxes, napkin holders, toilet paper dispensers and whatnot. It also carries artesanía from other parts of the country, like those fiber sandals and hats from Soatá, a village near Capitanejo. There's even pottery from Ráquira and ceramic chiva buses from the Tunja area. If the doors are closed, just give a knock—the family lives behind the shop. Carrera 9, 13-56. Tel: 7-661-7600. Updated: Feb 06, 2008.

Things to See and Do

Málaga and its region have plenty for all. There are numerous lagoons, páramo, waterfalls and caves. Adventure sportspeople can delve into the depths of Cueva de Calichal, practice torrentismo at Cascadas de Miranda, or rock climb Peñas del Cabío and Colorada, near Enciso. Several of the interesting small villages have *balnearios*, or swimming spas. Concepción is well-known for woollen textiles; Cerritos for its wind-swept páramo. Tequia ruins and Miranda make an enjoyable day hike, and there are indigenous cemeteries between the two. While in Málaga, go bowling, whether U.S. 10-pin in town or three-pin *bolo criollo* on the outskirts. Updated: Jan 15, 2008.

A Quick Bolo Primer

Every where in Colombia, along country roads and in the hearts of cities, you'll see signs announcing *bolo*, or bowling. There are two types of this very popular sport. *Bolo criollo* is what you will see most of the time at the outskirts of towns. At the end of an open-air, 18-meter (59-foot)-long court is a backboard, in front of which are three pins in a vertical line. A 300 to 500 gram (11- to 18-ounce) aluminum ball is tossed to a backboard, to knockdown the pins. This game has indigenous origins and is strictly for men. *Bolo americano*, or *boliche*, is good old 10-pin bowling as you find in the U.S. and elsewhere. Colombian woman are said to be quite good *bolicheras*, or bowlers. Updated: Feb 06, 2008.

Cueva de Calichal

Spelunkers, get ready for a bit of exploration. Cueva de Calichal—Calichal Cave—is awaiting you. The first chamber is easily accessed by anyone. Just slip through that fissure in the rocks. But if you really want to see the stalagmite and stalactite bowels of this piece of earth, get your ropes and clamps out. It takes a bit more expertise and devotion to get into those depths. While you're out this way at Vereda Calichal, enjoy the waterfall and the pool at its base, called the Cascada y Pozo Borbollón. Four kilometers from Málaga, follow the Cúcuta road to La Palma, from where a stone road leads to the road going to the electric plant. Take a left and soon you'll see the cave. For a more scenic route, before the bridge outside town, follow the *camino herradura* (stone road) that goes behind the monastery. Updated: Feb 06, 2008.

Bolo Americano

Ever wonder what ever happened to all those bowling alleys once the sport lost favor in the United States? Well, it appears everything was shipped to Colombia, lanes, shoes and balls. (The pinsetters, though, not—they're human, so watch for him to get on the rafters before you fire your ball down to those ten pins.) Bring back your childhood days; bowling in this country is affordable: $0.95 *per línea* (that is, per game, per person). You don't have to worry about anything—the balls are there (though few over 12 pounds) and shoes are rented (large sizes available; $0.25). Open up a brewski and join the friendly gang at Club Málaga Real for a round on its six lanes. Women are welcomed. In the front room and upstairs are billiards, also—but this sport is frowned upon for women. Club Málaga Real Carrera 8, 10-33. Tel: 7-660-5787. Updated: Feb 06, 2008.

Adexpegar

Adexpegar—Asociación para la Promoción y Práctica de los Deportes Extremos y de Aventura del Nororiente Colombian—is a new company formed by SENA students. The only tour operator in Málaga, Adexpegar specializes in adventure sports: rappelling, *torrentismo* (rappelling in waterfalls; $3.20, all equipment provided), *canotaje* (rafting) on the Río Chicamocha (from Málaga $18.65; from Capitanejo, on the river, $10.50). They also provide other adventures—but only for those aged 14 to 50. Excursions are guaranteed on weekends; during the week, only when groups of 10 or more are interested. Hours (either location): Monday-Friday 8 a.m.-noon, 2-6 p.m. Carrera 8, 12-05, Magallanes, piso 2; also Calle 13, 6A-66, Centro Comercial Santander, Local 4. Cell: 311-442-7028. Updated: Jan 15, 2008.

Málaga Lodging

Málaga has a very pleasant surprise awaiting its visitors: not only a variety of types of hotels, but also all of them with good prices.

Even the town's best options in the zona rosa, are comfortable in all aspects, from amenities to rates. Eco- and agro-tourism are beginning to get a foot-hold in the surrounding countryside, offering visitors alternatives to the standard hostel. Updated: Jan 15, 2008.

Hotel-Restaurante El Viajero

(BED: $3) The Hotel-Restaurante El Viajero is one of the two very inexpensive, very basic hotels right on Málaga's main square, Parque García Rovira. It is only $2.65 per person. All rooms are dark, with no windows, with thin walls separating them, and share the common, cold-water baths. But the rooms are spacious and clean. Calle 13, 8-56. Tel: 7-660-7416. Updated: Feb 15, 2008.

Granja Agroecoturística Los Guaduales

(ROOM: $5-9) Get out into the country to a self-sustaining farm. Located 11 kilometers (7 miles) from Málaga on the road to Capitanejo, Granja Agroecoturística Los Guaduales offers its visitors lodging in a hotel-like house, or camping, and food straight from the fields. To relax, there's a swimming pool, fishing, video bar and hiking trails. You can even roll up your sleeves and get your hands dirty helping out. If you want to get a bit more of a rush, the folks at the farm can take you rafting on the Chicamocha River or rappelling on four nearby waterfalls (torrentismo). Vereda El Espinal, San José de Miranda. Cell: 311-210-0540 / 314-316-4786, E-mail: granja.losguaduales@hotmail.com, URL: www.senaturistico.blogspot.com. Updated: Feb 06, 2008.

Hotel Santander

(ROOM: $8-16) Hotel Santander is a bargain, just a half-block from Parque García Rovira, in Málaga's zona rosa. The modern rooms are clean and good-sized. All have cable TV and private baths with gas-heated hot showers. To top it off, the friendly family serves you free coffee and orange juice in the morning. If there's anything you need, just pick up the phone in your room and they will attend you. Carrera 8, 13-42. Tel: 7-660-7121, Cell: 311-217-2210, Fax: 7-661-7586. Updated: Feb 15, 2008.

MÁLAGA RESTAURANTS

Restaurants in Málaga fall into two general categories: fast food and *comida criolla* (home-cooking). The only international cuisine choices are attempts at pizza. Come evenings, it is difficult to get a comida corriente; most dining establishments serve it only for lunch ($1.85-3.20). Vegetarians, you'll find eating a bit trying here, but you can pick up fixings at local supermarkets (Venus is right on the plaza), the innumerable bakeries and at one of the shops featuring local dairy products. The daily *mercado municipal* swells on market days, Wednesday and Saturday. Calle 14 and Carrera 7.

Málaga has a quaint zona rosa located just off the main plaza, along Carrera 8. Here you will find bars and discos—and yes, even karaoke. However, most are open only on the weekends. Oh, by the way, all those cafeterias and *fuentes de soda* you see around town aren't quite exactly coffee and soft drink joints. They are where most locals go to nurse a beer (or something stronger) while catching up on the news. Updated: Jan 15, 2008.

La Esperanza—Restaurante Típica

La Esperanza brings a hungry traveler's stomach the best in typical Santandereano food. Try the freshest meats from local farms: trout, other fishes and other seafood ($8-18.50), chicken ($4.75-7.40) and meats, including goat ($5.80-9.25). There are even sampler platters, if you don't quite know what to order ($8-9.25). Main dishes come with salad, yucca, potatoes and dessert. La Esperanza also serves breakfast ($2.10-3.20) and luncheon specials ($3.20-4.75). On the drink list is not only the usual alcoholic and non-alcoholic drinks, but also Colombian wine. Open Monday-Saturday 7 a.m.-9 p.m., Sunday 9 a.m.-3 p.m., holidays 7 a.m.-3 p.m. Carrera 8, 13-56. Tel: 7-660-8457, E-mail: restaurantelaesperanza@hotmail.com. Updated: Feb 15, 2008.

Restaurante y Cafetería Las Delicias

Down an alley alongside the market is Restaurante y Cafetería Las Delicias. At the noon hours, this place is packed with workers and families sitting down to a typical, home cooked comida corriente of soup, main dish with meat, beans, rice and drink ($1.85). Don't be shy about sharing a table with a perfect stranger—in fact, it'll be the only choice you have. Las Delicias also serves breakfast. Open daily 7 a.m.-2 p.m. Carrera 6A between Calles 12 and 13. Updated: Feb 15, 2008.

Pizza y Lasagna

This restaurant announces on its banner that it also has Mexican food like burritos and tacos. But most days your only choice will be pizza (Hawaiian or chicken and mushroom, $1.50 per slice) or lasagna ($3.70). The only vegetarian option is special-ordered pizza, but you'll have to pay for the whole thing ($10.60). Pizza y Lasagna does its own spin on the classic fast food: cheesy, flaky-crust pizza. No beer or juices are on the drink menu—just sodas. Despite the limited menu, this small, four-table establishment is popular with all *malagueños*, whether teens or families, out for a quick bite in the evening. Open Wednesday-Monday from 5 p.m. on Carrera 9, 11-53. Updated: Feb 15, 2008.

Málaga Nightlife

Bar Karaoke Fuego Verde

Attention, attention: Tonight's off-key singing to music videos is being preempted by the Nacional-La Equidad soccer game on the big-screen TV. Indeed, sometimes some things are much more important that karaoke and Fuego Verde recognizes that. And at some special times of the year, like Mother's Day, it'll even bring in a mariachi band to play. But most nights you can join the gang here for a few drinks and get crazy pretending you're Shakira, Ricky Martin or Vicente Fernández. Just look for the Tigo sign on the street. As soon as you step into the doorway, you'll see the bar's placard at the foot of the staircase. There's no cover or minimum consumption. Open daily 7:30 p.m.-3 a.m. Carrera 8, 13-14. Updated: Feb 06, 2008.

Jirafas Bar

For a laid-back vibe, head to Jirafas bar. If you're into a bit of dancing, hop on the dance floor and groove to salsa, vallenato and the like. Unfortunately, this is like most clubs in Málaga, open only on weekends. It's up on the second floor of a building in the heart of the city's zona rosa. Open Friday and Saturday, 7 p.m.-3 a.m. Address: Carrera 8, 13-29. Updated: Feb 15, 2008.

San José de Miranda and Tequia

Alt: 1,980m Pop: 5,450 City Code: 7

Tequia was founded in 1539, but due to lack of water and being only two kilometers from Málaga, Padre Isidro Miranda moved the town four kilometers further on to the Valle de Cutaligua. A few still live in Tequia, caretaking the ruins of the old parish church and the fresh-water swimming pools (even one for children). Hiking up a side road into the mountains, you can visit two ancient indigenous cemeteries, one at Vereda de Yerbabuena (preserved in situ at Señor Luis Jesús Gómez' house) and the other at Vereda de Lucusguta. A rough dirt road to the left of the church ruins will take you past farms and brick kilns down to the main "highway" again and into San José de Miranda. A faux-High-Gothic church sits on the main plaza like a pastel-iced cake. Follow Carrera 4 out of town. To the right after about 500 meters (300 feet) is Balneario Rosales, another spring-fed pool with a eucalyptus-fired sauna. About seven kilometers (four miles) down the left of Carrera 4, heading towards Bogotá, is Termales de Salado Bravo at Las Cuevas, undeveloped natural hot spring pools. Miranda celebrates its patron saint, Nuestra Señora de los Remedios, in February and the Fiesta de la Gallina (hen feast) in June. There are basic restaurants and an inn in Miranda. The Balneario de Tequia has a refreshment stand.

The balnearios are guaranteed to be open Friday-Sunday and Monday holidays, though they are often open during the week, also. Entries: Balneario de Tequia—$0.80 adults, $0.50 children. Balneario Rosales—pool, $1.05; sauna, 1 hour $2.65, 2 hours $5.50. Termales de Salado Bravo—free.

A taxi to Tequia costs $2.65 one way; colectivo taxi to Miranda is $0.65. Or walk to Tequia, the road begins from Calle 1 and Carrera 6C in Málaga. Updated: May 20, 2008.

Concepción

Alt: 2,005 m Pop: 7,000 City Code: 7

Concepción is a weaving center not too far from Málaga. Here, small workshops create blankets, jackets, ponchos and other items from virgin wool—a perfect place to pick up some warm clothing before heading to Parque Nacional Natural El Cocuy. This village is considered the heart of Colombian textiles, hosting the National Wool Fair every December. The home of Salón Wilches, a late-19th-Century liberal politician, is preserved. If you want to take a soak, choose between the fresh-water pools at Balneario Natural de la Quebrada Manaria or the warmer ones of Balneario Natural de Aguas Calientes. You can also visit the indigenous community, Samoré. Collective taxis leave when full from the corner of Carrera 8 and Calle 13; $5.30. Updated: May 20, 2008.

CAPITANEJO

Alt: 1,172m Pop: 7,800 City Code: 7

A paved highway traverses about 170 kilometers (102 miles) from Tunja, up into the eastern Cordillera, to Capitanejo. This is the Bogotá-Cúcuta route preferred by trucks and many bus companies, as opposed to the trajectory by way of Bucaramanga. It is shorter and has no tollbooths. On the southern limit of Capitanejo is the turn-off for the Sierra Nevada de El Cocuy and its hamlets.

Capitanejo is on the Río Chicamocha and serves as an alternative point to raft through that river gorge. The village enjoys a hot, dry climate, perfect for warming up after trekking in Parque Nacional Natural El Cocuy. The highway forms the main street, Carrera 4. One block west is Plazoleta Municipal Pedro Antonio Ruiz Prada, the main square whose name is as big as the plaza itself, in which most of Capitanejo's population could probably fit. Around this is the church, Palacio Municipal, bank, two nightclubs and a hotel. In the center is a large ceibo tree, which stands over a hidden lagoon and whose origin, according to legend, is lost in the mists of time. At a 1997 proposal to chop it down, the people rose to protect it. Decorating the plazoleta is a mosaic depicting the products for which Capitanejo is known: tobacco and goat. Indeed, this is the goat, tobacco and melon capital of Colombia. Goats make their appearance on the comida corriente menu and all-dolled-up for the patron saint processions in August. Updated: Jan 16, 2008.

HISTORY

The indigenous peoples who lived in the Capitanejo region were the Lacha. The Spaniards called them Chitareros, as their hair was cut to the mould of the gourd used for preparing *chicha* (alcohol made from fermented grains, corn or fruit). In 1541, Gerónimo de Aguayos, who had founded Málaga, and 70 other whites arrived in this area. Two years later, don Juan Rodríguez Parra received these lands along the Río Chicamocha and enslaved the Lacha. It wouldn't be until the following century, in 1630, that Capitán Cristóbal Verde de Aguilar would give Capitanejo its present name. At the turn of the 21st Century, paramilitary forces occupied the village; inhabitants recount the massacres and massive exodus that occurred. The Colombian military moved into Capitanejo in 2003, thus securing it. *Capitanejanos* have since been returning. Updated: Jan 16, 2008.

Photo by Lorraine Caputo

When to Go

The driest months in Capitanejo are December, January, June and July. The rainiest are April and May. The hottest months, with temperatures in the upper 30°s Celsius (upper 90s-lower 100°s Fahrenheit), are January and February. January is also the best month for *canotaje*, or whitewater rafting. Updated: Jan 16, 2008.

Holidays and Festivals

The New Year starts off with the Festival del Río, a time to hit the beaches along the Chicamocha River and to raft down its canyon. In July is the Fiesta de la Virgen del Carmen, patron of all taxi, bus and truck drivers. Goats dressed in earrings and skirts parade through the town as part of the commemorations to San Bartolomé, Capitanejo's patron saint. Honor is paid to those Capra denizens with the Festival del Cabrito, the third week of December. The year closes with the Fiestas del Retorno y Matachines, which include the aguinaldo novena leading up to Christmas, young boys dressed in costumes whacking challengers with inflated

EASTERN COLOMBIA

cows' bladders and the burning of Old Man Year. Updated: Jan 16, 2008.

Getting To and Away from Capitanejo

Capitanejo has no central bus terminal. Most of the transport company offices are on Carrera 4. All departures times are approximate, as the buses are passing through. Many companies only offer trips every other day, so be sure to check schedules carefully.

Here are various bus companies and their addresses: Coflonorte / Libertadores: Carrera 4, 5-32. Concorde: Carrera 4, 4-19. Copetrán: Calle 5, 4-84. Cotrans: Carrera 4, 4-12. Expreso Paz del Río / Gacela: Carrera 4, 4-39.

Arrive	Departure	Time	Price
El Cocuy	2 a.m., 3 a.m., 2 p.m., 3:30 p.m.	4 hours	$5
Bogotá (via Tunja)	3 a.m. - 10 p.m.	7 - 8 hours	$16 -19
Bucaramanga	3 a.m., 4:30 a.m., 10 a.m.	7 hours	$20
Yopal (Casanare)	1 a.m.	7 hours	$17
Cúcuta (via Pamplona)	3 a.m -10:30 p.m.	7 hours	$19
Güicán	2 a.m., 3 a.m., 2 p.m., 3:30 p.m.	4 hours	$6

Updated: Jan 16, 2008.

Safety in Capitanejo

Everyone assures the visitor that the town and surrounding countryside are perfectly safe now from the presence of guerrilla and paramilitary forces. There is a fortified Policia Nacional station in the village, and motorcycle patrols secure the highway. Cases of dengue have been reported in Capitanejo. Updated: Jan 16, 2008.

Capitanejo Services

Tourism Office

The tourism office is in the Palacio Municipal. Monday-Friday 8 a.m.-noon. Calle 5, between Carrera 5 and 6, Plazoleta Municipal.

Money

Banco Agrario has a branch in Capitanejo; however, it has no ATM or other services for the traveler (Calle 4, between Carreras 5 and 6, Plazoleta Municipal). Capitanejo has no casa de cambio, so come with plenty of pesos.

Keeping in Touch

Telecom is not only the sole international call center, it is also one of two internet "cafés" in Capitanejo ($1.05 per hour) (Carrera 3 4-18). The other place to hop on the web is at the public library, Biblioteca Pública Juan de J. Wilches (Calle 3, between Carrera 3 and 2). Several shops along the main street, Carrera 4, offer local and national calls. Skype is non-existent here.

For mailing letters or receiving general delivery, Adpostal is in an unsigned building next to the Palacio Municipal (Monday-Friday 8 a.m.-noon, 1-5 p.m., except when the señora pops out to run an errand. Calle 5, 5-28).

Medical

Capitanejo's public health facility is Hospital San Bartolomé (Carrera 4, vía Bogotá, at the entrance to town, Tel: 7-660-0015). Several pharmacies are on the same carrera in town.

Camera

Estudio Godoy is the only photo store in town. However, its sole raison d'etre is taking photographs. It carries no camera supplies. Updated: Jan 16, 2008.

Things to See and Do

Capitanejo may seem just a scorching town straddling a highway, but it does hide a few cool spots beneath that dust. For the traveler interested in religious attractions, there is the village church, San Bartolomé, the Centro de Peregrinación El Carmen and the Santuario del Sagrado Corazón, with great views over the river valley. Down near the Puente La Palmera spanning the Río Chicamocha, are beaches where you can take a free dip. For a more structured swim, go to one of the balnearios. Hike out to La Chorrera waterfall, raft down the Chicamocha, drop your line in at the Hacienda La Alejandría for some trout, or rock climb El Tablón and Las Juntas. There's a bit of everything in Capitanejo. Updated: Jan 16, 2008.

Balnearios

To beat the heat in Capitanejo, head for one of the balnearios, or swimming holes. There's one for every budget. Brisas del Chicamocha has a large pool with a slide for adults, a shallow pool for children, dressing rooms, shaded seating around the pools and a restaurant. This is the balneario closest to town. (Daily 9 a.m.-6 p.m. Carrera 4, via Málaga, just past Restaurante La Pola. Entry: $1.05 adults, $0.80 children under 8). Avilmar is near the banks of the Río Chicamocha, one kilometer from the village (motorcycle taxi from Calle 4 and Carrera 4, $0.50). Considered a more upscale balneario, it has not only a separate pool for the kiddies, but also a playground. Its facilities include sauna and restaurant. (Daily 9 a.m.-6 p.m. Carrera 4, via Bogotá. Entry: $1.60 adults, $1.05 children 12 and under). On the banks of the river itself is Playas de Chicamocha. Conditions for swimming here depend on the river's strength. Seek local counsel before taking a dip here (Entry: Free). Up in the mountains, near La Chorrera waterfall, is yet another option, at Hacienda Loma Linda. Updated: Feb 06, 2008.

Whitewater Rafting

Rushing down from the Sierra Nevada del Cocuy, the Servitá and Chicamocha Rivers merge at Capitanejo, their waters swirling and foaming, leaping through a canyon on their way to join the Río Magdalena. Rafting on these rapids is more well-known as an activity in the San Gil-Bucaramanga region. However, you can also do it here. Capitanejo is becoming more and more popular as an alternative launching point for pursuing this river. However, all depends on conditions—the snowmelt from the Sierra Nevada might make the river too low or ragingly strong. January is the most certain month but be sure to check with tour operators in Capitanejo or Málaga about taking you on such an expedition. Updated: Feb 06, 2008.

La Chorrera

Toppling 60 meters (197 feet) down a rock face is La Chorrera waterfall. A motorcycle taxi can take you as far as the Chorrera school ($5.30) if you don't want to walk the approximately 10 kilometers (6 miles) from town. Still, it's a one-hour hike further into the mountains to see these waters cascading down towards the Río Nevado, eventually mixing with those of the Río Chicamocha. To cool off after this trek, plunge into the pool at Balneario Hacienda Loma Linda. Updated: Feb 06, 2008.

Acolture

Acolture—Asociación Coldinista de Turismo y Recreación—is a project of the local SENA program. Primarily this tour operation is focused on taking groups of 20 or more rafting on the Chicamocha or to visit local attractions like La Chorrera waterfall. However, Professor Miriam Deysi can help line up a guide if you are only one or two travelers, price to be negotiated. The office can also provide information on hotels, restaurants and other tourist services in the village. Hours: Monday-Friday 8 a.m.-noon, 2-6 p.m., Saturday 8 a.m.-noon. Carrera 3, between Calles 3 and 4. Tel: 7-660-0098, Cell: 311-513-9450, E-mail: deysymcapi18@hotmail.com. Updated: Jan 16, 2008.

Capitanejo Lodging

Hotels in Capitanejo are all pretty basic, with only fans to cool your room and cold water showers (though with the heat in Capitanejo, this is barely a hardship). All have the typical, tropical Latin American construction. Ventilation is provided through latticed concrete blocks which are unscreened, as are the windows. This, needless to say, allows mosquitoes to come in search of the exotic visitor. Reservations are highly recommended for holiday times. Updated: Jan 16, 2008.

Hotel Cordobés

(ROOM: $4-11) A basic hostel run by the amiable older couple, Luis and Irene, with clean rooms that are simply furnished—beds, large table, nightstand—but suitable for your Capitanejo stay. All the rooms are around the back patio, just off the kitchen. Don Luis and doña Irene are always ready to invite you to sit down and chat over a *tinto* (coffee) in the morning, or to watch an evening telenovela with them. Hotel Cordobés is a long-time favorite among budget travelers deciding to experience Capitanejo hospitality for a day or two. Calle 4, 3-58. Tel: 7-660-

0403, Cell: 311-842-6220 / 313-205-2035. Updated: Feb 22, 2008.

Hotel Oasis

(ROOM: $5-16) Three generations of women have been housing visitors since 1953 at the Hotel Oasis. It is one of the few hotels in Capitanejo that has a dual price list: one for the *temporada baja*, low season, and another for the *temporada alta*, high season. All the large, simply dressed rooms have windows and private bath with water *al tiempo*, or room temperature. The tank is on the roof, so the day's climate will influence the temperature. Those rooms upstairs have TV and fan. Calle 5 and Carrera 5, Plazoleta Municipal. Tel: 7-660-0036. Updated: Feb 06, 2008.

Hotel Colonial

(ROOM: $8-15) Located a half-block from the Plazoleta Municipal on a quiet street, Hotel Colonial provides its guests with comfortable, clean rooms. Beds are super-fresh, not being made up until you arrive. All upstairs rooms have windows, mostly over the street, private cold-water bath, TV and fan. Meals are available in the restaurant upon request. Carrera 5, 3-20. Tel: 7-660-0230. Updated: Feb 22, 2008.

Capitanejo Restaurants

The menu is quite limited in Capitanejo: the comida corriente is primarily *cabro* (goat) and sometimes *gallina criolla* (range-raised hen), and is significantly more expensive than in other parts of Colombia. Having said that, the *cabro con pitoria* (rice made with goat's blood and finely chopped innards) is less than a third the price here than in restaurants elsewhere featuring it as a plato típico. So, if you want to try this traditional Santandereano dish, wait until you come here. However, take care. Not all of the eating establishments prepare their drinks with boiled or otherwise treated water. The weekly market is on Sunday.

Asadero Rokoko

If you get tired of the cabro lunches and can't quite afford a meal of range-raised hen, then pop across the street to Asadero Rokoko. Here, a quarter of roasted chicken costs $1.85. Dip the accompanying yucca and potatoes in the delicious, fresh, homemade chili sauce. The cooler has just about every kind of soft drink on the market in Colombia. Plastic disposable mitts are provided to keep your picking fingers clean. (Which means, unfortunately, you can't lick 'em clean—and this is finger-lickin' good chicken!) Open daily 9 a.m.-10 p.m. Carrera 4, 4-53. Tel: 7-660-0019, Cell: 311-215-9105. Updated: Feb 06, 2008.

Restaurante La Piragua

Restaurante La Piragua offers excellent, home-cooked meals that go on cloven hoof, wing and—occasionally—fin. The Santandereano classic dish, cabro, is served up traditional-style: *pipitoria* (rice with goat innards and blood), yucca and potatoes ($2.65-3.70). Gallina criolla, or range-fed chicken, is also on the menu ($3.70), as well as trout in season ($6.65). This eatery is tremendously popular with locals and folks passing through town, so go early to catch a lunch table. Restaurant La Piragua also fixes eggs and *caldo de papa* (potato soup) for breakfast. Open daily 6 a.m.-6 p.m. Carrera 4, 4-36. Tel: 7-660-0040. Updated: Feb 06, 2008.

Restaurante Chef

Another comedor that gets crowded at lunch time, Restaurante Chef serves Capitanejo's typical comida corrientes, or blue-plate specials: cabro (large order $3.70, small order $2.65) and gallina criolla ($3.70 small serving, $6.65 large). Yes, the menu is limited, but this is your chance to try goat at a very reasonable price. A medium-sized dining establishment, Restaurante Chef is open daily 11:15 a.m.-5 p.m. Carrera 4, between Calle 4 and 5. Tel: 7-660-0042. Updated: Feb 06, 2008.

Capitanejo Nightlife

During the week, if you want to have a beer, hang out at one of the two pool halls in town (men only—Colombian culture frowns on women in such establishments) or a cafetería. Some of the *estaderos* (adult drinking clubs) may be open. The only disco and only real bar operate just on weekends Friday, Saturday and Sunday—to close out the market day). Updated: Jan 16, 2008.

La Rumba

Outside the front door, doña Agustina sits on a stool welcoming tonight's imbibers and dancers. She charges no entry nor requires a minimum consumption in her corner discothèque of several dimly lit rooms. Her staff will put on anything the customers request, whether it be salsa, merengue, ranchero, vallenato or americano. It's a healthy place, she proudly proclaims, you take a table and no-one else will bother you if you don't want, not even if you're a woman alone. She'll even reserve one for you. Open Friday-Sunday and Monday holidays 7 p.m.-1 a.m. Calle 5, 5-70 (corner of Carrera 5), Plazoleta Municipal. Updated: Feb 06, 2008.

Pubs Blue Bar

Soft light bathes the dark blue walls of Pubs Blue Bar. No, this drinking hole doesn't specialize in Blues music. You're more likely to hear vallenato, salsa, merengue and the like at a volume too loud for this small space. Early in the evening there are only a few couples in dark corners holding hands, their beers beading in the day's waning heat. Later this pub will be full of sweating bodies throbbing to that music—after all, locals say this is the better dance hall. No admission is charged, nor is there a *consumo mínimo*, save that you must have at least one drink. Open Friday-Sunday 7 p.m.-3 a.m. Calle 4, between Carreras 5 and 6, next to Banco Agrario, Plazoleta Municipal. Updated: Feb 22, 2008.

Parque Nacional Natural El Cocuy

This national park is officially called Parque Nacional Natural de Sierra Nevada del Cocuy, Chita y Güicán, but most people just call it Parque Nacional Natural El Cocuy.

Its 306,000 hectares are located in Boyacá, Arauca and Casanare Departments. On this western side of the range, the park boundary is etched at the 4,000-meter (13,120-foot) line. The Sierra Nevada has 21 peaks, several over 5,000 meters (16,400 feet). Ritacu'wa (Ritacuba) Blanco is the highest, at 5,330 meters (17,483 feet). This region is delicate páramo and has been heavily impacted by farming populations. The park service is working with these communities in restoration of the ecosystem and in the development of sustainable alternatives, like eco-tourism. This area abounds with opportunities for trekking and climbing enthusiasts, and for those who just want a feel of the snow. The snowline is, at closest, only a three-hour hike away. This part of the park is divided into three general access points: Las Lagunillas or Alto de la Cueva; La Capilla or La Esperanza; and Rutaku'was (Ritacubas).

At the east side of PNN El Cocuy plunges to its lowest point, 600 meters (1,968 feet) in the Colombian llanos. Climbing the sheer rock here is only for experts. Because of the remoteness of the region and its dense vegetation, it has been less impacted by the human hand. The northern sector of PNN El Cocuy is part of indigenous U'wa territory. This area is the best preserved, in large part due to the U'wa's respect for nature. However, their culture and lands are endangered due to the presence of possible petroleum fields.

Fauna species found in PNN El Cocuy include the spectacled bear, puma, chinchilla, mountain tapir, white-tailed deer and dozens of bird species, among them the condor and the *águila real* (golden eagle). Flora is equally diverse, owing to the many ecosystems embraced by the park: *frailejón*, cardoon cactus, and *sietecueros* trees, numerous varieties of mosses and lichens, and *cojines*.

The Park contains the largest expanse of glacier fields in northern South America but they are quickly receding due to global warming. Scientists estimate that at the present rate of melting, the snow pack will disappear in 15 to 20 years. The Sierra Nevada del Cocuy is the birthplace of rivers flowing both to the Río Magdalena and the Orinoco.

For more information on PNN El Cocuy, visit: http://parquesnacionales.gov.coor / www.elcocuy.info/sierra_nevada.htm. Updated: Jul 02, 2008.

History

The history of PNN El Cocuy begins in the Cretaceous period, when this was a vast inland sea. Then, some 15 to 20 million years ago, the land began to rend, mountains uplifted, slowly growing into the Pliocene and Quaternary epochs. An ice field that formed that throughout this new eastern Cordillera extended from Laguna de Tota, across the Santander páramo to Norte de Santander Department. In recent centuries, those glaciers have been receding, more rapidly now with global warming.

Parque Nacional Natural El Cocuy, Colombia's fifth largest national park, was established in 1977. During the mid-1980s, the entire region (including the park and villages) was occupied by FARC and ELN guerrillas. In 2003 the Colombian military closed in and began clearing out the insurgents from the area. By 2005 all on the western side of the Sierra Nevada del Cocuy was secure. Updated: Jul 02, 2008.

When to Go

Weather wise, the best months to go into PNN El Cocuy are December to February when it is drier. June and July are also not too bad. The worst months are April, May, August and September when it rains.

Needless to say, these clearer nights are also the coldest, with temperatures dipping below freezing (it's even more frigid deeper within the park). As well, this is a popular destination for vacationing bogotanos, especially in early January. Updated: Jul 02, 2008.

Getting To and Away from PNN El Cocuy

From Bogotá and Tunja two routes are possible: one through Duitama, Soatá, La Uvita, Guacamayas and Panqueaba; the other through Capitanejo and on to Cordoncillo. The road at Cordoncillo divides, going right to El Cocuy village and left to Güicán. Both of these towns serve as entries into PNN El Cocuy and have national park offices where you obtain your permit.

From the north you can arrive from Cucarmanga, Pamplona or Cúcuta, by way of Málaga and Capitanejo, to El Espino and the Cordoncillo crossroads. A web of rough roads run in the area immediately adjacent to the national park, leading to hacienda and guide lodges. You can transit this in your own or a hired vehicle or in the lechero. Express services arranged with the lodges cost $26.50-42 per vehicle. The daily *lechero* (milk truck) leaves El Cocuy at 6 a.m. and Güicán at about 5:30 a.m. ($1.05 for Colombians, $2.65 for foreigners, regardless of distance). The distance from El Cocuy village to Guaicany is 25 kilometers (15 miles); Guaicany to La Capilla (health post, phone, store), 6 kilometers (3.6 miles); La Capilla to Kanwara turn-off, 7.1 kilometers (4.25 miles); Kanwara turn-off to Güicán, 13.6 kilometers (8.2 miles). From Kanwara is a dirt track leading down into the llanos. Updated: Jul 02, 2008.

Permits

Before entering PNN El Cocuy you must obtain your permit from the park office in El Cocuy village or Güicán. You will be asked on which day you plan to enter and on which you plan to leave. You can be flexible on the first, but not the second. If you do not return by that date and report to a park office, search and rescue operations will begin. You can, theoretically, extend the date before expiration, but communications are difficult (including cell phones). You will also be asked which areas you will be going to.

To go into the northern sectors of the park, you need to apply to the U'wa nation (office in Bogotá), as this is part of its territory. Granting of this permission is not guaranteed.
Entry to PNN El Cocuy is prohibited for those under 12 years or over 60 years, pregnant women, and persons with cardiovascular or pulmonary problems.

The permit is $2.10 for national students (including university, with ID), $4.20 for Colombians and $12.10 for foreigners. Updated: Jul 02, 2008.

Safety in PNN El Cocuy

Since the military takeover of the region in 2003, Parque Nacional Natural El Cocuy and surrounding villages are now considered safe. Trekkers report seeing army units patrolling the park interior. However, the plains side of the park, going down into the Arauca and Casanare Departments, is still within the *zona caliente*, (hot zone) of the country's civil war. Additionally, much of this area is dense virgin growth and unmapped. People have disappeared.

Military patrols may ask for your identification. A park official in El Cocuy said a notarized photocopy of your passport could be used in lieu of the original document.

Consider the altitude you are at. The lodges of the park are just below 4,000 meters (13,120 feet), and the park itself is at 4,000 meters or more. If traveling from Bogotá, you will gain significant altitude in a very short time. Do not push yourself to begin any hiking or trekking immediately after arriving. Properly acclimatize. High mountain sickness and pulmonary edema are serious threats, the latter resulting in at least one death per year. Also take precautions for hypothermia, snow blindness, dehydration and sunburn. Use 30+ factor sun screen and UV-protector sun glasses. Temperatures can drop dramatically, and snow or sleet storms can start with a moment's notice. Have thermal clothing and rain gear at all times. Use sturdy boots. If you bring a cellular phone, Comcel is recommended and you should turn it off and on every four hours to avoid signal problems. It can be difficult to receive cell phone signal in the park itself or the neighboring lodges.

As always, be sure to seek local advice about conditions, of both the environmental and political climates. Updated: Jul 02, 2008.

Medical and Rescue

At La Capilla, about midway on the park road, is a basic *puesto de salud*, or health post. Hospitals exist in the two main villages, with the better being in Güicán. The nearest airport for emergency medical evacuation is in Málaga.

If a person does not return by the end of his/her permit time, the national park service contacts the Cruz Roja to begin search and rescue operations. The Red Cross then coordinates its team (some of whom have had high-mountain rescue training), local farmers and military to look for the missing visitor. Don't expect any helicopter rescue if you run into problems. Updated: Jul 02, 2008.

Things to See and Do

If mountaineering and appreciating rare, natural beauty is your cup of tea, then you better start planning now to climb Sierra Nevada del Cocuy. Pico Iyer listed the mountain range with 18 snow-covered peaks as one of the "20 Places to See Before They Die" in the May 2007 issue of Condé Nast magazine—a study in 2005 gave some of the glaciers in the mountain range only 25 years 'til they melt away. This is an especially precarious dilemma since Iyer says that many of the locals in the area depend on the glaciers for a fresh supply of water.

Mountaineering, hiking and trekking in Sierra Nevada del Cocuy is considered one of the top activities in all of Colombia. If you are looking for companies to take you trekking, check out Sierra Nevada del Cocuy at www.sierranevadadelcocuy.com or Climbing, Skiing and Trekking Holidays in the Andes at www.andes.org.uk. These companies will give you time to acclimatize, especially before bringing you on the snow climb up to the highest peak, Ritacuba Blanco at 5,410 meters (17,749 feet). The treks all happen in the sunny season, December to March, but you'll still get to trek on glaciers and use an ice-pick.

You should probably only attempt this kind of climb if you have done something similar and simpler before, though the trekking companies should be able to adapt the trek based on your skills and needs. Updated: Jul 02, 2008.

Trekking

Another prime activity in PNN El Cocuy is trekking across its plains. A series of old trails traverse the wind-swept landscape rimed with snow-covered mountains. The solitude makes it a wonderful experience. A highlight is the Valle de Cojines, an area of huge pillows of *Plantago rigido* carpeting the earth. One–day treks include those to Las Lagunillas, Cueva de Cuchumba and the snow line of Ritaku'wa Blanco. The longest excursion is the Vuelta a las Sierras, or the Sierra Circuit, which can be combined with mountain climbing. A half-circuit can be done around the north sierra, returning through Ratoncito Valley (three days). Treks can also be done to Laguna Verde, Laguna de las Lajas, Laguna Grande de Pachacual or Laguna Grande de la Sierra. Updated: Jul 02, 2008.

Because all the trekking is at over 4,000 meters (13,120 feet) altitude, it is important to acclimatize first upon arriving to the park. Passes are at 4200-4900 meters (13,776 -16,072 feet). The weather can change quite suddenly, with sleet and snow storms. Read the Safety section for more information. You can obtain topographical maps with passes and campsites marked from the national park office in El Cocuy or from the Instituto Geográfico Agustín Codazzi in Bogotá.

If you are properly equipped and have substantial experience at high altitude and alpine/polar trekking, you can do the circuits on your own. A guide, though, is recommended. Pack horses can be hired at many of the lodges.

Vuelta a las Sierras / The Sierra Circuit

The most challenging of the treks in PNN El Cocuy is around the base of the Sierra Nevada del Cocuy, which is 22 kilometers (13.2 miles) by approximately five kilometers (3 miles). The excursion takes five to 10 days.

A medical doctor with over ten years experience trekking in Cocuy suggests this demanding five- to six-day circuit: Day 1—Through Las Lagunillas district, over Cusirí (4400 m / 14,432 ft) and Patio Bolos passes to Laguna La Plaza campsite. Day 2—To Laguna del Pañuela, over Paso Balcones (4400 m/14,432 ft). Day 3—To Laguna del Rincón, over Paso de El Castillo (4600 m/15,088 ft). If you are up to making it a very long day, you can continue to Valle de los Cojines and Laguna El Avellanal, crossing the 4600-meter (15,088-foot) Paso de la Sierra. Day 4—Over the mountain passes De los Frailes (4200 m / 13,776 ft) and de Cardenillo (4100 m / 13,448 ft) to Laguna de los Verdes. Day 5—To Kabañas Kanwara. Each day you will be hiking eight to nine hours. Updated: Jul 02, 2008.

Cueva de Cuchumba

Not too far from Hacienda La Esperanza, along the Quebrada El Cóncavo, is Cueva de Cuchumba. This cave with a waterfall within was once an important ceremonial center for the U'wa. It was here that they kept the image of a woman on cloth that a tall white man with a long white beard, dressed in white, had given them many generations earlier. They kept a fire of wax and *failejón* illuminating it. In 1736, Padre Miguel Blasco was catechizing to the U'wa and gifted them with a small painting of Our Lady of the Rosary. The U'wa responded, "We already have one, much more beautiful and splendorous." The priest had the U'wa textile moved to the church in Güicán, where you can see it today. The magical cave with its cascade bathing the stone walls is still there, though, near the Quebrada El Concavo.

From Hacienda La Esperanza, the walk takes about 10 minutes; from Cabañas Guaicany, one hour. A path from Güicán also goes to the Cueva. Updated: Jul 02, 2008.

Las Lagunillas

An easy one-day hike road trip is to Las Lagunillas. The road is well defined along the Río Lagunillas, a small stream flowing across the plain, sculpting the ancient, rock-strewn earth into mounds and forming small crystalline lagoons across the valley. After about 45 minutes you'll arrive to the first of the magical lagoons strung together, Laguna La Pintada, backdropped by Campanilla Negra. The trail climbs through a small pass, on to three more lagoons: La Cuadrada, La Atravesada and La Parada. The road begins at Alto de la Cueva, one kilometer (0.6 miles) from Cabañas Guaicany. One way, the trek is nine kilometers (5.4 miles). Updated: Jul 02, 2008.

Rock Climbing

For those who get their adrenaline rush hugging the faces of cliffs, feeling for the next hand hold, PNN El Cocuy has some special treats. Perhaps the most popular is El Púlpito del Diablo, a 5,100-meter (16,728-foot), two-pitch challenge of not only rock, but also ice. Other places to climb include Portales (5,100-meter / 16,728 feet, three pitches) and Morrenas, rising amid glaciers. The most death-defying escarpments lie on the west face of the Sierra Nevada del Cocuy, going down into the eastern plains. On this side of the range are vertical climbs of over 700 meters (2,300 feet), only for the most experienced rock climbers. The views over the llanos are said to be breathtaking.

A guide is necessary. Contact an operator in El Cocuy, Güicán or elsewhere. Basic experience is needed; skill levels are from easy to very difficult. Unfortunately, the prime area for rock climbing lies in the red zone of the country's civil war, an area in which activities cannot be recommended at this time. Updated: Jul 02, 2008.

Mountain Climbing

One of the biggest draws to PNN El Cocuy is the mountain climbing. The Sierra Nevada del Cocuy is considered to be one of the most beautiful ranges in the country and the lack of tourists makes for an un-crowded, quiet adventure. These peaks were first summited by a Swiss team in 1928. Colombians preparing for Himalayan and Southern Andes expeditions train here. The almost sheer, vertical rises provide challenges for even the most experienced mountaineer.

The Sierra Nevada has 21-plus peaks over 4,900 meters (16,072 feet). Some of the mountains to conquer are Ritaku'wa Blanco (5,330 m / 17,482 ft), Ritaku'wa Negro (5300 m / 17,384 ft), San Pablín Norte (5,200 m / 17,056 ft), El Concavo (5,200 m / 17,056 ft), and El Castillo (5,030 m / 16,500 ft). El

Puntiaguado (5,200 m / 17,056 ft) is a curious formation of a stone cube crowned by a stone spire. Plan on four to five days for your expedition. The mountains have many crevasses. Rope, ice axe and crampons are essential equipment (these will most likely be supplied by your guide). Guides in El Cocuy have excursions for those with no experience, as well as a mountain climbing school. Contact an operator in El Cocuy, Güicán or elsewhere. Updated: Jul 02, 2008.

Fishing

Don't forget to pack your rod and reel when coming to Parque Nacional Natural El Cocuy. You can whip loose your fly and take a hand at the trout swimming in the icy depths of Laguna Grande de Pachacual, Laguna de la Parada, or in the rivers slicing the plains. To fish in the lagoons, you must have a permit (obtainable from the national park office in El Cocuy village). To cast a line into the rivers, no special permission is needed. Also, some of the lodges at the edge of the park have stocked ponds. Updated: Jul 02, 2008.

PNN El Cocuy Tours

Guides and horses are available at all of the lodges at the edge of the national park. The park office in El Cocuy village maintains a list of the current prices of each. Depending on the destination, horse rental costs $10.50-26.50 per day and guide services $8-32 per day. Cabañas Guaicany is the most expensive. Prices are set among the guide lodges. Park rules establish that a guide (*guía*) is needed for each group of six persons and that a guía may only work seven hours per day. El Cocuy and Güicán have tour operators that can make all arrangements for you.

PNN El Cocuy Lodging

Cabaña-style hotels are concentrated in three areas of the park: Alto de la Cueva (Las Lagunillas), where Cabañas Guaicany and the inns of the Herrera (Miguel and Alejandro) brothers are; La Esperanza (La Capilla); and Ritaku'was, featuring Kabañas Kanwara, Cabañas Peñas Blancas and Posada Sierra Nevada. The majority do not have heat or chimneys. Many have camp sites. Make reservations December-January and June-July.

Camping is also possible within the park at several official campsites: El Hotelito, Laguna de la Plaza, Laguna Grande de la Sierra, Laguna de Panuelo, Laguna de los Verdes and other places. A tent with a good rain-fly and a -10°C (12°F) sleeping bag with insulation sleep pad are essential.

Cabaña Gaicany

(BED: $3-11) In a three-story, A-frame chalet, Juan Carlos Carreño and his family provide simple rooms with bunk beds for up to 35 guests. On the third floor are two rooms, each with a double bed. Up there is also a sitting area for everyone's pleasure with a view onto the snowy peaks. No rooms are heated. There are no private bathrooms. The one shower has an electric heater that barely takes the icy edge off the water. A new dining room and living room with fireplace are presently under construction. The Carreño family rents camping and climbing equipment. They hire guides and horses to all the major attractions in the southern and central range. Alto de la Cueva (Las Lagunillas) sector. Tel:1-563-5405 (Bogotá), Cell: 310-566-7554, E-mail: cab_guaicany@yahoo.es / guaicany@hotmail.com. Updated: Jul 02, 2008.

Hacienda La Esperanza

(BED: $5.30) After being abandoned for a spell, Hacienda La Esperanza has undergone renovation at the loving hand of Marco Artura Valderrama, once more giving shelter to weary explorers. Its highly polished floors gleam. The thick earthen walls of this 200-year-old farmhouse keep the three, multi-bed guest rooms toasty warm. The beds come with several wool blankets. The new bathrooms spout hot water showers. Off the central courtyard is a kitchen where you can order meals and a sitting room with fireplace. Hacienda La Esperanza provides guides and horses to Laguna Grande de la Sierra (horse $13.15 per day, guide $16 per day) and other points. The lechero will drop you off at La Capilla, from where it is two kilometers (1.2 miles) to Hacienda La Esperanza. Tel:1-263-8712 (Bogotá), Cell: 310-334-0218 / 310-200-4214, E-mail: haciendalaesperanza@gmail.com. Updated: Jul 02, 2008.

Cabañas Kanwara

(BED: $18) Kabañas Kanwara is probably the most luxurious inn in the park district. The three cabañas have five rooms each (one to three beds each, plus table) and hot water shower. Their balconies have a fine view of the Ritaku'was and the cordillera. Two of the lodges have kitchenettes, but no stove (use your camper). You can even warm up your feet in front of the fireplace before crawling into your blanket-laden bed. The restaurant serves excellent food ($3.70 per meal). Horses and guides are available for treks to Ritacu'wa Blanco ($13.15 and $16 per day respectively) and Laguna de los Verdes ($16 and $18.65 per day respectively), as well as to Laguna San Pablín, Púlpito del Diablo and Laguna Grande de la Sierra. Mountain climbing expeditions can also be arranged. Kabañas Kanwara's shop sells weavings by the U'wa and Hormiguitas de la Sierra weaving cooperative in Güicán. From the Kanwara turn-off to Kabañas Kanwara is 4.8 kilometers (3 miles). The rough road is steep, climbing 340 meters (550 feet). You can phone the lodge to meet you at the crossroads where the milk truck will drop you off ($2.60 charge). Cell: 311-231-6004 / 237-2260 / 316-835-4683, E-mail: infokanwara@gmail.com. Updated: Jul 02, 2008.

PNN El Cocuy Restaurants

All lodges within PNN El Cocuy serve meals, usually of the high-starch variety. Campers pitching their tents at such establishments may be able to use the kitchen, depending on the inn's policies. Otherwise bring along a camp stove.

If backcountry camping, purchase all necessary food and fuel supplies in the nearest villages before coming out to El Cocuy National Park. You may be able to buy some items from locals, but don't bank on it—and very few people live on the eastern side of the range. White gas is scarce in all of Colombia. You can stock up on it in Bogotá or Bucaramanga. Else bring a stove that uses multi-fuel or canisters. *Gasolina roja* (car petrol) is available at the gas stations in El Cocuy village and Güicán.

El Cocuy

Alt: 2,750m Pop: 7,610 City Code: 8

The road from Cordoncillo to El Cocuy is unpaved. This colonial town with white and sea-green buildings is the most touristy of the two entries into the Parque Nacional Natural El Cocuy, with better hotel, shopping and nightclub infrastructure. In the main plaza is a diorama of the entire Sierra Nevada del Cocuy mountain range. Otherwise, there isn't much to see or do in El Cocuy village itself. The daily milk truck, into the park begins its route here. Updated: Jun 29, 2008.

History

El Cocuy was the fourth Spanish town founded in Nuevo Reino de Granada, in 1541 by Captain Gonzalo García Zorro. Before the conquistadors arrived, indigenous Cacique Cocuy ruled the region. Once the Spaniards arrived, they used El Cocuy as a base for explorations for El Dorado in the llanos region. The indigenous were relocated to the warmer, lower regions to work as slaves on farms. El Cocuy was officially declared a residence for Spanish and mestizos in 1720.

In recent decades, El Cocuy and the surrounding region has been affected by Colombia's civil war. Native sons of El Cocuy include José Santos Gutiérrez, president from 1868-1870, engineer Olimpo Gallo Espinel, who discovered the iron mines at Paz del Río, and painter Roberto Arango. Updated: Jun 30, 2008.

When to Go

December and January are the best months to come to El Cocuy; nights are colder but the weather is dryer. The wettest months are April, May, August and September. Christmas season and New Year's Eve draw the most tourists to El Cocuy, so make reservations during these times. Updated: Jun 30, 2008.

Holidays and Festivals

El Cocuy is a typical village with its share of dates important to its people. A few festivals worth checking out are:

Month	Event
March-April	**Semana Santa**—The processions of the devout are quite a display of religious vigor, with extreme fasting and flagellation.
June	**Corpus Christi**—Cocuyanos decorate their Parque Principal with arcades of the region's fruits and a mini zoo.

Month	Event
July	**16: The feast of Virgen del Carmen**
December	**7-12: Nuestro Señor de las Misericordias** – El Cocuy honors its patron saint with an animal fair, artisan exhibits, bull fight- and much more.

Updated: Jun 30, 2008.

Getting To and Away From El Cocuy

All transportation to the village of El Cocuy arrives and departs from Carrera 5 along the Parque Principal. All the bus companies have their offices on this block. Buses only leave for Güicán and other small nearby villages and for Bogotá. To go north to Málaga, Bucaramanga, Pamplona or Cúcuta, go first to Capitanejo with a Bogotá-bound bus. Main bus companies include Gacela/Libertadores and Concorde.

From El Cocuy:

Arrive	Departure	Price
Capitanejo	4 - 5 a.m., 6 - 7 p.m.	$6
Bogotá (via Soatá)	5:30 p.m., 4 a.m., 5 a.m.	$20

The post office, El Correo, which runs between El Cocuy and Güicán, is operated by Cootradatil. It leaves once daily El Cocuy at 4 p.m. The fare is $1.30. Updated: Jun 30, 2008.

Safety in El Cocuy

There are armed government forces in El Cocuy village to maintain safety. Assassin bugs (which carry Chagas disease) and non-lethal scorpions are found in this area. Updated: Jun 30, 2008.

El Cocuy Services

Tourism Office

The national park office is the first place to visit upon arriving in El Cocuy. Not only can the friendly staff help to orientate you on the park's attractions, but they can also supply you with information on transportation, hotels and restaurants in El Cocuy and Güicán villages, and the current prices of lodging, meals, horse rental and guide services of inns located at the edge of the park. (Monday-Saturday 8 a.m.-noon, 2-5 p.m., Sunday 8 a.m.-noon. Corner of Carrera 5 and Calle 8, Tel.: 8-789-0359, E-mail: pnncocuphp@yahoo.com / pnncocuy@hotmail.com, URL: parquesnacionales.gov.co). The village's official website is www.elcocuyboyaca.com.

Money

Banco Agrario is the only money institution in El Cocuy. It has no ATM or other exchange services (Calle 8, between Carrera 3 and 4). Obtain plenty of pesos before coming to the region. Tunja and Málaga are the nearest cities with facilities.

Keeping in Touch

The Telecom office in El Cocuy village is closed indefinitely. Local shops charge $0.15 per minute for local and national calls. The lone internet café in El Cocuy has a slow connection costing $1.05 per hour (Monday-Saturday afternoons. Calle 7, 3-60).

If the internet fails you, send your loved ones a postcard through Adpostal (Monday-Friday 8 a.m.-noon, 2-5 p.m., Saturday 8 a.m.-noon. Carrera 3, 7-55).

Medical

Hospital San José (Tel.: 8-789-0011) and the Cruz Roja (8-789-0042) are at the entrance to El Cocuy village on Calle 11 and Carrera 6. The hamlet has few pharmacies: one at Calle 7, between Carreras 5 and 6 on the plaza.

Camera

Galería Cocuyana, the only camera shop in the PNN El Cocuy area, is in El Cocuy village and is owned by photographer Pío Avedaño. He keeps black and white, slide and 100ASA color film in stock, and has cameras for sale. You can also purchase calendars, posters and key chains with his graphic work. Sometimes the gallery may be closed, when Señor Avedaño is out in the field (daily 8 a.m.-7 p.m. Calle 5, 4-20, Tel: 8-789-0167, Cell: 311-513-9214). Updated: Jun 30, 2008.

Shopping

Artesanías de Mi Colombia

Artesanías de Mi Colombia specializes in crafts lovingly made in workshops all over

Boyacá Department. Pick up a ruana woven in Güicán or El Espino, other woollens from El Cocuy village, or some colorful baskets from Guacamayas. The shop also has a fine selection of fique bags made by the U'wa, cornhusk dolls from Tunja and pottery from Ráquira. Artesanías de Mi Colombia also sells postcards and posters of the national park. Carrera 3, between Calles 7 and 8. Tel: 8-789 0377, Cell: 310 494 5076 / 312 352 9121. Updated: Jun 30, 2008.

Tejidos Katly

Tejidos Katly sells a good selection of ruanas, the short wool ponchos that just about everyone wears in El Cocuy. To pick one up before venturing into the cold hinterlands of PNN El Cocuy, head to this shop. All Tejidos Katly's ruanas are made of natural-colored virgin wool and prices start at $10. Tejidos Katly sells plenty more to keep you warm, including jackets, ski masks, gloves and socks. Margarita Correño will be happy to take a break from her knitting to help you suit up. If the shop isn't open, ring up Doña Margarita. Carrera 5, 6-29. Cell: 311-474-0270. Updated: Jun 30, 2008.

Chirros y Gorras

Chirros y Gorras is your one-stop shopping for hats from every cranny of Colombia, including native and non-native styles, such as ball caps and pith hats. There's a wide variety of materials to choose from, including felt, leather and paja straw, which is used to make the classic, two-tone *sombrero* typical of Colombia. The prices aren't too bad, either, from $7 up. After dropping by Chirros y Gorras you'll find yourself fitting right in with the townsfolk, since hats are a favorite accessory. Carrera 5, 5-78. Updated: Jun 30, 2008.

Things to See and Do

The village of El Cocuy doesn't have many attractions of its own. It has no museums, no hot springs and no cultural centers. It seems to be willing to play a supporting role to the national park and its glories, in providing good services to the tourist preparing for trekking and mountain climbing. One activity, though, is paragliding from Maohama, a high bluff outside of this hamlet. Updated: Jun 29, 2008.

Paragliding in El Cocuy

To the west of El Cocuy village a dark cliff looms out of the greened landscape. This peak is called Maohama. It is easiest spot to access in PNN El Cocuy for practicing paragliding. Any time of the year is good for leaping off its heights and soaring like a condor over the crumpled earth of this corner of Colombia. The best month, though, is July when El Cocuy hosts a parapentismo festival. Contact the national park office or Coopserguías in El Cocuy to arrange an excursion with guide. Take note that a guide is mandatory for this type of excursion. Updated: Jun 30, 2008.

El Cocuy Tours

Coopserguías

Coopserguías is a cooperative of locals residing within Parque Nacional Natural El Cocuy. The down-to-earth souls of Coopserguías know the region like the back of their grizzled hands, and now are pooling together their resources and decades of knowledge to provide services to Cocuy explorers. They offer lodging, horses, equipment for rent and guides for treks and mountain climbing. Coopserguías works in cooperation with the national park service. The sign over the door says Oficina Ecoturismo—AENCO (Asociación Ecoturístico Nevado El Cocuy). The office has irregular hours, so it is best to call or e-mail. Calle 7 and Carrera 6, Parque Principal. Cell: 313 293 8313 / 311 880 0875, E-mail: coopserguias@hotmail.com, URL: www.coopserguias.com / www.colombiatrek.com. Updated: Jun 30, 2008.

Rodrigo Arias

For many years Rodrigo Arias has been exploring the Sierra Nevada del Cocuy, as well as mountain ranges from California to Patagonia. Hostels in many parts of Colombia often recommend his services to those wanting to experience the grandeur of Cocuy National Park. Arias offers all-inclusive packages for one person or small groups for day hikes, the eight-day circuit trek around the base of the sierra, scaling Ritaku'wa or the other mountains and climbing El Pulpito. He also teaches courses in mountaineering, rock climbing and rescue, and can arrange special excursions. Rodrigo Arias is now working in conjunction with Coopserguías, a cooperative in PNN El Cocuy. Cell: 313 293 8313, E-mail: arias_rodrigo@hotmail.com, URL: www.colombiatrek.com. Updated: Jun 30, 2008.

El Cocuy Lodging

El Cocuy village has a growing number of hotels. All are good value and even the budget places have hot water. The options are often in the hamlet's oldest structures, in various states of repair, with only common bathrooms located off the back patio (not within the main building). Newer hostels, aimed at travelers with more refined tastes, are still surprisingly affordable. Make reservations for the high seasons, especially the months of December, January, June and July. Updated: Jun 29, 2008.

Hotel Restaurante Casa Vieja

(ROOM: $4) Hotel Restaurante Casa Vieja is a bit of a misnomer, since it no longer has a restaurant. However, internationally renowned local artist Roberto Arango still opens the doors of his worn colonial home to the weary traveler, offering large rooms in various states of repair around the main courtyard. The courtyard makes up for what the sparsely furnished rooms lack. The garden is full of more varieties of geraniums than you thought existed and the portico is a gallery of Arango's Cocuy landscape paintings. The renovated hot water baths are at the back of the house. Carrera 6, between Calles 7 and 8, Parque Principal. Updated: Jul 01, 2008.

Hotel Villa Real

(ROOM: $6-11) An appealing, family-run inn, Hotel Villa Real is a comfortable place to stay in El Cocuy—both in price and in ambience. The rooms—all on the upper stories—are finely decorated and come in a variety of sizes (one to six beds) depending on your traveling group. The rooms share the clean common baths with hot showers. A sole quarter has its own bathroom. After your park excursion your rest is assured lying back on these good mattresses to zone out with the TV. Downstairs you can conveniently have your meals or grab a drink at the family's store. Calle 7, 4-50. Tel: 8-789-0038, Cell: 311-475-6495 / 311-810-2808, E-mail: hotelvillareal@hotmail.com. Updated: Jul 01, 2008.

Hotel Casa Muñoz

(ROOM: $11) The newest hotel in El Cocuy, Casa Muñoz has sharp rooms in a new annex of a colonial-era house. Each room, named after one of the mountains in the national park, has cable TV and baths with gas-heated hot water. Upstairs rooms have lofts with more mattresses, which are sure to be a hit with the kids. This inn has only one room with a single bed; the others are multi-bed. A restaurant will soon be a part of Casa Muñoz' services. Carrera 5, 7-28, Parque Principal. Tel: 8-789 0328 / 789 0028, Cell: 313 829 1073 / 332 1980, E-mail: hotelcasamunoz@yahoo.com / hotelcasamunoz@hotmail.com. Updated: Jul 01, 2008.

Cocuy Restaurants

Eating options in the village of El Cocuy are fairly slim. Some of the hotels have or plan to have restaurants. In the evenings, stands set up around the central park selling cheese *arepas* and other fast food. The market is at Carrera 5 and Calle 5. It and the dining section are active weekend mornings, with the principal market day being Friday. The village has several stores where you can purchase canned goods before heading into the national park.

A traditional dish served only at Christmas and New Years is *tamales*. These are much different than the Tolimense ones served in most of Colombia. Here, cornmeal mush is filled with pork, beef, chicken and pork skin (all marinated in herbs, spices and beer), garbanzos, onion and carrot. The tamale is steamed in a *hoja de raíz*, also called *bijao* (Calathea lutea).

Cafetería y Comidas Rápidas Donde Lilia

Cafetería y Comidas Rápidas Donde Lilia is the place to go for a late breakfast or a quick mid-morning snack. This small, no-frills snack stand serves a basic menu of empanadas and *rellenos*, a black sausage filled with potato and rice ($0.50-1). To wash it down, there are coffee and soft drinks. Open Monday-Saturday 9 a.m.-noon, closed Sunday. Calle 7, between Carreras 4 and 5. Updated: Jul 01, 2008.

Asadero Nortibrasas

Asadero Nortibrasas is a good choice for a break from the hotel-restaurant scene and their typical Colombian fare. In the front room, a large rotisserie rotates chickens over coals. Ask for your plate of roasted chicken and potatoes: a quarter-chicken costs $1.60, half is $3.20 and the whole bird is $6.40. If you want more of a traditional meal, order the grilled chicken breast or fish with rice, potatoes, plantains and salad ($3.70). Open daily 10 a.m.-8 p.m. Carrera 5, between Calles 8 and 9. Updated: Jul 01, 2008.

Restaurant Hotel Villa Real

Steam rising from the pots bathes doña Marta's face as she dishes up another bowl of soup. Her family is out in the five-table dining rooms, bustling from one customer to another. The main dish comes next with meat, rice and veggies. With a drink made from bottled water, this lunch (or dinner) costs $2.10. Mornings, doña Marta also serves *caldo de papa* (potato soup) or eggs to order with hot chocolate for $1.30. This is one of El Cocuy's most popular restaurants. Open daily 7 a.m.-8 p.m., although you may ask for earlier or later service. Calle 7, 4-50. Tel: 8-789-0038, Cell: 311-475-6495 / 311-810-2808, E-mail: hotelvillareal@hotmail.com. Updated: Jul 01, 2008.

NIGHTLIFE

The village of El Cocuy has few places for letting off steam and partying down. The only real disco is just open on Fridays, after the weekly market closes. However, there are other places where you can kick back and have a drink. Better still, save up the energy you would otherwise blow on rumbeando, for the treks and climbing you'll be doing in PNN El Cocuy. Updated: Jun 29, 2008.

Disco T-K

Join the locals in closing out a Friday market day at Disco T-K Fogata, the town's only discoteca. It's time to celebrate that done deal, to cut loose after long hours stooped over the stall and calling out your wares. Everyone keeps warm during the chilly nights dancing to the salsa, merengue, reggaetón, electrónica, vallenato or whatever else the crowd requests. There's no cover charge or minimum consumption. Open Friday only, 7 p.m.-2 a.m. Carrera 5, between Calles 7 and 8, Parque Principal. Updated: Jul 01, 2008.

Café-Bar Escocés

Café-Bar Escocés is a newly-opened intimate meeting place on the corner of the plaza in El Cocuy. Low rainbow lights play across the paintings of hometown legend Roberto Arango. The drink menu has cocuyano favorites such as *canelazo*, aguardiente and beer, plus wine for the international customers. Coffee, teas and sodas are also available. If the music inside gets loud, just pull up one of the benches out front and join in on a jawing session with the locals. Open daily 4 p.m.-midnight. Carrera 6 and Calle 8, next to Hotel-Restaurante Casa Vieja. Updated: Jul 01, 2008.

GÜICAN

Alt: 2,928m Pop: 9,644 City Code: 8

From Cordoncillo, a paved road goes to Güicán, which has a more wild-west feel to it than its neighbor El Cocuy. Perhaps Güicán's distinctive atmosphere is because it is the younger of the two main villages, not only in founding date, but also because it was rebuilt after an 1860 fire. Perhaps the difference lies in a closer relationship with the U'wa.

From the heights of El Peñol de los Muertos just outside the village, much of the nation jumped to their deaths upon arrival of the Spaniards. The modern-day U'wa territory is not too far from Güicán as the condor flies, and at times you can see them in town. Shops around the plaza sell bags and other artesanía created by them. Even though it is the larger village, it has a much more limited selection of hotels and restaurants. Oddly enough, however, it is richer in attractions. Updated: Jun 30, 2008.

HISTORY

This sliver of mountain valley was inhabited by U'wa (Güicanes). When their cacique Güaicaní heard the dreaded Spanish were approaching, he lead his people in jumping from El Peñol de los Muertos to escape a life of slavery and disease at the hands of the invaders. The Jesuits subsequently established Güicán on February 26, 1756. Some of the natives fled into the mountains and formed a resistance movement against the Spanish rule. A fire destroyed the village in 1860. After independence, Güicán became a hub of agricultural trade between the highlands and the eastern plains. At the vespers of the 21st Century, Güicán found itself in the heated center of the country's civil war and was occupied by the various forces. In 2003, the Colombian military began a clean-up operation of the entire region, and by 2005 the village was once more securely in the government's hands. Updated: Jun 30, 2008.

When to Go

As in other parts of the region, the best time to come to Güicán is when the weather is clear and dry, from December to February. This is also when nights are coldest and the number of national tourists blossoms. June and July are other good months to visit. The worst months are during the rainy season: April, May, August and September. Updated: Jun 30, 2008.

Holidays and Festivals
Güicán's patron saint is the Virgen Morenita whose feast day is February 2 (Candelaria), during which faithful make a romería, or pilgrimage to the Virgin. On this night the traditional Danza de la Clizneja, similar to the maypole dance, is performed. For the next half-week, from February 3 to 6, the town celebrates its *Fiestas Reales* with processions, horse races, a gastronomic fair and other activities. Updated: Jun 30, 2008.

Getting To and Away from Güicán

Buses leave only for El Cocuy and other small nearby villages, and direct for Bogotá. To journey north to Málaga, Bucaramanga, Pamplona or Cúcuta, go first to Capitanejo with a Bogotá-bound bus. In Güicán all bus offices are around the town's square. Coflonorte / Libertadores and Gacela / Paz del Río are both on Calle 3, and Concorde at Calle 4 and Carrera 4. The Bogotá bus charges the same fare from Güicán as from El Cocuy. They arrive in this village one hour later from the capital and depart one hour earlier. See El Cocuy for full information.

El Correo, the mail run, is operated by Cootradatil. It leaves three times per day from Güicán to El Cocuy at 7 a.m., 11 a.m., and 2 p.m. ($1.30).

To travel along the park access road, you can either arrange an Expreso service with a lodge ($26.50-42 per vehicle) or catch the daily lechero, leaving Güicán at 5:30 a.m. ($1.05 for Colombians, $2.65 for foreigners regardless of distance). Updated: Jun 30, 2008.

Safety in Güicán

The village and surrounding countryside is generally safe due to the national police and military patrols, though few people go out after 10 p.m. Scorpions (non-lethal) and assassin bugs are present in Güicán. Updated: Jun 30, 2008.

Things to See and Do

Even though Güicán has considerably less tourist infrastructure than El Cocuy village, it does have several attractions nearby: Peñol de los Muertos, where U'wa jumped to their deaths upon the arrival of the Spaniards; an incredible monument honoring that indigenous nation; petroglyphs, or rock paintings; and several hot spring pools. An alternative path to Cueva de Cuchumba, near Hacienda La Esperanza within the national park, can be hiked from Güicán. It begins at the end of Carrera 4, at Calle 1. Ask for directions frequently for La Capilla, as the road is not signposted. Updated: Jun 30, 2008.

Aguas Termales

After all the trekking in Parque Nacional Natural El Cocuy, your muscles may need a bit of relaxation. Near Güicán are Aguas Termales which will be just the trick for you—and help warm you after the frigid temperatures of the park. In an old farm are two pools. The smaller, shallower one is warmer. If the Aguas Termales happen to be closed, you're not out of luck. About five meters (20 feet) before the hacienda, on the right side of the dirt road, is El Chorrerón, a small cascade of hot water falling into a natural rock pool. Walk along the highway towards Cordoncillo or take the *camino deshecho*. Also, transport from Güicán heading to El Cocuy town or Soatá passes by the turn-off for the hot springs ($0.50). The Aguas Termales are open in the low season only Saturday and Sunday 8 a.m.-6 p.m.; in the high season they are open daily 8 a.m.-6 p.m. You can enjoy El Chorrerón daily from dawn to dusk. 4 kilometers (2.4 miles) from Güicán. Updated: Jun 30, 2008.

The Camino Deshecho and Petrographs

An alternative route down to the hot springs is what the locals call the Camino Deshecho (the unmade road). And that is precisely what this trail is: an old stone road, dating from who knows when, beaten by centuries of foot and hoof-trod. It is a pleasant walk downhill through the forest, past the very occasional house tucked behind giant boulders. Keep an eye out, as you can see reminders of the indigenous ancestors along the way. *Pinturas repestres* (rock paintings) decorate the stone outcroppings. The highway is narrow with blind curves and has no shoulders. Beware of approaching vehicular traffic. Updated: Jun 30, 2008.

Monumento a la Dignidad de la Raza U'wa

On the road out of Güicán is a monument facing north towards the indigenous nation it honors. This is Monumento a la Dignidad de la Raza U'wa (monument to the dignity of the U'wa race), created in 2007 by Delfín Ibáñez Carrero. It captures one of the most important events in U'wa history: the mass suicide at El Peñol de los Muertos. From the towering arms of Mother Earth tattooed with petrographs leap bodies of men, women and children. A condor takes flight, indigenous faces peering through its feathers. Engraved on its base is a U'wa proverb for us to remember: "God sleeps in the rocks, breathes in the plants, dreams in the animals, whispers in the waters and awakens in man."Carrera 5 direction Cordoncillo. Walk down Carrera 5 to the edge of town. The monument is on a roundabout island. Updated: Jun 30, 2008.

Peñol de los Muertos

And it occurred that men with faces of greed
Overthrew and erased our villages
Imposing their way of life by force.
Liberty is a gift that is born with life,
It justifies its existence.
Without it, Mother Earth reclaims us.
And to her breast we return conscious
We have fought for life, the race, for our presence.

—U'wa history

In the mid-18th Century, dust raised by horse hoof began whirling through this valley. The infamous Spaniards were approaching. Cacique Güaicaní knew what this meant for the U'wa people. They had to make a choice. Either live physically enslaved by these white invaders, dying of hunger and their plagues—or to live spiritually in freedom, returning to Mother Earth. An untold multitude chose to leap from El Peñol de los Muertos. Others fled deep into the mountains and to the plains on the other side, thus preserving U'wa culture to this day. Their struggle, however, continues against those men with faces of greed, now lusting after black gold, petroleum. In 1996 and 2003, U'wa threatened to once more leap from El Peñol as Occidental Petroleum exploited resources in U'wa territory. By the road, about 1.5 kilometers (1 mile), in the direction of the park. Updated: Jun 30, 2008.

Shopping

Artículos Religiosos La Morenita

Artículos Religiosos La Morenita sells much more than just rosaries, prayer books and other religious articles, most of which are made by Güicán artisans. This shop just around the corner from the church also has what must be Güicán's largest stock of woolen goods—ruana ponchos, hats, gloves and what-not—produced by a collective in this town. You can also pick up on a pamphlet explaining the legend of La Morenita and Cuchumba cave (from the Catholic point of view, of course). Carrera 5, between Calles 4 and 5. Updated: Jun 30, 2008.

Güican Tours

Güicanes

Victor Correa heads up Güicanes, a collective of professional Sierra Nevada guides ready to lead you in a discovery of their homeland. Correa and his colleagues offer a five-day mountaineering excursion of Ritaku'wa Blanco. Also on their agenda are a four-day trek to Laguna de la Sierra and a five-day jaunt to Laguna de la Plaza. Güicanes also can take you to Suesca for some climbing. Calle 4, 3-91. Tel: 1-240-5869 (Bogotá) / 8-789-7155 (Güicán), Cell: 316-228-7041, E-mail: guicanes@gmail.com / guaicani@gmail.com, URL: www.guaicani.com. Updated: Jun 30, 2008.

Güican Lodging

Your choice of accommodation in Güicán is mighty slim. You don't even have to use one hand to count the number of hotels here. Even though few in number, they do cover the whole range of quality, save high-luxury spas. Prices are budget to low-mid-range. Reservations are necessary at Christmas / New Year and during the summer (June-July) holidays. Updated: Jun 30, 2008.

Hotel El Frailejón

(BED: $4) Hotel El Frailejón isn't anything special, but it does have two advantages: it's centrally located near the bus offices and it's Güicán's cheapest inn. Perhaps that is why it is frequently full. The rooms are up a narrow staircase, above the restaurant-shop. The quarters are large with little furnishings, including a worn bed or two. Some have a window overlooking the plaza, a few come with none. The old common baths are sufficiently clean. Carrera 4, 3-34. Tel: 8-789-7037. Updated: Jul 01, 2008.

Hotel La Sierra

(BED: $6) No sign marks the presence of Hotel La Sierra. However, this house a few blocks downhill from the plaza is a hostel where for years the knowledgeable Profe has offered rooms to trekkers and others heading into the national park. Inside are several floors of rooms with private hot-water baths and televisions. The rooms on the upper floors are airier. If the Profe is around he can fill you in on the park and give knowledgeable advice. Calle 5, 6-20. Tel: 789 7109 / 7074. Updated: Jul 01, 2008.

Hotel Brisas del Nevado

(ROOM: $6-8) Hotel Brisas del Nevado is a pleasant inn located just a half-block from the main plaza and bus stops. Its clean, simply furnished rooms in the main building are bright with natural light and have one to four beds. Most share the sparkling common baths. Out in the garden is a new duplex cabaña with a front patio and private baths. The setting and privacy of these accommodations are a delight—but unfortunately, they are only for larger groups. Carrera 5, 4-57. Tel: 8-789-7028 /1-671-6642 (Bogotá), Cell: 300-273-3190. Updated: Jun 30, 2008.

Güican Restaurants

If the eating options are slim in El Cocuy village, they are even more sparse in Güicán. Almost all of the diners are attached to the few hotels. The municipal market is at Carrera 4 and Calle 2. Güicán is famous for its cheeses. The factory here has no store, instead the product is distributed to shops in the town. At times (especially in the high season) the cheese quickly sells out.

Comidas Rápidas Selecta

Comidas Rápidas Selecta fills with Güicán residents looking for a quick bite to eat in the evening. This snack stand offers the finest selection of hot dogs, hamburgers, sandwiches, empanadas and fruit salads ($0.50-2.65). You can keep your inner kid happy with a cup of gelatin topped with cream for dessert. Open daily 6:30-8:30 p.m. Carrera 5, near Calle 5. Updated: Jul 01, 2008.

Restaurant, Hotel La Sierra

Hotel La Sierra looks like an old garage, but at mealtimes its five cloth-covered tables are crammed with people. Breakfast is potato soup, or eggs with bread, cheese and coffee or hot chocolate ($1.30-1.85). Comida corriente is served for lunch or dinner. This set plate comes with rice, beans or potatoes, meat and salad. At noon it's accompanied by a fruit drink, in the evening by a hot agua de panela ($1.85 main dish only, $2.10 with soup). Open daily 6-9:30 a.m., noon-2:30 p.m., 5-8:30 p.m. Calle 5, 6-20. Tel: 8-789-7109 / 7074. Updated: Jul 01, 2008.

Restaurant, Hotel Brisas del Nevado

Hotel Brisas del Nevado's restaurant is a surprising member of Güicán's meager dining scene. Its two rooms are smartly decorated in a country style, and the doorways onto the streets are screened with glass and wood inserts accented with a wrought-iron vine motif. In the evening, candlelight illuminates these intimate spaces, creating a romantic place to have a last repast before leaving the Cocuy region behind. All meals cost $2.65. Open 7-8 a.m. for breakfast, noon-1:30 p.m. for lunch and 7-8 p.m. for dinner. Carrera 5, 4-57. Tel: 8-789 7028. Updated: Jul 01, 2008.

Güican Nightlife

Güicán has very few night clubs or drinking establishments and all are rough-and-tumble types of places that even Colombian tourists won't frequent. Updated: Jun 30, 2008.

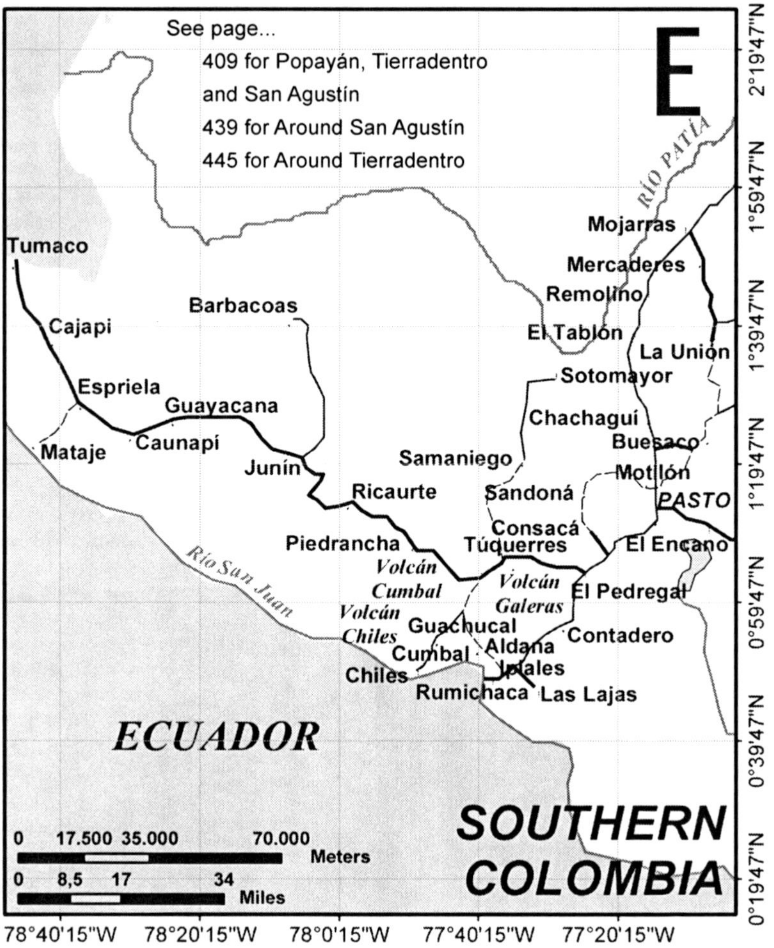

Southern Colombia

Stretching from the southern edge of the Valle de Cauca to the border with Ecuador, Southern Colombia contains everything your imagination can conjure: high-altitude *páramo* plains and snowy volcanoes, mangrove covered coastline and sultry jungle.

Popayán is a beautiful colonial city, renowned for its *Semana Santa* processions. Stroll through the narrow streets, stopping in its numerous churches and museums. Popayán serves as the gateway to two of Colombia's premier archaeological sites, both of unknown cultures: Tierradentro, brilliantly painted, human-carved burial caves; and San Agustín, many sites of incredible statuary. The countryside surrounding both sites provides great hiking opportunities.

Between the two lies Parque Nacional Puracé. After hiking around the Volcan de Coconucos or scaling Volcán Puracé, you can soak your strained muscles in several local hot springs.

Further south on the Pan-American Highway, you arrive at Pasto. This city, overlooked by the smoldering Galeras volcano, also has pleasant colonial-era architecture and plazas, as well as an interesting gold museum.

Just north of the Rumichaca border with Ecuador is Ipiales. Eight kilometers away is the Santuario de Nuestra Señora de las Lajas, a

neo-Gothic church spanning a river gorge. Also near Ipiales is the indigenous village Cumbal, shadowed by two icy volcanoes.
On the Pacific coast is Tumaco, a largely Afro-Colombian city. Birdwatch in the surrounding mangroves, scuba dive, go fishing, or just soak up some rays on El Morro beach. Tumaco is also a port for an alternative sea crossing into Ecuador.

The Putumayo is a vast expanse of near-pristine jungle stretching along the Colombia-Ecuador border. Accessible from Pasto is the country's largest lake, Laguna La Cocha.

Further inland is Puerto Asís, another border crossing into Ecuador, and Parque Nacional La Paya. The entire region has experienced guerrilla and paramilitary activity in recent years. For more info, see the Southern Colombia Safety section. Updated: Sep 25, 2007.

Highlights

Parque Nacional Puracé (p.424), at over 3,000m above sea level, will literally take your breath away with nearly a dozen volcanoes and thermal springs.

The **forests of statues (p.428)** in San Agustín are silent witnesses to the country's history. They guard the verdant valleys laced with waterfalls and caverns.

The spectacularly painted **subterranean burial chambers (p.441)** scattered across the hilltops of Tierradentro are a must-see inthis remote region.

A wonderful example of Andalusia-Mozarab colonial architecture, the White City of **Popayán (p.409)** stands the test of time and several natural disasters.

Just outside of Ipiales the spectacular neo-Gothic church **Nuestra Señora de las Lajas (p.459)** is a top destination for Colombian and Ecuadorian pilgrims.
Updated: Nov 26,2007

History

Before the European conquest of the Americas, the Tumaco culture (or La Tolita) reigned from north of present-day Tumaco to northern Ecuador. Little remains of their civilization, having been consumed by the mangrove jungle. In the central cordillera region are the statues and burial tombs of the mysterious culture we now call San Agustín-Tierradentro, the ancestors of today's Nasa (Páez). The inter-valley area between the two mountain ranges was home to the many Pasto nations whose traditions are kept alive in small villages like Cumbal, Saldoná and Túquerres.

The Spanish began making inroads into Southern Colombia in the 1530s. Under orders of Sebastián de Benalcázar (Benalcázar), Ipiales, Pasto and Popayán were founded as base camps for the exploration for El Dorado. These population centers fell under the Real Audencia de Quito, thus giving them a closer cultural and political nexus to Ecuador than to Bogotá and the rest of modern Colombia. One of the first independence uprisings occurred in the late 18th Century near Tumaco. African slaves escaped into the mangroves to become maroons and form the Pacific coast Afro-Colombia culture.

As the colonies' wars intensified in the early 19th Century, Southern Colombia witnessed the movements of troops from both sides. Pasto remained a royal supporter and suffered quite severely at the hands of Simón Bolívar's forces. When the nascent Gran Colombia split into the countries we know today, Nariño Department wished to leave with Ecuador but was prevented. In the modern era, Popayán has produced 11 presidents of Colombia.

During the present civil war which has lasted over 50 years, the FARC has been active. However, under President Uribe's clean-up program and Plan Colombia, they and coca production has been pushed towards the nether regions of the Colombia-Ecuador border. This has caused a tremendous growth in the number of *desplazados*, or refugees. Updated: Nov 26, 2007.

When to Go

The Southern region—Nariño, Cauca and Huila Departments—have three distinct climates. Tumaco and other places along the Pacific coast are said to be some of the rainiest on earth. The wettest months are May to July; the driest are April, May and August. Temperatures year-round range from 25° to 35°C (77°-95°F). Pasto, Popayán and other population centers in the valley between the Eastern and Central mountain ranges have four seasons of two distinct types of weather: January through March it is sun and warmth, and again from June to August, when it is also windy.

The rainy season occurs during April and May, and from September to December. Most of this region enjoys spring-like climate year round, though Popayán at a lower altitude is a bit hotter in the summer. In Central mountain range, which includes such attractions as Parque Nacional Natural Puracé, Tierradentro and San Agustín, November, December and January are the best months to visit. The clear weather brings the warmest days, but likewise cold nights. The windiest months are July and August, which are also cold. Rain is common the rest of the year; the wettest months are September, October, February and March. Temperatures depend on altitude. Updated: Nov 26, 2007.

Safety in Southern Colombia

The Southern Colombia region has seen much guerrilla and paramilitary activity for more than a decade, especially away from the Pan-American Highway. The jungles to the east and west of the road are also affected by the fumigations of Plan Colombia. Many of the roads are now heavily patrolled by the Colombian military. Checkpoints are common. This includes the roads out to Tumaco, and to San Agustín. Nighttime travel is still not advised by some locals, including between Ipiales, Popayán and Cali. However, many buses do travel at night along the Pan-American Highway. In some areas, buses do not travel during dark hours.

Travel into the Putumayo is still problematic. The weeks leading up to elections can also provide adventures beyond the norm; traditionally this has been when activity by and between the armed factions have increased. Consider twice before going off the well-worn Panamericana path at these times. Always seek local advice before heading to your destination.

If going to the Tumaco area, be sure to take precautions against malaria and dengue. Updated: Sep 25, 2007.

Things to See and Do

Southern Colombia has much to offer, whether you are interested in adrenaline or culture.

Three parque nacional crown jewels rest in the folds of the south: Sanquianga, with mangrove forests; Volcán Galeras; and Puracé National Park, with páramo, volcanoes and thermal springs.

Other hiking and climbing options include the Cumbal, Chili and Azufral volcanoes, and historic routes like Circuito Ancestral and the Camino Natural. You can spend days walking the countryside, exploring the enigmatic tombs and statues of San Agustín and Tierradentro, two premiere archaeological sites that silently testify to the great nation that once inhabited this region.

Listen up shoppers—Cumbal, Sandoná and Silvia have indigenous markets where you can pick up a *ruana* (poncho) or other *artesanía*. The beautiful *barniz* of Pato may be the perfect gift to take home.

Southern Colombia has beautiful colonial architecture, especially in Popayán, and numerous churches and museums. Stunning modern edifices also invite you, like Santuario Nuestra Señora de las Lajas.

Sports aficionados, you aren't left out of the scene here either; there's *chaza* in Pasto, *tejo* (with a curious twist) in San Agustín, and some mighty fine trout fishing at Coconuco and Paletará. Updated: Nov 26, 2007.

Southern Colombia Tours

In much of Southern Colombia, tourist infrastructure is still lacking as far as tour operators are concerned. Most agencies sell airline tour packages to prime destinations like Cartagena. They also book flights. SENA—Servicio Nacional de Aprendizaje—trains guides in Tumaco and Popayán in anticipation of growing tourism there.

Parque Nacional Natural Puracé is working with the *resguardos indígenas* (indigenous communities) within the park boundaries to provide guiding services there. This provides jobs for the local community so it does not have to rely on illegal hunting and log-

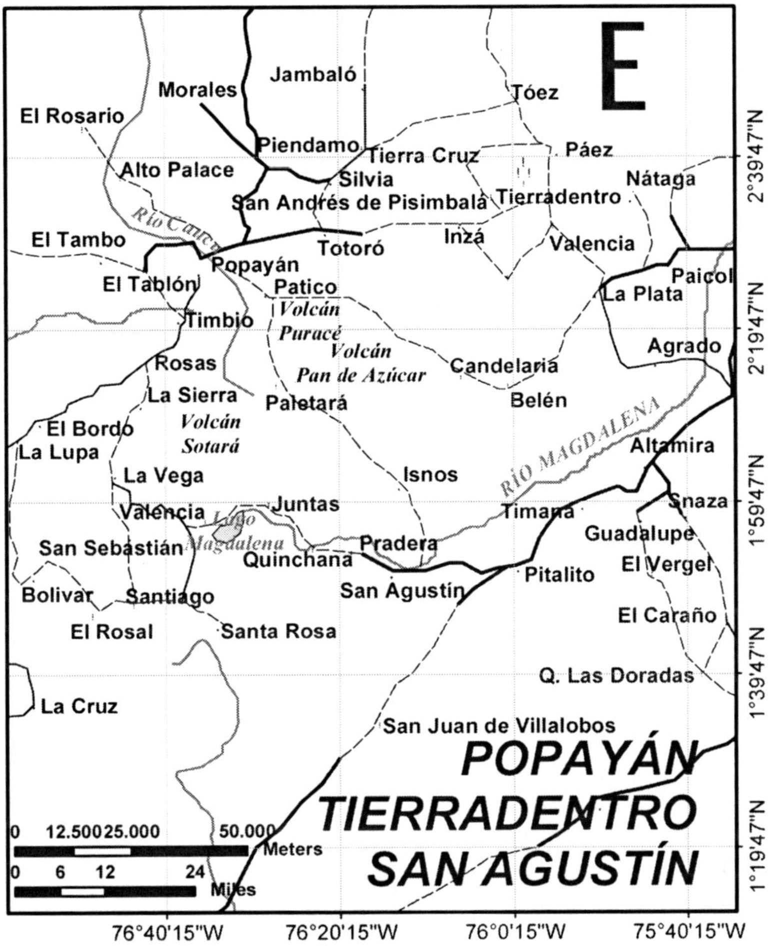

ging to make a living. As San Augustín has long been a tourist destination, it has dozens of independent guides (few of whom are certified) and now several tourist operator offices. Updated: Nov 26, 2007.

Southern Colombia Lodging

Much of Southern Colombia has a surprisingly limited range of lodging options, particularly luxury hotels. Popayán has some of the finest, located in colonial buildings. In cities like Ipiales and Pasto, the trend is moving toward providing for this clientele. Even in San Agustín, a long-popular tourist destination amongst foreigners, deluxe vacation homes are popping up. Many smaller villages—San Agustín, Tierradentro and Puracé, among others—are a budget traveler's paradise, with rooms below $5 per night.

In some of these villages, only the most basic hotels are available. Campgrounds are becoming more common in the region. You'll be able to break out your tent if heading for Playa El Morro on the coast, Parque Nacional Natural Puracé, San Agustín and Tierradentro. Updated: Nov 26, 2007.

Popayán

Alt: 1,737m Pop: 258,653 City Code. 2

The Pan-American Highway twists and turns for 248 kilometers (149 miles) north from

Pasto, arriving at Popayán in the Valle de Pubenza. To the south, east and north of this city are verdant plains studded with mountains. To the southeast is Volcan Puracé and the national park named for it.

Popayán is nicknamed *Ciudad Blanca*, or the White City. Its narrow streets are lined with two-story buildings constructed in rococo Andalusian-style architecture. Their whitewash is almost blinding on a sunny day. The cathedral is styled in clean, classic Roman lines. The central plaza, Parque Caldas, is a pleasant place to seek shade beneath palms and flowering trees. Here, musicians and comedians frequently entertain the crowds.

Traveling north towards Cali (142 kilometers/85 miles away) you then enter the humid Valle del Cauca, surrounded by mountain ranges on either side. During this journey you can occasionally see Nevado del Huila. Updated: Nov 05, 2007.

History

Popayán was another of the Colombian cities founded by orders of Sebastián de Benalcázar in 1536. It was initially governed by the Audencia Real de Quito, but then transferred under the administration of the Audencia Real de Bogotá. In the modern era, the city serves as the capital for Cauca Department. Eleven of the nation's presidents were patojos, or natives of Popayán. One, Francisco José de Caldas (1771-1815), was also a scientist and director of the newly established observatory in Bogotá. He discovered how to calculate altitude by the temperature at which water boils.

Popayán has suffered from numerous earthquakes over the centuries. One, in 1736, destroyed most of the city. In March 1983 the city was once more leveled by a strong tremor. The colonial sector of Ciudad Blanca has been carefully restored to its previous splendor. Some reconstruction work is still going on. Updated: Nov 05, 2007.

When to Go

Popayán has four seasons of two distinct types of weather. From January to March expect sunny days, and again from June through August, when it is also windy, especially in the last month. Those August winds bring two festivals to the Popayán area: the *Festival de las Cometas*, when kites dance across the azure skies, and paragliding events in Balboa, west of the city. The rainy season comes heavy in April and May, and once more with afternoon showers from September to December. The average temperature in the Ciudad Blanca is 18°C (64°F). Evenings are cool.

Holidays and Fiestas

Like Pasto and other southern Andean towns in Colombia, Popayán celebrates Carnival, or the *Fiesta de los Blancos and Negros*, on January 5 and 6. The city's observance of *Semana Santa*, Easter Week, is renowned throughout the country; at this time, lodging prices rise sharply and reservations are necessary far in advance. Mid-April to May is *Fiesta de Ecce Homo*; on the first day of the festival, a procession of women carries the statue of the Ecce Homo Christ down from the Belén church and on May 1 men return the Christ back to its temple.

Another August festival is the *Fiesta del Verano*, marked in the villages around the Ciudad Blanca. September is the *Festival Gastronómico*, or the Gastronomic Festival. *Día de los Ánimas*, Day of the Dead (November 1-3) is when *payusos* commemorate their dearly departed with special masses and cemetery events. The first part of December, until Christmas Eve, chirimías (music groups) pass through Popayán's streets day and night playing drum and flute music. Updated: Nov 05, 2007.

Getting To and Away from Popayán

Minibuses run up and down the narrow streets of Popayán ($0.65). Catch Transpubenza Ruta 5 from Calle 8 and Carrera 6 for the bus terminal or airport (one block away). Taxis cost about $3.

Traveling the hairpinning Ipiales-Popayán highway in a mini-van or other small vehicle can provoke motion sickness, even for those not prone to such.

Air

The airport is behind the bus terminal, about a 20-minute walk from the center. Avianca has direct flights to Bogotá, with connections to anyplace else in Colombia or the world (Monday-Friday, 8 a.m.-noon, 2-6 p.m., Saturday 9 a.m.-1 p.m. Carrera 5, 3-85. Tel:

2-824-3379, Cel: 315-463-3343, Fax: 2-824-4505, E-mail: agventasspn@avianca.com). Satena flies daily to Bogotá and Medellín, and twice-weekly to Guapi and Cali (Viajes Paletra/Satena: Monday-Friday, 8 a.m.-noon, 2-6 p.m., Saturday 8 a.m.-noon. Carrera 9, 4-14. Tel: 2-822-0217, 2-823-6728, URL: www.viajespaletara.mimejorsitio.com)

Bus

The bus terminal is a 15-minute walk from downtown. It has a luggage keep, restaurants, internet, phones, bathrooms and ATM (Visa, Plus, Mastercard, Cirrus). The bus companies servicing Popayán are Cootranshuila, Sotrancauca, Transipiales, Cootranor, Magdalena and Bolivariano. See following bus schedule.

From Popayán

Arrive	Departures	Time	Price
Silvia	Sun, Tues, 9 a.m. daily noon	1.25 hours	$2.35
Puracé	4:30 a.m., 6:45 a.m., noon, 2:30 p.m	1 hour	$2.65 - 3.15
Tierradentro	10:30 a.m.	5 hours	$7.90
Coconuco	hourly 6:30 a.m.-5:30 p.m.	1.5 hours	$1.60
San Agustín	6 a.m., 11 a.m., 1 p.m., 3 p.m.	6 hours	$13.10
Tumaco	10 p.m., 11 p.m.	11 hours	$23.70
Cali	every half hour	2 hours	$5.30 - 6.30
Medellín	6, 8, 11 p.m., midnight	11 hours	$28.40 -30.50
Bogotá	4, 5, 7, 7:30, 8, 9:30 p.m.	12 hours	$34-36

From Popayán, you can also travel overland to Pitalito, Puerto Asís, Mocoa, Timbío, Neiva and other points. Updated: Nov 05, 2007.

Safety in Popayán

The Valle del Cauca witnessed intense guerrilla activity for several decades. Travel is safer now under Uribe's road patrol; however, some Colombians still prefer not to travel on the Ipiales-Cali stretch of the Pan-American Highway at night. Within the city of Popayán, take extra care in the market and bridge areas. A visit to Barrio Alfonso López is not recommended. The El Tambo area west of Popayán has recently experienced FARC, ELN and AUC activity. Updated: Nov 05, 2007.

Popayán Services

Tourism Office

The Oficina de Turismo Popayán is located on a side street, two blocks from Parque Caldas, across from Santo Domingo church (Monday-Friday, 8:30 a.m.-12:30 p.m., 2:30-6:30 p.m., Saturday 9 a.m.-noon, 2-5 p.m., Sunday 9 a.m.-1 p.m. Carrera 5, 4-68. Tel: 2-824-2251, Cel: 311-307-2299, E-mail: oficinaturismopopayan@hotmail.com, URL: www.turismopopayan.com).

For any maps you might need, go to the Instituto Geográfico Agustín Codazzi (Monday-Friday, 8-11:15 a.m., 1:30-4 p.m. Calle 3, 7-08). Permits for Parque Nacional Puracé and other national parks in Southern Colombia may be obtained from Parques Nacionales Naturales de Colombia Surandina (Monday-Friday, 8-11:30 a.m., 2-4 p.m. Carrera 9, 25N-06. Tel: 2-823-1279 / 1212, URL: www.parquesnacionales.gov.co).

Money

Bancolombia changes only American Express travelers checks with a small commission; come with a photocopy of your passport's front pages and entry stamp. Its ATM handles Mastercard, Visa, Amex and Cirrus (Monday-Friday 8-11:30 a.m., 2-4:30 p.m. Carrera 6, 4-49, on Parque Caldas.) Santander can also do travelers cheques, and its ATM does Visa, Mastercard, Plus, Cirrus and other networks (Monday-Thursday, 8-11:30 a.m., 2-4 p.m., Friday 8-11:30 a.m., 2-4:30 p.m. Carrera 6, 5-52). Other banks near Parque Caldas include AV Villas and BBVA. Western Union/ Giros y Finanzas is in the Centro Comercial Colonial (Monday-Friday, 9 a.m.-12:30 p.m., 2-6 p.m., Saturday 9 a.m.-1 p.m. Calle 3 and Carrera 7, Suite 208). MoneyGram/Cambiamos can be found in the Centro Comercial Rodrival (Monday-Saturday, 8 a.m.-6 p.m. Carrera 7 and Calle 6, Local 9).

Activity ●
1 Iglesia Belén B1
2 Iglesia El Carmen B1
3 Iglesia Encarnación B2
4 Iglesia La Ermita B2
5 Iglesia San Agustín B1
6 Iglesia San Francisco B1
7 Iglesia Santo Domingo B1
8 Museo Arquidiocesano de Arte Religioso B1
9 Museo Casa Mosquera B1
10 Museo Casa Negret B1
11 Museo Casa Valencia B1
12 Museo de Historia Natural B2
13 Museo Iberoamericano de Arte Moderno B1
14 San José B1

Eating
15 Cafetería Santo Domingo La 4a B1
16 Carbonera Parrilla B1
17 Comedor Vegetariano Bio-Integrales Kanda B1
19 El Portón del Patio B2
20 Helados de Paila B1
21 La Cave B2
22 La Viña Parillada B1
23 Madeira Café B1
24 Mey Chow B2
25 No name Restaurant B1
26 Platería San Augustín B1
27 Restaurante China B1
28 Restaurante la Oficina B1
29 Restaurante Pizzería Italiano B1

Nightlife
30 Bar la Casona del Virrey B1
31 Imperio B1

Service ★
32 Banco Colombia B1
33 Correos de Colombia/Apostal B2
34 Diseño y Estructura Jorge Velásquez y Asociados B1
35 Foto Morillo B1
36 Hospital Nivel II Susana López B1
37 Instituto Geográfico Agustín Codazzi B1
38 Intercopias B1
39 Moneygram B1
40 Santander B1
41 Telecom B1
42 Tourism Office B2

Shopping
43 Artesanías Manas de Oro B1
44 Mercado B1
45 Supermercado Ley B1

Sleeping
46 Hospedaje Barú B1
47 HostelTrain Guesthouse B1
48 Hotel Boston B1
49 Hotel Camino Real B1
50 Hotel Capital B1
51 Hotel Colonial B1
52 Hotel Dann Monasterio B1
53 Hotel El Paso B1
54 Hotel la Casona del Virrey B1
55 Hotel la Plazuela B1
56 Hotel Los Portales B1
57 Hotel Panamá B1
58 Hotel Pass Home B1

Tour ♦
59 Luna Paz B1
60 SENA Student Guides B1

Transportation
61 Terminal Trans Intermunicipal A1

Keeping in Touch

Telecom charges $0.50 and up per minute for international calls (Monday-Saturday, 8 a.m.-noon, 2-5:30 p.m. Carrera 4 and Calle 3). STE Telecolom offers cheaper international services, $0.30 per minute to the U.S. and $0.60 to the U.K.; it also has internet at $0.80 per hour, local phone services and prepaid phone cards (Calle 5 7-11). For inexpensive internet, head over to Carrera 5, where several businesses charge $0.60 per hour: Diseño y Estructura Jorge Velásquez y Asociados (Monday-Friday, 8:30 a.m.-7 p.m., Saturday 8:30 a.m.-2 p.m. Carrera 5, 3-21) and Intercopias (Monday-Friday, 8 a.m.-12:30 p.m., 2-7 p.m., Saturday 9 a.m.-12:30 p.m. Carrera 5, 3-31), which also has Skype. You can send postcards from Correos de Colombia/Apostal at Calle 4, 2-56 (Monday-Friday, 8-11 a.m., 2-5 p.m.).

Medical

Popayán has two public hospitals: Hospital Nivel II Susana López de Valencia (Calle 15 17A-196, Tel: 2-821-1721) and Hospital Universitario San José (Carrera 6N, 142, Tel: 2-823-4508). The tourism office says there are English-speaking doctors at the Clínica La Estancia, which has emergency services and specialists (Calle 15N, 2-256. Tel: 2-823-3950 / 9553, E-mail: info@clinestancia.com, URL: www.clinestancia.com). Pharmacies, or droguerías, are very common, about one every block.

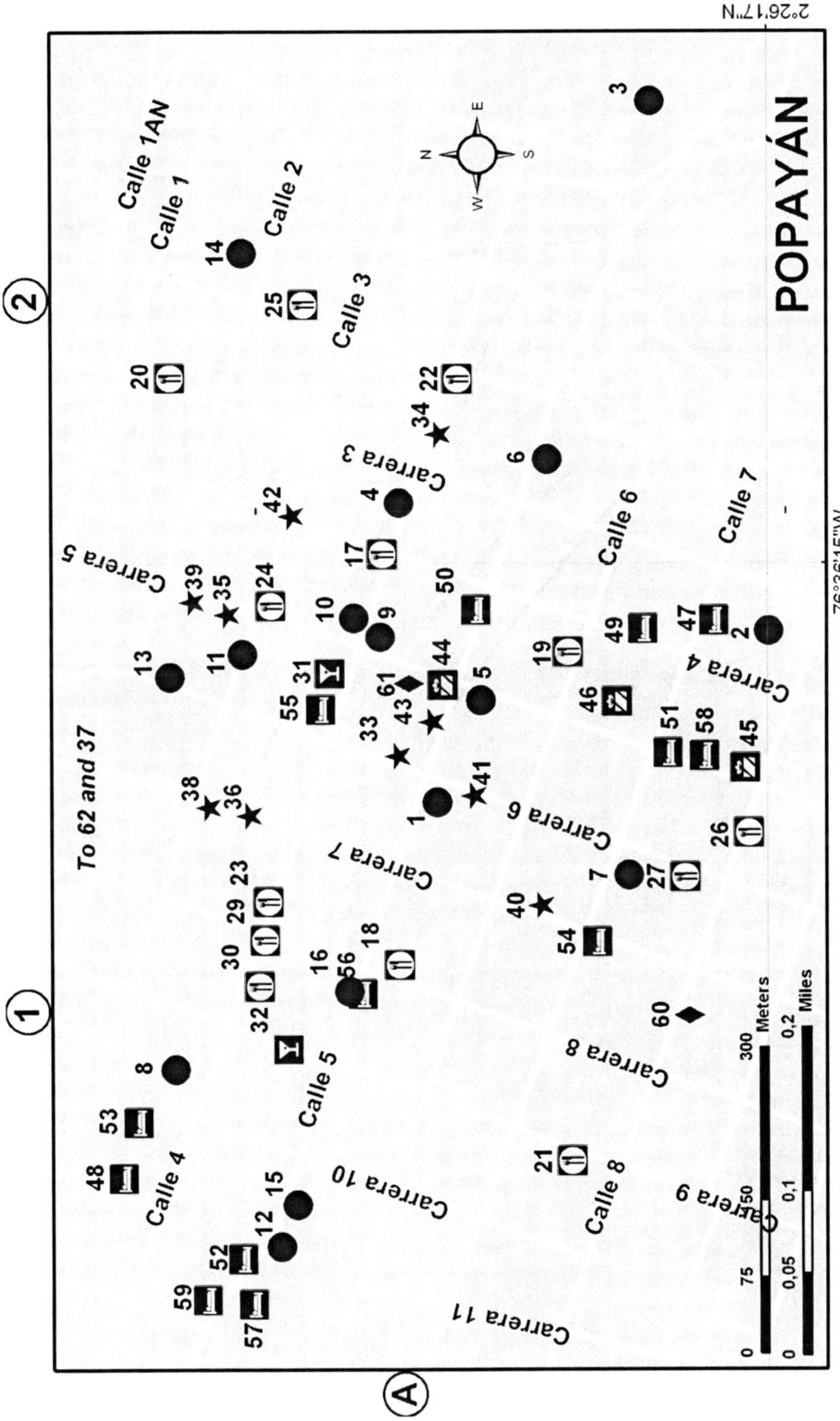

SOUTHERN COLOMBIA

Camera Repair

Most camera shops are located on Carrera 7 or Calle 5 in the center of town. Compact flash cards can be difficult to find; try Foto Morillo, which has five outlets (Main store: Monday-Saturday, 8 a.m.-7 p.m., Sunday 8 a.m.-1 p.m. Carrera 7, 4-80, on Parque Caldas. Tel: 2-824-0355). Updated: Nov 05, 2007.

Shopping

Artesanías Manos de Oro

Artesanías Manos de Oro brings together the works of Cauca's best artisans under one roof. Browse through the two pleasant showrooms, journeying from village to village, and admire the crafts each is renowned for. Woolen ruanas, silk and cotton shawls, items of hand-made paper and ceramic miniatures of homes and churches can be purchased here. If you haven't time to get to the pueblos, you still can take home a bit of artistry made by golden hands. Calle 5, 4-51. Tel: 2-822-0040, 820-6962. E-mail: sstartesanias@emtel.net.co. Updated: May 16, 2008.

Platería San Agustín

Since 1991, Albeiro Pérez has been crafting fine jewelry. Using sterling (.925) silver from Colombia, Italy, Thailand and Mexico, he creates all sorts of personal ornaments, some with semi-precious stones or glass beads. His filigree work is very delicate. There is bound to be a necklace, bracelet, ring or pair of earrings that strikes your fancy. Don Albeiro also does special orders, if you have a design in mind. Additionally, he repairs jewelry. Carrera 6, 7-54. Tel: 2-824-0528, Cel: 315-270-5332. Updated: Dec 19,2007.

El Taller de Esperanza Polanco F.

Esperanza Polanco forms clay by hand into wonderful candlesticks and lamps, chess sets and nativity crèches, mysterious masks, figurines and miniature scenes. She does tiles also, of original patterns—whether from her own imagination or yours. This small, crowded shop additionally has works by other patojo artisans, or from neighboring Patia village. There are woven ruana ponchos and bags, wrought iron work, basketry and other domestic wares from vegetable fibers. If you

	Description	Hours	Address	Contact	Price
Casa Mosquera	The 18th Century home of José María Mosquera y Figueroa, whose four sons came to be prominent figures.	Monday-Friday, 8 a.m.-noon, 2-6 p.m., Saturday, Sunday and holidays, 8 a.m.-noon, 2-5 p.m.	Calle 3, 5-14	Tel: 2-824-0683	$1.05
Casa Valencia	Home of poet-writer-politician-orator Guillermo Valencia.	Tuesday-Sunday and holidays, 10 a.m.-noon, 2-5 p.m.	Carrera 6. 2-69	Tel: 2-820-6160	$0.25 - 1.05
Museo Arquidiocesano de Arte Religioso	Divided into six halls devoted to specific artists, schools or topics, over 110 pieces are on exhibit here.	Monday-Friday, 9 a.m.-12:30 p.m., 2-6 p.m., Saturday 9 a.m.-2 p.m.	Calle 4, 4-56	Tel: 2-824-2759	$0.80 - 1.60
Museo de Historia Natural	An excellent introduction to what you will see in Parque Nacional Natural Puracé.	Daily 8 a.m.-noon, 2-5:30 p.m.	Carrera 2A, 1A-25	Tel: 2-820-9861, ext. 2602	$1.05 - 1.60
Museo Martínez	Set in a colonial house, this was paintor Efraín Martínez' favorite space.	Tuesday to Sunday, 10 a.m. to noon and 2 p.m. to 5 p.m.	Carrera 3, Los Tejares	Tel: 2-822-3364	$0.80 - 1.60

Updated: May 16, 2008.

can't come to Popayán for Easter Week, you can take home a miniature Semana Santa procession. Whatever item you purchase is guaranteed to be an exclusive design of high quality. Calle 4, 10-21. Tel: 2-824-4588, Cel: 300-613-3562, E-mail: esperanzapol@hotmail.com. Updated: May 16, 2008.

Things to See and Do

Strolling over Popayán's historic bridges, Puente de Humilladero and Puente Chiquito, is a great way to enjoy the sunshine. Spend rainy afternoons in the Ciudad Blanca's fine collection of churches and museums. Homes of some of Popayán's illustrious citizens have been turned into museums. Especially noteworthy are the Casa Negret and its Museo Iberoamericano de Arte Moderno, as well as the Museo de Arte Religioso and the excellent Museo de Historia Natural.

Popayán's Semana Santa commemorations are famous. Every night until *Viernes Santo* (Good Friday), candlelit processions wend the narrow streets. The following week are the children's processions. In this season, the Religious Art Museum exhibits the most precious artworks of the city's churches. Due to the university presence, Popayán also has a thriving theater and art-house scene. The beginning of October is the annual Festival de Teatro and Encuentro de Cuenteros, an international meeting of theater and storytelling. During the rest of the year, you can catch theatrical productions and films at the Centro Cultural Bolívar.

Near Popayán are a number of interesting villages, including Silvia, which houses a weekly indigenous market. Several tour routes allow you to visit these towns by foot or on horseback. To the east is Parque Nacional Puracé with good trekking and climbing. Coconuco, on the south edge of the park, has two hot springs which can be visited as a day trip from Popayán.

Along the same road is Paletará which has a trout fishing tournament every October. Don't forget the kite-flying and paragliding festivals in the windy month of August! Updated: Nov 05, 2007.

Museums of Popayán

Another place to get out of Popayán's rains are its museums. Many are the historical homes of past illustrious citizens, though a few premier art museums like Museo de Arte Religioso and the Museo Iberoamericano de Arte Moderno atract plenty of visitors. The Museo Casa Negret and Museo Iberoamericano de Arte Moderno are currently closed for renovation.

Museo Arquidiocesano de Arte Religioso

The Museo de Arte Religioso was founded in 1972 by the city's Archdiocese to protect and conserve the most valuable artwork of Popayán's churches. Divided by artist, school or topic, over 110 pieces are on exhibit in six halls. You may not photograph any of the works in the collection. Exhibit explanations are in Spanish only; Spanish-language guides are available.Calle 4, 4-56. Tel: 2-824-2759. Updated: May 16, 2008.

Museo de Historia Natural

Under the auspices of the Universidad de Cauca, the Museo de Historia Natural is a nice break from the usual art and miscellanea-housing historical museums. With splendid collections explaining the geology, paleontology, zoology and botany of the region, this is an excellent introduction to what you will see in Parque Nacional Natural Puracé. On the second floor is a new botanical garden. Carrera 2A, 1A-25. Tel: 2-820-9861, ext. 2602. Updated: May 16, 2008.

Centro Cultural Bolívar

The Central Cultural Bolívar screens art films from Colombia and around the world in this small theater just a few blocks from Parque Caldas. You can also catch documentaries or theater productions; check the websites for scheduled events. The center also hosts the annual Festival de Teatro and Encuentro de Cuenteros every October. A small snack stand sells teas, juices and regional munchies. Art films screened Thursday - Saturday, 7 p.m. and Sundays, 6 p.m. Calle 7, 3-17. Tel: 2-824-0016, E-mail: teatrobolivar@popayancultural.com, URL: www.popayancultural.com. Updated: May 16, 2008.

The Churches of Popayán

Take refuge from Popayán's afternoon showers in the sanctuary of one of its churches. The schedule of masses and church hours is in the telephone book.

Catedral Basílica Nuestra Señora de la Asunción—Calle 5, between Carreras 6 and 7, Parque Caldas.
La Encarnación—This temple was designed by Jesuit Simon Schenherr, who designed many South American churches. Calle 5 and Carrera 5.
San José—Another Simón Schenherr creation. Calle 5 and Carrera 8.
La Ermita—Calle 5, between Carreras 2 and 3.
Belén—The home of the Ecce Homo Christ statue affords great views over the city. Up hill at the end of Calle 4.
El Carmen—Calle 4, between Carreras 3 and 4.
Santo Domingo—The exterior is a good example of Rococo Andalusian architecture. Calle 4 and Carrera 5.
San Francisco—Calle 4 and Carrera 9.
San Agustín—In a side chapel is an impressive statue of Christ kneeling upon a silver globe. The altar screen is repousséed silver, and its Virgen Dolorosa is adorned in silver. Calle 7 and Carrera 6.Updated: Dec 19, 2007.

Catedral Basílica Nuestra Señora de Asunción

Popayán's cathedral is a testament to the clean lines of Roman architecture. The whitewashed exterior is accented only by towering columns with Ionic capitals. The interior of this sanctuary is painted ivory, pale blue and light grey with gold details. The barrel vaulting bands are intertwining vines; a gilded rosette adorns their apices. The aisle walls are treated with *fleur-de-lis* in high relief on the walls, low relief within the span of the arches. Fine silver work is evidenced in the silver sacristy, and the accoutrements of the Virgin of the Apocalypse. A modern screen with a textured gold background, depicting the Immaculate Conception, adorns the altar. Calle 5, between Carreras 6 and 7, Parque Caldas. Updated: Dec 19, 2007.

Semana Santa

Easily the most important holiday in Popayán, and one that has been celebrated annually for more than 450 years, Semana Santa transforms Popayán into a colorful procession of Catholic tradition, bringing in hundreds of visitors every year.

Following the model of Seville, Spain, the processions in Popayán are all nocturnal, except for the one on Palm Sunday, in which the triumphant entrance of Jesus Christ into Jerusalem is represented with the images of Saint Ecce Homo and El Señor Caído, taken from the chapel of Belén to the Basílica.

On Holy Tuesday white flowers adorn the procession that carries four images from the church of San Agustín to downtown. The procession on Wednesday uses pink flowers in representation of the joy of humanity for his immediate redemption. Holy Thursday is celebrated with a procession of red flowers at the 18th century church of San Francisco. Holy Friday begins at the church of Santo Domingo. A symbolic representation of the drama of The Passion is given with purple flowers and a group of men carrying hammers and other tools. Men wear white handkerchiefs with a small purple crown on their shoulders. Updated: May 09, 2008.

Silvia

At Silvia's Tuesday morning market, you can see the Guambiano indigenous in traditional dress. Afterward, join the Ruta Etno-Ecoturística, featuring nature trails, typical foods (especially trout), artesanías and indigenous villages. The route traverses the countryside from Piédamo to Silvia to Las Delicias to El Pueblito, before ending in La Campana. If you want to spend a few days exploring this area northeast of Popayán, Silvia has basic lodging. To rent horses, contact Freddy, a guide that rents them for $2.50 per hour (Cel: 312-758-6963).

It is possible to travel from Silvia to Tierradentro. On market day, transport runs frequently until early afternoon for Totoró. There, hop on a bus going to Inzá. Several times a day pick-up trucks go to Tierradentro and San Andrés de Pisimbalá. Sotrancauca has buses from Popayán to Silvia on Sunday and Tuesday at 9 a.m., and daily at noon ($2.35; 1.25 hours). Updated: May 20, 2008.

Circuito del Maíz

Traveling west of Popayán, you enter the Circuito del Maíz, or the Corn Circuit, a gastronomic tour of the region. Sample homemade arepas, tamales, sweets, chicha and other typical foods made from Zea in the villages of El Charco, Santa Ana and Cajete. You then end your journey at the La Lajita Spa to take a dip in the refreshing La Lajita creek. For more information, visit the tourism office in Popayán. Updated: May 20, 2008.

Circuito Ancestral

The Circuito Ancestral is a tour of small villages east of Popayán. This ancient route was used by Mosquera to travel from his plantation to the big city. On horseback or on foot, your can enjoy the ecological paths, the headwaters of the Río Molino and the indigenous reservation in Poblazón. Your journey begins in La Unión, also known as La Cabrera, where you can rent horses. It is just a 15 minute bus ride from Popayán. The historic trail then cuts three kilometers (two miles) crosscountry to Santa Helena. From there continue to Poblazón (five kilometers/three miles) and Santa Barbara (3 kilometers/two miles). From Santa Helena, you can take a two-kilometer (1.5-mile) detour to the birthplace of the Molino River. The complete 15-kilometer circuit takes about four hours. Try the goodies made from locally grown blackberries. The Popayán tourism office can give you more details on the Circuito Ancestral. Updated: May 20, 2008.

Cascada de Río Bedón

More or less parallel to the Popayán-La Plata road, which passes along the north edge of Parque Nacional Natural Puracé, is the Bedón River. Just past Kilometer 35 the río plunges from 3,060 meters (10,037 feet) altitude to less than 3,000 meters (9,840 feet) before continuing its course eastward through large-leafed foliage. The waters of Cascada de Río Bedón foam white not from the 60-meter (197-foot) fall, but from the sulfur swirling within its depths. You witness its force from the overlook built just 10 meters (33 feet) from the road. Take a bus along the road to Kilometer 35, or walk from one of the other attractions along the north road. Popayán-La Plata road, Kilometer 35, Parque Nacional Natural Puracé. Updated: Dec 19, 2007.

Termales San Juan

Sulfur-laden waters bubble from out of the earth, rushing to a brook winding across the páramo at 3,200 meter (10,496 feet) altitude. Deep emerald mosses and red lichens carpet the banks. The rocks in the stream are lacquered pale yellow from the minerals. Tall, thin grasses sway in the gentle wind. In the distance rise cragged mountain peaks. You have arrived at Termales San Juan. Sit in the thatched hut for a while and listen to the breeze, the birds, the frogs. Wander the trail that weaves among these waters. As inviting as these pools are, visitors cannot dip into them. Many animals come here and our smell in the waters and earth can scare them.

An uneven stone path next to the ranger station goes one kilometer (0.6 miles) to the thermal pools. Along the way, signs point out special features of the journey, including orchids, a mountain tapir crossing and a view of Pan de Azúcar Volcáno.

The complex on the Bedón River side of the road, which had a fine restaurant and an excellent geology-ethnographic museum, is presently closed; hopes are to secure funds for the repair of these buildings. Meals and drinks can be had at a small shack on the south side of the road, next to the ranger station. Popayán-La Plata road, Kilometer 37, Parque Nacional Natural Puracé. Updated: Dec 19, 2007.

Volcán Puracé

The star of this 803,600-hectare national park is Volcán Puracé. A near-perfect cone peak, it rises 4,760 meters (15,613 feet). A well-defined trail leads from the Pilimbalá ranger station through high mountain and páramo ecosystems to its summit; near the top, loose cinders make the going a bit tough. Even though the volcano last erupted in 1949, its fumeroles still emit sulfur fumes. The trail begins at 3,350 meters (10,988 feet) altitude and no special climbing equipment is needed. However, you are climbing at high altitude and through a landscape that is unrelenting. Clouds and rain can move in at any moment.

The ranger station here has lodging available, which is a convenient place to stay if surmounting the volcano. A simple restaurant serves breakfast, lunch and dinner. Even though the military reports all land mines have been removed from the volcano, the park service still recommends you stay on the path. The rangers further recommend you go accompanied, in a group and/or with a guide, as the climate and terrain provide special challenges, and that you begin the climb before 10 a.m. and the descent no later than 4 p.m. Pay attention to the signs warning of fumeroles. Do not enter the crater.

Volcán Puracé is most easily accessed from the north side of the park. A signed trail begins behind the Pilimbalá ranger station. To get to Pilimbalá, see the Puracé: Getting To and Away section.Updated: Dec 19, 2007.

V!VA Member Review- Parque Nacional Natural Puracé

A fantastic, charming, relaxing place. Definitely a place to return to! Slovenia, Apr 28, 2008.

Cadena Volcánica de Coconuco

The Cadena Volcánica de Coconuco is like a necklace of rough, uncut jet stones draping the páramo. Beginning at Pan de Azúcar, a volcano towering 4,670 meters (15,318 feet), nine more volcanic craters form a chain across the lunar-like landscape within the hinterlands of Parque Nacional Natural Puracé. A two-and-a-half-day trek can be made around their imposing presence, camping on the wild, wind-swept plains. You may be lucky and encounter some of the park's more elusive residents like the mountain tapir, puma and spectacled bear.

To get there, two routes are possible: beginning at and returning to Pilimbalá or Termales San Juan, or starting at Paletará and ending at Pilimbalá or Termales San Juan.

Contact Parques Nacionales Naturales de Colombia Surandina, in Popayán, to make a reservation and find out about present conditions. It can also help you to arrange the services of a local guide from the indigenous community. The park entry fee is paid at either Pilimbalá or Termales San Juan. Updated: Dec 19, 2007.

Camino Natural

Out of the three roads going into the park, the Camino Natural traces inside of it from San Sebastián in Cauca to San Agustín in Huila. This pre-Hispanic road takes the average hiker two days to complete, staying the night in San Antonio. Before you start asking if you are there yet, take into consideration it's only an eight-hour walk, but you'll want to stop and talk to fellow travelers along the way. Camino Natural is stone-paved and a secure route, no longer used by guerrillas. You'll need a guide and a park permit, both of which you can get from the Surandina office in Popayán. Don't miss the chance to take this ancient road through pristine landscapes, visiting indigenous villages along the way and finishing the walk at the site of the mysterious Agustine peoples' stoic statues. Updated: Dec 19, 2007.

Popayán Tours

Despite the number of attractions in Popayán, few tour operators have offices here. The tourism office keeps a list of independent, licensed guides who can show you around the city or take you to places of interest in the area. Many speak English as well as Italian, French, German or another language. Travel agents on or near Parque Caldas can help you make reservations for flights or purchase an airline excursion package to popular destinations in other parts of Colombia.Updated: Nov 05, 2007.

SENA Student Guides

Servicio Naciónal de Aprendizaje, SENA, and the Oficina de Turismo Popayán are training guides to fill the growing tourism demand of the region. The students, of economically disadvantaged backgrounds, are also receiving language training; many speak English as well as another language. Rates for their services are arranged between the client and the student-guide. For more information, contact Carmen Leonor Acosta, SENA instructor and director of the Oficina de Turismo Popayán. Carrera 5, 4-68. Tel: 2-824-2251, E-mail: oficinaturismoPopayán@hotmail.com, URL: www.turismopopayán.com. Updated: Jan 08, 2008.

Luna Paz

Ask in Popayán for a tour guide, and many will mention Jairo Paz, owner of Luna Paz. Señor Paz conducts ecotours to some of the region's most delectable destinations, including the burial tombs at Tierradentro, hotsprings in Parque Nacional Natural Los Nevados, the colonial city of Boyacá and the fincas of the Zona Cafetera (Coffee Zone). He also can take you to Cartagena, Capurganá or Sapzurró on the Caribbean coast or Juanchaco on the Pacific coast, where you can watch whales. Calle 8, 7-61. Cel: 315-513-9593,

Fax: 2-821-9595, E-mail: lunapaztour@hotmail.com, URL: www.lunapazecoturismo.tk Updated: Jan 08, 2008.

Resguardo Indígena Guides

What better way to see Parque Nacional Natural Purace than with a local from the Resguardo Indígena of the Coconuco-Nasa (Páez) people? They know the idiosyncrasies of this land's weather and terrain like noone else. In fact, Surandina prefers you use their services, instead of those of an outsider, for your own safety on the treacherous páramo highlands. Furthermore, you will be helping to create employment for these inhabitants of the park who otherwise might have to turn to illegal hunting, logging or other activities to earn money. The national park office in Popayán can help you arrange a guide. You negotiate the price with the guide yourself. The usual rate is $8-11 per day. Carrera 9, 25N-06. Tel: 2-823-1279 / 1212, URL: www.parquesnacionales.gov.co. Updated: Nov 01, 2007.

Popayán Lodging

In Popayán there's a place in the Centro Histórico for any budget, from bottom-dollar dives to luxury hotels in colonial buildings. Most absolute budget places are concentrated between Carreras 3 and 5, and Calles 6 to 8. For those able to spend a dollar or two more per night, or who are traveling as a couple, there are more low-cost options. Room prices triple during Semana Santa and hotels fill up—book well in advance. Updated: Nov 05, 2007.

Budget

Hotel Boston

(BED: $4.20-5.30) For journeyers on a tight budget, the Hotel Boston is one of several good options in the inexpensive sector of the city. As price is charged by bed, not per person, it is especially appealing: the rooms with shared bathroom cost only $4.20 whether you are a solo traveler or a couple. There is only one room with private bath, at $5.30 per bed. Be advised that apparently this hostel accepts hourly guests. Updated: Nov 12, 2007.

Hospedaje Barú

(BED: $4.20-5.30) Another possible budget traveler choice, the Hospedaje Barú has three patios, as is typical with old architectural style. The first two have seating areas filled with plants and tables; in the back, the former service courtyard, you can do your laundry. All three are surrounded by rooms, some with rustic private baths. Others share the clean-enough common bathrooms, with cold-water only showers. This hostel has many long-term guests, including teachers, students and families. Monthly rates are available: $68.50, common bath: $79, private bath. Calle 7, 3-39. Tel: 2-824-1220. Updated: May 16, 2008.

Hotel Panamá

(BED: $5.30-8) It's cheap, it's clean and the beds aren't bad. The rooms are small, though—not even big enough to swing a cat in—and the ground floor rooms are dark. There's only common-bath with cold-water showers and a laundry basin. You're guaranteed a Latin American lodging experience if your room faces the front patio, thanks to the loud TV that's on from early morning until late night. Still, the Hotel Panamá is probably the better choice among the budget hotels in Popayán. Carrera 5, 7-33. Updated: May 16, 2008.

Hotel Capital

(BED: $6.35-8.50) If you can afford to spend a dollar more, Hotel Capital is a comfortable choice for budget travelers. All rooms have common baths, but here there is deliciously hot water. The back courtyard garden is a wonderful place to swing from the hammock or sit around with doña María del Carmen and the other women, chatting a rainy afternoon away. You can ask to use the kitchen. While you're there, teach Rebeca, the resident parrot, a few new words. Carrera 5, 7-11. Tel: 2-838-8363. Updated: May 16, 2008.

Hotel Pass Home

(BED: $8) Located four blocks from the bus terminal and five from the historic center, Hotel Pass Home is a convenient place to stay in Popayán. It is a bare-bones inn, with white walls and small, cot-like beds. All rooms have television and spic-and-span bathrooms with hot water showers. There is a laundry area where you can wash your own clothes. The English-speaking owner prefers you make a reservation. Calle 5, 10-114. Cel: 316-448-9513. Updated: May 16, 2008.

HostelTrail Guesthouse

(BED: $8-18) A brand new backpacker house with all the facilities a traveler could want. Hot water, WiFi internet, 24 hour access, privates and dorm rooms, self-catering kitchen and DVD collection. Carrera 11, 4-16. Cel: 314-686-1866, E-mail: info@hosteltrail.com. URL: www.hosteltrail.com. Updated: Dec 19, 2007.

Cabañas

(BED: $10.50) Escape to the tranquility of Parque Nacional Natural Puracé. At Pilimbalá ranger station there are three A-frame cabañas for rent. After spending all day scaling Volcán Puracé or hiking in the park, cuddle up in front of the sitting room fireplace. There are two bedrooms, the first floor with bunk beds for six, and on the top floor, double mattresses for up to four more companions. A private bath is also at your disposal (cold-water shower). Sheets and blankets are provided. For travelers on a tighter budget, the park also has campsites and hammock huts for $2.10 per site, plus $2.65 per person. Office hours are Monday-Friday, 8-11:30 a.m., 2-4 p.m. Carrera 9, 25N-06. Tel: 2-823-1279 / 1212, URL: www.parquesnacionales.gov.co. Updated: Dec 19, 2007.

Hotel Colonial

(ROOM: $16-21) As its name implies, the Hotel Colonial is a building from the early centuries of this city. A small inn, the lobby is tastefully adorned with original artwork and flower-filled vases. The rooms are set off two narrow courtyards, and have wood furniture with wrought-iron accents, as well as private bathrooms with hot-water showers. The beds are firm. This lodge is a pleasant choice for those who are working with a mid-range budget. Calle 5, 10-97. Tel: 2-831-7848, Fax: 2-820-5178. Updated: May 16, 2008.

Mid-Range

El Paso

(ROOM: $18.50-31.50) On the second floor of a colonial-era building is the Hotel El Paso, a good mid-range hostel choice in Popayán. Furnished with solid, carved wood furniture (including a dressing table), all rooms have private bath with hot water and toilets dressed in frilly covers. The wooden doors are thick, guaranteeing to block out any noise from the many sitting areas. A large common balcony overlooks the street corner. This inn is quite popular with Colombian businessmen. Carrera 7, 7-14. Tel: 2-824-0227. Updated: May 16, 2008.

La Casona del Virrey

(ROOM: $22.50-38) Hotel La Casona del Virrey, a stylish inn set in a colonial-era building, is a surprisingly affordable alternative right in the heart of Popayán. This is the perfect place to watch the Semana Santa processions from the balconies; however, expect to pay for this privileged view. A broad spiral staircase leads up to the second floor with large, finely furnished guest rooms that have private bathrooms and cable TV. (Here's a secret: there is one three-bed room with an exterior bath that costs only $16 per person.) Calle 4, 5-78. Tel: 2-824-0836, Fax: 2-824-4237, E-mail: hotellacasonadelvirrey@hotmail.com. Updated: May 16, 2008.

Los Portales

(ROOM: $23-29) Take a seat in one of the rocking chairs around the front courtyard and listen to the water spilling from the fountain. Your room will look out upon this patio or one of the other three that Los Portales has. All the rooms have private bathrooms with hot water showers (with a glass doors, not curtains). Warm and sensible, you will be guaranteed a tranquil rest at this hostel. Calle 5, 10-125. Tel: 2-821-0139 / 5484, Fax: 2-821-0259, E-mail: losportaleshotel@yahoo.com. Updated: May 16, 2008.

La Plazuela

(ROOM: $52-72) A first-class hotel just across from Iglesia San José, Hotel La Plazuela is in a 1742 building rescued after the 1983 earthquake. Beautiful period pieces furnish the common sitting areas, and original watercolors adorn the walls. You can choose a room off the patio or with a street-side balcony. All have carved wood furniture, excellent beds, small refrigerator, cable TV and private bath with hot water. This is a perfect romantic getaway for you and your mate, or just to pamper yourself. Calle 5, 8-13. Tel: 2-824-1084, Fax: 2-824-0912, E-mail: hotellaplazuela@hotmail.com. Updated: May 16, 2008.

V!VA Member Review- La Plazuela

My in-laws stayed at this hotel and they had a very good experience. Washington DC, Mar 17, 2008.

Camino Real

(ROOM: $77-125) Foodies will want to stay at Hotel Camino Real; the hotel's restaurant has been recognized with multiple gastronomy awards and the menu covers a variety of plates. History buffs will also appreciate that completed in 1591, the building was first used as a center to teach high soceity women electing to become nuns to read and write. It became a hotel in 1982, and the décor reflects styles from both the Victorian age and the 1980s. Prices include tax and breakfast.Calle 5, 5-59. Tel: 2-824-3595 / 4514, Fax: 2-824-0816, E-mail: hotelcaminorealpopayan@caucanet.net.co, URL: www.hotelcaminoreal.com.co. Updated: May 16, 2008.

Hotel Dann Monasterio

(ROOM: $116-174) Hotel Dann Monasterio is the cream of the Popayán hotel crop. This Franciscan monastery-turned-hotel is the only accommodation around with a swimming pool. The gourmet restaurant serves local and international food. Wander through the open-air corridors and lounge in the well-kept garden. The hotel includes a bar, in-room satellite TV and breakfast. Calle 4A, 19-44. Tel: 2-824-2191, E-mail: centralreservas@hotelesdann.co, URL: www.hotelesdann.com. Updated: Apr 11, 2008.

Popayán Restaurants

Popayán offers visitors not only great Colombian food and parrillas (BBQ), but also an impressive selection of international food. Many eating establishments are closed on Sunday, and even more so on Sunday evening. *Almuerzos* and *comidas corrientes* range from $1.10-$3.70; the cheapest can be found on Calle 8, between Carreras 5 and 6. September is *chonta duro* season, a palm fruit that is served with salt and honey. Pick one up from the many street vendors. If you are self-catering, you can get supplies at the daily market at Calle 8N and Carrera 6, or at the Ley supermarket (Monday-Friday, 8 a.m.-8:30 p.m., Saturday 8 a.m.-9 p.m., Sunday and holidays 8:30 a.m.-3 p.m. Carrera 5, 6-33).

Helados de Paila

On those blindingly hot *payanés* days, drop by Helados de Paila for homemade ice cream made in a large copper bowl snuggled in a bed of ice. Blackberry, papaya and a variety of other natural fruit flavors await your taste buds (from $0.80 and up). A fresh fruit salad will also cool you down. You can come by on a rainy day, too, and warm up with a chicken or beef empanada ($1.05) and a hot drink. On Friday, Saturdays and Sundays the house specialty, pork ribs, is served. Closed Sundays. Carrera 9, 7-60. Tel: 2-824-3436. Updated: Dec 19, 2007.

La Cave

La Cave proves why Popayán was named the 2005 UNESCO World City of Gastronomy. The baked goods, particularly the cheesecake is arguably the best in the country. Aside from fresh baked goods, La Cave cooks up some fine pasta, crepes and other menu items. Neatly tucked into a quiet corner of the historical center of the city, your stomach will surely thank you for finding this Italian and French styled eatery. Calle 4, 2-07. Cel: 316-753-7670. Updated: May 29, 2008.

Comedor Vegetariano Bio-Integrales Kanda !

(LUNCH: $1.85) Ah, vegetarians, does Popayán have a surprise for you! A real, honest-to-goodness vegetarian restaurant with flavorful, nutritionally well-balanced meals. The *comida corriente* comes with lots of veggie sides and a salad bar, as well as brown rice with beans and/or soy meat. You can choose between a fruit drink or soy milk to accompany your meal. The ambiance is equally delicious, with several small rooms in which to dine and soothing flute music playing in the background. The regular set-plate meal is $1.85 and the executive, which comes with dessert, is $2.35. Unfortunately, Kanda is only open for lunch (11 a.m.-2:30 p.m.). Calle 6, 4-52. Tel: 2-839-4900, Cel: 311-372-6093. Updated: Dec 19, 2007.

Cafetería Santo Domingo La 4ª

(LUNCH: $1.60) Cafetería Santo Domingo is a small, simply furnished café. Its lunch special sells out quickly--and for good reason.

Not only is the meal tasty and inexpensive ($1.60), but the presentation has a special touch: all is served in black-fired pottery and wicker baskets. If you want just a quick snack, there are tamales and empanadas, as well as coffee, teas, malts, juices and beer. A word of warning to the tall diner: the second floor balcony has a low ceiling. Calle 4, 5-08. Updated: May 16, 2008.

Madeira Cafe

(ENTREES: $0.50-2.65) You can join locals for a quick cup of coffee or tea in this small, corner café. Perhaps you'd like to have that accompanied by a brownie or other sweet, or a sandwich ($0.50-$1.70). On a hot payanés day, a juice or malt (in chocolate, coffee, amaretto of fruit flavor) can be the thing to cool you down ($1.05-$2.35). On chill evenings, a *canelazo* or special coffee with liquor can warm your bones ($1.85-$2.65). The earth-tone interior is furnished with wood and wrought iron tables and chairs. Not only is there ground-floor seating, but also a small balcony for more intimate dining. Madeira has a shop next door selling local artesanía, chocolates and coffee. Open Monday to Friday, 9 a.m. to 8:30 p.m.; Saturday 2 to 8:30 p.m. Calle 3, 4-91. Updated: May 16, 2008.

No-Name Restaurant

On Calle 8 you can find several cheap restaurants. But this no-name, family-run eatery stands out from its neighbors in the quality of food it prepares (even boiling their water.) Even at the crowded lunch hour, service is quick and friendly here. The standard comida corriente is what's on the menu: soup, the main dish of a choice of meats, rice, beans and salad, plus refreshment made of fresh fruit. The only disadvantage is that it is closed on Sundays. Calle 8, 5-25. Updated: May 16, 2008.

El Portón del Patio

(ENTREES: $1.60) After spending a few hours in the Museo de Historia Natural, stop by El Portón del Patio for a quick bite to eat. The menu includes not only the standard comida corriente for meat-eaters or vegetarians ($1.60), but also crepes, mexican tacos and *arepas* with a variety of fillings ($1.05-2.10). Try the *marranita*, a green plantain filled with meat. Or just sit in the quiet, high-walled courtyard and have a cup of coffee beneath the old trees. If an afternoon shower hits, the porch is also a fine place for your break. El Portón del Patio is open Monday to Saturday for breakfast, lunch and dinner, from 8 a.m. to 8 p.m. Carrera 3, 1-83. Tel: 2-838-0044, Cel: 316-727-7004. Updated: May 16, 2008.

Comedor

(LUNCH: $2.10) While the restaurant at the Pilimbalá ranger station is under renovation, doña Blanca and her neighbors are continuing to cook up meals in a large hut on the other side of the thermal pools. (Don't get your hopes up too much; due to a 1995 earthquake, the heat and flow of these springs greatly diminished.) From dawn until 8 p.m., these women are serving up standard comidas corrientes for $1.60 (breakfast) to $2.10 (lunch and dinner). While waiting for your plate, you can stroll down the Sendero de Orquídeas right behind the restaurant and admire the orchids in bloom. The central fireplace is a wonderful place to warm up on those cold, rainy afternoons. Updated: Dec 19, 2007.

La Oficina

(LUNCH: $2.65) The interior of La Oficina is a bit incongruous with its name: the decorations are rustic, a bit humble, with pink cloths draping the tables—not quite like an office. Nonetheless, this is another favorite lunch spot for payaneses escaping from the doldrums of their offices ($2.65). The evening menu offers classic Colombian cuisine, such as *bandeja pisa, sancocho de gallina* and *frijoles antioqueños* ($4.20-6.35). Calle 4, 8-01. Tel: 2-824-0380. Updated: May 16, 2008.

Carbonera Parrilla

(ENTREES: $2.10-7.40) Carbonera Parrilla is for meat eaters only. A generous portion of chicken, pork, fish or succulent beef is served hot off the grill on a wooden plank to your picnic table ($2.10-7.40). If you can't make up your mind, you can order a combination platter. Alongside comes potatoes in bechamel sauce, rice, salad and—to dip your meat into—homemade chimichurri and barbecue sauce. To drink, there are juices and sodas ($0.35-1.05). But, hey, what's a BBQ without a beer ($0.80-1.15)? Open Monday to Saturday, noon to 9:30 p.m.; Sunday, noon to 4 p.m. Carrera 8, 5-15. Tel: 2-831-8581. Updated: May 16, 2008.

La Viña Parrillada

(LUNCH: $3.20) People drop in here to catch up on gossip over breakfast ($2.65). Come afternoon, the place hops with business people and office workers settling down to the scrumptious comida corriente ($3.20). Evenings you can dine until late, choosing from a wide array of à la carte dishes ($3.20-10.30); junior portions are available ($3.70-4.75). You can order wine by the glass or beer on tap. La viña means the vineyard, and this motif is carried throughout the restaurant, down to the grape-vine-printed tablecloths. For a more secluded space, retire to the balcony where there are only a few tables. Open daily from 8 a.m. to midnight. Calle 4, 7-79. Tel: 2-824-0602 / 3799. Updated: May 16, 2008.

Restaurant China

As you can guess by its name, Restaurant China dishes up Chinese food prepared with chicken, pork, beef or seafood and served with steamed white rice ($6.90-10.60). Vegetarian options are limited to chop suey or chow mein. Multi-course family menus are offered, which are more economical if you have a dining partner. The large interior is vacuous and bright. Despite the bright-red table cloths, clean-lined wood furniture and Chinese silk artwork, this restaurant has an undistinguished feel to it. Open daily 10 a.m. to 11 p.m. Calle 4, 13-31. Tel: 2-830-6734, 2-821-9639 / 9637. Updated: May 16, 2008.

Restaurante Pizzaría Italiana

(LUNCH: $3.70) This Italian café, decorated with Montreaux Jazz Festival posters, is a great spot for hearty, affordable dishes. Pull up a wood-and-leather seat at one of the tables and soon the wait staff will be with you. A pizza or pasta ($5-9.50) or tasty meat dish ($6.35-10.60) are all tasty options. The pastas come with a small salad, delectable garlic-parsley-onion dressing on the side, and bread. Wine is an expensive accompaniment to your meal ($3.60 for a scant-half glass). Restaurante Pizzaría Italiano also offers a set-lunch plate for $3.70. Open daily, noon to 10 p.m. Calle 4, 8-83. Tel: 2-824-0607. Updated: Dec 19, 2007.

Mey Chow

(ENTREES: $3.70-8) Upon entering Mey Chow through the plain wood doors, you are not immediately exposed to the grace of this establishment. Step out of the vestibule, past the sandstone reception, and its elegant simplicity is apparent. The central room is a skylighted courtyard with booths (for up to a dozen or so persons) and tables. Two side rooms provide more secluded dining. All is decorated in green, red and gold. On the back patio there is a leafy garden and peace cascade. The menu is limited, but has some offerings not seen elsewhere in Popayán, including Moo Goo Gai Pan and Szechuan Chicken ($3.70-$8). Any dish can be made vegetarian. Open Monday to Saturday, 6 to 11 p.m.; Sunday, noon to 3 p.m., 6 to 9 p.m.; closed Tuesday. Carrera 2, 2-23. Tel: 2-824-2761, 2-822-2043. Updated: Dec 19, 2007.

Popayán Nightlife

Whether your taste is for dancing to the latest salsa and reggaeton vibes, or to Latin golden oldies, or just chilling over a glass of wine and listening to cool jazz and bossa nova, you will find a place to sit and relax after a day catching the sights of Popayán. Many nightclubs, discos and bars are located right in the Historic Center, so you will not have to worry about catching a cab home. Updated: Nov 05, 2007.

Viejoteca, Rancho Grande

A discoteca where the DJ spins Latin golden oldies. Viejoteca draws a more mature crowd, reminiscing to the cumbia, salsa and merengue hits of their youth, the songs perhaps they fell in love to. But even if you are young, you can join in the shaking and swaying. Everyone is given a paper heart to pin on, the color designating civil status (single, engaged, married). On Thursdays there are dance parties starting at 9 p.m., until 3 a.m. Buses transit only until 11 p.m. ($0.60). To return home after that time, take a taxi ($2.65). Autopista Norte, 32N-50. Tel: 2-820-5219, Updated: Dec 19, 2007.

Bar La Casona del Virrey

For a more sophisticated evening out, have a drink at the lounge of the Hotel La Casona del Virrey. The low lights and soft music make for a pleasant retreat from the throbbing discos. On Friday evenings, a live trio performs boleros or tangos. Saturdays feature vallenatos or other types of laid-back music. No cover is charged for guests of the hotel; all others pay $2.65. Open Wednesday and Thursday, 5 p.m. to 11 p.m.; Friday, 5 p.m. to 3 a.m.; Saturdays, 7 p.m. to 3 a.m. Calle 4, 5-78m. Tel: 2-824-0836. Updated: Dec 19, 2007.

Imperio

This is the place to go for the young and young-at-heart. Imperio is a typical Latin discoteca with the latest reggaetón, electronic, salsa, merengue and vallenato hits, everyone dancing the night away until almost dawn. Open Thursday, Friday and Saturday from 9 p.m. to 3 a.m. The cover is $4.20; ladies, if you come before 10 p.m., you get in free. Carrera 9, between Calles 4 and 5. Updated: May 16, 2008.

PURACÉ

Alt: 2,381m Pop: 5,264 City Code:2

A road heads east from Popayán towards Parque Nacional Natural Puracé. After 18 kilometers (11 miles) it forks: one branch goes to La Plata and Garzón, the other to Pitalito. The largely unpaved La Plata road skirts the northern edge of the national park. Puracé is at Kilometer 12.
Almost 11km (7mi) beyond is the Cruce de Mina, the turn-off to a sulfur mine and the main ranger station at Pilimbalá (altitude: 3,350m/10,988ft).

Continuing along, you encounter other attractions of this sector of Parque Nacional Puracé: a condor observation point (Km 25), Laguna de San Rafael (Km 31), Cascada Bedón (Km 35), Termales San Juan (Km 37) and Cascada San Nicolás (Km 41). This finally arrives at La Plata, 147 kilometers (88 miles) from Popayán.

The southern fork is paved until Coconuco (altitude: 2,734 meters), where there are two hot springs: Agua Herviendo and Aguas Tibias. Twenty-four kilometers (14 miles) further along is Paletará. Both villages have good trout fishing and are also access points for Parque Nacional Puracé; from Paletará you can reach Laguna del Buey in the park. The next 62 kilometers (37 miles) of road is very rough until Isnos, near some of the archaeological and natural beauties of the San Agustín region. Twenty-seven kilometers (16 miles) beyond is the Cruce de San Agustín, the crossroads to that village. After another 27 kilometers (16 miles), the main road ends at Pitalito.

Puracé National Park has Andean forests, high Andean forests and páramo. Within its territory are the headwaters of Colombia's mightiest rivers: Cauca, Magdalena, Caquetá and Patía. It is home to over 160 species of birds, spectacled bear (Tremarctos ornatus), mountain tapir or danta de montaña (Tapirus pinchaque) and puma, among other mammals. In the 1990s, the San Diego Zoo in California helped to reintroduce the Andean condor to the region. A study is underway to document the number of orchid species here. Most of the park is *resguardo indígena*, or indigenous reserve lands, of the Coconuco, part of the Nasa (Páez) nation.

Reservations must be made with the national park office, Parques Nacionales Naturales de Colombia Surandina, in Popayán. The $7.40 entry fee is paid at Pilimbalá and Termales San Juan. Updated: Nov 08, 2007.

HISTORY

Parque Nacional Natural Puracé was founded in 1961, the first national park in Cauca Department. During the 1990s the FARC used the park as a base camp. The Colombia military, as a response, established bases on Volcán Puracé and other areas to combat the FARC. Since 2002, with President Uribe's campaign to eradicate the guerrilla movements, Puracé National Park has been cleaned of the forces—according to reports. After five years of virtually no tourism, Surandina is repairing service infrastructure in anticipation of visitors soon returning. Updated: Oct 31, 2007.

When to Go

November, December and January are the best months to visit Parque Nacional Natural Puracé and the surrounding region. The clear weather brings the highest daytime temperatures (14-16°C/57-61°F) but likewise, the coldest nighttime temperatures, sometimes dropping below freezing.

The windiest, coldest months are July and August. The rest of the year, be prepared for rain that can last all day and all night.

The wettest months are September-October, and February-March.

Holidays and Festivals

The hamlets neighboring the national park all have their festivals. Puracé village's patron saint is San Miguel Arcangel, celebrated from September 24-30. Sporting, cultural and culinary events, processions, pyrotechnic *vacas locas* and castles, and cock fights all take place during these days.

Coconuco celebrates San Pedro and San Pablo in June.

Paletará's annual rainbow trout fishing tournament is the second weekend of October.

Coconuco and Puracé celebrate Semana Santa with indigenous processions. In homes, foods such as corn, potatoes and rice, along with a wallet, are placed before a small light, a petition that food and money never be scarce for the family. Updated: Oct 31, 2007.

Getting To and Away from Puracé

Parque Nacional Natural Puracé and its villages are most easily accessible from Popayán, though you can reach them from Tierradentro (by way of La Plata) or San Agustín.

The North Road (Puracé and Pilimbalá)

From Popayán: Several companies run frequent buses to La Plata (Huila). The fare is $2.65 to the town of Puracé (1 hour); it is another $0.50 (30-45 minutes) to Cruce de Mina (beware of overcharging) and $1.05 (1.5 hours) to Termales San Juan. From the Cruce, walk one kilometer uphill to the turn-off for Pilimbalá (signed), then another 800 meters to the ranger station. The last bus passing by Cruce de Mina for Puracé village is at 5 p.m. From Puracé to Pilimbalá, you can also take the mining company bus at 7 a.m., leaving you about one kilometer from the ranger station. If you are coming from Tierradentro, take the direct Popayán bus or go to Cruce de San Andres de Pisimbalá and await a bus to that city; get off at Cruce de Mina (for Pilimbalá) or at Puracé village. To travel between Puracé and Coconuco, catch a bus or jeep at the fork of the two roads (Puracé-crossroads $1.05, crossroads-Coconuco $0.80).

The South Road (Coconuco and Paletará)

From Popayán: Sotrancauca—hourly to Coconuco 6:30 a.m.-5:30 p.m., $1.60, 1.5 hours. For Paletará, take a San Agustín or Pitalito bus and get off at the village. If coming from San Agustín, catch a Popayán-bound bus, which passes through Paletará and Coconuco. Updated: Nov 09, 2007.

Safety in Puracé

Parque Nacional Puracé is now safe. The military claims all landmines have been removed on Volcán Puracé; nonetheless, it is advised you stay on the trails any place in the park boundaries. The weather on the páramo can change rapidly. Temperatures reach freezing in some months, so bring plenty of warm clothing. Take precautions against hypothermia. Also have gear to protect against rain. Rubber boots are recommended. Folks in the neighboring villages say all is quiet and safe. The military presence is quite noteable in all the towns. Updated: Oct 31, 2007.

Puracé Services

Tourism Office

Before arriving to Parque Nacional Natural Puracé, you must contact Parques Nacionales Naturales de Colombia Surandina, in Popayán (Monday-Friday, 8-11:30 a.m., 2-4 p.m. Carrera 9, 25N-06, Tel: 2-823-1279 / 1212, URL: www.parquesnacionales.gov.co). The office will fill you in on present safety and weather conditions. It can also help you arrange for a guide. The rangers at the Pilimbalá station can also tell you about the park. In Puracé village, stop by the restaurant Micho for any information you may need about hiking in the area or about the national park.

Money

There are no banks, ATMs or places to change cash in any of the villages bordering the national park. Bring plenty of pesos with you.

Keeping in Touch

The Pilimbalá ranger station has a telephone and radio to communicate with the outside world. In Puracé, the Telecom office is on Carrera 7, a half-block from the church; at the time of writing, it had no service. In Coconuco, the company's office is on Carrera 2, the main street. In all the towns people rent their cellular phones for local or national calls, charging $0.15 per minute. The entire area is devoid of post offices. In some villages the only internet is at the high school, with connection for a few hours, Monday to Friday; priority is given to students. There is a privately run internet café in Coconuco (Daily 8 a.m.-9 p.m. Carrera 3, 2-99. $1.10 per hour).

Medical

When hiking or trekking in Parque Nacional Natural Puracé, carry along a first aid kit with basic medications. The park itself has no medical facilities. The Centro de Salud in Puracé village has 24-hour emergency and ambulance services (Carrera 6 3-50). There is a pharmacy behind the hospital, as well as at the house across the street at Calle 4 5-18, with the fotocopias sign. Coconuco's Centro de Salud is located at Carrera 2 5-59; it also has emergency attention. There is a pharmacy one block away (Monday-Friday, 8 a.m.-noon, 2-6 p.m., Saturday 8 a.m.-noon. Carrera 2, 4-15). Updated: Nov 01, 2007.

Things to See and Do

If you are bored of museums and churches and are ready to get out of the cities, dig out the hiking boots and head to Parque Nacional Natural Puracé. You can climb Volcán Puracé (4,640 meters/15,219 feet) or do the two-day trek around Pan de Azúcar (4,670 meters/15,318 feet) and the Cadena Volcánica de Coconuco. The pre-Hispanic Camino Nacional is also an off-the-beaten track adventure. The attractions along the north road make a great day excursion. For bird watchers, there are Andean condors and over 160 other species of birds. After days of hiking or trekking, you can soak in the hot springs in Coconuco. For those who like fishing, cast your line in Coconuco or Paletará for some of their famous rainbow trout. Updated: Nov 01, 2007.

Trout Fishing

Your fly lands softly in the crystalline water of Río Aguasilencio—Silent Water River—or one of its tributaries. A subtle breeze passes through the trees and grasses as sunlight dapples the landscape. Tonight you will be frying up the tender rainbow trout you catch here. But for now, it is the meditation of casting and waiting for the gentle tug on the line. If you are in Paletará some last week of October, you can challenge Colombians at the annual rainbow trout fishing tournement. Coconuco is 30 kilometers (18 miles) from Popayán by paved road, and Paletará 24 kilometers (14.5 miles) further on. You can also reach Coconuco and Paletará from San Agustín. See the Getting To and Away section for Puracé. Updated: Dec 19, 2007.

Hot Springs

After days of exploring the natural wonders of Puracé National Park and trekking across the cold, windy páramo, what better way to relax strained muscles than to soak in hot springs? Head down to Coconuco, on the south boundary of the park, where two thermal waters await you. Agua Herviendo is the hotter, bubbling out of the earth at 90°C (194°F)—enough to boil an egg in five minutes, it's said—and mixed with fresh spring water to a perfect temperature. This spa, owned and operated by the Coconuco-Nasa indigenous community, has three large pools and five "personal"-sized ones (the two closest to the source are very hot). The other hot springs are the privately owned Aguas Tibias. This place is more park-like, with thermal lagoons and pools, a water slide and thermal "jacuzzis" with mineral mud. Agua Herviendo has changing rooms, but no lockers. Next to the pools are several seating kiosks where you can place your belongings while soaking; keep an eye on them.

The hot springs are very crowded during holidays; if you want a more peaceful experience, avoid these times.

Both aguas termales have restaurants and lodging. At Agua Herviendo, a cabaña for up to six persons with private bath is $26.50 and a small one for up to four persons with shared bath is $16; camping costs $2.65 per tent per night. All options include free, 24-hour access to the pools. Aguas Tibias also has cabañas; camping is $8 per site.

Coconuco is 30 kilometers (18 miles) from Popayán by paved road, thus making this a nice day trip from the city. Agua Herviendo is one kilometer from the village by paved road (walk, or catch a collective pick-up truck from the main street $0.50 per person, $3.20 whole vehicle). Alternately, take the grassy cow trail that begins just past the Hotel Comfandi through pasturelands to Agua Herviendo, though beware patties and bulls (30 minutes). Aguas Tibias is four kilometers down the Coconuco-Paletará road. Updated: Dec 19, 2007.

Puracé Tours

Parque Nacional Natural Puracé is beginning to come back onto the radar screen of travelers. A few tour companies and guides in Popayán, San Agustín and Puracé village offer expeditions into the park. Better yet, there are local guides from the indigenous communities within the park who intimately know its terrain; the national park office in Popayán can help arrange their services for you. Updated: Nov 01, 2007.

Marino Garces

Prefer to stay in Puracé hamlet? You can still climb Puracé volcano in one day. Señor Marino Garcés can load you and your friends up in his four-wheel-drive Nissan and guide you to the top and back. He can also take you to visit Termales San Juan. For either excursion he charges a flat rate of $37 for up to eight persons. Bring along your own food and drink (if going to San Juan, you can eat there). For the volcano trek, remember to also have warm clothing, hat, gloves, good shoes or boots and raingear. Calle 2, 7-28. Tel: 2-847-7032. Updated: Nov 01, 2007.

Puracé Lodging

Accomodations in the area of Parque Nacional Natural Puracé are basic. There are only two options in the town of Puracé, which serves as a base for visiting the attractions along the north road. Within the park itself are cabanas, a cheaper hostel (under renovation at present time) and a campsite, which are more convenient for scaling Volcán Puracé. Of the villages on the south perimeter of the park, Coconuco has more choices, as it is a destination in its own right thanks to the hot springs, where lodging and camping are also available. At vacation times, reservations are necessary, especially for Coconuco. December and January are busy months in the park. Updated: Nov 01, 2007.

Estanco Oficial Residencias

(BED: $5.30) The cheapest place to stay in Coconuco is Estanco Oficial Residencias: Oficial Liquor Store Inn. In the front is where the locals and tourists hang to have a drink (especially popular on weekends and holidays). Beyond another door, along one side of the back courtyard, are the rooms to let. During the week, you can get a restful sleep here. The rooms are spacious and clean, the beds comfy. The four rooms share one clean, cold-water bathroom. Carrera 3, 4-23, Coconuco. Updated: Dec 19, 2007.

Residencias Cubita

(BED: $5.30) This small, four-room hotel is simple and plain, but the rooms are large, each with two beds. A few potted plants brighten up the patio. The common baths are clean--but brace yourself for the cold-water shower. Extra blankets are available for those nights when it gets frigid. The owners, Marlí and Marino, are hospitable. There is also secure parking for cars or motorcycles, and a laundry area. Calle 2, 7-28, Puracé village. Updated: Dec 19, 2007.

No-Name Hospedaje

(BED: $8-13.15) Simple, simple, simple describes this Coconuco hotel. A non-descript green building with a second-floor balcony and carved doors, it is a popular choice for vacationing Colombians—despite the fact that all the basic rooms share the common baths, which have only cold-water showers. But with two hot springs in Coconuco, you can always warm up there. Carrera 2 6-21, half-block from the church, Coconuco. Updated: Dec 19, 2007.

Puracé Restaurants

Your eating options in the Parque Nacional Natural Puracé region are fairly simple and limited. The menus are restricted almost exclusively to the comida corriente, or blue plate specials. Local trout also makes its appearance on the menus. At both Pilimbalá and Termales San Juan, there are small restaurants operated by the indigenous community. Basic supplies can be picked up at general stores or at the weekly markets in the villages. Updated: Nov 01, 2007.

Micho

Open afternoons into the evenings, Micho is the place to hang out for chicken wings, empanadas or other Colombian snacks while playing parcheesi, dominoes or chess. In one back room is a ping-pong table. At any hour you can view a movie from the 100-plus DVD collection on hand. The "theater" is a bare, white-washed lean-to with four plastic lawn chairs. The walls full of popular sayings and riddles are also an interesting way to pass the odd hour in this hamlet ("Does Colombia law prohibit you from marrying your widow's sister?"). Calle 2, 5-50, Puracé. Updated: Dec 19, 2007.

No-Name Restaurant

With whatever might be available in this small village, doña Elma whips up simple meals. Breakfast might be eggs, rice, potatoes and coffee ($1.30). Your lunch or dinner will, of course, have soup—and the main dish, meat or local trout, rice, yucca, tomatoes and a drink ($1.60). This eatery is very popular with the young soldiers stationed in Puracé. Calle 2, 6-15, Puracé. Updated: Dec 19, 2007.

Hato Viejo

Behind the green and orange bamboo "picket" fence is the front patio of the Hato Viejo restaurant. Take a table here, or inside in the light and airy dining room. The breeze passing through the large, open windows make the many wind chimes sing. Soon you will have your daily special in front of you ($1.95). Or perhaps today you're in the mood for some fresh rainbow trout. This eatery is popular with the village's doctors. Carrera 3 and Calle 5, Coconuco. Updated: Dec 19, 2007.

San Agustín

Alt: 1640m Pop: 30,000 City Code. 2

Like silent sentinels guarding the green mountains of southern Colombia, the pre-Columbian statues of San Agustín have long beckoned travelers to wander off the beaten track. The journey can be difficult, but the reward for these sojourners is days of walking through the countryside, exploring the numerous archaeological sites that bestow the name "Archaeological Capital of Colombia" to San Agustín.

The landscape also holds attractions: the nascent Río Magdalena, canyons, waterfalls and caves. The road from Popayán skirts the south boundary of Parque Nacional Natural Puracé; it is paved as far as Coconuco, after which it is poor to El Cruce, 27 kilometers (16 miles) from Pitalito. The road from Bogotá, by way of Neiva, Garzón and Pitalito, is completely paved. Life is laid-back in the village of San Agustín, so much so that many foreigners have decided to stay here to live.

Be prepared to spend a bit of time here learning about the enigmatic culture that a millennium ago carved monoliths (every one has a theory), hiking and just relaxing.Updated: Jan 10, 2008.

Photo by Dan Anderson

History

The people who carved the monoliths that populate the rolling lands of San Agustín remain a mystery. Today we call their civilization Agustinian, but its real name has been lost in the mists that swirl around these mountains. They are assumed to be the ancestors of the present-day Nasa (Páez) nation of the region. According to radiocarbon dating, the Upper Magdalena area had been inhabited since at least 4,000 years before Christ. The Agustinian culture is usually divided into two periods: the Formative, 1000 B.C.-1 A.D., and the Regional Classical, 1-900 A.D. This latter era was when most of the funerary sites were elaborated. Archaeologists believe the peoples of the pre-Columbian San Agustín and Tierradentro areas were of the same culture; remnants of roads lie beneath the jungle growth.

The Spanish settlement San Agustín was founded by Lucas de Herazo Mendigaña in 1790. It was always a sleepy town, until the latter part of the 20th century, when the civil war took root in the surrounding areas. Travelers' tales of encounters with the guerrilleros abounded. However, those days appear to be over with increased Colombian military presence, and once more San Agustín slips back into its quiescence. Updated: Jan 10, 2008.

When to Go

November, December and January are the best months to visit San Agustín, as there is less rain. July and August experience winds and cool temperatures. Rain is common the rest of the year, the wettest months being September, October, February and March.

San Agustín is once more gaining popularity amongst Colombians as a vacation destination. Keep this in mind if traveling there in July, August, December, January, Semana Santa and three-day holiday weekends.

San Agustín's principal patron saint is Saint Augustine, whose feast day is August 28. The village also commemorates San Pedro in June. Three noteworthy festivals take place here: In October is the Encuentro Nacional de Cultura, the National Cultural Encounter, and in November the Feria Equine (Horse Fair) and the Feria Artesanal y Comercial, highlighting the artisan and other production of the region.Updated: Jan 10, 2008.

Getting To and Away from San Agustín

Buses for the Parque Arqueológico leave from the Central Park every half-hour between 6 a.m. and 6 p.m. ($0.50, 20 minutes). Taxis run only until about 9 p.m. and charge $1-3, depending on the distance and time of day. Most transportation leaves from Calle 3, between Carreras 10 and 12.

To Pitalito—Pick-ups leave frequently from Calle 3, 5 a.m.-6 p.m., $2.10, 35-45 minutes.

Pitalito to La Plata—7 a.m., 10 a.m., 2 p.m., 4 p.m., $8.50, 3 hours. Or go to Garzón (bus $4.75, collective taxi $5.30), then to Pitalito (buseta $4.20, collective taxi $5.30). From La Plata you can go to Tierradentro. See that section for more details. From Pitalito service is more frequent to Neiva, Bogotá, Isnos and Popayán.

To Neiva—Taxis Verdes—4 a.m., 5 a.m., 8 a.m., 1 p.m., $10.50, 4 hours.

To Bogotá—Taxis Verdes—7 a.m., 7 p.m., $21, 9 hours. Coomotor—5 a.m., 6:30 p.m., 7:30 p.m., $22-27.30, 10 hours.

To Popayán—Coomotor—6 a.m., 9 a.m., 11 a.m., 3 p.m., 5 p.m., 7:30 p.m., $14.70, 6 hours. Cootranshuila (by way of Coconuco)—7 a.m., 10 a.m., 4 p.m., $13, 6 hours. Coming from Popayán, the bus may leave you at El Cruce, the crossroads for San Agustín. Catch a pick-up truck coming from Pitalito for San Agustín ($0.80).

Chivas: For neighboring villages, depart from near the market or from Calle 5.

Safety in San Agustín

In years past, many travelers reported their nighttime bus being stopped by FARC guerrillas and the passengers receiving a political lecture, but those days seem to be over. Since early this present millennium the Colombian military has occupied the town, surrounding countryside and roads. In terms of personal safety, it is safe to do at least the closer walks alone; some locals also say the longer hikes (e.g., to Alto de los Ídolos) are also okay. Updated: Jan 10, 2008.

San Agustín Services

Tourism Office

The municipal tourist office gives out good maps, but the service is a bit lacking (Monday-Friday, 8 a.m.-noon, 2-6 p.m., weekends and holidays, closed. Calle 3 and Carrera 12, in the Alcaldía building, Tel: 8-837-3062, E-mail: webmaster@sanagustin.com.co, alcaldia@sanagustin-huila.gov.co, URL: www.sanagustin.com.co). If the official tourism office is closed, stop by one of the tour operator offices. World Heritage Travel has many years experience orientating visitors to San Agustín.

Money

Banco de Bogotá has a Mega Red ATM (accepts all cards) open 24 hours on the main drag at Calle 3, 12-73. To change U.S. cash dollars, go to Almacén De Todos (daily 8 a.m.-7 p.m. Calle 3, 12-28) or Tienda Don Lazo (Calle 3, 11-62); both give well-below market rates. If you are journeying with travelers checks, you are out of luck in San Agustín; stock up on pesos before coming. Neither Moneygram nor Western Union have offices in San Agustín; the nearest are in Neiva and Popayán.

Keeping in Touch

San Agustín does have internet—four cafés, in fact. Internet Galería Café is the cheapest, at $0.70 per hour, and has a digital camera card reader. While pounding away on the keyboard, you can enjoy a coffee, beer or smoke, or let your eyes rest on the artwork decorating the walls. (Daily, 8 a.m.-10 p.m. Calle 3, 12-24). Enter.net charges more, $0.95, but has Skype; this non-smoking establishment sells no refreshments (Daily 8 a.m.-10:30 p.m. Carrera 11, 3-10). Other communications services in San Agustín seem to hide out in stores. Make local, national and international calls from Telecom in the t-shirt silk-screening shop near the Alcaldía (Monday-Friday, 8 a.m.-noon, 2-6 p.m., Saturday 2-4 p.m. Calle 3). Adpostal, the post office, is in the Maxitodo de la 13 store (Monday-Friday 8 a.m.-noon, 2-6 p.m. Carrera 13, 4-09).

Medical

Hospital Arsenio Repizo, the public hospital for San Agustín, is at Calle 3 and Carrera 3. There are many pharmacies on Calle 3, especially between Carreras 9 and 13.

Camera

It appears there's only one camera shop in San Agustín: Foto Color. Besides developing your film in one hour, it also carries 100, 200 and 400 ASA Kodak and Fuji 110 film; digital camera cards; and disposable, analog and digital cameras. However, it does not repair cameras (Monday-Friday, 8-11:30 a.m., 2-6 p.m., 7:30-10 p.m., Saturday 2-6 p.m.). Updated: May 20, 2008.

Shopping

Artesanías Bambú

Walking down the street near Parque Bolívar, you may hear the strands of *charango* music coming from a shop. Welcome to Artesanías Bambú, where director Manual Una will lay aside his instrument as you enter. The walls are strewn with jewelry, bags and multitudes of items that he and area artisans create from bamboo, clay, wood, guadua and other natural fibers. Or perhaps one of the stone carvings—replicas of this valley's statuary—strikes your fancy. Want a charango like don Manual plays? Hand-crafted instruments of all sorts are also for sale. For a special celebration, hire don Manual to perform. Carrera 13, 3-06. Cel: 310-759-3408, URL: www.howlingearth.com. Updated: Apr 14, 2008.

Taller de Cestería

Through the open doors, sunlight dapples the white-washed adobe walls of a small workshop. Within, strands of *vejuco alín*, a plant fiber, wave through the air as don Segundo weaves them into baskets and vases. Many times he carefully threads a bead onto the filament, adding colorful touches to his original creations. So he passes his days, waiting for you to arrive to purchase one of these cestas to take home. Also leaning against these ancient walls are hand-carved bamboo walking sticks, the perfect item to steady your pace as you hike to San Agustín's many wonders. Calle 5, 15-07. Cel: 311-242-9374. Updated: Apr 14, 2008.

Activities ●

1 Cancha de Tejo el Recreo B3
2 Centro el Templete A3
3 Iglesia NS de Lourdes B3
4 Iglesia San Agustín B2
5 Parque Arqueológico B1
6 Piscina Municipal Las Moyas A1
7 Plaza Cívica B3
8 Plaza de Ferias B2

Eating

9 Casa de Tarzán B3
10 Hotel Colonial Asadero B2
11 Pizza Manía B3
12 Restaurant Café Bar el Rancho B3
13 Bar La Casona de San Agustín B1
14 Cafetería Hotel Los Ídolos B3
15 Restaurant Brahama B2
16 Restaurant La Terraza B2

Services ★

17 Adpostal B2
18 Tourism Office B3
19 Banco de Bogotá ATM B2
20 Enter.net B3
21 FotoColor B2
22 Hospital Arsenio Repizo B4
23 Telecom B2

Shopping

24 Artesanías Bambú B2
25 Market B3
26 Solo Cuero (Just Leather) B3
27 Taller de Cestería B2

Sleeping

28 Casa de Nelly B3
29 Finca El Maco A1
30 Hospedaje El Jardín B3
31 Hotel Cambi B2
32 Hotel Central B3
33 Hotel Colonial B3
34 Hotel Los Ídolos B3
35 Hotel Yalconia B1
36 San Agustín Internacional B3

Tours ♦

37 Magdalena Rafting B2
38 Viajes Lanky Balcony B3
39 World Heritage Travel B3

Sólo Cuero

A large sign hanging above the door of this small workshop displays naively drawn saddlebag, machete sheaths and boots. In bold print, it announces Only Leather—Manufacture of: coverings, bags, belts, sandals, boots and other horse tackle. Indeed, whether you are preparing for the long journey to Ecuador on a steed or just want to pick up some of

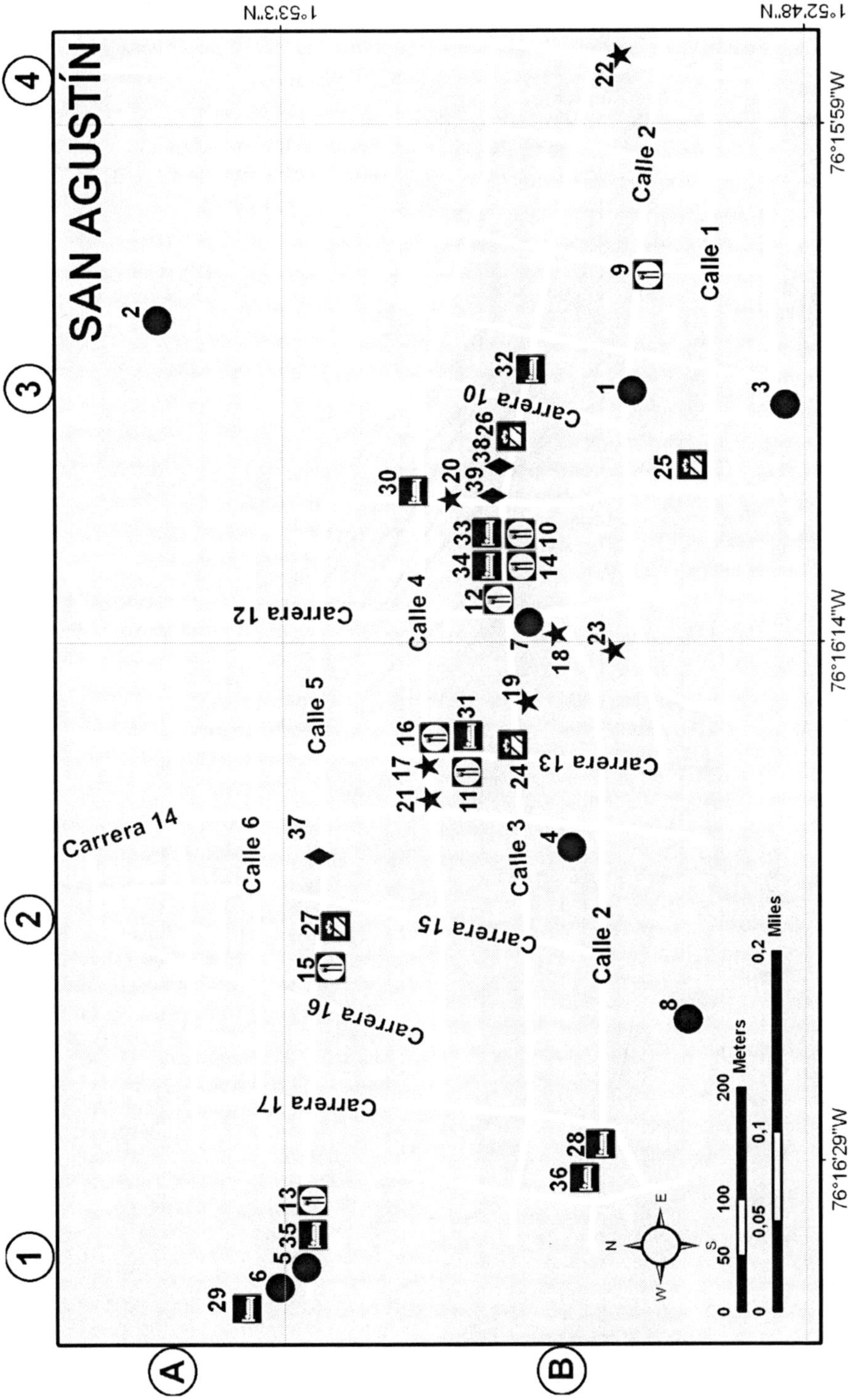
SAN AGUSTÍN
1°53'3"N
1°52'48"N
76°15'59"W
76°16'14"W
76°16'29"W
Carrera 10
Carrera 12
Carrera 13
Carrera 14
Carrera 15
Carrera 16
Carrera 17
Calle 1
Calle 2
Calle 3
Calle 4
Calle 5
Calle 6
0 50 100 200 Meters
0 0,05 0,1 0,2 Miles
N S E W
1 2 3 4
A B

Colombia's renowned leatherwork at reasonable prices, Solo Cuero is the place to come. Wooden boards in the doorway display an assortment of sporty sandals. If nothing quite strikes your fancy or meets your needs, Don Isidro can fill your special order. Calle 3, 10-59. Tel: 8-837-3518. Updated: Apr 14, 2008.

Dulce de Pata

On Calle 3, near Hotel Los Ídolos, doña María Córdoba passes the day seated on a stool. With two wooden paddles, she works a taffy-like substance into the perfect texture. Occasionally someone stops to buy a wooden stick or small cupful of this tasty sweet called *dulce de pata*, which literally translates into hooves' sweet. Doña María boils cows' hooves to remove the gelatin, then adds *panela* (raw sugar) and cooks it until it is thick and molasses-colored. She brings a kettle of this with her everyday and sits right here, working the liquid until it becomes off-white taffy. Go on, don't be squeamish—try a bit. Updated: Apr 11, 2008.

Things to See and Do

Be prepared to spend at least a couple of days in San Agustín. The area is perfect for hiking or horseback riding, with the reward of statues, tombs and petroglyphs. Some well-known sites include La Chaquira, Obando, Alto de los Ídolos and Alto de las Piedras. Take the challenge, though, to get to some of the less-visited ones, like Lavaderos or Alto de la Guacas. The Parque Arqueológico encompasses four sites and provides a good introduction. The scenery is equally stunning with dozens of waterfalls like Saltos del Mortiños and de Bordones tumbling through the jungle to join the nascent Río Magdalena, to whose headwaters you can trek or horsback ride. Other adventures include walking the Macizo Colombiano or riding all the way to Ecuador on horse. Sports are not to be forgotten. There's white water rafting, a huge city swimming pool, and a Colombian favorite, *tejo*—with an interesting twist. Updated: Jan 10, 2008.

Horseback Riding

Imagine mounting a beautiful mare to traverse these emerald hills, exploring the silent sentinels that still guard the San Agustín region, or the many lagoons and waterfalls hidden within the folds of this landscape. Prices per hour ($4.20) and per excursion are set by the municipality. The five-hour trip to El Tablón, La Chaquira, La Pelota and El Purutal is about $13, plus another $13 for your accompaniment's horse. Another adventure several travelers have undertaken is to ride with a guide all the way to Otavalo, Ecuador; this takes a major investment of time and money, however. One guide frequently lauded is Pacho Muñoz (Cel: 311-827-7972, E-mail: pachitocampesinito@yahoo.es). Maps provided by the tourism office and travel agencies show the network of trails in the region. Ask for specifics and about safety before heading out. Check your horse to be sure it is in healthy condition. If you take a guide, you will have to pay for his horse as well as his services. Updated: Apr 14, 2008.

Hiking around San Agustín

You can spend weeks hiking through San Agustín's verdant countryside. Trails lead to many of the archaeological sites, making for good day trips. Several—day treks, like the Macizo Colombiano—take you to crystalline lagoons sparkling on the páramo and the headwaters of the Magdalena River. A popular ramble is the El Purutal-to-El Tablón circuit. Another all-day excursion, now said to be quite safe, is the wending sendero to Alto de los Ídolos. Less-visited sites, such as Alto de las Guacas and the caves at Lavaderos are also worth looking into. Break out the boots and take a hike—scores of adventures await you in these mountains. Updated: Apr 14, 2008.

Rafting on the Magdalena

As Colombia's greatest river, the Magdalena winds 1540 kilometers (924 miles) and boils through many canyons before eventually ending in the Caribbean Sea. You can begin this sojourn with the río riding on class-II to IV white waters. The most popular course is an 11-kilometer (6.6-mile) run through class II and III rapids, suitable for the whole family. Another route features 30 torrents within 28 kilometers (17 miles). The roughest adventure, for experienced sojourners only, is a 20-kilometer (12-mile) sprint through a canyon, with class III and IV rapids. Two- and three-day excursions can also be arranged. Aptly, the indigenous name for the Magdalena is Guacaayo, meaning River of Tombs. Contact one of the local tour operators to set up your rafting adventure. Most operators require a minimum age of 12 years and an ability to swim. Make sure the tour operator provides you with proper safety equipment that is in good condition. A wet suit is necessary, as the water of the Magdalena is quite cold. Updated: Apr 14, 2008.

Parque Arqueológico

The main attraction in San Agustín is the Parque Arqueológico, which encompasses four artificially leveled hills containing tombs and sculptures that are hallmarks of the Agustinian culture. Between these hills are Fuente de Lavapatas, hand-carved pools used for ceremonial purposes, and Alto de Lavapatas, home of more tombs and sculptures. A path near the museum leads into the Bosque de Estatuas (Forest of Statues), which displays over 30 carvings. The museum houses pottery, jewelry and other finds from this site, dating from 1000 B.C.-900 A.D., as well as explains the society and culture of these mysterious people. It takes at least four hours to visit all the sites in the Parque Arqueólogico. Guides for hire, some of whom speak several languages, wait near the ticket office ($16 for group of 1-10). Some of the explanatory signs are in English and Spanish.Located three kilometers (1.8 miles) from San Agustín. Busetas leave from Parque Bolívar (daily, every 20 minutes 6 a.m.-6 p.m., $0.50). Mesetas and Fuente de Lavapatas are open from 8 a.m.-5 p.m., Alto de Lavapatas 8 a.m.-4 p.m., Museum 9 a.m.-5 p.m., Ticket Sales 8 a.m.-4 p.m. Updated: Apr 14, 2008.

Piscina Municipal Las Moyas

Once the sun begins to shine in San Agustín, it gets downright hot. The perfect way to cool down after visiting the Parque Arqueológico or doing the El Tablón-to-El Purutal circuit is to swing by the Piscina Municipal Las Moyas. A more-than-Olympic-sized swimming pool full of cool, fresh spring water awaits your laps. There's even a slide to sweep you off your tired feet. After drying off, shoot a few games of billiards in the ranchito. Off-road to Parque Arqueológico. Head out of town on Calle 5; the marked turn-off for the pool is 400 meters (1300 feet) along the road to the Parque Arqueológico; the piscina is a further 100 meters (320 feet) up the side road. You can also take a buseta from Parque Bolívar ($0.50). Updated: Apr 14, 2008.

Tejo

After going through the stands of the market on a lazy Sunday, you might find yourself staring at a sign that reads "Cancha de Tejo El Recreo." Through the courtyard of the rough, tin-roofed cancha, you'll find men in various stages of drunkenness throwing a 2.5-pound (1.125- kilo) lead weight at an up-right board 18m (59ft) down court. Tejo is a popular sport in Southern and Eastern Colombia, often played for a set price that includes a beer. Men and women play in different courts (women's courts are smaller), where you sip on your beer waiting for your turn to throw the weight as hard as you can. In other places, though, the target is called a bocín, which has small packets of gun powder attached to it; the object is to explode these. It seems the resourceful citizens of San Agustín have found a new use for the landmines that were laid in the backcountry during the Civil War actions in their area. Calle 2, 9-40. Updated: Apr 14, 2008.

San Agustín Tours

Dozens of guides work in San Agustín; however, few of them are officially licensed or speak anything other than Spanish. With the area now under the control of the Colombian military, more tour operators have opened their doors in anticipation of increased numbers of national and foreign tourists. At the Parque Arqueológico there are official guides for hire, many of whom speak English. They charge $16 for groups of one to ten people. Luis Alfredo Salazar guides in seven languages, including Japanese. Updated: Jan 10, 2008.

Magdalena Rafting

Magdalena Rafting is very highly recommended by travelers seeking the adventure of the rapids of the Upper Río Magdalena. With over 20 years experience on different rivers around the world, owner Amid provides his clients with all the safety equipment—neoprene suits to protect against the frigid waters, helmets and lifejackets—to make the run down Colombia's mightiest waterway three times daily, whether in raft or kayak. He also offers other trips, including the 20-kilometer (12-mile) one through the Magdalena River canyon and two or three day excursions. Don't know how to paddle? No sweat, Magdalena Rafting can pull the strokes for you, or teach you how to in special courses. Calle 5, 14-12, or stop by Creperie François Restaurant on the left-hand side of Calle 5, just before the Parque Arqueológico. Cel: 311-271-5333, E-mail: info@magdalenarafting.com, URL: www.magadalenarafting.com. Updated: Apr 14, 2008.

World Heritage Travel Office / Viajes Patrimonio Mundial

World Heritage Travel Office is San Agustín's oldest tour operator, partly owned and operated by the town's former tourism officer. It is a good alternative for receiving information about the attractions in the region. World Heritage offers everything from hikes or horseback riding to the nearby sites, to rafting the Río Magdalena. The all-day jeep trip is popular, taking in the Narrows of the Magdalena River, Obando, Alto de los Ídolos, Alto de las Piedras and several waterfalls for $13.00, including driver and transportation, but not lunch, entry fees or guide. Multi-lingual guides are available. Calle 3, 10-84. Tel: 8-837-3940, Cel: 311-292-4241, E-mail: viajespatrimoniomundial@yahoo.es. Updated: Apr 14, 2008.

Viajes Lanky Balonky

Juan Arbey, a SENA-certified guide, operates Viajes Lanky Balonky, one of San Agustín's newer tour providers. He offers a one-day package that takes in a wide-range of experiences in the San Agustín region: in the morning, horseback riding the El Tablón-La Chaquira-La Pelota- El Purutal circuit ($13-24, depending on number of persons), and in the afternoon a jeep trip to the Obando-Altos de los Ídolos-Alto de las Piedras circuit, taking in a waterfall and the Parque Arqueológico to boot. Lanky Balonky also provides multi-day ecological tours to Parque Nacional Natural Puracé on horse ($210 for one person, $132 per person for three or four participants). Calle 3, 10-62. Cel: 312-423-9995, 311-234-9448, E-mail: juanarbey@yahoo.com / lankybalonkysa@yahoo.es. Updated: Apr 14, 2008.

SAN AGUSTÍN LODGING

San Agustín is a budget traveler's haven. Most places charge about $5 per person. You can choose to lodge in town or out in the countryside on a ranch. Quite a few places are foreign-owned. Camping is mostly on the road on the way to the Parque Arqueológico, along which higher-price-ranged hotels are also located. Mid-range inns are almost non-existent. If staying outside the village, consider you will be walking home in the dark after a late dinner or drink, as taxis cease to run after 9 p.m. Updated: Jan 10, 2008.

Finca El Maco

(BED: $4.20-10.50) René has created the wonderful ecological Finca El Maco for those budget travelers who want to stay in fresh country air, eat excellent pizza and relax while checking out all San Agustín has. Creative lodging choices—how about a night in a tipi with a fire pit?—add to your adventure here. For a little splurge, have a massage to ease your muscles after a day of hiking or horseback riding. Try the organic dairy products made right on the farm. All is run with the attention for which the Swiss are renowned. Spanish, English, German and Italian are spoken. Tipi Cabaña (with common bath) $7.40, Chalet (with private bath) $9.50 (low season), $10.50 (high season). 1km (0.6 mi) from the village. Tel: 8-837-3437, Cel: 311-271-4802, E-mail: info@elmaco.ch, URL: www.elmaco.ch. Updated: Apr 16, 2008.

Hospedaje Cambi

(BED: $4.20-10.50) Just a half-block from Parque Bolívar, Magola Pérez welcomes San Agustín visitors to these inexpensive, simple, clean rooms in an old colonial building. Nearly all the rooms have TV and private bath; however, three singles with common bath await the solo budget traveler—one of the cheapest options in town. Most importantly, in the cool nights of this village, the quarters are warm and the common baths have hot water. Sitting areas in the flower-filled back patio invite relaxing on sunny days. During low season, a common bath costs $4.20 per person and $8 for a private bath and cable TV. The high season starts off at $5.30 per person or $10.50 for the private arrangement. Carrera 13, 3-36. Tel: 8-837-3357, Cell: 310-782-4958, E-mail: magolita2@hotmail.com. Updated: Apr 16, 2008.

Hotel Colonial

(BED: $5.30-8) On the main street of San Agustín, right where the collective taxis and pick-ups arrive, you can find Hotel Colonial. Set in another classic, aged building, this inn tenders ample, tidy rooms with private or common hot-water bath. Service is attentive and the staff knowledgeable about what to do and see in the region. For those discovering Colombia on motorbike, there's parking for your wheels. On the ground floor is a good restaurant serving up inexpensive set meals. Calle 3, 11-25. Tel: 8-837-3159, Cel: 311-459-3314. Updated: Apr 16, 2008.

Hotel Los Ídolos

(ROOM: $5.30-10.60) Hotel Los Ídolos is definitely the cheapest place to stay in San Agustín if you have a traveling partner. Be warned, however, that the rooms are claustophically small and stuffy, with only a small window set high. These wood-paneled spaces are hot during the day and cold at night. The only furniture is the beds, but even so the rooms are cramped. Nonetheless, if you are only using them as sleeping quarters, they are tolerable. Calle 3, 11-47. Tel: 8-831-3079. Updated: Apr 16, 2008.

Hospedaje El Jardín Casa Colonial !

(BED: $5.30-6.35) The Muñoz family opens the doors of its home in this well-preserved colonial building on a quiet side street in San Agustín village. The first thing that strikes you is the restaurant patio, full of hammocks, potted plants, stone replicas of Augustinian statues, a fireplace and aviary. The rooms are just as impressive, all with spectacular views of the surrounding mountains. Some of the rooms have a balcony. The bathrooms, both common and private, have hot water. Carrera 11, 4-10. Tel: 8-837-3455, Cel: 312-295-0398, E-mail: eljardin@hosteltrail.com/eljardin, URL: www.hosteltrail.com/eljardin. Updated: Apr 16, 2008.

Hotel Casa de Nelly

(BED: $5.30-10.50) Since the mid-1980s, French-owned Casa de Nelly has provided fine cabañas amidst a beautiful forest. Cats and dogs stroll through the terraced gardens and aviary. Nice touches abound in the sharply decorated, rattan-furnished rooms whose walls are painted with murals. Cabañas have a sitting area for curling up after a long day of visiting ruins. Even the dorm room is quite spacious, fitting only four guests. The Tudor-styled main house serves as lodge and restaurant. If you are on a budget, a common kitchen is also available. 2km (1.2 mi) from the village, off the Vereda La Estrella. Cel: 311-535-0412, 312-565-8339, E-mail: hotelrestaurantebarcasadenelly@yahoo.com.

Hotel Central

(BED: $6.35-8) This colonial-era hotel is tranquil, despite being on San Agustín's main street. With a family atmosphere, Hotel Central is the preferred choice of some travelers, thanks to its convenient location to restaurants and bus companies. The wood passageways have lots of seating, tables and plants to while away rainy days. All the rooms are large and adequately furnished, with windows either onto the patio or the street. Those quarters in front have classic wood balconies to watch the village's comings and goings. Unfortunately, only cold water flows from the bathroom taps. Calle 3, 10-32. Tel: 8-837-3027. Updated: Apr 16, 2008.

La Casa de Francois

(BED: $7.50-15) Friendly owner Francois will make your stay on his Gaudi-inspired estate well worth remembering. In fact, many guests of La Casa think they will stay for a few days and end up there for weeks, basking in the gorgeous San Agustín town and country views. Francois, who has owned the farm for fifteen years, went with a colorful and classy theme for his three bamboo and cob cottages. The dorm room is impeccably designed with wine bottles in the walls and holds up to eight people. For a bit more luxury and space, the bamboo hut houses three double beds. There are also two private rooms with hammocks to enjoy the view. All rooms share clean bamboo bathrooms with hot water. Meals can be prepared in Francois's creative, communal kitchen made from glass mosaics. Head up the hill on Carrera 13. Take the second right turn on the steep, dirt road, following the signs for "Hotel." A bit further up the hill, you will find La Casa de Francois on the left. Tel: 8-837-3847, Cel: 316-359-5618, URL: www.hosteltrail.com/lacasadefrancois. Updated: May 29, 2008.

Camping San Agustín

(SITE: $7.95-18.65) Camping San Agustín is a broad grassy expanse that allows not only tent, but also vehicle camping. If you don't have your own tent, you can rent one, complete with pad, air mattress, sheets and pillow ($5.30). Under the trees is a cook area, but you have to supply your own wood. In the main house of Camping San Agustín there are also rooms to rent, either sharing the cold-water showers with the campers or with its own bath. Out back is a three-bedroom cabaña for eight persons with a private, hot water bath. The camping site fee is $6.35 plus $1.60 per person. Tent rentals go for $5.30, or you can get a room with a shared bath for the same price, or one with a private bath for $8. Cabins are $18.65 per person. Two hundred meters (650 ft) down the road behind the Hotel Yalconia, across from the Piscina

Municipal Las Moyas. Follow Calle 5 out of town towards the Parque Arqueológico. Turn right on the first road after Hotel Yalconia. Tel: 8-837-3804.Updated: Apr 16, 2008.

Hotel Yalconia

(ROOM: $31-50) Hotel Yalconia is San Agustín's oldest luxury-class hotel. Of modern architecture, this two-story building provides all of the comforts one would want while enjoying the wonders of this region. The sitting areas are bright and airy, as are the guest rooms. The tiled bathrooms are immaculate. All are decorated with furnishings of the Bauhaus era, yet nothing shows its age. The pool out back is perfect for Agustinian sunny days. The hotel offers packages, which include a floor show of Andean music. Vía al Parque Arqueológico, 400m (quarter mile) from town. Tel: 8-837-3013, Cel: 316-304-8353, Fax: 8-837-3001, E-mail: hyalconia@gmail.com, URL: www.inturcol.com. Updated: Apr 17, 2008.

San Agustín Internacional Hotel

(ROOM: $63-160) These dream houses, perfect for families, are set in estate-like grounds with stone-lined lagoons and emerald lawns. Have you ever fantasized about staying in a typical Mediterranean house, or a Scandinavian? Or how about a TV-perfect U.S. home, or a Colombian hacienda just like on the telenovelas? Soon your family can also choose an Arabian one straight out of 1001 Nights, or a pagoda. Also under construction is a traditional indigenous maloka that'll have individual rooms for let. Vía Vereda La Estrella (end of Calle 2, at Carrera 19). Cel: 312-433-2510, 311-445-2615, E-mail: inturcol@gmail.com / hyalconia@gmail.com, URL: www.inturcol.com. Updated: Apr 17, 2008.

San Agustín Restaurants

The eating scene in San Agustín is pretty boring—just good old Colombian food and little else. A comida corriente usually costs $1.85. The public market at Carrera 11 and Calle 2 is a great place to grab a cheap meal. The weekly markets, when folks come in from neighboring villages, are Sunday and Monday. While in San Agustín, be sure to try dulce de pata or gelatina, a taffy-like sweet made of boiled cows' hooves and sugar.

Few choices for nightlife are to be found in San Agustín. Several of the bars and discos are said to be rough-and-tumble types of places. Nonetheless, there are a few more chilled-out places where you can kick back and relax after a long day of hiking. Almost all are located in the village; remember that if you are staying out in the country, taxis stop running at 9 p.m. and you'll have a long, dark walk home. Updated: Jan 10, 2008.

Hotel Colonial Asadero y Restaurante

The Asadero y Restaurante of the Hotel Colonial fixes up one of the best comida corrientes—whether breakfast, lunch or dinner—in San Agustín, and at one of the better prices to boot, only $1.85. For those who prefer something a bit lighter, skip the soup and it'll cost $1.60. The Asadero also has specialty dishes: chicken breast, catfish, mojarra fish, trout, pork and beef steak hot off the grill ($6.50-8). Calle 3, 11-25. Tel: 8-837-3159, Cel: 311-459-3314. Updated: Apr 17, 2008.

Pizza Mania

(ENTREES: $6.90-14.70) Just a half-block from the main square, under soft, hot-pink light, one of San Agustín's few forays into international cuisine is just opening up. This is Pizza Mania, a small, three-table affair. Grab a slice of pizza, whether Hawaiian, meat, chicken with mushrooms, margarita or vegetarian. If a day of hiking has your stomach growling, a whole pie costs $6.90-14.70. Saturdays and Sundays, the French-German owner whips up a special lasagna. To wash it all down, she can serve you beer, soda or juice. Open daily 6-10 p.m. Carrera 13, 3-47. Updated: Apr 17, 2008.

Brahama

As you're heading out one early morning to the Parque Arqueológico, stop by Restaurante Brahama for pancakes with chocolate or your choice of fruit. Later in the day, its home-cooked vegetarian set lunch hits the spot. If your dining companions are avowed carnivores, they won't feel too out of place. This vegetarian restaurant also serves the blue-plate special with meat for the same price. Á la carte plates and fruit salads are available any time of day. The three green rooms are a bit worn; off the large one in back there is a gate inviting you to the garden. Open daily 7 a.m.-7 p.m. Calle 5, 15-11. Updated: Apr 17, 2008.

La Terraza

Upstairs, above the Banco Agrario, a large orange and white space greets you, made even brighter by the great windows around two sides. Many folks, both local and foreign, chow down on Restaurante La Terraza's specials, which come with a choice of meats at any time of day. A few opt for regular menu items or broasted chicken. The service is quick here, though unfortunately the big-screen TV can be very loud at times. Calle 4, on the corner of Carrera 13, 2nd floor, Banco Agrario. Cel: 314-229-3796. Updated: Apr 17, 2008.

La Casona de San Agustín !

One of San Agustín's finest restaurants has sophistication from the furnishing to the menu. Cuisine covers the gamut of poultry to red meats to local fish, all prepared fresh and served with house salad and French fries or rice. Take a seat on the front patio, or in the back room with a balcony overlooking the Quebarada Las Moyas. While waiting for your order (the menu advises it'll take 20-30 minutes) challenge your dining partner to a game of chess at the giant board on the back balcony. La Casona also serves breakfast. Calle 5, 21-125, vía Parque Arqueológico (on right side of road, just past Hotel Yalconia). Tel: 8-837-9416. Updated: Apr 17, 2008.

Cafetería Hotel Los Ídolos

In the front-covered courtyard of the Hotel Los Ídolos is another cheap San Agustín eatery. The friendly women here serve up down-home Colombian meals. The full-helping set lunch is a comfortable $1.60, but the bargain half meal still has quite ample portions for those travelers watching their pennies. This Restaurante-Cafetería is also a good place to stop off for a juice (made with purified water) to recharge your batteries from all the sightseeing. Calle 3, 11-47. Tel: 8-831-3079. Updated: Apr 17, 2008.

Casa de Tarzan

With rough-paneled walls and tree trunks towering inside this bar, you might be tempted to go swinging from one of the rope-vines hanging from the branches after downing a beer here. But better to just sit back and swap tales with other travelers, or catch the movie or soccer game on the big-screen TV. Open Monday-Saturday, 8 p.m. until whenever; Sundays and holidays from 2 p.m. Calle 2, 8-04, across from the Bomberos fire station, Tel: 8-837-3457, Cel: 310-781-8797, 312-200-5124. Updated: Apr 17, 2008.

Restaurante-Café-Bar El Rancho

To get to the restaurant or café, then head down the stairs. To savor a Colombian beer or drink, climb the staircase where a large open space greets you. Pull up one of the leather-covered chairs at a wooden table (the ones on the balcony with a view of Calle 3 are fine for watching the evening Augustinian happenings) and check out the paintings, animal skins and Andean musical instruments bedecking the brick walls. Soon the bartender will be with you not only to ask for your drink order, but also your request for music. Open daily 4 p.m.-2 a.m. Calle 3, 11-60. Updated: Apr 17, 2008.

NEAR SAN AGUSTÍN

San José de Isnos

San José de Isnos (Quechua for Sacred Rock) is a small village 26 kilometers (15.5 miles) north of San Agustín. Five kilometers (3 miles) west is one of the most important Agustinian sites, Alto de los Ídolos, consisting of 37 funerary monuments dating from 1st Century B.C.-6th Century A.D. Some of the sculptures at this crescent-shaped site still retain their paint.

Five kilometers (3 miles) east of Isnos is Alto de las Piedras, a 9th Century B.C. site that is home to the famed Doble-Yo (Double- or Dual-I) figure. This orchid-adorned place contains nine burial mounds with statuary. Another nine kilometers (5.5 miles) along the same road, just before Bordones village, Salto de Bordones, a 300-meter (984-foot) high, chocolate-colored waterfall, plummets through the jungle. A broken stone trail leads to its base (one hour down).

You can also choose to stay in San José and use it as a base for visiting these sites and others. It has several hotels and restaurants. Major celebrations are the Carnaval Blanco y Negro the first week of January and Holy Week; the patron saint day, in honor of San José, is March 19. Market day is Saturday. 26 km (15.5 mi) north of San Agustín.

All-day jeep tours include Alto de los Ídolos, Alto de las Piedras and Salto de Bordones. Alternately, you can try to visit these sites on your own. First go to the crossroads below San Agustín, then to San José de Isnos ($2.10 total). Signs at both archaeological sites are only in Spanish. You can hire a guide at Alto de los Ídolos (extra charge). Jeep tours do not include the entry fees, the lunch in San José de Isnos, or a visit to the Museo Etnográfico at Bordones. Updated: May 20, 2008.

El Tablón

Between San Agustín and the Parque Arqueológico are several quite interesting sites. El Tablón, only 1.5 kilometers (1 mile) from the village, is said to be dedicated to the Moon Deity, with five statues and an ethnographic museum. A dirt path wends almost 2 kilometers (1.2 miles) through the countryside and across a creek to the Río Magdalena. In a spectacular setting mid-way down a canyon are the massive rock carvings of La Chaquira. Continuing the circuit, you arrive next at La Pelota with statuary (including a warrior, and an eagle with a serpent). On the next rise several hundred meters away is El Purutal, a possible ceremonial site, whose statues still retain the colorful paints of their creators.

The entire 15- kilometer (9-mile) hike takes six to seven hours. To begin at El Tablón, walk up Carrera 14 over the hill to the sign.

The paths can be quite muddy. You can break the hike up into two days, visiting El Purutal and La Pelota one day, and El Tablón and La Chiquira (two hours round trip) the other. To save time, you can take a buseta ($0.50) to either the turn-off for El Tablón or El Purutal, or hire horses. Refreshments are available only near El Tablón. Updated: May 20, 2008.

El Macizo Colombiano

If you are yearning to get off the beaten track and experience rural Southern Colombian charm, then go take a hike—from San Agustín to Quinchana and on to Valencia. The five-day trek on a Camino Real (stone and dirt trail) takes you across the Páramo de las Papas (3685 meters / 11,976 feet above sea level), passing by farm fields and through small villages. On the way is Laguna de la Magdalena, the birthplace of the Río Magdalena, located 81 kilometers (48.6 miles) from San Agustín. Flora and fauna along the way include orchids, birds and spectacled bear.

It is also possible to do the trip on horseback, which will take three days. The area is now heavily patrolled by the military, along with indigenous guards armed with clubs.

Photo by Dan Anderson

You can do the trek in the opposite direction, from Valencia (reachable from Popayán, 8 hours, $15) to San Agustín. Guides and lodging (Posada Nativa, $4.20 per person) are available in Valencia. For more information on doing it from this village, ask at the Popayán tourism office.

On the road to the Parque Arqueológico is a turn-off heading towards Quichana and Páramo de las Papas. However, because of the environmental conditions, a guide is highly advisable. Updated: May 20, 2008.

Obando: El Estrecho del Magdalena, petroglyphs and Parque Arqueológico de Obando

Traveling towards the small village of Obando, you'll cross the Magdalena River at the Estrecho, or Straits, the narrowest point—only 2.2 meters (7 feet) wide. Up a few hundred meters, on the other side of the dirt road, is a signed path to some not-often visited petroglyphs. After a further 2.5-3 kilometers (1.5-1.8 miles) the main camino arrives at Obando village, where excavations on burials dating from 11th-2nd Century B.C. began in 1992. The painted tombs are now part of the Parque Arqueológico de Obando, which also includes a museum. El Estrecho del Magdalena and nearby petroglyphs are open from dawn to dusk; Parque Arqueológico de Obando is open daily, 8 a.m.-noon, 1-5 p.m. All-day jeep tours include Estrecho del Magdalena and Parque Arqueológico de Obando (minus entry fee) on their route.

At the Parque Arqueológico de Obando, explanatory signs are in English and Spanish. There is a gift shop with locally produced artesanía. You can also visit these sites on your own, although public transportation is a bit more problematic. From Calle 5 and Carrera 14 in San Agustín leave infrequent buses for Obando ($1.60). You can get off

SOUTHERN COLOMBIA

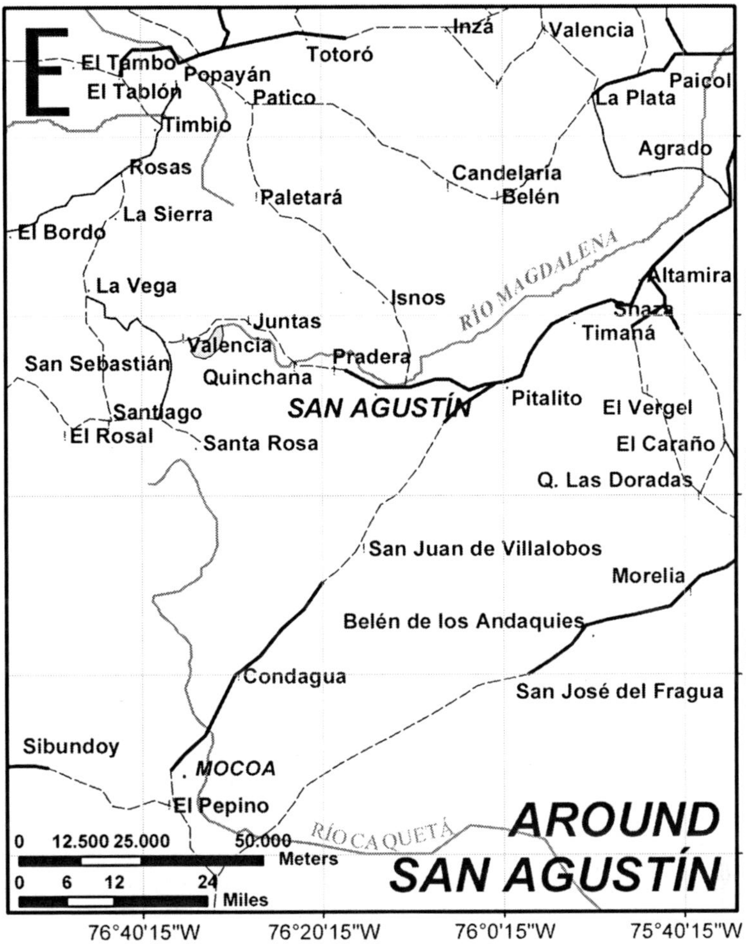

at the Estrecho, walk to the Petroglyphs and to Obando, then catch a bus back to San Agustín. Updated: May 20, 2008.

Tierradentro

Alt: 2,,464m Pop: 6,066 City Code. 2

Deep within the heart of the hilly countryside around Tierradentro lies one of Colombia's great archaeological gems: mysterious subterranean tombs painted in white-black-red-ochre geometrical patterns. It is a difficult journey to arrive there, especially in the rainy season. You will be rewarded, though, with incredible walking opportunities to explore the ruins and villages of this "Land Within."

A road runs from Popayán to La Plata, passing through Tótoro. The turn-off for Tierradentro is Cruce de Pisimbalá, also called Cruce de San Andrés, near the town of Guadalejo. The Popayán-La Plata road is paved only from El Pital, east of Guadalejo, to La Plata. (Note: this is a different road than that along the north edge of Parque Nacional Natural Puracé.)

From the crossroads, the road heads north towards the "Land Within," Tierradentro. The principal town is San Andrés de Pisimbalá. Two and a half kilometers before that village is Parque Arqueológico, the entrance and museums of this famed archaeological site. The settlement has the major concentration of lodging and restaurants in the area. The road continues uphill to San Andrés, where there are other hotels and eateries. Parque Arqueológico de Tierradentro is part of the Resguardo Indígena de Andrés, an indigenous reservation of the Nasa (Páez) nation. Inzá, a town just west of Guadalejo, has its market day on Saturday, when you can see many Nasa in traditional dress. Updated: Nov 08, 2007.

History

The Chibcha-speaking people arrived in these mountains about 7th-9th Century A.D. An agricultural society, they crafted weavings, stone carvings and ceramics. Worship focused on death and ancestors. Due to the lack of violent depictions, archaeologists believe the Nasa ancestors were a peaceful nation. Tierradentro and San Agustín were contemporary societies; their sculpture and housing are similar and their settlements were connected by roads.

When the Spaniards arrived here in the mid-15th Century, they called this land of rugged terrain, isolated villages and difficult travel Tierradentro, or "Land Within." In 1994, Nevado de Huila erupted, causing an avalanche that swept through the valley of the Páez River, killing over 1,000 people. Today, Tierradentro encompasses 21 indigenous reserves. Updated: Nov 06, 2007.

When to Go

As in other parts of this region, November, December and January are the best months to visit Tierradentro. The clear weather brings warm days, but cold nights. The windiest months are July and August, which are also cold. Rain is common the rest of the year; the wettest months are September, October, February and March (when rains are heaviest).

Tierradentro is a popular destination for vacationing Colombians at major holiday times, especially in December. At this time lodging will be full; likewise, more services, such as restaurants, will be open.

San Andrés has its patron saint ceremonies in mid-November. In the village of Calderas, one hour from San Andrés, you can catch traditional Nasa (Páez) indigenous music and dance during the Tumbichucue celebration held each year on December 31st. The weekly indigenous markets in Inzá and Belalcazar are both on Saturday, beginning at dawn; Guadalejo's market is on Sunday. Updated: Nov 06, 2007.

Getting To and Away from Tierradentro

Arriving at Tierradentro is a trip that can be beset by muddy roads and landslides in the rainy season. Vehicles are often overcrowded, with people riding atop and hanging off the back. It is most directly reached from Popayán. However, many visit it in the same breath as San Agustín, which is a full day's journey away; for more details, see below. If you miss a direct departure for your destination, then take a local pick-up or jeep to Cruce de Pisimbalá, a.k.a. Cruce de San Andrés, and catch other transport there. Both Popayán and La Plata serve as hubs for transportation. When arriving in Tierradentro, tell the driver you want to be dropped off at the Parque Archaeologico, if that is where you will be staying, as San Andrés village is another 2.5 kilometers further uphill.

To Popayán—Sotrancauca - 5:30 a.m., $7.90, 5 hours; from Popayán 10:30 a.m. Or go to the Cruce and catch a La Plata-Popayán bus.

To La Plata—Pick-up trucks—daily 6 a.m., 8 a.m., noon, 4 p.m. Chiva—Sunday, Wednesday 7 a.m., Friday 5 a.m. Both take 1.5-2 hours and cost $4.20.

The route between Tierradentro and San Agustín will—with a bit of luck—only take about six hours. But if you don't hit the connections right, you will probably have to spend the night in one of the transit points. The route is Tierradentro-La Plata-Pitalito-San Agustín. If you miss a direct La Plata-Pitalito bus, then go to Garzón, from where there are frequent minibuses for both towns. The new La Plata bus terminal is quite a distance from town; city buses connect the two ($0.35).

From La Plata to Tierradentro (San Andrés de Pisimbalá)—Cootransplateña—Daily 6:30 a.m., 10:30 a.m., 1 p.m., 4 p.m., 2 hours, $4.20. Chivas leave from downtown Sunday, Wednesday, Friday.

To Bogotá—Cootranshuila—9:30 p.m., 8 hours, $21. Coomotor—8:30 a.m., 9 p.m., 8 hours, $21; 11 a.m., $18.65.

Pitalito to La Plata—7 a.m., 10 a.m., 2 p.m., 4 p.m., 3 hours, $8.50. Or go to Garzón (bus

$4.75, collective taxi $5.30), then to Pitalito (buseta $4.20, collective taxi $5.30). From Pitalito there is also service to Neiva, Bogotá, Isnos and Popayán. Updated: Nov 06, 2007.

Safety in Tierradentro

The area is safe for hiking, even alone; however, locals will advise you not to walk at night. Further afield, deep into the mountains, the FARC is present, but never reportedly in the Tierradentro region itself. Transportation can be dangerously overcrowded. To guarantee a seat, go into San Andrés to catch transport out of Tierradentro; from La Plata to Tierradentro, buy your ticket in advance. Updated: Nov 06, 2007.

Tierradentro Services

Tourism Office

In the Parque Arqueológico part of Tierradentro, a shop offers regional tourist information (daily, 8 a.m.-8 p.m. Green house with the orange door, across from Hospedaje Ricabet). This store sells locally produced bags, necklaces and other items, and has a restaurant.

Money

Neither Tierradentro nor San Andrés de Pisimbalá have banks, places to change cash or travelers checks, nor money wiring services.

Keeping in Touch

As in many villages in this "Land Within," the high school has internet for several hours per day, Monday to Friday, with priority given to students. Many shops in both the Parque Arqueológico and San Andrés village have phone service, charging $0.10 per minute; look for the Minutos sign. Neither section of Tierradentro has a post office.

Medical

The local medical clinic is the Puesto de Salud San Andrés at the entry of San Andrés village (Monday-Friday, 8 a.m.-noon, 2-6 p.m., Saturday 8 a.m.-noon. Tel: 314-662-4446, 311-644-9071). Updated: Nov 06, 2007.

Things to See and Do

The main attraction of Tierradentro is its painted, pre-Columbian tombs. A trail connects four sites: Segovia, El Duende, El Tablón (which has statues stylistically similar to San Agustín) and Los Altos de San Andrés. Another burial, Aguacate, lies high in the mountains. The village of San Andrés de Pisimbalá has a thatched-roof church. The Parque Arqueológico also has two museums on either side of the road: one displays archaeological finds and the other explores the ethnography of the Nasa (Páez) peoples of the region. To the west and north of Tierradentro are several stone roads connecting hamlets such as Guanacas, Inzá, Silvia, Chinas and Lame. As security stabilizes, these will make for great off-the-beaten-track hiking. The region also hides multitudinous caverns, waterfalls and other natural wonders. Updated: Nov 16, 2007.

The Tombs of Tierradentro

Four major archaeological sites, all dating from 600 to 900 A.D., comprise Tierradentro: three burial and one of statues. The tombs were carved by hand from volcanic rock. Some are up to 3 meters (ten feet) deep. Most are painted within, with geometric and figurative designs in red, black, orange, grey, purple and yellow on white. A few also contain burial urns. Segovia, the first site from the museum, is the crown jewel of the complex. Thirty tombs are open; only 16 are lit. Numbers 8 to 12 are the most impressive. Alto del Duende, the next site, consists of four crypts. The third grouping, El Tablón, holds statues stylistically similar to those of San Augustín. Beyond San Andrés Pisimbalá is Alto de San Andrés with more tombs. Flash photos of the tombs are not allowed. Only a few tombs are lit, and only those at Segovia.

The time it takes to go between sites are as follows: Museo Etnográfico to Segovia, 20 minutes; Segovia to El Duende, 15 minutes; El Duende to El Tablón, 40 minutes; El Tablón to Alto de San Andrés, 30 minutes. The turn-off for the path to Alto de San Andrés is midway between Parque Arqueológico and the village; this can be done as a separate hike. If you do the trek reversed, going from San Andrés de Pisimbalá to El Tablón, Alto del Duende and Segovia, then the walk will be mostly downhill.

Check at Parque Arqueológico for availability of horses (be sure they are in good condition); typical charge is $2.10 per hour. Updated: Dec 19, 2007.

The Museums of Tierradentro

When the rain comes, pass the time in the two fine museums Tierradentro Archaeological Park offers. On the river side of the road is the Museo Etnográfico, describing the history and culture of the Nasa (Páez) peoples of the region. On the other side of the camino is the Museo Arqueológico, displaying artifacts from the tombs. One section explains the cultural connection with the area's other great archaeological site, San Agustín. The guard will accompany you on your exploration and answer your questions (Spanish only; exhibition signs in Spanish only).

The museums are located at the entrance of the Parque Arqueológico hamlet, on either side of the road, three kilometers before San Andrés de Pisimbalá. Updated: Dec 19, 2007.

Hiking to the Aguacate Tombs

Historians and Indiana Jones lovers will enjoy hiking to the ruined tombs of Aguacate, near the towns of Tierradentro and San Andrés Pisimbalá.

Starting just to the left of La Portada bar/restaurant in San Andrès Pisimbalà, the four-hour trek climbs hillsides, traverses ridges, and climbs and dips until, astride a mountain, the path reaches the tombs themselves. It's easy to see why people with power once chose to be buried there: if you weren't going anywhere for a few million years, you'd want a view that good, too.

The tombs themselves comprise more than a dozen dramatic and massive holes in the ground, most of which lead to caves of various sizes. Some are painted, others have large columns, and a few are only filled with spiders and dirt. Many have been grave-robbed, and the site is less archeologically important than

	Description	Hours	Address	Contact	Price
Museo de Oro	Small collection of pre-Columbian stone, textile, ceramic work, and requisite gold pieces.	Tuesday-Saturday, 10 a.m.-5 p.m.	Calle 19 21-27	Tel: 09-2-721-9108 / 721-5777, ext. 255 / 261	Free
Museo Juan Lorenzo Lucero	A 17th Century priest's collection of daily life objects, musical instruments and art.	Monday-Friday, 8-10 a.m., 2-3:30 p.m.	Calle 18 28-27	Tel: 09-2-731-4414	$1.10
Museo Luciano Rosero	Once-private collection of religious and secular art, archaeology, numistics and natural history.	Daily, 8 a.m.-6:30 p.m.	Calle 23 17-52	Tel: 310-396-3289.	$1.10
Museo Alfonso Zambrano	Collection of indigenous, colonial and Quiteño-school art.	Monday-Saturday, 8 a.m.-noon, 2-4 p.m.	Calle 20 29-79	Tel: 09-2-731-2837.	Free
Casona Taminango de Artes y Tradiciones Populares	Crafts executed in Nariño Department: woodworking, blacksmithing, copper and other metalwork, wool and paja weaving.	Monday-Friday, 8 a.m.-noon, 2-4 p.m. Saturday, 9 a.m.-1 p.m.	Calle 13 27-67	Tel: 09-2-723-5539	$0.55 -1.10
Centro Cultural Pandiaco	If you can't join pastusos for the Carnaval in January, you can revel in the color here.	Call for appointment	Oficina Municipal de Cultura	Tel: 09-2-731-4598	Free

Updated: Dec 19, 2007.

Segovia, but it is remarkable nonetheless, especially when you first see the tombs laid out before you, wrapped in an incredible vista.

The trail continues on, mostly downhill, and comes out right by the museums in Tierradentro. Luckily, the uphill neighbor of the museum is La Tienda Jugo Rico, and after four hours of walking, their delicious juices hit the spot perfectly.

The path is marked at most important forks, and wrong turns down unmarked splits never take long to terminate at farms or fields. Still, to save a bit of time stick to the larger choice when the trail splits.

If you want to keep hiking, you can continue back up to San Andrès Pisimbalà via another trail which passes by Secovia, Duende and El Tablon, the remaining sites. The second 'half' needs only two hours and isn't as beautiful, but is easier and is still a pleasant hike. Cross the main road and ask at the other museum, and they'll point you to the continuation of the trail. Both sides can be walked in the other direction, as well, of course. The museums and the three other sites require an inexpensive 3-day pass. Wear suitable shoes, clothing, and sunscreen. Bring water and a camera. Expect a bit of mud here and there. Climb the hill, a bit after the tombs, that rises up to the right of the path: there are sometimes horses hanging out atop it among a smattering of trees. To get there from Tierradentro, go to San Andrés de Pisimbalá. From San Andrés, go to La Portage restaurant, and take the path just on the left. Updated: Dec 19, 2007.

Ritual de Refrescamiento y Limpieza

After months of being on the road, you may need to have Ritual de Refrescamiento y Limpieza done. The Refresh and Cleansing Ritual is an ancient custom of the indigenous peoples here that is still being preserved. Agriano Piñacue and Victoriano Quinto, two traditional *curanderos* (medicine persons) of the Nasa nation do these ceremonies. Appointments must be made at least two to three days in advance, as the ritual is timed to the moon phases. To make arrangements for a Refresh and Cleansing Ritual, contact Doctor Carmen Leonor Acosta, director of the office of tourism in Popayán. She speaks English. Monday-Friday, 8:30 a.m.-12:30 p.m., 2:30-6:30 p.m., Saturday 9 a.m.-noon, 2-5 p.m., Sunday 9 a.m.-1 p.m. Carrera 5, 4-68. Tel: 2-824-2251, Cel: 311-307-2299, E-mail: oficinaturismoPopayán@hotmail.com, URL: www.turismoPopayán.com. Updated: Dec 19, 2007.

Las Pirámides

Las Pirámides is the ideal place to film an action-adventure movie. Most tourists do not budget enough time for a visit here, but if you have an afternoon free, you should stop by for a visit. On the way back, do a little browsing at the artisan store, which stocks handmade and naturally colored crafts, sweaters and bags.

Find guides Pedro or José, who linger around Hospedaje Ricabet or the hotel next door. They require an $8 rental fee for motorcycle transport there and back, plus a $2 guide fee. There is no official entrance fee to see Las Pirámides, but you should tip the caretaker $1, since they supply the tunnel lights and general upkeep of the place. All of these fees are well worth a visit to a very unknown but spectacular site. Updated: May 28, 2008.

Tierradentro Lodging

Most lodging options are found in the Parque Arqueológico section of Tierradentro. Besides a few formal inns, many families also rent rooms in their homes to tourists. In San Andrés de Pisimbalá there are three additional hotels. At present all hostels are basic; there are no upper-end hotels operating. San Andrés has a heavy military presence, which other travelers have found uncomfortable. The Parque is a more relaxing place to stay. Updated: Nov 06, 2007.

Casa de Señora Marta

(BED: $4) Perfect for travelers looking for an authentic experience while meeting interesting fellow travelers, señora Marta's place could belong to any quirky grandmother with beds to spare. House plants abound on ledges across from a cabinet of knick-knacks in the main communal room (which only has three walls) through which an eclectic but steady stream of international travelers has passed through over the last 24 years—more if you include the time in her old location. Señora Marta herself is friendly, neat, welcoming and unobtrusive, and she will cook up cheap and delicious food, including vegetarian dishes, given notice. There's no sign above her door, but anyone in town will tell you where she is. As a fellow traveler said, "staying with her mixes the best of staying in a hostel with the best of a homestay."Ask for la casa de señora Marta. Updated: Dec 19, 2007.

Hospedaje Lucerna

(BED: $4.20) Austere on the outside, with only small lettering announcing its presence, Hospedaje Lucerna is big on service. Inside, the rooms are grouped around the flower-filled garden. All share the common bath with hot water (give 20 minutes notice beforehand) and have shuttered windows. Mornings, sit down with the lovely elderly couple who open their home to travelers. Don Secundario will tell you about Tierradentro's history while you sip on a free cup of organic coffee from his neighboring farm. Doña Carmelita can also squeeze you up a glass of fresh orange juice—yes, organic, from their own orchard. You can even wash your clothes here. They also offer camping space with full use of the facilities. On the river side of the main road, next to the Museo Etnográfico, Parque Arqueológico. Updated: Dec 19, 2007.

Hospedaje Los Lagos

(BED: $4.20-5.25) For those preferring to stay in San Andrés Pisimbalá itself, Hospedaje y Restaurante Los Lagos is one of several options. Located at the end of the village's main road to the right, Los Lagos is a very basic inn. The guest rooms come only with beds—no other furnishings appear. One room has a private bath and double bed. All bathrooms have cold-water-only showers. The restaurant is reputed to be good, but advance notice must be given if you wish to dine here. Carrera 2A, 3-17. Updated: Dec 19, 2007.

Hospedaje Pisimbalá

(BED: $4.20-8) Hospedaje Pisimbalá is another old standby for journeyers to Tierradentro. Also a small, family-run inn, this place offers three rooms with shared bathroom and three rooms with private bath. Only one room has a solitary bed; the others are crowded with three beds each, making space to place your packs awfully tight. Hot-water showers are available. Camping is additionally offered, whether in your own tent or camper-van. The front garden is quite nice, with a bamboo gazebo. On the main road, about 200 meters from the Museo Arqueológico. Updated: Dec 19, 2007.

Hospedaje Mi Casita

(ROOM: $4-5) This sweet little hospedaje run by a young family rents out three rooms in what would otherwise just be their private home. Rooms here are spacious enough and the beds are comfortable. The shared bath has a clean toilet (with seat cover!) and hot water shower. Recuerdo, the resident black labrador retriever, lazes around all day to "keep guard" or just provide entertainment for the kids in the house. The owner's sister runs the shop and juice store next door and will even provide you a home-cooked meal for just $1.50, if you ask nicely. Look for the light blue house between the two juice stores in town; also across the street from Hospedaje Lucerne. Updated: May 28, 2008.

Hospedaje Ricabet

(ROOM: $6-8) Located at the upper edge of town, just before the curve heading up the hill to San Andrés center, is Hospedaje Ricabet, a mid-range option for travelers looking for a little more than a basic room. Six rooms are situated around a small courtyard—some of which have a private bath with hot water. The rate here is about $3 more expensive and a grade more comfortable than the other options in town. Up the hill from the Tierradentro park entrance, on the right hand side just before heading farther up to San Andrés town. Updated: May 28, 2008.

Tierradentro Restaurants

It is very difficult to find a place to eat in Tierradentro. Many places advertising themselves as restaurants in the Parque Arqueológico area don't open or have food in the off-season. It is best to make meal plans in advance with an establishment. More dining choices are had in the village, 2.5 kilometers away. In San Andrés de Pisimbalá there's a bakery and a few small stores in the Parque Arqueológico area. Friday is market day in San Andrés. Updated: Nov 06, 2007.

Jugos Ricos

Their name doesn't lie: Jugos Ricos serves some of the tastiest juice in South America, and not much else. Lots of flavors are available with chilled water or milk bases. Seventy five cents for a glass and a half, roughly—make sure you get the extra bit from the jug! Jugos Ricos Tienda is perfect for an afternoon cool-off or a between-museum, people-watching break. Cash only, tax included. Updated: Dec 19, 2007.

La Portada Restaurante-Bar

La Portada Restaurante-Bar is one of the few dining choices in San Andrés village open out-of-season. This restaurant is light and airy, with a large, covered veranda constructed of giant bamboo and brick, with brick-tiled floors. Open from 6 a.m. to 8 p.m. Monday through Saturday, and 5 to 8 p.m. Sunday evenings, you can get a set breakfast here for $1.60, or lunch or dinner for $1.85 (main dish only) to $2.40 (soup and main dish). La Portada also whips up good vegetarian options. If you are staying in the Parque Arqueológico sector, remember it is 2.5 kilometers (1.5 miles) away, a dark walk home after dusk. On the left side of the main road, at the entrance to San Andrés Pisimbalá village. Updated: Dec 19, 2007.

Restaurante Pisimbalá

Restaurante Pisimbalá, located in the the inn of the same name, is virtually your only dining choice in the Parque Arqueológico sector of Tierradentro. The señora makes up a good meal of whatever happens to be at hand, usually consisting of the day's soup, and a main dish or rice, beans, meat, salad and yucca or plátano—all for a simple $1.85. You can dine

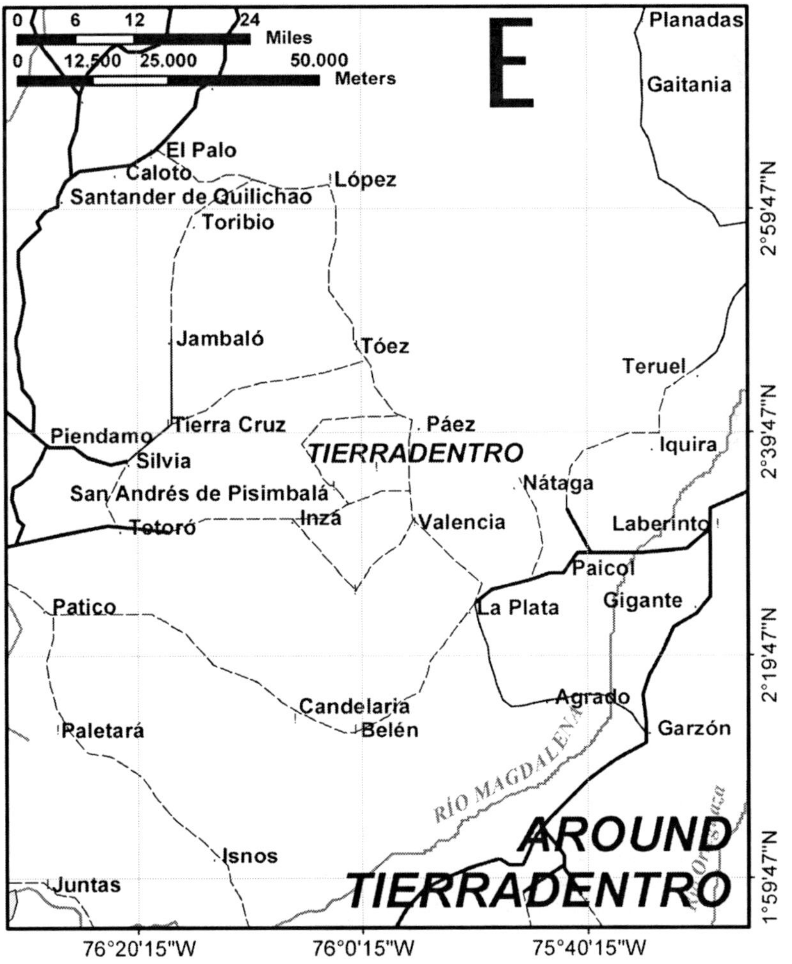

inside or, if the weather is nice, in the gazebo in the front garden. Be sure to give advance notice and set a time if you plan on dining here. In Hospedaje Pisimbalá, on the main road, about 200 meters from the Museo Arqueológico. Updated: Dec 19, 2007.

PASTO

Alt: 2,527m Pop: 400,000 City Code: 2

Located atop a plateau surrounded by verdant hills to the east and Volcán Galeras to the west, Pasto is 88 kilometers from the Ecuador border, on the Pan-American Highway. This capital of Nariño Department is a pleasant place to spend a few days. With impressive churches, architecture, museums and nearby villages to explore and natural reserves only several hours away, there is something for everyone's taste. Strolling through the streets, you can soon see why Pasto is nicknamed "La Ciudad de los Balcones"—The City of Balconies. Fine woodworking in many styles decorates these personal vantage points over the narrow colonial streets.

If you can, come in time for the city's renowned Black and White Carnival, celebrated in January—but wear your oldest clothes, like the locals do. It's said to be quite a messy party.

Pasto identifies itself culturally more with northern Ecuador than Colombia; during colonial times, trade routes connected this city with population centers further south. Updated: Oct 17,2007.

HISTORY

Like other Spanish cities in Southern Colombia, San Juan de Pasto was founded under orders of Sebastián de Benalcázar and was part of the Audencia Real de Quito. First established in 1539 by Capitán Lorenzo de Aldana at Guacanquer, Pedro de Puelles moved it the following year to its present location.

During the Independence Wars, Pasto remained a staunch Royalist supporter. Local historians say the city suffered tremendously at the hands of Simón Bolívar's troops. In 1830, Gran Colombia prevented Pasto and Nariño Department from joining the nascient country Ecuador.

In recent years, this city was chosen by the national government as a resettlement center for demobilized paramilitary forces. Updated: Oct 17, 2007.

When to Go

Pasto's altitude gives the city a spring-like climate year round. Anytime is fine to visit, but expect rain showers in any month. The months of June, July and August are windy. The city has a number of festivals worth attending. The most famous is the Festival de Blancos and Negros, or Carnaval. Spanish colonists gave slaves a vacation every January 5, which is why Carnaval is celebrated, but the modern celebration lasts much longer. Beginning on December 28, Day of the Innocents, a ceremony purifies the spirits. New Year's Eve is the Años Viejos, when effigies representing the past year are burnt in the streets. January 2 is Pericles Carnival and January 3 is the Indigenous Carnival—the streets throng with drum troupes, music, dance and horse parades. Then the two great days of celebration: Black Day and White Day, January 5 and 6 respectively, marked with parades, musicians, drum troupes and grease and talcum powder fights.

As if to get everyone cleaned up from the Carnaval, Pasto has a Fiesta de Aguas—a huge, city-wide water fight—on February 5.

Pasto commemorates its saint, San Pedro, with firework castles, religious processions and *guaguas de pan* (bread babies) the last Sunday of June and the first Sunday of July. Updated: Oct 17, 2007.

Getting To and Away from Pasto

Pasto has a good city bus network. Busetas ($0.20) begin running at 6 a.m.; most routes operate only until 7:30-8 p.m., with a few until 10 p.m. Rutas 4, 6, 7, 9 and 10 connect the bus station with downtown, passing by Calle 17 and Carrera 21.

Taxi fares are set by law. For routes within the city the cost is $1.60 per person; for the airport it is $3.60 per person.

Pasto's central bus terminal is located about 3 kilometers from the center, at Carrera 6 and Calle 16. The handicap-accessible building has an information booth, restaurants, shops, phones, an ATM (Visa, Cirrus, Plus), and even casinos and a pool hall.

Cheaper trucks and chivas leave regularly from the terminal at Carrera 9 16-10.

From Pasto

Arrive	Departures	Time	Price
Sandoná	6:30 a.m., 11 a.m., 4:30 p.m., 5:45 p.m.	2 hours	$2.10
Túquerres	5:30 a.m., 7:30 a.m.	2 hours	$2.60
Popayán	Hourly 5:30 a.m. - 11:30 p.m.	5-6 hours	$10.50 -13.60
Cali	Hourly 5:30 a.m. -11:30 p.m.	8 hours	$14.70 -18.35
Bogotá	Hourly 9:30 a.m. 10 p.m.	18 hours	$34 -40.30

Updated: Oct 17, 2007.

Aeropuerto Antonio Nariño de Pasto provides direct and connecting services to all of Colombia. It is located 30 kilometers from the city, at Cano.

Safety in Pasto

Pastusos proudly claim their city is safe; however, one community historian asserts that relocated, demilitarized paramilitary forces are rearming and thus the face of this town has changed. One area that's a bit dodgy and where you should take particular care is from Carrera 21 to the bus terminal after dark. Despite the frequent bus service, some locals still prefer not to travel the Ipiales-Pasto-Popayán-Cali route at night. Updated: Oct 17, 2007.

Pasto Services

Tourism Office

The extremely helpful tourism office has information on things to do and see in the city and surrounding region, as well as several excellent booklets on the artesans, painters and culinary traditions (including recipes) of Nariño (daily, 7 a.m.-noon, 2-6 p.m. Calle 18, 25-25, Tel: 2-723-4962). It also has a kiosk at the bus terminal. For any maps you might need, go to the Instituto Geográfico Agustín Codazzi (Monday-Friday, 8-11:15 a.m., 1:30-4 p.m. Carrera 21B, 18-40).

Money

Bancolombia (Calle 19, facing Parque de Nariño) changes Amex travelers cheques only on weekdays (Monday-Friday, 8 a.m.-4:30 p.m.); its branch at Calle 19, 25-57 changes them on Saturday mornings. Both branches have ATMs. Santander, also on Calle 19 on the Parque, changes dollar or Euro Amex travelers checks, but only in the morning (Monday-Thursday, 8-11:30 a.m., 2-4 p.m., Friday, 8-11:30 a.m., 2-4:30 p.m.) Pasto has both a Western Union agent, Giros and Finanzas (Monday-Friday, 8 a.m.-noon, 2-5:30 p.m., Saturday, 9 a.m.-1 p.m. Pasaje del Liceo, corner of Calle 17 and Carrera 26, Local 128) and a MoneyGram agent, Cambiamos (Monday-Saturday, 8 a.m.-6 p.m. Pasaje del Liceo, Local 228).

Keeping in Touch

Internet is common throughout Pasto, and runs anywhere from $0.80-1.30 per hour. Internel (daily, 10 a.m.-10 p.m. Centro Comercial Colombia, Calle 17, 21A-54, Local 103, Tel: 2-721-6812) is one of the few places that has Skype. Make international calls from Telecom; prices begin at $0.50 per minute (Monday-Saturday, 7 a.m.-7 p.m., Sunday, 8 a.m.-noon. Calle 17 and Carrera 23). Local and national calls can be made from any shop with a sign announcing phone calls; the cost is $0.10 per minute. Mail letters and postcards from Correos de Colombia/Apostal (Monday-Friday, 8 a.m.-noon, 2-6 p.m., Saturday 8 a.m.-noon. Calle 15, 23-60).

Medical

Pasto has two Level-III public hospitals: Hospital Departamental (Calle 22, 7-93, Parque Bolívar, Tel: 2-721-4625) and Hospital San Pedro (Calle 16, 42-00, Tel: 2-723-4349). Pharmacies, both national chains and locally-owned stores, are quite common; many can be found on Calle 18, if you are in need of emergency medications.

Laundry

It is hard to find a wet-wash laundry in Pasto; but there are plenty of dry cleaners. One that offers to do a regular wash is Lavandería Perlmatic, but only by piece; an expensive option at $1-2 per garment (Monday-Saturday, 8

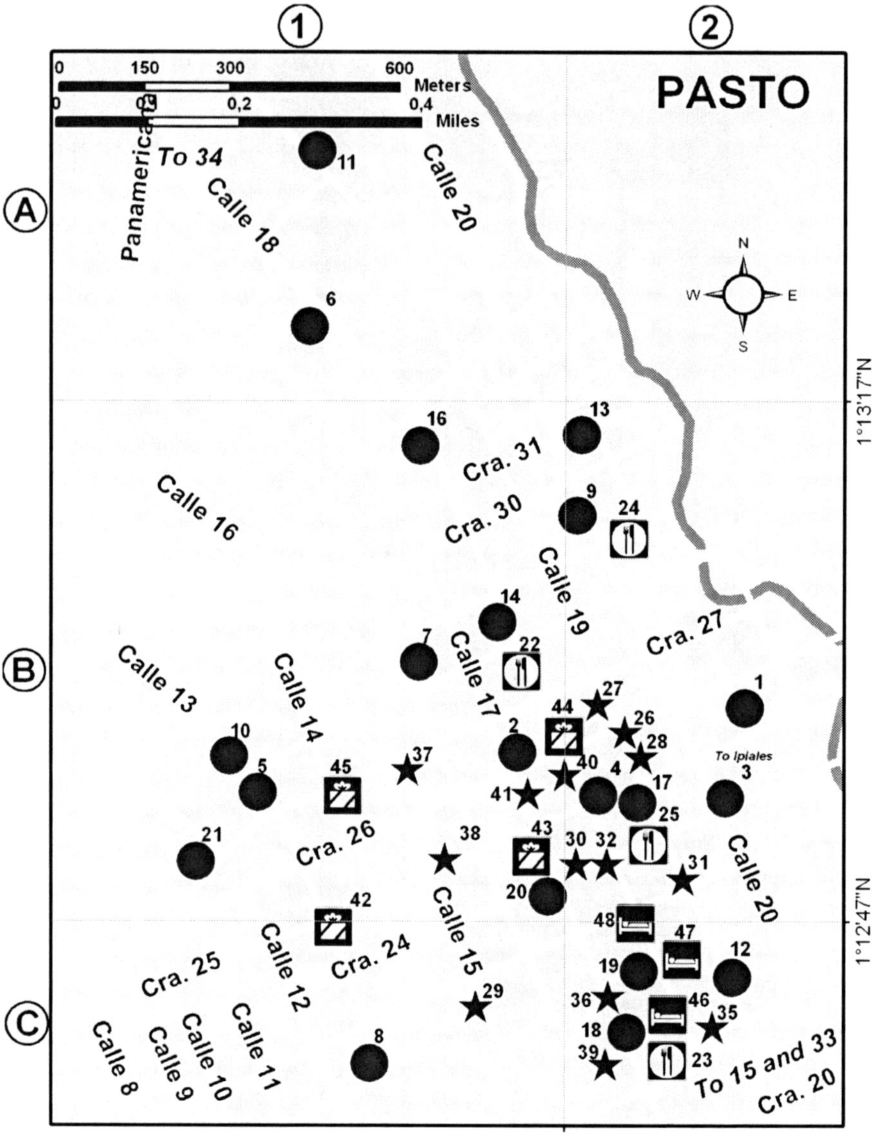

Activity ●

1 Museo Taller Relieves EBC B3
2 Catedral B2
3 Iglesia de Cristo Rey B3
4 Iglesia de San Juan B3
5 Iglesia Lourdes B2
6 Iglesia Mariadaz A2
7 Iglesia San Andrés B2
8 Iglesia Santiago Apóstol C2
9 Museo Alfonzo Zambrano B3
10 Museo Casona Taminango de Arte B2
11 Museo del Carnaval A2
12 Museo del Oro C3
13 Museo Fotográfico Luis Bernard B3
14 Museo Juan Lorenzo Lucero B2
15 Museo Luciano Rosero C3
16 Museo Madre Caridad Brader B2
17 Plaza de Nariño B3
18 Teatro Colombia C3
19 Templo de la Merced C3
20 Templo de San Augustín B2
21 Templo de San Felipe B2

Eating
22 Mestizo Peña Bar B2
23 Restaurante Casa López C3
24 Salud Pan B3
25 Tienda del Cafe del Parque B3
Service
26 Banco Colombia B3
27 Banco Colombia B3
28 Banco de Santander B3
29 Correos de Colombia/Adostal C2
30 Foto Almacén Tricolor C3
31 Foto Canon Digital C3
32 Foto Japón C3
33 Hospital Departamental C4
34 Hospital San Pedro A1
35 Instituto Geográfico Agustín Codazzi C3
36 Internet C3
37 Lava Mejor B2
38 Lavandería Perlmatic B2
39 Telecom C3
40 Tourism Office B3
41 Western Union and Moneygram B2
Shopping
42 Casa del Barniz de Pasto C2
43 Ecotema B2
44 Supermercado Ley B3
45 Vicens B2
Sleeping
46 Hotel Casa López C3
47 Hotel Manhattan C3
48 Koala Inn C3

a.m.-12:30 p.m., 2-7 p.m. Carrera 25, 15-40. Tel: 2-723-3025). Lava Mejor has one-day service, and charges by kilogram: $0.80 for wash and dry, $2.50 with ironing (Monday-Saturday, 8 a.m.-noon, 2-6 p.m., Sunday, closed. Carrera 27, 15-08, Tel: 2-722-8088).

Camera

Many of your photographic needs can be met right in the heart of Pasto, on Parque Nariño. Foto Japón, on the corner of Calle 18 and Carrera 24, has 100 ASA Kodak and Fuji film. Foto Almacén Tricolor, a half-block from the Parque, carries digital cameras and photo cards, and 100, 200 and 400 ASA Kodak film (Monday-Saturday, 8 a.m.-7:30 p.m. Carrera 24, 17-82. Tel: 2-722-3214). Foto Canon Digital offers the same items, but has an extra service: here you can download and print your digital photos or burn them to CD (Monday-Saturday, 8 a.m.-7 p.m. Calle 19, 23-61. Tel: 2-723-3818). Updated: Oct 17, 2007.

Shopping

Casa del Barniz de Pasto

Barniz de Pasto is an ancient technique practiced in this region since before the Europeans arrived on these shores. The seed of the mapo mapo tree is boiled in water to extract a rubber-like resin that is kneaded until it is flexible, colored with natural dyes, and then applied by hand to carved wood. The Casa del Barniz de Pasto showcases the work of a collective of these artists. Traditionally a men's craft, a few women are making inroads, with more delicate designs. The items are surprising affordable. Calle 13, 24-92. Tel: 2-723-8584, E-mail: casabarniz@hotmail.com. Updated: May 16, 2008.

Vicens

Colombia is renowned for its leather work, and Vicens proudly proclaims it creates "natural designs in leather." If you really want to get dressed up for a night at the discos and desire something special, then drop in at this shop. In its on-site workshop, the craftspersons of Vicens make everything from pants to jackets, vests to micro-mini skirts of fine, glove leather. Want gear a bit more traditional? Try on the hats or belts. For something smaller, there are also wallets, purses and hair barrettes. Carrera 27, 14-04. Tel: 2-729-8856, Cel: 315-501-0030, E-mail: vicenscuero@yahoo.com. Updated: May 19, 2008.

Ecotema

For more than 32 years Ecotema has been clothing Pasto's populace with beautiful, natural-color shawls, ruanas, ponchos, sweaters and shoulder bags. This cooperative of local weavers uses merino sheep wool in their crafts, though only sweaters of synthetic fibers are available. Hand embroidery and appliqués trim some pieces. Doña Yolanda can also show you towels, hot pads and other items to decorate your kitchen. Shop: Calle 17, 24-77; Factory: Calle 30, 19-120, Barrio Corazón de Jesús. Shop Tel: 2-729-2494; Factory Tel: 2-721-8386. E-mail: coopecotema@yahoo.com. Updated: Dec 19, 2007.

Things to See and Do

From colonial churches displaying an impressive variety of architectural styles to museums exhibiting arts and history, Pasto has enough to fill any cultural devotee's hours for many days.

For those aching to get out of the city, there are small villages to visit around the base of Volcán Galeras, including Sandoná with its weekly market. A few hours away are several nature preserves: Reserva Natural Biotopo Selva Húmeda and Reserva Natural La Planada. Túquerres is another village with an interesting weekly mercado; hike to its Volcán Azufral and Laguna Verde.

Going towards the Putumayo are Laguna La Cocha and the Santuario de Fauna y Flora Isla de la Carota. In this region are a number of Reserva Natural Privadas, community-based reserves you can visit or stay at.

Sports addicts can check out La Chaza, a pre-Columbian ball game played in city parks on the weekends.

Dying to see a flick? Check out what's on the weekly bill at Teatro Colombia. Munch on *crispetas* (popcorn) while watching the latest subtitled Colombian, Hollywood and international releases (daily, 3:15, 6:30, 9 p.m. Centro Comercial Colombia, Calle 17, 21A-54. Tel: 2-721-5450. Entry: $2.30, Thursday two-for-one). Updated: Oct 17, 2007.

Museums

Whether your interest is in colonial, graphic, photographic or traditional arts, or natural history, archaeology or ethnography—or even Carnaval—you have some place to spend a few hours. A couple of the museums are by appointment only: Casa-Museo Taller Relieves EBC, on Calle 21, 25-40. Tel: 2-723-3275, and Museo Fotográfico Luis Bernardo Esparza on Carrera 31C, 19-72. Tel: 2-731-0102.

Museo de Oro

This small collection of pre-Columbian stone, textile, ceramic work, and requisite gold pieces, including some very fine, 2,500-year-old filagree pieces, provides excellent explanations about pre-Conquest, indigenous trade routes in the Americas, and the cultural beliefs and practices of the Proto-Pasto (Piartal and Capulí) peoples (Spanish only). At lunch hours, live classical music accompanies your explorations of these galleries on the third floor, and those of modern art located one story below. The Banco de la Nación library is in the same building. Calle 19, 21-27, Centro Cultural Leopoldo López Álvarez. Tel: 2-721-9108 / 5777, ext. 255 / 261. Updated: May 16, 2008.

Museo Casona Taminango de Artes y Tradiciones Populares de Nariño

The casona in which the Taminango museum is housed, built in 1623, is not only the oldest house in Pasto, but also one of the oldest ones in the nation. The guide (Spanish only) will lead you through each room, explaining each of the crafts executed in Nariño Department: woodworking and carving, weaving, blacksmithing, copper and other metalwork, wool and paja weaving. If any craft catches your fancy, you can pick some up in the small, on-site shop. Calle 13, 27-67. Tel: 2-723-5539. Updated: May 16, 2008.

The Churches of Pasto

Catedral—A red-brick building of simple, classic Roman basilica design. Two Art Deco angels hold the baptismal font. Calle 17 and Carrera 26.
San Juan Bautista—The city's original cathedral, in an amazing Mozarabic style. Calle 18 and Carrera 25.
La Merced—A spiral staircase without a central axis pole. Calle 18 and Carrera 22.
Cristo Rey—Stunning neo-High Gothic architecture. Calle 20 and Carrera 24.
San Andrés—Calle 16 and Carrera 28.
Lourdes—A typical Latin American parish church. Calle 13 and Carrera 28.
San Felipe—Carrera 27, 11-31.
Santiago Apóstol—Calle 12, 22F-16.
Mariadaz—Calle 18, 32A-01, across from Universidad Mariana.

Iglesia del Cristo Rey

Whereas the Iglesia de San Juan displays one style of medieval architecture, that of Arab-influenced Spain, a few blocks away the Iglesia the Cristo Rey shows us the architecture of northern Europe of the same period. This church, built in the 1930s, is a stunning example of neo-High Gothic architecture. Light through the clerestory and apse windows floods the large, open interior. Quadpartite vaulting crowns the ceiling; but that of the transcept is octpartite with a rose design. The golden altar is like a giant reliquary coffer. All the interior sculpture and stained glass are ombian or Ecuadorian Jesuit artists. Calle 20 and Carrera 24. Updated: Dec 19, 2007.

Iglesia de San Juan

Walking into Iglesia de San Juan's interior is like entering a mosque. Built within a century of the Spanish conquest of the Americas, this temple, Pasto's original cathedral, exhibits a pure Mozarabic style of Islamic-era Spain. Note the almost complete absence of human figures within, the walls instead receiving an interlaced vine-design treatment. The arches are peak-arched with scalloped edges, as in Arab architecture. The ceiling of the apse is mudjedar: a giant wood jigsaw puzzle held together with no glue, nails or pegs. The windows in that part of the church, as well as in the left-hand chapel are covered with wooden, carved screens. Calle 18 and Carrera 25. Updated: Dec 19, 2007.

Volcán Galeras

Early Pastuso mornings you can catch a glimpse of Galeras, when the clouds lift enough to see it sending up smoke signals. Located only seven kilometers from Pasto, the volcano has high Andean páramo and sub-parámo ecosystems woven by over 120 rivers and four lagoons. Butterflies, deer, foxes, squirrels, cusumbo, raposa and 95 species of birds make their home on these flanks. Two hiking trails begin from the ranger station: Sendero Achichay (4060 meters) and Sendero Frailajón (3360-3960 meters). Since reawakening from a deep slumber in 1989, Galeras has been closed to hiking and climbing. You can, however, visit towns at its base in the Circumvalar de Galeras. Updated: May 16, 2008,

Túquerres

On the road to Tumaco, 72 kilometers from Pasto, is Túquerres. Founded in 1541 by Miguel de Muñoz at an altitude of 3051 meters, this village enjoys a cool climate. On Thursday mornings, Túquerres bustles with its weekly market. If you're looking for a *ruana* (poncho), this is the place to be. Traditionally, paila bowls and other copperware were forged here; but due to the high cost, this craft has all but disappeared.

Overshadowing the village is Volcán Azufral (3400 m). Within its crater are three lagunas: La Negra, La Barrosa and the moon-shaped La Verde. Ten fauna species and 476 floral are found in the area. Guides can be hired in Pasto, Popayán or Túquerres to take you up the two-hour trail that begins from San Roque neighborhood. Túquerres has basic hotels and restaurants, if you want to spend the night here.

Túquerres can be reached from either Pasto or Ipiales; just take any bus heading to Tumaco and alight at this town. Some companies also have several runs per day specifically to Túquerres ($2.60, 2 hours). Updated: May 20, 2008.

The Circumvalar de Galeras

The Circumvalar de Galeras (or Ruta Dulce de Nariño) around the base of Volcán Galeras samples historical, colonial villages with long artisan traditions: Nariño, La Florida, Sandoná, Consacá, Yacuanquer and Tangua. The most famous of these is Sandoná, 48 kilometers northwest of Pasto, on the other side of the volcano. It is an indigenous town with a Saturday market. The Panama hats drying in the streets are made by this village's women from *paja toquilla* (Carludovica palmate) fiber. Several guides offer the Circumvalar tour, or ask the Pasto tourism office for specifics on how to do the circuit yourself. To arrive at Sandoná on your own, take buseta 12 (Universidad de Nariño) ($0.20) or taxi ($1.60) to the Parqueadero. Updated: May 20, 2008.

La Chaza

Sundays, men of all ages partake in Chaza de Bombo, a ball game where four-to-eight-man teams hit a tennis ball with wooden rackets stretched with hide. When the ball hits the rackets, it sounds like the beating of drums. The game follows the rules of tennis, but with no net. In Chaza de Tabla, the racket head is wooden, studded with rubber. Then there is Chaza de Mano, in which the ball is hit with the bare hand. In these two forms of the game, the 800-gram ball is made of solid rubber. This game is traditionally played by men only, since before the Spanish ever arrived to this side of the world. From Calle 17, between Carrera 21 and 22, catch buseta Ruta 18 "Barrio Florida" to Parque Bolívar; the Estadio de Chaza is across from Ferretería Argentina. To watch a game of chaza de tabla or chaza de mano, catch Ruta 6 as it passes along Calle 15. Updated: May 16, 2008.

Pasto Tours

For the number of things to do in and around Pasto, there are surprisingly few tour operators. As in other parts of Southern Colombia, most agencies are devoted only to the booking of air flights. A few officially registered guides can take you to tour Sandoná and other small villages to visit around the base of Volcán Galeras, or to hike and bird watch in Reserva Natural Biotopo Selva Húmeda, Laguna La Cocha and Isla de la Carota, and Volcán Azufral and Laguna Verde. Updated: Oct 17, 2007.

Camino del Viento

Registered guide Orfa Marina Ascuntar specializes in ecological tourism. She can take you on a one-day hiking tour to Túquerres' Volcán Azufral and Laguna Verde, summitting Cumbal's volcanoes, visiting the villages on the skirts of Galeras volcano or soaking in Tajumbía's hot springs. If you want to spend a few more days afield, Ms. Ascuntar will show you the pleasures of the beaches at Tumaco and Bocagrande on the Pacific Coast or the diversity of birds and wildlife at the Reserva Natural Biotopo. She can also design tours specifically to your interests. Tel: 2-730-4287, E-mail: caminodelvientoTE@hotmail.com. Updated: Jan 08, 2008.

Turismo Aventura

If you are looking to join the condors in soaring over the mountains of Southern Colombia, you can give Carlos Yepes a ring. This professional pilot runs a paragliding outfit out of Pasto. He offers three and four-day packages, all inclusive, of paragliding over the valleys of Nariño Department and around its impressively active Galeras volcano. He also teaches courses in flying, unfortunately only in Spanish. For more information on activities offered or fees, check out his website. Tel: 2-731-2951, Cel: 300-617-7304, E-mail: carlosyepes@turismoaventura.com, URL: www.turismoextremo.com.co. Updated: Jan 08, 2008.

Pasto Lodging

Most of Pasto's lodging options are concentrated in two areas: near the bus terminal and in the Centro Histórico. A wider variety is found in the Historic Center—there are some very low-key, beautiful B&Bs, popular budget hostels and a few high-rise, luxury hotels shadowing the Parque de Nariño. Updated: Oct 17, 2007.

Hotel Manhattan

(BED: $5.30-8) With over 30 years of experience, Hotel Manhattan provides travelers with a restful spot to stay in the colonial heart of Pasto. The eclectically furnished rooms surrounding the sitting-area patio of this second-floor inn are spacious and warm; all come with cable TV and balconies. The wood floors throughout are polished and the common bathroom is kept clean. The ground-floor back patio has a laundry area. This is definitely a bargain. Calle 18, 21B-14. Tel: 2-721-5675. Updated: Dec 19, 2007.

Koala Inn

(ROOM: $7.40-16) On the outside, the Koala Inn looks nondescript. But once up the stairs, you find yourself embraced by classic solar architecture. The rooms, like the exterior, are also a bit plain and showing the wear of more than a decade of travelers from around the world who have made it the place to stay in Pasto. The hotel offers restaurant and laundry service (no self laundry washing allowed). It has recently changed ownership. Calle 18, 22-37. Tel: 2-722-1101. Updated: Dec 19 ,2007.

Hotel Casa López

(ROOM: $37-47) A very understated sign, a solitary H, marks the Casa López. The López family have lovingly converted this home that has belonged to them for over 70 years. The natural woodwork and floors of the Republican-era building are polished to a warm sheen. The interior has been designed by a fine hand, with nice touches like glass vases full of calais lilies. All six rooms come with private hot water bath, cable TV, phone and alarm clock radio. Breakfast is served in a separate, second-floor dining room. Adjoining Casa López is the Restaurante Victoria Regia with inside and patio seating. The López family prides itself on providing European-style service to their guests. Calle 18, 21B-11. Tel: 2-720-8172, 2-733-0223, E-mail: hcasaLópez@yahoo.com. Updated: May 16, 2008.

Pasto Restaurants

Pasto offers a smorgasbord of dining options. Unfortunately, the city is lacking in good, affordable vegetarian restaurants. The best restaurants are quite a distance from the downtown district, on the Panamericana and on Avenida de los Estudiantes. For those on a budget, the cheapest eateries are along Carrera 22 between Calles 16 and 18, and along Calle 17. The city market is located out near the bus terminal. A Ley supermarket right in the heart of the city can also fill your self-catering needs (Monday-Saturday, 8:30 a.m.-

8:30 p.m., Sundays and holidays, 9 a.m.-6 p.m. Corner of Calle 18 and Carrera 26).

Manhattan

You don't have to be a guest to enjoy one of the good meals doña Miriam whips up at the Hotel Manhattan. The restaurant is located in the large, skylighted patio. With a smile, she'll serve you a breakfast of eggs, bread or arepa, rice and hot chocolate for only $1.30. The lunch and dinner set meals are $1.60, the cheapest you can find in this city. So pull up a stool at the counter and chat with doña Miriam while you dine, or grab one of the lace-clothed tables in the alcove to enjoy a more intimate meal. You definitely will not be disappointed. Calle 18, 21B-14. Tel: 2-721-5675. Updated: Dec 19, 2007.

Salud Pan

This is the only option for vegetarians in downtown Pasto--and unfortunately, only at lunchtime. The midday meal comes with soup, the main plate (with gluten or beans, salad and rice) and drink or soy milk; a half-portion will cost a hungering vegan $1.85, the full-helping $2.35. In other hours, Salud Pan's bakery has whole-grain breads, sweets and flours. Choose between quinoa, soy, oat and multi-grain goodies. Be sure to taste the unusual radish bread. Open Monday-Saturday, 8 a.m.-7 p.m.; closed Sunday. Carrera 29, 20-34. Tel: 2-723-1406, Updated: Dec 19, 2007.

Tienda del Café del Parque

Tienda del Café del Parque is a salute to nariñense coffee and culture. The only coffee it serves is organically grown from Nariño Department, in a two-story shop that itself is a work of art—from the canvases on the walls, right down to the chairs painted with landscapes, abstracts and portraits. Downstairs is a bookshop selling literature by regional writers. Besides serving coffee, Tienda del Café also has hot cocoa, teas and non-caffeinated drinks, as well as pastries and sandwiches. The second-floor has a full-service bar, and balcony seating overlooking Nariño park. The ground story has a street-side patio from where you can also watch the daily life of pastusos. Friday nights features live music: jazz, classical or salsa. You can even enjoy this rich coffee back home, thousands of miles away--just grab a sack of coffee on your way out. Open Monday-Friday, 9 a.m.-9 p.m., Friday 9 a.m.-1 a.m., holidays 9 a.m.-noon; closed Sunday. Carrera 24, 18-62, Parque Nariño (next to the Plaza Casino). Cel: 300-657-7115. Updated: May 16, 2008.

Pasto Nightlife

The rumba in Pasto only happens on Thursday, Friday and Saturday nights. Most of the dance clubs are on Avenida de las Américas and in the Zona Rosa (Calle 20, between Carreras 27 and 28). The other nights of the week, you'll have to settle for having a drink at a bar—but not on Mondays, when many are closed. Some of the more down-home joints have canchas de sapo, if you want to try your hand at a Colombian version of darts: tossing coins into a metal frog's mouth. If you are going out for the night, check the bus schedule beforehand, or take a taxi home. Updated: Oct 17, 2007.

Mestizo Peña-Bar

Okay, folks--it's time to join an Andean hoedown! If you've gotten bored with the same ol' salsa-cumbia-reggeton at the other clubs, then there is a great alternative in Pasto. Every Thursday, Friday and Saturday night Mestizo Peña-Bar presents the best of Andino music live—and occasionally shakes up the mix with a llanera or Afro-Colombian band ($1.10 door charge, no minimum consumption). The locals hit the large dance floor to shake the work-week doldrums away. Don't know the steps? Well, on Wednesday nights, 6-8 p.m., there's classes to get you into the groove for the weekend ($1.10). Other nights, you can enjoy a drink in this bamboo-paneled space adorned with indigenous artwork. Open Monday-Saturday, 6 p.m.-1 a.m.; closed Sunday. Calle 18, 27-67. Tel: 2-729-3395, E-mail: mestizopb@hotmail.com. Updated: Dec 19, 2007.

Laguna de la Cocha

Alt: 2,760m Pop: 5500 City Code: 2

On the Eastern slopes of the Nudo de los Pastos, where the Andes branch into the Cordillera Occidental and the Oriental, the road begins to descend towards Macoa, capital of Putumayo Department. In the cloud-misted highlands is Laguna de la Cocha, a place of mystery and legend, a holy place for the ancient indigenous Quillacinga, or People of the Moon. In the icy depths there is said to be a lost city. Ley lines of positive energy converge on its central island, Isla de Corota.

Located 25 kilometers (15 miles) southeast of Pasto, Laguna de la Cocha is nestled in the world's lowest páramo ecosystem, at only 2760 meters (9053 feet) altitude, thanks to the lagoon's unusual geomorphic characteristics. (Typically páramo zones begin at 3000 meters / 9840 feet.) It is Colombia's second-largest lake and one of the best preserved in the Andes. From this cradle flows Río Guamuéz, its waters rushing to Río Putumayo and the Amazon. The isle is home to the Santuario de Flora y Fauna Isla La Corota.

On the shores of this marsh lake are 32 private reservas run by local communities where you can learn about the area's wildlife, conservation efforts, ecological farming techniques and natural medicine. The entire area affords premier bird watching. Boats connect settlements and the islands around the lake. Updated: May 19, 2008.

History

In ancient times, the Laguna and its Isla La Corota were sacred sites for the Quillacinga and other indigenous cultures. Centuries later, the Jesuits arrived on these shores and constructed a chapel to Our Lady of Lourdes on the Isla. Eventually, the Universidad de Nariño, recognizing the unique and fragile ecosystem of the isle, took it over and established a research center. In 1977, Isla La Corota was declared a Santuario de Flora y Fauna, and in 2000, 40,000 hectares of the lagoon's region fell under a Ramsar Convention, giving it protection as a páramo ecosystem of international importance. Updated: May 19, 2008.

When to Go

The climate of Laguna de la Cocha is cold and humid, with an average temperature of 12°C (54°F), and can drop to 3°C (38°F). Rain is a frequent occurrence here; normally December and January are dryer. In August there are high winds; according to local lore, this is a being that emerges from the lake's waters to overturn unsuspecting boats and drown its passengers.

The second Sunday of February, pilgrims come to visit the Capilla de la Virgen de Lourdes on the Isla de Corota.Updated: May 19, 2008.

Getting To and Away from Laguna de la Cocha

From the El Encano crossroads, a dirt road goes to Vereda El Puerto on the north shore of Laguna de la Cocha. From there, the camino splits. The west fork leads to Vereda Romerillo; the east fork traverses as far as Vereda Santa Teresita.

Departing from Pasto's cuartel, white collective taxis to Vereda El Puerto cost $8-10; busetas leave from Calle 20 and Carrera 20. You can also take a Sibundoy or Macoa-bound bus as far as El Encano and walk the last five kilometers (3 miles).

Vereda El Puerto is the port for boat transport to Isla La Corota and hamlets surrounding the lagoon. The five-minute ride out to the island costs about $7 per person (depending on the number of passengers). Updated: May 19, 2008,

Safety in Laguna de la Cocha

Even though the civil war wages not too far away, in the Putumayo, locals assert that El Encano and other settlements around Laguna de la Cocha are safe and tranquil. Because of the constant cold, wet climate of the region, warm clothing and raingear are essential. Eat high energy foods. Updated: May 19, 2008,

Things to See and Do

The peace of these high mountain humid forests might be enough to draw some people, just looking for a rest from the road. While you are here, though, enjoy a hike in the Santuario de Flora y Fauna Isla La Corota or visit a natural reserve run by the indigenous and campesino residents of the lake. Bird watchers, bring along your binoculars because many of those inhabitants await your checklists. Or, to pass a real lazy afternoon, drop a line into these pristine waters and hook a rainbow trout—an introduced species. Updated: May 19, 2008.

Santuario de Flora y Fauna Isla La Corota

A woman, bewitched by jealousy, was made into an island that to this day floats in the middle of Laguna de la Cocha. The fruit of her womb is the water that bathes her shores...or so legend tells us. This island was a sacred place for the Quillacinta and other indigenous nations. Today it embraces two sanctuaries: a nature one, Santuario de Flora y Fauna Isla La Corota, and a shrine to Our Lady of Lourdes.

The smallest of Colombia's national parks, Santuario de Flora y Fauna Isla La Corota comprises only eight hectares. A half-kilometer path leads up to the island's highest point, at 2,839 meters (9,312 feet). Its ecosystem is low mountain humid forest, exhibiting a great diversity of birds, amphibians and vegetation. At least 32 species of fowl roost here, including pullets, turtledoves, hummingbirds, ducks, wood pigeons, wrens, finches, tanagers, blackbirds and sparrows.

Over 500 species of plants carpet the small island, among them myrtle, alder, orchids, mosses and ferns.The environment is quite sensitive. Do not stray off the path. Do not pick any flowers or plants. Take out all your trash. A curious custom is 50 meters (165 feet) before the summit of the island, where visitors will take off their shoes, watches and metal items and go hug the Wish Tree. Some claim to be healed of illnesses. To get there, take a boat from Vereda El Puerto (approximately $7, 5 minutes).Updated: May 19, 2008.

Reservas Naturales de la Cocha

Since being declared a Ramsar protected area, local indigenous and campesino communities around Laguna de la Cocha have been taking an active role in conservation and the development of eco-tourism. All told, 32 hamlets are now reservas naturales, practicing sustainable agriculture and teaching environmental education. La Sombra de un Árbol and El Arrayán specialize in traditional and herbal medicine. Raíces Andinas preserves genetic resources, including the seeds of more than 30 varieties of potato. El Vicundo has an interpretation trail for birdwatching; La Casa del Buho has a museum. Most reservas make home-cooked meals for their visitors; some have basic lodging. Updated: May 19, 2008.

Laguna de la Cocha Lodging

Although Laguna de la Cocha is an easy day trip from Pasto, you may want to spend more time to soak in the tranquility and positive vibes of this corner of the Andes. Around the shores of the lake are several places where you can pass the night. The most formal and luxurious of these is Hotel Sindamanoy, of Swiss-chalet-styled architecture, and the Hotel Guámez. To enjoy Nariñense hospitality, you can also stay in one of the reservas naturales that offer lodging, like Raíces Andinas, Refugio Cristalino or Encanto Andino; El Vicundo has a camping area. Updated: May 19, 2008.

Laguna de la Cocha Restaurants

Scores of restaurants dot the roadsides at El Encano and El Puerto. The most common item on the menu is rainbow trout fresh out of the lake's icy waters. The family and community-run natural reserves also provide meals with farm-fresh products—including cuy (guinea pig.) Most of them can feed large groups. Updated: May 19, 2008.

Ipiales

Alt: 2,898 Pop: 72,000 City Code: 2

A Sunday morning stroll around Ipiales belies the reality of this city. Quiet streets soon bustle with travelers and merchants crossing the border, and Ecuadorian and Colombian pilgrims on their way to the Santuario de Nuestra Señora de Las Lajas.

Located on the Pan-American Highway just three kilometers north of the Rumichaca border crossing into Ecuador, Ipiales is only a transit point for many. However, it is worth passing a few days here. Services are improving in this Southern Colombian city; unfortunately, however, it still lacks a tourism office to orientate visitors—a shame, as there are interesting places to get to know. The city has several pleasant parks where you can people watch, and churches to visit. The incredible neo-Gothic Santuario de Nuestra Señora de Las Lajas that spans the Río Guáitra is only eight kilometers from Ipiales. Not too far from that pilgrimage site are some petroglyphs of the ancient Pasto indigenous culture. The village of Cumbral presents you with not only incredible vistas of two snow-capped volcanoes, but also walking and climbing opportunities.

So, don't be so hasty in flying through Ipiales to your other destinations in Colombia. Take a break to visit some of the surprises this region hides from fleeting eyes. Updated: Sep 25, 2007.

History

Several indigenous nations, principally of the Pasto who held off the Inca northward, called this region home before the Spanish conquest. Ipiales means People of White Smoke, deriving from Ipial, a Pasto cacique, plus the -es suffix, which means "people." The Villaviciosa de la Concepción de Ipiales was founded in 1537 by Pedro de Puelles, one of several captains sent by Benalcázar (a.k.a. Benalcázar) to found cities as base camps for the search for El Dorado. In the 1570s, the original city was totally destroyed by fire; at a new site several kilometers away it was rebuilt, with the name Villaje de Ipiales. It was administered by the Audencia Real de Quito. Ipiales joined the fight for independence from Spanish rule in 1809. The Libertador, Simón Bolívar, passed through the city on a number of occasions. Updated: Oct 14, 2007.

When to Go

Ipiales and Nariño Department have an agreeable spring-like climate, due to the high altitude of this southern Colombian region. From June to September it is cold and rainy. The other months see intermittent clear skies and sunshine.

No matter the season, the nights are surprisingly crisp. Ipiales has several festivals. El Festival de los Blancos y Negros (Festival of the Blacks and Whites) occurs January 3-6. Be sure to wear your oldest clothes, as it gets pretty nasty: on Black days, people cover themselves—and everyone else—with grease; on Blanco days, talcum powder flies.

Semana Santa (Holy Week) begins on the Wednesday before Easter. Every morning the via crucis wends through the city's streets, and in the evenings are processions. Many people also make the pilgrimage to Las Lajas at this time.

The Sacred Heart of Jesus is Ipiales' patron saint, celebrated sometime between the end of May and the end of June. The city is extremely crowded the first fortnight of September during the observance of the feast days of the Virgin of Lajas, culminating September 15.

On New Year's Eve, effigies representing events and noteworthy personalities of the past year are burnt in the streets. Updated: Sep 25, 2007.

Getting To and Away from Ipiales

The bus terminal is at Carrera 3 and Calle 6, seven blocks from Parque La Pola. You can catch any buseta passing along Carrerra 5 -$0.65,- a taxi (up to five persons, $1.40) or walk it. Combis to the Rumichaca border leave from Calle 14, between Carrera 7 and 10, when full ($0.80), and taxis from one block further up on Calle 14 ($3).

Ipiales has national and international flights leaving from Aeropuerto de San Luís, six kilometers from the city, directly to Bogotá, Puerto Asís, Cali and Neiva, with connections to all other points in the country. Sam, Tame, Aces and Avianca are some of the companies providing service. A sample of one-way fares are: Bogotá, $131; Cali, $94-100; Puerto Asís, $52; Medellín, $153-180; Cúcuta, $145; Cartagena, $138. Taxes and other fees are extra.

From Ipiales

Arrive	Departure	Time	Price
Tumaco	9 a.m., 10:30 a.m., 11:30 a.m., 1 p.m., 1:30 p.m.	5-6 hours	$10.25 11.30
Pasto	Hourly	1.5 hours	$3
Popayán	Hourly	8 hours	$13 14.40
Cali	Half-hourly	10 hours	$18
Medellín	10 a.m., 3 p.m., 7 p.m.	20 hours	$39
Bogotá	Hourly 8 a.m. -8 p.m.	22 hours	$42

Updated: Oct 08, 2007.

Safety in Ipiales

Ipiales, in general, is a safe town. However, like any city near a border, theft can be more likely than in other towns due to the constant movement of people, making it easy for a would-be thief to disappear. Use common sense: Keep an eye on your belongings at all times. Don't display large amounts of bills; keep only what you immediately need at hand—especially when changing money. Many locals travel only during the day, as guerrilla activity and robberies continue to be a problem (although less so than in the past due to the military's presence on the roads and checkpoints). A number of bus companies do offer overnight service to Pasto, Popayán and Cali. Updated: Oct 08, 2007.

Ipiales Services

Money

If coming from Ecuador, exchange only a little money at the border; you'll get a better exchange rate in Ipiales.
Bancolombia (Monday-Friday, 8 a.m.-4 p.m. Calle 14, on Parque La Pola) is the only bank in Ipiales that changes traveler's checks—and only American Express. Its ATM handles all banking networks, with a daily withdrawal limit of $600.

Other banks and exchange houses will change U.S. cash dollars to pesos. You will find many around Parque La Pola, and on Calles 14 and Carreras 5 and 6.

Most exchange houses are open 8 a.m.-6 p.m., some until 7 p.m. Restaurants and shops at the bus terminal may be able to change money, also.

For wiring money, the local Western Union office is at Giros and Finazas (Monday-Friday, 8 a.m.-noon, 2-5 p.m., Saturday, 8 a.m.-noon. Carrera 6, 13-23).

Keep in Touch

There are a fair amount of internet cafés scatter throughout Ipiales; most charge about $1 per hour. Mundo Net (Monday-Saturday, 8:30 a.m.-1 p.m., 2-8 p.m., Sunday, 8:30 a.m.-1 p.m. Carrera 7, 10-67) additionally has Skype and can burn your digital photos to CD.

To make a local or national phone call, just keep an eye out for the frequent "llamadas" signs; the going rate is $0.10 per minute.
For international calls, try Sai Telecom (Monday-Saturday, 8 a.m.-9:30 p.m. Calle 16, 6-47), which charges $0.80 per minute.
Snail mail can be posted at the Correo in the Alcaldía building complex on the Plaza de la Independencia (Monday-Friday, 8 a.m.-noon, 2-6 p.m., Saturday, 8 a.m.-noon).

Camera Repair

You can find a number of photo shops on Carrera 6, between the two plazas. They sell everything from print film to digital cameras. Foto Almacén Rollei (Daily, 8 a.m.-7 p.m., Carrera 6, 12-133, Tel: 2-773-3811) has 100 and 200 ASA film in stock, digital chips, camera batteries and a wide array of conventional and digital cameras. IOT can process your color-print film in one hour (24 exposures, $7.50) or burn your digital photos onto CD (unlimited number of images, $3.50, including CD). Foto Almacén Rollei also repairs both analog and digital cameras.

Shopping

Befitting a border town, the shops in Ipiales proffer almost anything you need. The city also has a number of droguerías, or pharmacies, to cure your ills.

For the market scene, head for the daily mercado on Carrera 10, between Calles 14 and 15. Here you can pick up on not only fruits and veggies, but also the latest in fashions. Ipiales is host to two weekly markets, both carrying out business the full length of Carrera 7. On Fridays is an indigenous market, featuring the produce and products from Colombia and Ecuador. A run-of-the-mill weekly market is on Saturdays.

If you are bicycling your way through the Americas, you can find parts for almost any type of bike, as well as repairs, at Bicicletería JJ (Monday-Saturday, 8 a.m.-12:30 p.m., 2-6:30 p.m. Carrera 7, 16-84, Tel: 2-725-1087; accepts Visa and MasterCard) and Ciclo Cadena (Monday-Saturday, 8 a.m.-noon, 2-6 p.m. Carrera 7, 16-73, Tel: 2-725-2149). Updated: May 16, 2008.

Things to See and Do

Ipiales is more than the last Colombian city on the way to the principle border crossing to Ecuador. It is also an important pilgrimage center for both Colombian and Ecuadorian Catholics. Eight kilometres away is the Santuario de Nuestra Señora de las Lajas, an impressive church built over a river gorge.

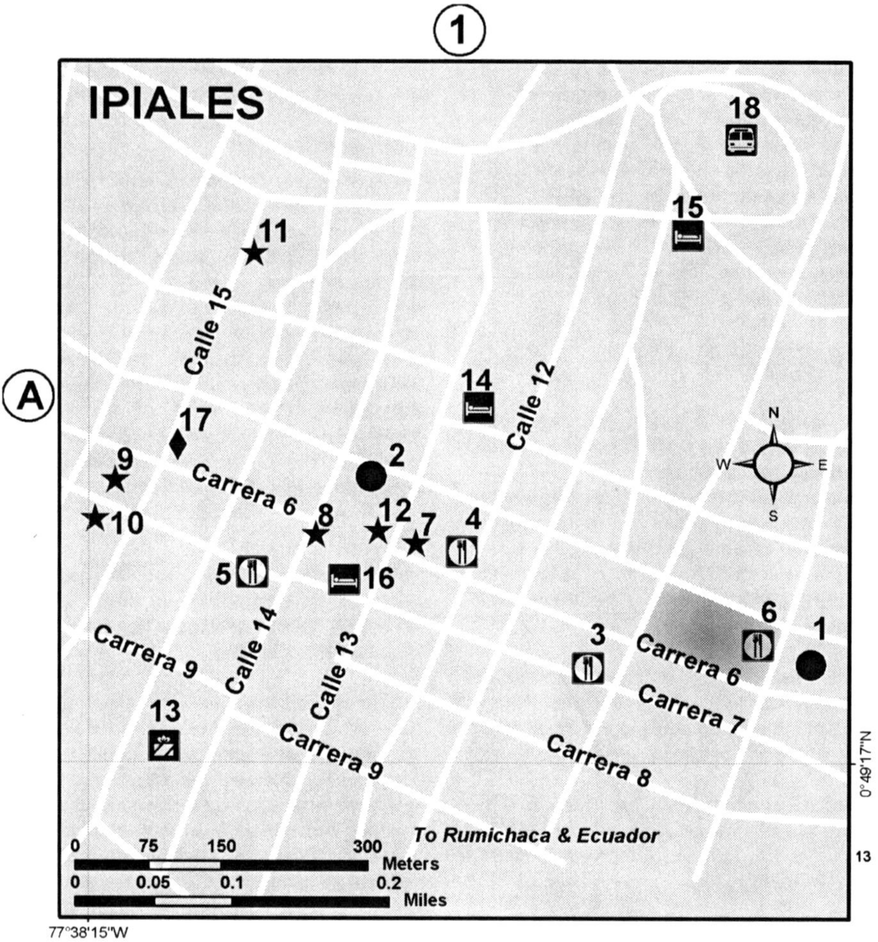

Activities
1 Parque de Independencia B2
2 Parque la Pola B2

Eating
3 Mundo Net B2
4 Pan Pan B2
5 Restaurante Mi Casita B2
6 Restaurante-Bar Rancho Grande B2

Services
7 Almacén Rollei B2
8 Banco Colombia B2
9 Ciclo Cadena B2
10 JJ Bicicletería B2
11 Sai Telecom B2
12 Western Union B2

Shopping
13 Mercado B2

Sleeping
14 Hotel Belmonte B2
15 Hotel Imperio B2
16 Hotel Internacional El Nogal B2

Tours
17 Valencia Torres B2

Transportation
18 Bus Terminal B2

SOUTHERN COLOMBIA

From the sanctuary, three kilometres along the Río Guáitra, there are the rock paintings of Piedra de los Monos, reminding us the area was also sacred to the Pasto ancestors of this region.

Numerous indigenous villages speckle the countryside around Ipiales. Visit the weekly market in Cumbal and dine on fresh trout at Laguna de Cumbal. If you're feeling an urge to do some climbing, Volcán Cumbal and Chilis are good challenges. Updated: Oct 08, 2007.

Churches and Plazas of Ipiales

Ipiales has two pleasant public squares: Parque de la Independencia (also known as Parque 20 de Julio), between Carreras 5 and 6, and Calles 8 and 9, and Parque La Pola, between Carreras 5 and 6, and Calles 13 and 14. Around Parque de la Independencia are the municipal buildings and the city's cathedral. A tall column atop which Lady Liberty stands on the back of a soaring condor is in the center of the park. The Catedral Bodas de Plata, dedicated to Saint Peter, was constructed in 1823. The church's red-brick exterior of classical lines rises into twin bell towers. Within, the clean style continues. Massive Ionic columns divide the nave from the side aisles, which are lined with chapel screens touched with gold gilt. The left aisle ends in a chapel. Large clerestory windows flood the nave with sunlight. The ceilings are of inlaid wood. (Monday-Friday, 7 a.m.-1 p.m., 2-7 p.m., Saturday and Sunday, 7 a.m.-7 p.m.)

Parque La Pola is more the center of Ipiales. Here is where you will find banks and places to exchange money. Combis from the border can drop you off at this park. The center of Parque La Pola is marked with the statue of another woman: independence heroine Policarpa Salavarrieta. She is breaking free from the chains that bind her to a pillar. The blue and white Iglesia de San Felipe Neri, of the same period as the Catedral, has an unusual touch: its two campaniles are topped with onion domes, reminiscent of Russian Orthodox architecture. Inside, the temple's nave is flanked by narrow aisles lined with chapel screens dedicated to various versions of the Virgin. The nave terminates in a square apse. Thick Corinthian columns support the painted, textured-tin ceiling. Small clerestory windows truncate the thick walls, making this church not as bright as its sister, the cathedral. Updated: Oct 19, 2007.

Santuario Nuestra Señora de las Lajas

One day in 1750 (more or less), María Mueses de Quiñónez was walking from Potosí to Ipiales. Upon her back she carried her young, deaf-mute daughter Rosa. They decided to rest at Pastarán cave on the banks of the Río Guáitra. When doña María awoke from a nap, she discovered her daughter had wandered off. Upon finding her, Rosa said, "Mamacita, the Mestiza called to me!" She pointed to an image of a woman holding a child and two men.

Thus begins the story of Santuario Nuestra Señora de las Lajas. A small adobe chapel was built to protect the image of the Virgin in the shallow cave, forming the "altar screen" of the temple. Over the centuries it expanded to the impressive neo-Gothic structure that now spans the Guáitra River. Many Colombians and Ecuadorians make the pilgrimage to this site, beseeching the Virgin Mary for her intercession. The cliff walls are covered with thousands of plaques thanking her for miracles. (The Vatican only recognizes one).

Pack a picnic lunch and come spend the day strolling the network of paths that interlace over the grounds. Take a bath in the healing pools at the foot of the waterfall. There's even a playground. The on-site museum has exhibits on the Sanctuary's history and on the Pasto indigenous.

To get there, colectivo taxis leave Ipiales from Carrera 6 and Calle 6 ($0.80). Up the hill, in Las Lajas village, are several hotels, from basic to grand ($3-10 per person, per night), or you can stay at the Casa Pastoral ($4 per night; Tel: 2-775-4463).

The Santuario is crowded at Easter (Semana Santa) and for the Virgen de las Lajas feast days during the first two weeks of September. On the way back, stop off in El Charco for roasted cuy, a regional specialty. Las Lajas village, eight kilometers from Ipiales. Tel: 2-775-4462 / 4428, E-mail: laslajas08@yahoo.es. Updated: May 20, 2008.

Piedra de los Monos

While at Santuario Nuestra Señora de las Lajas, take a hike down to what was certainly a holy site for the previous inhabitants of this region: Piedra de los Monos. Following a well-signed path from the Catholic sanctuary, along the Río Guáitra, you will arrive at these petroglyphs, after three kilometers.

In crimsom, white and shades of purple, the Pasto people decorated this rock overhang with animal and anthropomorphic figures, and their signature sun symbol. The entire "canvas" measures six meters by four meters. The age of these creations is not known.

Above, on the rim of this gorge, we can witness the ceremonies of the valley's modern inhabitants. But here, we can only speculate what types of rites the Pasto performed in the past. Take public transport to Lajas village (see Santuario Nuestra Señora de las Lajas). Three kilometers from Santuario Nuestra Señora de las Lajas. Updated: Dec 19, 2007.

Cumbal

This small indigenous village on the altiplano is quiet during the week, but on Sundays it is the place to be due to its bustling market. Stalls display fruits from highlands and low, or ruanas from local workshops.

It's worth a stay in one of the basic hotels, to set your plans for visiting the two snow-capped volcanoes that tower over the hamlet early most mornings. To climb Volcán Cumbal (4,780 m), ask the locals to accompany them on their daily harvests of ice and sulfur. From the top you'll see the snowy peaks of Ecuador to the south, and to the west, a vast emerald jungle expanse to the Pacific Ocean glittering on that distant horizon.

To summit Volcán Chiles (4600 m), go to the village of the same name on the volcano's slopes. There you may be able to find someone to guide you. It should take about six hours to reach the apex, which lies on the Colombia-Ecuador border. Inquire, also, about the nearby hot springs. Aguas Hediondas, on the southern slopes within Ecuador, are literally boiling sulphur waters set on a barren páramo plain where condors soar.

Collective taxis leave daily for Cumbal, when full, from the Ipiales bus terminal, 5 a.m.-5 p.m. The last vehicle leaves for Ipiales at 4:30 p.m. from the mercado plaza. (45 minutes, $2.50 one way). Transport to Chiles leaves from Cumbal. Updated: May 20, 2008.

Ipiales Tours

As Ipiales is more tuned to commerce than it is to tourism, there are no operators offering tours to the region's attractions. You are pretty much on your own here. Fortunately, you can easily reach them solo. If you want to save time on traveling to your next Colombia destination, several travel agencies await your business. These are located near the intersection of Carrera 7 and Calle 16. Updated: Oct 08, 2007.

Valencia Torres

If the prospect of extended bus travel in Colombia makes you wince, then consider flying. Valencia Torres can help you book tickets for anywhere you want to go. A small, no-frills office, the staff is helpful. Even though it is Ipiales' Avianca agency, Valencia Torres also books with Satena, Aires, Sam and other national airlines—and even Tame, in case you want to fly to Quito. This travel agency can also sell you airline tour packages to prime Colombian vacation spots. Valencia Torres also handles national and international courier services. Monday-Friday, 8 a.m.-noon, 2-6 p.m., Saturday 8 a.m.-noon. Calle 16, 6-43. Tel: 2-773-4523, Fax: 2-773-2247, E-mail: valenciatorres@etb.net.co. Updated: Oct 19, 2007.

Ipiales Lodging

Ipiales has a wide offering of lodging choices for all budgets. Many low-end hostels are located on Calle 13, near the Iglesia San Felipe Neri; expect to pay $5 or less per night. In the past few years, more luxury hotels catering to business travelers have appeared on the ipialeño scene; these are mainly concentrated on Carrera 7. Updated: Oct 08, 2007.

Belmonte !

(BED: $4.60-8.20) Doña Olga proudly states, "This is not a luxurious place. It's basic, secure, clean and cheap"—and that is precisely what the Hotel Belmonte is. The rooms are simply appointed with classic, heavily carved furniture; some rooms come with cable TV included in the price. All use the clean, common bathroom which has 24-hour hot water. Some of the rooms can be a bit noisy. This hostel is popular with backpackers and pilgrims alike. Doña Olga is helpful with tourist information. Carrera 4, 12-111. Tel: 2-773-2771. Updated: Dec 19, 2007.

V!VA Member Review- Belmonte

After that long trip from Quito, this is a great place to crash the night before heading to Lajas the next day. Oct 07, 2007.

Imperio Real

(ROOM: $9.25-12.50) After your long journey, just walk across the street to Hotel Imperio Real, no matter what the hour. Its dim, stone-inlaid hallways quietly lead you to your room. Open the door and walk into a bright room complete with your own private bath (with gas-heated hot water 24-hours a day) and cable TV. If you don't feel like dining downstairs, you can call room service and enjoy your meal in your suite. This hostel also offers laundry service. Carrera 3, 6-26. Tel: 2-773-4887. Updated: Dec 19, 2007.

Hotel Internacional El Nogal

(ROOM: $15.50-28) Hotel Internacional El Nogal is a new luxury hotel on the Ipiales scene. The tastefully decorated rooms have telephone, cable TV and private, hot water baths. Unfortunately, some of the rooms do not have windows. But, never mind, if you feel like you really need to unwind, head down to the free sauna and turkish baths. Also included in the price is a buffet American breakfast served in the second-floor restaurant. Other services are free parking in an attached, underground garage, internet, laundry, room service, transport to/from the airport and money exchange. Carrera 7, 13-77. Tel: 2-725-3983 / 3984, Fax: 2-725-3985, E-mail: hotelnogal_ipiales@yahoo.com. Updated: Dec 19, 2007.

IPIALES RESTAURANTS

For an inexpensive place to eat, check out the panaderías on Carrera 6 between Parque La Pola and the Plaza de la Independencia. Many serve set lunches and dinners for between $1.60 and $2.50. There are also cheap restaurants on Parque La Pola. Ipiales also has upscale restaurants specializing in traditional Colombian food; most are around Plaza de la Independencia and on Carrera 7. While visiting Las Lajas, be sure to stop off in El Charco to taste a specialty of the southern Colombian Andes: cuy roasted over a wood fire. Updated: Oct 08, 2007.

Pan Pan

Pan Pan is just one of the many bakeries that make much more then just breads and cakes. They also make blue-plate specials with hearty soups, followed by a main dish of meat, rice, beans, salad and patacones, washed down with a fresh fruit drink—for only $2-2.50 (slightly higher on Sundays). Be sure to pick up a cookie right out of the oven on your way out. Pan Pan also serves breakfasts for $1.60. Open Monday-Saturday, 7 a.m.-9 p.m., Sunday 8 a.m.-7 p.m. Carrera 6, 12-76, Tel: 2-773-3861. Updated: Dec 19, 2007.

Restaurante Mi Casita

An ipialeño tradition, Restaurante Mi Casita dishes up home-cooked, Colombian favorites. If hunger gnaws you early on, you can breakfast here ($2-2.50). Later in the day, choose a dish of meat, chicken or fish prepared with a variety of recipes and accompanied with rice, potatoes and salad for $4.60. Or try the traditional *bandeja paisa* for $6.70. If your wallet is feeling a bit slimmer than that, opt for the blue-plate special, offered at lunch and dinner, for $3. The only alcohol served here is beer. Open Monday-Sunday, 8 a.m.-8 p.m. Calle 9, 6-18. Tel: 2-773-2754. Updated: May 16, 2008.

Rancho Grande

Styled to look like a humble hut, Restaurante-Bar Rancho Grande sports green-painted bamboo outside and in. Sit down at one of the green-clothed tables and have an aperitif from the full bar while you study the menu. Meat or poultry main dishes cost $4.50-5. If seafood is more your speed, be prepared to pay $5-9. All entrées come accompanied with rice, potatoes and salad. Rancho Grande does not prepare a daily blue-plate special for lunch or dinner, but it does for breakfast ($2-2.50). Open daily, 7 a.m.-7 p.m. Carrera 7, 14-51. Tel: 2-773-2662. Updated: Dec 19, 2007.

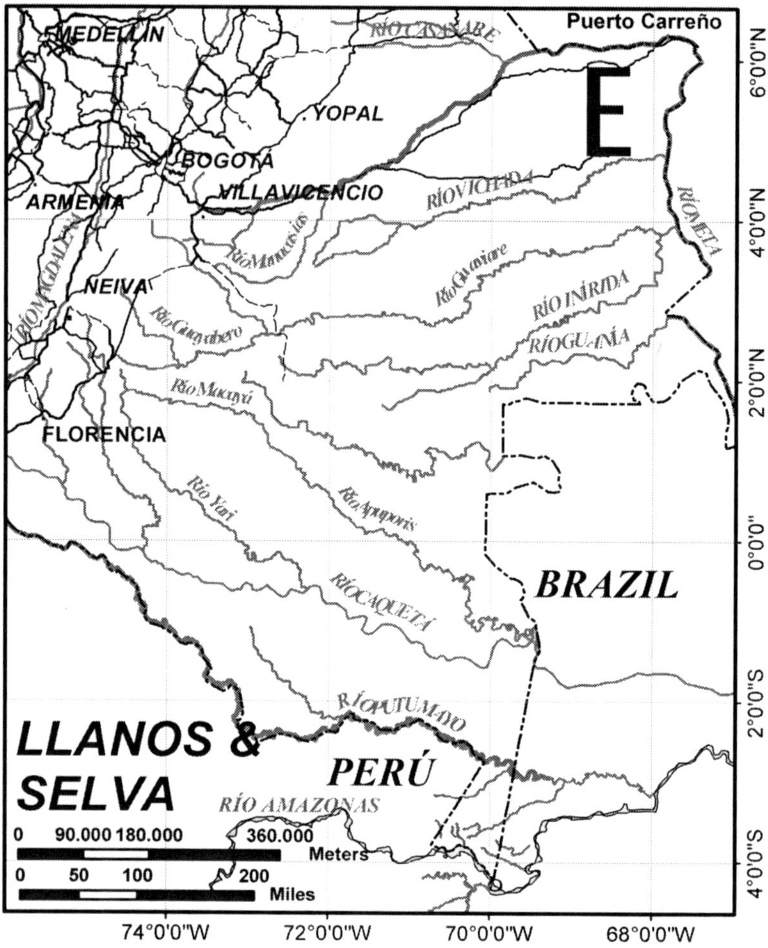

LLANOS AND SELVA

The Llanos (eastern plains) and Selva (jungle) constitute more than half of Colombia. Steeped in the history of the Spaniards' lust-driven quest for El Dorado, the regions' wilderness succeeded in keeping all but the hardiest out.

The Llanos, also known as the Región Orinoquia, encompasses the Colombian departments of Meta (capital, Villavicencio), Casanare (capital, Yopal), Arauca (capital, Arauca), Vichada (capital, Puerto Carreño) and Guainía (capital, Puerto Inírida). This area makes up part of the Orinoco River basin and borders Venezuela. The Selva, or the Región Amazonía, is made up of the departments of Putumayo (capital, Mocoa), Caquetá (capital, Florencia), Guaviare (capital, San José de Guaviare), Vaupés (capital, Mitú) and Amazonas (capital, Leticia). The most famous of these is Amazonas, where Leticia is the crossroads for the Amazon River, with connections to Peru and Brazil. Roads weave through the Llanos, connecting it to Bogotá and other cities on the western side of the Cordillera Oriental. Traveling by river down the Río Orinoco into Venezuela is one ageless dream of travelers. Traveling in the jungle is dictated by transportation, since there are no roads in most of the region, except those radiating out from Leticia and one connecting Puerto Asís and other Putumayo towns with Southern Colombia. Otherwise travel is restricted to boat on the many rivers lacing through the jungles.

The mystique of the Llanos and Selva has continued to the present day. It is still an unfathomable region—not only because of the blanketing, lush vegetation, but also because it is the epicenter of Colombia's civil war. It was here that Farclandia existed, a demilitarized zone under guerrilla FARC control at the turn of the millennium. It is also where the heaviest fighting continues to occur as the Colombian military recovers the territory bit by bit. Some places, though, are currently safe enough to visit, such as Villavicencio and Puerto López in the Llanos and Leticia with its neighboring villages and Sibundoy (Putumayo). Other areas are once more coming within the scope of travelers. Recently several foreigners have reported no problems in traveling from San Agustín to Pasto, by way of Mocoa—a journey that was impossible until about April 2008. Keep your ear to the ground to stay informed about the next possible area of exploration in this region. Updated: Jul 09, 2008.

Highlights

Visit the **Sibundoy (p.482)** in the Putumayo, an indigenous community famed for its mask carving.

Any Colombian Amazon journey begins in **Leticia (p.465)**, whether into the jungle, to Parque Nacional Amacayacu or floating on the great river's muddy water to Peru or Brazil.

Watch the pink dolphins leap out from the silver waters of **Lago Tarapoto (p.483)**, near Puerto Nariño.

Whitewater raft on the Río Ariari, Río Guatiquía and other rivers that slice through the eastern plains.

Dip into the **Caño Cristales** in Parque Nacional Natural La Macarena (p.480). Updated: Jul 09, 2008.

History

After Francisco de Orellana blazed a trail to the Amazon River in 1542, many mid-16th Century conquistadores, like Diego de Orduz, passed through the jungles and plains on the quest for El Dorado. This opened the way for the Catholic missionary orders—the Franciscans, Capuchins, Jesuits and Augustinians—to establish settlements throughout the region. At the time of the Spaniards' arrival, the Llanos were inhabited by independent indigenous Arawak villages, such as the Guahibos and Sálivas. Their inhabitants were displaced by the Spaniards and forced to live in Catholic missions. The same occurred to the Selva indigenous nations along the Napo, Caquetá, Putumayo and Amazon Rivers.

The indigenous tribes who live in the jungle met another great disaster with the rubber boom of the late 19th Century. Large swaths of the rainforest were destroyed and slavery was legalized. The Huitoto population, once the Amazon's largest group, suffered more than a 60 percent decrease. La Casa Arana, a major rubber company, is believed to have killed 50,000 indigenous workers with bad working conditions, whippings and murder.

Threats to the environment and the indigenous continued into the 20th Century. With the advent of motorized transportation in the 1930s, roads were built from highland cities like Pasto and Bogotá into the Llanos and Selva. The resulting migration pushed roads further and further into the jungle, not only for new settlers, but also for the extraction of valuable hardwoods and gold reserves. In the 1980s, deep sections of the jungle became home to vast plantations of marijuana and coca and mega-cocaine labs. Tranquilandia, one of the largest, had 14 labs, electricity, roads and an airfield, and processed 3500 kilograms (7,700 pounds) of pure white powder every month. Problems continued for the region into the next decade when the players of Colombia's civil war moved into the relative haven of the Llanos' and Selva's jungles. A 42,000 square kilometer demilitarized zone was established by peace accords between Colombian President Andrés Pastrana and the FARC guerrillas in 1999. Farclandia, as it was nicknamed, covered much of Caquetá and Putumayo Departments. San Vicente del Caguán was the capital. Pastrana rescinded the deal in 2002, due to continued kidnapping and other practices by FARC. With the new millennium and a new president, Álvaro Uribe, FARC strongholds in the Llanos and Selva have been systematically attacked. Updated: Jul 09, 2008.

Safety in Llanos and Selva

The security situation in the Llanos and Selva can be summed up in two words: war zone. This is where the FARC and other factions of the Colombian Civil War have their strongholds, and where the heaviest fighting between them and the Colombian military are presently taking place.

In the Llanos, the major cities are OK. Avoid traveling off the main roadways. Always ask local advice about the safety of any place you want to travel to further down the road. Expect many military checkpoints; have your documents at hand. River travel is said to be secure now because of heavy military patrols on the principal waterways. However, the roads to the river ports may not be secure.

Likewise, the Selva rivers also are reported to be heavily patrolled. The Leticia area is safe, but around Puerto Asís is considered problematic at this time. Near here is where in, March 2008, the Colombian military bombed Ecuadorian territory in an operation against the FARC. Residents on both sides of the border continue to report fighting.

In terms of more mundane hazards, like diseases, malaria and yellow fever are common in both the Selva and the Llanos. Take proper measures to protect against mosquitoes, and take malaria medication. A yellow fever vaccination is essential. Both regions are home to spiders, snakes and scorpions, so shake your clothing and shoes out before dressing. Keep insects, animals, poisonous plants and more in mind, and be aware of where you place your hand while in the wild, especially don't go around picking up any logs or rocks—you never know what lives underneath. If you are bleeding (including a woman's time of the month) or have any kind of open wound, keep in mind that piranha and other carnivorous fish feed in the early mornings and late afternoons, so avoid swimming in rivers or lakes. At night, be careful around

Glossary of Rodeo Terms

While in the Llanos region, take the opportunity to go to the rodeo—or, in local parlance, *el coleo*. To help you with the *llanero* (from the Llanos) terminology, here are some definitions of major events:

Carrera a Caballo ► Horse Racing: one-on-one and competitions of riders on the fastest horse.

Enlazada del Becerro ► Calf Roping: Each two-person team has to pursue a calf once it is let loose out of the chute, ride it down, lasso it and tie its feet together in the shortest time possible.

Herrada del Becerro ► Calf Branding: Each team, on foot, chases down the calf, lassos it and ties its feet together, then brands the calf in the shortest time possible.

Monta del Potro Cerrero ► Bareback Bronco Riding: The participant has to ride an unbroken (untamed) horse without saddle or bridle for the longest period of time.

Ordeño de la Vaca Mañosa ► Milking the Ornery Cow: This test, done on foot, consists of wrangling a rascally cow and milking her in the shortest time possible.

Monta del Potro Matrero ► Bull Riding: Considered the most dangerous of rodeo events, the winner must ride a bull bareback for at least eight seconds.

Coleo Criollo ► Calf Scramble: Practiced the traditional way, barefoot contestants have to pull the tail of a yearling and knock it down.

Llanerazo ► The Big Llano Event: The hexathlon, so to speak, of the rodeo world. The winner must demonstrate proficiency in the six above events (except cow milking), as well as in traditional llanero dancing and musical performance. Updated: Jul 09, 2008.

water, because caymans can be a dangerous threat. Updated: Jul 09, 2008.

Things to See and Do

The biggest attraction in the Llanos and Selva is the wildlife. Caymans, *babillas* (the more calm-spirited cousin of the cayman), *chigüiros* (the largest rodent in the world), *tití leoncitos* (the planet's smallest primate), anacondas, boas and pink dolphins are just a few of the intriguing creatures inhabiting these forests and rivers. Birdwatchers find paradise with macaws, harpy eagles, ibises, hummingbirds, cara caras, royal eagles and almost a thousand other species of birds.

Visit indigenous villages to learn about their culture and to purchase artisan work. In Leticia and Puerto Nariño annual festivals celebrate the indigenous culture. The Llanos has a *mestizo* culture distinct from other parts of Colombia. Here, Joropo dance and music reigns and international competitions are held twice a year. Catch another big feature on these plains of vast cattle ranches—the *coleo* (rodeo). The Llanos also offers rafting and rock climbing. Updated: Jul 09, 2008.

Llanos and Selva Tours

Currently, most excursions into the Selva or Llanos are arranged through companies based in Bogotá, mostly for convenience. But these trips are often much more expensive than arranging them with locally-based companies. In Leticia, there are many tour agencies that offer trips into the jungle and to lodges. Slowly, as the Llanos become more secure, tour operators are opening up shop in Villavicencio. These are providing white-water rafting and rock climbing, as well as expeditions to Parque Nacional Natural Sierra de la Macarena. In theory you don't need a tour agency for some activities, which can be done on your own. Nonetheless, because of environmental and security (war) considerations, it is highly advisable to go with a guide, preferably one from the area who should know the local situation in depth. Updated: Jul 09, 2008.

Llanos and Selva Lodging

Accommodation options in the Llanos and Selva tend to be more expensive than in other regions in Colombia, something budget travelers should take into consideration. In the jungle, camping with a tent is not possible due to snakes, though a hammock could come in handy, especially in smaller villages. Cheaper hotels usually have common bathrooms and fans. Rooms at mid- and upper-range hotels tend to have private bathrooms. Most accommodation of any classification only have room-temperature showers. Only the most expensive hotels have hot water. Air conditioning is a choice in mid-range and high-end hotels.

These two regions have accommodation alternatives distinct from other parts of Colombia. In the Llanos there are upscale country hotels complete with swimming pools and horseback riding, in addition to guest ranches. Near Leticia are several jungle lodges. Updated: Jul 09, 2008.

Leticia

Alt: 95m Pop: 35,000 City Code: 8

Welcome to the last outpost of Colombia, in the far southeastern corner of the country. Leticia forms part of the triple frontier, along with Tabatinga, Brazil, and Santa Rosa, Peru. Twenty-five kilometers (15 miles) downstream is Benjamin Constant, a major Brazilian port on the river and alternative point for taking a boat on the Amazon to Manaus. Leticia is the point where some travelers first step foot in Colombia. Others say their last goodbye before taking a boat upstream to Iquitos, Peru, or downstream to Brazil. Although the most developed of the three border cities, Leticia is still a small town. Everything is within walking distance. Parque Santander is the hub of social life. During dawn and dusk the trees are a riot of *pericos* (small green parrots). In this park, the Victoria Regia Amazonica pool has the largest water lilies in the world. Nearby are two wonderful sculptures: Alegoria Cómica del Amazona by Aida Orrego and one of leaping pink dolphins. Upon arriving in Leticia, you have to pay an entry tax of $8 and show your international yellow fever vaccination certificate. Updated: Jul 07, 2008.

History

The history of Leticia embraces many legends. One legend goes back to the Spanish and Portuguese exploration of the Amazon River, when Benigno Bustamante established

San Antonio in 1867 on orders from the Peruvian government (to prevent Colombia from staking a claim to the river). He named it San Antonio after a cross inscribed with this name found at the site, where a Portuguese explorer and his expedition had starved to death. Peru and Colombia had a number of confrontations in the region, which intensified from 1911 until the Salomón-Lozano Treaty of 1922. The treaty gave Colombia access to the Amazon River and at this point the town's name was changed to Leticia. The modern name is explained through the second legend. The tale says that a Colombian soldier fell in love with an indigenous woman with the name Leticia.

In 1933, 300 armed Peruvians invaded Leticia, proclaiming it as part of Peru once more. Another bilateral agreement was signed in 1934, which created a demilitarized zone around Leticia, unhindered navigation on the Amazon and Putumayo Rivers and a pledge of non-aggression on the part of both countries. To ensure Leticia would remain loyal to Colombia, the federal government populated the town with *bogotanos*. In the 1960s and 1970s, Leticia's economy boomed thanks to the drug trade. Once the drug cartel was controlled, Leticia fell onto hard times, and now relies heavily on tourism. Updated: Jul 08, 2008.

When to Go

Leticia has two distinct seasons. The dry season lasts from June to September. The rainy season begins in October with amounts of precipitation gradually increasing and the heaviest rains falling from January to May. Temperatures are fairly constant throughout the year, with days reaching 31-32°C (87-90°F) and nights reaching 21-22°C (70-72°F). The Amazon flows heaviest in May and the lowest in September. There is a 15-meter (49-foot) difference between the two stages.

Weekends are fairly busy with the shoppers who come in from Colombian, Peruvian and Brazilian river settlements. You might have a hard time finding a hotel room during weekends. Updated: Jul 08, 2008.

Holidays and Festivals

The big event on Leticia's calendar is the Festival Internacional de la Confraternidad Amazónica, which is celebrated every year from July 15 to 20. Participants come from Colombia, Peru and Brazil for this tri-country fair that includes cultural and sporting activities. Other holidays observed in Leticia are:

April 25—Leticia's founding.

July—Fiestas de San Pedro.

November—Festival Internacional de Música Popular Amazonense El Pirarucú de Oro, music and dances from the Amazon region.

December 31—Parade of Año Viejo (effigies) Updated: Jul 08, 2008.

Getting To and Away From Leticia

Leticia is accessible by river and air. The only road that exists is a dry-weather track to Tarapacá (with public transport only as far as Km 18) and to Tabatinga.

Boat

Leticia's port is at the end of Calle 8. The street is quite muddy in the rainy season. From the three floating docks, catch a launch to villages along the Amazon and its tributaries. Two types of boats work these routes. There's the fast boat with an enclosed passenger compartment and the *peque-peque*, which is an open canoe with a long-shafted outboard motor. In the past it was cheaper to take a boat from Puerto Asís to Leticia, but this route now goes right through the war zone, where there is heavy fighting and bombing occasionally reported.

For the following routes, go directly to the docks. There are launches that leave every 15 to 20 minutes.

To Santa Rosa—daily 6 a.m.-8 p.m., $1.05.

To Tabatinga—daily 6 a.m.-8 p.m., $1.05.

Ask around the docks for information about slow-boat peque-peques to the different villages.

To Puerto Nariño—twice weekly, $9.50, 6 hours or more.

Several agencies at the end of Calle 8 sell tickets for fast boats to Parque Nacional Natural Amacayacu, Mocagua and Puerto

Nariño, including Transportes Fluviales del Amazonas (daily 6 a.m.-6 p.m. Calle 8, 11-183. Tel: 8-592-5999). It is recommended to buy your passage the day before.

To PNN Amacayacu, Mocagua and Puerto Nariño—8 a.m., 10 a.m., 2 p.m., $10.50 / $11 / $11.50, 1.5-2 hours.

For information on international boats to Manaus, Brazil, and Iquitos, Peru, see "Colombia-Brazil-Peru Border Crossings."

Air

Leticia's Aeropuerto Internacional Vásquez Cobo is 1.5 kilometers (one mile) from downtown. Avenida Vásquez Cobo in front of the airport becomes Carrera 10. AeroRepública flies to Bogotá daily ($142-190 one way, including taxes) (Monday-Friday 8 a.m.-noon, 2-6 p.m., Saturday 8 a.m.-noon. Calle 7, 10-36. Tel: 8-592-7838). On Sundays you can buy your ticket at the airport. Satena also has flights to Bogotá three days per week ($77 with taxes) (Monday, Wednesday, Friday 2-6 p.m. Calle 11, 5-73. Tel: 8-592-4845). Flights are cheaper on some days rather than on others. Shop around and check the companies' websites. Updated: Jul 08, 2008.

Getting Around

Busetas leave from Parque Orellana to the Kilometer villages and the Lagos (5:45 a.m.-6:20 p.m. $0.50-1.85) and to Tabatinga and the Tikuna village Maria Azzu (6 a.m.-6:20 p.m., $0.80-1.05). *Mototaxis*, with you riding on back, charge $0.50 around town and $1.05 to the Policia Federal post in Tabatinga. Taxis cost $1.60-2.65, depending on the distance.

Renting a motor scooter is a different way to get around. Many shops along Calle 11, Avenida Internacional and Carrera 10 rent motorcycles. The going price is $2.65 per hour, $15.15 for a half day and $21 for 24 hours. Updated: Jul 08, 2008.

Safety in Leticia

Within the town of Leticia it is relatively safe, though residents advise against walking toward the airport, the river or the border after 10 p.m. It's recommended that visitors stay in the immediate downtown area. In terms of the civil war, people will tell you that "it's a whole jungle away."

As in any place in the tropics, mosquito-born diseases are a concern. Get the yellow fever vaccine at least 10 days before arriving. The tri-border region undergoes a fairly rigorous spraying program to control Aedes and Anopheles denizens. Nonetheless, take proper precautions against mosquitoes, especially if venturing into less populated areas. Updated: Jul 08, 2008.

Leticia Services

Tourism Office

Leticia's tourism office, Secretaría de Medio Ambiente y Desarrolo Productivo, has city maps in English or Spanish and information about things to do and see (Monday-Friday 8 a.m.-noon, 2-5 p.m. Calle 9, 10-86. Tel: 8-592-5944, URL: www.leticia-amazonas.gov.co). The Departamento de Fomento Ecoturístico (D.A.F.E.) has good pamphlets about eco-tourism in Leticia and other parts of Colombia (Monday-Friday 8 a.m.-noon, 2-5 p.m. Calle 8, 9-75. Tel: 8-592-7569). Other important offices include:

Parque Nacional Natural—Buy your Amacayacu ticket here, or apply to volunteer at one of the region's national parks (students, professionals or those with national park experience) (Monday-Friday 8 a.m.-noon, 2-5 p.m. Carrera 9, 6-100, piso 2. Tel: 8-592-7124).

Instituto Geográfico Agustín Codazzi—(Monday-Friday 7:30-11:30 a.m., 2-4 p.m. Carrera 11, 9-14).

DAS (Colombian immigration)—The office in town only handles extensions (Monday-Friday 8 a.m.-noon, 2-5 p.m. Calle 9, 9-62). For entry or exit stamps, go to the office at the airport (Monday-Friday 7:30 a.m.-noon, 1-6 p.m.; Saturday, Sunday, holiday 7:30 a.m.-noon, 1-4 p.m.).

Brazilian consulate—(Monday-Friday 8 a.m.-noon, 2-4 p.m. Carrera 9, 13-84).

Peruvian consulate—(Monday-Friday 8 a.m.-12:30 p.m. Calle 11, 5-32).

Money

No one in Leticia handles travelers checks. The banks do not exchange cash, either, go to an exchange house (casa de cambio).

Banco de Bogotá—ATM: ATH, Visa, MasterCard, Cirrus, Plus (corner of Carrera 10 and Calle 7).

BBVA—Gives cash advances on Visa; ATM: MasterCard, Visa, Plus, Cirrus (Monday-Friday 8-11:30 a.m., 2-4:30 p.m. Corner of Carrera 10 and Calle 7).

Money exchange house can change U.S. dollars, Euros, Colombian pesos, Brazilian reais or Peruvian soles. Shop for the best rates, which are slightly better than in Bogotá.

Cambios Alliance 3—(Monday-Friday 8 a.m.-noon, 2-6 p.m., Saturday 8 a.m.-noon Carrera 11, 7-50).

Amazonas Cambios—(Monday-Friday 8 a.m.-noon, 2-6 p.m., Saturday 8 a.m.-noon Calle 8, 10-95). There are also a number of exchange (cambios, *truco*) stands along Calle 8 past Carrera 11, toward the riverfront and on the left-hand side. For money wiring, Western Union is in Supermercado León (Monday-Friday 8 a.m.-noon, 2-6 p.m., Saturday 8 a.m.-noon. Calle 8, 9-60).

Keeping in Touch

Telecom charges $0.05 per minute for local and $0.10 per minute for national calls. Its rates for international calls are probably the best in town: $0.25 per minute to the U.S. and $0.30 per minute to the U.K. (Monday-Friday 8 a.m.-noon, 2-5 p.m., Saturday 8:30-11:30 a.m. Carrera 11 and Calle 9).

On average, shops charge $0.10 per minute for local / national calls. To mail postcards, head to Correos de Colombia / Adpostal (Monday-Friday 8 a.m.-noon, 2-6 p.m., Saturday 8 a.m.-noon Calle 8, 9-65).

There are plenty of places to use the internet, especially on Carrera 10, between Calles 11 and 13, and on Calle 9. Surprisingly, many are open until late and almost all have Skype. An hour of internet use costs $0.50-0.80.

Medical

Hospital San Rafael de Leticia is the region's medical facility (Carrera 10, 13-78. Tel: 8-592-7075, E-mail: hsanrafael1@telecom.com.co). There are several pharmacies on Carrea 10, around Calle 8.

Laundry

Lavandería Aseo Total will do up your wash according to your specifications. Depending on the type of service, (wash, dry, fold and / or iron) the cost is $0.90-1.05 per pound. If you get your duds in early enough, they'll be ready by the afternoon. Open Monday-Saturday 6 a.m.-9 p.m., Sunday 8 a.m.-1 p.m. Carrera 10, 9-32. Tel: 8-592-6051.

Camera

Leticia has several photo shops. However, there are limited options, so pick up high-speed film prior to your arrival.

Leticolor Digital has digital and disposable cameras, digital cards, 400ASA UltraMax Kodak film, batteries, camera cases and develops film. Open Monday-Friday 8 a.m.-12:30 p.m., 2-7 p.m., Saturday 9 a.m.-12:30 p.m., 2-7 p.m., holidays 9 a.m.-12:30 p.m., closed Sunday. Calle 8, 9-42. Tel: 8-592-4778, Cell: 311-440-1614, E-mail: camiloandrescastillo@yahoo.es.com.

Foto Reina offers repairs of conventional cameras, as well as an assortment of digital camera cards, 100 and 400ASA color film and batteries. Open Monday-Saturday 7 a.m.-7 p.m., Sunday 7 a.m.-noon, 1-7 p.m. Carrera 10, 8-14. Tel: 8-592-3882. Updated: Jul 07, 2008.

Shopping

Tienda Naturalista Artesanal El Manantial

On this front porch, Doña Edilma displays the crafts of Colombian and Peruvian settlements along the Amazon and its tributaries. There are many things you can take home as a memento of your trip: bows and arrows, dolphins and other wildlife hand-carved in precious woods, necklaces, earrings and other jewelry made of jungle seeds and the large, hard scales of the piricurú fish, walking canes, and paintings. She also has a wide assortment of natural medicines that is said to cure anything from high fever to low sex drive. Carrera 11, 6-96. Updated: Jul 07, 2008.

Pasaje Orellana

You're heading into the wilds of the Amazon, so you're in need of supplies. Steer over to the Pasaje Orellana. The shops have a good selection of hammocks and mosquito nets (try Cacharrería Mohemed). For sloshing through the omnipresent mud, there are plenty of gum boots. If boating on these silted waters is your adventure, grab a game for whiling away your time. Pick up anything else you need here, too, including toothpaste and flashlights. For reading materials, cut across the park to Cerrajería Asertec, which has books in English, Spanish, Portuguese and other languages. Open Monday-Saturday 7 a.m.-8 p.m., Sunday 7 a.m.-noon. Carrera 11, 7-60. Backside of Parque Orellana, one block from the river. Updated: Jul 08, 2008.

Casa Brasil Uirapuru

Casa Brasil has a full assortment of crafts from the indigenous and mestizo settlements along the Amazon River and its tributaries. There's a very fine assortment of bark paintings and hardwood sculptures of local wildlife, like jaguars and pink dolphins. But there's much more that will catch your eye. In the back is Museo Uirapuru, a collection of indigenous crafts and artifacts (no photos allowed). Casa Brasil accepts only MasterCard and Visa and can ship purchases overseas. Calle 8, 10-35. Tel: 8-592-7056 / 4649. Updated: Jul 08, 2008.

Things to See and Do

Once you begin scratching the surface, you discover there are so many things to do and see while waiting for a boat out of Leticia. Of course, there are tours into the jungle and visits to Parque Nacional Natural Amaracayu and Isla de los Micos. On the Brazilian and Peruvian sides of the rivers, there are jungle lodges where you can hang for a few days. Go canoeing or drop a fishing line into the tributaries at Lagos Yahuarcacas, where you can see the world's largest water lily. In Leticia is the Museo Etnográfico del Hombre Amazónico (The Ethnographic Museum of the Amazon Man), and there are free weekly movies at the university. On the road to Tarapacá, other sites to see are the Serpentario Armero-Guayabal (snake and reptile house), Amazonas and the Tikuna and Huitoto "Kilometer" villages. Puerto Nariño and Lago Tarapoto, homes of the pink dolphin, are just a few hours away, too. Updated: Jul 07, 2008.

Museo Etnográfico del Hombre Amazónico

Who are the indigenous nations living in the Amazon region? What are their customs? How did the arrival of the white man affect the nations? These and other answers are available at the Museo Etnográfico del Hombre Amazónico in the Banco de la República's cultural center. This museum also houses many fine examples of implements and crafts made and used by the Yucuna, Huitoto and Tikuna peoples. The collection is the effort of Franciscan Capuchin Mission monks. The Banco de la República's cultural center also has a library that has story hour for children and other programs (Monday-Friday 8 a.m.-noon, 2-6 p.m., Saturday 8 a.m.-noon) and hosts free exhibits and special events. The view of the river from the back terrace is wonderful, especially at sunset. Banco de la República Area Cultural Carrera 11, between Calles 9 and 10. Updated: Jul 08, 2008.

Serpentario Armero-Guayabal

Slinking through the dense underbrush, coiling around the boughs of trees, slithering through the rivers' roots are creatures whose eyes are watching you explore the Amazon. Some are venomous, others harmless and still others would love to give you a big hug before swallowing you whole. All of these serpents play a role in keeping the jungle healthy. To get a close-up view of these snakes, Serpentario Armero-Guayabal can help you do so safely and teach you about conservation efforts on their behalf. From Parque Orellana, catch a buseta to the Kilometer villages and hop off at Kilometer 11 (5:45 a.m.-6:20 p.m. $1.05). Calle 8, 9-18 (Tanimboca); Carrera 10, 11-69. Tel: 8-592-6692 (Tanimboca); 8-592-7679 / 5973, Cell: 311-204-3532 (Leticia), URL: www.nativa.org. Updated: Jul 08, 2008.

Reserva Tanimboca

Dosel is the term used for the highest part of the tree canopy, usually about 35-40 meters (115-130 feet). Climb up to those heights at Reserva Tanimboca and explore an 80-meter (300-feet) trail from tree-to-tree, through a neighborhood inhabited by lizards, birds and monkeys ($32 per person). Other activities include ecological land walks and kayaking on the Río Tacana ($11). Night excursions through the jungle ($24-37, depending on number of participants, including transportation) or in search of caymans are other options. Reserva Tanimboca also has lodging available in a treehouse (one person $80, two people $105, 3 people $126). From Parque

Orellana, catch a buseta to the Kilometer villages and hop off at Kilometer 8 (5:45 a.m.-6:20 p.m. $0.80). Many tour agencies also offer outings to Reserva Tanimboca. Kilometer 8, Vía Tarapacá. Tel: 8-592-76779, Cell: 310 774 5919, E-mail: doseltanimboca@hotmail.com. Updated: Jul 07, 2008.

Isla de los Micos

Isla de los Micos (Island of the Monkeys) is a standard stop on tours of the Amazon. Thirty-five kilometers (21 miles) upstream from Leticia, this 450-hectare island is home to our distant primate cousins, capuchin monkeys—a not-so-elusive bunch of creatures. Take an interpretive hike through primary tropical forest, observe the flora and fauna, go fishing and kayaking on Lago Tucuchira, or birdwatching is particularly rewarding. Tours visit Huitoto and Tikuna settlements on this island, too. Contact any of the tour agencies in Leticia about a day tour that includes Isla de los Micos. The price of tours includes transportation. Updated: Jul 08, 2008.

Parque Nacional Natural Amacayacu

Parque Nacional Natural Amacayacu is one of the most easily (and safely) accessible jungle national parks. Its 293,500 hectares on the banks of the Amazon and Amacayacu Rivers is home to more than 150 species of mammals, including pink and grey dolphins, *danta*, jaguar, manatee, *nutria* and the tití leoncita, the smallest primate in the world. This place is also a reptilian haven that's full of crocodiles, anacondas and boas. Parque Nacional Natural Amacayacu has one of the most diverse populations of birds, which includes almost 500 species and makes this a must-stop for birdwatchers. Amacayacu is one of the most virgin tropical forests, with thousands of species of plants and trees. You can explore the park by canoe up its many waterways or on foot along marked trails. Undertake the six-day hike from one extreme of the park to the other accompanied by a specialist guide.

The concessions (hotels, restaurants, tours) have been privatized, Decameron now administers everything. Lodging has improved, but prices have risen steeply. This is the only lodging option within the park. For shared accommodation, prices are from $46-55, and for a *maloka* cabin prices range from $120-145 for a single and $70-85 for a double occupancy. Prices are per person and include breakfast and dinner, but not boat transportation.

Buy your ticket from the national park office in Leticia. Contact a tour agency in Leticia or the Decameron Explorer at Hotel Decameron Ticuna for plans to visit the park. Steer away from agencies and take a public launch (see Getting to and away from Leticia for details).

A cheaper alternative for accommodations at the park, is staying in a neighboring *Resguarda Indígena* (indigenous village), like Mocagua. To do this, ask to speak with the head of the village upon arrival to ask permission to stay. Lodging in these villages cost approximately $6 per person.

Students and professionals of biological sciences / ecology and individuals with national park experience can apply at the national park office in Leticia to be a volunteer. The park is 60 kilometers (36 miles) upstream from Leticia. Updated: Jul 08, 2008.

Leticia Tours

Leticia certainly has no lack of agencies eager to take you into the jungle. Also, as soon as you step foot in Leticia, whether stepping out of the airport or onto the dock, you'll be greeted by independent guides offering their services. It's hard to know who has a good track record, so check around with other travelers.

Jugalvis "Juancho" Valenca Pérez is one highly recommended independent guide who does specialized trips. For example, he does a five-day, four-night excursion that focuses purely on medicinal plants ($1,050 for two persons, all inclusive). Carrera 11, 7-34. Cell: 311-206-6341. Updated: Jul 07, 2008.

Decameron Explorer

Decameron Explorer offers all types of options for getting to know the Amazon region. Jungle jaunts include boat trips to Lago Tarapoto to observe pink dolphins, hikes on Isla de los Micos, night safaris to search for caymans and special birdwatching excursions. If you feel a bit more energetic, they also take you kayaking on local lakes or canopying at Reserva Tanimboca. Cultural activities include trips to indigenous villages and sessions with medicine men. Visit the agency to see their complete menu of services. But the most important item on their list is managing the concessions at Parque Nacional Natural Amacayacu, including the lodging. Carrera 11, 6-11. Tel: 8-592-4196, Cell: 313-294-1428, E-mail: amazonas.receptivosexplorer@decameron.com. Updated: Jul 08, 2008.

Leticia Lodging

Budget accommodation isn't quite budget in Leticia. Remember, hotels do have you over the proverbial barrel here. The usually reliable standby, camping, is not a viable option due to climate and fauna factors. Be prepared to spend at least $10 per night per person. Some budget travelers prefer to hop on a boat to Puerto Nariño to spend a few days there. Most places will not have hot water, but will provide you with at least a fan. Air conditioning is also available, for a price. The more expensive hotels have swimming pools. Shop around, especially during the low season, when cheaper deals can be struck. Updated: Jul 07, 2008.

Budget

Mochileros

(BED: $9) Mochileros is a European-style backpacker hostel that came to Leticia as a wonderful idea. It has once-splendid facilities, including common rooms with a book exchange and board games, a common kitchen, laundry area and rooftop terrace. The dorms have sturdy wooden bunks and lockers for securing backpacks. Unfortunately, it's a bit neglected these days. If you want to check it out, call ahead because the front desk isn't staffed all the time. The administrator will meet you and give you a key. Carrera 5, 9-117. Tel: 8-592-5491, Cell: 314-280-6558, E-mail: javierespiritu@yahoo.es / jamersonx@hotmail.com. Updated: Jul 07, 2008.

MAHATU

(BED: $9-20) The jungle hostel MAHATU is deep in the Amazon jungle. The hostel offers its guests a jungle garden with an Indian maloka hut, a guest kitchen, bicycles, computer access and reliable information about the Amazon. Take a taxi from downtown Leticia to get to the hostel or contact the hostel for complimentary pickup from the port or airport. Carrera 7, 9 - 69. Tel: 8-539-1265, E-mail: gustavo@amazonaslife.com, URL: www.mahatu.com. Updated: Apr 14, 2008.

Residencias del Centro

(BED: $11) Officially it is now called Residencias del Centro, but everyone still calls it Residencias Colombia. The orange and green sign hanging out front takes a neutral stance on the issue. It just simply says "Residencias." It is still, though, the most centrally located of the cheaper hotels in Leticia. So, take a hike up the faded orange staircase to the hotel that has large rooms with a built-in bed, window and fan. The common baths are basic yet clean. The friendly owners are knowledgeable about the region and can assist you in finding an independent guide. Carrera 10, 8-52. Tel: 8-592-4311. Updated: Jul 08, 2008.

Mid-Range

Hospedaje Los Delfines

(BED: $16-27) This is a fine place to stay if you can afford to spend a bit more. All the rooms are nicely furnished and include a private bathroom, fan, mini-bar and screened windows. Hammocks abound in the courtyard and there is a TV in the common room. Hospedaje Los Delfines has something that distinguishes it from any hotel—it has its own water treatment plant, which is checked regularly by health officials. Carrera 11, 12-85. Tel: 8-592-7488, Cell: 310-309-9194, Fax: 8-592-7388, E-mail: losdelfinesleticia@hotmail.com. Updated: Jul 08, 2008.

Residencias Amira

(BED: $19-32) This place used to be one of the more economical hotels in Leticia, however, it recently upgraded. Now, Residencias Amira offers only rooms with private bathrooms and a mini-bar. All rooms have two to four beds—a mix of singles and doubles. The common balcony is a great place to sit to enjoy the cooler evenings. But, honestly, this place seems a bit overpriced when compared to similar-quality hotels in town. Calle 9, 9-69. Tel: 8-592-7767, Cell: 310-585-4114, E-mail: diverleones@hotmail.com. Updated: Jul 08, 2008.

High-End

Hotel Anaconda

(ROOM: $66-140) Although not the most expensive hotel in Leticia, the extras Hotel Anaconda piles on makes it excellent value. The 50 rooms all come with balconies, some with a view of the Amazon River. These large suites have good beds, private bathrooms with both cold and hot water, A/C, TV and mini-bar. The pool—with a slide—is open not only to guests, but also to the paying public (adult $3.20, child $2.35). Hotel Anaconda has its own water and energy plants, to guarantee its guests never go without. All of this and much more continue to make this well-established hotel a Leticia favorite. Carrera 11, 7-34. Tel: 8-592-7119 / 7891 / 7274, Fax: 8-592-7005, E-mail: reserves@hotelanaconda.com.co / leticia@hotelanaconda.com.co, URL: www.hotelanaconda.com.co. Updated: Jul 08, 2008.

Decalodge Ticuna

(BED: $95-186) The Ticuna had always been one of Leticia's premier hotels. Since Decameron has taken it over, it has blossomed into a spectacular lodge. It is like another world—the front room has a hammock and cane chairs and beyond is the bedroom decorated with regional artesanía and contemporary paintings. Before entering the hot water bathroom, there is a powder room with shelves stacked with snowy-white towels. The grounds include a pool with a fountain and lookout tower where you can watch the sun set over the Amazon. Prices depend on season and day of the week, and include breakfast, lunch and tax. Rates do not include use of in-room safe deposit boxes ($2.10 extra). Carrera 11, 6-11. Tel: 8-592-6600 / 4237 / 6949 / (toll free) 8000-51-0765, E-mail: contactus@decameron.com, URL: www.decameron.com. Updated: Jul 08, 2008.

Leticia Restaurants

Like accommodations, food in the heart of the jungle costs more, though you'll still be able to find a daily plate special, called a menu, for under $2. At the municipal market there is not only fresh produce and meats, but also inexpensive eateries, some with a river view. Be careful about drinks when dining at the market (daily 6 a.m.-4 p.m. Calle 8, half-block from the river). All along Calle 8 are general stores and supermarkets. And, it seems like the scent of fresh-baked goods wafts from the bakeries on every corner, which are great places to grab a cheap breakfast or snack. Then, at night check out the tent city of grill stands that sets up on the corner of Avenida Internacional and Calle 7. Stock up on purified water—Gaseosas Leticia has a 24-hour / seven-day dispenser. If you bring your own clean container, five liters costs $0.30 and 20 liters $0.60. It also sells full *garrafones* (jugs), five liters cost $1.60 and 20 liters for $9.75 (Calle 8, between Carreras 8 and 9).

While in Leticia, try some of the local delicacies, like *mojojoy* (a worm) or *pirarucú* and *gamitana* fishes. Another regional fish commonly found on your plate is *acarahuasú*, otherwise known to aquarium enthusiasts as the oscar (*cichlidae astronauts ocellatus*).

Mimo's

Cool down on a sultry day at Mimo's, the place to go for any kind of ice cream treat, including simple soft-freeze cones ($1.05-2.10) and gourmet sundaes ($2.25-4.45). There are even special creations for the kids, like the snowman and the Medusa with gummy-worm hair. No sweat for those on a diet, Mimo's has a full line of dietetic ice creams and sauces. Take home a liter of one of the 15 hand-dipped flavors. Open daily 10 a.m.-9:30 p.m. Carrera 11, 7-26, across from Parque Orellana. Tel: 8-592-5129. Updated: Jul 08, 2008.

Restaurante Sancho Panza

(LUNCH: $1.60-2.10) Restaurante Sancho Panza on Leticia's main drag is a favorite among budget eaters. The front veranda has a few tables, but daily plate specials are the only thing on the menu, which include the usual soup, meat-beans-rice-plátano tray and drink. Enough food to make sure even Sancho Panza (Don Quixote's squire) doesn't go away hungry. If you have an early boat to catch, breakfast is also served. All meals cost $1.60-2.10. Open daily 6 a.m.-9 p.m. Carrera 10, 8-72. Updated: Jul 08, 2008.

Restaurante Tropical

(LUNCH: $2.65) The décor of Restaurante Tropical is just as delightful as the food it serves and the jungle kitsch abounds among the plants and aquariums. The jaguar with the safari helmet is a kick. The tables out on the front porch are a delightfully cool place to enjoy breakfast ($2.65-3.20), blue plate special ($2.65) or a sandwich or burger with fried potatoes ($1.60-2.65). Besides the usual fruit drinks and beer, Restaurante

Tropical also mixes up caipirinhas ($1.60). Carrera 10, 8-80. Tel: 8-592-7934. Updated: Jul 07, 2008.

Restaurante El Sabor

(LUNCH: $3.20-6.35) Restaurante El Sabor is one of the old standbys for visitors and for locals, too. It offers no lunch special—just foods straight off the BBQ. Pull up a table on the front palm-thatch patio or in the large inside room and order up a serving of pork, beef or chicken ($3.20-4.45) or fish ($6.35). All meals come with soup, salad bar and a pitcher of Amazon fruit drink made with purified water. A vegetarian plate can also be requested (beans, rice, vegetables, salad and egg; $2.65). Open Tuesday-Sunday, 6 a.m.-10 p.m. Calle 8, 9-16. Updated: Jul 07, 2008.

Cozinha Fazenda

(ENTREES: $2.65-10.50) A truly international restaurant at the triple border and one of the few vegetarian options in Leticia. It has a Portuguese name in Spanish-speaking Leticia and a menu that offers French toast and pancakes for breakfast ($1.60 for one, $3.20 for a stack of three). Other times of the day, there are pizzas with your choice of toppings (small $5.30, medium $8, large $10.50). Sandwiches are another major feature, with meats, four cheeses or the Romeo y Julieta (cheese and guava paste) ($2.65-3.20). The only mixed drinks are caipirinha and *caipiroska*. Open daily 6 a.m.-11 p.m. Carrera 9, 7-48. Updated: Jul 07, 2008.

Tierras Amazónicas

(ENTREES: $4.20-9) The menu at Tragadero y Beberdero Tierras Amazónicas is a plank of wood, befitting this old jungle space. Its full bar offers such regional drinks as caipirinha cocktails ($2.65) and *chuchuwasa* (an aphrodisiac drink made from a bark). Turn over the plank to see that the establishment is much more than a mere drinking hole. It is a restaurant that offers a full Colombian-Brazilian-Peruvian menu with 16 ways to prepare your fish fresh out of the Amazon, whether pirarucú or piranha ($4.20-9). Open Tuesday-Sunday noon-3 p.m., 6:30-11 p.m. (food until 10:30 p.m.). Calle 8, 7-50. Updated: Jul 08, 2008.

Leticia Nightlife

Leticia has a pretty active nightlife scene. Although, if you are around on a Tuesday night, most in-town establishments are closed. The most grooving nights are Wednesday to Saturday. There are all types of places, from the sit-down bars to cumbia-samba-vallenato-reggaetón discos. Along Avenida Internacional, heading to the border, are establishments that are open all week and until dawn. However, be advised that these double as strip joints and brothels. Updated: Jul 07, 2008.

Club de Billar y Cafetería Barbacoas

Folks are at Club de Billar y Cafetería Barbacoas before the parrots begin their morning song and way after they return to the roosts. People talk over coffee or a drink on the sidewalk café or shoot a game of pool inside. If you're looking for a wake-up brew, or a night cap, this is the place to stop. Women who sit alone, be warned that service will be a longer wait for you. Open Monday-Saturday 5 a.m.-2 a.m., closed Sunday. Cafeteria service only until 10 p.m. Carrera 10, 8-28. Updated: Jul 08, 2008.

Mosshe's Bar

This corner bar is where people meet to have a drink at the end of a long, hot day. Outside there is a sidewalk café and inside a red sofa wraps around the sinuous walls. There are chic black and chrome fixings throughout and the ambience is drenched by a mix of rap, blues, tropical and contemporary Brazilian music. Most liquors come by shot ($1.85-$4.20), half-bottle or full-bottle ($21-105). Mosshe's even has Bailey's Irish Cream on hand, as well as cocktails like martinis, screwdrivers, Manhattans, caipirinhas and piña colada ($4.20-6.35). Open Sunday-Thursday 5 p.m.-2 a.m., Friday and Saturday 5 p.m.-4 a.m., closed Tuesday. Carrera 10, 10-12, across from Parque Santander. Tel: 8-592-7422. Updated: Jul 08, 2008.

Villavicencio

Alt: 465m Pop: 384,000 City Code: 8

Villavicencio is the gateway to where the sun paints a mango-colored sky over the flat lands of the eastern plains of Colombia at the end of the day. Just on the other side of the Cordillera Oriental, two hours from Bogotá, is where the birds and wildlife paint a silhouette against the sky as dusk falls.

The new highway from the nation's capital to Villavicencio is quite an exhilarating experience. The 86-kilometer (52-mile) superhighway climbs out of Bogotá to an altitude of over 3,100 meters (10,168 feet). It then plunges down over 50 bridges and through five tunnels to Villavicencio at 467 meters (1532 feet), a descent of almost 2,600 meters (8530 feet). Túnel de Boquerón, the second tunnel, is 2.4 kilometers (1.5 miles) long and the last one, Túnel de Buenavista, is over 4.5 kilometers (2.7 miles).

Once arriving in Villavicencio, you have entered what *villavos* call the *Territorio de Paz* (Territory of Peace). This town along the banks of the Río Guatiquía is the most important cultural and commercial center of the Colombian Llanos. Villavicencio is a town of simple pleasures and a complex history. Many of the men wear traditional llanero clothing (a poncho folded over one shoulder), a hat and boots. You have come to Colombia's version of the Wild West, right down to the rodeos. Updated: Jul 08, 2008.

History

Villavicencio was on one of the principal routes for Spaniards on the El Dorado quest. The city was founded on April 6, 1840 by Antonio Villavicencio y Verastegui. The original settlement was the farmland of Guamalote, which was on a principal cattle train route from the plains to Bogotá. It was part of the Estado de Cundinamarca until 1868, when the Territorio de San Martín de los Llanos was established and Villavicencio was the capital. In 1909 the name of the territory was changed to Meta, and in 1959 its status was upgraded to a department. In the latter part of the 20th Century and into the new millennium, the town suffered occupations by civil war factions, including paramilitaries. Updated: Jul 04, 2008.

When to Go

You will probably encounter a shower or two anytime in Villavicencio. The town has a huge 220 days of rain per year. The temperatures rise as high as 35°C (95°F) and evenings can be as cool as 19°C (66°F). Relative humidity is on average a muggy 78 percent.

Villavicencio is not on the vacation-destination list of most Colombians. Nonetheless, you will still find that some of the country hotels charge more during holiday times. Updated: Jul 04, 2008.

Holidays and Festivals

Toward the end of March is the annual Concurso Mundial de la Mujer Vaquera, or International Women's Rodeo (www.mujervaquera.com). Participants come from Colombia, Chile, Brazil, Mexico, Guatemala, Panamá, Costa Rica, U.S. and other countries. A second rodeo event, Encuentro Mundial de Coleo (www.mundialcoleo.com.co), is held October 14 to 17. The famed Jaropo music festival happens twice a year, from June through July and in December.

Out of all the religious observances, check out Villavicencio's Easter Week, observed from Palm Sunday to Easter Sunday with processions and a sacred music concert series, or the Novenas de Aguinaldos from December 16 to 24. The feast days of the patron saint, Nuestra Señora del Carmen, are held in July. Updated: Jul 04, 2008.

Getting To and Away From Villavicencio

Anything from rains to earthquakes can cause landslides on the road from Bogotá to Villavicencio. To know the present conditions, visit www.coviandes.com. For additional information, the highway has 103 SOS call boxes and three tollbooths.

Bus

The bus terminal is approximately seven kilometers (four miles) from downtown, on the Anillo Vial, midway between Calle 35 and Carrera 22. It is easily accessible by buseta. It has the usual services, like snack stands and rest rooms, as well as a tourist information booth in the front.

Collective pickups and jeeps for Restrepo and other points leave from Calle 37E and Carrera 28.

Additionally there is a bus service to Yopal, Arauca, Tame, Puerto Carreño and San José de Guaviare.

From Villavicencio

Arrive	Departure	Time	Price
Bogotá	Every 15-20 mins	2-3 hours	\$11
Puerto López	Hourly, 7 a.m.-7 p.m.	1.5 hours	\$5
Puerto Gaitán	Hourly, 7 a.m.-7 p.m.	3.5 hours	\$13
Granada	Every 20 mins	1.5 hours	\$5

Air

Aeropuerto Vanguardia is approximately four kilometers (2.4 miles) from the city, off the road to Restrepo (a right turn at the Monumental de las Harpas). Villavicencio Aires (Calle 41, 32-34. Tel: 8-662-9411) has daily flights to Bogotá and Satena (Carrera 31, 39-27, Piso 2. Tel: 8-662-1260) flies to Bogotá, Puerto Inírida and Puerto Carreño. Updated: Jul 04, 2008.

Getting Around

The Instituto de Turismo del Meta has a list of the official prices for taxis. A sample of fares is: normal run (including bus terminal-downtown), \$1.85; downtown-airport, \$3.85; bus terminal-airport, \$4.90; and, downtown-Parque de las Malocas, \$2.40. City busetas also go to points throughout town and many pass near Parque del Hacha or one block down on Carrera 29 (\$0.65)Updated: Jul 04, 2008.

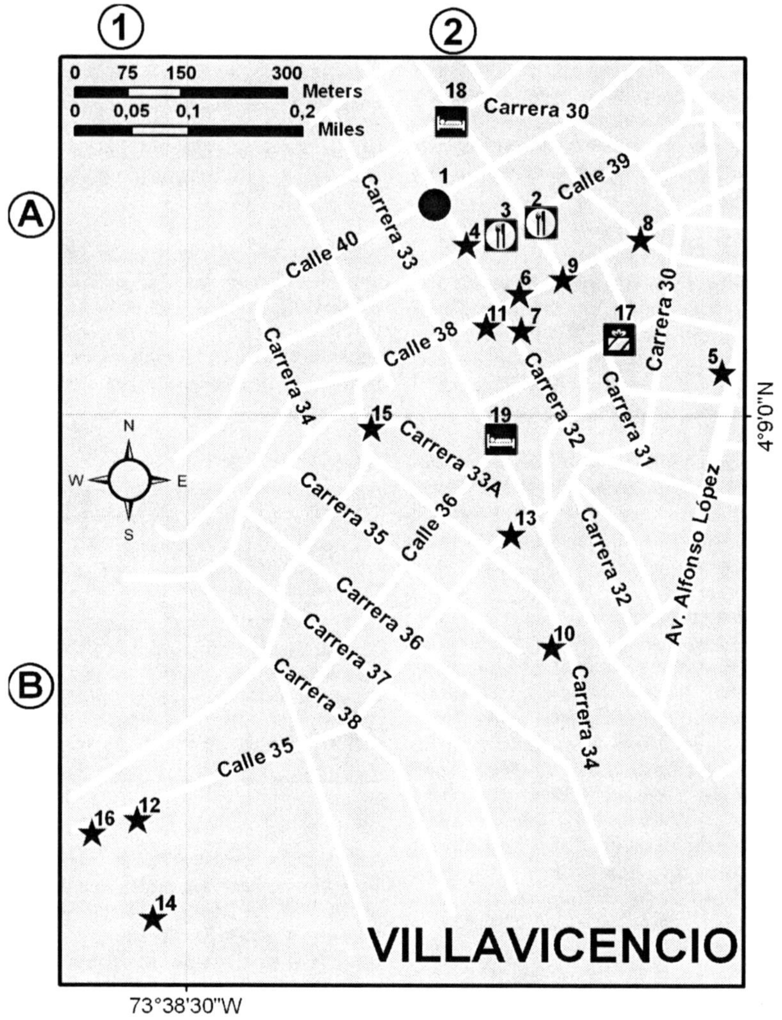

Activity ●

1 Casa de la Cultura Jorge Elíecer Gaitán A2

Eating

2 El Saman del Parque A2
3 Restaurante Govindas A2

Service ★

4 Adpostal A2
5 Almacén de Discos El Joropo A2
6 Banco Colombia A2
7 Banco de la República A2
8 Banco Popular A2
9 BBNA A2
10 Chinchorros Saidez B2
11 Cosmonet A2
12 DAS B1
13 El Gran Llanerazo B2
14 Hospital San Antonio B1
15 Instituto Geográfico Agustin Codazzi B2
16 Telecom B1

Shopping

17 Centro Comercial Centauro A2

Sleeping

18 Hotel Savoy A2
19 Hotel Tabary B2

Safety in Villavicencio

For travelers with their own car or on bike, be aware that the highway from Bogotá has a very steep, downhill grade.

Villavicencio is relatively safe during daylight hours. Parque de los Fundadores is OK on weekends, but consider it off limits during times when no one is around and after dark. Updated: Jul 04, 2008.

Villavicencio Services

Tourism Office

Instituto de Turismo del Meta has excellent information on the attractions in Meta Department (Monday-Friday 8 a.m.-noon, 2-6 p.m., Saturday 8 a.m.-noon. Carrera 32, 38-70, Edificio Romarco. Tel: 8-671-6666, URL: www.turismometa.gov.co). Better maps of the city and region, however, are obtained at the **Punto de Información Turística** in Parque El Hacha (Monday-Friday 7:30 a.m.-6 p.m., Saturday and Sunday 8 a.m.-6 p.m. Carrera 32, between Calles 35 and 36).

Other offices of importance include:

DAS (Colombian immigration)—Calle 37, 42-34. Tel: 8-672-5188.

Instituto Geográfico Agustín Codazzi—Carrera 33A, 37-14, oficina 401. Tel: 8-662-6967.

Money

Many of Villavicencio's banks are on Calle 38, including:

BBVA—ATM: MasterCard, Visa, Plus (Calle 38, 31-74).

Bancolombia—changes American Express travelers checks; ATM: MasterCard, Visa, Plus, American Express (Monday-Friday 8 a.m.-4:30 p.m. Calle 38, 32-27).

Banco Popular—ATM: MasterCard, Visa, Plus, Cirrus (Calle 38, near Carrera 30A).

The city has a lot of money exchanges, which are mostly located in the Centro Comercial Centauros (Carrera 31, 37-32), i.e. EuroDivisas. Open daily 8 a.m.-1 p.m., 2-7 p.m. Local 79, second level, Tel: 8-662-8361. This mall is also where you will find Western Union / Giros y Finanzas (Monday-Friday 8 a.m.-noon, 2-5 p.m., Saturday 8:30 a.m.-1 p.m. Locals 64-65).

Keeping in Touch

The local Telecom office has been closed for renovation (Calle 37, 42-12); luckily, Villavicencio doesn't lack for other purveyors of local and national call services. Adpostal is still providing services to mail letters (Monday-Friday 8 a.m.-noon, 2-6 p.m., Saturday 8 a.m.-noon. Calle 39, 32-02). Internet is somewhat common, and most places are on Calle 38, past the main plaza, and charge $0.80 per hour. Cosmonet has international calls starting at $0.30 per minute, as well as broad band internet (Calle 38, 33-62). Be advised that Skype is scarce.

Medical

The principal healthcare provider in Villavicencio is the Hospital Regional de Villavicencio (Calle 37A, 28-53, Tel: 8-670-5032, E-mail: hospital@hospitalvillavicencio.gov.co). Others serving the needs of villavos are the Hospital San Antonio (Carrera 42 and Calle 33) and Hospital San Luis (Calle 35 and Carrera 44D). Pharmacies are especially concentrated on Calle 38, between Carreras 30 and 32.

Camera

You'll find several photo shops on Calle 38, between Carreras 33A and 30. Many are open on Sunday. Updated: Jul 04, 2008.

Shopping

El Gran Llanerazo

El Gran Llanerazo has a tremendous selection of crafts from the Meta and Casanare Departments. The most predominant items are *cotizas* (sandals) made of cow or pig leather or embroidered jute. For a different fashion statement, try on the ones made of *babilla*, or spectacled cayman. (Farm-raised, of course, since it is illegal to hunt them in the wild). There are also a wide assortment of leather belts, hats, key chains, sculptures and products made from wood and horn. Carrera 34, 35-60. Tel: 8-667-4038. Updated: Jul 04, 2008.

Almacén de Discos El Joropo

The Llanos of Colombia and Venezuela are renowned for their music and dance—see the box on "Joropo." Almacén de Discos El Joropo has everything you need to enjoy or perform this musical genre, like recordings, sheet music, instruments and accessories. Even award winners of the annual Festival de Joropo shop here. The store can put you directly in touch with workshops that make traditional joropo musical instruments, including harps and guitars. Carrera 29, 36-30/36. Tel: 8-671-5134 / 311-475-9413. Updated: Jul 04, 2008.

Chinchorros Saidez

The *chinchorro* is the most comfortable piece of furniture made for a home in the Llanos. These broad hammocks are woven as a close-mesh net. Cool on a sultry day and large enough to cocoon yourself in on a chilly night, it is the most perfect hammock one could ever imagine. Cinchorros Saidez has a fine selection with a simple single costing $53 and a more elaborately worked one for $125. Doubles (for two people) begin at $140. If you would like to snuggle down with the entire family, family-sized chinchorros are also available. Special orders take one week. ASMEVILL (Asociación de Microempresarios de Villavicencio) market, Calle 33B, 34-10. Tel: 8-672-7905, Cell: 312-314-7326 / 314-392-4807. Updated: Jul 04, 2008.

Things to See and Do

Villavicencio does have a few things to occupy your time, like the international festivals held from time to time at the Casa de la Cultura Jorge Eliécer Gaitán. Or, check out the Museo Eduardo Carraza (Carrera 32 and Calle 40. Tel: 8-671-4947 / 662-6327, Cell: 310-286-5945). The Banco de la República features concerts and exhibits (Carrera 32, 37-67). There are also many parks that scatter the city like emeralds, as well as statues saluting the Llano culture and way of life. One especially spectacular one is Monumento a las Arpas, which has three gigantic harps (10 meters high by seven meters wide), each with 32 strings of water. Look for this statue two kilometers along the Ruta del Piedemonte, at the turnoff for the airport.

Several tourist routes extend out of Villavicencio. Along these routes are quaint villages, hot springs and other glimpses of the Llanos. You can go horseback riding, hiking, birdwatching, whitewater rafting and take wildlife tours. Updated: Jul 04, 2008.

Parque de los Fundadores

Local families hang out on Saturday and Sunday afternoons at the Parque Los Fundadores, on the south side of Villavicencio. The masterpiece of the park is the Monumento a los Fundadores, which is the last work executed by renowned Colombian sculptor Rodrigo Arenas Betancourt. In the center of the park is a fountain that has lights playing off its cascades. Between are several small plazas where you can catch street theater or comedy, enjoy a fresh juice, have your photo taken on a horse or buy artisanal work. If the excitement wears you out, stretch out on the expanses of grass. The park is not considered safe after dark, it is best to go when villavos go—over the weekend. To get to Parque Los Fundadores, catch a bus that says "Porfía" from the corner of Parque del Hacha of Carrera 32 and Calle 35A, near the *bomberos* station, then to Vía Puerto López, past Unicentro Llano and Carrera 4.

Parque Lineal is another green space, which is on the way to Parque de los Fundadores. It is half way along the road leading out of town to Puerto López, which begins past the Unicentro shopping mall. Updated: Jul 04, 2008.

Bioparque Los Ocarros

Bioparque Los Ocarros teaches about the creatures of the Orinoco River Basin and follows the zoo trend to create natural spaces for the animals. Spread throughout 5.7 hectares, there are 181 species that include land and waterfowl and the majestic jaguar, inquisitive monkeys and the fearsome cayman and its laid-back cousin the babilla. Discover the fish of these rivers on the Aquarium Island and the many snakes on the Serpetarium Isle. All the animals on exhibit have been rescued from traffickers or are donations from people who had them as pets. Signs give excellent explanations about the ecological importance, status and habitat of each animal (in Spanish), but provide the taxonomic and common English names for the species.

Bioparque Los Ocarros also is a research center and clinic. The park is wheelchair accessible. Remember that the animals take a siesta come early afternoon, during the hottest part of the day. If you want to see the animals up and about, come visit in the morning or late afternoon. From Calle 37E and Carrera 28, catch a collective jeep heading toward

Festival Nacional de Joropo

The quintessential expression of life on the Llanos is the Joropo, both a musical genre and a dance form. The music is played on a harp, *bandola* (similar to the mandolin) and *cuatro* (a small, four-string guitar), with a continuous beat kept up by maracas. The songs' couplets bespeak love, life, loss and adventures. During the dance, women's full skirts swirl as men stamp to the rhythm. The music is a mix of the people who populate the Llanos: indigenous, European and African. Every year contestants arrive from all over Colombia and Venezuela for the Festival Nacional de Joropo, which started in 1960. For a week that spans the end of June and the beginning of July, Villavicencio's streets fill up with competitions in musical performance, dance and poetry. There are also beauty pageants and horse shows, arts and crafts exhibits and a gastronomic fair. Updated: Jul 04, 2008.

Restrepo and tell the driver to drop you off at Bioparque Los Ocarros ($1.30). The road marked by a sign that goes to the entrance of the park is on the other side of the highway. It is three kilometers (1.8 miles) north of Villavicencio, Ruta del Piedemonte Llanero. Tel: 8-670-9094, Fax: 8-664-8490, URL: www.bioparquelosocarros.com, www.corpometa.com. Updated: Jul 04, 2008.

Ruta Piedemonte Llanero

Ruta Piedemonte Llanero follows the eastern edge of the Cordillera Oriental. On one side, the mountains scrape the sky and on the other the endlessly flat land merges with the heavens. The route passes through Bioparque Los Ocarros and Centro-Cultural Etno-turístico El Maguare of the Uitoto indigenous. Restrepo (Km 16) has an interesting church, and nearby are the salt flats Salinas de Upín (3 kilometers / 1.8 miles away) and natural pools in the Río Caney. Cumaral (Km 23) has the best rodeo ring in the department, and other close attractions include Río Guacavia and Lagos de Samacanda. Some 70 kilometers (42 miles) further are two hot springs spas: Termales Aguas Calientes and Termales de Guaicaramo.

If traveling in your own vehicle, follow Highway 65 northeast out of Villavicencio. Just outside of the city are two tollbooths, and then a third beyond Cumaral. For public transportation, hop on a collective pickup from Calle 37E and Carrera 28 in Villavicencio. Updated: Jul 04, 2008.

Ruta del Amanecer Llanero

Sunsets and sunrises blaze over these eastern plains. The Ruta del Amanacer goes deep into the flatlands, teeming with cattle farms and wildlife, like capybaras and caymans, as well as multitudes of birds. Upon leaving Villavicencio, you will pass the Monument to the Fallen Combatant before passing the military base and oil installations at Apiay. Merecure, Latin America's largest agro-ecological park, is at Kilometer 47, and has lodging, camping, fishing and a zoo. The highway continues to Puerto López, near the geographical center of the nation. All along the way are agro- or eco-tourist country hotels, and more hotels in Puerto López.

If in your own vehicle, follow Highway 40 east out of Villavicencio (one tollbooth). Using public transport, there are buses for Puerto López and other points that leave from the bus terminal. Some agencies in Villavicencio offer tours along this route. Updated: Jul 04, 2008.

Ruta del Embrujo Llanero

The Route of Llanero Enchantment (*Embrujo*) begins its southward journey on Highway 65 from Villavicencio. The first town of note, Acacias (Km 22) is the tourism capital of the Meta Department and has a *malecón* (riverwalk). In mid-October Acacias celebrates a llanero music festival. Guamal (Km 41) is a vacation spot on the shores of Río Humadea. The road cuts through plains, marshes and African palm plantations, over which herons swoop. At Kilometer 67 is San Martín, the region's oldest city and heart of the cattle-raising and rodeo district. Mid-November is the International Llano Folklore and Equestrian Ballet Festival in San Martín. The journey is declared safe as far as Granada on the Río Ariari. Further on are Fuente De Oro, San Juan De Arama (where there is a waterfall and the Termales de Santo Domingo hot springs), Lejanias, Mestas, Vista Hermosa, La Uribe and La Macarena.

If traveling in your own vehicle, follow Highway 65 south out of Villavicencio. Before Acacias there is a tollbooth and there is another between San Martín and Granada. Collective pickups and jeeps heading for towns along the route depart from Calle 37E and Carrera 28. Updated: Jul 04, 2008.

Parque Nacional Natural Sierra de la Macarena

Those few travelers who ever make it to Parque Nacional Natural Sierra de la Macarena describe crystal-imbedded rock outcroppings from the Cenozoic Era that glitter in the Llano sun. The mountain range is 150 kilometers (90 miles) long and 35 kilometers (21 miles) wide and gives birth to the Duda, Guayabero, Losada and Güéjar rivers. The only part of the park presently accessible is Caño Cristales, a series of pools and waterfalls. From April to June, its rocks are matted with green algae, then from June to November, those carpets turn a brilliant purple.

Overland travel to La Macarena village and the park is not recommended at this time. Some travel agents in Villavicencio arrange fly-in tours complete with lodging to the one corner of the national park where it is said to be safe.

The Sierra de la Macarena is in the red zone of Colombia's civil war fighting, and the area is largely controlled by the FARC. Trekking and climbing is not recommended at this time due to probability of land mines. Go only with an organized tour, which should guarantee some degree of security. Also check with the national park office in Bogotá about current conditions.

The delicate algae that grows at Caños Cristales is a protected species, so be careful not to disturb it. Do not take any rocks or plants home as a souvenir. Stay on the paths and follow your guide's instructions. Carry out your trash. Updated: Jul 04, 2008.

Villavicencio Tours

At present, there are only a few tourist agencies that operate in Villavicencio and offer to take national and international visitors to magical places in the Llanos. As safety improves, don't be surprised to see even more operators jumping into the field, since the attractions—especially whitewater rafting and rock climbing—will undoubtedly make it one of the hottest places to visit in Colombia. Already you can enjoy some of them, like excursions out into the plains to see its unique wildlife and magnificent sunsets. Updated: Jul 04, 2008.

Vergel Aventura Servicios Turísticos del Llano

Imagine rafting on the white waters of a Llanos river as it flows from the Cordillera Oriental to these plains. Vergel Aventura takes you on just such an adventure, shooting the Class III rapids of Río Ariari in Parque Nacional Natural Sumapaz. The trip also involves crossing the river on a *tarabita* (cable car), a hike through the jungle and swimming in the crystalline pools of two waterfalls ($80 per person, including lunch, snacks, guides and transport; $50 per person without transport). Vergel Aventura also rafts the Río Guatiquía. Combine a rafting excursion with canopy, rappelling, paragliding or horseback riding. This company has a three-day/two-night package to Caño Cristales in Parque Nacional Natural La Macarena (two to eight people, all inclusive with flight, $470 per person). Hotel del Llano, Carrera 30, 49-77. Tel: 8-682-5353, Cell: 300-264-3760 / 311-281-9328. E-mail: reservas@vergelaventura.com, URL: www.vergelaventure.com. Updated: Jul 04, 2008.

Llanos Travel

Llanos Travel has a full plate of tours to offer its clients. Hop onto the one-day tours along the tourist Rutas Embrujada (as far as Granada), Llanera (as far as Puerto López) or Piedemonte (to Restrepo). The tours costs $55-90, including guide, transportation and lunch. Llanos Travel can take you to the prime attractions in town, like Parque Las Malocas or Bioparque Los Ocarros. If you can scare up 25 people, hire their bus complete with a band to take you around the city. Hotel del Llano, Carrera 30, 49-77. Tel: 8-671-3278 / 3245 / 664-1120, Cell: 325-327-7824, E-mail: llanostravel@gmail.com. Updated: Jul 04, 2008.

Villavicencio Lodging

The lodging scene in Villavicencio is a bit unusual in comparison to other Colombian cities. It has scores of luxury hotels, but comes up a bit short on mid-range choices. Those hostels that are in the budget category also double as pay-by-the-hour joints. Outside the city, there are many country-club style hotels, with bungalows, restaurants and swimming pools. Many of these hotels also have horse stables. Updated: Jul 04, 2008.

Hotel Savoy

(ROOM: $22-45) The Hotel Savoy is a popular place with business travelers looking for a finer hotel at a comfortable price. The large lobby is beyond the reception area, which creates a sense of exclusivity. The clean and modestly decorated guest rooms are medium in size with cable TV and private bathroom. Hotel Savoy's restaurant serves a vegetarian set lunch ($4) (Monday-Saturday noon-2 p.m.), though come early as it often sells out. Calle 41, 31-02. Tel: 8-662-2666 / 2667 / 5007. Updated: Jul 04, 2008.

Hotel del Llano

(ROOM: $100-120) For years, this place has been considered one of the finest and most respected luxury hotels in Villavicencio. Its rooms are ample with comfortable beds, private bathrooms, cable TV and many other pleasurable touches. The back patio not only has an Olympic-size swimming pool, but also a splash area for children. Hotel del Llano plays frequent host to the city's festival contestants and visiting dignitaries. Prices include American breakfast, taxes and insurance. Carrera 30, 49-77. Tel: 8-671-7000 / 3278 / 3245, E-mail: hotellan@etell.net.co. Updated: Jul 04, 2008.

Villavicencio Restaurants

Prices tend to be a bit higher in Villavicencio than in other parts of Colombia. Daily plate specials run from $1.85 to $4.20. The city market is along Calle 37A, between the Ley supermarket and Carrera 26 and sprawls into the sidestreets. The Ley supermarket is set in the area (Monday-Saturday 9 a.m.-8 p.m., Sunday 9 a.m.-6 p.m. Calle 37B, 29-83).

While in Villavicencio, be sure to try the most typical of llanero foods—*carne a la vara*, or seasoned meat roasted on an upright spit. Some restaurants are permitted to serve farm-raised capybaras. One recommended place is Asadero y Restaurante El Cabrestero. Anillo Vial, across the 7a Brigada military base.

El Saman del Parque

For any meal of the day, drop by El Saman del Parque, just a few doors down from Villavicencio's cathedral. This small café is often full with locals dropping by for a coffee prepared with *panela*. A popular quick snack is the *arepa de choclo con queso* (ground sweet corn and cheese) that is prepared in the beehive oven at the door and served on a banana leaf. Breakfasts are served with eggs as you wish, bread, juice and coffee. For lunch, there's a plate special and snack foods, beer and *tragos* (drinks) in the evenings. Monday through Saturday live music entertains the house. Open daily 7 a.m.-10 p.m., Fridays and Saturdays until 11 p.m. Calle 39, 32-76. Cell: 312-522-1746. Updated: Jul 04, 2008.

Asadero Hato Grande

(ENTREES: $5.80) Meat-and-potato lovers can get their fill of their favorite dish, Colombian style, at Asadero Hato Grande. This place serves authentic beef from the plains, cooked on an upright spit over a wood fire. The plate teems with meat, potatoes and yucca. For those travelers on a budget, order the plate special, which comes with the roasted meat, beans, rice, pasta and salad. The restaurant also cooks up *sancocho de gallina* and has *tamales* on the weekends. To get there from downtown, Catch the "Ceiba" buseta in front of the fire station near Parque El Hacha. Open daily 6 a.m.-10 p.m. Calle 35, 17-07. Tel: 8-666-5317. Updated: Jul 04, 2008.

Restaurante Govindas

In a worn dining room, the young man pulls himself away from the video about natural healing to take your order. Like Govindas restaurants all over Colombia, this dining hall offers only vegetarian fare. This one, though, is bare of any plants or other decorations. Only a few posters of Krishna bless the patrons. The set-plate lunch, too, is presented simply. The shop sells whole grain baked goods. Govindas also offers yoga and meditation classes and therapeutic massages. Lunch is Monday to Friday noon to 2 p.m. If you'd like something from the bakery, just ring the bell. Carrera 32, 39-42. Tel: 8-662-2557, Cell: 311-888-3370. Updated: Jul 04, 2008.

Villavicencio Nightlife

Nightlife is hot only on weekends and holidays, and clubs usually open at 6:30 p.m., though the scene doesn't get going until after 9 p.m. To catch some live llanero music, some recommended clubs are El Botlón on the highway toward Puerto López and El Pentagrama del Llanero in the Unicentro mall on Avenida Puerto López. Restaurants on the outskirts of town often have live bands on the weekends. Updated: Jul 04, 2008.

Puerto López

Alt: 178m	Pop: 17,000	City Code: 8

From Villavicencio, traverse the Ruta del Amanecer Llanero due east 78 kilometers (47 miles) and you arrive at Puerto López. This is Meta Department's principal port on the broad Río Meta. From Alto de Menegua, you can see the plains spreading to all horizons, intertwining with the river. Near the city are Laguna Mozambique and El Ombligo de Colombia (the Bellybutton of Colombia)—the geographical center of the country. One of the most important celebrations here is the Festival de las Colonia, December 26-30. Various hotels of different classes, including country hotels, as well as camping are available. Updated: Jul 04, 2008.

Getting To and Away From Puerto López

Buses leave from Villavicencio to Macarena, Arimena and Autollanos on the hour from 7 a.m. to 7 p.m.
Bolivariano—11:30 a.m., 2:30 p.m. All companies charge $5.30 and take 1.5 hours.
Puerto López is a principal port on the Río Meta, which flows into the Río Orinoco. With patience, it is possible to catch a boat downstream. Plus, the rivers are said to be heavily patrolled by the Colombia military. Updated: Jul 04, 2008.

Sibundoy

Alt: 2,000m	Pop: 13,500	City Code: 8

Heading from Pasto eastward, the highway passes through Laguna de la Cocha and then enters the Putumayo and continues to that department's capital, Mocoa, before turning north toward Pitalito, near San Agustín. For several years the only part of the Putumayo safe to visit was the Valley of Sibundoy, a largely indigenous area with roots deep in the *Nudo de los Pastos* (the Knot of the Pastos), which unravel into the Cordillera Oriental and Occidental. The origins of multitudes of streams flow eastward to join the Putumayo and Amazon Rivers. The village existed long before the Spaniards' first visit in 1534. Inca Huayna Cápac had conquered the local indigenous in 1492 and established a Quechua-speaking settlement here, which were the ancestors of the modern-day Ingas. The population is still largely indigenous and wears long blue and violet ponchos. Every year in February there is the Return of the First People Carnaval, which includes traditional music and dance. Sibundoy is renowned for its artisan work, especially mask carving. Sibundoy's principal park is full of fallen tree trunks carved with symbols and the mythology of the Inga and Kamsá nations. There are also several basic hotels around town that provide lodging.

The war zone looms not too far from Sibundoy. At the beginning of this millennium travel was only possible as far as Sibundoy, 80 kilometers (48 miles) west of Mocoa. Recent traveler reports indicate that the entire Pitalito-Pasto circuit can now be safely traveled. Updated: Jul 07, 2008.

Getting To and Away From Sibundoy

Sibundoy is accessible by public transportation from Pasto (several companies with daily departures, 3 hours, $5) and from Pitalito by way of Mocoa (10 hours, $12). Updated: Jul 07, 2008.

Puerto Nariño

Alt: 110m	Pop: 2,000	City Code: 8

At the confluence of Río Loretoyacü, 75 kilometers (45 miles) west of Leticia is Puerto Nariño, the *Pesebre del Amazonas* (Cradle of the Amazon). This small village surrounded by jungle is a tranquil place to hang your hat for a few days. Its biological and ethnic diversity give ample opportunity for exploration, including walking trails and canoeing on the slow Loretoyacü to Lago Tarapoto in search of the mystical pink dolphin. It is part of the Ticoya indigenous reserve of the Tikuna, Cocoma and Yagua peoples, who make up 90 percent of the town's population.

Puerto Nariño is on the itinerary of tours that go to Lago Tarapoto and is increasingly popular among backpackers, since it is quieter and less expensive than Leticia. The town begins with a flat, narrow plain on the waterfront, then the land begins to rise like a many-tiered cake. No cars venture the streets of Puerto Nariño, because in truth, there are no streets, just a well-laid out, well-signed grid of sidewalks. Puerto Nariño is a national model of an ecological village, with a recycling and organic waste management programs and development of eco-ethno-tourism. Updated: Jul 08, 2008.

Things to See and Do

For such a small village, Puerto Nariño has an amazing amount of things to do and see. It is a good base for getting to know the jungle and indigenous villages, and it's more economical than Leticia. One of the most astounding features of Puerto Nariño is the museums. There also are paths for learning about the medicinal and agricultural uses of the jungle, and there are *miradores* (lookout towers) to watch the rivers flow past. Nearby are indigenous villages possible to visit.

The biggest attraction, however, is Lago Tarapoto where you can observe pink dolphins and the majestic Victoria Regia water lily. Don't forget that just a half-hour down-river is the Parque Nacional Natural Amacayacu. Updated: Jul 08, 2008.

Senderos and Miradores

A network of trails and *miradores* help you to appreciate the natural beauty of this region.

Mirador Naipata—From Naipata, Casa en el Árbol, just outside Puerto Nariño you can see the Río Loretoyacü flow into the Amazon.

Mirador Mowa—This tower overlooking the Río Amazonas and jungle is located in the indigenous village 20 de Julio, a 30-minute walk or 10-minute boat ride from Puerto Nariño.

Sendero Ecológico—A path leading through the forest that shows medicinal, fruit, hardwood and ornamental plants.

Sendero Ecológico Mitológico—A project of the students at the Internado de San Francisco. A guided tour of this trail will teach you about the ecology and mythology of the jungle flora.

Sendero Ecológico Nama Aruku—The Path of Knowing is designed and maintained by students of INEAGRO to show the botanical richness of the region and the ancestral uses of plants.

Sendero Interpretativo Puerto Nariño San Martín—This trail through secondary growth rainforest leads to the Tikuna village of San Martín on the edge of Parque Nacional Natural Amacayacu. Updated: Jul 08, 2008.

Lago Tarapoto

The Río Loretoyacü bulges a bit to one side, creating Lago Tarapoto, a beautiful lake sur-

Museum	Description	Hours	Address	Price
Ethnocultural Museum House of the Monkeys	Exhibits the craftsmanship and the culture of the Tikuna, Cocama and Yagua.	Monday-Friday 7 a.m.-noon, 2-5:45 p.m.	Carrera 7 and Calle 5	Free
Casa Artesanal Tachiwagü	A maloka that teaches the indigenous world vision.	Monday-Friday 9 a.m.-noon, 2-5 p.m.	Carrera 6 between Calles 5 and 6	$0.50
Centro de Interpretación Natütama	A non-profit organization working on conservation issues and eco-education that welcomes visitors. The center has more than 70 life-size carvings of plant and animal species of the Río Amazonas waterways.	Wednesday-Monday 8 a.m.-noon, 2-5 p.m., closed Tuesday	On south bank of Quebrada Menoe as it enters the Río Loretoyacü	

Updated: Jul 08, 2008.

LLANOS AND SELVA

rounded by jungle, speckled with mangrove islands. Along its shores are isolated indigenous hamlets secreted in the dense vegetation. This is a place of magic, where pink dolphins leap from the silvered waters. Here, along the shallow, quiet waters of channels branching off the lake, is Victoria regia, the world's largest water lily. Explore this magical realm by boat, swimming in the cool waters or dropping a line in for piranha.

To see the river and Lago Tarapoto, you can hire a boat with guide. Paddle canoes are most ecological ($12-15). Peque-peques (a canoe with a long-propeller motor) are the next best ($21 for 4-5 persons, with guide). They are slow, but fuel efficient.

Try to avoid taking a tour with a speed boat, as it disturbs the pink dolphins and other aquatic life. You have a better chance of seeing dolphins in early morning and late afternoon. Victoria regia water lilies grow in the backwaters of the lake. Updated: Jul 08, 2008.

Fundación Omacha

Taking its name from the Tikuna word for the pink dolphin, this organization works on the conservation of the Amazon's aquatic denizens. It accepts volunteers, so check out its website for more information. Village side of the Quebrada Menoe as it enters the Río Loretoyacü. E-mail: info@omacha.org / moralula@yahoo.com.mx, URL: www.omacha.org.

Indigenous Villages

Accessible by path or by boat from Puerto Nariño are several indigenous villages you can visit where you can buy artisan work. Sendero Interpretativo Puerto Nariño San Martín leads to the Tikuna hamlet of San Martín, not too far from Parque Nacional Natural Amacayacu. Unfortunately, it has become affected by tourists, and people are now charging for photos. Mocagua, another Tikuna settlement near the national park, is more traditional. A traditional Tikuna village, 20 de Julio, is known for its artisan work and has a mirador. San Juan del Socó on Río Loretoyacü is another village you can boat to.

San Martín and 20 de Julio are accessible by path from Puerto Nariño. Follow the signs from Carrera 6. For the other two, check with villagers about a canoe to take you there, or go in one of the boats leaving three times daily. Some of these hamlets, like Mocagua, allow overnight stays. Speak with the *curaca* (village leader) if you are interested. Updated: Jul 08, 2008.

Puerto Nariño Lodging

In the realm of lodging, Puerto Nariño surprisingly has a half-dozen inns offering a peaceful night's rest. Most are simple hostels, though even those vacationers looking for a bit more luxury have a place to hang their hats, too. Budget travelers generally head for Puerto Nariño if they want to stay a while in the Leticia area. Hotels are cheaper here and closer to many of the prime attractions, including virgin jungle. The town has electricity only until 10 p.m., so be sure to keep a flashlight and candles at hand. Updated: Jul 08, 2008.

Alto del Águila

(BED: $8) Fray Hector has created a tranquil retreat overlooking the Río Loretoyacü. The three cabañas are airy and comfortable. Watch the sunset from the tower, which you'll have to share with two possessive macaws. Evenings are pleasurably spent on the back porch, conversing with Fray Hector. The brother is a most gracious host. If he's full, he can arrange for you to stay at the Hermana Vicentinas' cabañas at the Internado de San Francisco. A curfew of sorts exists, as the sisters let guard dogs loose at night.

From Carrera 6, follow the signs for Internado de San Francisco. Upon reaching the school, cut across the grounds to the grassy trail that leads to Alto del Águila. Also, you can hire a boat from the village to take you to the dock just below the hostel. One kilometer (0.6 miles) from the village, just past Internado de San Francisco school. Cell: 311-502-8592, E-mail: altodelaguila@hotmail.com. Updated: Jul 08, 2008.

Hospedaje Manguare

(BED: $8) An inexpensive option in the heart of Puerto Nariño. It is convenient for exploring the trails and miradores of the area. In this small hostel at the back of her home, doña Isabel offers simple rooms, some with several beds, sharing a clean common bath. After hiking around, you might need to clean your muddy clothes. Conveniently, the *señora* allows guests to wash clothes, which is a plus in this town with no Laundromat. Calle 4, 5-68. Cell: 311-276-4873 / 531-0063. Updated: Jul 09, 2008.

Hotel Casa Selva

(ROOM: $16-80) This hotel has blossomed into the most expensive and luxurious place in Puerto Nariño. This two-story, white beauty has 12 rooms around the interior patio. Shuttered windows and balconies make these quarters bright and airy. All come with private bath and fan. A common room with hammocks is the perfect place to rest after a day of sightseeing. Catch the sunset over the Río Loretoyacü from the mirador on the grounds. Carrera 6, 6-78. Cell: 315-333-2796, E-mail: casaselvahotel@yahoo.es.

Across the way is Hostal Asaí, also run by Casa Selva. This hostel is more economical, costing only $16 per person. Carrera 6, 6-65. Tel: 8-592-6656, Cell: 311-477-8973, E-mail: hostalasai@yahoo.es. Updated: Jul 09, 2008.

Puerto Nariño Restaurants

You can pretty much count on one hand the number of restaurants in Puerto Nariño. You haven't much choice, especially in the evening. Most have set hours for serving meals, so you will have to plan accordingly. In general, food is a bit more expensive here.

In the back part of the Perros Fredy building are several rustic eateries that serve lunch. The place to pick up groceries in town is the general store on Carrera 7, between Calles 7 and 8, near the waterfront. A basic market sets up during the day at Carrera 7 and Calle 8. Updated: Jul 08, 2008.

Perros Fredy

(LUNCH: $2.65) More than just hotdogs and hamburgers, Perros Fredy has some simple á la carte dishes, like *bifstek a la plancha*. Perros Fredy additionally serves a standard comida corriente with drink that is made with purified water. You can choose to sit inside at the short counter and chat with the señora, or at the table out on the porch. This is the only restaurant that doesn't close during the afternoon. Open 6 a.m.-10 p.m. Carrera 7, between Calles 6 and 7. Updated: Jul 09, 2008.

Restaurante Tucunare

(LUNCH: $2.65) This restaurant is nothing fancy—just a large, simply-dressed eatery serving nothing but down-to-earth meals. It is also one of the more economical restaurants in Puerto Nariño—its breakfasts cost $2.10 and the luncheon specials are $2.65. Unfortunately, Restaurante Tucunare is not open for dinner. Open 7-9 a.m. for breakfast, noon-2 p.m. for lunch. Carrera 6, between Calles 6 and 7. Updated: Jul 09, 2008.

Restaurante Margaritas

(LUNCH: $3.70) This diner is haughtily proud of the fact that many tour groups stop here on trips to Lago Tarapoto. The quality of its service and its prices reflect it. Breakfasts cost $2.65. Lunch is a standard fish, beans, rice, yucca and patacones, accompanied by soup and drink ($3.70). For dinner you can choose between the á la carte menu ($4.20) or the set meal ($3.70). Open 7-9 a.m., noon-2 p.m., 6:30-8 p.m. Calle 7, between Carreras 6 and 7. Updated: Jul 09, 2008.

Colombia-Peru-Brazil Border Crossing

Leticia may be the end of the road for Colombia, but it is also the crossroads of the Amazon jungle. From here many adventurers set sail for Brazil or Peru, fulfilling a life-long dream of traveling on one of the world's greatest rivers, the Amazon—or as the locals call it, the Río Amazonas. Get ready to embark for your next destination, whether upstream to Iquitos, Peru, or downstream to Manaus, Brazil.

Immigration

Regulations and procedures frequently change. Check with your ticket agent to see if the boat stops for *migración* (immigration). If not, you may need to take care of these formalities the day before your boat leaves. See the respective cities for addresses and hours.

Colombia—Get your passport stamped at the airport DAS office. If you need a visa to enter there is a consulate in Tabatinga.

Peru—The immigration post is in Santa Rosa, on the other side of the river from Leticia.

Brazil—Immigration formalities are handled by the Policia Federal in Tabatinga.

Colombia-Brazilian border—Brazil has a consulate in Leticia. Citizens of some countries need a visa for this country, including those from the U.S., Canada and Australia. You'll need the form, a 5 x 7 cm photo, your yellow fever vaccination certificate, an on-going ticket (or credit card or sufficient funds), and pay the fee ($25.50 for Aussies, $167 for U.S. citizens). The consul speaks Spanish and English, as well as Portuguese.

If you are only making a day trip into a neighboring town, you will not need to go through immigration. If you are going to a jungle lodge in a neighboring country, check with your tour operator to see if you will need to go through the bureaucracy. This is especially important for nationalities needing a visa for Brazil.

Transportation

The three river towns all are connected to larger cities in their respective countries by air and by river. A few things to keep in mind if you choose to do the age-old way, by boat:

► Speak only with the captain of the boat. Confirm departure date and time, and prices.

► Compare prices with different boats, and inspect the vessel for cleanliness. Pay only the captain or another authorized person, and obtain a receipt. You can also purchase your ticket from an authorized agent.

► Larger boats have cabins (some even with A/C). However, these are more expensive than hammock space on the deck, and tend to be hot and stuffy. If you opt to travel swinging along in your hammock, be sure to choose a spot away from the fumes and noise of the engines, the insect-attracting lights, and the bathrooms. Have rope not only to hang your *hamaca*, but also to hang cloth for privacy. Board early (often it is possible to do so the night before) to land a choice spot.

► Use a mosquito net and repellent, and don't forget to take your malaria medication.

► Secure your belongings very well. Lock your bags, and always keep the key with you. Be particularly vigilant when the boat pulls into a port village during the trip because this is when most thefts happen.

► Food will be provided, as will drinks (often made with river water). Bring along fresh fruits, comfort foods and purified water. Have your own cup, as well, plus some diarrhea medication, just in case.

► It gets remarkably cool at night on the river. Light, warm clothing and a blanket (or cloth hammock) will keep you warm.

Iquitos, Peru

Getting To and Away From Iquitos

Boat

Most cargo ships to Iquitos depart from Santa Rosa rather than from Islandia a bit further down river. Every day a boat leaves in the evening, usually between 6 and 9 p.m. Take a good look at the ship before you commit yourself. Do all your negotiations with only the authorized ticket seller or at the ship's administration office aboard (hammock $16-20, cabin $23-27, 3 nights / 2 days).

Fast boats (*rápidos*) also ply this route, departing from Tabatinga and Leticia. In Leticia, you can purchase your ticket in advance at Almacén El Repuesto (Calle 7, 10-72. Tel: 8-592-7156 / 311-217-6770; in Iquitos: Raimundi 390. Tel: 065-241-468), in Tabatinga from Pirarucu Turismo and in Santa Rosa. Tickets may be paid with U.S. dollars, Peruvian soles, Colombian pesos or Brazilian reals. Passage includes breakfast, lunch and sodas. Tuesday-Sunday, 4-5 a.m., $60, 9 hours.

Air

North American Airlines has a charter flight from Santa Rosa to Iquitos on Sunday at 10 a.m. More information can be obtained at the rápidos ticket office in Santa Rosa, just before the immigration post.

Santa Rosa, Peru

Alt: 50m Pop: hundreds Code: 51+65

On an island directly across from Leticia is the smallest of the triple border towns, Santa Rosa. In reality, it is so small, it doesn't seem to be worth the census-taker's time to make a call and count. The town isn't much, but it is the jumping-off point for travelers looking for a boat up the Amazon River to Iquitos. A paved way parallels the riverbank. The walk frays into dirt paths disappearing into the dense vegetation. This main "street," though is as far as you ever need to go in Santa Rosa. Your launch from Leticia or Tabatinga will pull up among the many other canoes shoved against the shore. To the left is where the next boat for Iquitos may be loading up. Also along this stretch are the Peruvian migración post, about a half-dozen basic hotels, a handful of restaurants and other businesses. From the street vendors you can pick up a comic book or other last-minute item for your sojourn. Updated: Jul 07, 2008.

Getting To and Away from Santa Rosa

The only way to get to or from Santa Rosa is by launch, leaving from the main street. To Leticia: daily 6 a.m.-8 p.m., $1.10. To Santa Rosa: daily 6 a.m.-8 p.m., $2.80. Santa Rosa is a more convenient departure point for cargo ships than Islandia is, and as such most leave from here. Several agencies on the main drag sell tickets for the rápido boat and the weekly flight to Iquitos. See Colombia-Brazil-Peru Border Crossings for more information. Updated: Jul 09, 2008.

Santa Rosa Services

The most important office in Santa Rosa is immigration, about 50 meters (180 ft) to the right of the boat docks, past Hotel Diana (Monday-Saturday 8 a.m.-noon, 2-6 p.m.). There are no banks in Santa Rosa. Hospedaje El Mirador, about 120 meters (400 ft) from the boat dock changes money. To stay in touch with the outside world, the main phone office is 30 meters (100 ft) to the right of immigration, in the Snack Bar Sabor Peruano "mall." There is no internet in Santa Rosa. Updated: Jul 09, 2008.

Manaus, Brazil

Getting To and Away from Manaus

Boat

Tabatinga has two river ports: the principal one, Porta da Feira, at the end of Rua Santo Dumont in the market area, and the Porto Fluvial de Tabatinga at the end of Rua Duarte Coelho, at which Manaus boats also dock. Some of the ships plying the Manaus route are Voyagers III and IV, Fenix, Manuel Monteiro and Coracão de Jesus (better). All have the choice of hammocks on deck or cabins. Suites have all the comforts, including TV, mini-fridge and A/C. Brazilian boats now purport to prepare drinks with purified water. Buy your ticket directly from the administrator on board or from Pirarucu Turismo in Tabatinga. Other slow boats leave from Benjamin Constant, Brazil, 1.5-two hours downstream from Tabatinga.

From/To	Departure	Time	Price
Tabatinga /Manaus	Wednesday, Sunday 2 p.m., Friday 8 a.m.	30-72 hours	$53 -320
Manaus / Tabatinga	Wednesday-Saturday 3 p.m., Wednesday 7 a.m.	2-7 days	$121 -530

Air

Planes leave from Tabatinga's airport, about four kilometers (2.4 mi) south on Avenida Amizade. Busetas from Leticia's Parque Orellana go there (5:45 a.m.-6:20 p.m. $1.85), or you can arrive by taxi ($2.65). Flights are to Manaus or to Tefe, from which connections to Manaus can be made. Tickets may be purchased at CNM Câmbio e Turismo. Monday-Friday, 8 a.m.-noon, 2-4 p.m. Avenida Amizade 2017, in the yellow ochre shopping center. Tel.: 97-3412-2600, Fax: 97-3412-3055, E-mail: cbnmtur@yahoo.com.br.

To Manaus—Through Rico Airlines you can leave on Tuesday, Thursday, Saturday at 11:40 a.m. for $330. The flight lasts 2.5 hours.

Manaus-Tabatinga—With a stop in Tefé, flights leave on Wednesday, Thursday, Sunday 8 a.m. trip. On Sunday, Wednesday and Friday flights depart at 4:20 p.m. for $330. On Sunday, Wednesday and Friday there are flights at 11 a.m.

Tabatinga, Brazil

Alt: 85m Pop: 45,300 City Code: 97

On the other side of the border, just a kilometer (0.6 miles) from downtown Leticia, is that Colombian city's Brazilian cousin,

Tabatinga (pronounced ta-ba-CHEEN-ga). If you want just to sample Brazil's cooking and fine Garota chocolates, you don't need to do any formal border procedures. Just walk down Avenida Internacional in Leticia southward. At the border it becomes Avenida Amizade. Its principal port, Porta da Feira down by the market, bustles with peque-peques arriving from indigenous villages and the next Manaus-bound boat loading up. If you're heading down river, do stop into the Policia Federal to get your passport stamped. Although it is the larger city, Tabatinga has fewer services than Leticia, where most travelers prefer to stay. However, there are hotels and restaurants as well as money and communication facilities. Many people here speak Spanish, or at least *portunhol* (a mix of Portuguese and Spanish). Updated: Jul 07, 2008.

Getting To and Away From Tabatinga

Tabatinga has two ports: Porta da Feira (at the end of Rua Santos Dumont down by the market) and Porto Fluvial de Tabatinga (past the Marinha do Brasil naval base at the end of Rua Duarte Coelho). Boats for Benjamin Constant and Manaus leave from both ports. Local boats depart from the Porta da Feira to arrive in Leticia and Santa Rosa. Boats to Leticia leave daily at 6 a.m.-8 p.m. for $1.10. To get to Santa Rosa take a daily boat at 6 a.m.-8 p.m. for $2.80. Catch a buseta from Avenida Amizade for Leticia, Tabatinga's airport or the Tikuna village Maria Azzu (6 a.m.-6:20 p.m., $0.80-1.05). Mototaxis ($0.50) and taxis ($1.60-2.65, depending on distance) also ply these routes. Tabatinga's airport is about four kilometers (2.4 miles) along Avenida Amizade. Rico Airlines and Trip Airlines fly to Tefé and Manaus several times a week. See Colombia-Brazil-Peru Border Crossings for more information. Updated: Jul 09, 2008.

Tabatinga Services

Tourism Office

Tabatinga has no tourism office. An important institution in town is the Policia Federal to have your passport stamped upon arriving from (or leaving for) Manaus (daily 8 a.m.-noon, 2-6 p.m. Avenida Amizade 650). If you need a visa for Colombia, there is a consulate in Tabatinga (Monday-Friday 8 a.m.-1 p.m. Rua General Sanpaio 623).

Money

Banco do Brasil has an ATM that accepts Visa, MasterCard and Cirrus (Avenida Amizade and Rua Marechal Mallet). To change dollars, Euros or reais, go to CNM Câmbio e Turismo. Monday-Friday, 8 a.m.-noon, 2-4 p.m. Avenida Amizade 2017, in the yellow ochre shopping center. Tel: 97-3412-2600, Fax: 97-3412-3055, E-mail: cbnmtur@ahoo.com.br.

Keeping in Touch

You can find a few internet cafés on Avenida Amizade. The Correios (post office) is on this same boulevard, between Rua Santos Dumont and Rua Coronel Berg (Monday-Friday 8 a.m.-4 p.m.). Updated: Jul 09, 2008.

Tabatinga Tours

Pirarucu Turismo

Pirarucu Turismo in Tabatinga is the principal seller in the Triple Border region of tickets for the all big boats to Manaus. It also sells passages for the rápidos to Manaus or to Iquitos. But this tour operator has much more on its menu. Pirarucu Turismo offers day excursions to Benjamin Constant, Brazil ($30), Puerto Nariño, Colombia ($35), and Cavallo Cocha, Peru ($53). Through these trips you visit indigenous communities and enjoy nature of those places (prices include transportation, guide and lunch). This agency also has a two-night / two-day package to their jungle lodge in Cavallo Cocha ($70-95 per person, depending on the number of tourists). Rua Santos Dumont 02, across from the market. Tel: 97-9151-5936 / 0594, E-mail: pirarucuturismotbt@hotmail.com, URL: www.pirarucuturismo.com. Updated: Jul 08, 2008.

Tabatinga Lodging

Hotel Internacional Bagpackers

(BED: $8-16) Formerly Travelers' Jungle Home, Hotel Internacional Bagpackers has moved from Tony's home to a larger, more central location. If your boat from Manaus gets in after dark, this budget backpacker's hostel is three blocks from Tabatinga's Porta da Feira. With a dorm room and several rooms with private bath, this inn is bare-boned and apparently still unpacking from the move. Hotel Internacional Bagpackers has a common kitchen and a place to hang out. Rua Pedro Texeira 9, second floor. Cell: 312-585-8855. Updated: Jul 09, 2008.

Index

A

INDEX

B

INDEX

C

INDEX

H

INDEX

N

O

P

INDEX

INDEX

U

INDEX

Y

Z

Environmental Tips for Travelers

By Nicola Robinson, Nicola Mears and Heather Ducharme, Río Muchacho Organic Farm, Ecuador.

While traveling in a foreign country, it is important to minimize your impact. Here are some tips you should keep in mind while on your trip. Some of this advice may be more difficult to take on board while traveling than it would be to incorporate into your daily lives at home. However, even if you only put into practice three or four of the suggestions, on the road or at home, it will certainly help reduce your impact on the planet.

Garbage

• Carry a water bottle and always check if there is somewhere to fill it up at your hotel / restaurant—most hotels and restaurants have purified water in 20-litre bottles called *botellones*. These places usually also sell water in small bottles and might be reluctant to begin with as they think they are losing a sale. Of course you will need to pay for the refill also. If you have to buy bottles, buy the biggest you can and just refill from there, especially if you plan to be in the same place for a while.

• Purify your own water to avoid creating garbage.

• Try to avoid excessive wrapping and plastic bags which are all too readily dished out for each small purchase. If you can, explain to the shop keeper why you want to give the bag back. If you shop in a local market, take your own bag or have them place everything in one large plastic bag instead of numerous small ones.

• Use a digital camera instead of film. The process of developing film can produce a lot of waste, and unwanted photos are non recyclable and often end up in the trash.

• Use a reusable container for soap so you can use your own instead of the small hotel soaps, which come individually wrapped. If you use hotel soap, use one and take the remainder with you—it will just be thrown out.

• Avoid using excessive cosmetic products such as hairspray, mousse, aftershave and perfume, or try to find effective environmentally-friendly alternatives such as biodegradable shampoos and crystal deodorants, which last longer (most containers for these products are non recyclable). Avoid using disposable products such as plastic razors and single-use contact lenses.

• Try to use rechargeable batteries or eliminate use of batteries entirely. For example, use a wind-up or solar torch or radio.

• Use recycled paper for letters home, trip diaries and toilet paper.

• Buy in bulk if you are traveling in a large group to reduce packaging.

• Recycle whatever you can in the country you are traveling. Some products that can not be recycled in the host country can be recycled in your home countries (such as batteries), so please take them home if possible.

Food and health

• Avoid eating foods that you know are from endangered or threatened species (research these before you come to the country). Buy and eat locally grown and locally processed foods wherever possible, rather than food shipped from long distances, which use more energy and packaging.

• Consider using alternative natural medical products for common travelers' illnesses. This may be healthier for you and keeps you from leaving behind pharmaceuticals in the local water and soil (this is becoming a detectable problem in first world countries, thought to affect aquatic organisms like fish and frogs).

Nature, Flora and fauna

• Avoid buying souvenirs of local fauna. Many stores sell cases of bright colored butterflies, spiders and insects which are caught by the hundreds in the Amazon. The sales people will tell you that they are not caught but that they raise them—it is not true!

• Avoid buying souvenirs that are made with endangered species or species that have to be killed to be made into a craft. Support crafts made from renewable resources.

• Don't collect insects, flora and fauna without a permit. Leave them for everyone to enjoy.

• When walking, stay on the trails and close gates behind you.

Camping and Water

• Use toilets where they exist. If there are no toilets, bury human waste in a hole 20 centimeters deep. Human waste should be buried at least 50 meters from water sources.

• Use biodegradable soaps and detergents.

• Don't wash shampoo and detergent off directly in rivers, but rather as far away as you can (4 meters minimum).

• Avoid making fires.

• Use a T-shirt when snorkeling as sunscreen is harmful to marine life.

Transport

• Use public transport instead of private (e.g. bus instead of rental car) when possible to reduce fossil fuel use. Share rental cars and taxis with others. If possible, walk or use a bicycle. It not only helps the planet, but it keeps you in shape as well!

Electricity

• Lights, fans, TVs, radios, or computers: If you are not using it, turn it off!

Traveling with children and babies

• Try and teach your child about the local environmental issues. Point out good and bad practices.

• Encourage your child to snack on fruit, which has a biodegradable wrapper!

• If traveling with a baby, why not use cotton diapers? Disposable diapers are becoming a major waste issue in developed countries and are becoming a desirable product in the developing world. Using cotton will set a good example to others and reduce the promotion of disposable diapers.

Local environmental issues

• Try to learn about the important environmental issues in the country. Good environmental practices (e.g. reduce, reuse, recycle!) are often the same in different countries, but the specific issues are often different (e.g. different recycling options, different endangered habitats and species, different laws and policies, etc.)

• Think about where you are eating and staying, and support the more environmentally friendly businesses. If you stay in an ecolodge, talk to the owners / managers, ask how they manage their garbage (including human waste), if they recycle and if they use grey water systems to reuse their water. Where do their building materials, food, and power come from? Do they practice or contribute to conservation? Do they support the local community? Be constructive rather than critical if you don't get a good response—some people truly think that it can be called an ecolodge if it is built with natural materials.

• Many countries have interesting volunteer opportunities with environmentally oriented organizations, and volunteering is an option. Research carefully—some volunteer opportunities are not what they say they are. The Web site www.volunteersouthamerica.net has links to several free and low-cost volunteer opportunities around South America.

The following is a list of helpful environmental Web sites for further information:

WWW.ECOMALL.COM and WWW.GREENHOME.COM both contain advice and links to places you can buy environmentally friendly products.

WWW.MINAMBIENTE.GOV.CO Ministry of the Environment, Colombia (in Spanish)

WWW.IUCNREDLIST.ORG A list of endangered species around the world by the International Union for Conservation of Nature and Natural Resources

PACKING LISTS

(* indicates something that might not be available in Colombia)

General packing list

There are a number of items that every traveler should consider bringing to Colombia as follows:

- ☐ **Medicines and prescriptions** (Very important. Bringing all relevant medical info and medicines may well save you a lot of grief in Colombia)
- ☐ **Photocopies of passport** and other relevant ID documents
- ☐ Paperback novels (sometimes you'll be sitting on buses, in airports, or somewhere else for a long time. It is possible to find and /or exchange books in several places in Colombia, but don't count on much selection if you don't read Spanish)
- ☐ Plug converter (many older buildings in Colombia have 2-prong outlets only, although the voltage is the same)
- ☐ A good camera (see photography section)
- ☐ Water bottle (bottled water is readily available in Colombia, but you may want your own bottle)
- ☐ Sunglasses
- ☐ Motion sickness medicine
- ☐ Lip balm
- ☐ *Tampons (difficult to find outside the major cities)
- ☐ Sun hat
- ☐ Condoms and other contraceptives
- ☐ *Foot powder
- ☐ Antacid tablets, such as Rolaids
- ☐ Mild painkillers such as aspirin or ibuprofen
- ☐ *GPS device (especially for hikers)
- ☐ Watch with alarm clock
- ☐ Diarrhea medicine (i.e. Imodium)
- ☐ Warm clothes (The highlands are cooler than you think)

BACKPACKER PACKING LIST:

- ☐ All of the above, plus:
- ☐ Rain poncho
- ☐ Plastic bags
- ☐ *Swiss army knife/Leatherman
- ☐ Toilet paper
- ☐ *Antibacterial hand gel
- ☐ Small padlock

CARIBBEAN COAST PACKING LIST

- ☐ Extra film/camera supplies
- ☐ Waterproof disposable camera for snorkeling
- ☐ Sunscreen
- ☐ Good, wide brimmed hat
- ☐ Long pants, lightweight
- ☐ Long-sleeved shirt, lightweight

RAINFOREST PACKING LIST

- ☐ Rubber boots (most jungle lodges have them, call ahead)
- ☐ *Bug spray (with Deet)
- ☐ Flashlight
- ☐ Waterproof bags
- ☐ Rain poncho
- ☐ First aid kit
- ☐ *Compass
- ☐ Whistle
- ☐ Long-sleeved shirt and pants
- ☐ Malaria/yellow fever medicine
- ☐ Original passport
- ☐ Mosquito net (if your destination does not have one; call ahead)
- ☐ Biodegradable soap

Additional Items

- ☐ ____________________
- ☐ ____________________
- ☐ ____________________
- ☐ ____________________
- ☐ ____________________
- ☐ ____________________
- ☐ ____________________
- ☐ ____________________

Anti-packing list: Things NOT to bring to Colombia

x Expensive jewelry. Just leave it home.

x Nice watch or sunglasses. Bring a cheap one you can afford to lose.

x Go through your wallet: what won't you need? Leave your drivers' license (unless you're planning on driving), business cards, video-club membership cards, 7-11 coffee club card, social security card and anything else you won't need at home. The only thing in your wallet you'll want is a student ID, and if you lose your wallet you'll be grateful you left the rest at home.

x Illegal drugs. You didn't need us to tell you that, did you?

x Stickers and little toys for kids. Some tourists like to hand them out, which means the children pester every foreigner they see.

x Really nice clothes or shoes, unless you're planning on going to a special event or dining out a lot.

V!VA Travel Guides brings you a tear-out list of useful contacts in Colombia.

Feel free to photocopy this sheet for your use, to give to your dog or to wallpaper your room.

Emergency Numbers

All emergencies	112 or 123	Immediate attention center	156
Fire	119	Red Cross	132

Medical

Fundación Santa Fe de Bogotá
Calle 119 No. 9-33, Bogotá
Tel: 1-603-0303
URL: www.fsfb.org.co

Medihelp Services, Cartegena
Carrera 6a, 5-101, Bocagrande, Cartagena
Tel: 5-665-2255
URL: www.medihelpservices.com

Dentist (Bogotá): Antonio Flórez—Calle 134 No.13 - 83, Office 806, Edifício El Bosque, Bogotá. Tel: 1-520-0108, Cel: 1-310-878-5179, Fax: 1-626-7868, E-mail antonioefa2004@yahoo.com. Speaks Spanish and English.

English-Speaking Lawyers (Criminal)

Chávez-Herrera & Morano International P.A.
Calle 32, 5-09, Oficina 315, Cartagena
Tel: 1-286-8305 / 288-9466
Fax: 1-288-9466
E-mail: chhm@coldecon.net.co

Rodrigo Martínez-Torres
Calle 37, 15-78, Bogotá
Tel: 575-664-4584 / 7128
Fax: 1-664-2659
E-mail: rmartinezt@etb.net.co

Traveler Guidance

V!VA Travel Guides: www.vivatravelguides.com

South America Explorers' Club
E-mail: don@saexplorers.org
www.saexplorers.org

Tourist Information Office
Carerra 8, 9-83, Plaza de Bolívar, Bogotá
Tel: 1-327-4916

Post Office (Correos)

Bogotá—Carrera 7 and Calle 13, Ed. Murillo Toro

Cartagena—Carrera 7, 8B-20

Int'l Country Codes

United States and Canada—1

United Kingdom—44
Australia—61

Transport

Taxis: In Bogotá—Compañía Taxis Verdes, Tel: 355-5550, or Abandera Radio Taxi, Tel: 288-8888. In Cartagena—Comunicamos Tele Taxi, Tel: 660-0000.

Complete the sections below for your convenience:

My Tour Operator:

My Hotel Address:

Taxi Directions to My Hotel:

Airlines in Bogotá:

Aerogal (Ecuadorian)
Calle 92, 15-48 Local 209
Tel: 1-618-0511, Fax: 1-621-0657
E-Mail: reservasbog@aerogal.com.ec
URL: www.aerogal.com.ec

American Airlines (US)
Calle 71 A, 5-90, Local 101
Tel: 1-439-7777
URL: www.aa.com

Avianca (Colombian)
Avenida 19, 4-37, Local 2
Tel: 2-845-649
www.avianca.com

Continental Airlines (US)
Carrera 7, 71-21, Torre A Local 2
01.800.944.0219
URL: www.continental.com

COPA (Panamanian)
Carrera 9 A, 99-02, Local 108
Tel: 01-800-550-7700
URL: www.copaair.com

Iberia (Spanish)
Carrera 19ª, 85-11
Tel: 1-610-5066, Fax: 1-218-3733
URL: www.iberia.com

Lan Chile (Chilean)
Calle 100 8A-49, Torre B, Piso 7, Of. 708
Tel: 1-651-3970, Fax: 1-611-5560
URL: Lan.com

Satena (Colombian)
Avenida El Dorado, entrada 1, interior 11
Tel: 1-605-2222
E-mail: webmaster@satena.com
URL: www.satena.com

Taca (El Salvador)
Calle 113, 7- 21, Local 124
Tel: 01-800-951-8222
URL: www.taca.com

Varig (Brazilian)
Carrera 7, 33-24
Tel: 1-350-8300
URL: www.varig.com

Embassies in Bogotá:

Australia (Consulate)
Carrera 16, 86A-05
Tel: 1-236-2828, Fax: 1-610-9707

United Kingdom
Carrera 9 No. 76-49, Floors 8 and 9
Tel: 1-326-8300, Fax: 1-326-8302
URL: ukincolombia.fco.gov.uk

Canada
Carrera 7, 114-33, Floor 14
Tel: 1-657-9800
E-mail: enqserv@dfait-maeci.gc.ci
URL: Colombia.gc.ca

France
Carrera 11, 93-12
Tel: 1-638-1400, Fax: 1-638-1430

Germany
Carrera 4, 72-35, Floor 6
Tel: 1-212-0511

Ireland (Consulate)
De Las Americas 56-41
Tel: 1-446-6114, Fax: 1-446-6120
E-mail: carlos.gomez2@co.smurfitgroup.com

Japan
Carrera 7, 71-21, Torre B, Floor 11
Tel: 1-317-5001, Fax: 1-317-4989
E-mail: info@embjp-colombia.com
URL: www.colombia.emb-japan.go.jp

Netherlands
Carrera 13, 93-40
Tel: 1-638-4200, Fax: 1-623-3020
E-mail: bog@minbuza.nl
URL: colombia.nlembajada.org

Spain
Calle 92, 12-68
Phone: 1-622-0090, Fax: 1-621-0809
E-mail: embespco@correo.mae.es

Switzerland
Carrera 9A, 74-08, Floor 11
Tel: 1-349-7230, Fax: 1-349-7195
E-mail: bog.vertretung@eda.admin.ch
URL: www.eda.admin.ch/bogota

United States
Carrera 45, 24B-27
Tel: 1-315-0811, Fax: 1-315-2197
E-mail: asktheembassybogota@state.gov
URL: bogota.usembassy.gov

Israel
Calle 35, 7-25, Caxdac building, Floor 14
Tel: 1-327-7500, Fax: 1-327-7555
E-mail: info@bogota.mfa.gov.il
URL: bogota.mfa.gov.il

Russia
Carrera 4, 75-00 Apartado Aereo
Tel: 1-212-881 / 5560, Fax: 1-210-4694
E-mail: embajadarusia@cable.net.co /
rusposol@cable.net.co

Useful Spanish Phrases

Conversational

Hello	Hola
Good morning	Buenos días
Good afternoon	Buenas tardes
Good evening	Buenas noches
Yes	Sí
No	No
Please	Por favor
Thank you	Gracias
It was nothing	De nada
Excuse me	Permiso
See you later	Hasta luego
Bye	Chao
Cool	Chévere
How are you (formal)	¿Cómo está?
" " (informal)	¿Qué tal?
I don't understand	No entiendo.
Do you speak English?	¿Habla inglés?
I don't speak Spanish.	No hablo español.
I'm from England	Soy de Inglaterra
" " the USA	Soy de los Estados Unidos.

Health/Emergency

Call....	¡Llame a...!
an ambulance	una ambulancia
a doctor	un médico
the police	la policía
It's an emergency.	Es una emergencia.
I'm sick	Estoy enfermo/a
I need a doctor	Necesito un médico.
Where's the hospital?	¿Dónde está el hospital?
I'm allergic to...	Soy alérgico/a a
antibiotics	los antibióticos.
penicillin	penicilina
peanuts	maní
shellfish	los mariscos
milk	leche
eggs	huevos
wheat	trigo

Getting Around

Where is...?	¿Dónde está...?
the bus station	la estación de bus?
a bank	un banco
an ATM	un cajero automático
the bathroom	el baño
Where does the bus leave from?	¿De dónde sale el bus?
Left, right, straight	Izquierda, derecha, directo.
One city block	Un cuadro
Ticket	Boleto

Accommodation

Where is a hotel?	¿Donde hay un hotel?
I want a room.	Quiero una habitación.
Single / Double / Marriage	Simple / Doble / Matrimonial
How much does it cost per night?	¿Cuanto cuesta por una noche?
Does that include breakfast?	¿Incluye el desayuno?
Does that include taxes?	¿Incluye los impuestos?
Is there 24-hour hot water?	¿Hay agua caliente veinticuatro horas al día?